# MODERN SYNOPSIS OF
## COMPREHENSIVE TEXTBOOK OF
# PSYCHIATRY/IV

### FOURTH EDITION

# MODERN SYNOPSIS OF
## COMPREHENSIVE TEXTBOOK OF
# PSYCHIATRY/IV

### FOURTH EDITION

## Harold I. Kaplan, M.D.

Professor of Psychiatry, New York University School of Medicine;
Attending Psychiatrist, University Hospital of the New
York University Medical Center;
Attending Psychiatrist, Bellevue Hospital, New York, New York

## Benjamin J. Sadock, M.D.

Professor of Psychiatry, New York University School of Medicine;
Attending Psychiatrist, University Hospital of the New
York University Medical Center;
Attending Psychiatrist, Bellevue Hospital, New York, New York

WILLIAMS & WILKINS
Baltimore • London • Los Angeles • Sydney

*Editor:* Sara A. Finnegan
*Associate Editor:* Victoria M. Vaughn
*Copy Editor:* William Vinck
*Design:* JoAnne Janowiak
*Illustration Planning:* Lorraine Wrzosek
*Production:* Raymond E. Reter

Accurate indications, adverse reactions, and dosage schedules for drugs are provided in this book, but it is possible that they may change. The reader is urged to review the package information data of the manufacturers of the medications mentioned as to recommended dose, contraindications for administration and side effects. This recommendation is of particular importance in response to new or infrequently used drugs.

*Made in the United States of America*


First edition, 1972
Second edition, 1976
Third edition, 1981


Foreign Editions
  Portuguese
  Spanish


**Library of Congress Cataloging in Publication Data**

Kaplan, Harold I.
  Modern synopsis of Comprehensive textbook of psychiatry/IV.

  Includes bibliographies and index.
  1. Mental illness. 2. Personality. 3. Psychotherapy. I. Sadock, Benjamin J., 1933- . II. Comprehensive textbook of psychiatry/IV. III. Title. [DNLM: 1. Mental disorders. WM 100 K172m]
  RC454.K35 1985      616.89      84-5260
  ISBN 0-683-04513-X


87 88 89    10 9 8 7 6 5

*Dedicated to our wives, Nancy Barrett Kaplan*
*and*
*Virginia Alcott Sadock,*
*without whose help*
*this book would not have been possible*

# Preface

Psychiatry stands for the humanity that should exist among all people but is often lacking. Modern-day psychiatry emphasizes the interaction between doctor and patient and is devoted to the humane and compassionate aspects of medicine. This textbook is dedicated to that humanism which is often lost in technically based modern-day medical practice. Equally, those considerations are often forgotten in the interaction between medical school faculty and students, with the result that we tend to produce computer-like, robotic physicians.

In the United States, psychiatry is the only medical school course taught in all 4 years of the curriculum. If taught properly, this course should be a dramatic reminder to all of medicine of its mission—diagnosis, treatment, and the elimination of pain, suffering, and disease through the treatment of the whole person.

The *Modern Synopsis* of the fourth edition of the *Comprehensive Textbook of Psychiatry* (CTP-IV) is not simply a shortened version of the larger book, although the contents of that edition are heavily weighted in this book.

Rather, this edition is a rewritten distillation of the three previous editions of the *Comprehensive Textbook* and the *Modern Synopsis*. The authors have included not only the most important recent advances in psychiatry but also have added sections that are new and different from those in the previous books. Moreover, this edition is not simply a summary of CTP-IV but is a companion volume to be used as a supplementary text by medical students, psychiatric residents, residents in other areas of medicine, practicing psychiatrists, and workers in related behavioral fields.

The *Modern Synopsis* forms part of a tripartite effort by the authors to encompass the teaching of psychiatry and the behavioral sciences. Another aspect of that effort is the *Comprehensive Textbook of Psychiatry*, now in its fourth edition, available in either one or two volumes, which is global in depth and scope although hardly as portable as this book. The final part of the system is the *Study Guide of the Modern Synopsis of the Comprehensive Textbook of Psychiatry* which consists of multiple-choice questions derived from and keyed to the *Modern Synopsis*. A book of multiple-choice questions gives recognition to the importance and contributions of the National Board of Medical Examiners and the American Board of Psychiatry and Neurology on whose published curricula all of our books are based. Their examinations are given in multiple-choice question format, which is the type of question and teaching technique used in the *Study Guide*.

While the authors recognize the enormous importance and positive contributions of those Boards, there is controversy about their enormous influence and power, albeit constructive, on our educational system. Similarly, the nosology used in this textbook is based on the American Psychiatric Association's *Diagnostic and Statistical Manual of Mental Disorders* (DSM-III), which since 1980 has been the "law of the land" in American psychiatry. While the authors have reservations about the utility and validity of DSM-III, which is an innovative but questionable improvement over the previous manual, DSM-II, the student must know DSM-III until it is predictably changed when the next version, DSM-IV, is published. *Modern Synopsis* is neither a review book nor an outline of psychiatry and it is more than a diagnostic manual. It is a comprehensive and fully integrated textbook which is what the field of psychiatry both deserves and requires.

The authors want to acknowledge the original contributors to the fourth and previous editions of the *Comprehensive Textbook of Psychiatry*. Our debt to those contributors is both obvious and considerable; however, we recognize and take responsibility for this book, including whatever shortcomings may exist.

We especially want to thank Virginia Alcott Sadock, M.D., who is Clinical Associate Professor of Psychiatry and Director of Graduate Education in Human Sexuality at New York University Medical Center. As in all our former books, including the *Comprehensive Textbook of Psychiatry,* she has served as assistant to the editors and actively participated in every editorial decision. Her enthusiasm, sensitivity, comprehension, and depth of psychiatric knowledge were of immeasurable importance to the authors. She has ably represented not only the viewpoint of women in medicine and psychiatry but also has made many contributions to the content of this textbook. We are deeply appreciative of her outstanding help and assistance.

Peter M. Kaplan, M.D., who is Resident in Psychiatry at New York University Medical Center, served as a key assistant to the editors in the preparation of this book. Not only did he represent the viewpoint of the modern-day medical student and psychiatric resident but he helped enormously in all aspects of the writing, editing, and substance of this textbook. He made particular contributions in the field of psychopharmacology which is his area of expertise.

A skilled and devoted staff was necessary to complete the enormous task involved in the production of this book. We want to thank Norman Sussman, M.D., Phillip Kaplan, Nancy Barrett Kaplan, James Sadock, and Victoria Sadock for their help. Linda Didner Platt was in charge of our secretarial and office staff and Brian Shaw provided important literature research. At William & Wilkins we want to thank Sara Finnegan, President of the Book Division, who played a key role in every stage of production. Others who helped in production were Vicki Vaughn, Norvell Miller, and William Vinck. William M. Passano, Jr., Chairman of the Board and President of Waverly Press Inc., has continued to offer us every assistance for which we are most grateful.

Finally, we wish to express our sincere appreciation to Robert Cancro, M.D., Professor and Chairman of the Department of Psychiatry at the New York University Medical Center, for his full support and encouragement throughout this project.

Harold I. Kaplan, M.D.

Benjamin J. Sadock, M.D.

New York University Medical Center
New York City

# Acknowledgments

The authors wish to acknowledge the following individuals, most of whom contributed to one or more of the four editions of the *Comprehensive Textbook of Psychiatry* and whose material was synopsized providing much of the basis for this book.

Nancy C. Andreasen, Ph.D., M.D.
Haroutun M. Babigian, M.D.
Arthur J. Bachrach, Ph.D.
James B. Bakalar, J.D.
Lorian Baker, Ph.D.
Aaron Beck, M.D.
Arthur L. Benton, Ph.D.
Jeffrey Boyd, M.D.
James A. Boydstun, M.D.
John Paul Brady, M.D.
H. Keith H. Brodie, M.D.
Richard W. Brunstetter, M.D.
Robert Butler, M.D.
Justin Call, M.D.
Magda Campbell, M.D.
Robert Campbell, M.D.
Robert Cancro, M.D.
Dennis P. Cantwell, M.D.
Arthur C. Carr, M.D.
Stella Chess, M.D.
Alan Crocker, M.D.
Leon Cytryn, M.D.
John M. Davis, M.D.
John Donnelly, M.D.
Lloyd O. Eckhardt, M.D.
David Elkind, Ph.D.
W. Dennis Engels, M.D.
Sherman C. Feinstein, M.D.
Stephen Fleck, M.D.
Vincent J. Fontana, M.D.
Alfred Freedman, M.D.
Anastasius Georgatas, M.D.
John F. Greden, M.D.
Wayne H. Green, M.D.
Milton Greenblatt, M.D.
Lester Grinspoon, M.D.
Ernest M. Gruenberg, M.D.
Samuel B. Guze, M.D.
Katherine A. Halmi, M.D.
Harry F. Harlow, Ph.D.
Saul I. Harrison, M.D.

Ernest L. Hartmann, M.D.
Marc H. Hollender, M.D.
Steven E. Hyler, M.D.
Jerome Jaffe, M.D.
Jeannette Jefferson Jansky, Ph.D.
Francis J. Kane, M.D.
Steven Katz, M.D.
Steven Keller, Ph.D.
Otto F. Kernberg, M.D.
Mitchell L. Kietzman, Ph.D.
Susan T. Kleeman, M.D.
Gerald L. Klerman, M.D.
Peter H. Knapp, M.D.
Irvin A. Kraft, M.D.
Markus Kruesi, M.D.
Donald G. Langsley, M.D.
Ruth L. Lavietes, M.D.
Heinz E. Lehmann, M.D.
Dorothy Otnow Lewis, M.D.
Melvin Lewis, M.B., B.S. (London)
Robert Liberman, M.D.
Louis Linn, M.D.
Zbigniew J. Lipowski, M.D.
Reginald S. Lourie, M.D.
Joseph D. Matarazzo, Ph.D.
Philip R. A. May, M.D.
John E. Meeks, M.D.
William W. Meissner, S.J., M.D.
Jon K. Meyer, M.D.
George Mora, M.D.
Patrick F. Mullahy, M.A.
John C. Nemiah, M.D.
Donald Oken, M.D.
J. Christopher Perry, M.D.
Cynthia Pfeffer, M.D.
Chester M. Pierce, M.D.
George H. Pollock, M.D., Ph.D.
Dane G. Prugh, M.D.
Joaquim Puig-Antich, M.D.
John D. Rainer, M.D.
Judith Rapoport, M.D.

ix

Lynn Whisnant Reiser, M.D.
Morton F. Reiser, M.D.
H. L. P. Resnik, M.D.
Virginia A. Sadock, M.D.
Joseph Schildkraut, M.D.
Steven Schleifer, M.D.
Abraham Schmitt, D.S.W.
Clarence Schultz, M.D.
Melvin L. Selzer, M.D.
Peter E. Sifneos, M.D.
Larry Silver, M.D.
Albert J. Silverman, M.D.
Robert Simon, M.D.
George Simpson, M.D.
Ralph Slovenko, LL.B., Ph.D.
Iver F. Small, M.D.
Joyce E. Small, M.D.
Solomon H. Snyder, M.D.
Albert Solnit, M.D.
Philip Solomon, M.D.
David Spiegel, M.D.
Herbert Spiegel, M.D.
Herzl R. Spiro, M.D., Ph.D.
Robert L. Spitzer, M.D.

Bonnie Spring, Ph.D.
Marvin Stein, M.D.
Robert L. Stewart, M.D.
Robert J. Stoller, M.D.
Charles F. Stroebel, Ph.D., M.D.
Albert J. Stunkard, M.D.
Stephen Suomi, Ph.D.
Norman Sussman, M.D.
Alexandra Symonds, M.D.
Martin Symonds, M.D.
Ludwik Syzmanski, M.D.
Troy L. Thompson, M.D.
George E. Vaillant, M.D.
J. Ingram Walker, M.D.
Jack Weinberg, M.D.
Herbert Weiner, M.D.
Myron Weiner, M.D.
Richard D. Weiner, M.D., Ph.D.
Myrna Weissman, Ph.D.
Charles E. Wells, M.D.
Sidney Werkman, M.D.
Janet B. W. Williams, D.S.W.
Edward A. Wolpert, M.D., Ph.D.
Joseph Zubin, Ph.D.

# Contents

## Chapter 23
## Other Psychiatric Disorders

## Chapter 24
## Sleep and Sleep Disorders

## Chapter 25
## Psychiatric Emergencies

## Chapter 26
## Psychotherapies

## Chapter 27
## Organic Therapies

# 1

# The Life Cycle

## Introduction

Systematic study of the human life cycle began early in the 20th century as an outgrowth of dynamic psychiatry's concern with the course and process of personality development. Initial formations examined the role of inner psychic events and emphasized the overwhelming impact of childhood development on the adult personality. Subsequent conceptualizations, including much of the more recent work, have extended the focus of interest to include the influence of interpersonal processes and the nature of change during later phases of life. The charting of the cycle from birth to death now seems essential to a more complete understanding of the complexities of human behavior and is especially useful in predicting the difficulties that arise in the course of human development.

## Features of Life Cycle Theories

A number of underlying assumptions characterize models of the human life cycle. The fundamental notion is that development occurs in successive, clearly defined stages. This sequence is considered to be invariant; that is, it occurs in a constant order. A second proposition, the epigenetic principle, first described by Erik Erikson, maintains that each stage of the life cycle is characterized by events or crises that must be satisfactorily resolved in order for development to proceed smoothly. If resolution is not achieved within a given life period, the epigenetic model states that all subsequent stages will reflect that failure in the form of physical, cognitive, social, or emotional maladjustment. A third notion, one implicit in most formulations, is that each stage contains a dominant feature, complex of features, or crisis point that distinguishes it from phases that come before or that follow.

The most significant differences between various models of the human life cycle involve the developmental criteria cited. For instance, individual schemes may emphasize such diverse elements as biological maturity, psychological capacities, adaptive techniques, defense mechanisms, symptom complexes, role demands, social behavior, or cognitive style. Another common difference between life cycle theories involves language: There is no standard vocabulary used to describe the major developmental phases. A phase of the life cycle may be described by terms such as stage, season, period, era, epoch, and life stage. In general, though, those terms are conceptually congruent and can be used interchangeably.

## Past and Present Contributions to Life Cycle Theory

Current thinking about the human life cycle has been shaped by a handful of highly influential sources. The dominant work on the subject remains the developmental scheme introduced by Freud in 1915. His theory, focused on the period of childhood, was organized around his libido theory and stated that childhood phases of development corresponded to successive shifts in the investment of sexual energy to areas of the body usually associated with eroticism: the mouth, the anus, and the genitalia. Accordingly, he discerned developmental periods that were classified as follows: oral phase, age 0–1 or 1½ years; anal phase, age 1½–3 years; and phallic phase, age 3–5 years.

Freud also described a fourth period, latency, which extends from age 5 until puberty. Latency is marked by a diminution of sexual interest, which is reactivated at puberty. The basic outlook expressed by Freud was that successful resolution of those childhood phases is essential to normal adult functioning. By comparison, what happens in adulthood is of comparatively little consequence.

Many followers of Freud modified or built upon his conceptualizations while adhering to his focus on sexual energy as the distinctive quality that separates the stages of development. Karl Abraham, for example, further subdivided the phases of psychosexual development. He separated the oral period into a sucking phase

1

and a biting phase; divided the anal phase into a destructive-expulsive (anal sadistic) phase and a mastering-retaining (anal erotic) phase; and divided the phallic period into an early phase of partial genital love (true phallic phase) and a later mature genital phase. In addition, Abraham linked certain adult personality types to difficulties in resolving one of those specific periods.

Melanie Klein, although also adhering to Freud's basic formulations, saw developmental events as occurring more rapidly. She maintained that superego development is already under way during the first and second years of life, rather than the fourth. She also placed the onset of the oedipal conflict in the first months of life. The basic premise of Klein's work—like that of Freud's and Abraham's—is that internal processes are the fundamental determinants of personality development and are thus the moving forces in the human life cycle.

Carl Jung, on the other hand, viewed external factors as playing an important role in personal growth and adaptation. He further held that personality development occurs throughout life—it is not firmly determined by early childhood experiences.

Harry Stack Sullivan took that view even further. He approached the issue of the life cycle by stating that human development is largely shaped by external events, specifically by social interaction. His influential model of the cycle states that each phase of development is marked by a need for interaction with other people. The quality of that interaction then determines the personality of the person. Sullivan distinguished the stages or eras of normal development as follows: Infancy, from birth to the beginning of language (1½ to 2 years); childhood, from language to the need for compeers (2 to 5 years); juvenile era, from the need of compeers and the beginning of formal education to preadolescence (5 to 8 or 9 years); preadolescence, from the beginning of the capacity for intimate relationships with peers of the same sex until genital maturity; adolescence, early phase, which extends from the eruption of true genital interest to the patterning of sexual behavior, and late phase, which extends from the patterning of preferred genital activity to the establishment of a fully human or mature repertory of interpersonal relationships; and maturity, development of self-respect and capacity for intimate and collaborative relationships and loving attitudes.

Erik Erikson's approach to the life cycle embodies elements of both an intrapsychic viewpoint and an interpersonal viewpoint. While accepting Freud's theory of infantile sexuality, he also saw developmental potentials at all stages of life. Indeed, Erikson constructed a model of the life cycle consisting of eight stages that extend into adulthood and old age. The succession of stages is summarized below, along with the dominant issue or maturational crisis that Erikson cited as arising during each period:

1. Oral-sensory stage: trust versus mistrust
2. Muscular-anal stage: autonomy versus shame and doubt
3. Locomotor-genital stage: initiative versus guilt
4. Stage of latency: industry versus inferiority
5. Stage of puberty and adolescence: ego identity versus role confusion
6. Stage of young adulthood: intimacy versus isolation
7. Stage of adulthood: generativity versus stagnation
8. Stage of maturity: ego integrity versus despair

Margaret Mahler studied early childhood object relations and made a significant contribution to the understanding of personality development. She described the separation-individuation process, resulting in a person's subjective sense of separateness from the world around him. The separation-individuation phase of development begins in the fourth or fifth month of life and is completed by age 3.

Mahler delineates four subphases of the separation-individuation process. They are:

1. Differentiation: child is able to distinguish between self and other objects.
2. Practicing period: in the early phase, the child discovers the ability to physically separate himself from his mother by crawling and climbing but still requires the mother's presence for security. The later phase is characterized by free, upright locomotion (7 to 10 months until 15 to 16 months).
3. Rapprochement: increased need and desire for the mother to share the child's new skills and experiences. Also, a great need for the mother's love (16 until 25 months of age).
4. Consolidation: achievement of a definite individuality and attainment of a certain degree of object constancy (25 to 36 months of age).

Other approaches, emphasizing neither the psychodynamic nor the environmental aspects of development, have also influenced the study of the life cycle. Jean Piaget presented elaborate formulations about the qualitative differences in cognition during development. His work has been instrumental in understanding the development of thought processes. He discerned three major periods of intellectual development; sensorimotor, birth to 2 years; concrete operations, 7 to 12 years; and formal operations, 12 years through adulthood. Piaget described a further division of the period of concrete operations into a preconceptual phase (ages 2 to 4) and an intuitive or preoperational phase (ages 4 to 7).

Arnold Gesell has described developmental schedules that outline the qualitative sequence of motor, adaptive, language, and personal-social behavior of the child from the age of 4 weeks to 6 years. Those milestones of development allow for comparison between the development of a particular child and a normative standard. Gesell's schedules are widely used in both pediatrics and child psychiatry.

Among the important trends in more recent life cycle research has been the replacement of theoretical models with clinically derived models, the extension of interest to include adulthood, and the continuing subdivision of the life stages into even smaller segments of time.

One important study has been conducted by Daniel Levinson and his co-workers at Yale University. That study set out to clarify the issues and characteristics of male personality development in early and middle adulthood. A total of 40 men, whose ages at the start of the investigation ranged from 35 to 45 years, were studied; the resulting observations caused Levinson to postulate a new scheme of the adult phases of the life cycle. He suggested that the life cycle is composed of four major eras, each lasting about 25 years, with some overlap, so that a new era is starting as the previous one is ending. Levinson was able to identify a typical age of onset—that is, the age at which an era most frequently begins. The evolving sequence of eras and their age span as described by Levinson are: childhood and adolescence, age 0–22; early adulthood, age 17–45; middle adulthood: age 40–65; and late adulthood: age 60 and up.

Levinson also identifies 4- to 5-year transitional periods between each era. Those periods function as boundary zones in which a person terminates the outgoing era and initiates the incoming one.

A second major study of adulthood has been reported by George Vaillant, who studied a group of 95 men over a period of 35 years. Some of the results of the investigation are summarized below.

A happy childhood was found to significantly correlate with positive traits in middle life. That was manifested by few oral-dependent traits, little psychopathology, the capacity to play, and good object relations.

Vaillant noted that a hierarchy of ego mechanisms was constructed as the men advanced in age. Defenses were organized along a continuum that reflected two aspects of the personality: immaturity-maturity and psychopathology-mental health. It was found that the maturity of defenses correlated with both psychopathology and objective adaptation to the external environment. Moreover, there were shifts in defensive style as a person matured.

Vaillant concluded that adaptive styles mature over the years and that the maturation is more dependent on development from within than on changes in the interpersonal environment. He also concluded that the model of the life cycle outlined by Erikson appears valid.

## Overview of the Human Life Cycle

In view of the several different models for conceptualizing the phases of the life cycle (see Table I), it has become customary to organize the periods of development into an outline that reflects contributions made by each of the disparate models and studies. The most commonly cited stages are:

> Infancy
> Toddler period
> Preschool (oedipal) period
> Juvenile period
> Preadolescence
> Adolescence
> Young adulthood
> Middle adulthood
> Late adulthood (old age)

What follows is a brief overview of the features that are generally recognized as being associated with each of these periods.

### Infancy

Infancy refers to the period from birth until about the age of 18 months. During the first month of life, the infant is termed a neonate or newborn. Infancy is considered to end when the use of language develops.

Infants are born with a number of reflexes, many of which were once needed for survival. Experts assume that the genes carry messages for those reflexes. Among the reflexes are the Moro reflex—flexion of the extremities when startled; the rooting reflex—turning toward the touch when the cheek is stroked; the sucking reflex, which occurs when any object is placed in the mouth; and the Babinski reflex—spreading of the toes with an up-going big toe when the sole of the foot is stroked.

Infants are also born with an innate reflex pattern, endogenous smiling, which is unintentional. Later, exogenous smiling occurs as a reaction to outside stimuli.

TABLE I
LIFE CYCLE IN DEVELOPMENTAL STAGES*

| Age (yr) | Epigenetic States of Erikson | Psychosexual Stages of Freud | Stages of Cognitive Development of Piaget | Major Emotional and Developmental Disorders |
|---|---|---|---|---|
| 0–1 | Trust vs. mistrust: Basic feelings of being cared for by outer-providers | Oral (merges into oral-sadistic) | *Sensorimotor:* Infant moves from an indifferent stage to awareness of self and the outside world. Object permanence not yet developed (birth to 2 yr) | Rumination, pylorospasm. Stranger anxiety at 8 months, infantile autism, failure to thrive |
| 1–3 | Autonomy vs. shame, doubt (begins at 18 mo): Rebellion, clean-dirty issues, compulsive behavior | Anal (divided into anal-expulsive and anal-retentive) | Object permanence develops 18–24 mos. | Sleep disturbances, pica, negativism, temper tantrums, toilet-training problems. Night terrors, separation anxiety, phobias |
| 3–7 | Initiative vs. guilt: Competitiveness develops, self-confidence emerges | Phallic (includes urethral eroticism and Oedipal-Electra complex) | *Preoperational thought:* A prelogical period in which thinking is based on what child wants, not what is (3–7 yr) | Somnambulism. School phobias, encopresis, enuresis, dyslexia, gender identity disorders. Tics |
| 7–13 | Industry vs. inferiority: Peer relations important, risk-taking behavior begins | Latency | *Concrete operations:* Child appears rational and able to conceptualize shapes and sizes of observed objects (7–13 yr) | Psychosomatic disorders, personality disorders, neurotic disorders, antisocial behavioral patterns, anorexia nervosa, bulimia |
| 13–18 | Identity vs. role diffusion: Develops sense of self, role model important | Genital phase | *Formal operations:* Person is able to abstract and can deal with external reality. Can conceptualize in adult manner and evaluate logically. Ideals develop (12 or 13 yr through adulthood) | Suicidal peak in adolescents, schizophrenia, identity crisis. Neurotic disorders |
| Early adulthood | Intimacy vs. isolation: Love relationships, group affiliations important | Genital phase consolidation | | Anxiety states. Bipolar disorder |
| Middle adulthood | Generativity vs. self-absorption or stagnation: Contributing to future generations, acceptance of accomplishments | Maturity | | Mid-life crisis. Dysthymia |
| Late adulthood | Integrity vs. despair: Learning to accept death, maintaining personal values | | | Highest suicide rates, organic mental disorders |

* For the behavioral and physical landmarks of the infant and child up to 5 years, see Section 28.1, "Normal Child Development."

Growth is so rapid during infancy that developmental landmarks are measured in terms of weeks. Most of the landmarks are readily observed. Examples of some major developmental events and their approximate time of appearance are: ocular control, 4 weeks; balance, 16 weeks; grasping and manipulation, 28 weeks; sitting alone, creeping, poking, and ability to say one word, 40 weeks; standing with slight support, cooperation in dressing, and verbalization of two or more words, 12 months; and use of words in phrases, 18 months.

Three major periods of change appear at 2 months, 6 months, and 8 months. At those times, changes are seen in brain development, in skills and perceptions, and in sociability. At 2 months the infant smiles and stares at his own hand. Around 6 months of age the thumb-forefinger approximation begins and, later, the hand-eye-mouth coordination. At 8 months the infant develops a sense of separate identity, and stranger anxiety and separation anxiety emerge at this time.

Infants are able to differentiate different sensations. Babies as young as 12 hours old gurgle with satisfaction when sugar water is placed on the tongue and grimace at a drop of lemon juice. An infant smiles at the smell of bananas and protests at the smell of rotten eggs. At 8 weeks of age, he can differentiate between the shapes of objects and colors. Stereoscopic vision begins to develop at 3 months.

Although that list is only part of the observable process of change during infancy, it reveals the utter helplessness characteristic of this period. The dependency on others is total, a fact that has important psychological effects. Specifically, there is an extreme sensitivity to the mother; both the overt and the more subtle aspects of maternal behavior profoundly affect the infant. According to Erikson, the development of what he termed *basic trust* is a result of consistent and affectionate maternal behavior during infancy.

By the end of infancy there is a threefold gain in weight, and the first teeth have appeared.

## Toddler Period

Two major milestones occur during the toddler period: the development of language and the beginnings of locomotion. Negativistic behavior develops, including constant repetition of the word "no." Internalization of rules begins, as well as the beginnings of the superego. A major issue is separation anxiety and the fear of the loss of the mother's love and approval. That fear comes from the conflict between the wishes of the child and the desires of the parent.

By age 3 years, most children are able to talk in sentences. They can tell stories and communicate clearly.

The development of social behavior is characterized by the child's learning to feed himself, to take himself to the toilet, and to make an effort to dress himself. Although fantasy life and play dominate this developmental period, there is a shift toward play with other children. The term "object constancy" refers to the process by which the mental representation of the mother—the "need-satisfying object" becomes organized and maintained in the child's mind so that the representation can be evoked as a memory, even when the mother is absent. As the toddler matures, that ability develops. Gender identity—the sense of maleness or femaleness—is firmly established by age 2½ or age 3. If sex has been wrongly assigned—as sometimes happens with ambiguous external genitalia—a gender identity disorder usually develops.

## Preschool (Oedipal) Period

The preschool period lasts from about the age of 3 until about the age of 5 or 6. During that time the child becomes less egocentric, loosens bonds with the mother, spends more time in imaginative play, and masters most bodily functions. Dressing and feeding, for example, can be done without assistance by the end of the preschool era. The child begins identifying with the parent of the same sex. At the same time, there may be anger directed at that parent because of the presence of the oedipal conflict. The child may try to physically separate the parents.

A fear of bodily injury and issues of bodily integrity are of prime importance. This is the "Band-Aid phase," in which every injury needs to be examined and taken care of by the mother.

Preoccupation with the genitals is common. According to Freud, when children realize that not everyone is the same, they develop a fear of genital mutilation. Freud postulated that castration anxiety in boys and fear of genital penetration and mutilation in girls develop during this period.

Transient phobias are seen at this age, but they disappear as the child matures. There is a spurt in the development of cognitive capacity that, along with the growing ability to control emotional impulses, sets the stage for entry into school.

## Juvenile Period

Beginning at age 5 or 6 and continuing until puberty, the child experiences a shift in focus away from the home and toward school and friends. School phobia and enuresis are common at this age. During this period there is apparent cessation of sexual preoccupation and a blockade of libido. Boys and girls are inclined to choose friends and to join groups of their own sex, even though sex role behavior between boys and girls becomes more apparent. Boys tend to reject overt signs of physical affection on the part of their mothers, and girls may become "mother's little helper." There is an emphasis on three tasks during this period: learning, development of the intellect, and a sense of belonging to a peer group.

### Preadolescence

The preadolescent period has an onset and a termination that are highly variable from one child to another. Generally the period encompasses the ages between 11 and 13 for boys and between 10 and 12 for girls. Preadolescence is marked by several outstanding emotional characteristics, such as regression, diffusion, shifting cathexis, instability of mood and temperament, normative crisis (affects and behavior become more fluid and unpredictable in response to biological and psychological demands), and intensification of heterosexual interest.

Thinking becomes more logical, abstract, and judgmental, and there is an even more pronounced shift in the focus of relationships away from the home and toward peers.

Among the common defense mechanisms of this period are repression, reaction formation, and displacement.

Biological signs in boys that mark the end of preadolescence are the enlargement of the testes and scrotum, along with pigmentation and thinning of the scrotum. For girls, breast signs include budding, widening of the areola, elevation of the mound of subareolar tissue, and the presence of erect papilla. In both boys and girls, the appearance of hair in the genital area is a sign of puberty. In addition, the appearance of axillary hair usually precedes the appearance of pubic hair. The reappearance of masturbation occurs as the preadolescent begins to experience sexual tension.

### Adolescence

The onset of the aforementioned secondary sexual characteristics marks the beginning of adolescence. The age of onset may range from age 7 to 17; termination may range from age 17 to age 25. A marked shift away from parents and toward the peer group for support and approval occurs. An overt interest in sex develops as does an increase in the desire to experiment with sexuality.

Adolescence is generally divided into three phases: early adolescence (12 to 15 years), middle adolescence (14 to 18 years), and late adolescence (17 to 21 years). These subdivisions are based on the characteristic aspects of those phases. For example, early adolescence is marked by the dissolution of intense ties to parents, siblings, and parental surrogates; increased anxiety and depression, acting out behavior; and occasional delinquent acts. Teenagers obtain about 300,000 legal abortions and give birth to about 600,000 babies per year. There is a diminution in sustained interest and creativity. Middle adolescence is marked by efforts at mastering simple issues concerned with object relationships. The late adolescent phase—which is marked by resolution of the separation-individuation tasks of adolescence—is characterized by vulnerability to crisis, particularly with respect to personal identity (Erikson's *identity crisis*).

### Young Adulthood

The period of young adulthood is a stage of life that extends from the early twenties until the early or middle forties. This is perhaps the most poorly defined of all developmental periods. Characteristically, most of the important decisions that will affect the remainder of one's life are made during this stage. These decisions include choice and entry into a job or profession, courtship and marriage, the establishment of enduring friendships, and a sacrifice of activities that were considered play. The major issue of this period that must be resolved is that of intimacy. Vaillant, addressing himself to this fact, noted that a difficulty in conceptualizing intimacy was the dominant motif of complaints among patients in the young adult years. The emotional disorders that selectively affect this group, he further observed, "reflect anguish or protest against failures at intimacy." Indeed, Erikson identified the crisis of this period as being intimacy versus isolation.

### Middle Adulthood

The terms "middle adulthood," "middle life," "midlife," and "middle age" are used to describe a period that—depending on the author—may range from the age of 30 to 65. The age of 50 has been called the old age of youth and the youth of old age. The onset of middle adulthood, as marked by psychological processes, occurs somewhat earlier in women than in men.

Mogul has enunciated a working definition of middle age, defining it as a period when "previous choices in important life areas and the ensuing successes, failures, satisfactions, and disappointments are reviewed and reworked in the context of old aspirations and wishes, the current recognition of limitations in oneself, and the finiteness of opportunities and of time itself."

Significantly, that definition emphasizes the psychosocial aspects of this period. Although there are certain physiological changes—in the form of bodily declines and increased development of chronic illness—these are highly variable as opposed to the almost fixed midlife occurrences of increased financial responsibilities, establishment of social roles, and development of identity. During middle adulthood the person who is a parent must often relate to his grown children, as well as to his own parents; he is squeezed between two generations.

Midlife is marked by the use of certain defensive maneuvers. Specifically, the defenses that dominate during those years are dissociation, repression, sublimation, and altruism.

A number of practical concerns arise during middle age that tend to be different for men and women. For married women, important issues relate to the movement of children away from the home and into the adult world, whereas unmarried women reflect on the family they might have had. Indeed, some definitions of middle age mark the onset of the period by the termination of the parental role. And, though menopause has long been considered the central event of middle age, recent evidence suggests that the impact of lost reproductive capacity is not as significant as had been previously suspected. Returning to work after being tied to the home also represents a major source of upheaval for an increasing number of women.

For men, generativity is a major issue, as is consolidation of career. There may also be concern about a decrease in sexual desire.

### Late Adulthood

Eleven percent of the population is over 65 years of age; by 2020, fully 20 percent of the population will be over 65, with most of them being women. Less than 20 percent of men over 65 are at work, and the percentage of women at work is lower.

Of people over 65, one-quarter live alone, and only 5 percent are in nursing homes. Fifteen percent of the population over 65 suffer from either a functional or an organic brain disorder, such as Alzheimer's disease and Pick's disease. Approximately one-half of the 1½ million Americans living in nursing homes are said to have Alzheimer's disease.

Late adulthood, or old age, is marked by the emergence of new issues. Many of those issues are related to the physical manifestations that accompany the aging process—a decline in physical health and reduced sensory acuity. Negative stereotypes about being old—held by society and the elderly themselves—are important aspects of this period.

A primary task of this period is the need to adapt to major losses, such as work, friends, or a spouse. Old age may present special difficulties for women, who are widowed longer than men, institutionalized more frequently, and usually poorer than men of the same age. For both sexes there is, as Neugarten described, "the yielding of a position of authority and the questioning of one's former competence; the reconciliations with significant others and with one's achievements and failures; the resolution of grief over the death of others and of the approaching death of self; the maintenance of a sense of integrity in terms of what one has been, rather than what one is, and concern over legacy and how to leave traces of oneself."

### Death

According to Kübler-Ross, the dying person experiences five psychological stages before death—denial, anger, bargaining, depression, and acceptance. Those stages are not necessarily sequential, however, and a person may shift back and forth among the stages at any time.

In the words of Omar Khayyam, "The Moving Finger writes; and, having writ, Moves on: nor all your Piety nor Wit, Shall lure it back to cancel half a Line, Nor all your Tears wash out a Word of it." The life cycle comes to its natural end with death. People must accept that inevitability. Having done so, they enter the final stages of the life cycle, as Erikson said, with a sense of integrity, rather than a sense of despair.

**REFERENCES**

Arthur M B, Bailyn L, Levinson D J, Shepard H: *Working with Careers.* Center for Research in Career Development, Columbia University, New York, 1984.

Erikson E H: The life cycle. In *International Encyclopedia of the Social Sciences.* Macmillan and Free Press, New York, 1968.

Gutmann D: Psychoanalysis and aging: A developmental view. In *The Course of Life: Psychoanalytic Contributions Toward Understanding Personality Development.* S I Greenspan, G H Pollock, editors, vol 3. US Department of Health and Human Services, Mental Health Study Center, Adelphi, Maryland, 1981.

Jacques E: Death and the mid-life crisis. Int J Psychoanal *46:* 502, 1965.

Levinson D J, Darrow C N, Klein E B, Levinson M

H, McKee B: *The Seasons of a Man's Life.* Alfred A Knopf, New York, 1978.

Levinson D J, Gooden W L: The life cycle. In *Comprehensive Textbook of Psychiatry*, ed 4, H I Kaplan, B J Sadock, editors, p 1. Williams & Wilkins, Baltimore, 1985.

Lidz T: *The Person: His and Her Development Throughout the Life Cycle.* International Universities Press, New York, 1983.

Neugarten B L, editor: *Middle Age and Aging: A Reader in Social Psychology.* University of Chicago Press, Chicago, 1968.

Ortega y Gasset J: *Man and Crisis.* W. W. Norton, New York, 1958.

Van Gennep A: *The Rites of Passage.* University of Chicago Press, Chicago, 1960.

White R W: *The Enterprise of Living.* Holt Rinehart & Winston, New York, 1972.

# 2

# Science and Human Behavior: Contributions of the Biological Sciences

## 2.1 GENETICS AND PSYCHIATRY

### Introduction

In the last decade, the science of genetics has made major conceptual and technical advances, and today it unites molecular biology, biochemistry, and cell biology toward the goal of explaining the transmission, expression, and variation of gene-coded information in developing organisms. Psychiatry, both in research and practice, has forged closer bonds with genetics: this union has come about with the growth of psychiatry as a responsible medical specialty and biological discipline in an interdisciplinary framework, as well as with increasing sophistication in the techniques and formulations of human genetics, including the principles of dynamic interaction with the environment.

It took nearly a century for the convergence of psychiatry and genetics to come about. Caught up in the ancient dichotomies of nature-nurture and mind-matter, most psychiatrists tended to distinguish and choose between biological and psychological approaches to etiology and treatment. There is an interplay of all the factors affecting human development, whether genic, chromosomal, biochemical, embryological, metabolic, experiential, or social. The goal of psychiatric genetics as a science may be considered, in the broadest sense, to be the clarification of the mechanisms of human variation and development not only in psychiatric disorders but also in normal behavior.

### Genetics of Psychiatric Disorders

#### Schizophrenia

In reviewing the status of schizophrenia genetics, it can be said that the cumulative evidence for a necessary genetic vulnerability is generally accepted, regardless of uncertainties about diagnosis and hence the validity of particular research data, the nature and role of environmental factors, the mode of inheritance, the development of symptoms in individuals at risk, and, ultimately, the biological nature of the genotype. Taken together, research data support an essential genetic component and have not been otherwise adequately explained.

**Studies Using Individual Pedigrees.** Because schizophrenia is a relatively common disorder, little information can be gained by the anecdotal reporting of a few families. In the early pre-Mendelian and pre-Kraepelinian era, such observations were prevalent and achieved a certain notoriety. If, however, schizophrenia is considered to be a heterogeneous syndrome, there is a value in studying individual large pedigrees, more apt to be homogeneous in etiology, using current methods that incorporate biological variables. There is also information in pedigrees that is not available in pooled population-risk data, and methods of segregation analysis are being exploited in the attempt to define the modes of inheritance. Neither of these approaches has yet yielded specific genetic markers or settled on a definitive pattern of inheritance, but is clearly useful to supplement population risk studies with research designs using the individual family as the unit.

**Studies of Risk in Relatives.** This approach, known as the proband or morbidity risk method, was one of the first to be applied to schizophrenia genetics following the rediscovery of Mendel's genetic laws and Kraepelin's diagnostic reformulations. Even in the early findings of Rüdin and Schulz, the expectancy for the siblings of patients was higher than the general population rate and, among these siblings, was relatively higher if the probands had an insidious onset, relatively lower if the probands had an acute onset, precipitating cause, and benign course. A 2-fold goal was thus early established for this mode of investigation: (1) to substantiate a genetic influence and (2) to validate, on genetic grounds, distinctions between clinical subtypes.

In the 1930s, one of the largest of the earlier studies was conducted in Berlin by Kallmann, and it reviewed the families of 1,087 patients. The over-all expectancy for siblings was 11.5 percent and for children 16.4 percent, as compared with 0.85 to 2 percent in the general population. For both relationship groups, there was a higher risk for relatives of catatonic and hebephrenic (nuclear) patients than for relatives of paranoid or simple (peripheral) types. Second-degree relatives—grandchildren, nephews, and nieces—showed a risk of about 3 percent in Kallmann's study. Pooled results of other family studies yielded comparable if somewhat lower figures, with 8.7 percent as the minimal expectancy in siblings, 12 percent in children of one schizophrenic parent, and from 35 to 68 percent in children of two schizophrenic parents.

These data give strong evidence of a necessary, although not sufficient, genetic factor, although they can neither separate genetic environmental factors nor conform to any specific form of inheritance. In practice, they are of use chiefly as empirical risk figures and are of value in genetic counseling.

Two important observations from family risk data should not be overlooked: (1) that the children of schizophrenic mothers have the same risk as the children of schizophrenic fathers and (2) that the children of two schizophrenic parents have a risk as high as 40 percent. These facts are inconsistent with a purely intrafamilial environmental theory.

**Studies of Twins.** Twin studies have not given definitive answers to what is inherited, how it is inherited, and what the significant environmental factors are. Nevertheless when their data are combined with the data of other research designs, they have been useful not only for what they foreshadowed but also for their contribution to the search for genetic markers and to problems of nosology, severity, and penetrance.

The classical twin studies, reported between 1928 and 1961 in Europe, Japan, and the United States, were based mostly on hospitalized index cases with severe and usually chronic illness. There was noteworthy agreement among many investigators; the concordance for monozygotic twins of schizophrenic patients, without age correction, ran from 60 to 70 percent, and for dizygotic twins of the same sex from 13 to 18 percent.

The largest series of twin index cases, over 900, was reported by Kallmann in 1946 and 1953 and yielded uncorrected over-all concordance rates of 69 percent and 10.3 percent for monozygotic and dizygotic twins respectively. With age correction, these rates yielded the well-known expectancies of 86 percent for monozygotic twins and 15 percent for dizygotic twins. More recent studies also used newer methods of zygosity analysis, particularly blood groups, thus reducing possible sources of error, although it had been shown that errors of zygosity determination have been rare and could not have been crucial even in the older reports.

Although the absolute concordance rates were lower in the newer studies, the monozygotic rates were significantly higher than the dizygotic, and they were higher for the co-twins of more seriously ill cases than of cases with milder course. One survey was based on all 25,000 pairs of twins born in Norway between 1901 and 1930. Concordance rates for pairs with schizophrenia in one twin ranged from 25 to 38 percent for monozygotic pairs and from 4 to 10 percent for dizygotic pairs, depending on the severity of illness and the strictness of diagnostic criteria. Another study reporting on all twins treated as outpatients or short-stay inpatients at the Maudsley Hospital in London between 1948 and 1964, found over-all concordance rates of 50 percent for monozygotic twins and 10 percent for dizygotic. The rates rose up to 77 percent if the index case had been hospitalized for 2 or more years. In Denmark, a review of the children of monozygotic twins was conducted from pairs with schizophrenia in one or both members. It was noteworthy that the risk of schizophrenia in such children was similar to the known risk for children of one schizophrenic parent. The risk did not vary significantly whether the twin who was the child's parent was schizophrenic or not or came from a concordant or discordant pair. This result would appear to establish a heritable vulnerability factor independent of state.

Finally, a survey of 274 pairs with a diagnosis of schizophrenia in one or both twins, who were chosen from a register of over 15,000 male U.S. veterans who were twins, yielded concordance rates of 27.4 percent for monozygotic and 4.8 percent for dizygotic twins. Limited to a group already screened for relative health, these figures continue the trend for lower concordance rates in less chronic schizophrenia, but the ratio of monozygotic to dizygotic concordance rates is maintained even in this group.

**Studies of Adoptees and Their Families.** Adoption studies were designed to throw light on gene-environmental interaction and on problems of diagnosis. In the area of interaction, they could deal with the role of stress, rearing, and parent-child relationships; in the diagnostic areas, with concepts of diathesis, spectrum diagnosis, psychotic equivalents, and borderline and schizotypic states.

The prototype of adoption studies in schizophrenia was conducted in Oregon and reported in 1966. A survey of 47 children born to schizophrenic mothers and separated at birth were matched with a group of 50 controls for sex, placement, and time in foundling institutions, but with no record of the mother having been in hospital. Because the illness of the mothers preceded and continued during pregnancy, there was the possibility that some intrauterine noxious factor played a role. Also, most of the parents who adopted the index children knew of the mothers illness, although none refused to adopt on these grounds. After reaching adulthood, the experimental group had an age-corrected schizophrenia rate of 16.6 percent, very much in line with earlier family risk data, while the control group had no schizophrenia cases. In addition, the experimental group showed excess of sociopathic personality and institutionalization in prison or psychiatric hospital. It is noteworthy that outcome was not affected by the social class of childhood homes or by the length of time spent in foster or foundling homes prior to adoption.

Soon after, there began to appear reports from the extensive NIMH Danish studies. These studies were of three basic designs in which (1) children of schizophrenic biological parents were reared by adoptive parents and compared with a matched group of adoptees whose biological parents had no psychiatric history; (2) the biological parents and extended families of schizophrenic adoptees were compared with the biological families of matched nonschizophrenic control adoptees; and (3) the biological and adoptive parents of schizophrenic adoptees were studied for disturbed behavior. In the latter two designs, additional control groups—biological parents of schizophrenic nonadoptees; biological parents who reared difficult but nonschizophrenic children, e.g., nongenetic retardates; and adoptive parents—were variously studied.

In the first design, the prevalence of schizophrenia and schizophrenia-like disorders was greater in the adopted-away offspring of schizophrenics than in the adopted-away offspring of nonschizophrenics. In the second design, diagnoses in the schizophrenia spectrum were concentrated in the biological relatives of adoptees who became schizophrenic. Importantly, there

was a significant excess of schizophrenia diagnoses in the paternal half siblings of schizophrenic adoptees, thus excluding intrauterine influences or early mothering experiences as contributing environmental factors. In the same studies, no instances of schizophrenia-like disorder were found in the relatives of probands with a diagnosis of acute schizophrenia, thus supporting the tendency to consider that syndrome genetically unrelated to the others. In the third design, biological parents of schizophrenia adoptees showed a higher rate of disorder and a lower mental health rating than the adopting parents of schizophrenics or a group of parents burdened by the difficulty of rearing a mentally retarded child. Also reported was a cross-fostering study, in which a group was added whose biological parents were free of illness but whose adoptive parents included a diagnosis related to schizophrenia. This latter group showed no increase in illness, while the index group, with illness in the biological but not in the adoptive family, did show significantly increased pathology.

**Longitudinal Studies of Predisposed Individuals.** For purposes of economy, prospective studies can identify children for observation who have presumed risk factors, rather than attempt to follow in detail an entire birth cohort expected to yield only one or two patients out of every 100. One group known to be at high risk on the basis of family expectancy rates is represented by the offspring of schizophrenic parents. With a 10 to 15 percent risk with one affected parent and a 40 percent risk with two, such children represent strategic populations for study. The environmental impact of family disruption due to hospitalization of a parent has to be controlled by including children in families with severe but nonschizophrenic parental pathology, as well as children of normals. One current study is focusing on measures of attention, motor and neurological impairment, and intelligence test scores as indicators of vulnerability to schizophrenia.

**Genetic Markers.** Genetic polymorphisms may serve as markers for use in linkage studies in multigenerational pedigrees. So far, the technique has not yielded definitive results in schizophrenia, largely because of inadequacy of diagnostic data and of analytic methods.

Among associated genetically controlled risk factors, monoamine oxidase (MAO) activity as measured in blood platelets has received much consideration. This enzyme activity is a heritable and stable trait, it is significantly lower in chronic schizophrenics than in normal controls, and it discriminates between ill and well relatives of schizophrenic index cases. The over-all decrease in enzyme activity is modest, however, and there is a considerable overlap between affected and unaffected individuals. Low MAO activity may nevertheless contribute to vulnerability in select cases, which may then merit special study.

**Genetic Counseling in Schizophrenia.** Even if the mode and mechanism of the heritable factor in schizophrenia has not been defined, there exist empirical risk figures and the experience of investigators to guide genetic counseling. Such counseling is best provided by psychiatrists or other professionals who have firsthand experience with diagnostic and interviewing techniques and are aware of nosological distinctions and alternate forms of schizophrenia-like illness. The highest empirical risk in counseling, about 40 percent, is to the offspring of two schizophrenic parents. If one potential parent is schizophrenic, the risk is in the 10 to 15 percent range. Often it is only the brother or sister of one of the couple who is ill; assurance can be given to the couple that the risk for their children is probably in the 2 to 3 percent range, not appreciably greater in absolute value than for the general population. Evidence from twin and family studies is that acute schizophrenia carries a lower risk than other forms. As in all genetic counseling, environmental factors must be considered, including the stability of the marriage and home, the nurturing ability of the parents, and the effect of a healthy or unhealthy child on the parents' own difficulties. Genetic counseling should ideally be done by persons who combine familiarity with the frontiers of genetic research, clinical background leading to appreciation of the course and heterogeneity of the illness, experience in the management of family problems, and aptitude for empathic communication with families seeking help.

## Genetics of Affective Disorders

Older studies of family risk and twin concordance in affective disorder neglected to distinguish between bipolar and unipolar disease. Kraepelin found large numbers of relatives of manic-depressives had the same illness, and other family studies reported rates of 10 to 15 percent in siblings, less in parents and children. Studies of twins indicated a concordance rate of about 70 percent in monozygotic pairs. Almost all family studies showed complete differentiation of manic-depressive and schizophrenic psychoses.

A clinical distinction was made in 1959 between bipolar illness, with periods of mania, and unipolar illness, with recurrent depression alone. Since then, genetic studies have been directed at investigating the biological validity of this distinction and determining empirical risks and modes of inheritance for both forms. Twin studies were reviewed, and most pairs in the literature were either both unipolar or both bipolar; bipolar monozygotic pairs had a higher concordance rate (about 70 percent) than unipolar pairs (45 percent). Some bipolar twins, however, had unipolar co-twins, which coincided with many family studies where bipolar probands had an excess of unipolar relatives. These observations have prompted investigators to consider that unipolar symptoms may sometimes be a manifestation of the bipolar phenotype, with the manic symptoms not expressed. Application of the liability threshold model to affective disorders has addressed the problem of the genetic relationship of the different clinical forms. Some models using forms of affective illness as threshold determinants with schizoaffective, bipolar I (mania), bipolar II (hypomania), and unipolar disease representing decreasing vulnerability have suggested that they fall on a continuum and have shown compatibility with a multifactorial mode of inheritance.

Bipolar disease, the less common form, has the higher risk for first-degree relatives if unipolar disease when found in such relatives is considered a genetically equivalent condition. With a general population estimate of about 1 percent, the risk for such relatives of bipolar probands ranges in various studies from 15 to 21 percent. About half the relatives have unipolar symptomatology. Females have a higher risk in most surveys, as do relatives of probands with early onset and a preponderance of manic symptoms.

In the case of probands with unipolar disease, the risk of the same illness in first-degree relatives averages about 9 percent in males and 14 percent in females, compared with 1.8 percent and 2.5 percent, respectively, for males and females in the general population. Bipolar illness among these relatives is rare.

Unipolar illness has been divided by some into depressive spectrum disease—with early onset and a family history of depression, alcoholism, and sociopathy—and pure depressive illness—with late onset and only depression in the family. The former has been described as more common in women, sometimes manifesting itself as alcoholism in males; the latter has been described as more common in males. Bipolar illness has been divided into cases with severe manic episodes (bipolar I) and those with hypomanic episodes (bipolar II), into rapid-cycling and slow-cycling forms, into cases with early rather than late onset, and into cases with and without family history. If preponderantly manic cases with early onset appear to have a higher genetic risk, they also seem to show a better response to lithium treatment, an example of a possible pharmacogenetic approach to genetic distinctions.

A study of the parents of adult bipolar probands who had been adopted early in life has provided further evidence of genetic influence. The biological parents of this group show an incidence of affective disorder—bipolar, unipolar, and schizoaffective—equal to that in biological parents of bipolar nonadoptees. They also show a much higher incidence than the adoptive parents of these same children than three control groups consisting of biological and adoptive parents of normal adoptees and biological parents of patients with poliomyelitis. The last group controls for the effect on parents of rearing a difficult handicapped child.

Stemming from the observation that affective disorder is more common in women, there have been attempts to establish a locus on the X chromosome for a gene transmitted as an X-linked dominant factor; such a pattern would preclude father-to-son transmission. Because such transmission does occur, presumably in the absence of assortative mating, there must clearly be families in which the X-linked pattern does not obtain. In a number of studies of informative families, evidence for linkage of bipolar illness with color-blindness loci on the G6PD locus has been presented; other studies have found no linkage, and the positive results have also been criticized on the basis of nonrandom ascertainment and insufficient correction for penetrance and age of onset. A recent analysis attempted to reconcile these findings by demonstrating heterogeneity, with clear separation between the groups that showed linkage and those that did not.

No definitive genetic markers for vulnerability to affective disorders have been currently identified, although a recent report suggests increased cholinergic receptor (binding site) activity in fibroblasts from patients and ill relatives.

Genetic counseling in affective disorders is often sought by parents, one or both of whom themselves have had depressive and possibly manic spells. This situation is different from the case in schizophrenia where in practice it is more often unaffected relatives who seek advice. Although empirical risk figures for offspring of affected parents are higher than in schizophrenia, one is able to point out the episodic nature of the attacks and the potential for successful treatment. A major problem does arise when a prospective mother is taking lithium, as there is sufficient evidence of teratogenic, chiefly cardiac, effect during early pregnancy. This situation requires expert counseling and careful clinical monitoring. Although the controversial evidence on X-linkage with color blindness is not strong enough for use in counseling, the search for biochemical markers linked or associated with genetic vulnerability continues.

### Sociopathic Behavior and Criminality

Antisocial personality disorder is characterized by a history of continuous and chronic antisocial behavior of a defined nature with onset before the age of 15 and in the absence of symptoms of severe mental retardation or schizophrenic, schizoaffective, or manic disorder. In this syndrome it is especially difficult to separate the effect of family and social environment, including such factors as alcohol and drug abuse, from genetic predisposing factors. Early studies abroad revealed a high concordance for criminalty among monozygotic twins, but the rate for same-sexed dizygotic twins was not much lower. In general, the distribution of concordance rates in siblings, opposite- and same-sexed dizygotic twins, and monozygotic twins has led most genetic investigators to suspect a large environmental role in the pathogenesis of criminal behavior.

Studies of adoptees have tried to separate the effects of genetic and environmental influences, although they suffer from the usual problem of diagnosis, even more difficult in this heterogeneous group.

In one study, the adopted-away children of female offenders when compared to controls showed a significant increase in criminality and antisocial personality, although most of the arrests were for property crimes, and incarceration was infrequent. An adoption study, using the converse design, reported on the biological relatives of psychopathic adoptees and matched controls. The frequency of all mental disorders was found to be higher in the biological relatives of the psychopathic probands than among their adoptive relatives or among either group of relatives of the controls. The difference was even greater when only psychopathic spectrum disorders were considered, and it was highest of all among biological fathers.

Interaction between genetic and environmental influences has been suggested in cross-fostering studies where criminality in adoptive fathers has been noted to increase the risk in the biological offspring of criminals. Social class and alcoholism have been also noted as contributing or interacting factors.

## Organic Mental Disorders

### Alzheimer's Disease

This syndrome, characterized by senile plaques and by loss of mental function without focal defects, may occur in the senile or presenile period. A dominant form of inheritance has been suggested in the latter form. In women with the senile variety, a higher frequency of chromosomal loss (aneuploidy) and an excess of SCE's has been described.

### Huntington's Disease

This disease is a classical example of a dominantly inherited disease with neurological and psychiatric symptoms and a variable age of onset. Although some cases appear in early adulthood or in late middle life, the mid-40s is the average age. Unless a parent has died young, there will be a family history in the direct line, and each child of an affected parent will have a 50 percent risk of inheriting the gene. Naturally, the older the children in question are without becoming ill, the lower their remaining risk becomes. Nevertheless, without a reliable biochemical or neurological test for gene carriers in the preclinical stages, such persons may have to decide on marriage and parenthood while they are still in doubt as to their own status. Huntington's disease is one of the conditions for which linkage with DNA fragment polymorphisms is being sought.

### Tourette's Disorder

This disorder of uncertain cause is characterized by multiple motor and vocal tics. Although Tourette considered the condition to have a hereditary component, genetic and biological aspects have been largely ignored until recently. One study reports a high concordance rate in monozygotic twins. About a third of Tourette patients have a family history of tics. Females, the less frequently affected sex, have a higher genetic loading, with more affected relatives than males. These data have been interpreted in terms of a two-threshold single major locus model of inheritance incorporating sex effect.

### Lesch-Nyhan Syndrome

This behavioral disorder, inherited as an X-linked recessive trait, is based on a known enzyme lack. A deficiency in the enzyme hypoxanthine guanine phosphororibosyltransferase leads to hyperuricemia with mental retardation, spastic cerebral palsy, choreoathetosis, and self-destructive biting of fingers and lips. This bizarre behavior also includes aggression against others. Children with this syndrome feel pain, do not want to bite themselves, and welcome restraint. In this illness, a distinct genetically controlled enzymatic defect is associated with stereotyped behavior patterns. Although certain pharmacological and behavioral modification approaches have been used for treatment with some success, illnesses such as this may soon be treated definitively through prenatal detection and gene replacement. The fact is thus illustrated that knowledge of genetic causation is not synonomous with therapeutic nihilism, but may actually lead to more effective cures.

### Alcoholism

This substance-abuse disorder is influenced by both heredity and environment. Severe drinking problems are found more in sons of alcoholics than in controls, even when both groups were separated from their biological parents early in life. Moreover, sons are no more apt to become alcoholic if reared by their alcoholic parents than if adopted away. Alcoholism is much less common in women, a fact that is reflected in the comparatively lower rates for daughters of alcoholic parents. Some data suggest an overlap of depression and alcoholism in daughters raised by their own alcoholic parents, and other data suggest a possible spectrum, with early onset depression in women and increase in alcoholism and sociopathy without depression in male first-degree relatives.

Aside from the cultural influences, alcoholism may be determined by metabolic differences. An atypical form of alcohol dehydrogenase, as found in many Japanese persons, may cause flushing after ingestion of alcohol and possibly may make such an individual drink less.

## Anxiety and Personality Disorders

Family and twin studies of neurotic illness have shown an increase of a like kind among relatives and monozygotic twins, particularly in obsessional and anxiety disorder, less so in the heterogeneous category of hysteria. Studies based on psychological tests have involved general neurotic traits, as well as factors within the normal range of personality variation. Heritability on the Minnesota Multiphasic Personality Inventory Test (MMPI) was highest on the scales of depression, social introversion, and psychopathic deviation and was lowest on hypochondriasis, hysteria, paranoia, and pathological sexuality. Diagnostic imprecision and lack of biological validation have hampered quantitative studies in this area; further genetic analysis of such phenomena as lactate-induced phobic anxiety attacks and their prevention by tricyclic antidepressants may lead to better understanding of the underlying defect in such disorders.

### Psychosexual Syndromes

In animals there is evidence that prenatal hormonal influences may affect sexual behavior, e.g. androgens may masculinize both morphology and species-specific sexual activity. For humans, gender assignment and parental rearing practices generally take precedence.

The role of sex chromosomal anomalies in determining behavior depends on key interactions with social and educational factors. In Klinefelter's syndrome, for example, some cases of homosexuality, transvestitism, and pedophilia have been reported but are not typical.

Androgen insensitivity syndrome is a term applied to individuals with male (XY) chromosomal constitution whose tissues, because of genetic defect, do not respond to testosterone. They have the external genitalia and appearance of normal females, are usually raised as girls, and consider themselves as feminine. Conversely, females (XX) with adrenogenital syndrome are influenced by fetal androgens, so that their genitalia are masculinized; they often exhibit tomboyish, although not homosexual behavior.

Male homosexuals show no evidence of chromosomal abnormality. Early twin studies showed monozygotic twin concordance rates, with dizygotic co-twins showing no increase over general population statistics. These findings were interpreted as suggesting a gene-controlled disarrangement in psychosexual maturation patterns. In this formulation, homosexuality would be part of the personality structure, rather than physically determined. An ability to perceive and respond to sexual stimuli, to recognize satisfaction and success in heterosexual performance, and to use those experiences as integrating forces may be crucial to sexual role development. Vulnerability factors in these areas may influence sexual choice, which is then reinforced accidentally or by family or social surrounding. A few monozygotic twin pairs discordant for homosexual behavior also showed important intrapair similarities, principally in psychological test findings that indicated sexual and body-image confusion. Divergent patterns of behavior and sexual identification may be influenced by such factors as differences in the twins' relationship with their parents and frustration in sexual contacts. In the same context, a biological-genetic basis for transsexualism has been hypothesized, but its role or importance is as yet poorly understood.

### Intelligence and Mental Defect

The role of heredity in intelligence is the subject of much discussion and is surrounded by a number of difficult problems, conceptually and practically. The issues include the value of compensatory education, the nature of learning, and the problems of underprivileged groups. The nature of intelligence is debated: Is it a stable quality, how can it be measured, and can it be measured free from cultural influences? Diagnostic tools vary from standard I.Q. tests and many other forms of test to teacher's estimates of learning ability and occupational status achieved in society. Other factors making genetic studies difficult are nongenetic nutritional, familial, social, and educational influences and assortive mating for factors subsumed under intelligence.

Intelligence scores, largely consisting of I.Q.'s, do indeed show remarkable correlation with genetic closeness within families. Extrapolation from such data to hypotheses about I.Q. differences between socioeconomic or ethnic groups with wide environmental differences is, however, a dubious procedure.

Mental defect, as distinguished from below-average intelligence, may be due to infection, birth trauma, or specific gene mutations and chromosomal aberrations; however, such specific factors account for barely half of all persons with an I.Q. below 70. Polygenic inheritance is probably responsible for most of the others, with social deprivation usually playing a secondary or modifying role. It has been estimated that five-sixths of these retarded persons in the United States are the offspring of a retarded parent or of a normal parent with a retarded sibling.

Other intriguing questions regarding the role of genetics in intelligence are the similarity of performance I.Q. in twin pairs in which one member suffers from early total deafness; the stability of similarities in twins' I.Q., even into advanced years; and the possibility of gene linkages or biological associations. In connection with the search for mechanisms, it has been variously suggested that myopia, torsion dystonia, retinoblastoma, hyperuricemia, and adrenogenital syndrome are associated with decreased intelligence.

## Chromosomal Aberrations

### Autosomal Defects

Lejeune reported the presence of an extra small chromosome in patients with Down's syndrome, later identified as chromosome 21 in the standard nomenclature (see Fig. 1). This condition, known as *trisomy* arises through a process of nondisjunction, usually in the formation of the ovum or, rarely, the spermatocyte. In the process of meiosis, one chromosome of each pair ordinarily goes to each of the daughter cells. If, instead, the two chromosomes travel together and both enter one of the daughter cells, that gamete will have an extra chromosome. When it combines in fertilization with a normal gamete, a zygote or single-cell-stage individual is formed with the extra chromosome, or a total of 47 chromosomes.

Down's syndrome, formerly misnamed mongolism, presents with typical physical features and mental retardation. It was known for a long time to occur more often in children born of older mothers, and it had a concordance rate in identical twins of close to 100 percent. These findings, plus the generalized nature of the signs

and symptoms, foreshadowed an early germinal, possibly chromosomal, defect. In fact, Waardenburg predicted a chromosomal defect in 1932, but had no way of testing his hypothesis.

With an over-all rate of 1 per 1,000 but with a progressive risk in later ages up to 1 in 50 for mothers over the age of 45, it is now recommended that pregnancies in women over the age of 35 be monitored by amniocentesis. In this process, some amniotic fluid containing fetal epithelial cells is removed during the first trimester, the cells are grown in culture, and the presence or absence of trisomy 21 is established, giving the family the option of abortion if a Down's syndrome karyotype is established.

Some children with Down's syndrome present with a count of 46 chromosomes, but with one of extra length. By inspection and banding patterns, it is clear that the translocation chromosome consists of the long arm of one chromosome, such as 13, 14, 15, 21, or 22 plus most or all of the extra chromosome 21; thus, the karyotype is essentially trisomic. In such cases, one parent may have a balanced translocation—45 chromosomes, with the translocation chromosome present but with one of the unattached

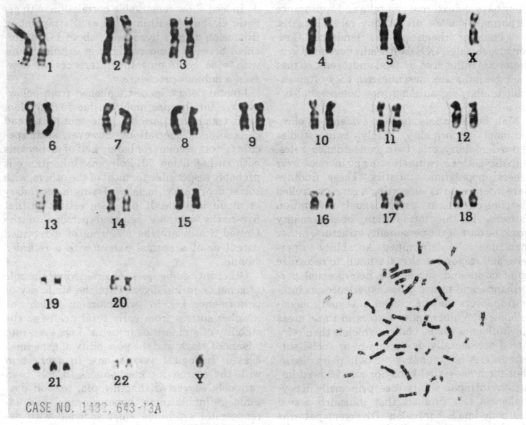

CASE NO. 1432, 643-13A

FIGURE 1. Karyotype of male with 21 trisomy (Down's syndrome), Giemsa (G−) banding.

chromosomes 21 absent, leaving the karyotype effectively normal. These distinctions are important in counseling. If a child with Down's syndrome is a trisomy or if the child is a translocation but both parents are normal (de novo translocation), the risk of recurrence for future children is only slightly increased, taking maternal age into account. If, however, either parent is a balanced translocation carrier with any chromosome combination other than 21/21, there is an empirical risk for each child to be affected about 10 to 15 percent if the mother is the carrier and 3 to 8 percent if the carrier is the father. In the case where the translocation is 21/21, the risk for each child is 100 percent. Again, amniocentesis is available in all these cases for prenatal diagnosis.

Many other forms of autosomal trisomy and other chromosomal rearrangements have been reported, some giving rise to typical birth anomaly syndromes. One example described first by Lejeune is deletion of the short arm of chromosome 5, producing a child with low birth weight, retardation, and a striking cry like that of a cat. This disorder is known as cri-du-chat syndrome.

### Sex Chromosome Defects

Some of the typical syndromes caused by sex chromosome aberrations are of psychiatric interest. Klinefelter's syndrome is occasionally marked by various degrees of weak libido, mental subnormality, and nonspecific personality disorders, ranging from inadequate personality to schizophrenic-like behavior. Physically, such persons are tall males and have gynecomastia and small testicles. Other findings include a communicative deficit, marked by a reduction in verbal I.Q., possibly associated with a left-hemisphere deficit. Although a Barr body (see Fig. 2) indicates the presence of two X chromosomes, karyotype analysis confirms that a Y chromosome is also present (47,XXY). The XXY karyotype occurs as frequently as 2 to 3 per 1000 male newborns. It is not certain whether behavior disorder, when it occurs, results from the chromosome imbalance or whether the chromosomal syndrome precipitates an otherwise determined psychosis by adding an additional biological or social burden, perhaps connected with body frame or eunuchoid habitus.

Among females with an extra X chromosome (47,XXX), which has a frequency at birth of 1 in 1000, some persons have been found in clinics and hospitals who are mildly retarded and socially withdrawn; they usually suffer from menstrual disturbances. No specific behavior correlate can be postulated, although there are reports of a proportion of XXX cells (mosaicism) in some schizophrenic women.

Turner's syndrome is represented by females with various physical symptoms, such as short stature, webbing of the neck (lymphedema), shield-like chest, and streaked gonads with primary amenorrhea. Sexual immaturity and body defects do not seem to result in any emotional disturbance; in fact, these girls and women have been described as resilient to adversity, stable in personality, and maternal in temperament. They are not mentally retarded, but have been reported to show a specific defect in space-form appreciation and constructional skills, one of the few examples of a specific intellectual correlate of a karyotypic defect, possibly associated with a right hemisphere deficit. Turner's syndrome is comparatively rare in living infants—about 1 in 2500—although the (45,XO) karyotype is frequent in abortions.

A special interest centered for a time on the 47,XYY genotype. This karyotype was originally reported to be significantly more frequent in tall males who were institutionalized for criminal activity—usually against property—and who had low intelligence. Sensational at first, this finding was subsequently questioned on the basis of sampling bias. Some intensively studied cases seemed to show episodic impulsive behavior, triggered by environmental stimuli, with their usual makeup being mild, passive, docile, and inadequate; a relation of this episodic behavior to seizure-like activity in the brain has been suggested. In considering the effect of the XYY chromosome anomaly, one must note its incidence in newborns is about 1 in 1000, so that only longitudinal studies of such infants or large-scale population sampling could reveal the true range of phenotypes and the interaction of genetic and environmental factors in the development of children with an extra Y chromosome. Yet, to focus attention on such infants may do them harm. Even when the condition is discovered as an incidental finding in amniocentesis, careful explanation to the parents is essential to help them make their choices and to avoid damage.

### Genetic Counseling

In daily practice, the clinical application of increased knowledge in the areas of genetics and family guidance is the responsible provision of marriage and parenthood counseling in the presence of a gene-borne condition in the concerned family. When doubt exists regarding important and emotion-laden decisions as to marriage and parenthood, people need to have access to trained professional advisers who are able not

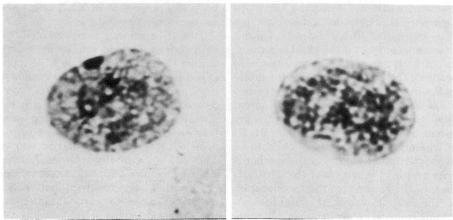

FIGURE 2.   Sex chromatin in buccal epithelial cells (thionin stain). *Left*, chromatin positive. *Right*, chromatin negative. The dark-staining mass of chromatin found in the cell nucleus of the female (X-chromatin) is known as a Barr body.

only to elicit facts and evaluate them scientifically but also to resolve fears and misunderstandings and to be aware of the impact of their procedures on their patients.

Genetic counseling can actually be considered as a short-term course of psychotherapy based on psychological understanding and conducted according to established techniques of psychiatric intervention. Counselors should be equipped to diagnose psychiatric disorder and to be aware of nosological distinctions and alternate forms of the same syndrome. They need also to understand the impact of knowledge and discovery on the individuals or couples, depending on their level of maturity, guilt and conflicts, defense mechanisms, and ego strengths and weaknesses. Of equal importance are the medical, legal, and psychological implications of such procedures as amniocentesis, contraception, sterilization, abortion, artificial insemination, and adoption.

If at all possible, genetic counseling must be done face-to-face, not by telephone or mail. As in all psychotherapy, the emotional reactions of the counselors have to be considered, as well as their prejudices or blind spots. Counseling varies in its technique and its impact with the time it is given relative to marriage, parenthood, or the birth of a child. Risk estimates need to be understood in relation to benefit, leading to the concept of burden, something with both subjective and objective components. The counselor has to be ready to deal with depression, while not preventing the persons counseled from expressing their wishes, fears, and emotions.

From the clinical point of view, responsible genetic counseling provides the most direct ap-

plication of medical knowledge in the field of genetics to patients and their families.

### Social and Ethical Problems

Many social problems associated closely with the dynamics of population growth and evolutionary change are raised by advances in medical genetics. If psychiatrists are concerned with individual and community mental health, as well as some of the broader questions of social planning, they cannot avoid attending to these issues. Dysgenic trends in human populations include wars, certain differential reproductive patterns, improvement in the efficiency of therapeutic procedures not accompanied by attention to reproductive trends, and such mutagenic procedures as exposure to chemical substances or radiation. At the same time, diversity in the human genotype may increase human adaptability to present and future environment.

In the narrower area of clinical psychiatric genetics, the scientific as well as the ethical and legal issues involved in genetic screening, genetic counseling, and the handling of genetic information need wide discussion by geneticists, psychiatrists, philosophers, clergymen, and lawyers.

Genetic engineering—the transfer of DNA fragments into the gene structure of another organism—has great potential for definitive treatment of much genetic disease; the dangers of such experimentation appear to have been exaggerated. Cloning of humans, if it ever becomes technically possible, poses problems not only of control but also of ethics in creating a human identical to another, with all of its psychological implications.

## REFERENCES

Gershon E S, Matthysse S, Breakefield X O, Ciarenillo D D, editors: *Genetic Research Strategies in Psychobiology and Psychiatry.* Boxwood Press, Pacific Grove, CA, 1981.

Gottesman I I, Shields J: *Schizophrenia: The Epigenetic Puzzle.* Cambridge University Press, New York, 1982.

Kallmann F J: *Heredity in Health and Mental Disorder.* W. W. Norton, New York, 1953.

Lewin B: *Genes.* John Wiley & Sons, New York, 1983.

President's Commission for the Study of Ethical Problems in Medicine and Biomedical and Behavioral Research: *Screening and Counseling for Genetic Conditions.* US Government Printing Office, Washington DC 1983.

Rainer J D: Genetics and psychiatry. In *Comprehensive Textbook of Psychiatry,* ed 4, H I Kaplan, B J Sadock, editors, p 25. Williams & Wilkins, Baltimore, 1985.

Schmitt F O, Bird S J, Bloom F E, editors: *Molecular Genetic Neuroscience,* Raven Press, New York, 1982.

Slater E, Cowie V: *The Genetics of Mental Disorders.* Oxford University Press, London, 1971.

---

# 2.2 BASIC SCIENCE OF PSYCHOPHARMACOLOGY

### Introduction

A large number of disciplines have been involved in the study of the basic science and action of psychotropic drugs, including biochemistry, physiology, neuroanatomy, and clinical psychiatry. All these disciplines aid in understanding how drugs act on the mind. A fundamental understanding of psychopharmacology demands a familiarity with central nervous system (CNS) neurotransmitters.

### Neurotransmitters

Interactions of psychotropic drugs with the catecholamines, norepinephrine and dihydroxyphenylethylamine (dopamine), have been discovered by numerous investigators and seem to account for the actions of numerous drugs. But, quantitatively, those compounds are all only minor transmitters in the brain, although they may have particular importance in the areas of the brain concerned with emotional behavior. Even in the corpus striatum, the area of the brain with the highest concentration of dopamine, only about 15 percent of the nerve terminals use dopamine as their transmitter. In the hypothalamus, the brain region richest in norepinephrine, only about 5 percent of the nerve terminals are noradrenergic. In the brain as a whole, the two catecholamines probably account for synaptic transmission at no more than about 1 to 2 percent of synapses. Serotonin is the transmitter at considerably fewer synapses than the catecholamines. Although such estimates are more difficult to obtain for acetylcholine, it is likely that no more than 5 to 10 percent of the synapses in the brain are cholinergic. There is now considerable evidence that histamine is a neurotransmitter in "emotional" areas of the brain, such as the hypothalamus. However, its levels in the brain are substantially lower than those of serotonin and the catecholamines, and it probably accounts for fewer synapses than the other biogenic amines.

What, then, are the major neurotransmitters in the CNS? It is likely that a variety of amino acids are transmitters at the major excitatory and inhibitory synapses. In various brain regions $\gamma$-aminobutyric acid (GABA) probably accounts for transmission at between 25 and 40 percent of synapses. GABA inhibits the firing of neurons and is, therefore, a major inhibitory transmitter. In the spinal cord and brain stem, the amino acid glycine, in addition to its other metabolic functions, seems to be a prominent inhibitory transmitter at about the same percentage of synapses as GABA. The identity of the major excitatory neurotransmitters is somewhat less certain; however, glutamic and aspartic acids, which uniformly excite neurons, satisfy many characteristics demanded of the prominent excitatory neurotransmitters.

### Opioid Peptides

A major recent development has been the awareness that numerous peptides may also be neurotransmitters. The most studied peptide transmitters are the opiate-like peptides, the enkephalins.

The opiate-like substance is a mixture of two peptides, five amino acids in length and differing only in one amino acid. They are referred to as methionine-enkephalin (met-enkephalin) and leucine-enkephalin (leu-enkephalin), respectively.

The pituitary gland contains substantial levels of a 31-amino-acid peptide, called $\beta$-endorphin. $\beta$-Endorphin has potent actions at opiate receptors, but its function is unclear. Peptides do not readily enter the brain from the pituitary glands; therefore, $\beta$-endorphin's physiological site of action is probably in the periphery.

$\beta$-Endorphin is released during stressful stimuli together with ACTH. It is not clear whether the peripheral target organ of $\beta$-endorphin, like ACTH, is the adrenal cortex. High affinity binding sites for $\beta$-endorphin not responding to opiate drugs have been identified on lymphocytes. Indeed, it is probable that the opiate-like action of β-endorphin is an epiphenomenon and that the physiological role of β-endorphin as a pituitary hormone is not related to any opiate-like effects.

Low levels of β-endorphin occur in the brain Cell bodies in the hypothalamus project to the limbic system and brain stem. Because the localization of β-endorphin in the brain does not match that of opiate receptors, β-endorphin in the brain presumably does not mediate the kinds of actions typically associated with opioid effects. Nevertheless, as discussed below, the close coincidence of enkephalin localization and opiate receptors establishes that enkephalin is the normally ocurring neurotransmitter of the opiate receptor.

Immunohistochemical techniques have proved valuable for clarifying the functions of opioid peptides. Antibodies are raised against the peptides usually linked to a carrier protein. Opiate receptors can also be visualized microscopically by means of autoradiographic techniques. Maps localizing opiate receptors and enkephalin neurons coincide fairly closely and involve brain structures whose functions are linked to opiate actions.

Localizations of opiate receptors and enkephalins can explain many of the pharmacological actions of opiates. For instance, small enkephalin-containing interneurons in the dorsal spinal cord influence opiate receptors localized to nerve endings of sensory neutrons, inhibiting their release of sensory pain neurotransmitters, such as substance P. Enkephalin tracts and opiate receptors in the limbic system, which regulate emotional behavior, may explain euphoric effects of opiates. Respiratory depression, which accounts for lethal effects of opiates, may involve receptors in the solitary nucleus of the brain stem, which regulates visceral reflexes, including respiration. One can even explain pupillary constriction produced by opiates based on high localizations of opiate receptors and enkephalin neurons in the pretectal area and the superior colliculus.

### Other Neuropeptides

**Neurotensin.** Numerous other peptides in the brain may have functions as interesting as those of the enkephalins. Neurotensin, a 13-amino-acid peptide, was isolated on the basis of the ability of brain extracts to lower blood pressure. There are extremely potent analgesic effects of neurotensin when injected directly into the brain. Neurotensin-elicited analgesia is unrelated to the opiate system because it is not blocked by opiate antagonists, such as naloxone. Thus, drugs that mimic neurotensin may have

analgesic properties without typical opiate side effects.

**Substance P.** Next to enkephalin, substance P is the most studied brain peptide. Its localization throughout the brain resembles that of neurotensin and enkephalin. Substance P's role as the sensory transmitter of pain has been extensively supported. Substance P occurs in 20 percent of dorsal root ganglia cells, with some processes extending to the skin and others entering the spinal cord and giving rise to terminals in the substantia gelatinosa. Because substance P is a neurotransmitter of pain pathways, the blockade of its release in spinal cord by opiates may account in part for analgesia, at least as mediated at the spinal cord level.

**Cholecystokinin.** Cholecystokinin (CCK) was originally isolated from the duodenum as a substance that contracts the gallbladder, hence its name.

CCK is unique among the neuropeptides in its high concentration in the cerebral cortex where there are many CCK-containing cells. Indeed, of the neuropeptides, CCK and vasoactive intestinal polypeptide (VIP) are the only two with major cell groups in the cerebral cortex.

One localization of CCK of relevance to psychiatry is its coexistence with dopamine in certain cells. The coexistence of a neuropeptide and a biogenic amine in the same neuron is by no means restricted to CCK and dopamine. There exist numerous other examples, including the colocalization of serotonin and substance P in some neurons. It is, in fact, possible that the storage together of multiple neurotransmitters in any neuron may turn out to be the rule, rather than the exception.

Drugs that block CCK receptors may relieve schizophrenic symptoms in the same way as neuroleptics, but without the extrapyramidal side effects associated with blockade of dopamine receptors in the corpus striatum.

For CCK there may be an interesting link between its intestinal and central localizations. Very low doses of CCK-8 injected peripherally cause satiety in previously hungry animals; CCK reduces appetite in humans as well. The satiety elicited by CCK occurs with lower doses when it is injected peripherally than when it is administered directly into the brain. It is thought that CCK acts on specific receptors located on the vagus nerve in the stomach and liver and that information from the vagus then enters the brain to suppress appetite.

**Vasoactive Intestinal Polypeptide (VIP).** VIP was first identified in the intestine and subsequently shown to occur in the brain. VIP and CCK appear to be excitatory neurotransmitters.

**Bradykinin.** Bradykinin was first discovered in the plasma, although it probably serves functions in the intestine as well as the brain. Bradykinin is the most potent pain-producing substance known.

**Carnosine.** The dipeptide carnosine ($\beta$-alanylhistidine) is the smallest of the neurotransmitter candidate peptides in the brain. It is highly concentrated in the primary olfactory pathway.

Besides the peptides already discussed, numerous other peptides with functions throughout the body also occur in the brain. Among these are angiotensin, insulin, glucagon, and vasopressin. As already mentioned, pituitary peptides, such as ACTH, luteinizing hormone (LH), thyroid-stimulating hormone (TSH), and prolactin (PRL), also occur in the neuronal systems in the brain. Hypothalamic-releasing hormones, such as thyrotropin-releasing hormone (TRH), gonadotropin-releasing hormone (GnRH or LRH), corticotropin-releasing factor (CRF), somatostatin, and growth hormone releasing factor (GRF) also have been localized in neuronal systems in the brain.

### Amine Tracts

A major advance in understanding the functions of the amines in the brain occurred when histochemical techniques were developed to localize neurons containing norepinephrine, dopamine, and serotonin (see Fig. 1).

**Norepinephrine.** There are two major norepinephrine tracts—a ventral and dorsal pathway in the CNS. It is likely that the ventral norepinephrine pathway, with terminals in the pleasure centers in the lateral hypothalamus, subserves such affective behaviors as euphoria and depression. One may speculate that the dorsal norepinephrine pathway to the cerebral cortex is associated with alerting actions of these neurons.

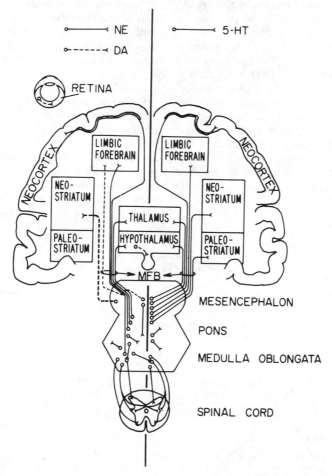

FIGURE 1.   Pathways of serotonin (*5-HT*), norepinephrine (*NE*), and dopamine (*DA*) neuronal systems in the central nervous system. (Adapted from Anden N E, Dahlstrom A, Fuxe K, Larsson K, Olson K, Ungerstedt U: Ascending monoamine neurons to the telencephalon and diencephalon. Acta Physiol Scand 67: 3131, 1966.)

Other norepinephrine pathways with cell bodies in the brain stem send axons down in the lateral sympathetic columns of the spinal cord, terminating at various levels. These neurons influence a variety of spinal cord reflexes. It is conceivable that, in this way, norepinephrine pathways mediate apparent emotional influences on muscle tone in such conditions as anxiety and tension.

**Dopamine.** There are several discrete dopamine pathways. The most prominent pathway has cell bodies in the substantia nigra and gives rise to axons that terminate in the caudate nucleus and putamen of the corpus striatum. This pathway is degenerated in Parkinson's disease, accounting for major symptoms of the condition. Restoration of the depleted dopamine by treatment with its amino acid precursor dihydroxy-L-phenylalanine (L-dopa) greatly alleviates the symptoms of Parkinson's disease. Neuroleptic drugs, by blocking dopamine receptors, elevate plasma prolactin. There are also dopamine neurons in the retina whose function is obscure but tantalizing, inasmuch as the retina contains no norepinephrine or serotonin fibers.

**Serotonin.** Serotonin is so highly concentrated in raphe nuclei that almost all their cells are probably serotonergic. Selective destruction of the raphe nuclei in animals results in insomnia. Restoring the depleted serotonin with tryptophan or 5-hydroxytryptophan, the amino acid precursors of serotonin, puts such insomniac animals to sleep. Similarly, stimulation of the raphe nuclei at physiological frequencies makes animals somnolent. Thus, serotonin neurons play some role in regulating sleep-wakefulness cycles.

### Amine Metabolism

Understanding the metabolic pathways of the biogenic amines greatly enhances one's ability to appreciate their interactions with psychotropic drugs. The amino acid tyrosine is the dietary precursor of the catecholamines (see Fig. 2). The first enzyme in the biosynthetic pathway of the catecholamines is tyrosine hydroxylase, which converts tyrosine into dihydroxyphenylaline. Tyrosine hydroxylase is believed to be the major rate limiting enzyme in catecholamine biosynthesis, because increasing or decreasing its activity produces corresponding changes in the levels of the catecholamines. Dopa is then decarboxylated by the enzyme dopa-decarboxylase to dopamine. Dopa-decarboxylase is often referred to as aromatic amino acid decarboxylase, because it acts on any aromatic amino acid, with important consequences when certain amino acids are used as drugs. For instance, if one treats a patient with 5-hydroxytryptophan, which is an aromatic amino acid that is decarboxylated into serotonin, the catecholamine neurons form serotonin from 5-hydroxytryptophan just as efficiently as do the serotonin neurons, so that after such treatment serotonin accumulates as a false transmitter in catecholamine neurons.

Catecholamines are metabolically degraded primarily by two enzymes, monoamine oxidase and catechol-O-methyltransferase (COMT) (see Fig. 3). Monoamine oxidase oxidatively deaminates dopamine or norepinephrine to the corresponding aldehydes. Those aldehydes, in turn, can be converted by aldehyde dehydrogenase to corresponding acids. The aldehydes may also be

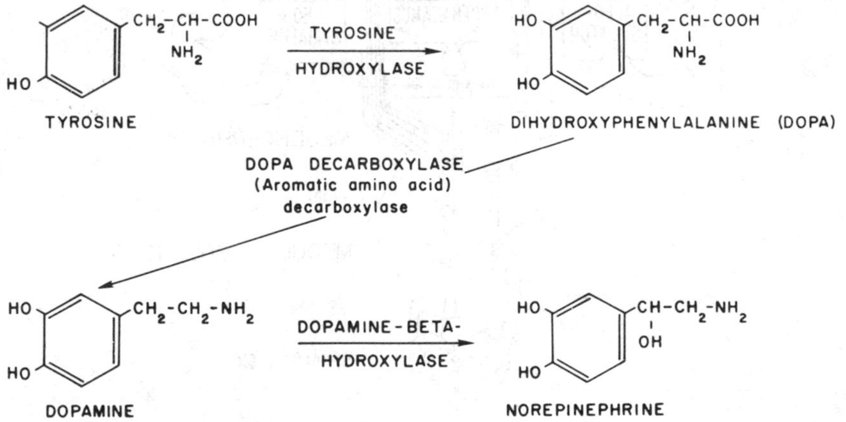

FIGURE 2. Pathways of catecholamine synthesis. (From Snyder S H: New developments in brain chemistry: Catecholamine metabolism and its relationship to the mechanism of action of psychotropic drugs. Am J Orthopsychiatry *37:* 864, 1967.)

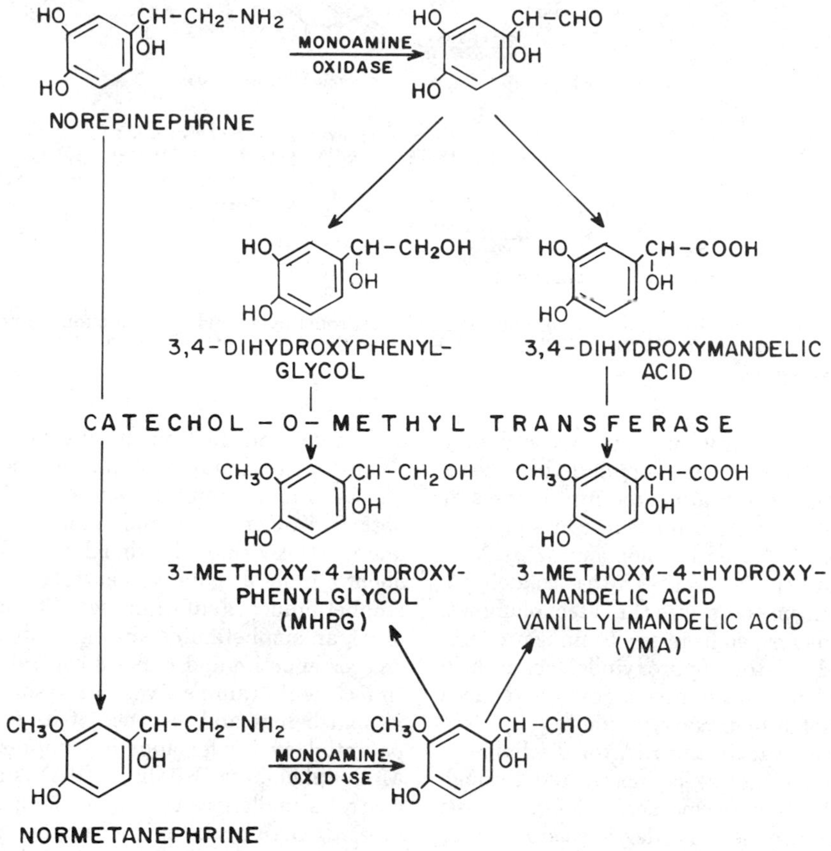

FIGURE 3.    Pathways of catecholamine catabolism. (From Snyder S H: Catecholamines and serotonin. In *Basic Neurochemistry*, R W Albers, G I Siegal, R Katzman, B W Agranoff, editors, p 89. Little Brown and Co, Boston, 1972.)

reduced to form alcohols. Dietary factors, such as the ingestion of ethanol, can determine the relative amounts of catechol acids or alcohols formed from the catecholamines because ethanol also competes for aldehyde dehydrogenase.

In the peripheral sympathetic nervous system, the O-methylated acid product of norepinephrine degradation is called vanillylmandelic acid (VMA). Its levels are measured in clinical laboratories as an index of sympathetic nervous function and to diagnose tumors that produce norepinephrine or epinephrine, such as pheochromocytomas and neuroblastomas. Dopamine O-methylation and deamination gives rise to homovanillic acid.

In the brain, reduction of the aldehyde formed from the action of monoamine oxidase on norepinephrine or normetanephrine predominates, so that the major metabolite in the brain is an alcohol derivative called 3-methoxy-4-hydroxylphenylglycol (MHPG). The MHPG formed in the brain is conjugated to sulfate. Because MHPG can diffuse from the brain to the general circulation, estimates of its levels in the urine might be thought to reflect directly the activity of norepinephrine neurons in the brain. However, although MHPG is proportionately only a minor breakdown product of norepinephrine in the periphery, quantitatively it seems that a significant portion of urinary MHPG still derives from the periphery, with a variable amount coming from the brain. Nonetheless, measuring urinary MHPG seems to be a valuable tool in estimating the function of brain norepinephrine neurons and has value in predicting the response of depressed patients to antidepressant drugs.

**Serotonin.** Tryptophan, the dietary amino acid precursor of serotonin, is hydroxylated by the enzyme tryptophan hydroxylase to form 5-hydroxytryptophan (see Fig. 4). 5-Hydroxytryptophan is decarboxylated to serotonin. When parkinsonian patients are treated with L-dopa, dopamine is formed not only in dopamine neu-

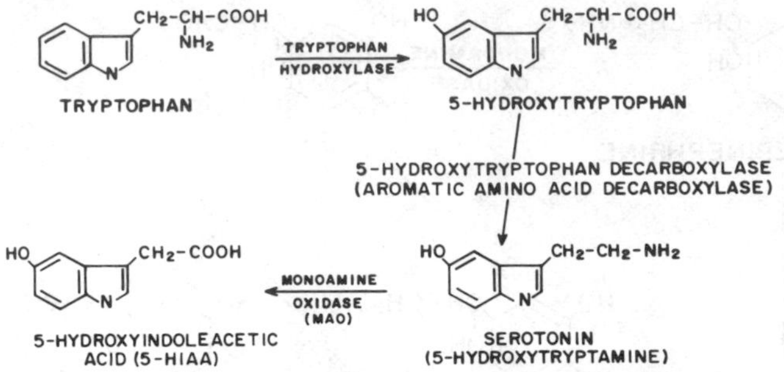

FIGURE 4. Pathways of serotonin synthesis and degradation. (From Snyder S H: Catecholamines and serotonin. In *Basic Neurochemistry*, R W Albers, G I Siegal, R Katzman, B W Agranoff, editors. p 89. Little Brown and Co, Boston, 1972.)

rons but also in serotonin neurons and may displace serotonin so that dopamine becomes a false transmitter in brain serotonin neurons of those patients, with unknown consequences. Serotonin is destroyed by monoamine oxidase, which oxidatively deaminates it to the aldehyde, just as the enzyme does with the catecholamines. The aldehyde formed from serotonin is predominately oxidized to 5-hydroxyindoleacetic acid (5-HIAA), although a limited amount is reduced to the alcohol, 5-hydroxytryptophol.

**Reuptake Inactivation.** After discharge at synapses, acetylcholine is inactivated through hydrolysis by the enzyme acetylcholinesterase. None of the enzymes that degrade serotonin or the catecholamines seems to be responsible for their synaptic inactivation. Instead, these amines are predominantly inactivated by reuptake into the nerve terminals that released them. Highly efficient and specific uptake systems have been demonstrated for all the neurotransmitter candidates in the CNS—for norepinephrine, dopamine, serotonin, GABA, glutamic and aspartic acids, and glycine, but not for histamine and acetylcholine. It seems likely that reuptake inactivation is the universal mechanism for neurotransmitter amine and amino acid inactivation and that enzymatic degradation in the case of acetylcholine is an exception to the rule. Interference with reuptake inactivation is a major mechanism of action of several psychotropic drugs.

## Psychotropic Drug Action

### Stimulants

Amphetamines and related stimulants bear striking structural resemblances to the catecholamines (see Fig. 5). Pharmacologists have generally assumed that amphetamines act through one of the two catecholamines in the brain.

Amphetamine facilitates synaptically released catecholamines. The extent to which specific dopamine and norepinephrine pathways account for the stimulant, euphoric, and anorectic effects of amphetamines is unclear. Of the two optical isomers of amphetamine, *d*-amphetamine (Dexedrine, Smith Kline & French) is about 5 times as potent a central stimulant as *l*-amphetamine. Fenfluramine (Pondimin, Robins), an amphetamine analogue, effectively decreases appetite and is not a central stimulant. In fact, fenfluramine gives rise to somnolence in human beings and, because of its lesser abuse potential, is a safer appetite-suppressing drug. Methylphenidate (Ritalin, CIBA) is a powerful central stimulant with very little appetite-suppressing activity. It is the amphetamine analogue of choice in the treatment of hyperactive children for whom loss of appetite would be a serious side effect. The mechanism of this paradoxical action of amphetamines in hyperactive children is unclear. Some investigators think that the drug is not paradoxical at all. Instead, by its alerting effect, amphetamine enables children to focus their attention and hence be less distractible and hyperactive.

There is evidence that single doses of amphetamine do produce euphoria in those patients who subsequently display a favorable therapeutic response to tricyclic antidepressants. In this way, amphetamine affords a test substance to determine therapeutic response to antidepressant drugs. Conceivably, amphetamine has a potential for alleviating certain aspects of depression, but perhaps because of its dynamics of action—directly releasing catecholamines into the synaptic cleft, besides blocking their uptake—it produces adverse psychic effects that counteract its therapeutic actions.

Amphetamine addicts—speed freaks—self administer huge amounts of amphetamine intravenously. Such persons frequently develop an acute paranoid psychosis, which may be clinically indistinguishable from acute paranoid schizophrenia and which provides the best drug model of schizophrenia. Accordingly, understanding brain mechanisms in the mediation of amphetamine psychosis may shed light on the pathophysiology of schizophrenia. Indirect evidence suggests that brain dopamine mediates the symptoms of amphetamine psychosis. Besides producing a model schizophrenia, small doses of amphetamine administered intravenously to schizophrenics exacerbate symptoms in some patients, but paradoxically, they alleviate somewhat the symptoms of other patients.

### Antidepressant Drugs

The two major classes of antidepressant drugs were discovered at about the same time: the monoamine oxidase inhibitors and the tricyclic antidepressants (see Fig. 6). Monoamine oxidase inhibitors comprise a group of agents that have

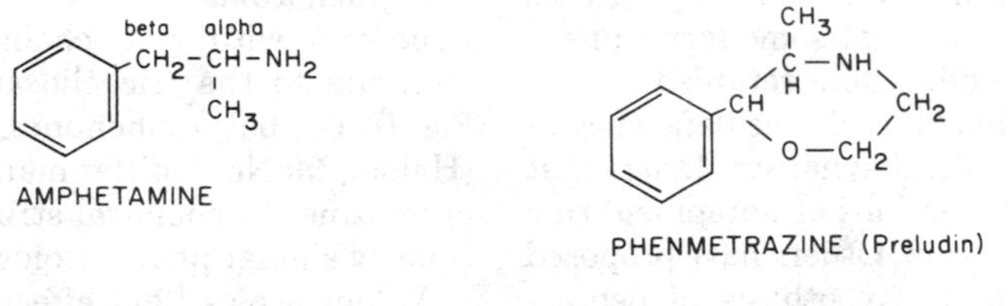

FIGURE 5. Structures of amphetamine and related drugs.

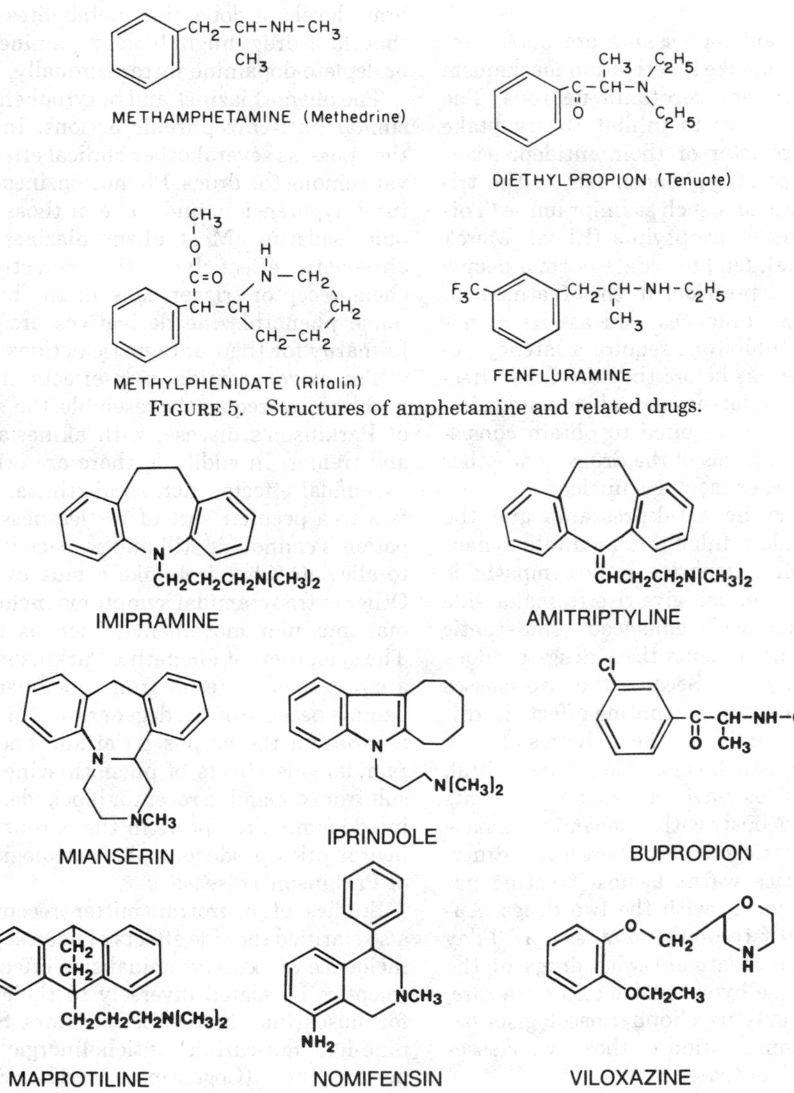

FIGURE 6. Antidepressant drug structures.

widely varying chemical structures but that have in common the ability to inhibit monoamine oxidase. Inhibition of that enzyme results in an accumulation of the monoamines norepinephrine, dopamine, and serotonin within nerve terminals. At a certain point, the amines start leaking out into the synaptic cleft, so that the drugs facilitate the actions of all monoamines.

There is no direct evidence as to which monoamine is crucial for the antidepressant actions of those drugs. The norepinephrine hypothesis of depression postulates that some forms of depression, especially endogenous retarded depressions, are attributable to a relative deficiency of norepinephrine at central synapses. Drugs that enhance the synaptic actions of norepinephrine tend to relieve depression. Others have proposed an analogous serotonin hypothesis of depression.

The tricyclic antidepressants are potent inhibitors of the reuptake inactivation mechanism of catecholamine and serotonin neurons. The ability of those drugs to inhibit the reuptake process is a predictor of their antidepressant efficacy. Like certain phenothiazines, the tricyclic antidepressants, such as imipramine (Tofranil, Geigy) and amitriptyline (Elavil, Merck Sharp & Dohme), tend to sedate normal people and yet relieve depression. In the treatment of depression, these drugs, as well as the monoamine oxidase inhibitors, require a latency period of 1 to 3 weeks before they are fully effective. Whether this latency period is related simply to the duration required to obtain consistently high brain levels of the drugs or whether it is related to other factors is unclear.

Both the tricyclic antidepressants and the monoamine oxidase inhibitors facilitate synaptic actions of norepinephrine in the sympathetic system. This action can give rise to major side effects associated with enhanced sympathetic function. In some patients these drugs produce marked hypertension. Because the two classes of drugs facilitate norepinephrine effects in different ways, they enhance the activities of each other in a synergistic fashion. Severe, even fatal, hypertensive crises have occurred in patients treated simultaneously with monoamine oxidase inhibitors and tricyclic antidepressant drugs. American practice warns against treating patients simultaneously with the two drugs. Authorities generally recommend at least a 10-day interval between treatment with drugs of the two classes. These hypertensive crises are rare, however, and many psychopharmacologists believe that the combination of those two classes of drugs is relatively safe.

## Antischizophrenic Drugs

The most important drugs in psychiatry are probably the antischizophrenic phenothiazines and butyrophenones, which are generally referred to as neuroleptics. Abundant evidence supports the contention that these drugs exert a selective antischizophrenic action, so that neuroleptics have been used as tools to discern abnormal brain mechanisms in schizophrenia. The phenothiazines are complex three-ringed structures with side chains quite similar in structure to the tricyclic antidepressants (see Fig. 7). The butyrophenones, such as haloperidol (Haldol, McNeil), differ markedly from the phenothiazines in chemical structure, but have extremely similar pharmacological activities.

As long ago as 1963, effects of neuroleptics on brain levels of dopamine metabolites suggested that these drugs might block dopamine receptors or deplete dopamine intraneuronally.

The phenothiazines and butyrophenones have similar antischizophrenic actions. In addition, they possess several other clinical effects, which vary among the drugs. Phenothiazines elicit postural hypotension, and some of those drugs are quite sedating. Most phenothiazines exert an antiemetic effect by acting directly on the chemoreceptor trigger zone in the brain stem. Some phenothiazine derivatives are marketed primarily for their antiemetic actions.

The extrapyramidal side effects of the phenothiazines frequently resemble the symptoms of Parkinson's disease, with akinesia, rigidity, and tremor. In addition, there are other extrapyramidal effects, such as akathisia, which refers to a peculiar sort of restlessness in which patients cannot sit still and so pace in an effort to alleviate what feels like a muscular itching. Other extrapyramidal symptoms include abnormal muscular movements, such as torticollis. The symptoms of idiopathic Parkinson's disease are presumed to result from a deficiency of dopamine because of the degeneration of dopamine neurons in the corpus striatum. The extrapyramidal side effects of phenothiazine drugs result from dopamine receptor blockade. By blocking dopamine receptors in the corpus striatum, neuroleptics produce a pharmacological model of Parkinson's disease.

Studies of neurotransmitter receptors have also clarified the side effects of neuroleptics. The incidence of extrapyramidal side effects of neuroleptics is related inversely to their affinities for muscarinic cholinergic receptors. Such atropine-like muscarinic anticholinergic drugs as benztropine (Cogentin, Merck Sharp &

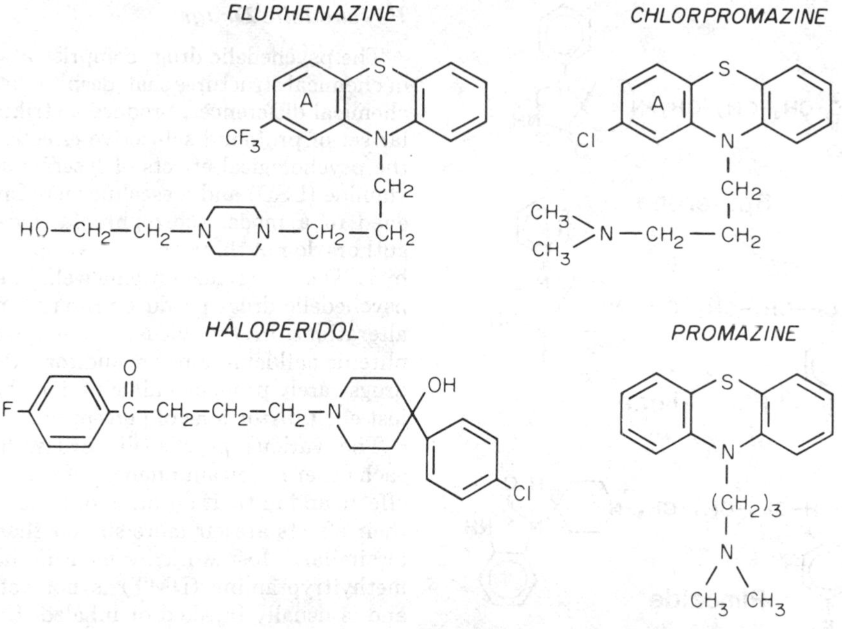

FLUPHENAZINE

CHLORPROMAZINE

HALOPERIDOL

PROMAZINE

FIGURE 7.  Structures of phenothiazines and haloperidol.

Dohme) and trihexiphenidyl (Artane, Lederle) are effective antiparkinsonian agents and block the extrapyramidal effects of neuroleptics. Neuroleptics all have some muscarinic anticholinergic properties. Those neuroleptics with greater anticholinergic potency, such as thioridazine (Mellaril, Sandoz) produce fewer extrapyramidal effects than do the weaker anticholinergics, such as fluphenazine (Prolixin, Squibb) and haloperidol.

The sedative-hypotensive effects of the neuroleptics appear related to blockade of $\alpha$-noradrenergic receptors. Neuroleptics that, at therapeutic doses, block a greater proportion of central $\alpha$-receptors, such as promazine and chlorpromazine, are more sedative-hypotensive than those occupying fewer $\alpha$-receptors, such as haloperidol and fluphenazine.

Patients treated for a long period of time with phenothiazines develop a side effect that seems to be the opposite of the parkinsonian-like side effects of the drugs, namely tardive dyskinesia. Tardive dyskinesia involves a hypermotility of facial muscles and the extremities. Even though tardive dyskinesia follows prolonged phenothiazine treatment, phenothiazines and butyrophenones can relieve these symptoms. This suggests that the mechanism responsible for tardive dyskinesia is an overcompensation of dopamine systems for the dopamine receptor blockade. After prolonged treatment with phenothiazines,

dopamine receptors may become supersensitive to the effects of dopamine.

Despite their clinical utility, neuroleptics are not a panacea in the treatment of schizophrenia. They are most effective in relieving the positive symptoms of schizophrenia, including hallucinations, delusions, and major thought disorders. They are much less effective in dealing with the negative symptoms of schizophrenia, including poverty of speech, affect, and intellectual performance. There has recently been greater interest in these negative symptoms of schizophrenia, which predominate in patients with more severe illness and poor prognosis, sometimes referred to as simple schizophrenics or chronic undifferentiated schizophrenics. The greater interest has stemmed from studies employing pneumoencephalography or computed tomography (CT) scanning that indicate that 20 to 30 percent of schizophrenics have enlarged cerebral ventricles. This subpopulation of schizophrenics displays a preponderance of negative symptoms and a poor prognosis; moreover, these patients also respond poorly to conventional neuroleptics.

Although most phenothiazine and butyrophenone neuroleptics fail to influence markedly negative symptoms of schizophrenia, some neuroleptics of the diphenylbutylpiperidine class, not yet introduced in the United States, do relieve negative symptoms. Examples of the

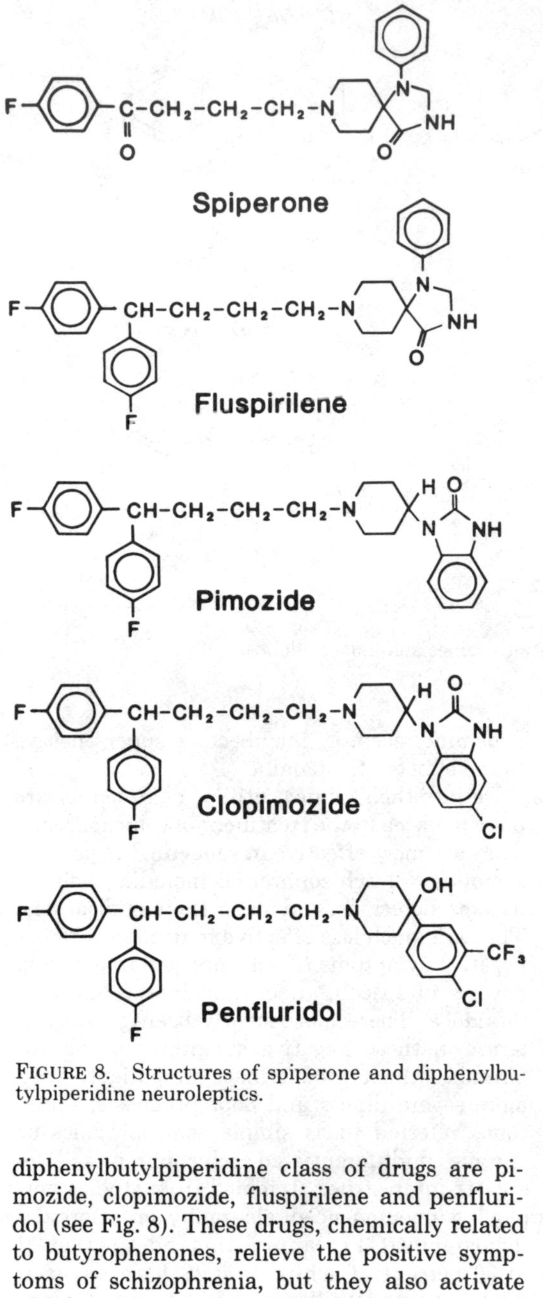

FIGURE 8. Structures of spiperone and diphenylbutylpiperidine neuroleptics.

diphenylbutylpiperidine class of drugs are pimozide, clopimozide, fluspirilene and penfluridol (see Fig. 8). These drugs, chemically related to butyrophenones, relieve the positive symptoms of schizophrenia, but they also activate withdrawn patients, increase socialization, and thus appear to be effective in dealing with the negative symptoms of schizophrenia.

Phenothiazines can be metabolized by a large number of pathways. More than 100 metabolites of chlorpromazine have been reported in the urine. There are wide individual variations in blood levels of chlorpromazine after fixed doses, deriving largely from variable absorption but also from inter-individual differences in drug metabolism.

### Psychedelic Drugs

The psychedelic drugs comprise a wide range of chemical structures that, despite their marked chemical differences, produce a strikingly similar set of profound subjective effects. Although the psychological effects of lysergic acid diethylamide (LSD) and mescaline were initially likened to a model schizophrenia, most current authors do not think that the symptoms elicited by LSD mimic schizophrenia well. For instance, psychedelic drugs produce primarily perceptual alterations in the visual sphere, but schizophrenic hallucinations are auditory. Psychedelic drugs rarely produce hallucinations but usually just elicit distortions of perception.

The various psychedelic drugs differ from each other in certain nuances of their subjective effects and in their duration of action; however, their effects are far more similar than they are dissimilar. Most work by mouth, although dimethyltryptamine (DMT) is not active orally and is usually injected or inhaled. LSD effects persist for about 8 hours; mescaline is a little longer lasting. DMT is the shortest-acting psychedelic drug; its effects persist for only about 1 hour. Certain methoxyamphetamines, such as 2,5-dimethoxy-4-methylamphetamine, or DOM (STP), are less susceptible to metabolism than is mescaline, from which they are derived. They are active in much smaller doses, and their effects continue for long periods, sometimes for as long as 24 hours.

### Antianxiety Agents

The notion of prescribing a sedative drug to reduce emotional tension and promote mild skeletal muscle relaxation is a long-standing one in clinical medicine. Phenobarbital has been a favorite drug for this use since its introduction in the early part of the 20th century. Of the many available barbiturates, phenobarbital seems to be the most valuable drug in this regard, primarily because of its slow onset and long duration of action. Barbiturates with shorter durations of action, such as secobarbital, are better sleeping medications, but are less satisfactory as tranquilizers.

In the early 1950s meprobamate (Miltown, Wallace; Equanil, Wyeth) was introduced as a novel agent to alleviate anxiety without causing sedation (see Fig. 9). It was thought that meprobamate might be less liable to elicit physical dependence and less dangerous in overdoses than barbiturates. Although meprobamate appears not to be as selective in antianxiety effects nor as safe as first projected, the benzodiaze-

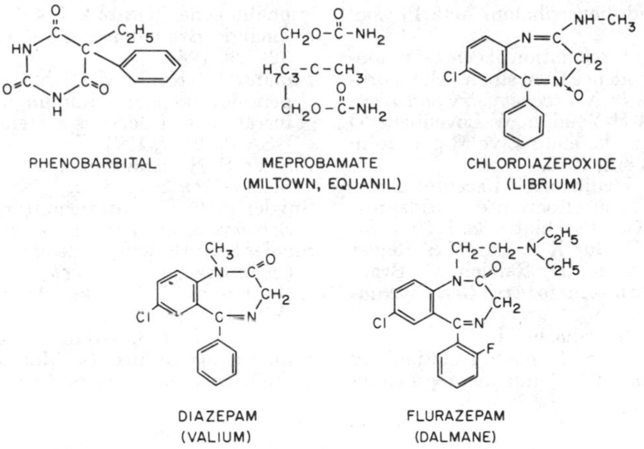

FIGURE 9. Structures of antianxiety drugs.

pines do largely fulfill this promise. In both animal and human studies, they exert selective anxiolytic actions and have very little dependence liability. Even large overdoses are rarely lethal except in combinations with other depressants, such as alcohol. Dependence does occur with benzodiazepines when they are prescribed for a long or indefinite period. When used for a self-limited time to treat a specific anxiety episode, they present minimal addictive danger.

All benzodiazepines exert sedative, antianxiety, muscle relaxant, and anticonvulsant effects.

Pharmacologically, there is considerable overlap of alcohol, barbiturates, meprobamate, chlordiazepoxide, and diazepam. The symptoms of withdrawal from all those drugs are similar, with insomnia, tremulousness, anxiety, convulsions, and a confusional psychosis resembling delirium tremens. For that reason, one can relieve withdrawal symptoms from one drug by the administration of any of the others. Diazepam is highly effective in treating the symptoms of delirium tremens or of barbiturate withdrawal.

Discovery of specific benzodiazepine receptors in the brain has shed light on the mechanisms of benzodiazepine action. The relative potencies of benzodiazepines in competing for binding sites parallels closely their pharmacological activity. Research into benzodiazepine receptors has produced important advances in synaptic biology. This research may have therapeutic relevance in the development of novel, less sedating and possibly less dependence-producing benzodiazepine-like agents.

Pharmacological evidence indicates that benzodiazepines facilitate synaptic actions of the inhibitory neurotransmitter GABA. GABA enhances benzodiazepine receptor binding and various GABA derivatives do this in proportion to their GABA-like synaptic actions. GABA receptors themselves have recognition sites for benzodiazepines whereby benzodiazepines alter GABA receptor-binding activity. Thus, GABA and benzodiazepine recognition sites appear to exist on the same macromolecular receptor protein.

Benzodiazepine receptor research may clarify the differences in antianxiety effects, sedation, muscle relaxation, and anticonvulsant actions elicited by various benzodiazepines. Recently, pharmacological and molecular techniques have distinguished two subtypes of benzodiazepine receptors, type I and type II receptors. In some parts of the brain, type II receptors are associated with nerve endings of GABA neuronal pathways, whereas type I receptors are postsynaptic to GABA synapses and occur on postsynaptic densities within neurons. The most widely employed therapeutic benzodiazepines do not differ markedly in their effects on type I and type II receptors. Some experimental benzodiazepines vary in their effects on the two sites, but is not yet clear to what extent the two subtypes of receptors differentially mediate various drug effects.

The possibility for more effective and safer benzodiazepine related agents represents one of the more exciting aspects of modern molecular psychopharmacology research.

**REFERENCES**

Anden N E, Dahlstrom A, Fuxe K, Larsson K, Olson K, Ungerstedt U: Ascending monoamine neurons to the telencephalon and diencephalon. Acta Physiol Scand *67:* 3131, 1966.

Aghajanian G K: Feedback regulation of central monoaminergic neurons: Evidence from single cell recording studies. In *Essays in Neurochemistry and Neuropharmacology*, M B H Youdim, W Lovenberg, D F Shavman, J R Lagnado, editors, vol 3 p 1. John Wiley & Sons, New York, 1978.

Charney D, Menkes D, Heninger G: Receptor sensitivity and the mechanism of action of antidepressant treatment. Arch Gen Psychiatry *38:* 1160, 1981.

Gur R E, Scholnick B E, Gur R C, Caroff S, Reiger W, Obrist W D, Younkin D, Reivich M: Brain function in psychiatric disorders. *Arch Gen Psychiatry* 41: 695, 1984.

Noda M, Teranishi Y, Takahashi H, Toyosato M, Notake M, Nakanishi S, and Numa S: Isolation and structural organization of the human preproenkephalin gene. Nature *297:* 431, 1982.

Seeman P: Brain dopamine receptors. Pharmacol Rev *32:* 229, 1981.

Simantov R, Kuhar M J, Uhl G R, Snyder S H: Opioid peptide enkephalin: Immunohistochemical mapping in rat central nervous system. Proc Natl Acad Sci USA *74:* 2167, 1977.

Snyder S H: Brain peptides as neurotransmitters. Science *209:* 976, 1980.

Snyder SH: Neurotransmitters and CNS disease: Schizophrenia. The Lancet *2:* 970, 1982.

Snyder S H: Basic Science of psychopharmacology. In *Comprehensive Textbook of Psychiatry*, ed 4, H I Kaplan, B J Sadock, editors, p 42. Williams & Wilkins, Baltimore, 1985.

Tallman J, Paul S, Skolnick P, Gallager D: Receptors for the age of anxiety: Molecular pharmacology of the benzodiazepines. Science *207:* 274, 1980.

# 3

# Science of Human Behavior: Contributions of the Psychological Sciences

## 3.1    PERCEPTION AND COGNITION

### Perception

Perception, according to a generally accepted definition, is the process of organizing and interpreting sensory data by combining them with the results of previous experience. This definition indicates that perception is a complex process involving not only the past as well as the present, but an external stimulus as well as an internal response.

Perception stretches from the biological sciences on one side to the social sciences on the other, and it includes data and ideas from physics and philosophy. The study of perception involves the physical properties of stimuli, the individual's nervous system, his background, and his experiences. The physical properties of stimuli—wavelengths of light, frequencies of sound, and the like—are fundamental in determining the nature of the sensory data. The individual's nervous system is the locus of the sensation and the perception, and its functional strengths and deficiencies relate to what is sensed and what is perceived. The individual's family background, general social milieu, and experiences contribute to his interpretation of the sensory data that he receives.

There are various sensory modalities through which organisms are stimulated, and the sense organ that is stimulated yields only a particular type of sensation. This last point was first enunciated as the doctrine of the specific energy of nerves by Johannes Müller in the 19th century.

A great deal of the work on the influence of the stimulus field in perception has been done in the visual area. This is probably because what is perceived visually is strongly determined by the ordering of the stimulus components in

space, and this ordering is rather easy to manipulate. For example:

****************

is a row of 16 asterisks. By manipulating the spatial relationships, one can enhance the probability that they will be seen as eight pairs of asterisks:

** ** ** ** ** ** ** **

Such situations led to the enunciation of a principle to the effect that the whole is different from the sum of its parts. One explanation of this principle defines stimulus organization, or Gestalt, as an additional property of the stimulus field.

**Individual Development and Experience.** One tends to perceive the more important stimuli rather than the less important. Since the attribute of importance is based on individual experience and interests, two people in the same situation may perceive very different things, and yet both may be accurate. What each perceives is a function of his own learning and experience. For example, the letter A would simply be a collection of lines to someone who does not know how to read.

An experience that predisposes an individual to certain types of perceptions is called a set. The more ambiguous the stimulus, the more its perception is determined by the set or proclivities of the subject. And, the stronger the set of the individual, the more it determines his perception. The meaning attributed to a particular stimulus by an individual is a function of the ambiguity of the stimulus and the strength of his set.

The major application of these principles in psychiatry has been in projective testing, in which ambiguous stimuli are presented to individuals, and their responses are analyzed in terms of their emphasis and patterning. Extrapolated from this analysis is a description of the individual's personality in terms of his perceptual proclivities. Perhaps the best known projective test is the Rorschach test, a collection of 10 inkblots.

The needs of the individual influence the content of what is perceived. Overall psychological needs, as well as immediate physical needs, influence perception. The Thematic Apperception Test (TAT) is based on this proposition. The stimuli for this test consist of pictures of people in various situations. The situations are ambiguous enough to allow for a variety of interpretations. The subject is asked to tell a story about each picture, and his story is interpreted in terms of his particular needs and drives.

Many experiments have indicated that people can be influenced in their own perceptual judgments by the judgments of others. The degree of influence depends on the consistency of others' judgments, the status of the other judges, and the expertise attributed to them.

Much of perception is learned behavior. A series of studies of people who were blind from birth and who, at varying ages, underwent successful surgery for the removal of cataracts demonstrated that they had great difficulty in perceiving objects, and even greater difficulty in distinguishing one object from another. Most of the young subjects were able to acquire adequate visual perception with time and practice, but many of the older subjects sustained an apparently permanent visual handicap.

**Psychopathology and Perception.** If the motivational and need states of the organism influence his perception of his environment, it follows that psychopathological disturbance will have a profound effect on perceptual functioning. An individual who has a pathological fear or need to avoid certain categories of people or experience can be expected to block out perception of threatening stimuli.

The relationship between perception and psychopathology is a fruitful area for further psychiatric study.

## Cognition

Cognition is the process of knowing and becoming aware of perceptions, and ordering these perceptions into concepts and broader abstractions.

Cognition develops in interaction with the circumstances of the individual's life, proceeding from the more concrete to the more abstract. When any part of man's symbolic language system is impaired, as by psychopathology, his thinking or problem-solving process is adversely

affected. Indeed, disturbed thought processes characterize most forms of mental illness. Through analysis of these thought processes, much insight can be gained into the nature of the individual's pathology and, by extrapolation from many such studies, into the nature of various types of disturbance.

Studies of thought processes and methods of problem-solving in the nondisturbed individual also yield information that relates to personality organization and type. One aspect of individual differences lies in the capacity to solve problems, a capacity sometimes referred to as intelligence.

In a sense, cognition includes recognition, recall, and symbolization (labeling). Implied in these skills is the development of the individual in interaction with his environment.

## Language

Language may be considered the currency of cognition, at least for humans: we manipulate objects symbolically by labeling them.

**Verbal Mediators.** Adding language to apparently nonlinguistic problems facilitates their solution. For example, when labels are given to nonsense figures, it takes less time to learn their sequence. Similarly, when prepositions are interjected between pairs of words that are to be learned, the number of repetitions needed to learn them decreases. For example, if the subject is to learn to say "table" after the experimenter says "hat," he learns the association faster if he adds "on the" to himself; "hat on the table" is learned faster than simply "hat . . . table."

**Acquisition of Language.** Language and its forms come to the child from his environment. He learns to speak the language of the people who surround him, even though his capacity for language learning and use are a part of his biological endowment. If language plays a major role in thought, and if language is environmentally stimulated and its content environmentally determined, then it follows that environmental stimulation has much to do with thought. A child who is reared in a largely nonverbal environment may be perfectly capable of learning as fast as a more privileged child, but without the verbal facility he may be handicapped in the solution of many different types of problems.

**Use of Language.** It has been concluded that the kinds of occupational, social, and environmental conditions that go along with certain social class levels describe the type of verbal behavior seen in people. Lower class families tend to show restrictive speech codes, and middle class families tend to speak in elaborated codes. The two speech types differ from each other in the complexity of syntax, sentence length, richness of vocabulary, and several other categories. The middle class groups have, therefore, a means for expressing more complicated thoughts.

Mothers who speak in restricted codes are likely to be status-oriented in their relationships with their children, but mothers with more elaborated speech codes tend to be person-oriented. The status-oriented mother disciplines her child in terms of "because I say so." The person-oriented mother is more likely to give reasons for actions and for discipline that are within the child's experience and his own motivations.

### Development of Cognition

Many theorists define a series of stages in cognitive growth. Usually, these theories indicate that one stage grows out of the next and that the stages follow a certain invariable sequence. Most, but not all, of the theories include the supposition that each stage expands on and replaces the prior one, although there can be vestigial remnants.

**Piaget's Theories.** A major theorist in this regard is Jean Piaget, a Swiss psychologist whose exhaustive and ingenious observations of his own three children provided the foundation for an elaborate developmental theory with cognitive development at its base.

According to Piaget, during the entire developmental period, the child is involved in building schemata, or organizations of behaviors relevant to each other. The child's responses to the world are made up of schemata, though not exclusively. Schemata are acquired by the dual process of assimilation and accommodation. The first refers to the introjection of knowledge about the environment, which is then incorporated into the child's existing body of knowledge. In this incorporation, the existing body is modified somewhat to accommodate the new elements: this modification is termed accommodation.

In the first developmental period, the sensorimotor stage, the infant first responds to his environment in an undifferentiated manner. Later in this stage he displays a relatively coherent organization of sensory-motor actions vis-à-vis his immediate environment.

In the next stage, the preoperational thought period, the child first begins to understand and use symbols, although he is able to do so only in unitary ways; double classifications elude him. For example, he can understand that a particular person can be Johnny's mother, but he is unable to see the same person as Mary's teacher. By the end of the preoperational stage, the child is able to think in terms of classes, see relationships, and handle number concepts.

The stage of concrete operations includes increasing ability to handle numbers, development of a real logic, and ability to relate external events to each other, independent of the self. The child can now classify the same person or object along more than one dimension.

The last developmental stage that Piaget defines is the period of formal operations, from about 11 to about 15 years. The child develops true abstract thought and is able to make hypotheses and test them logically.

**Stimulation and Cognition.** The concept that intelligence is determined by the operation of internal processes, presumably genetically determined, is controversial. Some theorists still hold to portions of it, but the majority view intelligence as a function that develops in the relationship between the individual and his environment, that draws on various tools such as language, and that grows or declines as a consequence of environmental encounters.

There is evidence that, in the absence of special intervention, children in a nonstimulating environment show a drop in intelligence test scores.

### Psychopathology and Cognition

**Comparisons with Children and Primitives.** The fact that children, patients with brain damage, and those with various forms of psychopathology are all concrete in their thought processes, has tempted many theorists to compare the latter clinical groups to developing children. Cross-cultural studies, too, at times relate primitive concrete thought to the concretism found in children in our culture. Some workers label all these comparisons false. They point out that there is an essential difference between the concretism of the developing child and the regression to concretism that characterizes the disturbed or organically impaired adult. The primitive man lives in a world to which he is admirably adjusted; the pathological individual tries to adjust himself by means of primitive behavior to a world for him inadequate and nonprimitive.

**Schizophrenic Cognition.** There is a voluminous literature on thought processes in mental disease. The only point of agreement has been the conviction that schizophrenic thought is somehow different from normal thought.

Research has indicated that schizophrenics are not necessarily unable to form concepts, and that the concepts which they form are not significantly concrete or infantile. Rather, schizophrenics may be concerned with bizarre and personal concepts that they are unwilling to communicate or that they communicate in a private language. Other theorists have demonstrated that schizophrenic concept-formation ability can be raised to a normal level by decreasing the number of distracting stimuli.

Schizophrenics have often been observed to include irrelevant and extraneous factors in their response to a conceptual task. Such a phenomenon has been explained on the basis of a schizophrenic inability to select only those stimuli that are relevant to the task being performed. However, schizophrenics, including the chronic population, have performed normally on a variety of conceptual tasks when time pressure and distractions are eliminated, and when cues and motivation are increased.

### Memory

Experimental studies of memory indicate that what is remembered is related to the experience that intervenes between the initial learning and the recall. The closer in nature that the intervening experience is to the learning situation, the more interference there is with the initial learning and with recall.

Accuracy of memory varies also with the method used to test it. The most difficult circumstance in which to remember something is in response to an open-ended question that gives no information itself; for instance, "Name the rivers of Africa." If one were asked to name four rivers in Africa that begin with the letter N, the task would be easier.

There are also differences between immediate memory, and memory for events that occurred in the more distant past. The senile person has a much superior memory for remote events than for recent events.

Certain drugs apparently enhance or interfere with memory functions. Scopolamine, for example, causes forgetfulness and amnesia. The neurochemical aspects of learning and memory are described in detail in Section 3.3 on learning theory.

### REFERENCES

Broadbent D E: *Decision and Stress.* Academic Press, New York, 1971.
Chapman L J, Chapman J P: *Disordered Thought in Schizophrenics.* Appleton-Century-Crofts, New York, 1973.
Lindsay P H, Norman D A: *Human Information Processing,* ed. 2. Academic Press, New York, 1977.
Kietzman M L, Sutton S, Zubin J: *Experimental Approaches to Psychopathology.* Academic Press, New York, 1975.
Kietzman M L, Zubin J, Steinhauer S: Information processing in psychopathology. In *Perspectives in Psychological Experimentation: Towards the Year 2000,* V Sarris, A Parducci, editors. Erlbaum Associates, Hillsdale, NJ, 1983.
Kietzman M L, Spring B, Zubin J: Perception, cognition, and information processing. In *Comprehensive Textbook of Psychiatry,* ed 4, H I Kaplan, B J Sadock, editors, p 157. Williams & Wilkins, Baltimore, 1985.
Magaro P A: *Cognition in Schizophrenia and Paranoia: The Integration of Cognitive Processes.* Erlbaum Associates, Hillsdale NJ, 1980.
Nuechterlein K H: Reaction time and attention in schizophrenics: a critical evaluation of the data and theories. Schizophr Bull *3:*373, 1977.
Zubin J, Magaziner J, Steinhauer S R: The metamorphosis of schizophrenia: from chronicity to vulnerability. Psychol Med *13:*551–571, 1983.

## 3.2    JEAN PIAGET

### Introduction

Jean Piaget (1896–1980) is the Swiss psychologist whose discoveries concerning children's thinking have earned him a permanent place among the first rank of psychologists and social scientists (see Fig. 1). Like Freud, Piaget and his work have had effects outside the boundaries of social science. In fields such as chemistry, physics, mathematics, and philosophy, Piaget's work is well known and is being applied, particularly in designing new curriculums for high school and college courses in these subjects. Jean

FIGURE 1.   Jean Piaget. (By permission of the Jean Piaget Society, Temple University, Philadelphia.)

Piaget has shown that developmental psychology is a true science, because it has significance for many different domains of research investigation.

## Piaget's Theory

The first and perhaps the most important of Piaget's premises is that human intelligence is an extension, albeit at a higher level, of biological adaptation. Second, Piaget argued that adaptation—at whatever level of organization, from protozoa to humans—has a logical substructure. And, third he assumed that human intelligence evolves in a series of stages that are related to age. At each successive stage, intellectual adaptation is more general and shows a higher level of logical organization than at the previous stages.

**Intelligence as Biological Adaptation.** Piaget insisted on the continuity between biological and psychological processes of adaptation, arguing that the processes of adaptation are the same from the lowliest organisms to the highest. Far from being reductionistic, however, Piaget's theory is a testimony to the extraordinary complexity of even the simplest biological adaptation.

It is in this respect that Piaget's position differed from that of much of psychological learning theory. Though learning theory also postulates a continuity between biological and psychological processes of adaptation, these processes are seen as elementary connections between measurable behaviors and stimuli. Piaget, however, viewed the stimulus and the response as abstractions made for the benefit of the investigator. These abstractions are constructed by the child's mental activity, and they cannot be defined objectively and without reference to the child's own mental activity.

Central to Piaget's theories is an understanding of epigenesis, of which he advocated a sophisticated version. In biology, epigenesis is the position that growth and development are not preformed but, rather, are sequentially created. At each stage in development, the preceding structure writes the program for the next succeeding structure.

Piaget's was a sophisticated epigenesis because he went beyond a descriptive acceptance of the concept and tried to understand its mode of operation. For Piaget, however, neither biological nor psychological answers sufficed; in his view, behavioral adaptations result in phenocopies or translations into the genetic programs that make possible a kind of selection at the genetic level that parallels selection at the behavioral level. This internal selection process, triggered by the organisms behavioral adaptations, helps to account for behavioral progress.

**Logical Substructure of Behavior and Knowledge.** For Piaget, knowledge was first and foremost human. Whether the discipline is mathematics or sociology, the accumulation of information is carried on by human minds. If there is a unity to human knowledge, therefore, it must be sought not in the resulting knowledge—although that can provide guidelines—but in the processes of human knowing. It is when one looks at the processes involved in constructing knowledge that one begins to discern the unity of the sciences.

Regarding knowledge, Piaget was a structuralist. He argued that, in any domain of human knowledge, one can find three principles in operation—wholeness, self-regulations, and transformations. In Piaget's view these characteristics hold true both for human thought and for the various disciplines of knowledge. This parallelism is not accidental or fortuitous, but a direct consequence of the fact that any system of knowledge must reflect, in some ways, the intellectual system of those who created it.

*Wholeness.* The structures or systems that characterize human knowledge, as well as human thinking, are organized wholes. Piaget distinguished between a whole and an aggregate. Although the aggregate is a mere collection of parts, the whole has parts that are dynamically related one to the other.

*Transformation.* What distinguishes wholes from aggregates is that the system can undergo transformations without losing its identity. If, for example, the population of people eating at a restaurant changes, the aggregate changes as well: the group eating there one day has no systematic relationship to the group eating there the next day. In contrast, the kinship group remains a group, even after they have dispersed: spatial transformations do not destroy the group's wholeness. A true whole embodies principles of transformation that permit changes to occur within the system that do not, at the same time, destroy the system.

*Self-regulation.* The third property of structured wholes is that of self-regulation. This means that the transformations that characterize a whole are such as to keep the system intact. Although the transformations permit changes to occur, they do not permit changes that would produce new elements that could not be incorporated into the system. Piaget argued that self-regulation takes many different forms in different disciplines; and his structuralism made patent the parallelism between the structures of knowledge and the structures of knowing.

### Stages in the Development of Intelligence

In his extensive studies of children's thinking, Piaget found four major stages leading to the attainment of adult thought, each stage a necessary prerequisite for the one that follows. Similarly, each stage is characterized by a system of operations that has the characteristics of all true structures—namely, wholeness, transformation, and self-regulation.

**Sensorimotor Period (Birth to 2 Years).** The critical achievement of this period is the construction of object concepts. To the adult, objects such as balls, cars, houses, and other people have an existence that is independent of the adult's own immediate experience. The adult believes that objects are there, even though he is not able to see them. This belief is not innate; it could hardly have been part of his biological heritage. Nor was the idea simply learned, because object permanence is not taught.

Objects and one's sense of their permanence are constructed during the first year or so of life by the progressive coordination of sensorimotor schemata—elementary concepts—that result from the infant's actions on the world and from his or her growing mental abilities and motor skills. For example, as children gain better control over their heads, eyes, and hands, they can begin to coordinate touching and seeing. They can begin to look at objects they touch, and touch objects they see. In this way, they begin to coordinate visual and tactile schemata to form elaborate object concepts that are both seeable and touchable.

As the infant becomes more mobile, he or she can elaborate new schemata as the spatial, visual, and tactile world expands. In addition, new motor and mental abilities permit new and more elaborate coordinations. Such attempts reflect not only a beginning sense of objects and their relations, but also a sense of intentionality. By the end of the first year, the child's sense of objects as permanent has advanced to the point at which he or she will look for them even when they are hidden.

Toward the end of the second year of life, the child's object world is fairly well elaborated, as is the sensorimotor system of intelligence. The structural nature of this system is reflected in the infant's behavior. When the child touches one object to get another, these actions are part of an organized whole and are not random, isolated acts. Likewise, at the end of the second year, the infant can look for and find an object that was displaced two times. The concealment and the displacements are transformations, and the young infant's ability to deal with these

transformations is indicative of the fact that his or her mental system is a transformed one.

Self-regulation is also evident in the child's behavior vis-à-vis objects. Indeed, the 2-year-old's ability to follow a double displacement indicates that the child sees the act of hiding the object as reversible. This is evidence that his or her mental system has the characteristic of self-regulation.

One consequence of the construction of object permanence has to do with the development of attachment. The attachment of a child to a parent presupposes object permanence: the object will continue to exist when it is no longer present to the senses. True attachment to parents apparently does not happen until the last trimester of the first year of life.

A second consequence of the construction of object permanence has to do with the child's self-concept. Just as the infant begins to construct object concepts, so does he or she construct a concept of the self as object. This object self is primarily a body self, consisting of the parts of the body the child can see, activate, and manipulate.

**Preoperational Stage.** During the second year of life, children begin to give evidence of having attained a new, higher order level of mental functioning that manifests wholeness, transformations, and self-regulation at a higher level. These characteristics are shown not only in the child's language but in his or her play, dreams, and imitative behavior as well. These behaviors are symbolic: they are processes by which the child re-presents objects and activities in their absence. The attainment of object permanence, which involves representation of an imaginary variety, marks the transition from sensorimotor to preoperational or intuitive intelligence.

The progressive elaboration of language offers one example of the structures of the period. With respect to wholeness, the young child's verbal utterances quickly begin to show grammatical regularities that suggest that they are not generated at random. After the child's initial one-word utterances, his two-word utterances are usually noun-verb or noun-adjective constructions. These utterances also reflect transformations in the sense that the child can substitute words in his or her constructions. A child may say "Bobby up" and "Bobby eat." Self-regulation is shown by the fact that the child's new linguistic constructions, such as the words children make up, are speakable within the language system that he or she is operating in.

Children's play during the period shows the same features, and transformations are also in evidence. Self-regulation is evident in the limited range of play variations that children allow themselves to engage in.

Children at this stage have a system of mental regulations and functions that anticipate a true logical system. Functions operate much as do the functions of arithmetic: things are represented in terms of their functions.

From a clinical point of view, the preoperational period bears witness to the constructions of a symbolic self. The child symbolizes not only the world but also the self. "Me" and "mine" and the child's name become a powerful foci of feelings and emotion. Like the body self constructed in infancy, the symbolic self constructed in early childhood is distorted. The boundaries are unclear, as are the functions of self vis-à-vis the functions of others.

In addition, the modes of thinking at this stage—phenomenalistic causality (events that happen together cause one another), animism, and nominal realism (belief that words partake of the object or quality they represent)—pertain to the self as well. The symbolic self has loose boundaries and has a closer participation with the immediate world than is true for adults. The young child feels more at the mercy of external forces and also feels that he or she has more control over them than is true at later stages of development.

**Concrete Operational Stage.** Toward the age of 5 or 6, children give evidence of having attained another, higher level system of mental structures that Piaget called concrete operations. These operations resemble, in their mode of functioning, the operations of arithmetic. Concrete operations enable children to engage in syllogistic reasoning, which in turn permits them to acquire and to follow rules. In addition, concrete operations enable young people to construct unit concepts (a unit, such as a number, is both like and different from every other number) and thus to quantify their experience. This period of development is characterized by the construction of what may be called the lawful world.

Concrete operations also manifest the characteristics of wholeness, transformation, and self-regulation; indeed, in concrete operations these characteristics are prominent.

The child at the concrete operational stage arrives at a concept of a lawful self as one who can make and follow rules. Children who become overly invested in this facet of themselves may show obsessive-compulsive symptoms, whereas children who resist this facet often seem willful and immature. The most desirable outcome is for the child to develop a healthy respect for rules but to come to understand that there are legitimate exceptions.

**Formal Operational Period.** At about the age of 11 or 12, most children begin to give evidence of having attained a new system of mental structures that Piaget called formal operations. Formal operations are not as universally attained as are concrete operations. The formal operations are more abstract than are the concrete operations and, in effect, constitute a second-order system that operates on the first. Whereas concrete operations enable children to reason about things, formal operations enable young people to reason about reasoning or thinking.

Because formal operational thought is, to a considerable extent, freed from content, it can soar. With formal operations young people can conceive of ideal worlds, ideal people, and many possible careers. An ideal, by definition, does not take concrete limitations into account and assume that they do not exist. Formal operations thus account for the idealism of youth, for their intellectualism, and for their capacity to reflect on their own and other people's thinking.

Formal operations, like the other systems of mental structures, show the characteristics of wholeness, transformation, and self-regulation, but at a higher, more abstract level. Formal operations make possible the construction of a reflective self, and enables young people to distinguish between the ideal self and the real self, both facets of this reflective self.

## REFERENCES

Ginsburg H: Jean Piaget. In *Comprehensive Textbook of Psychiatry*, ed 4, H I Kaplan, V B J Sadock, editors, p 178. Williams & Wilkins, Baltimore, 1985.

Ginsburg H, Opper S: *Piaget's Theory of Intellectual Development.* ed 2. Prentice-Hall, Englewood Cliffs, NJ, 1979.

Liben L: *Piaget and the Foundations of Knowledge.* Erlbaum Associates, Hillsdale, NJ, 1983.

Piaget J: *The Grasp of Consciousness.* Harvard University Press. Cambridge, MA, 1976.

Piaget J: *Judgment and Reasoning in the Child.* Harcourt. New York, 1926.

Piaget J: *The Language and Thought of the Child.* Routledge and Kegan Paul, London, 1926.

Piaget J: *The Moral Judgment of the Child.* Harcourt Brace and World. New York, 1932.

Piaget J: *The Origins of Intelligence in Children.* International Universities Press, New York, 1952.

Piaget J: *Play, Dreams, and Imitation in Childhood.* W. W. Norton. New York, 1951.

## 3.3     LEARNING THEORY

### Introduction

Basic to every form of behavioral interaction—therapy and teaching in particular—is the concept that a change takes place in the person's behavior and that this change is, in large measure, a result of learning. What factors contribute to the success of learning as a behavioral change, and how they can be measured, improved, and applied, have become crucial enterprises for researchers and clinicians.

Learning is a change in behavior that results from practice, with learning representing an intervening process or variable that links organismic states before and after a change in behavior occurs. The definition of learning always assumes a permanent change in behavior, excluding changes resulting from such factors as maturation, sensory adaptation, and fatigue.

The central question has always been that of differentiating learning from performance. The organism may acquire capabilities to perform some act through learning, but the act itself may not occur. Thus, *learning* refers to long-term changes of the organism produced by practice, whereas *performance* refers to translation of learning into behavior. Practice alone does not produce learning; it is necessary for some maintaining event to occur. It is necessary to add reinforcement, which is any event, contingent upon the response of the organism, that alters the future likelihood of this response.

Learning, then, may be defined as a change in behavior potential, resulting from reinforced practice. Reinforcement, as so considered, becomes an example of an empirical law of effect that is basic to much of contemporary learning theory. The law of effect, as stated by Thorndike, says that acts followed by a situation which the individual does not avoid, and which he often tries to preserve or attain, are selected and fixated, while acts followed by situations which the individual avoids or attempts to change are eliminated. Rewarded responses are always strengthened, but punished responses do not always diminish in strength. There is thus an emphasis on reward as a primary determinant of behavior.

### Conditioning

Most theorists accept a rough dichotomy between two types of conditioning: classical (Pavlovian) and instrumental (operant). Attempts to explore the interactions between these two types of conditioning have shown potential relationships, but the differences in procedure existing in the two approaches is emphasized.

**Classical Conditioning.** Ivan Pavlov (see Fig. 1) the Russian physiologist, observed in his work with gastric secretions in dogs that stimuli that were often present at the time the dogs were offered food came to evoke salivation in the animals, even in the absence of food. For example, the footsteps of the experimenter as he entered the room came to evoke salivation in dogs, even though the dogs could not see or smell food. Pavlov assumed that the stimulus of the footsteps came to be associated with food. His research was directed toward an analysis of this event, which he called the "conditional reflex"—the reflex that would occur, given certain conditions—later somewhat mistranslated as the more familiar "conditioned reflex" or "conditioned response."

In a typical Pavlovian experiment, a stimulus that, before training, had no capacity to evoke a particular type of response, becomes able to do so. For example, under normal circumstances, a bell sounded near an animal probably does no more than evoke exploration, such as a turning of the head toward the sound or, perhaps at most, a startle response. Also, under normal circumstances, a hungry animal may be expected to salivate in the presence of food. Pavlov's conditioned reflex experiment was a training experiment in which the previously neutral

FIGURE 1.   Ivan Pavlov (1849–1936).

stimulus of a bell was made, by pairing it with the food, to evoke the response of salivation, which it normally would not do. To diagram this:

*Preconditioning:* $S \rightarrow R$
(bell) (exploration)
$S \rightarrow R$
(food) (salivation)
*Conditioning:* $S$ (bell) $\rightarrow S$ (food) $\rightarrow$
$R$ (salivation)

Bell sounds are followed by the presentation of food. The animal salivates at the sight of the food and ultimately pairs $S$ (bell) and $S$ (food).

*Postconditioning:* $S$ (bell) $\rightarrow R$(exploration)
conditioned
$S$ (food) $\rightarrow R$ (salivation)
(unconditioned stimulus)
(unconditioned response)

Because the food naturally produces salivation, it is referred to as an unconditioned stimulus. Because the bell was originally unable to evoke salivation but came to do so when paired with food, it is referred to as a conditioned stimulus.

*Stimulus Generalization and Discrimination.* In the process of conditioning, Pavlov noted that animals would respond to stimuli similar to the stimulus to which they were conditioned. This event, noted by other experimenters, was called by Thorndike "response by analogy" and by Pavlov "generalization."

Generalization is at the basis of higher learning, inasmuch as it is possible through stimulus generalization to learn similarities. For example, one need not learn individual street sign characteristics (on a curb, on a pole, on a building). There is sufficient stimulus similarity in such events to allow for generalization to occur. However, for a balance in learning, stimulus discrimination must also occur. To learn differentiation of similar stimuli is also the beginning of higher learning. For example, a child may refer to any quadruped as "doggie," but he learns to discriminate among quadrupeds so that he can differentiate a dog, from a cow, from a cat, and ultimately, as finer discrimination occurs, a boxer, from a beagle, from a basset.

A good deal of disordered behavior illustrates problems of this balance between generalization and discrimination. A patient may have negative affective reactions to a person with a moustache, presumably based on a traumatic earlier experience. To have a faulty generalization to all men with moustaches shows that discrimination training, presumably in therapeutic experience, has not been successful.

In sum, learning becomes a balance of generalization and discrimination, with conditioning leading to generalization of similar stimuli to the one conditioned, and with discrimination leading to an extinction of responses to those stimuli similar to the original, but not the actual conditioned stimulus.

**Instrumental Conditioning.** In contrast to classical conditioning, in which the organism is usually restrained—in a Pavlovian harness, for example—and in which the response is elicited by the experimenter, instrumental conditioning is an experimental technique in which a freely moving organism emits behavior that is instrumental in producing a reward. For instance, a cat in a Thorndike puzzle box must learn to lift a latch in order to escape from the box; a monkey in an experimental chair must press a lever to effect the presentation of food.

Sanford listed four kinds of instrumental conditioning, which are outlined in Table I.

Generally, it is assumed that most learning occurs as a result of instrumental responding, rather than as an elicited consequence of classical conditioning. But both classical and instrumental conditioning techniques have begun to occupy a central place in the theoretical and practical behaviors of a growing group of clinicians who consider their methods to be clearly based on experimental laboratory procedures, therapists who derive their techniques and principles from learning theory as based in the laboratory. The clinicians—represented by such theorists as Mowrer, Wolpe, and the followers of methods developed by Skinner—refer to themselves as "behavior therapists," "learning therapists," and "conditioning therapists," such appellations being virtually interchangeable and synonymous.

## Hull's Learning Theory

Hull sought to establish a theory of behavior, which he equated with learning, that could be quantified and tested in accordance with scientific method. He described the learning process this way: "Just as the inherited equipment of reaction tendencies consists of receptor-effector connections, so the process of learning consists in the strengthening of certain of these connections as contrasted with others, or in the setting up of quite new connections." These connections occurred internally and were mediated by nervous system stimulation. The establishment of a connection occurs as:

$$S \rightarrow s \rightarrow r \rightarrow R$$

An external stimulus, $S$, has as its function the stimulation of an efferent system, $s$, which, in

TABLE I
FOUR KINDS OF INSTRUMENTAL CONDITIONING

| | |
|---|---|
| 1. Primary reward conditioning | Simplest kind of conditioning. The learned response is instrumental in obtaining a biologically significant reward, such as a pellet of food or a drink of water |
| 2. Escape conditioning | The organism learns a response that is instrumental in getting him out of some place he prefers not to be |
| 3. Avoidance conditioning | The kind of learning in which a response to a cue is instrumental in avoiding a painful experience. A rat on a grid, for example, may avoid a shock if he quickly pushes a lever when a light signal goes on |
| 4. Secondary reward conditioning | The kind of learning in which there is instrumental behavior to get at a stimulus which has no biological utility itself but which has in the past been associated with a biologically significant stimulus. For example, chimpanzees will learn to press a lever to obtain poker chips, which they insert in a slot to secure grapes. Later they will work to accumulate poker chips even when they are not interested in grapes |

turn, effects a motor impulse, $r$, within the nervous system. The final response, external $R$, does not have to occur for learning to take place. The critical connection is the $s$-$r$ connection, leading to a habit.

**Habit Family Hierarchy.** The habit, for Hull, is an established connection within the nervous system, but these connections are not limited. The concept of the habit family hierarchy allows for the transfer of learning or generalization to occur. Thus, a given stimulus, $S$, may evoke a number of different responses in varying levels of strength, but this stimulus evokes a response or set of responses within the nervous system that anticipates a goal response. For Hull, the goal response is antedated by fractional responses in the establishment of a habit. The fractional response then becomes a mediating element between $S$ and $R$. An example of this is salivation occurring before the consummatory goal response to eating.

**Hull's Concept of Drive.** Thorndike's law of effect used the concept of satisfaction to account for reinforcing effects of certain responses. Hull, however, stated that attaining the goal response reduces the drive associated with the aroused need, strenghtening the behaviors that led to the reduction in tension. This strengthened sequence becomes the habit.

**Inhibition.** Hull postulated that neural impulses (afferent receptor discharges) "occurring at about the same time interact and so modify each other." He called this afferent interaction, and viewed it as a basis for the reduction or elimination of a response through the presence of an extra or foreign stimulus in a conditioned stimulus compound, which can reduce the excitatory potential. An example is the interference of "irrelevant stimulations resulting from an emotional upset" that may disrupt a child's classroom performance.

Hull saw this as equivalent to Pavlov's external inhibition. Pavlov's concept of internal inhibition is similar to Hull's conditioned inhibition, which resulted from reactive inhibition, a negative drive state similar to fatigue or physiological impairment resulting from activity. Hull's conditioned inhibition is an interfering set of events.

Thus, Hullian learning theory was largely based on neurophysiological postulates and concerned itself with drive and drive reduction as basic to reinforcement.

**Wolpe's Conditioning Theory**

In 1950, Wolpe defined neurotic behavior as behavior that "consists of persistent habits of learned (conditioned) unadaptive behavior acquired in anxiety-generating situations." It is no coincidence that Wolpe invoked the term "habit" to describe neurotic behavior in this regard. The Hullian influence becomes clear again in the light of Wolpe's observation about anxiety responses; namely, that they necessarily produce anxiety drive (with concomitant central neural excitation) as an antecedent. Wolpe also reflected this neural approach to learning when he noted that learning is subserved by the development of conductivity between adjoining neurons. Here one sees the Hullian concepts of learning as being mediated by central nervous system activity, the neurophysiological basis of drive, and anxiety as a drive leading, presumably, to activity at drive reduction.

**Reciprocal Inhibition.** Wolpe also reflected a Hullian orientation in his important principle of reciprocal inhibition, which may account for anxiety drive reduction. This principle states that if a response inhibitory to anxiety can be instigated in the presence of anxiety-evoking stimuli, it will weaken the connection between these stimuli and the anxiety responses. Relaxation, for example, is considered to be incompatible with anxiety and, therefore, inhibitory to it.

**Anxiety Hierarchy.** Wolpe also used Hull's concept of habit family hierarchy in an interesting clinical fashion when he established anxiety hierarchy relationships among anxiety-evoking stimuli. Assuming that varying stimuli may evoke the response of anxiety, Wolpe asked his patient to imagine, usually under hypnosis, the least disturbing item of a list of potentially anxiety-evoking stimuli, then to proceed up the list to the most disturbing stimuli. For example, a patient with a fear of death might rank the sight of a coffin lower in the hierarchy then a corpse (highest intensity), with perhaps a tombstone ranked somewhere in between.

Wolpe's technique of desensitization is a counterconditioning technique in which responses designed to inhibit the anxiety response are evoked at each level along the hierarchy. Reciprocal inhibition of the fear response is thus conditioned.

FIGURE 2. B. F. Skinner.

### Skinner's Learning Theory: Operant Conditioning

Proponents of an experimental analysis of behavior based on operant conditioning techniques and reinforcement theorists form a group of behaviorists who tend largely to minimize theoretical considerations and to concentrate on an analysis of the functional relationships among events. For example, instead of dealing with the represssion of unacceptable thoughts, as psychoanalysts do, Skinner (see Fig. 2) suggested that it is more important to avoid the inner causes and to emphasize the questions that ask why the response surfaced in the first place, why it was punished, and what current variables are active.

The term "operant" refers to a class of responses that is emitted by the organism, rather than elicited by some known stimulus. Operant responses are also frequently referred to by such terms as "voluntary," as opposed to "involuntary" or reflex behavior. Reflex responses are elicited as in classicial conditioning and are called "respondents." Thus, respondents, such as pupillary reflexes, are differentiated from operants. An example of an operant response is reaching for a telephone.

Skinner differentiated two types of conditioning, which he called type $S$ and type $R$. Type $S$ conditioning "is defined by the operation of the simultaneous presentation of the reinforcing stimulus and another stimulus."

In type $R$ conditioning, the reinforcing stimulus "is contingent upon a response." This distinction between classical (respondent, involuntary, type $S$) and instrumental (operant, voluntary, type $R$) conditioning is not entirely accepted by many learning theorists, on the grounds that the criteria are too ambiguous. Psychophysiological interactions, for example, are not clearly differentiated into operant and respondent.

**Reinforcement.** A key concept in operant conditioning is that of reinforcement. In operant conditioning the term "positive reinforcement" is used to describe an event consequent upon a response that increases the probability of this response recurring. A "negative reinforcement" is an event likely to decrease the probability of this response's recurrence. A negative reinforcement is an event that strengthens the response that removes it; for example, if a punishing consequence attaches to a response, any behavior that avoids or escapes the punishment will be strengthened—that is, increased in probability.

**Response Frequency.** Another important concept is the use of response frequency as a basic formulation. The frequency with which a response is emitted is a clear, observable measure of behavior. Skinner observed that personality descriptions are couched in frequency terms; to say that a person is "an enthusiastic skier," "an inveterate gambler," or "hostile" reduces to a statement of a perceived frequency with which a certain class of behavior is emitted, presumably with some normative conceptualization in mind. Aggressive behavior is emitted by most people; to say that a person is hostile suggests that this class of response occurs with a higher level of frequency than is usually expected.

**Shaping Behavior.** A fundamental concept in operant conditioning is that of shaping, by which the experimenter, having specified the response he desires from the organism, successfully brings the organism closer to the chosen terminal behavior. In establishing this behavior, he begins with the mass of responses available to the organism he is manipulating. By clearly defining the terminal response, the experimenter must then identify the steps by which this terminal response will be shaped. By successive approximation—that is, leading the organism to the desired behavior—shaping occurs.

For example, if an experimenter wishes a pigeon to peck at a translucent plastic key on a wall of an experimental box, he most likely starts by reinforcing the pigeon for facing the particular wall on which the key lies. Then he reinforces the pigeon when he moves toward the wall, when he ultimately pecks at the wall, and, finally, when the pigeon pecks at the plastic key. The terminal response of key pecking was shaped from a large number of possible responses.

It is critical in shaping that the reinforcement occur immediately after the response, inasmuch as a delay in reinforcement may be accompanied by other responses that are not desired, and these responses, in turn, may be accidentally reinforced.

**Chaining.** Responses can be built on other responses to develop a complex chain. Complex behavior may be conditioned response by response. In one experiment, a rat was first trained to eat from a food tray, then to press a lever to obtain food that was delivered by means of a solenoid activating a hopper. Once his bar-pressing response for food reinforcement was established, it was possible to shape a number of responses chained in a complex fashion (see Fig. 3).

**Stimulus Control.** Basic to the question of stimulus complexity and stimulus presentation is the concept of stimulus control. There is reason to assume that although behavior is established through reinforcement in a stimulus situation, the maintenance of once-established behavior is more a function of stimulus control than of continuing reinforcement. Stimulus generalization and stimulus discrimination are powerful aspects of maintaining behavior once conditioned: the control of behavior by stimuli is

something taken for granted. A rudimentary example of stimulus control is one familiar to most people. Assume for the moment that you have been sitting in room A and need an object that is located in room B. You go to room B to secure the object and, when you enter the room, forget what it was you went to get, whereupon you return to room A, where the object is not but where the stimuli that evoked the searching behavior are.

Stimulus control emphasizes the importance of environmental stimuli in the study of behavior. In recent years, the interest in architectural psychology in analyzing the impact of such environments as hospital wards and classrooms on human behavior reflects an important application of stimulus control.

**Programming (Schedules of Reinforcement).** A final important concept of the operant paradigm is that of programming, or schedules of reinforcement. Behavior is developed to specification by these schedules of reinforcement, which are centered on the contingent relationship between response and reinforcement. Under conditions of shaping behavior, a continuous reinforcement schedule is usually in effect; for every desired response emitted by the organism, food or another reinforcer is presented. This one-to-one continuous reinforcement is referred to as the "crf schedule."

**Adventitious Reinforcement.** There are times when responses are reinforced accidentally by a coincidental pairing of response and reinforcement. An early experiment by Skinner illustrates this. Skinner placed a pigeon in an experimental box and left it there for a brief period every day. Every 15 seconds, no matter what the bird was doing, a food hopper appeared, allowing the bird access to food. The appearance of food was completely independent of the bird's actions. Despite this, certain well defined responses of stereotyped nature, such as turning counterclockwise in a box two or three times between reinforcements, began to appear in the bird's behavior. Skinner noted that if the bird happens to be executing some response as the hopper appears, it tends to repeat this response which he referred to as adventitious reinforcement.

### Mowrer's Two-Factor Learning Theory

Mowrer theorized that much learning can be explained on the basis of acquired fear (anxiety), and that responses that reduce this anxiety are learned and maintained.

**Contiguity and Drive Reduction.** Mowrer suggested that anxiety responses are learned by contiguity. An adventitious association of a neu-

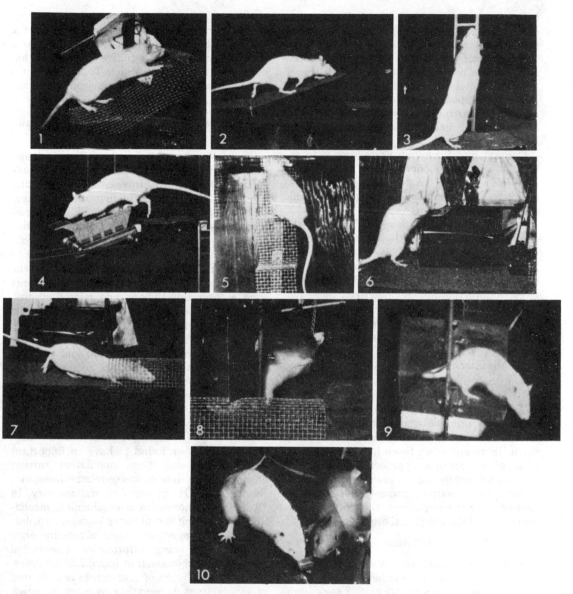

FIGURE 3. Demonstration of chained responding. (Courtesy of A. J. Bachrach, Ph.D.)

tral stimulus with a painful stimulus conditions something taken for granted. A rudimentary fear by contiguity in a fashion related to stimulus substitution in classical conditioning. In other words, a stimulus that in itself is not fear evoking is accidentally presented at the same time as a painful stimulus; by simple conditioning, what Mowrer then called sign learning, the neutral stimulus becomes a conditioned aversive stimulus.

Any response that results in the avoidance of elimination of such a conditioned aversive stimulus, as an anxiety-producing event, is reinforced, even in the absence of other reinforcement, because the response reduces anxiety (drive). Once learned, these avoidance responses persist.

Mowrer thought that these were different from other types of conditioned responses in that there was no need for continued reinforcement to maintain the response. Other conditioned responses extinguish in the absence of reinforcement. Mowrer felt that conditioned anxiety responses do not need the reinforcement of repetition of the original trauma. Although the responses were conditioned by contiguity, they are maintained by the reinforcing effects of drive reduction. Classical conditioning of fear by contiguity is maintained by the subsequent conditioning (instrumental) of avoidance behavior by drive reduction.

**Autonomic Responses.** Another differentiation Mowrer assumed in his two-factor theory was that fear responses are entirely autonomic. Emotional responses are involuntary and largely autonomic; instrumental responding is voluntary and largely under the control of the central nervous system.

Operant and Pavlovian procedures with respect to autonomic conditioning were brought into focus by Neal Miller, who presented research on the operant conditioning of autonomic responses, such as heart rate.

Mowrer also invoked a model in which the stimuli conditioned to the onset of painful events acquire certain drive (anxiety) characteristics, but those stimuli associated with the avoidance of or escape from pain become positively reinforcing. Mowrer described these two events as responses of fear and hope. In recent years, Mowrer's theorizing has centered largely on the development of neurosis and, in particular, the centrality of guilt and anxiety in emotional disorders.

### Cognitive Learning Theory

The learning theorists so far discussed have all been essentially S-R associationists, no matter what differences existed between and among them. In recent years there has been a resurgence of interest in an approach that, according to many of its proponents, goes beyond a mechanistic view of learning and behavior and takes into account the cognitions, thoughts, and expectations of the individual organism.

### Tolman

Tolman's learning theory is very much a sign-learning approach, and he believed that what an organism learns is not simply an S-R assocation, no matter how conditioned, but, rather, an expectancy of signs. His organism is goal directed and purposive. "Purposive," for Tolman, describes a behavior pattern and states that learning results from the acquisition of information about the environment, rather than the attachment of particular responses to particular stimuli. This acquisition of information about the environment considers a stimulus, for example, as a sign for food and thus creates an expectancy that food is in its environment. The Pavlovian model of bell-food conditioning, therefore, is viewed in a cognitive fashion as a sign learned to produce an expectancy for food. Another crucial abstraction is that of demand. The need for food creates a demand that, coupled with the

signs acquired as information about the environment, enables the individual to engage in the purposive behavior of food seeking. Finally, a concept unique to the cognitive approach is that of a cognitive map, by which Tolman meant a learned representation of the environmental situation.

### Neurochemical Aspects of Learning and Memory

Two research efforts in neurochemical and neuroelectric factors in brain functioning have occurred which have proved to be fertile and exciting developments. The first of these is neurochemical exploration by the PET scan (positron-emission tomography) a metabolic brain-imaging technology which has enabled researchers in an *in vivo, in situ* manner precisely to identify areas in the brain associated with the metabolic activity that takes place during events such as cognition. These, and related studies, have occasioned a significant reevaluation of the localization of brain function, recognizing, among other findings, that such functions are distributed throughout the brain and that the traditional division of right hemisphere/left hemisphere control is not as clear-cut as may have been conceived.

The second major development in recent years is the discovery of the opioid peptides, the morphine-like chains of amino acids termed *endorphins* which were found to have an important role in stress and stress modulation, further elucidating the role of stress-related hormones (such as ACTH) in learning and memory. In 1970 Kety conceived a neurochemical mechanism in learning and memory storage, postulating a diffuse projection system of noradrenergic neurons reinforcing information (associated with stress and arousal) at individual synapses. Subsequently, years of research have indicated catecholamines do modulate memory, although not needed for memory formation. The distinction between memory formation and memory consolidation is an important research focus, with the role of hormones strongly supported. There is evidence to strongly support the view that hormones, released by stimulation, act to modulate the strength of the memory of the experience and that central modulating influences on memory interact with the influences of peripheral hormones.

Much of the foundation for such positions derives from detailed studies of the effects of chemical agents on learning and memory. With regard to catecholamines there is a body of data supporting, in general, the findings that antagonists of catecholamine metabolism (such as reserpine, chlorpromazine, and propranolol) measurably interfere with processes of learning and memory, while catecholamine agonists (such as amphetamine, epinephrine, norepinephrine, and dopamine) can facilitate performance.

Pituitary hormones such as ACTH and vasopressin appear to enhance learning and resemble the activity of catecholamine agonists. Vasopressin, for example, has been shown to improve the learning of long lists of objects.

Arousal is frequently associated with the activation of central noradrenergic systems and the release of hormones such as epinephrine, ACTH, and vasopressin suggesting that these neurohumoral processes modulate memory. Research findings suggest that retention of learned experiences is influenced by post-training treatments affecting peripheral adrenergic functioning and that the effects of the treatments may involve the release of epinephrine from the adrenal medulla. The findings support the view that epinephrine may normally be involved in the endogenous modulation of memory storage.

A review of certain aspects of neurochemical research can only provide ideas for the learning theorist and the clinician. Ongoing research will be elucidating neurochemical mechanisms of learning, memory consolidation and reactivation, the role of stress stimulation in learning and memory as reflected in stress-released hormones and the interaction of the pituitary-adrenal and catecholaminergic system.

**REFERENCES**

Bachrach A J: *Psychological Research: An Introduction*, ed. 4. Random House, New York, 1980.
Bachrach A J, Quigley W A: Direct methods of treatment. In *An Introduction to Clinical Psychology*, I A Berg, L Pennington, editors, ed. 3, p 482. Ronald Press, New York, 1966.
Bachrach A J: Learning theory. In *Comprehensive Textbook of Psychiatry*, ed 4, H I Kaplan, B J Sadock, editors, p 184. Williams & Wilkins, Baltimore, 1985.
Davis H, Hurwitz H M B: *Operant-Pavlovian Interactions*. Erlbaum Associates, Hillsdale, NJ, 1977.
Dunn A J: Neurochemistry of learning and memory: an evaluation of recent data. Ann Rev Psychol *31:* 343–390, 1980.
Hull C L: *Principles of Behavior: An Introduction to Behavior Theory*, Appleton-Century-Crofts, New York, 1943.
Lief H I: Sensory association in the selection of phobic objects. *Psychiatry 18:* 331, 1955.
McGaugh J L: Preserving the presence of the past: hormonal influences on memory storage. Am Psychol *38:* 164–174, 1983.
Mowrer O H: A stimulus-response analysis of anxiety and its role as a reinforcing agent. Psychol Rev *46:* 553, 1939.
Rescorla R A, Holland P C: Behavioral studies of associative learning in animals. Ann Rev Psychol *33:* 265–308, 1982.
Skinner B F: *Science and Human Behavior*. Macmillan, New York, 1953.
Wolpe J: The experimental foundations of some new psychotherapeutic methods. In *Experimental Foundations of Clinical Psychology*, A J Bachrach, editor, p 554. Basic Books, New York, 1962.

---

# 3.4 ETHOLOGY

## Introduction

The dictionary defines ethology as the systematic study of animal behavior. Originally, ethologists were primarily interested in the detailed analysis of the behavior of intact animals in their natural environment or closely related environments, using direct observation as the basic technique for behavioral measurement. With the passage of time, ethologists added experimental modifications to the natural environment and initiated experimental laboratory investigations.

## Contributions to Psychiatry

Ethological data and theory have allegedly been used to support basic constructs of psychoanalysis. Freud postulated psychic energy as the basic motivating force underlying human behavior. It has been suggested that an objective explanation or description of psychic energy may be provided in terms of Lorenz's action-specific energy hypothesis, which implies that external inhibition of instinctive behavior patterns acts as a powerful intrinsic motivational factor insofar as the behavior is concerned. Once an animal's specific reservoir of energy is completely drained or depleted as a result of continuous activation of a particular response, a time interval is required for the energy supply to be replenished.

According to Hess, the action-specific energy hypothesis is illustrated by the phenomenon of displacement, in which a conflict between two instinctive behavior patterns results in the release of a third instinctive behavior pattern. In the stickleback fish, conflict between attack and flight is often resolved by nest-building behavior. This transition from the purely physical behavior patterns of animals to the physical and psychic relationships characterizes the developmental motivational changes from the animal to the human level. Furthermore, at the human level, the psychic energy that may be invested in the sexual and aggressive drive may be cathected to the mental representations of these objects, as determined by individual experience.

A complex interpretation of displacement activity has been presented by some workers. They hypothesize that the gratification of sexual instincts takes different forms during different periods of development and that the mechanism that leads from one form to another functions in the same way that displacement activities function in lower animals. As one form of gratification is inhibited, the instinct accepts another form of gratification.

Hess has strongly indicated that Freudian theory is closely related to ethology by way of the concept of imprinting, which places an enormous emphasis on the importance of early learning. Imprinting refers to the early, rapid, specific, and persisting learning, seen particularly in birds, by which the neonatal animal becomes attached to the mother and, by generalization, to members of the animal's own species. The term "imprinting" was given to this phenomenon by Konrad Lorenz (see Fig. 1) although the phenomenon or a similar phenomenon had previously been described. Unlike most learning, imprinting is facilitated by punishment or painful experience.

Body contact or some similar mechanism is now generally accepted as a primary, if not the primary, mechanism binding the baby to the mother. However, analysts are unwilling to accept any further ethological-psychological affectional theory, since it contradicts or does not relate to Freud's four developmental stages: oral, anal, phallic, and genital. Another matter of concern to analysts is that biological theories assume generalization, whereas analytical treatment is an individual matter of more concern to the analysts than are generalized scientific laws.

On the basis of observation and study of normal and autistic children, the Tinbergens explicated basic rules, long employed in ethological practice, that they felt should be observed in socially contacting and treating the autistic human infant. Social approach and contact with the child should be achieved by averting the eyes, since direct stare is a biologically threatening gesture. Also, any successful gestural approach should be followed and extended by cautious step-by-step procedures. The Tinbergens believed that every attempt should be made to avoid overintimidation of the autistic child, that intense observation and attention should be given to nonverbal interactions, and that intense social bonding should be achieved without extreme or sudden intrusion.

### Induced Subhuman Psychopathology

The first scientist to study induced psychopathology in a laboratory animal was the neurophysiologist Ivan Pavlov in Russia. Pavlov inadvertently produced the abnormal phenomenon, which he labeled "experimental neurosis," by use of a conditioning technique. He taught dogs to discriminate between a circle and an ellipse and then progressively diminished the ratio between the diameter of the circle and the length of the ellipse. When the difference was reduced to approximately 10 percent, the neurotic symptoms of extreme and persistent agitation, with continual struggling and howling appeared and apparently remained for a long time in most animals. Pavlov attributed the neurosis to a collision in time or space of the processes of excitation, or reinforcement, and inhibition, or nonreinforcement.

Other investigators, using a wide variety of animals, have succeeded in attaining more precise liminal discriminations in a wide variety of visual problems without severe psychopathology. It is true that driving an animal to achieve liminal discriminations may produce some emo-

FIGURE 1. In a famous experiment, Lorenz demonstrated that goslings would respond to him as if he were the natural mother. (Reprinted by permission from Hess, E. H. Imprinting: An effect of early experience. Science 130: 133, 1959.)

tional stress, but the Pavlovian technique has never become the method of choice for achieving nonhuman psychopathology or experimental neuroses.

Gantt and Liddell in America used similar techniques to produce behavior disorders in subhuman animals forced into conflictual learning situations. Gantt used the term "behavior disorders" to describe his dogs' complex and variegated autonomic responses. Liddell described the stress responses he obtained in sheep, goats, and dogs as "experimental neurasthenia," and this condition was obtained in some cases by merely doubling the number of daily test trials in an unscheduled manner. It was also achieved by conflict between food and pain. Liddell believed that the experimental neurasthenia represented a primitive, relatively undifferentiated state, rather than mimicking any human psychopathological condition.

Massermann studied abnormal behavior produced by motivational conflict situations in cats and monkeys. The subjects were trained to obtain food pellets from boxes and were then subjected to blasts of air on an irregular schedule when they approached food. Masserman also studied methods designed to extinguish the abnormal behaviors through disuse, stimulus satiation, reconditioning, and alcoholic therapy.

### Nurturance of Normality

The only way to demonstrate induced psychopathic behavior in laboratory animals is to compare the abnormal animals with others that are normal or, at least, as normal as can be achieved. The Harlows have defined the social, as contrasted to the physical, essentials that create a normal environment—laboratory or feral. These essentials are provided by particular people as gifts of affection.

An obvious criterion for the social adequacy of any particular environment is the degree to which it prohibits or limits social interactions, particularly affectional interactions, between or among its inhabitants during or throughout any or all stages of social development. Doubtless there are many other variables of secondary importance, particularly those related to the physical environment.

Throughout most of the primate order, there exist five basic affectional systems. One is the system of mother love. A second, closely synchronized system is that of infant love for the mother. The third system is peer love or agemate love or playmate love. The fourth system develops from and is a normal sequence of peer love and is heterosexual love. In primates heterosexual love in normal form depends on the establishment of the antecedent affectional systems. The fifth love or affectional system is that of paternal love.

Most feral environments provide opportunities for the development of all these forms of love or affection to the members of the primate order. No monkey laboratory environment made all these forms of love available to all monkey participants until the creation of the nuclear family apparatus by the late Margaret K. Harlow. This apparatus produced nuclear families of rhesus monkeys with a single father and mother and their infants. The family members lived in such a manner that both parents were accessible to each other and to all the parental groups.

The structure of the nuclear family apparatus is illustrated in Figure 2. Four nuclear families were housed in each apparatus. The nuclear family apparatus provides all family members full opportunity for social and sexual expression, and the primary missing feral variable is the predator.

The Harlows have studied the effects of various forms of social environment on the social development of young monkeys. These studies have convinced them that development must be a combined function of emotional learning, social learning, and maturation.

By and large, monkeys mature 4 or 5 times as fast as humans in many aspects, and at birth a monkey is comparable to a 1-year-old human being in terms of body and bone structure. Female monkeys are sexually mature at about 3 years of age, even though most females must wait another year for the advent of their offspring. Male monkeys are spermatically competent at an equal age, even though the anatomical adornments of maturity, the large canine teeth and temporal muscles, do not achieve pubertal perfection for 6 or 7 years.

Like people, monkeys attain full intellectual age at approximately full sexual age. Curiosity in the monkey matures by 30 days of age, even though its full potentialities have not yet been realized, and early curiosity is regulated and restrained by maternal ministrations. The all-important primate behavior pattern of play matures at aproximately 90 days of age, as shown in Figure 3. Social fears appear at approximately 80 to 100 days of age, similar to Spitz's 9-month anxiety in human beings, an anxiety that really matures between 6 and 13 months of age.

It is now known that virtually every rhesus monkey infant born in the wild or in a "good" laboratory rearing environment will spend most

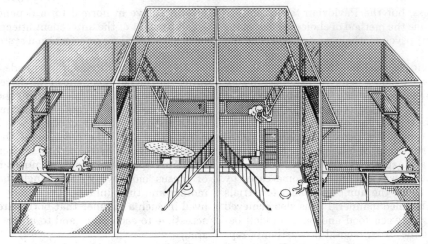

FIGURE 2.   Nuclear family living apparatus.

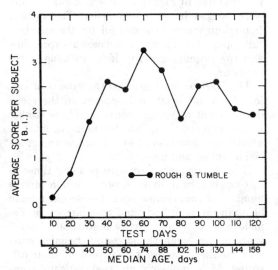

FIGURE 3.   Development of social behavior in monkeys.

of its first weeks of life on or in close proximity to its mother. During this time the infant is dependent on its mother not only for nourishment but also for physical warmth and emotional security, or "contact comfort" as Harlow first termed it in 1958 (see Fig. 4). The mother also provides the infant with protection from predators and other potential threats to its survival.

## Advent of Abnormalities

### Total Social Isolation

Probably the most dramatic and destructive abnormal environment is that of total social isolation. Monkeys may be raised from birth onward under such conditions. Here, for some predetermined period of time, an animal has no

social partners and can consummate no social interactions.

**Three-Month Total Social Isolation.** Two studies conducted at the Wisconsin Primate Laboratory on the effect of total isolation in monkeys from birth through the first 3 months of life yielded similar results. When removed from their early world of social nothingness and exposed to the world of monkeys and manipulanda, some of the infants went into a state of deep shock. Two died of self-imposed anorexia, and another was on the verge of starvation until saved by forced feeding.

The infants that survived, and most did, made a remarkable social adjustment by the development of play. When allowed to interact with equal-age, normally reared rhesus monkeys, the isolates were playing effectively within the first week or so. By the end of the first month and throughout the second month, the behavior of the 90-day isolates was normal, as indicated by the frequency of play and threat gestures.

**Six-Month Total Social Isolation.** Raising monkeys in total social isolation from birth throughout the first 6 months of life produced dramatic developmental differences in the isolated monkeys. The early infantile responses of self-clasp and huddle remain consistently low in socially raised monkeys. But these infantile behaviors increased progressively in the isolated monkeys and attained a level that was clearly abnormal and significantly greater than the level of infantile responses made by the controls.

Similar results were obtained for the level of rocking responses and stereotype responses. Rocking responses remained at a near-normal level throughout the first 4 isolation months and then exploded upward with increasing frequency. Stereotypy progressively increased from

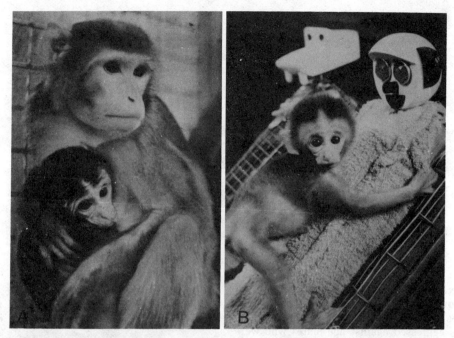

FIGURE 4. Contact comfort in infant rhesus monkeys. (A) Normal ventral contact between mother and infant; (B) Harlow's classic surrogate mother experiment in 1958 demonstrated that monkey infants preferred a cloth-covered surrogate mother that provided contact comfort to a wire-covered surrogate that provided food but no contact comfort.

the second month onward. Neither rocking nor stereotypy is a normal infant response; both apparently depend on prolonged deprivation.

When removed from the isolation chambers, these 6-month isolates were terrified by relatively normal social age-mates. Representatives from the normal and abnormal groups were then tested 5 days a week for 2 months in social groups of two isolates and two controls in a standardized playroom situation.

The isolate monkeys exhibited a very low level of threat responses, whereas the controls showed a high incidence of threat. Situational and social fears had matured in all the animals, but the isolates had had no social opportunities to develop natural and normal defense mechanisms. One cannot learn in a social vacuum. Threat responses were essentially nonexistent in the isolate monkeys. Levels of threat behavior by the isolate and control subjects remained essentially unchanged during the first and second months.

Play in the isolates was essentially nonexistent. The failure of the isolate monkeys to develop any play probably stems from the isolates' fear of their normal age-mates. The lack of play was not the result of aggressive physical assault on the part of the normal monkeys, since this was not observed. Aggression, even relatively weak aggression, does not mature in monkeys

until or slightly after the end of the first year of life. However, social fears had matured long before these isolate monkeys were allowed any social interaction with peers. Play requires freedom of movement and freedom of social interaction, and play and fright give rise to antithetical responses. Play can be inhibited almost as effectively by the threat of aggression as by aggression itself.

Representative members of the 6-month totally isolated monkeys were maintained in the laboratory under conditions of partial social isolation for 3 or more years, and, when they were socially tested under these inadequate social conditions, their social responses to each other became more impaired. When these long-term isolates were paired with equal-aged macaques or even monkeys half their age, they assumed violent and grotesque postures of terror such as the monkey lying on its back supine and frozen with terror (see Fig. 5). This is a posture never assumed by a normal monkey.

The long-term effects of 6 months of total social isolation produced the paradoxical position of creating adolescent monkeys that were both abnormally aggressive and abnormally fearful. The 6-month isolates aggressed or attempted to aggress against all other monkeys. They aggressed or threatened infants, an activity beneath the dignity of any normal rhesus

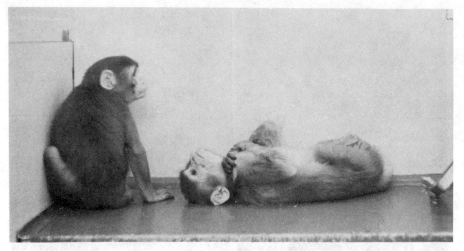

FIGURE 5.   Frozen fear postures in isolate monkeys.

monkey. Furthermore, during these acts of threat or assault, the isolates indicated, by their gestures, feelings of fear and apprehension. The isolates aggressed against age-mates who were far more physically adept. These aggressions were fraught with fear, and the physical encounters were massacres. Even worse, the 6-month isolates often made one suicidal aggressive assault against a member of a group of large, mature, aggressive males, illustrating the ultimate combination of paradoxical fear and hate. Such aggressions seldom occurred twice since even the isolate monkeys could learn in this situation to compensate for their emotional deficiencies or hypersufficiencies.

**Twelve-Month Total Social Isolation.** A group of macaque monkeys for the first 12 months of life, a period roughly equivalent to 5 or 6 human years were isolated. These monkeys were totally unresponsive to the new physical and social world with which they were presented when the screens of their isolation world were raised (see Fig. 6). The researchers measured play of the most nonsocial type—that of individual or activity play. The control monkeys showed a high level of activity throughout the entire 10-week test period, whereas the 12-month isolates started with a very low level, which progressively languished with the passage of time. Since the isolates were devoid of play, the researchers did not expect them to be full of passion, and they were correct. Nevertheless, the researchers tested these isolates for both threats and social play and obtained the expected—nothing.

### Partial Social Isolation

Under partial social isolation, each animal lives in a wire cage that is usually one in a rack

FIGURE 6.   Twelve-month total social isolate upon removal of isolation screen.

of several cages. Actually, monkeys, and doubtless other animals, have been housed in this manner for many decades without thought being given to the fact that these animals were being socially deprived. Indeed, before researchers became aware of the social predicament of monkeys raised in partial social isolation, the monkeys were described as control subjects or even normal subjects for various experimental groups.

Monkeys raised in partial social isolation can see, hear, and doubtless smell other monkeys. But partially isolated monkeys can never make any physical contact with other monkeys, and without physical contact, monkeys can experience none of the normal affectional or love sequences.

During the first and second years of life by partially isolated monkeys, totally infantile responses of rock and huddle and self-mouth wane with age, whereas self-bite and stereotypy wax. In other words, the extremely infantile responses drop out and are superseded by more complex responses.

Totally isolated monkeys tend to exhibit a depressive type posture, including such patterns as self-clutch, rocking, and depressive huddling. Partially isolated monkeys assume, with increasing frequency, postures that are more schizoid. These postures may include extreme stereotypy and sitting at the front of the cage and staring vacantly into space. Occasionally, the arm of a monkey starts to rise, and, as it extends, the wrist and fingers flex. While this takes place, the monkey ignores the arm, but, when it is extended, the monkey may suddenly respond to the arm, jump as if frightened, and even attack the offending appendage (see Fig. 7).

Maturation of aggression progresses systematically in monkeys raised in bare wire cages over a period of years—both externally directed aggression and self-directed aggression. All monkeys were tested in two conditions, a passive condition, when the observers sat 8 feet from the subjects and only observed and scored, and an active condition, when an experimenter ran a large black rubber glove over the cage top.

FIGURE 7.  Partial social-isolate monkey attacking offending appendage.

Externally directed aggression was apparent in the male at 2 years and not apparent in the female until year 4. The frequency of aggressive responses matured progressively in the male and the female, but aggression was stronger in the male before the fifth year of life. Self-aggression matured later than did externally directed aggression in both the male and the female, and it was never as frequent as was externally directed aggression.

### Privation and Deprivation

In privation, the animal experiences no social companionship from birth until some predetermined period. Deprivation results when animals are isolated after social relationships have been established. Invariably, deprived or late-isolate groups have shown far less behavioral deficit than the early-isolate or privation animals. Furthermore, when the late-isolate deprivation monkeys returned to social living, they often appeared to be meaninglessly hyperaggressive.

## Induction of Depression

### Anaclitic Depression

In the first formal Harlow study of induced nonhuman anaclitic depression, the test situation was designed so that each of two mother-infant pairs lived in home cages, with an infant play area in between. The infants were free to wander at will from the home cages to the mutual play area, but the mothers were restrained in the home cages by the size of the apertures into the play area. Play by these infants, like all rhesus infants, matured at about 90 days of age and was near maximal at 180 days, which was the age chosen to begin maternal separation. This separation was achieved by dropping transparent Plexiglas screens in front of both home cages while the two infants were romping in the play area.

All monkeys tested in this situation exhibited a complete or nearly complete picture of human anaclitic depression. At initial separation the rhesus infants exhibited a protest stage, as illustrated by violent attempts to regain maternal contact, plaintive vocalization, and a persistent high level of random behavior. The protest stage changed to despair during the subsequent 48 hours. Despair was characterized by a drastic reduction in vocalization and movement and by the frequent assumption of prone postures, with the head and body wrapped in the arms and legs. The most dramatic measure of the despair stage was that of the near-total suppression of play. Play was almost abolished during the 3-week period of maternal separation and then rose rapidly after maternal reunion.

When many human children are reunited with their mothers, their responses toward the maternal figure are those of rejection; Bowlby called this reunion stage "detachment." This phenomenon of detachment is far less common and far less intense in monkey infants than in the human infants reported by Bowlby. One of the first infant monkeys tested showed some maternal detachment upon reunion, and one mother showed some transient reluctance to accept her infant. Temporary detachment by the infant to the mother was exhibited by one of four infants in a replication study. However, the separated monkey infants typically reattached to the monkey mother vigorously and rapidly when the separation phase ended. Bowlby has expressed doubts about the universality of the detachment stage in human infants.

**Repeated Separation of Infant Monkey Peers.** Suomi measured the effects of repeated separation of infant pairs that had been separated from their mothers and raised in a spacious cage as part of a group of eight infants. At 90 days of age, the first of a series of 20 separations was begun, with monkeys being separated for 4 days and reunited for 3 days in each of the 20 separations completed over a 6-month period.

During the course of every separation, the separated age-mate pairs displayed the three conventional stages of anaclitic depression—protest, despair, and reattachment (detachment). However, infantile behaviors of self-mouth and self-clasp, which normally drop out by the fourth month, persisted in undiminished frequency and remained throughout the 9-month test period. Furthermore, complex social behaviors of environmental exploration and particularly play, which should become progressively more frequent and precise from 3 months to 9 months, remained unchanged in their formlessness and remained at a near-nonexistent frequency throughout the entire 9-month period. Thus, multiple peer separations did more than cause distress and depression. The separations eradicated the entire normal behavioral maturational process.

### Depression in Adolescent Monkeys

McKinney measured the effects of age-mate separation in one group of socially sophisticated monkeys more than 3 years of age and also measured the effect of vertical chamber confinement in a similar group.

Age-mate separation produced no depression in the socially sophisticated adolescents. Positive but slightly puzzling results were obtained

from the vertically chambered animals. After release, these monkeys tended to show depressed locomotions, and the members of a pair frequently sat close to each other without attempting effective social interactions and without showing the conventional infantalized responses of self-clasp, huddle, rock, and stereotypy.

### Behavioral Rehabilitation

### Time

An approach to psychopathology that may be considered either a method or a control is the manipulation of no variable other than time. It is doubtful whether time is ever the therapeutic method of primary choice. Time's efficacy may be an illusory factor, since in many cases it is the natural and normal social forces acting on the animal during the temporal interval that facilitate the cure, rather than time itself.

After 6 months of social isolation, monkeys placed with normal peers were socially inadequate. Subsequently, the isolates lived alone for 3 or more years. Time alone worked wonders for these animals, but in a negative direction: the original behavioral deficits not only remained but were exaggerated. Actually, there is no objective record of a monkey psychopathology being cured by time.

### Treatment of Specific Symptoms

All basic affectional patterns of mother love, infant love, peer love, heterosexual love, and even paternal love are based on responses involving bodily contact. Social isolation denies the monkey any contact comfort during both its personal and its social development. When social contact became accessible to isolated rhesus monkeys after isolation had ended, they did not make systematic attempts to achieve or maintain bodily contact with their simian associates. In fact, they went out of their way to avoid contact with fellow-species members.

To test contact comfort rehabilitation, Suomi first placed a group of rhesus monkeys in total isolation for 6 months. The isolates were then put in individual cages with a heated, simplified surrogate—a false model of a monkey mother mode of wire and cloth. Subsequently, six pairs of isolates and their surrogates were placed in a large group living cage for 8 weeks. The data showed that the monkeys given surcease from social sorrow by surrogate satisfaction subsequently showed a marked decrease in self-directed disturbance activities, including self-clasp, self-mouth, rock, and stereotypy. Contingent on the reduced frequency of display of these behaviors, there was an increase in frequency of environmental exploration and peer contact.

Obviously, increased frequency of environmental exploration and peer contact is not total rehabilitation, which should involve multiple peer interactions, various forms of peer play, and real or at least attempted heterosexual behavior. It appears that experience with the warm surrogate imparted considerable social security to the isolated monkey, as it can impart security during the social development of the normal infant. Contact with surrogates changed the isolated monkeys from animals devoid of security when with their confreres into animals capable of maintaining some social contacts. Social contact training, nevertheless, failed as a total rehabilitation process. The isolated monkeys never achieved the full gamut of monkey realization, involving active, sex-typed play and appropriate sexual responsiveness.

### Social Behavior Therapy

Four males were reared for the first 6 months of life in total social isolation, then removed and allowed to interact with four normal female "therapist" monkeys that were housed in quad cages. Each of the normal monkeys had previously had 2 daily hours of early social experience with another infant, and the pairings of social partners were systematically rotated.

When first socially tested in the home cage, the isolates were 180 days of age and the "therapists" were 90 days of age. This age differential was deliberately chosen so that the isolated monkeys would not be terrified by their new companions. Also, increasingly complex play develops in normal monkeys from 90 days onward, and these behaviors were judged best to gradually indoctrinate isolate monkeys into increasingly complex social interactions.

At this time two "therapist" females and two isolate monkeys were housed in diagonal corners of the home cage, and a "therapist" and an isolate were allowed 2 daily hours of social interaction, the various members of each group being systematically rotated. The quad cages were home cages when rehabilitation was instituted, and home cages are minimally disturbing environmental situations. Pairs of normal and isolate monkeys were subsequently tested in strange playrooms for 2 hours a day with increasing frequency throughout the rehabilitation process.

Successful therapy in the home cage was indicated by the progressive reduction of abnormal behaviors by the isolate monkeys of self-clasp, huddle, rock, and stereotypy. All these infantile or abnormal behaviors were progressively reduced under behavior therapy, and the frequency of these deviant derelictions fell to a normal level in the relatively strange playroom situation.

Although the decrease in frequency of abnormal behaviors is an indicator of rehabilitation, the most important measure of successful behavior therapy is that of the development of adequate, positive social behaviors, such as social contact, particularly play. Social contact by the isolated monkeys in both the home cage and playroom environments reached normal levels by the end of the planned period of rehabilitation.

Although frequency of play progressively increased throughout the 6-month planned rehabilitation period, it did not quite attain normal levels in the playroom. Since there had been no rationale for the period of therapy, an additional 6-month period of behavior therapy was instituted. At the end of the 12-month period of therapy, no differences existed between isolated and control monkeys in the observed frequency of any behavioral forms, including social behaviors of social contact and play.

Through accidents of time or birth, the four "therapists" were females and the four isolates were males. Normative monkey studies have shown that males and females play differently. Male play is rough, tough, and contactual; female monkey play is gentle, chasing, and basically noncontactual. The only play the female "therapists" could have taught the isolates was gentle, noncontact play; but, when the male monkeys were rehabilitated, their play was masculine, contactual monkey play. Thus, when the males were converted to behavioral normality, they achieved their full heritage of monkey masculinity.

**REFERENCES**

Bowlby J: *Attachment and Loss: Attachment.* Basic Books, New York, 1969.
Harlow H F: The nature of love. Am Psychol *13:* 673–685, 1958.
Levine S: A psychobiological approach to the ontogeny of coping. In *Stress, Coping, and Development in Children,* N Garmezy, M Rutter, editors. McGraw-Hill, New York, 1982.
Pavlov I P: *Conditioned Reflexes* (G. V. Arrep., Trans.). Oxford University Press, London, 1927.
Suomi S J: Social development in rhesus monkeys: consideration of individual differences. In *The Behaviour of Human Infants,* A Oliverio, M Zappella, editors. Plenum Press, New York, 1983.
Suomi S J: Ethology. In *Comprehensive Textbook of Psychiatry,* ed 4, H I Kaplan, B J Sadock, editors. p 226. Williams & Wilkins, Baltimore, 1985.
Suomi S J, Harlow H F: Social rehabilitation of isolate-reared monkeys. Dev Psychol *6:* 487–496, 1972.
Suomi S J, Immelmann K: On the process and product of cross-species generalization. In *Observing Man Observing Animals,* D W Jajecki, editor. Erlbaum Associates, Hillsdale, NJ, 1983.
Suomi S J, Ripp C: A history of motherless mother monkey mothering at the University of Wisconsin Primate Laboratory. In *Child Abuse: The Nonhuman Primate Data,* M Reite, N Caine, editors. Alan R. Liss, New York, 1983.

# 4

# Science of Human Behavior: Quantitative and Experimental Methods in Psychiatry

## 4.1 EPIDEMIOLOGY

### Introduction

Epidemiology is the study of health conditions in a population, in relation to any factors existing in or affecting that population, which may influence the origin of the health state or affect its distribution in that population. The object of such study is to ameliorate any factors that contribute to ill health, to enhance any that contribute to health, and to draw generalizations that can be applied to other populations to contribute to health in general.

### History

The origins of the science of epidemiology are very ancient. Probably the first discovery was the fact that disease tends to be a greater threat when the wastes of human living accumulate. Certainly by the time it was possible to encode the Mosaic laws (ca. 1200 B.C.), a great deal of epidemiology was already known. Indeed, in almost all civilizations prior to the Renaissance, health and disease were closely bound to the religious systems of the people.

#### Epidemic Constitution

Much thought was given to why waves of disease struck at particular times and intervals. These rather vague thoughts found expression in terms such as "epidemic constitution," offered at different times and by different people to explain the influence of climate and other cosmological factors.

Nonspecific but nevertheless effective action based on epidemiological concepts perhaps reached its highest point in the famous Broad Street pump incident in London in 1854. At that time John Snow realized that cholera was being spread by water from a particular pump, and

prevented the use of this water by dismantling the pump, thereby retarding the epidemic.

#### Specificity

The next step in epidemiology came with improvement in diagnosis. The most important figure in this was Sydenham, who recognized many illnesses in the 17th century. He recognized that such broad generalizations as the epidemic constitution could not deal equally well with all questions of disease spread; each disease might well have its own laws of spread and, by implication, of control. This is a concept applied too long to mental diseases; there is still a tendency to talk about the prevention of mental illness, as though paresis, pellagrous psychosis, various postencephaletic states, alcoholism, mongolism, depression, and schizophrenia were all the same.

Sydenham's work led to the recognition that specific illness required specific preventive measures. The same lesson of specificity is only now being learned in psychiatry. In every case in which a mental illness has been prevented, a clear-cut causative factor related to a definable syndrome was discovered. The decline of syphilitic psychosis with the emergence of effective treatment for syphilis is an example of this.

The discovery of the importance of bacteria in disease led to the development of the modern epidemiology. With the discovery of obligatory causative agents, the development of the epidemiology of the "one overwhelming cause" took place. For a number of years, concern was almost exclusively centered on causes of disease and the control of causative agents, either directly or through immunological reactions. There were always individuals in the population who were known to be infected but who did not become ill, and there were always those who recovered while others died. And, there were many diseases

54

in which the model of infection did not fit the cases, notable among them being some arthritic conditions, arteriosclerosis, and, among the mental diseases, schizophrenia, depression, neurosis, alcoholism, and the character disorders. These unsolved problems led, under the leadership of Dubos and others, to a renewed consideration of the host factors in disease, or those factors within the individual patient that determine his vulnerability. The disease that precipitated much of this thinking was tuberculosis, and, as Felix expressed it, schizophrenia is like tuberculosis without the mycobacterium entering the picture. Except for those mental illnesses known to have obligatory causes—and they are numerically small in proportion to the others—the epidemiology of the mental illnesses falls in the same category as the epidemiology of arthritis, coronary thrombosis, and arteriosclerosis.

## Study Methods

### Diseases with Obligatory Causes

The shape of the ascending epidemic curve depicting the proportion of a population affected by a disease over a period of time appears to depend primarily on such factors as the length of time between exposure and onset of disease for the particular illness under question, and the method of transmission of the disease. The descending arm of the epidemiological curve depends on the exhaustion of the supply of susceptible persons in the population. Also, both ends of the curve depend on the prior history of the disease in the population, the type of immunity resulting from having the disease, and any immunizing measures that may have been used. Particular shapes of curves are typical for certain groups of illnesses, and the epidemic curve may lead to the determination of the diagnosis in some epidemics, and can lead to information useful in identifying the obligatory causative agent.

Experimental and mathematical methods have been useful in diseases that occur in waves and then disappear or reach a low ebb of sporadic occurrence. They have thus far been less helpful in the study of diseases that vary little in their rates over time, or that do not result in death or recovery within a relatively short period.

### Chronic Diseases

Chronic diseases require other methods of study, particularly when no obligatory causative factor is known. Changes in rate of occurrence are likely to be rather slow, and this makes them hard to interpret, particularly since medical sci-

ence is likely to have changed in quality of diagnosis and treatment while any change in rate has been occurring. This is particularly true when the causative factor has to act over a long period of time to produce its effect. The best example of this kind of problem is the association between cigarette smoking and lung cancer.

The tool most useful in studies of chronic illness for which no obligatory cause is known is the life table. Essentially, the life table is a composite of the experience of a group of people who share certain factors believed to be related to a pathological process, in contrast to a group without these factors.

For many diseases the end point of the life table is death; in other diseases the end is a form of disability. In psychiatry the measure is often hospitalization, the point at which society will no longer tolerate the sick person in its midst. Although the concept has certain advantages for dealing with psychiatric illnesses, the tolerance of societies does not stay constant, and advances in treatment may result in improved behavior without affecting the underlying disease process. Nevertheless, the life table method presents many still unexploited possibilities for the study of psychiatric illnesses.

### Diseases without Known Causative Factors

The life table method is also applicable in studying illness states in which no causative factor can be postulated. Various sorts of events occurring in people's lives can be used as the basis for forming contrasting groups, which can then be followed to some other event, such as the appearance of disease, social or productive death, or death itself. The method can also be applied with some risk to retrospective data.

### Diseases with Multiple Causes

The life table method allows the testing of a wide range of possible relationships between events and what follows them. In individual cases, the method was introduced by Adolf Meyer as the life chart. Others have worked out various ways of evaluating behavior at successive points in time, so that interesting events may be related to later behavior. From this sort of study of the lives of individual patients, hypotheses arise that can then be tested by life table methods.

### Mental Diseases

Methods of epidemiology are applicable to psychiatric diseases, provided that the data can be properly quantified. This means that diagnosis must be replicable, if not valid, and that life events involved in hypothesis testing must be somewhat quantifiable.

These desiderata are important, but helpful concepts may be developed through work done before they are fully met. The clear-cut proof that a kind of retardation is associated with the absence of an enzyme necessary in the metabolism of phenylalanine logically leads to the testing of all infants and the inauguration of special diets for those lacking the essential enzyme. Meanwhile, the as yet unproved assumption that children deprived of a broad preschool experience constitute a high proportion of the mildly mentally retarded cannot be neglected. Epidemiology does not insist on absolute proof of relationship. But it does help place some responsibilities for selection of methods, and for marshaling available facts concerning actions taken to relieve the problems of the various mental illnesses.

For the most part, the epidemiology of the mental disorders is at a primitive level, particularly with regard to its most important problems: schizophrenia, depression, and the various neuroses. Studies of schizophrenia and depression have been largely descriptions of the prevalence of the illness in various populations and the comparison of the sick, by various characteristics, to the total population. Hypotheses have been based on such findings, but exceedingly few if any studies have been directed toward the testing of these hypotheses.

### Definitions

Various terms are used in epidemiologic studies that require definition.

The proportion of a population that has a condition at one moment in time is called the *prevalence rate*. The proportion of a population that begins an episode of a disorder during a year's time (new cases) is called the *annual incidence rate*. In a stable situation, the prevalence rate is approximately equal to the annual incidence rate times the average duration, measured in years, of the condition. The risk of acquiring a condition at some indefinite time in the future represents the accumulation of age-specific annual incidence rates over a period of time.

In Table I, the prevalence rates of various mental disorders are presented.

### Clinical Picture and Syndrome Identification

The clinical picture of a condition may be significantly altered when the perspective is broadened by searching out cases not in active treatment. Patients may be followed after they have stopped treatment, or cases that have not come to clinical attention may be located.

Without systematic data gathering, clinicians sometimes think of manic-depressive illness as relatively benign. Yet some 9 percent of a cohort followed by Lundquist developed a chronic course. And, in the early 1930s, Derby found a death rate of 22 percent in hospitalized acute manic cases. Lundquist found the risk for multiple attacks to be higher for manics, particularly those who had an onset before age 20.

The *social breakdown syndrome* includes a variety of decompensations in personal and social functioning. Most episodes of social breakdown syndrome are short-lived, start in the community, and end shortly after a hospital admission. But some cases last for years, representing extreme social disability and wasted lives. This kind of picture is characteristic of chronically deteriorated psychotic patients.

Psychiatric patients have more physical disorders than do most people. Babigian and Odoroff found the relative risk of death in the mentally ill to be 2½ to 3 times that of the general population. When the chronically ill, the aged, and the alcoholics, who are high-risk groups, are removed, the relative risk remains 1½ to 2 times that of the general population.

Some features of the deteriorated functioning previously thought to be an ineluctable consequence of psychosis have been shown to be largely preventable sociogenic complications. On the other hand, mental disorders may be only one facet in the spectrum of ill health suffered by some patients.

### Causes

Clinical observations, laboratory research, and epidemiology feed one another with new knowledge, new investigative techniques, and new insights into disease pathogenesis. Sometimes the breakthrough comes through purely epidemiological data. This was true with pellagra and fetal rubella's causation of fetal anomalies, including mental retardation. More often, epidemiology comes in when clinical observations or laboratory findings need field testing to implement programs designed to reduce the impact of a condition on the population.

#### Preventive Trials

The planned preventive trial determines whether a planned modification of cirumstances actually lowers the incidence of disease. It provides more definite information about causes than any other kind of method. It generally comes as the last in a series of investigations

TABLE I
MENTAL DISORDER PREVALENCE RATES PER 1,000†

| Author | Site and Date | Total Mental Disorders | Psychoses | Schizophrenia | Affective Psychoses | Neuroses | Personality Disorders | Mental Retardation | Impaired | Comments |
|---|---|---|---|---|---|---|---|---|---|---|
| *Treated cases plus identified through nonmedical records or key informants* | | | | | | | | | | |
| Cohen, Fairbank | Eastern Health District, 1933 | 44.5 | 8.18 (age over 15) | | | 2.0 | | | | After Plunkett and Gordon table |
| Lemkau et al. | Eastern Health District, 1936 | 60.5 | 6.6 | | | 3.10 | 4.61* | | | Age-adjusted rates. Population age over 10 |
| *Same plus intensive survey of subsample population* | | | | | | | | | | |
| Rosanoff | Nassau County, 1916 | 13.74 | 2.39* (functional) | | | | | 5.46 | | Intensively surveyed area's total mental disorder rate: 36.4 |
| Roth, Luton | Tennessee, 1938 | 69.4 | 6.32* | 1.73* | 1.65* | 4.0* | 37.8* | 8.20* | | Intensively surveyed area's total mental disorder rate: 123.7 |
| Lin Leighton | Formosa, 1946–1948 | 10.8 | 3.8 | 2.1 | 0.7 | 1.2 | 0.5 | 3.4 | | Persons with more than one symptom pattern were counted for each, and diagnoses' specific rates exceed total rate |
| | Bristol, 1952 | 690 | 10 | | | 570 | 290 | 110 | 420 | |
| *Surveys of total populations* | | | | | | | | | | |
| Bremer | Norway fishing village, 1939–1944 | 232.4 | 35.9 | | | 58.0 | 93.5 | 55.6 | 193.6 | (chronic) |
| Essen-Möller | Lundby, Sweden, 1947 | Evident and probable 179.0 Conceivably ill 180 | 19.5* | 7 | 10.2* | 58.8* | Major 64* Minor 210* | 9.8 | | Lifetime prevalence rates calculated on total population |
| Hagnell | Lundby, Sweden, 1957 | | 17 | | | 131 | | 12 | | Lifetime prevalence rates |
| Eaton, Weil | Hutterites, 1950 | 46.5* | 12.4* | 2.1 | 9.3 | 16* | 12* | | | Base population 15 and over; lifetime prevalence |
| *Surveys of probability sample populations* | | | | | | | | | | |
| Leighton | Stirling County, 1948–1950 | 570 | | | | | | | 240 | Population over 18 |
| Rennie, Srole | Midtown Manhattan, 1953–1954 | 815 | | | | | | | 234 | Interviewed population's age: 20–59 |

† Courtesy of E. M. Gruenberg, M.D. Values followed by an asterisk are calculations made by Dr. Gruenberg.

that have clarified a casual hypothesis, but preventive trials can also come very early in the course of investigations.

Another form of preventive trial occurs when a major reform is introduced with the intent of preventing a specific form of disorder. It cannot be designed to include a control group because the reform involves the reorganization of all the mental health services of a community.

### Stress

Stress is an ill-defined concept used in different ways by researchers of various scientific backgrounds who do not always explain their specific meaning. This lack of definition produces methodological difficulties.

In recent years, attention has been focused on life events. Whether they are good or bad, life events demand adaptive changes. Persons with many significant life events are more likely to become ill than are those who experience few and minor events.

### Early Physical Environment

Knobloch and Pasamanick demonstrated the relationship between prenatal factors and mental retardation, and between organic and functional disorders in children. They also correlated season of birth and incidence of mental deficiency. Significantly, more children born in the winter months were admitted to the Columbus State School in Ohio. This finding was particularly true for those children born in years when the average temperature in the third month after their conception had been the highest of the summer. This finding suggests that pregnant women may then have decreased their protein intakes to levels low enough to impair the developing brains of their unborn children. Malnourished populations have been shown to have handicaps of central nervous system development.

### Sociopsychological Hypotheses

Faris and Dunham found a concentric distribution of schizophrenia rates, with the highest rates at the center of Chicago and the lowest at the periphery of the city. Manic-depressive psychoses had a random pattern throughout the city, and there was a tendency for such cases to come from a higher socioeconomic level than did schizophrenics. Organic psychoses, alcoholic psychoses, and drug addiction had different patterns. The authors advanced the hypothesis that social isolation produced the abnormal traits of behavior and mentality characteristic of schizophrenia.

The drift hypothesis, which holds that impaired persons slide down the social scale because of their illness, was not supported by their data. Young patients who had little time to drift were concentrated in the same manner as older patients. Wender's study of the socioeconomic status of schizophrenic adoptees and their biological and adoptive parents found that only part of their data supported the drift hypothesis.

The hypothesis of differential tolerance explains higher schizophrenic admission rates in some communities on the basis of familial and cultural attitudes. The segregation hypothesis holds that, instead of helplessly drifting downward, the schizophrenic actively seeks city areas where anonymity and isolation protect him against the demands that more organized societies make. Another sociogenic hypothesis is that belonging to a lower social class, with the problems that it entails, fails to inhibit—and possibly triggers or exacerbates—existing psychopathology.

Durkheim related increasing industrialization and urbanization to a rise in secularism and individualism, and a decreased sense of community affiliation. He coined the term "anomie" to describe this phenomenon. He believed that suicide rates were an index of a population's anomie. Durkheim showed that suicide rates across nations and over time increased with Protestantism and secularization.

### Familial Aggregations

Clinicians have been impressed with the high frequency of mental disorders among the relatives of their patients. It was long assumed that, when family histories of particular conditions were being studied, one was studying the transmission of genetic material through the germ plasm. The earliest morbidity surveys tended to show the existence of a very definite familial aggregation of cases of schizophrenia and of manic-depressive psychosis.

When it became clear that the familial patterns of schizophrenia could not be accounted for by any simple Mendelian mechanisms, psychogenetic theories became more popular and persuasive. By the end of World War II, a spate of articles of familial rearing patterns in relationship to the later development of schizophrenic syndromes in children had begun to appear. These investigators tended to ignore the fact that parents and children come from the same genetic pool and have more in common than their emotional relationships to one another.

Böök postulated that familial clusters of schizophrenia could be accounted for by a recessive gene with very low penetrance. A low penetrance implies that environmental factors play important roles in determining which persons carrying the gene become affected.

It is known that genetic factors play a crucial role in the etiological complex responsible for schizophrenia and manic-depressive illness. It is also known that somatic insults—such as stress, prematurity, and malnutrition—and such unfavorable environmental circumstances as poverty and emotional deprivation, are associated with psychopathology.

## REFERENCES

Dohrenwend B P, Dohrenwend B S: Perspectives on the past and future of psychiatric epidemiology (The 1981 Rema Lapouse Lecture). Am J Public Health 72: 1271, 1982.
Hollingshead A B, Redlich F C: *Social Class and Mental Illness.* John Wiley & Sons, New York, 1958.
Kleinbaum D G, Kupper L L, Morgenstern H: *Epidemiologic Research: Principles and Quantitative Methods.* Lifetime Learning Publications, Belmont, CA, 1982.
Leighton D C, MacMillan A M, Harding J S, Macklin D B, Leighton A H: *The Character of Danger*, Basic Books New York, 1963.
Regier D A, Burke J D: Epidemiology. In *Comprehensive Textbook of Psychiatry*, ed 4, H I Kaplan, B J Sadock, editors, p 295. Williams & Wilkins, Baltimore, 1985.
Regier D A, Goldberg I D, Taube C A: The de facto U.S. mental health services system: A public health perspective. Arch Gen Psychiatry 35: 685, 1978.
Robins L N, Helzer J E, Croughan J, Ratcliff K S: National Institute of Mental Health diagnostic interview schedule: Its history, characteristics, and validity. Arch Gen. Psychiatry 38: 381, 1981.
Srole L, Langner T S, Michael S T, Opler M K, Rennie T A C: *Mental Health in the Metropolis: The Midtown Manhattan Study.* McGraw-Hill, New York, 1962.

# 4.2    SENSORY DEPRIVATION

### History

Instances of aberrant mental behavior in explorers, shipwrecked sailors, and prisoners in solitary confinement have been known for centuries. Toward the end of World War II, startling confessions, induced by brainwashing in prisoners of war, caused a rise of interest in the psychological phenomena brought about by deliberate diminution of sensory input in the human being.

To test the hypothesis that an important element in brainwashing is prolonged exposure to sensory isolation, Hebb and his co-workers in Montreal brought solitary confinement into the laboratory and demonstrated that volunteer subjects—under conditions of visual, auditory, and tactile deprivation for periods of up to 7 days—reacted with increased suggestibility. See Figures 1 to 3 for a similar experiment. Some of the subjects also showed symptoms that have since become recognized as characteristic of the sensory deprivation state: anxiety, tension, inability to concentrate or organize one's thoughts, increased suggestibility, vivid sensory imagery—usually visual, sometimes reaching the proportions of hallucinations with delusionary quality—body illusions, somatic complaints, and intense subjective emotional distress. The term "indeterminate stimulus experience" has been

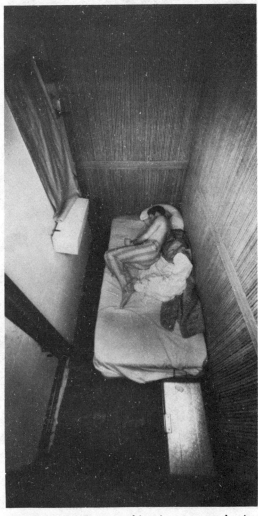

FIGURE 1.   A volunteer subject in a sensory deprivation experiment. The special room is soundproofed and pitch black. (The photograph was taken with the use of infrared light.) The subject wears gloves to blunt the sense of touch. (Yale Joel, Life Magazine, © Time, Inc.)

FIGURE 2.   Just after his release, the subject tries in vain to hold a small rod in a hole without touching the sides. (Yale Joel, Life Magazine, © Time, Inc.)

applied to this general group of symptoms and has been defined as "a syndrome of experiences for which no appropriate environmental stimulus can be detected." In this section, the term "sensory deprivation symptoms" is essentially synonymous with indeterminate stimulus experience.

### Theoretical Explanations

The two most popular theories for the phenomenon of sensory deprivation are the psychological and the physiological.

### Psychological Theories

Psychological explanations were anticipated by Freud, who wrote: "It is interesting to speculate what could happen to ego function if the excitations or stimuli from the external world were either drastically diminished or repetitive. Would there be an alteration in the unconscious mental processes and an effect upon the conceptualization of time?"

Indeed, under conditions of sensory deprivation, abrogation of the ego's secondary process (perceptual contact with reality and with organ-

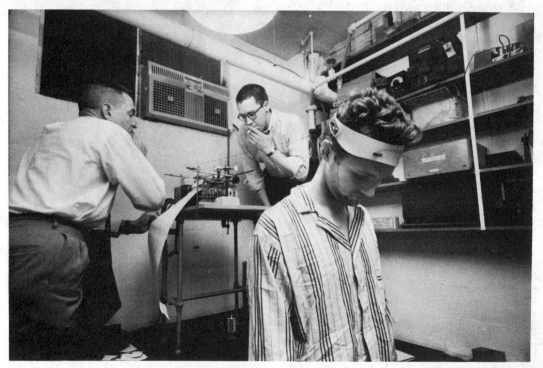

FIGURE 3.   Immediately after his release, the volunteer was subjected to a battery of tests. Although most volunteers could perform simple memorization in confinement, tests showed their comprehension ability to be impaired just after release. It took most volunteers about a day to return to normal. (Yale Joel, Life Magazine, © Time, Inc.)

ized, logical thinking) brings about the emergence of the primary process—irrationality, regression, confusion, disorientation, fantasy formation, primitive emotional responses, hallucinatory activity, and wish-dominated, pseudopathological mental reactions.

A number of investigators have found it useful to use psychoanalytic terminology to make the results of their work more understandable. Rapaport stressed the concept of ego autonomy as crucial in a subject's ability to tolerate sensory deprivation, and Goldberger and Holt agreed that ego strength as measured by them could predict individual tolerance in their experiments. The concept of regression in the service of the ego was also used. Many pointed out that a patient being psychoanalyzed is in a kind of sensory deprivation mental room (soundproofing, dim lights, couch), and is encouraged to free associate and otherwise invite primary process mental activity. In the sensory deprivation situation, the subject becomes even more dependent on the experimenter, and must trust him for the satisfaction of such basic needs as feeding, toileting, and physical safety. In water tank sensory deprivation there is also the similarity to the womb with its amniotic fluid.

### Physiological Theories

Presumably the maintenance of optimal conscious awareness and accurate reality testing depends on a necessary state of alertness, which, in turn, depends on a constant stream of changing stimuli from the external world, mediated through the ascending reticular activating system in the brain stem. In the absence or impairment of such a stream, as occurs in sensory deprivation and in sensory monotony, alertness falls away, direct contact with the outside world diminishes, and the balance of integrated activity tilts in the direction of increased relative prominence of impulses from the inner body and the central nervous system itself. For example, idioretinal phenomena, inner ear noise, and somatic illusions may take on a hallucinatory character.

Reverberating circuits from the association areas and proprioceptive systems, previously inhibited and kept from greater spread by the exteroceptive and activating systems, find themselves released and able to dominate the brain. The result is an increased tendency to rehearsal of memory, meditative thought, reverie, excessive preoccupation with somatic stimuli, stimulus-bound thinking, and body image awareness and distortions. Material previously repressed and relatively unconscious is given an impetus

to appear in consciousness. The breakthrough, when it occurs, is experienced as unwilled or spontaneous, because the material involved has been relatively inaccessible to willful utilization.

### Other Theories

Among numerous other theories, those of particular interest are the following.

**Personality.** Personality theories attempt to explain not the phenomena of sensory deprivation, but the variation in these phenomena from subject to subject. For example: Why do some volunteers in experiments quit sooner than others? Different approaches are offered by different investigations, and these approaches include introversion-extroversion, body-field orientation, and optimal stimulation level.

**Instinctual Drive or Need.** These theories are based on hypothetical needs or drives built into the organism, allied to inquisitiveness, curiosity, investigative or search behavior, and information seeking for stimulus hunger, optimal satisfaction, and oversatiation.

**Expectation.** These hypotheses involve social influences, including the important role played by the experimenter. Modern researchers place great emphasis on anticipation, instructional set, and the demand characteristics of the experimental situation (tacit and overt suggestion).

**Cognitive.** These theories, allied to the neurophysiological, lay stress on the organism as an information-processing machine whose purpose is optimal adaptation to the perceived environment. With insufficient information, the machine cannot form the cognitive map against which to match current experience, and there is resultant disorganization and maladaptation. Continuous feedback is necessary to monitor the organism's own behavior and to attain optimal responsiveness. Without this feedback, the person virtually lives inside a Rorschach inkblot, forced to project outward individually determined themes having little relationship to the reality situation. This is similar to what many psychotics do.

### Areas of Application

Although there are many unsolved problems regarding sensory deprivation—how it works and why it works—there can be little doubt that sensorily impoverished, monotonous environments can produce a serious and sometimes dangerous disruption of the mind. As this fact has become more widely known, numerous instances of its application to problems of everyday experience have been found.

## Public Health

The dangers of long-haul trucking over monotonous superhighways have been recognized as being related to inherent sensory deprivation and its symptoms. Increased accident rates and errors in judgment in boring assembly-line work have been similarly implicated. It is becoming increasingly understood that automation for greater production, with the elimination of supposedly distracting stimuli on the remaining workers, carries its price in sensory deprivation symptoms and human fallibility.

Modern architecture applied to industrial and business plants sometimes has the deleterious effect of producing an environment devoid of adequate sensory stimulation for workers. Lack of natural light has been shown to disturb the performance of workers in underground factories.

## Military

Reference has already been made to the pertinence of sensory deprivation in the brainwashing of prisoners of war. The possibilities for increasing human suggestibility and persuasibility have continued to attract investigators, largely from the disciplines of psychology and sociology, but also from psychiatry.

Sensory deprivation has been recognized as an important causative factor in situations in which isolation and monotony are intrinsic to the military duty. Men assigned in small groups to constricted or remote stations—polar parties, radar watches, submarine duty, space vehicles, silo sites, even fallout shelters—may develop temporarily distorted perceptions and disorganized thinking, such as a gray-out or break-off phenomenon in high-flying jet pilots, especially when the horizon cannot be seen; a kind of catatonic-like immobilization of the eyes or screen-fascination in radar observers; rapture of the deep, a form of space disorientation and confusion in deep-sea divers; and white-out, in polar bases.

## Nursing

A relatively recent development in the field of nursing has been the discovery that sensory deprivation is a feature of ordinary hospital bed rest and, as such, plays an important part in the appearance of sensory deprivation symptoms. Conversely, an excessive noise level in hospital acute care units has a masking effect (sensory overload), and can be as disturbing to patients as is sensory deprivation.

## Medicine

Sensory deprivation is now frequently recognized as an important feature in the care of some patients with transient psychotic states or sensory deprivation symptoms, especially in hospitalized patients and in those with severe handicaps, such as blindness, deafness, and paralysis. Although it may be seen in all branches of medicine, it occurs more often and tends to show special aspects in the following fields.

**Internal Medicine.** The so-called cardiac psychosis may be a form of sensory deprivation symptoms and may be quite unrelated to the actual state of the patient's hemodynamic physiology or medication. The well-meaning physician's hospital orders may turn out to be a sentence of sensory deprivation, with excessive or too long-enduring absolute bed rest, silence, and no visitors. The patient may be found wandering in the corridors—usually at night, when the wards have become quiet—confused, thinking he is at home, and being unable to find a familiar room. Sensory deprivation has loosened his hold on reality and has made him prey to fantasy.

**Geriatrics.** Mental functioning in the elderly may deteriorate, not only for organic neurological reasons but also because of pitiful social isolation and sensory deprivation. An increasing number of persons among the elderly live out their lives in single, desolate, barren rooms.

Boore, a lecturer in nursing at the University of Edinburgh, wrote of her experience in preventing sensory deprivation in old people. She addressed herself to the special limitations of many old people—restricted visual fields and other visual faults, confinement in bed, tactile restriction to bedsheets, dulled taste and smell perceptions, unfamiliar hospital sounds, minimal kinesthetic stimulation, and restricted social environment. These patients need a great deal more light, including night lights, than most people realize, she said, and those over 85 need eight times as much as normal. Their glasses should be cleaned frequently, hearing aids should be more freely furnished and regular attention paid to their batteries, and food for the elderly should be spiced and seasoned more than usual. Their calendars and clocks should be large and prominent, and the clocks should chime. Also, rooms and corridors should be painted in attractive and different colors for better orienting value, and to increase the pattern of sensory input. Additionally, television sets and radios are helpful, and nothing can match the value of attending people—the ministering nurse, friends, relatives, and hospital volunteers. As Boore wrote, "The methods for improving sensory input are limited only by one's imagination."

**Surgery.** In recent years, postoperative psychosis has become an increasingly disturbing complication in surgery, largely in prolonged and especially dangerous operations, such as open-heart and organ transplant work. It is now felt that the extensive isolation and immobilization in postoperative recovery rooms and intensive care units may play an important causative role by means of sensory deprivation.

**Ophthalmology.** The mental disturbance that sometimes follows operations for cataract or other eye disorders, and that is characterized by confusion and disorientation, has been known for years as cataract delirium. Weisman and Hackett preferred to call it black patch delirium, because they believed it is more related to the patching than to the cataract or the operation. Bandaging only one eye or allowing a central peephole in the patches has been found frequently corrective or preventive. However, there have been dissenting opinions as to whether the condition should be attributed in a major way to sensory deprivation.

**Orthopedics.** Patients with some forms of orthopedic problems require long periods of immobilization in body casts, head tongs, and other severely restricting apparatuses. Some of these patients develop sensory deprivation symptoms, amounting at times to psychotic states that interfere seriously with orthopedic treatment. Although immobilization alone can sometimes produce mental disturbances, it is reasonable to assume that the addition of other elements of sensory deprivation in the same patient can become additive. In any event, corrective sensory stimulation as part of the therapy in these cases has been found to be of practical value.

**Neurology.** In the days when poliomyelitis was a fearful and rampant illness, the bulbar form of it often required treatment in a respirator to sustain life. Some of the patients who had to remain in the respirator (iron lung) for long periods of time developed peculiar hallucinatory states that disappeared promptly when the patient was removed from the respirator. In these states, the patient often imagined that he was traveling about in a strange vehicle resembling the respirator. The states were found to be due not to poor oxygenation, toxicity, fever, drugs, or progression of the poliomyelitis, but to the condition of life in a tank-type respirator—staring at one spot on the ceiling, hearing little but the constant and monotonous drone of the motor, and being hardly able to move, even if one

were not paralyzed—in fact, life in extreme sensory deprivation.

Other neurological diseases sometimes requiring treatment in a respirator and thus being subject to sensory deprivation include polyneuronitis, myasthenia gravis, and bulbar palsy. Sensory deprivation has also been described in a patient with paraplegia.

**Mental Hospital Psychiatry.** The element of sensory deprivation is surely important in delirium tremens, in which the best sedative is a sympathetic, attentive nurse. Sensory deprivation is probably also a vital factor in the deterioration of the chronic back-ward inmate. When this type of sensory deprivation is neutralized by the many attentions that accompany a new drug study, some previously neglected patients may seem to get well. Likewise, when wards for chronic patients are emptied by zealous physicians, sometimes at the behest of economy-minded authorities, the resultant flood of unaccustomed stimulation may have a nonspecific beneficial effect on these patients and on their sensory deprivation symptoms, the reaction being in addition to the usual favorable responses to the doctor's personal attention and expectations.

*Psychology*

In addition to cutaneous stimuli, a variegated sensory environment is necessary for the normal development of the infant. Mental retardation may be the result of sensory deprivation, as well as of biochemical and physiological factors. Animal studies have also shown that early sensory deprivation leads to lowered resistance to stress in later life.

Psychoanalysis, in its theoretical aspects a branch of psychology, has also profited from sensory deprivation research. Rapaport drew implications of value from sensory deprivation work for his psychoanalytic ego psychology. Schmale and Freedman both used anecdotal data from sensory deprivation reports in their theoretical formulations regarding affect. References were made to "big eye" (pervading insomnia) and "long eye" (a state of mental blankness: "A 20-foot stare in a 10-foot room"), both encountered in South Pole expeditions and reported by Shurley. Cited also were the reports on autistic children treated, in part, by 40 to 80 days of confinement in a dark environment with a minimum of intrusions or demands. The children were reported as markedly improved, but this work has not been duplicated. Harlow's well-known work with infant monkeys deprived of their mothers and raised on wire mesh or terry cloth surrogate mothers was discussed, as well as experiments of nature, such as the congenitally deaf or blind, and the boy, recently deceased, who was being raised in a germ-free plastic bubble because of congenital defect in his immunological system. Sensory input in one modality can offset deprivation in another, and certain kinds of infant care—skin contact, embracing, cuddling—previously held essential are not critical for the development of a wide range of affective capacity.

### Psychiatric Treatment

Mentally ill patients have been placed in sensory deprivation and surprisingly, instead of the production of the usual sensory deprivation symptoms with negative feelings, most of these patients reported positive feelings, some persisting long after the study was completed. There were improvements in motivation, increased desire to socialize, loosening of defenses, subsidence of such pathological symptoms as depressive ruminations and hallucinations, and increased awareness of inner conflicts and anxieties. Presumably because of temporary regression and then improved ego functioning, these patients became more receptive to psychotherapy. The same technique with three obsessive-compulsive neurotics, however, resulted in no improvement.

Sensory deprivation has also been used in combination with other psychotherapeutic techniques to treat patients with various neurotic disorders. Cooper and co-workers used sensory deprivation, followed by systematically planned role playing on the part of the therapist, in patients with intransigent hypochondriacal personality disorder. They felt that their results were good, compared with the lack of change in members of a control group.

Suedfeld has spent much of his energy toward the task of curing addicted smokers, by using sensory deprivation along with other psychotherapeutic measures. Taped messages about the hazards of smoking are read to the subjects during sensory deprivation, and their attitude structures are thus modified. Sensory deprivation is the unfreezer (a term attributed to Lewin). Permanance of no smoking then requires a refreezing in the new pattern, and this apparently is more difficult, depending as it does on many external factors.

### REFERENCES

Barabasz A F: Restricted environmental stimulation and the enhancement of hypnotizability: pain, EEG alpha, skin conductance and temperature responses. Int Clin Exp Hypn *30:* 147, 1982.

Borrie R A, Suedfeld P: Restricted environmental stimulation therapy in a weight reduction program. J Behav Med *3:* 147, 1980.

Fine T H, Turner J W, Jr: The effect of brief restricted environmental stimulation therapy in the treatment of essential hypertension. Behav Res Ther *20:* 567, 1982.

Heron W, Bexton W H, Hebb D O: Cognitive effects of a decreased variation in the sensory environment. Am Psychol *8:* 366, 1953.

Solomon P, Kleeman S T: Sensory deprivation. In *Comprehensive Textbook of Psychiatry,* ed 4, H I Kaplan, B J Sadock, editors, p 321. Williams & Wilkins, Baltimore, 1985.

Solomon P, Rossi A M: Sensory deprivation. In *Modern Perspectives in World Psychiatry,* J G Howells, editor, p 222. Oliver and Boyd, London, 1968.

Suedfeld P, Ballard E J, Murphy M: Water immersion and flotation: from stress experiment to stress treatment. J Environ Psychol *3:* 147–155, 1983.

Zubek J P, editor: *Sensory Deprivation: Fifteen Years of Research.* Appleton-Century-Crofts, New York, 1969.

# 5

# Theories of Personality and Psychopathology: Classical Psychoanalysis

## 5.1 SIGMUND FREUD

### Introduction

Concepts derived from psychoanalysis are applied so widely in psychiatric training and practice that they have become a fundamental part of the approach to mental and emotional disorders. Obviously then, it is imperative that the student develop a clear understanding of classic psychoanalytic theory and the work of its founder, Sigmund Freud.

Traditionally, classic or orthodox psychoanalysis has referred primarily to Freud's libido and instinct theories; it has come to include the concepts of ego psychology as well. Essentially, it is based on the free association method of investigation, which yielded the data used by Freud to formulate the key concepts of unconscious motivation, conflict, and symbolism.

Psychoanalytic theory, like all personality theory, is concerned primarily with the elucidation of those factors that motivate behavior. Psychoanalysis is unique, however, in that it considers these motivating forces to derive from unconscious mental processes. Freud's demonstration of the existence of an unconscious mind and his concept of psychic determinism are generally regarded as his greatest contributions to science, and they remain the fundamental hypotheses of psychoanalytic theory.

### Early Life of Freud

Sigmund Freud was born of Jewish parents on May 6, 1856, in Freiburg, a small town in Moravia, which has since become part of Czechoslovakia. When he was 4 years old, his father, a wool merchant, brought the family to Vienna where Freud lived most of his life until he was forced to flee to England in 1938, when the Nazis annexed Austria. He died in 1939.

### Medical Training

Freud was a medical student from 1873 to 1881. During this period, the biological researches of Darwin and his associates, and the investigations in physiology and physics by Helmholtz and his school were producing a new scientific climate that played a significant role in Freud's intellectual development. This new orientation emphasized natural law, the unity of science, and scientific exactitude, as opposed to the romanticism and mysticism that pervaded scientific thought in Central Europe after the Napoleonic Wars. For 5 years while he was at medical school, Freud studied in the physiological laboratory of Ernst Brücke, a founder of the scientific movement known as the Helmholtz school of medicine.

### Medical Career

Freud continued to work in Brücke's laboratory for a year after he graduated from medical school. It was there that he developed the physiological framework into which he later tried to cast his psychological theories, before he became resigned to the fact that lack of relevant physiological data precluded the explanation of mental phenomena, in terms of the physicochemical nature of brain function.

During the year that he spent at Brücke's Institute of Physiology, Freud did several highly creditable pieces of histological and neuroanatomical research. He found research particularly congenial, and he hoped to continue with his theoretical work, but financial considerations made this impossible. Despite a deep aversion for the practice of medicine as such, Freud was forced by his personal economic situation to leave the laboratory setting in 1882 and to begin work in the General Hospital in Vienna, first on the surgical service and then in Theodor Meynert's psychiatric clinic.

In 1885, he received a traveling grant that allowed him to visit Paris, where he studied at the Salpêtrière for 19 weeks under the great French neurologist Jean-Martin Charcot. During the time that he spent in Charcot's clinic, Freud was able to observe a wide variety of neurological syndromes. However, he was most impressed by Charcot's radical approach to hysteria. As a result of Charcot's influence, Freud became deeply interested in the problem of hysteria, and he came to be firmly convinced that hysterical phenomena were genuine.

The psychological explanation for hysterical phenomena was not investigated by Charcot. However, the possibility that such phenomena were psychological in origin did occur to Freud when Charcot was able to precipitate hysterical paralyses, seizures, and other characteristic symptoms through hypnotic suggestion.

Freud returned to Vienna from Charcot's clinic in Paris in 1886 with the avowed intention of giving up his laboratory studies so that he might devote all his time to the clinical practice of neurology.

See Figures 1 through 7 for highlights in the life of Freud.

## Beginnings of Psychoanalysis

From 1887 to 1897, the period in which Freud began to study seriously the disturbances of his hysterical patients, psychoanalysis can be said to have taken root. These slender beginnings had a three-fold aspect: the emergence of psychoanalysis as a method of investigation, as a therapeutic technique, and as a body of scientific knowledge based on an increasing fund of information and basic theoretical propositions. These early researches flowed out of Freud's initial collaboration with Josef Breuer, and then increasingly out of his own independent investigations and theoretical developments.

### The Case of Anna O.

Josef Breuer was a prominent Viennese physician with whom Freud formed a close friendship while he was working at Brücke's Institute. Breuer's treatment of "Anna O."—specifically his communication to Freud of the details of the case—was one of the factors that led to the development of psychoanalysis.

Breuer treated "Anna O." (Bertha Pappenheim) from December 1880 to June 1882. The patient was an intelligent girl of 21 who had developed a number of hysterical symptoms in association with the illness of her father, of whom she was passionately fond. These symptoms included paralysis of the limbs, contrac-

tures, anesthesias, disturbances of sight and speech, anorexia, and a distressing nervous cough. Her illness was further characterized by two distinct phases of consciousness. During one, she was normal; during the second, she took on another, and more pathological, personality. The transition between these states of consciousness was effected by autohypnosis, which Breuer subsequently supplemented with artificial hypnosis. Anna had shared with her mother the duties of nursing her father until his death. During her altered states of consciousness, she was able to relate the vivid fantasies and intense emotions that she had experienced while tending her father. And, to the great amazement of the patient—and Breuer—her symptoms could be made to disappear if she could recall, with an accompanying expression of affect, the scenes of circumstances under which they had arisen. Once she had become aware of the value of this "talking cure" or "chimney sweeping," Anna proceeded to deal with each of her manifold symptoms, one after another.

In the course of treatment, Breuer had become increasingly preoccupied with this unusual patient, and his wife had grown increasingly jealous and resentful. When he realized this, Breuer abruptly terminated treatment. Only a few hours had elapsed, however, before he was recalled to Anna's bedside. He found the patient, whom he had believed to be greatly improved, in a state of acute excitement. Anna, who had never alluded to the forbidden topic of sex during the course of treatment, was then experiencing a hysterical childbirth (pseudocyesis). The phantom pregnancy was the logical termination of the sexual feelings she had developed in response to Breuer's therapeutic efforts, a development of which he had been quite unaware. Breuer managed to calm her through hypnosis. However, the experience unnerved him and served to restrict his further participation in Freud's investigations into the unknown, and therefore unpredictable and dangerous, sphere of the mind.

### Studies on Hysteria

The collaboration with Breuer finally brought about the publication of "Preliminary Communication" in 1893. Essentially, Freud and Breuer extended Charcot's concept of traumatic hysteria to a general doctrine of hysteria. Hysterical symptoms were related to determined psychic traumata, sometimes clearly and directly and sometimes symbolically.

The authors observed that individual hysterical symptoms seemed to immediately disappear when the event that provoked them was clearly brought to life and the patient was able to describe the event in great detail, and put the accompanying affect into words. The basis of hysteria was described as a state of dissociated consciousness.

"Preliminary Communication" was followed in 1895 by *Studies on Hysteria*, in which Breuer and Freud reported on their clinical experience in the treatment of hysteria and proposed a theory of hysterical phenomena. The volume included "Preliminary Communication," a report by Breuer of his work with Anna O., a series of cases reported by Freud, a lengthy theoretical section written by Breuer, and, finally, a section on the psychotherapy of hysteria, which was contributed by Freud.

Out of his cases, Freud constructed the following sequence of steps in the development of hysteria:

1. The patient has undergone a traumatic experience, one that stirred up intense emotion and excitation and that was intensely painful or disagreeable to the patient.

2. The traumatic experience represented to the patient some idea or ideas that were incompatible with the dominant mass of ideas constituting the ego.

3. This incompatible idea was intentionally dissociated or repressed from consciousness.

4. The excitation associated with the incompatible idea was converted into somatic pathways and resulted in the hysterical manifestations and symptoms.

5. What is left in consciousness is merely a mnemonic symbol that is connected with the traumatic event only by associative links, which are frequently disguised.

6. If the memory of the traumatic experience can be brought into consciousness, and if the patient is able to release the strangulated affect associated with it, the affect is discharged, and the symptoms disappear.

### Technical Evolution

As a result of his early interest in hypnosis and his exposure to hypnotic technique in the clinics of Charcot and Liébault, Freud began to use hypnosis intensely in treating his patients when he opened his own practice in 1887. In the beginning, his use of hypnosis was primarily as a means of getting the patient to rid himself of his symptoms by means of hypnotic suggestion. It was soon obvious, however, that even though the patient responded to hypnotic suggestion and acted, under hypnosis, as if the symptoms did not exist, the symptoms asserted themselves during the patient's waking experience. In 1889, Freud turned to the cathartic method in conjunction with hypnosis in order to retrace, as Breuer had in the case of Anna, the history of the symptom. The first time that he employed this method, in the case of Frau Emmy von N., he adhered quite strictly to the concept of the traumatic origin of hysterical phenomena. Accordingly, the goal of treatment was limited to the removal of symptoms through recovery and verbalization of the suppressed feelings with which they were associated. This procedure has since been described as abreaction.

The beneficial effects of this hypnotic treatment were transitory: they lasted only as long as the patient remained in contact with the physician. Freud suspected therefore that they were in fact dependent upon the personal relationship between patient and physician. Freud's suspicion was confirmed when one day the patient awoke from a hypnotic sleep and suddenly threw her arms around his neck. Unlike Breuer, he was not frightened by this experience. Rather, he attempted to explore its significance.

From this point on, Freud understood that the therapeutic effectiveness of the patient-physician relationship, which had so mystified him, could be attributed to its erotic basis. These observations were to become the basis of the theory of transference. In any event, these experiences served to underscore his dissatisfaction with hypnosis. He wanted to be free of hypnosis because it had become increasingly apparent that the hypnotic method owed its success to the fact that the patient acted out of love for her doctor: that is, she remembered traumatic experiences and feelings at his command and appeared to recover from her illness in order to please him. He had also found that many of the patients that he encountered in private practice were refractory to hypnosis. Freud continued to use hypnosis when indicated until he had refined the technique of free association to his entire satisfaction. When he reached this point in 1896, he never used hypnosis again.

### Concentration Method

Bernheim had said that the experiences recalled under hypnosis could once again be recalled in states of consciousness if the physician asked the patient leading questions and urged him to produce these crucial memories. In Freud's concentration method, the patient was asked to lie down on a couch and close his eyes. He was then instructed to concentrate on a particular symptom and to try to recall memo-

FIGURE 1.   Sigmund Freud as a young man. (Austrian Information Service, New York, N. Y.)

FIGURE 2.   Sigmund Freud's office in Vienna. (Austrian Information Service, New York, N. Y.)

FIGURE 3.   Berggasse 19, the building in which Freud had his offices and which now houses the Freud Museum. (Austrian Information Service, New York, N.Y.)

FIGURE 4.   Sigmund Freud and his father. (Austrian Information Service, New York, N. Y.)

ries. Freud pressed his hands on the patient's forehead in order to facilitate the emergence of such memories, and he urged the patient to remember and continued to question him.

### Free Association Method

The use of free association evolved very gradually from 1892 to 1895. The first step in its development came about when a patient, Elisabeth von R., remarked that she had not expressed her thoughts because she was not sure what Freud wanted to hear. From this point on, Freud no longer tried to direct the patient's thinking but encouraged her to ignore all censorship and to express every idea that occurred to her, no matter how insignificant, irrelevant,

or shameful it might seem. At a later point in treatment, the patient complained that Freud had interrupted her train of thought by his persistent questions and that she found his habit

FIGURE 7. Mrs. Paula Fichtl, Freud's last maid, with some personal items: hat, cane. (Austrian Information Service, New York, N. Y.)

FIGURE 5. Sigmund Freud and his mother in 1872. (Austrian Information Service, New York, N. Y.)

FIGURE 6. Sigmund Freud at his desk in his Vienna office. (Austrian Information Service, New York, N. Y.)

of pressing his hand on her forehead an unnecessary distraction.

By the late 1890s, both Freud and his patients had come to feel that the urging, pressing, and questioning which were part of the concentration method actually interfered with the free flow of thought. Accordingly, these procedures were abandoned, and eventually patients were no longer instructed to close their eyes. However, the use of the couch continues to play a central role in classic psychoanalysis, and the fundamental rule of the free association method has remained unchanged.

Freud discovered that his patient's train of memory extended well beyond the traumatic event that had precipitated the onset of illness. He found that his patients were able to produce memories of their childhood experiences, of scenes and events that they thought had long been forgotten. This discovery led to the conclusion that frequently these memories had been inhibited because they involved sexual experiences or painful incidents in the patient's life. Moreover, the recollection of such experiences could evoke intense excitement, moral conflict, feelings of self-reproach, or fear of punishment. Since these childhood experiences remained so vivid, they must exert a predisposing influence in relation to the development of psychoneurosis. Freud continued to acknowledge the role of heredity in determining a person's future susceptibility to neurosis, but he assigned much of the responsibility for the cause of the psychoneuroses, which had hitherto been attributed to heredity, to unfavorable childhood experiences.

Freud discovered early in his practice that his patients were often unwilling or unable to recount memories that later proved to be significant. He defined this reluctance as resistance. Later, he found that in the majority of his patients resistance was due to active forces in the mind (of which the patients themselves were often unaware) which led to the exclusion from consciousness of painful or distressing material. Freud described this active force as repression. In a broad sense, Freud considered repression to be at the core of symptom formation.

### Theory of the Instincts

Freud used the term "libido" to refer to "that force by which the sexual instinct is represented in the mind." He recognized that the sexual instinct does not originate in finished form. Rather, it undergoes a complex process of development during which it has many manifestations apart from the simple aim of genital union. The libido theory referred to the investigation of all of these manifestations and the complicated paths they might follow in the course of development.

### Infantile Sexuality

Freud had become convinced of the relationship between sexual trauma and disturbances of sexual functioning. He originally viewed these conditions as related to the misuse of sexual function.

As his clinical experience increased, Freud was able to reconstruct the early sexual experiences and fantasies of his patients. These data provided the framework for a developmental theory of childhood sexuality. Perhaps an even more important source of information was his own self-analysis, which he had begun in 1897. The realization of the operation of infantile sexual longings in his own experience suggested to Freud that these phenomena might not be restricted to the pathological development of neurosis, but that essentially normal persons may undergo similar developmental experiences.

The earliest manifestations of sexuality arise in relation to bodily functions that are basically nonsexual, such as feeding and the development of bowel and bladder control. During the oral phase, which extends into the second year of life, erotic activity centers on the mouth and lips and is manifested in sucking, biting, and chewing. During the anal phase, when the child is increasingly preoccupied with bowel function and control from ages 2 to 4, the dominant erotic activity shifts from the oral to the anal and rectal regions. The phallic phase of sexual development begins during the third year of life and continues until approximately the end of the fifth year. Erotic activity at this time is linked both psychologically and physiologically with the activities and sensations associated with urination.

Freud described the erotic impulses that arise from the pregenital zones as component or part instincts. Ordinarily, in the course of development, these component instincts undergo repression or retain a restricted role in sexual foreplay. The failure to achieve genital primacy may result in various forms of pathology. The persistent attachment of the sexual instinct at a particular phase of pregenital development was termed a fixation.

Freud further discovered that, in the psychoneuroses, only a limited number of the sexual impulses that had undergone repression and were responsible for creating and maintaining the neurotic symptoms were of a normal kind. For the most part, these were the same impulses that were given overt expression in the perversions, or paraphilias as they are now called. The neuroses, then, were the negative of perversions.

### Development of Object Relationships

Throughout his description of the libidinal phases of development, Freud made constant reference to the significance of the child's relationships with crucial figures in his environment. Freud postulated that the choice of a love object in later life, the love relationship itself, and object relationships in other spheres of activity depend largely on the nature and quality of the child's object relationships during the earliest years of life.

At birth the infant has no awareness of the external world of objects. At most, he is capable of an undifferentiated sensitivity to pain and pleasure. Hunger, cold, and pain give rise to tension and to a corresponding need to seek relief from these painful stimuli in sleep. At the same time, the human infant cannot achieve relief from painful stimuli without help from outside. Object relationships of a primitive kind are established when the infant begins to grasp this fact. Because he is aware only of his own tension and relaxation and is unaware of the external world, longing for the object exists only as long as disturbing stimuli persist and the object is absent. Once the object appears and the infant's needs are gratified, the longing disappears.

**Oral Phase.** The infant's first awareness of an object in a psychological sense comes from his longing for something that is already familiar, for something that gratified his needs in the past but is not immediately available. Essentially, it is hunger that compels the infant to recognize the outside world. In this context, the infant's primitive reaction to objects, his desire to put them in his mouth, becomes understandable. The infant judges reality in terms of whether something will provide satisfaction and should therefore be swallowed, or whether it will create tension and should consequently be spit out.

At this point, the mother becomes more than an anonymous agent whose ministrations keep the infant alive. She is recognized as the source of nourishment and of the erotogenic pleasure the infant derives from sucking. As such, she becomes the first love object.

**Anal Phase.** In a broad sense, the infant's role during the oral phase of development is a passive one. The onus is on the mother to gratify or frustrate his demands. In contrast, during the anal period the child is expected for the first time to relinquish one aspect of his freedom: he is expected to accede to his mother's demand that he use the toilet for the evacuation of feces and urine. The primary aim of anal eroticism is the enjoyment of the pleasurable sensation of excretion. Later on, the stimulation of the anal mucosa through retention of the fecal mass may be a source of more intense pleasure.

The connection between anal and sadistic drives may be attributed to two factors. First, the object of the first anal-sadistic activity is the feces themselves, and their pinching off is perceived as a sadistic act. Subsequently, people are treated as the feces were. The sense of social power that evolves from sphincter control constitutes the second sadistic element. The child exerts his power over his mother by giving up or refusing to give up his feces.

The first anal strivings are autoerotic. Pleasurable elimination and, at a later point, pleasurable retention do not require the outside help of an object. At this stage of development, defecation is invested with omnipotence, and the feces, which represent the agent of such pleasure, become a libidinal object by virtue of their narcissistic evaluation. Although they have become external, they have ego quality, for they represent part of what was once one's own body. Hence there is a tendency to reintroject what was once eliminated in order to restore narcissistic equilibrium. Thus the feces become an ambivalently loved object: they are loved and retained (or reintrojected), and they are hated and pinched off.

**Phallic Phase.** The fundamental task of finding a love object belongs to the phallic period, at which time the pattern for later object choices is set down. Freud used the term Oedipus complex to refer to the intensive love relationships formed during this period.

In boys, the development of object relationships during the phallic phase is relatively simple because the boy remains bound to his first object, the mother. The boy's interest in the mother as the source of nourishment continues, and he develops a strong erotic interest in her and a desire to possess her exclusively. These feelings usually become manifest at the age of 3 and reach a climax in the fourth or fifth year of life.

With the initial appearance of the Oedipus complex, the boy begins to court his mother almost as a lover would, expressing his wish to sleep in her bed, proposing marriage, and taking advantage of any opportunity to watch her dress or undress. Competition from his siblings for the mother's affection is intolerable. But, above all, he wants to eliminate his arch rival: her husband and his father. The child anticipates retaliation for his aggressive wishes toward his father. He begins to feel that, if he continues to show sexual interest in his mother, his penis will be removed. The idea of such deprivation in association with the male organ was identified by Freud as the castration complex. Confronted by the threat of castration, especially from his father, the boy must renounce his oedipal love for his mother. He then identifies with his father and incorporates within himself his father's prohibitions.

As in the boy's case, the little girl forms an initial attachment to her mother as the source of fulfillment of her vital needs. But unlike the boy, for whom the mother remains the love object throughout, the girl is faced with the task of shifting this primary attachment from the mother to the father, in order to prepare herself for her future sexual role.

Fundamental differences between the boy's and the girl's psychosexual development emerge when the girl discovers, during the phallic period, that the clitoris with which she is endowed is inferior to its male counterpart, the penis. The little girl reacts to this discovery with an intense sense of loss and injury and with envy of the male, i.e. penis envy. At this point the mother, who had previously been an object of love, is held responsible for bringing her into the world less well equipped. With the further discovery that the mother lacks this vital organ as well, her inadequacy becomes even more profound. In an attempt to make up for her inadequacy, the little girl turns to her father in the hope that he will give her a penis or a baby in place of the missing penis. This is called Electra complex. The girl's sexual love for her father later diminishes because of his failure to satisfy her demands and because she fears her mother's disapproval.

**Latency Stage.** This is the stage of relative quiescence or inactivity of the sexual drive during the period from the resolution of the Oedipus complex until pubescence (from about 5 to 6 years untilabout 11 to 13 years).

The institution of the superego at the close of the oedipal period and the further maturation of ego functions allow for a considerably greater degree of control over instinctual impulses. Sexual interests during this period are generally thought to be quiescent. This is a period of primarily homosexual affiliations for both boys and girls and a sublimation of libidinal and aggressive energies into energetic learning and play activities, exploring the environment, and becoming more proficient in dealing with the world of things and persons around them. It is a period for development of important skills. The relative strength of regulatory elements often gives rise to patterns of behavior that are somewhat obsessive and hypercontrolling.

**Genital Stage.** The genital or adolescent phase of psychosexual development extends from the onset of puberty in about the eleventh to thirteenth years until the adolescent reaches young adulthood.

The physiological maturation of systems of genital (sexual) functioning and attendant hormonal systems leads to an intensification of drives, particularly libidinal drives. This intensification produces a regression in personality organization, which reopens conflicts of previous stages of psychosexual development and provides the opportunity for a reresolution of these conflicts in the context of achieving a mature sexual and adult identity.

The primary objectives of this period are the ultimate separation from dependence on and attachment to the parents and the establishment of mature, nonincestuous, heterosexual object relationships. Related to these objectives are the achievement of a mature sense of personal identity and acceptance and integration of a set of adult roles and functions that permit new adaptive integrations with social expectations and cultural values.

## Narcissism

Prior to the psychoanalytic application of the concept of self-love, the term narcissism was applied in a restricted sense to designate a sexual perversion of the type demonstrated by the Greek youth Narcissus, who fell in love with his own reflection. In 1908, Freud observed that, in cases of dementia precox (schizophrenia), libido appeared to have been withdrawn from other persons or objects, and he concluded that this might account for the loss of contact with reality that was typical of such patients. He then speculated as to where this libido had been invested instead. The megalomanic delusions of these patients appeared to indicate that the libido they had withdrawn from external objects was then invested in themselves, in their own egos. Freud also became aware of the fact that the phenomenon of narcissism was not limited to the psychoses: it might occur in neurotic and normal persons as well as under certain conditions, such as in physical illness and sleep.

Freud's observations of the narcissistic behavior of young children provided incontrovertible evidence of the role of narcissism in development, and led him to incorporate such considerations into his libido theory. Freud postulated that a state of primary narcissism existed at birth: that is, the neonate is entirely narcissistic; his libidinal energies are devoted entirely to the satisfaction of his needs and the preservation of his well-being. Later, as the infant gradually begins to recognize the person immediately responsible for his care as a source of tension relief or pleasure, libido is released for investment in that person, usually the mother. Thus, the development of object relations parallels this shift from primary narcissism to object attachment. However, some narcissistic libido is normally present throughout adult life; this is considered healthy narcissism and finds expression in the person's sense of well-being. Moreover, Freud observed that in a variety of traumatic situations—such as injury or the threat of injury, object loss, or excessive frustration—libido is withdrawn from objects and reinvested in the self.

Narcissism differs from autoeroticism in that autoeroticism refers to eroticism in relation to the person's own body or its parts; narcissism refers to the love of something more abstract, either the self or the person's ego.

A love object may be chosen in adult life because she resembles the person's idealized self-image or his fantasied self-image, or because she resembles someone who took care of him during the early years of his life. Persons who have an intense degree of self-love, especially certain beautiful women, have, according to Freud, an appeal over and above their esthetic attraction. Such women supply for their lovers the lost narcissism that was painfully renounced in the process of turning toward object love. A homosexual object relationship represents still another example of a narcissistic object choice. In this case, the person's choice of an object is predicated on sexual resemblance.

## Aggression

In 1915, in *Instincts and Their Vicissitudes,*

Freud arrived at a dualistic conception of the instinct as divided into sexual instincts and ego instincts. He recognized a sadistic component of the sexual instincts, but this aspect still lacked a sound theoretical basis.

Increasingly, Freud saw the sadistic component as independent of the libidinal, and he gradually separated it from the libidinal drives. It seemed, too, that there was sadism associated with the ego instincts as well as with the libidinal instincts. The notion of sadism was gradually broadened to include other characteristics under the heading of aggressiveness. At this point in his thinking, Freud attributed aggressiveness to the ego instincts and thus separated the sadistic components from the sexual instincts. Sexual sadism was then explained by the fusion between ego instincts and sexual instincts.

But putting the aggressive instinct in the category of ego instincts had its difficulties. On the basis of clinical evidence of self-destructive tendencies of depressed patients and self-inflicted injuries among his masochistic patients, along with his observations of the wanton destructiveness normally manifested by small children, Freud concluded that in many instances aggression or aggressive impulses did not serve self-preservative purposes.

With the publication of *The Ego and the Id* in 1923, Freud gave aggression a separate status as an instinct with a separate source, which he postulated to be largely the skeletomuscular system, and a separate aim of its own, destruction. The ego was left with its own ego instincts, the nature of which at this point remained unspecified.

### Life and Death Instincts

Freud introduced his theory of the dual life and death instincts, Eros and Thanatos, in 1920. This classification of the instincts is more abstract and had broader applications than his previous concept of libidinal and aggressive drives. The life and death instincts were thought to represent the forces that underlie the sexual and aggressive instincts.

Freud defined the death instinct as the tendency of organisms and their cells to return to an inanimate state. In contrast, the life instinct, or Eros, refers to the tendency of particles to reunite, of parts to bind to one another to form greater unities, as in sexual reproduction. Inasmuch as the ultimate destiny of all biological matter, with the exception of the germ cells, is to return to an inanimate state, the death instinct was thought to be the dominant force.

### Pleasure and Reality Principles

The pleasure principle, which Freud considered to be largely inborn, refers to the tendency of the organism to avoid pain and to seek pleasure through tension discharge. In essence, the pleasure principle persists throughout life, but it must be modified by the reality principle. The demands of external reality, called the reality principle, necessitate the postponement of immediate pleasure, with the aim of achieving perhaps even greater pleasure in the long run. The reality principle is largely a learned function; therefore, it is closely related to the maturation of ego functions, and it may be impaired in a variety of mental disorders that are the result of impeded ego development.

### Topographic Theory

The topographic theory, as set forth in *The Interpretation of Dreams* in 1900, represented an attempt to divide the mind into three regions, the unconscious, the preconscious, and the conscious, which were distinguished from one another by their relationship to consciousness.

**The Unconscious.** The unconscious contains repressed ideas and affects and is characterized as follows.

1. Ordinarily, its elements are inaccessible to consciousness and can become conscious only through the preconscious, which excludes them by means of censorship or repression. Repressed ideas may reach consciousness when the censor is overpowered (as in psychoneurotic symptom formation), relaxes (as in dream states), or is fooled (as in jokes).

2. The unconscious is associated with the particular form of mental activity that Freud called the primary process, or primary process thinking. The primary process has as its principal aim the facilitation of wish fulfillment and instinctual discharge; thus it is intimately associated with the pleasure principle. It disregards logical connections, permits contradictions to coexist, knows no negatives, has no conception of time, and represents wishes as already fulfilled. Primary process thinking is characteristic of very young children, who are dedicated to the immediate gratification of their desires.

3. Memories in the unconscious have lost their connection with verbal expression. However, when words are reapplied to the forgotten memory trace, it can reach consciousness once more.

4. The content of the unconscious is limited

to wishes seeking fulfillment. These wishes provide the motive force for dream and neurotic symptom formation.

5. The unconscious is closely related to the instincts. It contains the mental representatives and derivatives of the instinctual drives, especially the derivatives of the sexual instinct.

**The Preconscious.** This region of the mind is not present at birth but develops in childhood. The preconscious is accessible to both the unconscious and the conscious. Elements of the unconscious can gain access to consciousness only by first becoming linked with words and reaching the preconscious. However, one of the functions of the preconscious is to maintain repression or censorship of wishes and desires. The type of mental activity associated with the preconscious is called secondary process, or secondary process thinking. Such thinking is aimed at avoiding unpleasure, delaying instinctual discharge, and binding mental energy in accordance with the demands of external reality and the person's moral precepts or values. It respects logical connections and tolerates inconsistencies less well than does the primary process. Thus the secondary process is closely allied with the reality principle, which governs its activities for the most part.

**The Conscious.** Freud regarded the conscious as a kind of sense organ of attention that operated in close association with the preconscious. Through attention, the person can become conscious of perceptual stimuli from the outside world. Within the organism, however, only elements in the preconscious enter consciousness; the rest of the mind is outside of awareness.

**Significance of the Topographic Theory.** The topographic theory's main deficiencies lay in its inability to account for two important characteristics of mental conflict. First, many of the defense mechanisms that patients employed to avoid pain or unpleasure were themselves not initially accessible to consciousness. Obviously, then, the agency of repression could not be identical with the preconscious, inasmuch as this region of the mind was by definition accessible to consciousness. Second, patients frequently demonstrated an unconscious need for punishment. However, according to the topographic theory, the moral agency making this demand was allied with the anti-instinctual forces available to awareness in the preconscious.

These criticisms were among the important considerations that led Freud to discard the topographic theory insofar as it was concerned with the assignment of specific processes to specific regions of the mind. He came to realize that what is more important is whether these processes belong to the primary or the secondary system. The concepts included in Freud's topographic theory that have retained their usefulness refer to the characteristics of primary and secondary thought processes, the essential importance of wish fulfillment, the tendency toward regression under conditions of frustration, and the existence of a dynamic unconscious.

### The Interpretation of Dreams

Freud first became aware of the significance of dreams in therapy when he realized that, in the process of free association, his patients frequently described their dreams of the night before or of years past. He then discovered that these dreams had a definite meaning, although it was disguised. And, he found that encouraging his patients to free-associate to dream fragments was more productive than their associations to real life events, insofar as it facilitated the disclosure of unconscious memories and fantasies.

In *The Interpretation of Dreams*, published in 1900, Freud concluded that a dream, like a neurotic symptom, is the conscious expression of an unconscious fantasy or wish that is not readily accessible in waking life. Although dreams were considered one of the normal manifestations of unconscious activity, they were shown later to bear some resemblance to the pathological thoughts of psychotic patients in the waking state. The dream images represent unconscious wishes or thoughts disguised through symbolization and other distorting mechanisms.

The analysis of dreams elicits material that has been repressed or otherwise excluded from consciousness. The manifest dream, which embodies the experienced content of the dream and which the sleeper may or may not be able to recall after waking, is the product of the dream activity. The unconscious thoughts and wishes that, in Freud's view, threaten to awaken the sleeper are described as the latent dream content. Freud referred to the unconscious mental operations by which the latent dream content is transformed into the manifest dream as the dream work. In the process of dream interpretation, Freud was able to move from the manifest content of the dream by way of associative exploration to arrive at the latent dream content, which lies behind the manifest dream and which provides it with its core meaning.

In Freud's view, a variety of stimuli initiated dreaming activity—nocturnal sensory stimuli, day residues, and repressed infantile drives. Contemporary understanding of the dream process, however, suggests that dreaming activity takes place more or less in conjunction with the psychic patterns of central nervous system activation that characterize certain phases of the sleep cycle. What Freud thought to be initiating stimuli may, in fact, be incorporated into the dream content.

### Significance of Dreams

The study of dreams and the process of their formation became the primary route by which Freud gained access to the understanding of unconscious processes and their operation. He maintained that every dream somehow represents a wish fulfillment, a form of gratification of an unconscious instinctual impulse in fantasy form. In the state of suspended motility and regressive relaxation induced by the sleep state, the dream permits a partial and less dangerous gratification of the instinctual impulse.

### Dream Work

The theory of dream work became the fundamental description of the operation of unconscious processes. Unconscious instinctual impulses that were continually pushing for discharge had been repressed because of their unacceptable or painful nature. These impulses had to be attached to neutral or innocent images to be allowed into conscious expression. This was made possible by selecting apparently trivial or insignificant images from the residues of the dreamer's current psychological experience, and linking these trivial images dynamically with the latent unconscious images, presumably on the basis of some resemblance that allowed the associative links to be established. The dream work used a variety of mechanisms, including symbolism, displacement, condensation, projection, and secondary revision.

**Symbolism.** Symbolism is a complex process of indirect representation. The symbol is a manifest expression of an idea that is more or less hidden or secret. Freud discovered that the ideas or objects represented in this way were highly charged with inappropriate feelings and burdened with conflict. The forbidden meanings of these symbols remained unconscious. Although the symbol disguises what is unacceptable, it can also offer partial gratification of underlying wishes or can signify, and thus partially retain, lost objects.

**Displacement.** The mechanism of displacement refers to the transference of emotions from the original object to which such emotions are attached, to a substitute or symbolic representation of that object in the dream. Whereas symbolism refers to the substitution of one ob-

ject for another, displacement facilitates the distortion of unconscious wishes through the transference of affect from one object to another. For example, the mother may be represented visually in the dream by an unknown woman or one who has less emotional significance for the dreamer.

**Projection.** Through the process of projection, the dreamer's unacceptable impulses or wishes are perceived in the dream as emanating from another person. Moreover, the person to whom these unacceptable impulses are ascribed is often the one toward whom the dreamer's own unconscious impulses are directed. For example, a person who has a strong but repressed wish to be unfaithful to his wife or sweetheart may dream that she has been unfaithful to him.

**Condensation.** Condensation is the mechanism by which several unconscious wishes, impulses, or attitudes are combined and expressed in a single image. In a child's dream an attacking monster may represent not only the dreamer's father but also some aspects of his mother, and the monster may stand for his own primitive impulses as well.

**Affects in Dreams.** Repressed emotions may not appear in the dream at all, or they may be experienced in somewhat altered form. For example, repressed rage toward another person may take the form of a mild dislike. Or, a repressed longing may be represented by a manifest repugnance.

**Secondary Revision.** Secondary revision is the mechanism through which the absurd, illogical, and bizarre characteristics of the dream—the distorted effects of symbolism, displacement, and condensation—acquire the coherence and rationality required by the dreamer. Secondary revision employs intellectual processes resembling the thought processes that govern states of consciousness.

**Anxiety Dreams.** Symbolism, displacement, condensation, projection, and secondary revision serve a dual purpose: they facilitate the discharge of latent impulses, and they prevent the direct discharge of instinctual drives, thereby protecting the dreamer from the excessive anxiety and pain that would accompany such discharge. Of course, these mechanisms may fail. Then the ego reacts to the direct expression of repressed impulses with severe anxiety.

**Punishment Dreams.** In the punishment dream, the ego anticipates superego condemnation if repressed impulses find direct expression in the dream. In anticipation of the terrible consequences of the loss of the ego's control over the instincts in sleep, the demands of the superego are satisfied by giving expression to punishment fantasies.

### Structural Theory of the Mind

Freud abandoned the topographic model and replaced it with the structural model of the psychic apparatus. The structural model was formulated and presented in *The Ego and the Id*, which appeared in 1923.

From a structural viewpoint, the psychic apparatus is divided into three provinces: id, ego, and superego, which are distinguished by their different functions. The main distinction lies between the ego and the id. The id is the locus of the instinctual drives. It is under the domination of the primary process; therefore, it operates in accordance with the pleasure principle, without regard for reality. The ego, on the other hand, represents a more coherent organization whose task it is to avoid unpleasure and pain by opposing or regulating the discharge of instinctual drives, in order to conform with the demands of the external world. In addition, the discharge of id impulses is opposed or regulated by the third structural component of the psychic apparatus, the superego, which contains the internalized moral values and influence of the parental images.

**Id.** Freud conceived of the id as a completely unorganized, primordial reservoir of energy, derived from the instincts, that is under the domination of the primary process. Freud postulated that the infant is endowed at birth with an id, that is, with instinctual drives that seek gratification. The infant does not, however, have the capacity to delay, control, or modify these drives. And, in the matter of coping with the external world, he is completely dependent on the egos of other persons in his environment.

**Ego.** No more comprehensive definition of the ego is available than that which Freud gave toward the end of his career in 1938 in *Outline of Psychoanalysis*: "Here are the principal characteristics of the ego. In consequence of the preestablished connection between sense and perception and muscular action, the ego has voluntary movement at its command. It has the task of self-preservation. As regards external events, it performs that task by becoming aware of stimuli by storing up experiences about them (in the memory), by avoiding excessively strong stimuli (through adaptation), and finally by learning to bring about expedient changes in the external world to its own advantage (through activity). As regards internal events in relation to the id, it performs that task by gaining control over the demands of the instinct, by deciding whether they are to be allowed satisfaction, by postponing that satisfaction to times and circumstances favorable in the external world, or by suppressing their excitations entirely. It is guided in its activity by consideration of the tension produced by stimuli, whether these tensions are present in it or introduced into it."

Freud believed that the modification of the id occurs as a result of the impact of the external world upon the drives. The pressures of external reality enable the ego to appropriate the energies of the id to do its work. In the process of formation, the ego seeks to bring the influences of the external world to bear upon the id, to substitute the reality principle for the pleasure principle; it thereby contributes to its own further development. Freud emphasized the role of the instincts in ego development, particularly the role of conflict. At first this conflict is between the id and the outside world; later it is between the id and ego itself.

At first, the infant is unable to differentiate his own body from the rest of the world: the ego begins with the child's ability to perceive his body as distinct from the external world.

Gratification and frustration of drives and needs in the early months of life affect the future fate of the ego. Adequate satisfaction of the infant's libidinal needs by the mother or mother surrogate is crucially important. And, although it is less clearly understood and appreciated, a certain amount of drive frustration in infancy and early childhood is equally important for the development of a healthy ego. Maternal deprivation at significant stages of development leads to the impairment of ego functions to varying degrees. However, overindulgence of the child's instinctual needs interferes with the development of the ego's capacity to tolerate frustration, and consequently with its ability to regulate the demands of the id in relation to the outside world.

The loss of the loved object or of a particularly gratifying relationship with the object is a painful experience at any stage of life, but it is particularly traumatic in infancy and early childhood, when the ego is not yet strong enough to compensate for the loss. Yet in the early years of life, the child is constantly subjected to such deprivation. In the normal course of events, the young child does not suffer the actual loss of his parents, but he must endure constant alterations in his relationship with them. Moreover, at each stage in his development, he must endure the loss of the kind of gratification that was appropriate to the previous phase of his maturation but that must then be given up.

Increasing internalization permits an increasing capacity for delay and detour, increasing independence from the pressure of immediate stimuli, and a more developed capacity for flexibility of response. Internalization, therefore, increases the organism's range of adaptive functions and enlarges its resources for coping with environmental stresses. It includes those processes by which the inner psychic world is built up, including incorporation, introjection, and identification.

Incorporation seems to involve a primitive oral wish for union with an object, which loses all distinction and function as object. The external object is completely assumed into the inner world of the subject. Incorporation is operative in relatively regressive conditions. It can be regarded as the mechanism of primitive, primary internalization and is probably operative in severely regressed psychotic states involving loss of self-object differentiation, permeation of ego boundaries, and psychotic identifications.

Introjection was originally described by Freud in *Mourning and Melancholia* as a process of narcissistic identification, in which the lost object is retained as a part of the internal structure of the psyche. Freud later applied this mechanism to the genesis of the superego, so that introjection became the primary internalizing mechanism by which parental images were internalized at the close of the oedipal phase. The child tries to retain the gratifications derived from these object relationships, at least in fantasy, through the process of introjection. By this mechanism, qualities of the person who was once the center of the gratifying relationship are internalized and re-established as part of the organization of the self.

Since introjects are responsive to and derivative from instinctual drive components, they can serve important defensive functions. Developmentally, their function is, in part, that of binding and mastering and thus modifying the impact of instinctual drives on the emerging ego apparatus. But they can become involved more deeply in the response to and modification of drive pressures, so that they become the foci of internal defensive functions. This defensive function of introjective organizations within the psyche makes them highly susceptible to drive influences and relatively more susceptible to regressive drive pulls. When these defensive pressures predominate in the development of introjects, the result is an impediment to further consolidation and building of internal psychic structure, a susceptibility to regressive pulls, and a liability to projective forms of defense.

The process of introjection can lead not only to the development of a pathological organization within the psyche, but also to the development of internal structures that are compatible with the development of healthy object relationships. Identification with the aggressor is a defensive maneuver based on the child's need to protect himself from the severe anxiety experienced in relation to the object. The child protects himself by introjecting the characteristics of the feared person, who is perceived by the child as his attacker and on whom the child is dependent. The perception of the object as attacking is usually due in part to the prior projection of the child's own hostile and destructive impulses onto the object by way of the defensive maneuver of projection. The child defends himself from his own hostile and destructive wishes by allying himself with the aggressor, rather than allowing himself to be the victim. Thus, he can share in the aggressor's power, rather than be helpless and powerless before him.

Such introjections, however, may impoverish the ego by burdening it with negative (aggressive, ambivalent) introjects. These introjects, by reason of the susceptibility to projection, distort and impede the development of object relations and the subsequent capacity for more mature and meaningful relations, and also impede the capacity for healthier and more constructive internalizations by way of identification.

Identification is an active structuralizing process that takes place within the ego, by which the ego constructs the inner constituents of regulatory control on the basis of selected elements derived from the model. What constitutes the model of identification can vary considerably, and can include introjects (internalized transitional-like objects), structural aspects of real objects, or even value components of group structures and group cultures.

The lines that differentiate identification from introjection should be kept clear. Introjection operates as a function of instinctual forces—both libidinal and aggressive—so that, in conjunction with projection, it functions intimately in the vicissitudes of instinctual and drive derivatives. Identification, however, functions relatively autonomously from drive derivatives. Introjection is indirectly involved in the transformation and binding of energies. Hence, introjection is much more influenced by drive energies, and its binding permits greater susceptibility to regressive pulls and to primary process forms of organization. The result of binding through identification, however, is more autonomous, more resistant to regressive pulls, and organized more specifically in secondary process terms. Identification, therefore, is specifically the mechanism for the formation of structures of secondary autonomy.

FUNCTIONS OF THE EGO. Several functions are generally conceded to be fundamental to the ego's operation. Many advances have been made in studying the ego, and this study makes up the important field of "ego psychology."

*Control and Regulations of Instinctual Drives.* The development of a capacity to delay immediate discharge of urgent wishes and impulses is essential if the ego is to assure the integrity of the individual, and fulfill its role as mediator between the id and the outside world. The development of the capacity to postpone instinctual discharge, like the capacity to test reality, is closely related to the progression in early childhood from the pleasure principle to the reality principle.

This progression parallels the development of the secondary process or logical thinking, which aids in the control of drive discharge. The evolution of thought from the initially prelogical primary process thinking to the more logical and deliberate secondary process thinking is one of the means by which the ego learns to postpone the discharge of instinctual drives. For example, the representation in fantasy of instinctual wishes as fulfilled may obviate the need for urgent action that might not serve the realistic needs of the individual. And, the capacity to figure things out or anticipate consequences represents thought processes that are essential to the realistic functioning of the individual. Obviously, then, the ego's capacity to control instinctual life and to regulate thinking is closely associated with its defense function.

*The Relation to Reality.* Freud always regarded the ego's capacity for maintaining a relationship to the external world as among its principal functions. The character of its relationship to the external world may be divided into three components: (1) the sense of reality, (2) reality testing, and (3) the adaptation to reality.

1. The Sense of Reality. The sense of reality originates simultaneously with the development of the ego. The infant first becomes aware of the reality of his own body dimensions. Only gradually does he develop the capacity to distinguish a reality outside his body.

2. Reality Testing. The ego's capacity for objective evaluation and judgment of the external world depends on the primary autonomous functions of the ego, such as memory and perception. Because of the fundamental importance of reality testing for negotiating with the outside world, its impairment may be associated with severe mental disorder. The development of the capacity to test reality (which is closely related to the progression from the pleasure to the reality prin-

ciple), and to distinguish fantasy from actuality, occurs gradually. Once gained, this capacity is subject to regression and temporary deterioration in children, even up to grade school age, in the face of anxiety, conflict, or intense instinctual wishes. However, this deterioration should not be confused with the breakdown of reality testing that occurs in adult psychopathology.

3. Adaptation to Reality. The capacity of the ego to utilize the individual's resources to form adequate solutions is based upon previously tested judgments of reality. Thus it is possible for the ego to develop good reality testing in terms of perception and grasp, at the same time that it develops an inadequate capacity to accommodate the individual's resources to the situation as perceived. Adaptation is closely allied to the concept of mastery in respect to both external tasks and the instincts. It should be distinguished from adjustment, which may entail accommodation to reality at the expense of certain resources or potentialities of the individual. The function of adaptation to reality is closely related to the defensive functions of the ego.

*Object Relations.* The development of a capacity for mutually satisfying object relationships is one of the fundamental functions of the ego. The relationship with a need-satisfying object begins when the infant is 6 months old, and under normal circumstances undergoes progressive development from then on. This process may be disturbed by retarded development or regression or, conceivably, by inherent—that is, genetic—defects or limitations in the capacity to develop object relationships. The development of object relationships is closely related to the evolution of drive components and the phase-appropriate defenses that accompany them.

*Synthesis.* The synthetic function—the ego's integrative capacities, its tendency to bind, unite, coordinate, and create, and its tendency to simplify or generalize—is concerned with the over-all organization and functioning of other ego functions in the course of its operation.

*Primary Autonomous Functions.* Primary autonomous ego functions are based on rudimentary apparatuses that are present at birth; they develop outside the conflict with the id. Hartmann has included perception, intuition, comprehension, thinking, language, certain phases of motor development, learning, and intelligence among the functions in this conflict-free sphere. However, each of these functions may become involved in conflict secondarily in the course of development. For example, if aggressive, competitive impulses intrude on the impetus to learn, they may evoke inhibitory reactions on the part of the ego.

*Defense Functions.* A systematic and comprehensive study of the defenses employed by the ego was presented for the first time by Anna Freud's (see Fig. 8), contribution on *The Ego and the Mechanisms of Defense.* Miss Freud maintained that everyone, normal as well as neurotic, employs a characteristic repertoire of defense mechanisms to varying degrees.

In the early stages of development, defenses emerge as a result of the ego's struggles to mediate between the pressures of the id and the requirements and strictures of outside reality. At each phase of libidinal development, associated drive components evoke characteristic ego defenses. For example, introjection, denial, and projection are defense mechanisms associated with oral sadistic impulses, whereas reaction formations, such as shame and disgust, develop in relation to anal impulses and pleasures. Defense mechanisms from earlier phases of development persist side by side with those of later periods. When defenses associated with pregenital phases of development tend to become predominant in adult life over more mature mechanisms such as sublimation and repression, the personality retains an infantile cast.

Defenses are not of themselves pathological. On the contrary, they may serve an essential function in maintaining normal psychological

FIGURE 8. Anna Freud.

well-being. Nonetheless, psychopathology may arise as a result of alterations in normal defensive functioning. Table I presents a brief classification and description of the most important basic defense mechanisms.

**Superego.** The superego is concerned with moral behavior based on unconscious behavioral patterns learned at early pregenital stages of development. Frequently, the superego allies itself with the ego against the id, imposing demands in the form of conscience or guilt feelings. Occasionally, however, the superego is allied with the id against the ego. This happens in cases of severely regressed reaction, when the functions of the superego may become sexualized once more or may become permeated by aggression, taking on a quality of primitive (usually anal) destructiveness, thus reflecting the quality of the instinctual drives in question.

The superego comes into being with the resolution of the Oedipus complex. The dissolution of the Oedipus complex and the concomitant abandonment of object ties lead to a rapid acceleration of the introjection process. Introjections from both parents become united and form a kind of precipitate within the self, which then confronts the other contents of the psyche as a superego. This identification with the parents is based on the child's struggles to repress the instinctual aims that were directed toward them, and it is this effort of renunciation that gives the superego its prohibiting character. It is for this reason, too, that the superego results to a great extent from an introjection of the parents' own superegos. Because the superego evolves as a result of repression of the instincts, it has a closer relation to the id than does the ego. The superego's origins are more internal; the ego originates to a greater extent in the external world and is its representative.

Throughout the latency period and thereafter, the child (and later the adult) continues to build on these early identifications through contact with teachers, heroic figures, and admired persons, who form his moral standards, his values, and his ultimate aspirations and ideals. The child's conflicts with his parents continue, but now they are largely internal, between the ego and the superego. The standards, restrictions, commands, and punishments imposed previously by the parents from without are internalized in the child's superego, which now judges and guides his behavior from within, even in the absence of his parents. This initially punitive superego must be modified and softened, so that eventually it can permit adult sexual object choice and fulfillment. The task of adolescence

TABLE I
DEFENSE MECHANISMS

**Denial.** A mechanism in which the existence of unpleasant realities is disavowed. The term refers to a keeping out of conscious awareness any aspects of either internal or external reality that, if acknowledged, would produce anxiety.

**Displacement.** A mechanism by which the emotional component of an unacceptable idea or object is transferred to a more acceptable one.

**Dissociation.** A mechanism involving the segregation of any group of mental or behavioral processes from the rest of the person's psychic activity. It may entail the separation of an idea from its accompanying emotional tone, as seen in dissociative disorders.

**Identification.** A mechanism by which a person patterns himself after another person; in the process, the self is more or less permanently altered.

**Identification with the aggressor.** A process by which a person incorporates within himself the mental image of a person who represents a source of frustration from the outside world. A primitive defense, it operates in the interest and service of the developing ego. The classic example of this defense occurs toward the end of the oedipal stage, when a boy, whose main source of love and gratification is his mother, identifies with his father. The father represents the source of frustration, being the powerful rival for the mother; the child cannot master or run away from his father, so he is obliged to identify with him.

**Incorporation.** A mechanism in which the psychic representation to another person or aspects of another person are assimilated into oneself through a figurative process of symbolic oral ingestion. It represents a special form of introjection and is the earliest mechanism of identification.

**Intellectualization.** A mechanism in which reasoning or logic is used in an attempt to avoid confrontation with an objectionable impulse and thus defend against anxiety. It is also known as brooding compulsion and thinking compulsion.

**Introjection.** The unconscious, symbolic internalization of a psychic representation of a hated or loved external object with the goal of establishing closeness to and constant presence of the object. It is considered an immature defense mechanism. In the case of a loved object, anxiety consequent to separation or tension arising out of ambivalence toward the object is diminished; in the case of a feared or hated object, internalization of its malicious or aggressive characteristics serves to avoid anxiety by symbolically putting those characteristics under one's own control.

**Isolation.** In psychoanalysis, a mechanism involving the separation of an idea or memory from its attached feeling tone. Unacceptable ideational content is thereby rendered free of its disturbing or unpleasant emotional charge.

**Projection.** Unconscious mechanism in which a person attributes to another those generally unconscious ideas, thoughts, feelings, and impulses that are in himself undesirable or unacceptable. Projection protects the person from anxiety arising from an inner conflict. By externalizing whatever is unacceptable, the person deals with it as a situation apart from himself.

**Rationalization.** A mechanism in which irrational or unacceptable behavior, motives, or feelings are logically justified or made consciously tolerable by plausible means.

**Regression.** A mechanism in which a person undergoes a partial or total return to earlier patterns of adaptation. Regression is observed in many psychiatric conditions, particularly schizophrenia.

**Repression.** A mechanism in which unacceptable mental contents are banished or kept out of consciousness. A term introduced by Freud, it is important in both normal psychological development and in neurotic and psychotic symptom formation. Freud recognized two kinds of repression. (1) repression proper—the repressed material was once in the conscious domain; (2) primal repression—the repressed material was never in the conscious realm.

**Sublimation.** A mechanism in which the energy associated with unacceptable impulses or drives is diverted into personally and socially acceptable channels. Unlike other defense mechanisms, sublimation offers some minimal gratification of the instinctual drive or impulse.

**Substitution.** A mechanism in which a person replaces an unacceptable wish, drive, emotion, or goal with one that is more acceptable.

**Suppression.** Conscious act of controlling and inhibiting an unacceptable impulse, emotion, or idea. Suppression is differentiated from repression in that repression is an unconscious process.

**Symbolization.** A mechanism which one idea or object comes to stand for another because of some common aspect or quality in both. Symbolization is based on similarity and association. The symbols formed protect the person from the anxiety that may be attached to the original idea or object.

**Undoing.** A mechanism by which a person symbolically acts out in reverse something unacceptable that has already been done or against which the ego must defend itself. A primitive defense mechanism, undoing is a form of magical action. Repetitive in nature, it is commonly observed in obsessive-compulsive disorder.

---

is to modify the oedipal identifications with the parents.

### Theory of Anxiety

For many years, Freud approached anxiety from the standpoint of the drives, and he regarded neurotic anxiety as transformed libido. In 1926 he attacked the problem of anxiety from the standpoint of the ego. Both real anxiety and neurotic anxiety were viewed as occurring in response to a danger to the organism. In real anxiety the threat emanates from a known danger outside the person; neurotic anxiety is precipitated by an unknown danger.

Freud distinguished two kinds of anxiety-provoking situations. In the first, for which the phenomenon of birth is the prototype, anxiety occurs as a result of excessive instinctual stimulation that the organism does not have the capacity to bind or handle. The excessive accumulation of instinctual energy overruns the protective barriers of the ego, and a panicky state, or trauma, results. These traumatic states are most likely to occur in infancy or childhood, when the ego is immature; however, they may also occur in adult life, notably in psychotic turmoil or panic states when the ego organization is overwhelmed.

In the more common situation, which occurs after the defensive system has matured, anxiety arises in anticipation of danger rather than as its result, although the affect may be experienced as if the danger had already occurred. In these situations the anxiety may arise because the person has learned to recognize, at a preconscious or unconscious level, aspects of a situation that were once traumatic. Signal anxiety mobilizes protective measures to avert the danger and prevent a traumatic situation from arising. The person may employ avoidance mechanisms to escape from a real or imagined danger from without, or he may bring to bear psychological defenses on the part of the ego from within to guard against or reduce the quantity of instinctual excitation.

According to this theory, neurotic symptoms—phobias, for example—indicate an imperfection in the psychic apparatus. The defensive activity of the ego has not succeeded in coping adequately with the unwelcome drive. As a result, mental conflict persists, and the danger that actually arose from within is now treated as though it had its origins in the external world. In psychosis, this failure of defensive function is more complete, greater portions of external reality are perceived as dangerous, and greater distortions of the ego become necessary in order to accommodate distortions in the view of the outside world.

### Character

In 1913, Freud made an important distinction between neurotic symptoms and character traits. Neurotic symptoms come into being as a result of the failure of repression; character traits owe their existence to the success of repression or, more accurately, of the defense system, which achieves its aim through a persistent pattern of reaction formation and sublimation. In 1923, Freud observed that the replacement of object attachment by identification (introjection), which set up the lost object inside the ego, also made a significant contribution to character formation. In 1932, Freud emphasized the particular importance of identification (introjection) with the parents for the construction of character, particularly with reference to superego formation.

Psychoanalysis has come to regard character as the pattern of adaptation to instinctual and environmental forces that is typical or habitual for a given person. Character is distinguished from the ego by the fact that character refers largely to directly observable behavior and styles of defense, acting, thinking, and feeling.

Innate biological predisposition, the interaction of id forces with early ego defenses and environmental influences, and various early identifications and imitations of other human beings leave their lasting stamp upon character. The degree to which the ego has developed a capacity to tolerate delay in drive discharge and to neutralize instinctual energy determines, for example, the degree to which such character traits will later emerge as impulsiveness.

The exaggerated development of certain character traits at the expense of others may lead to character disorders or produce a vulnerability or predisposition to the psychoses.

### Psychoanalytic Classification of Neurosis and Psychosis

In this chapter, the classical psychoanalytic diagnostic classification of Freud is being followed. This differs from the more descriptive nosology now in use in DSM-III. The reader is referred to Chapter 9, "Classification in Psychiatry," to determine the equivalent terms.

### Theory of Neurosis

Neuroses develop under the following conditions. (1) There is an inner conflict between drives and fears that prevents drive discharge. (2) Sexual drives are involved in this conflict. (3) The conflict has not been "worked through" to a realistic solution. Instead, the drives which seek discharge have been expelled from consciousness through repression or another defense mechanism. (4) The repression has merely rendered the drives unconscious; it has not deprived them of their power and made them innocuous. Consequently, the repressed tendencies—disguised neurotic symptoms—have fought their way back into consciousness. (5) A rudimentary neurosis based on the same type of conflict existed in early childhood.

Maternal deprivation in the first few months of life may impair ego development. Failure to make the necessary identifications, either because of overindulgence or because of excessive frustration, interferes with the ego's task of mediating between the instincts and the environment. Lack of capacity for equitable expression of drives, especially aggressive ones, may lead the child to turn them onto himself and to become overtly self-destructive. Inconsistency, excessive harshness, or undue permissiveness on the part of the parents may result in the disordered functioning of the superego. Instinctual conflict may impair the ego's capacity for sublimation, resulting in excessive inhibition of its autonomous functions. Severe conflict that cannot be dealt with through symptom formation may lead to severe restrictions in ego functioning and to the impairment of the capacity to learn and develop new skills.

When the ego has been weakened, a shock or traumatic event that seems to threaten survival may break through the ego defenses. A large amount of libido is then required to master the resultant excitation. But the libido thus mobilized is withdrawn from the supply normally applied to external objects and from the ego itself, and this withdrawal further diminishes the strength of the ego and produces a sense of inadequacy. Disappointments or frustrations of adult strivings can revive infantile longings that may be dealt with through symptom formation or further regression.

### Secondary Gains of Neurosis

The reduction of tension and conflict through neurotic illness is the primary purpose or gain of the disorder. The ego, however, may try to gain advantages from the external world by provoking pity in order to get attention and sympathy, by manipulating others, or even by receiving monetary compensation. These are the secondary gains of the illness.

Each form of neurosis has its characteristic form of secondary gain. In phobias there is a regression to childhood, when one was still protected. Gaining attention through dramatic acting out and, at times, deriving material advantages, are characteristic of conversion hysteria. In compulsive neurosis, there is frequently a narcissistic gain through pride in illness. In psychosomatic states, psychic conflicts are denied by projecting them onto the physical sphere. In the psychoses, the warding off of a painful idea, experience, or frustration in the outside world leads to severe regression and loss of reality testing.

### Symptomatic Neurotic States

**Hysteria.** Hysterical states are described in two major forms, depending on whether conver-

sion symptoms or dissociative reactions are predominant in the pathology.

Conversion disorder, which usually occurs in women but may also be seen in men, is characterized by bodily symptoms that resemble those of physical disease—paralysis, anesthesia, blindness, convulsions, pathological blushing, fainting, headaches, and other types of painful bodily experience—but that have no somatic basis. Unless these symptoms occur in very mild form in an otherwise well-adjusted personality, they may be positive indications for analysis. The typical course of treatment in such cases is the early alleviation of symptoms and the recognition of basic conflicts produced by genital wishes. Analysis of these conflicts usually leads to fundamental changes in the personality, in addition to permanent symptomatic relief. But a few cases of hysteria are difficult to analyze or may even be unanalyzable, particularly cases of hysteria in women whose personalities are exceptionally infantile, and some chronic cases in which the pleasure derived over long periods of time from secondary gain is too great to be renounced.

The dissociative type of hysteria occurs in a variety of complex forms that are often difficult to distinguish sharply, but that are characterized by the fact that a group of recent related mental events—which may consist of memories, feelings, or fantasies—are beyond the patient's power of conscious recall but still remain psychically active and ultimately capable of conscious recovery. The usual forms of dissociative disorder are somnambulism, various forms of amnesia (which can be quite localized or general), a variety of fugue states, and the unusual condition of multiple personality. Other forms of dissociative phenomena that have been described include various trance states, automatic writing, Ganser's syndrome, and some forms of mystical states of experience.

Hysteria provides a defense against overintense libidinal stimulation by transformation of psychical excitation into physical innervation. There is regression to the phallic stage of psychosexual development. As a result, various alterations of motor function or sensation may occur.

The choice of the afflicted region may be determined by the unconscious sexual fantasies and the corresponding erogeneity of the afflicted part, by physical injury or a change in the part which increases its susceptibility, by the nature of the situation in which the decisive repression occurred, and by the ability of the organ to express symbolically the unconscious drive in question. Hysteria may imitate a wide variety of diseases, which complicates the clinical picture considerably.

**Phobia.** Phobia is an abnormal fear reaction caused by a paralyzing conflict resulting from an increase of sexual excitation attached to an unconscious object. The fear is avoided by displacing the conflict onto an object or situation outside the ego system. The ego fights off the anxiety through states of inhibition or it avoids objects that have become connected with unconscious conflicts either through historical associations or through their symbolic significance.

The patient's history, the nature of the drives warded off, and the mechanisms of defense employed determine the clinical symptoms. Phobias about infection and touching often express the need to avoid dirt, and they show that the patient has to defend himself against anal-erotic temptations. Fear of open streets and stage fright may be defenses against exhibitionistic wishes. Anxieties about high places, closed places, falling cars, trains, and airplanes are developed to fight pleasurable sensations connected with stimulation involving the equilibrium.

In adults, the onset of various phobias typically occurs at a time of crisis in the sexual life. Fixation at the phallic stage, sexual frustrations, the presence of an external factor that may weaken the ego, increases in libidinal excitement, and a particular susceptibility to anxiety reactions are the most common causative factors.

**Obsessional Neurosis.** The obsessional or obsessive compulsive disorder is characterized by persisting or urgently recurring thoughts and repetitively performed behavior that bear little relation to the patient's realistic requirements, and that are experienced by him as foreign or intrusive. This syndrome is characterized by rumination, doubting, and irrational fears. All these symptoms can be accompanied by morbid anxiety when the intruding thoughts or the repetitive acts are prohibited or otherwise interfered with. Other symptoms are a strong tendency to ambivalence, a regression to magical thinking (particularly in relation to the obsessional thoughts), and indications of rigid and destructive superego functioning. The conflicts involved in obsessional neurosis usually lie closer to the prephallic phase of psychosexual development than to the phallic-oedipal phase.

The obsessional neurosis comes about as a result of the separation of affects from ideas or behavior by the defense mechanisms of undoing and isolation, by regression to the anal-sadistic level, or by turning the impulses against the self. As a defense against a painful idea in the unconscious, the affect is displaced onto some other indirectly associated idea, one more tolerable, which in turn becomes invested with an inordinate quantity of affect.

The onset of obsessive compulsive neurosis occurs relatively late in childhood because it depends on the formation of the superego. The introjection of the parents into the superego explains the relative predominance of punitive and expiatory symptoms.

**Depressive Neurosis.** The basic psychoanalytic approach to depressive states was laid down by Freud in *Mourning and Melancholia* in 1917. The basic mechanism he described there is the introjection of a lost object and a turning against the self of the aggressive impulses originally directed against the ambivalently loved object. A common theme in depressive states is the undermining or diminution of self-esteem.

Neurotic depressions usually involve a reactive component and are to be distinguished from more severe depressive syndromes, such as major depressions and manic-depressive states, in which the degree of regression is considerably more severe and in which the impairment of reality testing and of interpersonal functioning is much greater.

The patient in a depressive state often complains of disturbances of mood, which are described as involving sadness, unhappiness, and hopelessness. He usually experiences a loss of interest in his usual activities or complains of difficulties in concentration. The patient feels lonely, empty, guilty, worthless, inferior, or inadequate. The depressive symptoms often serve the purpose of eliciting sympathy and support. But at times, his complaints are so hostile and demanding that he frustrates his own purpose by irritating or alienating potential sources of affection. Suicidal ideas are frequently a component of depressive syndromes.

Depressive neurosis usually involves reaction to loss or failure. The loss may be the death of a loved person or a disappointment by a love object. A depression can also be triggered by failure to live up to one's own standards or to achieve specific personal or vocational goals.

Important factors affecting self-esteem seem to be the following: First, the patient has a poor self-image, usually based on early pathological development of his concept in an unfavorable or rejecting family atmosphere. Second, the discrepancy between behavior and the values maintained by the superego and the resulting punishment by the superego is experienced as guilt.

Third, if the ego-ideal is excessively grandiose, it places excessive demands on the ego. Fourth, the capacity for effective functioning of the ego itself is undermined.

Insufficient parental acceptance and affection, excessive parental devaluation, excessive frustration experienced prematurely, and a sense of ineffectiveness in the early social and independent performance of activities can undermine self-esteem. Loss of the parent in childhood has long been established as a predisposing factor to depression. During and after childhood, self-esteem can be adversely affected by illness, disfigurement, unattractiveness, or poor social, vocational, or educational performance.

**Hypochondriasis.** Hypochondriasis rarely appears as an isolated neurosis. More frequently, it appears as a complication in the picture of some other psychopathological condition, such as a compulsion neurosis or depression, or it appears as a stage in the development of or recovery from a psychotic condition. Sadistic and hostile impulses, withdrawn from objects and represented in the form of organic complaints, may play a particularly pronounced role in hypochondriacal syndromes. The typical hypochondriac is a conspicuously narcissistic, seclusive, monomaniacal person who is often in a transitional state between reactions of a more hysterical character and those that are delusional and clearly psychotic.

**Impulse Disorders.** The disorders of impulse control involve impulsive actions that, although not necessarily overtly sexual, serve the purpose of avoiding or mastering some type of pregenital anxiety that is intolerable to the ego. The strivings for security and for instinctual gratification are characteristically combined in the impulsive actions. Running away, conduct disorders, kleptomania, pyromania, gambling, substance abuse, and alcoholism are examples of irresistible impulsive activities. The impulse-ridden person, who is frequently encountered in psychiatric practice, eventually discharges tension or avoids inner conflict by urgent activity, which is sometimes of a destructive or self-destructive nature.

**Organ Neuroses.** These syndromes, also known as psychosomatic disorders, are characterized by functional and even anatomical alterations. Peptic ulcer, asthma, and ulcerative colitis are regarded as typical examples of physical conditions affected by psychological factors.

Many theories have been advanced to explain the origins of these phenomena. Psychosomatic symptoms have been described as affect equivalents, which represent dammed-up emotions, or as their symbolic representations, which can-

not be discharged through behavior or speech and which find expression in structural or functional alteration of an organ or organ system. Although it has some validity, the theory of affect equivalents is generally regarded as an oversimplified explanation of the multitude of complex interrelationships between psychological and somatic processes.

Other workers maintain that if a person has a predisposition or susceptibility to psychosomatic disorders, the inhibition of specific affects may lead to certain hormonal secretions, to changes in physical functions, and eventually to alteration in the tissues themselves.

**Paraphilias.** The paraphilias include such behavioral entities as fetishism, transvestism, exhibitionism, voyeurism, and sadomasochism. Freud used the term perversion, which is now obsolete, to refer to this group of disorders. The general mechanism of these disorders is thought to be a defensive flight from castration anxiety connected with fears of oedipal retaliation. They are disorders that are manifestly sexual in character. When the pathological impulses are released, orgasm is achieved. In fetishism, the anxiety is avoided by displacement of instinctual libidinal impulses to an inanimate object that symbolizes parts of the body of the loved person. Consequently, neurotic interest is attached to an object or body part that is inappropriate for normal sexual gratification. The transvestite finds sexual excitement in dressing in garments of the opposite sex. Exhibitionism is the deliberate exposure, usually compulsive, of sex organs, whereas the voyeur achieves sexual gratification by watching the sexual activities of others.

Sadism and masochism often appear early in childhood, and represent a tendency to seek out or to inflict physical or mental suffering as a means of achieving sexual arousal or gratification contingent on physical or mental pain, such as beatings, threats, humiliations, or subjugation at the hands of the sexual partner. The sadist gains sexual gratification by inflicting such torment on the sexual partner.

### Character (Personality) Disorders

In its psychoanalytic sense, character refers to the ego's habitual mode of bringing into harmony the tasks presented by internal demands and the external world. A particular character pattern or type becomes pathological when its manifestations are so exaggerated that behavior destructive to the individual or to others results, or the functioning of the person becomes distorted or restricted and a source of distress to himself or others.

**Phobic Character.** This person limits this reactive behavior to the avoidance of the situations for which he originally yearned. Thus certain external situations are avoided, as is true of neurotic phobic behavior. In addition, internal reactions, such as rage, love, or all intense feelings, may be subjected to phobic avoidance.

**Compulsive Character.** Reaction formations, isolation, and intellectualization are characteristic. The compulsive character attempts to overcome sadism by kindness and politeness, to conceal pleasure in dirt by rigorous cleanliness. As the result of isolation, there is a lack of adequate affective response and a restriction in the number of available modes of feeling. Object relationships are of an anal-sadistic nature.

**Hysterical Character.** The hysterical character has been described as a person who is inclined to sexualize all relationships and who tends toward suggestibility, irrational emotional outbreaks, chaotic behavior, dramatization, and histrionic activity.

**Cyclic Character.** This type of person exhibits periodic mood swings from depression to varying degrees of elation, and he is particularly concerned with unresolved oral needs and conflicts.

**Depressive Character.** This type may show the characteristics of the depressive neurosis on a more enduring and chronic, if more low-keyed, basis. Chronically low self-esteem and feelings of worthlessness are characteristic of this syndrome. Very often there is a history of early object loss or severe deprivation, often involving the loss of a parent. The syndrome of depressive character relates to ego deficiencies and inadequacies.

**Passive-Aggressive Character.** Passive-aggressive personalities are characterized by passive or submissive behavior as ways of expressing hostile or destructive feelings or intentions. Such behaviors are usually directed at others on whom they feel dependent or subordinate. They include disinterest, withdrawal, negativism, obstructionism, inefficiency, procrastination, sabotage, perfunctory behavior, errors of omission, indifference, foot dragging, lack of initiative, literalness in compliant behavior that frustrates the outcome, and a variety of other passive behaviors. Any hostile or negative intent is denied, although there may be angry outbursts from time to time.

**Narcissistic Character.** This type presents a pathological picture characterized by an excessive degree of self-reference in interaction with others, an excessive need to be loved and admired by others, and apparently contradictory attitudes of an inflated concept of themselves and an inordinate need for tribute and admiration from others.

**Schizoid Character.** This type often presents a complaint of depression. They complain of feeling cut off, of being isolated and out of touch, of feeling apart or estranged from people and things around them; of feeling that things are somehow unreal, of diminishing interest in things and events around them, of feeling that life is futile and meaningless. Patients often call this state of mind "depression," but it lacks the inner sense of anger and guilt often found in depression. Moreover, depression is essentially object-related. The schizoid character has renounced objects; external relationships have been emptied by a massive withdrawal of libidinal attachment. The schizoid's major defense against anxiety is to keep emotionally out of reach, inaccessible, and isolated. The schizoid condition is based on the internalization of hostile, destructive introjects.

### Borderline States

Such patients represent a stable form of personality organization that is intermediate between neurotic levels of integration and the more primitive psychotic forms of personality organization. Anxiety is usually chronic and diffuse. Neurotic symptoms are multiple. Sexuality is frequently promiscuous and often perverse. Personality organization tends to be impulsive and infantile, and the imperative need to gratify impulses breaks through episodically, giving the borderline life-style an acting-out quality. Narcissism is often a predominant element in the character structure. Underlying these elements is often a core of paranoia based on projection of rather primitive oral rage. The underlying character dimensions may also take the form of severe depressive-masochistic pathology.

The inner organization of the borderline personality reveals the weakness in the structure of the ego. The patient shows a marked lack of tolerance for even low degrees of anxiety, has poor capacity for impulse control, lacks suitable channels for sublimation, has a poor capacity for neutralization, and often shows a generalized shift toward primary-process cognitive organization.

It is difficult for the patient to engage in a productive therapeutic relationship. Frustration tolerance is low, and narcissistic expectations are high. The therapeutic interaction is often distorted by attempts to manipulate the therapist in order to gain needed gratification. The manipulation often takes the form of a suicidal gesture aimed at getting the therapist to comply with the patient's wishes.

### The Psychoanalytic Theory of Psychosis

Freud postulated that in paranoia the need to project coincided with an unconscious need for homosexual love that, although of overwhelming intensity, was consciously denied by the patient. He also suggested that paranoid delusions represented sexual conflicts concerning persons of the same sex that had been projected onto some other person of force, which was then perceived as persecuting.

Freud also stated that psychosis was characterized by the patient's incapacity for normal emotional interest in other people and things. The energy withdrawn from impoverished love relationships produces an abnormal, excessive interest in the bodily functions and psychic attributes of the self, and the psychotic patient's use of language indicates an emotional interest in the verbal symbol rather than in the object that the word represents. Many of the more obvious symptoms of psychosis are secondary to this primary loss of the capacity to love others. Freud concluded that delusions, hallucinations, and certain forms of disorganized behavior represent rudimentary efforts on the part of the patient to restore his lost feelings for objects.

Subsequent investigations have followed Freud's suggestion that the conflicts that result in psychotic adaptations occur primarily between the individual and his environment. In contrast, the conflicts in neurosis are primarily within the personality, between unconscious infantile wishes and adult attitudes. The psychoses are seen as resulting from defects in the ego's integrative capacities; from a defect in the ego's capacity for fusion and, consequently, from limitations in the ego's capacity to neutralize instinctual energies; from the ineffectiveness of those functions essential to the capacity for establishing real object relations; and from the impairment of functions essential for controlling intense infantile wishes by normal or neurotic mechanisms.

The psychotic adjustment uses more primitive types of defense, particularly denial, distortion, and projection. The primitive defenses are reflected in flight, social withdrawal, and the simple inhibition of impulses. These defense mechanisms are much less highly organized than the mechanisms of repression and reaction formation.

### Melancholia

Freud emphasized the fact that the pain in mourning is limited to loss of an external object. In contrast, in melancholia the ego itself is impoverished because it has experienced an internal loss. The orally dependent person, who requires constant narcissistic supplies from outside, is most likely to manifest this reaction in its severe form. The prototype of depression is the deprivation of vital narcissistic supplies— love, affection, and care—at the oral stage. It is the excessive duration and domination of the organism by depressive affect, rather than its occurrence, that is pathological.

Depression is characterized by a decrease in self-esteem, a sense of helplessness, the inhibition of ego functions to varying degrees, and a subjective feeling of sadness or loss of varying intensity. Psychotic depressions are marked by their greater intensity, and by the degree of fragmentation and helpless vulnerability that characterizes the ego response to the depressive affect. The intensity of the aggression released is more primitive in psychotic states, and psychotic depressions are almost universally accompanied by profound suicidal ideas or serious suicidal attempts. Psychotic depression has also been described as a basic affective state in which the ego feels totally incapable of fulfilling its aims or aspirations, although these aims persist as desired goals. The ego is thus thrown into a state of continuing and total hopelessness. Persons prone to depression often display a pseudoindependence and self-assurance, which is a reaction to early severe deprivation and is intended to serve as a defense against the threat of further deprivation or rejection.

### Manic-Depressive Disorder

The manic-depressive person manifests a particular kind of infantile narcissistic dependency on his love object. To offset his feelings of unworthiness, he requires a constant supply of love and moral support from a highly valued love object, which may be an individual, an organization, or a cause to which he feels he belongs. As long as this object lasts, he is able to function with high efficiency. But because of his strong self-punitive tendencies, the object choice of the manic-depressive person is masochistically determined and is bound to disappoint him. Thus he himself sets the stage for his illness. When he is disappointed by the love object, ego functioning is impaired at every level.

The depressive phase subsides and gives way to temporary elation (mania) when the narcissistically important goals and objects appear to be within reach once again, when they have become sufficiently modified or reduced to be realistically attainable, when they are renounced completely, or when the ego recovers from its narcissistic shock and regains its self-esteem with the help of various recuperative agencies.

Mania represents a way of avoiding awareness of inner depression. It includes denial of painful inner reality and flight into external reality. Since the manic person does not want to become aware of his own feelings, he cannot permit himself to empathize with others; he is emotionally isolated.

## Schizophrenia

Psychoanalytic concepts regarding schizophrenia continue to undergo modification and revision. Originally, Freud postulated that the onset of schizophrenia signified a withdrawal of libido from the outside world. This libido, he thought, was subsequently absorbed into the ego, producing a state of megalomanic grandiosity, or it was returned to the outside world in the form of delusions.

Recent clinical interest in schizophrenia has centered on the intense ambivalence characteristic of schizophrenic patients, their retaliation (persecutory) anxiety, and the infantile ego mechanisms they typically use in their relationship with objects. The failure of these mechanisms results in the patient's decompensation or regressed state. Two stages are particularly conspicuous in the clinical picture of schizophrenic regression: first, the break with reality; second, the attempts to re-establish contact with reality.

Schizophrenic regression is usually precipitated by loss or frustration of object needs. The effect of loss results in the supremacy of negative affects, thus dislocating the delicate balance between introjective components in the patient's self-organization. There is a loss of equilibrium between the positive good introjects and the negative bad introjects that compose the structure of the self. The inundation with diffused and deneutralized destructive and negative feelings necessitates a regression to a point of deepest fixation—namely, the narcissistic position—where the patient not only is a potential victim but also operates for self-consolidation. At this level, the patient's regressive disorganization is accompanied by a dedifferentiation of boundaries between self and object. Only in that position can the patient achieve release of the internal tension. The path of regression varies according to whether the losses are acute and overwhelming or slow and cumulative and according to the patient's structural organization.

Admittedly, the preschizophrenic ego is weak in terms of the development of mature defense mechanisms, but, with the onset of psychosis, elements of mature mechanisms that have become established become admixed with infantile patterns. The acute onset of schizophrenia is related to an increased intensity of paranoid (persecutory) anxiety, feelings of omnipotence, and intolerable depressive anxieties—all of which had previously been warded off by narcissistic ego patterns of behavior. In addition, the patient typically demonstrates perceptual distortion, self-hatred, and a reliance on infantile and highly dependent patterns of object relatedness.

## Treatment

Freud realized that the success of treatment depended on the patient's ability to understand the emotional significance of an experience on an emotional level, and to retain that insight. Psychoanalysis tries to bring repressed material back to consciousness so that the patient, on the basis of his greater understanding of his needs and motives, may find a realistic solution to his conflict. Freud elaborated a treatment method that attaches minimal importance to the immediate relief of symptoms, moral support from the therapist, and guidance counseling. The goal of psychoanalysis is to pull the neurosis up by its roots, rather than prune off the top.

## Patient Selection

The capacity for mature adjustment is limited in some persons, even though they do not have a particularly severe neurosis. Often there is no evidence of strong drive to combat the more infantile aspects of their personalities. Analysis is contraindicated in extreme cases of this kind, since there is no element of personality that will strive to use the treatment for eventual maturity.

Apart from the capacity for logical thought and a certain degree of ego strength, fundamental vigor of personality is a prerequisite. The analytical patient undergoes a difficult experience. From time to time he must be able to accept a temporary increase in unhappiness or anxiety in the expectation of eventual benefit. When there is some question as to the patient's qualifications in this regard, a short period of trial analysis may be recommended to evaluate the problems and potentialities of the patient more completely.

A youthful mind (less in terms of actual years than in terms of elasticity of functioning) is essential. In general, however, treatment proceeds more quickly to an effective result when patients are in their twenties and thirties. Often an important element in patients lives is that they have been able to preserve and maintain some area of successful ego functioning in a consistent and productive manner. Honest skepticism about analysis is usually a good prognostic sign, as long as it is not extreme.

Potentially analyzable neurotic patients have

been able to sustain significant object relations with both parents through the latency years, after the resolution of the oedipal complex. Classical psychoanalysis is the treatment of choice for potentially mature patients in whom the developmental difficulties lie on the level of the mastery of genuine internal conflicts. Patients who are unable to tolerate anxiety or depression (such as borderline personalities) are rarely able to work through a transference neurosis. The more significant difficulty for such patients is their inability to terminate any form of therapy successfully.

### Analytical Process

The analytical process refers to the regressive emergence, working through, interpretation, and resolution of the transference neurosis. The analytical situation, on the other hand, refers to the setting in which the analytical process takes place—specifically, the positive real relationship between patient and analyst based on the therapeutic alliance.

The regression induced by the analytical situation allows for a re-emergence of infantile conflicts and thus induces the formation of a transference neurosis. In the transference neurosis the original infantile conflicts and wishes become focused on the person of the analyst and are re-experienced and relived. In the analytical regression, earlier infantile conflicts are revived and can be seen as a manifestation of the repetition compulsion.

The analytical process can be usefully divided into three phases. The first phase involves the initiation and consolidation of the analytical situation. The second phase involves the emergence and analysis of the transference neurosis. The third phase involves the carrying through of a successful termination and separation from the analytical process. Each phase requires different capacities in the patient and focuses on different developmental aptitudes. The analyst must determine the relative aptitude of the patient to meet the demands of each phase.

In the first phase the patient must have a capacity to maintain basic trust in the absence of gratification; he must be able to maintain self-object differentiation in the absence of the object; he must retain a capacity to accept the limitations of reality, to tolerate frustrations, and to acknowledge his own limitations and lack of omnipotence. In the second phase the patient must be able to regress sufficiently to allow the transference neurosis to emerge and be analyzed and to work through its various elements. The third phase involves the patient's capacity to

tolerate separation and loss, and to integrate affects constructively in a pattern of positive identification with the analyst.

### Techniques

The cornerstone of the psychoanalytic technique is free association. The primary function of free association, besides the obvious one of providing content for the analysis, is to induce the necessary regression and passive dependence that are connected with establishing and working through the transference neurosis. The use of free association in the analytical process is a relative matter. Although it remains the basic technique and the fundamental rule by which the patient's participation in the analysis is guided, there are frequent occasions in which the process of free association is interrupted or modified, according to the defensive needs or the developmental progression taking place within the analysis.

The analysis becomes a recurring conflict between transference and resistance, manifested by involuntary inhibitions of the patient's effort to free-associate that may last for moments or days. This conflict is a repetition of the sexuality-guilt conflict that produced the neurosis itself. The analysis of resistance is the analyst's prime function, and interpretation is his chief tool. The analyst not only paraphrases the patient's verbal reports but indicates at appropriate moments what he is not reporting. As a general rule, analytic interpretation does not produce immediate symptomatic relief. On the contrary, there may be a heightening of anxiety and the emergence of further resistance. It is not so much the analyst's insight into the patient's psychodynamics that produces progress in the analysis, but his ability to help the patient to gain this insight for himself by reducing unconscious resistance to such self-awareness through appropriate, carefully timed interpretation.

In the course of his analysis, the patient undergoes two processes, remembering and reliving, which constitute the dynamics of the treatment procedure. Remembering refers to the gradual extension of consciousness back to early childhood, at which time the core of the neurosis was formed. Reliving refers to the actual reexperiencing of childhood events in the context of the patient's relationship with the analyst.

The patient displaces the feelings he originally directed toward the participants in these early events onto the analyst, who becomes, alternately, a friend or an enemy, one who is nice to him, or frustrates his needs and punishes him and is correspondingly loved or hated. To an increasing extent, the patient's feelings toward the analyst replicate his feelings toward the specific people that he is talking about. This object displacement, which is an inevitable concomitant of psychoanalytic treatment, is called transference. As unresolved childhood attitudes emerge during transference, the patient begins to see himself as he really is, with all his unfulfilled and contradictory needs spread before him.

### Results

No analyst can eliminate all of the personality defects and neurotic factors in a patient, no matter how thorough the treatment. On the other hand, mitigation of the rigors of a punitive superego is an essential criterion of the effectiveness of treatment. Psychoanalysts do not usually regard alleviation of symptoms as the most significant index of therapeutic change. The absence of recurrence of the illness or of further need for psychotherapy are more important indices of the value of analysis. However, the chief basis of evaluation remains the patient's general adjustment to life: his capacity for attaining reasonable happiness, contributing to the happiness of others, dealing adequately with the normal vicissitudes of life, and his capacity to enter into and sustain mutually gratifying and rewarding relationships with other people in his life.

### REFERENCES

Fenichel O: *The Psychoanalytic Theory of Neurosis.* W. W. Norton, New York, 1945.
Freud A: *The Ego and the Mechanisms of Defense.* International Universities Press, New York, 1946.
Freud S: *Standard Edition of the Complete Psychological Works of Sigmund Freud.* Hogarth Press, London, 1953–1966.
Greenberg J R, Mitchell S A: *Object Relations in Psychoanalytic Theory.* Harvard University Press, Cambridge, MA 1983.
Hartmann H; *Essays on Ego Psychology.* International Universities Press, New York, 1964.
Jones E: *The Life and Work of Sigmund Freud,* 3 volumes. Basic Books, New York, 1953–1957.
Meissner W: Classical psychoanalysis. In *Comprehensive Textbook of Psychiatry,* ed 4, H I Kaplan, B J Sadock, editors, p 337. Williams & Wilkins, Baltimore, 1985.
Weisman A D: *The Existential Core of Psychoanalysis.* Little, Brown, Boston. 1965.
Zetzel E R: *The Capacity for Emotional Growth.* International Universities Press, New York, 1970.
Zetzel E R, Meissner W W: *Basic Concepts of Psychoanalytic Psychiatry.* Basic Books, New York, 1973.

## 5.2    ERIK ERIKSON

### Introduction

Erik Erikson (see Fig. 1), born in 1902, brought Freud's psychoanalytic theory out of the bounds of the nuclear family, focusing his interest beyond the molding power of the child's early life and the oedipal family romance, to the wider milieu of the social world, where children interact with peers, teachers, national ethics, and expectations. He added to Freud's theory of infantile sexuality by concentrating on the child's development beyond puberty, thus rejecting the notion that childhood experience is the sole determinant of lifelong behavior patterns and personality.

In considering the healthy personality, Erikson selected the ego as the tool by which a person organizes outside information, tests perception, selects memories, governs action adaptively, and integrates the capacities of orientation and planning. Erikson introduced the term *epigenesis* to refer to the stages of ego and social development.

### Theory of Personality

Erikson is probably best known for his positing of eight stages of ego development, which cover the entire life-span from birth to death (see Table I). These stages, which roughly parallel Freud's psychosexual stages, have both positive and negative aspects, are marked by emotional crises, and are very much affected by the person's particular culture and by his interaction with the society of which he is a part.

**Oral-Sensory Stage; Basic Trust versus Mistrust.** During the first months of life, the mouth is the most sensitive zone of the body.

FIGURE 1.   Erik Erikson.

TABLE I
ERIKSON'S DEVELOPMENTAL STAGES AND
PSYCHOSOCIAL CRISES

| Developmental Stage | Psychosocial Crisis |
| --- | --- |
| I. Oral-sensory (infancy) | Basic trust versus mistrust |
| II. Muscular-anal (early childhood) | Autonomy versus shame, doubt |
| III. Locomotor-genital (play age) | Initiative versus guilt |
| IV. Latency (school age) | Industry versus inferiority |
| V. Puberty and adolescence | Identity versus role confusion |
| VI. Young adulthood | Intimacy versus isolation |
| VII. Adulthood | Generativity versus stagnation |
| VIII. Maturity | Integrity versus despair |

The infant incorporates, taking in food, a nipple, a finger. There is hunger for nourishment and for stimulation of the sense organs and the whole surface of the skin. Depending on what happens between the baby and the mother, who is also a bearer of the values of the society, the baby develops either a basic feeling of trust that his wants will be frequently satisfied, or a sense that he is going to lose most of what he wants.

During the second 6 months, the dominant social mode moves from getting to taking, manifested orally in biting. However, the nursing child finds the nipple removed if he bites. Weaning begins, and sorrow or nostalgia begin too. But if his basic trust is strong, he can draw from a built-in and lifelong spring of hope instead of a well of doom.

**Muscular-Anal Stage: Autonomy versus Shame and Doubt.** In the second and third years of life, the child learns to walk by himself, to feed himself, to talk, and to control his anal sphincter muscles. He then has a choice of social modes: to keep or let go. Also, the walking child struggles for mastery of his whole self in contradiction to such restraining forces as gravity and parental wishes.

If parents encourage a child to rely on his own abilities and provide a framework that is not arbitrary, whimsical, or too difficult, he gains a certain confidence in his autonomy. However, if his feces are called bad, or if he is overrestrained, he then feels enraged at his impotence, and he feels foolish and shamed. Once shamed, he mistrusts his own rightness and comes to doubt himself.

**Locomotor-Genital Stage: Initiative versus Guilt.** At age 3, the child moves out into the world, where his learning becomes instructive; he grabs with eagerness and curiosity. However, the child shows his first initiative at home, where he expresses passionate interest in the parent of the opposite sex. Of course, he is disappointed. He may simultaneously be trying to wrest a place for himself in the affection of parents against siblings.

He develops a division between what he wants to do, and what he is told he should do. The division increases until a gap grows between the infant's set of expanded desires, his exuberance at unlimited growth, and his parent's set of restrictions. He gradually turns these parental values into self-obedience, self-guidance, and self-punishment. This stage ends at about 6 years.

**Stage of Latency: Industry versus Inferiority.** The child can become confident of his ability to use adult materials during the period of latency, when he is waiting, learning, and practicing to be a provider. Or, he can forsake the attempt, forsake industry itself, and come to the conclusion that he is inferior and cannot operate the things of the world. This stage runs from ages 6 to 11.

**Stage of Puberty and Adolescence: Identity versus Role Confusion.** The teenage years (ages 11 to 18) summon up the question of whether a child will opt for the career that his parents want him to choose, or whether he will choose another. If another, what? Indecision and confusion often cause young people to cling to each other in a clannish manner. A youth is in suspension between "the morality learned by the child and the ethics to be developed by the adult." This suspension Erikson calls a moratorium.

Characteristic of the development period of adolescence and youth is the *identity crisis*, the term introduced by Erikson to describe the inability of the adolescent to accept the role he believes is expected of him by society.

**Stage of Young Adulthood: Intimacy versus Isolation.** A young adult either shares himself in intense and long term relationships, or becomes self-interested and self-indulgent. Without a friend or a partner in marriage, a sense of isolation grows to dangerous proportions.

In true intimacy, there is mutuality. If love and sex become united rather than separated, the young adult is able to make love that can be shared with another person and that goes back to the world through their children.

**Stage of Adulthood: Generativity versus Stagnation.** Generativity means a vital interest outside the home in establishing and guiding the oncoming generation or in bettering society. The childless can be generative; however, adults living only to satisfy personal needs and to acquire comforts and entertainment for themselves are engaged in the self-absorption that is stagnation. These decades span the middle years of life.

**Stage of Maturity: Integrity versus Despair.** When death has come within the range of daily thought, the mature adult develops a set of feelings stemming from despair. He may be able to triumph over it by ego integrity: that is, by a strong sense of self and of the value of past life. Strength comes from looking back to a life that has produced satisfaction. Without this, there is a fear of death, a despair, and despair's mask, disgust.

## Abnormal Development and Functioning

Erikson's theory of zones and modes forms the skeleton by which certain types of malfunctioning can be understood. The social modes are those of getting, taking, holding, letting go, and being "on the make" or "making it." The physical modes underlying these are the physical actions by which the zone under question is capable of performing. Passive and active incorporation, retention, elimination, and intrusion are Erikson's five physical modes of action.

A zone can become too prominent, causing an adult to be aware of the oral or the anal, for instance, in a way that is out of proportion to his stage of life. Or a mode can become too habitual; elimination, for example, can start with spitting, move on to uncontrolled bowels, and then to many but incomplete orgasms in women or to premature ejaculation in men.

**Lying and Sitting Stage.** If the mother does not supply the newborn with food when he wants it—withdrawing the nipple for fear of being bitten, for instance—the child may try to hang on even harder, causing the nipple to be even more forcibly removed. The infant may develop a biting reflex prematurely and a frustrating sense that he will lose what he wants. His resentment at being manipulated can make him compulsive and obsessive as he later turns his willfulness toward the manipulation of others.

If trust does not develop and mistrust does, fertile ground for schizophrenia exists. Trust involves mutuality: if either partner is withdrawn, the gap between them widens, and the infant may begin a flight into a schizophrenic withdrawal.

The infant may feel empty, starved not just for food but for sensual and visual stimulation. He may become, as an adult, a seeker after stimulating thrills that do not involve intimacy. At the weaning or biting stage, the enraged infant may develop a sadistic and masochistic confusion. A drastic, sudden weaning and loss of mother can lead to infantile and lifelong depression.

At the time of bowel and bladder control, the baby's fear of loss of autonomy becomes a fear of being robbed by outsiders or by inner saboteurs. A paranoid fear that evil lurks nearby or even within the body can originate at this time. If the baby cannot resist being manipulated, he may develop such a rage against manipulation that he tries to control everyone and every event in a compulsion neurosis.

**Standing Stage.** In becoming upright, the child experiences in a new way his sense of smallness. When he looks forward, he sees the eyes of others examining him. Feeling small, he may not be ready for that exposure. If shaming is experienced continuously, the child can ultimately develop extreme and sustained defiance after realizing that he cannot be all bad.

The child cannot see his own buttocks, but others do. A feeling develops that others can dominate the backside, even invade and lay low one's autonomy. Paranoid fears of unseen and hostile people can come into being. Others can condemn the feces that seemed acceptable when leaving the body, and a doubt begins that what one produces and leaves behind is inadequate. Paranoid fears of threats from within are based on this sense.

When the child finally walks, he fears losing that ability or becoming imprisoned or immobile. He also fears having no guidance, no borders. Without being told when familiar ground ends, the child does not know against whom he must arm himself or when he can relax.

As sexual fantasies are accepted as unrealizable, a child may punish himself for these fantasies by fearing harm to his genitals. Under the brutal assault of the developing superego, he may repress his wishes and begin to deny them. If this pattern is carried forward, paralysis, inhibition, or impotence can result. Or, in fear of not being able to live up to what others expect, the child may turn to psychosomatic disease.

**School Stage.** Erikson talks of two dangers during the elementary school years. One risk is that of considering oneself less of a workman and provider than the next person. A child who acquired trust, autonomy, and initiative at home can come to school and find himself discriminated against or told that he is inferior. This can cause him to go back to the personal scene in the home, where he will always remain small. The other hazard is that of making work the whole of life.

**Adulthood.** If adult identity is not secure, a

person may shun the process of sharing friendship, orgasm, or affiliation of any kind. He avoids intimacy and retreats into self-absorption or isolation.

The adult who has no interest in guiding or establishing the oncoming generation is likely to look obsessively for intimacy that is not truly intimate. Such people may marry and even produce children, but all within a cocoon of self-concern and isolation. These persons pamper themselves as if they were the children, becoming prey to psychosomatic invalidism.

If, looking back on his life, a person feels that he never acquired the things he wanted and did not do anything meaningful, he is open to panic at seeing his time run out and his chances used up.

### Treatment

The infant normally develops basic trust as the cornerstone on which all other ego characteristics depend. The neurotic or psychotic person who lacks it may be given his second chance for building this trust by the therapist. Mutuality, so important in Erikson's system of health, is also vital to the cure. He urges that the relationship of the healer to the sick person be one of equals.

Erikson discusses four dimensions of the job of the psychoanalyst. The patient's desire to be cured and the analyst's desire to cure him run along an axis of cure-research. It is to be a common research; there is mutuality in that

patient and therapist are motivated by cure, and there is a division of labor.

The second dimension Erikson calls objectivity-participation. The therapist must keep his mind open. "Neuroses change," says Erikson. New generalizations must be made and arranged in new configurations.

The third dimension runs along the axis of knowledge-participation. The therapist "applies selected insights to more strictly experimental approaches."

The fourth dimension is tolerance-indignation. The expression of indignation by a controlling therapist is harmful: it increases inequality and makes more difficult the realization of that recurrent idea in Erikson's thought, mutuality.

### REFERENCES

Coles R: *Erik H. Erikson: The Growth of His Work.* Little, Brown, Boston, 1970.
Erikson E: Identity and the psychosocial development of the child. In *Discussion on Child Development,* vol. 30. International Universities Press, New York, 1958.
Erikson E.: *Young Man Luther: A Study in Psychoanalysis and History.* W. W. Norton, New York, 1958.
Erikson E: *Insight and Responsibility.* W. W. Norton, New York, 1964.
Erikson E.: *Identity: Youth and Crisis.* W. W. Norton, New York, 1968.
Erikson E: *Gandhi's Truth.* W. W. Norton, New York, 1969.
Meissner W: Classical psychoanalysis. In *Comprehensive Textbook of Psychiatry,* ed 4, H I Kaplan, B J Sadock, editors, p 337. Williams & Wilkins, Baltimore, 1985.

# 6

# Theories of Personality and Psychopathology: Cultural and Interpersonal Schools

## 6.1    KAREN HORNEY

What is known as the Horney theory systematizes the concepts formulated by Karen Horney (1885–1952) (see Fig. 1) between 1937 and 1952. The need for a theory that differed from Freud was based on (1) differences in the symptoms of neurosis characteristic of the 19th century as compared with the symptoms that predominated during the 20th century and differences in the symptoms that were typical of Europe as compared with those in the United States; (2) the fact that the variation in symptoms from one patient to another could not be adequately explained on a purely biological basis; and (3) dissatisfaction with classical psychoanalytic therapeutic results.

### Theory of Personality

The individual is seen holistically, as a unit within a social framework, ever influencing and being influenced by his environment. Functionally, personality may be said to consist of the attributes that characterize the constantly changing organization of the individual. These include his biological and social needs, behavioral traits, feelings, attitudes toward others and self, self-evaluations and concepts, social values, expectations, inhibitions, and conflicts. Each attribute is simultaneously created by the individual and acts upon him, demanding satisfaction, producing strivings, or pressing toward action. One attribute may reinforce or conflict with another. Attributes are learned from the family.

Partly because of this holistic, functional, dynamic view of personality, Freud's structural theory of personality and his economic theory of a fixed quantity of psychic energy were held untenable. According to the Horney theory, motivating factors derive from current personality attributes rather than from infantile libidinal strivings that are carried over from childhood through the repetition compulsion.

Understanding the triple concept of self—the actual self, the real self, and the idealized self—is crucial to the understanding of the Horney theory. The actual self refers to the individual as the sum total of his experience. Temperamental factors are recognized as contributors, but their role is less important in neurotic development than are neurotogenic, environmental, and intrapsychic factors. The real self is a central inner force or principle common to all, yet unique in each individual. It is equated with healthy integration and the sense of harmonious wholeness. Horney maintained that, given such optimal environmental circumstances as parental warmth and acceptance and a certain amount of healthy friction, the child who is normal physiologically and neurologically will develop a healthy personality. She opposed the notion of the death instinct and considered the individual's destructive tendencies as neurotic rather than innate. The idealized self, the third concept, is solely a neurotic manifestation.

### Theory of Psychopathology

Horney conceived of neurosis as a disturbance in the total personality that (1) has its source in distorted parent-child relationships and is subsequently self-perpetuated, (2) is characterized by distortions in the individual's relationships with others and self, which stem from emotional conflicts and anxiety, and (3) results in discrepancy between potential and achievement, in rigidity and suffering, and in impairment of function in most areas of living.

The formation of the neurotic personality involves both intrapsychic and interpersonal (cultural) factors. As culture bearers, parents determine the child's generic values, self-concepts,

FIGURE 1.　Karen Horney. (From the Association for the Advancement of Psychoanalysis, New York.)

and some behavior patterns. However, whether the child conforms to these influences or rebels depends on intrapsychic processes. Cultural influences in conflict with the child's natural tendencies may blur or otherwise undermine his identity. In a broad sense, cultural influences determine what is considered healthy or neurotic for a particular society. And specific neurotic conflicts between cultural values—for example, competition and success versus brotherly love and humility—may produce neurosis.

Early childhood experiences play a crucial role in the genesis of neurosis. This is not to be confused with direct causality. The adult does not simply repeat childhood reactions; individual neurotic growth patterns are superimposed on these childhood reactions.

### Genesis of Anxiety and Conflict

The child who is exposed to rejecting parental attitudes reacts with vague feelings of loneliness, helplessness, and fear of the potentially hostile world that surrounds him. This reaction is called basic anxiety. To avoid this anxiety he develops attitudes toward his parents that are either compulsively submissive, aggressive, or detached. These attitudes are called neurotic trends or drives. When one predominates, the others are

repressed but continue to exert a dynamic force. Such attitudes create basic intrapsychic conflict, which generates further anxiety.

The preceding description challenges the classic psychoanalytic theory of psychosexual development, including the concepts of fixed biological phases of development that are related to specific body regions, the sexual nature of child-parent relationships (Oedipus complex), and regression. Horney attributes excessive preoccupation with a genital (or other) organ function to a parental attitude, such as maternal overconcern or rigidity regarding this function. She ascribes the adolescent's feelings of sexual attraction for the parent of the opposite sex or homosexual tendencies to parental seductiveness or unconscious rejection of the child's given sexual role rather than to inherent libidinal tendencies. Sexuality and the conflicts surrounding it are not considered causes of neurosis. On the contrary, neurosis may cause disturbances in sexual feelings, attitudes, and behavior.

### Characterological Defenses against Neurotic Trends

To allay anxiety and resolve the conflict between neurotic trends, the child, and later the adult, must institute further protective measures, which form the basis for the self-perpetuated neurotic development. These measures consist of characterological defenses or solutions to conflict, in contrast to the Freudian symptomatic defense mechanisms such as repression and denial, which are more limited and focused.

**Major Solutions.** The three major solutions or approaches to inner harmony—self-effacement, expansiveness, and resignation—extend and expand the original compulsive trend into a new way of life. The patient may have some awareness of his use of these solutions, but their ramifications, intensity, resistance to change, and implications are largely unconscious.

*Self-effacement.* In the self-effacing solution, love has the greatest appeal for solving life's difficulties. The individual needs to be loved, to give in rather than argue. He is oversensitive to and fears criticism, rejection, and abandonment. He inhibits any expression of aggression, initiative, competitiveness, striving toward success. His attitudes often cause him to be taken advantage of, and he unconsciously invites such treatment.

*Expansiveness.* The expansive solution requires mastery over life and over others in the neurotic sense of domination and self-glorification. Such an individual needs to control and gain prestige. He shuns affection, sympathy, and trust as weaknesses; he is afraid to admit to error or imperfection, even illness, for these represent negative values.

*Resignation.* The resigned person strives not only for freedom from conflict but for freedom from all emotional feelings. He wants to be self-sufficient and independent. He fears influence, obligation, intrusion, coercion, pressure, change. His need for detachment renders emotional ties intolerable.

**Auxiliary Solutions.** The total neurotic superstructure remains fragile, giving rise to disruptive feelings of strain and tension. Auxiliary measures to preserve inner harmony become necessary.

Externalization consists of experiencing inner processes or feelings as occurring outside the self. It is particularly evident in those persons who show a paucity of inner emotional experiences.

Compartmentalization or psychic fragmentation is the experiencing of self as consisting of unconnected parts and of one's attitudes as without interrelationship.

Alienation from self is both a defensive measure and a consequence of the neurotic process. It is active, achieving the relief of tension by blurring genuine wants, feelings, and beliefs that conflict with neurotically idealized qualities.

Automatic control, which is largely unconscious, checks the generation of impulses and feelings and their expression. Instead, these impulses and feelings may be expressed somatically.

Supremacy of the mind (intellectualization) refers to the use of intellect to avoid experiencing emotional conflict. This mechanism, which involves logic and reasoning, may prevent free association in therapy. It may also trigger panic when the individual is abruptly threatened with loss of control by anesthesia or intoxication or when he is forced to let go in sexual activity.

### Actualization of the Idealized Self

The attempt to attain a greater degree of unity, however spurious, requires the actualization of the idealized self: a means of avoiding psychic conflict by rising above it. Initially, the glorified image is conscious: it is often experienced in fantasy or daydreams. However, it progressively encompasses more of the personality and becomes partly or totally unconscious.

**Neurotic Claims and Demands.** The neurotic expects to be treated by the outside world in accordance with his glorified self-concept. Irrational needs, based on fears, inhibitions, and feelings of deprivation, are transformed into claims. Unaware of his self-exaggeration, he is not conscious of the excessiveness of his expectations.

The neurotic molds and drives himself to live up to his irrational self-concept through a system of "shoulds," "musts," demands, and expectations. These inner dictates are largely unconscious.

This construct has been compared with the classic psychoanalytic concept of the superego, but there are differences between them. In Freudian theory, the superego represents internalized parental cultural values; it corresponds to conscience. The "shoulds," however, do not constitute a genuine moral code, nor do they represent an attainable ideal. Aimed at some form of irrational perfection, they are always neurotic.

**Pride System.** The idealized image achieves intense value and hold on the individual as it becomes invested with pride. Genuine pride in realistic achievement provides a solid feeling of self-worth; but the neurotic's false pride, based on exaggerated self-concepts and spurious values, is brittle, vulnerable to challenge or threat, as when a claimed attribute is disproved by reality. Neurotic pride may take various forms: pride in prestige, intellect, will power, strength, honesty, lofty standards, lovability, appearance, sexual prowess. The typical hurt-pride reaction consists of shame (failure from within) or humiliation (action from without).

The neurotic feels contempt for what he is, for his actual self. Pride and self-hatred, two sides of the same coin, form the pride system. It manifests itself in relentless demands on self, merciless self-accusation, self-contempt, self-frustration, self-torture, and self-destructive behavior.

**Central Inner Conflict.** Self-hatred is also directed against the real self. Since positive tendencies are threatening to the neurotic idealized self-image, they must be avoided or denied. Taboos are imposed on such qualities as enthusiasm, spontaneity, productive effort, curiosity, and creativity. During the final phases of analysis, such attributes emerge and the restrictive neurotic superstructure is weakened, producing a special form of intrapsychic discord, a central inner conflict. All the patient's symptoms become more intense, but they are less rigid and less threatening and incapacitating. Anxiety may increase periodically, but the patient seems better able to handle it.

**Alienation from Self.** The various neurotic mechanisms—compulsive distorted self-concepts, "shoulds," claims, self-hatred—all combine to lead to alienation. The individual moves away from his experiential center and genuine identity to create a pseudoidentity and pseudoself. Some manifestations are objectively observable; others are subtle and subjective.

### Symptom Formation

Specific symptoms can be understood only in the context of the total personality.

**Anxiety.** The anxiety-producing conflict is not seen simply as ego versus id. Any pride-invested aspect of self that has subjective compulsive value may be endangered, either by a contradictory internal tendency or by disapproval from without.

**Fear.** Whereas anxiety is the imminent coming to awareness of a threatening, conflict-producing factor, fear is the reactive feeling to the very possibility of such emergence. Fear may be generalized, e.g. exposure of pretense or duplicity, or it may be more directly related to special neurotic attitudes, e.g. fear of success in the self-effacing neurotic.

**Panic.** Panic is due to the sudden collapse of a major aspect of the idealized image accompanied by the sudden threatened emergence of intense repressed conflicting drives.

**Psychosomatic Symptoms.** Psychosomatic symptoms arise with the emergence of a repressed conflict, acutely experienced as a dilemma, or a repressed affect that cannot be totally experienced. Such symptoms are nonspecific: the same symptom may be related to different affects, or different ones may relate to the same affect at different times.

### Treatment

Symptom relief is no longer a primary therapeutic goal. Nor is social adjustment a therapeutic goal; viewed psychologically, it often embraces compulsive conformity with little regard for the real self. The concept of curing neurosis makes no sense, since past development cannot be undone. But removal of stifling, distorting influences allows growth potentials to expand. The aim is movement toward self-realization. Emphasis in therapy is on the here and now. It is essential that the analyst have knowledge of the patient's personality. To make conscious that which is unconscious is still a basic goal.

### Therapeutic Techniques

**Free Association.** Free association is desirable but not essential. It does not imply uttering everything that comes to mind, as classically stated, but refers to uncensored, spontaneous reporting of all inner experiences at the same time that attention is directed on such productions.

The patient's attitudes toward the analyst involve more than transference of child-parent attitudes. The analyst is experienced in complex ways, derived from the patient's unique neurotic needs, expectations, and claims, which change at different times. Current life situations are emphasized.

**The Analyst's Role.** The analyst plays an active role in the treatment; he is not the detached, evaluating observer with the classic mirror function. There is a repeated emotional movement between the patient and the analyst. The analyst's reactive feelings can help indicate unconscious maneuvers of the patient. However, he should be able to distinguish his own neurotic residual feelings.

**Interpretations.** The analyst's interpretations should be questioning and tentative, intended to stimulate. They may be explicit remarks or implicit signs.

**Dreams.** Dreams are a primary tool for furthering analytic insight. The first dream related in the analysis, whether a present or a past recurrent one, is crucially significant. It is the purest, tersest, and most meaningful, often expressing the patient's entire personality structure and attitudes toward life and the analysis.

**Limitations of Therapy.** The limitations of Horney therapy are determined by the goals, the degree to which any patient can avail himself of it, and the lack of experience of its practitioners with specific diagnostic conditions. It is long-term therapy requiring much time and money; thus it is limited in the number it can reach, although low-cost clinics and group analysis are increasing this number. An overwhelmingly unfavorable past or present environment may limit the extent of change. A certain capacity for psychological thinking and awareness is required. Also favorable are a certain moral toughness, a tolerance for anxiety or psychic pain, ability to stay with a problem, a basic desire to change, and a certain intelligence and imagination. Advanced age is a relative limitation, rigidity of attitude and behavior being more important than chronological age. Use of this therapy with children is still limited. Application to the psychoses and sociopathic or acting-out personalities is largely unexplored.

**REFERENCES**

Horney K: *The Neurotic Personality of Our Time*. W. W. Norton, New York, 1937.
Horney K: *New Ways in Psychoanalysis*. W. W. Norton, New York, 1939.
Horney K: *Self-Analysis*. W. W. Norton, New York, 1942.
Horney K: *Our Inner Conflicts*. W. W. Norton, New York, 1945.
Horney K, editor: *Are You Considering Psychoanaly-*

*sis?* W. W. Norton, New York, 1946.

Horney K: *Neurosis and Human Growth.* W. W. Norton, New York, 1950.

Symonds A: Emotional conflicts of the career woman. Am J Psychoanal *43:* 21, 1983.

Symonds A, Symonds M: Karen Horney. In *Comprehensive Textbook of Psychiatry*, ed 4, H I Kaplan, B J Sadock, editors, p 419. Williams & Wilkins, Baltimore, 1985.

## 6.2 HARRY STACK SULLIVAN

Harry Stack Sullivan (1892–1949) received his training in psychiatry during the early years of Freud's profound influence on American psychiatry. However, he did not go to Vienna for his psychoanalytic experience and training, as did so many of his colleagues. Instead, he worked in the United States with Adolf Meyer and with William Alanson White. Both his analytic training and his personal analysis were in the classic tradition. But Sullivan (see Fig. 1) worked closely with a group of psychoanalysts and social psychologists who were moving away from the classic psychoanalytic theories because of the biological and instinctual bias of those theories.

Sullivan was dissatisfied with psychoanalytic concepts that could not be validated because they were based on experiences beyond recall or because they required prior acceptance of certain variables, such as the aggressive or death instinct, as universal human attributes. Consequently, he insisted on formulating his concepts entirely from observable data.

Sullivan defined psychiatry as the study of interpersonal relations that were manifest in observable behavior. Although he had great interest in what transpired inside an individual, he felt that the individual could be studied only in terms of his interactions with others.

### Theory of Personality

#### Basic Theoretical Concepts

Sullivan formulated four basic postulates as the foundation for all of his theories.

**Biological Postulate.** This stated that man, as an animal, differs from all other animals in his cultural interdependence. Man's cultural development is a function of his psychological as well as his physiological dependence. It stems from his growing capacity for tenderness, from his ability to develop an interest in another human being that is equal to his interest in himself.

**Man's Essentially Human Mode of Functioning.** Man, in the performance of his most diverse activities, is still closer to the human

FIGURE 1. Harry Stack Sullivan. (Courtesy New York Academy of Medicine.)

mode of functioning than to animals. This does not obviate the value of animal studies or comparisons between animal and human behavior. It only refines and restricts the application of the findings derived from such studies.

**Significance of Anxiety.** This refers to the central role of anxiety in human development. It emphasizes the presence of anxiety to varying degrees in all human functioning but postulates the impossibility of absolute states of anxiety and of absolute states of euphoria. The varying amounts of anxiety present in an individual determine his variable state of euphoria.

**Tenderness Postulate.** Tenderness in all its various manifestations is an interpersonal development rather than an innate feeling present in the form of an instinct or a God-given virtue. Sullivan states that "the activity of an infant which arises from the tension of his needs produces tension in the mothering one which is felt by her as tenderness." Thus Sullivan recognizes that anxiety does not always exert a disintegrating effect, nor does it always constitute an obstacle in interpersonal functioning.

#### Goals of Human Behavior

All human beings have major goals, which Sullivan called end states. The first goal is to fulfill the biological needs of the organism in terms of food, air, sex, etc. The second goal relates to man as a cultured social being and involves those needs that go beyond the purely physiological necessities, such as the need for status and the need for a relationship with others. The first goal is called the need for satisfactions, and the second is called the need for security.

These needs are manifested as inner tensions, and the characteristic ways in which the individual strives to fulfill them are called dynamisms. The infant's cry, for example, is the simple dynamism used to fulfill his multiple needs. As his needs become more complex, the dynamisms that he employs become more complicated and varied.

The dynamism used involves a bodily zone such as the mouth or the genitals. This concept of Sullivan's bears some similarity to Freud's theory of the phases of psychosexual development, but there are marked differences. Freud considered these bodily zones to be the central determinant of behavior as specific phases of development. These apertures were important to Sullivan because they were the areas through which the individual established interpersonal contact. Thus the infant, whose biological needs are paramount and to whom the mouth plays a crucial role as a vehicle for the satisfaction of his nutritional needs, tends to relate to the environment almost exclusively on an oral level. This factor, rather than the accumulation of libido in the oral area, makes the oral aperture a significant area of personality development.

When a dynamism manages to achieve or fulfill a particular need, the tension of the need is removed; the situation is described as having been integrated, satisfied, or resolved. However, many needs are either unfulfilled or only partially fulfilled by the dynamism. The complete fulfillment of a need, particularly a need for security, is frequently interrupted by the presence or development of anxiety.

In an affluent society, man's tensions are almost exclusively related to his need for security, which can be satisfied only through meaningful interpersonal relationships. If an individual has notable success in fulfilling both his biological and psychological needs and if he experiences a minimum of disintegrating situations, he will feel only a minimum of anxiety. The increasing power and confidence that he feels with regard to his security will give rise to a feeling that Sullivan called self-esteem. A minimal amount of self-esteem is required to deal with the realistic feelings of powerlessness and helplessness

that are evoked in a man in the course of his lifetime.

### Modes of Experience

Various modes of experiencing, which depend on the development of cerebral capacities and physiological skills, permit the development of such psychological functions as differentiation, symbol formation, and other complex intellectual processes. Since much learning occurs in an interpersonal context, the individual's capacity to comprehend such relationships and his mode of experiencing them influence his learning capacity.

**Prototaxic Mode.** The prototaxic mode of experiencing consists of raw, undifferentiated momentary states. There is no connection between experience and the feelings or ideas within or outside oneself; consequently, such experiences seem to have cosmic and universal connections. Such experiencing is characteristic of infancy and occurs in mental illness, particularly schizophrenia.

**Parataxic Mode.** In the parataxic mode events appear to be causally related because of temporal relationships and serial connections. However, there need not be any logical relationships. This kind of distorted thinking is an essential ingredient in the thinking of the paranoiac.

**Syntaxic Mode.** In the syntaxic or logical mode events are related through logical or rational thinking. It is the most mature type of experiencing and represents the highest cognitive capacity of which man is capable.

### Learning

Freud conceived of learning almost entirely in terms of the pain-pleasure principle. Sullivan placed particular emphasis on learning as a way of minimizing anxiety. He described a number of factors that are essential to the learning process, such as empathy, self-sentient activity, trial and error, reward and punishment, learning through imitation, and ultimately deduction and conceptualization. Learning, he maintained, was accelerated by lowering the anxiety gradient. On the other hand, the initiation and motivation of the learning process depends on the presence of a certain amount of anxiety.

### Anxiety

Anxiety is the focal issue in personality development for the neo-Freudians, as it was for Freud himself. As with all other concepts developed by Sullivan, anxiety was seen as an interpersonal phenomenon and was described as the response to the feelings of disapproval from a significant adult. Thus it can occur only in an interpersonal context, even if the other person is not real but a fantasied image.

The feeling that he is disapproved of can be communicated to and interpreted by the individual in a variety of ways, or it can be falsely interpreted, as in prototaxic and parataxic experiencing. In any event, since anxiety is a most distressing feeling and may be accompanied by a variety of somatic symptoms and psychological feelings of impending doom, it cannot be tolerated for long. It must be dealt with.

Sullivan views personality development as a process of learning to handle anxiety by the use of adaptive maneuvers and defense techniques designed to gain approval from significant people. When anxiety is widespread, the individual attempts to limit the opportunities for the further development of anxiety by restricting his functioning to familiar, well-established patterns of activity.

## Role of Sex

In contrast to Freud, who maintained that sexual factors were of major significance from the earliest years, Sullivan felt that sex played its most significant role in the later development eras. Nor did he view sex as the primary source of neurotic and psychotic disturbances. But the early experiences of the individual may produce serious obstacles in the development of adequate sexual behavior. In this way Sullivan accounted for homosexuality and other sexual disorders as symptoms, rather than causes, of personality disorders.

## Stages of Personality Development

Personality is a collection of processes that occur as an outgrowth of interpersonal experiences rather than the unfolding of intrapsychic forces. Sullivan described five stages.

**Infancy.** This period of development, from birth to the beginning of language at about the age of 2, is characterized by utter helplessness and dependence on the benevolence of other humans, particularly the mothering person. The infant's cry and his capacity to arouse tenderness in others are his only tools for satisfying his needs. The oral zone is the area of interaction with the world, and the development of feelings of security and self-esteem depend entirely on the infant's capacity to fulfill his needs.

Anxiety makes its first appearance during this period as a result of the infant's failure to achieve satisfaction of his primary needs. The infant also experiences feelings of security or

anxiety through a process of empathy. The self-system—Sullivan's term for personality—begins to develop in infancy and becomes a technique for avoiding anxiety. The self-system is a reflection not only of maternal and parental attitudes but of any accumulated set of experiences that begin in infancy and continue for a long period of time.

**Childhood.** From 2 to 5 years of age is the period of acculturation. The problem of becoming educated into the requirements of one's culture is often extremely difficult, not only because of unfavorable experiences in infancy but because of the contradictory demands of the culture. Willful activity rather than compliant behavior becomes a prominent part of dealing with powerful adults. Tenderness is transformed into malevolence, and the child becomes surrounded by a sea of hostility that he can deal with only by hostile or paranoid rejoinders.

**Juvenile Era.** When the child begins to manifest a need for compeers, he has entered the juvenile era. Generally, this occurs when he is about 5 years old. His interpersonal range moves beyond his own home and his own parents. He must share a common parental figure in the form of teacher and deal with other individuals who have equal claims upon her. He must learn to deal with new authorities and to cooperate, compete, and compromise with his peers. During this period, the child develops a clear-cut personality and characteristic ways of dealing with others.

**Preadolescence.** This period, ranging from approximately 8 to 12 years of age, is notable for the development of the capacity for love and collaboration with another human being of the same sex. It is devoid of sexual exchanges, however, since gonadal maturation has not yet occurred.

Difficulties begin to manifest themselves toward the end of the era as the sexual apparatus begins to mature and friendships dissolve due to interest in the opposite sex. If there is unequal maturing or if one chum is unequal to the task of moving into heterosexual relationships, an individual may cling to preadolescent intimacy, which may become complicated by lust, producing homosexual behavior.

**Adolescence.** Even if one enters this period with a fairly solid self-system as an outgrowth of good earlier experiences, adolescence is a most difficult transition. If, however, one arrives at this juncture with weak self-esteem and a tendency toward anxiety in interpersonal encounters, the transition to heterosexuality and adulthood will be extremely difficult.

Intimacy with another human being is now complicated by lust. The adolescent must separate himself from his family dependencies at a time when he is not entirely independent either economically or emotionally. He must decide on a career and develop standards and values for the future. He must reach compromises in accepting the values of the adult world. While he is struggling with all of these issues, he is expected to be acquiring and perfecting scholastic or technical skills that will provide him with future economic security. It is a tumultuous period in which one seeks one's identity as a human being.

When heterosexual patternings are established and adult roles are assumed, the period of adolescence draws to a close and the individual has arrived at adulthood. However, adulthood is not always synonymous with maturity, which is achieved by only a fortunate few. Maturity involves a self-respect that permits one to meet most situations with a capacity for intimate and collaborative relationships and loving attitudes—an understandably difficult achievement.

## Theory of Psychopathology

Anxiety, the dynamic, propelling force for personality development, is also the essential element in the production of the neuroses, a psychoses, and other psychopathological phenomena. The self-system, by discharging tensions in acceptable ways and preventing more massive outbursts of anxiety, maintains the individual as an effective functioning entity. However, under extreme stress imposed by external demands or the overwhelming pressures of internal needs, the protective armor of the self-system is inadequate to stem the tide and more massive disintegration occurs, producing the neuroses and psychoses.

### The Neuroses

Sullivan distinguishes between the substitutive (neurotic) and the disintegrative (psychotic) processes. In hysteria, for example, the major substitutive technique is a simple process of amnesia in which clear recognition of issues is avoided; somatic substitutions become the major area of relating to others.

When the process of substitution is used to maintain anxiety at a tolerable level, the individual uses other techniques as well, such as sublimation, which may be broadly defined as a way of making unacceptable impulses acceptable. In addition, there is the ubiquitous tendency toward selective inattention, in which aspects of experiencing that might upset or stimulate anx-

iety are simply not noticed. If this technique becomes too extensive, it may seriously impair perception and learning and be responsible for many major deficiencies in functioning.

Personality devices or techniques are used to keep out of awareness those responses, reactions, and impulses that, if admitted to awareness, would produce serious personality disorganization. The neurotic symptom, therefore, is an adaptive reaction whose major function is to prevent disintegration of personality and promote repair.

Sullivan's view of the obsessional disorder gives one a clear notion of his concepts of psychopathology. Freud viewed obsessive symptoms as a compromise attempt to deal with ambivalent feelings and to prevent the expression of unacceptable aggressive or sexual impulses. As he saw it, the symptom was not only a displaced substitute for the impulse but also a partial satisfaction of it. Sullivan, on the other hand, viewed the obsessional process as one in which the individual attempts to exert maximal control over himself and the universe to guarantee and protect himself against deep feelings of uncertainty and insecurity. He attempts to do this by the personal magic of compulsive ritual or obsessive, ruminative omniscient thinking. And he strives to achieve perfection, omnipotence, and omniscience so that he may be beyond criticism, rejection, or danger. He avoids commitment and involvement, since these contain emotional elements that cannot be controlled. The somatic disorders that frequently accompany obsessional states are the result of the inner tensions produced by these neurotic demands.

### The Psychoses

Psychosis results when the repressed aspects of personality emerge into conscious awareness. These aspects are alien to the ego and disruptive to conventional, acceptable social processes, or else they evoke a sense of loathing and shame. Consequently, their manifestation produces a violent reaction that results in panic, frequently followed by an extremely regressed catatonic reaction. In this state the individual withdraws from reality and becomes wholly preoccupied with fantasy in a cosmic struggle that usually consists of intense rage, stuporous immobility, or a combination of both.

If the individual attempts to reconstruct or reintegrate his self-system by repressing all doubts about himself or by bolstering his inadequate self-system by invalid referential processes, he may then experience a paranoid reorganization of personality. However, there are other possible solutions as well. Instead of an intellectually organized solution, such as the paranoid formulation, there can be a hebephrenic dilapidation, in which emotional deterioration seems to be central. The individual gives up any attempt to view the world in coherent, systematic terms, and it becomes a totally illogical and meaningless world.

### Treatment

Sullivan's focus in therapy was on anxiety and the interpersonal context in which it occurs. He viewed therapy as a succession of psychiatric interviews in which the psychiatrist is a participant in the exploratory process and an observer of trends in the patient that the patient's defensive patterns prevent him from noticing, thus the term which he introduced—participant observer. He recognized the value of free association, dream analysis, and other symbolic reconstructions, but his main emphasis was on the communicative process and what it could reveal regarding the patient's response to anxiety. The genetic reconstruction of the symptom took second place to data of recent origin, which were less prone to distortion.

Sullivan believed that the process of therapy required the active participation of the therapist; therefore, anonymity was not considered a virtue. He extended the notion of transference to include the multitude of distortions that develop out of parataxic interpretations of one's experience, not only with one's parents but also with other people. Because of the active role played by the therapist, countertransference becomes an important technique in the therapeutic process.

The therapeutic process was, for Sullivan, not only an exploratory process for uncovering repressed or dissociated material but also a learning process in which the restructuring of new patterns was assisted. Sullivan felt that therapy could be terminated when the patient's capacity to see himself was validated by the view that others had of him when he was free of substitutive devices and when his self-respect was adequate to withstand any view of himself by others.

### REFERENCES

Chapman A H: *Harry Stack Sullivan: His Life and His Work*. GP Putnam's Sons. New York, 1976.
Chatelaine K L: *Harry Stack Sullivan: The Formative Years*. University Press of America, Inc., Washington, DC, 1981.
Chrzanowski G: *Interpersonal Approach to Psychoanalysis: Contemporary View of Harry Stack Sullivan*. Gardner Press, New York, 1977.
Crowley R M: *Harry Stack Sullivan: The complete bibliography*. Contemp Psychoanal *11:* 83, 1975.
Greenberg, J R, Mitchell S A: *Object Relations in Psychoanalytic Theory*. Harvard University Press, Cambridge, MA 1983.
Havens L L: *Participant Observation*. Jason Aronson, New York, 1976.
Kvarnes R, Parloff G, editors: *A Harry Stack Sullivan Case Seminar: Treatment of a Young Male Schizophrenic*. W W Norton, New York, 1976.
Mullahy P: *The Contributions of Harry Stack Sullivan*. Hermitage House, New York, 1952.
Perry H S: *Psychiatrist of America: The Life of Harry Stack Sullivan*. The Belknap Press of Harvard University Press, Cambridge, MA, 1982.
Zaphiropoulos M L: Harry Stack Sullivan. In *Comprehensive Textbook of Psychiatry*, ed 4, H I Kaplan, B J Sadock, editors, p 426. Williams & Wilkins, Baltimore, 1985.

## 6.3　CARL JUNG

Carl Jung (1875–1961) differed from Freud in his concept of the unconscious as the original mold of the personality and not merely the repressed part. Jung (see Fig. 1) regarded the symbolic approach to dreams and other unconscious manifestations as the most rewarding means of comprehending the language of the psyche and of describing its dynamics. He believed that the psyche communicates through images rather than concepts, and that these images take the form of analogies and parables that represent the meaning of a given situation.

FIGURE 1.　Carl Jung (print includes signature). (National Library of Medicine, Bethesda, Maryland.)

## Objective Psyche

This term replaced Jung's earlier reference to the "collective unconscious," which had given rise to serious misunderstanding and misinterpretation. Jung defined the objective psyche as nothing less than the totality of a priori psychic prefigurations and predispositions, the whole substratum of autonomous psychic functioning. He held that this reservoir of psychic existence gives birth to consciousness; it exists prior to the conscious mind and continues to function together with or despite consciousness; it is autonomous and has laws unto itself. Although the objective psyche may contain many elements that were once conscious and have become unconscious again, through repression, for instance, the unconscious as a whole cannot be considered a mere relic of consciousness.

### The Personal Unconscious

Freudian and other schools of thought refer to experience that was once conscious but was subsequently rejected as repressed material. Jung refers to it as the personal unconscious. Attitudes, urges, and feelings that have been repressed as incompatible with one's ego ideal appear in personalized form in dreams and fantasies as the individual's unacceptable and repressed other personality.

### Introversion and Extroversion

The introverted life adaptation is equal in value to the extroverted one. Introversion is that approach to life experiences in which the individual's predominant sense of reality derives from the actions and reactions of his inner world: thoughts, intuitions, emotions, and sensations. Extroversion is the attitude in which the individual's concern with material objects and people predominates. Just as an overemphasis on introversion may result in inadequate external adaptation, extreme extroversion, which is fostered by prevailing cultural and educational values, may lead to depersonalization, loss of a sense of identity, and submersion of the individual in conformist herd psychology.

### Archetypes and Complexes

The two chief elements of the objective psyche are the archetypes and the complexes that surround them. The archetypes of the objective psyche are a priori energy-field configurations that express themselves in typical representational images and in typical human emotion and behavior patterns. They are analogous to the instinctual patterns observed in animal behavior. All psychic energy is channeled and directed into these basic forms of experience, behavior, and emotion. Thus the archetypes constitute the predispositions of the psyche or the basic motivations and drives around which the conscious personality organizes itself.

Complexes, defined as feeling-toned ideas, may develop as a result of long term conditioning of early traumatic experience. However, their structure derives from an archetypal model: that is, they are based on transpersonal and universal forms of human experiencing. To illustrate, the mother complex—one's unique manner of reacting to one's mother or one's way of being motherly—is determined not only by personal experience with one's mother but also by a preformed image that Jung called the mother archetype. The mother complex develops as the result of the conflict between archetypal expectation and actual experience with the real woman (or women) who function in a motherly role.

The archetypes, such as mother, father, child, and hero, are manifested as mythological or personalized images in dreams and fantasies, and they are invariably projected onto other people. The archetypal configurations encountered most frequently are the persona, shadow, animus, anima, and self.

**Persona.** Jung used this term to characterize expression of the archetypal drive toward conformity and external reality. The persona is the mask that covers the personality of the individual; it is the face that he presents to the outside world. In dreams the persona is represented in the form of images of clothing and as problems involving dress.

Overidentification with the persona results in a stereotyped, false personality based on early values and standards of performance that emphasized the need to conform. Conversely, an inadequate persona means an inadequate adaptation to collective and social demands.

**Shadow.** The shadow is represented in dreams as another person of the same sex as the dreamer. It personifies the dreamer's repressed personal unconscious qualities, his other personality. To the extent that the individual is not aware of his shadow, he ascribes those qualities that he rejects and cannot accept in himself to the others.

**Anima and Animus.** Anima and animus are archetypal representations not of personal qualities but of predispositions or potentials that have not yet become personalized or entered conscious awareness. They are universal basic human drives from which both conscious and unconscious individual qualities develop. Since they include a man's undeveloped femininity (anima) and a woman's undeveloped masculinity (animus), they appear in unconscious imagery as persons of the opposite sex.

**Self.** In contradistinction to Freud's use of the term "self" to refer to the empirical ego personality, Jung used the term to hypothesize a central archetype that embraces both conscious and unconscious elements. Since his idea of the unconscious extends to future potentialities as well as to all current and past experience, the self, as the center of a personality that is both actual and potential, represents not only what a person was and is but also what he is still to become.

### The Ego and the Unconscious

The archetypes and the complexes that form around them operate independently of the ego and are to varying degrees in conflict with the intents of the conscious personality; therefore, they are capable of causing psychic dissociation and fragmentation. The resultant threat to emotional stability can be overcome only if these archetypes and complexes are consciously confronted and understood in symbolic terms.

### The Process of Individuation

Jung described the process of individuation as the growth and expansion of personality that occurs by realizing and becoming what one intrinsically is. This process defines the purpose of therapy for both the neurotic and the psychotic patient, and it delineates the goal of the healthy person who is seeking a clearer or deeper understanding of the meaning of life.

### Libido Theory

Jung viewed the libido as every possible manifestation of psychic energy. It is not limited to sexuality or to the power drive but may express or include every possible expression of the psyche, including the religious or spiritual urge— the urge to find meaning in life.

### Analytic Principles

The aim of psychotherapy, as Jung defined it, is to bring about an adequate adaptation to reality. But reality includes the demands of the unconscious and the as yet unrealized potentialities of the inner world of the objective psyche as well as one's adaptation to society. The need for outward adaptation is well recognized and has been stressed in clinical practice; Jung's major contribution stems from his unique view of man's inner adaptation. He maintained that all psychic drives are amoral and ambivalent: that is, they do not fit into positive-good or negative-bad classifications. Rather, a person's conscious attitude toward these drives determines whether they play a constructive or destructive role in his life.

### Concept of Psychopathology

When drives, archetypal urges, talents, or qualities are repressed or not allowed to develop, they remain primitive, undifferentiated, unadapted, and negative. As such, they exert a potentially threatening or destructive influence on personality. When they interfere with reality adaptation, they manifest themselves in pathological obsessions or symptoms.

### Therapeutic Techniques

Jung's therapeutic approach aims at effecting a reconciliation of conscious and unconscious drives and goals through conscious observation of the symbolic statements of the objective psyche as they manifest themselves in dreams, fantasies, and artistic productions. The messages inherent in these phenomena must be integrated into conscious life and tested in terms of external values and adaptations.

### Goal of Treatment

The aim of Jungian treatment is to develop within each patient the creative potentialities, even if only the creative potentiality for living. The therapist must have no fixed ideas of what is right or normal and what is not. He must try to help his patient find new meanings within. To this end, the patient is not so much told about himself as put in touch with himself.

**REFERENCES**

Groesbeck C J: The archetypal image of the wounded healer. Anal Psychol 20: 122, 1975.
Groesbeck C J: When Jung was the analyst; a review of "A Secret Symmetry" by A. Carotenuto. Psychol Persp 14: 89, 1983.
Groesbeck C J: Carl Jung. In Comprehensive Textbook of Psychiatry, ed 4, H I Kaplan, B J Sadock, editors, p 433. Williams & Wilkins, Baltimore, 1985.
Jung C G: Problems of modern psychotherapy. In The Practice of Psychotherapy, p 53. Princeton University Press, Princeton, NJ, 1954.
Jung C G: A review of complex theory, in Structure and Dynamics of the Psyche, p 95. Princeton University Press, Princeton, NJ, 1967.
Jung C G: Symbols of Transformation, ed 2. Princeton University Press, Princeton, NJ, 1967.
Jung C G: Memories, Dreams, Reflections. Random House, New York, 1961.
Jung C G: Approaching the unconscious, in Man and His Symbols, p 18. Doubleday, Garden City, NY, 1964.
Langs R: Psychotherapy, A Basic Text. Jason Aronson, New York, 1982.
Perry J: The Self in Psychotic Process. University of California Press, Berkeley, CA, 1953.

## 6.4     ALFRED ADLER

### Introduction

Alfred Adler's (1875–1961) very first publication, a pamphlet on the health hazards of tailors, described two concepts that remained basic to all his later teachings: the relationship of the individual to his social environment, and the interrelatedness of body and mind.

### Theory of Personality

#### Unity of the Individual

Adler (see Fig. 1) was the first theoretician to describe man's psychological functioning as the combined product of organic factors and goal-directed psychological drives. The individual (*individium* = indivisible) and his behavior are the result of interwoven dynamic, somatic, psychological, and social processes. He also had a need to perceive himself as a unit subjectively. This sense of unity and continuity is the basis for his sense of identify, self-esteem, and self-acceptance. His theory is known as individual psychology.

#### Unified Concept of Motivation

The helplessness of the infant gives rise to universal feelings of inferiority, which supply the motivation for a compensatory striving for superiority. Consequently, the dynamic force behind all human activity is the striving toward superiority, perfection, and totality. He introduced the term inferiority complex, the idea that everyone is born with a feeling of inferiority secondary to real or fantasized organic or psychological deficits.

The individual's life goal is determined by his inventive and creative power: it is an expression of his uniqueness. The specific kind of superiority that the individual wants to attain, and the methods that he adopts toward its achievement, derive from the particular circumstances of his own life, particularly his biological endowment and his early environment.

#### Life Style

Life style is the individual's active adaptation to the social milieu. The growing child selects from among his experiences, and especially from his own interactions within his family and his observations of their social relations with others, those events that can fit into a consistent, coherent pattern. Events that do not fit into a coherent pattern are considered unimportant and are forgotten, as are thoughts and feelings that would painfully contradict his self-concept.

The life cycle develops in a step-by-step maturational process. Children concentrate on— and seem singularly preoccupied with— the behavior of the adults who surround them. These myriad, repeated primary experiences constitute the minute pieces of the mosaic created by the child in the first 5 years of his life, a mosaic which has as its eventual form a relatively stable scheme of apperceptions.

#### Social Context and Social Feeling

Just as the partial functions of the individual must be understood within the context of the unity of personality, so the total person must be considered within the broader context of society. If the child grows up under favorable circumstances, his early self-interest will be transformed into the desire for a socially meaningful life.

Adler conceptualized social feeling as a criterion for mental health. A healthy life style is directed toward achieving competence and social success by working toward the goal of social usefulness. Adler also pointed out that increased social feeling enhances man's intelligence, heightens his self-esteem, and enables him to adjust to unexpected misfortunes.

FIGURE 1.   Alfred Adler.

## Theory of Psychopathology

### Neurosis

A neurotic disposition stems from childhood experiences that are characterized by overprotection or neglect, or a confusing mixture of both. Out of these experiences, the growing child creates a negative self-image of helplessness, a conviction of his inability to develop mastery or to cope with the tasks of life. This distorted image of the helpless self is supplemented by his apperception of a social environment that is overtly hostile, punishing, and depriving or subtly demanding and frustrating. Self-protection becomes his primary objective.

Once the child's inner psychological world has developed, it is difficult for him to give up even the smallest segment of his distorted subjective creation. All of the pieces fit together, and any change would disrupt the only adaptive pattern that he has been able to construct from what appeared to be the crucial cues in his early environment.

Adler introduced the term masculine protest, which depicts a universal human tendency to move from a passive and feminine role to a masculine and active role. The doctrine is an extension of his ideas about organic inferiority. It became the prime motivational force in normal and neurotic behavior in the Adlerian system.

### Psychosis

From Adler's viewpoint, psychosis is due to a combination of somatic and psychological factors. He emphasized understanding the psychotic's private logic and recognizing its coherence in grandiose or depressing fantasies, despite a lack of common sense. Although the neurotic may suffer from a sense of failure, real or imagined, the psychotic does not recognize this, nor does he accept the ultimate criterion of social validity. Rather, his fantasies compensate for his sense of utter hopelessness and despair of ever achieving significance in the real world.

### Treatment

Therapeutic change is accomplished in several steps, which partly overlap and always dovetail. If the patient's mother failed to interpret society to the patient in childhood, the therapist must assume this responsibility as the first step in the therapeutic process, although he is heavily handicapped in his attempt to convince the adult patient to correct a scheme of perceptions developed in childhood. In the second phase, the therapist—and then the patient—learn to understand the patient's life style and goal. The therapist's understanding of the patient is essential if a reconstructive relationship is to develop and persist throughout therapy. On the other hand, the patient's increased insight into his motivations, intentions, and goals contributes to—but is not a perequisite—for therapeutic change. Insight may follow and not necessarily precede changes in behavior. In the third phase, the patient's inferiority feelings and fears diminish, he develops a positive self-image, and his social feeling is strengthened. In the fourth phase, the patient is encouraged to select and try out new ways of relating to people, and to enjoy new devices for coping with tasks of life.

**Psychotherapeutic Techniques.** Encouragement was Adler's main weapon in combating the patient's life style. The patient's exaggerated sensitivity can be overcome by the therapist's kindly and consistent interest in him, despite his bizarre and contradictory behavior. As a result of this experience in human relatedness, the patient becomes more hopeful that he will achieve some of his goals; he learns to feel less isolated and begins to feel that he is part of society.

Adler considered the Freudian concept of transference as misleading. He maintained that the patient's sexual involvement with the therapist was an unnecessary obstacle to therapeutic progress. On the other hand, despite his safeguarding operations, the patient expects his therapist to be trustworthy, reliable, warm, able, and interested in his welfare in the here-and-now situation. Adler was convinced that every human being with an aptitude for social interest needs and wants this kind of relationship.

The therapist understands the patient's resistance to change as a fear of giving up the attitudes developed in childhood. An active approach, based on the therapist's empathy and expressed awareness of how much courage the neurotic patient requires to seek an alternate life goal, will restore the patient's faith in himself, help him to realize his strength and ability, and foster his belief in his own dignity and worth. Without encouragement, neither insight nor change is possible.

**REFERENCES**

Adler A: *The Individual Psychology of Alfred Adler: A Systematic Presentation in Selections from His Writings,* H L Ansbacher, R R Ansbacher, editors. Basic Books, New York, 1956.

Adler A: *Problems of Neurosis: A Book of Case Histories,* P Mairet, editor. Harper & Row, New York, 1964.

Weiner M F: Other psychodynamic schools. In *Comprehensive Textbook of Psychiatry,* ed 4, H I Kaplan, B J Sadock, editors, p 451. William & Wilkins, Baltimore, 1985.

## 6.5     OTTO RANK

Early in his life, Otto Rank (1884–1939) was a member of Freud's inner circle. His departure from the orthodox camp began in the early 1920s when he questioned the wisdom of lengthy analyses. Rank's final break with Freud was precipitated by his publication in 1923 of *Trauma of Birth*. After 1926 Rank became increasingly critical of psychoanalysis, and he finally reached the point where he no longer considered himself a psychoanalyst.

### Theory of Personality

Rank (see Fig. 1) conceived of personality within a frame of reference that emphasized human values such as religion and art. He stressed the dynamic dualism in life—the polarities of male and female, individuation and conformity, impulse and inhibition—eschewing the one-sided approach that he considered characteristic of Freudian formulations. Rank's will psychology is essentially an ego psychology.

FIGURE 1.   Otto Rank. (Courtesy of New York Academy of Medicine.)

### Trauma of Birth

Freud had emphasized the powerful psychological reactions of birth as the prototype of later anxiety; but Rank correlated anxiety with separation from the mother; specifically, with separation from the womb, the source of effortless gratification. He hypothesized that this painful experience results in primal anxiety, which is then subject to primal repression. Any subsequent desire to return to the position of primal pleasure gives rise to anxiety. Indeed, any change from a pleasurable to a painful situation gives rise to feelings of anxiety. Rank suggested that childhood was devoted to the mastery of the birth trauma, although the original or primal anxiety was displaced onto other situations and objects.

### Infantile Sexuality

Rank interpreted infantile sexuality as the child's concern with where he came from and the anxiety that surrounds his desire to return. The boy clings to the notion that all human beings have a phallus, in order to avoid the primal anxiety that is associated with the knowledge of the existence of female genitalia, and homosexuality is rooted in the dread of female genitalia. Female penis envy is conceptualized as a reaction to male's possession of a penis and is similarly associated with the primal anxiety.

Rank reformulated the theory of the Oedipus complex as the attempt to master birth anxiety by accepting the mother's genitals as a source of pleasure rather than pain and anxiety. Sleep, dreams, and even cultural phenomena were similarly explained in terms of the birth trauma and the persisting desire to return to the mother's womb.

### Guilt and Fear

The child learns that he can say "no" to his parents and even to his own impulses. However, this counter will, which is essential to the process of individuation, tends to destroy unity with others, and so it tends to arouse feelings of guilt. Rank called the guilt that stems from this source "ethical guilt" to differentiate it from the moralistic guilt aroused by behavior that is contrary to social commandment.

In addition, the process of achieving individuality is beset with life fear: that is, the fear of giving up the support and comfort of symbiotic relationships analogous to that of the prenatal state. But the developing child is assertive and potentially creative and views any regression to the womb as a loss of individuality and a threat to life. This is manifested in the death fear, which drives him toward greater effort, just as life fear inhibits.

### Impulse, Emotion, and Will

Rank characterized the personality chiefly in terms of impulse, emotion, and will. The child's impulses seek immediate discharge and gratification. Emotion rises as a result of the blocking of impulse from without or within. But the child's real emotional life begins when he learns to master his impulses, as in toilet training; that is, when he begins the process of will development. The will, which is born out of the need to master one's impulse life, is also turned outward and manifested as stubbornness, willfulness, disobedience, inhibition, and denial.

### Theory of Psychopathology

Rank was not concerned with psychiatric nosology. References to various forms of neurosis were presented chiefly within the framework of personality types.

In the creative or artistic type, will is the organizing principle; inhibition prevails in the neurotic; impulse is pre-eminent in the antisocial person. Rank felt that the artist reconciled separation or individualization and the need for union in an essentially constructive manner. On the other hand, the neurotic is a frustrated artist type, one who has failed to achieve an integration of the opposing trends in life. Unable to adopt the approach of the average person, he may become completely involved in trivial experiences to avoid the pain of an independent act of willing, or he may become unduly compliant or consistently rebellious. The neurotic is dominated by a fear of life. He preserves a sense of wholeness by his totalistic, overwhelming relationship with others. The neurotic may become the detached antisocial type in an effort to maintain his ego intact. The death fear is dominant in this criminal or psychopathic type. Such a person dreads the loss of individuality threatened by any union with another.

### Treatment

The core of Rank's therapeutic technique is the concept of relationship. Rank emphasized the relationship between patient and therapist. The goal of treatment is to help the patient accept his separateness and will without guilt. Therefore, resistance is accepted as a valid expression of will. The patient must feel the support of the therapist in his new ventures toward independence, even when they do not meet with the therapist's full approval. Throughout the period of the therapy, the pa-

tient is given quiet assurance that he can be loved without feeling dominated.

As soon as a good working relationship is established, however early in the treatment, a definite date for termination of therapy is decided on, subject to change. This technique militates against the excessive dependence on the therapist that is so common in Freudian therapy. The patient accepts respnsibility for change, and his knowing in advance the time of termination makes the separation less traumatic.

### REFERENCES

Karpf F B: *The Psychology and Psychotherapy of Otto Rank*. Philosophical Library, New York, 1953.
Rank O: *Beyond Psychology*. Haddon Craftsmen, Camden, NJ, 1941.
Rank O: *Will Therapy and Truth and Reality*. Alfred A. Knopf, New York, 1950.
Rank O: *The Trauma of Birth*. Robert Brunner, New York, 1952.
Taft J: *Otto Rank*. Julian Press, New York, 1958.
Weiner M F: Other psychodynamic schools. In *Comprehensive Textbook of Psychiatry*, ed 4, H I Kaplan, B J Sadock, editors, p 451. Williams & Wilkins, Baltimore, 1985.

## 6.6    MELANIE KLEIN

In contrast to orthodox psychoanalytic theory, Melanie Klein (1882–1960) maintained that a primitive superego is formed during the first and second years. She believed that aggressive rather than sexual drives are pre-eminent during the earliest stages of development. She maintained that children 2 years old could be treated analytically without the cooperation of the child's parents. She described depression which occurred during the first year of life. She believed that environmental factors played a relatively minor role in development. And she traced the onset of the oedipal conflict to the earliest months of life.

### Theory of Personality

Klein emphasized the infant's autoeroticism and primary narcissism. She considered the infant capable of object relations despite his poorly defined ego boundaries. Toward the middle of the first year, oral frustration gives rise to his unconscious awareness that his parents enjoy sexual pleasure, which is initially conceived of in oral terms. This awareness produces oral envy and increased instinctual oral sadism, which stimulates oedipal impulses. At first, these impulses take the form of a desire to penetrate and destroy the mother's body. The child hopes thereby to orally incorporate the father's penis, which he fantasizes as having been incorporated by the mother.

In the girl, the impulse to destroy the mother's body gives rise to the fear that her own body will be destroyed in retaliation. In the boy, these aggressive impulses produce castration anxiety. The primitive superego emerges at this stage of development. the child's sadistic impulses are projected onto an external object that is subjected to attack.

The child also introjects objects that cause pain. These evoke a cruel superego which causes severe anxiety. Therefore, in the early anal-sadistic phase the child seeks to eject his superego and even his id.

These early anxieties and defenses are modified by the development of libido and real object relations. In the girl, the turning from the mother's breast to the father's penis is a precursor of the oedipal situation. A similar reaction in the boy may lead to homosexuality unless a reorientation toward the mother occurs.

The ejection of the superego in the early stage of anal development permits the reintrojection of good objects and alleviation of anxiety and phobias, which have a paranoid, projective character. In the later anal stage, the superego is no longer ejected: anxiety turns into guilt, and obsessional behavior appears.

At the time of weaning, the infant begins to recognize the mother as one person, both good and bad. The child is filled with anxiety lest the love object be lost through his own destructiveness—his ejection of the bad object. This conflict is the basis of the depressive position, in which guilt arises as the precursor of conscience. The guilty child uses magic in an effort to convert the bad mother into a good one and to protect the introjected good objects against the bad.

### Theory of Psychopathology

Klein considered sadism a determining factor in mental conflict. The paranoid and depressive positions are fixation points for possible psychotic disintegration. She believed that the presence of excessive anxiety in infancy and the predominance of a severe superego led to disturbances of ego development and to psychosis.

The ego deals with the depressive position in two ways. A flight to the good introject carries with it the danger of a later denial of reality and schizophrenic psychosis. A flight to the external good object is the characteristic forerunner of neurosis and a possible weakness in ego functioning, with marked dependency on the object.

Failure to identify with the introjected and real love objects can result in psychotic disorders, such as paranoia and manic-depressive states. The persistence of an extremely primitive superego may account for the antisocial personality.

### Treatment

On the hypothesis that the play of children might replace the free association technique that is the basis of the analysis of adults, Klein developed an analytical play technique, employing small toys of a primitive type. Careful observation revealed that the child expresses his fantasies and real life experiences in a symbolic fashion through play with these simple toys. This play can be analyzed in the same way that a symptom or dream can be analyzed. The child also talks while he plays, and these words have the value of the associations produced in the classic free association technique. The play elements are interpreted to the child in minute detail.

For successful treatment of a child, however young, Klein believed that the child should use language in the analysis to the full extent of his capacity. However, the direct interpretations described are adjusted to the child's level of development, in terms of speech and thought, to facilitate comprehension.

Klein believed that children form positive and negative transferences in the classic sense. Negative transference is manifested by fear in the younger child and by mistrust, dislike, and reserve in the older child. As anxiety is resolved through play and its interpretations, pleasure in play is renewed and positive transferences are formed.

**REFERENCES**

Kernberg O F: Melanie Klein. In *Comprehensive Textbook of Psychiatry*, ed 4, H I Kaplan, B J Sadock, editors, p 441. Williams & Wilkins, Baltimore, 1985.
Klein M: *Contributions to Psycho-Analysis, 1921–1945*. Hogarth Press, London, 1948.
Klein M: *The Psycho-Analysis of Children*, ed 3. Hogarth Press, London, 1949.
Klein M: *Our Adult World*. Basic Books, New York, 1963.
Klein M, Heimann P, Isaacs S, Riviere J: *Developments in Psychoanalysis*. Hogarth Press, London, 1952.

## 6.7     WILHELM REICH

Wilhelm Reich (1897–1957) completed his formal medical training at the University of Vienna in 1922 and quickly rose to prominence in the psychoanalytic movement. In the late

1920s, as director of the Vienna Seminar for Psychoanalytic Therapy, he initiated discussions of analytic technique that paved the way for modern ego psychology. But for most of his career Reich (see Fig. 1) was involved with the quest for the biological basis of the libido theory. In this search he made numerous pseudoscientific claims, including the discovery of orgone energy as the basis of life.

### Theory of Character Structure

Reich's basic concept is that character is a defensive structure, an armoring of the ego both against instinctual forces within and the world without. As a defense that becomes an automatic mode of reaction, it acquires a rigidity that produces a loss in psychic and physical elasticity. The degree of persisting elasticity determines the difference between the healthy and the neurotic personality. The affect-inhibited compulsive personality is the prototype of the rigid, neurotic character.

At the core of the formation of character are incestuous wishes and their inevitable frustration. Character formation represents an attempt to resolve the conflict. It is precipitated by the fear of punishment produced by early sexual education. Society imposes its demands for a certain solution, which produces a certain kind of character structure. The outcome of the oedipal phase determines whether the individual will be capable of a satisfactory sexual life free from neurotic problems. Neurosis can be prevented only by the development of character that permits genital sexual gratification.

### Theory of Psychopathology

The hysterical character is the result of fixation at the phallic stage of libido development. His movements are soft and sexually seductive, with a special kind of agility. He has little tendency toward sublimation or reaction formation and little actual sexual satisfaction. Sexual tensions are discharged somatically or in the form of anxiety.

The compulsive character is orderly and thrifty. Outwardly he is extremely controlled; inwardly he is distrustful and indecisive. His affective reactions are diminished almost to the point where affect is completely blocked. These characteristics are the result of fixation at the anal-sadistic level as a result of overstrict or premature toilet training.

The phallic-narcissistic character is confident and arrogant. These traits plus aggression and sadism are manifested overtly, since reaction formation is absent. He is attractive as a sexual object, although he may be orgastically impotent. The male always has contempt for the female and has great phallic pride, but the phallus is in the service of aggression, not love. The formation of this character type is usually attributed to frustration of the child's attempts to win the love object through display of the phallus and his consequent identification with the rejecting person.

Reich disagreed strongly with Freud's concept

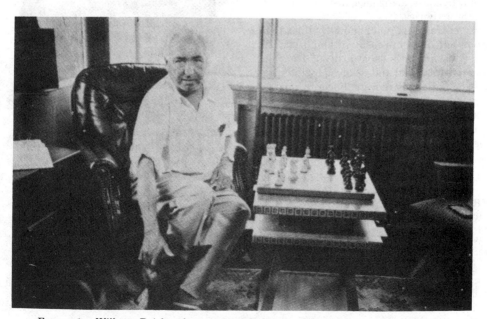

FIGURE 1.  Wilhelm Reich at home. (Photo courtesy of Farrar, Straus & Giroux, Inc.)

of a death instinct, and he was particularly opposed to Freud's reference to the death instinct as the basis for masochistic phenomena. The masochistic character, according to Reich, is the result of the repression of exhibitionistic impulses at the onset of the genital phase of development. However, the masochistic character rarely develops a masochistic perversion. Fear of an increase in pleasurable excitation inhibits any strong pleasure sensation and converts it into pain, adding to the store of rejection and displeasure that the masochist feeds on.

Reich distinguished several phases in the development of neurosis. During the infantile phase of development, there is a conflict between the fulfillment of libidinal needs and their frustration, in the course of which these needs are repressed. A breakthrough in this regression, through the formation of a phobia, for example, leads to a weakening of the ego. The phobia is overcome by a neurotic character trait. When adolescent conflict is complicated by the inadequacy of the character armor, the phobia or a corresponding symptom reappears. Reich considered the character neurosis to be more serious than the symptom neurosis.

### Treatment

Reich's most enduring contribution, the technique of character analysis, is based on his hypothesis that certain resistances are inherent in the character structure of the neurotic patient. These resistances are evident in the patient's specific ways of acting and reacting and may take the form of extreme passivity, ingratiation, argumentativeness, arrogance, distrust, and certain motor activities.

Character traits are much more complex than symptoms and are more easily rationalized. The character resistance is separated out from the total analytic material and resolved by interpretation. The patient is repeatedly confronted by his character traits until he begins to experience them as painful symptoms or foreign bodies requiring removal. Once the character resistance has been diminished or removed, the emphasis on the analysis of repressed infantile material begins.

### REFERENCES

Reich W: *The Function of the Orgasm.* Orgone Institute Press, New York, 1948.
Reich W: *Character Analysis,* ed 3. Orgone Institute Press, New York, 1949.
Weiner M F: Other psychodynamic schools. In *Comprehensive Textbook of Psychiatry,* ed 4, H I Kaplan, B J Sadock, editors, p 451. Williams & Wilkins, Baltimore, 1985.

## 6.8    ADOLF MEYER

Adolf Meyer (see Fig. 1) was born in Niederwenigen, Switzerland, on November 13, 1866, the son of a Zwinglian minister, and died in 1950. In medical school he was influenced by the psychiatrist August Forel, director of the Burghölzli Hospital for the Insane. In 1892, he emigrated to the United States to eventually become director of the Henry Phipps Clinic of Johns Hopkins Medical School.

In 1903, Meyer postulated that mental disorder often had its roots in a personality imbalance caused by the disorganization of habits. He viewed incomprehensible symptoms of mental illness as crude and inadequate attempts by the patient to cure himself, attempts that had to be guided rather than suppressed. Contrary to Kraepelin's stress on deterioration as the eventual outcome in dementia precox, Meyer believed that personality traits, such as withdrawal, preceded the appearance of the disease, and he suggested that prevention and recovery were possible.

FIGURE 1.   Adolf Meyer, 1866–1950. (National Library of Medicine, Bethesda, Md.)

Meyer recommended that the patient's school, family, and community attempt to intervene early in the development of the illness. The first applications of the principles of social work to occupational and recreational therapy with convalescent patients, and the organization of aftercare programs, were inspired by Meyer's work during this period.

As early as 1906, Meyer evaluated Freud's study of the infantile phase of development as pathologically important, and warned against premature rejection of psychoanalysis, although he objected to Freud's emphasis on the pathological and hypothetical, rather than on the healthy and verifiable aspects of mental functioning.

## Theory of Psychobiology

Meyer introduced the term "psychobiological interpretation" in 1909. In the broad context of psychobiological interpretation, Meyer explained, pathological personality reactions could be explained as regression to former, previously protective phylogenetic reactions that were incompatible with adaptation.

Psychobiology emphasized the importance of biographical study in order to understand the whole person. To Meyer, the clinical psychiatric examination included the following components: (1) identifying the motives or indications for the examination, with particular focus on presenting pertinent details in the patient's life history elicited through biographical study; (2) listing the obviously related personality items, factors, and reactions; (3) careful study of the physical, neurological, genetic, and social status and of the correlation between these variables and personality factors; (4) differential diagnosis; and (5) formulation of a therapeutic plan geared to each case. Symptoms were viewed as compensatory phenomena; that is, as reactions.

In interviewing a patient, Meyer considered it better to begin by focusing on his chief complaint, which directed attention to the situation that required immediate therapeutic intervention. Later, the psychiatrist determined the nature and extent of the disturbance in the context of the patient's overall functioning, his previous medical history, and the role played by such factors as constitution, development, and environment. Unconscious material elicited from the patient and information supplied by his family supplemented the psychiatrist's efforts.

Meyer introduced the concept of common sense psychiatry, which refers to understanding the patient in the simplest terms possible, without the confusing perplexities and obstructions that might otherwise confuse the therapeutic process.

## Treatment

Meyer believed that the psychiatrist began to treat the patient at the time of their initial contact, with the patient's exposition of his problem. This did not mean that diagnosis was not essential; however, the first step was evaluation of the patient's assets and liabilities.

Problems were approached on a conscious rather than an unconscious level, and therapy was administered in the course of ordinary face-to-face conversation. At the beginning of each therapeutic session, the patient was encouraged to discuss his experiences in the interval since the last interview, beginning with obvious and immediate problems. Eventually, these problems were explored in greater detail when deeper relevant material had been elicited from the patient through the use of spontaneous association, a term used by Meyer in preference to "free association" to describe the overcoming of the patient's resistance to verbalizing his basic problems in the unbiased atmosphere of the psychiatrist's office.

It was the psychiatrist's responsibility to reassure the patient so that he could function adequately between interviews. This reassurance was conveyed through casual comments and sensitive questioning. Under the guidance of the psychiatrist, the patient analyzed his personality problems and their relative importance, and then reconstructed the origin of his conflicts and devised healthier behavioral patterns.

Meyer believed that the essential goal of therapy was to aid the patient's adjustment by helping him to modify unhealthy adaptations. He called this "habit training." In the process of habit training, the psychiatrist used a variety of techniques—guidance, suggestion, re-education, and direction—always with emphasis on the current life situation. Psychobiological therapy was especially valuable with psychotics, although it was also recommended for neurotic disorders.

## REFERENCES

Meyer A: *Collected Papers of Adolf Meyer*, 4 vols. Johns Hopkins Press, Baltimore, 1948–1952.
Meyer A: *Psychobiology: A Science of Man.* Charles C Thomas, Springfield, IL, 1957.
Smith S: *Ideas of the Great Psychologists.* Harper & Row, Philadelphia, 1983.
Weiner M F: Other psychodynamic schools. In *Comprehensive Textbook of Psychiatry*, ed 4, H I Kaplan, B J Sadock, editors, p 451. Williams & Wilkins, Baltimore, 1985.

# 7

# Diagnosis and Psychiatry: Examination of the Psychiatric Patient

## 7.1    PSYCHIATRIC INTERVIEW

### Introduction

The interview is the main tool used by the psychiatrist to gain a knowledge of the patient and the nature of his problem. An understanding of the patient in health and in sickness comes chiefly from his account of his life events, attitudes, and emotions and of the development of his symptoms. Great emphasis is placed on encouraging the patient to tell his story in his own words. The diagnosis and prognosis are based on these data and the additional information obtained from the patient's relatives, the physical examination, psychological tests, and any other special examinations. With this knowledge, treatment objectives can be formulated, and a plan of therapy that is realistic for the patient can be instituted.

### Physician-Patient Relationship

The physician-patient relationship is the keystone of the practice of medicine. The relationship implies that there is an understanding and trust between the psychiatrist and his patient. With rapport, the patient feels that the psychiatrist accepts him and recognizes his assets, even though they may be outnumbered by his liabilities.

Failure of the physician to establish good rapport accounts for much of his ineffectiveness in the care of his patients. If a doctor dislikes a patient he is prone to be ineffective in dealing with him. If, on the other hand, the physician can handle the resentful patient with equanimity, the patient may become loyal and cooperative.

The reaction of the patient toward the psychiatrist is apt to be a repetition of the attitude he has had toward previous physicians or toward parents, teachers, or other authoritative persons who have figured importantly in his life. Not only individual experiences but broad cultural attitudes of patients affect their reactions. It is desirable for the physician to have as much understanding as possible of the subculture of the patient.

As a protective defensive pattern, the psychiatrist may assume a habitual attitude toward all patients. Such rigidity is frequently inappropriate to the particular patient and situation. The psychiatrist must avoid side-stepping issues that are important to the patient but that he finds boring or difficult to deal with.

When the psychiatrist can convey to the patient that he is receptive to hearing about any subject, discussion is facilitated. It is then easier for the patient to talk about topics that are commonly embarrassing or disturbing.

### Technique

The patient comes to the psychiatrist for expert assistance. He may have a relatively realistic attitude, or he may yearn for a parental type of guidance and expect magic from the psychiatrist. The psychiatrist may either reinforce this illusion of magic by using a suggestive type of approach or try to dissipate these beliefs through an analysis of the problem.

When the patient shows marked inhibitions, the examiner should aim to put him at ease and allow him to talk freely. If the patient has questions, they should be answered frankly. Explanations should be given in keeping with the patient's capacity to understand. If a patient does not wish to talk to the psychiatrist, it is advisable to discontinue the interview and resume contact at a later time.

If the patient is overbearing, it is likely that he is frightened. The interviewer needs to cope with this underlying fear to dissipate the over-compensatory anger. If the patient feels that the psychiatrist has empathy, he is likely to talk more freely. It is frequently possible to capitalize on the patient's sense of humor in getting him to talk more easily. Smiling with him helps him feel a sense of rapport.

In guiding the interview, the examiner should allow the patient free expression of thoughts and feelings, and he should let the patient tell his story. Gaps can be filled in later. Listening is a major tool. Minimum activity encourages the patient to expand on his thoughts and enables him to bring up relevant topics. Attention must be paid to what the patient omits as well as to what he says. Undue emphasis or exaggeration, overt signs of emotion, and changes in manner and tone of voice may give clues to a distortion.

Interviews should be conducted in privacy. Usually, they should not last longer than an hour, although with some alert, receptive patients the initial interview may be prolonged to an hour and a half. Longer subsequent interviews may also be scheduled, especially if it is not possible or appropriate to see the patient frequently. Fatigue and limited productivity indicate that the interview should be shortened.

### Question Techniques

Questions can be injected when the patient gives appropriate leads. Leading questions and interpretive comments should be avoided. The perceptive examiner asks questions that will help the patient develop understanding of himself as a person. The examiner avoids influencing the patient to comply with preconceived theories.

### Note-taking and Recording

It is usually desirable to record some verbatim statements. Notes should be taken as unobtrusively as possible and should not be so extensive as to interfere with the free flow of the patient's talk or the interviewer's capacity to listen to the patient. Reassurance that the notes are confidential should be given.

Psychiatrists should be alert to the reaction of the patient. If the patient objects to note-taking, it is best to discontinue it. On the other hand, many patient's consider note-taking as a sign of the physician's interest and appreciation of the importance of what is being said.

When notes are not taken during the interview, the physician should take the time to record the data immediately after the patient leaves, or he might consider audio or videotape recordings, which are more complete and interfere less with spontaneous, easy communication. The patient's permission should be given before a recorder is used.

### Attitudes of the Psychiatrist

The psychiatrist needs to listen without showing strong reactions, even though he may be reminded of his own disturbing problems or experiences.

However, complete passivity on the part of the psychiatrist leaves the patient feeling helpless. An authoritarian attitude on the part of the psychiatrist is uncalled for and interferes with the patient's ability to talk easily. Indeed, it is likely to constitute a traumatic repetition of a cultural or parental pattern.

### Initial Interview

Since patients are usually anxious and may find it difficult to talk, the setting should be quiet, private, and free from interruption. A comfortable chair should be provided for the patient. The psychiatrist should introduce himself and invite the patient to be seated. A courteous, interested, respectful, considerate, and tolerant attitude on the part of the psychiatrist helps put the patient at ease.

The psychiatrist should avoid seeming to be in a hurry, since such an attitude inhibits the patient. A stilted, detached, or cold attitude and evidences of anxiety, anger, or indifference alienate the patient. The psychiatrist may develop empathy by trying consciously to put himself in the patient's place.

Asking the patient about the chief problems that brought him to the psychiatrist or hospital is usually the best way to start the interview. The patient can then be encouraged to tell the story of his present illness in his own words.

The conversation should be guided, rather than pursued in the manner of a prosecuting attorney. Simple explanations, reassurance, and praise may be used to obtain information when the patient needs to have his anxiety alleviated. The use of simple English, rather than technical terms, helps overcome barriers in communication. The psychiatrist should avoid being moralistic, prejudicial, dictatorial, or punitive.

The patient is frequently more able to talk about himself during the first interview than later, when he has mobilized defenses and resistances. Quiet attentiveness on the part of the physician lessens the development of anxiety, which leads to blocking and silences. When the patient does stop talking the psychiatrist should ask a question or two; prolonged silences are apt to be disconcerting. In asking questions, the psychiatrist should repeat the patient's phrases as much as possible to minimize distortions.

There should be follow-through on the leads the patient gives. When the meaning is not clear to the psychiatrist, tactful inquiry is indicated. Intimate topics can be introduced by asking less emotionally charged questions, such as those concerning physical development. If the patient becomes unduly upset, the subject should be dropped and brought up again at a later interview. When the patient belabors a subject, the psychiatrist should change the topic.

Discussion of present problems gives the psychiatrist an opportunity to ask whether there have been similar problems in the past. This approach gives him insight into the origins of sensitivities. In the first contact with the patient, however, interpretations are usually avoided. It is better to let the patient reach his own conclusions. The psychiatrist should also avoid pointing out inconsistencies until later interviews, when rapport is well-established.

Near the end of the interview the psychiatrist may warn the patient that only a few minutes more time is available. Such a statement should be given during an appropriate pause, rather than injected in the middle of a discussion that seems highly meaningful to the patient. The psychiatrist may then ask the patient to raise questions of his own or to mention something else that he feels is particularly significant.

If no further interviews are anticipated, the psychiatrist can give a brief summary and recommendation. If further interviews are contemplated, the psychiatrist may state that there is need for more discussion, express continued interest, and suggest that the patient think over the topics covered and what he may wish to add during the next interview.

## Subsequent Interviews

Subsequent interviews should continue the understanding and therapeutic approach initiated in the first contact. If there is a lag in getting started, the psychiatrist may ask the patient what has been on his mind, how he has been feeling, or what has been happening. The patient may be encouraged to expand on topics introduced during the first interview, or inquiry may be made about areas that were insufficiently covered or were not discussed at all.

To avoid giving excessive direction, the psychiatrist should permit pauses so that the patient can organize his thoughts. If the pause becomes awkward, a question can be asked about the previous statement. When the patient is having difficulty bringing out pertinent data, questions that cover his background and clarify

his problems are indicated. A play-by-play account of his daily 24-hour pattern is useful.

If the patient shows some asocial behavior, the psychiatrist should continue an attitude of analyzing and understanding; he should not condone or condemn. There should be respect for his defenses and opinions. When rapport has become well-established, some challenging of the patient's ideas may be interjected.

## Special Types of Interviews

Interview techniques need to be varied according to the personality reactions of the patient, the type and degree of illness, and the objectives of the interview. Various degrees of permissiveness and directiveness may be used.

### Nondirective Interview

This method emphasizes minimal activity on the part of the interviewer. When there are pauses, the interviewer repeats the last words of the patient. However, extreme nondirectiveness leaves the patient feeling abandoned and is likely to create considerable anxiety. Only a limited number of well-oriented, intelligent patients appear to be suitable for a strictly nondirective approach.

### Consultation Interview

The consultant psychiatrist should discuss the patient's problems with the referring physician. The consultant must preserve the relationship of the patient to his doctor, use great discretion in answering the patient's questions, and help facilitate the medical or surgical treatment. The psychiatrist should discuss his findings with the referring physician.

When it is necessary to give an opinion after a limited period of interviewing time, a directive approach is required. As much essential information as possible must be obtained. However, such interviews usually lack depth of understanding and therapeutic value.

### Stress Interview

Certain patients are monotonously repetitious or show insufficient emotionality for motivation. Apathy, indifference, and emotional blunting are not conducive to a discussion of personality problems. In patients with such reactions, stimulation of emotions can be constructive. These patients may require probing, challenging, or confrontation to arouse feelings that further understanding.

### Interview using Drugs

The use of drugs is of value in interviews with some patients who have difficulty in expressing themselves freely. Sodium amytal has proved to be the most generally valuable drug. Drugs are also of value in helping to distinguish between psychogenic and structurally determined disease.

Drugs should not be used in this way with reluctant patients or those with severe physical disease. Caution should be used in those patients with paranoid reactions and in those who appear to be on the verge of a psychosis.

### Interview using Hypnosis

Hypnosis may be of value in certain patients who are unable to discuss important conflicts easily. During hypnosis, the patient should be encouraged, but not aggressively forced, to talk freely about important conflicts or memories that he may have forgotten or that he finds it difficult to discuss because of feelings of anger, anxiety, or shame. Since premature confrontation is likely to create undue anxiety and resistance, he may be told that after the hypnotic interview he will recall only those memories he consciously wishes to discuss.

### Interview with Anxious Patient

Attention should be paid to what thoughts and environmental strains precipitate or increase the anxiety. When the stresses are not evident, prolonged investigation may be necessary to elucidate the sources of the emotion. Free association, dream analysis, hypnoanalysis, and narcoanalysis may result in definitive insights.

### Interview with Patient Displaying Psychophysiological Symptoms

Study of the correlations among stresses, resultant feelings, and bodily symptoms leads to an understanding of the mechanisms. Enlisting the aid of the patient as a collaborator is helpful.

### Interview with Depressed Patient

Depressed patients have short attention spans and should have relatively brief interviews. Their tendency to reiterate in a destructive, self-deprecatory way may require active interruption by the psychiatrist. The possibility of suicidal preoccupation should be investigated. Many patients feel relieved to be able to talk to a confidant about such thoughts. Verbal expression may lessen the need to take action. Words of reassurance, such as a statement that many people frequently consider death as a possible solution to emotional problems, can be helpful.

The hopelessly ill or dying patient may have some degree of depression. The interviewer can ask the patient how he feels about his illness and allow him to talk about death if he wishes to do so, but should not ask prying questions of those who are not ready to discuss death.

### Interview with Delusional Patient

The psychiatrist should show interest, understanding, and receptiveness, but, since he should represent to the patient a person soundly based in reality, he must not subscribe to the patient's delusions. He should neither agree with nor contradict the patient. Rather, he should try to find out more about the nature of the delusional thoughts. A skeptical attitude may help raise doubts in the patient's mind and may eventually lead him to an understanding of the delusions.

### Interview with Withdrawn Patient

If a patient is absorbed with his inner world of fantasy and is unable to talk spontaneously about his feelings, the psychiatrist must be active in asking questions. He should pay close attention to the patient's verbal and nonverbal reactions and should change the subject when there is difficulty in discussing certain areas of conflict. In extreme withdrawal, there should be frequent, brief visits. When there is no response, the physician may explain in a kindly manner that he will be available when the patient is ready to communicate with him. The mute patient may be acutely aware of what is going on, so care needs to be exercised to avoid saying anything that may antagonize and further alienate him.

### Interview with Manic Patient

Good rapport is not possible with a highly excited patient. The examiner should maintain a calm, receptive attitude and note the thought content carefully. Overtalkative, disturbed patients give valuable information about underlying conflicts that they are not likely to bring up when they gain better control of themselves. Sometimes, especially when the patient is treated with tolerance and understanding, an underlying depression may break through the elation.

## Interviewing Relatives

It is essential to interview relatives of children, the mentally retarded, psychotic patients who cannot give a clear history, and patients with personality disorders who notoriously misconstrue or misrepresent facts. Relatives of patients with other illnesses can give significant supplemental information and express points of view that add to the understanding of the problem. When a patient has marital conflicts, it is often necessary to see the spouse.

The patient should usually be told about contemplated interviews with relatives before they are held and should be reassured that his confidences will not be betrayed. When the patient is strongly opposed to the psychiatrist's interviewing his relatives, the interviews should usually be deferred, conducted in the presence of the patient, or not held at all, unless the patient is a child or grossly psychotic. The psychiatrist must keep in mind that an understanding tolerance is due both his patients and their relatives.

A history obtained from relatives may have greater validity than that given by the patient. However, the patient's fantasies may be of greater significance than reality.

## REFERENCES

Deutsch F, Murphy N F: *The Clinical Interview.* International Universities Press, New York, 1955.
Ginsberg G L: Psychiatric interview. In *Comprehensive Textbook of Psychiatry,* ed 4, H I Kaplan, B J Sadock, editors, p 482. Williams & Wilkins, Baltimore, 1985.
Lewis N D C: *Outlines for Psychiatric Examinations,* ed 3. New York State Department of Mental Hygiene, Utica, NY, 1943.
MacKinnon R A, Michel R: *The Psychiatric Interview in Clinical Practice.* W. B. Saunders, Philadelphia, 1971.
Menninger K A: *The Vital Balance.* Viking Press, New York, 1963.
Spitzer R L, Fleiss J L, Burdock E T, Hardesty A S: The mental status schedule: rationale, reliability and validity. Compr Psychiatry 5: 384, 1964.
Stevenson I: *The Psychiatric Examination.* Little, Brown and Co., Boston, 1968.
Sullivan H S: *The Psychiatric Interview.* W. W. Norton, New York, 1954.

---

# 7.2 PSYCHIATRIC HISTORY AND MENTAL STATUS EXAMINATION

## Introduction

A psychiatric history is assembled by formulating questions to elicit the presenting complaints and assess the severity of associated impairments in social, biological and psychological functioning; to establish the chronology of changes and the relation of these changes to potentially stressful experiences; to ascertain whether the patient has had experiences that caused him to be concerned with his psychological well-being in the past; to determine whether and what kind of treatment he has received in the course of the current episode and, if there is a past history of psychiatric disorder, what, if any, treatment was helpful; to obtain the patient's medical history and the family history of both psychiatric and nonpsychiatric illnesses; to elicit the patient's personal history; and to explore his attitude, his reactions to various events, and his style of handling stresses.

The patient's mental status should be an evaluative statement, based entirely on the observations made and the responses given to specific questions or tests in the course of the examination, and should not be contaminated with historical data.

Interpretation of the information gathered and the observations made should be postponed until all the necessary evidence has been obtained and the clinician is ready to formulate the diagnosis and make recommendations. Both the clinical history and the mental status examination have time-limited validity. The length and the focus of the interview vary, but it must be sufficiently broad to document all actions that the clinician may take or refrain from taking. The clinician is always responsible for assessing the patient's level of anxiety, social competence, and impulse control.

### Psychiatric History

The order in which the various areas are covered depends on the presenting complaint, the patient's way of relating to the clinician, and the clinician's own preferences. Furthermore, the type of questions the psychiatrist asks will change as epidemiological studies and treatment trials provide new information on the natural history of illnesses and their response to treatment.

The history is usually elicited from the patient, his relatives, and his close friends. In exceptional circumstances, persons who have had an opportunity to observe the patient at work may also be questioned. Data obtained from collateral sources should be recorded separately, clearly indicating the relationship of the informant to the patient, and should be judged for reliability by the clinician.

The examiner must make sure that certain basic identifying data about the patient have been collected before the first meeting ends. Such information should include the patient's name, age, place of birth, religion, marital status, education, occupation, ethnic background, and home address, as well as the name, address, and telephone number of the patient's family physician and of his nearest relative or friend.

Although history taking usually begins with the patient's account of his problem, it is best to explore first the circumstances of the referral whenever the clinician knows or the patient's behavior suggests that he had been inadequately prepared for the examination.

The presenting complaints should be recorded in the patient's own words, even when he denies having any problems at all or makes illogical or bizarre statements. The examiner must establish the last time the patient felt well or reasonably well, the length of time he has experienced his current complaints, whether these complaints have changed in character or severity since they began, and what kind of relationship exists between the patient's complaints and major changes in his life situation.

The inquiry should include an assessment of the patient's social competence and psychobiological functioning. It is advisable to inquire whether the patient is currently under care for any nonpsychiatric illness and, if so, when he was last seen by his physician, what treatment he is receiving, and whether the state of his general health is at present stable, improving, or worsening.

Once the characteristics of the present illness have been delineated, the patient should be asked whether he had a psychological disorder in the past and whether the current episode is similar to one he experienced previously. The frequency and duration of past episodes, the age at which the patient was first seen in consultation for a psychological disorder, the treatment he received, the setting in which it took place, and, when there is a history of multiple episodes, the longest time interval the patient got along without psychiatric treatment—all provide important clues for the diagnosis and for future management. The patient should also be asked what information he was given about his condition in the past.

### Family History

The family history of psychiatric and nonpsychiatric conditions may be obtained by asking first if any friend or family member has or has had a similar condition. Questions about family history should cover any episode of attempted or completed suicide, mood disorder, psychiatric treatment and hospitalization, drinking problems, delinquency, mental retardation, peculiar or eccentric behavior, and history of any illness, psychiatric or nonpsychiatric, that has occurred in more than one member of the family.

### Medical History

The extent to which details of early development and childhood illnesses are dealt with var-

ies according to the patient's problem and age and the availability of collateral sources of information or access to medical records. In every instance, the patient's general health history should include a thorough review of his drug intake.

If the patient is of adolescent age or younger, the history of his early development, including the difficulties the patient's mother may have had with pregnancy and delivery, is very important. Medical and developmental data should include early sleep and feeding patterns, how the patient responded to physical discomfort or other stresses, and the approximate time when major developmental landmarks were completed. Information should also be obtained about such indices of subtle neurological dysfunctioning as choreiform movements and other peculiar or stereotyped activities, persistent somatic complaints, speech defects, and the quality of fine motor coordination.

Next, the inquiry should focus on illnesses and operations since infancy and should include the age at which they occurred, their complications and outcomes, and the patient's reactions to these events. The patient should be asked specifically whether he ever had a head injury, lost consciousness, or had symptoms indicative of central nervous dysfunctioning.

Questions about the patient's drug-taking habits may begin by asking him whether he is presently taking any medication and, if so, what kind and how often; whether he has ever had any allergic or idiosyncratic reaction to a drug and, if so, to what kind of drug and what kind of reaction he experienced; whether he has ever taken more medication than was ordered by the prescribing physician; whether he is currently using sedatives, sleeping pills, antianxiety drugs, alcohol, narcotics, pain killers, stimulants, marijuana, hashish and, if so, how frequently and for what reason; whether he ever experienced any symptoms of withdrawal that were severe enough to require medical attention; whether he was ever treated for acute intoxication; and whether he is a multiple-drug user.

### Family Environment

The questioning should begin by asking him to describe, in some detail, the environment he was reared in. Were there any major changes or stresses in the family environment? What were the characteristics of the paternal and maternal supervision and discipline? The attitudes of the parents should be explored in relation to the various developmental stages and life events.

It is also important to determine the patient's

view of his siblings and to explore whether the patient believes the parents' attitudes toward his siblings and other members of the family were different from their attitudes toward him. The patient's socialization patterns should be delineated in relation to the family environment to establish whether the patient's increasing independence was fostered or hindered by those who cared for him. Questions about the patient's attitude and ability to make and keep friends and handle kindergarten and school experiences are important, since separation anxiety in childhood is one of the chronic anxieties in adults. Equally important and far easier to verify is the patient's school performance. When the records show that the patient did not perform adequately in school, it is always worthwhile to investigate whether the patient's siblings had similar difficulties.

One should inquire whether the patient ever became a disciplinary problem in school and, if so, for what reason; if the patient showed evidence of antisocial behavior, did he tend to have any accomplices; did he choose playmates who were also unruly or in trouble; and was there any history of antisocial behavior in the siblings or other members of the family?

During adolescence, attitudes toward the family and peers undergo profound changes. Intimate friendships and dating patterns tend to develop, and assertive behavior is practiced on a much larger scale than before. The nature and the extent of the rebelliousness should be carefully delineated. Asking the patient to describe his views and attitudes about adolescent friendships and dating patterns provides a convenient starting point to trace the patient's sexual history and to get an idea of how he handled intimate relationships.

If the patient is married, what was the duration of his courtship; what attracted him to his mate; what was the age of both partners at the time of the marriage; what was the reaction of the respective families to the marriage? What, if any, are some of the major areas of dissatisfaction in the marriage? Has the patient or his spouse engaged in extramarital affairs, and, if so, how were they handled? If the patient has children, what is his relationship to them; do any of them present special problems or stresses for the marriage, and, if so, what are these problems? If the patient is divorced or separated, how many years did the marriage last, and what were the major areas of dissatisfaction that caused the split?

Even if there is nothing in the patient's report to suggest sexual problems, the patient should be tactfully questioned about his sexual prefer-ences, about the possibility of sexual problems; and about how these difficulties affect his relationship with his partner.

A female patient should be asked about her menstrual periods, pregnancies, abortions or miscarriages, and adoptions.

### Occupational History

If the patient is still a student, is he currently attending school? If not, when did he drop out, and at what point in his scholastic career did this occur and for what reason? Is the patient's level of education in harmony with his abilities, ambitions, and life goals?

Was the patient ever in military service or in a paramilitary service, and, if so, was there ever any disciplinary action taken against him; what type of discharge did he receive?

What kind of work has the patient done since leaving school? Are the patient's earning capacities and duties and responsibilities the same as they were when he was feeling well? If the patient is no longer employed, when was the last time he held a job, and what was the longest time he ever kept a job? If the patient is a housewife, did her effectiveness in attending to her household tasks change and, if so, in what way?

Who handles the financial responsibilities in the patient's household? Was the patient ever bankrupt? Does he gamble frequently? Is he receiving any financial help and, if so, from whom?

What are the patient's church, community, and leisure time activities? Does he belong to clubs and other organizations and, if so, did his participation in these activities change recently?

### Personality Style

The clinician must attempt to obtain enough information to determine whether the behavior patterns displayed represent a lifelong maladaptive style or symptoms of an intercurrent medical or psychiatric illness and what the patient's current and customary responses to stress are.

A few questions asked about the patient's usual way of feeling or behaving will give sufficient information about his level of anxiety, tendencies for phobias and obsessional thinking, social immaturity or excessive dependency needs, aloofness and withdrawal, proneness to cyclothymia, suspiciousness, or outright paranoid attitude. The inquiry should then proceed to determine how the patient handles difficult, frustrating, or otherwise unpleasant events, giving the clinician an opportunity to explore his proneness to suicide or aggressive and antisocial behaviors.

### Current Living Conditions

Does the patient live with anyone, or, if he lives alone, does he have any close friends or relatives he can turn to in times of distress? What is the emotional climate under which the patient is living? Are the significant others in his life able to tell when the patient is not feeling well? Do people close to him approve or disapprove of the patient's being in treatment for psychological problems?

## Mental Status Examination

The mental status is a record of current findings. It includes the description of the patient's appearance, general behavior, motor activity, speech, alertness, mood, cognitive functioning, the views he holds about his condition, and the attitudes he displayed throughout the examination, as well as the reactions evoked by the patient in the examiner.

### Appearance

The examiner's over-all impression of the patient should be followed by a description of the patient's dress and grooming, unusual features in his physical appearance, expression, and eye contact.

### Motor Activity

Is the patient ambulatory? Does he move around restlessly, keep still most of the time, or fluctuate between the two? Movements may be graceful or clumsy. He may appear to have an unusual gait or impairment. He may grimace, have tics, or display waxy flexibility.

### Speech Activity

The patient's speech may be unusually fast or slow. There may be sudden interruptions in the flow of speech. The volume of the patient's voice may be loud or scarcely audible. Intonation and modulation may be preserved or altered. His speech may be unusually vivacious, monotonous, or affected. He may have word-finding difficulty or a speech defect. Impairments in hearing or vision may be present or suspected.

If the patient communicates by gestures but does not speak, the clinician must resort to direct examination to determine whether the lack of verbal communication is an isolated event or merely one aspect of an over-all pattern of diminished responsiveness.

### Mood and Affect

The patient may express feelings of sadness or elation spontaneously or in response to specific questions, or his affect may be so constricted that it remains unaltered or flat, no matter what topics are discussed. The patient's mood may be constant or may fluctuate between elation and sadness throughout the interview. His affect may be appropriate or inappropriate.

### Alertness

The patient may be slightly drowsy or somnolent, or he may be watchful or even hyperalert. He may be intermittently alert and drowsy throughout the examination. Changes in alertness are always associated with inattention.

### Thought

The patient's thinking may be slowed down or accelerated, resulting in hesitation or blocking. The patient's thinking may be pedantic or incoherent. The content of the patient's thought may include realistic concerns as well as exaggerated ones to an actual life event or concerns that have no discernible connection to reality.

When the patient is invited to describe his nervousness, he may also report somatic symptoms or display observable manifestations of discomfort. The patient may also report having unrealistic fears or phobias, he may show evidence of hypochondriasis, or he may be troubled by obsessive ideas. Compelling ideas may reach delusional proportions.

A specific question always should be asked about suicide: Are you having or have you ever had thoughts of wanting to harm yourself or had thoughts that life was no longer worth living?

The patient should also be asked whether he harbors thoughts of wanting to harm another person.

### Perception

Distorted or otherwise altered perceptions may be experienced in reference to self or the environment. Illusions or hallucinations may also be perceived and can occur in any one of the sensory modalities. When the patient does not report abnormal perceptions, but, in the clinician's judgment, his general demeanor suggests that he is having hallucinatory experiences, a notation to this effect should be made.

### Intellectual Functioning

The clinician should conduct a formal examination to assess the patient's general fund of knowledge, orientation, memory, ability to perform simple mathematical operations, and capacity for abstract thinking. Questions and tests must be suitable for patients with little or no schooling or with modest intellectual endowment, as well as for patients whose intellectual achievements are considerable.

General fund of knowledge may be determined by asking the patient to name as many items as he can recall in each of the following categories: colors, animals, fruits, towns. Then the following four questions are asked: What are the colors in the American flag? What is a thermometer? How far is it from Los Angeles to New York? What are the names of three countries in the Middle East?

A generally accepted test for immediate recall is the digit span test, which is administered by asking the patient first to repeat three digits after the examiner, then to give them in reverse order; the same operation is then repeated with four, five, six, and seven digits. Recent memory is assessed by asking the patient to describe how he spent the last 24 hours or what he had to eat for the last meal. Memory for the remote past can be evaluated by inquiring about important dates in the patient's life. The answers must be verifiable.

Another simple and practical way of evaluating orientation and memory is to administer Kahn's 10-question mental status examination: (1) What is the name of this place? (2) Where is it located (address)? (3) What day of the week is it? (4) What is the month now? (5) What is the year? (6) How old are you? (7) When were you born (month)? (8) When were you born (year)? (9) Who is the President of the United States? (10) Who was the President before him?

A brief test for calculation consists of asking the patient to subtract 7 from 100; he is asked to repeat this operation until six successive subtractions are obtained.

The capacity for abstract thinking—that is, the ability to make valid generalizations—can be tested by asking the patient to interpret a common proverb, for example, "People in glass houses should not throw stones." A simpler and probably more reliable test for abstract thinking is an abbreviated object-sorting test, consisting of four toy vehicles, a set of four toy utensils, and four pieces of toy furniture. The patient is asked to group them according to their purpose and utility. The inability to create three distinct sorts is indicative of impaired ability for abstract thinking.

### Attitude

The patient may be neutral, displaying little or no feeling in telling his story or in replying to questions, or he may be fearful, perplexed, hostile, evasive, sarcastic, ingratiating, dramatic, seductive, or completely unresponsive, but rarely is any one of these attitudes consistently displayed. The clinician should, therefore, note whether the patient became more comfortable as the interview went on (or vice versa) and whether any of the changes in attitude occurred in relation to specific circumstances or topics discussed.

The patient may regard his condition as psychiatric or nonpsychiatric, he may attribute his condition to a certain cause or causes, or he may fail to acknowledge that he is ill. He may anticipate improvement in his condition or view it as a persistent handicap that will profoundly affect his long-term life plans.

### Examiner's Reaction

The clinician may find the patient likable, or he may be angered, irritated, anxious, or frustrated by the patient. If the examiner feels the patient is expressing underlying hostility but displays no overt antagonism, it should be so recorded, along with changes in the clinician's reactions toward the patient during the interview.

This section of the examination report should be concluded with a statement expressing the clinician's judgment regarding the accuracy of the information obtained and pointing out any inconsistencies.

### Summary and Recommendations

The clinician should critically examine and summarize his findings. He should state the estimated duration of the current episode and whether in his judgment the patient has improved or deteriorated since he first became ill; describe the course of the illness; summarize all relevant findings; state whether further diagnostic procedures are recommended or additional information is necessary and, if so, from what source.

When the clinician places the patient's illness in a given diagnostic category, he may list all the evidence gathered from the history and examination that is consistent with such a diagnosis, as well as all the evidence that is inconsistent with such a formulation or that points to the necessity of more than one diagnosis. Alternatively, the clinician may choose to defer the diagnosis until he is in a position to obtain and interpret the results of additional studies ordered, or he may conclude that he found no evidence of any psychiatric disorder. The diagnosis should be recorded in accordance with the code provided by the third edition of the American Psychiatric Association's *Diagnostic and Statistical Manual of Mental Disorders* (DSM-III).

In formulating the treatment plan, the clinician should note whether the patient requires psychiatric treatment at this time and, if so, what problems and target symptoms the treatment is aimed at; what kind of treatment or combination of treatments the patient should receive; and what treatment setting seems most appropriate. If hospitalization is recommended, the clinician should specify the reasons for hospitalization, the type of hospitalization indicated, the urgency with which the patient has to be hospitalized, and the anticipated duration of inpatient care.

The clinician should estimate the immediate and long-term prognosis of the patient's illness and the estimated length of treatment.

If either the patient or his family is unwilling to accept the recommendations for treatment and the clinician feels that the refusal of his recommendations may have serious consequences, the patient or a parent or guardian should be invited to sign a statement that the treatment recommended was refused.

**REFERENCES**

American Psychiatric Association: *Diagnostic and Statistical Manual of Mental Disorders*, ed 3. American Psychiatric Association, Washington, DC, 1980.
Bermer P, Gabriel E, Katschnig H, Kochler K, Lenz G, Simhandl C: *Diagnostic Criteria for Schizophrenia and Affective Psychoses*. World Psychiatric Association Press, Vienna, 1983.
Ginsberg G L: Psychiatric history and mental examination. In *Comprehensive Textbook of Psychiatry*, ed 4, H I Kaplan, B J Sadock, editors, p 487. Williams & Wilkins, Baltimore, 1985.
Lewis N D C: *Outlines for Psychiatric Examination*, ed 3. State Hospital Press, Utica, NY, 1943.
Spitzer R L, Skodo A E, Gibbon M, Williams J B S: *DSM-III Case Book*. American Psychiatric Association Press, Washington, DC, 1981.
Wallace E R: *Dynamic Psychiatry in Theory and Practice*. Lea & Febiger, Philadelphia, 1983.
Webb L J, DiClemente C C, Johnstone E E, Sanders J L, Parley R A, editors: *DSM-III Training Guide*. Brunner/Mazel, New York, 1981.

# 7.3    PSYCHIATRIC REPORT

The following summary represents an outline the student may use in writing a psychiatric report.

1. **Psychiatric history**
   A. *Preliminary identification:* name; age; marital status; sex; occupation; language if other than English; race, nationality, and religion insofar as they are pertinent; previous admissions to a hospital for the same or a different condition; with whom does the patient live
   B. *Chief complaint:* exactly why the patient came to the psychiatrist, preferably in the patient's own words; if this information does not come from the patient, note who supplied it
   C. *Personal identification:* brief, nontechnical description of the patient's appearance and behavior as a novelist might write it
   D. *History of present illness:* chronological background and development of the symptoms or behavioral changes culminating in the patient's seeking assistance; patient's life circumstances at the time of onset; personality when well; how illness has affected his life activities and personal relations—changes in personality; interests, mood, attitudes toward others, dress, habits, level of tenseness, irritability, activity, attention, concentration; memory, speech; psychophysiological symptoms—nature and details of dysfunction, location, intensity, fluctuation; relationship between physical and psychic symptoms; extent to which illness serves some additional purpose for the patient when dealing with stress—secondary gain; whether anxieties are generalized and nonspecific (free floating) or specifically related to particular situations, activities, or objects; how anxieties are handled—avoidance of feared situation, use of drugs or other activities for distraction
   E. *Previous illnesses:*
      1. Emotional or mental disturbances—extent of incapacity, type of treatment, names of hospitals, length of illness, effect of treatment
      2. Psychosomatic disorders: hay fever, rheumatoid arthritis, ulcerative colitis, asthma, hyperthyroidism, gastrointestinal upsets, recurrent colds, skin conditions
      3. Medical conditions, following the customary medical review of systems, if necessary; lues, use of alcohol or drugs
      4. Neurological disorders: history of craniocerebral trauma, convulsions, or tumors
   F. *Past personal history:* history (an-

amnesis) of the patient's life from infancy to the present to the extent that it can be recalled; gaps in history as spontaneously related by the patient; emotions associated with these life periods—painful, stressful, conflictual

1. Prenatal history: nature of mother's pregnancy and delivery: length of pregnancy, spontaneity and normality of delivery, birth trauma, whether patient was planned and wanted, birth defects
2. Early childhood (through age 3)
   a. Feeding habits: breast-fed or bottle-fed, eating problems
   b. Maternal deprivation, early development—walking, talking, and teething—language development, motor development, signs of unmet needs, sleep pattern, object constancy, stranger anxiety, separation anxiety
   c. Toilet training: age, attitude of parents, feelings about it
   d. Symptoms of behavior problems: thumb sucking, temper tantrums, tics, head bumping, rocking, night-terrors, fears, bed wetting or bed soiling, nail biting, masturbation
   e. Personality as a child: shy, restless, overactive, withdrawn, studious, outgoing, timid, athletic, friendly, patterns of play, reactions to siblings
   f. Early or recurrent dreams or fantasies
3. Middle childhood (ages 3 to 11): early school history—feelings about going to school, early adjustment, gender identification, conscience development, punishment
4. Later childhood (from puberty through adolescence)
   a. Social relationships: attitudes toward siblings and playmates, number and closeness of friends, leader or follower, social popularity, participation in group or gang activities, idealized figures; patterns of aggression, passivity, anxiety, antisocial behavior
   b. School history: how far the patient progressed, adjustment to school relationships with teachers—teacher's pet or rebellious—favorite studies or interests, particular abilities or assets, extracurricular activities, sports, hobbies, relationships of problems or symptoms to any school period
   c. Cognitive and motor development: learning to read and other intellectual and motor skills, minimal cerebral dysfunctions, learning disabilities—their management and effects on the child
   d. Particular adolescent emotional or physical problems: nightmares, phobias, masturbation, bed wetting, running away, delinquency, smoking, drug or alcohol use, anorexia, bulimia, weight problems, feeling of inferiority
   e. Psychosexual history
      i. Early curiosity, infantile masturbation, sex play
      ii. Acquisition of sexual knowledge, attitude of parents toward sex
      iii. Onset of puberty, feelings about it, kind of preparation, feelings about menstruation, development of secondary sexual characteristics
      iv. Adolescent sexual activity: crushes, parties, dating, petting, masturbation, wet dreams and attitudes toward them
      v. Attitudes toward opposite sex: timid, shy, aggressive, need to impress, seductive, sexual conquests, anxiety
      vi. Sexual practices: sexual problems, homosexual experiences, paraphilias, promiscuity
   f. Religious background: strict, liberal, mixed (possible conflicts), relationship of background to current religious practices
5. Adulthood

a. Occupational history: choice of occupation, training, ambitions, conflicts; relations with authority, peers, and subordinates; number of jobs and duration; changes in job status; current job and feelings about it

b. Social activity: does patient have friends, is patient withdrawn or socializing well; kind of social, intellectual, and physical interests; relationships with same sex and opposite sex; depth, duration, and quality of human relationships

c. Adult sexuality
   i. Premarital sexual relationships
   ii. Marital history: common-law marriages, legal marriages, description of courtship and role played by each partner, age at marriage, family planning and contraception, names and ages of children, attitudes toward the raising of children, problems of any family members, housing difficulties if important to the marriage, sexual adjustment, areas of agreement and disagreement, management of money, role of in-laws
   iii. Sexual symptoms: anorgasmia, impotence, premature ejaculation
   iv. Attitudes toward pregnancy and having children: contraceptive practices and feelings about them
   v. Sexual practices: paraphilias, such as sadism, fetishes, voyeurism; attitudes about fellatio, cunnilingus, and coital techniques

d. Military history: general adjustment, combat, injuries, referral to psychiatrists, veteran status

G. *Family history:* elicited from patient and from someone else, because quite different descriptions may be given of the same people and events; ethnic, national, and religious traditions; other people in the home, descriptions of them—personality and intelligence—and what has become of them since the patient's childhood; descriptions of different households lived in; present relationships between patient and other people who were in the family; role of illness in the family; history of mental illness

H. *Current social situation:* where does patient live—neighborhood and particular residence of the patient; is home crowded; privacy of family members from each other and from other families; sources of family income and difficulties in obtaining it; public assistance, if any, and attitudes about it; will patient lose job or apartment by remaining in the hospital; who is caring for children

I. *Dreams, fantasies, and value systems*
   1. Dreams: prominent ones, if patient will tell them; nightmares
   2. Fantasies: recurrent, favorite, or unshakable daydreams; hypnagogic phenomena
   3. Value systems: whether children are seen as a burden or a joy; whether work is seen as a necessary evil, an avoidable chore, or an opportunity.

II. **Mental Status:** sum total of the examiner's observations and impressions derived from the initial interviews
   A. *General description*
      1. Appearance: posture, bearing, clothes, grooming, hair, nails; healthy, sickly, angry, frightened, apathetic, perplexed, contemptuous, ill at ease, poised, old looking, young looking, effeminate, masculine; signs of anxiety—moist hands, perspiring forehead, restlessness, tense posture, strained voice, wide eyes; shifts in level of anxiety during interview or abrupt changes of topic
      2. Behavior and psychomotor activity: gait, mannerisms, tics, gestures, twitches, stereotypes, picking, touching examiner, echopraxia, clumsy, agile, limp, rigid, retarded, hyperactive, agitated, combative, waxy

3. Speech: rapid, slow, pressured, hesitant, emotional, monotonous, loud, whispered, slurred, mumbled, stuttering, echolalia; intensity, pitch, ease, spontaneity, productivity, manner, reaction time, vocabulary
4. Attitude toward examiner: cooperative, attentive, interested, frank, seductive, defensive, hostile, playful, ingratiating, evasive, guarded

B. *Mood, feelings, and affect*
1. Mood (a pervasive and sustained emotion that colors the person's perception of the world): how does patient say he feels; depth, intensity, duration, and fluctuations of mood—depressed, despairing, irritable, anxious, terrified, angry, expansive, euphoric, empty, guilty, awed, futile, self-contemptuous
2. Affective expression: how examiner evaluates patient's affects—broad, restricted, depressed, blunted or flat, shallow, anhedonic, labile, constricted, fearful, anxious, guilty; amount and range of expression; difficulty in initiating, sustaining, or terminating an emotional response
3. Appropriateness: is the emotional expression appropriate to the thought content, the culture, and the setting of the examination; examples if emotional expression is not appropriate

C. *Perceptual disturbances*
1. Hallucinations and illusions: does patient hear voices or see visions; content, sensory system involved, circumstances of the occurrence; hypnogogic or hypnopompic hallucinations
2. Depersonalization and derealization: extreme feelings of detachment from one's self or the environment

D. *Thought process*
1. Stream of thought; quotations from patient
   a. Productivity: overabundance of ideas, paucity of ideas, flight of ideas, rapid thinking, slow thinking, hesitant thinking; does patient speak spontaneously or only when questions are asked
   b. Continuity of thought: do patient's replies really answer questions; are they goal directed and relevant or irrelevant; are there loose associations; is there a lack of cause-and-effect relationships in patient's explanations; are statements illogical, tangential, circumstantial, rambling, evasive, perserverative; is there blocking or distractibility
   c. Language impairments: impairments that reflect disordered mentation, such as incoherent or incomprehensible speech (word salad), clang associations, neologisms
2. Content of thought
   a. Preoccupations: about the illness, environmental problems; obsessions, compulsions, phobias; obsessions, plans, intentions, recurrent ideas about suicide, homicide, hypochondriacal symptoms, specific antisocial urges; specific questions should always be asked about suicidal ideation
   b. Thought disturbances
      1. Delusions: content of any delusional system, its organization, the patient's convictions as to its validity, how it affects his life; somatic delusions—isolated or associated with pervasive suspiciousness; mood-congruent delusions—in keeping with a depressed or elated mood; mood-incongruent delusions—not in keeping with the patient's mood; bizarre delusions, such as thoughts of being controlled by external forces or thoughts being broadcast out loud
      2. Ideas of reference and ideas of influence: how ideas began, their con-

tent, and the meaning the patient attributes to them

3. Abstract thinking: disturbances in concept formation; manner in which the patient conceptualizes or handles his ideas; similarities, differences, absurdities, meanings of simple proverbs, such as, "A rolling stone gathers no moss"; answers may be concrete (giving specific examples to illustrate the meaning) or overly abstract (giving generalized explanation); appropriateness of answers should be noted

4. Information and intelligence: patient's level of formal education and self-education; estimate of the patient's intellectual capability and whether he is capable of functioning at the level of his basic endowment; counting, calculation, general knowledge; questions that have some relevance to the patient's educational and cultural background

5. Concentration: subtract 7 from 100 and keep subtracting 7's; if patient cannot subtract 7's, can easier tasks be accomplished—4 times 9; 5 times 4; whether anxiety or some disturbance of mood or consciousness seems to be responsible for difficulty

E. *Orientation*

1. Time: does patient identify the date correctly; can he approximate date, time of day; if he is in a hospital, does the patient know how long he has been there; does patient behave as though he is oriented to the present

2. Place: does patient know where he is

3. Person: does patient know who the examiner is; does he know the roles or names of the persons with whom he is in contact

F. *Memory:* impairment, efforts made to cope with impairment—denial, confabulation, catastrophic reaction, circumstantiality used to conceal deficit; whether the process of registration, retention, or recollection of material is involved

1. Remote memory: childhood

data, important events known to have occurred when the patient was younger or free of illness, personal matters, neutral material

2. Recent past memory: the past few months

3. Recent memory: the past few days, what did patient do yesterday, the day before; what did he have for breakfast, lunch, dinner

4. Immediate retention and recall ability to repeat six figures after examiner dictates them—first forward, then backward, then after a few minutes' interruption; other test questions; did same questions, if repeated, call forth different answers at different times; digit-span measures; other mental functions, such as anxiety level and concentration

5. Effect of defect on patient: mechanisms patient has developed to cope with his defect

G. *Impulse control:* is patient able to control hostile, aggressive, sexual, and amorous impulses

H. *Judgment*

1. Social judgment: subtle manifestations of behavior that is harmful to the patient and contrary to acceptable behavior in the culture; does the patient understand the likely outcome of his behavior and is he influenced by this understanding; examples of impairment

2. Test judgment: patient's prediction of what he would do in imaginary situations; for instance, what he would do if he found a stamped, addressed letter in the street

I. *Insight:* degree of awareness and understanding the patient has that he is ill

1. Complete denial of illness

2. Slight awareness of being sick and needing help but denying it at the same time

3. Awareness of being sick but blaming it on others, on external factors, on organic factors

4. Awareness that illness is due to something unknown in himself

5. Intellectual insight: admission that he is ill and that his symp-

toms or failures in social adjustment are due to his own particular irrational feelings or disturbances, without applying that
knowledge to future experiences
6. True emotional insight: emotional awareness of the motives
and feelings within himself of
the underlying meaning of
symptoms; does the awareness
lead to change in personality and
future behavior; openness to new
ideas about himself and the important people in his life
J. *Reliability:* estimate of examiner's
impression of patient's veracity or
ability to report his situation accurately

### III. Further diagnostic studies
A. *Physical examination*
B. *Additional psychiatric diagnostic interviews*
C. *Interviews with family members,
friends, or neighbors by social worker*
D. *Psychological tests by psychologist:*
type and purpose
E. *Specialized tests as indicated:* electroencephalogram, computed tomography scan, positive emission
tomography, laboratory tests, tests
of other medical conditions, reading
comprehension and handwriting
tests, tests for aphasia

### IV. Summary of positive findings: men-
tal symptoms, laboratory findings, psychological test results, if available; drugs
patient has been taking, including dosage and duration of intake

### V. Diagnosis: diagnostic classification ac-
cording to the third edition of the American Psychiatric Association's *Diagnostic and Statistical Manual of Mental Disorders* (DSM-III)—nomenclature, classification number, diagnoses to be ruled
out; DSM-III uses a multiaxial classification scheme consisting of five axes,
each of which should be covered in the
diagnosis
A. *Axis I:* consists of all clinical syndromes (i.e. affective disorders,
schizophrenia, generalized anxiety
disorder)
B. *Axis II:* consists of personality disorders and specific developmental
disorders

C. *Axis III:* consists of any existing
medical or physical illness (i.e. epilepsy, cardiovascular disease, gastrointestinal disease)
D. *Axis IV:* refers to psychosocial stressors (i.e. divorce, injury, death of a
loved one) relevant to the illness; a
rating scale with a continuum of 1
(no stressors) to 8 (catastrophic
stressors) is used
E. *Axis V:* relates to the highest level
of functioning exhibited by the patient during the previous year (i.e.
social and vocational functioning,
leisure time activities); a rating scale
with a continuum of 1 (superior
functioning) to 7 (grossly impaired
functioning) is used

### VI. Prognosis: opinion as to the probable
future course, extent, and outcome of
the illness; specific goals of therapy

### VII. Psychodynamic formulation: causes
of the patient's psychodynamic breakdown—influences in the patient's life
that contributed to his present illness;
environmental, genetic, and personality
factors relevant in determining patient's
symptoms; primary and secondary gains;
outline the major defense mechanisms
used by the patient

### VIII. Treatment plan: modalities of treat-
ment recommended, role of medication,
inpatient or outpatient treatment, frequency of sessions, probable duration of
therapy; individual, group, or family
therapy; type of psychotherapy; symptoms or problems to be treated

## 7.4 PSYCHOLOGICAL TESTING OF INTELLIGENCE AND PERSONALITY

### Introduction

Standard psychological tests provide a fairly
objective means for comparing a relatively controlled sample of the patient's behavior with
available normative data representative of a
larger reference group. Adequate standardization of tests has probably been achieved most
extensively in the area of intelligence testing.
Related to the standardization of any test are
the available data that presumably demonstrate

whether the test is both valid and reliable: Does the test measure what it purports to measure? Does the test yield consistent results over time with different examiners? Consistencies and inconsistencies between tests are helpful in establishing the level of confidence that can be held about any specific inference and in relating surface behavioral characteristics to their motivational origins.

In the test battery a broad range of stimuli on the continuum of structure-ambiguity is available for eliciting a patient's response samples. In contrast to specific or highly structured questions, such as those on an intelligence test, the projective techniques presumably have no right or wrong answers. The person being tested must give meaning to (interpret) the stimulus in accordance with his own inner needs, drives, abilities, defenses, impulses—in short, according to the dictates of his own personality. A basic assumption is that persons who show a certain kind of disturbance in a test situation of a given degree of ambiguity will in all probability show a similar reaction in a social situation of equal ambiguity. The test battery most widely used in clinical practice for evaluation of psychiatric patients generally includes an individual intelligence test, an association technique, a storytelling test, completion methods, and graphomotor tests.

### Referral Purposes

Intellectual evaluation can best be accomplished by an individual intelligence test, such as the Wechsler Adult Intelligence Scale (WAIS). Problems of differential diagnosis can best be answered by recourse to a full test battery in which relationships among tests may offer significant insight into the patient's total pattern of functioning.

Deficiencies that accompany organic brain malfunctioning are frequently highlighted by means of psychological tests. On occasion, they are most apparent in areas ordinarily conceptualized as intellectual. In the other instances, they are most apparent in graphomotor productions. Brain malfunctioning may often be apparent in responses to the projective techniques. Some psychologists have devised special tests and procedures solely for the purpose of detecting brain damage.

Elucidation of personality dynamics usually requires recourse to techniques that vary in the degree to which their stimulus value is obvious and clear. Where weak reality-testing abilities are revealed, supportive treatment is generally considered more advisable than intensive analytical treatments that may precipitate further decompensation of already weakened defenses.

Psychological tests may be helpful in answering specific questions related to a particular patient, such as whether there is evidence of suicidal ideation or whether the patient is likely to be dangerous or homicidal. And many specialized tests are designed to evaluate such issues as educational fitness, occupational interest, and vocational aptitudes.

### Classification of Tests

The usual distinctions involve whether the test was devised to evaluate intellectual and cognitive abilities or those other modes of responding assumed to be related to nonintellectual factors, such as personality. However, intellectual functioning may be intimately related to the psychodynamics of personality functioning.

Another traditional distinction involves whether the test is individually administered or given simultaneously to a group. Individual testing has the advantage of providing opportunity for the examiner to evaluate rapport and motivational factors as well as to observe and record the patient's behavior during testing. Careful timing of responses is also possible. Group tests, on the other hand, are usually more easily administered. They have generally been devised for easier scoring and more objective interpretation. But some tests can be administered in either individual or group forms.

Objective personality tests are typically pencil-and-paper tests based on items and questions having obvious meaning and the advantage of yielding numerical scores and profiles easily subjected to mathematical or statistical analysis. Projective tests, on the other hand, present stimuli whose meaning is not immediately obvious— that is, some degree of ambiguity forces the subject to project his own needs into or onto an amorphous, somewhat unstructured situation. Interpretation of the elicited free association data usually requires experience and knowledge of personality theory on the part of the examiner. The philosophy and the interpretative approach of the examiner are important in determining whether the given tool is used as an objective test, a projective technique, or something alternating between them.

### Intelligence Testing

#### General Background

Tremendous individual differences exist in people's ability to assimilate factual knowledge, to recall either recent or remote events, to reason logically, to manipulate concepts (either numbers or words), to translate the abstract to the literal or the literal to the abstract, to analyze and synthesize forms, and, in short, to deal meaningfully and accurately with problems and priorities deemed important in a particular setting.

Alfred Binet introduced the concept of the mental age (MA), which is the average intellectual level of a particular age. The intelligence quotient (I.Q.) is the ratio of MA over CA (chronological age) multiplied by 100 to do away with the decimal point. When chronological and mental ages are equal, the I.Q. is 100, that is, average. Since it is impossible to measure increments of intellectual power past the age of 15 by available intelligence tests, the highest divisor in the I.Q. formula is 15.

Another way of expressing the relative standing of an individual within his group is by percentile. The higher the percentile, the higher his rank within a group. For example, if a person is at the 80th percentile level, he exceeds 80 percent of the group in the trait measured and is exceeded by the remaining 20 percent. An I.Q. of 100 corresponds to the 50th percentile in intellectual ability for the general population.

The I.Q., as measured by most intelligence tests, is an interpretation or classification of a total test score in relation to norms established by some group. For this and other reasons, the I.Q. can be misleading, since it is an average of different abilities or levels of ability that themselves may show great variability.

The I.Q. is a measure of present functioning ability, not necessarily of future potential. Although under ordinary circumstances the I.Q. has a surprising stability through life, there is no absolute certainty about its predictive properties. A person's I.Q. must be examined in the light of his past experiences as well as his future opportunities.

The I.Q. itself conveys no meaning as to the origins of its reflected capacities, whether genetic (innate) or environmental. The most useful intelligence test must measure a variety of skills and abilities, including verbal and performance, early learned and recently learned, timed and untimed, culture-free and culture-bound. No intelligence test is totally culture-free, although tests do differ significantly in degree.

### Wechsler Adult Intelligence Scale (WAIS)

The WAIS is the best standardized and most widely used intelligence test in clinical practice today. The WAIS comprises 11 subtests (yielding a full-scale I.Q.), including six verbal subtests and five performance subtests (yielding a separate verbal I.Q. and performance I.Q.). Subtest raw scores are weighted so as to be comparable to each other. Intelligence levels are determined statistically, based on the assumption that intellectual abilities are distributed in terms of a normal-curve distribution throughout the population.

The subtests are presented in the following order: information, comprehension, arithmetic, similarities, memory for digits, vocabulary, digit symbol, picture completion, block design, picture arrangement, and object assembly. Raw subtest scores are prorated into subtest scores. Verbal and performance I.Q.'s, as well as the full-scale I.Q., are determined by the use of separate tables for each of the seven age groups from 16 to 64 years. Variability in functioning is thus revealed through discrepancies between verbal and performance I.Q.'s, between scaled subtest scores (intertest variability), and within any subtest, since items in each test are arranged in order of difficulty (intratest variability).

### Personality Testing

The tests in the psychological test battery used in most psychiatric settings are usually chosen in terms of how well they serve the purpose of a psychodynamic formulation of personality functioning. Basic to this selection is the assumption that behavior is often motivated by forces that vary as to their degree of accessibility to awareness and behavioral expression. The need for a battery of tests arises not because of the possible invalidity of any single test but because different tests detect different levels of functioning and because the relationships between tests reflect the person's multilevel system of functioning.

### Rorschach Test

Surveys over the years suggest that the Rorschach test is the most frequently used individual test, with the possible exception of the WAIS, in clinical settings throughout the United States. The Rorschach was devised by Hermann Rorschach (see Fig. 1), a Swiss psychiatrist, who began around 1910 to experiment with ambiguous inkblots (see Fig. 2). The Rorschach is a standard set of 10 inkblots that serve as the stimuli for associations. In the standard series the blots, administered in order, are reproduced on cards 7 by 9½ inches and are numbered from I to X. Five of the blots are in black and white; the remainder include other colors. A verbatim record is kept of the patient's responses, along with initial reaction times and

FIGURE 1.   Hermann Rorschach. (Courtesy of New York Academy of Medicine.)

FIGURE 2.   Plate I of the Rorschach Test. (Reprinted by permission, Hans Huber Medical Publisher, Berne.)

total time spent on each card. After completion of what is called the free association, an inquiry is then conducted by the examiner to determine important aspects of each response that will be crucial to its scoring.

Scoring of responses converts the important aspects of each response into a symbol system related to the following variables: location areas, determinants, and content areas. The location is scored in terms of what portion of the blot was used as the basis for the response. Grossest differentiations involve whether it was the whole blot (W), a large, usual detail of the blot (D), a small detail of the blot (d), or the white space (S). The determinants of each response reflect

what there was about the blot that made it look the way the patient thought it looked. Determinants include form (F), shading (K, t or c), color (C), movement either of humans or animals (M or FM), inanimate movement (m), and various combinations of these determinants with varying emphases. The content areas—human, animal, anatomy, sex, food, nature, and so forth—reflect breadth and range of interests.

The Rorschach is particularly useful as a diagnostic tool. The thinking and associational patterns of the patient are highlighted or brought more clearly into focus largely because the ambiguity of the stimulus provides relatively few cues for what may be conventional or standard responses. Recognizing the behavioral differences between hysterical and obsessive-compulsive patients, one could correctly infer that the hysterical patients have fewer and vague responses, are less systematic in approach, and use fewer small detail responses than do the obsessive-compulsive patients. The presumed emotional lability of the hysteric should also dictate that he will probably more freely show uncontrolled color responses (CF and C) on the Rorschach than does the obsessive-compulsive patient. And schizophrenia, which is sometimes difficult to detect through structured interviews only, may be expressed on the Rorschach by poor contact with reality, overgeneralization, unconventionality of thinking, idiosyncrasy of thought, peculiarities of language, suicide indicators, body-image and ego-boundary difficulties, and difficulties in interpersonal relationships.

### Thematic Apperception Test (TAT)

The TAT was designed by Henry Murray and Christiana Morgan as part of a case-study exploration of the normal personality conducted at the Harvard Psychological Clinic in 1943. It consists of a series of 30 pictures (see Fig. 3) and one blank card. Only 20 of the cards were originally expected to be used with an individual subject, with the choice of some pictures depending on the subject's sex and age. Today, fewer pictures are usually used, with the selection depending on the examiner's card preference and on what conflict areas he wishes to clarify with a particular patient.

Although most of the pictures obviously depict people, thus making the test stimuli more structured than the inkblots of the Rorschach test, there is ambiguity in all the pictures. Unlike the Rorschach blots, to which the patient is asked to associate, the TAT requires that he construct or create a story.

As the test was originally conceived, an im-

FIGURE 3.    Card 12F of the Thematic Apperception Test. (Reprinted by permission of the publishers from *Thematic Apperception Test* by Henry A. Murray, Cambridge, Mass.: Harvard University Press, copyright © 1943 by the President and Fellows of Harvard College; 1971 by Henry A. Murray.)

portant aspect of each story was the figure (the hero) with whom the storyteller seemed to identify and to whom he was presumably attributing his own wishes, strivings, and conflicts. The characteristics of people other than the hero were considered to represent the subject's view of other people in his environment. It is assumed that all the figures in a TAT story are equally representative of the subject, with more acceptable and conscious traits and motives being attributed to figures closest to the subject in age, sex, and appearance and the more unacceptable and unconscious traits and motives attributed to figures most unlike the subject.

The stories must be considered from the standpoint of unusualness of theme or plot. Whether the patient is dealing with a common or an uncommon theme, however, his story reflects his own idiosyncratic approach to organization, sequence, vocabulary, style, preconceptions, assumptions, and outcome. TAT cards have different stimulus value and can be assumed to elicit data pertaining to different areas of functioning. Generally, the TAT is most useful as a technique for inferring motivational aspects of behavior.

### Sentence Completion Test (SCT)

SCT responses are often most helpful in establishing level of confidence regarding predictions of overt behavior. The SCT is designed to tap the patient's conscious associations to areas of functioning in which the psychologist may be interested. It is composed of series of sentence stems (usually 75 to 100)—such as "I like ..."

"Sex is ..." "Sometimes I wish ..."—that the patient is asked to complete in his own words. Since such tests are easily constructed, many psychologists have devised their own form of this test, although copyrighted forms are available.

The patient may be encouraged to take all the time he needs, thus allowing him to consider thoroughly how he wishes to present himself. The text may also be administered verbally by the examiner, similar to the word association technique, in which the patient is told he should reply with the very first thing that comes to his mind. Sentence stems vary in their ambiguity, hence some items serve more as a projective test stimulus ("Sometimes I ..."). Others more closely resemble direct-response questionnaires ("My greatest fear is ...").

With the individual protocol, most psychologists use an inspection technique, noting particularly those responses that are expressive of strong affects, that tend to be given repetitively, or that are unusual or particularly informative in any way. Areas where denial operates are often revealed through omissions, bland expressions, or factual reports ("My mother *is a woman*). Humor may also reflect an attempt to deny anxiety about a particular issue, person, or event. Important historical material is sometimes revealed directly ("I feel guilty about *the way my sister was drowned*).

### Word-association Technique

The word-association technique consists of presenting stimulus words to the patient and having him respond with the first word that comes to his mind.

Complex indicators include long reaction times, blocking difficulties in making responses, unusual responses, repetition of the stimulus word, apparent misunderstanding of the word, clang associations, perseveration of earlier responses, and ideas or unusual mannerisms or movements accompanying the response. After the initial administration of the list, some clinicians repeat the list, asking the patient to respond with the same words that he used previously; discrepancies between the two administrations may reveal associational difficulties. Because it is easily quantified, the test has continued to be used as a research instrument, although its popularity has diminished greatly over the years.

### Minnesota Multiphasic Personality Inventory

The most widely used self-report inventory is the MMPI. The inventory consists of 550 statements—such as "I worried about sex matters," "I sometimes tease animals," "I believe I am being plotted against"—to which the testee has to respond with "True," "False," or "Cannot say." The test may be used in card or booklet form, and several programs exist to process the responses by computer.

The MMPI gives score on the following 10 scales: 1. Hs (hypochondriasis); 2. D (depression); 3. Hy (hysteria); 4. Pd (psychopathic deviate); 5. Mf (masculinity-femininity); 6. Pa (paranoia); 7. Pt (psychasthenia); 8. Sc (schizophrenia); 9. Ma (hypomania); 10. Si (social introversion).

Items of the scale differentiate between eight clinical groups. Other scales test for the reliability and consistency of the responses, which are, of course, subject to deliberate false reporting. The finally obtained 14 scores are plotted on a profile; any scores that are two standard deviations above the mean are considered potentially pathological. However, a correct interpretation of the MMPI results requires extensive clinical experience by the psychologist or a highly sophisticated computer program. One may not, for instance, simply diagnose schizophrenia on the basis of a high score on the schizophrenic scale. Cultural and age differences must be taken into account when interpreting MMPI results.

### Bender (Visual Motor) Gestalt Test

The Bender-Gestalt test is a test of visual motor coordination, useful for both children and adults. It was designed by Lauretta Bender, at Bellevue Psychiatric Hospital, who used it to evaluate maturational levels in children. Developmentally, a child below the age of 3 is generally unable to reproduce any of the test's designs meaningfully. Around 4 he may be able to copy several, but poorly. At about 6 he should give some recognizable representation of all the designs, though still unevenly. By 10 and certainly by 12, his copies should be reasonably accurate and well-organized. Bender also presented studies of adults with organic brain defects, mental retardation, aphasias, psychoses, neuroses, and malingering.

The test material consists of nine separate designs, adapted from those used by Wertheimer in his studies in Gestalt psychology. Each design is printed against a white background on a separate card (see Fig. 4). Presented with unlined paper, the patient is asked to copy each design with the card in front of him. There is no time limit. This phase of the test is highly structured and does not investigate memory function, since the cards remain in front of the patient while he copies them. Many clinicians include a subse-

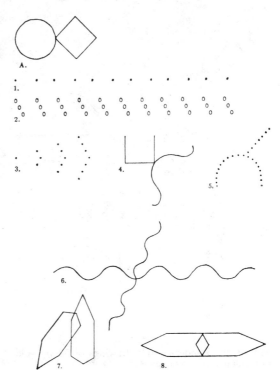

FIGURE 4. Test figures from the Bender Visual Motor Gestalt Test, adopted from Wertheimer. (From Bender, L. *A Visual Motor Gestalt Test and Its Clinical Use.* Research Monograph no. 3, American Orthopsychiatric Association, New York, 1938.)

quent recall phase, in which (after an interval of 45 to 60 seconds), the patient is asked to reproduce as many of the designs as he can from memory. This phase not only investigates visual memory but also presents a less structured situation, since the patient must now rely essentially on his own resources. It is often particularly helpful to compare the patient's functioning under the two conditions.

Probably the most frequent clinical use for the test with adults is as a screening device for detecting signs of organically based interference, especially in grosser forms. Evaluation of the protocol depends on the form of the reproduced figures and on their relationship to each other and to the whole spatial background (see Figs. 5 and 6).

### Draw a Person Test

The Draw a Person test (DAP) was first used as a measure of intelligence with children. The test is easily administered, usually with the instructions, "I'd like you to draw a picture of a person; draw the best person you can." After the completion of the first drawing, the patient is asked to draw a picture of a person of the opposite sex to that of his first drawing. Some

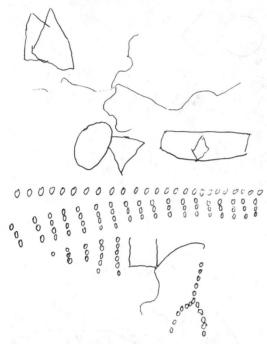

FIGURE 5. Bender-Gestalt drawings of 57-year-old brain-damaged female patient.

FIGURE 6. Bender-Gestalt "recall" of 57-year-old brain-damaged female patient.

clinicians use an interrogation procedure in which the patient is questioned about his drawings. ("What is he doing? What are his best qualities?") Modifications include asking also for a drawing of a house and a tree (house-tree-person test), of one's family, and of an animal.

A general assumption is that the drawing of a person represents the expression of the self or of the body in the environment. Interpretive principles rest largely on the assumed functional significance of each body part. Most clinicians use drawings primarily as a screening technique, particularly for the detection of organic brain damage.

### Integration of Test Findings

The integration of test findings into a comprehensive, meaningful report is probably the most difficult aspect of psychological evaluations. Inferences from different tests must be related to each other in terms of the confidence

the psychologist holds about them and of the presumed level of the patient's awareness or consciousness being tapped.

Most psychologists follow some general outline in preparing a psychological report, such as: test behavior, intellectual functioning, personality functioning (reality-testing ability, impulse control, manifest depression and guilt, manifestations of major dysfunction, major defenses, overt symptoms, interpersonal conflicts, self-concept, affects), inferred diagnosis, degree of present overt disturbance, prognosis for social recovery, motivation for personality change, primary assests and weaknesses, recommendations, and summary.

### REFERENCES

Bender L: *A Visual Motor Gestalt Test and Its Clinical Use.* American Orthopsychiatric Association, New York, 1938.
Berg M: Borderline psychopathology as displayed on psychological tests. J Pers Assess *47:* 120, 1983.
Carr A C: Psychological testing of personality. In *Comprehensive Textbook of Psychiatry,* ed 4, H I Kaplan, B J Sadock, editors, p 514. Williams & Wilkins, Baltimore, 1985.
Carr A C, Forer B R, Henry W E, Hooker E, Hutt M L, Piotrowski Z A: *The Prediction of Overt Behavior through the Use of Projective Techniques.* Charles C Thomas, Springfield, IL 1968.
Exner J E: *The Rorschach: A Comprehensive System,* vols 1, 2, and 3. John Wiley & Sons, New York, 1982.
Lylerly S B: *Handbook of Psychiatric Scales,* ed 2. National Institutes of Mental Health, Rockville, MD, 1978.
Matarazzo, J D: Psychological assessment of intelligence. In *Comprehensive Textbook of Psychiatry,* ed 4, H I Kaplan, B J Sadock, editors, p 502. Williams & Wilkins, Baltimore, 1985.
Rorschach H: *Psychodiagnostik.* Bircher, Bern, 1921.
Schafer R: *Psychoanalytic Interpretation in Rorschach Testing.* Grune & Stratton, New York, 1954.

## 7.5 PSYCHOLOGICAL TESTS FOR BRAIN DAMAGE

### Introduction

Disease or injury at the higher levels of the central nervous system is likely to be reflected in disturbances in mentation, feeling, and conduct. It is this basic fact that makes behavioral assessment an integral part of clinical neurological evaluation, particularly when the question of disease involving the cerebral hemispheres has been raised.

To a considerable degree, the aspects of behavior sampled by clinical observation and by neuropsychological tests are the same—for example, speed of response, level of comprehension, and use of language—but the test procedures assess these aspects of behavior with greater reliability and precision. The tests go on to sample other aspects of behavior, such as visual memory and psychomotor skill, that are not readily elicited in the general examination. Thus, neuropsychological tests both validate the impressionistic findings of the general clinical examination and provide additional information about other aspects of intellect and personality (see Table I).

## Neuropsychological Tests

### General Intelligence and Dementia

Patients with cerebral disease may show an over-all behavioral inefficiency and be unable to meet the diverse intellectual demands associated

TABLE I
TESTS FOR ASSESSING BRAIN DAMAGE

| Category | Subcategories | Remarks |
|---|---|---|
| General scales | Wechsler scales (WAIS, WISC, WPSSI)<br>Stanford-Binet<br>Halstead-Reitan battery | Given the availability of adequate normative standards in relation to the patient's educational and cultural background, a performance significantly below expectations should raise the question of cerebral damage. This generalization applies to both adults and children. |
| Reasoning and problem solving | Shipley abstractions<br>Raven progressive matrices<br>Gorham proverbs<br>Elithorn perceptual mazes<br>Porteus mazes<br>Goldstein-Scheerer sorting tests<br>Wisconsin card-sorting test | Performance level is closely related to educational background and premorbid intellectual level. In general, the clinical application of these tests is more useful in the case of educated patients. If specific language and perceptual defects can be ruled out as determinants of defective performance, failure suggests frontal lobe involvement or diffuse cerebral disease. |
| Memory and orientation | Repetition and reversal of digits<br>Visual memory for designs<br>Auditory memory for words or stories<br>Visual memory for words or pictures<br>Temporal orientation | For complete assessment, a number of memory tasks (auditory versus visual, verbal versus nonverbal, immediate versus recent) should be given. Defects in temporal orientation suggestive of impairment in recent memory may be elicited. |
| Visuoperceptive and visuoconstructive | Identification of hidden figures<br>Discrimination of complex patterns<br>Facial recognition<br>Inkblot interpretation<br>Block design construction<br>Stick arranging<br>Copying designs<br>Three-dimensional block construction<br>Responsiveness to double visual stimulation | These tasks are useful indicators of the presence of cerebral disease. Analysis of qualitative features of performance and comparison of performance level with the status of language and reasoning abilities often provide indications with regard to locus of the lesion. |
| Somatoperceptual | Finger recognition<br>Right-left orientation<br>Responsiveness to double tactile stimulation | These are useful indicators of the presence and locus of cerebral disease. |
| Language | Token test<br>Controlled word association<br>Illinois test of psycholinguistic abilities<br>Diagnostic reading tests | Test performance depends on educational background, and clinical interpretation must allow for this and other possibly significant factors. In adult patients, defective performance (particularly in relation to other abilities) suggests dysfunction of the cerebral hemisphere that is dominant for language. In children, defective performance does not have this localizing significance but does raise the question of the presence of cerebral damage. Performance on verbal reasoning tests, such as Shipley abstractions and Gorham proverbs, may also disclose specific impairment in language function. |
| Attention, concentration, and motor abilities | Simple and choice reaction time<br>Visual vigilance<br>Imitation of movements<br>Motor impersistence | These are useful behavioral indicators of the presence and sometimes the locus of cerebral disease that deserve more extensive clinical application. |

with the responsibilities of daily life. The normal counterpart of dementia or deterioration is general intelligence.

Dementia implies an over-all impairment in mental capacity with consequent decline in social and economic competence. There are, in fact, clinically distinguishable types of dementia—for example, an aphasic type, an amnesic type, a type showing prominent visuoperceptual and somatoperceptual defects, and a relatively pure type manifesting impairment in abstract reasoning and problem solving within a setting of fairly intact linguistic and perceptual capacity.

In this country, the Wechsler Adult Intelligence Scale (WAIS) is by far the most widely used test battery to assess general intelligence in adult subjects. In its clinical application, a number of procedures have been used to evaluate the possibility of a decline in general intelligence that may be ascribable to the presence of cerebral disease. The most direct approach is to compare the patient's obtained age-corrected I.Q. score with the age-corrected I.Q. score that might be expected in view of his educational background, cultural level, and occupational history. An obtained I.Q. below the expected I.Q. may be interpreted as raising the question of the presence of cerebral disease. However, many patients with unquestionable cerebral disease do not show an over-all decline in general intelligence of sufficient severity to be reflected in a significant lowering of their WAIS I.Q. score. Consequently, this procedure may be expected to yield a fair proportion of false-negative results.

A variant of this procedure is to compare obtained and expected I.Q. scores on the WAIS performance scale, which consists, for the most part, of nonverbal and relatively novel tasks. This comparison has proved to be practically as useful as the comparison of full scale I.Q. scores.

Since it has been found, at least in nonaphasic patients, that certain types of performance tend to be more seriously affected by cerebral damage than are others, a second approach has been to compare performance level of presumably less sensitive tasks with that on more sensitive tasks. Thus, verbal scale I.Q. is compared to performance scale I.Q., or performance on a set of insensitive tests, such as information or picture completion, is compared with performance on a set of sensitive tests, such as arithmetic or block designs.

### Reasoning and Problem Solving

Impairment of the capacity for abstract reasoning and reduction in behavioral flexibility when confronted with an unfamiliar situation are well-known behavioral characteristics of the brain-damaged patient. But one must rule out language and perceptual handicaps as determinants of a defective performance before making the inference that the performance indicates impaired reasoning or impaired problem-solving ability.

These tests are valuable for disclosing behavioral deficit in the neurologically negative patient with frontal lobe or beginning diffuse cerebral disease who shows no specific sensory, perceptual, language, or motor impairments and who, on initial encounter, appears to have a functional psychiatric disorder. Conversely, these tests are less useful for the specific purpose of inferring brain disease when applied to unintelligent or uneducated subjects or those suffering from psychosis.

### Memory

Impairment of various types of memory, most notably short-term and recent memory, is a prominent behavioral deficit in brain-damaged patients, and it is often the first sign of beginning cerebral disease and of aging.

Memory is a comprehensive term that covers the retention of all types of material over different periods of time and involving diverse forms of response. Consequently, the neuropsychological examiner is more inclined to give specific memory tests and evaluate them separately than to use an omnibus battery that provides for a brief assessment of a large variety of performances and yields a single score in the form of a memory quotient.

Immediate memory may be defined as the reproduction, recognition, or recall of perceived material within a period of not more than 5 seconds after presentation. It is most often assessed by digit repetition and reversal (auditory) and memory-for-designs (visual) tests. Both an auditory-verbal task, such as digit span or memory for words or sentences, and a nonverbal visual task, such as memory for designs or for objects or faces, should be given to assess the patient's immediate memory. Patients with lesions of the right hemisphere are likely to show more severe defect on visual nonverbal tasks than on auditory verbal tasks. Conversely, patients with left hemisphere disease, including those who are not aphasic, are likely to show more severe deficit on the auditory verbal tests with variable performance on the visual nonverbal tasks.

Recent memory refers to the reproduction, recognition, or recall of perceived material after a period of time (10 seconds or longer) has elapsed after the initial presentation. It is typically assessed by measuring the patient's memory for a story read to him, for items in a display of words or pictures or abstract forms, or for material he has learned, such as lists of words or pictures. This type of task provides one of the more sensitive indicators of the presence of cerebral disease. However, quality of performance depends closely on level of effort and attention.

It is commonly believed that remote memory is well-preserved in patients who show pronounced defects in recent memory. This is true only in a relative sense. In fact, the remote memory of senile and amnesic patients is usually significantly inferior to that of normal subjects of comparable age and education. Although events in the remote past are recalled, their placement within a temporal framework is likely to be imprecise, and uncertainty about such items as the dates of Presidential terms or wars or even the birth dates of their children is more the rule than the exception.

### Orientation

Orientation for person or place is rarely disturbed in the brain-damaged patient who is not psychotic or severely demented, but defects in temporal orientation, which can be considered to reflect the integrity of recent memory, are common. These defects are often missed by the clinical examiner because of his tendency to regard slight inaccuracy in giving the day of the week or of the month as inconsequential. However, about 25 percent of nonpsychotic patients with hemispheric cerebral disease are likely to show significant inferiority with respect to precision of temporal orientation.

### Perceptual and Perceptuomotor Performances

Many patients with brain disease show defective capacity to analyze complex stimulus constellations or inability to translate their perceptions into appropriate motor action. Unless the impairment is of a gross nature, as in visual object agnosia or dressing apraxia, or interferes with a specific occupation skill, these deficits are not likely to be the subject of spontaneous complaint. However, appropriate testing discloses a remarkably high incidence of impaired performance on visuoanalytic, visuospatial, and visuoconstructive tasks in brain-damaged patients, particularly in those with disease involving the right hemisphere. This type of impairment also extends to tactile and auditory perceptual task performances.

### Language Functions

Gross impairment in language functions in the form of frank aphasia can scarcely be over-looked by the psychiatrist, although the less experienced examiner may sometimes misinterpret paraphasic or jargon speech as a sign of dementia or psychosis. On the other hand, less severe disturbances of language expression and comprehension may go unrecognized for the simple reason that the interview or the application of a few simple tests for aphasia fails to bring them out. But relatively minor defects in the use of language may be valid indicators of the presence of brain disease, particularly if it involves the dominant hemisphere.

### Attention and Concentration

The capacity to sustain a maximal level of attention over a period of time is sometimes impaired in brain-damaged patients, and this impairment is reflected in oscillation in performance level on a continuous or repeated activity. There is some evidence that this instability in performance is related to electroencephalographic abnormality and that the occurrence of inexplicable declines in performance is related temporally to the appearance of certain types of abnormal electrical activity. Simple reaction time provides a convenient measure of variability and speed of simple responses and possibly is as discriminative and informative as assessments of performance on more complex and lengthy tasks.

### Behavioral Indices of Brain Damage in Children

The behavioral consequences, if any, of early brain damage may take many forms, of which the hyperkinetic or attention deficit disorder is only one. Early brain damage may result in little or no behavioral deficit, and, when such deficit does appear, it is usually less severe than that caused by a comparable lesion in adults. Thus, there is reason to believe that many brain-damaged children are not identified by current methods of behavioral assessment.

### General Intelligence

The most frequently used batteries are the Wechsler Intelligence Scale for Children (WISC), the Stanford-Binet, and the Wechsler Preschool and Primary Scale of Intelligence (WPPSI). A relatively low level of general intelligence is probably the most constant behavioral result of brain damage in children.

### Perceptual and Perceptuomotor Performances

Many brain-damaged children with adequate verbal skills show strikingly defective visuoperceptive and visuomotor performances. The test most frequently used is copying of designs, either from a model or from memory. About 25 percent of brain-damaged school children of adequate verbal intelligence perform defectively—that is, on a level exceeded by 95 percent of normal children of comparable verbal intelligence. The task discriminates between brain-damaged children and those suffering from presumably psychogenic emotional disturbance.

### Language Functions

There is considerable evidence that aphasic children—those who show a gross maldevelopment of oral language abilities as compared with general mental level—suffer from brain damage. Perinatal brain injury may be a causative factor in at least some cases of developmental dyslexia or more generalized learning disability. The finding of a relatively high incidence of electroencephalographic abnormality in children with learning disabilities points to the same conclusion.

### Motor Performances

Motor awkwardness and inability to carry out movement sequences on command or by imitation are commonly seen in brain-damaged children. A variety of tests are available for the assessment of manual dexterity—for example, manipulations with tweezers, paper cutting, and peg placing.

Motor impersistence—inability to sustain an action initiated on command, such as keeping the eyes closed or maintaining central fixation during confrontation testing of visual fields—is seen in a relatively small proportion of adult patients with cerebral disease. However, it is shown with remarkably high frequency by nondefective brain-damaged children. Many mental defectives also show excessive motor impersistence, particularly those with frank brain damage.

### REFERENCES

Benton A L: *The Visual Retention Test: Clinical and Experimental Applications*, ed 4. Psychological Corporation, New York, 1974.
Benton A L: Psychological testing for brain damage. In *Comprehensive Textbook of Psychiatry*, ed 4, H I Kaplan, B J Sadock, editors, p 535. Williams & Wilkins, Baltimore, 1985.
Benton A L, Hamsher K, Varney N R, Spren O: *Contributions to Neuropsychological Assessment*. Oxford University Press, New York, 1983.
De Renzi E, Vignolo L A: The Token Test: A sensitive test to detect receptive disturbances in aphasics. Brain *85:* 665, 1962.
Filskov S B, Boll T J: *Handbook of Clinical Neuropsychology*. Wiley-Interscience, New York, 1981.
Levin H S, Grossman R G, Kelly P J: Assessment of long-term memory in brain-damaged patients. J Consult Clin Psychol *45:* 684, 1977.
Levin H S, Benton A L, Grossman R G: *Neurobehavioral Consequences of Closed Head Injury*. Oxford Unversity Press, New York, 1982.
Lezak M D: *Neuropsychological Assessment*, ed 2. Oxford University Press, New York, 1983.

## 7.6   MEDICAL ASSESSMENT IN PSYCHIATRIC PRACTICE

### Introduction

Some psychiatrists contend that a complete medical work-up is essential for every patient; others maintain that for many patients it is unnecessary and that for a few it is even contraindicated. Nevertheless, the medical status of every psychiatric patient should be considered at the outset, and usually it is the psychiatrist who decides whether a medical evaluation is needed and, if so, what it should include.

### Selection of Patients for Medical Assessment

Complaints can be divided into three groups: those involving (1) the body, (2) the mind, and (3) social interactions.

If symptoms involve the body—as with headache, impotence, and palpitations—a medical examination is required to determine, insofar as possible, the part that somatic processes play in causing the distress. The same approach is indicated for symptoms involving the mind—such as depression, anxiety, hallucinations, and paranoid delusions—because they can be expressions of somatic processes. When the problem is clearly limited to the social sphere, there is no special indication for a medical examination.

It is not appropriate, except under special circumstances, for the psychiatrist to require a complete medical examination for a person without physical or mental complaints.

### Performance of the Medical Assessment

Psychoanalysts do not perform physical examinations on their analysands, nor should they. Unfortunately, this rule, like that of not confering with family members, has spilled over into situations for which it was never intended. Misapplication of this injunction, especially on the part of the neophyte, has resulted sometimes in an inappropriate hands-off policy, even in a hospital setting.

For practical reasons, most psychiatric patients who require a medical assessment should have it performed by an internist or a family practitioner, rather than by a psychiatrist. Although practical and technical reasons can be adduced to excuse psychiatrists from performing complete physical examinations routinely, they should still be expected to elicit a complete medical history and to use their visual, auditory, and olfactory powers fully.

### The Psychiatrist's Role in Medical Assessment

The objectives of the medical evaluation of a psychiatric patient are (1) the detection of underlying and perhaps unsuspected organic pathology that may be primarily responsible for psychiatric symptoms, (2) an understanding of demonstrated disease as a factor in over-all psychiatric debility, and (3) an appreciation of somatic symptoms that reflect primarily psychological, rather than organic, disease.

Patients reach psychiatrists for evaluation and treatment by various routes, and planning for proper medical examinations must take this diversity into account.

### The Referred Patient

When the patient is referred by a primary physician, the psychiatrist can turn to the referring physician for information about the patient's general health and the extent of physical pathology, if any.

Occasionally, the patient's psychological status suggests the possibility of a specific disease not identified during a recent medical examination. It may then be necessary to ask the primary physician if this possibility has been explored adequately; if not, the patient should be sent back for additional studies.

The patient aware of physical changes but who is told that there is no evidence of disease, and that any indisposition is imaginary or emotional, is likely to become depressed, precipitating a referral to the psychiatrist. In the early stages of myasthenia gravis or multiple sclerosis, for example, this phenomenon is not unusual. The physician must remember that diagnostic studies, however thorough, seldom exclude pathology with certainty. Therefore, if new signs or symptoms develop or if it seems that old ones were ignored, it is advisable to request another physical examination or perhaps additional laboratory studies.

A similar situation is presented by the patient with unexplained or unusual somatic symptoms who is referred for psychiatric treatment on the assumption that the complaints must, therefore, be psychological in origin. If the psychiatrist cannot adduce definite evidence of psychological problems, the patient should be returned to the referring physician for additional medical studies and continuing surveillance.

### The Emergency Room Patient

In most instances, the patient in the emergency room is seen first by a primary physician. Only if the findings are essentially negative and there is a suspicion of an emotional or mental disorder is the psychiatrist called.

In some instances, when the triaging person immediately labels the patient as psychiatric, the psychiatrist may be the first physician called. In these cases it is especially important that clues be sought that point to medical, as well as psychiatric, disorders, and that all appropriate studies be performed.

Acutely psychotic patients, especially if they are obstreperous or assaultive, may be precipitously labeled psychiatric by the primary physician who is eager to dispose of disruptive and unwelcome problems. The psychiatrist—mindful of how often delirium, encephalitis, and seizure disorders present in this manner—should perform a thorough examination.

### The Self-referred Patient

If the patient's complaints are clearly the result of faulty interactions or problems in living—especially if the problems are long-standing—a medical examination is not required. If, on the other hand, features of the history presented by the self-identified psychiatric patient suggest a physical disorder, the lead should be carefully pursued. For example, when a patient who has rarely experienced emotional upsets complains of depression, anxiety, and irritability that cannot readily be explained on a psychodynamic basis, an underlying disease that has triggered these symptoms should be suspected. In women whose symptoms come on 4 or 5 days before each period, the possibility of water retention, a phenomenon that also produces premenstrual weight gain, can be suspected.

### The Patient in Psychiatric Treatment

Because intercurrent illnesses may arise while patients are being treated for their psychological problems, it is essential for the psychiatrist to be alert to factors calling for additional diagnostic studies. It has been noted that patients in psychoanalysis may be all too willing to, or desire to attribute their illness to psychological problems. Attention should be paid to the possible use of denial, especially if the complaints do not seem to be related to the conflicts currently in focus.

Not only do patients attribute somatic disorders to psychological problems, but therapists sometimes do so, too. There is the danger of providing psychodynamic explanations for physical symptoms.

The appearance of symptoms such as dizziness and drowsiness, or signs such as skin eruption and gait disturbance, which are common side effects of psychotropic medications, calls for a medical reevaluation if the patient fails to respond in a reasonable period of time to changes in the kind or the dosage of the medications administered.

Early in an illness, paucity or an absence of significant physical or laboratory findings is common. In such an instance, and especially if there is glaring evidence of psychic trauma or emotional conflict, all symptoms are likely to be attributed to a psychiatric disorder and new symptoms seen in this light. Indicators for repeating the medical work-up may be missed unless the physician is alert to clues suggesting that some symptoms do not fit the original diagnosis and point, instead, to a medical illness. Occasionally, a patient with an acute illness, like encephalitis, is hospitalized with the diagnosis of schizophrenia, or a patient with a subacute illness, like carcinoma of the pancreas, is treated in private office or clinic with the diagnosis of depression. Although it may not be possible to make the correct diagnosis at the time of the initial psychiatric evaluation, continued surveillance and attention to clinical details usually provide clues leading to the recognition of the underlying disease.

The likelihood of intercurrent illnesses is greater with some psychiatric disorders than with others. An example is drug abuse, in which there is lowered resistance to infection and a heightened likelihood of trauma, dietary deficiencies, and skin diseases—such as scabies, impetigo, and pediculosis—commonly associated with poor hygiene.

When somatic and psychological dysfunctions are known to coexist, the psychiatrist should be fully conversant with the patient's medical status. In the presence of cardiac decompensation, peripheral neuropathy, or other physical disorders, it is essential to assess the nature and degree of impairment attributable to the physical disorder, and to establish a realistic baseline for physical endeavors. Does the patient exploit a disability, or is it ignored with resultant overexertion? If activity and complaints seem out of keeping with the physical disability, a psychiatric consultation is likely to be sought. To render a meaningful opinion, the psychiatrist should carefully review the medical findings and also take a detailed psychiatric history. One pitfall for medical practitioners, including psychiatrists, is to assume that a diagnostic label defines the extent of the disability. The situation is compounded if the physician imparts this viewpoint to the patient. It is essential for the psychiatrist to assess functional capabilities and limitations, rather than to make a sweeping judgment based on a diagnostic label.

With certain patients under care for psychophysiological disorders, it is necessary to be especially vigilant about their medical conditions. Such is the case with patients with ulcerative colitis who are bleeding profusely, and patients with anorexia nervosa who are losing appreciable weight. In these circumstances, there is the possibility that the patients' lives are endangered.

## The Medical Assessment

The medical assessment consists of more than the physical examination; it includes all the procedures conducted for patient evaluation. With each patient, the psychiatrist depends on history taking and observation to gauge general health. In selected instances, the information derived serves as a guide in conducting the physical examination and performing laboratory procedures (see Table I).

### History

When patients are seen for psychiatric evaluation, two aspects of the medical history should be developed: (1) facts about known physical disease and dysfunction, and (2) information about specific physical complaints. As a rule, it is not necessary to carry out a minutely detailed review of the bodily systems. An inquiry should be made into the present and past use of coffee, tea, tobacco, alcohol, other drugs, and medications. One should hesitate, for example, before using a medication such as chlorpromazine, with its potential for causing hypotension, in a patient with known cerebrovascular insufficiency, or imipramine or amitriptyline, with their cardiotoxic effects, in a patient with a history of myocardial irritability. These three medications may also be contraindicated in a patient whose hypertension is being controlled by guanethidine, because their actions are antagonistic to this particular antihypertensive agent.

Information about previous illnesses may provide valuable clues. For example, if the present disorder is paranoid in nature and there is a history of several similar episodes, each of which

responded promptly to diverse forms of treatment and left no residuals, the possibility of
amphetamine psychosis is strongly suggested. A
drug screen should be ordered to pursue this
lead.

An occupational history may provide essential
information. Exposure to inorganic mercury
may result in complaints suggesting a neurosis
or functional psychosis, and exposure to lead, as
in smelting, may produce an organic mental
disorder. The latter clinical picture may also
result from imbibing moonshine with a high lead
content.

More difficult and more variable is the second
aspect of history taking—eliciting information
concerning specific complaints presented by the
patient. The physician must be able to obtain
from the patient complaining of headache sufficient information to predict with considerable
certainty whether the pain is or is not the result
of cranial pathology. At the same time, the examiner should be alert enough to recognize that
the pain in the right shoulder of a hypochondriacal patient with abdominal discomfort may
be the classical referred pain of gallbladder disease.

The medical history should always include
information concerning medications currently
being taken by the patient. Many medications,
such as reserpine and isoniazid, may produce
side effects of a psychiatric nature. A prescribed
medication taken in therapeutic dosage may for
various reasons occasionally reach high blood
levels. Digitalis intoxication, for example, may
occur under such circumstances and result in an
impairment of mental functioning.

**Differential Diagnosis.** It is essential that
the psychiatrist listen to the recital of symptoms
not only in terms of diagnosing psychiatric disorders and understanding psychodynamic connections, but also in terms of diagnosing medical
diseases.

Awareness of how symptoms cluster into patterns typical of particular disorders is as important for the psychiatrist as it is for other physicians. For example, fleeting, periodic stabbing
pains in the left side of the neck may suggest
angina pectoris, coronary artery disease, or hyperventilation syndrome. Hyperventilation syndrome is most likely if other symptoms include
a few or all the following: onset at rest, sighing
respirations, apprehension, anxiety, depersonalization, palpitations, feelings of an inability to
swallow, numbness of the feet and hands, and
carpal pedal spasm.

**Diagnostic Aids.** Symptoms that are atypical for functional psychiatric disorders should
also be alerters. For example, if a patient with

hallucinations and delusions complains of a severe or excruciating headache at the onset of the
psychosis and during its early phase, the symptom should not be written off as being of little
consequence or as part of a schizophrenic process. Such a symptom suggests the possibility of
brain pathology and calls for careful and repeated neurological examinations. Similarly, if
a psychotic patient remains incontinent after
treatment for several days with psychotropic
medication, some cause other than schizophrenia should be suspected.

*Observation*

When psychiatrists-in-training are exhorted
to develop their powers of observation, it usually
means that they should learn to recognize unconsciously determined nonverbal clues. To the
same extent, they should also develop their powers of observation in assessing general health
and in recognizing manifestations of physical
illness.

**Visual Evaluation.** The scrutiny of the patient begins at the first encounter. In moving
from the waiting room to the interview room,
the gait is observed for telltale signs of dysfunction. Is there unsteadiness? Ataxia suggests diffuse brain disease, alcohol or other drug intoxication, chorea, spinocerebellar degeneration or
weakness based on general physical disease, or
on an esoteric underlying disorder, such as myotonic dystrophy. Does the patient walk without
the usual associated arm movements and turn
in a rigid fashion, like a toy soldier, as is seen in
early Parkinson's disease? Is there an asymmetry of gait, such as turning one foot outward,
dragging a leg, or absent swing of one arm,
suggesting a focal brain lesion?

As soon as the patient is seated, the examiner's attention should be directed to grooming.
Is the patient's hair combed, and are nails clean
and teeth brushed? Has clothing been chosen
with care, and is it appropriate? Although inattention to dress and hygiene is common in emotional disorders, it is also a hallmark of organic
brain disease, and particular lapses—such as the
mismatching of socks, stockings, or shoes—
should strongly suggest an organic brain disease.

The patient's posture and automatic movements—or the lack of them—should be noted.
Next, the appearance of the patient is scrutinized to assess general health. What is the status
of the patient's nutrition? Recent weight loss,
although often encountered in depression and
schizophrenia, may be due to gastrointestinal
disease, diffuse carcinomatosis, Addison's disease, hyperthyroidism, and many other somatic
disorders. Obesity may result from either emo-

TABLE I
MEDICAL PROBLEMS THAT MAY PRESENT AS PSYCHIATRIC SYMPTOMS*

| | Sex and Age Prevalence | Common Medical Symptoms | Psychiatric Symptoms and Complaints | Impaired Performance and Behavior | Diagnostic Problems |
|---|---|---|---|---|---|
| Hyperthyroidism (thyrotoxicosis) | Females 3:1, 30 to 50 | Tremor, sweating, loss of weight and strength | Anxiety if rapid onset; depression if slow onset | Occasional hyperactive or grandiose behavior | Long lead time; a rapid onset resembles anxiety attack |
| Hypothyroidism (myxedema) | Females 5:1, 30 to 50 | Puffy face, dry skin, cold intolerance | Anxiety with irritability, thought disorder, somatic delusions, hallucinations | Myxedema madness: delusional, paranoid, belligerent behavior | Madness may mimic schizophrenia; mental status is clear, even during most disturbed behavior |
| Hyperparathyroidism | Females 3:1, 40 to 60 | Weakness, anorexia, fractures, calculi, peptic ulcers | | | Anorexia and fatigue of slow-growing adenoma resemble involutional depression |
| Hypoparathyroidism | Females, 40 to 60 | Hyperreflexia, spasms, tetany | Either state may cause anxiety-hyperactivity and irritability or depression—apathy and withdrawal | Either state may proceed to a toxic psychosis; confusion, disorientation, clouded sensorium, etc. | None; rare condition except after surgery |
| Hyperadrenalism (Cushing's disease) | Adults, both sexes | Weight gain, fat alteration, easy fatigability | Varied; depression, anxiety, thought disorder with somatic delusions | Rarely produces aberrant behavior | Bizarre somatic delusions caused by bodily changes resemble schizophrenia |
| Adrenal cortical insufficiency (Addison's disease) | Adults, both sexes | Weight loss, hypotension, skin pigmentation | Depression—negativism, apathy; thought disorder suspiciousness | Toxic psychosis with confusion and agitation | Long lead time; weight loss, apathy, despondency resemble involutional depression |
| Porphyria, acute intermittent type | Females, 20 to 40 | Abdominal crises, paresthesias, weakness | Anxiety—sudden onset, severe; mood swings | Extremes of excitement or withdrawal; emotional or angry outbursts | Patients often have truly neurotic life styles; crises resemble conversion reactions or anxiety attacks |
| Pernicious anemia (Addisonian anemia) | Females, 40 to 60 | Weight loss, weakness, glossitis, extremity neuritis | Depression—feelings of guilt and worthlessness | Eventual brain damage with confusion and memory loss | Long lead time—sometimes many months; easily mistaken for involutional depression; normal early blood studies may give false reassurance |
| Hepatolenticular degeneration (Wilson's disease) | Males 2:1, adolescence | Liver and extrapyramidal symptoms, Kayser-Fleischer rings | Mood swings—sudden and changeable; anger—explosive | Eventual brain damage with memory and I.Q. loss; combativeness | In late teens, may resemble adolescent storm, incorrigibility, or schizophrenia |

| Condition | Demographics | Somatic symptoms | Psychiatric symptoms | | Remarks |
|---|---|---|---|---|---|
| Hypoglycemia (islet cell adenoma) | Adults, both sexes | Tremor, sweating, hunger, fatigue, dizziness | Anxiety—fear and dread, depression with fatigue | Agitation, confusion; eventual brain damage | Can mimic anxiety attack or acute alcoholism; bizarre behavior may draw attention away from somatic symptoms |
| Intracranial tumors | Adults, both sexes | None early; headache, vomiting, papilledema later | Varied; depression, anxiety, personality changes | Loss of memory, judgment, self-criticism; clouding of consciousness | Tumor location may not determine early symptoms |
| Pancreatic carcinoma | Males 3:1, 50 to 70 | Weight loss, abdominal pain, weakness, jaundice | Depression, sense of imminent doom but without severe guilt | Loss of drive and motivation | Long lead time; exact age and symptoms of involutional depression |
| Pheochromocytoma | Adults, both sexes | Headache, sweating during elevated blood pressure | Anxiety, panic, fear, apprehension, trembling | Inability to function during an attack | Classic symptoms of anxiety attack, intermittently normal blood pressures may discourage further studies |
| Multiple sclerosis | Females, 20 to 40 | Motor and sensory losses, scanning speech, nystagmus | Varied; personality changes, mood swings, depression; bland euphoria uncommon | Inappropriate behavior due to personality changes | Long lead time; early neurological symptoms mimic hysteria or conversion disorders |
| Systemic lupus erythematosus | Females 8:1, 20 to 40 | Multiple symptoms of cardiovascular, genitourinary, gastrointestinal, other systems | Varied; thought disorder, depression, confusion | Toxic psychosis unrelated to steroid treatment | Long lead time, perhaps many years; psychiatric picture variable over time; thought disorder resembles schizophrenia |

*Table by Maurice Martin, M.D.

tional distress or organic disease. The moon facies, truncal obesity, and buffalo hump are striking findings in Cushing's syndrome, as are symptoms of emotional distress. The puffy, bloated appearance of hypothyroidism and the massive obesity and periodic respiration of the Pickwickian syndrome are also easily recognized in those patients who may present psychiatric symptoms.

The skin frequently provides valuable information. The yellow coloration of hepatic dysfunction and the pallor of anemia are reasonably distinctive. Intense reddening may be due to carbon monoxide poisoning or photosensitivity resulting from porphyria or phenothiazines. Eruptions may be manifestations of disorders such as systemic lupus erythematosus, tuberous sclerosis with adenoma sebaceum, and sensitivity to drugs. A dusky purplish cast of the face, plus telangiectasia, are almost pathognomonic of alcoholism.

The psychiatrist may be involved in situations in which it is suspected that the patient is creating his or her own disease, whether it is a dermatitis, bleeding disorder, or hyperinsulinism. Careful observation may result in pursuing clues that lead to the correct diagnosis. For example, the location and the shape of the skin lesions and the time of their appearance may suggest the likelihood of dermatitis factitia.

**Auditory Evaluation.** Examiners should listen as intently as they look for evidence of physical disease. Slowed speech is characteristic not only of depression but of diffuse brain dysfunction; unusually rapid speech is characteristic not only of mania and anxiety, but also of hyperthyroidism. A weak voice with monotony of tone is heard in Parkinson's disease, and psychiatrists frequently see patients in an early stage of this disease who complain mainly of depression. A slow, low pitched, hoarse voice should suggest to the attentive listener the possibility of hypothyroidism.

Difficulty in initiating speech may be due to anxiety or stuttering, or it may be the hallmark of Parkinson's disease. Easy fatigability of speech, which may be a manifestation of an emotional problem, is also characteristic of myasthenia gravis, and these patients are sometimes seen by psychiatrists before the correct diagnosis has been made because their symptoms suggest a psychological, rather than an organic, disorder. Slurring of speech may result from alcohol, other drugs, or structural brain changes.

**Olfactory Evaluation.** Although the human sense of smell is neither so well developed nor so eminently useful as the senses of sight and hearing, it sometimes provides information of value. The unpleasant odor of a patient who fails to bathe makes one suspicious not only of depression but also of organic brain dysfunction. The odor of alcohol or of substances used to hide it is revealing in a patient who attempts to conceal a drinking problem. Similarly, recognizing the burnt-rope odor of marijuana smoke may be informative. Occasionally, a uriniferous odor calls attention to bladder dysfunction secondary to nervous system disease. Characteristic odors are also noted in patients with diabetic acidosis and uremia, or in hepatic coma.

### Physical Examination

**Psychological Considerations.** The effect on the patient of even a routine physical examination should be borne in mind. Instruments and procedures may be frightening. A simple running account of what is being done can prevent much needless anxiety. Moreover, if the patient is consistently forewarned of what will be done, there is not the dread of being suddenly and painfully surprised. Comments such as, "There's nothing to this" or, "You don't have to be afraid because this won't hurt" leave the patient in the dark, and are much less reassuring than a few words about what actually will be done.

Although the physical examination is most likely to stimulate or intensify a reaction of fear and anxiety, it can also stir up sexual feelings. A suspicious, hysterical woman with fantasies of being seduced may misinterpret an ordinary movement in the physical examination as an amorous advance. Similarly, a paranoid man with homosexual fears may perceive a rectal examination as a sexual attack.

In considering the implications of a procedure, the physician should remember that if he or she lingers over the examination of a particular organ because of scientific interest in an unusual but normal variation, the patient is likely to assume that a serious pathological process has been discovered. Such a reaction is most likely to be profound in an anxious or hypochondriacal patient.

The physical examination occasionally serves a psychotherapeutic function. An anxious patient may be relieved to learn that in spite of troublesome symptoms, there is no evidence of the serious illness that is feared. The young man or woman who complains of chest pain and is certain that this pain heralds a heart attack can usually be reassured by the report of a normal physical examination and electrocardiogram. The reassurance, however, relieves only the acute episode. Unless psychiatric treatment succeeds in dealing with the determinants of the reaction, recurrent episodes are likely.

Sending a patient who has a deeply ingrained fear of malignancy for still another study intended to be reassuring usually proves unrewarding.

During the performance of the physical examination, an observant physician may note indications of emotional distress. Indeed, this observation may be the starting point for a train of events leading to a psychiatric referral.

**Deferring the Physical Examination.** Occasionally, circumstances make it necessary or desirable to defer a complete medical assessment. An example is the paranoid or manic patient who is combative and resistive. In this instance a medical history should be elicited from a family member if possible; unless there is a pressing reason, the physical examination should be deferred until the patient is more amenable to being examined.

**The Neurological Examination.** A careful neurological examination is mandatory for each patient suspected of having organic brain dysfunction. During the history-taking process, the level of awareness, attentiveness to details of the examination, understanding, facial expression, speech, posture, and gait are noted. The neurological examination should then be performed with two objectives in mind: (1) to elicit signs pointing to focal, circumscribed cerebral dysfunction, and (2) to elicit signs pointing to diffuse, bilateral cerebral disease. The first objective is met by the routine neurological examination, which primarily reveals asymmetries in the motor, perceptual, and reflex functions of the two sides of the body due to focal hemispheric disease. The second objective is met by performing specific maneuvers designed to elicit signs of diffuse brain dysfunction. These signs include the corneomandibular, sucking, snout, palmomental, grasp, and toe grasp reflexes, and the persistence of the glabella tap response. Such signs strongly suggest diffuse brain dysfunction.

**Incidental Findings.** Psychiatrists should be able to evaluate the significance of findings uncovered by consultants. For example, the patient who complains of a lump in the throat (globus hystericus) may be found on examination of the pharynx to have hypertrophied lymphoid tissue. It is then tempting to think of a cause-and-effect relationship, and, indeed, some textbooks of otolaryngology have ascribed the sensation of the lump in the throat to the hypertrophied tissue. But how can one be sure that this finding is not incidental? Has the patient been observed to have hypertrophied lymphoid tissue at a time when no complaint is registered? And are there many persons who usually have hypertrophied tissue but never experience the sensation of a lump in the throat?

Another example is the patient with multiple sclerosis who complains of an inability to walk, but on neurological examination has only mild spasticity and unilateral Babinski's sign. Again, it is tempting to ascribe the symptom to the neurological disorder, but in this instance the findings are totally out of keeping with the manifest dysfunction.

Often, some lesion may be found that may account for a symptom, but the psychiatrist should make every effort to separate a causative lesion from an incidental one, to separate a lesion that produces the symptom from one that is merely found in the area of the symptom.

### Diagnostic Studies

Even in this era of defensive medicine, diagnostic studies should never be performed merely for the sake of completeness. To do so would subject patients to unwarranted discomfort and expense. Procedures recently performed and reported as negative should not be repeated unless new signs or symptoms appear or indications for follow-up reappear. Diagnostic procedures that involve a significant expense, that are likely to produce much discomfort, or that entail appreciable risk should be ordered only if there is reasonable likelihood that the findings may alter the plan of treatment, and thereby favorably influence the outcome.

If a procedure is pressingly indicated for medical reasons, it should be done regardless of the patient's emotional or mental state. Every effort, of course, should be made to assuage anxiety, reduce pain, and make the timing as favorable as possible.

**Selecting Diagnostic Procedures.** In patient care, the medical evaluation and the psychological evaluation should be addressed as separate processes, each having its own rules, procedures, and limitations. Thus, to evaluate somatic illness, the physician selects diagnostic tests to measure physical functions. Data obtained from the physical examination and from laboratory procedures do not serve as evidence for or against the existence of a psychological disorder. Conversely, data obtained from the psychological investigation do not serve as evidence for or against the existence of a somatic disorder. In practice, both aspects of the investigation should and usually do proceed concurrently but independently.

**Possible Organic Brain Disease.** Not infrequently, even after a thorough history and a neurological examination, the psychiatrist is still in doubt as to the presence or absence of organic brain dysfunction, and may have to turn for help to ancillary testing procedures. Psychological assessment is often the most useful of the available procedures. The clinical psychologist has tests capable of revealing small defects in function resulting from focal or diffuse brain disease, but the psychologist must be apprised of the problems so that he or she can make appropriate choices among the many tests available. The psychiatrist should also be familiar with the psychological tests used. The expectation then is not for the psychologist to make the diagnosis but, rather, to provide a set of observations helpful in reaching a definitive diagnosis. Regrettably, when the presence or absence of organicity is unclear on the basis of clinical observations, the uncertainty is often borne out, rather than resolved, by psychological testing. In such cases, a repeat psychological evaluation, after an interval of several months, often helps to resolve the problem.

The growing availability of computed cranial tomography (CT-scan) has greatly expanded the psychiatrist's capacity to explore the intracranial cavity for possible brain lesions. The following indications for CT-scans in psychiatric patients have been suggested: (1) a focal abnormality on neurological examination, (2) dementia, (3) a persistent or unexplained confusional state, (4) seizures, (5) a focal or generalized electroencephalographic abnormality, (6) a history of rage attacks or impulsive aggressive behavior, (7) psychological test findings that suggest organicity, and (8) an unusual headache history.

The diagnostic yield from routine skull radiography is low, but, since it is a relatively harmless procedure that occasionally reveals significant abnormalities, its use should be continued. The electroencephalogram (EEG) is another safe and painless procedure. For the psychiatrist, the EEG has its greatest usefulness in cases in which the distinction between delirium and functional psychosis is unclear, and in episodic disorders.

Definite evidence of organic dysfunction demonstrated by any of the diagnostic steps—interview, neurological examination, psychological testing, computed cranial tomography, skull X-rays, and electroencephalography—may point to the need for additional procedures such as spinal fluid examination, radioactive brain scan, radioiodinated serum albumin scan, or arteriography.

## Importance of Medical Illness in Psychiatric Patients

Numerous articles call attention to the need for thorough medical screening of patients seen in psychiatric hospital units and clinics. The medical literature abounds with descriptions of patients whose disorders were initially considered functional but ultimately proved to be organic, especially neurological. The most encouraging aspect of such reports is that a careful reading of the histories and clinical manifestations reveals features pointing toward organicity in almost every instance. Diagnostic errors arose not because there were no features to suggest organicity, but because such features were accorded too little weight.

## Special Considerations

### Medical Considerations for Psychiatric Treatment

Specific medical considerations arise immediately if psychotropic medications and electroconvulsive therapy are considered in planning psychiatric treatment.

**Medication.** The dangers of a particular medication must be weighed against its possible benefits. The chief contraindications of medications are cardiovascular, renal, and hepatic diseases, but diseases of other organs must also be considered. If medications with potential dangers are prescribed, precautions should be taken when possible. For example, if phenothiazines or other medications with anticholinergic action are given to patients with glaucoma, tonometry should be performed regularly to monitor the effect of the medications on the eyes, and a local miotic agent should be used as needed.

**Electroconvulsive Therapy.** Relatively few special medical considerations arise when electroconvulsive therapy is being considered. The physician should use electroconvulsive therapy cautiously in patients with myocardial disease, thrombophlebitis, hypertension, pulmonary disease, and bone disease, although some authors consider increased intracranial pressure the only absolute contraindication.

### The Medically and Psychiatrically Ill Patient

Occasionally, the psychiatrist treats a patient in need of hospital care who is suffering concurrently from a psychiatric disorder and a medical illness. It is then necessary to choose where the patient is to be treated. Although local circumstances vary, if the psychiatric disorder is such that it will not interfere with medical care, the patient should generally be hospitalized first on a medical unit, and then transferred to a psychiatric unit when medical needs become less pressing. However, if the patient's psychiatric status threatens to interfere seriously with the administration of medical care, hospitalization on a psychiatric unit may be necessary first.

## REFERENCES

Hall R C W, Popkin M K, Devaul R A, Faillace L A, Stickney S K: Physical illness presenting as psychiatric disease. Arch Gen Psychiatry *35:* 1315, 1978.
Hall R C W, Gardner E R, Stickney S K, LeCann A F, Popkin M K: Physical illness manifesting as psychiatric disease. II. Analysis of a state hospital inpatient population. Arch Gen Psychiatry *37:* 989, 1980.
Hall R C W, Gardner E R, Popkin M D, LeCann A F, Stickney S K: Unrecognized physical illness prompting psychiatric admission: A prospective study. Am J Psychiatry *138:* 629, 1981.
Hoffman R S: Diagnostic errors in the evaluation of behavioral disorders. JAMA *248:* 964, 1982.
Hollender M H, Wells C E: Medical Assessment in psychiatric practice. In *Comprehensive Textbook of Psychiatry*, ed 4, H I Kaplan, B J Sadock, editors, p 543. Williams & Wilkins, Baltimore, 1985.
Koranyi E R: Morbidity and rate of undiagnosed physical illnesses in a psychiatric clinic population. Arch Gen Psychiatry *36:* 414, 1979.
Leeman C P: Diagnostic errors in emergency room medicine: Physical illness in patients labeled "psychiatric" and vice versa. Int J Psychiatry Med *6:* 533, 1975.
Patterson C W: Psychiatrists and physical examinations: A survey. Am J Psychiatry *135:* 967, 1978.
Williams S E, Bell D S, Gye R S: Neurosurgical disease encountered in a psychiatric service. J Neurol Neurosurg Psychiatry *37:* 112, 1974.
Woods B T: C-T scanning in an adult psychiatric population. McLean Hosp J *1:* 150, 1976.

# 8

# Clinical Manifestations

## 8.1 CLINICAL MANIFESTATIONS OF PSYCHIATRIC DISORDERS

### Introduction

In the pages that follow, symptoms are considered from an adaptational point of view and are traced from their roots in essentially normal behavior through a variety of abnormal behavior patterns. The patient's overall behavior is explored: how he thinks, feels, and acts; the degree to which he is alert and oriented; how well he observes and remembers; his personal eccentricities; and the ways in which he relates to other persons, in his family, at work, at play, and in the community.

### Disturbances in Thinking

#### Normal Thought

Normal thought, or cognition, refers to ideational or informational experience, as contrasted to affects or feelings. It refers to a broad range of psychic phenomena, including abstract and concrete thinking, judgment, orientation, memory, perception, and imagery. In dreams, the prevailing mode of thought representation is visual, whereas in waking thinking the verbal or lexical mode predominates.

Normal rational thinking consists of a goal-directed flow of ideas, symbols, and associations, initiated by a problem and leading to reality-oriented conclusions. Normally, the attentive listener is able to follow logically the verbal and ideational sequences of speech. In actuality, a perfectly logical associative flow is rarely observed. Much more often, speech sequences are interrupted by the forgetting of a familiar name or fact, a slip of the tongue, a period of relative incoherence during which the thread of thought is momentarily lost, or a digression that is irrelevant to the main topic.

These lapses from logic (parapraxes), which are part of normal thinking, were described by Freud in *The Psychopathology of Everyday Life:*

"Slips of the tongue are the best examples of conflicts between strivings for discharge and opposing forces. Some tendency that has been warded off either definitely by regression or by a wish not to express it here and now finds a distorted expression counter to the opposing conscious will." The essence of the parapraxis, then, is that it constitutes a compromise or the solution to a problem arising from conflicting psychological drives.

Cognitive controls are the psychological mechanisms governing selective attention and inattention; in response to stress, they may lead to delays or detours in the thought process. In potentially traumatic situations, thoughts may be blocked entirely or distorted in characteristic ways that make up, in part, the defense mechanisms.

The flow of thought becomes available for clinical scrutiny when it is verbalized in speech or writing. In addition to thought content, evaluation of speech includes attention to volume, pitch, voice quality, rate, phrasing, fluency, emphasis, intonation, inflection, and articulation.

Dysprosody is a loss of normal speech melody. Inflection and rhythm are disturbed, resulting in speech that is monotonous, halting, and occasionally suggesting a foreign accent. It can be the result of organic brain disease, as in Parkinson disease for example. It can also be a psychological defensive device seen most markedly in schizophrenia and serving the function of maintaining a safe distance in social encounters.

At every point, the expressed flow of ideas is part of a dialogue in which the personal significance of the other member is crucial.

Dreaming represents another normal setting in which lapses from logical thought and expression occur. Although dreams often seem bizarre, meaningless, and illogical, Freud demonstrated that a characteristic organization or pattern of thinking can be identified within the dream. He used the term primary process to signify that the pattern of thinking is primary in the chronological sense that it occurs first in the developmental process. In primary-process thinking, there is a tendency toward concrete thinking, condensation of separate psychological items into one item, displacement of feelings from one item to another, and a disregard for time sequence, so that past and present may be treated simultaneously. There is also a considerable use of metaphor and symbolism. According to psychoanalytic theory, all these departures from logical thinking avoid painful feelings and fulfill forbidden pleasures.

Free association may be cited as an example of an artificially induced disturbance in association. In psychoanalytic psychotherapy, the patient is encouraged to express spontaneously every thought, without selection. In effect, he is encouraged to suspend the demands of logic and reality, at least on a purely verbal level, for the duration of the psychotherapeutic session. By this device, the normal associative stream is deliberately disrupted, and the flow of associations assumes qualities of unpredictability, strangeness, and disconnection with reality. Poets and stream-of-consciousness writers may also suspend the normal associative stream as a creative literary device.

In the loosening of the association, the flow of thought may seem haphazard, purposeless, illogical, confused, incorrect, abrupt, and bizarre. This seemingly illogical and confusing progression of thought results when the observer is not in tune with the patient's private frame of reference. When he cracks the code, he discerns that there is a communicative and self-defensive method in the patient's madness.

### Disturbances in Form and Stream of Thought

Dereism or dereistic thinking emphasizes the disconnections from reality. Autism emphasizes the preoccupation with inner thoughts, daydreams, fantasies, delusions, and hallucinations that occur after disconnection from reality. In common usage the two terms are interchangeable. Autistic trends may occur as a character trait, referring to persons who are bashful, shy, retiring, shut in, inaccessible, or introverted. As a consequence of the preoccupation with inner fantasies, autistic thinking is not readily subject to correction by reality and is not likely to be followed by action.

The schizophrenic repels intimacy by an almost endless variety of abnormalities of voice and speech. The manner of speech may be rendered conspicuously stilted by unusual choices of words or phrases, inaudibility or inappropriate shouting, extreme intellectualization, and so on.

Although these verbal mannerisms often have a clearly repelling effect, they also retain some communicative value. By regulating the balance of those opposite effects, the schizophrenic can carefully determine the emotional distance between himself and others, becoming maximally unintelligible when he is most threatened and even entirely normal with others—for example, with a skilled therapist or some other person whom the patient trusts.

Neologism is the coinage of new words, usually by condensing several other words that have special meaning for the patient. In extreme forms of neologism, a word salad ensues that is characterized most of all by its unintelligibility.

Magical thinking refers to the belief that specific thoughts, verbalizations, associations, gestures, or postures can in some mystical manner lead to the fulfillment of certain wishes or the warding off of certain evils. This type of thinking may occur normally in superstitious or religious beliefs that are appropriate in specific sociocultural settings. Young children are prone to this form of thinking as a consequence of their limited understanding of causality. It is a prominent aspect of obsessive-compulsive thinking. It achieves its most extreme expression in schizophrenia.

Intellectualization is a flight into intellectual concepts and words that are emotionally neutral, in order to avoid objectionable feelings or impulses of a sexual or aggressive nature. It may take the form of brooding or anxious pondering about abstract, theoretical, or philosophical issues. It often occurs in normal adolescence. It is also seen in obsessive-compulsive neurotics, as a cognitive style in certain character types, and as a mechanism of defense in some schizophrenics.

Circumstantiality is a disorder of association in which too many associated ideas come into consciousness because of too little selective suppression. The circumstantial patient eventually reaches his goal in spite of many digressions. Circumstantiality may thus be distinguished from tangential thinking, in which the goal is never clearly defined or ever reached. In circumstantiality, excessive detail is used to describe simple events, at times to an absurd or bizarre degree. Like intellectualization, circumstantiality often represents a way of avoiding objectionable impulses and feelings.

Tangential thinking involves verbal interjections that derail the dialogue. By moving at a tangent to the main orbit of the discussion, the patient avoids intimate interactions. A similar effect can result from punning, which is a form of tangential thinking.

Clang associations represent a thought disturbance in which the mere sound of the word, rather than its meaning, touches off a new train of thought. It is thus related to tangential thinking. It occurs most often in manic states with flight of ideas, and may result in a series of punning and rhyming nonsensical associations.

Stereotypy is the constant repetition of a speech or action from force of habit or limitations of choice. When stereotypy expresses itself as the reiteration of a specific word or phrase, it is called verbigeration. It may occur in either spoken or written form. It is most often seen in schizophrenia.

Perseveration is the persisting response to a prior stimulus after a new stimulus has been presented. It is most often associated with organic brain disease.

Abstract thinking, as described by Kurt Goldstein, includes the ability to assume a mental set voluntarily, to shift voluntarily from one aspect of a situation to another, to keep in mind simultaneously various aspects of a situation, to grasp the essentials of a whole and to break a whole into its parts, to abstract common properties, to plan ahead, to assume make-believe attitudes, to use symbolism in one's thoughts and actions, and to interpret proverbs. By means of a series of specialized tests, Goldstein was able to demonstrate that the capacity for abstract thinking is impaired in many patients with organic brain disease.

It has been erroneously assumed that in schizophrenia, too, the capacity for abstract thinking is impaired. This incapacity is purportedly demonstrated in the schizophrenic's impaired capacity to interpret proverbs. As a matter of fact, schizophrenics are often capable of a high order of abstract thinking in the context of mathematics and other scientific work. Their difficulties with the interpretation of proverbs are the result of a tendency to bizarre idiosyncratic thinking, particularly in relation to a strange examiner in a test situation, rather than a primary defect in the capacity to think abstractly.

Foreign-language patients who are depressed or frightened fall back on their mother tongues and seem incapable of speaking English. As such patients improve, they often surprise their physicians with the amount they do understand and the degree to which they can make themselves understood.

Blocking consists of sudden suppressions in the flow of thought or speech in the middle of a sentence. Commonly, the patient is unable to explain the reason for the interruption, which is usually the result of an unconscious mental intrusion. When, with conscious effort, the patient endeavors to continue the thought, new thoughts may crop up that neither the patient nor the observer can bring into connection with the previous stream of thought. The complete blanking out of the flow of thought, the effort to renew it, and the inability to account for the interruption create an unpleasant feeling state within the patient. Blocking is also known as thought deprivation. Although the phenomenon occurs intermittently in normal persons and in a variety of diagnostic categories, it occurs most strikingly in schizophrenia.

The rate at which thoughts are produced is an important clinical variable.

In depressed states, the flow of associations is slowed up—not intermittently in response to hallucinatory or delusional intrusions, as in blocking, but as an ongoing consequence of sadness. The patient thinks and speaks slowly. He is essentially unresponsive to his environment. The range of his thought is limited to a perseverative repetition of his pessimism and despair. Such a patient commonly complains that thinking requires considerable conscious effort, that his concentration is poor and his memory impaired. In extreme states of slowing due to depression, the clinical picture may resemble the mutism of a catatonic schizophrenic.

Blocking may progress to total mutism. In his loneliness and in his drive to recontact the world on less frightening terms, the schizophrenic may elaborate a "successful" psychotic system, on the basis of which his suffering is temporarily relieved. At this point, the patient may speak rapidly and animatedly, giving full expression to his delusional beliefs and responding actively to his hallucinations.

As depression lifts, the rate of thought and speech also accelerates. If the condition swings over to a manic state, pressure of speech occurs; that is, voluble speech difficult for the listener to interrupt. Pressure of speech may progress to flight of ideas, a nearly continuous high-speed flow of speech. The patient leaps rapidly from one topic to another, each topic being more or less meaningfully related to the preceding topic or to adventitious environmental stimuli, but his progression of thought is illogical, and the goal is never reached. The speed and cleverness with which the manic patient leaps from one idea to another can be dazzling. From a qualitative point of view, the manic patient's associations are not strange or absurd. In fact, the connections and identifiable events in the environment are usually understandable, amusing, and even convincing. Puns and witticisms are common.

The flight of ideas of a manic patient must be differentiated from the disturbance of association displayed in the rapid speech of schizophrenic catatonic excitement. The shifts in schizophrenic talk are confusing because of the indiscriminate overinclusion of material belonging to both shared social contexts and private fantasy contexts. It is the fact that the schizophrenic patient draws largely on an autistic reservoir for his ideas and verbal symbols that makes his productions strange, as contrasted to those of the manic patient.

In spite of these qualitative differences between the associative stream of the manic patient and that of the catatonic-excited schizophrenic patient, both show a pattern of flight from the pain of some intolerable external reality, even though one draws on an inner and essentially inaccessible repertoire, and the other on an outer and socially evident repertoire for the specific words and ideas that make up the associative flow.

Pressure of speech may occur more or less within the limits of normal conversation, and one then speaks of volubility. In certain neurotic disorders, talkativeness may acquire a compulsive quality that is called logorrhea. This talkativeness may be associated with peculiarities of speech rhythm in which the patient pauses for breath unexpectedly in the middle of a sentence and rushes on without pause to the next sentence, thereby cutting off the listener from the give and take of a normal dialogue. Logorrhea occasionally occurs episodically as a manifestation of temporal lobe epilepsy.

Organic brain disease is a major cause of disturbances in the flow of speech. Aphasia is a disturbance of language output, resulting almost always from damage to the left side of the brain. However distorted a patient's speech may sound, if his productions read as correct English sentences when transcribed, he is suffering not from aphasia but from some form of articulatory speech disability.

Geschwind observed that the most important distinction in disorders of language output is that between fluent aphasia and nonfluent aphasia. Patients with nonfluent aphasia produce little speech, and what is produced is uttered slowly, with great effort and poor articulation. Characteristically, the speech of such patients lacks the small grammatical words and endings, so that it may take on the quality of a telegram. Asked about the weather, such a patient may say, "Sunny." If urged to produce a full sentence, he may say, "Weather—sunny."

By contrast, patients with fluent aphasia effortlessly produce well-articulated long phrases or sentences with a normal grammatical skeleton, having normal rhythm and melody. Such patients often speak more rapidly than normal. Despite the many words produced, however, their speech is often remarkably devoid of content. Thus, a knob may become "what you use to open a door" or a "thing." A knife may become a "fork," a spoon a "spoot," a thumb an "Argentinian rifle." In some cases, the words produced are totally neologistic. One patient, for example, responded to all questions with animated but perserverative responses consisting of two nonsense words, "itsi potsi," repeated with various intonations and inflections (jargon aphasia).

Nonfluent aphasias result from lesions in Broca's area. These lesions generally involve the adjacent motor cortex and cause an associated hemiplegia, which is usually greater in the arm than in other areas; facial weakness is less prominent because the lower face has substantial bilateral innervation. By contrast, fluent aphasias result from lesions in Wernicke's area and typically have no associated hemiplegia.

Global aphasia is the result of a massive lesion affecting both Broca's area and Wernicke's area. A patient with global aphasia almost always has a severe hemiplegia and suffers from a grossly nonfluent aphasia, combined with a severe loss of comprehension and repetition.

Every patient who is aphasic in speech is also aphasic in writing, although there are rare patients who are aphasic in writing but not in speech. Therefore, if a patient is able to produce full normal language in a written form but does not speak, one must conclude that he is suffering not from aphasia but from some form of mutism. Mutism may occur in catatonic schizophrenia, severe depression, hysterical aphonia, and a variety of organic disorders involving the speech apparatus, as contrasted to the language areas of the left cerebral cortex. Patients with organic disorders of the speech apparatus may, on recovery, show dysarthria—that is, difficulty in articulation but not in word finding or in grammar.

Fluent aphasia is frequently misdiagnosed, since many physicians are unaware of the frequency of aphasia without hemiplegia. The patient may be called psychotic or confused, particularly when there is a rapid outpouring of abnormal speech.

Although aphasia has been discussed here in purely biological terms, the severity of the disorder may wax and wane within certain limits in response to changing object relationships. When brain-injured patients are pushed to perform tasks they can no longer do, they may respond with agitation, panic, and intensification of the neurological deficit, a response termed by Kurt Goldstein as the catastrophic reaction.

### Disturbances in Thought Content

Certain types of thought content are essentially nonverbal. They are probably manifestations of right brain functioning. The most outstanding example is the mystical experience. This phenomenon can occur fleetingly in normal persons during the induction phase of general anesthesia. It may be chemically induced in addicts. It can occur transiently in schizophrenia and in the experiences of religious mystics.

The mystical experience, whatever the circumstance that elicits it, has certain distinguishing qualities:

1. Ineffability. The person insists that his experience is inexpressible and indescribable, that it is impossible to convey what it is like to one who has never experienced it.

2. Noesis. The person feels that the mystery of the universe has been plumbed, that an immense illumination or revelation has occurred. Along with this feeling may go a curious sense of authority, the conviction that one is privileged to lead and to command. As for the revelation itself, it seems to consist of layer upon layer of truth that, as it unfolds, may find expression in some familiar or even commonplace thought that suddenly seems pregnant with new meaning. On occasion, the expressions of the truth may take the form of a document of poetic beauty and great moral significance, such as the writings of the biblical prophets. On the other hand, the revelation may be expressed in unintelligible words or nonsense syllables (glossolalia, speaking in tongues).

3. Transiency. The actual mystical state may last only a moment or go on for an hour or two; but, when the experience ceases, the particular quality of feeling it aroused is only imperfectly reproducible in memory. Yet it is unforgettable and highly treasured, and may color all subsequent activity.

4. Passivity. In the mystical state there is an abeyance of will, as if the person were in the grip of a superior power to whose direction he is highly responsive.

5. Unio mystica. There is a sense of mystic unity with an infinite power, an oceanic feeling in which opposites are reconciled, in which there are "darknesses that dazzle" and "voices of silence." There is a quality of timelessness, in which minutes and centuries are one and in which past and present are one.

The mystical experience seems to represent a specific state of consciousness, since it tends to occur in settings of exhaustion and toxicity in which full alert consciousness is impaired. It also seems to represent psychological regression at its most extreme.

A fantasy is a mental representation of a scene or occurrence that is recognized as unreal but is either expected or hoped for. There are two types of fantasy: creative fantasy, which prepares for some later action, and daydreaming fantasy, which is the refuge for wishes that cannot be fulfilled. Creative fantasy may start in inspirational moments that are rooted deep in the unconscious. However, it is then elaborated systematically and is translated into a realistic program of action. The daydream as a refuge for wishes that cannot be fulfilled is self-explanatory. It tends to diminish with psychological and biological maturation. Increasingly, daydreaming is replaced by direct sexual satisfaction with appropriate love objects and by sublimations at work and at play. Sublimation is the replacement of forbidden behavior with related activities that are personally satisfying and socially approved—for example, the choice of a medical career to replace death wishes toward an ailing parent or sibling. To some extent, daydreaming persists within normal limits throughout life. However, in autistic characters and in borderline psychotic states, daydreaming may preempt so much time and energy that it seriously impairs the person's capacity for normal relationships and responsibilities.

Pseudologia fantastica, or pathological lying, differs from normal daydreaming in that the person believes in the reality of his fantasies intermittently and for long enough intervals of time to act on them.

Such a patient tends to outrage the moral sensibilities of his victims and commonly provokes punishment. When confronted with damning evidence, the patient usually acknowledges his falsehoods readily. However, he has a compulsive need to act out his fantasies repeatedly. It is often difficult to ascertain whether the untruths are expressed with conscious or unconscious intent to deceive, or as part of an actual delusional distortion of reality.

The imposter is a type of pathological liar who seeks to gain some advantage by imposing on others various lies about his attainments, social position, or worldly possessions.

The imposter is obviously suffering from a severe identity problem. He is attempting to foist a false identity, but perhaps of greater significance is his need to reject his own real identity. Such persons are often quite gifted and capable of authentic success in the real world, but an unconscious fear of success causes them to misspend their talents. They tend to be self-defeating in their dramatizations and usually end up with humiliation and punishment.

A phobia is an exaggerated and invariably pathological dread of some specific type of stimulus or situation. Table I presents a small list of common phobias. Many others have been described, and phobias are probably limitless in number.

Whereas a setting that elicits pleasure evokes approach behavior, one that elicits fear evokes avoidance. There are probably biological differences in the readiness to respond with fear. Certainly, one can breed animals for more or less timidity. A few fear responses in humans seem to be innate. Around the eighth month of development, for example, a child usually becomes capable of distinguishing the familiar face of his mother. At this time, the infant reacts with anxiety to the face of a stranger (eighth-month anxiety, stranger anxiety). A crawling infant reacts with fear to perceived heights. Loud noises and sudden rough movements can elicit startle reactions at any age.

Fears become attached to specific situations as the outcome of a learning process. For example, a patient may develop a fear of sea or air travel as a result of specific traumatic experiences. A child may develop a school phobia because his fearful mother inculcates her own fear of separation. Punitive parents may inculcate childhood fears that emerge in adult life as a variety of sexual, eating, and excretory fears.

Psychoanalytic theory emphasizes the role of symbolism in phobia formation.

Sometimes the associative connections in phobias seem rather direct. A forbidden wish to suck, bite, or devour, for example, may result in a fear of eating specific foods or a fear of eating in specific places. A fear of loss of control of violent impulses may lead to a fear of all scenes of violence. A fear of sexual penetration may lead to a fear of being cut or stabbed, and this fear may lead to a fear of contact with all sharp instruments.

In other instances, the associative connections are more obscure. A fear of walking on the street (agoraphobia), for example, may be based on unconscious prostitution fantasies. The sexual excitement and fear of punishment connected with these fantasies may result in palpitation and breathlessness, which then presents clinically as a cardiac neurosis.

Phobic reactions that start in adult life are more resistant to treatment or to spontaneous remission. Many phobic patients who are otherwise immobilized by their fears can function if accompanied by some trusted person who is called a "phobic companion."

The foregoing discussion has emphasized those phobic reactions that have been learned and that are connected psychologically with specific objects (for example, animals, insects, knives, dirt, and vomitus), specific places (high places, closed places, hospitals), and social situations (public performances, such as eating, speaking, and signing one's name). These specific and circumscribed phobic reactions respond best to psychotherapy—analytic, supportive, or

TABLE I
PHOBIAS*

| Phobia | Dread of | Phobia | Dread of |
|---|---|---|---|
| Acro- | High places | Necro- | Dead bodies |
| Agora- | Open places | Nycto- | Darkness, night |
| Algo- | Pain | Patho- (noso-) | Disease, suffering |
| Astra- (astra-po-) | Thunder and lightning | Peccato- | Sinning |
| | | Phono- | Speaking aloud |
| Claustro- | Closed (confined) places | Photo- | Strong light |
| | | Sito- | Eating |
| | | Tapho- | Being buried alive |
| Copro- | Excreta | | |
| Hemato- | Sight of blood | Thanato- | Death |
| Hydro- | Water | Toxo- | Being poisoned |
| Lalo- (glosso) | Speaking | Xeno- | Strangers |
| Myso- | Dirt, contamination | Zoo- | Animals |

* Modified from Warren H C: *Dictionary of Psychology.* Houghton Mifflin, New York, 1934.

behavior modifying—and require enforced exposure to the frightening situation as part of the treatment plan. The phobias tend to arise early in life and may become incapacitating in early adult years. In addition, some phobic reactions associated with panic attacks occur unpredictably in a variety of settings that generate in the patient a fear of leaving home because he dreads having a panic attack away from home. This is classified as agoraphobia with panic attacks, and it often begins during the adult years. A purely psychological treatment approach is often unsuccessful. On the other hand, preliminary therapy with a tricyclic antidepressant usually brings the panic attacks under control, after which psychological treatment becomes more effective. Occasionally, the monoamine oxidase inhibitors are successful in controlling the panic attacks.

An obsession is the pathological presence of a persistent and irrresistible thought, feeling or impulse that cannot be eliminated from consciousness by any logical effort. Typically, the patient feels compelled to carry out specific ritualized or stereotyped acts, known as compulsions, in order to minimize their distressing effects—hence, obsessive-compulsive neurosis. Obsessive fears and doubts may overlap the phobias.

Whereas the phobic or hysterical patient dramatizes fantasies in the form of relatively simple fears and bodily sensations, the fantasies of the obsessional neurotic are converted into intellectually complex word games. Patients with the disorder invest words and thoughts with unrealistic power. They imagine that an inadvertent thought or comment, or some innocent act, may cause great harm to a loved one or punishment to one's self. Conversely, a given verbal formula may ward off danger to self or to others. Thus, much time and energy are spent by the obsessional patient in undoing with one set of thoughts or actions the harm he feels he has already accomplished with another set. Since words are powerful, it becomes necessary to choose one's words carefully. And, for the obsessional neurotic, no matter how carefully he chooses his words, he is never sure that he chose carefully enough, and so he repeats himself with verbal formulas of ever-increasing complexity. These formulas may take the form of prayers. Behind that preoccupation with seemingly magical but actually trivial words is concealed an intrapsychic struggle involving erotic and aggressive impulses in every conceivable combination of activity and passivity, of masculinity and femininity, of piety and blasphemy, of obedience and rebellion. Such verbal gymnastics demand a great mastery of language, which requires considerable intelligence. Conversely, whenever verbal skills are limited because of limitations of intelligence or education, obsessional defenses usually do not appear.

Scrupulousness is characterized by a pathological sense of guilt and a preoccupation with repetitious religious ritual and a caricatured concern for detail. Recognition of this disorder by clergy leads to psychiatric referral, rather than futile attempts at religious reassurance.

When thought content centers on a particular idea and is associated with a strong effective tone, the patient is said to be dominated by a trend or preoccupation—for example, a paranoid trend or a suicidal preoccupation.

When a patient ascribes personal significance to neutral remarks or comments, he is said to show referential thinking or to display ideas of reference. For example, these ideas arise when the patient attributes to others thoughts and feelings that he himself has imagined, a process called projection. The associated pattern of oversuspiciousness is called paranoid thinking. When a shy but essentially normal person enters a social situation, he may experience a series of self-observing, self-criticizing thoughts, which he succeeds in brushing aside in favor of the social encounter. Such thoughts, if intensified to the point of paralyzing shyness but recognized as unreasonable, are designated as neurotic hypersensitivity.

Between ages 3 and 6, a child often devises an imaginary companion. This companion typically appears after a traumatic event, like the birth of a sibling or the death of a grandparent. The imaginary companion may be a simple double who helps assuage loneliness, or a scapegoat who is the recipient of endless scoldings and punishments for misbehavior. With emotional maturation, the need for the companion subsides, and he is gradually forgotten. The imaginary companion can be likened to a transitional object. Persistent attachment to the transitional object into adolescence is evidence of a maturational lag.

A delusion is a false belief that arises without appropriate external stimulation, and that is maintained unshakably in the face of reason. Furthermore, the belief held is not one ordinarily shared by other members of the patient's sociocultural and educational group; for example, it is not a commonly believed superstition or a religious or political conviction. Delusions are pathognomonic of the psychoses. They occur most frequently in schizophrenia, but they can be observed in all psychotic states, including those of organic origin.

In some delusional states, persecutory feelings become attached to body feelings, such as intestinal movements or the sensation of stool in the rectum. Somatic delusions are characterized by their bizarre quality. For example, a patient may believe that his intestinal tract has become occluded with solid paraffin or that his internal organs are rotting and worm infested. These delusions are to be differentiated from the localized or circumscribed somatic symptoms of hysterics and the generalized physical complaints of hypochondriacs.

In erotomania or de Clérambault syndrome, the patient, always female, maintains a fixed delusional belief that a man, usually considerably older and of higher social status, is in love with her. The psychotic patient growing up with the belief that she is unloved or unlovable solves that narcissistic wound by the grandiose fantasy. The delusional system may overflow into complicating and socially embarrassing situations. It is particularly resistant to treatment.

Pathological jealousy may occur in marital settings in which a spouse has unconscious extramarital sexual impulses, either heterosexual or homosexual, which are then projected onto the marital partner and may emerge clinically as delusions of infidelity.

The difference between normal and pathological jealousy is similar to that between normal grief and pathological mourning. Every child suffers jealousy when a third person—whether father or sibling—intrudes between himself and his mother. The occurrence of pathological jealousy in adult life is related to unresolved early childhood attachments. At times, a pathological lack of jealousy can occur.

Litigiousness is a pathological tendency to take legal action because of imagined mistreatment or persecution. Delusions of persecution may involve a surgeon because of delusional fantasies concerning the surgical procedure. Hostile relatives may project their negative impulses onto the hospital staff. In compensation neurosis or accident neurosis, somatic complaints—initiated by an industrial accident or other situation involving compensation—may resist all therapeutic interventions and lead to endless litigations until a lump-sum settlement is made.

Ecstatic states may be associated with delusions of grandeur or megalomania, a delusionally exaggerated idea of one's importance. A male patient may express the idea that he is the Savior or a latter-day saint; a female patient may believe that she is the Virgin Mary and is about to give birth to the Baby Jesus. Delusions of grandeur may result in identifications with political or military figures of great power. The salvation of the world is the basic delusional goal. Often, that grandiose goal is to compensate for feelings of inadequacy. In manic states, inappropriate delusions of great wealth may result in crippling financial expenditures.

A shift of mood from elation to depression may result in the self-accusatory delusion of having committed an unpardonable sin. This delusion is associated with intense guilt and remorse. In place of the delusions of saving the world, there may appear the end-of-the-world fantasy, the delusional belief that the world is about to come to an end. The patient may be convinced that the salvation of the world depends on his own death; as a consequence, he may destroy or seriously multilate himself. In less bizarre terms, the depressed patient may feel that the world would be better off without him, and may have suicidal impulses or ideation on an altruistic basis. In contrast to the delusion of great wealth, there may be, in the depressed state, a delusion of poverty. The complaint, "I am poor," is characteristic of depression, almost independently of the patient's true economic state. In addition to feelings of guilt, worthlessness, and impoverishment, the patient may express a loss of interest in all previously satisfying spheres of activity. He may lose his appetite for food, family, sex, work, and play. Loss of appetite for food may be the result of delusions of poisoning.

Paradoxically, some patients invest the process of not eating and weight loss with such intense emotional satisfaction that they lapse into anorexia nervosa, which, on occasion, may lead to death by starvation, in spite of an apparent continued interest in other aspects of life. This condition is associated with a delusional denial of the cachectic state.

### Disturbances in Judgment

Judgment, from a psychiatric point of view, is the mental act of comparing or evaluating alternatives within the framework of a given set of values for the purpose of deciding on a course of action. The comparison may be in terms of magnitude, rightness, goodness, beauty, or economic worth. If the course of action decided on is consonant with reality as measured by mature adult standards, judgment is said to be good, intact, or normal. If, on the other hand, wish-fulfilling impulses predominate and lead to impulsive decisions based on the need for immediate infantile gratification, whether directly or as part of a psychotic delusional system, then judgment is said to be poor, impaired, or abnormal.

One of the developmental hurdles is to be able

to accept the fact that a person—one's mother, for example—who is judged to be good today is the same person judged to be bad tomorrow. Object constancy, the ability to maintain a positive loving relationship in spite of periods of frustration and separation, is a hallmark of the maturing mind. Some persons fail to achieve this fusion. They see others only in terms that are purely good or purely bad. Such persons, characterized clinically as suffering from borderline disorders, are constantly suffering from episodes of rage and depression because those on whom they depend are not unfailingly supportive.

Speech initiates a decisive step in the development of reality testing and judgment. Words permit more precise communication and more precise anticipations of trial actions.

The function of judgment, then, depends on maturation of the mental apparatus. Intelligence and education are required for the inculcation of values.

For good judgment to prevail, the sensory apparatus must be capable of accurate perception and discrimination. Memory must provide a reservoir of data as a basis for comparison. The motor apparatus must have the skills to carry out decisions and the inhibitory mechanisms for postponing action. Thus, a developmental process is automatically implied in the concept of judgment. Although rudimentary manifestations of judgment can be found in infancy and early childhood, judgment develops steadily with biopsychosocial maturation. It is maximal in the fully alert, emotionally mature adult: it is impaired in all circumstances associated with regression.

Adolescents display impaired judgment for many reasons. Through lack of education and experience, they may fail to recognize which situations or ideas merit attention. Adolescence, with its characteristic intensification of intrapsychic conflict, may be associated one moment with excellent reality testing based on adult goals and aspirations, and a moment later with impaired reality testing based on persistent, unmastered infantile longings. Undeveloped values and self-discipline may precipitate ill-advised actions. Thus, judgment in the adolescent is notoriously uneven and unpredictable.

Estimates of judgment may be based on responses to test questions or standard hypothetical situations. For example, a mentally defective patient with a long history of delinquency and fire setting was asked, "What would you do if you found a stamped, addressed and sealed envelope in the street?" He answered, "I would put it in the mailbox if it didn't have anything in it for me."

### Disturbances in Intelligence

Intelligence may be defined as the capacity to meet a novel situation by improvising a novel adaptive response. This capacity is composed of three factors: abstract intelligence, which is the capacity to understand and manage abstract ideas and symbols; mechanical intelligence, which is the capacity to understand, invent, and manage mechanisms; and social intelligence, which is the capacity to act reasonably and wisely in human relations and social affairs.

Efforts to quantify intelligence have been made by means of various tests that consist of questions or tasks the subject is required to answer or perform. Scores so obtained are then used as a basis for defining different levels of intelligence.

The most frequently used score for measuring intelligence is the intelligence quotient (I.Q.). The I.Q. is a numerical ratio, derived from a comparison of the score that a person makes on a given test of intelligence with the average score that subjects of his own age have attained on the same or a similar test.

Mental retardation is a lack of intelligence to a degree in which there is interference with social and vocational performance. Mild degrees of impairment (I.Q. of 50 to 70) are associated with trainability and the capacity to function in sheltered settings. Moderate impairment (I.Q. of 35 to 50), severe impairment (I.Q. of 20 to 34), and profound impairment (I.Q. below 20) are usually the result of gross organic brain disease and require ongoing supervision, usually in a specialized institution.

Reading ability is crucial to formal education. Dyslexia—a syndrome characterized by a specific difficulty in learning to read, spell, and write—can masquerade as an impairment of intelligence. Frequently, secondary emotional and behavioral disorders confuse the clinical picture even further. The ratio of boys to girls with dyslexia is about five to one.

Children and adolescents suffering from depression may surface clinically as academic underachievers, and must be differentiated from those with other causes of learning disability.

### Disorders of Consciousness

Consciousness has been defined as the distinguishing feature of mental life. It is synonymous with the quality of being aware and of having knowledge. Thus, it is a faculty of perception that draws on information from the outer world directly through the sense organs and indirectly through stored memory traces. The term "sensorium" is sometimes used as a synonym for consciousness. When a person is clearly aware of the nature of his surroundings, his sensorium is said to be clear or intact. For example, correct orientation is a manifestation of a clear sensorium. Conversely, a person whose contact with reality is impaired as a consequence of organic brain disease is said to have a cloudy, or an impaired, sensorium. Implicit in the concept of full consciousness is the capacity to understand information and to use it effectively to influence the relationship of the self to the environment. Consciousness may be said to have a sensory component or a degree of receptive awareness, which is measured as cognitive intensity or level of cognition, and a motor component or a degree of kinesthetic readiness to initiate and execute a voluntary act, which is conative intensity or level of conation.

### Levels of Consciousness

Consciousness may be said to exist on a continuum, with maximum alertness at one extreme and absolute unconsciousness or coma at the other extreme, with varying degrees of alertness in between. There is, indeed, a continuum, but striking discontinuities can also be recognized.

There is a variety of states of consciousness seen in hospitalized patients recovering from acute reversible brain disease—for example, on recovery from subarachnoid hemorrhage or encephalitis. Characteristically, patients display a euphoric reaction during the earliest stages of recovery, a paranoid reaction during the intermediate state, and a depressive reaction in the final stage of recovery.

Akinetic mutism, or coma vigil, is a syndrome usually associated with tumors of the third ventricle. Characteristically, the patient lies inertly in bed. He is able to swallow, but he has to be fed. Although essentially unresponsive to stimuli, the patient does follow the human face. Tracking movements of the eyes can be elicited by means of a two-dimensional pictorial representation of the face, as well as by the face itself. Sucking and grasping reflexes are also usually present. The phenomenon seems to represent a regression to an early developmental stage, when the infant tracks the mother's face and relates to her primarily with respect to feeding.

Attention is an aspect of consciousness that relates to the amount of effort exerted in focusing on certain portions of an experience so that they become relatively more vivid. One may speak of primary attention—which is passive, involuntary, automatic, instructive, or reflexive—and secondary attention, which is active or voluntary.

Attention may fluctuate in intensity from moment to moment in acute brain disorders and toxic metabolic states. Attention may remain alert and vigilant and shift flexibly from topic to topic. In distractibility, a person's attention is too easily drawn away from a given focus by extraneous stimuli. In its most extreme form it occurs in manic states. However, in milder forms it characterizes neurotic reactions of anxiety and depression and, in relation to depression, may play an important role in learning disabilities. Distractions may also be a result of the intrusion of fantasies, and those occur most intensely in schizophrenia. Attention span may be defined as the reciprocal of distractibility. In selective inattention, or denial, the person blocks out those environmental details that generate unpleasant feelings. An extreme form is seen in childhood schizophrenia as pain anosognosia, in which the child is not only unresponsive to pain but may inflict multilating wounds on himself.

Self-consciousness is typically associated with lowered self-esteem and the expectation of rejection by others. Although it may occur fleetingly in anyone, it occurs in neurotic states of anxiety and depression, as well as in schizophrenia and the depressive psychoses. In the psychotic states, the consciousness of self may become so extreme that one's own thoughts acquire the vividness of auditory hallucinations.

Suggestibility exists when a person responds compliantly and with unusual readiness. It can occur acutely when the person is overwhelmed by feelings of helplessness and passivity, as in the relationship of a frightened child to a parent or any adult in a psychologically traumatic situation.

Suggestibility can occur as an ongoing character trait in certain emotionally immature persons, and it expresses itself as gullibility. Extreme forms of suggestibility occur in catatonic stupor in the form of automatic obedience as echolalia, echopraxia, and waxy flexibility (cerea flexibilitas).

In catatonic stupor the patient is motionless, mute, and more or less nonresponsive to painful stimuli. The patient is aware of his environment with a clarity and intensity that is belied by his superficially stuporous appearance. After the stupor has subsided, the patient is able to give detailed retrospective accounts of the happenings during the catatonic episode. Thus, it is necessary to be circumspect in one's conversations in the presence of a catatonic patient.

Suggestibility also plays an important role in communicated insanity (*folie à deux*), a psychotic reaction in which two or more closely related and associated persons simultaneously show the same symptoms and in which one member seems to have influenced or suggested the clinical picture to the other. Cultism is a variant of *folie à deux* in which one person, the leader, inculcates a group with his private ideology and then creates living conditions which prevent reality-testing social contacts.

In hypnosis, the subject enters into a hyperattentive relationship with the hypnotist during which a trance state occurs, characterized by heightened suggestibility. As a result, a variety of hysteria-like sensory and motor abnormalities may be induced, as well as dissociative states and hypermnesia. Although the trance state may be superficially made to simulate sleep as a result of specific suggestions by the hypnotist, it is physiologically distinct from sleep.

Dissociation means a loss of the usual consistency and relatedness between various groups of mental processes, resulting in apparent independent functioning of one of them. Although dissociation and splitting are used more or less synonymously, "dissociation" usually refers to hysterical or hypnosis-induced dissociative states, whereas "splitting" is used with reference to schizophrenia.

Although dissociation underlies every symptom of hysteria, there are occasions when the splitting is so profound as to alter the whole personality and behavior of the patient. Double and multiple personalities are the terms applied when a person at different times appears to be in possession of entirely different mental contents, dispositions, and characters, and when one of the different phases seems to show complete ignorance of the other phase or phases. In trance states, which may occur spontaneously in hysteria or in response to hypnotic suggestion, the apparently sleeping subject may express the dissociative state in the form of automatic writing—that is, the subject may express in written form ideas and feelings that he will not recognize as his own when the trance state is ended. The performance of automatic writing and other actions during a trance state, in response to a command or a suggestion, is called command automatism. A command automatism may manifest itself after the trance state is presumably over as a posthypnotic suggestion.

Perhaps the most familiar example of a dissociative state is that experienced during a nightmare. At a particularly terrifying moment in the dream, the dreamer may suddenly reassure himself: "This is only a dream. You are not in real danger. You can wake up any time you want." And when he wakes up, he experiences the transition from a mental state that felt absolutely real just a moment ago, to a new mental state that the feeling of reality is now attached to.

Patients displaying dramatic dissociative states give the clinical impression of psychosis, although they usually retain a hold on reality through the basic personality, and can be worked with psychotherapeutically.

An automatism is an activity performed without conscious knowledge on the part of the subject and is usually followed by complete amnesia. It occurs most often after a grand mal seizure, head trauma, or pathological alcoholic intoxication. It may also occur as a posthypnotic suggestion.

Some teenagers display one moral code while at home or in school, and a completely dissociated (delinquent) code while with the gang. The ease with which they slip from one moral position to another suggests the term cassette-type superego, analogous to the ease with which one slips a new cassette into a tape recorder.

Students of mob psychology have studied the elation, impulsivity, general emotional regression, and personality dissociation that can occur in a seemingly normal adult when he becomes part of a mob.

## Sleep

Sleep is a complex state of altered consciousness, consisting of separate stages that have been variously labeled and classified.

Insomnia is a pathological inability to sleep. In catatonic or manic excitement, the patient may remain uninterruptedly sleepless for 24 to 48 hours at a time. These reactions of extreme excitement may go on to hyperthermia and death due to exhaustion.

Depressed patients usually complain of frequent awakenings during the night, but most of all of early-morning insomnia—that is, the patient wakes up too early and is often bathed in anguished perspiration. This sleep pattern is commonly associated with anorexia, weight loss, feelings of sadness, and suicidal ideation.

Inability to fall asleep is a form of insomnia characteristic of the neuroses. The patient often fears sleep because of nightmares. This phenomenon is particularly common in the traumatic neuroses induced by battlefield experiences. Sleep disturbances may result from circadian-rhythm disturbances; most commonly due to jet travel, they may be of unknown causes. Treatment may require alterations in the patient's life style—that is, accepting the necessity for periodic reversals in night-day wakefulness patterns or deliberately inducing nights of sleep deprivation. It is believed that some reactions of depression are connected with such circadian-rhythm disturbances.

Recent studies have shown that depressed

patients have significantly longer sleep latency—that is, the time it takes to fall asleep. Such patients also spend less time asleep than do other persons.

The detection of penile tumescence during sleep has been used to differentiate potency disturbances of functional origin from cases of organic impotence.

Somnambulism can be precipitated in adult patients taking large bedtime doses of the major tranquilizers, antidepressants, and antihistamines. There is often a premonitory period, during which the patient complains of too much dreaming.

EEG-monitored transcendental meditation (TM) shows that much of TM time is spent in sleep stages 2, 3, and 4. Thus, much of the refreshment reported after a TM seance may be the result of a much-needed nap.

The fact that dreaming sleep is triggered cyclically by a neurobiological clock and is associated with a period of nonresponsiveness to external waking stimuli requires a reconsideration of Freud's theory, particularly the implications of his proposition that dreams occur in response to waking stimuli and function primarily as guardians of sleep.

Hypersomnia or excessive sleeping is often seen in depressive disorders occurring in neurosis. It is commonly associated with other depressive equivalents, such as overeating, and a variety of other addictive states, as well as sexual and aggressive acting out and academic underachievement. It may also occur in the early stages of a psychotic depressive illness, before more advanced stages of decompensation have occurred.

Reversal of sleep habit is a common accompaniment of hypersomnia. The patient tends to sleep soundly through the early morning hours, wake up gradually in the early afternoon, and achieve full wakefulness at a time when most people are going to bed. This pattern is most likely a psychologically caused interpersonal distance-regulating device for a person whose pattern is one of avoidance and retreat.

Drowsiness is a state of consciousness that intervenes normally between sleep and waking. It is characterized by a tendency to concrete thinking and transient hallucinatory phenomena, auditory and visual, which can occur normally just before sleep (hypnagogic hallucinations) and just before waking up (hypnopompic hallucinations).

Somnolence is abnormal drowsiness. It occurs in a variety of toxic, metabolic, and inflammatory diseases of the brain, and with brain tumors that press on the floor of the third ventricle.

## Epileptic and Convulsive Disorders

The essence of epilepsy from the standpoint of diagnosis is the periodic recurrence of transient disturbances of consciousness.

Twilight states, or dream-like states of consciousness, can occur as independent seizure phenomena apart from grand mal seizures, and are called psychomotor epilepsy. If the associated EEG abnormality is confined to the temporal lobe, one may speak of temporal lobe epilepsy; if the twilight states are associated with unpleasant olfactory and gustatory hallucinations with tasting tongue and lip movements, one may speak of uncinate fits. They are also characterized by circumscribed periods of intellectual dulling, disturbance in consciousness, confusion, and disorientation. Brief auditory and visual hallucinatory symptoms and schizophrenic-like psychotic reactions have been described. Generally, there is an amnesia for actions during that period. Characteristically, all these seizure patterns are associated with electroencephalographic abnormalities, which coincide in duration with the duration of the abnormality in the state of consciousness.

Patients with episodes of unexplained paroxysms of abdominal pain that are associated with transient confusional reactions, syncope, or headache may show seizure patterns on the EEG. These are instances of abdominal epilepsy and may be relieved by appropriate antiseizure medication.

Because seizures may be precipitated by flickering lights, some patients are unable to tolerate television.

In monitoring delirium reactions with the EEG, one occasionally uncovers instances in which the mental disorder is the consequence of a petit mal status, with its characteristic sequence of spike-and-dome waves on the EEG. These reactions can be controlled with appropriate antiseizure medication.

It is sometimes said that seizure disorders are associated with a higher incidence of sociopathy—that is, with convictions for crime. Most likely, epilepsy itself is not the cause of sociopathy; rather, the social ostracism that is often the fate of the epileptic may lead to adaptational problems, including sociopathy.

### Disturbances of Orientation

Orientation may be defined as the ability to recognize one's surroundings and their temporal and spatial relationships to one's self, or to appreciate one's relations to the social environment. The capacity for orientation involves the following categories: (1) Time: knowledge of the hour, day of the week, date, month, season, year. (2) Place: name of present location and home address, reason for being in this place at this time; inquiries in this area may reveal pathological denial of physical illness and the existence of other types of delusional systems. (3) Person: identity of self and others in the immediate environment, including not only a knowledge of names but also an appreciation of the role of each person in that setting.

The capacity for orientation depends, in the main, on three factors: the availability of perceptual data from the outer world, the availability of the stored data of recent memory, and the demands of reality, which is part of the emotional equipment of the mature adult.

One may speak of a specific drive to seek out and maintain accurate orientation as a psychological quality characterizing the mature adult. Normally, the inability to establish one's bearings generates anxiety and appropriate orientation-seeking behavior. A normal person, for example, on awakening in strange surroundings from a deep sleep, may have a brief period of bewilderment, during which he scans his environment for clues, draws on his stored memory for recent events, and, finally, with a sense of relief, orients himself correctly. If he awakens from a particularly vivid dream characterized by a deep sense of the reality of the events in the dream, he may have a similar brief struggle to reestablish his orientation. If a patient wakes up from a coma, he may not be able to marshal sufficient data to orient himself. He may suffer from anxiety and bewilderment, and respond to specific inquiries concerning orientation with panic and requests for information, or by admitting that he does not know the answers to the questions.

In a variety of settings, persons abdicate their firm commitment to reality. Adults in normal recreational settings, for example, deliberately cultivate flight from reality as part of the recreational process. In the theater, surrender to the make-believe of the play may be so complete that it takes a period of active struggle to reestablish contact with the real world when the performance is over. Alcohol and other common central nervous system inhibitory substances encourage and temporarily make possible flights from reality, and facilitate rapprochement with the world of make-believe.

A vivid feeling of reality is not necessarily associated with actual contact with reality. The delusional patient, for example, reorganizes his entire comprehension of the surrounding world to conform to his psychotic system, a process called rationalization, the purpose of which is to reduce the feeling of cognitive dissonance.

Disorientations in different spheres tend to parallel and to support—that is, to rationalize— each other. Through secondary elaboration, an inner consistency is achieved, like that often characterizing a dream. If the time precedes the onset of the patient's illness, the place is apt to be consistent with that time. People are similarly misidentified, and the reason for everyone's being together at that time and in that place is rationalized by a complex delusional system. When the disorientations in the delusional system are logically organized so that they have a rational inner consistency, the delusional system has been systematized.

When systematized delusions occur in schizophrenia, they are generally expressive of chronicity. They are resistant to psychotherapeutic intervention and carry a poor prognosis.

For many years, the incorrect orientation answers of brain-injured patients were too briefly dismissed with, "The patient is confused" or "The patient shows memory impairment." On close observation, orderly patterns can be discerned within the over-all picture of disorientation.

### Disorientation for Time

Hospitalized patients without organic brain disease commonly lose track of the date, the day of the week, and even the month. Thus, correct answers may be expressive of an alert and intact sensorium, but errors in these categories are not diagnostic of organic brain disease. An error in the year, on the other hand, is of diagnostic significance. It is in relation to the year that one commonly encounters a persistent pattern of misremembering.

A patient may give the year as 1984, and, even though he is corrected repeatedly, on each subsequent questioning he persists in stating that the year is 1984. Thus, he remembers quite dependably the wrong year. To characterize that misremembering as a simple lapse of memory is to miss the point that the patient is remembering what he wishes to remember—that is, he is responding to a wish or to a feeling that he is living in a year that was, perhaps, the last time he was in good health. The incorrect response, "The year is 1984," expresses a wish to be well, rather than a simple failure of memory.

Errors for the time of day are not significant as evidence of organic brain disease unless the error crosses a mealtime. Brain-injured patients commonly show errors for time of day if awakened from a nap—thinking, for example, that lunch or supper is actually breakfast.

In giving his personal history, a patient often condenses incidents in time that should actually be separated. A patient giving a psychiatric history may report the birth of a younger sibling and the occurrence of an operation, such as a tonsillectomy, as taking place in the same year, when, in fact, the younger sibling was born when the patient was age 3 and the operation took place at age 6. In some such instances, it is possible to demonstrate that guilt over sibling rivalry on the one hand, and the childish misinterpretation of an operative procedure as a punitive act on the other, although temporally separated, are condensed as a retrospective temporal falsification, so that crime and punishment become fused in memory as a single event.

Neurotic problems involving rebellious attitudes or a need to avoid painful reality may result in patterns of persistent tardiness. The affective state also plays a role in temporal orientation. During moods of elation, time seems to move quickly, whereas depressive moods are associated with a feeling that time is dragging.

Some anxious patients are unable to tolerate free time and have a need to fill all the temporal nooks and crannies of the day with prearranged activities. Such patients often suffer from a fear of loss of impulse control and defend themselves against acting out by overscheduling themselves. On the other hand, some patients, with a fear of their own passivity, complain that they are too tightly scheduled. The outer controlling elements are experienced as potentially dangerous forces capable of overwhelming the victim. Such patients are incapable of tolerating authority, and may present particular problems in relation to school and military service, where punctuality is a sine qua non for successful performance.

### Disorientation for Place

The brain-injured patient in a general hospital may express the wish to be well by insisting that he is not in a hospital but in his home. When one such patient was asked to explain the presence of the doctors and nurses who were all around her, she answered, "These people have taken over my home and have made it over to look like a hospital, but it is really my home." Other patients give the name of the institution correctly but characterize it as a hotel, a restaurant, or a convalescent home—that is, in various ways they deny the gravity of the illness by denying that they are in a hospital. On occasion, the patient gives the name of the hospital correctly but places the hospital close to home, saying, "I live a block away" or "I live across the street," when, in fact, home may be miles away. At times the patient locates himself in another hospital in which he was treated many years ago for a relatively minor illness from which he recovered. In this spatial dislocation he is expressing a *déjà vu*. He says, in effect, "I've been here before, and I went home in good health." Temporal disorientation commonly accompanies the pattern of spatial disorientation.

These meaningful alterations, which are clear in the case of the patient with diffuse brain disease, provide the clue for the disorientations in place encountered without organic brain disease. Schizophrenic patients may be disoriented for place in less predictable ways than are patients with organic brain disease, but their delusions are always meaningful.

### Disorientation for Person

A married female patient displaying disorientation for person may give her maiden name and insist that she is not married. Such denials often express elements of marital disharmony from which the patient wishes to take flight. They may also be associated with temporal disorientation, representing regression to a time preceding the onset of illness.

Anosognosia is a disorder in which patients tend to misidentify in a manner that enables them to deny the illness. The hospital doctor in a white coat may be identified as a fish peddler and the place of their encounter as a fish market. Some physical or characterological trait in a doctor or a nurse may be the basis for a persistent misidentification of that person as a friend from the past who has no connection with illness. The doctor may be identified under such circumstances as a former teacher or an insurance salesman.

The tendency to divide the world into good and bad elements and then to create delusional systems that, in effect, embody that split, resulted in a delusion expressed by a woman with one son named William. She claimed she had two sons, one named Bill, who was a good son, and one named Willie, who was bad.

Duplication may involve not only the entire person but part of a person. For instance, a hemiplegic patient may insist that he has two left arms, one good left arm and one bad left arm.

In patients without organic brain disease, the concept of self may be so chaotic that the vulnerable patient tends to be highly suggestible and to identify with any dominant person he is with. He may incorporate specific mannerisms of speech and dress and self-destructive patterns of behavior, such as narcotic addiction. This instability of self-concept is particularly conspicuous in teenaged girls. For this reason, they are vulnerable to mass hysterical behavior, as television audiences know from watching their responses to popular public performers. The chaotic concept of self most characteristic of adolescents is what Erikson referred to as the identity crisis. Confronted with an essentially insoluble dilemma concerning one's role in life, some teenagers go beyond experimental introjections and identifications and take flight into psychosis.

A teenaged girl could not decide whether to be a successful writer and civic-spirited citizen like her father or a beautiful, narcissistic woman like her mother. The patient had a prominent nose that caused her to resemble her father. A plastic surgeon modified her nose, achieved an excellent cosmetic result, and succeeded in emphasizing delicate feminine features resembling those of her mother. Postoperatively, she went into an acute schizophrenic state, characterized by delusions that she was a sought-after beauty who had a great vision to save the world as a second Florence Nightingale.

## Disturbances of Memory

Memory is based on three essential processes: (1) registration, the ability to establish a record of an experience in the central nervous system; (2) retention, the persistence or permanence of a registered experience; and (3) recall, the ability to arouse and report in consciousness a previously registered experience.

A good memory involves the capacity to register data swiftly and accurately, the capacity to retain those data for long periods of time, and the capacity to recall them promptly in relation to reality-oriented goals.

Although a good memory is one of the factors in the complex of mental capacities that make up intelligence, phenomenal feats of memory are occasionally encountered in settings of apparent mental retardation. These feats of memory usually involve rote memory, the capacity to retain and reproduce data verbatim, without reference to meaning. In logical memory, on the other hand, problem solving in relation to a reality-oriented goal is paramount.

In addition to quantitative, there are also qualitative differences in memory. Some persons are particularly well endowed with visual memory and can recall images with virtual hallucinatory intensity. They are called eidetic persons, and the reproduced memories are called eidetic images. This eidetic capacity tends to occur in childhood and subside with age, so that it is rare after adolescence. Eidetic mental retardates tend to retain that quality longer than do normal persons.

### Disturbances in Registration

Registration depends on the level of consciousness. Anything that diminishes consciousness, such as alcoholism or concussion, interferes with registration. A prizefighter may go on for several rounds to win a fight after a dazing blow to the head, and yet have no recoverable memory for events after the blow. A circumscribed memory loss of that kind occurring during the time after an acute brain injury is called anterograde amnesia. An alcoholic may behave in a socially acceptable manner for an entire evening and yet have no recoverable memory of the events of that evening (alcoholic blackout). Disturbed states of consciousness lasting for weeks and months associated with encephalitis, subarachnoid hemorrhage, and severe brain trauma may be followed by a permanent inability to recall the events experienced during that period. In all these instances, the subsequent defect in recall starts with primary defects involving registration and retention.

There are conditions in which registration seem to be impaired because the patient appears to be totally nonreactive. This impairment occurs in catatonic schizophrenia and in severe panic states. However, when the brain is intact from an organic point of view but perceived experiences are repressed or denied for purely emotional reasons, registration is normal. In these instances, seemingly nonobserved events can be recalled later, either directly or with the use of specific techniques for eliciting forgotten or repressed memories, such as hypnosis, narcoanalysis, and psychoanalysis.

### Disturbances in Retention

In the establishment of lasting memories, there is a preliminary learning stage during which the memory trace is unstable. The memory curve, or the curve of forgetting, is a graphic representation of the relative amounts of memorized material that can be recalled after various intervals of time. For persons with good memories, memory traces are quickly established, and the curve of forgetting is prolonged and may extend over the entire lifetime of the person. In some instances of organic brain disease, the curve of forgetting is accelerated. In Korsakoff's psychosis, memory for recently acquired facts may decay in a matter of seconds, without any residual capacity for recall.

### Disturbances in Recall

Amnesia is the partial or total inability to recall past experiences. Any process that interferes with the formation of a short-term memory or its fixation into long-term memory results in complete or permanent amnesia. This type of amnesia may also be called registration amnesia. Chronic brain disease impairs both registration and recall. This is seen in Korsakoff's syndrome, vascular disease, senile dementia, and brain tumor. When memories are presumed to have been formed and stored permanently but access to them is somehow prevented, the result is an amnesia that in many cases is temporary and treatable. This is referred to as recall amnesia.

The sharp distinction between amnesia of organic origin and amnesia of emotional origin is made for purposes of description and clarification. Most amnesias seen in relation to organic brain disease are, in fact, mixed amnesias in which organic deficits and emotional interference with recall both play a role.

Hysterical amnesia is a loss of memory for a particular period of past life or for certain situations associated with great fear, rage, or shameful humiliation. This form of amnesia is highly selective and systematized to fulfill the patient's specific emotional needs.

The brain-injured patient who is highly motivated may succeed in overcoming organically determined impairments of recall by a variety of mnemonic devices. For example, in response to a request to name an abstract work or concept, he may start with a concrete visual image that is charged with highly personal significance. In his search for the correct word, he may then go on to make writing movements with his head. Finally, after much effort exerted over that tortuous path, he arrives at the abstract word for which he is searching. Thus, in order to discover subtle memory defects in brain-injured patients, one must inquire into the mechanism of recall, as well as the actual content of what is remembered.

In contrast to the aphasic impairments of recall, which are highly circumscribed and involve specific words or actions, is the impairment of recall associated with the hysterical fugue state, a form of dissociative reaction that sets in after a severe emotional trauma.

Paramnesia is a distortion of recall resulting from the inclusion of false details, meanings, or emotions or wrong temporal relationships. It is also known as *fausse reconnaissance* and retrospective falsification.

Distortions in recall are encountered in normal persons. Witness' errors in the courtroom are examples of this. There is in everyone a readiness to distortion whenever accurate recall elicits painful affects. The presence of diffuse organic brain disease has the effect of facilitating and fixating that universally present tendency toward paramnesia.

Confabulation is the unconscious filling in of memory gaps by imagined experiences. It is characteristic of diffuse organic brain disease. These recollections change from moment to moment and are easily induced by suggestion. A simple test for confabulation is to ask the hospitalized patient, "Where were you last night?" This question is usually enough to elicit the phenomenon if it is present.

*Déjà vu* is an illusion of recognition in which a new situation is incorrectly regarded as a repetition of a previous memory. It can occur in normal persons, particularly in settings generating anxiety. It is more common in neurotic states and occurs occasionally in the aura of grand mal epilepsy. In *jamais vu* there is a feeling of unfamiliarity with a situation that one has actually experienced.

Related to *déjà vu* is *déjà entendu*, in which a comment never heard before is incorrectly regarded as a repetition of a previous conversation, and *déjà pensé*, in which a thought never entertained before is incorrectly regarded as a repetition of a previous thought.

Hypermnesia is the capacity for an exaggerated degree of recall. It can be elicited episodically in a hypnotic trance, particularly when regression in time is specifically suggested to the subject. It is seen as an ongoing state in certain prodigies, obsessive-compulsive neurosis, paranoia, and mania.

### Disturbances in Perception

Perception is the awareness of objects, qualities, or relations that follows the stimulation of peripheral sense organs, as distinct from the awareness that results from memory. Thus, perception is the necessary precursor of memory, and is connected with memory through the process of memory registration.

There are as many categories of perceived data as there are types of end organs, including visual, auditory, olfactory, gustatory, tactile, and kinesthetic. Accurate perception depends, first of all, on an intact perceptual apparatus at every level of organization, and impairments in perception set the stage for delusions, hallucinations, and a variety of misinterpretations of reality.

Perception does not consist of simple somatic responses. It depends on a complex maturational process with psychological and social components. A complex mental barrier against traumatic stimuli, known as the *Reizschutz*, is developed gradually in the mother-child interactions of infancy. Schizophrenic children do not develop this perceptual shield, and for them ordinary stimuli exert a traumatic effect and give rise to a chronic posture of negativism and retreat.

Apperception is conscious awareness of the significance of a percept. It is based on the complex psychological components that determine its total impact.

Perception may be the result of relatively simple, affectively neutral stimuli, presented one at a time or two at a time (double simultaneous stimulation). Stimuli may be complex, involving both visual and kinesthetic factors in making a discriminatory judgment, as in binocular vision; or stimuli may be a combination of visual, olfactory, and gustatory in an essentially gustatory perception.

Between the presentation of a stimulus and its recognition by the observer, there is a time lapse called the perception time. This lapse involves time for the transmission of the nerve impulse from the sensory receptor to the appropriate brain centers. More significant is the time involved to overcome an emotionally determined barrier to perception, a barrier that exists to protect the person against traumatic stimuli.

Whereas emotionally induced fainting eliminates all perception, circumscribed eliminations of perception may occur as a device for coping with traumatic stimuli. In negative hallucination, a person with a physiologically intact nervous system fails to perceive a stimulus. It can be induced through hypnosis. When the nonperceived stimulus is excluded from conscious awareness because it is traumatic, it is usually part of the syndrome of hysteria.

Any modality of perception may be disordered in hysteria. Total anesthesia can occur, but diminution in sensation is more common. These perceptual disturbances do not follow recognizable neuroanatomical distributions but involve, rather, a part of a limb (glove-and-stocking distribution), half the body, and the mucous membranes (vagina, rectum, nose, mouth, and pharynx). Peculiar to the hysterical anesthesias is the simultaneous involvement of all forms of sensation, superficial and deep, without the sensory dissociation that frequently characterizes organic sensory disturbances. If the sensory loss is limited to half the body, it is found to stop exactly at the midline, a condition contrary to the normal cutaneous innervative overlapping. Similarly, psychogenic loss of sensation is attested to by the hysteric's perception of the tuning fork on only one side of the sternum or on only one side of the head, an obvious impossibility in view of the normal bone conduction of vibrations.

Repeated testing of visual fields in hysteria may result in a spiral contraction of the visual field. Hysterical blindness may occur.

Macropsia is a condition characteristic of hysteria in which objects appear larger than they really are. They may assume terrifying proportions.

Micropsia is a condition in which objects appear smaller than they really are. The condition may alternate with macropsia in hysteria, but it has also been described as an aura in some cases of epilepsy.

Hysterical patterns of perceptual disturbance do not by any means rule out organic disease. The perceptual disturbances often seem to emerge in response to repeated sensory testing. This is not at all the result of a conscious intent to deceive the examiner but more likely the outcome of a naive appeal for help.

Brain-injured patients with left hemiplegia, hemianesthesia, and hemianopsia often steadfastly neglect the entire left side of the visual field. For example, they eat all the food on the right side of the hospital tray up to the midline; they write only on the right half of the page; they read the right half of a word. In drawing the human figure, they draw only the mirrored representation of the right half of the body, neglecting entirely to draw the other half. In all these instances, there seems to be a selective inattention to the sick side, an inattention that manifests itself as an essentially hysterical disturbance in vision. The relationship of the hysterical disturbance to denial of illness seems quite clear. "The sick side does not exist."

Patients with organic hearing impairments have selectively more difficulty than do others in hearing emotionally disturbing auditory stimuli. In a sense, those patients with mixed (organic and functional) hearing disturbances are expressing in a selective and more circumscribed fashion the same phenomenon that is encountered in complete hysterical deafness without organic hearing impairment—namely, a blocking out of potentially traumatic auditory percepts.

Hysterical anesthesia has been described as a kind of localized fainting. Anorgasmia, also known as frigidity, including all degrees of anesthesia of the vagina and external genitalia, is a common defense against sexual excitement. In each circumstance there is a withdrawal of attention from potentially traumatic external events. Hysterical anesthesia of the nasopharynx leads to absent gag reflex, commonly observed in hysteria.

Just as withdrawal of attention from a body part can reduce perception to the point of complete anesthesia, so can a sensory end organ be overinvested with attention because of anxiety. In the latter instance, there may be areas of hyperalgesia to touch, and to headaches and other body pains. In spite of verbal expressions of great suffering, the hysterical patient may show a characteristic attitude of unconcern (*la belle indifference*). Complaints of pain may be associated with rigidity of muscles and occasionally bizarre flexion deformities of the extremities and spine.

Although the physical complaints typically do not conform to recognizable clinical syndromes, actual physical disease, past or present, may set the stage for use of a specific body part in symptom formation that is without organic basis. The return to a previous symptom, or the perpetuation and intensification of a present organic symptom in the formation of a hysterical symptom, is termed somatic compliance. The preoccupation with headache after a head injury in an industrial accident involving compensation is an example of somatic compliance.

In all the perceptual disturbances of hysteria, it is not enough to demonstrate that the pattern of sensory abnormality is impossible from the point of view of known neuroanatomical facts. One must also search out the emotional meaning of the perceptual disturbance in adaptational terms, recalling that anesthesia, hyperesthesia, and paralysis commonly serve to defend the patient against sexual or violent impulses that he fears may get out of control, or serve as a cry for help in patients whose verbal skills are limited.

### Hypochondriasis

A generalized withdrawal of attention from external objects is almost always followed by an increase in the attention focused on the self as an object. If the retreat from the world of real objects is complete enough, a pathological awareness of body feelings emerges, and that awareness is the basis for hypochondriasis. One normally encounters a transiently increased awareness of somatic sensations on drifting off to sleep—an awareness of the heart beat, various visual phenomena, and so on.

Hypochondriasis is the unshakable belief that widespread physical disease is present, in the face of all evidence to the contrary. As a symptom, it occurs in many forms of mental illness. It is most common in the depressions, particularly those of the involutional period. It may take bizarre forms in schizophrenia, in which case one may speak more appropriately of somatic delusions. It may occur in a chronic, low-grade form over a period of years as part of a neurotic reaction.

Abnormal body feelings associated with hysteria tend to be localized and serve to protect the person against the still longed for but potentially traumatic encounters with circumscribed portions of the outer world. Abnormal body feelings associated with hypochondriasis, on the other hand, tend to be generalized, in the sense that the entire body is involved, and result from a relatively complete withdrawal from external objects. Thus, an important difference between the hysteric and the hypochondriac is the degree to which contacts with real objects in the external world have been retained or surrendered.

### Illusions

In an illusion, there is perceptual misinterpretation of a real external sensory experience.

In a state of anxiety and loneliness, a traveler is apt to mistake a tree trunk for a menacing adversary, or a mist for a terrifying apparition. This tendency does not necessarily imply psychopathology. However, a schizophrenic patient may hear an insulting remark in the chime of a clock or feel the sinister hand of death in a casual handshake. This kind of misinterpretation is also known as an illusion.

Illusions may occur in certain toxic states. For example, in the stage of alcohol withdrawal syndrome just preceding hallucinosis, the sound of a match striking can elicit a startled leap into the air, with fear and trembling. Such frightened reactions to ambiguous or neutral stimuli indicate that the patient is projecting and is on the threshold of ideas of reference.

### Hallucinations

A hallucination is the apparent perception of an external object when no corresponding real object exists—that is, an internal psychological event is mistakenly attributed to an external source. A dream is a simple example of a hallucination in normal experience.

Any modality of perception may be involved. Within the framework of normal hallucinatory experience, hypnagogic and hypnopompic hallucinations should be mentioned. Hypnagogic hallucinations occur in the drowsy state preceding deep sleep. They may contain both auditory and visual elements with great clarity and intensity. At times, they are associated with paresthesias in the mouth and hand, the sound of murmured voices, and vague visual images of large objects approaching and receding. These hypnagogic hallucinations have been called the Isakower phenomenon and are seen to represent a reawakening of the memory of early nursing experiences.

Although it is said that hypnagogic hallucinations occur most often in persons suffering from hysteria, they can also occur in normal persons, particularly during childhood and early adolescence. What has been said of hypnagogic hallucinations is also true of hypnopompic hallucinations, except that hypnopompic hallucinations occur during the drowsy state, after deep sleep and before awakening. They also occur as part of the syndrome of narcolepsy.

When the schizophrenic patient is wide awake by all neurophysiological criteria, he may experience hallucinations as vivid as those experienced by normal people during dreams. He often acts on these inner perceptions, as though they were more compelling than the external realities that compete for his attention. He may incorporate illusions into his hallucinations, so that the hallucinations occur along side external perceptions and even intermingle with them.

Hallucinosis is a psychotic state in which the patient seems to be alert and well oriented, in spite of the fact that he is hallucinating. Such patients may slip in and out of the hallucinatory state, with intervals of insight and lucidity—hence, Hughlings Jackson's term "mental diplopia."

A group of hallucinogenic psychotomimetic drugs characteristically elicit hallucinosis—that is, hallucinations in a setting of relatively clear consciousness. Mescaline and lysergic acid diethylamide (LSD) are well-known representatives of this group of drugs. The person's relative alertness makes it possible for him to communicate his hallucinations in considerable detail in an experimental situation.

Under mescaline, visual hallucinations, combined with visual illusions, are most frequently reported. These visual phenomena are vivid and change rapidly. Auditory hallucinations also occur but less frequently than do visual illusions. In LSD toxicity, a patient may experience a colorful hallucination after hearing a loud voice, or he may have an auditory hallucination in response to a bright light (synesthesia). There is also the LSD phenomenon known as trailing, a perceptual abnormality in which moving objects are seen as a series of discrete and discontinuous images, reminiscent of a stroboscopic photograph with multiple exposures.

After repeated ingestions of LSD, one may precipitate a disorder, called flashbacks, that may last for months after the last usage. The disorder is characterized by spontaneous recurrences of illusions and visual hallucinations similar to those experienced during the acute toxic state. There may be bursts of color and visions of formed objects. Depersonalization, perceptual distortions, hallucinations, and episodes of catatonia may occur. The trailing phenomenon, too, may make its reappearance.

Generalized organic brain disease of almost any cause can be associated with hallucinatory states that are at times indistinguishable from schizophrenia. These reactions may be expressive of drug sensitivities. Atropine and its derivatives may cause characteristic Lilliputian hallucinations in drug-sensitive adults receiving relatively small quantities in the form of eyedrops, or in children being treated for enuresis with atropine derivatives. In Lilliputian hallucinations, the hallucinated objects, usually people, appear greatly reduced in size. Although they occur most characteristically in psychotic reactions to a variety of drugs and toxic-metabolic states, they can, on occasion, occur in psychotic reactions without organic brain disease. They are to be differentiated from micropsia, a hysterical phenomenon in which real objects in the environment appear reduced in size.

Similarly, relatively small doses of alcohol or marijuana can produce hallucinations in sensitive subjects. Even the major tranquilizers, which are administered to decrease psychotic manifestations, may intensify hallucinations or elicit new ones in patients hypersensitive to anticholinergic substances.

Patients who are chronically habituated to any sedative substance—such as alcohol, barbiturates, meprobamate, or diazepoxide—often experience hallucinations when these drugs are withdrawn (abstinence syndrome or withdrawal reaction). These hallucinatory states are commonly associated with great terror.

Brain tumors, subarachnoid hemorrhage, uremia, strokes, a broad range of endocrine abnormalities, and a variety of drugs may all play a role in initiating hallucinatory states. Different chemical agents may have the same hallucinatory effect on a given person, and, conversely, a given chemical may produce widely varying responses in different persons.

In addition, the effect of a given chemical agent varies with the mood, the social setting, and the physical condition of the patient.

In describing a hallucinatory state, one should consider several elements described below.

**Projection to the Outer World.** At times, hallucinations are perceived with great intensity; at other times, they are perceived as barely audible whispers or barely visible shadows. At times, the hallucination is clearly placed in the outer world; at other times, it is experienced within the body—a picture or a voice located in the head, the chest, or some other part of the body. The images and words may be distinct or blurred. They shade off from unmistakable sensory experiences at one extreme, through vivid imaginations and inspired thoughts, to ordinary thoughts and ideas at the other extreme. Thus, hallucinations and delusions occur on a continuum and are measured by the degree of the patient's conviction of the objective reality of a bizarre experience.

**Sensory Modality.** A basic hallucination is one associated with the sensation of touch. Although it may occur in schizophrenia, it is more common in delirium tremens, in which those cutaneous hallucinations are commonly associated with visual hallucinations of tiny, crawling animals. Creeping sensations under the skin are known as formication. Among cocaine users, the phenomenon is known as the cocaine bug. Olfactory and gustatory hallucinations of bad tastes and odors may be encountered as part of the aura of temporal lobe epilepsy (uncinate fit). They may also occur in schizophrenia, with complex delusional elaborations of being poisoned. The auditory sphere is probably the most frequently involved sensory modality in the hallucinations of schizophrenia. Reflex hallucinations may occur in one sensory sphere as the result of irritation in another; for example, a toothache may stimulate an auditory hallucination. Kinesthetic hallucinations may occur in amputees, as part of the phantom-limb experience.

**Circumstances That Have Elicited the Hallucinations.** A careful history and physical and laboratory examinations identify some organic hallucinatory states otherwise indistinguishable from schizophrenia. Toxic delirium is apt to occur at night. Acute hallucinatory states may be precipitated in certain schizoid persons by the enforced physical intimacy of army barracks life.

**Insight.** Insight is most likely to be present in the early stages of any psychosis and during the period of recovery. In either case, its presence tends to be associated with a good prognosis, and patients showing insight are usually cooperative for treatment.

**Emotional and Ideational Content of the Hallucinations.** The acute reactions of withdrawal from drugs and the toxic deliriums are typically associated with great terror. Reactions of flight are common, and the patient, if unattended, may leap out of a hospital window.

During psychotic states of ecstasy and elation, hallucinatory experiences may involve sexual excitement and feelings of being infused with impregnating rays. In paranoid states, voices may be threatening. Rays may "cause" diseases, poisonings, or strange feelings. Voices may order the patient to commit acts of violence to save himself or the world from unspeakable sin. In depressive states, voices may be derisive and humiliating. They may accuse the patient of sexual perversion and order him to commit some expiatory act of self-mutilation or self-destruction.

As in dreams, memory traces constitute the building blocks of hallucinations. Indeed, it has been theorized that hallucinations may be the result of abnormalities in the memory retrieval system. The past history of each patient provides the clue for understanding hallucinatory content. The content reflects the effort to master anxiety and to fulfill various wishes and needs. Whereas patients with organic brain disease tend to express simple ideas related to the wish to be well and to be home, patients with functional psychoses express more complex ideas based on interactions with imagined partners, and concern themselves primarily with sexual and aggressive drives that the patient has been unable to master in real life.

## Disturbances in Affect

Affect is the feeling tone, pleasurable or unpleasurable, that accompanies an idea. Affect determines the general attitude, whether of rejection, acceptance, flight, fight, or indifference. Thus, the affects provide the motivational drive or psychodynamic component in relation to every life situation and play a determining role in the thoughts and actions of a person in health and disease. Affect may be described as shallow or inadequate (emotional flatness), inappropriate (when the emotion does not correspond to the stimulus), or labile (changeable).

Euphoria refers to the first, moderate level in the scale of pleasurable affects. It has been defined as a positive feeling of emotional and physical well-being. When it occurs in a manifestly inappropriate setting, it is indicative of mental disorder. Although it is usually psychogenic, it may be observed in organic brain disease.

Elation may be thought of as a second level in the scale of pleasurable affects. It is characterized by a definite affect of gladness in which there is an air of enjoyment and self-confidence, and motor activity is increased. This affect belongs within the limits of normal life experience, yet it may be indicative of mental disorders when it occurs in a manifestly inappropriate setting.

Various pharmacological agents may induce euphoria or elation. Alcohol, narcotics, and the amphetamines may be cited as examples. Underlying most cases of addiction is an anxious-depressive state that drives the patient to use agents that relieve the painful affective state. These substances enable the person to repress or deny the existence of painful affects. Brain lesions may have a similar impact on painful affects.

Exaltation may be defined as extreme elation; it is usually associated with delusions of grandeur. It merges into ecstasy, which represents a peak state of rapture. These affects in inappropriate circumstances are found almost exclusively in relation to psychosis, as in schizophrenia. They are also encountered in religious emotional transports, which may occur in certain persons as private mystical experiences, or they may be mass induced in revivalist ceremonies.

It was once thought that lesions of the frontal lobe specifically elicited a mood of euphoria. It is now known that any brain impairment—anywhere, and from any cause—that lowers the level of consciousness can have that effect. A small lesion involving the floor of the third ventricle may have a greater mood-elevating effect than does a much larger lesion occurring elsewhere. Affability encountered in patients with senile dementia is an example of mood elevation associated with diffuse organic brain disease.

Research has identified normally occurring brain substances—enkephalins and $\beta$-endorphins—that mimic the effects of opiates, that may have the effect of relieving physical and mental pain during traumatic emergencies, and that may also contribute to states of mental well-being. It has also been hypothesized that opiate dependency states result from a deficiency in the supply of normally available endorphins.

So far, the role of drugs and toxic and organic factors as affect-elevating agents has been emphasized. Some patients are able to eliminate painful affects from consciousness without the aid of chemical consciousness-impairing agents. By using the psychological defense mechanism of denial or selective inattention, they avoid confrontations with traumatic percepts, and, by means of repression, they avoid confrontations with painful memories. If these mechanisms are sufficiently successful, a psychotic state supervenes. The manic patient does not feel deprived; he feels elated. In place of pessimism and despair, he has feelings of unwarranted optimism and self-confidence, and he is physically overactive and high spirited. He feels that he has unlimited resources and, as a result, squanders money with reckless abandon. This pattern is called the manic reaction or mania. When less intense, the behavior is described as a hypomanic reaction.

## Depression

Depression is one of the most common illnesses to which humans are subject. Paradoxi-

cally, it is probably the most frequently overlooked symptom, and, even when recognized, it is probably the single most incorrectly treated symptom in clinical practice. Not only are the signs and symptoms of depression multiple and complex at any given stage of the disorder, but there are many stages and different problems in varying age groups. Its symptoms at onset, for example, differ considerably from those that develop later on and from those that appear penultimately in the depressed patient who commits suicide. There is also the age factor. The manifestations in the teenager differ considerably from those seen in late life.

From a purely descriptive point of view, the phenomena associated with depression are often indistinguishable from those seen in bereavement—that is, in the normal reaction of grief and mourning.

In addition to depression of psychological and social origin, biological inputs must not be overlooked. Certain medications can precipitate a severe depression in a previously well functioning person. Reserpine and corticosteroids in high doses and phenothiazines are familiar examples. Retroperitoneal neoplasms, such as lymphoma and carcinoma of the pancreas, can precipitate depression. Depressive illness may set in after certain viral infections, such as hepatitis, infectious mononucleosis, and influenza. In addition, there is evidence for a biologically based hereditary factor in vulnerability to depression, particularly in the recurrent depressions of manic-depressive illness.

Premenstrually, many women are subject to mood swings. Depression and anger are common, as well as suicidal behavior and sociopathy. There may be a breakthrough of compulsive symptoms. The phenomenon undoubtedly has both psychological and endocrinological causative components.

**Depression Equivalents and Masked Depression.** Certain depressive symptoms are best understood as cries for help. When depression first appears, the victim often displays a reaction of protest. A grade-school child, for instance, may show hyperkinetic behavior, fire setting, accident proneness, and enuresis. The adolescent may indulge in conspicuous displays of antisocial behavior that compel the adult world to pay attention. All too often, these cries for help are misinterpreted and dealt with punitively, with resultant intensification of the depression. An older person often seeks out his physician with physical complaints because he does not know how else to express his cry for help.

Deviations in sexual behavior may occur episodically and acutely in response to situations that impair self-esteem. For example, homosexual cruising, the compulsive search for a promiscuous partner, may occur in a bisexual man after a marital quarrel. Perverse exhibitionistic behavior may occur when the birth of a new child gives rise, in the father, to feelings of being rejected. One patient had transvestite episodes as an anniversary mourning reaction to the childhood loss of his mother. By dressing like her, he could make believe that she was still alive.

The somatic complaints commonly seen in depression are of several varieties. They may have symbolic connections with a loved one from whom separation is dreaded or has already occurred. In these instances one is dealing primarily with conversion phenomena. In other instances the patient may complain of an existing relatively mild physical disorder, such as an inguinal hernia, in the hope that hospitalization will provide an escape from an unbearable conflict or compel attention that is not otherwise obtainable. Access to medical echelons of help may be achieved through injuries "accidentally" incurred at work.

**Clinically Overt Depression.** When the breakthrough occurs—as it inevitably must—what emerges are the commonly recognized symptoms of depression. The very appearance of the victim changes: He looks old and sad. His face is lined. His posture is stooped and bent. Indeed, the gait and facial expression may bear a superficial resemblance to the signs of parkinsonism. In so-called simple depression, psychological and motor spontaneity are lost. The patient tends to be slowed-up and mute. His voice is low; his replies to questions are brief and monosyllabic. All previous interests are lost. There is anorexia with weight loss. There is loss of sexual desire and a loss of interest in recreation, work, family, and friends. The patient complains of an indescribable misery that he sometimes locates in his chest or abdomen. He is filled with self-reproach and is convinced that he is a failure, that his money is gone, that he is old, and that he has become stupid. He expresses feelings of pessimism, poverty, hopelessness, and futility. He is filled with guilt and shame. He expects punishment. He has suicidal thoughts and impulses. In addition, he displays characteristic somatic concomitants: dryness of the mouth with *fetor oris*, sighing respiration, and constipation. In place of a prior tendency to hypersomnia, insomnia sets in and is most commonly associated with frequent waking spells during the night and early-morning agitation, with sweating and feelings of anguish. As interest in the outer world is withdrawn, there comes an intensified awareness of the body, with hypochondriasis and somatic delusions. Many patients describe a deeply felt need to weep but complain of an inability to do so and say, "I believe I'd feel better if I could only cry." On the other hand, there may be periods of uncontrollable sobbing. In contrast to the foregoing picture of the psychological and motor-slowing characteristic of simple depression, some patients display a state of agitated depression characterized by much pacing, wringing of the hands, weeping, and loud vocalizations of despair.

Anaclitic depression refers to the syndrome shown by infants during the first years of life if they are deprived of the attentions of a suitable mothering figure. Anaclitic means "leaning on" and is a psychoanalytic term denoting an infant's dependency on his mother for his sense of well-being. On separation from the mother, the infant goes through a characteristic sequence of changes. There is an initial phase of protest, characterized by intense crying and struggling. If the state of deprivation continues, the infant lapses into the phase of despair. At this point his behavior suggests hopelessness. Struggling decreases, and his crying is monotonous and softer than before. In children's hospitals, this quieter state is commonly misinterpreted as a state of diminished distress. Actually, it is a state of mourning. Some of these infants fail to thrive. They may stop eating and then waste away and die, a state called marasmus. Most survive but lapse into a phase of detachment in which the infant withdraws from human relationships and becomes preoccupied with inanimate objects or his own body parts, engaging in masturbation, fecal smearing, head banging, or rocking.

Geriatric patients often show a mixture of organic brain defect, usually aphasia and apraxia, combined with depression. The effect of the depression may be to intensify the manifestations of organicity. The combined picture is the pseudodementia often seen in late-life depression. Unwarranted pessimism may lead to therapeutic nihilism, whereas adequate antidepression treatment may result in striking improvement in the depression and, indeed, in some reversal of the organic deficits.

The appearance of depressive symptoms may also signal the onset of recovery from an acute schizophrenic episode, as if the delusional state represented a respite from life's problems; as a consequence, recovery is associated with a sense of loss. Some schizoaffective patients retreat into manic grandiose psychotic states as a life-saving escape from an intolerably depressing situation.

Depression can appear paradoxically as the aftermath of some great success in those who are destroyed by success. Many instances may be cited in current literary history in which the production of a successful novel or play was followed by severe depression and suicide. The depression appears when success is unconsciously symbolized as a destruction and displacement of the father. To avoid this kind of depression, patients are characteristically self-defeating, or they may assume an imposter role that makes it possible to deny the actuality of one's achievements.

A change in the mood not only changes one's whole life outlook, but may change the content of delusions and alter the entire symptom complex. A schizophrenic who believed he was saving the world when he was in an exalted mood felt he was responsible for the end of the world when he became depressed. A male patient who would derive sexual excitement from fantasies of being whipped on the buttocks during depressed moods would excite himself sexually with fantasies of receiving an enema from a loving mother in more elated moods. A superstitious patient, who saw all kinds of evil omens in a depressed mood, felt himself surrounded by lucky signs and omens when elated.

*Suicide.* Suicide is an important consideration in the problems of depression. It is the primary issue in deciding whether to treat a given patient as an outpatient or in an inpatient setting. The physician must ask the depressed patient if he has suicidal thoughts or impulses. Some physicians hesitate to do so for fear that they will plant the thought in the patient's mind de novo; the contrary is true. Patients appreciate the inquiry as an expression of concern, particularly if the examining physician explains that the prognosis in depression is good and that he does not want harm to befall the patient before improvement can be effected.

It often happens that a patient who threatens suicide while he is an outpatient is more comfortable in an inpatient setting. He then presses for discharge and evinces no interest in further psychiatric care. One may draw a superficial impression of clinical improvement and sanction discharge to an unchanged and essentially intolerable life situation. The result is an unusually high suicide rate in that patient group. Active clinical contact should be maintained for at least 6 months, the period of maximum suicidal danger.

One often hears the cliché, "The period of improvement from depression is the time of the greatest suicidal danger." There is a small grain of truth in this, in the sense that some depressed patients are so immobilized by lack of energy and drive that those depressive symptoms do

exert some lifesaving function. However, more often the improvement referred to is pseudoimprovement, which occurs in the sheltered hospital setting, and death is the result of inadequate posthospital treatment planning.

It is erroneous to regard clinical depression as the only or even the major cause of suicide. In a general hospital, the delirious patient who is either postoperative or suffering from some toxic metabolic disorder presents the greatest suicidal risk of all, particularly at night. Schizophrenic patients may commit suicide or some act of self-mutilation in the delusional belief that they are saving others in so doing.

Hysterical patients who are prone to suicidal gestures may die accidentally. Patients with perverse sexual practices involving playing at tying themselves and hanging themselves may die accidentally (autoerotic asphyxiation).

Suicidal patients sometimes plan well in advance of the act, setting their affairs in order and writing a suicidal note. On occasion, the note becomes a full-fledged novel. A work of art sometimes fulfills needs that may have the effect of averting the suicidal act.

### Anxiety

Anxiety may be defined as a disagreeable emotional state in which there are feelings of impending danger, characterized by uneasiness, tension, or apprehension. The cause is usually unconscious or unrecognized intrapsychic conflict. Anxiety is associated with a characteristic pattern of autonomic nervous system discharge involving altered respiration rate, increased heart rate, pallor, dryness of the mouth, increased sweating, and musculoskeletal disturbances, involving trembling and feelings of weakness. Every organ system in the body, including the orgasm mechanism, may participate in the expression of anxiety.

Anxiety is to be differentiated from fear, in which the foregoing combination of feelings and nervous discharges occurs as a reaction to a real, conscious, and external danger that is present or that threatens to materialize.

Panic is a state of extreme, acute, intense anxiety accompanied by disorganization of personality and function.

Free-floating anxiety is the nucleus and key symptom of neurosis. It consists of a feeling of dread that the patient cannot logically assign to a specific cause. In the quest for causality, patients suffering from free-floating anxiety are always ready to attach it to some suitable ideational content.

Generalized anxiety disorder is a neurotic state based primarily on free-floating anxiety. It is characterized by irritability, anxious expectation, pangs of conscience, and episodes of panic. There is a hypersensitivity to ordinary sights and sounds, as a result of which startle reactions occur frequently and with minimal sensory provocation. Cardiac palpitation, breathlessness, giddiness, nausea, dryness of mouth, diarrhea, compulsive eating, urinary frequency, seminal emissions, blurring of vision, general physical weakness, and other physical manifestations may occur chronically as part of anxiety neurosis. In an effort to reduce the unpleasant feelings associated with anxiety, the person evolves a variety of defensive devices that in their entirety constitute many of the clinical manifestations of psychiatric disorder.

Conversion disorders, for example, is a well-known pathological device for reducing or eliminating free-floating anxiety. It is a neurosis characterized by sensory and motor deficits without a corresponding structural organic lesion. The effect of a hysterical paraplegia, for example, may be to prevent access to a situation feared by the patient because of unconsciously desired and rejected erotic or aggressive impulses. Often, the physical symptom is so effective in alleviating the anxiety that the patient displays an attitude of calm (*la belle indifférence*) that contrasts strangely with the extent of the physical disability.

Social phobia and simple phobia occur when the patient develops fears or phobias, in relation to specific situations that may stimulate erotic or aggressive impulses unconsciously desired and rejected by the patient. A similar anxiety-relieving role can be made out for many of the symptoms of obsessive-compulsive neurosis and schizophrenia.

In the following case, a young woman was brought into the emergency room of a general hospital by her sister with an adductor spasm of both legs and an inability to walk. The motor abnormality was without accompanying organic disease. The emergency room physician gave her a small quantity of amobarbital sodium (Amytal) intravenously, with the strong suggestion that her leg muscles would relax and return to normal when he finished counting to 10. At the appropriate signal, the patient relaxed, got off the table, and walked out of the emergency room, apparently elated. Four hours later she was returned to the emergency room in a catatonic stupor, for which she had to be hospitalized. At this point, information was elicited for the first time that the patient had recently moved into her sister's household and had suffered from guilt and anxiety as a result of illicit sexual play with her brother-in-law. Thus, removal of the hysterical defense (adductor spasm) caused her to regress to a psychotic defense (catatonia).

In classifying the anxiety disorders, DSM-III emphasizes in particular those cases in which panic attacks occur in an essentially unpredictable way with respect to time, place, or social circumstances. This is particularly characteristic of agoraphobia with panic attacks. It is also true of panic disorder. Most phobic states with panic are mixtures—that is, they are associated with panic in specific phobia-generating situations, as well as with the seemingly nonspecific episodes of panic. From the point of view of clinical management, differential diagnosis is important, since the nonspecific panic reactions respond rather specifically to the tricyclic and monoamine oxidase inhibitor antidepressants.

## Aggression

Aggression is defined as a constellation of specific thoughts, feelings, and actions that are mobilized by frustration of a wish or need, and whose goal is to remove the frustration in order to permit drive discharge.

Not all the specific thoughts, feelings, and actions characteristic of aggression are manifest. For example, one may feel rage and have no conscious thoughts that rationally explain it. One may kill in cold blood without feelings of anger. One may consciously harbor angry thoughts and feelings and commit no overt act. Or one may repress the entire process so completely that its only overt expression is a psychosomatic disorder whose psychological component can be made manifest only through psychotherapy.

In pathological mother-child relationships, a spectrum of rage reactions may be discerned, with postpartum depression and suicide at one end of the scale and child battering and infanticide at the other. Schizophrenic mothers may have infanticidal impulses (Medea syndrome) because the newborn child may symbolize a hated sibling or other family member. These same women may be capable of normal mothering behavior in relation to someone else's child.

Episodes of violence may occur as manifestations of a seizure disorder. To make the diagnosis, one has to demonstrate temporally related electroencephalographic abnormalities.

Schizophrenics may become violent when confronted with unwanted intimacies from which they feel that they cannot escape. Violence may erupt when a naive therapist does not understand or respect the schizophrenic patient's need to maintain a safe interpersonal distance—that is, a need to avoid intimacy.

Violence associated with criminal acts of breaking and entering may be connected with perverse sexual impulses. Sadistic and masochistic fantasies may inadvertently lead to violence, as in the accidental suicides of patients with bonding fantasies.

Irritability is a chronic diffuse state of anger that occurs as an interpersonal distance-regulating device. It may occur in paranoid personality disorder. It is commonly encountered in adolescents who are warding off sexually charged encounters with parents or siblings.

Vandalism is an act of indiscriminate violence that has many qualities in common with a child's temper tantrum. It represents a displacement from the true target of the rage and is associated with a personal feeling of impotent fury. It may occur in privacy as the act of one person. More often, it occurs semipublicly in socioeconomically deprived areas. It is directed at community property in general and is associated with a prevailing cultural attitude of approval of the behavior. It may also occur episodically in settings of mob violence, and may be associated with looting and a general mood of festivity.

Ambivalence refers to the coexistence of antithetical emotions, attitudes, ideas, or wishes toward a given object or situation. Usually, only one attitude emerges into consciousness, the other remaining unconscious. Ambivalence is encountered in all instances of affective instability. Thus, it plays a role in the mood swings that occur within normal limits. However, it is fundamental to many pathological mental states. There is the familiar doing and undoing characteristic of obsessive-compulsive neurosis, and the pathologically prolonged mourning that takes place when there is ambivalence toward the lost object. However, the most dramatic aspects of ambivalence are seen in schizophrenia, and for Bleuler ambivalence was one of the primary symptoms of this disease.

Underlying the ambivalence of the schizophrenic is the need-fear dilemma and the unending search for a suitable human relationship. The schizophrenic's interpersonal needs are so highly specialized that a suitable person is not easily come by; if one is found, the schizophrenic clings with abnormal intensity. Such relationships are filled with ambivalence and instability. Any suggestion of intimacy immediately moves the patient to dread and the need to retreat. The partner's retreat terrifies the patient and leads to intensified clinging. This is the nightmare fate of the schizophrenic—to swing eternally between the two poles of unendurable loneliness and of an unendurable dread of intimacy.

Alcohol intoxication remains the most important contributer to many episodes of destructive dyscontrol. The amphetamines, cocaine, a variety of hallucinogens, the barbiturates, the tricyclic antidepressants, and the prolonged use of benzodiazepines have all been implicated in episodes of violent dyscontrol.

The act of rape is essentially an expression of rage and the wish to dominate the victim. In rape, male sexuality is always in the service of other nonsexual needs.

Aggression turned against the self, such as extreme forms of self-mutilation, is sometimes seen in adult schizophrenics who enucleate their eyeballs, castrate themselves, inflict burns, eviscerate surgical incisions, and stab themselves to death with frightful wounds. Smaller degrees of self-inflicted wounds—notably wrist slitting, as contrasted to wrist cutting with serious suicidal intent, and trichotillomania (compulsive hair pulling)—occur more often in women than in men. Severe self-inflicted injuries are seen in childhood schizophrenia and the Lesch-Nyhan syndrome, an X-linked recessive defect in purine metabolism associated with severe mental retardation.

Children may display tantrum-like attacks of rage on reunion with their parents after enforced periods of physical separation. Adolescents may react with tantrum-like violence against inappropriately intimate physical approaches by parents, particularly in settings of marital disturbance.

Perhaps the most impressive clinical fact about violent behavior is its unpredictability. Many patients show a potential for violence on psychological testing and may even threaten it verbally over a period of years, and yet do not erupt overtly as long as the patient's supportive social network remains intact. Sudden loss or rejection by a loved one or some other event that sharply reduces self-esteem may provoke violent behavior. Many patients who have been protected from violent outbursts in the sheltered inpatient setting of a mental hospital are often embroiled in antisocial acts involving violence and police action as a result of unsupervised deinstitutionalization.

### Compound Emotions

In addition to the primary emotional states already described, there are many compound emotional states. The list of emotions in Table II is by no means exhaustive.

For example, smugness is compounded of self-satisfaction, self-absorption, and a reduced

TABLE II
CATALOGUE OF THE EMOTIONS

| | | |
|---|---|---|
| Anger | Envy | Petulance |
| Anxiety | Faith | Poise |
| Arrogance | Fear | Querulousness |
| Bitterness | Gloating | Rage |
| Boredom | Gratitude | Sadism |
| Cheating | Grief | Sarcasm |
| Confusion | Guilt | Shame |
| Curiosity | Gullibility | Shyness |
| Cynicism | Hate | Smugness |
| Depression | Homesickness | Teasing |
| Derision | Hope | Trust |
| Disillusionment | Jealousy | Uncanny feelings |
| Elation | Masochism | Vengefulness |
| Enthusiasm | Nostalgia | |

awareness of the environment. With it, there is also greediness and grasping, without associated guilt. There is also a characteristic pleased look about the mouth of the smug person. A negative reaction to smugness, based on envy and rivalry, is present to some degree in everyone. Enviousness designates a behavior pattern that elicits envy in others. It occurs characteristically in people with strong narcissistic needs who provoke others into attitudes of grudging admiration, in an unending quest for new inputs to bolster their fragile self-esteem. Bitterness is a feeling of resentment over what appears to be a justified grievance. It is associated with demands for redress. Confusion occurs when one cannot resolve the normally present ambivalence that creates a split attitude of love and hate, good and bad, toward most objects. Boredom is a state of dissatisfaction and disinclination to act. Time drags, as it does in depression, but the feeling in boredom is one of emptiness or apathy. Some instances of seemingly unmotivated violence in adolescents may represent an attempt to overcome boredom. Pathological jealousy has been compared to normal jealousy, as pathological mourning is compared to normal mourning. Pathological jealousy is compounded of grief, hatred, loss of self-esteem, and ambivalence. It may have its roots in unconscious homosexual attachments and merge into paranoid delusional thinking. Vengefulness is a striving toward an object, as in love, but for the purpose of ensuring its destruction. It is associated with a desire to get even and is calculated to assuage guilt and to relieve feelings of fear and hatred. Curiosity is a feeling state that gives rise to exploratory behavior. It is a drive to generate and increase anticipatory pleasure. In a creative person it can prevail over hunger, fear, pain, or pleasure. It is a craving for increasing tension that is as urgent as the quest for tension relief or satiety that follows consummatory pleasure.

## Mechanisms for Maintaining Mood Control

Mood is a sustained and prevailing emotional set. Since emotional set determines the direction and the intensity of behavioral response, a large part of mental functioning is related specifically to mood control.

Psychogenic fainting or loss of consciousness in response to an emotionally traumatic event is a model for the mechanisms of defense in the sense that it is a way of breaking off contact with an excessively painful reality. Similarly, a child may cover his eyes or ears to exclude unpleasant impressions. The defense mechanisms that evolve with emotional maturation provide a repertoire of techniques for controlling the emotional impact of events. These techniques include repression, denial, projection, sublimation, intellectualization, rationalization, regression, suppression, reaction formation, undoing, introjection, identification, isolation, and displacement.

Depersonalization is a mental phenomenon characterized by a feeling of unreality and strangeness about one's self. The patient says, in effect, "This experience does not hurt me because I am not me." The term "depersonalization" includes feelings of unreality, estrangement, amnesia, multiple personality states, and distortions in the body image. Depersonalization may be partial or complete, transient or long lasting. It may be encountered in hysteria or as part of the aura of epilepsy, but in schizophrenic states it tends to be more complete and lasting than in other disorders.

Derealization is a mental phenomenon characterized by the loss of the sense of reality concerning one's surroundings. The patient says, in effect, "This environment is not dangerous to me because this environment does not really exist." Derealization includes distortions of spatial and temporal relationships so that an essentially neutral environment seems strangely familiar (déjà vu) or strangely unfamiliar (jamais vu), or otherwise strange and distorted. Like depersonalization, to which it is closely related, derealization can be partial or complete, transient or long lasting. Similarly, it may occur in hysteria or as part of the aura of epilepsy, but derealization, too, tends to be most complete and persistent in schizophrenic states.

Although depersonalization and derealization occur as adaptational mechanisms to reduce unpleasant affects, they may in their own right create a feeling of impending catastrophe. Depersonalization and derealization are sometimes seen in atypical depressive reactions. A tendency to misconstrue them as schizophrenic phenomena may led to the inappropriate use of major tranquilizers, with intensification of the symptomatic relief.

The concept of an interpersonal distance-regulating mechanism seems closer to the clinical facts than is the more static concept of defense.

Defense or distance-regulating mechanisms may be established during a developmental period, when they fulfill a more or less useful adaptational function. With further maturation, these mechanisms may outlive that function and become counterproductive. A childhood fear of dogs, for example, may become an institutionalized part of an ongoing life style that impairs freedom of action and reduces self-esteem. The removal of such a symptom with behavior therapy is easily accomplished. However, some mechanisms fulfill an important distance-regulating function, even in adult life. The removal of such mechanisms can result in depression or substitute symptom formation, or may necessitate alterations in basic relationships.

## Disturbances in Motor Aspects of Behavior

**Conation**, or the conative aspect of mental functioning, refers to the capacity to initiate action or motor discharge and concerns the basic strivings of a person as expressed through his behavior. The affective component of an idea determines the force and the direction of the action that follows that idea. Thus, conation cannot be considered apart from affects, and conversely, all affects represent potential energy through their conative components.

The schizophrenic has difficulty initiating goal-directed activity. He may in some instances be capable of useful work if it is initiated for him and carried out under supervision, as in a sheltered workshop or state hospital or any other setting where self-support and independent functioning are not expected of him. Indeed, the lack of a self-starting mechanism—that is, the inability of a schizophrenic to initiate and carry out goal-directed behavior in any sphere, whether it be vocational, recreational or familial—is a hallmark of schizophrenia and is associated with a poor outcome in any activities program, unless hospital staff leaders are constantly and actively on the scene to keep the activity in progress.

Lacking the capacity to initiate their own actions, some schizophrenics respond to suggestions automatically and uncritically (command automatism) or by echolalia, which is the pathological repetition by imitation of the speech of another person; by echopraxia, the pathological repetition by imitation of the movements of another person; or by waxy flexibility (cerea flexibilitas), the maintenance by a patient of imposed postures with increased muscle tone, as when a limb remains passively in the position in which it is placed, however long or uncomfortable. Waxy flexibility is most characteristic of catatonic schizophrenia. Catalepsy is often used as a synonym for waxy flexibility; it is also used in a wider sense to include the intense muscular rigidities that can be induced by hypnotic suggestion.

A mannerism is a gesture or other form of motor expression peculiar to a given person. It is used interchangeably with stereotypy and posturing, the assuming of specific physical attitudes.

Some persons display a mannerism of staring upward to the right or the left while lost in thought. This same posture may occur in a schizophrenic listening to an auditory hallucination. An inappropriately fixed smile may occur as a mannerism in schizophrenia.

The startle reaction is a reflex response to an unexpected stimulus of great intensity. It is associated with a sudden increase in the level of consciousness and a diffuse motor response involving flexion movements of the trunk and extremities, hence, in German, *Zusammenschrecken* reflex. It occurs in normal people, but it may be elicited more readily and with a greater motor excursion in posttraumatic stress disorder, as occurs after a traumatic battlefield experience during wartime.

### Overactivity (Psychomotor Excitement)

Some persons are endowed biologically with a tendency to increased motor output, which can be demonstrated in fetal movements studied in utero.

Children and adolescents suffering from depression often show hyperactivity. Depressed adolescents may be reckless, antisocial, and sexually promiscuous.

Agitation refers to a state of pacing, hand wringing, and verbalized complaints of suffering, which occurs in agitated depression.

Hysterical convulsions usually consist of pantomimic expressions of sexual and aggressive fantasies. Occasionally, a hysterical patient mimics a grand mal seizure with extraordinary fidelity. The differential diagnosis depends on the absence of electroencephalographic abnormalities during the seizure and the absence of abnormal reflexes immediately thereafter.

Neurotic reactions of the obsessive-compulsive type are characterized by obsessive thoughts and by complex compulsive rituals. Most common are compulsive hand washing, counting, and repetitive ceremonial rituals, including the recitation of prayers and the repeated checking of door locks, water faucets, gas jets, and windows. In each instance, the compulsive act simultaneously carries out a forbidden wish and then undoes it. The endlessly repeated cycle of anxiety by carrying out the compulsive act, and the need to undo the act characterizes the compulsive symptoms.

Other types of compulsive acts are not usually connected with obsessive-compulsive neurosis— for example, alcoholism (dipsomania), compulsive stealing (kleptomania), compulsive fire setting (pyromania), and compulsive sexual acting out in a woman (nymphomania). Included in this category too, is compulsive gambling.

Compulsive drinking of great quantities of water in a relatively short span of time is occasionally seen in schizophrenia in response to specific delusions or hallucinations. This is called water intoxication. For example, the Virgin Mary "commanded" a psychotic patient to drink holy water. Another patient momentarily expected to be sucked into the sun and had to drink much water in preparation for that dehydrating ordeal. Severe electrolyte disturbances with grand mal seizures can occur in those instances. The electrolyte imbalance can itself be a cause of a toxic-metabolic psychotic reaction that complicates the basic schizophrenic disorder and can on occasion result in a fatal outcome.

The compulsive eating of scaling wall paint in children is called pica. It has been hypothesized that an underlying nutritional deficiency is the cause. For example, it is often contended that an iron deficiency is regularly found in those cases. On the other hand, in a study of families in an inner-city walk-up apartment house complex, pica occurred most often in children living above the third floor, who seemed to have less opportunity for out-of-doors play than did children living on lower floors.

A tic is an intermittent spasmodic twitching of the face or other body part that is repeated at frequent intervals, and without external stimulus.

Gilles de la Tourette's disease, *maladie des tics*, now known as Tourette's disorder, is a disorder characterized by a facial tic, which may spread to involve the head, neck, and upper and lower extremities. The tic is associated with stereotyped gestures, echolalia, coprolalia (compulsive use of obscene spoken words), and complusive thoughts. It usually begins between the ages of 7 and 15. The muscular movements begin in the face and extend to the rest of the body.

The patient opens his mouth, spits, jerks his head, claps his hands, scratches, jumps, and dances. Articulation and phonation are affected, and barking noises are often made. The patient repeats certain words or phrases, frequently expressing compulsive ideas.

Most patients with anorexia nervosa tend to be hyperactive before, during, and after hospitalization. The threat of enforced physical restriction often stimulates a cachectic anorectic patient to start eating, and enlargement of the sphere of activity may be used as the reward to encourage further eating and weight gain. Curiously, many anorectic patients retain the pattern of physical hyperactivity in posthospital settings, and the weight gain is successfully maintained. Such patients may give a clinical impression of depression.

Bulimia (compulsive overeating) is commonly associated with anorexia nervosa and occurs with self-induced vomiting for purposes of weight control.

Institutionalized patients who are retarded and psychotic may indulge in self-injurious behavior—for example, head slapping and head banging.

Manic patients may talk, sing, dance, and joke with apparently inexhaustible energy and good spirit. In agitated depression, there may be crying, pacing, and wringing of hands. In catatonic excitement, the pattern of overactivity is extreme from a quantitative point of view and bewildering from the point of view of content. Talking, which may be loud and voluble, is in response to delusions and hallucinations. The talk may consist of endless repetitions of sentences or phrases, the meaning of which is obscure. The severe ambivalence characterizing the schizophrenic process may result in great mood swings, ranging from abject terror to exaltation. There may be sudden eruptions of terror and rage, in response to which the patient may become homicidal. There may be moments of deep guilt and an urge to self-sacrifice, which may result in acts of self-mutilation. The excited catatonic patient may execute various gestures that have the intent of influencing the world by means of magic. Catatonic excitement, because of extreme intensity and prolongation, may result in severe exhaustion states, with dehydration, hyperthermia, and sudden death. The use of physical retraint tends to increase terror, intensify excitement, and increase the dangers of exhaustion and death. In addition, the major tranquilizers commonly used in treating catatonic excitement affect temperature control through hypothalamic suppression, further increasing the danger of hyperthermal death.

### Underactivity (Psychomotor Retardation)

Just as there are persons constitutionally predisposed to hyperkinesis, so there are others who react to stress with motor inhibition. In childhood and early adolescence, generalized patterns of inhibition and retreat tend to have a graver clinical significance than they do in later years, and they suggest a potential for a schizophrenia.

Simple depression, in contrast to agitated depression, is characterized by the absence of anxiety and by decreased motor activity. There is a feeling of pronounced fatigue and great difficulty in initiating any activity, including speech. Responses to stimuli are slowed up on an ideational, verbal and motor level. The patient's posture is expressive of the underlying affect of hopelessness and futility.

Hysterical motor disturbances can affect any of the voluntary muscle groups in patterns calculated to ward off forbidden sexual and aggressive discharges or to avoid situations of physical danger. They may present themselves clinically as paralysis or muscular weakness (asthenia); abnormal posture, such as torticollis, camptocormia, pseudocontractures, and stiffness; gait disturbances ranging from hysterical paraplegia to astasia-abasia. The speech apparatus may be affected with aphonia, hoarseness, and stammering. Blepharospasm may occur in relation to forbidden scoptophilic wishes. The muscular abnormalities of hysteria are usually associated with an increase in muscular tonus. If sustained, they may produce painful orthopedic and gynecological disorders. For example, hysterical spasm of the muscles of the pelvic floor may cause vaginismus. Concerning the physical findings in hysterical paralysis, Freud wrote: "The hysteric acts in his paralyses and other manifestations as if anatomy were nonexistent or as if he had no knowledge of it."

Although hysterical paralyses are usually associated with increased muscle tone and rigidity, on some occasions a total flaccidity, except for the retention of normal reflexes, is encountered. On occasion, an attitude of ambivalence expresses itself in variations in muscle tone.

In schizophrenic children, in particular, there are wide and unpredictable changes in muscle tone, so that a child being carried holds himself with inappropriate stiffness at one moment, and goes totally limp at another.

Cataplexy, commonly associated with narcolepsy, is characterized by sudden loss of motor tone, with profound weakness of the arms, legs, neck, and speech apparatus. These attacks are brought on by unexpected strong emotional reactions involving laughter, anger, surprise, or pleasure.

In schizophrenic catatonic stupor, the patient is immobile. His face may be mask-like. He is unresponsive to questions and commands, except occasionally when he manifests echolalia or echopraxia. When an attempt is made to bend his arm at the elbow, he may vigorously extend it. He may close his eyes tightly when asked to open them. These qualities, which may be regarded as contrariness or countersuggestibility, are manifestations of a generalized oppositional attitude called negativism. Ambivalence may modify the muscle tonus of the patient with catatonic stupor to the extent that he permits bending of his arm but against a resistance, so that a characteristic tonus quality emerges known as waxy flexibility.

Speech disturbances may express themselves as motoric inhibitions—for example, hysterical hoarseness and mutism.

Stammering is a disorder characterized by spasmodic, halting, or hesitating speech. Stuttering is a more severe degree of stammering. It tends to have an explosive quality, based on violent expulsive respiratory movements associated with the production of speech. It usually appears between the ages of 2 and 6 years. It occurs much more frequently in males than in females, and is said to be more frequent in those who are left-handed than in the right-handed.

## Disturbances of Personality

Personality refers to the sum total of the thoughts, feelings, and actions that a person habitually uses in his ongoing adaptations to life. Personality is essentially synonymous with character. Deeply ingrained behavior patterns are clearly recognizable by adolescence and occasionally earlier. The element of continuity is perhaps the most distinguishing element of personality, as contrasted with the episodic or discontinuous nature of most other diagnostic categories.

Although personality development entails a certain loss of freedom of thought and action, it also protects against trauma and overt symptom formation. This protective function of personality has given rise to the term "character armor."

The structural rigidities of personality may conceal deep-seated psychopathology. For example, a patient with a schizoid personality may function satisfactorily in civilian life as long as he is permitted to work on the night shift in the post office and to lead a hermit-like existence by day. If drafted into the armed forces, with its group living and inescapable physical intimacy, an acute schizophrenic episode may erupt. Or a woman with a passive-dependent personality disorder may live for decades in a satisfactory symbiosis with a strong, controlling father figure of a husband, and then collapse with a depressive psychosis when her husband dies.

Thomas and Chess delineated the following categories of temperament that are identifiable in early childhood and that influence personality development: activity level (the proportions of active and inactive periods during the day); rhythmicity (the predictability of such functions as hunger, feeding pattern, elmination, and the sleep-wake cycle); approach or withdrawal (speed and ease with which behavior is modified in response to altered environment); intensity of reaction (energy level); threshold of responsiveness (to sensory stimuli, the environment, and human relationships); quality of mood (pleasant and sociable versus unpleasant and unsociable); distractibility; and attention span and persistence.

DSM-III lists a number of identifiable personality disorders: paranoid, introverted, schizoid schizotypal, histrionic, narcissistic, antisocial, borderline, avoidant, dependent, compulsive, and passive-aggressive.

In addition to the official rubrics, there are other suggested personality classifications.

From a psychosomatic point of view, type A and type B personalities have been identified. Type A people show excessive ambition, a tendency to be overscheduled, overwhelming aggression, and impatience. They are particularly prone to myocardial infarction and probably many other somatic disorders. In contrast is the more easy-going, relaxed type B personality.

The Rip van Winkle personality defect occurs in one who has been out of touch with his environment for many years because of illness, family peculiarities, or social circumstance. When the patient comes to, he discovers that he is a stranger in a strange land, with a broken family, no social ties, and lost occupational skills. In certain family settings, the defect may present as an inhibition in the development of specific skills—social, athletic, mechanical, musical. These developmental omissions may contribute to lowered self-esteem. Successful treatment may call for a catching-up process by means of direct education.

"Existential neurosis" is associated with the conviction that life is meaningless, or with the chronic inability to believe in the importance or usefulness of anything one does. It is a state of nihilism, and is associated with the feeling that one is deliberately and self-consciously playing out a series of essentially empty roles to fulfill social obligations and body needs.

## Disturbances in Appearance

Excessive fastidiousness may suggest an obsessive-compulsive disorder. Deterioration from a previous normal level of neatness may be an early sign of depression or schizophrenia. When a female patient seeks to arouse sexual desire by her seductive dress and manner, a hysterical character disorder may be suspected. A sexually fearful woman may deliberately choose neutral or drab clothing to discourage the interest of potential sexual partners. Regressive clinging to childhood may be expressed in childish patterns of dress.

Rejection of normal sexual identity may be implied in the way adolescent boys and girls dress. Repulsive body odor due to lack of bathing has been called the "skunk maneuver," which is calculated to keep a frightening world at a safe distance. Paranoid patients may wear dark glasses so that they can spy on others without themselves being spied on. Eccentric patterns of dress, including unkempt beards, may become a badge of rebellion or conformity for membership in teenage groups.

Transvestites are sometimes acting out complex fantasies involving a wish to recapture a lost parent figure. Schizophrenic patients may first reveal the delusion of body change by complaining that a hat or a pair of eyeglasses no longer fits properly. Powerful automobiles and other possessions may be ego prostheses and serve to compensate for feelings of inferiority.

## REFERENCES

Barsky A J, Klerman G L: Hypochondriasis, bodily complaints and somatic styles. Am J Psychiatry *140:* 273, 1983.
Bender M B: *Disorders of Perception.* Charles C Thomas, Springfield, IL, 1952.
Bleuler E: *Dementia Praecox: The Group of Schizophrenias.* International Universities Press, New York, 1950.
Geschwind N: Aphasia. N Engl J Med *284:* 654, 1971.
Hollender M H, Callahan A S III: Erotamnia or de Clérambault syndrome. Arch Gen Psychiatry *32:* 1574, 1975.
Kety S S: What is schizophrenia? Schizophr Bull *8:* 597, 1982.
Kovacs M, Beck A T: Maladaptive cognitive structures in depression. Am J Psychiatry *135:* 525, 1978.
Linn L: Clinical manifestations of psychiatric disorders. In *Comprehensive Textbook of Psychiatry,* ed 4, H I Kaplan, B J Sadock, editors, p 550. Williams & Wilkins, Baltimore, 1985.
McLaughin J T: Primary and secondary process in the context of cerebral hemispheric specialization. Psychoanal Q *47:* 237, 1978.
Parkes C M: *Bereavement: Studies of Grief in Adult*

*Life.* International Universities Press, New York, 1972.

Stern R S, Cobb J P: Phenomenology of obsessive-compulsive neurosis. Br J Psychiatry *132:* 233, 1978.

Thomas A, Chess S, Birch H G, Korn K: *Behavioral Individuality in Early Childhood.* New York University Press, New York, 1963.

Thompson L J: Learning disabilities: an overview. Am J Psychiatry *130:* 393, 1973.

Weinstein E A, Kahn R L: *Denial of Illness.* Charles C Thomas, Springfield, IL, 1955.

Wing J K: The social context of schizophrenia. Am J Psychiatry *135:* 1333, 1978.

Winncott D W: Transitional objects and transitional phenomena. Int J Psychoanal *34:* 89, 1953.

## 8.2 TYPICAL SIGNS AND SYMPTOMS OF PSYCHIATRIC ILLNESS

I. **Consciousness:** state of awareness
   Apperception: perception modified by one's own emotions and thoughts
   Sensorium: state of functioning of the special senses
   Psychotic: gross impairment of reality testing
   A. *Disturbances of consciousness*
      1. Disorientation: disturbance of orientation as to time, place, or person
      2. Clouding of consciousness: incomplete clearmindedness with disturbance in perception and attitudes
      3. Stupor: lack of reaction to and unawareness of surroundings
      4. Delirium: bewildered, restless, confused, disoriented reaction associated with fear and hallucinations
      5. Coma: profound degree of unconsciousness
      6. Coma vigil: coma in which eyes remain open
      7. Dreamy state (twilight): disturbed consciousness with hallucinations
   B. *Disturbances of attention:* the amount of effort exerted in focusing on certain portions of an experience
      1. Distractibility: inability to concentrate attention
      2. Selective inattention: blocking out things that generate anxiety
   C. *Disturbances in suggestibility:* compliant and uncritical response to an idea or influence

1. *Folie á deux* (or *folie á trois*): communicated emotional illness between two (or three) persons
2. Hypnosis: artificially induced modification of consciousness

II. **Emotion:** A complex feeling state with psychic, somatic, and behavioral components that is related to affect and mood.
   A. *Affect:* the subjective and immediate experience of emotion attached to ideas. Affect has outward manifestations.
      1. Inappropriate affect: disharmony between the emotional feeling tone and the idea, thought, or speech accompanying it.
      2. Appropriate affect: emotional tone in harmony with the accompanying idea, thought, or speech.
      3. Blunted affect: a disturbance in affect manifestated by a severe reduction in the intensity of externalized feeling tone.
      4. Flat affect: absence or near absence of any signs of affective expression.
      5. Labile affect: rapid changes in emotional feeling tone, unrelated to external stimuli.
   B. *Mood:* a pervasive or sustained emotion
      1. Dysphoric mood: an unpleasant mood
      2. Euthymic mood: normal range mood
      3. Expansive mood: expression of one's feelings without restraint
      4. Irritable mood: easily annoyed and provoked to anger
      5. Mood swings: oscillations between periods of euphoria and depression or anxiety
      6. Elation: air of confidence and enjoyment associated with increased motor activity
      7. Exaltation: intense elation with feelings of grandeur
      8. Ecstasy: feeling of intense rapture
      9. Depression: psychopathological feeling of sadness
      10. Grief or mourning: sadness appropriate to a real loss
      11. Alexithymia: inability or difficulty in describing or being aware of one's emotions or moods
   C. *Other emotions*
      1. Anxiety: feeling of apprehension due to unconscious conflicts

2. Fear: anxiety due to consciously recognized and realistic danger
3. Agitation: anxiety associated with severe motor restlessness
4. Tension: increased motor and psychological activity that is unpleasant
5. Panic: acute intense attack of anxiety associated with personality disorganization
6. Free-floating anxiety: pervasive fear not attached to any idea
7. Apathy: dulled emotional tone associated with detachment or indifference
8. Ambivalence: coexistence of two opposing impulses toward the same thing in the same person at the same time
9. Depersonalization: feeling of unreality concerning oneself or one's environment
10. Derealization: distortion of spatial relationships so that the environment becomes unfamiliar
11. Aggression: forceful goal-directed action that may be verbal or physical and that is the motor counterpart of the affect of rage, anger, or hostility

III. **Motor behavior (conation):** the capacity to initiate action or motor discharge that concerns the basic strivings of a person as expressed through that person's behavior
   A. *Disturbances of conation*
   1. Echolalia: psychopathological repeating of words of one person by another
   2. Echopraxia: pathological imitation of movements of one person by another
   3. *Cerea flexibilitas* (waxy flexibility): state in which one maintains body position into which one is placed
   4. Catalepsy: state of unconsciousness in which immobile position is constantly maintained
   5. Command automatism: automatic following of suggestions
   6. Catatonic behavior: motor anomalies in non-organic disorders
      a. Excitement: excited motor activity
      b. Rigidity: assumption of an inappropriate posture
   7. Automatism: automatic performance of acts representative of unconscious symbolic activity
8. Cataplexy: temporary loss of muscle tone and weakness precipitated by a variety of emotional states
9. Stereotypy: continuous repetition of speech or physical activities
10. Negativism: frequent opposition to suggestions
11. Mannerisms: stereotyped involuntary movements
12. Verbigeration: meaningless repetitions of speech
13. Overactivity
   a. Psychomotor agitation: overactivity, usually nonproductive and in response to inner tension
   b. Hyperactivity (hyperkinesis): restless, aggressive, destructive activity
   c. Tic: spasmodic, repetitive motor movements
   d. Sleepwalking (somnambulism): motor activity during sleep
   e. Compulsion: uncontrollable impulse to perform an act repetitively
      (1) Dipsomania: compulsion to drink alcohol
      (2) Egomania: pathological self-preoccupation
      (3) Erotomania: pathological preoccupation with sex
      (4) Kleptomania: compulsion to steal
      (5) Megalomania: pathological sense of power
      (6) Monomania: preoccupation with a single subject
      (7) Nymphomania: excessive need for coitus in female
      (8) Satyriasis: excessive need for coitus in male
      (9) Trichotillomania: compulsion to pull out one's hair
      (10) Ritual: automatic activity compulsive in nature, emotional in origin
14. Hypoactivity (hypokinesis): decreased activity or retardation, as in psychomotor retardation; slowing of psychological and physical functioning
15. Mimicry: simple imitative motion activity of childhood

IV. **Thinking:** goal-directed flow of ideas, symbols, and associations initiated by a problem or tasks and leading toward a reality-oriented conclusion; when a logical sequence occurs, thinking is normal

A. *Disturbances in form of thinking*
  1. Formal thought disorder: thinking characterized by loosened associations, neologisms, and illogical constructs
  2. Illogical thinking: thinking containing erroneous conclusions or internal contradictions
  3. Dereism: mental activity not concordant with logic or experience
  4. Autistic thinking: thinking that gratifies unfulfilled desires but has no regard for reality; term used somewhat synonymously with dereism

B. *Disturbances in structure of associations*
  1. Neologism: new words created by the patient for psychological reasons
  2. Word salad: incoherent mixture of words and phrases
  3. Circumstantiality: digression of inappropriate thoughts into ideational processes, but patient eventually gets from desired point to desired goal
  4. Tangentiality: inability to have goal-directed associations of thought; patient never gets from desired point to desired goal
  5. Incoherence: running together of thoughts with no logical connection, resulting in disorganization
  6. Perseveration: psychopathological repetition of the same word or idea in response to different questions
  7. Condensation: fusion of various concepts into one
  8. Irrelevant answer: answer that is not in harmony with question asked
  9. Loosening of associations: flow of thought that is vague, unfocused, and illogical
  10. Derailment: gradual or sudden deviation in train of thought without blocking

C. *Disturbances in speed of associations*
  1. Flight of ideas: rapid verbalizations so that there is a shifting from one idea to another
  2. Clang associations: words similar in sound, but not in meaning, call up new thoughts
  3. Blocking: interruption in train of thinking, unconscious in origin
  4. Pressure of speech: voluble speech difficult to interrupt
  5. Volubility (logorrhea): copious, coherent, logical speech
  6. Poverty of speech: restriction in the amount of speech used
  7. Muddled speech: fluent speech in which elements of different thoughts are muddled together

D. *Disturbances in type of associations*
  1. Motor aphasia: disturbance of speech due to organic brain disorder in which understanding remains but ability to speak is lost
  2. Sensory aphasia: loss of ability to comprehend the meaning of words or the use of objects
  3. Nominal aphasia: difficulty in finding correct name for an object
  4. Syntactical aphasia: inability to arrange words in proper sequence

E. *Disturbances in content of thought*
  1. Magical thinking: belief that thoughts, words, or actions can prevent an occurrence by some mystical means
  2. Poverty of content of speech: speech that gives little information due to vagueness, empty repetitions, or obscure phrases
  3. Overvalued idea: false belief maintained with less than delusional thinking
  4. Delusion: false belief, not consistent with patient's intelligence and cultural background, that cannot be corrected by reasoning
    a. Bizarre delusion: an absurd, false belief
    b. Mood-congruent delusion: delusions whose content is mood appropriate
    c. Mood-incongruent delusion: delusions whose content is mood inappropriate
    d. Nihilistic delusion: false feeling that self, others, or the world is nonexistent
    e. Delusion of poverty: false belief that one lacks material possessions
    f. Somatic delusion: false belief involving functioning of one's body

g. Systemized delusion: false belief united by a single event or theme

h. Delusion of grandeur: exaggerated conception of one's importance

i. Delusion of persecution: false belief that one is being persecuted; often found in litigious patients

j Delusion of reference: false belief that the behavior of others refers to oneself; derived from ideas of reference in which one falsely feels one is being talked about by others

k. Delusion of self-accusation: false feeling of remorse

l. Delusion of control: false feeling that one is being controlled by others

m. Delusion of infidelity: false belief derived from pathological jealousy that one's lover is unfaithful

n. Paranoid delusions: oversuspiciousness leading to persecutory delusions

5. Trend or preoccupation of thought: centering of thought content around a particular idea, associated with a strong affective tone

6. Hypochondria: exaggerated concern over one's health that is not based on real organic pathology

7. Obsession: pathological persistence of an irresistible thought, feeling, or impulse that cannot be eliminated from consciousness by logical effort

8. Phobia: exaggerated and invariably pathological dread of some specific type of stimulus or situation

   a. Acrophobia: dread of high places
   b. Agoraphobia: dread of open places
   c. Algophobia: dread of pain
   d. Claustrophobia: dread of closed places
   e. Xenophobia: dread of strangers
   f. Zoophobia: dread of animals

V. **Perception**: awareness of objects and relations that follows stimulation of peripheral sense organs

A. *Disturbances associated with organic brain disease:* agnosia—an inability to recognize and interpret the significance of sensory impressions

B. *Disturbances associated with hysteria*: illnesses characterized by emotional conflict, the use of the defense mechanism of conversion, and the development of physical symptoms involving the voluntary muscles or special sense organs

   1. Hysterical anesthesia: loss of sensory modalities resulting from emotional conflicts
   2. Macropsia: state in which objects seem larger than they are
   3. Micropsia: state in which objects seem smaller than they are

C. *Hallucinations*: false sensory perceptions not associated with real external stimuli

   1. Hypnagogic hallucination: false sensory perception occurring while falling asleep
   2. Hypnopompic hallucination: hallucination occurring while awakening from sleep
   3. Auditory hallucination: false auditory perception
   4. Visual hallucination: false visual perception
   5. Olfactory hallucination: false perception in smell
   6. Gustatory hallucination: false perception of taste, such as unpleasant taste due to an uncinate fit
   7. Tactile (haptic) hallucination: false perception of movement or sensation, as from an amputated limb (phantom limb), crawling sensation on the skin (formication)
   8. Lilliputian hallucination: perception of objects as reduced in size
   9. Mood-congruent hallucination: hallucination whose content is mood appropriate
   10. Mood-incongruent hallucination: hallucination whose content is mood inappropriate

D. *Illusions:* false sensory perceptions of real external sensory stimuli

VI. **Memory:** function by which information stored in the brain is later recalled to consciousness

A. *Disturbances of memory*
   1. Amnesia: partial or total inability

to recall past experiences
2. Paramnesia: falsification of memory by distortion of recall
   a. *Fausse reconnaissance:* false recognition
   b. Retrospective falsification: recollection of a true memory to which the patient adds false details
   c. Confabulation: unconscious filling of gaps in memory by imagined or untrue experiences that patient believes but that have no basis in fact
   d. *Déjà vu:* illusion of visual recognition in which a new situation is incorrectly regarded as a repetition of a previous memory
   e. *Déjà entendu:* illusion of auditory recognition
   f. *Jamais vu:* false feeling of unfamiliarity with a real situation one has experienced

3. Hypermnesia: exaggerated degree of retention and recall

VII. **Intelligence:** the ability to understand, recall, mobilize, and integrate constructively previous learning in meeting new situations
   A. *Mental retardation:* lack of intelligence to a degree in which there is interference with social and vocational performance: mild (I.Q. of 52 to 67), moderate (I.Q. of 36 to 51), severe (I.Q. of 20 to 35), or profound (I.Q. below 20); obsolescent terms are idiot (mental age less than 3 years), imbecile (mental age of 3 to 7 years), and moron (mental age of 8 or more)
   B. *Dementia:* organic loss of mental function
   C. *Pseudodementia:* clinical features resembling a dementia not due to organic brain dysfunction, most often due to depression

# 9

# Classification in Psychiatry

## Introduction

Classification is the process by which the complexity of phenomena is reduced by arranging them into categories according to some established criteria for one or more purposes. A classification of mental disorders consists of a list of categories of specific mental disorders grouped into various classes on the basis of some shared characteristics.

## Validity

The validity of classification of mental disorders is the extent to which the entire classification and each of its specific diagnostic categories achieve the purposes of communication, control, and comprehension.

The literature dealing with the validity of mental disorders rarely distinguishes among the different types of validity. When certain types of validity are discussed, such as concurrent validity, the terminology is borrowed from the psychometric literature and applied in an inconsistent manner and without an appreciation of the differences in the subject matter to which it *is applied.* In psychometrics one is generally interested in how valid a particular procedure, such as an intelligence test, is for measuring a particular dimension of behavior, such as intelligence. That is different from the problem of assessing the validity of a classification of mental disorders in which it is necessary to distinguish between the validity of the procedure for making a diagnosis, such as the clinical diagnostic evaluation, and the validity of each of the categories themselves, such as schizophrenia and affective disorder.

Predictive validity is the extent to which knowledge that a person has a particular mental disorder is useful in predicting some aspects of the future for that person, such as subsequent course of the illness, complications, and response to treatment. Clearly, that kind of validity is most directly related to the major practical purposes of a classification of mental disorders, management and treatment.

Historically, it was largely on the basis of predictive validity that Kraepelin distinguished manic-depressive psychosis from dementia precox according to their differences in course. A more recent example is the demonstration of the relative specificity with which persons with bipolar disorder respond to treatment with lithium carbonate, providing predictive validity for the unipolar-bipolar distinction in the classification of affective disorders.

## Reliability

The reliability of a classification of mental disorders or of a specific diagnostic category is the extent to which users can agree on diagnoses applied to a series of cases. Strictly speaking, reliability is the extent to which subjects can be discriminated from each other. For that reason, a series of cases is required. If one examines the extent to which clinicians classify a single case in the same way, only agreement is determined.

Although a classification can be used reliably but may not be valid, the validity of a classification is limited by the extent to which it can be used reliably. If reliability is totally lacking, the system can have no validity. If reliability is present but only fair, there can be some validity, but that validity is limited. For that reason, it is not logical to require that reliability be good before a category is included in a classification of mental disorders for general use, as long as the category seems to have some type of validity. For example, even if a diagnosis of schizophrenia could be judged with only fair reliability, its inclusion in a classification is justified by the important treatment considerations implicit in making the diagnosis.

## DSM-III

### Basic Features

The official classification system as outlined in the American Psychiatric Association's *Diagnostic and Statistical Manual of Mental Disorders* (DSM-III), is generally atheoretical with regard to etiology with the exception of those few disorders in which the etiology or pathophysiological processes are known, such as the organic mental disorders. Thus, DSM-III attempts to describe comprehensively what the manifestations of the mental disorders are, and only rarely attempts to account for how the disturbances come about, unless the mechanism is included in the definition of the disorder. This general approach can be said to be descriptive in that the definitions of the disorders by and large consist of descriptions of the clinical features of the disorders.

**Diagnostic Criteria.** Specified diagnostic criteria are provided for each specific mental disorder. The only exception is the category of schizoaffective disorder.

**Multiaxial Evaluation.** DSM-III is a multiaxial system for evaluation that includes the following five axes: Axis I, clinical syndromes, and conditions not attributable to a mental disorder that are a focus of attention or treatment; Axis II, personality disorders and specific developmental disorders; Axis III, physical disorders or conditions; Axis IV, severity of psychosocial stressors; and Axis V, highest level of adaptive functioning during the past year.

Axes I and II comprise the mental disorders and conditions not attributable to a mental disorder that are a focus of attention or treatment. Axis III permits the clinician to indicate any current physical disorder or condition outside of the mental health disorders section of the World Health Organization's *International Classification of Diseases, Injuries and Causes of Death* (ICD-9). Table I outlines the DSM-III classification of mental disorders. Table II outlines the ICD-9 classification.

Axis IV provides a seven-point rating scale for coding the over-all severity of stress that is judged to have been a significant contributor to the development or exacerbation of the current disorder. Each scale level is anchored with examples for adults and for children and adolescents. The person's prognosis may be better when a disorder develops as a consequence of marked stress than when it develops after minimal or no stress (see Table III).

The rating of severity of stress should be based on the clinician's assessment of the stress that an average person with similar sociocultural values and circumstances would experience from the psychosocial stressors. That judgment involves a consideration of the amount of change in the person's life due to the stressor, the degree to which the event is desired and under the person's control, and the number of stressors. In addition, in certain settings it may be useful to note the specific psychosocial stressors. This

TABLE I
DSM-III CLASSIFICATION: AXES I AND II
CATEGORIES AND CODES

*All official DSM-III codes and terms are included in ICD-9. However, in order to differentiate those DSM-III categories that use the same ICD-9 codes, unofficial non-ICD-9 codes are provided in parentheses for use when greater specificity is necessary. The long dashes indicate the need for a fifth-digit subtype or other qualifying term.*

**DISORDERS USUALLY FIRST EVIDENT IN INFANCY, CHILDHOOD OR ADOLESCENCE**

**Mental retardation**
(Code in fifth digit: 1 = with other behavioral symptoms [requiring attention or treatment and that are not part of another disorder]; 0 = without other behavioral symptoms
317.0(x)  Mild mental retardation, __
318.0(x)  Moderate mental retardation, __
318.1(x)  Severe mental retardation, __
318.2(x)  Profound mental retardation, __
319.0(x)  Unspecified mental retardation, __

**Attention deficit disorder**
314.01 with hyperactivity
314.00 without hyperactivity
314.80 residual type

**Conduct disorder**
312.00 undersocialized aggressive
312.10 undersocialized, nonaggressive
312.23 socialized, aggressive
312.21 socialized, nonaggressive
312.90 atypical

**Anxiety disorders of childhood or adolescence**
309.21 Separation anxiety disorder
313.21 Avoidant disorder of childhood or adolescence
313.00 Overanxious disorder

**Other disorders of infancy, childhood or adolescence**
313.89 Reactive attachment disorder of infancy
313.22 Schizoid disorder of childhood or adolescence
313.23 Elective mutism
313.81 Oppositional disorder
313.82 Identity disorder

**Eating disorders**
307.10 Anorexia nervosa
307.51 Bulimia
307.52 Pica
307.53 Rumination disorder of infancy
307.50 Atypical eating disorder

**Stereotyped movement disorders**
307.21 Transient tic disorder
307.22 Chronic motor tic disorder
307.23 Tourette's disorder
307.20 Atypical tic disorder
307.30 Atypical stereotyped movement disorder

**Other disorders with physical manifestation**
307.00 Stuttering
307.60 Functional enuresis
307.70 Functional encopresis
307.46 Sleepwalking disorder
307.46 Sleep terror disorder (307.49)

**Pervasive developmental disorders**
Code in fifth digit: 0 = full syndrome present; 1 = residual state.
299.0x Infantile autism,

299.9x Childhood onset pervasive developmental disorder, —
299.8x Atypical, —

**Specific developmental disorders**
**Note: These are coded on Axis II.**
315.00 Developmental reading disorder
315.10 Developmental arithmetic disorder
315.31 Developmental language disorder
315.39 Developmental articulation disorder
315.50 Mixed specific development disorder
315.90 Atypical specific developmental disorder

**ORGANIC MENTAL DISORDERS**
**Section 1. Organic mental disorders whose etiology or pathophysiological process is listed below (taken from the mental disorders section of ICD-9).**

**Senile and presenile dementias**
Primary degenerative dementia, senile onset,
290.30 with delirium
290.20 with delusions
290.21 with depression
290.00 uncomplicated
Code in fifth digit: 0 = uncomplicated; 1 = with delirium; 2 = with delusions; 3 = with depression.
290.1x Primary degenerative dementia, presenile onset, —
290.4x Multi-infarct dementia, —

**Substance-induced**
**Alcohol**
303.00 intoxication
291.40 idiosyncratic intoxication
291.80 withdrawal
291.00 withdrawal delirium
291.30 hallucinosis
291.10 amnestic disorder
Code severity of dementia in fifth digit: 1 = mild; 2 = moderate; 3 = servere; 0 = unspecified.
291.2x Dementia associated with alcoholism, —
**Barbiturate or similarly acting sedative or**
**hypnotic**
305.40 intoxication (327.00)
292.00 withdrawal (327.01)
292.00 withdrawal delirium (327.02)
292.83 amnestic disorder (327.04)
**Opioid**
305.50 intoxication (327.10)
292.00 withdrawal (327.11)
**Cocaine**
305.60 intoxication (327.20)
**Amphetamine or similarly acting sympathomimetic**
305.70 intoxication (327.35)
292.81 delirium (327.32)
292.11 delusional disorder (327.35)
292.00 withdrawal (327.31)
**Phencyclidine (PCP) or similarly acting arylcyclohexylamine**
305.90 intoxication (327.40)
292.90 mixed organic mental disorder (327.49)
**Hallucinogen**
305.30 hallucinosis (327.56)
292.11 delusional disorder (327.55)
292.84 affective disorder (327.57)
**Cannabis**
305.20 intoxication (327.60)
292.11 delusional disorder (327.65)
**Tobacco**
292.00 withdrawal (327.71)
**Caffeine**
305.90 intoxication (327.80)

**Other or unspecified substance**
305.90 intoxication (327.90)
292.00 withdrawal (327.91)
292.81 delirium (327.92)
292.82 dementia (327.93)
292.83 amnestic disorder (327.94)
292.11 delusional disorder (327.95)
292.12 hallucinosis (327.96)
292.84 affective disorder (327.97)
292.89 personality disorder (327.98)
292.90 atypical or mixed organic mental disorder (327.99)

**Section 2. Organic brain syndrome whose etiology or pathophysiological process is either noted as an additional diagnosis from outside the mental disorders section of ICD-9 or is unknown.**
293.00 Delirium
294.10 Dementia
294.00 Amnestic syndrome
293.81 Organic delusional syndrome
293.82 Organic hallucinosis
293.83 Organic affective syndrome
310.10 Organic personality syndrome
294.80 Atypical or mixed organic brain syndrome

**SUBSTANCE USE DISORDERS**
Code in fifth digit: 1 = continuous; 2 = episodic; 3 = in remission; 0 = unspecified.
305.0x Alcohol abuse, —
303.9x Alcohol dependence (Alcoholism), —
305.4x Barbiturate or similary acting sedative or hypnotic abuse, —
304.1x Barbiturate or similarly acting sedative or hypnotic dependence, —
305.5x Opioid abuse, —
304.0x Opioid dependence, —
305.6x Cocaine abuse, —
305.7x Amphetamine or similary acting sympathomimetic abuse, —
304.4x Amphetamine or similary acting sympathomimetic dependence, —
305.9x Phencyclidine (PCP) or similarly acting arylcyclohexylamine abuse, — (328.4x)
305.3x Hallucinogen abuse, —
305.2x Cannabis abuse, —
304.3x Cannabis dependence, —
305.1x Tobacco dependence, —
305.9x Other, mixed or unspecified substance abuse,

304.6x Other specified substance dependence, —
304.9x Unspecified substance dependence, —
304.7x Dependence on combination of opioid and other non-alcoholic substance, —
304.8x Dependence on combination of substances, excluding opioids and alcohol, —

**SCHIZOPHRENIC DISORDERS**
Code in fifth digit: 1 = subchronic; 2 = chronic; 3 = subchronic with acute exacerbation; 4 = chronic with acute exacerbation; 5 = in remission; 0 = unspecified.
Schizophrenia,
295.1x disorganized, —
295.2x catatonic, —
295.3x paranoid, —
295.9x undifferentiated, —
295.6x residual, —

**PARANOID DISORDERS**
297.10 Paranoia
297.30 Shared paranoid disorder
298.30 Acute paranoid disorder
297.90 Atypical paranoid disorder

TABLE I *continued*

## PSYCHOTIC DISORDERS NOT ELSEWHERE CLASSIFIED
295.40 Schizophreniform disorder
298.80 Brief reactive psychosis
295.70 Schizoaffective disorder
298.90 Atypical psychosis

**NEUROTIC DISORDERS: These are included in Affective, Anxiety, Somatoform, Dissociative and Psychosexual Disorders. In order to facilitate the identification of the categories that in DSM-II were grouped together in the class of Neuroses, the DSM-II terms are included separately in parentheses after the corresponding categories. These DSM-II terms are included in ICD-9-CM and therefore are acceptable as alternatives to the recommended DSM-III terms that precede them.**

## AFFECTIVE DISORDERS
**Major affective disorders**
Code major depressive episode in fifth digit: 6 = in remission; 4 = psychotic features (the unofficial non-ICD-9-CM fifth digit 7 may be used instead to indicate that the psychotic features are mood-incongruent); 3 = with melancholia; 2 = without melancholia; 0 = unspecified

Code manic episode in fifth digit: 6 = in remission; 4 = with psychotic features (the unofficial non-ICD-9-CM fifth digit 7 may be used instead to indicate that the psychotic features are mood-incongruent), 2 = without psychotic features, 0 = unspecified.
    **Bipolar disorder,**
296.6x mixed, —
296.4x manic, —
296.5x depressed, —
    **Major depression,**
296.2x single episode, —
296.3x recurrent, —

**Other specific affective disorders**
301.13 Cyclothymic disorder
300.40 Dysthymic disorder (or Depressive neurosis)

**Atypical affective disorders**
296.70 Atypical bipolar disorder
296.82 Atypical depression

## ANXIETY DISORDERS
    **Phobic disorders (or Phobic neuroses)**
300.21 Agoraphobia with panic attacks
300.22 Agoraphobia without panic attacks
300.23 Social phobia
300.29 Simple phobia
    **Anxiety states (or Anxiety neuroses)**
300.01 Panic disorders
300.02 Generalized anxiety disorder
300.30 Obsessive compulsive disorder (or Obsessive compulsive neurosis)
    **Post-traumatic stress disorder**
308.30 acute
309.81 chronic or delayed
300.0 Atypical anxiety disorder

## SOMATOFORM DISORDERS
308.81 Somatization disorder
300.11 Conversion disorder (or Hysterical neurosis, conversion type)
307.80 Psychogenic pain disorder
300.70 Hypochondriasis (or Hypochondriacal neurosis)

300.70 Atypical somatoform disorder (300.71)

## DISSOCIATIVE DISORDERS (OR HYSTERICAL NEUROSES, DISSOCIATIVE TYPE)
300.12 Psychogenic amnesia
300.13 Psychogenic fugue
300.14 Multiple personality
300.60 Depersonalization disorder (or Depersonalization neurosis)
300.15 Atypical dissociative disorder

## PSYCHOSEXUAL DISORDERS
**Gender identity disorders**
Indicate sexual history in the fifth digit of Transsexualism code; 1 = asexual; 2 = homosexual; 3 = heterosexual; 0 = uspecified.
302.5x Transsexualism, —
302.60 Gender identity disorder of childhood
302.85 Atypical gender identity disorder

**Paraphilias**
302.81 Fetishism
302.30 Transvestism
302.10 Zoophilia
302.20 Pedophilia
302.40 Exhibitionism
302.82 Voyeurism
302.83 Sexual masochism
302.84 Sexual sadism
302.89 Atypical paraphilia

**Psychosexual dysfunctions**
302.71 Inhibited sexual desire
302.72 Inhibited sexual excitement
302.73 Inhibited female orgasm
302.74 Inhibited male orgasm
302.75 Premature ejaculation
302.76 Functional dyspareunia
306.51 Functional vaginismus
302.79 Atypical psychosexual dysfunction

**Other psychosexual disorders**
302.00 Ego-dystonic homosexuality
302.90 Psychosexual disorder not elsewhere classified

## FACTITIOUS DISORDERS
300.16 Factitious disorder with psychological symptoms
301.51 Chronic factitious disorder with physical symptoms
300.19 Atypical factitious disorder with physical symptoms

## DISORDERS OF IMPULSE CONTROL NOT ELSEWHERE CLASSIFIED
312.31 Pathological gambling
312.32 Kleptomania
312.33 Pyromania
312.34 Intermittent explosive disorder
312.35 Isolated explosive disorder
312.39 Atypical impulse control disorder

## ADJUSTMENT DISORDER
309.00 with depressed mood
309.24 with anxious mood
309.28 with mixed emotional features
309.30 with disturbance of conduct
309.40 with mixed disturbance of emotions and conduct
309.23 with work (or academic) inhibition
309.83 with withdrawal

309.90 with atypical features

## PSYCHOLOGICAL FACTORS AFFECTING PHYSICAL CONDITION
Specify physical condition on Axis III.
316.00 Psychological factors affecting physical condition

## PERSONALITY DISORDERS
**Note: These are coded on Axis II.**
301.00 Paranoid
301.20 Schizoid
301.22 Schizotypal
301.50 Histrionic
301.81 Narcissistic
301.70 Antisocial
301.83 Borderline
301.82 Avoidant
301.60 Dependent
301.40 Compulsive
301.84 Passive-Aggressive
301.89 Atypical, mixed or other personality disorder

## V CODES FOR CONDITIONS NOT ATTRIBUTABLE TO A MENTAL DISORDER THAT ARE A FOCUS OF ATTENTION OR TREATMENT
V65.20 Malingering
V62.89 Borderline intellectual functioning (V62.88)
V71.01 Adult antisocial behavior
V71.02 Childhood or adolescent antisocial behavior
V62.30 Academic problem
V62.20 Occupational problem
V62.82 Uncomplicated bereavement
V15.81 Noncompliance with medical treatment
V62.89 Phase of life problem or other life circumstance problem
V61.10 Marital problem
V61.20 Parent-child problem
V61.80 Other specified family circumstances
V62.81 Other interpersonal problem

## ADDITIONAL CODES
300.99 Unspecified mental disorder (nonpsychotic)
V71.07 No diagnosis or condition on Axis I
799.91 Diagnosis or condition deferred on Axis I

V71.08 No diagnosis on Axis II
799.92 Diagnosis deferred on Axis II
  * From American Psychiatric Association: *Diagnostic and Statistical Manual of Mental Disorders*, ed 3. American Psychiatric Association, Washington, DC, 1980. Used with permission.

information may be important in formulating a treatment plan that includes attempts to remove the psychosocial stressors or to help the person cope with them.

Axis V permits the clinician to indicate his or her judgment of the person's highest level of adaptive functioning, for at least a few months, during the past year. A seven-point rating scale is provided, and it is anchored with examples for adults and for children and adolescents. Adaptive functioning is conceptualized as a composite of three major areas: social relations, oc-

TABLE II
ICD-9 CLASSIFICATION OF MENTAL DISORDERS

## ORGANIC PSYCHOTIC CONDITIONS
**Senile and pre-senile organic psychotic conditions**
290.0 Senile dementia, simple type
290.1 Pre-senile dementia
290.2 Senile dementia, depressed or paranoid type
290.3 Senile dementia with acute confusional state
290.4 Arteriosclerotic dementia
290.8 Other
290.9 Unspecified

**Alcoholic psychoses**
291.0 Delirium tremens
291.1 Korsakov's psychosis, alcoholic
291.2 Other alcoholic dementia
291.3 Other alcoholic hallucinosis
291.4 Pathological drunkenness
291.5 Alcoholic jealousy
291.8 Other
291.9 Unspecified

**Drug psychoses**
292.0 Drug withdrawal syndrome
292.1 Paranoid and/or hallucinatory states induced by drugs
292.2 Pathological drug intoxication
292.8 Other
292.9 Unspecified

**Transient organic psychotic conditions**
293.0 Acute confusional state
293.1 Subacute confusional state
293.8 Other
293.9 Unspecified

**Other organic psychotic conditions (chronic)**
294.0 Korsakov's psychosis (non-alcoholic)
294.1 Dementia in conditions classified elsewhere
294.8 Other
294.9 Unspecified

## OTHER PSYCHOSES
**Schizophrenic psychoses**
295.0 Simple type
295.1 Hebephrenic type
295.2 Catatonic type
295.3 Paranoid type
295.4 Acute schizophrenic episode
295.5 Latent schizophrenia
295.6 Residual schizophrenia
295.7 Schizo-affective type
295.8 Other
295.9 Unspecified

**Affective psychoses**
296.0 Manic-depressive psychosis, manic type
296.1 Manic-depressive psychosis, depressed type
296.2 Manic-depressive psychosis, circular type but currently manic

TABLE II *continued*

296.3 Manic-depressive psychosis, circular type but currently depressed
296.4 Manic-depressive psychosis, circular type, mixed
296.5 Manic-depressive psychosis, circular type, current condition not specified
296.6 Manic-depressive psychosis, other and unspecified
296.8 Other
296.9 Unspecified

**Paranoid states**
297.0 Paranoid state, simple
297.1 Paranoia
297.2 Paraphrenia
297.3 Induced psychosis
297.8 Other
297.9 Unspecified

**Other nonorganic psychoses**
298.0 Depressive type
298.1 Excitative type
298.2 Reactive confusion
298.3 Acute paranoid reaction
298.4 Psychogenic paranoid psychosis
298.8 Other and unspecified reactive psychosis
298.9 Unspecified psychosis

**Psychoses with origin specific to childhood**
299.0 Infantile autism
299.1 Disintegrative psychosis
299.8 Other
299.9 Unspecified

**NEUROTIC DISORDERS, PERSONALITY DISORDERS, AND OTHER NONPSYCHOTIC MENTAL DISORDERS**
**Neurotic disorders**
300.0 Anxiety states
300.1 Hysteria
300.2 Phobic state
300.3 Obsessive-compulsive disorder
300.4 Neurotic depression
300.5 Neurasthenia
300.6 Depersonalization syndrome
300.7 Hypochondriasis
300.8 Other
300.9 Unspecified

**Personality disorders**
301.0 Paranoid
301.1 Affective
301.2 Schizoid
301.3 Explosive
301.4 Anankastic
301.5 Hysterical
301.6 Asthenic
301.7 With predominantly sociopathic or asocial manifestations
301.8 Other
301.9 Unspecified

**Sexual deviations and disorders**
302.0 Homosexuality
302.1 Bestiality
302.2 Paedophilia
302.3 Transvestism
302.4 Exhibitionism
302.5 Transsexualism
302.6 Disorders of psychosexual identity
302.7 Frigidity and impotence
302.8 Other
302.9 Unspecified

**303.     Alcohol dependence**

**Drug dependence**
304.0 Morphine type
304.1 Barbiturate type
304.2 Cocaine
304.3 Cannabis
304.4 Amphetamine type and other psychostimulants
304.5 Hallucinogens
304.6 Other
304.7 Combinations of morphine type drug with any other
304.8 Combinations excluding morphine type drug
304.9 Unspecified

**Nondependent abuse of drugs**
305.0 Alcohol
305.1 Tobacco
305.2 Cannabis
305.3 Hallucinogens
305.4 Barbiturates and tranquilizers
305.5 Morphine type
305.6 Cocaine type
305.7 Amphetamine type
305.8 Antidepressants
305.9 Other, mixed or unspecified

**Physical conditions arising from mental factors**
306.0 Musculoskeletal
306.1 Respiratory
306.2 Cardiovascular
306.3 Skin
306.4 Gastro-intestinal
306.5 Genito-urinary
306.6 Endocrine
306.7 Organs of special sense
306.8 Other
306.9 Unspecified

**Special symptoms or syndromes not elsewhere classified**
307.0 Stammering and stuttering
307.1 Anorexia nervosa
307.2 Tics
307.3 Stereotyped-repetitive movements
307.4 Specific disorders of sleep
307.5 Other disorders of eating
307.6 Enuresis
307.7 Encopresis
307.8 Psychalgia
307.9 Other and unspecified

**Acute reaction to stress**
308.0 Predominant disturbances of emotions
308.1 Predominant disturbances of consciousness
308.2 Predominant psychomotor disturbance
308.3 Other
308.4 Mixed
308.9 Unspecified

**Adjustment reaction**
309.0 Brief depressive reaction
309.1 Prolonged depressive
    reaction
309.2 With predominant
    disturbance of other
    emotions
309.3 With predominant
    disturbance of conduct
309.4 With mixed disturbance of
    emotions and conduct
309.8 Other
309.9 Unspecified

**Specific nonpsychotic mental
disorders following organic
brain damage**
310.0 Frontal lobe syndrome
310.1 Cognitive or personality
    change of other type
310.2 Postconcussional
    syndrome
310.8 Other
310.9 Unspecified

**311. Depressive disorder,
not elsewhere classified**

**Disturbance of conduct not
elsewhere classified**
312.0 Unsocialized disturbance
    of conduct
312.1 Socialized disturbance of
    conduct
312.2 Compulsive conduct
    disorder
312.3 Mixed disturbance of
    conduct and emotions
312.8 Other
312.9 Unspecified

**Disturbance of emotions
specific to childhood and
adolescence**
313.0 With anxiety and
    fearfulness
313.1 With misery and
    unhappiness
313.2 With sensitivity, shyness
    and social withdrawal
313.3 Relationship problems
313.8 Other or mixed
313.9 Unspecified

**Hyperkinetic syndrome of
childhood**
314.0 Simple disturbance of
    activity and attention
314.1 Hyperkinesis with
    developmental delay
314.2 Hyperkinetic conduct
    disorder
314.8 Other
314.9 Unspecified

**Specific delays in
development**
315.0 Specific reading
    retardation
315.1 Specific arithmetical
    retardation
315.2 Other specific learning
    difficulties
315.3 Developmental speech or
    language disorder
315.4 Specific motor retardation
315.5 Mixed development
    disorder
315.8 Other
315.9 Unspecified

**316. Psychic factors
associated with
diseases classified
elsewhere**

**317. Mild mental
retardation**

**Other specified mental
retardation**
318.0 Moderate mental
    retardation
318.1 Severe mental retardation
318.2 Profound mental
    retardation

**319. Unspecified mental
retardation**

---

\* From World Health Organization: *Manual of the
International Classification of Diseases, Injuries, and
Causes of Death*, rev. 9. World Health Organization,
Geneva, 1978. Used with permission.

cupational functioning, and the use of leisure
time (see Table IV).

An example of the results of a DSM-III multiaxial evaluation follows:

Axis I: 303.92 Alcohol dependence, episodic

Axis II: 301.60 Dependent personality disorder

Axis III: Alcoholic cirrhosis of liver

Axis IV: Psychosocial stressors: anticipated
retirement and change in residence with loss of
contact with friends. Severity: 4 moderate

Axis V: Highest level of adaptive functioning
past year: 3 good

**Systematic Description.** The text of DSM-
III systematically describes each disorder in
terms of current knowledge in the following
areas: essential features, associated features, age
at onset, course, impairment, complications,
predisposing factors, prevalence, sex ratio, familial pattern, and differential diagnosis.

### Classification of Mental Disorders

Table I presents the DSM-III classification of
mental disorders (Axes I and II). Table II presents the ICD-9 classification of mental disorders. There are 16 major diagnostic classes and
a total of 187 specific diagnostic categories in
DSM-III. Although one of the criticisms of
DSM-III has been the proliferation of diagnostic
categories, DSM-II had 146 specific categories.
Thus, the difference between DSM-II and DSM-
III is rather small, far smaller than the average
increase in the number of specific diagnostic
categories for other sections of ICD-8 and ICD-
9 CM.

**Disorders Usually First Evident in In-
fancy, Childhood, or Adolescence.** The disorders in this section are those that usually arise

TABLE III

USE OF AXIS IV: RATING EXAMPLES OF PSYCHOSOCIAL STRESSORS*†

| Code | Term | Adult Example | Child or Adolescent Example |
|------|------|---------------|------------------------------|
| 1 | None | None Apparent. | None Apparent. |
| 2 | Minimal | Small bank loan; minor violation of the law. | Vacation with family. |
| 3 | Mild | Change in residence; change in working hours or conditions. | New school year; change in day care center; insufficient parental control. |
| 4 | Moderate | Death of close friend; new career; sexual difficulties. | Change to new school; birth of a sibling; illness of close relative. |
| 5 | Severe | Personal injury or illness; marriage; marital separation; major financial loss; fired from job. | Divorce of parents; hospitalization; major illness in family member; arrest; harsh and persistent parental discipline. |
| 6 | Extreme | Divorce; death of a spouse or child; jail term. | Death of parent or sibling; physical or sexual abuse, severe injury or illness resulting in paralysis or loss of a limb. |
| 7 | Catastrophic | Devastating natural disaster; multiple family deaths; concentration camp experience. | Multiple family deaths. |
| 0 | Unspecified | No information or not applicable. | No information or not applicable. |

* These examples represent relative severity of stressors, not their cumulative effect.
† From Webb L J, et al.: editors: *DSM-III Training Guide*. Brunner/Mazel, New York, 1981.

TABLE IV
USE OF AXIS V: RATING SCALE AND EXAMPLES FOR USE OF AXIS V*

| Level | Adult Example | Child or Adolescent Example |
|---|---|---|
| **1 SUPERIOR**—Unusually effective functioning in social relations, occupational functioning, and use of leisure time. No distress associated with occupational functioning. | A single parent functions extremely well on the job, takes excellent care of the children, has several close friends, and pursues an interest in music. | A 12-year old gets excellent grades in school, has numerous friends, and excels in soccer and swimming. |
| **2 VERY GOOD**—Better than average functioning in social relations, occupational functioning, and use of leisure time. | A single parent does all of the above but complains of feeling stressed on the job. | A 12-year-old does all of the above but complains of some distress in keeping up with both school and sports. |
| **3 GOOD**—No more than slight impairment in either social or occupational functioning. | A single parent functions well on the job, takes excellent care of the children, has several close friends, but has no leisure interests or pursuits. | A 12-year-old participates in school activities and sports, has numerous friends, but has some difficulty maintainng a C average in school. |
| **4 FAIR**—Moderate impairment in either social relations or occupational functioning, or some impairment in both. | A single parent has difficulty carrying through with job assignments and has several acquaintances, but no close friends. | A 12-year-old gets average grades in school, has only one friend, and does not participate in any social activities. |
| **5 POOR**—Marked impairment in either social relations or occupational functioning, or moderate impairment in both. | A single parent has difficulty keeping a job for more than a few weeks. | A 12-year-old has no friends and is getting failing grades in two subjects at school. |
| **6 VERY POOR**—Marked impairment in both social relations and occupational functioning. | A single parent has difficulty keeping a job for more than a few weeks, has no close friends or acquaintances, and has frequent angry outbursts with neighbors and family. | A 12-year-old has no friends and is failing in all subjects at school. |
| **7 GROSSLY IMPAIRED**—Gross impairment in virtually all areas of functioning. | A single parent is unable to care for the home or children, does not attend to personal hygiene, and is usually incoherent. | A 12-year-old is unable to attend school, is unable to attend to personal hygiene, and refuses to talk to family or friends. |
| **0 UNSPECIFIED** | No information. | No information. |

* From Webb L J, et al.: editors: *DSM-III Training Guide*. Brunner/Mazel, New York, 1981.

and first manifest themselves in infancy, childhood, or adolescence. This class appears first in the classification to encourage clinicians to first consider these disorders when diagnosing adults. And, disorders from the other sections of the classification are often appropriate for children or adolescents. In ICD-9 the disorders that relate to childhood are not grouped together.

The minor classes of disorders in this section can be grouped into the following five major groups, based on the predominant area of disturbance: (1) intellectual (mental retardation); (2) behavioral (overt) (attention deficit disorder, conduct disorder); (3) emotional (anxiety disorders of childhood or adolescence; other disorders of infancy, childhood, or adolescence); (4) physical (eating disorders, stereotyped movement disorders, other disorders with physical manifestations); and (5) developmental (pervasive developmental disorders, specific developmental disorders).

**Organic Mental Disorders.** The essential feature of all these disorders is a psychological or behavioral disturbance that is due to transient or permanent dysfunction of the brain. DSM-III recognizes the following organic brain syndromes: (1) delirium and dementia, with relatively global cognitive impairment; (2) amnestic syndrome and organic hallucinosis, with relatively selective areas of cognitive impairment;

(3) organic delusional syndrome and organic affective syndrome, with features resembling schizophrenic or affective disorders; (4) organic personality syndrome with features affecting the personality; (5) intoxication and withdrawal, associated with drug ingestion or cessation and not meeting the criteria for any of the previous syndromes; strictly speaking, these two categories are defined by etiology rather than syndromally; and (6) other organic brain syndrome, a residual category for any other organic brain syndrome not classifiable as any of the previous syndromes.

The organic mental disorders contain two sections. Section 1 includes those disorders in which the etiology or the pathophysiological process involves either aging (senile and presenile dementias, such as multiinfarct dementia) or the ingestion of a substance (substance-induced organic brain syndromes, such as opioid intoxication). Section 2 includes organic brain syndromes whose etiology or pathophysiological process is either noted as an additional diagnosis from outside the mental disorders section of ICD-9—for example, delirium due to pneumonia—or is unknown. ICD-9 does not specifically recognize many of the DSM-III organic mental syndromes such as organic affective and organic delusional syndromes.

**Substance Use Disorders.** This section of the classification includes disorders in which behavioral changes are caused by taking substances that affect the central nervous system, and that in almost all subcultures are viewed as extremely undesirable. The categories of substance abuse are defined by a minimal duration of use (1 month), social complications of use (such as impairment in social or occupational functioning), and a pathological pattern of use (such as the inability to cut down or stop use, remaining intoxicated throughout the day). Substance dependence is generally defined by the presence of either tolerance or withdrawal.

**Schizophrenic Disorders.** As defined in DSM-III, at some time during the illness a schizophrenic disorder always involves at least one of the following: delusions, hallucinations, or certain characteristic disturbances in the form of thought. No single clinical feature is unique to schizophrenia or evident in every case or at every phase of the illness, except that, by definition, the diagnosis is not made unless the period of illness, including the prodromal and residual phases, has persisted for at least 6 months.

The following phenomenological subtypes are recognized: disorganized, catatonic, paranoid, undifferentiated, and residual. In addition, the course of the illness is coded as subchronic, chronic, subchronic with acute exacerbation, chronic with acute exacerbation, and in remission.

In ICD-9, the concept of Schizophrenia is much broader than in DSM-III. First of all, there is no duration requirement and presumably the diagnosis can be made on the basis of a cross-sectional symptom picture. Secondly, there is no requirement of an active psychotic phase and thus both simple and a latent subtype are included for such cases. (Those cases would probably be diagnosed in DSM-III as having schizotypal or borderline personality disorder.) In ICD-9 there is a schizoaffective type of schizophrenia whereas in DSM-III schizoaffective disorder is classified separately from both schizophrenia and affective disorder.

**Paranoid Disorders.** The essential feature is a clinical picture in which the predominant symptoms are persistent persecutory delusions, or delusions of jealousy that are not explainable by some other psychotic disorder. There are three specific paranoid disorders: paranoia, shared paranoid disorder, and acute paranoid disorder.

In ICD-9, paranoid disorders are not limited to persecutory delusions or delusions of jealousy and can be diagnosed on the basis of grandiose or somatic delusions as well. ICD-9 includes within the group of paranoid states paraphrenia, for paranoid psychoses in which there are conspicuous hallucinations and no deterioration in personality functioning. Such cases in DSM-III would probably be diagnosed as having atypical psychosis, since the presence of prominent hallucinations would rule out the diagnosis of a paranoid disorder.

**Psychotic Disorders Not Elsewhere Classified.** This is a residual class for psychotic disorders that are not classified as an organic mental disorder, a schizophrenic disorder, a paranoid disorder, or an affective disorder. It contains three specific categories: schizophreniform disorder, brief reactive psychosis, and schizoaffective disorder.

**Affective Disorders.** The essential feature of this group of disorders is a disturbance of mood accompanied by related symptoms. This major class contains two specific minor classes. The first, major affective disorders, includes bipolar disorder and major depression. Bipolar disorder is subdivided according to the current episode as mixed, manic, or depressed. Major depression is subdivided according to whether the disturbance is a single episode or recurrent.

There is also provision for further characterizing the current episode as in remission, with psychotic features, with or without melancholia (for a major depressive episode), and without psychotic features (for manic episodes). The second minor class, other specific affective disorders, includes cyclothymic disorder and dysthymic disorder (chronic mild depression).

In ICD-9, most of the affective disorders are called manic-depressive psychoses and are grouped together under the rubric of affective psychoses. Thus, the unipolar-bipolar distinction of DSM-III is not used. Other affective disorders in ICD-9 are scattered throughout the classification and include neurotic depression, affective personality disorder, and brief and prolonged depressive reactions. Whereas DSM-III encourages the use of the adult category of major depression for children when appropriate, in ICD-9 there is a separate category for such cases, disturbances of emotions specific to childhood and adolescence with misery and unhappiness.

**Anxiety Disorders.** In this group of disorders, some form of anxiety is the most predominant disturbance, or is experienced if the person tries to resist giving in to his or her symptoms.

Phobic disorders are characterized by persistent avoidance behavior secondary to irrational fears of a specific object, activity, or situation. In anxiety states, the predominant disturbance is the experience of anxiety itself, which may be episodic, as in panic disorder, or chronic and persistent, as in generalized anxiety disorder. In obsessive-compulsive disorder, there are recurrent obsessions or compulsions or both. In post-traumatic stress disorder, the essential feature is the development of characteristic symptoms after experiencing a psychologically traumatic event or events that are outside the range of human experience usually considered to be normal.

**Somatoform Disorders.** In this class, all the disorders involve physical symptoms suggesting physical disorder for which no demonstrable organic findings are adequate to explain the symptoms, and for which positive evidence or a strong presumption indicates that the symptoms are linked to psychological factors or conflicts. The first disorder in this category is somatization disorder, a chronic polysymptomatic disorder that begins early in life. The second disorder is conversion disorder, in which the predominant disturbance is conversion symptoms that are not symptomatic of another disorder. Psychogenic pain disorder is for psychologically induced pain not attributable to any other mental or physical disorder. Hypochon-

driasis involves an unrealistic and persistent interpretation of physical symptoms or sensations as abnormal, leading to the preoccupation with the fear or belief of having a serious disease.

**Dissociative Disorders.** The essential feature of these disorders is a sudden, temporary alteration in the normally integrated functions of consciousness, identity, or motor behavior. This class includes psychogenic amnesia, psychogenic fugue, multiple personality, and depersonalization disorder.

**Psychosexual Disorders.** There are four minor classes: gender identity disorders, characterized by the person's feelings of discomfort and inappropriateness about his or her anatomical sex and by persistent behaviors generally associated with the other sex; paraphilias, characterized by arousal in response to sexual objects or situations that are not part of normative arousal-activity patterns; psychosexual dysfunctions, characterized by inhibition in sexual desire or the psychophysiological changes that characterize the sexual response cycle; and other psychosexual disorders, which include ego-dystonic homosexuality.

In ICD-9 all of the sexual disorders are grouped together; in ICD-9 the class is called sexual deviations and disorders. Whereas in DSM-III homosexuality per se is not a mental disorder unless it is ego-dystonic, in ICD-9 the clinician is instructed to code the presence of homosexuality "whether or not it is considered as a mental disorder."

**Factitious Disorders.** These disorders are characterized by physical or psychological symptoms that are produced by the person and are under his or her voluntary control. The judgment that a particular piece of behavior is under voluntary control is made by the exclusion of all other possible causes for the behavior. Factitious disorders are distinguished from acts of malingering, in which the "patient" is also in voluntary control of the symptom production but for a goal that is obviously recognizable with a knowledge of the environmental circumstances, rather than of his or her psychology.

**Disorders of Impulse Control Not Elsewhere Classified.** This is a residual category for disorders of impulse control that are not classified elsewhere as, for example, substance use disorders or paraphilias. A disorder of impulse control is characterized by a failure to resist an impulse to perform some action that is harmful to the person or to others; there is an increasing sense of tension before performing the act; and, at the time of performing the act, there is an experience of pleasure, gratification, or release. This class includes pathological gambling, kleptomania, pyromania, intermittent explosive disorder, and isolated explosive disorder.

**Adjustment Disorder.** This category is for maladaptive reactions to identifiable life events or circumstances that do not meet the criteria for—and are not merely exacerbations of—one of the other mental disorders, and that are expected to remit when the stressor ceases or when a new level of adaptation is reached. Predominant symptoms, such as depressed mood, can be coded.

**Psychological Factors Affecting Physical Condition.** This category documents the certainty with which a clinician judges psychological factors to be contributory to the initiation or the exacerbation of a physical condition. The physical condition is noted on Axis III. The judgment that psychological factors are affecting the physical condition requires evidence of a temporal relationship between the environmental stimulus and the meaning given to it, on the one hand, and the initiation or exacerbation of the physical condition, on the other.

**Personality Disorders.** The essential features are deeply ingrained, inflexible, maladaptive patterns of relating to, perceiving, and thinking about the environment and oneself that are of sufficient severity to cause either a significant impairment in adaptive functioning or subjective distress. The personality disorders have been grouped into three clusters. The first cluster includes paranoid, schizoid, and schizotypal personality disorders. Persons with these disorders often seem odd or eccentric. The second cluster includes histrionic, narcissistic, antisocial, and borderline personality disorders. Persons with these disorders often seem dramatic, emotional, or erratic. The third cluster includes avoidant, dependent, compulsive, and passive-aggressive personality disorders. Persons with these disorders often seem anxious or fearful. A residual category for atypical, mixed, or other personality disorders can be used for other specific personality disorders, or for cases with mixed features that do not qualify for any of the specific personality disorders described in DSM-III.

ICD-9 does not have equivalent categories to the DSM-III categories of narcissistic, borderline and avoidant personality disorder. ICD-9 has a category, affective personality disorder, that corresponds to the DSM-III categories of dysthymic disorder and cyclothymic disorder.

**V Codes.** This category includes codes for conditions that are a focus of attention or treatment but are not attributable to any of the mental disorders noted previously. In some instances, one of those conditions is noted because, after a thorough evaluation, no mental disorder is found to be present. In other instances, the scope of the diagnostic evaluation was not such as to adequately determine the presence or absence of a mental disorder, but there is a need to note the reason for contact with the mental health care system. Or, a person may have a mental disorder, but the focus of attention or treatment is a condition that is not due to the mental disorder. For example, a person with bipolar disorder may have marital problems that are not directly related to the manifestations of the affective disorder but are the principal focus of treatment.

## The Revision of DSM-III

In May 1983, the American Psychiatric Association appointed a Work Group to Revise DSM-III based on the clinical experience gained since the publication of DSM-III in 1980. That revision is not expected to be published for several years.

## Diagnostic Criteria

It is generally agreed that the most important advance of DSM-III is its provision of specified diagnostic criteria for virtually all of the mental disorders. This methodologic advance has been adopted by research investigators associated with various national schools of psychiatry, such as the French and German schools. The availability of alternative sets of diagnostic criteria for the same disorders has led to what has been called the "polydiagnostic method" for studying the comparative validity of these criterion sets. Applying the polydiagnostic method to schizophrenia, several studies have examined different definitions of the disorder and have generally found the DSM-III definition to have the highest predictive validity with regard to long-term outcome.

As expected, some of the specific diagnostic criteria in DSM-III have been found to be in need of revision because they are unclear. For example, the DSM-III criteria for dysthymic disorder state that "during the past two years the individual has been bothered most or all of the time by symptoms characteristic of the depressive syndrome...." It is unclear whether "most" of the time referred to the proportion of each day or of the year. Other criteria are conceptually unsound. For example, the DSM-III class of paranoid disorders is limited to illnesses with either persecutory delusions or delusions of jealousy. There is no apparent basis for this limited concept of paranoid disorders since traditionally, the concept has also included other monosymptomatic delusions, such as delusions of reference or delusions of grandeur.

## DSM-IV and ICD-10

Hopefully, some day there will be only one internationally accepted classification of mental disorders. Given the presence of various national schools of psychiatry and the still inadequate data base for basing a classification of mental disorders, it is extremely unlikely that DSM-IV and ICD-10, both expected in the early 1990s, will be identical. However, work on the mental disorders chapter of ICD-10 began in 1983 with the goal of reaching international agreement on the major diagnostic classes so that, at least in this regard, ICD-10 and DSM-IV will be closer to each other than is DSM-III to ICD-9.

## REFERENCES

American Psychiatric Association: *Diagnostic and Statistical Manual. Mental Disorders*, ed 3. American Psychiatric Association, Washington, DC, 1980.

Feighner J P, Robins E, Guze S B, Woodruff R A, Winokur G, and Munoz R: Diagnostic criteria for use in psychiatric research. Arch Gen Psychiatry 26: 57, 1972.

Kendell R E: *The Role of Diagnosis in Psychiatry*. Blackwell, Oxford, 1975.

Rosenhan D L: On being sane in insane places. Science 179: 250, 1973.

Spitzer R L: More on pseudoscience in science and the case for psychiatric diagnosis: a critique of D. L. Rosenhan's "On Being Sane in Insane Places" and "The Contextual Nature of Psychiatric Diagnosis." Arch Gen Psychiatry 33: 459, 1976.

Spitzer R L, Williams J B W: Classification of mental disorders. In *Comprehensive Textbook of Psychiatry*, ed 4, H I Kaplan, B J Sadock, editors, p 591. Williams & Wilkins, Baltimore, 1985.

Spitzer, R L, Endicott J, Robins E: Research diagnostic criteria: rationale and reliability. Arch Gen Psychiatry 35: 773, 1978.

Spitzer R L, Williams J B W, Skodol A E: DSM-III: the major achievements and an overview. Am J Psychiatry 137: 151, 1980.

Spitzer R L, Williams J B W, Skodol A E: *International Perspectives on DSM-III*. American Psychiatric Press, Washington, DC, 1983.

World Health Organization: *International Classification of Diseases*, rev 9. World Health Organization, Geneva, 1977.

# 10

# Schizophrenic Disorders

## Introduction

Schizophrenia is a syndrome that is heterogeneous in its cause, pathogenesis, presenting picture, course, response to treatment, and outcome. The syndrome is nevertheless assumed to be an illness or disorder, rather than a socially unacceptable set of behaviors. The clinical picture is seen as a modestly homogeneous end state that derives from different initial conditions through different biosocially influenced pathways.

## History

The symptoms of what is now called schizophrenia have fascinated physicians and philosophers for thousands of years. However, the search for the causes and the cures of schizophrenic manifestations was impeded by the fact that what is now known as schizophrenia was not even described as a disease entity until 1896, when Emil Kraepelin (see Fig. 1) brought together, under the term dementia precox, a variety of psychotic syndromes previously believed to represent separate diseases. Kraepelin's description of dementia precox included the prognostic factor of final deterioration and the observed clinical phenomena, such as hallucinations, delusions, stereotypies, and disordered affect. These phenomena were a substantial aid to diagnosis; but, to arrive at a definitive diagnosis, the clinician might well have to wait for several years to observe the outcome in dementia, and to confirm the presumptive diagnostic impression of dementia precox.

In 1911 Eugen Bleuler (see Fig. 2) broke through this impasse with his new conceptualization of the whole problem, and the new term "schizophrenia" for dementia precox. Translated literally, schizophrenia means split-mindedness, and Bleuler saw the splitting of the personality, rather than the outcome, as the central feature of the disease. He no longer considered incurability and terminal deterioration to be necessary features of schizophrenia. To him, schizophrenia was both a disease entity and a psychopathological reaction, a syndrome. Consequently, he expected some patients to deteriorate and others to recover with or without defect. Bleuler's fundamental contribution was the introduction of a hierarchy of symptoms to replace the mere description of unweighted clinical phenomena.

Kraepelin described three basic types of dementia precox: catatonic, hebephrenic, and paranoid. Bleuler described a fourth type: simple schizophrenia. These four types are still generally accepted today as basic schizophrenic syndromes, although there has been some debate whether simple schizophrenia as a diagnostic entity should be retained. Later investigators added a number of new subtypes, including schizoaffective, latent, borderline, undifferentiated, residual, and pseudoneurotic schizophrenia among others. A more extensive discussion of these types will be found below under the heading of "Clinical Syndromes."

## Epidemiology

### Incidence

The true incidence rate of schizophrenia is difficult to obtain. In addition to the lack of objective diagnostic methods that complicate the process of identification of cases, complete identification entails both the detection of every person afflicted by the disease in a well-defined community, and the ability to determine the actual date of onset of the illness. The age groups investigated also vary, with most studies considering the segment of the population aged 15 and over.

The incidence rates for schizophrenia from the studies that considered all ages varied from a low of 0.43 per 1,000 population to a high of 0.68 per 1,000. For the age group 15 and over, the rates ranged from a low of 0.30 per 1,000 to a high of 1.20 per 1,000.

In summary, pooled studies show an incidence of 1 per 1,000.

**Prevalence.** The variation in prevalence rates from studies around the world is much

FIGURE 1. Emil Kraepelin, 1856–1926. (Courtesy National Library of Medicine. Bethesda, Maryland.)

higher than the variation in incidence rates. European and Asiatic investigators record lifetime prevalence rates through surveys. They consider treated and untreated cases and count all persons who have had a schizophrenic episode, whether they are under active treatment or not during the survey period. The lifetime prevalence rates for European studies ranged from a low of 1.9 per 1,000 to a high of 9.5 per 1,000; the range was much smaller for Asiatic studies, 2.1 to 3.8 per 1,000. Two North American studies of lifetime prevalence provide low rates of 1.0 and 1.9 per 1,000 respectively. Other studies in the United States gave period prevalence rates for treated cases, and they ranged from 2.3 to 3.6 per 1,000.

Summarizing the prevalence data available in the United States, one can state that between 0.23 percent and 0.47 percent of the total population are likely to receive psychiatric treatment for a schizophrenic illness during any particular year, provided adequate mental health care facilities are available in all communities. This means that a minimum of 500,000 and a maximum of 1 million persons will need treatment

annually for the illness. For 62 percent of each group, treatment will involve at least one hospitalization during the year. With a lifetime prevalence of about 1 percent—about 2 million Americans may be suffering from a mental disorder that would be classified as schizophrenia today.

**Risk of Death.** There is an excess mortality among schizophrenics and other patients with mental illness that is not readily explainable. Institutional care, which in the past was one of the major factors involved in the high mortality rates among schizophrenics, does not appear to be a major contributor to death in this population.

**Reproduction Rates.** Incidence and prevalence rates of schizophrenia are affected by the mortality and reproduction rates of schizophrenic populations. Mortality rates affect mainly prevalence; reproduction rates influence both incidence and prevalence. The expectation of becoming schizophrenic for members of a

FIGURE 2. Eugen Bleuler, 1857–1939. (Courtesy National Library of Medicine. Bethesda, Maryland.)

family increases if one of them is already suffering from schizophrenia. With the advent of psychoactive drugs, open-door policies, the emphasis on rehabilitation, and community-based care for the schizophrenic, increased rates of marriage and fertility have been observed. A study compared the marriage and reproductive patterns among schizophrenics admitted to New York state hospitals between the years 1934–1936 and 1954–1956. This study found a substantial increase in marriage and reproduction rates both before and after the onset of illness in the 1954–1956 sample as compared with the 1934–1936 sample. The combined reproduction rate for male and female schizophrenics increased from about 57 to 94 children per 100 patients. For female schizophrenics, the increase was from 70 to 130 children per 100 women. Women schizophrenics produce more children than do men schizophrenics. The increases in reproduction and marriage rates for schizophrenics were relatively larger than those reported for the general population. Even these reported increases may seriously underestimate schizophrenic marriage and reproduction.

**Mental Hospital Beds.** A significant proportion of mental hospital beds are occupied by schizophrenic patients. Patterns of hospitalization for schizophrenic patients have changed over the past 2 decades. The duration of each hospital experience diminished, and the number of readmissions increased. Patients are now being hospitalized more often for shorter periods of time. The probability for readmission within a 2-year period after discharge from the first lifetime hospitalization for a schizophrenic is about 40 percent. Between 15 and 25 percent of discharged schizophrenics will eventually be readmitted and receive continued care for a prolonged period of time.

Schizophrenia is the most expensive of all mental disorders from the standpoints of direct treatment costs, loss of productivity, and expenditures for public assistance. It is estimated that the annual cost of schizophrenia in the United States is about 2 percent of the gross national product. The direct delivery of psychiatric care accounts for only 20 percent of this figure. The remaining costs reflect the loss in productive capacity resulting from the disorder's early onset, hospitalization, and unemployment.

Declines in the number of resident inpatients and shorter hospital stays have contributed to a reduction in the direct costs of treatment, but over-all expenditures have not fallen, due in part to welfare and disability payments and rehabilitation. The total cost of schizophrenia to society continues to escalate.

**Socioeconomic Status.** One of the most consistent findings in epidemiological studies of schizophrenia is the presence of a disproportionate number of schizophrenics in the lower socioeconomic classes.

Two major hypotheses have been proposed to explain the relationship of social class to schizophrenia. The first hypothesis is generally known as the social causation hypothesis, which assumes that the social and economic stresses experienced by the lower classes are causatively related to schizophrenic illness. The second hypothesis is generally known as the social selection or drift hypothesis, which claims that low social class membership rates in schizophrenia are more a function of schizophrenic illness, and that schizophrenic patients tend to be downwardly mobile. Neither of these hypotheses has been definitely proved, nor has the extent of the contribution of either hypothesis been demonstrated.

**Other Factors.** Several other factors have been proposed as having some influence on the rates of schizophrenia; however, the results from different investigations have not substantiated the influence of these factors conclusively. The first of these factors is migration. Some studies suggested that immigrants have higher rates of first hospital admissions for schizophrenia than their counterparts who remained at home. The second factor considered is industrialization, because higher rates of schizophrenia are attributed to highly industrialized societies. The prevalence of schizophrenia has also been found to rise among third-world populations as contact with technologically advanced cultures increases. A third related factor is the influence of sociocultural factors and of culture change on the rates of schizophrenia. This factor, often neglected as an explanation for disease, was discussed by Murphy, who provided suggestive hypotheses for the importance of culture in understanding cross-national variations in the incidence and the chronicity of schizophrenia. He argued that cultures may be more or less schizophrenogenic, depending on how mental illness is perceived, the content of the patient role, the system of social supports, and the complexity of social communication. He also suggested that culture affects the microstructure of the brain and hence the vulnerability to schizophrenia. He cited drug trial data indicating that schizophrenics who were identical except for cultural background responded differently to the same drug administered in a uniform manner. Although the causative role of culture in the disease process has not yet been unequivocally established, Murphy offers persuasive arguments that greater attention should be given to the evocative aspects of culture in the genesis of schizophrenia.

## Etiology

### Genetic Hypotheses

**Studies of Relatives.** Studies of relatives report, on the basis of hospital records, that, in the general population and in stepsiblings, the morbid risk for schizophrenia is from 0.3 to 2.8 percent; in parents of schizophrenic probands, it is 0.2 to 12 percent; in full siblings, it is 3 to 14 percent; for children with one schizophrenic parent, it is 8 to 18 percent. If both parents are schizophrenic, the risk for the children is between 15 and 55 percent. For second-degree relatives, the median risk value is 2.5 percent.

In summary, pooled results of family studies show about a 9 percent risk in siblings, 12 percent in children of one schizophrenic parent and about 50 percent in children of two schizophrenic parents.

**Studies of Twins.** The preferred method for testing genetic theories is the study of concordance rates for schizophrenia in monozygotic and dizygotic twins. These rates have ranged from 0 to 86 percent and from 2 to 17 percent, respectively. Franz Kallmann pointed out that the concordance rate for monozygotic twins who had not lived together for some years before his study was 77.6 percent, but that the rate for those twins who had not been separated was 91.5 percent. He also found that many more female twins than male twins were concordant for schizophrenia, whether they were monozygotic or not. The results of these twin studies also indicate that the more severely ill the index twin is, the greater the concordance rate for schizophrenia in the other twin.

Concordance rates in hospitalized twins have been shown to be higher if one selects samples from a hospital population, rather than from consecutive admissions to the hospitals; the best of these studies yield concordance rates of 40 to 50 percent for monozygotic and 9 to 10 percent for dizygotic twins.

In summary, pooled studies show expectancy rates of about 80 percent for monozygotic twins and 15 percent for dizygotic twins.

**Adoption.** Seymour Kety and his co-workers reported on the distribution of schizophrenia in the biological and adoptive relatives of children given up for adoption and who later in life had to be hospitalized for a schizophrenic illness. Schizophrenia did not occur with any greater frequency in the adoptive relatives of index cases, i.e. adopted away children who became

schizophrenic, than in the control cases. Biological paternal half siblings of the schizophrenic adoptees are more likely than usual to be schizophrenic. These paternal half siblings obviously do not share the same intrauterine or extrauterine family environments as their adopted half siblings. Biological parents of schizophrenic children had more severe psychiatric illness than did their adoptive parents, who had more psychopathology than the adoptive parents of children who were not schizophrenic. Adopted children of a schizophrenic parent are twice as likely to be psychiatrically ill as the children in other groups. Finally, adopted away children of schizophrenic parents develop schizophrenia at higher rates than the general population.

These studies have lent strong support to the contention that genetic factors play a role in schizophrenia. However, most schizophrenic patients do not have psychotic parents. No accurate figures exist that would allow anyone to assess how prevalent the presence of psychosis is in the parents of schizophrenic children.

**Predisposition and Learning.** Still another series of theories focuses on both genetic predisposition and learning in schizophrenia. The validation of such theories usually requires the study of psychophysiological variables, but one theoretical proposal states that the predisposition to schizophrenia is characterized by excessively strong physiological reactions to mild stress, easy or rapid acquisition of conditioned responses, unusually slow recovery from autonomic imbalance, and excessive stimulus generalization reactiveness. In the patient with acute schizophrenia, an increase in anxiety is correlated with an increase in the level and breadth of stimulus generalization. As a result, many new stimuli become potentially capable of arousing anxiety, and a vicious cycle is set up. As generalization widens, atypical and tangential thought sequences intrude, and perceptions are distorted. The chronic schizophrenic state is characterized by learning avoidant and irrelevant thoughts that seek to reduce anxiety whenever it occurs. If these thoughts successfully defend against anxiety, they become self-reinforcing.

### Developmental Hypotheses

A number of hypotheses have been proposed to account for the disturbances in behavior and psychological functioning in schizophrenia in either developmental or psychophysiological terms. Psychologists and psychiatrists agree that, because of basic deficits in ego functioning, schizophrenic persons are unable to handle their personal conflicts and to cope with their environment. Schizophrenics find everyday tasks stressful not because the tasks themselves are necessarily pressured, but because these persons perceive the tasks as threats. In addition, their conflicts sensitize them to certain classes of life experiences, such as separation from the home. Any theory of schizophrenia must account for the failure in the capacity to adapt and to resolve conflict on the basis of impaired psychological functioning.

No resolution of the controversy among psychogenic theorists of schizophrenia has occurred. Some believe that the primary defect in schizophrenia is in ego functioning; others believe that in schizophrenia ego functions are disrupted by impulses, conflict, and massive anxiety. In any case, the conflicts that schizophrenic patients demonstrate are not specific to them; rather, the severity of the conflicts and the schizophrenics' incapacity to defend against them is pathogenetic.

### Environmental Hypotheses

In the past few years particular emphasis has been placed on the study of the parents and families of schizophrenic patients, with the hope of isolating certain variables—such as some aspects of the behavior, personality, or attitudes of one or both parents—or of specifying modes of family interactions that seem to play an etiological role in schizophrenia. In addition, recent publications have dealt with the relationship between the formal aspects of a parent's cognitive style and the cognitive style of the schizophrenic child.

For many complex reasons, workers in the United States tend to favor environmentalist theories that place the burden for the predisposition to schizophrenia on the parents and family. Genetic or predisposing factors tend to be overlooked, disregarded, or dismissed as insignificant. Rather, it is stressed that the familial or social environment causes certain children to become schizophrenic, and the intervening variables are the categories of life experience that precipitate their schizophrenic reactions. This is the basis for the theory that schizophrenia is not a disease, and that there are only schizophrenic persons, who have been molded in this manner by experience.

The behavior of some of the parents of schizophrenic children may differ in intensity, but not in quality, from the behavior of parents of nonschizophrenic children. Therefore, the mechanisms whereby life experience molds the schizophrenic child are either conflicts created in the child, or irrational reactions and ways of thinking learned by imitation or identification. The asocial manner of schizophrenic persons is explained by the fact that social learning may also fail in these children because of their pathological environment, leading to a lifelong aversion to other people.

It is clear, however, from the data so far reviewed that genetic factors predispose to psychopathology, if not to schizophrenia. It is also clear that the inheritance of the gene or genes does not inevitably lead to schizophrenic illness. There must be unidentified environmental factors that, in addition to the genotype, produce the schizophrenic phenotype. It is, therefore, entirely legitimate to seek these factors in the family and in the cultural, economic, and social environment of the child who becomes schizophrenic sometime in his life. If these factors are found, and if what is inherited is a predisposition to psychopathology, it is important to identify the specific experiences that are instrumental in producing the schizophrenic phenotype, and not some other form of psychopathology.

### Initiating Factors

Although a person must be predisposed to schizophrenic illness for some stress or event to initiate the illness, one cannot disregard such initiating factors in any etiological theory.

Many factors, including drugs—such as alcohol, LSD, the amphetamines, and cannabis—may initiate the schizophrenia. In addition, many schizophrenic patients become ill after being rebuffed, brutalized, or raped.

Loss or rebuff has a portentous meaning to these patients. Divorce, death of a parent, child or spouse often precipitate the illness. Many of the schizophrenic symptoms can be understood as a way of expressing this loss and of compensating for it in highly personal metaphors. But, clearly, the patient cannot cope with the loss or rebuff in the manner that most people do—by grieving or by finding a surrogate for the lost person. Their manner of dealing with the loss or rebuff is by denial, projection, total identification with the lost person, or some other primitive means.

### Biological Factors

The etiological theory most stubbornly clung to over time states that schizophrenia is a physical disease due to a structural or functional defect in some organ system or in some biochemical mechanism.

**Dopamine Hypothesis.** The dopamine hypothesis of schizophrenia relates the specific behavioral symptoms of the disorder to an increased amount of dopamine available at synapses or to a hyperactivity of the dopamine pathways. Clinical and laboratory evidence supporting this concept is abundant.

The idea that schizophrenia is associated with dysfunction in the dopamine system was based on the observation that all clinically effective antipsychotic drugs increase dopamine metabolite levels and thus, it was inferred, cause a central elevation of dopamine activity. The mechanism responsible for the phenomenon, it was speculated, is a drug-induced blockade of dopamine receptors, which triggers an increased production of the transmitter.

The dopamine hypothesis is also supported by the fact that chloropromazine and other antipsychotic drugs block both norepinephrine and dopamine receptors and allows for a buildup of dopamine at nerve endings.

Studies repeatedly demonstrated an acceleration of dopamine turnover and dopamine neuron firing rate after the administration of phenothiazines or other neuroleptics. It was further demonstrated that these drugs inhibit dopamine-sensitive adenylate cyclase in certain receptor membranes. Normally, cyclase activity increases when dopamine stimulation provokes biological activity.

Antipsychotic agents have been shown, through the use of X-ray crystallography, to assume molecular configurations similar to that of dopamine. It has also been shown that these drugs do, in fact, compete with dopamine and exhibit an affinity for stereospecific dopamine-binding sites. This ability has been correlated with their clinical potency.

Other evidence supporting the dopamine hypothesis is that agents that increase amounts of catecholamines in the brain increase psychotic symptoms. The long-known ability of amphetamines to induce clinical symptoms similar to those seen in schizophrenia supports that observation as does the fact that amphetamine worsens the symptoms of schizophrenia. Dopamine and dopamine agonists, such as apomorphine, produce symptoms that resemble the amphetamine-induced psychosis. When the dopamine tracts are lesioned, however, high doses of both amphetamines and dopamine-like drugs fail to produce stereotyped behavior.

As convincing as this evidence is, the precise nature of the underlying defect of the dopamine system has not yet been elucidated. Many researchers think that the hyperdopaminergia is merely the most evident expression of another pathophysiological defect.

**Transmethylation Hypothesis.** Schizophrenia may result from abnormal transmethylation—specifically aberrant $O$-methylation—of catecholamines, yielding dimethoxyphenylethylamine (DMPEA), a compound closely related to mescaline. Researchers also reported finding DMPEA in the urine of schizophrenics and not in normal control subjects, and they were also able to demonstrate the conversion, in vitro and in vivo, of dopamine in schizophrenic patients to the urinary excretion product of DMPEA.

Research conducted by other workers has failed to confirm the initial findings of a relationship between urinary DMPEA and schizophrenia. Perhaps the most serious challenge to the proposed mechanism has been the observation that DMPEA in the urine is closely related to diet, raising the question as to whether it is an endogenous metabolite or an artifact of exogenous origin. The pink spot seen in chromatographic studies, supposed to represent DMPEA, has similarly been implicated as an artifact, being produced by the ingestion of phenothiazines or tea drinking.

**Indolamine Hypothesis.** A defect in the methylation of indolamines, most notably serotonin, has also been investigated for the possible significance of their role in schizophrenia. The theory has been referred to as the psychedelic model of schizophrenia. It is based on the observation that two substances, bufotenine and dimethyltryptamine (DMT)—the $N$-methylated derivatives of serotonin and tryptamine, respectively—both have hallucinogenic properties. Early investigations demonstrated increased blood and urine levels of methylated indolamines in schizophrenic patients, and showed that an enzyme that mediates the methylation of tryptamine to DMT—indolamine-$N$-methyltransferase—is present in the human brain. The feasibility of the hypothesis was enhanced by clinical studies that demonstrated that normal persons, given large doses of the two amino acids, tryptophan and methionine, or a combination of the two, experience an excited state. The same regimen in schizophrenics produces a recurrence and exacerbation of psychosis, with the disorder being more severe if there is concurrent administration of a monoamine oxidase inhibitor (MAOI). This experimental technique, termed precursor loading, is of particular value in elucidating the biochemical reactions underlying observed behavioral changes. Methionine, for example, is a methyl donor that can combine with either tryptophan or serotonin. The provision of exogenous tryptophan or the accumulation of endogenous serotonin, through the action of MAOI, produces an excess of substrate with which methyl groups can combine. The enzyme described may then divert synthesis toward the pathway that results in bufotenine or DMT.

**Monoamine Oxidase Hypothesis.** Researchers have reported a somewhat lower mean activity of monoamine oxidase (MAO) in blood platelets of chronic schizophrenic patients than in normal control subjects. Subsequent attempts to replicate the original observations have produced conflicting results. At present, low MAO activity does not seem to be a specific feature of schizophrenic disorders or of vulnerability to the development of schizophrenia.

**Electrolyte Hypothesis.** A relationship between malignant catatonia and high calcium levels has been noted. Describing the clinical course of one patient over a 25-year period, concurrent hyperthermia during catatonic episodes was observed, a phenomenon linked to increased muscle calcium levels.

Calcium affects neurotransmitter activity and competes with neuroleptic drugs at the neuronal membrane site. Calcium and magnesium levels are decreased by antipsychotic treatment. It was found that serum calcium levels increased markedly at the onset of catatonic episodes, and it has been hypothesized that elevations of serum calcium levels are temporarily involved in the switch process of affective state changes.

**Endorphins.** Some neurotransmitters such as β-endorphin have exacerbated symptoms of schizophrenia in certain patients, and increased levels of endorphins have been found in the spinal fluid of some patients. The meaning of the role of endorphins, however, is not yet clear.

### Neurophysiologic Theories and Findings

**Abnormalities in Children.** Neurological abnormalities have been reported for a number of years in schizophrenic children. These abnormalities have either been ascribed to perinatal complications, including viral infections of the pregnant mother, or to lags or arrests in the maturation of the brain. Several kinds of abnormalities have been noted; however, there are serious problems in reliably assigning various kinds of neurological abnormalities to children who are already psychotic.

When predictions are made, on the basis of a physical examination, that a child will become psychotic and the prediction is borne out to a significant degree, support is found for the idea that a physical alteration of the brain—due either to genetic, intrauterine, or perinatal fac-

tors—impairs neural and psychological development. Infants who from the age of 1 month manifested disturbed regulation of physiological patterns—such as vasomotor instability, disturbed sleep patterns, poor temperature control, poor muscle tone—and of alertness and uneven patterns of growth, with retardation or precocity in motor, perceptual, and language skills and in the social sphere, were found to be predisposed to schizophrenia in later childhood. Peculiarities of gait, motor awkwardness, postural disturbances, changes in muscle tone, and sudden unexplained movements have been described in schizophrenic children. Whirling movements and the vestibular control of posture may be disturbed. Intelligence tests indicate a considerable inferiority in intelligence. A preference is shown by schizophrenic children for proximal rather than distance receptors. Auditory and visual information cannot be integrated by such children. A high prevalence of impaired hand-to-hand integration exists from 4 to 9 months of age. Not only is visuomotor integration impaired, but also visual-proprioceptive integration is poorly integrated in children of hospitalized schizophrenic mothers.

The incidence of neurological abnormalities in various series of schizophrenic children varies considerably, however, and such abnormalities also occur in nonschizophrenic children. Perinatal complications are frequently a part of the histories of children with reading difficulties, mental deficiency, and cerebral palsy; they are not specific to the later development of a schizophrenic illness.

### Structural Alterations of the Brain

**Ventricle Enlargement.** The search for an anatomical basis for schizophrenia has a long and checkered history. Structural alterations have been sought at the macroscopic, microscopic, and ultrastructural levels. Therefore, it was inevitable that with the development of the computed tomography (CT) scan, the search for a gross anatomical defect in the brains of schizophrenic patients would be resumed.

The basis for these claims is that some schizophrenic patients have enlarged lateral ventricles of the brain, increased sulcal fluid volumes, reversal of the normal asymmetrics of the brain, or atrophy of the anterior vermis of the cerebellum. Studies supporting these findings, however, are not consistent.

Several studies have reported ventricular enlargement in patients with bipolar affective disorders, and sulcal enlargement has recently been reported. The lateral ventricles and sulci enlarge normally with age; by the age of 40, they regularly show such changes and continue to widen with advancing age. Positive correlations have been reported between advancing age, increasing cognitive impairment, and ventricular enlargement. Clearly, age is a factor accounting for a progressive shrinkage of the brain parenchyma. It is not surprising, therefore, that in one report small differences in the ventricular-brain ratio was found between schizophrenic patients and normal controls.

Evidence at this time that CT scans will reveal gross anatomical changes in the brains of patients is highly questionable.

**Defect in Energy Metabolism.** With the development of new techniques for measuring cerebral blood flow by the xenon technique and cerebral glucose metabolism by positron emission tomography (PET), new findings are being reported (see Fig. 3). These techniques allow measurements of regional differences in blood supply and metabolism of the brain, respec-

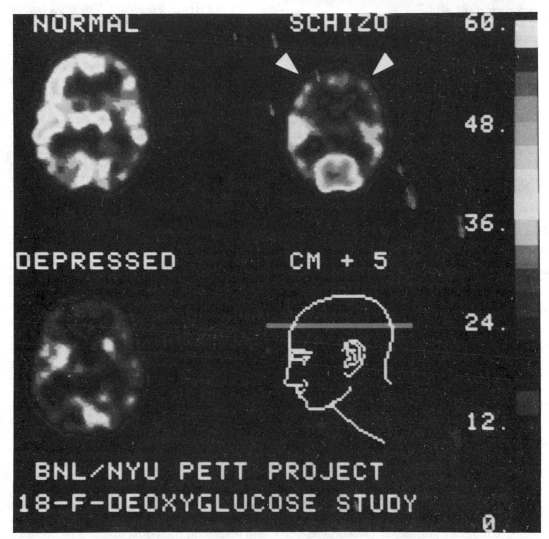

FIGURE 3. Representative positron emission tomographic (PET) scans of three subjects in a plane through the lateral ventricles, thalamic nuclei, and basal ganglia. The occipital pole is at the bottom of the section. The *arrows* indicate the dimunition of cerebral energy metabolism in the frontal cortex that is associated with the chronic stage of the schizophrenic process. Temporal cortical activity is also significantly decreased. Neuroleptic treatment does not normalize the "hypofrontal" pattern. Primary affective disorders have not yet been investigated in a large series. A scan of a person with major depression (DSM-III) shows in the *lower left*. There is a generalized lowering of glucose metabolism in this subject. Other applications of this technique are the examination of cerebral metabolism under states of cognitive and emotional stress, the study of receptors and their properties, and the effect of drugs and other somatic therapies on brain functional neuroanatomy. (Courtesy of the Brookhaven National Laboratory, New York University Medical Center, and Alfred P. Wolf, Ph.D., and Jonathan D. Brodie, M.D.)

tively. Differences in flow in normal and schizophrenic patients who were on neuroleptic drugs have been observed. Inactive, autistic, or catatonic patients showed a diminution of blood flow in the precentral regions of the brain, whereas hallucinating patients and patients with disorders of thinking had relatively high flows in the postcentral, temporal, and latero-occipital regions of the cerebral cortex. Mean hemispheric and over-all blood flow and cerebral oxygen consumption were the same in schizophrenic and normal subjects.

Abnormal glucose tolerance curves and the retarded metabolism of lactate, which were frequently reported in schizophrenia in the past, have since been ascribed to a relative deficiency of vitamins of the B group. More recently, defects in oxidative phosphorylation and of the metabolism of phosphorus in erythrocytes have been reported. Schizophrenic patients have been said to have a serum factor producing hyperglycemia, possibly due to an antagonist of insulin present in blood. In comparison with the plasma of normal control patients, the plasma of schizophrenic subjects is said to contain a substance that, when incubated with chick erythrocytes, increases the lactate to pyruvate ratio in the medium.

**Eye Movements.** The schizophrenic patient pursues an object moving in a pendular manner with jerky, interrupted movements. Not all unmedicated schizophrenic patients have this aberration of eye movements, but 50 to 85 percent do. Forty-five percent of their first-degree relatives and 7 percent of the general population also have the aberration, suggesting that these eye movement abnormalities are under genetic control.

This aberration, whose intrinsic physiology is not understood, seems more related to the etiology than to the pathophysiology of schizophrenia. An inspection of the pursuit movements of twin pairs is especially interesting as the patterns show a startling similarity.

Smooth-pursuit movements are used to follow moving targets. Saccadic (jerky) movements are mobilized to place this target on the fovea quickly and accurately; they correct the point of gaze and interrupt pursuit movements or replace them if inaccurately carried out. The saccadic movements are qualitatively intact in schizophrenic patients, but are increased in number. Eye-tracking movements in schizophrenic patients who are ill or in remission show more back and forth saccades.

**Galvanic Skin Response.** Teams of investigators have variously reported that a group of schizophrenic subjects has a higher resting level of galvanic skin response (GSR), blood pressures, or heart rates. One cannot assume, on the basis of such findings, that there is some intrinsic deviation in the autonomic nervous system in schizophrenia. The higher resting level may simply reflect the subject's heightened physiological response to the novelty of the experimental situation, to some aspect of the social setting of the experiment, or to the experimenters themselves.

**Evoked Brain Potential.** The EEG tracing is influenced by stimuli which when computed and averaged, give a tracing called the average evoked potential. The findings from the evoked potentials in schizophrenics suggest that they have a general inefficiency in discovering the meaning in information signals, and that they could not maintain an effective control strategy for processing information.

There are many studies showing that schizophrenic patients have difficulty in attending selectively, in perceiving redundant or multiple inputs, and in processing signals as quickly or correctly as normal people.

### Immune Theories

**Immunoglobulins.** There have been several reports on changes in immunoglobulin levels in the serum of schizophrenic patients. There are five main classes of immunoglobulins, and within each class there is considerable chemical heterogeneity. These classes are now called immunoglobulin A, D, E, G, and M. Each class has different physiological properties. In addition to being involved in the various kinds of antigen-antibody reactions, immunoglobulins are known, under certain conditions, to acquire antigenic properties within the body and then to be responded to by other antibodies to form antibody-antibody complexes. Examples of such complexes are the so-called rheumatoid factors, some of which consist of a complex of an immunoglobulin G (IgG) and an immunoglobulin-M (IgM). These factors are present in the serum of patients with a wide variety of illnesses, in addition to being present in the serum of most patients with rheumatoid arthritis. They are also present in the serum of 1 to 5 percent of a normal population of people.

**Autoimmune Hypotheses.** Two autoimmune hypotheses exist about schizophrenia. A general hypothesis says that autoimmune phenomena play a role, and a specific hypothesis proposes that (auto)antibodies are present in schizophrenia against brain cells. To detect antibodies against antigens in the brain, the difficult techniques of direct and indirect fluorescence are used. Reports have been published that schizophrenia is associated with the presence of a circulating immunoglobulin, taraxein, which is bound to nuclei of oligodendroglia of septal area neurons in the human brain. The injection of fractions of the IgG component of serum of patients who were schizophrenic or the injection of antibodies from sheep immunized with extracts of the septal caudate nuclear region of human and monkey brains induced behavioral and electroencephalographic changes in the septal region of monkeys.

### Schizotaxia

One of the most influential and conceptually the most satisfying theories of the etiology of schizophrenia proposed a defect in neural integration (schizotaxia) as the genotype. Social learning, imposed on this genotype, leads to a type of personality organization predisposed but not inevitably prone to decompensate into schizophrenic illness. This personality organization is characterized by four traits consisting of (1) different degrees of a thought disorder (cognitive slippage), (2) an inability for enjoyment, (3) ambivalence, and (4) an aversion to human relationships.

There is much to be said for this hypothesis, which integrates genetic and experiential factors, albeit in learning theory terms. It is also one of the very few hypotheses that points out that the schizophrenogenic mother may herself be either a schizotype or schizophrenic. Although she may pass on a gene or genes for schizophrenia, the child still must live with her; thus, the environment in which the child is raised is conducive to eliciting the genotypic predisposition to schizophrenia.

### Diagnosis

#### Strategies

A number of different diagnostic strategies have achieved general clinical acceptance. The fundamental altered signs of Bleuler are broadly used throughout Western psychiatry. Those include primary and secondary symptoms. The primary symptoms are: flat or inappropriate affect, loose associations, ambivalence, and autism (the so-called four A's). The secondary symptoms include hallucinations and delusions. Despite their wide acceptance, this approach had recurrent problems. Ambivalence is not unique to the schizophrenic syndrome and hallucinations and delusions occur in other psychiatric disorders. Furthermore, the determination of the presence of ambivalence or autism at a level

that exceeds that found in nonschizophrenic populations requires a high degree of clinical inference.

Schizophrenic patients manifest alterations of affect in terms of the range of display, intensity, lability, and appropriateness. If any affective feature is unique to the schizophrenic syndrome, it is the inappropriateness of the affect when compared to the ideation. But the assessment of this feature requires refined clinical judgment, except in the most extreme cases. The same is true of association or thought disorder.

Gabriel Langfeldt, unlike Bleuler, derived his criteria from empirical experience, rather than a theoretical formulation. Langfeldt divided the disorder into true schizophrenia and schizophreniform psychosis. The diagnosis of true schizophrenia rests on the findings of depersonalization, autism, emotional blunting, insidious onset, and feelings of derealization and unreality. True schizophrenia is often referred to as nuclear schizophrenia, process schizophrenia or nonremitting schizophrenia.

Kurt Schneider described a number of so-called first-rank symptoms of schizophrenia that he considered in no way specific for the disease but of great pragmatic value in making a diagnosis. Schneider's first-rank symptoms include the hearing of one's thoughts spoken aloud, auditory hallucinations that comment on the patient's behavior, somatic hallucinations, the experience of having one's thoughts controlled, the spreading of one's thoughts to others, delusions, and the experience of having one's actions controlled or influenced from the outside.

Schizophrenia, Schneider pointed out, also can be diagnosed exclusively on the basis of second-rank symptoms, along with an otherwise typical clinical appearance. Second-rank symptoms include other forms of hallucination, perplexity, depressive and euphoric disorders of affect, and emotional blunting.

Schneider did not mean these symptoms to be rigidly applied, and he warned the clinician that the diagnosis should be made in certain patients, even though they failed to show first-rank symptoms. Unfortunately, this warning is frequently ignored, and the absence of such symptoms in a single interview is taken as evidence that the person is free of a schizophrenic disorder.

### DSM-III Classification

DSM-III reflects the idea that the category of schizophrenia includes a group of disorders, and specifies the followng as essential characteristics: disorganization from the previous level of daily functioning in at least two areas, such as work, social relations, and self-care; the presence of at least one symptom from a list of six during the active phase of the illness; at least a 6-month duration of illness, during which the symptom or symptoms necessary for making the diagnosis are present; onset of illness before age 45; and not due to organic mental disorder or mental retardation. The symptom list in DSM-III for the diagnosis of a schizophrenic disorder includes six items. Three are delusional in nature, two are hallucinatory, and the last item is thought disorder accompanied by affective disorder, delusions or hallucinations, disorganized behavior, or catatonic symptoms. DSM-III places great diagnostic significance on what it terms characteristic delusions and hallucinations (see Table I).

ICD-9 lists the basic four types, but comments on simple schizophrenia that its schizophrenic symptoms are not clear-cut and that it should, therefore, be diagnosed sparingly, if at all. Other schizophrenic subtypes listed in ICD-9 include acute schizophrenic episode, latent schizophrenia, residual schizophrenia, schizoaffective type, other, and—to be used only as a last resort—unspecified. DSM-III lists only five types under schizophrenic disorders: disorganized (hebephrenic), catatonic, paranoid, undifferentiated, and residual. It does not include simple schizophrenia, and neither ICD-9 nor DSM-III lists the pseudoneurotic type, which, according to ICD-9, can be recorded under the category of latent schizophrenia. DSM-III does provide a special diagnostic category for the schizoaffective disorders, thus indicating that these disorders cannot be readily included under either the schizophrenic disorders or the affective disorders. DSM-III also provides a separate diagnostic category for schizophreniform disorder, using Langfeldt's concept of a diagnostic entity for any schizophrenic condition that has lasted less than 6 months (see Table II).

## United States-United Kingdom Diagnostic Project

The United States-United Kingdom schizophrenia project has established that the American concept of schizophrenia has been considerably widened during the last 30 years and that the European—more specifically, the British—concept of the disease has remained more restricted, in accordance with the original Kraepelinian concept of dementia precox. Thus, the comparatively greater number of patients in the United States classified as schizophrenic reflects expanding diagnostic habits, rather than an increased incidence of schizophrenia.

TABLE I
DIAGNOSTIC CRITERIA FOR A SCHIZOPHRENIC DISORDER*

A. At least one of the following during a phase of the illness:

(1) bizarre delusions (content is patently absurd and has *no* possible basis in fact), such as delusions of being controlled, thought broadcasting, thought insertion, or thought withdrawal

(2) somatic, grandiose, religious, nihilistic, or other delusions without persecutory or jealous content

(3) delusions with persecutory or jealous content if accompanied by hallucinations of any type

(4) auditory hallucinations in which either a voice keeps up a running commentary on the individual's behavior or thoughts, or two or more voices converse with each other

(5) auditory hallucinations on several occasions with content of more than one or two words, having no apparent relation to depression or elation

(6) incoherence, marked loosening of associations, markedly illogical thinking, or marked poverty of content of speech if associated with at least one of the following:
(a) blunted, flat, or inappropriate affect
(b) delusions or hallucinations
(c) catatonic or other grossly disorganized behavior

B. Deterioration from a previous level of functioning in such areas as work, social relations, and self-care.

C. Duration: Continuous signs of the illness for at least 6 months at some time during the person's life, with some signs of the illness at present. The 6-month period must include an active phase during which there were symptoms from A, with or without a prodromal or residual phase, as defined below.

*Prodromal phase:* A clear deterioration in functioning before the active phase of the illness not due to a disturbance in mood or to a Substance Use Disorder and involving at least *two* of the symptoms noted below.

*Residual phase:* Persistence, following the active phase of the illness, of at least *two* of the symptoms noted below, not due to a disturbance in mood or to a Substance Use Disorder.

*Prodromal or Residual Symptoms*
(1) social isolation or withdrawal
(2) marked impairment in role functioning as wage-earner, student, or homemaker
(3) markedly peculiar behavior (e.g. collecting garbage, talking to self in public, or hoarding food)
(4) marked impairment in personal hygiene and grooming
(5) blunted, flat, or inappropriate affect
(6) digressive, vague, overelaborate, circumstantial, or metaphorical speech
(7) odd or bizarre ideation, or magical thinking, e.g. superstitiousness, clairvoyance, telepathy, "sixth sense," "others can feel my feelings," overvalued ideas, ideas of reference
(8) unusual perceptual experiences, e.g. recurrent illusions, sensing the presence of a force or person not actually present

*Examples:* Six months of prodromal symptoms with 1 week of symptoms from A; no prodromal symptoms with 6 months of symptoms from A; no prodromal symptoms with 2 weeks of symptoms from A and 6 months of residual symptoms; 6 months of symptoms from A, apparently followed by several years of complete remission, with 1 week of symptoms in A in current episode.

D. The full depressive or manic syndrome (criteria A and B of major depressive or manic episode), if pres-

TABLE I—*Continued*

ent, developed after any psychotic symptoms, or was brief in duration relative to the duration of the psychotic symptoms in A.

E. Onset of prodromal or active phase of the illness before age 45.

F. Not due to any Organic Mental Disorder or Mental Retardation.

---

* From American Psychiatric Association: *Diagnostic and Statistical Manual of Mental Disorders*, ed 3. American Psychiatric Association, Washington, DC, 1980. Used with permission.

TABLE II
NOSOLOGY OF TYPES OF SCHIZOPHRENIA*

| DSM-III | ICD-9 |
| --- | --- |
| Catatonic | Catatonic |
| Disorganized | Hebephrenic |
| Paranoid | Paranoid or Paraphrenic |
| Undifferentiated | (No equivalent term in ICD-9) |
| Residual | Residual |
| Schizophreniform (Brief Reactive Psychosis) | Acute Schizophrenic Episode (Oneirophrenia) (Schizophreniform) |
| (No equivalent term in DSM-III)† | Latent (Borderline) (Prepsychotic) (Prodromal) (Pseudoneurotic) (Pseudopsychopathic) |
| (No equivalent term in DSM-III) | Simple |
| Schizoaffective | Schizoaffective |

* Terms in parentheses may be subsumed under the major heading.
† Schizotypal and borderline personality disorders are sometimes used by American psychiatrists as equivalent to latent schizophrenia; but this is not consistent with DSM-III.

### Hallucinations and Delusions as Diagnostic Criteria.

Another reason for the greater tendency to diagnose schizophrenia in North America than in other areas is that many North American psychiatrists take it for granted that a patient who is hallucinating or who expresses paranoid delusions must be schizophrenic if no organic brain disease can be detected.

Sensory and perceptual disorders, such as hallucinations, may, indeed, give good diagnostic clues. However, not all types of hallucinations point toward schizophrenia. There are important qualifications regarding the modality, the time, and the content of the hallucination. Experiences of being controlled by outside forces or of having strange, continuous, somatic (cenesthetic) hallucinations or auditory, verbal hallucinations, particularly if the voices are coming from God or the devil or address the patient in the second person or talk about him, may support a diagnosis of schizophrenia. Perceptual distortions of time or objects in space point toward a diagnosis of schizophrenia, but only if they have been present at least several days; otherwise they may well be of toxic origin. The time factor applies also to the symptoms of loss of ego boundaries, the experience of being fused with the universe, and the experience of having one's thoughts spread to others.

The presence of delusions provides strong presumptive evidence for schizophrenia only if these delusions have strange, magical, esoteric, or bizarre content.

### Signs and Symptoms

The presence of some key symptoms for schizophrenia weighs heavily in favor of a diagnosis of schizophrenia.

**Loosening of Associations.** The loosening of associations—the specific thought disorder of the schizophrenic—is perhaps one of the most valuable diagnostic criteria. But a good knowledge of psychopathology is required to be sure of its presence, and to avoid confusing it with other forms of disturbed thinking, such as manic flight of ideas, disintegration of thought processes due to clouding of consciousness, and impaired reasoning due to fatigue or distraction. It is not sufficient to ask a patient the meaning of a proverb and then, on the basis of one's personal impression, declare that the patient has a pronounced schizophrenic thinking disturbance. It is sometimes impossible to distinguish, on the basis of a proverb test, between the disordered thinking of a schizophrenic and a manic patient, except for the greater verbosity of the manic.

**Bizarre Behavior.** The patient's behavior may furnish significant clues for the diagnosis of schizophrenia. Bizarre postures and grimacing are certainly characteristic of schizophrenic conditions, but what constitutes a bizarre posture is not always easy to establish unequivocally (see Fig. 4). Religious rituals and special positions for meditation or rock-and-roll dancing with which the observer is not familiar may be called bizarre.

True catalepsy may be almost pathognomonic of schizophrenia, but it is not a common symptom. A stupor is highly suggestive of catatonic schizophrenia, but hysteria or a depressive stupor must be carefully ruled out in the differential diagnosis.

The deterioration of social habits, even involving the smearing of feces, is not sufficient grounds for the diagnosis of schizophrenia. Such deterioration can occur in various toxic and organic psychoses, temporarily in hysterical twi-

FIGURE 4. A 44-year-old chronic schizophrenic woman showing characteristic mannerism and facial grimacing. (Courtesy of New York Academy of Medicine.)

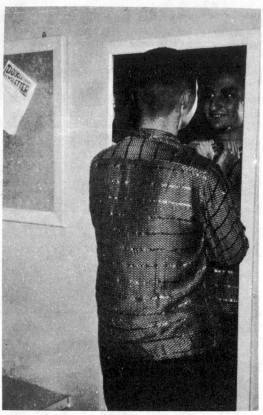

FIGURE 5. Hebephrenic patient. Posturing, grimacing, and mirror gazing are symptomatic of the disease. (Courtesy of Heinz E Lehmann, M.D.)

light states, and even at the peak of a manic attack in manic-depressives.

Pronounced social withdrawal also occurs under many conditions, ranging from simple sulking to anxiety and depression. Sustained passivity and lack of spontaneity should suggest the diagnosis of schizophrenia only if organic and depressive conditions can be definitely ruled out.

Stereotypies and verbigeration strongly suggest schizophrenia. But they occur almost exclusively in chronic institutionalized patients and are rarely seen today. Frequent and lengthy staring into a mirror and other odd mannerisms are also highly suggestive of a diagnosis of schizophrenia (see Fig. 5).

**Hallucinations.** Sensory experiences or perceptions without corresponding external stimuli are common symptoms of schizophrenia. Most common are auditory hallucinations, or the hearing of voices. Most characteristically, two or more voices talk about the patient, discussing him in the third person. Frequently, the voices address the patient, comment on what he is doing and what is going on around him, or are threatening or obscene and very disturbing to the patient. Many schizophrenic patients experience the hearing of their own thoughts. When they are reading silently, for example, they may be quite disturbed by hearing every word they are reading clearly spoken to them.

Visual hallucinations occur less frequently than auditory hallucinations in schizophrenic patients but they are not rare. Patients suffering from organic or affective psychoses experience visual hallucinations primarily at night or during limited periods of the day, but schizophrenic patients hallucinate as much during the day as they do during the night, sometimes almost continuously. They get relief only in sleep. When visual hallucinations occur in schizophrenia, they are usually seen nearby, clearly defined, in color, life size, in three dimensions, and moving. Visual hallucinations almost never occur by themselves but always in combination with hallucinations in one of the other sensory modalities.

Tactile, olfactory, and gustatory hallucinations are less common than visual hallucinations.

Schizophrenics often experience cenesthetic hallucinations, or sensations of altered states in body organs without any special receptor apparatus to explain the sensations—for example, a burning sensation in the brain, a pushing sensation in the abdominal blood vessels, or a cutting sensation in the bone marrow.

The present-day schizophrenic is much less likely to discuss his hallucinations openly than he was only 20 years ago.

**Dream Content.** Studies of the dream content of schizophrenic patients have shown that dreams of schizophrenics are less coherent and less complex—also less bizarre—than are the dreams of normal persons. Unpleasant emotions are more common in the dreams of schizophrenics than in the dreams of normals.

**Delusions.** By definition, delusions are false ideas that cannot be corrected by reasoning, and that are idiosyncratic for the patient—that is, not part of his cultural environment. They are among the most common symptoms of schizophrenia.

Most frequent are delusions of persecution, which are the key symptom in the paranoid type of schizophrenia. The conviction of being controlled by some unseen mysterious power that exercises its influence from a distance is almost pathognomonic for schizophrenia. It occurs in most, if not all, schizophrenics at one time or another, and for many it is a daily experience. The modern schizophrenic whose delusions have kept up with the scientific times may be preoccupied with atomic power, X-rays, or spaceships that take control over his mind and body. Also typical for many schizophrenics are delusional fantasies about the destruction of the world.

**Disturbances of Thinking.** The schizophrenic disturbance of thinking and conceptualization is one of the most characteristic features of the disease.

The one feature common to all manifestations of schizophrenic thought disorder is that the schizophrenic patient thinks and reasons on his autistic terms, according to his own intricate private rules of logic. The schizophrenic may be highly intelligent, certainly not confused, and he may be very painstaking in his abstractions and deductions. But his thought processes are strange and do not lead to conclusions based on reality or universal logic.

One investigator emphasized the fact that the schizophrenic may consider two things identical merely because they have identical predicates or properties. A schizophrenic patient may reason: "John is Peter's father, therefore, Peter is John's father." Such symmetrical reasoning is sometimes justified. For instance, John is Peter's brother; therefore, Peter is John's brother. But at other times such symmetrical conclusions are not justified, and the schizophrenic does not seem to know when he may apply them and when he may not.

A concretization of thought and a loss of the abstract attitude are typical of schizophrenic thinking. The patient loses his ability to generalize correctly, and he exhibits, in the ordering of his concepts, a defect similar to a loss of the figure-ground relation in perceptual performance. This defect is often brought out by the simple clinical test of asking the patient to interpret a well-known proverb. One schizophrenic interpreted the saying "A stitch in time saves nine" as "I should sew nine buttons on my coat"—an overly personalized and concrete explanation.

Overinclusion is a typical feature of the schizophrenic thought disorder. The schizophrenic tends to include many irrelevant items in his ideational and verbal behavior. Relatively few chronic schizophrenics present this symptom. It usually develops within the setting of a delusional mood, when things look different, sensations are more intense, and everything seems to have some strange special significance.

Schizophrenics are not capable of holding a set as well as a normal person is. This inability becomes evident when schizophrenics are tested for their reaction time in responding to a stimulus that is preceded by a ready signal. In a normal person, the introduction of the ready signal shortens the reaction time to the stimulus that may follow the signal within 10 to 15 seconds. But the schizophrenic's reaction time remains the same whether or not he is warned of the coming stimulus. They also generally have an increased arousal level and show greater responsivity to nonrelevant stimuli, and less responsivity to relevant stimuli, than do normal persons.

The schizophrenic is more dependent on immediate stimuli, and more determined in his behavior by them, than by long-range goals.

Another characteristic symptom of schizophrenia is the abrupt blocking of the stream of thought, or sometimes of all psychic activity. The patient's thoughts seem to stop suddenly and without warning. He ceases to speak in the middle of a sentence; after such a blocking episode, which may last seconds or minutes, he may be perplexed and have difficulty in coordinating his behavior. When he is questioned about his experience, he is likely to report that he had the physical sensation of somebody's taking his thoughts out of his head.

**Excessive Concreteness and Symbolism.** The one common factor running through the schizophrenic's preoccupation with invisible forces, radiation, witchcraft, religion, philosophy, and psychology is his leaning toward the esoteric, the abstract, and the symbolic. Consequently, a schizophrenic's thinking is characterized simultaneously by an overly concrete nature and an overly symbolic nature (see Fig. 6).

**Incoherence.** For the schizophrenic, language is primarily a means of self-expression, rather than a means of communication. His verbal and graphic productions are often either empty or obscure (see Figs. 7 and 8). Schizophrenic speech uses a larger number of words that do not belong, and schizophrenics tend to repeat words more frequently than do normals in long speech samples.

**Neologisms.** Occasionally, the schizophrenic creates a completely new expression, a neologism, when he needs to express a concept for which no ordinary word exists.

**Mutism.** This functional inhibition of speech and vocalization may last for hours or days, but, before the era of modern treatment methods, it often used to last for years in chronic schizophrenics of the catatonic type. Many schizophrenics tend to be monosyllabic and to answer questions as briefly as possible. They attempt to restrict contact with the interviewer as much as

**FIGURE 6.**    A 25-year-old schizophrenic man produced this eerie-looking mixture of commercial poster and existential quandary about time. (Courtesy of Heinz E Lehmann, M.D.)

FIGURE 7.   Bizarre drawing by a 26-year-old male schizophrenic patient, who provided no explanation of its meaning. (Courtesy of Joel Barg, Art Therapy, Douglas Hospital, Montreal, Canada.)

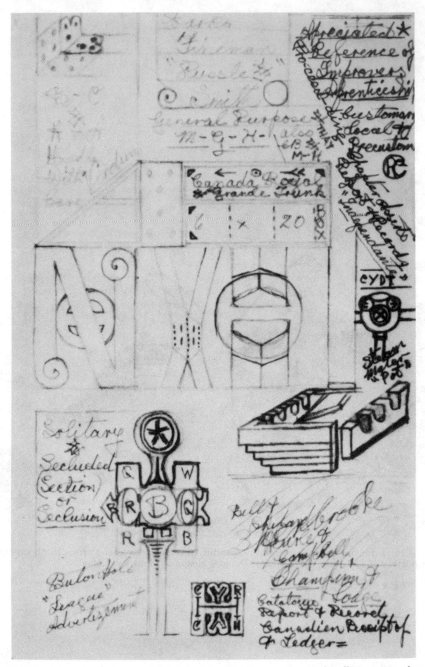

FIGURE 8.   This drawing, carefully executed by a schizophrenic woman, graphically expresses her incoherent thinking and her tendency to perseveration of ideas, combined with an ability to accomplish quite complex drafting. Similar drawings may be produced when normal people doodle while their attention is not focused on what they are doing. (Courtesy of Heinz E Lehmann, M.D.)

possible without being altogether uncooperative (see Fig. 9).

**Echolalia.**  Occasionally, the schizophrenic patient exhibits echolalia, repeating in his answers to the interviewer's questions many of the same words the questioner has used. "For in-

stance: Examiner: "How did you sleep last night?" Patient: "I slept well last night." Examiner: "Can you tell me the name of your head nurse?" Patient: "The name of my head nurse? The name of my head nurse is Miss Brown.""

Echolalia seems to signal two facts—that the

FIGURE 9. "Schizophrenic withdrawal." (Sid Bernstein, Research Facility, Orangeburg, New York.)

patient is aware of some shortcomings in his ideation, and that he is striving to maintain an active rapport with the interviewer. He acts much like somebody who is learning a new language and who, in answering his teacher's questions, uses as many of the teacher's words in the strange language as he can possibly manage.

**Verbigeration.** This rare symptom is found almost exclusively in chronic and very regressed schizophrenics. It consists of the senseless repetition of the same words or phrases, and it may, at times, go on for days. Like neologisms and echolalia, verbigeration is a rare symptom today and is almost restricted to long-term, institutionalized schizophrenics. Many psychiatrists working with schizophrenics in the community may never encounter these manifestations of schizophrenic deterioration.

**Stilted Language.** Some schizophrenics make extraordinary efforts to maintain their social relations in order to maintain their relatively stable adjustment. But they may betray their rigidity and artificiality in their interper-

sonal relations by a peculiarly stilted and grotesquely quaint language.

**Mannerisms.** Mannerisms of speech and movements are typical for many schizophrenics (see Fig. 10). So is grimacing, which can sometimes be noticed only by an experienced observer but is sometimes carried to a grotesque degree. In its more subdued form, grimacing may appear as tic-like movements, particularly in the perioral area.

**Stuporous States.** These states used to be common in the catatonic subtype of schizophrenia. Today, modern physical treatment methods permit therapists to interrupt stupors, usually within a few days, either by electroconvulsive treatment or by pharmacotherapy, and the stuporous patient has become a rare phenomenon.

Also rare today is catalepsy, or waxy flexibility (cerea flexibilitas), which was present in many patients 40 years ago. It consists of a wax-like yielding of all the movable parts of the body to any efforts made to place them in certain positions. Once placed in position, the arm, leg, or head remains in that position for a long time, sometimes for hours, even if the position is uncomfortable for the patient (see Fig. 11).

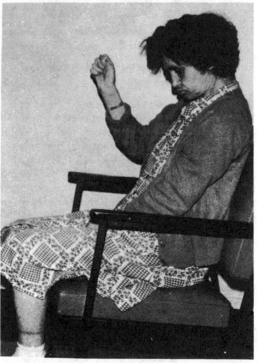

FIGURE 10. Chronic catatonic patient. This patient is immobile, demonstrating waxy flexibility. Her arm is in an uncomfortable position, elevated without support, and her stony facial expression has a *Schnauzkrampf* or frozen pout. (Courtesy of Heinz E Lehmann, M.D.)

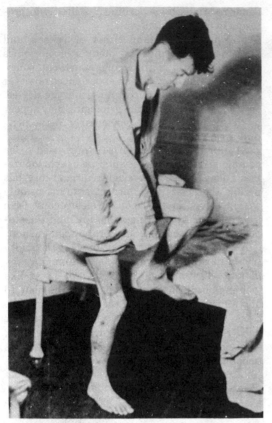

FIGURE 11.  A chronic schizophrenic stands in a cataleptic position. He maintained this uncomfortable position for hours. (Courtesy of New York Academy of Medicine.)

Many chronic schizophrenics still show a pronounced lack of spontaneity and move rarely or only when specifically asked to do certain things. However, a patient who shows almost no response to his environment is definitely capable of acutely perceiving what is going on around him. Even a patient in a complete stupor may, several months later, recall every word of a conversation carried on in front of him while he appeared to be in state of unconsciousness.

**Echopraxia.** This motor symptom is analogous to echolalia in the verbal sphere—imitation of movements and gestures of a person the schizophrenic is observing.

**Automatic Obedience.** Another symptom sometimes observed in catatonic patients is automatic obedience. A patient may, without hesitation and in a robot-like fashion, carry out most simple commands given to him.

**Negativism.** The term negativism refers to a patient's failure to cooperate, without any apparent reason for that failure. The patient does not appear to be fatigued, depressed, suspicious, or angry. He is obviously capable of

physical movement. But he fails to carry out even the simplest requests. Sometimes he may even do the opposite of what he is asked; for instance, he lowers his hand when one asks him to raise it.

**Stereotyped Behavior.** This behavior is occasionally seen in chronic schizophrenics, and not only in the back wards of old-time mental hospitals. It may present itself as repetitive patterns of moving or walking, perhaps pacing in the same circle day in and day out, or it may be the repetitive performance of strange gestures. Or, the patient may again and again, sometimes over a period of years, use the same phrases, ask the same questions, and make the same comments.

Most stereotyped behaviors of schizophrenic patients can be prevented and counteracted effectively by personal attention and through the use of various psychosocial therapies.

**Deteriorated Appearance and Manners.** Schizophrenic patients tend to deteriorate in their appearance. Their efforts at grooming and self-care may become minimal, and they may have to be reminded to wash, bathe, shave, change their underwear, and so on.

In general, schizophrenics show poor regard for the social amenities.

**Reduced Emotional Responses.** The quantitative change invariably consists of a reduction in the intensity of emotional responses. Many schizophrenics seem to be indifferent or, at times, totally apathetic. Others, with less marked emotional restriction or blunting, show, at least, some emotional shallowness or a certain lack of depth of feeling.

**Anhedonia.** Anhedonia is a particularly distressing symptom of many schizophrenics. The anhedonic person is incapable of experiencing or even imagining any pleasant emotion. Without being actually depressed, he feels emotionally barren. This hopeless, empty feeling drives some schizophrenics to commit suicide.

**Inappropriate Responses.** A typical emotional reaction of the schizophrenic is an incongruous or inappropriate response to life situations. A schizophrenic patient may talk about his child's death with a broad smile, or he may react with rage to a simple question about how he slept last night. The splitting or dissociation of the affective response from the cognitive content is almost pathognomonic for schizophrenia.

The degree of emotional blunting and inappropriateness of a schizophrenic's emotional reactions are among the most telling measures of the extent to which the schizophrenic process has invaded the personality. Emotional blunting also reflects the prognosis and the degree of personality deterioration in a chronic schizophrenic. Conversely, appropriate emotional reactions and a well-preserved emotional response are always favorable prognostic signs in schizophrenia.

**Abnormal Emotions.** Schizophrenia not only alters emotional reactions to external stimuli, but may induce strange emotions and moods that are seldom, if ever, experienced under normal conditions. For instance, states of exaltation with feelings of omnipotence, oceanic feelings of oneness with the universe, religious ecstasies, terrifying apprehensions about the disintegration of one's own personality or body, anxious moods when the catastrophic destruction of the universe seems to be impending—all these are emotional experiences occurring in different stages of schizophrenia, but they are most frequently encountered in the acute phases of the breakdown.

**Somatization.** There are no specific somatic manifestations in schizophrenia. However, in the early stages of the disease, patients often complain of a multitude of symptoms—headache, rheumatic pains in the shoulders, back strain, weakness, and indigestion. They are sometimes treated for months for neurasthenia, or are thought to be hypochondriacs or malingerers.

**Sensitivity.** All schizophrenics are, at least originally, more sensitive than the average person. It is likely that the increased sensitivity and heightened responsiveness to sensory and emotional stimulation is present in schizophrenics from an early age, possibly from birth. Schizophrenia may be characterized by a genetic hypersensitivity that leaves the patient vulnerable to an overwhelming onslaught of stimuli from without and within.

**Social Withdrawal.** Almost without exception, schizophrenic patients are characterized by social withdrawal, by the emotional distance one experiences in their presence, and by a lack of capacity for establishing rapport with others.

**Loss of Ego Boundaries.** A characteristic feature of most schizophrenic conditions is the so-called loss of ego boundaries. This symptom may give the patient the delusional conviction that he is reading other people's minds or being controlled by other people's thoughts. It also renders him extremely vulnerable to any kind of external stimulation. His own identity may fuse with that of any object in the universe around him, and he may suffer personally when he becomes aware that some object in his environment is being attacked. The loss of ego boundaries and identity produces feelings of depersonalization, followed by experiences of de-

realization. The resulting loss of contact with reality is the core symptom of any psychosis.

One specific symptom related to a loss of identity is the uncertainty many schizophrenics feel about their gender.

**Variability.** Another strange but fundamental characteristic of schizophrenia is its unpredictable variability or inconsistency. A schizophrenic patient may be incapable, at a certain time, of carrying on a rational, simple conversation, and yet half an hour later he may write a sensible and remarkably well-composed letter to a relative.

**Precox Feeling.** The precox feeling consists of an intuitive experience by the examiner that determines whether it is possible to empathize with the patient. Only those patients whose emotional distance makes it impossible to establish an empathic rapport should be classified as schizophrenic; all other conditions should be diagnosed as schizophreniform.

## Negative Symptoms

Negative symptoms of schizophrenia include blunted affect, autism, social isolation, withdrawal, and decreased initiative. They are compared to the so-called positive symptoms such as delusions, hallucinations, ideas of reference and agitation. The terms are used by psychopharmacologists, who are more successful managing the positive symptoms with neuroleptics than they are in affecting the negative symptoms.

## Prepsychotic Personality

The typical but not invariable history is that of a schizoid or schizotypal personality—quiet, passive, with few friends as a child; daydreaming, introverted, and shut in as an adolescent and adult. The child is often reported as having been especially obedient and never in any mischief. In school he was good in spelling but poor in arithmetic. He made few friends as a child, and his deficient friendship pattern was particularly noticeable in adolescence.

The typical preschizophrenic adolescent has few dates, does not usually learn to dance, and has no close boyfriends or girlfriends. He is not interested in petting or other heterosexual or homosexual activities but is often disturbed about masturbation. He avoids all competitive sports, but he likes to go to the movies, watch television, or listen to stereo music. He may be an avid reader of books on philosophy and psychology.

Typically, schizophrenics have had many different jobs but held none for long. It is usually difficult to ascertain why they did not stay longer in any position.

### Suicide and Homicide

Dramatic self-mutilation in schizophrenic patients—for example, the gouging out of an eye or the cutting off of the penis—occurs in probably less than 1 percent of all cases. It has been referred to as the Van Gogh syndrome and may sometimes be the expression of dysmorphophobic delusions, the irrational conviction that a serious bodily defect exists, or reflect other complex, unconscious mechanisms.

Suicide is a danger for schizophrenics that must never be forgotten. Probably more schizophrenics than manic-depressives commit suicide, although the immediate risk of suicide is relatively greater among manic-depressives. A schizophrenic may commit suicide because he is deeply depressed—for instance, during a schizoaffective reaction. Or, he may kill himself in response to the relentless commands he is receiving from hallucinatory voices.

Some chronic schizophrenics have unpredictable suicidal impulses during brief spells of dejection. Suicide rates were reported to be as high as 4 percent in a group of schizophrenics followed over a period of years.

In many cases, the psychiatrist and the nurses who knew a patient or his family for a long time are unable, in retrospect, to recognize any change in his condition that might have been considered a warning signal of the impending tragedy.

Probably the greatest number of schizophrenic suicides occurs among those suffering from the beginning stages of schizophrenia. Sometimes, when the disease is in an early stage of development, even the victim's family and best friends have virtually no inkling of the terrible problem with which the patient is grappling. Many of the unexplained suicides among students on a university campus are probably committed by young persons who have become aware of a malignant, insidious process that threatens to destroy their minds. Rather than seek psychiatric treatment or confide their feelings of uncontrollable disintegration to their friends, they choose to end their lives.

It is exceedingly difficult to prevent most schizophrenic homicides, since there is usually no clear warning. Most of the homicides come as a horrifying surprise. Patients who are known to be paranoid with homicidal tendencies should not, as a rule, be allowed to move about freely as long as they retain their delusions and their aggressive tension. The homicidal schizophrenic patient may appear to be relaxed, even apathetic; then, within a day or two, he kills somebody.

A careful analysis of these unpredictable suicides and homicides leads to the conclusion that the most significant single factor in most of them is a traumatic experience of rejection. The schizophrenic's pathological sensitivity makes him extraordinarily vulnerable to all common life stresses. For him, rejection, particularly by members of his own family, seems to be more traumatic than most other stresses.

### Clinical Syndromes

The types of schizophrenia which are officially accepted in DSM-III are listed in Table II. Other types are recognized in ICD-9. Still others can be found in the psychiatric literature. This section outlines the more accepted types of schizophrenia.

### Catatonic

Catatonic schizophrenia (see Table III) occurs in two forms: inhibited or stuporous catatonia and excited catatonia. The essential feature of both forms is the marked abnormality of motor behavior.

**Stuporous Catatonia.** The stuporous catatonic may be in a state of complete stupor, or he may show a pronounced decrease of spontaneous movements and activity. He may be mute or nearly so, or he may show distinct negativism, stereotypies, echopraxia, or automatic obedience. Occasionally, catatonic schizophrenics exhibit the phenomenon of catalepsy or waxy flexibility.

A patient in a state of complete catatonic stupor usually can be roused from it in a dra-

TABLE III
DIAGNOSTIC CRITERIA FOR CATATONIC TYPE*

A type of Schizophrenia dominated by any of the following:

(1) catatonic stupor (marked decrease in reactivity to environment and/or reduction of spontaneous movements and activity) or mutism
(2) catatonic negativism (an apparently motiveless resistance to all instructions or attempts to be moved)
(3) catatonic rigidity (maintenance of a rigid posture against efforts to be moved)
(4) catatonic excitement (excited motor activity, apparently purposeless and not influenced by external stimuli)
(5) catatonic posturing (voluntary assumption of inappropriate or bizarre posture)

* From American Psychiatric Association: *Diagnostic and Statistical Manual of Mental Disorders*, ed 3. American Psychiatric Association, Washington, DC, 1980. Used with permission.

matic manner by the intravenous injection of a short-acting barbiturate. In many instances he becomes, for an hour or two, relatively lucid.

**Excited Catatonia.** The excited catatonic is in a state of extreme psychomotor agitation. He talks and shouts almost continuously. His verbal productions are often incoherent. Patients in catatonic excitement urgently require physical and medical control, since they are often destructive and violent to others, and their dangerous excitement can cause them to injure themselves or to collapse from complete exhaustion.

Today most patients can be carried safely through the critical period of acute excitement with modern pharmacotherapy and electroconvulsive treatment.

**Periodic Catatonia.** A rare but intriguing form of catatonia is periodic catatonia also known as Gjessing's disease. Motor functions, ideation, and perception in periodic catatonia are closely linked to the patient's changing levels of positive or negative nitrogen balance. Patients affected with the disease have periodic recurrences of stuporous or excited catatonic states. Each recurrence of catatonic behavior is associated with an extreme shift in the patient's metabolic nitrogen balance. Relapses in such patients can be prevented by regulating their nitrogen balance through the continuous administration of thyroxin. However, these metabolic and therapeutic observations apply only to patients suffering from periodic catatonia, and most schizophrenic patients who present catatonic symptoms do not fall into this category. Most of the rare cases of periodic catatonia seen in recent years responded well to neuroleptic medication, and relapses were usually prevented by neuroleptic maintenance medication.

**Catatonia as a Nonspecific Syndrome.** In recent years, several investigators have drawn attention to the fact that catatonia is not a disease entity or exclusively a subtype of schizophrenia but, rather, a nonspecific syndrome that occurs quite frequently in other psychiatric conditions.

### Disorganized (Hebephrenic)

The disorganized or hebephrenic subtype (see Table IV) is characterized by a marked regression to primitive, disinhibited, and unorganized behavior. The onset is usually early, before age 25. The hebephrenic patient is usually active but in an aimless, nonconstructive manner. His thought disorder is pronounced, and his contact with reality is extremely poor. His personal appearance and his social behavior are dilapidated.

His emotional responses are inappropriate, and he often bursts out laughing without any apparent reasons. Incongruous grinning and grimacing are common in this type of patients, whose behavior is best described as silly or fatuous.

### Paranoid

The paranoid type of schizophrenia (see Table V) is characterized mainly by the presence of delusions of persecution or grandeur. Paranoid schizophrenics are usually older than catatonics or hebephrenics when they break down; that is, they are usually in their late twenties or in their thirties. Patients who have been well up to that age have usually established a place and an identity for themselves in the community. Their ego resources are greater than those of catatonic and hebephrenic patients. Paranoid schizophrenics show less regression of mental faculties, emotional response, and behavior than do the other subtypes of schizophrenia.

A typical paranoid schizophrenic is tense, suspicious, guarded, and reserved. He is often hostile and aggressive. The paranoid schizophrenic usually conducts himself quite well socially. His intelligence in areas not invaded by his delusions may remain high.

### Paraphrenia

Although paraphrenia is not included as a diagnostic entity in DSM-III, it appears as a synonym for schizophrenia, paranoid type, in

TABLE IV
DIAGNOSTIC CRITERIA FOR DISORGANIZED TYPE*

A type of Schizophrenia in which there are:

   A. Frequent incoherence.

   B. Absence of systematized delusions.

   C. Blunted, inappropriate, or silly affect.

\* From American Psychiatric Association: *Diagnostic and Statistical Manual of Mental Disorders*, ed 3. American Psychiatric Association, Washington, DC, 1980. Used with permission.

TABLE V
DIAGNOSTIC CRITERIA FOR PARANOID TYPE*

A type of Schizophrenia dominated by one or more of the following:

   (1) persecutory delusions
   (2) grandiose delusions
   (3) delusional jealousy
   (4) hallucinations with persecutory or grandiose content

\* From American Psychiatric Association: *Diagnostic and Statistical Manual of Mental Disorders*, ed 3. American Psychiatric Association, Washington, DC, 1980. Used with permission.

ICD-9. When it is not used to denote a nosological entity in its own right, the term "paraphrenia" is often used to describe chronic schizophrenic conditions characterized by the presence of well-systematized delusions. Paraphrenic patients are characterized by the unrealistic, fantastic, sometimes bizarre, and never plausible nature of their delusions. The personalities of paraphrenic patients, on the other hand, are usually well preserved, and the patients are often quite happily adjusted to their life situations, In fact, some paraphrenics seem to derive considerable satisfaction from their delusions, which are more often of a grandiose than of a persecutory nature.

### Simple

Simple schizophrenia does not appear in DSM-III as a subtype of schizophrenia. However, schizophrenia, simple type, is listed in ICD-9, although clinicians are cautioned to resort to the diagnosis only rarely.

The simple schizophrenic's principal disorder is a gradual, insidious loss of drive, interest, ambition, and initiative. He is usually not hallucinating or delusional, and, if these symptoms do occur, they do not persist. He withdraws from contact with other people, tends to stay in his room, avoids meeting or eating with other members of the family, stops working, and stops seeing his friends. If he is still in school, his marks drop to a low level, even if they were consistently high in the past.

The patient avoids going out into the street during the day, but may go for long walks by himself early in the morning or at odd hours. He tends to sleep until noon or later, after staying up alone most of the night. During the early stages of his illness, the patient may have many somatic complaints, variously diagnosed as fatigue, nervousness, neurosis, psychosomatic disease, and laziness. He is often treated for a year or more before the correct diagnosis is made. Later, in many cases, the simple schizophrenic turns into a tramp, hobo, or street person. He becomes increasingly shallow in his emotional responses and is quite content to drift aimlessly through life as long as he is left alone.

Although he appears to be indifferent to his environment, he may react with sudden rage to persistent nagging by members of his family. The immediate reason for admission of a simple schizophrenic to a hospital is often an outburst of violence directed against his mother or father for a trivial reason.

Simple schizophrenics may resemble pathological personalities of the inadequate or schizoid type. But the distinguishing feature in that

simple schizophrenia makes its appearance at some time during or after puberty and from then on, as a rule, goes on to definite deterioration; personality deviations usually start earlier and then remain the same over the years.

### Schizoaffective

In the schizoaffective disorders, a strong element of either depressive or euphoric affect is added to otherwise schizophrenic symptoms. Schizoaffective patients may be depressed, retarded, and suicidal. At the same time, they may express absurd delusions of persecution, complain of being controlled by outside forces, and have a distinct schizophrenic thought disorder. Or patients with various schizophrenic symptoms may be euphoric, playful, and overactive. In the diagnosis of these cases, however, the presence of schizophrenic symptoms is the decisive factor.

The prognosis for schizoaffective patients is generally better than that for other schizophrenics, but it is usually worse than the prognosis for manic-depressives. The chronic course of the illness and the marked deterioration are more characteristic of schizophrenia than of affective disorder.

The schizoaffective subtype of schizophrenia is listed as a schizophrenic disorder in the ninth revision of ICD-9; however, the American Psychiatric Association, in DSM-III, lists schizoaffective disorder as a diagnostic entity by itself, and includes it neither under schizophrenic disorders nor under affective disorders, but under psychotic disorders not elsewhere classified.

### Undifferentiated

Frequently, patients who are clearly schizophrenic cannot be easily fitted into one of the other subtypes, usually because they meet the criteria for more than one subtype. Some acute, excited schizophrenic patients—diagnosed in ICD-9 as suffering from acute schizophrenic episode—and some inert, chronic patients fall into this category, for which DSM-III provides the designation "undifferentiated" (see Table VI).

### Latent

Latent schizophrenia is diagnosed in those patients who may have a marked schizoid personality and who show occasional behavioral peculiarities or thought disorders, without consistently manifesting any clearly psychotic pathology. The syndrome is also known as borderline schizophrenia.

Latent schizophrenia is not listed in DSM-III, but is listed in ICD-9, although it is not a

TABLE VI
DIAGNOSTIC CRITERIA FOR UNDIFFERENTIATED
TYPE*

A.  A type of Schizophrenia in which there are: prominent delusions, hallucinations, incoherence, or grossly disorganized behavior.

B.  Does not meet the criteria for any of the other listed types or meets the criteria for more than one.

    * From American Psychiatric Association: *Diagnostic and Statistical Manual of Mental Disorders*, ed 3. American Psychiatric Association, Washington, DC, 1980. Used with permission.

TABLE VII
DIAGNOSTIC CRITERIA FOR RESIDUAL TYPE*

A.  A history of at least one previous episode of Schizophrenia with prominent psychotic symptoms.

B.  A clinical picture without any prominent psychotic symptoms that occasioned evaluation or admission to clinical care.

C.  Continuing evidence of the illness, such as blunted or inappropriate affect, social withdrawal, eccentric behavior, illogical thinking, or loosening of associations.

    * From American Psychiatric Association: *Diagnostic and Statistical Manual of Mental Disorders*, ed 3. American Psychiatric Association, Washington, DC, 1980. Used with permission.

diagnosis recommended for general use. In DSM-III latent schizophrenia most nearly corresponds to schizotypal personality disorder.

### Residual

Residual schizophrenia (see Table VII) is a chronic form of schizophrenia which follows an acute episode of illness. Latent schizophrenia is the stage before a schizophrenic breakdown, and residual schizophrenia is the stage after the attack. Residual schizophrenia is also known as ambulatory schizophrenia.

### Childhood

Childhood schizophrenia is diagnosed when schizophrenia makes its appearance before puberty. Schizophrenia can occur in very young children. The prognosis for a person who develops schizophrenia before puberty or in his early teens is usually poor.

In most cases, the schizophrenic child has a disturbed body image; he may, for instance, literally not know where his feet are. He may show poor motor coordination and exhibit peculiar motor behavior, such as spinning and twirling. Schizophrenia in childhood is characterized primarily by a primitive plasticity—that is, uneven development caused by a maturational lag at an embryological level.

### Late-onset

Although schizophrenia is typically a disease of adolescence or young adulthood, it may, particularly in its paranoid form, make its first appearance in the fifth, sixth, or even seventh decade of life. German psychiatrists classify as late schizophrenics many psychotics who, in America, would be classified as suffering from involutional psychosis.

### Pseudoneurotic

In 1949, Hoch and Polatin described a clinical variety of schizophrenia to which they gave the name "pseudoneurotic schizophrenia." Pseudo-

neurotic schizophrenics are, as the name implies, patients who present predominantly neurotic symptoms. But, on close and careful examination, they may reveal schizophrenic abnormalities of thinking and emotional reaction. Sometimes these abnormalities are so well compensated that it is all but impossible to demonstrate schizophrenic symptoms in clinical examinations, in psychological tests, or even in the history.

The pseudoneurotic schizophrenic is characterized by pan-anxiety, pan-phobia and chaotic sexuality. The diffuse pan-anxiety is probably the most specific diagnostic criterion. The phobias are not fixed and may amorphously affect all areas of life over a period of time. Unlike patients suffering from anxiety neurosis, the pseudoneurotic schizophrenic has anxiety that is always free floating and that hardly ever subsides, even temporarily. The existence of this diagnostic category of schizophrenia has been contested, and it is used mainly on the North American continent, although not in DSM-III. Its use may have the practical value of reorienting the therapeutic strategy in certain patients from unsuccessful psychotherapy to physical treatment methods—in particular, pharmacotherapy.

### Oneiroid

Oneiroid states in schizophrenic patients were first described by Mayer-Gross. In the oneiroid state, the patient feels and behaves as though he were in a dream. (*Oneiros* is the Greek word for dream.) He may be deeply perplexed and not fully oriented in time and place. During that state of clouded consciousness, he may experience feelings of ecstasy and rapidly shifting hallucinated scenes. Illusionary distortions of his perceptional processes, including disturbances of time perception, and the symptomatic picture, may resemble those of a hysterical twilight state. During oneiroid reactions, the observer can most clearly observe the schizophrenic's peculiar "double bookkeeping," as it has been called. The patient may be convinced that he is traveling through space on a satellite and, at the same time, conscientiously follow the regular hospital routine. The oneiroid schizophrenic acknowledges everyday realities but gives priority to his world of hallucinatory and delusional experiences, whereas the normal person with a vivid fantasy life always gives priority to contingencies of reality. Oneiroid states are usually limited in duration and occur most frequently in acute schizophrenic breakdowns. They are usually called brief reactive psychotic episodes in DSM-III (see Table VIII).

### Bouffée Délirante (Acute Delusional Psychosis)

In French psychiatry, the condition known as acute delusional psychosis, or *bouffée délirante*, is not included in the diagnosis of schizophrenia. Rather, *bouffée délirante* is considered to be a disease entity in its own right, a psychiatric disorder that does not require maintenance pharmacotherapy.

Dongier, in 1978, listed the following essential criteria for the diagnosis of *bouffée délirante*, not all of which need to be present: (1) frequent background of personality disorder; (2) absence of a schizoid premorbid personality; (3) acute onset; (4) duration of less than 3 months; (5) spontaneous return to premorbid level of adjustment, even without specific antipsychotic treatment; (6) polymorphous symptoms, a disorderly (kaleidoscopic) succession of differing delu-sional contents; (7) a fascinating intensity of the delusional experience; (8) oscillations between insight and delusion; (9) mood alterations and fluctuations; (10) increase of delusions in sleep-related states; and (11) sudden termination after days or weeks (rarely months). The secondary criteria are: (1) similar heredity (acute delusional psychosis and not schizophrenic process); (2) a reactive quality (emotional stress, fatigue, infectious disease); (3) any of Schneider's first-rank symptoms; (4) some clouding of consciousness; (5) little effect from phenothiazines apart from sedation; (6) worsening under the effect of intravenous amobarbital sodium; (7) normal event-related slow potentials; and (8) night sleep electroencephalographic recording with some specific features.

Accordingly, *bouffée délirante* episodes belong to the schizophrenic spectrum diseases. In American clinical practice, these episodes are usually diagnosed as schizophreniform disorder, schizoaffective disorder, or brief reactive psychosis. French psychiatrists report that about 40 percent of patients with the diagnosis *bouffée délirante* are later reclassified as suffering from schizophrenia.

### Process Schizophrenia

The Scandinavian psychiatrist Langfeldt distinguished a strict concept of schizophrenia known as process, nuclear or nonremitting schizophrenia. Process schizophrenia has an insidious onset and a deteriorating course. The disorder involves blunted affect, disordered thinking, autistic preoccupation and loosening of associations.

TABLE VIII
DIAGNOSTIC FEATURES OF BRIEF REACTIVE PSYCHOSIS*

| Essential Features | Associated Features | Other Features† |
|---|---|---|
| Recognizable stressful event preceding the appearance of symptoms | Perplexity | Disorder is often unofficially called hysterical psy- |
| Emotional turmoil and at least one of the following: | Bizarre behavior | chosis |
| 1. Incoherence; markedly illogical thinking | Inappropriate, volatile affect | |
| 2. Delusions | Disorientation; clouding of consciousness | |
| 3. Hallucinations | Poor insight | |
| 4. Grossly disorganized behavior | Patient is usually incapacitated and dependent on the | |
| Duration of disorder more than a few hours but less than 1 week | close assistance of others | |
| Disorder may be superimposed on other disorders, such as personality disorder | Sometimes followed by mild depression | |
| Rule out organic mental disorder, manic episode, and factitious illness with psychological symptoms (Ganser's syndrome) | | |

* Adapted from American Psychiatric Association: *Diagnostic and Statistical Manual of Mental Disorders,* ed 3. American Psychiatric Association, Washington, DC, 1980.
† Not cited as a clinical feature in DSM-III but may be present in this disorder.

*World Health Organization Diagnostic Study*

A major study has been made by the World Health Organization (WHO), which launched in 1965 one of the most ambitious and comprehensive research efforts ever undertaken in the diagnosis of schizophrenia, the International Pilot Study of Schizophrenia.

The following are some of the key WHO findings and observations:

Within groups of units of analysis, auditory hallucinations seem to be one of the most valuable symptoms for the diagnosis of schizophrenia; this symptom not only ranks high in discriminatory power, but also has a high frequency of occurrence (74 percent) and a high reliability (0.86). The experience of being controlled rated highest in reliability. Delusions and qualitative disorders of formal thinking, such as erroneous logic, were rated of medium reliability. Flatness of affect and incongruity of affect were of comparatively low reliability.

A striking finding was that the interrater reliability of the patients' own reports, such as auditory hallucinations and experiences of being controlled, tended to be consistently higher than the reliability of observations of patient behavior—for instance, qualitative disorder of form of thinking or flatness of affect—although the differences were sometimes small. Most of the symptoms of lowest reliability were observations by the interviewers.

**Specificity of Symptoms.** More significant than sheer statistical frequency of occurrence and even reliability of symptoms is their diagnostic discriminatory power—the specificity of symptoms. For example, a symptom such as the use of neologisms may be rarely observed. However, it is highly specific and almost pathognomonic for schizophrenia. In fact, the presence of the single symptom of neologisms gives a 97 percent probability that the condition would be diagnosed anywhere in the world as schizophrenia. On the other hand, lack of insight is frequently observed in schizophrenics, as it is in all psychotics, but it is among the least specific symptoms of schizophrenia. Flatness of affect is frequently reported and is a quite specific symptom, but, unfortunately, its reliability is low. It is often difficult to reach agreement among different examiners as to whether or not the particular symptom is present.

In the area of specificity, the following is a list of six of the most frequently reported symptoms in the concordant schizophrenic group that were not found among the 15 most frequent symptoms in the discrepant schizophrenic

groups: auditory hallucinations (frequency, 74 percent), flatness of affect (80 percent), voices speaking to the patient (65 percent), thought alienation (52 percent), thoughts spoken aloud (50 percent), and delusions of control (48 percent). These may be considered the core symptoms of schizophrenia, as revealed by the WHO study.

Conversely, the following are six of the most frequent symptoms that appeared in the discrepant group but were not among the 15 most frequently reported symptoms in the concordant group: poor rapport (frequency, 46 percent), depressed mood (37 percent), gloomy thoughts (34 percent), sleep problems (27 percent), hopelessness (27 percent), and hypochrondriacal preoccupations (23 percent). These symptoms, although not altogether atypical for schizophrenia, seem to be peripheral symptoms.

Tables IX and X summarize the WHO findings.

## Differential Diagnosis

### Neurotic Symptoms in Schizophrenia

Hysterical symptoms are common in acute schizophrenic breakdowns: thus, the presence of hysterical, dissociative, or even conversion symptoms does not rule out a diagnosis of schizophrenia. Every schizophrenic breakdown is preceded by a period of marked tension and anxiety, which may last only a few days or may extend over many months. During the acute and subacute stages of a schizophrenic attack, anxiety and depression may color the clinical picture significantly, again without excluding the overruling diagnosis of schizophrenia, which, in such cases, has not yet diminished the patient's emotional reaction to the onslaught of the psychotic attack. Obsessive symptoms are common in

TABLE IX
FREQUENCY OF SYMPTOMS IN A POOLED SAMPLE OF CORE SCHIZOPHRENIC PATIENTS EXAMINED IN NINE INTERNATIONAL CENTERS*

| Symptom | Frequency (%) |
| --- | --- |
| Lack of insight | 97 |
| Auditory hallucinations | 74 |
| Verbal hallucinations | 70 |
| Ideas of reference | 67 |
| Suspiciousness | 66 |
| Flatness of affect | 66 |
| Voices speaking to patient | 65 |
| Delusional mood | 64 |
| Delusions of persecution | 64 |
| Inadequate description of problems | 64 |
| Thought alienation | 52 |
| Thoughts spoken aloud | 50 |

* Adapted from Sartorius N, Shapiro R, Jablensky A: The International Pilot Study of Schizophrenia. Schizophr Bull *1:* 21, 1974.

| Units of Analysis | | |
|---|---|---|
| 0.93: High | 0.62–0.60: Medium | 0.59–0.47: Low |
| Suicidal | Change of interest | Stereotyped behavior |
| Elated thoughts | Dissociation of speech | Increased libido |
| Ideas of reference | Perplexity | Negativism |
| Delusions of grandeur | Lability | Perseveration |
| Thought hearing | | Body hallucinations |
| Derealization | | Morose mood |
| Lack of concentration | | |
| Hopelessness | | |
| Delusions of persecution | | |
| Delusions of reference | | |

* Adapted from World Health Organization: *Report of the International Pilot Study of Schizophrenia.* World Health Organization, Geneva, 1973.

schizophrenic conditions, and an obsessive-compulsive clinical picture can develop into schizophrenia.

### Bipolar Disorder versus Schizophrenia

The differential diagnosis between schizophrenia and manic-depressive disorder should not, as a rule, present many difficulties. The behavior of an excited catatonic patient is directed primarily by his own qualitatively disordered mental processes. His actions are unpredictable and appear senseless, his affect is difficult to understand, and his verbal productions may be irrational and incoherent. A manic patient, on the other hand, is always distractible, and most of his actions are determined by his immediate environment.

Depressive conditions should never be diagnosed as schizophrenic unless there are also some unmistakably schizophrenic symptoms present. In schizoaffective disorders, which may resemble manic-depressive conditions, the presence of clearly schizophrenic symptoms, such as schizophrenic thought disorder, places the reactions in the diagnostic category of schizophrenia.

### Paranoid Disorders versus Paranoid Schizophrenia

Since paranoid delusions of persecution or grandeur are essential symptoms in both the paranoid subtype of schizophrenia and in paranoid disorders, the differential diagnosis between the two conditions must be carefully considered when paranoid symptoms prevail. The diagnostic decision must be based on the presence or absence of the essential features of schizophrenia and its paranoid subtype, as outlined in Tables I and V. A positive diagnosis of a paranoid disorder can be made only when the patient's condition fulfills the criteria of that disorder without any schizophrenic symptomatology, such as autism, loosening of associations, hallucinations and so on.

### Schizophrenia in the Adolescent

Any psychiatric disorder that occurs during adolescence assumes a certain schizophrenic coloring, since many of the features characteristic of nonschizophrenic adolescent turbulence—exaltation, intense preoccupation with abstract ideas, unpredictable variations of mood, daydreaming, introspection, shyness—are often seen in schizophrenia. Therefore, it is not unusual to misdiagnose a manic or depressive phase of a manic-depressive disorder as schizophrenia if the patient's first attack occurs in late adolescence. Also, the usual rule that manic-depressive disorder does not occur at that early an age simply is not always true.

### Psychological Tests

In most clinical centers, certain psychological test batteries are routinely used to indicate, confirm, or rule out a diagnosis of schizophrenia.

A diagnosis of schizophrenia is supported if these tests reflect unusual or bizarre perceptual and conceptual processes (Rorschach, TAT, drawing tests, and WAIS, particularly the Similarity Subtest). Other typical findings are variability and uneven scattering of test scores (WAIS), and disturbances of concept formation—in particular, overinclusive and autistic thought processes (Object-Sorting and Concept-Formation Tests). Self-report personality inventories (MMPI) allow for objective and even automated scoring, and can be helpful in the differential diagnosis of doubtful cases.

### Prognosis and Course

The more acute the onset of a schizophrenic attack, the better are the chances for a good remission or complete recovery. If a precipitating event has clearly triggered the breakdown, the chances for a favorable outcome are also relatively better.

The younger a patient is at the onset of his schizophrenic psychosis, the worse is his prognosis. Patients who break down in childhood or early puberty seldom recover completely.

A history of good adjustment in the important areas of social, sexual, and occupational functioning before the breakdown also indicates a favorable prognosis. Married schizophrenics have a better prognosis than do single, divorced, or widowed patients; the fact that they are married is evidence that interpersonal bonds may serve as a bridge for a return to the community. A patient who relates easily to people in his environment and who is capable of emotional warmth and natural emotional reactions has a good chance for reintegration. The presence of depression as a feature of the schizophrenic syndrome also makes for a better prognosis. Conversely, sustained emotional withdrawal and aloofness, or shallow and inappropriate affective responses, are ominous prognostic signs.

An extended follow-up study of schizophrenic patients showed that most of them seemed to reach a plateau about 5 years after their first breakdown, and that those who had not remitted after 2 to 3 years faced a gloomy outlook.

## The Family

The patient's family plays an important role in his prognosis. A number of studies in recent years have established the fact that many schizophrenics come from deeply disturbed families. The patient who lives in a family with high levels of tension is more likely to relapse than the patient whose family is more tolerant with one another and with the patient.

## Preventing Relapses

A prognostic factor is the patient's cooperation and degree of conscientiousness in following prescribed drug maintenance therapy. Many schizophrenic patients today can be rendered symptom free within a few weeks or months, but about 60 percent of them can be maintained in this condition only with continued drug therapy after they have been discharged into the community. Placebo-controlled maintenance studies have established this point. The more often a patient neglects to take his maintenance medications—that is, the worse his compliance—the more likely he is to suffer a relapse.

## Deterioration

The risk of personality deterioration increases with each schizophrenic relapse. Schizophrenic recoveries are often called remissions because many of the patients later relapse. Although they may remit again, there is, with each schizophrenic attack, a greater probability of some permanent personality damage. This risk of personality deterioration increases rapidly after the second relapse.

However, chronic schizophrenia does not inevitably lead to intellectual deterioration. And, contrary to widely held convictions throughout the psychiatric profession, the schizophrenic process may be reversible over long periods of time.

## Final Outcome

There are five possible outcomes for the schizophrenic patient: full and permanent remission; remission, with one or more future relapses; social remission, with personality defect and with the patient either capable of self-care and self-support, or dependent on protection and supervision; stable chronicity; and deterioration to a terminal stage. This last stage—a vegetable-like existence—is a rare phenomenon among schizophrenics who have become ill during the past 25 years. Modern physical and social treatment methods are in most cases successful in preventing at least the terminal stage of deterioration, which was the most probable outcome of schizophrenia in Kraepelin's time, and which was probably due more to the ravages of institutionalization than to schizophrenia.

DSM-III has suggested a classification of the course of the illness which is outlined in Table XI.

## Clinical Management

It is essential to specify therapeutic goals because one person's failure would be considered another person's success. A generally agreed on goal of treatment is psychotic symptom reduction. The most rapid and cost-effective method of achieving this goal is through the use of psychopharmacological agents. The clinician should master a few such drugs, preferably one from each major class, and avoid the common errors of polypharmacy and using too small a dose. Drugs, however, do not alter the personality organization or enhance psychological growth, and deficiencies in these areas may leave the patient at an increased risk for a subsequent decompensation. The various methods that have proved to be useful in influencing behavior can

TABLE XI
CLASSIFICATION OF COURSE*

The course of the illness is coded in the fifth digit:
  (1) *Subchronic.* The time from the beginning of the illness, during which the individual began to show signs of the illness (including prodromal, active, and residual phases) more or less continuously, is less than 2 years but at least 6 months
  (2) *Chronic.* Same as above, but greater than 2 years.
  (3) *Subchronic with Acute Exacerbation.* Reemergence of prominent psychotic symptoms in an individual with a subchronic course who has been in the residual phase of the illness
  (4) *Chronic with Acute Exacerbation.* Reemergence of prominent psychotic symptoms in an individual with a chronic course who has been in the residual phase of the illness
  (5) *In Remission.* This should be used when an individual with a history of Schizophrenia, now is free of all signs of the illness (whether or not on medication). The differentiation of Schizophrenia In Remission from no mental disorder requires consideration of the period of time since the last period of disturbance, the total duration of the disturbance, and the need for continued evaluation of prophylactic treatment

* From American Psychiatric Association: *Diagnostic and Statistical Manual of Mental Disorders*, ed 3. American Psychiatric Association, Washington, DC, 1980. Used with permission.

be applied toward the goal of personality change. They include individual, group, and family therapy used alone and in various combinations.

## Milieu Therapy

The relative value of milieu therapy for the schizophrenic patient has not been conclusively demonstrated by objective research. In the past, it was often assumed that the good results reported by certain hospitals could be attributed to their better milieu. However, there is now evidence that the good results may be primarily the result of admitting patients with better prognoses, and that the ward atmosphere may depend on differences in the patients' prognoses, rather than vice versa.

The hospital environment should be carefully regulated, with discriminating respect for the schizophrenic's limited perceptual and cognitive resources. Indeed, there is good reason to believe that structured and authoritative support—with well-defined roles and expectations, scrupulous respect for personal distance, and firm but reasonable limits, flavored with a touch of good-natured humor may be appropriate for a schizophrenic patient.

Controlled research clearly indicates that drugs are effective at all levels of milieu care and that, in general, an intensive milieu program alone is less effective than drug therapy, even

drug therapy in a relatively custodial setting. With current methods, there are still a number of hard core, treatment-resistant patients, for some of whom long-term hospital care is properly indicated. But, with the use of modern psychotropic drugs, the hospital can be, for the average schizophrenic patient, essentially a center for relatively brief crisis treatment until he is psychologically ambulatory. Deeper insights or new social patterns and techniques should not be sought at the price of the detrimental effects and added cost of prolonged hospitalization, which deprives the patient of the sustaining and satisfying ego-organizing influence of work, family, and friends.

Milieu therapy is enhanced by group meetings of patients and staff, separately and together, that focus on social functioning, rather than on psychopathology. In general, a therapeutic community encourages self-reliance and rewards the patient progressively for efforts toward social readaptation. The patient is expected to participate in planning his own treatment program and in helping other patients, and to assume responsibility in ward affairs and the outside world.

A wide range of rehabilitation services is needed to give appropriate domestic and social support—in-hospital living facilities, hostels, half-way houses, communal group-living arrangements, family care, foster homes, lodgings, apartments, hotels, ex-patient social clubs, and Schizophrenics Anonymous—and to provide a suitable work setting, vocational counseling, job training, in-hospital work-for-pay programs, sheltered workshops in the hospital or in the community, trial work placement, communal and cooperative patient-operated businesses, and protected positions in industry.

## Psychotherapy

Today, it is generally held that schizophrenic patients can be reached by psychotherapy and that a relationship can be readily established, although the relationship is intensely charged and quite different from that encountered in the treatment of neurosis. The main distinction between neurotic and psychotic (narcissistic) transference is that the psychotic has lost his internal object representations and can no longer differentiate between the self and the object world. He attaches (projects) his delusional complexes onto the therapist.

In general, orthodox formal psychoanalysis has no place in the treatment of overt psychosis, although some rare patients may recover sufficiently to be suitable for analysis if restitution is complete and consolidated. Nor is formal psychotherapy of the kind commonly used for neurotics likely to be of much help in the treatment of the hospitalized or still psychotic patient.

Establishing a relationship is often a peculiarly difficult matter, for the schizophrenic is desperately lonely yet defends against closeness and trust, and is likely to become suspicious, anxious, hostile, or regressed when someone attempts to draw close. Simple directness, sincerity, a scrupulous observation of distance and privacy, and sensitivity to the unspoken significance of social conventions are preferable to premature informality and the condescending use of first names or timid appeasement. Exaggerated warmth or professions of friendship are out of place and likely to be perceived as attempts at bribery, manipulation, or exploitation.

Within the context of a professional relationship, flexibility is essential. At times, the therapist may have meals with the patient, sit on the floor, go for a walk or out to a restaurant, accept and give gifts, play table tennis, remember the patient's birthday, allow him to telephone the therapist at any hour, or just sit silently with him. The main aim is to convey the idea that the therapist wants to understand the patient and will try to do so, and that he has faith in the patient's potential as a human being, no matter how disturbed, hostile, or bizarre he may be at the moment. Manfred Bleuler stated that the correct therapeutic attitude toward a schizophrenic patient is to accept him as a brother, rather than watch him as a person who has become unintelligible and different from the therapist.

**The Therapist and Countertransference.** In the literature of psychotherapy for schizophrenia, one gains an understanding of the massive resistances and impasses presented by schizophrenics, of the frustrations and disappointments of working with them, and of the dedication and persistence required.

The treatment of schizophrenic patients is always a stressful experience, especially for the therapist who regards primary-process manifestations as alien and frightening, and who is upset by confusing communications or easily threatened by disturbed behavior. It requires considerable aplomb to deal with patients who make the therapist feel angry, irritated, embarrassed, hopeless, guilty, frustrated, or inadequate and who may chop him down, frighten him, deluge him with obscenity and vituperation, or engage in wildly disruptive behavior that wards off closeness. Things are not made easier by the schizophrenic's seemingly uncanny ability to sense and observe the therapist's anxiety and to comment on his weak points. Therapists often respond by defensive and argumentative security operations or, perhaps even worse, by placating or reassuring the patient that he is not psychotic. Contrary to general belief, most patients are relieved to find someone who recognizes their psychosis and takes it seriously, provided he is not overwhelmed by it and appears to be reasonably confident.

Countertransference can be used constructively if the therapist is able to recognize and accept it without burdening the patient with ill-advised security operations; the therapist's reaction may then be used as a signal that he has the same anxiety as the patient.

**Intervention Techniques.** Once a relationship has been established, the patient may be willing to relinquish his symptoms and defenses. Some therapists believe that, if the relationship can be sustained, no specialized technical maneuvers are required. Bleuler, for example, defined three essential principles. The first principle is a steady, quiet appeal to the patient's healthy ego, to his sense of responsibility and dignity. The second principle is the use of surprise and shock to shake the patient out of his autism—for example, suddenly confronting him with a new and surprising social situation, giving him an unexpected responsibility or a sudden interpretation, or discharging him unexpectedly from the hospital. One of the qualities of many therapists who seem to work most successfully with schizophrenic patients is the ability to dramatize a situation and get the patient's attention. They also dramatize reality for the staff and for the patients' families; they dramatize reality for everyone. The third principle is the use of quiet and orderly surroundings and the avoidance of overstimulation, to calm down excitation.

Others do more, the type of intervention depending on the therapist's school and personal style. Two divergent trends can be identified—primary-process intervention and secondary-process intervention—representing opposite poles on a continuum between therapists who become heavily involved in the psychosis in a fluid way, and those who see therapy as a corrective learning experience.

*Primary-process Intervention.* Primary-process techniques are generally not suitable for the usual therapist, for they require both an extraordinary amount of time and unusual personal qualities. Perhaps the most widely known primary-process technique is John Rosen's direct analysis, which is now mainly of historical interest. In that approach Rosen made interpretations of unconscious material, e.g. such as telling the schizophrenic that he hated his father and wanted to kill him.

*Secondary-process Intervention.* The first advocate of this approach may have been Paul Federn, who emphasized the need to repress what has broken through into consciousness; to interpret defenses, rather than impulses; and to focus on reality, rather than on unconscious content. There is a cooperative exploration of the patient's internal and external relationships and behavior to examine what he does to reality; education to help him identify sources of danger and anxiety and to help him react appropriately, rather than defensively; and improvement in emotional modulation and frustration tolerance.

*Nonverbal Intervention and Body Ego.* Attention has been focused on the essentially nonverbal character of primary-process communication and the central importance of disturbances in body image, particularly in regressed patients. The concept of recovery as a progressive definition and demarcation of ego boundaries through increased cathexis of body limits and the bodily self has led to the development of body ego methods, largely nonverbal procedures that reestablish the experience of body self and reality contact, concentrating on body image, identity, posture, and movement. Such techniques may have value in making contact and establishing a relationship, and in preparing the way for a more verbal phase of treatment. This is similar to the symbolic realization therapy advocated by Margaret Sachehaye.

### Group Therapy

In general, the balance of the experimental evidence indicates that group therapy, combined with drugs, produces somewhat better results than drug treatment alone, particularly with outpatients. Positive results are more likely to be obtained when treatment focuses on real-life plans, problems, and relationships; on social and work roles and interaction; on cooperation with drug therapy and discussion of its side effects; or on some practical recreational or work activity. There is considerable doubt whether dynamic interpretation and insight therapy have much value for the usual schizophrenic patient. But the social interaction, sense of cohesiveness, identification, and reality testing are highly therapeutic group processes for schizophrenics.

### Family Therapy

The family plays an important role in the treatment of the schizophrenic patient, and his illness is usually accompanied by serious family problems. Indeed, some therapists deal with schizophrenia as an illness not of the patient alone but of the entire family. In any case, appropriate active involvement with the family and significant others is usually essential, both while the patient is in the hospital and after his release. The psychiatric social worker and the psychiatrically trained public health nurse can often play major and decisive roles in this area, and they must do so if effective treatment is to be extended to more than a handful of patients.

### Drug Therapy

A few therapists still believe that drugs have no place in the treatment of schizophrenia and that drugs are incompatible with psychotherapy and psychosocial methods of treatment. However, this resistance is steadily passing into history.

Well-controlled studies have established that drugs have real value in the treatment of schizophrenia, that they reduce both primary and secondary symptoms. Drugs will never be all that there is to the treatment of schizophrenic patients. Optimal and long-term therapeutic response usually necessitates the use of psychotherapeutic group, vocational, social, and other treatment modalities. One of the major objectives of skilled psychopharmacotherapy is to enable the patient to participate fully in these forms of therapy. Moreover, although the efficacy of pharmacotherapy in the treatment of schizophrenia has been solidly established, not all schizophrenic patients need it.

In general, only one drug should be used at a time. Polypharmacy is seldom indicated, for it exposes patients not only to the known hazard of side effects from each drug separately, but also to largely unknown interaction effects. For a more complete discussion of the use of antipsychotic drugs, see Section 27.1.

### Behavior Therapy

Behavior therapy has been able to make psychotics less psychotic by reducing the frequency of bizarre, disturbing, and deviant behavior and by increasing adaptive, normal behavior. Thus, the behavioral approach has had qualified success.

Conditioning is not a panacea. Many chronic schizophrenics have too scanty a behavioral repertoire for the easy use of behavioral techniques; others either do not respond to available reinforcing stimuli or have life situations that undo any success that is gained. Some patients respond poorly or not at all to behavioral efforts. Most therapists believe that it is also necessary to make changes in the environment, so that it can support the ex-patient's functioning and maintenance of gains.

One cannot expect behavioral modification to cure schizophrenia in the sense of reversing the assumed biological or psychological defect. But a direct attack on behavior and training social skills can provide prosthetic and remedial support.

Behavioral modification is not limited to inpatient settings It has been used successfully with outpatients, and one of the most promising areas for its use is in working with the patient and his family to modify some of their counterproductive and negative interactions.

### Insulin Coma Therapy

A course of insulin treatment, consisting of a series of deep comas produced daily by large doses of insulin, was widely used in the past for the treatment of schizophrenia. It is now virtually obsolete in this country, since drugs apparently produce the same or better results and are less expensive, less dangerous, and more acceptable to patients and to staff.

### Electroconvulsive Therapy

The status of electroconvulsive therapy (ECT) is unclear. Although it is widely used, its efficacy in schizophrenia has seldom been assessed by controlled investigation, particularly by comparisons with drug therapy. It is highly questionable in the treatment of schizophrenia. See Section 27.6 for a discussion of ECT.

### Psychosurgery

Drugs have almost entirely replaced psychosurgery as a treatment method for schizophrenia, although there has been no controlled experimental comparison of the results achieved by the two methods. This lack is readily understandable, as psychosurgery has been generally considered a last resort for seemingly desperate cases. Nevertheless, it would be unfortunate to relegate psychosurgery entirely to limbo. Neurosurgical intervention in certain selected cases may have beneficial effects, and carefully controlled research in this area seems worthwhile.

### Nicotinic Acid Megavitamin Therapy

Claims that large doses of niacin (3 gm. or more a day) are effective in the treatment of schizophrenia have yet to be substantiated by acceptable objective evidence. At present they are considered of little or no value. For a discussion of miscellaneous organic therapies and their role in the treatment of schizophrenia see Section 27.8.

### REFERENCES

Babigian H N: Schizophrenia: epidemiology. In Comprehensive Textbook of Psychiatry, ed 4, H I Kaplan, B J Sadock, editors, p 643. Williams & Wilkins, Baltimore, 1985.
Bellack A S, editor: Treatment and Care of Schizophrenia. Grune & Stratton, New York, 1984.
Bleuler M: What is schizophrenia? Schizo Bull 10: 8, 1984.
Endicott J, Nee J, Fleiss J, Cohen J, Williams J B B, Simon R: Diagnostic criteria for schizophrenia: reliabilities and agreement between systems. Arch Gen Psychiatry 39: 8, 1982.
Hornykiewicz O: Brain catecholamines in schizophrenia: a good case for noradrenaline. Nature 299: 484, 1982.
Kane J M, Rifkin A, Woerner M, Reardon G, Sarantakos S, Schiebel D, Ramos-Lorenz J: Low-dose neuroleptic treatment of outpatient schizophrenia. Arch Gen Psychiatry 40: 893, 1983.
Lieberman R P, Falloon I R H, Wallace C J: Drug-psychosocial interactions in the treatment of schizophrenia. In The Chronically Mentally Ill: Research and Services. SP Publications, New York, 1983.
May P R A: Treatment of Schizophrenia: A Comparative Study of Five Treatment Methods. Science House, New York, 1968.
Schultz C G: Schizophrenia: individual psychotherapy. In Comprehensive Textbook of Psychiatry, ed 4, H I Kaplan, B J Sadock, editors, p 734. Williams & Wilkins, Baltimore, 1985.
Weiner H: Schizophrenia: etiology. In Comprehensive Textbook of Psychiatry, ed 4, H I Kaplan, B J Sadock, editors, p 650. Williams & Wilkins, Baltimore, 1985.

# 11

# Paranoid Disorders

## Definition

The dominant symptoms of paranoid disorders are persistent persecutory delusions or delusions of jealousy that cannot be explained by other psychiatric disorders. The delusions are not bizarre or scattered, but are generally developed logically and are well-systematized. The emotional response to these delusions appears appropriate; the personality remains intact or deteriorates minimally over a prolonged period of time.

## History

In 1818, Heinroth introduced the current concept of paranoia when he described disorders of the intellect under the term *verrücktheit*. In 1838, the French psychiatrist Esquirol coined the term monomania to characterize delusions with no associated defect in logical reasoning or general behavior. Kahlbaum, in 1863, used the term paranoia to designate these disorders. DSM-III separates paranoid schizophrenia from paranoid personality disorder and the paranoid disorders—which include paranoia, shared paranoid disorder, and paranoid states.

## Epidemiology

It is difficult to make accurate estimates of the incidence of paranoid disorders. Everyone uses denial, projection, and paranoid ideation to a certain extent in daily living. The lack of valid statistics on the syndrome of the paranoid disorders lies in poor definition, imprecise instruments, and haphazard investigation. A study of patients with various diagnoses who exhibited paranoid symptoms found that 10 percent had paranoid disorders. The only large-scale systematic study dealing with non-schizophrenic paranoid psychoses showed that paranoid psychoses were found in 12 percent of patients.

Kraepelin reported that 70 percent of the patients studied with paranoia were male. In involutional paranoia, females predominate in a seven to one ratio. There is often a negative family history for psychiatric illness.

## Causes

No conclusive evidence indicates that hereditary factors or neuropathological abnormalities explain the condition. Psychological factors appear to be important in the development of paranoid disturbances.

### Freud's Contributions

In 1896, Freud described projection as the main defense mechanism in paranoia. Later, Freud read *Memoirs of My Nervous Illness*, an autobiographical account by the gifted jurist Daniel Paul Schreber. Freud demonstrated from his review of the autobiography how unconscious homosexual tendencies were defended against by denial and projection. Because homosexuality is consciously inadmissible to some paranoid patients, the feeling "I love him" is denied and changed by reaction formation into "I do not love him, I hate him," and this feeling is further transformed through projection into "It is not I who hates him, it is he who hates me." In a full-blown paranoid state this feeling is elaborated into "I am persecuted by him." The patient is then able to rationalize his anger by consciously hating those he perceives to hate him. Instead of being aware of passive homosexual impulses, the patient rejects the love of anyone except himself. In erotomanic delusions, the patient changes "I love him" to "I love her," and this feeling, through projection, becomes "She loves me."

Freud also believed that unconscious homosexuality is the cause of delusions of jealousy. In an attempt to ward off threatening impulses, the patient becomes preoccupied by jealous thoughts; thus, the patient asserts, "I do not love him, she loves him." Freud believed that the man the paranoid patient suspects his wife of loving is a man to whom the patient feels homosexually attracted. The dynamics of unconscious homosexuality are the same in the female patient as in the male patient in classic psychoanalytic theory.

Clinical evidence has not consistently supported Freud's thesis. Some paranoid patients are not homosexually oriented; other overtly homosexual persons never develop paranoid delusions.

### Lack of Trust

Clinical observations indicate that the paranoid person experiences difficulty in establishing a warm and trusting relationship with the parenting figures. The mother of the paranoiac is frequently described as overcontrolling, seductive, and rejecting, and the father as distant, rigid, and sadistic, or weak and ineffectual. If the parental figures cannot be relied on to help the child deal with disappointments, humiliations, and frustrations, the child soon develops an attitude that the environment is consistently hostile and becomes hypersensitive to imagined slights, so that all relationships become characterized by lack of trust.

Paranoiacs primarily use the defense mechanisms of reaction formation, denial, and projection. Reaction formation is used as a defense against aggression, dependency needs, and feelings of affection. The need for dependency is transformed into staunch independence. Denial is used to avoid awareness of painful reality. Consumed with anger and hostility and unable to face responsibility for this rage, resentment and anger are projected onto others.

Hypersensitivity causes others to avoid the paranoiac, and this reaction tends to amplify his hostile and suspicious attitude. Intolerant of criticism, he readily criticizes others. Overaggressive, the paranoiac sees an aggressor in everyone around him; thus, the paranoiac treats others as projections of his own unconscious hostility. Such alienating behavior incurs the hostility of others, resulting in a spiral of psychopathology. A psychotic delusional system results as a defense against feelings of rejection and inadequacy. Feelings of inferiority are replaced by delusions of superiority, grandiosity, and omnipotence, and delusional erotic ideas replace feelings of rejection.

### Overdetermined Goals

The preparanoid child is often expected to perform impeccably. Undeserved and unjustified punishment may be doled out whenever the child fails to meet the parents' expectations. When great expectations for outstanding achievement are encouraged by the parent, the insecure child may develop secretly elaborated fantasies as a way of enhancing his self-esteem.

### Superego Projection

Superego projection is exemplified by the patient who is fearful of being watched, as a child may be fearful of being watched by parents. Likewise, critical and frightening delusions are often projections of superego criticism. The delusions of female paranoid patients often involve accusations of prostitution. As a child, the female paranoiac turned to her father for the maternal love that she was unable to receive from her mother. Incestuous desires developed. Later heterosexual encounters are an unconscious reminder of the incestuous desires of childhood; these desires are defended against by superego projection, accusing the female paranoiac of prostitution.

### Paranoid Pseudocommunity

Norman Cameron described at least seven situations that favor the development of paranoid disorders: (1) an increased expectation of receiving sadistic treatment; (2) situations that increase distrust and suspicion; (3) social isolation; (4) situations that increase envy and jealousy; (5) situations that lower self-esteem; (6) situations that cause a person to see his own defects in others; and (7) situations that increase the potential for rumination over probable meanings and motivations. When frustration from any combination of these conditions exceeds the limits that the paranoid personality can tolerate, the patient becomes withdrawn and anxious; he realizes that something is wrong but cannot explain it. The crystallization of a delusional system offers a solution to the problem. Elaboration of the delusion to include imagined persons, and to ascribe malevolent motivations to these real and imagined people, results in organization of the "pseudocommunity." This delusional entity binds together projected fears and wishes to justify the paranoic's hostile aggression and give it a tangible target.

### Other Mechanisms

Paranoid states are common in migratory minority and immigrant groups, possibly because of the adaptational experiences of learning a new language and the developing feelings of loneliness and isolation. When the migratory and immigrant persons return to their native countries, the paranoid ideas frequently disappear.

## Clinical Features

DSM-III defines the essential feature of paranoid disorders to be persistent persecutory delusions or delusions of jealousy not explained by other psychotic disorders. Differences among paranoid schizophrenia, paranoid personality disorder, and the paranoid disorders are matters of degree that are quantitative, rather than qualitative, and the boundaries among these disorders are unclear. The delusions of the paranoid disorders usually involve a single theme or a series of connected themes; these themes may be simple or elaborate. Associated features found in the paranoid disorders include anger, ideas or delusions of reference, social isolation, seclusiveness, eccentricity, suspiciousness, and hostility that may lead to violence. Litigious activity is common. To meet the diagnostic criteria for a paranoid disorder (see Table I), the patient must not have any of the characteristic schizophrenic symptoms, manic or depressive symptoms should be absent, there should be no evidence of an organic mental disorder, and the duration of the illness should be at least 1 week from an onset of a noticeable change in the patient's usual condition. Paranoid disorders are divided into paranoia, shared paranoid disorder, and paranoid states.

## Paranoia

The essential feature of paranoia (see Table II) is a permanent and unshakable delusional system accompanied by the preservation of clear and orderly thinking. Generally, there is an insidious development; emotion and behavior are explainable by the delusional system.

The incidence of classical paranoia in a sample of psychiatric admissions ranged from 0.1 percent to 0.4 percent, depending on the rigidity of the criteria. Onset was most often after 30 years of age. The true incidence of paranoia is unknown, because many patients function well enough in society so as not to come to the attention of psychiatrists.

Like all paranoid disorders, paranoia is a defense against ego disintegration. It differs from other paranoid disorders in that the delusional system is so well-encapsulated that the remainder of the personality is able to operate relatively normally, and good object relations are maintained. Patients are able to continue with their business and professional work, maintain adequate socialization, and undergo no ego disorganization.

**Conjugal Paranoia.** Conjugal paranoia, a variant of classical paranoia, is characterized by delusions that involve only the spouse. Initial minor criticism of the marital partner slowly progresses through suspiciousness to frank delusions revolving around thoughts of the spouse's infidelity. Conjugal paranoia is distinct from pathological jealousy, which is a symptom that occurs in other illnesses, such as alcoholism, schizophrenia, affective psychoses, and the organic mental disorders.

**Hypochondriacal Paranoid Psychosis.** Hypochondriacal paranoid psychosis is a descriptive term emphasizing hypochondriacal delusions as the main delusion. Hypochondriasis can be found in schizophrenia, obsessive and phobic disorders, depression, organic psychoses, and personality disorders. When hypochondriacal symptoms are delusional in nature and do not fit any of the above categories, they should be classified under the paranoid disorders.

When an exhaustive physical work-up shows

TABLE II
DIAGNOSTIC CRITERIA FOR PARANOIA*

A. Meets the criteria for Paranoid Disorder.

B. A chronic and stable persecutory delusional system of at least six months' duration.

C. Does not meet the criteria for Shared Paranoid Disorder.

* From American Psychiatric Association: *Diagnostic and Statistical Manual of Mental Disorders*, ed 3. American Psychiatric Association, Washington, DC, 1980. Used with permission.

TABLE I
DIAGNOSTIC CRITERIA FOR PARANOID DISORDER*

A. Persistent persecutory delusions or delusional jealousy.

B. Emotion and behavior appropriate to the content of the delusional system.

C. Duration of illness of at least 1 week.

D. None of the symptoms of criterion A of Schizophrenia, such as bizarre delusions, incoherence, or marked loosening of associations.

E. No prominent hallucinations.

F. The full depressive or manic syndrome (criteria A and B of major depressive or manic episode is either not present, developed after any psychotic symptoms, or was brief in duration relative to the duration of the psychotic symptoms.

G. Not due to an Organic Mental Disorder.

* From American Psychiatric Association: *Diagnostic and Statistical Manual of Mental Disorders*, ed 3. American Psychiatric Association, Washington, DC, 1980. Used with permission.

no organic causes for the symptoms, the patient is convinced that the physician is as incompetent as those who failed him in the past. Reassurance that nothing is wrong physically only increases the patient's rage and insistence on more detailed studies. Offering medications or other treatment modalities may relieve the symptoms briefly, but they quickly return in more exaggerated form. The patient becomes so preoccupied with his physical symptoms that he quits his job, stops seeing his few friends, and devotes much of his time to his illness.

Hypochondriasis can be psychodynamically explained as a regression to the infantile narcissistic state in which the patient withdraws emotional involvement with other people and fixates on his physical self. Generally, the symptom choice symbolically represents the patient's ambivalent identification with a parenting figure.

**Erotic Paranoid Reactions.** In erotic paranoid reactions, the patient has the delusion that someone loves him or her, but that the person is unable to communicate the love because of extenuating circumstances. Often, the delusions focus on a prominent public figure of the opposite sex. In erotic paranoid reactions, the love is usually a projected narcissistic love used as a defense against low self-esteem and severe narcissistic injury. Occasionally, the delusions are a defensive maneuver against homosexuality. Some patients with erotic paranoid reactions act on the delusions by sending letters or meeting the supposed lover in person, urging that the love between them be acknowledged. Others feel themselves persecuted by love. Some treat the situation similarly to normal love, except that the delusion goes unrequited.

**Grandiose Paranoid Reactions.** Delusions of grandeur are less frequent than are delusions of persecution. Delusions of grandeur represent a regression to the narcissistic feelings of omnipotence of early childhood, in which feelings of undenied and undiminished powers predominated. The most prevalent themes are derived from the surrounding culture and popular stories; thus, the patient may believe himself to be a talented scientist, inventor, or prophet. Patients with political and religious delusions of grandeur have a tremendous need to free themselves of hostile aggression; the delusion is of someone who can bring universal peace or universal destruction.

**Persecutory Paranoid Reactions.** Persecutory paranoid reactions are the most common of the paranoid states. They develop out of a reaction to a deep distrust of others and an unusually strong propensity to deny hostility. Patients with these reactions characteristically project their hostility and gradually formulate a paranoid pseudocommunity.

**Paranoid Litigious State.** The litigious paranoid state is usually found in an obstinate person who is insistent on his rights. Frequently, the litigious activities do not appear until after some unsatisfactory legal experience causes the patient to initiate further ill-advised legal action.

**Paranoid Disorders of the Elderly.** Although involutional paranoid state has been dropped from DSM-III, some investigators believe that it should be classified as a separate and distinct entity.

Paraphrenia is a term used to include the paranoid disorders of the elderly in which signs of organic demential or primary affective illness cannot explain the symptoms. Ten percent of all psychiatric admissions aged 60 years or more fell into this category. Frequently, the prepsychotic personalities of these patients were abnormal, with paranoid and schizoid features predominating.

### Shared Paranoid Disorder (Folie à Deux)

The essential feature of shared paranoid disorder is a paranoid delusional system that develops as a result of a close relationship with another person who already has an established paranoid psychosis (see Table III). One of the two patients is generally a dominant paranoid person with fixed delusions; the other is likely to be a dependent, suggestible person who incorporates the dominant one's delusions while they are together, but gives them up rather easily when they are separated and given therapeutic help. The most common pairs are two sisters. A husband and a wife, a mother and a child, two brothers, a brother and a sister, and a father and a child represent other frequent pairs. The condition is thought to be exceedingly rare. *Folie à deux* occurs in exceptional conditions. Not only does one person have to be the dominant one, but the two persons involved must have lived a very close existence for a long time in the same

TABLE III
DIAGNOSTIC CRITERIA FOR SHARED PARANOID DISORDER*

A. Meets the criteria for Paranoid Disorder.

B. Delusional system develops as a result of a close relationship with another person or persons who have an established disorder with persecutory delusions.

* From American Psychiatric Association: *Diagnostic and Statistical Manual of Mental Disorders*, ed 3. American Psychiatric Association, Washington, DC, 1980. Used with permission.

environment, relatively isolated from the outside world. This syndrome is found more frequently among women than among men. Occasionally, more than two persons are involved.

### Acute Paranoid Disorder

Rarely, paranoid disorders may be acutely precipitated and entirely clear within a 6-month period. These cases would be classified as acute paranoid disorders; paranoid psychosis in immigrants (cultural-bound paranoid states), and prison psychoses are the most common examples of paranoid conditions that may last only briefly (see Table IV).

**Paranoid Psychosis in Immigrants (Cultural-bound Paranoid States).** The development of suspiciousness and paranoid ideas is commonly found in immigrants. Surrounded by strange people whose ways of emotional reaction are much different, the immigrant's appearance, way of speaking, and mannerisms often become objects of contempt or ridicule. Uncertainty in the new environment tends to increase isolation. The incidence of paranoid psychosis is about 5.5 percent among native-born American patients, as opposed to 16.5 percent among foreign-born patients. The increased incidence of paranoid disorders in immigrants may be due to an increased immigration of persons with unstable personalities.

**Prison Psychosis.** Because of the high rate of homosexual attack and criminal abuse inside prisons, it is often difficult to tell whether the thoughts of prisoners are based on reality or are entirely delusional. In those patients who develop a paranoid psychosis arising in the course of confinement, stress seems to act as a precipitating factor in the prepsychotic personality.

### Atypical Paranoid Disorder

Atypical paranoid disorder includes those paranoid disorders that fail to meet the criteria for other paranoid conditions. The conditions would include the esoteric paranoid states, as well as those disorders with an acute onset lasting longer than 6 months.

TABLE IV
DIAGNOSTIC CRITERIA FOR ACUTE PARANOID DISORDER*

A. Meets the criteria for Paranoid Disorder.

B. Duration of less than 6 months.

C. Does not meet the criteria for Shared Paranoid Disorder.

* From American Psychiatric Association: *Diagnostic and Statistical Manual of Mental Disorders*, ed 3. American Psychiatric Association, Washington, DC, 1980. Used with permission.

### Course and Prognosis

Because most patients with classical paranoia show a certain amount of self-control, they seldom enter a hospital, and the community learns to tolerate them as "crackpots." Patients with conjugal paranoia fare better than paranoiacs. Most are eventually considered cured. Patients have a better prognosis when the delusions are not fixed. Patients having a fully encapsulated delusional system are less amenable to pharmacotherapy or psychotherapy than are those patients with paranoid symptoms associated with schizophrenia or the affective disorders. Factors considered to have a good prognosis are female sex, married, onset before age 30, acute onset, less than 6 months' duration of the psychosis before hospitalization, and presence of precipitating factors.

### Diagnosis

The diagnosis of paranoid disorder should be made only after finding the positive criteria that delineate this psychosis. The cardinal feature is the presence of persistent persecutory delusions, or delusions of jealousy. To establish the diagnosis, one must eliminate schizophrenia, affective disorders, brief reactive disorders, and organic mental disorders.

There is often a history of social isolation, seclusiveness, or eccentricities of behavior. A mental status examination reveals an angry, suspicious person who complains of ideas of reference. During the history and mental status examination, the physician should be alert for symptoms and signs that may suggest other possible diagnoses.

Routine laboratory studies may be necessary to rule out somatic disease. If there is a suspicion of an early organic mental disorder, psychological testing, such as the Bender-Gestalt and the Wechsler Memory Scale, may be in order. If findings justify it, an electroencephalogram, a brain scan, a spinal fluid examination, or a neurological consultation may be indicated.

### Assessment for Violence

The assessment of the potential for violence is in many ways quite similar to the assessment of suicidal risk. The therapist should not hesitate to ask the patient about his homicidal plans and preparations for their completion. Destructive aggression is more common in patients with a past history of violence. If aggressive feelings existed in the past, the patient should be asked how he managed them. Persons accompanying the patient, including police officers, should always be interviewed. If hospitalization is necessary, the therapist can foster the therapeutic alliance by openly discussing how hospitalization can help the patient obtain additional control in restraining his impulses.

## Differential Diagnosis

The essential feature of paranoid personality disorder is a long-standing mistrust of people. Patients with this disorder are hypersensitive and continually alert for environmental clues that will validate their original prejudicial ideas. Often sullen, withdrawn, humorless, haughty, arrogant, cold, and calculating, they tend to view life negatively and exaggerate insignificant slights into hidden motives and special meanings, but delusions are absent. Although occupational difficulties are common and the patients have grossly impaired interpersonal relationships, with special difficulty in relating to authority figures, patients with paranoid personality disorder rarely seek psychiatric help. Under stress, these patients can easily develop a full-blown paranoid delusion and are then classified under the paranoid disorder.

The delusions of paranoid schizophrenia are bizarre and fragmented, in contrast to the better-organized delusions of the paranoid disorders. In those few patients who have hallucinations in conjunction with a paranoid disorder, the hallucinations are associated with the delusions; hallucinations in the schizophrenic are not necessarily connected with delusions. Patients with paranoid disorders lack the Schneiderian first-rank symptoms of schizophrenia.

Paranoid disorders should be distinguished from psychotic depressions. Although patients with psychotic depressions may have delusions with somatic delusions predominating, they also exhibit the biological signs of depression, which are not present in paranoid disorders. If a paranoid patient has a depressed affect, the affect is secondary to the delusional system; in a depressed patient, however, the converse is true—that is, the delusions are secondary to the depression (see Tables V–VII).

Manic patients who present with hostile aggression may be mistaken for patients with acute paranoid reactions. The angry mood of the manic patient quickly passes; in the paranoid disorder, the haughty, complaining, and hostile behavior remains. Often, the manic patient is easily distracted, whereas the paranoiac is adamant.

Paranoid states can be secondary to physical disease, such as uremia, cerebral malaria, lead poisoning, pernicious anemia, endocrine disorders, presenile psychoses, and cerebral arteriosclerosis. Paranoid states seen in organic mental

TABLE V
DIFFERENTIAL DIAGNOSIS*

| | |
|---|---|
| Paranoid personality disorder | Pervasive and long-standing suspiciousness of other people |
| Paranoid disorder | Delusions of jealousy or persecution |
| Schizophrenia | One symptom from the following: Delusions of being controlled Thought broadcasting Thought insertion Thought withdrawal Fantastic or implausible delusions Other delusions without persecutory or jealous content Auditory hallucination in which a noise keeps up a running commentary on the patient's thoughts or behavior Auditory hallucination not associated with depression or elation or limited to two words Delusions of any type accompaned by hallucination of any type Loosening of association combined with inappropriate affect |
| Manic episode | Elevated, expansive, or irritable mood with pressured speech and hyperactivity |
| Depressive episode | Pervasive loss of interest or pleasure combined with at least four of the following: Change in weight when not dieting Sleep difficulty Psychomotor agitation or retardation Loss of energy Decrease in sex drive Feelings of self-reproach or excessive guilt, either of which may be delusional Indecisiveness Suicidal thoughts |
| Organic mental disorder | Disordered memory and orientation Impairment in judgment, and impulse control Perceptual disturbance—simple misinterpretations, illusions and hallucinations Clinical features that may fluctuate rapidly |

* Adapted from American Psychiatric Association: *Diagnostic and Statistical Manual of Mental Disorders*, ed 3. American Psychiatric Association, Washington, DC, 1980.

disorders are characterized by forgetfulness, impairment of memory, defects in judgment, and disorientation. In the paranoid states, memory and orientation are intact, and no organic defects can be observed.

TABLE VI
DIFFERENCES IN DELUSIONS

| | |
|---|---|
| Paranoid disorder | Delusions of jealousy and persecution |
| Schizophrenia | Delusions of being controlled; bizarre delusions; sometimes delusions of persecution |
| Mania | Grandiose delusions |
| Depression | Delusions of guilt; somatic delusions |
| Organic mental disorder | Delusions secondary to perceptual disturbances |

TABLE VII
SUBTYPES OF PARANOID DISORDERS*

Paranoia (essential features):
  Insidious development of an unshakable delusional system
  Preservation of clear and orderly thinking
  Emotion and behavior consistent with the delusional system
Shared paranoid disorder (*folie à deux*):
  A paranoid delusion that develops as a result of a close relationship with another person who already has an established paranoid psychosis; if the two paranoiacs are separated, the delusion beliefs in the second person diminish or disappear.
Acute paranoid disorder:
  Sudden onset of paranoid disorder, usually precipitated by stress; last less than 6 months

* Adapted from American Psychiatric Association: *Diagnostic and Statistical Manual of Mental Disorders*, ed 3. American Psychiatric Association, Washington, DC, 1980.

## Treatment

### Hospitalization

The initial problem in treatment is determining whether the patient requires hospitalization. If the delusions have exerted an important influence on his behavior in the past and the delusions seem to be controlling the patient to act on them in an aggressive way toward others, then hospitalization is indicated. In addition, if the patient is reacting to the delusions in a way that prevents adequate social functioning, hospitalization is probably best. If the physician is convinced that the patient would best be treated in a hospital, an attempt should be made to persuade the patient to accept hospitalization; if this attempt fails, legal commitment may be initiated. Often, if the physician convinces the patient that he firmly believes hospitalization is necessary, the patient voluntarily enters a hospital to avoid legal commitment. Although the patient soon begins to test the potential for early discharge, a brief period of hospitalization may decrease his anxiety, so that his paranoid delusions become less severe; the patient may come to tolerate hospitalization by establishing a meaningful therapeutic relationship with the physician.

### Chemotherapy

Paranoiacs are particularly suspicious of chemotherapy and can easily incorporate the administration of medications into their delusional system. Nevertheless, an antipsychotic drug is often indicated for the control of the patient's acute agitation and anxiety. The initial aim of attenuating anxiety, agitation, and psychotic delusions is accomplished by using one of the major antipsychotic drugs. The evaluation of several parameters can be helpful in selecting an antipsychotic medication. The patient's previous response to medication and his physical condition are important considerations. For example, a paranoid patient with insomnia may respond best to the sedative effects of chlorpromazine, but a malnourished elderly paranoid patient may suffer from this drug's hypotensive side effects.

In initiating antipsychotic medication in the paranoiac, the clinician should prescribe a small test dose. If no major side effects develop, the dose may be gradually increased until therapeutic benefits or toxicity develop. Occasionally, after an adequate trial of 2 to 3 weeks, a patient may fail to respond to a particular antipsychotic drug. If this occurs, the patient should be switched to an antipsychotic medication of a different class. Generally, however, the most common cause of drug failure is patient noncompliance. A long-acting parenteral piperazine, such as fluphenazine enanthate (with a duration of action of 10 to 14 days) or fluphenazine decanoate (with a duration of 14 to 21 days), can be used if the patient is not reliable enough to take oral medication, or if it is suspected that the medication is poorly absorbed when given orally. About 25 mg of enanthate or decanoate given every other week is equal to 5 mg of oral fluphenazine administered once daily.

In acute paranoid emergency situations, parenteral administration can be used. Haloperidol, 2 to 5 mg intramuscularly administered, is a good choice because it is least cardiotoxic, has minimal hypotensive effects, and does not suppress respiration. After agitation has been controlled, the patient may be shifted to the oral route, the amount depending on the prominence of the psychotic symptoms. After 4 to 6 weeks of therapy, the medication may be reduced to half the initial amount. The next month, another reduction by half can be made, and this reduction is gradually repeated until the patient is completely off the medication or is maintained on a minimal dose. Some patients require medication for a long period of time; observation and frequent examinations are the key to appropriate psychopharmacological management of the paranoid disorders.

## Psychotherapy

The essential element in effective psychotherapy is establishing a relationship in which the patient begins to trust the therapist. Initially, the therapist should neither agree with nor challenge the patient's delusion. The therapist begins by trying to elicit the psychodynamic reason for the particular delusion and the adaptive purpose that it serves. The physician may stimulate the patient's motivation to receive help by emphasizing a willingness to help him with his insomnia, anxiety, or irritability, without challenging the delusions or suggesting that the delusions be treated.

The unwavering reliability of the therapist is essential. The therapist should always be on time and make appointments as regularly as possible, with the goal of developing a solid, reliable, and trusting relationship with the patient. Overgratification actually increases the patient's hostility and suspiciousness because of the core realization that all demands cannot be met. With each gratification, demands increase; there can be no possible future in this kind of relationship. The therapist should avoid overgratification by not extending the appointment time for longer than has been previously designated, by not giving extra appointments unless absolutely essential, and by not being lenient about the fee.

The therapist in the beginning must emphasize the good aspects of the patient's past relationships, no matter how tenuous they were. The therapist should avoid disparaging remarks about the patient's delusions or ideas, but can sympathetically indicate to the patient that his preoccupation with the delusion both distresses himself and interferes with a constructive life. When the patient begins to waver in his delusional belief, the therapist may increase reality testing by asking the patient to clarify his concerns.

Neutralizing the aggressive drives, a complex metapsychological problem, is a vital concept in treating the paranoiac. Basically, neutralization consists of controlling love and hate by internalizing good relations with others. One of the tasks of the therapist is to provide a soothing function that helps neutralize the patient's primitive aggression. In the climate of being a good-enough therapist, the drives become neutralized in the intertwined process of building a trusting relationship, encouraging verbalization in the place of action, and promoting autonomy and independence.

Because homosexual trends are often regressive fantasies caused by sexual inadequacy with the opposite sex—such as impotency, fear of rejection, or inadequate feelings—the therapist should first deal with the patient's heterosexual fears, rather than making disparaging interpretations concerning homosexuality.

Through a relationship with the therapist, the patient begins to neutralize his drives, and his ego is strengthened, so that he attains his own identity. Trust is developed, defenses are shored up to handle anxiety and agitation, and the presenting conflict begins to resolve. The patient may learn to adjust to the delusions that remain intact.

## Group Therapy

Because of their hypersensitivity, suspiciousness, and tendencies to misinterpret events, paranoid patients generally do not do well in group therapy. Other patients may not be aware of the paranoiac's sensitivity, and innocuous statements may be devastating to the paranoiac. The paranoid patient may silently simmer with his hate or explode in a violent attack on the innocent, although offending, patient.

## Evaluation of Therapy

Although the prognosis of the paranoid disorders has traditionally been considered poor, two-thirds of all paranoid patients improve with a combination of therapy and medication. A good outcome depends on the therapist's ability to respond to the patient's mistrust of others and the resulting interpersonal conflicts, frustrations, and failures. A satisfactory social adjustment determines the success of treatment, rather than whether or not the patient's delusions abate.

## REFERENCES

American Psychiatric Association: *Diagnostic and Statistical Manual of Mental Disorders*, ed 3. American Psychiatric Association, Washington, DC, 1980.

Freud S: Psychoanalytic notes upon an autobiographical account of a case of paranoia (dementia paranoides). In *Collected Papers*, vol 3, p 387. Hogarth Press, London, 1925.

Freud S: Some neurotic mechanisms in jealousy, paranoia, and homosexuality. In *Standard Edition of the Complete Psychological Works of Sigmund Freud*, vol 18, p 221. Hogarth Press, London, 1955.

Kendler K S: The nosologic validity of paranoia (simple delusional disorder), a review. Arch Gen Psy-

chiatry *37:* 699, 1980.
Manschreck T C: The assessment of paranoid features. Compr Psychiatry *20:* 370, 1979.
Meissner L J W W: *The Paranoid Process.* Jason Aronson, New York, 1978.
Retterstol N: *Prognosis in Paranoid Psychoses.* Charles C Thomas, Springfield, IL, 1970.
Swanson D P, Bohnert P J, Smith J H: *The Paranoid.* Little Brown and Co. Boston, 1970.

Walker J I, Brodie H K H: Paranoid disorders. In *Comprehensive Textbook of Psychiatry*, ed 4, H I Kaplan, B J Sadock, editors, p 747. Williams & Wilkins, Baltimore, 1985.
Walker J I, Cavenar J O Jr: Paranoid symptoms and conditions. In *Signs and Symptoms in Psychiatry*, pp 483–510. J. B. Lippincott, Philadelphia, 1983.
Winokur G: Delusional disorder (paranoia). Compr Psychiatry *18:* 511, 1977.

# 12

# Schizoaffective Disorders

## Introduction

DSM-III does not define or give diagnostic criteria for schizoaffective disorders. Instead, the diagnosis is included among Psychotic Disorders Not Elsewhere Classified, to indicate strong reservations about its validity as a separate disorder.

## Definition

Schizoaffective disorders are defined here as a syndrome of depressive or manic features that develop before or concurrently with certain psychotic symptoms, such as a preoccupation with a mood-incongruent delusion or hallucination. The psychotic symptoms are such as to be considered unusual in an uncomplicated affective disorder. The diagnosis of schizoaffective illness is not made if the illness is due to any organic mental disorder.

Two kinds of psychotic symptoms define schizoaffective disorders. The first kind includes those that are part of the criterion list for schizophrenia, such as delusions of control and certain types of auditory hallucinations, and that would suggest schizophrenia, if there were no accompanying affective syndrome. The second kind includes those that arise in the context of an affective syndrome without an apparent relationship to depression or elation. Otherwise, the clinical features consist of various mixtures of affective and schizophrenia-like symptoms.

## Epidemiology

Most patients with depression who consult psychiatrists do not report psychotic symptoms. Probably no more than a quarter to a third of depressed patients experience delusions, hallucinations, or prominent ideas of reference.

An estimate of 1.6 percent may be taken as an approximate maximum frequency of schizoaffective conditions. However, the frequency of schizoaffective illness, as defined in DSM-III, is considerably less, because intercurrent affective episodes during the course of schizophrenia are excluded, as are many patients whose psychotic features seem clearly part of an affective illness. A reasonable estimate of the prevalence of schizoaffective disorders, as defined here, may be no more than 1 percent.

Close relatives of patients with schizoaffective disorders show a lower prevalence of schizophrenia than is seen in relatives of schizophrenics; instead, the relatives of patients with schizoaffective disorders show an increased frequency of affective illness, a frequency similar to that seen in the relatives of patients with affective disorders. Most of the ill relatives of schizoaffective patients suffer from uncomplicated, straightforward affective illnesses. At the same time, an increased frequency of schizoaffective conditions may be seen among the relatives.

No striking sex differences in the frequency of schizoaffective disorders have been reported.

## Causes

Little is known concerning the causes of all functional psychoses, including schizoaffective disorders.

## Clinical Features

All patients present with a mixture of affective features, depressive or manic, and one or more clearly evident hallucinations or delusions that are unusual in uncomplicated affective disorders.

Typically, the psychosis begins abruptly, either coincident with an affective disturbance, or after an affective syndrome has been evident for some days or weeks. It is often difficult to be sure which feature began first. The affective and psychotic components of the illness may parallel each other in intensity throughout, or one may wax and wane while the other holds steady.

A common sequence is for the affective and the psychotic features to begin more or less simultaneously; then the delusions or hallucinations subside, leaving the patient with a typical depression or mania. The psychotic features are usually dramatic and overt, creating disturbances for relatives, friends, and neighbors.

Such episodes may last very briefly, but they usually run a course of weeks to months. Some patients experience repeated episodes, separated by months or years of apparently normal psychological functioning. Others have several similar episodes that are then followed by other episodes of typical depression or mania. In yet others the episodes are supplanted by a persistent illness that is indistinguishable from typical chronic schizophrenia, with or without associated periods of disturbed mood.

Suicidal thinking and completed suicide are common in these patients. An unanswered question is what proportion of young persons who commit suicide are suffering from schizoaffective disorders, rather than from uncomplicated schizophrenia. The suicide risk, like the familial illness pattern, has lent support to the view that many, if not most, schizoaffective illnesses are, in fact, atypical cases of depression or mania, rather than cases of schizophrenia.

## Course and Prognosis

The long-term course and outcome of schizoaffective disorders cannot be discussed separately from the course and outcome of schizophrenia itself. The course of schizoaffective disorders may be quite variable, but it seems on average to be significantly better than the course of schizophrenia.

Typically, the psychotic features develop acutely, and the patient is brought for professional help within weeks of their onset, because the patient's family or the patient himself recognizes that a significant change in functioning has taken place.

## Diagnosis

The diagnosis of schizoaffective disorders follows directly from their definition and the clinical picture. The findings on psychiatric examination may be quite variable. In one patient, the psychotic features may be more prominent than the affective features; in another patient the situation may be reversed. In any single patient, these two types of features may fluctuate together or independently. Generally, however, the delusions or hallucinations are quite striking and present no problems in recognition. Patients are disturbed and create considerable difficulty for their families and friends. In general, the more floridly disturbed the patient, the more likely is the illness to be schizoaffective, rather than schizophrenic. The affective features are similar to those seen in uncomplicated depression and mania. See Table I for a list of the signs and symptoms of schizoaffective disorders.

## Differential Diagnosis

The differential diagnosis should cover affective disorders, schizophrenia, organic mental disorders, and certain substance-use disorders, particularly those associated with the abuse of amphetamines, lysergic acid diethylamide (LSD), and other hallucinogens.

Substance abuse should always be considered when confronted by an acutely psychotic patient, including one with striking affective symptoms. Outside history, blood and urine screening for appropriate metabolites, and careful observation usually permit the correct diagnosis. The great majority of substance-abuse illnesses subside within a few days after discontinuation of the drug, and very rarely last more than 10 to 12 days after discontinuation.

## Psychological Tests

Psychological test results, not surprisingly, show a mixture of features associated with both

TABLE I
DIAGNOSTIC FEATURES OF SCHIZOAFFECTIVE DISORDERS

| Essential Features | Associated Features |
|---|---|
| Depressive or manic syndrome<br>One or more of these symptoms:<br>  1. Delusions of control<br>  2. Thought broadcasting<br>  3. Thought insertion<br>  4. Thought withdrawal<br>  5. Auditory hallucinations: voices commenting on patient or conversing with each other<br>  6. Auditory hallucinations: not related to depression or elation, more than one or two words<br>  7. Preoccupation with delusion or hallucination that is not related to depression or elation<br>  8. Delusions for at least 1 month after resolution of affective disturbance<br>  9. Repeated incoherence, unless concurrent with manic syndrome<br>Depressive or manic symptoms simultaneous with above symptoms<br>Duration of illness at least 1 week<br>Not due to organic mental disorder | Course of illness; episodic, chronic, or in remission |

schizophrenia and affective disorders. Few studies have taken schizoaffective disorders, as a separate classification, into consideration.

## Treatment

Most patients with schizoaffective disorders require hospitalization because of their psychotic features, affective disturbances, or risk of suicide. Antipsychotic agents (such as the phenothiazines and butyrophenones), tricyclic antidepressants, antimanic drugs (such as lithium and the phenothiazines), and electroconvulsive therapy are the mainstays of treatment.

Most patients are helped by the available treatments. For many, drugs or electroconvulsive therapy or a combination results in prompt recovery, and the ability to return to work or school. To what extent the continuation of an antipsychotic or antimood drug prevents relapse is not clear, but some evidence indicates that such a prophylactic effort is helpful, at least in some cases. Unfortunately, some patients relapse after only a brief remission and must be treated vigorously to achieve a more lasting remission. A minority of patients show very little improvement, despite the application of all treatments, and they progress to a chronic state of illness.

## REFERENCES

Brockington I F, Leff J P: Schizoaffective psychosis: Definitions and incidence. Psychol Med 9: 91, 1979.

Clayton P J: Schizoaffective disorders. J Nerv Ment Dis 170: 646, 1982.

Fowler R C, Liskow B I, Tanna V L, Lytle L, Mezzich J: Schizophrenia-primary affective disorder discrimination. I. Development of a data-based diagnostic index. Arch Gen Psychiatry 37: 811, 1980.

Fowler R C, Mezzich J, Liskow B I, Van Valkenburg C. Schizophrenia-primary affective disorder discrimination. II. Where unclassified psychosis stands. Arch Gen Psychiatry 37: 815, 1980.

Goodwin D W, Guze S B: Psychiatric Diagnosis, ed 3. Oxford University Press, New York, 1984.

Goplerud E, Depue R A: Affective symptoms, schizophrenia, and the conceptual ambiguity of postpsychotic depression. Schizophr Bull 5: 554, 1979.

Guze S B: Schizoaffective disorders. In Comprehensive Textbook of Psychiatry, ed 4, H I Kaplan, B J Sadock, editors, p 756. Williams & Wilkins, Baltimore, 1985.

Johnson D A W: Studies of depressive symptoms in schizophrenia. I. The prevalence of depression and its possible cause. Br J Psychiatry 139: 89, 1981.

Langfeldt G: The prognosis in schizophrenia. Acta Psychiatr Neurol Scand (Suppl), 110, 1956.

Pope H G, Jr, Lipinski J F, Cohen B. M., Axelrod D T: "Schizoaffective disorder": An invalid diagnosis? A comparison of schizoaffective disorder, schizophrenia, and affective disorder. Am J Psychiatry 137: 921, 1980.

# 13

# Major Affective Disorders

## History

Depression has been recorded since antiquity and descriptions of what we now call the affective disorders can be found in many ancient documents.

The Old Testament story of King Saul describes a depressive syndrome as does the story of Ajax's suicide in Homer's *Iliad*.

About 450 B.C. Hippocrates used the terms mania and melancholia to describe mental disturbances. Cornelius Celsus described melancholia in his work *De Medicina* about 100 A.D. as a depression caused by black bile and the term continued to be used by other medical authors including Aretaeus (120–180 A.D.), Galen (129–199 A.D.), and Alexander of Tralles in the sixth century.

In the middle ages medicine remained alive in the Islamic countries and Rhazes, Avicenna and the Jewish physician Maimonides considered melancholia a distinct disease entity (see Fig. 1). The modern day psychiatrist must look to Emil Kraepelin who in 1896 developed the classification of manic-depressive insanity, which we use today and which was built on the knowledge of that disorder by French and German psychiatrists who preceded Kraepelin.

In 1854 Jules Falret (see Fig. 2) described a condition called *folie circulaire* in which the patient experienced alternating moods of depression and mania. About the same time another French psychiatrist Jules Baillarger described the condition *folie à double forme*, in which the patient would become deeply depressed and fall into a stuporous state from which he would eventually recover. And in 1882, the German psychiatrist Karl Kahlbaum described mania and depression as a stage of the same disease.

Kraepelin's description of manic-depressive insanity contained most of the criteria which psychiatrists use currently to establish the diagnosis. In the various editions of his textbook, *Psychiatry*, he proposed that the entire group of manic-depressive disorders be considered as one illness which did not end in dementia or deterioration.

FIGURE 1. "Melancholia" by Albrecht Dürer, (1471–1528) showing a winged figure in the typical depressive posture surrounded by scattered rubble of a meaningless world.

Kraepelin also described a type of depression which began after menopause in women and during late adulthood in men which came to be known as involutional melancholia; but eventually that came to be seen as a variant type of affective disorder.

Since Kraepelin, many attempts have been made by generations of psychiatrists (including our own) to improve the classification of depressive disorders. Typical of those schemes are the St. Louis Criteria, Research Diagnostic Criteria, and the DSM-III classification.

## Classification

The affective disorders are a group of clinical conditions, whose common and essential feature is a disturbance of mood accompanied by related

FIGURE 2.  Jean Pierre Falret, (1794–1870) (Courtesy of Osler Library, McGill University, Montreal.)

TABLE I
DSM-III CLASSIFICATION OF AFFECTIVE DISORDERS*

*Major affective disorders*
Code depressed episode in fifth digit: 6 = remission, 4 = with psychotic features (the non-ICD-9-CM fifth digit 7 may be used to indicate that the psychotic features are mood-incongruent), 3 = with melancholia, 2 = without melancholia, 0 = unspecified.

Code manic episode in fifth digit: 6 = remission, 4 = with psychotic features (the non-ICD-9-CM fifth digit 7 may be used to indicate that the psychotic features are mood-incongruent), 2 = without psychotic features, 0 = unspecified.

|  | Bipolar disorder |  |
|---|---|---|
| 296.6x | mixed, | _____ |
| 296.4x | manic, | _____ |
| 296.5x | depressed, | _____ |
|  | Major depression |  |
| 296.2x | single episode, | _____ |
| 296.3x | recurrent, | _____ |

*Other specific affective disorders*
301.13  Cyclothymic disorder
300.40  Dysthymic disorder (Depressive neurosis)

*Atypical affective disorders*
296.70  Atypical bipolar disorder
296.82  Atypical depression

\* From American Psychiatric Association: *Diagnostic and Statistical Manual of Mental Disorders*, ed 3, American Psychiatric Association, Washington, DC, 1980. Used with permission.

cognitive, psychomotor, psychophysiological, and interpersonal difficulties.

Mood usually refers to sustained emotional states that color the whole personality and psychic life. It is a pervasive or prevailing emotion that affects the total personality.

Mood may be normal, elevated, or depressed. Patients with elevated mood show expansiveness, flight of ideas, decreased sleep, heightened self-esteem, and grandiose ideas. Patients with depressed mood show loss of energy and interest, guilt feelings, difficulty in concentrating, loss of appetite, and thoughts of death or suicide.

The DSM-III category of affective disorders groups all the affective disorders together. Within that group, the subcategory "major affective disorders" includes bipolar disorder (mixed, manic, or depressed) and major depression (single episode or recurrent). There are two additional categories of affective disorder: other specific affective disorders (cyclothymic disorder and dysthymic disorder) and atypical affective disorder (atypical bipolar disorder and atypical depression) (see Table I).

Various other subclassifications of depression have been described, such as neurotic, reactive, psychotic, and endogenous. Although some of those subclassifications are discussed in this chapter, the student needs to be aware that confusion exists in the field, and it is best to think of depression as falling into two major categories of bipolar disorder (defined by one or more manic episodes) and major or unipolar depression (defined by one or more depressions without manic episodes).

The classification of manic-depressive illness, introduced by Kraepelin, is almost the same as bipolar disorder, but it is not exactly synonymous with the DSM-III classification. Some of Kraepelin's manic-depressive patients never had episodes of mania, whereas patients classified as having bipolar disorder do have one or more episodes of mania. Most clinicians use the two terms synonymously, however. The patient is classified at the time of examination as being manic, depressed, or in a mixed state (mania alternating with depression).

## Depression as a Normal Human Emotion

Depression refers to a normal human emotion, as well as to a group of syndromes or disorders. The term "depression" has different meanings in various scientific fields, such as neurophysiology, pharmacology, psychology, and psychiatry. For the neurophysiologist, depression refers to any decrease in electrophysiological activity—for example, cortical depression. For the pharmacologist, depression refers to the effect of drugs that decrease the activity of the target organ. Thus, the central nervous system depressants include drugs, such as the barbiturates and the anesthetics, that decrease responsiveness to stimuli by producing sleep or coma. For the psychologist, depression refers to any decrement in optimal cognitive, perceptual, or motor performance. For the clinical psychiatrist, however, depression covers a wide range of changes in emotional states, ranging in severity from the normal mood fluctuations of everyday life to severe psychotic episodes.

The use of the term "depression" in a number of scientific fields has tended to lend support to the view or, perhaps more accurately, the wish that common mechanisms underlie the neurophysiological, pharmacological, psychological, and clinical phenomena. As a result, many clinicians and investigators have postulated that clinical depressive symptoms are the result of a reduction of some generalized or specific central nervous system function and, therefore, are treated best with a drug that has a countereffect—that is, a stimulant drug. Clinical experience demonstrates, however, that psychotherapeutic methods are often effective in treating some depressive states, lending support to the psychoanalytic and psychological theories of depression as also having validity.

### Epidemiology

#### *Incidence and Prevalence*

The affective disorders, particularly depression, are among the most frequently occurring or prevalent psychiatric disorders in adults. The meaning of such statements can vary, however, and statistics and reports of the frequency of occurrence are derived from a variety of measures (see Table II).

Incidence refers to the number of new cases, and prevalence refers to the total number of cases a year found at a given period or point in time. A risk factor is any factor that increases the chances of a person's developing a particular disorder.

The lifetime expectancy of developing an affective disorder of any type is about 20 percent for females and 10 percent for males. For Western nations, if attention is limited to bipolar disorder, lifetime expectancy is about 1 percent for both sexes. If broadly defined depressions of all types are included, however, lifetime expectancy rates increase markedly, going as high as 30 percent in some estimates.

A considerable proportion of persons with depression never see a physician. In all categories of depression, only 20 to 25 percent of depressed people receive treatment. Reported prevalence and incidence figures must be viewed as minimum estimates.

#### *Sex*

An almost universal trend, independent of country, is the greater prevalence of depression among women than among men. The incidence

TABLE II
EPIDEMIOLOGY OF AFFECTIVE DISORDERS IN WESTERN INDUSTRIALIZED NATIONS

|  | *Major Depression (Unipolar)* | *Bipolar Disorder* |
|---|---|---|
| Prevalence (No. of cases at a point in time) | 2–3 cases/100 men (2–3 percent) 5–9 cases/100 women (5–9 percent) | 0.6–0.9 cases/100 men and women combined |
| Incidence (No. of new cases per year) | 82–201 new cases/100,000 per year for men 247–598 new cases/100,000 per year for women (Only 20–25% of people receive treatment for depression) | 9–15.2 cases/100,000 per year for men (0.009–0.015 percent) 7.4–30 cases 100,000 per year for women (0.007–0.030 percent) |
| Sex | 2:1, women:men | No apparent difference |
| Age | Peaks in women at ages 35–45 and peaks in men after 55 and then increases with age | Onset usually before age 30 |
| Social class | No pattern | More frequent in upper socioeconomic class |
| Race | No conclusive data for blacks and whites | No relationship |
| Family history | Increased risk with family history of depresssion or alcoholism | Increased risk with family history of bipolar illness |
| Childhood experiences | Increased risk with parental loss before age 11 | Inconclusive |
| Marital status | Increased risk in those who lack close relationship with another person | More common among divorced persons |
| Lifetime expectancy | 10 percent for men 20 percent for women | 0.9–1.1 percent for men 0.6–1.3 percent for women |

of depressions is twice as great in women as in men for reasons that are unclear. Some suggested explanations include different stresses, childbirth, learned helplessness, and hormonal variations. In bipolar disorder, however, the rates are equal between the sexes.

### Social Class

In bipolar disorder there appears to be a slightly higher incidence among the upper socioeconomic class than among other classes. Major depression has no correlation with social class.

### Marital Status

Hospital admission rates for affective disorders are slightly higher than usual for those who lack a close intimate relationship with another person or who are single or divorced. Bipolar disorder may be more common among divorced persons than among others.

### Age

Bipolar disorder has an early age of onset, in late adolescence or before age 30. In unipolar depressions women reach a peak from 35 to 45 years, and men peak after age 55.

### Race

There is no conclusive evidence for any differences among blacks and whites. However, more blacks are hospitalized for affective disorders than are whites.

### Family History

The first degree relatives of unipolar depressives show a lifetime risk of 20 percent for affective disorder. The first degree relatives of bipolar patients show a lifetime risk of 25 percent for an affective disorder.

### Recurrence

Fifty to sixty percent of patients who are in remission from bipolar or unipolar depression will have another attack. Episodes usually recur ever 3 to 9 years.

### Causes

Any discussion of the causes of the major affective disorders must take into account both the biological factors and the social factors involved in the disease process.

### Biological Factors

**Genetics.** Family studies found relatives of bipolar patients to have a significantly higher risk for bipolar illness than for unipolar illness, but relatives of unipolar patients were more at risk for unipolar illness than bipolar illness. Twin studies indicate significantly greater risk in monozygotic twins than in dizygotic twins for similar affective disease processes. Monozygotic twins reared apart show about a 65 percent concordance rate for affective disorder.

Other genetic factors are possible linkages between the X chromosome and bipolar or manic-depressive illness. The direct study of X-linked markers, such as deutan color-blindness and the $XG_a$ blood group, suggest that bipolar affective disorder is transmitted by an X-linked dominant gene. HLA (human leukocyte antigen) associations with bipolar affective disorder have also been reported. However, doubt is thrown on the significance of those X-linkage findings by repeated findings of sick father-son pairs, a finding directly contradicting the hypothesis. Recent work demonstrates father-to-son transmission of membrane lithium transport abnormalities in red blood corpuscles.

Two genetic subgroups of bipolar disease may exist: a classical early-onset group (mean age of onset, 25 years) and a late-onset group (mean age, 39 years). Those in the first group show positive family histories, but those in the second group do not. Thus, bipolar affective disorder seems to be under different genetic controls in different patients. In some patients, it behaves like an X-linked genetically controlled illness; in other patients, it behaves as if it is transmitted in a pattern of autosomal dominant inheritance with variable expressivity; and in still other patients, it behaves as if it is not genetically controlled.

Two subgroups of major depression patients—early-onset females (onset before age 40) and late-onset males (onset after age 40) have been described. Those subgroups demonstrate family members with very different illnesses. In the families of late-onset male probands, one finds depression as often in the males as in the females, and one finds little alcoholism or sociopathy in male relatives. In the families of early-onset female probands, on the other hand, one finds more depression in female relatives than in male relatives, and one finds more alcoholism and sociopathy in male relatives than in the other families. Those findings have been generalized to form two prototype subgroups: depression spectrum disease (early-onset females) and pure depressive disease (late-onset males). The findings require further confirmation.

**Other Biological Factors.** In addition to genetic factors in transmission, other biological factors may be significant in the cause and pathogenesis of affective disorders. Those factors include electrolyte disturbances, especially of sodium and potassium; neurophysiological alterations based on findings from electrophysiological studies using electroencephalography and evoked potential methods; dysfunction and faulty regulation of autonomic nervous system activity; neuroendocrine abnormalities, including hypothalamic, pituitary, adrenal cortical, thyroid, and gonadal changes; and neurochemical alterations in the neurotransmitters, especially in the biogenic amines, which serve as central nervous system and peripheral neurotransmitters.

BIOGENIC AMINES. The biogenic amines include three catecholamines: dopamine, norepinephrine and epinephrine. Indolamine is another biogenic amine represented by serotonin. And acetylcholine is also a biogenic amine.

*Catecholamines.* The catecholamine hypothesis is based, in part, on the observations that drugs such as the monoamine oxidase inhibitors and tricyclic antidepressants, which potentiate or increase brain catecholamines, cause behavior stimulation and excitement and have an antidepressant effect. Conversely, drugs that deplete or inactivate central amines produce sedation or depression. Lithium carbonate, effective in the treatment of mania, decreases the release and increases the reuptake of norepinephrine.

Some studies have shown that there may be a shortage of brain norepinephrine in depression. A metabolite 3-methoxy-4-hydroxyphenylethylene glycol (MHPG) has been found to be decreased in the cerebrospinal fluid and urine of depressed patients. Drugs that reduce norepinephrine levels, such as methyldopa, propranolol, and reserpine, may cause depression, and amphetamine, which causes synaptic release of norepinephrine, cause elevated mood.

In mania, a few studies have indicated that there may be higher concentrations of norepinephrine as measured by MHPG levels. The fraction of MHPG in humans that is derived from the brain has been the subject of controversy, and the clinical utility of using MHPG as a measure of the presence or absence of depression has yet to be determined.

*Acetylcholine.* The relationship of acetylcholine and catecholamines has also been implicated in depression because some depressed patients become more depressed when acetylcholine central nervous system activity is increased. The cholinergic system plays a role in REM sleep and the reduced REM latency in depression may reflect CNS hyperactivity of acetylcholine.

*Serotonin.* Serotonin, another biogenic amine,

is distributed in the central nervous system, and some depressed patients have been found to have a decreased serotonin metabolite, 5-hydroxyindoleacetic acid (5-HIAA), in their cerebrospinal fluid. The findings are not consistent, however, in that the amount of 5-HIAA derived from brain tissue or from non-central nervous system sites has not been determined.

Another piece of evidence that suggests the involvement of serotonin in depression is the observation that tryptophan, a serotonin precursor, relieves depression in some patients. Also, reserpine depletes brain serotonin and antidepressants increase brain serotonin activity.

Other studies have shown a possible altered serotonin rhythmicity, rather than an absolute deficiency, in particular subgroups of depression. It has been reported that platelet serotonin, which shows a normal diurnal rhythmicity, was desynchronized in unipolar depressives, especially among postmenopausal women.

*Endocrine Disorders.* Involvement of the endocrine system in depression has been suspected for many years. Among the observed somatic symptoms suggestive of endocrine changes in affective disorders are decreased appetite, weight loss, insomnia, diminished sex drive, gastrointestinal dysfunction, and predictable diurnal variations of mood. Newly developed, highly sensitive assay techniques have been able to detect marked alterations of hormone activity concurrent with depressive events.

Mood changes have been clinically associated with a variety of endocrine disorders. The paranoid depressive states of hyperadrenalism (Cushing's disease), the hyperactivity and elation of hyperthyroidism (thyrotoxicosis), the depression sometimes associated with exogenous estrogen therapy—all suggest such a relationship. Depression is common in the postpartum period, when hormonal levels change.

*Growth Hormone.* Basal secretions of growth hormone (GH) by the pituitary gland are normally augmented in response to a drop in blood sugar, starvation, stress, exercise, and estrogens. A conventional test of GH activity involves the administration of insulin, followed by the measurement of the expected rise in plasma GH levels. Using this method, investigators have repeatedly demonstrated that, in many instances of depression, there is a diminished response to such insulin-induced hypoglycemia. The phenomenon is noted most often in unipolar depressions. In bipolar depressions the response is normal or enhanced. GH release is impaired in a significant percentage of postmenopausal women with diagnosed unipolar depression. A number of clinical and laboratory investigations have demonstrated an association between maternal deprivation and inhibition of GH secretion. It is noted among human infants with the failure-to-thrive syndrome. Similar findings have been noted in rat pups who are removed from their mothers soon after birth. When the pups are returned to their mothers, there is a rapid reversal of the deprivation-induced GH abnormality.

Control of GH release seems to reside in catecholinergic neurons. GH release is increased by dopaminergic stimulation.

*Cortisol.* Many depressed patients exhibit hypersecretion of cortisol. The sequence of events leading to the elevation of the adrenal steroid hormone probably begins with an increased hypothalamic corticotropin-releasing factor (CRF) discharge. Normally, noradrenergic tracts inhibit CRF release. In depressed states, diminished activity by those neurons results in disinhibition of CRF. With the absence of restraint, CRF levels rise, sparking the function of the adrenal cortex and the resulting release of adrenocorticotrophic hormone (ACTH).

The finding that hypersecretion of cortisol is present in some depressed patients, has been used in the dexamethasone suppression test (DST) in that dexamethasone is an exogenous steroid that suppresses the blood level of cortisol.

The dexamethasone suppression test (DST) is a laboratory test used to determine the endogenous depressive state (major depression with melancholia). The test consists of administering at bedtime 1 mg. of oral dexamethasone and collecting several serial plasma samples on the following day, usually at 8 A.M., 4 P.M., and 11 P.M. Approximately 98 percent of normal patients show a suppressed level of cortisol. That is considered a negative finding. In 50 percent of endogenous depressed patients, however, that suppression does not occur. In those patients cortisol escapes the suppressive action of dexamethasone, and the finding is considered positive. A serum cortisol level greater than 4.5 to 5 $\mu$g/dl for any of the blood samples is abnormal. The test is believed to reflect changed activity in the hypothalamic-pituitary-adrenal axis in certain depressed patients.

False-positive results occur in a variety of conditions, such as Cushing's disease, renal and hepatic illnesses, and anorexia nervosa. The findings are also affected by medications such as phenobarbital, meprobamate, benzodiazepine, and steroids. Therefore, the DST is best used as a research tool at the present time (see Table III).

TABLE III
MEDICAL CONDITIONS AND PHARMACOLOGIC AGENTS THAT MAY INTERFERE WITH RESULTS OF THE DEXAMETHASONE SUPPRESSION TEST*

False-positive results are associated with:
 Phenytoin
 Barbiturates
 Meprobamate
 Glutethimide
 Methyprylon
 Methaqualone
 Carbamazepine
 Cardiac failure
 Hypertension
 Renal failure
 Disseminated cancer and serious infections
 Recent major trauma or surgery
 Fever
 Nausea
 Dehydration
 Temporal lobe disease
 High-dosage estrogen treatment
 Pregnancy
 Cushing's disease
 Unstable diabetes mellitus
 Extreme weight loss (malnutrition, anorexia nervosa)
 Alcohol abuse
False-negative results are associated with:
 Hypopituitarism
 Addison's disease
 Long-term synthetic steroid therapy
 Indomethacin
 High-dosage cyproheptadine treatment
 High-dosage benzodiazepine treatment

\* From Young M, Stanford J: The dexamethasone suppression test for the detection, diagnosis, and management of depression. Arch Int Med *100:* 309, 1984. Used with permission.

*Other Hormones.* A significant proportion of depressed patients exhibit an absent or diminished thyroid-stimulating hormone (TSH) response to thyrotropin-releasing hormone (TRH) challenge.

Additional changes in neuroendocrine activity have been discerned. Prolactin levels may exhibit irregular circadian rhythm, and luteinizing hormone (LH) secretion is often diminished in depressed postmenopausal women.

CHRONOPSYCHOBIOLOGY. Periodic variations in physiological and psychological functions occur. Circadian rhythm shows a periodicity of about 24 hours. Sleep is one such periodic state, divided into REM and non-REM periods.

Polysomnograph studies show that in a major depression there is decreased total sleep time, an increased percentage of dream time, and a decreased REM latency (the time between falling asleep and the first REM period). There is also a very long first REM period.

In mania there is a decreased percentage of dream time. That finding has led to the idea of depriving depressed patients of dream time

(REM sleep) to see if their mood improves. When depressed patients are deprived of sleep for one or two nights (and thus of dreaming), mood does appear to improve somewhat.

### Psychosocial Factors

**Life Events and Environmental Stress.** Most American clinicians and investigators have long been convinced that a relationship exists between stressful life events and clinical depression. Clinical case discussions often include statements relating stress, especially from life events, to the onset of depressive episodes. In such discussions, life events are thought to play an important role in the causation of depression—at least its precipitation, as evidenced by such statements as "The depression arose in relation to . . ." and "The depression was precipitated by. . . ." Some clinicians even believe that life events play the primary or major role in depressions; others are more conservative, limiting the role of life events to contributing to the onset and timing of the acute episode.

The theory of an environmental cause of affective disorders has multiple sources: Adolf Meyer's general psychobiological approach, psychological observations on reactions to loss, and psychopathological studies relating the presence or absence of precipitating events to the assignment of patients along the endogenous reactive continuum.

In general, the research confirms the relationship between life events and depression.

**Personality and Psychodynamic Factors.** It is widely believed that persons prone to depression are characterized by low self-esteem, strong superego, clinging and dependent interpersonal relations, and limited capacity for mature and enduring object relations. Although those traits are common among depressives, no single personality trait, constellation, or type has been established as uniquely predisposed to depression. All humans, of whatever personality pattern, can and do become depressed under appropriate circumstances, although certain personality types—the oral-dependent, the obsessive-compulsive, and the hysterical—may be at greater risk for depression than the antisocial, the paranoid, and certain other types who use projection and other externalizing modes of defense.

Psychodynamic formulations are concerned not only with ongoing dynamic conflicts—evident in guilt, reactions to loss, and hostility turned against the self—that may be involved in the manifest depressive episode but also with features that may antedate the acute depressive episode and, therefore, may be regarded as causal. Some of those features are rooted in personality, since a major psychodynamic hypothesis focuses on the predisposition of certain personality types to depression.

At the present time, the psychodynamic hypotheses are primarily of great heuristic value, contributing to case formulation, guidance of psychotherapeutic practice, and the design of future research.

**Psychoanalytic Factors.** Karl Abraham thought that episodes of manifest illness are precipitated by the loss of a libidinal object, eventuating in a regressive process in which the ego retreats from its mature functioning state to one in which the infantile trauma of the oral-sadistic stage of libidinal development dominates because of a fixation process in earliest childhood.

In Freud's structural theory, the introjection of the lost object into the ego leads to the typical depressive symptoms diagnostic of a lack of energy available to the ego. The superego, unable to retaliate against the lost object externally, flails out at the psychic representation of the lost object, now internalized in the ego as an introject. When the ego overcomes or merges with the superego, there is a release of energy that was previously bound in the depressive symptoms, and a mania supervenes with the typical symptoms of excess.

Later analytic writers have elaborated the basic Abraham-Freud conceptualization in various ways. Although most analytic writers pay lip service to the concept that the disease has an underlying neurophysiological substrate, few attempt to conceptualize that state in any but psychological terms.

Heinz Kohut made significant contributions to the psychology of the self and the treatment of narcissistic personality disorders. Narcissistic personality disorder is one of the frequent differential diagnostic considerations in manic-depressive patients, because patients with narcissistic personality disorder frequently demonstrate transient periods of elation and depression, often with grandiosity and euphoria in one phase and self-depreciation in a succeeding phase, just as is seen in classic manic-depressive disorder.

**Premorbid Personality Factors.** A premorbid personality organization exists in some depressed patients. Depressed patients frequently decompensate under stress, are not socially facile, require excessive environmental support, and tend to be obsessive personalities. They are also introverted, dependent, narcissistic, and insecure, and they feel guilty.

Manic patients tend to have more normal premorbid personalities than do depressed patients. Some studies indicate that patients can be taught to learn more adequate ways of coping with stress and maladaptive patterns of behavior. Aaron Beck, who devised cognitive therapy, relies on the patient's capacity to learn new coping mechanisms. Patients also learn their negative view of themselves and their past experience, and they unlearn their negative expectation of the future.

**Learned Helplessness.** In some animal experiments in which dogs were exposed to electric shocks from which they could not escape, the dogs reacted with helplessness and made no attempt to escape future shocks. They learned to give up and appeared to be helpless. In humans who are depressed, one can find a similar state of helplessness. If the psychiatrist can instill in a depressed patient a sense of control and mastery of the environment, the depression frequently lifts. Similarly, reward and positive reinforcement from one's environment can often help the patient overcome depression. Those behavioral techniques are used in individual and group therapy.

### A Unified Theory

Today, it seems fruitful to conceive of the major affective disorders as genetically controlled disorders in which spontaneous shifts of activity cycles cause typical symptoms of the disorder. Alternately, specific psychogenic factors meaning "loss" act as triggers and can precipitate an episode, either manic or depressed. Once started, the episode does not usually respond to interpretation, and in appropriate subgroups, one or another chemical treatment is indicated. Once the episode is controlled chemically, psychological treatment may be necessary to help the patient deal with the secondary consequences of his illness, to help remove the effects of specific psychogenic triggers, or to deal with psychological problems diagnostic of a second disorder. Thus, some patients with bipolar illness need lithium carbonate and psychological help with handling psychological losses, and some need lithium carbonate and psychological treatment of a coexisting narcissistic or other personality disorder.

### Diagnosis and Clinical Features

Major affective disorders are characterized by one or more episodes of major illness involving a prominent and persistent disturbance in mood, either manic or depressed, clearly distinguished from prior functioning. The essential feature of a manic episode is an elevated, expansive, or irritable mood associated with such symptoms as hyperactivity, excessive involvement in activities without the use of judgment, pressured speech, inflated self-esteem, distractibility, flight of ideas, and decreased need for sleep. The essential feature of a depressed episode is a depressive mood or pervasive loss of interest or pleasure associated with symptoms of sleep and appetite disturbance, change in weight, psychomotor agitation or retardation, decrease in energy, a feeling of guilt or worthlessness, and thoughts of suicide. Any given episode may be characterized as manic, depressed, or mixed in symptoms and with or without psychosis in intensity. When the symptoms disappear, the resulting picture is said to be in remission.

### Bipolar-Unipolar Distinction

Patients with a history of manic episodes (the bipolar group) are separated from those patients who have had only recurrent episodes of depression (the unipolar group). Among the various nosologic approaches, the bipolar-unipolar distinction has achieved considerable acceptance. DSM-III is consistent with evidence pointing to the importance of the distinction between unipolar and bipolar forms of affective disorder.

Considerable evidence of possible genetic, familial, personality, biochemical, physiological, and pharmacological differences between bipolar and unipolar affective disorders has been presented. Patients with bipolar disorder show a far higher frequency of positive family history than do patients with only depression. Psychopharmacological studies also indicate differences in the response of bipolar patients and depressed patients to psychoactive drugs, especially lithium. Patients with bipolar disorder are more likely to develop hypomanic responses to dopa or to imipramine and other tricyclics than are patients with depression.

Although the concept of bipolar disorder is well defined and amply substantiated by research and by clinical experience, the status of a unipolar manic disorder is still uncertain. In DSM-III, the diagnosis of bipolar disorder is made when there is a manic episode, whether or not there has been a depressive episode.

### Major Depression

The essential feature of major depression is a distinct period of decreased psychophysiological activation. In that state, the predominant mood is depressed, or the patient shows a pervasive loss of interest or pleasure. The patient is frequently not aware of or does not complain of the mood disturbance, and what is evident is a withdrawal from usual activities. Symptoms that may be present include sleep disturbance (usually early-morning awakening), loss of appetite, cognitive disturbance (including inability to concentrate or to make decisions), slowed thinking, decreased energy, feelings of worthlessness and guilt, and thoughts of suicide and death. Sexual interest is greatly diminished (see Table IV).

When the depression is mild, environmental changes may lead to some amelioration of the condition; but, when the depression is severe, no such effect is found.

There are certain age-associated features of major depression. In early childhood, separation anxiety may lead to clinging behavior and school phobia. In latency and early-adolescent boys especially, negative and antisocial behavior may occur (depressive equivalents). Sexual acting out, truancy, and running away are seen in older boys and girls. In the elderly, pseudodementia—that is, depression presenting primarily as a loss of intellectual functioning—must be carefully differentiated from true dementia caused by organic mental disorder.

Major depressive episodes may be recurrent or single. Some studies have shown that the average depressive episode usually lasts from 3 to 6 months.

Major depressions may be associated with melancholia or may have psychotic features (see Fig. 3).

**Major Depression with Melancholia.** This classification of depression has shown a positive response to both tricyclics and electroconvulsive therapy (ECT) and a negative response to psychotherapy. Among inpatients, about 50 percent of those who have a major depressive episode have melancholic symptom features (see Table V).

This classification has also been called endogenomorphic or endogenous depression. The syndrome has at least four component hypotheses: (1) There is a co-variation of symptoms, so that a central group of symptoms—including retardation, early-morning awakening, weight loss, guilt, and unreactivity—occur together. (2) There is difficulty in soliciting a history of recent life events and precipitating events. Hence, there has developed the concept of the reactive depression, which occurs in response to recent loss, disappointment, stress, and other external events. The implication is that those depressions without a recent history of external stress result from some intrinsic biological process; hence, they have acquired the label of endogenomorphic. (3) There is a correlation with age; old patients are more likely to be endogenous, and young patients are more likely to the reactive. (4) There is a correlation with personality; the endogenous patients show

TABLE IV
DIAGNOSTIC CRITERIA FOR MAJOR DEPRESSIVE EPISODE*

A. Dysphoric mood for loss of interest or pleasure in all or almost all usual activities and pastimes. The dysphoric mood is characterized by symptoms such as the following: depressed, sad, blue, hopeless, low, down in the dumps, irritable. The mood disturbance must be prominent and relatively persistent, but not necessarily the most dominant symptom, and does not include momentary shifts from one dysphoric mood to another dysphoric mood, e.g., anxiety to depression to anger, such as are seen in states of acute psychotic turmoil. (For children under 6, dysphoric mood may have to be inferred from a persistently sad facial expression.)

B. At least four of the following symptoms have each been present nearly every day for a period of at least two weeks (in children under 6, at least three of the first four).

(1) poor appetite or significant weight loss (when not dieting) or increased appetite or significant weight gain (in children under 6, consider failure to make expected weight gains)
(2) insomnia or hypersomnia
(3) psychomotor agitation or retardation (but not merely subjective feelings of restlessness or being slowed down) (in children under 6, hypoactivity)
(4) loss of interest or pleasure in usual activities, or decrease in sexual drive not limited to a period when delusional or hallucinating (in children under 6, signs of apathy)
(5) loss of energy; fatigue
(6) feelings of worthlessness, self-reproach, or excessive or inappropriate guilt (either may be delusional)
(7) complaints or evidence of diminished ability to think or concentrate, such as slowed thinking, or indecisiveness not associated with marked loosening of associations or incoherence
(8) recurrent thoughts of death, suicidal ideation, wishes to be dead, or suicide attempt

C. Neither of the following dominate the clinical picture when an affective syndrome (i.e., criteria A and B above) is not present, that is, before it developed or after it has remitted:

(1) preoccupation with a mood-incongruent delusion or hallucination (see definition below)
(2) bizarre behavior

D. Not superimposed on either Schizophrenia, Schizophreniform Disorder, or a Paranoid Disorder.

E. Not due to any Organic Mental Disorder or Uncomplicated Bereavement.

* From American Psychiatric Association: *Diagnostic and Statistical Manual of Mental Disorders*, ed 3. American Psychiatric Association, Washington, DC, 1980. Used with permission.

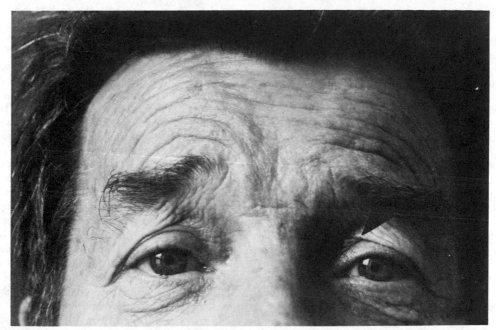

FIGURE 3. The Swiss neuropsychiatrist Veraguth has described a peculiar triangle-shaped fold in the nasal corner of the upper eyelid (*arrow*). This fold is often associated with depression and referred to as Veraguth's fold. The photograph illustrates this physiognomic feature in a 50-year-old man during a major depressive episode. Veraguth's fold may also be seen in individuals who are not clinically depressed, usually while they are harboring a mild depressive affect. Electromyographically it has been shown that distinct changes in the tone of the corrugator and zygomatic facial muscles accompany depression. (Courtesy of Heinz E. Lehmann, M.D.)

TABLE V
DSM-III CRITERIA FOR MELANCHOLIA*

Loss of pleasure in all or almost all activities, lack of reactivity to usually pleasurable stimuli (doesn't feel much better, even temporarily, when something good happens), and at least three of the following:
1. Distinct quality of depressed mood—that is, the depressed mood is perceived as distinctly different from the kind of feeling experienced after the death of a loved one
2. The depression is regularly worse in the morning
3. Early-morning awakening (at least two hours before usual time of awakening)
4. Marked psychomotor retardation or agitation
5. Significant anorexia or weight loss
6. Excessive or inappropriate guilt

* From American Psychiatric Association: *Diagnostic and Statistical Manual of Mental Disorders*, ed 3. American Psychiatric Association, Washington, DC, 1980. Used with permission.

a more stable nonneurotic form of premorbid personality than do the reactives.

**Major Depression with Psychotic Features.** Although the traditional meaning of the term "psychotic" emphasized loss of reality testing and impairment of mental functioning—manifested by delusions, hallucinations, confusion, and impaired memory—two other meanings have evolved during the past 50 years. In the most common American usage of the term, "psychotic" became synonymous with severe impairment of social and personal functioning, manifested by social withdrawal and inability to perform the usual household and occupational roles. The other use of the term specifies degree of ego regression as the criterion for psychotic

illness. As a consequence of those multiple meanings, in current clinical and research practice the term has lost its precision.

Depressions with psychotic features are relatively infrequent in current clinical practice. Only 10 percent of large samples show delusions, hallucinations, confusion, and other manifestations of impaired reality testing.

For clinical description, however, the term "psychotic" does have some limited clinical usefulness. The description of a psychotic depression implies severe impairment, high suicidal risk, and possible need for hospitalization. Patients with psychotic depressions are difficult to treat and are often refractory to antidepressants, neuroleptics, and electroconvulsive therapy.

When hallucinations or delusions are present in a psychotically depressed patient, they may be classified as either mood-congruent or mood-incongruent.

The term "mood-congruent" refers to psychotic features that are consistent with a depressed mood—that the patient has committed a grave sin or a heinous crime for which he should be punished, for example. "Mood-incongruent" refers to delusions or hallucinations in which the content is not consistent with the depressed mood. A patient may believe himself to be the Messiah, for example—a grandiose belief apparently unrelated to his depressed state of mind.

The clinical significance of whether or not the psychotic features are congruent or incongruent with depressed mood is unclear at the present time. However, the clinician may suspect a schizophrenic process in the latter situation—that is, if mood-incongruent delusions or hallucinations are present (see Table VI).

### Bipolar Disorder

In bipolar affective disorder, the patient's history is one of recurrent discrete periods of illness in which episodes of mania occur alone or alternate with episodes of depression.

The essential feature of a manic episode is a distinct period of intense psychophysiological activation. In that state the predominant mood is either elevated or irritable, accompanied by one or more of the following symptoms: hyperactivity, the undertaking of too many activities, lack of judgment of the consequences of actions, pressure of speech, flight of ideas, distractibility, inflated self-esteem, and hypersexuality.

The elevated mood is euphoric and often infectious in nature. Although uninvolved people may not recognize the unusual nature of the patient's mood, those who know the patient recognize it as not usual for the patient, or it is characteristic of the patient when high. Alternatively, the mood may be irritable, especially when the patient's activities are thwarted. Often, a patient who suffers from recurring manic episodes exhibits a change of predominant mood from euphoria early in the course of the illness to irritability later in the process (see Table VII).

In addition to mood disturbance, speech is often disturbed. As the mania gets more intense, formal and logical speech considerations are overthrown, and speech becomes loud, rapid, and difficult to interpret. As the activated state increases, speech becomes full of puns, jokes, plays on words, and irrelevancies that are at first amusing; but, as the activity level increases still more, associations become loosened. Increasing distractibility leads to flight of ideas, word salads, and neologisms. In acute manic excitement, speech may be totally incoherent and indistinguishable from that of a schizophrenic in acute catatonic excitement.

Self-esteem is inflated during a manic episode, and, as the activity level increases, the feelings about the self become increasingly disturbed. Delusional grandiose symptoms are in evidence, and the patient is willing to undertake any project possible.

Nocturnal electroencephalographic findings in mania are of a decreased total sleep time and a decreased percentage of dream time, as well as an increased dream latency. Those findings may be interpreted as supportive of the hypothesis that circadian rhythm activities are delayed in mania because of an increase in the activity of the intrinsic pacemaker.

Associated features found in mania include lability of mood, with rapid shifts to brief depression. Such a finding accounts for those patients who present loosened associations and who alternately laugh and cry. In addition, hal-

TABLE VI
MAJOR DEPRESSION WITH PSYCHOTIC FEATURES*

This category should be used when there apparently is gross impairment in reality testing, as when there are delusions or hallucinations or depressive stupor (the individual is mute and unresponsive). When possible, specify whether the psychotic features are mood-incongruent. (The non-ICD-9-CM fifth-digit 7 may be used instead to indicate that the psychotic features are mood-incongruent; otherwise, mood-congruence may be assumed.)

*Mood-congruent Psychotic Features:* Delusions or hallucinations whose content is entirely consistent with the themes of either personal inadequacy, guilt, disease, death, nihilism, or deserved punishment; depressive stupor (the individual is mute and unresponsive).

*Mood-incongruent Psychotic Features:*
Delusions or hallucinations whose content does not involve themes of either personal inadequacy, guilt, disease, death, nihilism, or deserved punishment. Included are such symptoms as persecutory delusions, thought insertion, and delusions of being controlled, whose content has no apparent relationship to any of the themes noted above.

* From American Psychiatric Association: *Diagnostic and Statistical Manual of Mental Disorders*, ed 3. American Psychiatric Association, Washington, DC, 1980. Used with permission.

TABLE VII
DIAGNOSTIC CRITERIA FOR MANIC EPISODE*

A. One or more distinct periods with a predominantly elevated, expansive, or irritable mood. The elevated or irritable mood must be a prominent part of the illness and relatively persistent, although it may alternate or intermingle with depressive mood.

B. Duration of at least one week (or any duration if hospitalization is necessary), during which, for most of the time, at least three of the following symptoms have persisted (four if the mood is only irritable) and have been present to a significant degree:
 (1) increase in activity (either socially, at work, or sexually) or physical restlessness
 (2) more talkative than usual or pressure to keep talking
 (3) flight of ideas or subjective experience that thoughts are racing
 (4) inflated self-esteem (grandiosity, which may be delusional)
 (5) decreased need for sleep
 (6) distractibility, i.e., attention is too easily drawn to unimportant or irrelevant external stimuli
 (7) excessive involvement in activities that have a high potential for painful consequences which is not recognized, e.g., buying sprees, sexual indiscretions, foolish business investments, reckless driving

C. Neither of the following dominate the clinical picture when an affective syndrome (i.e., criteria A and B above) is not present, that is, before it developed or after it has remitted:
 (1) preoccupation with a mood-incongruent delusion or hallucination
 (2) bizarre behavior

D. Not superimposed on either Schizophrenia, Schizophreniform Disorder, or a Paranoid Disorder.

E. Not due to any Organic Mental Disorder, such as Substance Intoxication.

* From American Psychiatric Association: *Diagnostic and Statistical Manual of Mental Disorders*, ed 3. American Psychiatric Association, Washington, DC, 1980. Used with permission.

lucinations of any type, ideas of reference, and frank delusions may be present. Unlike the delusions seen in schizophrenia, those seen in mania are often fleeting and related to the level of activity of the mood, rather than to long-lasting psychological conflict.

The first episode in a bipolar disorder may be in the form of a severe depression. If a sudden switch to mania is noted, the correct diagnosis of bipolar disorder is easily made. Sometimes the patient cycles or "switches" in and out of mania (see Table VIII).

A diagnosis should be made only after finding the typical positive criteria defining episodes of the illness and only if the episode of manifest illness is clearly distinguishable from the patient's usual functioning. If the disturbance of affect is depressed, the depression must be sustained for at least 2 weeks; the diagnosis of manic episode requires a disturbance of affect lasting at least 1 week.

A manic episode is characterized by a change of mood from a usual normal mood to a predominantly elevated, expansive, or irritable mood. If the mood is elevated or expansive, at least four of the following seven symptoms should be present; if the mood is irritable, five symptoms are necessary: (1) increased activity socially, sexually, and at work; (2) increased talkativeness; (3) flight of ideas by objective examination or subjective report of racing thoughts; (4) grandiosity, at times to a delusional degree; (5) decreased need for sleep; (6) distractibility; and (7) poorly thought-out involvement in projects or activities.

TABLE VIII
DIAGNOSTIC CRITERIA FOR BIPOLAR DISORDER, MIXED*

A. Current (or most recent) episode involves the full symptomatic picture of both manic and major depressive episodes, intermixed or rapidly alternating every few days.
B. Depressive symptoms are prominant and last at least a full day.

* From American Psychiatric Association: *Diagnostic and Statistical Manual of Mental Disorders*, ed 3. American Psychiatric Association, Washington, DC, 1980. Used with permission.

A depressive episode is characterized by a change of mood from a usual normal mood to a predominantly dysphoric mood or by a loss of interest or pleasure in all or almost all of the patient's usual activities. At least four of the following symptoms should be present: (1) striking change of weight; (2) sleep difficulty, either measurable insomnia or measurable hypersomnia; (3) decreased energy; (4) psychomotor retardation or agitation, objectively observable; (5) decreased interest in usual activities or in sexuality; (6) excessive self-reproach or guilt; (7) decreased ability to think or concentrate; and (8) suicidal action or recurrent thoughts of suicide.

### Differential Diagnosis

Major affective disorders are characterized by one or more episodes of illness involving a prominent and persistent disturbance in mood, either manic or depressed, clearly distinguished from prior functioning.

The major affective disorders present with a clear and precise point of onset, and the period of illness is clearly circumscribed from the pre-illness and post-illness functioning of the patient. A major affective disorder is clearly distinguishable from dysthymia or depressive neurosis in that, in the minor affective disorder, the disturbance of affect is long-lasting (usually more than 2 years), and there seems to be a gradual and unclear point of onset of the illness. A patient with a depressive neurosis may have a superimposed major affective disorder.

The diagnosis of a major affective disorder is not made if the affective state is secondary to a known organic disorder, such as a hypomanic or manic response to steroids, or if the affective state accompanies a primary thought disorder, such as schizophrenia. However, some somatic disorders release an affective illness previously not expressed and the patient may have an affective disorder and a thought disorder simultaneously (see Tables IX–XI).

### Other Causes of Manic Episodes

**Somatic Disease.** Certain substances used to treat somatic illnesses may trigger a manic response. In those instances, the most common of which is the manic response to steroids, the disorder is diagnosed as an affective syndrome. However, cases exist in which spontaneous manic and depressive episodes originated some years later in patients whose first illness episode seemed to be triggered by the steroids used to treat an organic illness. Other drugs are also known to have the potentiality for initiating a manic syndrome—for example, amphetamines and tricyclic antidepressants.

**Psychological Disease.** Two general groups of patients have manic and hypomanic-like reactions, to be differentiated from true manic episodes: schizophrenics and patients with narcissistic personality disorders.

Mania is excluded if any of the following symptoms of schizophrenia are present: (1) delusions of control from outside; (2) delusions of broadcasting thoughts; (3) delusions of insertion of thoughts into the patient's mind; (4) experience of withdrawal of thoughts from the patient's mind; (5) auditory hallucination of a commentary on the patient's behavior or thoughts or of a conversation between voices; (6) auditory hallucination not related to levels of depression

TABLE IX
SOMATIC DISORDERS THAT MAY BE CAUSALLY RELATED TO DEPRESSIVE SYNDROMES

| Disease | Depression |
|---|---|
| Cardiovascular | Over 60% of hospitalized cardiac patients are depressed; 18 months after a myocardial infarction, one third of patients develop a depression. |
| Gastrointestinal | It may be diffcult to recognize what comes first—gastrointestinal or depressive symptoms. |
| Neurological | Symptoms of Huntington's disease, brain tumors and primary dementias are frequently preceded by or associated with depression. As many as 25 percent of patients with multiple sclerosis may be depressed. |
| Diseases of the pancreas | |
| Hypothyroidism | |
| Hyperthyroidism | In the form of apathetic thyrotoxicosis. |
| Hyperparathyroidism | |
| Addison's or Cushing's disease | |
| Rheumatoid arthritis | Between 40 and 50 percent of patients show depressive features. |
| Infectious diseases | Particularly virus diseases, e.g. mononucleosis. |
| Various neoplasms | Depression is sometimes the first manifestation. More than 40 percent of cancer patients, especially those receiving chemotherapy, show depressive symptoms. |
| Malnutrition | Elderly people, because of poor eating habits and impaired absorption, are highly susceptible to protein and vitamin (B) deficiencies and resulting depression. |

TABLE X
COMMONLY USED DRUGS THAT MAY BE CAUSALLY RELATED TO DEPRESSIVE SYNDROMES

| Drug | Depression |
| --- | --- |
| Psychotropic drugs | Antipsychotic agents (phenothiazines; butyrophenones); barbiturates; meprobamate; benzodiazepines; a variety of "street" drugs. |
| Corticosteroids | Also may induce manic states. |
| L-Dopa | Also may induce manic states. |
| Digitalis | More frequently induces toxic psychosis. |
| Antihypertensive drugs | Most frequently reserpine (in about 10 percent); $\alpha$-methyldopa; propranolol; hydralazine; guanethidine; clonidine. |
| Cocaine | May induce manic states. |

TABLE XI
PHARMACOLOGIC AGENTS THAT CAN PRODUCE DEPRESSION

| Product Category | Chemical Name | Product Name and Pharmaceutical Company |
| --- | --- | --- |
| Antineoplastics | Mitotane | Lysodren (Bristol) |
|  | Asparaginase, MDS | Elspar (Merck, Sharp, & Dohme) |
| Antiparkinosonism drugs | Levodopa-carbidopa | Sinemet (Merck, Sharp, & Dohme) |
|  | Amantadine hydrochloride | Symmetrel (Endo) |
| Adrenal cortical steroids | Cortisone acetate | Cortisone Acetate Tablets (Upjohn) |
| Antibacterials | Cycloserine | Seromycin (Lilly) |
| Cardiovascular preparations | Propranolol | Inderal (Ayerst) |
|  | Metoprolol tartrate | Lopressor (Geigy) |
|  | Prazosin hydrochloride | Minipress (Pfizer) |
|  | Rescinnamine | Moderil (Pfizer) |
|  | Pindolol | Visken (Sandoz) |
|  | Atenolol | Tenormin (Stuart) |
|  | Quanabenz acetate | Wytensin (Wyeth) |
| Progestational agents | Norethindrone acetate | Norlutate (Parke-Davis) |
|  | Norgestrel | Ovrette (Wyeth) |
| Estrogen agents | Estradiol | Estrace (Mead Johnson) |

or elation; (7) monoideatic delusions or hallucination other than those related to delusions of poverty, guilt, and self-depreciation; (8) persistence of delusions or hallucinations 1 month after the resolution of the affective state within which they were experienced.

Narcissistic personality disorder often presents with periods of euphoria and depression quite similar in content to the phenomena seen in the major affective disorders. In the personality disorder, however, the affective disturbance is solely initiated by a failure of empathy on the part of a significant object, it is fleeting, it is not as intense as in the major affective disorders, and it is amenable to interpretation.

### Other Causes of Depressive Episodes

**Somatic Disease.** Depressive syndromes are known to occur after substance use—for example, reserpine-induced depression—and in organic illnesses—for example, cancers of all types and infectious diseases. In both cases, the dis-

order is considered an organic affective syndrome secondary to the known causative agent. If a full-blown affective syndrome develops in reaction to a functional impairment secondary to a physical illness, the syndrome is a full-blown affective disorder, and the physical disorder is also diagnosed.

Senile, presenile, and multi-infarct dementia must be differentiated from depressive episodes in the elderly. In the case of pseudodementia, the depression presents with symptoms mimicking an organic state that clears with appropriate treatment of the depression. In the dementias, treatment of the depression is not rewarding.

**Psychological Disease.** Any psychological illness may present with symptoms of depression. Chronic depressive, schizophrenic, and cyclothymic disorders may have superimposed depressive episodes. That situation may also be true of patients with alcoholism, somatization disorder, and anxiety disorders, including children with separation anxiety disorders that develop the full-blown clinical syndrome.

Uncomplicated bereavement is not considered a mental disorder, even if the full depressive syndrome develops, unless resolution of grief does not occur.

### Treatment

The treatment of the major affective disorders is one of the most rewarding for the psychiatrist. Specific treatment is now available in the acute phase to prevent the recurrence of both manic and depressive episodes. Nevertheless, it remains true that the therapist must always be on guard against the possibility of suicide, a possibility likely to occur when the patient begins to come out of a depression and has the energy available to act on the suicidal impulse he talked about when he was deeply depressed but lacked the energy to carry out. Because the prognosis for each individual episode is good, despite any negative results of initial treatment efforts, optimism is always warranted and welcomed by both patient and family (see Fig. 4).

### *Hospitalization*

The first and most critical decision the physician must make is whether to hospitalize the patient or to attempt outpatient treatment. In this era, when hospitalization is discouraged by governmental authorities and third-party intermediaries, it is critical that the physician make this judgment on the basis of clinical considerations. In the presence of acute mania or acute depression, hospitalization is imperative. Acute manic excitements are life-threatening, and immediate supportive measures must be instituted to prevent a fatal outcome. In the presence of a history of rapidly progressing symptoms and rupture of the usual support systems in the environment, hospitalization is also strongly indicated.

Mild depression or mild hypomania may be safely treated in the office if the physician evaluates the patient frequently, if there are no signs of lapses of judgment or of weight loss and insomnia, and if the environmental support system is considered strong and neither overinvolved with nor withdrawing from the patient. Situations between those extremes require careful and frequent evaluation. The dictum that, in the presence of the history of a previous episode, the current episode will be of the same or greater severity and duration may be misleading. Some

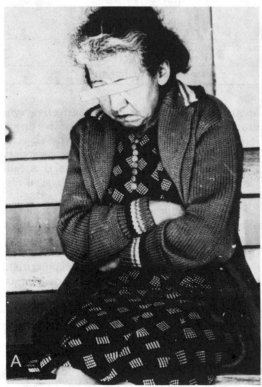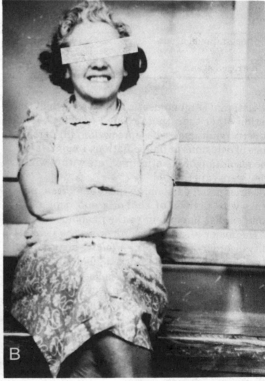

FIGURE 4.   A 38-year-old woman (*A*) during a state of deep retarded depression and (*B*) 2 months later, after recovery. Note the turned-down corners of the mouth, the stooped posture, the drab clothing and hair-do during the depressed episode. (Courtesy of Heinz E. Lehmann, M.D.)

interpret such a dictum too literally and do not evaluate the day-to-day situation as carefully as possible. In all cases, any sign of a change for the worse in symptoms, external behavior, or attitude of the environment toward the patient is sufficient to warrant hospitalization.

### Somatotherapies

**Electroconvulsive Therapy.** Electroconvulsive therapy (ECT) is regarded by many as a specific therapy for those retarded depressions characterized by somatic delusions and delusional guilt, accompanied by a lack of interest in the world, suicidal ideation, and weight loss. It is also used in less severe depression that is resistant to antidepressant drugs. Historically, the emergence of antidepressant drugs lessened the use of ECT in depression. In many respects that was unfortunate, for, although ECT has the reputation among some persons of being brutal, morbidity and mortality after its use have been reported to be lower than that seen after the use of antidepressants. In addition, ECT is used to terminate a mania when all other measures fail.

**Psychopharmacological Agents.** The pharmacological treatment of these disorders is discussed in Section 27.2 dealing with antidepressant drugs and Section 27.4 dealing with lithium therapy. The reader is referred to those sections for an extensive discussion of the important role of psychopharmacology in the treatment of depression.

### Psychotherapy

Psychotherapy is essential to at least supplement drug treatments in those cases in which the patient seems to suffer from a basically physiological form of the illness, and psychotherapy is absolutely central to the treatment of those patients who seem to have a psychological illness in addition to the physiological disorder. Some self-destructive, ambitious, early-onset bipolar manics easily manipulate their doses of lithium in an apparent attempt to increase their energy level while actually sabotaging their work efforts. Without effective psychotherapy, those patients destroy their careers. Other patients need to isolate a loss experience, triggering an episode of illness to detoxify such experiences. Thus, psychotherapy may range from analytic procedure to supportive care and may be combined with drug therapy. In some cases, the psychiatrist's treatment of the manic with lithium resembles the internist's treatment of the diabetic with insulin.

### Types of Psychotherapy

**Psychoanalytic Therapy.** Freud described that a vulnerability to depression caused by an interpersonal disappointment very early in life led to future love relationships marked by ambivalence. Actual or threatened interpersonal losses in adult life would trigger a self-destructive struggle in the ego that would be manifested as depression. Such individuals are inordinately dependent on others for narcissistic gratification and for maintenance of self-esteem. Frustration of their dependency needs leads to a plummet in self-esteem and to subsequent depression. In general, the goal of psychoanalytic psychotherapy is to effect a change in personality structure or character, and not simply to alleviate symptoms. Improvement in interpersonal trust, in intimacy and generativity, in coping mechanisms, in ability to experience a wide range of emotions, and in the capacity to grieve are some of the aims. Treatment may often require the patient to experience heightened anxiety and distress during the course of therapy, which usually continues for several years.

**Short-term Therapy.** The short-term therapies differ from classical psychoanalysis in their emphasis on the identification of a specific dynamic focus. A particular issue, usually an interpersonal problem, is selected, and both the patient and therapist agree to deal primarily with this problem during therapy. This focus is considered dynamic because it is used as a link with core conflicts arising from early life. This technique actively uses the current conflict as a microcosm for the more substantial and long-lasting conflicts in the patient's life.

**Interpersonal Therapy (IPT).** IPT is a short-term psychotherapy, normally consisting of anywhere from 12 to 16 weekly sessions, and it was developed specifically for the treatment of nonbipolar, nonpsychotic ambulatory depressives. It is characterized by an active approach on the part of the therapist and by an emphasis on current issues and social functioning in the life of the patient. Intrapsychic phenomena, such as defense mechanisms or internal conflicts, are not addressed in the therapy. Discrete behaviors, such as lack of assertiveness, social skills, or distorted thinking may be addressed, but only in the context of their meaning or effect on interpersonal relationships.

**Behavior Therapy.** Several behavior therapies have been developed for the treatment of depression. Although they vary in terms of specific techniques and focus, these therapies have certain assumptions and strategies in common:

1. The treatment program is highly structured and generally short-term.

2. The principle of reinforcement is seen as the key element in depression.

3. Changing behavior is considered to be the most effective way to alleviate depression.

4. The focus is on articulation and attainment of specific goals. Some behavioral treatments are characterized by multicomponent treatment approaches combining a variety of behavioral techniques, where the use of techniques may be tailored to the individual needs of each patient. Normally there are core ingredients, considered essential, in conjunction with a number of optional techniques.

**Cognitive Therapy.** The cognitive theory of depression posits that cognitive dysfunctions are the core of depression and that affective and physical changes, and other associated features of depression, are consequences of the cognitive dysfunctions. For example, apathy and low energy are results of the individual's expectation of failure in all areas. Similarly, paralysis of will stems from the individual's pessimism and feelings of hopelessness.

The goal of cognitive therapy which was developed by Aaron Beck is to alleviate depression and to prevent its recurrence by helping the patient (1) to identify and test negative cognitions; (2) to develop alternative, more flexible schemas and more positive ways of thinking; and (3) to rehearse both new cognitive and new behavioral responses. The goal is also to change the way an individual thinks and subsequently to alleviate the depressive syndrome.

### Family Therapy

Family therapy is not generally viewed as a primary therapy for the treatment of depression, but its use is indicated in cases where (1) an individual's depression appears to be seriously jeopardizing that person's marriage or family functioning or both, or (2) an individual's depression appears to be promoted and maintained by marital or family interaction patterns or both. Family therapy examines the role of the depressed member in the over-all psychological well-being of the whole family; it also examines the role of the entire family in the maintenance of the depression. This approach has especial salience when the depressed individual is the mother of young children. In general, however, diagnosis of family dynamics should be approached cautiously when one of the members is acutely depressed. Family interaction patterns may have been substantially disrupted by the depression.

### Combination Psychotherapy and Medication

Depression is a complex group of disorders that involve many body systems. Medications may be advisable in certain depressions, whereas psychotherapeutic approaches are preferred in others. In many cases, a combination of drugs and psychotherapy may be best. There is some evidence to support the notion that drugs tend to affect the specific somatic and vegetative symptoms of depression, whereas psychotherapies affect interpersonal and cognitive aspects. Therefore, a comprehensive approach would involve both modalities complementing one another.

### Evaluation of Treatment

Generally, the literature indicates that severe acute depression responds well to ECT, less severe depression responds well to tricyclics, and lithium or tricyclics can be useful prophylactic agents against depression. Acute mania responds to neuroleptics and lithium, and lithium is prophylactic against recurrences of mania. In general, psychotherapy combined with drug treatment offers the best prognosis in most affective disorders.

### REFERENCES

Ban T A, Gonzales R, Jablensky A S, Sartorius N A, Vartanian F E, editors: *Prevention and Treatment of Depression*, p 89. University Park Press, Baltimore, 1981.

Bech P: Rating scales for affective disorders: their validity and consistency. Acta Psychiat Scand Suppl *295:* 5, 1981.

Binitie A: The clinical manifestations of depression in Africans. In *Prevention and Treatment of Depression*, T A Ban, R Gonzalez, A S Jablensky, N A Sartorius, F E Vartanian, editors, p 83. University Park Press, Baltimore, 1981.

Dorus E, Cox N J, Gibbons R D, Shaughnessy R, Pandey G N, Cloninger C R: Lithium ion transport and affective disorders within families of bipolar patients. Arch Gen Psychiatry *40:* 557, 1983.

Freud S: *Mourning and Melancholia*, Vol 14, p 243. Hogarth Press, London, 1957.

Georgotas A, Cooper T, Kim M, Hapworth W: The treatment of affective disorders in the elderly. Psychopharmacol Bull *19:* 226, 1983.

Georgotas A, Friedman E, McCarthy M, Mann J, Krakowski M, Siegel R, Ferris S: Resistant geriatric depressions and therapeutic response to monoamine oxidase inhibitors. Biol Psychiatry *18:* 195, 1983.

Gershon E S: The genetics of affective disorders. In *Psychiatry Update*, Grinspoon L, editor, vol 2. American Psychiatric Association Press, Washington, DC, 1983.

Gershon E S, Hamovit J, Guroff J J, Dibble E, Leckman J F, Sceery W, Targum S D, Nurnberger J I, Jr, Goldin L R, Bunney W E, Jr: A family study of schizoaffective, bipolar I, bipolar II, unipolar, and normal control probands. Arch Gen Psychiatry *39:* 1157, 1982.

Lehmann H E: Affective disorders: clinical features. In *Comprehensive Textbook of Psychiatry*, ed 4, H I Kaplan, B J Sadock, editors, p 786. Williams & Wilkins, Baltimore, 1985.

Nurnberger J I Jr, Gershon E S: Genetics of affective disorders. In *Neurobiology of Mood Disorders*, R Post, J Ballenger, editors. Williams & Wilkins, Baltimore, 1984.

Spitzer R L, Endicott J, Robins E: *Research Diagnostic Criteria (RDC) for a Selected Group of Functional Disorders*. New York State Psychiatric Institute, New York, 1977.

Van Valkenburg C, Lowry M, Winokur G, Cadoret R: Depression spectrum disease versus pure depressive disease. J Nerv Ment Dis *165:* 341, 1977.

# 14

# Other Specific Affective Disorders: Dysthymic Disorder and Cyclothymic Disorder

## Introduction

Most patients experience affective disorders as episodic; after a time-limited period of symptoms, they return to their normal state. A majority of patients with episodes of affective disorder, whether depression or mania, experience them as brief episodes.

In recent years, it has become increasingly recognized that a significant proportion of patients suffer from chronic affective disorders, either dysthymic or cyclothymic disorder. Although the two disorders are grouped together in terms of their common clinical course, there is no presumption as to common causes or single treatment.

## Dysthymic Disorder (Depressive Neurosis)

Clinical experience and numerous studies have shown that most depressions are episodic. Although a large proportion of adults experience acute depressions—usually without coming to the attention of physicians, let alone psychiatrists—a significant percentage experience their condition as chronic.

Most chronic depressions probably represent the inadequately recognized and poorly treated residual of unresolved or partially remitted acute depressions. About 15 to 20 percent of patients experiencing acute depressions do not make a complete recovery, but show some intermittent fluctuating, and chronic symptoms, often persisting for years.

### Definition

The creation of a separate category in DSM-III for patients with dysthymic disorder (depressive neurosis) represents an important step forward. This advance in diagnosis is particularly important in the era of community psychiatric treatment, inasmuch as most of the patients are not institutionalized and are able to continue in the community.

The essential feature of dysthymic disorder is a chronic nonpsychotic disturbance, involving depressed mood or a loss of interest or pleasure in all or almost all usual activities and pastimes. Usually, associated symptoms are not of sufficient severity to meet the criteria for major depression.

Dysthymic disorder is defined as a long-standing illness of at least 2 years' duration with either sustained or intermittent disturbances in depressed mood and associated symptoms. The disorder may begin in early adult life, often without a clear onset. In the past, patients with this disorder included those with depressive neurosis. Subgroups include patients with masked depression or depressive equivalents.

### Epidemiology

Since this is a relatively new diagnostic category, precise data as to incidence and prevalence are lacking. However, a number of studies have indicated that it is a relatively common condition. A lifetime prevalence has been reported of about 45 per 1,000, using criteria for depressive personality, that are similar to the clinical characteristics for dysthymic disorder in DSM-III. This incidence is also attested to by the fact that most admissions to the psychiatric wards of general hospitals fall into one of the depressive disorders.

### Causes

The theories and hypotheses proposed as to causation follow those for affective disorders in general.

**Personality Characteristics.** The large number of patients with depression whose onset is in the late teens and young adulthood suggests psychodynamic features, particularly those related to faulty personality and ego development

255

culminating in difficulty in adaptation to adolescence and young adulthood.

Undue interpersonal dependency and obsessionality often predispose to depression. Several pervasive personality traits, especially low self-esteem and introversion, are strongly associated with "the depressive character." Personality features such as dependency, guilt, and passivity may not return to normal levels, even though symptom relapse and remission occur.

**Psychosocial Factors.** Differences of opinions exist as to the role of psychosocial stressors as precipitants of chronic episodes. One hypothesis is that the chronic disorder represents the poorly treated or partially resolved residue of prior acute depressions in adult life that likely had psychosocial precipitants.

**Physiological Causes.** Many of the chronic conditions may present the residual effects of secondary depressions due to the chronic use of alcohol, amphetamines, or barbiturates or may be related to long-standing medical illness, such as gastrointestinal, arthritis, thyroid, and other endocrine disorders.

### Clinical Features

The essential feature of dysthymic disorder is a long-standing nonpsychotic symptom complex of at least 2 years' duration. The major predominant symptom is that of depressed mood. In addition, there is often a loss of interest or pleasure in all or almost all usual activities, pastimes, and sources of pleasure (see Table I).

The depressed mood may be characterized by the patient's reporting himself as feeling sad, blue, down in the dumps, or low. Life may be described as dark, black, or bleak. The depressed mood and associated features may be either relatively persistent in which case the disorder is considered chronic, or intermittent, in which case the periods of symptoms are separated by intervals of normal mood, with the capacity to enjoy pleasure and function at some normal level of social activity. The relatively normal periods may last from a few days to a few weeks.

In distinguishing the dysthymic disorder from cyclothymia, one must ascertain whether the return to normal is experienced as a relief from depression or whether there are positive signs of euphoria, increased activity, and poor judgment, in which latter case the patient should be considered cyclothymic.

The patient may have manifestations of the nonpsychotic features of the depressive syndrome, such as impaired self-esteem, slowing of speech and thinking, and loss of appetite. These features are usually experienced by the patient as discontinuous and ego-alien changes from his usual or former self.

TABLE I
DIAGNOSTIC CRITERIA FOR DYSTHYMIC DISORDER*

A. During the past two years (or one year for children and adolescents) the individual has been bothered most or all of the time by symptoms characteristic of the depressive syndrome but that are not of sufficient severity and duration to meet the criteria for a major depressive episode (although a major depressive episode may be superimposed on Dysthymic Disorder).

B. The manifestations of the depressive syndrome may be relatively persistent or separated by periods of normal mood lasting a few days to a few weeks, but no more than a few months at a time.

C. During the depressive periods there is either prominent depressed mood (e.g., sad, blue, down in the dumps, low) or marked loss of interest or pleasure in all, or almost all, usual activities and pastimes.

D. During the depressive periods at least three of the following symptoms are present:

(1) insomnia or hypersomnia
(2) low energy level or chronic tiredness
(3) feelings of inadequacy, loss of self-esteem, or self-deprecation
(4) decreased effectiveness or productivity at school, work, or home
(5) decreased attention, concentration, or ability to think clearly
(6) social withdrawal
(7) loss of interest in or enjoyment of pleasurable activities
(8) irritability or excessive anger (in children, expressed toward parents or caretakers)
(9) inability to respond with apparent pleasure to praise or rewards
(10) less active or talkative than usual, or feels slowed down or restless
(11) pessimistic attitude toward the future, brooding about past events, or feeling sorry for self
(12) tearfulness or crying
(13) recurrent thoughts of death or suicide

E. Absence of psychotic features, such as delusions, hallucinations, or incoherence, or loosening of associations.

F. If the disturbance is superimposed on a preexisting mental disorder, such as Obsessive Compulsive Disorder or Alcohol Dependence, the depressed mood, by virtue of its intensity or effect on functioning, can be clearly distinguished from the individual's usual mood.

* From American Psychiatric Association: *Diagnostic and Statistical Manual of Mental Disorders*, ed 3. American Psychiatric Association, Washington, DC, 1980. Used with permission.

During the depressive periods, there are usually the various nonpsychotic and mild features of the depressive disorder. The presence of delusions and hallucinations is by definition inconsistent with the diagnosis of dysthymic disorder. Among the associated symptoms are those commonly associated with depressive episodes, including poor appetite, weight change, sleep difficulty (particularly early-morning wakening), loss of energy, fatigability, psychomotor retardation, loss of interest or pleasure in activities, decreased sexual drive, decreased sexual performance, feelings of guilt and self-reproach, obsessive preoccupation with health, complaints of difficulty in thinking, indecisiveness, thoughts of suicide, feelings of helplessness and hopelessness, and pessimism.

Although the clinical presentation with predominant depressive mood, as described above, is most common, it is important to recognize a number of major variants, including the following:

**Masked Depressions.** In patients with masked depressions, the mood disturbance may not be readily apparent, but the patient may present with chronic pain, insomnia, weight loss, or other bodily complaints. This mode of presentation is most often seen by psychiatrists working in general hospitals and as consultants to medical practitioners.

**Hypochondriacal and Somatic Complaints.** A large number of patients with recurrent diagnosed medical complaints, often called hypochondriacs or crocks, are unrecognized intermittent or chronic depressives whose ticket of admission to the health care system is through their bodily complaints. They are usually middle-aged and elderly patients, most often women.

**Pessimism and Hopelessness.** Patients with helplessness, pessimism, and discouragement represent another mode of presentation. The difficulties may be directed against the self—as with feelings of self-reproach, low self-esteem, and feelings of failure in life—or inadequate functioning at work or in marriage. Such patients may be labeled as masochistic personalities. On the other hand, their pessimism may be directed outward, with tirades against the world and feelings of having been treated poorly by relatives, children, parents, work, colleagues, or the system.

**Alcohol Abuse.** Clinicians must recognize that a high percentage of chronic alcoholics develop secondary depressions. The rates range from 25 to 50 percent.

**Drug Ingestion.** Selected drugs—particularly the steroids, amphetamines, barbiturates, and central nervous system depressants—are known to produce depression after periods of heavy use. A chronic depression secondary to heroin use or long-term methadone use has also been described.

### Course and Prognosis

**Age of Onset.** A review of the clinical course reveals important differences related to the age of onset.

Many patients report that their depressive symptoms began in late adolescence or young adulthood, and that the symptoms have been of a chronic nature for such long periods as to have become ingrained as part of their characters. In patients with onset early in life, it is important to reconstruct the history carefully, seeking episodes of acute onset, especially in the transition from adolescence to young adulthood. The family history is also valuable to detect a history of affective disorders, since dysthymic patients may have mild forms of major depression whose severity has not been sufficient to reach the criteria for classification as major depression.

The most common period of onset is in maturity and middle age. Such patients give a history of a relatively good social adjustment and normal mood through adolescence and young adulthood, with a gradual or insidious onset of depressive symptoms or poorly remembered episodes of acute depression or residual symptoms after the grief reaction to the death of a parent, sibling, or child. A careful history may reveal that there has, in fact, been an impairment of marital functioning, with disputes, irritability, and poor sexual functioning; impairment of parental functioning, particularly with teenage children; or impairment of occupational functioning.

Onset in old age is often a difficult diagnostic problem because of the need to differentiate depressive pseudodementia from dementia. Many elderly patients present with an impairment of cognitive functions, complaints of decreased memory, inability to concentrate, poor attention, and slowing of functioning. The differential diagnosis of dementia due to central nervous system disorders, such as Huntington's chorea or—more often—senile brain disease, may be difficult. The disorders may coexist, and the issue is not so much dementia versus depression as the coexistence of the two disorders.

**Suicide.** In all affective disorders, there is an increased risk of suicide. Attention should be given to probing for potential suicide, reconstructing the history of previous suicide attempts, eliciting suicidal ideation, and exploring suicidal fantasies. If they exist, attention should be given to the history of the use of medication, particularly since suicide-prone patients are often heavy users of the health care system. They show a tendency to accumulate partially used bottles of medicine. Attention should also be given to accident proneness, particularly in automobile driving.

**High Risk for Medical Illnesses.** Patients with chronic and intermittent depressions are probably at greater risk for serious medical illnesses than are other persons. Studies indicate a higher than average death rate, often due to cardiovascular disease. Some suggestions have been made that such patients may be more prone than average to cancer; perhaps there is no true increase in incidence but an increased mortality because depressed persons delay seeking medical attention or are misdiagnosed because of their previous history of chronic complaints.

**Hospitalization.** Mental hospitalization for dysthymic disorder is currently uncommon, although such hospitalization did occur in the era before the development of modern somatic treatments.

**Impairment of Social Functioning.** Currently, the most common impairments lie in the areas of social functioning, manifested by a reduced ability to sustain emotional intimacy, a reduction of sexual interest, lowered sexual performance (often manifested by impotence), and a decreased frequency of intercourse. Moreover, there may be difficulty in maintaining usual levels of social activity, with reduced interest in hobbies and games and less participation in sports or social activities than before the depression developed. There are periods of social withdrawal and lowered initiation of social activities. Divorce, unemployment, and business or professional failure may often be the consequence of dysthymic disorder.

**Prognosis.** The most important determinant of the course and outcome of dysthymic disorder is whether or not the disorder is recognized. If they are left to themselves, patients often have continuing episodes of chronic or intermittent symptoms, with gradual impairment of social functioning. They may have frequent hospitalizations or visits to emergency rooms because of suicide attempts or the aggravation of somatic complaints. When the depression is recognized and treated intensively, the prognosis improves greatly in the majority of cases.

### Diagnosis

The essential criteria for diagnosis were given in the description of the mood disturbance. The associated symptoms are those of major depressive episodes except that, by definition, the presence of delusions and hallucinations precludes the diagnosis of dysthymic disorder.

The most difficult differential diagnosis involves the personality disorders, especially histrionic personality disorder, formerly called hysterical personality. Sometimes patients with dysthymic disorder are called borderline, dependent, or narcissistic personalities. The diagnosis of a personality disorder is often consistent with the patient's having an acute or intermittent depression. Some evidence indicates that certain types of personality patterns—such as compulsive, dependent, or histrionic personal-

ity—are predisposed to depression with greater frequency than is the general population.

Patients with somatoform disorders, sometimes called hysteria or conversion disorders, may also have a predisposition to depression, and reports about patients with Briquet's syndrome indicate that about 20 percent of them experienced depressive episodes in the course of their clinical functioning.

### Treatment

A number of psychological and somatic therapies have been proposed for treating dysthymic disorder. Among the psychological treatments, the most widely described are those derived from psychoanalytic and psychodynamic theories of personality. An analysis of the patient's symptoms must be combined with an analysis of character structure. Psychoanalytic hypotheses relate the development and the maintenance of depressive symptoms and maladaptive personality features to unresolved conflicts from early childhood.

A number of psychotherapeutic techniques are recommended for dealing with the dependency and manipulation manifested in the therapeutic relationship. Some of these techniques focus on the long-term maladaptive interpersonal maneuvers used by the chronic depressive to sustain his or her characteristic modes of interpersonal relations. These maladaptations serve to manipulate the key figures in the patient's environment, thus protecting the patient from having to undertake any significant changes in life style or relationships. Attempts to get the patient to change are met with increased symptoms and veiled threats of suicide or regression, which serve to perpetuate the pattern of interpersonal relations, often to the frustration of the patient and those in his or her immediate life space.

The efficacy of a number of the techniques has been established for long-term maintenance treatment of chronic patients, and those likely to relapse or have recurrences after an acute episode. They indicate the value of psychotherapy alone in modifying interpersonal relations and personal satisfaction, as well as psychotherapy's enhanced efficacy when combined with tricyclic drug therapy.

Interpersonal therapy, cognitive therapy, and behavior therapy as used in the treatment of depression have been described in the preceding section on major affective disorders.

Among the somatic therapies, particular attention should be given to the tricyclic antidepressants. These drugs remain the main form of pharmacotherapy with demonstrated efficacy for depressions.

Monoamine oxidase inhibitors (MAOIs) may be of particular value for subgroups of depressed patients who do not show response to tricyclics, especially patients with atypical features marked by anxiety, hysterical, and depersonalization symptoms. Alprazolam (Xanax) has also been found to be of use in this subgroup and has the advantage of having less side effects than MAOIs.

Although there is controversy about the use of amphetamines and amphetamine-like drugs for depression, some clinicians have found, that in selected cases, the judicious use of those drugs are of value, although this use is not recommended by the United States Food and Drug Administration (USFDA).

Amphetamine can be used to gauge the potential effectiveness of certain tricyclics in depressed patients. A positive response as measured by improved mood to a 2 or 3 day trial of amphetamine usually means that a tricyclic is likely to be effective.

In addition, amphetamine has been found useful in some patients with involutional depression and of value in medically ill depressed patients. A beneficial synergistic effect using desipramine (Norpramin) and methylphenidate (Ritalin) in combination for the treatment of depression has been reported, and methylphenidate has been found to be of value in a selected group of depressed patients after cardiac surgery.

In view of the above and other significant studies, the authors believe a more flexible utilization of amphetamine and amphetamine-like drugs such as methylphenidate is indicated and it is not appropriate for governmental agencies such as the USFDA, the Drug Enforcement Administration (DEA), and the various state licensing boards to interfere in the responsible and judicious practice of medicine by restricting the use of such drugs because of the abuse potiential, especially when their value has been so clearly demonstrated.

## Cyclothymic Disorder

### Definition and History

The term "cyclothymia" was first coined by Kahlbaum in the mid-19th century for what was then called circular insanity. The common usage is to regard cyclothymia as a personality condition manifested by a chronic nonpsychotic disturbance involving numerous periods in which there are symptoms characteristic of either the manic or the depressive syndrome or both. Usually, these periods are not of sufficient intensity to meet the full criteria for bipolar disorder. Furthermore, the patient usually experiences them as ego-syntonic and usually does not present himself for psychiatric treatment. However, members of his family, relatives, and co-workers may be disturbed by the patient's mood swings and behavior fluctuations, and recommend treatment.

With the recent success of lithium in the treatment of full-blown manic episodes and in the prevention of recurrence in patients with bipolar disorder, increasing numbers of patients with cyclothymic disorder are coming to the attention of psychiatrists, and there is a new focus on patients with the disorder.

### Epidemiology

The only epidemiological study is the one called the New Haven Community Study. The authors reported a lifetime prevalence of cyclothymia of less than 1 percent. This figure is likely a major underestimate because of the variability of the diagnostic criteria and the reluctance of persons with cyclothymic disorder to identify themselves as patients.

### Causes

There is a general consensus that cyclothymia is a mild or attenuated form of bipolar disorder. This consensus is based on a number of sources of evidence, including: (1) the symptomatic and phenomenological similarity between symptoms and the behavior of persons with cyclothymic disorder and the full-blown bipolar disorder; (2) the distribution of affectively disordered biological relatives among family members; and (3) observations based on follow-ups that a significant proportion evolve into the clinical picture of bipolar disorder, showing pharmacological similarities in response to treatment, including the tendency for hypomanic response to tricyclic therapy and favorable response to lithium.

There is an increased frequency of cyclothymic personality disorders in the biological relatives of probands with bipolar affective disorders.

In the psychodynamic theories, emphasis is placed on early childhood experience, often with the postulation of trauma and fixation during the early oral stages of infant development. Attempts are made to describe a specific family constellation, but the differentiation of cyclothymic disorder from other forms of bipolar disorder is not clear.

TABLE II
DIAGNOSTIC CRITERIA FOR CYCLOTHYMIC DISORDER*

A. During the past two years, numerous periods during which some symptoms characteristic of both the depressive and the manic syndromes were present, but were not of sufficient severity and duration to meet the criteria for a major depressive or manic episode.

B. The depressive periods and hypomanic periods may be separated by periods of normal mood lasting as long as months at a time, they may be intermixed, or they may alternate.

| | |
|---|---|
| C. During depressive periods there is depressed mood or loss of interest or pleasure in all or almost all, usual activities and pastimes, and at least three of the following: | During hypomanic periods there is an elevated, expansive, or irritable mood and at least three of the following: |
| (1) insomnia or hypersomnia | (1) decreased need for sleep |
| (2) low energy or chronic fatigue | (2) more energy than usual |
| (3) feelings of inadequacy | (3) inflated self-esteem |
| (4) decreased effectiveness or productivity at school, work, or home | (4) increased productivity, often associated with unusual and self-imposed working hours |
| (5) decreased attention, concentration, or ability to think clearly | (5) sharpened and unusually creative thinking |
| (6) social withdrawal | (6) uninhibited people-seeking (extreme gregariousness) |
| (7) loss of interest in or enjoyment of sex | (7) hypersexuality without recognition of possibility of painful consequences |
| (8) restriction of involvement in pleasurable activities; guilt over past activities | (8) excessive involvement in pleasurable activities with lack of concern for the high potential for painful consequences, e.g., buying sprees, foolish business investments, reckless driving |
| (9) feeling slowed down | (9) physical restlessness |
| (10) less talkative than usual | (10) more talkative than usual |
| (11) pessimistic attitude toward the future, or brooding about past events | (11) overoptimism or exaggeration of past achievements |
| (12) tearfulness or crying | (12) inappropriate laughing, joking, punning |

D. Absence of psychotic features such as delusions, hallucinations, incoherence, or loosening of associations.

E. Not due to any other mental disorder, such as partial remission of Bipolar Disorder. However, Cyclothymic Disorder may precede Bipolar Disorder.

* From American Psychiatric Association: *Diagnostic and Statistical Manual of Mental Disorders*, ed 3. American Psychiatric Association, Washington, DC, 1980. Used with permission.

## Clinical Features

The essential features of cyclothymic disorder are chronic disturbances involving frequent periods during which there are nonpsychotic symptoms characteristic of both depressive and manic syndromes (see Table II). However, the symptoms are usually not of sufficient severity or duration to meet the criteria for a full-blown manic or depressive episode. Usually, the manifestations of the mood cycles alternate biphasically, or they may be intermixed. In other cases there may be periods as long as several months of relatively normal mood. During the periods of affective change, the symptoms related to either depression or mania are present in a mild form. During the elated phase, the patient may have an elevated, expansive, or irritable mood.

There may also be decreased sleep need, increased productivity, unusual self-imposed working habits, a sense of increased capacity for attention and concentration, and sharpened or unusual creative thinking. Characteristic of the hypomanic or elated phase are episodes of buying sprees, with financial extravagance, gifts, and excessive indulgence. The sprees may be so severe as to produce business failure and bankruptcy. There may be frequent job changes, periods of sexual promiscuity, or religious or political changes.

## Course and Prognosis

The typical manifestations of the personality changes begin to appear in mid- to late adolescence. During this developmental phase, the patient is often described as moody, with periods of being high and low. The moods may be experienced as aggravations or accentuations of normal adolescent development. There is a variability in the intensity of either the elated phase or the depressive phase, and in the duration and the degree of periodicity.

During adulthood, these patients may be very adaptive, particularly during the hypomanic or elated phase, when their optimism, social gregariousness, good humor, high drive, and ambition may make them successful in business, professional life, public service, or academic pursuits. However, there may be excessive periods of maladaptive features. During the depressed phase, the patient may be underactive, have difficulty in concentrating, be underresponsive, and perform at lower levels than normal. Conversely, during the periods of elation or hypomania, the patient may behave inappropriately socially, with excessive sexual behavior, poor management of funds, and poor judgment in family, business, and social activities. As the patient proceeds through adulthood, the periods of depressive or hypomanic mood swings may become so intense or so long as to make the clinical diagnosis possible.

## Diagnosis

The diagnosis is usually readily obtained by getting a history from the patient or his relatives and friends as to the degree of mood swing. However, there may be important differential diagnostic features, particularly from histrionic, antisocial, and sociopathic personalities. The histrionic features may be particularly difficult to differentiate from cyclothymic disorder because of elements of increased sexuality, changes in mood, and sociability in each condition. The family history may be helpful in the differential diagnosis, as may be the patient's response to treatment, especially lithium.

Important differential diagnostic considerations apply to mood swings associated with the ingestion of drugs, particularly steroids, amphetamines, and drugs of the hallucinogenic type. Mood swings have also been described as part of the secondary affective disorder related to chronic alcoholism.

In patients over the age of 40 showing the onset of mood swings, attention should be given to searching for organic features.

## Treatment

There are reports of occasional attempts at psychotherapy, particularly long-term psychotherapy, with cyclothymic disorder, but no systematic studies are available. The most significant treatment advance has been the advent of lithium. Several investigations report positive results after its use in cyclothymic disorders.

## REFERENCES

Akiskal H S: Dysthymic disorder: psychopathology of proposed chronic depressive subtypes. Am J Psychiatry *140:* 11, 1983.

Akiskal H S, Djenderedjian A H, Rosenthal R H, Khani M K: Cyclothymic disorder. Validating criteria for inclusion in the bipolar affective group. Am J Psychiatry *134:* 1227, 1977.

Arieti S, Bemporad J: *Severe and Mild Depression: The Psychotherapeutic Approach.* Basic Books, New York, 1978.

Bonime W: Dynamics and psychotherapy of depression. In *Current Psychiatric Therapies*, J Masserman, editor, p 137. Grune & Stratton, New York, 1962.

Drimmer E J, Gitlin M J, Gwirtsman H E: Desipramine and methylphenidate combination treatment for depression: case report. Am J Psychiatry *140:* 212, 1983.

Kaufmann, M W, Murray G B, Cassem N H: Use of psychostimulants in medically ill depressed patients. Psychosomatics *23:* 817, 1982.

Klerman, G L: Combining drugs and psychotherapy in the treatment of depression. In *Depression: Biology, Psychodynamics, and Treatment*, J O Cole, A F Schatzberg, S H Frazier, editors, p 213. Plenum Publishing Corp., New York, 1978.

Weissman M M, Klerman G L: The chronic depressive in the community: Unrecognized and poorly treated. Compr Psychiatry *18:* 523, 1977.

# 15

# Other Affective Disorders

## 15.1 ATYPICAL AFFECTIVE DISORDERS: ATYPICAL DEPRESSIVE DISORDER AND ATYPICAL BIPOLAR DISORDER

### Introduction

The majority of patients with one or another of the various affective disorders present with the fairly typical symptoms classified in DSM-III. However, a residual category of patients have features that are not readily classified because of the unusual combinations of symptoms or mode of presentation.

There are two subcategories of atypical affective disorder—atypical depression and atypical bipolar disorder.

### Atypical Depression

#### Definition

Atypical depression is a residual category for classifying patients with depressive features that cannot be classified as a major affective disorder or dysthymic disorder, or as an adjustment disorder. Examples include (1) a disorder that does not satisfy the symptomatic criteria for a major affective disorder, and that is apparently not reactive to psychosocial stress, so that it cannot be classified as an adjustment disorder; (2) a disorder that fulfills the criteria for dysthymic disorder with the exception that there have been intermittent periods of normal mood lasting more than 2 months; (3) a pattern of recurrent short-lived depressive reactions after personal rejection or some other loss of romantic attachment; during one form of the condition, the person is likely to show such symptoms as overeating, excessive sleeping, and lethargy in the absence of significant endogenous features; the syndrome, when seen in a person with histrionic personality disorder, has been referred to by some as hysteroid dysphoria; and (4) a distinct and sustained episode of depression in a patient with schizophrenia, residual type, that develops without an activation of the psychotic symptoms, and is not an apparent reaction to a psychosocial stressor.

#### Epidemiology

Because atypical depression is a new category, defined mainly by its residual quality, it is not possible to generate specific information about its epidemiology, prevalence, sex ratio, and familial patterns.

#### Causes

Nor is it possible to describe with any specificity the disorder's causes. It is unlikely that atypical depression represents a single condition, or is capable of being explained by one theory of causation. It is likely, however, that it represents unusual modes of clinical presentation and natural history of the major forms of affective disorder. With this likelihood, the theories of causation discussed previously also apply.

#### Clinical Features

There have been a number of discussions in the literature of atypical forms of clinical depressive disorders. Several of these descriptions merit explanation.

The advent of psychotropic drugs made it likely that clinicians would note unusual relationships between clinical symptom patterns and responses to psychotherapeutic drugs. A number of investigations have attempted to correlate symptom patterns with treatment response, in order to increase the specificity and the predictability of psychopharmacotherapy.

#### Clinical Course

The clinical course is often determined by the age of onset. Among adolescents and young adults, atypical depression may be quite common because of the developmental nature of the patient's circumstances. Mood swings are a normal part of adolescent development. On the other hand, patients with mood disturbances may involve themselves in risk-taking behavior, such as excessive speed in automobile driving, sexual promiscuity, experimentation with drugs and alcohol, avoidance of responsibility, and various forms of identity confusion or identity crises, as described by Erikson. Various forms of delinquency and antisocial behavior have also been attributed to underlying masked or unrecognized affective states.

During adulthood, the most common forms of atypical depression are those described earlier as masked depressions, neurasthenia, and hypochondriasis. Unexplained insomnia may also have an atypical onset in adulthood. When the sleep disturbance is that of early-morning awakening, attention should be given to the existence of other endogenous-like symptoms, such as weight loss, guilt, and psychomotor retardation. On the other hand, patients may report difficulty in falling asleep or troubled sleep; only after careful mental status examination does the associated mood disturbance become apparent. Many patients are prescribed barbiturates and sedative hypnotics on the basis of the presenting symptom of insomnia alone, when the more appropriate treatment would be an antidepressant drug.

Among elderly patients, atypical forms of affective disorders often involve pseudodementia. The patients complain of slowed thinking, difficulty in concentration, and impaired memory, and manifest slowed movements during interview and in social behavior. There may even be weight loss, sleep difficulty, and, at times, incontinence of urine and feces. The differential diagnosis from senile dementia is of major clinical importance. The most common diagnostic error is to assume automatically that all clinical disorders arising in the elderly are senile dementia and to miss the diagnosis of depression. This is particularly important, since the depressive conditions of the elderly are highly respondent to treatment and are often reversible.

## Diagnosis

The most important prerequisite for treatment is an adequate diagnostic representation. During diagnosis, physicians should be alert to the possibility of atypical depression in patients with insomnia, chronic pain, atypical facial pain, backache, headache, or any other persistent bodily complaint, fatigue state, or neurasthenia. The most important diagnostic efforts should involve careful probing for the symptom complex, particularly for depression and related mood disorders, and for associated symptoms, such as guilt, self-reproach, and loss of interest in hobbies and activities (anhedonia).

## Treatment

Attention during treatment should be given to a trial with a tricyclic antidepressant or a monoamine oxidase inhibitor (MAOI's). If the symptom complex is that of atypical features with the absence of endogenous features, an initial trial with MAOI's may be indicated, particularly when phobic and anxiety symptoms predominate. Alprazolam (Xanax) is also useful in this type of atypical depression. On the other hand, if physiological somatic complaints predominate, particularly those suggestive of endogenous features, a trial with tricyclic antidepressants may also be indicated. With both classes of antidepressant drugs, MAOI's and tricyclics, as well as with alprazolam, attempts should be made to push the dose to higher levels and to monitor platelet MAO levels, in the case of treatment with MAOI's, or plasma levels of the tricyclics. Treatment with barbiturates, sedative hypnotics, and minor tranquilizers is not recommended. A number of studies have reported good results in atypical depression with the judicious use of small doses of amphetamine and methylphenidate especially in combination with tricyclics.

## Atypical Bipolar Disorder

Atypical bipolar disorder is a residual category for classifying persons who have features of both manic and depressive symptoms in their clinical history, but whose manifestations do not meet the criteria for bipolar disorder or cyclothymic disorder. One example might be a person who previously had a depressive episode, and who now has an episode of illness with some manic symptoms, but features not sufficient to meet the criteria for a manic episode.

## Diagnosis

Increased attention to the diagnosis of affective disorders and the availability of lithium treatment has prompted a number of descriptions of atypical bipolar disorder.

Among adolescents, the diagnosis may be particularly difficult. Adolescents who are initially admitted with schizophrenic diagnoses, and who fail to respond to neuroleptics may be depressed, not schizophrenic. They often manifest atypical behavior patterns, bizarre features, psychotic manifestations, labile mood, overactivity, flight of ideas, pressured speech, and distractibility. Response to lithium in such cases may be excellent.

About 15 percent of manic psychotic patients have delusions of persecution. Aggression, destruction of property, hostility, and hallucinations and delusions may predominate in the manifest psychopathology period. However, reconstruction of the episode usually reveals that in its early phases the patient was euphoric, grandiose, overactive, and jovial, and that only gradually, as the manic episode progressed, did the joviality and elation give way to irritability, hostility, anger, and paranoid features.

A moderate percentage of manic patients, often initially diagnosed as schizophrenic because of gross disordered conduct, psychotic thinking, perhaps first-rank Schneiderian symptoms, and delusions and paranoid features in the course of an acute episode, prove responsive to lithium, and a review of their clinical courses indicates episodes of remission, with return to normal clinical functioning.

The boundary with normality is most often seen in patients with various forms of personality disorders. It is now recognized that there are mild variants of major affective disorders, including cyclothymic disorder and atypical bipolar disorder.

Patients with affective disorders may also have a variety of personality disorders. These personality features may be extensions of normal personality functioning, or they may be of sufficient intensity or duration, or have enough maladaptive consequences, as to warrant being called disorders. Certain types of personality disorders may predispose to developing affective disorders. They include compulsive personality, histrionic personality, and narcissistic and borderline personalities.

Mild forms of affective disorder may blend with the personality or, if they become chronic, are likely to be incorporated into the personality and, rather than being experienced as symptoms, are experienced as part of the person's character.

### Treatment

Psychotherapy is widely used and advocated for patients with atypical bipolar disorder, particularly because of their maladaptive personality features and interpersonal difficulties. In the absence of controlled clinical trials, however, there is considerable doubt as to the long-term efficacy of such treatments, particularly when they are not combined with drug therapy—that is, with lithium.

A number of drugs should not be used with these patients, most notably amphetamines, tricyclic antidepressants, and MAOI's, which are likely to aggravate the manic predisposition and intensify latent psychotic features. The treatment of choice is lithium, either alone or in combination with psychotherapy.

**REFERENCES**

Angst J, Felder W, Lohmeyer B: Schizo-affective disorders: results of a genetic investigation, I. Affective Disord 1: 137, 1979.

Bertelsen A: A Danish twin study of manic-depressive disorders. In Origin, Prevention and Treatment of Affective Disorders, M Schou, E Stromgren, editors, p 227. Academic Press, London, 1979.

Erikson, E H: Identity: Youth and Crisis. W. W. Norton, New York, 1968.

Hirschfeld, R M A, Klerman G L: Personality attributes and affective disorders. Am J Psychiatry 136: 67, 1979.

Kernberg O: Borderline personality organization. J Am Psychoanal Assoc 15: 641, 1967.

Kielholz P: Masked Depression. Hans Huber, Bern, 1973.

Kovacs M: Psychotherapies for depression. In Psychiatry Update, L Grinspoon, editor, vol 2. American Psychiatric Association, Washington, DC, 1983.

Lesse S: Psychotherapy in combination with antidepressant drugs in patients with severe masked depressions. Am J Psychiatry 31: 185, 1977.

Robinson D S, Nies A, Ravaris L, Lamborn K R: The monoamine oxidase inhibitor, phenelzine, in the treatment of depressive-anxiety states: a controlled treatment of depressive-anxiety states: a controlled clinical trial. Arch Gen Psychiatry 29: 407, 1973.

## 15.2 GRIEF, MOURNING BEREAVEMENT, AND THANATOLOGY

### Introduction

Ideal usage would reserve the word "grief" for the subjective feelings and affect that are precipitated by loss; the word "mourning" to refer to the processes (grief work) by which grief is resolved; and the word "bereavement" to the state accompanying the mourning process. Not all the professional literature follows this usage. The German word "trauer" used by Freud in his classic 1917 paper, Mourning and Melancholia, can mean both the affect of grief and its outward manifestations, but was rendered in translation as mourning. In 1961, Bowlby used "mourning" to refer to the psychological processes initiated by the loss of a loved object but "grief" to refer to the subjective states accompanying it.

### Normal Grief

Although there are many variations in the patterns found in individuals experiencing grief, there are sufficient similarities to warrant characterization of grief as a syndrome that has a course with an expected resolution.

Initial grief is often manifested as a state of shock that may be expressed in a feeling of numbness and a sense of bewilderment or a sense of being stunned. This apparent inability to comprehend what has happened may be short-lived, followed by expressions of suffering and distress most usually indicated by sighing and crying, although in Western culture this expected feature of grief is less common among men than among women. Other physical expressions of grief may include the following: feeling of weakness; decreased appetite; weight loss; and difficulty concentrating, breathing, and talking. Sleep disturbances may include difficulty going to sleep, waking up during the night, or awakening early. Dreams of the deceased often occur, with the dreamer awakening with a sense of disappointment in finding that the experience was only a dream. Preoccupation with thoughts of the deceased are a specific identifying feature of grief, as the person relives experiences shared with the deceased or tries instead to avoid all thoughts of the deceased. Simultaneously, a withdrawal of interest in the outside world may include decreased interest in eating, manner of dress, and usual social activities. Seemingly out of keeping with the sense of despair may also be expressions of anger, on occasion toward the deceased, but also directed to doctors, nurses, friends, relatives, and even God, who may be blamed in some way for what has happened. Self-reproaches are not unusual, although these are less common and less intense in normal grief than in pathological grief and usually center on some relatively minor act of omission or commission toward the deceased. Forms of denial occur throughout the entire period of bereavement, with the bereaved person becoming aware of inadvertently thinking or acting as if the loss had not occurred. Efforts to perpetuate the lost relationship are evidenced by an investment in objects that may have been treasured by the deceased or that remind the grief-stricken person of the deceased (linkage objects). A sense of the presence of the deceased may be so intense as to constitute an illusion or a hallucination, although in normal grief the person recognizes that it is a false impression. As part of what has been labeled identification phenomena, the person may take on the qualities, mannerisms, or characteristics of the deceased person, as if to perpetuate that person in some concrete way. This maneuver can reach potentially pathological expression with the development of physical symptoms similar to those experienced by the deceased or to ones suggestive of the illness from which the deceased died.

Some authorities have discerned a sequence to the stages of grief; they are as follows: shock; emotional release; utter depression, loneliness, and a sense of isolation; physical symptoms of distress; panic; guilt in relation to the loss; hos-tility; initial attempts to return to normal activities; overcoming of grief; and readjustment. In 1970, John Bowlby hypothesized four stages: An early phase of numbness or protest (stage 1) that may be interrupted by outbursts of distress, fear, or anger being soon followed by a phase of yearning and searching for the lost figure (stage 2) that may last several months or even years. This phase is characterized by preoccupations with the lost person, a physical restlessness, and a perceptual set that leads the griever to interpret these personal experiences as reflections of the presence of the deceased. Weeping and anger are characteristic expressions of this search. Gradual recognition and integration of the reality lead to a subsequent phase of disorganization and despair (stage 3). Restlessness and aimlessness may now characterize inefficient and ineffective efforts to initiate and perpetuate productive patterns of behavior, interpersonal or otherwise. Finally, with the establishment of new patterns, objects, and goals, the bereaved person reaches a phase of greater or lesser degree of reorganization (stage 4) during which grief recedes into cherished memories.

These stages are not as discrete as their characterizations might imply, because there are great variations from individual to individual. Nevertheless, in usual cases the diverse manifestations of grief tend to subside over time. Traditionally, it has been assumed that grief expends itself within 1 or 2 years as the person has the opportunity to experience the calendar year at least once without the lost person. It has become increasingly apparent, however, that the signs and symptoms of grief may persist much longer than 1 or 2 years, and the person sometimes continues to have varying grief-related feelings, symptoms, and behavior indefinitely and even throughout life. Even if never totally unaffected by the loss, however, the person in normal bereavement does in time return to a state of productivity and relative well-being.

## Mourning and Melancholia

An enduring differentiation of normal grief (mourning) and abnormal reactions to loss (melancholia) was provided by Freud in 1917. In his definition of mourning was the recognition that it is a reaction that is the result not only to the death of a loved person but one that may arise from less obvious losses, even to that of some abstraction, such as an ideal that has taken the place of a loved person. It was obviously the idea of loss per se of which Freud wrote, although still maintaining it within an interpersonal context.

Freud characterized the distinguishing features of mourning as including profound dejection, a lack of interest in the outside world, a diminished capacity to love, and an inhibition of activity, all of which are viewed as normal in spite of their departure from usual attitudes. Melancholia, however, involves all these with one other feature—a lowering of self-esteem viewed as valid today; that is, an exaggerated loss of self-esteem is not a prominent aspect of normal grief, however profound the dejection and sense of loss.

### Anticipatory Grief versus Delayed, Inhibited, or Denied Grief

Patterns that may alter the expression of acute grief at the time of the loss include the roles either of anticipatory grief or of delayed, inhibited, or denied grief.

The concept of anticipatory grief has been applied to grief expressed in advance of a loss that is perceived as inevitable, as distinguished from grief that occurs at or after the loss. By definition, anticipatory grief ends with the occurrence of the anticipated loss, regardless of what reactions follow. Unlike conventional grief, which diminishes in intensity with the passage of time, anticipatory grief may increase in intensity as the expected loss becomes more imminent. In some instances, however, particularly when the occurrence of the loss is delayed, anticipatory grief may be expended, leaving the individual showing fewer of the manifestations of acute grief when the actual loss occurs. Once anticipatory grief has been expended, it may be difficult to reestablish the prior relationship, as has been demonstrated with the return from combat or concentration camps of persons previously thought to be dead.

Patterns of response differ greatly, depending on the personality style of the griever, as well as the nature of the loss. The loss of aged or long-suffering patients, for example, may be experienced as a blessing when it occurs, whereas the death of a young child may elicit acute grief that is extreme, regardless of whether or not anticipatory grief has taken place. Anticipatory grief may be muted by hope that the loss will not occur, although a long period of anticipation may add to the grieving person's ambivalence about the anticipated loss, thus complicating the relationship, as well as the later course of bereavement. Anticipatory grief also occurs in professional caretakers for their patients perceived as terminally ill, a factor that may complicate and also diminish the quality of the care offered.

Delayed, inhibited, or denied grief refers to the absence of evidence of grief when it ordinar-

ily would be expected. In some instances grief is simply being delayed until it no longer can be avoided. Often the first reaction to a loss that has not allowed opportunities for anticipatory grief is temporary shock or denial, with details of arrangements for funeral and burial distracting the person from fully experiencing the magnitude or implications of what has happened.

Individuals vary greatly as to their need to hide their grief, there being marked differences as to whether it is the showing or the concealing of grief that is considered shameful and embarrassing. Familial and cultural influences also affect how the mourner will behave in public. The "stiff upper lip" admired by one group contrasts dramatically with the weeping, wailing, and fainting that another group accepts as the norm. Hence, it may be difficult to gauge the extent of another's grief from outward appearances unless one has some understanding of the setting from which the person comes.

Potentially pathogenic is grief that is inhibited or denied expression because the person is simply not dealing with the reality of the loss. A false euphoria may prevail, suggesting that bereavement is on a pathological course. Inhibited or denied grief reactions contain the seeds of such unfortunate consequences as the person's experiencing persisting physical symptoms similar to those of the deceased, or unaccountable reactions on the anniversary of the loss or on occasions of significance to the deceased. Denied or inhibited grief may also reach expression by being displaced to some other loss that, although seemingly insignificant in its own right, may symbolize the original loss. Overreaction to another person's trouble may be one manifestation of displacement.

Finally, of course, it must be recognized that some relationships, regardless of their public view, are sufficiently negative as to render reduced or absent grief a totally normal and appropriate response, albeit often confusing or seemingly inappropriate to onlookers. Although the professional literature abounds with case histories illustrating the detrimental consequences of the loss of a spouse or parent, discretion has dictated that less prominence be given to instances where the consequences are extraordinarily positive.

### Psychodynamics

The psychodynamics of grief, mourning, and bereavement, like those of any symptom or syndrome, are concerned essentially with the functional significance of the emotional and motivational aspects of behavior, including both conscious and unconscious determinants. The universality of the grief response raises the question of what constellation of forces operate within people to explain the similarities and variations among them at the time of a loss.

Purely related to conscious motivations and influences, the magnitude and nature of the loss does bear some direct relationship to the kind of reaction that is elicited by it. In general, for example, a loss through death of a loved one—the most common precipitant of a grief reaction—has an irreversibility about it that does not characterize separations and rejections from living persons. Hence, denial as a defense is constantly confronted or challenged by a reality that is difficult to transcend if reality testing ability is to be still maintained.

Psychoanalytic theorists have stressed the role of unconscious dynamics operating in the mourning process, with the general assumption being that the greater the role of factors that are unconscious and inaccessible to awareness, the more is the likelihood that the reaction will be an untoward one. Although Freud recognized the difficulty of explaining the grief in terms of individual psychodynamics, he proposed a model consistent with his libido theory of that time, explaining mourning as similar to melancholia in that a withdrawal of libido from its attachment to the lost object occurs with both—a painful matter because libidinal positions are never easily abandoned. In mourning, the loss is clearly perceived and reality ultimately prevails, although requiring the passage of time because withdrawal of libido does not occur wholesale but through every memory and expectation to which libido is bound. In melancholia, however, the loss is not clearly perceived; that is, the person does not recognize fully what was lost even when aware of who was lost. Hence the mourning of the melancholic appears excessive both to the outside observer and to the person.

In 1961, Bowlby proposed the theory that many aspects of the mourning process can be understood as separation anxiety elicited by the disruption of the attachment behavior that is part of the person's instinctive equipment. Although attachment behavior is especially characteristic of children, it remains active throughout life, leading to the inevitability of separation anxiety when the person loses the object of the attachment. Most of the symptoms of bereavement can be understood as attempts to search for and to regain the lost object, efforts that serve a successful purpose in most separations by reuniting the person with the object of attachment; that is, expressions of crying or anger serve to bring the mother to the child just as they do to bring back an errant lover in adult-

hood. The very facial expression characteristic of adult grief, in fact, has been considered the result of the inhibition of the tendency to scream like an abandoned child. It is only when the separation stems from a loss that is irreversible that such behavior seems purposeless, although carried out with the same conscious or unconscious objectives as with temporary separations where the behavior is likely to be rewarded. Because the grief behavior does not elicit its usual response, the person's sense of frustration and anger is further intensified.

Regardless of the purposeful role of anger, all authorities agree that it occurs in normal mourning much more frequently than is generally supposed, often reaching conscious overt expression in spite of the cultural taboos against it at the time of bereavement. Whether as a reaction to grief and thus designed to alleviate it, or whether an essential causative component of it, the presence of anger must be taken for granted.

Agreement also exists on the role of childhood experiences in setting the model for later separation experiences. In psychoanalytic thinking, prominent roles have been given to the concepts of incorporation, identification, and introjection for explaining the reactions of a depressed person as similar to those of the young child adjusting to its first major loss. The validity of these concepts has been supported in the dreams and fantasies of patients in psychoanalysis.

Some persons may develop physical symptoms similar to those accompanying the fatal illness of the dead person. After some attempts motivated by the desire to bring back the lost person, the bereaved person will also retain a link to the lost object through fond memories, recollections, and perhaps even through symbolic representations of the person in the form of preserved possessions. With the passage of time the person becomes free to seek some other replacement. Such a mature use of identification as a means of adjusting to a loss is possible only when a sense of self-identity, or firm ego boundaries, has been established before the loss.

In a reaction to a loss that results in a pathological depression, processes are analogous to those involved in incorporation and introjection, a less adaptive and more primitive way of adjusting to a loss than that which characterizes the process of identification. In introjection, the object is incorporated, but is neither integrated and assimilated into the personality through the more mature process of identification, nor is it ever fully relinquished. A fusion of ego boundaries occurs between the self and nonself (the incorporated image or object), because the ability to make this distinction was never adequately developed.

The introjection of an object toward which there was intense ambivalence gives rise to depression, self-accusations, and feelings of worthlessness that reflect the previously unacceptable aspects of the original relationship. That is, the ambivalence, originally directed to the incorporated object, is now expressed against the self because the object and the self are not distinguished. The self-accusations of a depressed person can thus be the unconscious accusations the person is directing at someone else (the incorporated object). In a cry for attention, love, and service, the person may also be acting out an unconscious desire to punish someone else. Further guilt and depression ensue.

These psychodynamics of mourning were enunciated by Sigmund Freud and Karl Abraham.

### Management of Grief

Individuals in normal grief seldom seek psychiatric assistance, because they accept their reactions and behavior as appropriate to the extent of their loss. When professional assistance is sought, it most usually involves requests for sleeping medication, rather than release from the general depressed state that they accept as quite normal. Such requests are most usually made to the family physician, rather than to a psychiatrist.

Whether requested by the grief-stricken person or not, medications of any kind should probably be used cautiously. Most authorities do not recommend the use of antidepressants when the person is experiencing an appropriate expression of grief, for example, nor are antianxiety agents generally considered necessary. At most a mild sedative to facilitate sleep is probably all that is warranted. It can be held that the person should not be deprived of an opportunity to experience a process that ultimately can be rewarding and maturing in its effect. With the recognition that grief cannot be permanently postponed and is going to reach expression in some way, however circuitous, ventilation of feelings is to be encouraged, rather than to be "narcotized," because the more sustained the inhibition of feelings the more intense will they be likely to be when finally expressed.

Outcomes are likely to be most favorable if soon after bereavement the bereaved person experiences interactions with others as being positive ones. Surveys document the fact that bereaved persons often do not feel that friends, relatives, and clergymen have been particularly helpful to them and that they view the most

significant psychosocial support as coming from the funeral director in a relationship that usually ends with the deceased's burial. Friends and relatives may indeed be unintentionally thoughtless or at least not particularly helpful. In various ways they may tend to discourage free expression of feelings, especially grief and anger; although trying to be sympathetic, they may insist on how badly they feel, as if to tell the bereaved that they are the ones who need comfort; they may try to shut off conversations about the deceased, presumably for the other person's benefit, but most usually to avoid their own discomfort; after initial expressions of support and sympathy, they may simply avoid the bereaved, feeling the person is an impediment to their own enjoyment; or they may now assume that the person is sexually available because no longer commited to another. Like the divorcee, perhaps, the recent widow or widower may be ready prey as objects to people one's fantasies, whether sexual, financial, or otherwise.

Particularly helpful have been efforts to bring the similarly bereaved together, to share expressions of loss and to offer companionship, social contacts, and emotional support. These efforts include such formal organizations as the Widowed Persons Service, Parents Without Partners, and Compassionate Friends (for parents who have lost a child) that are available in most large cities. Sometimes such opportunities are available through church or senior citizen groups.

### Thanatology

Thanatology may be defined as that discipline which investigates death, dying, life-threatening behavior, grief, bereavement, suicide, and fatal illness. The field can hardly be circumscribed since it also includes death-oriented institutions and customs, all designed to contain mankind's dread of its own extinction.

### Stages of Dying

Elizabeth Kubler-Ross has described dying as typified by five stages: denial, anger, bargaining, depression, and acceptance.

Denial is accompanied by shock, the patient may refuse to believe that he is going to die or has a fatal illness. Anger is characterized by the patient venting his frustration about death on family, friends, or physicians. In the bargaining stage the patient promises something—such as giving to charity—in exchange for a respite from death or a change in the diagnosis of his illness. Depression ranges from feelings of sadness about events to acute suicidal impulses or attempts. With acceptance, the patient is able to deal with his impending death and often requests to be left alone or to be with one or two loved ones.

The trajectory of death however, is hardly smooth. There are many fluctuations due to impersonal, intrapersonal, and interpersonal factors related to disease, personality, and social supports. Stages, phases, and dimensions of a chronic fatal illness represent a confluence of psychosocial factors rather than distinct stages.

### Psychiatric Management of the Dying Patient

Very few preterminal patients need, demand, or accept intensive psychotherapeutic interventions. They have more urgent matters with which to cope. Physical distress puts a distance from psychological issues, a phenomenon also indicated by remissions from depression and from delusional states during a severe physical illness.

Psychiatrists offer most to the dying when they provide resources for support or renewal of relationships that have faltered. Mainly, the psychiatrist recognizes a time-honored obligation to provide support and comfort for the sick person facing imminent death. This means compassionate concern, coupled with clarification of major problems and insistence upon ensuring continuing support, security, and safety for patients and caregivers. The term "death with dignity" has become so sloganized that hardly anyone knows what it means. Dignity does not mean formality and artificial behavior. It does mean respect for the individuality of a dying patient who has courageously endured inroads of illness, as well as many disappointments.

Prerequisites for a good death are (1) care and support, (2) participation and knowledge of what is happening and being done, (3) composure and control of unwarranted mood swings, (4) ample communication with others on medical and nonmedical topics, (5) continuity and linkage of past and present without dwelling on the unchangeable, and (6) blending timeliness and timelessness into a final closure. As a result, the time seems right; the best that is and is available has been conferred.

**Precepts for the Therapist.** Although no set of instructions fits everyone and is suitable for every therapist who would intervene in management of terminal illness, there are certain caveats to observe. It is mistaken to believe that terminal patients are principally preoccupied with existential matters; many patients have already come to terms with their allotment of time, despite distress. Therapists should avoid gratuitous platitudes, mystical formulas, unso-

licited reassurance, and empty phrases that alienate and do not reach what a patient is actually feeling. There is no requirement to feel guilty, nor to console arbitrarily. Neither should the therapist hide feelings, if this is likely to help.

Pain and other physical symptoms must be controlled amply in order to provide the bedrock for an appropriate death. How sedated a patient should be during final hours and days is an individual question. Some patients prefer tranquility; others prefer interaction for as long as possible. Few patients or families ask for miracles, if pain and other symptoms are controlled and caregivers heed proper psychosocial guidelines.

### The Hospice Movement

By far, the most convincing, practical demonstration of concern for the terminally ill is found in the hospice movement. It is psychosocial thanatology in action, joined to better care for families and patients who have gone beyond the benefits of therapeutic medicine.

Beginning with a small residential unit in the early 1960s, Dame Cicely Saunders and her backers generated a movement that has vastly altered the options available for those facing inexorable death. There is scarcely a city or town in the United States, for example, where various volunteer organizations calling themselves hospices cannot be found.

A hospice refers to a place that is neither a fully equipped acute hospital nor a nursing facility that offers little more than custodial services and much medication. It usually means an inpatient service or home care by experienced physicians, nurses, and aides who often volunteer their services. Primary emphasis is on the psychosocial unit of family and patient, in contrast to inconsistent palliative care previously given by a busy local physician or by a regional nurse who was already overworked.

Among the advantages of the hospice concept are (1) better care for both the family and the patient through an established, supervised program; (2) an effective alternative to unnecessary, expensive hospitalization or consignment to a substandard custodial facility; (3) consistent control over pain medication; (4) prevention of social isolation and neglect; (5) possible prevention of morbid grief reactions among the survivors.

Recently, certain governmental agencies and third-party insurers have supported various hospices because hospice and home care are more economical than regular hospitalization. The advantage of third-party support is obvious.

Family practitioners and visiting nurses may find that at least partial remuneration could compensate for a very taxing and unrewarding effort. Third-party requirements also insist on uniform standards, better procedures, and more professional evaluations than in a wholly voluntary organization.

## REFERENCES

Averill J A: Grief: Its nature and significance. Psychol Bull *70:* 721, 1968.

Bowlby J: Process of mourning. Int J Psychoanal *42:* 317, 1961.

Bowlby J: *Attachment and Loss. III: Sadness and Depression.* Basic Books, New York, 1980.

Bowlby J, Parkes C M: Separation and loss. In *International Yearbook for Child Psychiatry and Allied Disciplines.* E J Anthony, C Koupernik, editors. Wiley-Interscience, New York, 1970.

Carr A C: Grief, mourning and bereavement. In *Comprehensive Textbook of Psychiatry,* ed 4. H I Kaplan, B J Sadock, editors, p 1286 Williams & Wilkins, Baltimore, 1985.

Kutscher A, Carr A, Kutscher L, editors. *Principles of Thanatology.* Columbia University Press, New York, 1984.

Clayton P, Desmarais L, Winokur G: A Study of normal bereavement. Am J Psychiatry *125:* 168, 1968.

Freud S: Mourning and melancholia (1917). In *The Standard Edition of the Complete Psychological Works of Sigmund Freud,* vol 14, Hogarth Press and the Institute of Psychoanalysis, London, 1957.

Gonda T A, Ruark J E: *Dying Dignified: The Health Professionals Guide to Care.* Addison-Wesley, Menlo Park, CA, 1984.

Hansen L, McAleer C: Terminal cancer and suicide: the health care professional's dilemma. Omega *14:* 241, 1984.

Jacobson E: Normal and pathological moods: Their nature and functions. In *The Psychoanalysis Study of the Child.* R S Eissler, A Freud, H Hartmann, E Kris, editors, vol 12, p 73. International Universities Press, New York, 1957.

Lindemann E: Symptomatology and management of acute grief. Am J Psychiat *101:* 141, 1944–1945.

Parkes C M: *Bereavement.* International Universities Press, New York, 1972.

Schoenberg B, Carr A C, Perez D, Kutscher A H, editors: *Loss and Grief: Psychological Management in Medical Practice.* Columbia University Press, New York, 1970.

Weisman A D: Thanatology. In *Comprehensive Textbook of Psychiatry,* ed 4. H I Kaplan, B J Sadock, editors, p 1277. Williams & Wilkins, Baltimore, 1985.

# 16

# Organic Mental Disorders

## Introduction

It is an odd paradox that despite their increasing frequency and importance, organic mental disorders constitute the most neglected area of clinical psychiatry in this country. Only in the past few years have psychiatrists started to pay attention to this area. They have been compelled to do so by the growing frequency of organic mental disorders that are related to the aging of the population (some 23 million Americans are currently aged 65 years or over), to the abuse of alcohol and other substances, to the advances in critical care medicine that allow the survival of many brain-damaged persons, and to the so-called diseases of medical progress—that is, cerebral complications of modern drugs and surgical treatments for cardiovascular, renal, and other diseases.

## Definition

Organic mental disorders are a class of disorders of mental functioning and behavior caused by permanent damage to the brain, or by temporary dysfunction of the brain, or by both these factors. The underlying cerebral disease or disorder may be primary—that is, originating in the brain—or secondary to systemic disease. It may be diffuse or focal, or both. The resulting psychopathological manifestations reflect destruction or metabolic derangement of brain structures subserving cognitive functions, emotions, and motivation of behavior. Organic brain syndromes represent clusters of psychological or behavioral abnormalities or symptoms that show a tendency to occur together; these constitute the class of mental disorders designated "organic." These syndromes share a common feature in that a cerebral disorder constitutes a necessary condition for their occurrence. Their essential clinical characteristics, however, differ widely and reflect such variables as the degree of spread, the localization, the rate of onset and progression, and the nature of the underlying pathological process in the brain. Further, the clinical picture displayed by any given patient is modified to some extent by his or her personality structure, intelligence, education, emotional state, interpersonal relationships, and other psychological and social factors.

## Classification

The whole class of conditions caused by or associated with cerebral disease or dysfunction is designated "organic mental disorders." The disorders encompass nine purely descriptive clusters of psychopathological symptoms referred to as "organic brain syndromes." The nine syndromes include four groups: (1) those with relatively global cognitive impairment—delirium and dementia; (2) those characterized by relatively circumscribed cognitive impairment or abnormality—amnestic syndrome and organic hallucinosis; (3) those that are predominantly manifested by personality disturbances or that closely resemble some of the functional mental disorders—organic personality syndrome, affective syndrome, and delusional syndrome; and (4) those that are associated with ingestion (intoxication) or reduction (withdrawal) in the use of a substance.

Delirium and dementia are typically associated with relatively widespread cerebral pathology, which in the case of delirium tends to be transient, and in the case of dementia tends to be prolonged and, in many but not all cases, permanent. Amnestic syndrome, organic hallucinosis, and organic personality syndrome are usually associated with localized cerebral damage or dysfunction. Organic affective syndrome and delusional syndrome have no known structural correlates; they constitute the most controversial feature of the classification.

## Causes and Pathogenesis

A great many potential causes of cerebral damage and dysfunction exist and may induce one or more organic brain syndromes. For example, a brain tumor may give rise to delirium, dementia, amnestic syndrome, and hallucinosis. The intervening variables include the localiza-

271

tion, the degree, and the rate of spread of the tumor, and the presence of increased intracranial pressure. Also, an age of 60 years or more increases susceptibility to organic mental disorders. Both delirium and dementia are particularly frequent in the elderly, and preexisting brain damage of any origin enhances susceptibility to delirium. Reduced ability to metabolize drugs is a factor predisposing elderly patients to the development of delirium in response to even therapeutic doses of medical drugs.

Certain features of the environment may facilitate the occurrence of an organic mental disorder, especially delirium or dementia. Social isolation, interpersonal conflicts and losses, unfamiliarity of the environment, and deficient or excessive sensory inputs may have such an influence.

### Clinical Features and Psychopathology

No single set of psychological abnormalities may be regarded as characteristic or pathognomonic of the class of organic mental disorders as a whole. Only those symptoms that are most commonly and predictably associated with demonstrable cerebral disease are discussed here.

#### Cognitive and Intellectual Impairment

The most common and, hence, clinically the most important psychopathological manifestations of brain pathology involve the impairment of one or more cognitive functions, including memory, thinking, perception, and attention. The following list includes the most common manifestations of impaired cognitive functions and information processing.

1. Memory impairment, especially that manifested by the impaired recall of relatively recent events and by the inadequate formulation of new memories and, thus, by impaired ability to learn;

2. Impairment of abstract thinking, manifested by the reduced ability to generalize, synthesize, differentiate, reason logically, form concepts, solve problems, and plan action;

3. Impairment of ability to perform novel tasks and to sustain cognitive performance, especially under time pressure and in the face of irrelevant stimuli or distraction;

4. Decrement of over-all intellectual functioning;

5. Impairment of judgment—that is, reduced ability to anticipate and appreciate likely adverse consequences of one's action, especially in a social context;

6. Attention disturbance, such as impaired ability to mobilize, focus, sustain, or shift attention;

7. Impaired spatiotemporal orientation;

8. Impaired ability to calculate;

9. Impaired ability to grasp the meaning of information inputs;

10. Impaired or distorted perception of one's body and one's environment, and of the self-environment boundary, with consequent perplexity and tendency to misperceptions or body image disorders or both.

The loss of abstraction, of reasoning ability, and of capacity to understand the nature of a problem, constitutes the most common manifestation of impaired brain function found on psychological testing. The deterioration of efficiency in performance on intellectual and cognitive tasks is another such manifestation.

The impairment of abstraction, memory, and efficiency in intellectual and cognitive performance is the hallmark of relatively widespread brain pathology, reversible or not. The presence of these cognitive abnormalities in a given patient constitutes presumptive evidence of cerebral damage or dysfunction, and should lead to appropriate investigations of the presumed brain disorder by nonpsychological techniques—radiographic, electroencephalographic, and so on.

Perplexity, distractibility, and fatigue are among the most common and troublesome manifestations of brain damage in adults.

#### Altered Emotionality and Impulsivity

Verbal and nonverbal expressions of emotions, drives, and impulses are often changed and inappropriate in patients with cerebral disease. Apathy, euphoria, and irritability are common emotional concomitants of cognitive impairment and of organic personality disorder. The patient with brain damage tends to exhibit emotional lability—that is, undue readiness to cry, laugh, or show anger—and a tendency to shift rapidly from one form of emotional expression to another. Such reduced capacity for the control and fine modulation of emotional expression is the most common form of emotional pathology in the patient with an organic mental disorder.

Control of the expression of needs, drives, and appetites is often impaired. Virtually any type of drive or impulse may be expressed by the patient with little restraint or regard for social consequences.

#### Disturbances of Alertness and Wakefulness (Vigilance)

A typical feature of an acute or transient and widespread cerebral disorder is a disturbance of awareness of self and the environment. Basic to this disturbance is a disorder of wakefulness and of alertness—that is, readiness to respond to stimuli. This type of psychopathology is often referred to in the literature as "disturbances of consciousness." Terms such as clouding, reduction, alteration, and narrowing of consciousness are commonly used in this context.

### Compensatory and Protective Symptoms

Patients with cerebral damage or dysfunction tend to exhibit characteristic behavior patterns aimed at maintaining adequate performance and avoiding distress engendered by its failure. These compensatory and protective coping strategies are referred to here as symptoms, whether they are adaptive or maladaptive.

### Reactive Symptoms

A person suffering from an organic mental disorder tends to react to it cognitively, emotionally, and behaviorally. These reactions reflect the subjective meaning of the disorder for the patient and his or her personality, value system, social and economic situation, and other psychosocial variables. Specifically, psychotic symptoms represent the most severe form of reactive pathology. For example, a habitually suspicious and mistrustful person may develop frank paranoid delusions of persecution, jealousy, or somatic change. Another patient may display delusions of grandeur or of poverty accompanied by appropriate affect. As a general rule, reactive psychopathology is most likely to accompany relatively mild or moderate cognitive impairment or abnormality. It may be difficult or even impossible to distinguish reactive symptoms from those more directly related to cerebral damage or dysfunction.

### Diagnosis

The diagnosis of an organic brain syndrome includes two necessary components: first, essential psychological features of the given syndrome must be present, and, second, there must be independent or nonpsychological evidence of an antecedent or concurrent cerebral disorder that is judged to be a necessary condition for the syndrome exhibited by the patient.

## Delirium

### Definition

The term delirium denotes a transient organic mental disorder characterized by the global impairment of cognitive functions, acute onset, and widespread disturbance of cerebral metabolism.

The patient's ability to receive, process, store, and recall information, and to maintain organized mental activity, is reduced. This impairment tends to fluctuate during the day and to be most marked at night. The sleep-wakefulness cycle is usually disorganized.

Delirium corresponds to the acute confusional state and the acute brain syndrome of other classifications. It also includes many so-called toxic psychoses and encephalopathies. It would improve communication if only one term, delirium, were used to denote the syndrome described here.

### Epidemiology

Some 5 to 15 percent of patients on general medical and surgical wards are likely to manifest delirium of some degree of severity. The incidence of delirium in surgical intensive care units has been reported to range from 18 to 30 percent. The incidence in coronary and general medical intensive care units is variously reported to be from 2 to 20 percent. The incidence of postanesthetic or emergence delirium is about 6 percent, but can reach 20 percent among patients premedicated with scopolamine hydrobromide. The incidence of delirium after open-heart and coronary-bypass surgery is about 30 percent. Of severely burned patients, about 20 to 30 percent become delirious.

The incidence and the prevalence of delirium among the aged are higher than in other age groups.

Delirium is one of the most common mental disorders diagnosed by liaison psychiatrists in general hospitals. At least 20 percent of patients seen by them in psychiatric consultation exhibit an organic brain syndrome, most often delirium.

### Causes

The cause of delirium is multifactorial. A necessary condition for its occurrence is the presence of widespread derangement of cerebral metabolism, resulting in a disorganization of higher brain functions and mental activity. The occurrence, the severity, and the clinical features of delirium are influenced by certain predisposing and facilitating factors.

A large number of diseases, both cerebral and systemic, and toxic agents introduced into the body from outside, can result in delirium (see Table I).

Predisposing factors include: (1) age 60 years or more; the elderly are especially susceptible to the development of delirium in response to almost any physical illness or drug; (2) addiction to alcohol or drugs or both; (3) cerebral damage

TABLE I
ORGANIC CAUSES OF DELIRIUM*

1. Intoxication
    A. Drugs: anticholinergic agents, sedative-hypnotics, digitalis derivatives, cimetidine, methyldopa, levodopa, opiates, salicylates, anticonvulsants, antiarrhythmic agents, phencyclidine, etc.
    B. Alcohol
    C. Addictive inhalants: gasoline, glue, ether, nitrous oxide
    D. Industrial poisons: carbon monoxide and disulfide, organic solvents, methyl chlorides, heavy metals
2. Alcohol and drug withdrawal
    A. Alcohol—delirium tremens
    B. Sedatives and hypnotics: barbiturates, chloral hydrate, benzodiazepines, ethchlorvynol, methyprylon, glutethimide, meprobamate, paraldehyde
    C. Amphetamines—occasionally
3. Metabolic encephalopathies
    A. Hepatic, renal, pulmonary, pancreatic insufficiency or failure
    B. Hypoxia
    C. Hypoglycemia
    D. Vitamin deficiency: nicotinic acid, thiamine, cyanocobalamine, folate
    E. Endocrinopathies: hyperinsulinism, hyperthyroidism, hypothyroidism, hypopituitarism, Addison's disease, Cushing's syndrome, hypoparathyroidism, hyperparathyroidism
    F. Disorders of fluid, electrolyte, and acid-base balance: hypernatremia, hyponatremia, hyperkalemia, hypokalemia, hypercalcemia, hypocalcemia, hypermagnesemia, hypomagnesemia, alkalosis, acidosis, dehydration, water intoxication
    G. Errors of metabolism: porphyria, carcinoid syndrome
4. Infections
    A. Systemic: pneumonia, typhoid, typhus, acute rheumatic fever, malaria, influenza, mumps, diphtheria, brucellosis, Rocky Mountain spotted fever, infectious mononucleosis, infectious hepatitis, Legionnaires' disease
    B. Intracranial: viral, bacterial, fungal, protozoal encephalitis and meningitis, postvaccinial and postinfectious encephalomyelitis, trichinosis
5. Epilepsy
6. Head injury
7. Vascular diseases
    A. Cerebrovascular: hypertensive encephalopathy; arteritis—systemic lupus erythematosus, rheumatoid vasculitis, polyarteritis nodosa; temporal arteritis; thrombosis, embolism, subarachnoid hemorrhage
    B. Cardiovascular: myocardial infarction, congestive heart failure, cardiac arrhythmias
    C. Migraine
8. Intracranial tumor
    A. Neoplasm
    B. Abscess
    C. Subdural hematoma
    D. Aneurysm
    E. Parasitic cyst
9. Cerebral degenerative diseases
    A. Multiple sclerosis
    B. Alzheimer's disease—senile dementia
10. Injury by physical agents
    A. Hyperthermia
    B. Hypothermia
    C. Electric injury
11. Diseases due to hypersensitivity
    A. Serum sickness
    B. Food allergy

* Modified from Lipowski Z J: *Delirium: Acute Brain Failure in Man.* Charles C Thomas, Springfield, IL, 1979.

of any origin; and (4) individual susceptibility to a particular agent, such as allergy to a drug, or to the development of delirium in general.

### Clinical Features

The essential features of delirium include a rapid onset; concurrent disturbances of attention, memory, thinking, orientation, perception, and psychomotor behavior; a disorder of the sleep-wakefulness cycle; and a tendency for cognitive abnormalities to fluctuate unpredictably in the course of a day (see Table II).

The onset of delirium may be ushered in by prodromal symptoms, such as anxiety, restlessness, hypersensitivity to light and sound, slight difficulty in thinking coherently, insomnia, and vivid dreams or even transient visual hallucinations during the night. Full-blown delirium may first become manifest at night, when the patient wakes up and experiences confusion about his or her whereabouts, situation, and the dividing line between dream, veridical perceptions, and hallucinations. Attention is difficult

TABLE II
DIAGNOSTIC CRITERIA FOR DELIRIUM*

A. Clouding of consciousness (reduced clarity of awareness of the environment), with reduced capacity to shift, focus, and sustain attention to environmental stimuli.

B. At least two of the following:

    (1) perceptual disturbance: misinterpretations, illusions, or hallucinations
    (2) speech that is at times incoherent
    (3) disturbance of sleep-wakefulness cycle, with insomnia or daytime drowsiness
    (4) increased or decreased psychomotor activity

C. Disorientation and memory impairment (if testable).

D. Clinical features that develop over a short period of time (usually hours to days) and tend to fluctuate over the course of a day.

E. Evidence, from the history, physical examination, or laboratory tests, of a specific organic factor judged to be etiologically related to the disturbance.

* From American Psychiatric Association: *Diagnostic and Statistical Manual of Mental Disorders*, ed 3. American Psychiatric Association, Washington, DC, 1980. Used with permission.

to focus, maintain, and shift voluntarily. Alertness is abnormally increased or decreased. The patient is often distractible or easily distracted by irrelevant stimuli. His or her ability to think coherently is reduced, and thinking becomes slowed or abnormally accelerated, disorganized, and more concrete. Reasoning and problem solving become difficult or impossible, and unbidden images and thoughts, sometimes highly disturbing to the patient, may be experienced. Memory is impaired to some extent. There is impaired recall of memories formed before the onset of delirium, and defective registration and probably retention of current percepts. Recall of the experiences during delirium after its resolution is characteristically spotty, and the patient may refer to it as a bad dream or a nightmare that is only vaguely remembered.

As a rule, orientation is impaired. The patient is rarely unaware of his or her own identity. Disorientation reflects basic cognitive deficits and, in the case of positive misidentification, an attempt to compensate for them.

Perceptual discrimination is impaired. The patient is less able than before to relate ongoing stimuli to past knowledge, and hence to grasp the meaning of information inputs. His or her ability to screen out irrelevant stimuli and to extract relevant stimuli is diminished.

Cognitive impairment in delirium tends to fluctuate unpredictably and often rather rapidly during the daytime, and is typically most pronounced during the night. So-called lucid intervals, during which the patient is more attentive and rational and is in better contact with his or her surroundings, may appear at any time and last for minutes to hours.

Psychomotor behavior is usually abnormal. The patient is either predominantly hypoactive and lethargic or, on the contrary, hyperactive to the point of exhaustion. There may be unexpected shifts, from a relatively quiet state to agitation, and vice versa.

There is often emotional disturbance. The most commonly observed emotions are fear or anxiety, depression, and apathy. If fear is intense—for instance, and a result of frightening illusions and hallucinations—the patient may make determined attempts to escape without regard to possible injury to self or others. At times, an angry attack occurs. A deeply depressed patient may attempt suicide, but a delirious patient is much more likely to sustain an injury as a result of a wild flight.

### Course and Prognosis

Delirium is, by definition, a transient disorder. This implies that the syndrome is never chronic, but it does not follow that its outcome is always one of restitution of premorbid mental functioning. The duration of delirium averages a week, less often several weeks, and rarely a few months. Delirium may be intermittent—that is, it may recur at varying intervals. If the underlying cerebral disorder persists, however, delirium shades over into dementia—that is, a more chronic brain syndrome in which the fluctuating level of awareness and related symptoms are replaced by a relatively stable cognitive impairment, reversible or not.

The outcome of delirium may be one of four kinds: (1) full recovery of premorbid functioning, the most common outcome; (2) death; (3) transition to dementia or another organic brain syndrome; or (4) transition to a nonorganic mental disorder, such as paranoia or schizophrenia—a rare event.

### Diagnosis

Delirium is diagnosed at the bedside and not in the psychological laboratory. A history of the sudden onset of the essential features is highly suggestive. Diurnal fluctuations and nocturnal exacerbation of symptoms are highly characteristic. The presence of a known physical illness or a history of head trauma, alcoholism, or drug addiction increases the probability of delirium. The onset at night is also especially suggestive.

The diagnosis requires a demonstration of multiple cognitive deficits on the mental status examination.

Delirium needs to be distinguished from other organic brain syndromes, especially dementia (see Table III); from brief reactive, schizophreniform and atypical psychoses; from factitious illness with psychological symptoms; and from dissociative disorders.

### Treatment

A cardinal rule of the treatment of delirium is to identify its cause and to remove or treat it, applying appropriate medical or surgical therapeutic techniques. In addition to causative treatment, the management of delirium involves symptomatic and general measures aimed at the relief of distress and the prevention of complications, such as accidents.

Nutrition and electrolyte and fluid balance must be maintained.

An adequate intake of vitamins is important, since their deficiency may contribute to delirium.

An optimal sensory, social, and nursing environment should be provided. The patient is best cared for in a quiet, well-lighted room. It is good policy to leave on a dimmed light at night.

TABLE III
CLINICAL DIFFERENTIATION OF DELIRIUM AND DEMENTIA*

|  | Delirium | Dementia |
|---|---|---|
| Onset | Acute | Usually insidious; if acute, preceded by coma or delirium |
| Duration | Usually less than 1 month | At least 1 month, usually much longer |
| Orientation | Faulty, at least for a time; tendency to mistake unfamiliar for familiar place, person | May be correct in mild cases |
| Thinking | Disorganized | Impoverished |
| Memory | Recent impaired | Both recent and remote impaired |
| Attention | Invariably disturbed, hard to direct or sustain | May be intact |
| Awareness | Always reduced, tends to fluctuate during daytime and be worse at night | Usually intact |
| Alertness | Increased or decreased | Normal or decreased |
| Perception | Misperceptions often present | Misperceptions often absent |
| Sleep-wakefulness cycle | Always disrupted | Usually normal for age |

* After Lipowski Z J: *Delirium: Acute Brain Failure in Man.* Charles C Thomas, Springfield, IL, 1979.

Psychiatric consultation is usually required, since physicians tend to overlook the early symptoms of delirium and often allow it to progress to a point at which it becomes a psychiatric emergency. Liaison psychiatrists are familiar with delirium, its causes and its treatment, and can usually offer helpful advice.

An agitated, restless, and fearful or belligerent delirious patient needs to be sedated to prevent complications and accidents. No single psychotropic drug available today is recommended for all cases of delirium. As a general rule, haloperidol (Haldol) is the drug of choice in most cases. Depending on the patient's age, weight, and physical condition, the initial dose may range from 2 to 10 mg intramuscularly, to be repeated hourly if the patient continues to be agitated. The effective total daily dose may range between 10 and 60 mg for most delirious patients. As soon as the patient is calm, oral medication in the form of tablets or liquid concentrate should begin. Two daily oral doses should suffice, with two-thirds of the dose being given at bedtime. The oral dose should be about 1.5 times higher than the parenteral dose to achieve the same therapeutic effect. A mildly to moderately agitated patient may be given oral haloperidol from the start in two daily doses of 2 to 10 mg. Patients with anticholinergic delirium are best treated with physostigmine. Hepatic encephalopathy is best managed with a benzodiazepine, such as oxazepam or diazepam.

## Dementia

### Definition

Dementia is an organic brain syndrome, characterized by an acquired decrement of intellectual abilities sufficiently severe to impair social or occupational performance, or both. A fully developed case features impairment of memory, abstract thinking, and judgment, and some degree of personality change—that is, either an accentuation or an alteration of the patient's habitual character traits. The disorder may be progressive, static, or reversible, and is caused by a relatively widespread cerebral damage or dysfunction.

### Epidemiology

About a million Americans over age 65 have a significant degree of intellectual impairment justifying the diagnosis of dementia. About 65 percent of them suffer from Alzheimer's type of dementia. These estimates do not take into account dementia of various causes occurring in people less than 65 years old. Each year, approximately 10 million Americans sustained head injuries of sufficient severity to require medical attention, and 633,000 persons have cerebral lacerations, contusions, or subdural or epidural hematomas, so head trauma alone is likely to contribute significantly to the incidence and the prevalence of dementia. Alcoholism is another cause, of an unknown, but probably considerable, magnitude.

### Causes

Dementia, like delirium, is a behavioral manifestation of relatively widespread cerebral pathology, and has multifactorial causation. A necessary condition for its occurrence is a relatively widespread damage or dysfunction of the brain, due to any one of a large number of cerebral and systemic diseases. The cause of dementia is multifactorial in the sense that psychological and social factors influence its occurrence, severity, and course. Table IV lists diseases and conditions that may be associated with dementia.

Psychosocial factors co-determine the degree of severity of the dementia, and possibly its onset. Premorbid personality, intelligence, and education seem to influence the patient's motivation and capacity to compensate for his or her intellectual deficits and thus, the degree of functional disability. These factors are most clearly at play when the extent of the cerebral pathology is relatively minor, and when the site of the lesion does not result in a change of the patient's personality and motivation. Furthermore, a rapidly progressive disease is liable to reduce the modifying effects of psychological factors. The current emotional state of the patient, whether related to the awareness of cognitive deficits or reactive to some environmental event or situation, is likely to influence the degree of severity of intellectual impairment. Anxiety and depression are particularly important in this regard, since they tend to reduce the patient's efficiency in performance.

### Clinical Features

The hallmark of dementia is the deterioration of efficiency in intellectual or cognitive performance, of sufficient severity to interfere with the patient's social or occupational functioning or both. The deteriorated or impaired performance reflects cognitive deficits in the areas of memory, abstract thinking, problem solving, and the learning of new knowledge and skills. Additional essential features include the impairment of judgment, defective control of impulses and emotions, and personality change—that is, either an accentuation or an alteration of premorbid personality traits.

In mild or early cases of dementia, difficulties in sustaining mental performance may be observed, with early appearance of fatigue and a tendency for the patient to fail when the task is novel or complex, or both, or if it requires shifts in problem-solving strategy. As the disorder progresses, failures to perform become increasingly more frequent and spread to simple everyday tasks, so that the patient is rendered incapable of taking care of his or her basic needs.

Memory impairment is typically an early and prominent feature. There is usually general forgetfulness or anterograde amnesia, reflecting difficulty in learning new material and in retaining current experiences.

Memory impairment is at least partly respon-

TABLE IV
DISEASES AND CONDITIONS CAUSING DEMENTIA*

Degenerative diseases of the central nervous system
  Alzheimer's disease
  Senile dementia
  Simple cortical atrophy
  Pick's disease
  Huntington's chorea
  Parkinson's disease
  Progressive supranuclear palsy
Vascular disorders
  Multiinfarct dementia
  Carotid artery occlusive disease
  Cranial arteritis
  Subarachnoid hemorrhage
  Arteriovenous malformation
  Cerebral embolism
  Binswanger's disease
Metabolic, endocrine, and nutritional disorders
  Hepatic, renal, or pulmonary failure
  Dialysis dementia
  Endocrinopathies: hypothyroidism, hypopituitarism, hypoparathyroidism, hyperparathyroidism, Addison's disease, Cushing's syndrome, hyperinsulinism
  Chronic disorders of electrolyte metabolism: hypercalcemia, hypocalcemia, hyponatremia, hypernatremia, hypokalemia
  Hypoxia or anoxia of any origin, such as secondary to cardiac arrest or congestive heart failure
  Hepatolenticular degeneration (Wilson's disease)
  Paget's disease
  Porphyria
  Avitaminosis: cyanocobalamine, folate, nicotinic acid, thiamine
  Vitamin intoxication: vitamins A and D
  Remote effects of carcinoma and lymphomas
Intracranial space-occupying lesions
  Neoplasm, benign or malignant
  Aneurysm
  Colloid cyst
  Chronic subdural hematoma
  Chronic abscess
  Parasitic cyst
  Tuberculoma
  Lymphoma and leukemia
Head trauma
Epilepsy
Infections
  Meningitis of any cause
  Encephalitis of any cause
  Brucellosis
  Syphilis
  Subacute sclerosing panencephalitis
  Creutzfeldt-Jakob disease
  Kuru
  Multifocal leukoencephalopathy
Intoxication
  Alcohol
  Heavy metals: mercury, lead, arsenic, thallium
  Carbon monoxide
  Medical drugs, such as barbiturates
Normal-pressure hydrocephalus
Heat stroke
Electric injury
Disorders of the hematopoietic system
  Erythremia
  Thrombotic thrombocytopenic purpura
Miscellaneous diseases of unknown origin
  Sarcoidosis
  Histiocytosis X
  Multiple sclerosis

* Table by Z J Lipowski, M.D.

sible for faulty orientation in space and time. The patient with advanced dementia tends to get lost in familiar surroundings—that is, he displays spatial disorientation. Impaired orientation for time may appear early and always precedes disorientation for place and person.

The patient exhibits a reduced ability to apply what Kurt Goldstein called the abstract attitude: the patient displays difficulty in generalizing from a single instance, in forming concepts, in grasping similarities and differences between concepts, in distinguishing essential from nonessential properties of things or situations, in solving problems, and in planning action. Further, the ability to calculate, to reason logically, and to make sound judgments is more or less defective.

Defective control of impulses and emotions, altered emotionality, and personality change constitute an integral part of dementia, and influence the patient's relationships with other people.

Emotional, cognitive, and behavioral responses to subjective awareness of intellectual deficits, attempts at compensating for the defects, and strategies used to avoid failures in intellectual performance, constitute the associated features of dementia. They include compensatory, protective, and reactive symptoms.

### Course and Prognosis

Intellectual deterioration with an onset after the age of 18 should be designated as dementia. If the clinical picture of dementia develops before the age of 18 in a person who had previously had normal intelligence, both mental retardation and dementia should be diagnosed. Onset before the age of 40 is relatively uncommon, and the frequency of onset increases after the age of 60.

The onset of dementia may be sudden or acute, as a result of head trauma, cardiac arrest, or encephalitis. More often, however, the onset is insidious or gradual, as in Alzheimer's disease, senile dementia, cerebrovascular disease, and hypothyroidism.

The syndrome may gradually recede over a period of weeks, months, or even years, in response to treatment or as a result of the natural healing processes. It may progress relentlessly and steadily, or in a stepwise fashion, or it may remain relatively stationary after a single acute insult. This variability of the onset, course, and prognosis of dementia must be emphasized, since the term dementia has come to connote progressive and irreversible intellectual deterioration. This connotation has, no doubt, originated in an erroneous equation between dementia, a syndrome, and presenile and senile dementias, a group of typically progressive and incurable cerebral diseases.

The earliest symptoms of dementia are manifold and subtle and may escape the attention of people in the patient's environment. The patient's personality is apt to undergo a more or less marked change in the direction of accentuation or alteration of his or her personality characteristics. In the case of accentuation, personality traits are exhibited in bolder relief, sometimes to the point of caricature.

Alcohol is poorly tolerated by demented persons, and may precipitate grossly disinhibited behavior.

As dementia progresses or is temporarily severe, the symptoms tend to become more conspicuous, and new ones may appear. Intermittent or constant defects in orientation, memory, judgment, and thinking become clearly evident. At this stage, the family or the employer is liable to become alarmed, but the patient is likely to be oblivious of his or her deterioration. He or she may display insomnia with agitated and psychotic behavior, and with a tendency to wander away from home. The patient may get lost in surroundings familiar to him or her and be picked up wandering helplessly in the streets. Control of impulses and emotions is clearly defective. Emotions tend to be blunted, labile, and inappropriately expressed. Perceptual discrimination is reduced, and misperceptions—that is, illusions and hallucinations—may appear, especially at night. Social judgment is grossly impaired, and the patient may act in a socially embarrassing or even in a frankly antisocial manner. In the end, the patient becomes an empty shell of his or her former self—fully disoriented, incoherent, amnesic, and incontinent of urine and feces.

### Diagnosis

The diagnosis of dementia involves two aspects: recognition of the syndrome on clinical grounds and identification of its cause. An early diagnosis is of utmost importance.

Clinical diagnosis of dementia is based on information derived from the history obtained from the patient and any available witnesses, and a mental status examination. Evidence of change in the patient's accustomed performance and behavior in ordinary life situations is looked for. Any report of such a change in a person known to suffer from some form of cerebral pathology, or even in one not known to be physically ill, should raise the question of dementia, especially if the patient is more than 40 years old and lacks a positive psychiatric history.

Complaints by the patient about intellectual impairment and forgetfulness should be noted, as should the frequently present evasions, denials, and rationalizations aimed at concealing cognitive deficits. A patient who becomes angry or sarcastic, or who changes the subject when asked about his or her intellectual performance, should prompt the clinician to pursue a determined search for possible cognitive detects.

An evaluation of a patient's mental status is carried out throughout the psychiatric interview. The diagnosis of dementia rests on finding the presence of its essential features (see Table V).

The patient's appearance and behavior should be noted. A dull, apathetic, or vacuous facial expression and manner, an overly easy change of emotions, sloppy grooming, uninhibited remarks, or silly jokes, all suggest the presence of dementia.

Once dementia has been diagnosed on clinical grounds, with or without the aid of a neuropsychological examination, a determined attempt must be made to establish its cause. The question that should be foremost in the clinician's mind is whether a treatable cause is responsible for the dementia in the patient.

Dementia needs to be distinguished from other organic brain syndromes, and from nonorganic mental disorders.

The distinction between delirium and dementia may be difficult and at times impossible to make at a given time. Delirium is distinguished by rapid onset, generally brief duration, fluctuation of the cognitive impairment during the course of the day, nocturnal exacerbation of symptoms, marked disturbance of the sleep-wakefulness cycle, and prominent disturbances of attention and perception. Hallucinations, especially visual ones, and transient delusions are more common in delirium than in dementia. Intellectual deterioration lasting without interruption for more than 1 month is more likely to represent dementia than delirium.

The main diagnostic problem, one most important, clinically, concerns the separation of dementia from an affective disorder, especially depression. A depressive disorder frequently accompanies dementia and may be one of its presenting features. Pseudodementia is a term used to refer to functional psychiatric disorders when they feature cognitive dysfunction resembling dementia (see Table VI).

Occasionally, dementia needs to be differentiated from chronic schizophrenia or a factitious illness with psychological symptoms. Diagnostic reasoning in such cases follows a direction similar to the one just suggested for depression.

TABLE V
DIAGNOSTIC CRITERIA FOR DEMENTIA*

A. A loss of intellectual abilities of sufficient severity to interfere with social or occupational functioning.

B. Memory impairment.

C. At least one of the following:

(1) impairment of abstract thinking, as manifested by concrete interpretation of proverbs, inability to find similarities and differences between related words, difficulty in defining words and concepts, and other similiar tasks

(2) impaired judgment

(3) other disturbances of higher cortical function, such as aphasia (disorder of language due to brain dysfunction), apraxia (inability to carry out motor activities despite intact comprehension and motor function), agnosia (failure to recognize or identify objects despite intact sensory function), "constructional difficulty" (e.g., inability to copy three-dimensional figures, assemble blocks, or arrange sticks in specific designs)

(4) personality change, i.e., alteration or accentuation of premorbid traits

D. State of consciousness not clouded (i.e., does not meet the criteria for Delirium or Intoxication, although these may be superimposed).

E. Either (1) or (2):

(1) evidence from the history, physical examination, or laboratory tests, of a specific organic factor that is judged to be etiologically related to the disturbance.

(2) in the absence of such evidence, an organic factor necessary for the development of the syndrome can be presumed if conditions other than Organic Mental Disorders have been reasonably excluded and if the behavioral change represents cognitive impairment in a variety of areas

\* From American Psychiatric Association: *Diagnostic and Statistical Manual of Mental Disorders*, ed 3. American Psychiatric Association, Washington, DC, 1980. Used with permission.

### Treatment

Treatment of dementia should be directed at its cause. Unfortunately, in more than one-half of the cases of dementia in the elderly, no effective treatment of the underlying cerebral disorder is available. This does not mean that nothing can be done to alleviate the patient's distress to some extent; on the contrary, therapeutic nihilism is detrimental to the patient's welfare, as it ignores the capacity for better adjustment, for coping with deficits, and for compensation for the deficits the patient exhibits.

### Amnestic Syndrome (Amnesic Syndrome, Korsakoff's Syndrome)

#### Definition

Amnestic syndrome is an organic mental disorder characterized by an impairment of memory as the single or predominant cognitive defect. The memory pathology is of two types; retrograde amnesia—that is, a pathological loss

TABLE VI
DIFFERENTIATION OF DEMENTIA FROM DEPRESSIVE PSEUDODEMENTIA*

| | Dementia | Pseudodementia |
|---|---|---|
| Onset | Intellectual deficits antedate depression | Depressive symptoms antedate cognitive deficits |
| Presentation of symptoms | Patient minimizes or denies cognitive deficits, tries to conceal them by circumstantiality, perseveration, changing topic of conversation | Patient complains vocally of memory impairment and poor intellectual performance, exaggerates and dwells on these deficits |
| Appearance and behavior | Often neglected, sloppy; manner facetious or apathetic and indifferent; catastrophic reaction may be evoked; emotional expression often labile and superficial | Facial expression sad, worried; manner retarded or agitated, never facetious or euphoric; bemoans or ridicules own impaired performance but no true catastrophic reaction |
| Response to questions | Often evasive, angry, or sarcastic when pressed for answers, or tries hard to answer correctly but just misses | Often slow, "I don't know" type of answer |
| Intellectual performance | Usually globally impaired and consistently poor | Often confined to memory impairment; inconsistent; if globally impaired, it is so because patient refuses to make effort |
| Sodium amobarbital interview | All cognitive deficits accentuated | Performance improved |

* Table by Z J Lipowski, M.D.

of memories established before the onset of the illness—and anterograde amnesia—that is, reduced ability to recall current events. The disorder is caused by focal damage or dysfunction involving the cerebral substrate of memory.

### Causes

A number of organic pathological factors and conditions can give rise to the amnestic syndrome. The most common cause in this country is probably thiamine deficiency associated with chronic alcoholism.

In the absence of epidemiological data, no definite statement about the frequency of the various causative associations can be given. Most factors and disorders known to be associated with the amnestic syndrome are listed in Table VII.

### Clinical Features

The core feature of the amnestic syndrome is the impairment of memory. Regardless of the cause, there is an impairment of recent memory, with preservation of the ability for immediate recall, as tested by digit span, for example. Remote memories are preserved. The ability to learn new material is defective, the patient is unable to learn and remember such information as the name of the hospital or of his or her physician, and the recall of events of the past decade or longer is defective. There is, thus, both anterograde amnesia and retrograde amnesia.

Disorientation to some extent is often present in the Wernicke-Korsakoff syndrome, but it is not an invariable feature of the amnestic syndrome of other causes. Confabulation is also a

TABLE VII
CAUSES OF AMNESTIC SYNDROME*

Thiamine deficiency (Wernicke-Korsakoff's syndrome) usually due to alcoholism
Head trauma with damage of the diencephalic or temporal regions; postconcussive states; whiplash injury
Brain tumor involving the floor and the walls of the third ventricle or both hippocampal formations
Subarachnoid hemorrhage
Intoxication: carbon monoxide, isoniazid, arsenic, lead
Vascular disorders: bilateral hippocampal infarction due to thrombosis or embolism occluding posterior cerebral arteries or their inferior temporal branches
Intracranial infections: herpes simplex encephalitis, tuberculous meningitis
Cerebral anoxia: after unsuccessful hanging attempt, cardiac arrest, inadequate aeration or prolonged hypotension during general anesthesia
Degenerative cerebral diseases: Alzheimer's disease, senile dementia
Bilateral temporal lobectomy with bilateral hippocampal lesions
Surgery for ruptured aneurysm of the anterior communicating artery
Electroshock treatment
Epilepsy
Transient global amnesia

* Table by Z J Lipowski, M.D.

common but not a constant characteristic. Lack of insight into memory deficits is frequently prominent, and the patient tends to minimize, rationalize, or even explicitly deny their presence. Minor deficits in perception and concept formation may be found in alcoholic Korsakoff patients. Lack of initiative, emotional blandness, and apathy are common. The patient is typically alert and responsive, and has no impairment of grasp of surroundings, or of communications addressed to him or her. He or she is able to reason and solve problems within the limits imposed by the forward memory span.

### Course and Prognosis

The mode of onset, the course, and the prognosis of the amnestic syndrome depend on its cause in the given case. The syndrome may be transient or persistent, and its outcome may be complete or partial recovery of memory function, or an irreversible or even progressive memory defect. Typically, Wernicke's encephalopathy comes on subacutely in a patient with a history of many years of alcohol abuse, and is accompanied or followed by amnestic (Korsakoff's) syndrome. Wernicke's encephalopathy features quiet delirium, ataxia of gait, nystagmus, and ophthalmoplegia. Delirium clears up within a month or so, and, in about 85 percent of all survivors of the encephalopathy, the amnestic syndrome either becomes manifest or has been evident all along. A small minority of patients develop the amnestic (Korsakoff's) syndrome without a preceding episode of Wernicke's encephalopathy.

Transient amnestic syndrome may result from a head injury, carbon monoxide poisoning, temporal lobe epilepsy, vascular insufficiency—for example, transient global amnesia and migraine—electroconvulsive therapy, intake of such drugs as isoniazid and barbiturates, brain tumor, cardiac arrest, or a subarachnoid hemorrhage. Permanent amnestic syndrome of some degree of severity occasionally follows a head trauma or carbon monoxide poisoning. Persistent memory impairment may also result from a subarachnoid hemorrhage, cerebral infarction, herpes simplex encephalitis, and tuberculous meningitis. Slowly progressive amnestic syndrome should suggest a brain tumor, Alzheimer's disease, or senile dementia.

### Diagnosis

The diagnosis of amnestic syndrome rests on finding its essential features (see Table VIII).

The amnestic syndrome needs to be differentiated from delirium and dementia, and from psychogenic loss of memory. In both dementia and delirium, there is memory impairment of some degree of severity, which is, however, only one component of global intellectual or cognitive dysfunction. Psychogenic loss of memory characterizes certain dissociative disorders, such as psychogenic amnesia and fugue, which feature sudden onset of retrograde amnesia for personally significant memories, usually accompanied by a loss of sense of personal identity of which

TABLE VIII
DIAGNOSTIC CRITERIA FOR AMNESTIC SYNDROME*

A. Both short-term memory impairment (inability to learn new information) and long-term memory impairment (inability to remember information that was known in the past) are the predominant clinical features.

B. No clouding of consciousness, as in Delirium and Intoxication, or general loss of major intellectual abilities, as in Dementia.

C. Evidence, from the history, physical examination, or laboratory tests, of a specific organic factor that is judged to be etiologically related to the disturbance.

* From American Psychiatric Association: *Diagnostic and Statistical Manual of Mental Disorders*, ed 3. American Psychiatric Association, Washington, DC, 1980. Used with permission.

the patient may or may not be aware. There is usually evidence of a subjectively stressful or conflict-arousing precipitating event. Anterograde amnesia is rarely psychogenic. Psychogenic amnesia or fugue may be precipitated by a head trauma, an epileptic seizure, or acute alcohol intoxication, and those factors may make diagnosis difficult on occasion. In the psychogenic memory disorders, the patient's responses are typically inconsistent and indicate an intact memory for personally neutral information. A sodium amobarbital interview may help distinguish amnestic syndrome from psychogenic amnesia by bringing out the motivation for the psychogenic amnesia.

### Treatment

Treatment of the amnestic syndrome must first of all be directed at its cause. It is particularly important to try to prevent the development of Wernicke's encephalopathy in the alcoholic patient by treating the alcoholism and urging the patient to take vitamins regularly. Once encephalopathy has developed, it must be treated vigorously to prevent or minimize the amnestic syndrome that is likely to follow. Thiamine, 50 mg parenterally daily until the patient is able to resume a normal diet, is recommended. In addition, the patient should receive other B-complex vitamins.

## Organic Hallucinosis

### Definition

Organic hallucinosis is a mental disorder in which recurrent or persistent hallucinations in a state of full wakefulness are the predominant or only symptom, and are attributed to some clearly defined organic factor.

## Causes

Organic hallucinosis is probably uncommon, but relevant epidemiological data are lacking. It is most likely to be encountered in a setting of chronic alcoholism or hallucinogen abuse, or as a toxic side effect of such drugs as levodopa. Conditions associated with hallucinosis are listed in Table IX.

## Clinical Features

Hallucinations in one or more sensory modalities that are either recurrent or persistent, and are experienced in a state of full wakefulness and alertness, constitute the essential feature.

Insight into the experience of hallucinations may range in degree from full to none. In the case of no insight, the patient has the delusional conviction that his or her hallucinations are true perceptions, and he or she tends to act accordingly. Insight may fluctuate in the same patient and is not to be viewed as a simple all-or-none feature. Delusions must be restricted to the existence or the content of the hallucinations, or both, if the diagnosis of organic hallucinosis, rather than a diagnosis of organic delusional syndrome, is to apply.

Any sensory modality may be involved in hallucinosis, but auditory hallucinosis is probably the most common form, followed by the visual and tactile forms.

In alcoholic hallucinosis, there are typically threatening, criticizing, or insulting voices of people speaking about the patient in the third person. Visual hallucinosis often takes the form of scenes involving diminutive (Lilliputian) human figures or various small animals. As a rule, the patient is fully oriented, but may display a mild intellectual deficit. Rare musical hallucinosis typically features religious songs.

## Course and Prognosis

The course and the prognosis depend on the underlying pathology. The onset is usually acute, and the average duration is days to weeks. In some patients hallucinosis becomes chronic, and schizophrenic features may appear. Some cases of acute hallucinosis progress to delirium.

## Diagnosis

Hallucinosis is diagnosed on the basis of the patient's history, and, on psychiatric examination, on the absence of the features of delirium, dementia, organic delusional syndrome, and organic affective syndrome. The appearance of hallucinosis in a patient should prompt the search for organic causative factors. Visual hallucinosis should raise the question of a focal cerebral lesion, hallucinogen abuse, side effects of medical drugs, migraine, or temporal arteritis. Auditory hallucinosis should prompt an inquiry about alcohol abuse.

Organic hallucinosis needs to be distinguished from delirium, in which the fluctuating impairment of attention and cognitive functions may be accompanied by hallucinations. In dementia, hallucinations may occur but are overshadowed by intellectual deficits. In the organic delusional syndrome, hallucinations may be present, but delusions, extending beyond the content and the veridical nature of the hallucinations, are in the foreground. In the amnestic syndrome, it may be difficult to tell hallucinations from confabulations, but memory impairment is the most prominent symptom. Epilepsy, especially of the temporal lobe type, may feature auditory or visual hallucinations, or both. Such hallucinations are usually part of an ictus, are accompanied by other ictal phenomena, are paroxysmal, and occur in a setting of reduced and not clear awareness. Diagnostic criteria for this syndrome are presented in Table X.

## Treatment

Treatment depends on the underlying condition. An anxious or agitated patient needs to be reassured that he or she is suffering from what is likely to be a temporary mental disorder. The content of the hallucinations may provide clues about the patient's inner conflicts and fears that may need to be dealt with by psychotherapy. It is best to hospitalize and sedate a markedly fearful and delusional patient, such as one suffering from alcoholic hallucinosis.

TABLE IX
CAUSATIVE FACTORS IN ORGANIC HALLUCINOSIS*

Substance absue
  Alcohol (acute alcoholic hallucinosis)
  Hallucinogens: LSD, psilocybin, mescaline, morning glory seed
  Cocaine
Drug toxicity: levodopa, bromocriptine, amantadine, ephedrine, pentazocine, propranolol, methylphenidate
Space-occupying lesions of the brain:
  Neoplasm: craniopharyngioma, chromophobe adenoma, meningioma of the olfactory groove, temporal lobe tumors
  Aneurysm
  Abscess
Temporal arteritis
Migraine
Hypothyroidism
Neurosyphilis
Huntington's chorea
Cerebrovascular disease
Disease of sense organs: bilateral cataracts, glaucoma, otosclerosis

* Table by Z. J. Lipowski, M.D.

TABLE X
DIAGNOSTIC CRITERIA FOR ORGANIC HALLUCINOSIS*

A. Persistent or recurrent hallucinations are the predominant clinical feature.

B. No clouding of consciousness, as in Delirium; no significant loss of intellectual abilities, as in Dementia; no predominant disturbance of mood, as in Organic Affective Syndrome; no predominant delusions, as in Organic Delusional Syndrome.

C. Evidence, from the history, physical examination, or laboratory tests, of a specific organic factor that is judged to be etiologically related to the disturbance.

*From American Psychiatric Association: *Diagnostic and Statistical Manual of Mental Disorders*, ed 3. American Psychiatric Association, Washington, DC, 1980. Used with permission.

## Organic Delusional Syndrome

### Definition

Organic delusional syndrome is a mental disorder characterized by the predominance of delusions in a state of full wakefulness and alertness that are attributed to some clearly defined organic factor.

### Causes

A variety of chemical substances and a number of cerebral and systemic diseases may induce the syndrome. The syndrome often—but not always—lifts after the toxic agent has been withdrawn or the physical illness has subsided. Greater than chance association seems to exist between amphetamine intoxication and paranoid psychosis, and between lesions involving the limbic system and schizophreniform psychosis.

### Clinical Features

The essential feature of the organic delusional syndrome is the presence of delusions in a state of full wakefulness and alertness that are attributed to a clearly defined organic factor. The delusions may be systematized or not, and their content may vary—that is, they may be persecutory delusions, delusions of jealousy, and so forth. The disorder does not meet the criteria for delirium, dementia, or organic hallucinosis.

Hallucinations of any type, and various other features of schizophrenic disorders, may be present. Passivity feelings, thought disorder, and auditory and tactile hallucinations are significantly less common in schizophrenia-like psychoses than in schizophrenic disorders, but catatonic symptoms are more common in schizophrenia-like psychoses than in schizophrenic disorders. Affective and anxiety symptoms, excitement, depersonalization, and body image disturbances may occur. A mild cognitive impairment, insufficient for the diagnosis of dementia, may be present.

### Course and Prognosis

The course and the prognosis depend to some extent on the underlying cause. Symptoms may outlast the remission of the cerebral disorder by varying periods of time, and may even become chronic. On the whole, however, their prognosis seems to be more favorable than that of schizophrenic disorders, especially in the younger age groups.

### Diagnosis

Diagnosis of the syndrome involves two indispensable components: (1) establishing the presence of the essential features by means of a psychiatric history and examination and (2) finding evidence of an organic factor antedating the onset of the syndrome and judged to be of causal significance (see Table XI).

The syndrome needs to be distinguished from schizophrenic, schizophreniform, and paranoid disorders. This distinction depends on finding evidence of a specific organic factor judged to be causatively significant. Organic hallucinosis is differentiated by the absence of delusions or, if delusions are present, by their close relationship to hallucinations. Admittedly, in some cases such a distinction is difficult to make, as the two syndromes may shade into one another.

### Treatment

Management of the syndrome depends on its underlying cause, which should be identified and treated. Otherwise, symptomatic treatment follows the general guidelines applicable to schizophrenic and paranoid disorders.

## Organic Affective Syndrome

### Definition

Organic affective syndrome is a mental disorder characterized by either a depressive or a manic mood disorder that is attributed to a clearly defined organic factor.

### Causes

A number of somatic disorders and drugs have been implicated in the causes of depressive and, to a smaller extent, manic disorders. A depressive syndrome of some degree of severity is a common concomitant of physical illness, including cerebral disease, and may be viewed as a

TABLE XI
DIAGNOSTIC CRITERIA FOR ORGANIC DELUSIONAL SYNDROME*

A. Delusions are the predominant clinical feature.

B. There is no clouding of consciousness, as in Delirium; there is no significant loss of intellectual abilities, as in Dementia; there are no prominent hallucinations, as in Organic Hallucinosis.

C. There is evidence, from the history, physical examination, or laboratory tests, of a specific organic factor that is judged to be etiologically related to the disturbance.

*From American Psychiatric Association: *Diagnostic and Statistical Manual of Mental Disorders*, ed 3. American Psychiatric Association, Washington, DC, 1980. Used with permission.

psychopathological response to the meaning of the illness and its consequences for the patient. If such a meaning is construed as a loss of personally cherished values, a depressive disorder of some degree of severity may ensue. However, it can be hypothesized that in some cerebral disorders of various causes, a depressive, or occasionally a manic, syndrome may be induced by direct interference with the neurophysiological and biochemical processes subserving normal mood. In such cases, an affective disorder may arise without the interposition of the meaning of illness for the patient. This hypothesis is compatible with the current tendency to view the causes of depressive disorders as heterogeneous. Conditions that have been reported to be associated with depressive or manic features are listed in Table XII.

### Clinical Features

Disturbances of mood closely resembling those observed in either a depressive or a manic episode are the predominant and essential clinical feature (see Table XIII). These disturbances are attributed to a clearly defined organic factor, whose onset must antedate that of the affective syndrome, and which is judged to be causally related to the affective syndrome. The essential features of delirium, dementia, organic hallucinosis, and organic delusional syndrome are absent. The syndrome may vary in severity from mild to severe or psychotic, and may be descriptively indistinguishable from an affective disorder, depressive or manic.

Delusions and hallucinations, and other associated features of the type encountered in affective disorders, may be present.

### Course and Prognosis

The onset may be acute or insidious, and the course varies, and depends to some extent on the underlying cause. The removal of the cause need not result in the patient's prompt recovery from the affective syndrome, since the syndrome has considerable momentum of its own, and may persist for weeks or months after the successful treatment of the underlying physical condition or the withdrawal of the implicated toxic agent.

TABLE XII
CONDITIONS ASSOCIATED WITH ORGANIC AFFECTIVE SYNDROME*

Drugs: reserpine, corticosteroids, methyldopa, levodopa, cycloserine, ethionamide, oral contraceptives, amphetamines, hallucinogens
Endocrine diseases: hypothyroidism, Cushing's syndrome, Addison's disease, hyperparathyroidism
Infectious diseases: influenza, infectious mononucleosis, infectious hepatitis, viral pneumonia
Pernicious anemia
Carcinoma of the pancreas
Brain tumor
Systemic lupus erythematosus
Parkinsonism
Carcinoid syndrome
Neurosyphilis

*Table by Z J Lipowski, M.D.

### Diagnosis

Diagnosis involves two essential components: (1) establishing the presence of the essential features by means of a history and psychiatric examination and (2) identifying the organic factor judged to be responsible for the disorder. Such judgment is based on the finding that the putative organic causal factor antedated the onset of the affective disorder and is known to be associated with the disorder.

### Treatment

Management of the organic affective syndrome involves treatment of the physical disorder and the affective symptoms. Psychopharmacological treatment may be called for and should follow the guidelines applicable to the treatment of affective disorders, with due regard to the coexistent physical conditions. Psychotherapy may be indicated as an adjunct to the other treatments.

## Organic Personality Syndrome

### Definition

Organic personality syndrome designates a change in personality style or traits manifested primarily by reduced drive or by an impaired control of behavioral expressions of emotions and impulses or both. There must be evidence of an organic factor antedating the onset of the

TABLE XIII
DIAGNOSTIC CRITERIA FOR ORGANIC AFFECTIVE SYNDROME*

A. The predominant disturbance is a disturbance in mood, with at least two of the associated symptoms listed in criterion B for manic or major depressive episode.

B. No clouding of consciousness, as in Delirium; no significant loss of intellectual abilities, as in Dementia; no predominant delusions or hallucinations, as in Organic Delusional Syndrome or Organic Hallucinosis.

C. Evidence, from the history, physical examination, or laboratory tests, of a specific organic factor that is judged to be etiologically related to the disturbance.

* From American Psychiatric Association: *Diagnostic and Statistical Manual of Mental Disorders*, ed 3. American Psychiatric Association, Washington, DC, 1980. Used with permission.

syndrome and judged to be causally significant for its occurrence.

## Causes

The conditions most often associated with the syndrome are listed in Table XIV. Head trauma is probably the most important cause of the syndrome. Subarachnoid hemorrhage, especially with anterior communicating artery aneurysm, is another significant cause.

## Clinical Features

Change in the personality style and behavior manifested primarily by the impaired control of the expression of emotions and impulses is the cardinal feature. Emotions are characteristically labile and shallow, with euphoria or apathy predominant. Euphoria may mimic hypomania, but true elation is absent, and the patient may admit that he or she does not really feel happy. There is a hollow and silly ring to the patient's excitement and facile jocularity. Such euphoria may readily give way to frank apathy and unconcern or to anger. Apathy may give a superficial impression of depressed mood, but true sadness and depression are uncommon. Temper outbursts with little or no provocation may occur, especially after alcohol ingestion, and may result in violent behavior. The expression of impulses is characteristically disinhibited and may be manifested by inappropriate jokes, a coarse manner, improper sexual advances, or even by frankly antisocial conduct resulting in conflicts with the law, such as assaults on others, sexual misdemeanors, and shoplifting. The degree of disinhibition may vary in severity from patient to patient, but it has to be sufficiently pronounced to be recognized as a change from the patient's characteristic style of interacting with his or her social environment. Foresight and the ability to anticipate the social or legal consequences of one's actions are typically diminished. Many patients exhibit low drive and initiative, and have difficulty in completing initiated actions that demand sustained motivation to be consummated. Concurrently, psychomotor

TABLE XIV
CONDITIONS ASSOCIATED WITH ORGANIC PERSONALITY SYNDROME*

Head trauma
Subarachnoid hemorrhage and other vascular accidents
Space-occupying lesions of the brain: neoplasm, aneurysm, abscess, granuloma
Temporal lobe epilepsy
Postencephalitic parkinsonism
Huntington's chorea
Multiple sclerosis
Endocrine disorders
Chronic poisoning: manganese, mercury
Drugs: cannabis, LSD, steroids, etc.
Neurosyphilis
Arteritis, such as in systemic lupus erythematosus

* Table by Z J Lipowski, M.D.

activity is generally reduced but may be episodically increased to the point of overactivity.

Mild disorders of cognitive function often coexist, but do not amount to intellectual deterioration. Patients tend to be inattentive and may exhibit disorders of recent memory that seem to be due to a lack of initiative or motivation to recall what he or she actually remembers. With some prodding, however, the patient is likely to recall what he or she claims to have forgotten.

## Course and Prognosis

Both the course and the prognosis of organic personality syndrome depend on its cause. The syndrome may follow a period of coma and delirium in cases of head trauma or vascular accident, and may remain permanently. It may be succeeded by dementia in cases of brain tumor or Huntington's chorea. It may be reversed in cases of chronic intoxication or in postencephalitic parkinsonism treated with levodopa. Some patients require custodial care or, at least, close supervision in order to meet their basic needs, avoid repeated conflicts with the law, or protect them and their families against the hostility of others or against destitution resulting from impulsive and ill-conceived actions.

### Diagnosis

Diagnosis of the organic personality syndrome comprises two aspects: (1) establishing a change in the person's customary behavior that fulfills the essential criteria and is accomplished by a psychiatric history and examination and (2) identifying an organic factor judged to be responsible for the change in behavior (see Table XV).

### Treatment

Management of the organic personality syndrome involves treatment of the underlying organic condition if the condition is treatable. Psychopharmacological treatment of the symptoms may be indicated in some cases—for example, imipramine for organic emotionality and lithium for violent behavior. The effectiveness of psychotropic drugs in the condition has not yet been sufficiently demonstrated.

The patient may need counseling to help him or her avoid difficulties at work, or to prevent social embarrassment. A change of job or even premature retirement may be indicated. The patient's family, as a rule, needs emotional support and concrete advice on how to help minimize the patient's tendency to undesirable conduct. Alcohol should be avoided. The patient should not be left in charge of minors. Social engagements should be curtailed if the patient has a tendency to act in a grossly offensive manner. Indeed, the clinician must not abrogate his or her therapeutic obligations just because the patient is unlikely to gain insight or to improve substantially.

### Intoxication and Withdrawal

As used in DSM-III, the concept of intoxication is a residual category for a clinical picture that does not correspond to any of the specific organic brain syndromes. An essential feature is maladaptive behavior; also, it is a substance-specific syndrome that is due to the recent use and presence in the body of an intoxicating substance. Common examples of intoxication might be maladaptive behavior caused by cannabis, amphetamines, or alcohol. Table XVI summarizes the criteria for intoxication, and the diagnostic criteria for withdrawal are presented in Table XVII. As with intoxication, the withdrawal syndrome that develops varies according to the substance involved.

Intoxication and withdrawal from opiates, nonnarcotic agents, and alcohol are all discussed in Chapter 19, Drug Dependence. Table XVIII outlines the criteria for the DSM-III diagnostic category "Atypical or Mixed Organic Brain Syndrome."

### Dementias Arising in the Senium and Presenium

This is a classification of mental disorder which encompasses a single category called primary degenerative dementia. The category is subdivided according to the age of onset for the purpose of historical continuity and to maintain continuity with ICD as follows: primary degenerative dementia, senile onset (after age 65), and primary degenerative dementia, presenile onset (age 65 and below). Formerly dementia associated with Alzheimer's disease was called senile dementia and Pick's was called presenile dementia; however that division no longer applies because almost all dementias occurring in the senium and presenium are caused by Alzheimer's disease and the differentiation is made on histopathological grounds rather than clinical grounds.

### Primary Degenerative Dementia

Primary degenerative dementia is a clinical disorder characterized by a severe loss of intel-

TABLE XV
DIAGNOSTIC CRITERIA FOR ORGANIC PERSONALITY SYNDROME*

A. A marked change in behavior or personality involving at least one of the following:

   (1) emotional lability, e.g., explosive temper outbursts, sudden crying
   (2) impairment in impulse control, e.g., poor social judgment, sexual indiscretions, shoplifting
   (3) marked apathy and indifference, e.g., no interest in usual hobbies
   (4) suspiciousness or paranoid ideation

B. No clouding of consciousness, as in Delirium; no significant loss of intellectual abilities, as in Dementia; no predominant disturbance of mood, as in Organic Affective Syndrome; no predominant delusions or hallucinations, as in Organic Delusional Syndrome or Organic Hallucinosis.

C. Evidence, from the history, physical examination, or laboratory tests, of a specific organic factor that is judged to be etiologically related to the disturbance.

D. This diagnosis is not given to a child or adolescent if the clincial picture is limited to the features that characterize Attention Deficit Disorder.

TABLE XVI
DIAGNOSTIC CRITERIA FOR INTOXICATION*

A. Development of a substance-specific syndrome that follows the recent ingestion and presence in the body of a substance.

B. Maladaptive behavior during the waking state due to the effect of the substance on the central nervous system, e.g., impaired judgment, belligerence.

C. The clinical picture does not correspond to any of the specific Organic Brain Syndromes, such as Delirium, Organic Delusional Syndrome, Organic Hallucinosis, or Organic Affective Syndrome.

*From American Psychiatric Association: *Diagnostic and Statistical Manual of Mental Disorders*, ed 3. American Psychiatric Association, Washignton, DC, 1980. Used with permission.

TABLE XVII
DIAGNOSTIC CRITERIA FOR WITHDRAWAL*

A. Development of a substance-specific syndrome that follows the cessation of or reduction in intake of a substance that was previously regularly used by the individual to induce a state of intoxication.

B. The clinical picture does not correspond to any of the specific Organic Brain Syndromes, such as Delirium, Organic Delusional Syndrome, Organic Hallucinosis, or Organic Affective Syndrome.

*From American Psychiatric Association: *Diagnostic and Statistical Manual of Mental Disorders*, ed 3. American Psychiatric Association, Washington, DC, 1980. Used with permission.

TABLE XVIII
DIAGNOSTIC CRITERIA FOR ATYPICAL OR MIXED ORGANIC BRAIN SYNDROME*

A. The disturbance occurs during the waking state and does not fulfill the criteria for any of the previously described Organic Brain Syndromes.

B. Evidence, from the history, physical examination, or laboratory tests, of a specific organic factor that is judged to be etiologically related to the disturbance.

*From American Psychiatric Association: *Diagnostic and Statistical Manual of Mental Disorders*, ed 3. American Psychiatric Association, Washington, DC, 1980. Used with permission.

lectual function in an elderly patient for which no other cause is found. It is progressive and insidious. Clinically, the diagnosis remains one of exclusion, and the disorder can be differentiated from normal senescence only by considering the degree of dementia. The differentiation from other forms of dementia (such as multi-infarct dementia) requires a thorough general evaluation, a neurological evaluation, and such laboratory tests as are indicated.

In the United States, first admissions to state and county mental institutions for elderly patients—that is, those more than 65 years of age—are preponderantly for organic brain disease.

The cause of primary degenerative dementia remains unclear. Some authors have suggested that it is merely a progression of normal senescence; others have reported that a hereditary factor is important. It is possible that there is more than one causative factor in this common disorder.

The brain is atrophied with widened cortical sulci, and the third and lateral ventricles are enlarged (see Fig. 1). Although atrophy is most marked in the frontal and temporal lobes, the entire brain is atrophied.

The specific lesions found in primary degenerative dementia include senile plaques, granulovacuolor degeneration of neurons and neurofibrillary tangles (see Fig. 2). These lesions are classically described in Alzheimer's disease. Rare cases have the histological features of Pick's disease. In Pick's disease, the frontal and temporal lobes are usually the most seriously affected, the occipital lobes being less affected, and the parietal lobes still less so (see Fig. 3). The neurofibrillary changes and senile plaques that characterize Alzheimer's disease and senile dementia are absent in Pick's disease.

Primary degenerative dementia may begin at any age, but it is most common in later life. It begins insidiously. Usually, the patient presents with an impairment of recent memory and then an impairment of judgment. These symptoms are generally associated with some slowing and rigidity of movement and often with a slow and shuffling gait. The illness is progressive and commonly lasts for 1 to 10 years. As it progresses, no one feature is characteristic of the dementia. Later, it may be associated with specific intellectual changes, such as aphasia, apraxia, and agnosia. Late in the illness, myoclonic or generalized seizures may develop, and

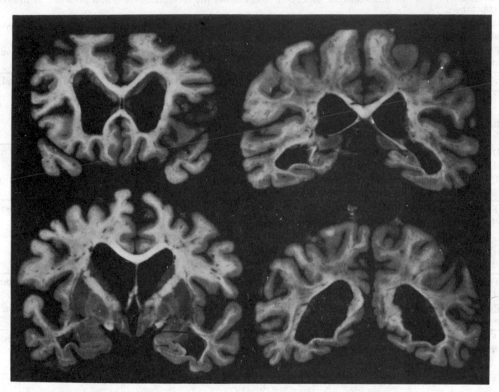

FIGURE 1.   Senile dementia (Alzheimer's disease): diffuse cerebral atrophy with dilatation of the ventricles and widening of the cortical sulci. (Courtesy of Dr. Thomas Reagan, Mayo Clinic, Rochester, Minnesota).

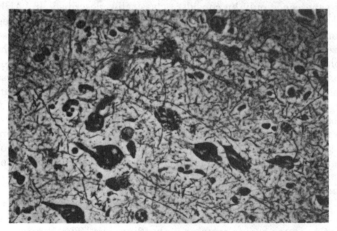

FIGURE 2.   Senile dementia (Alzheimer's disease): senile plaques and neurofibrillary degeneration (Bodian stain, ×238). (Courtesy of Dr. Thomas Reagan, Mayo Clinic, Rochester, Minnesota.)

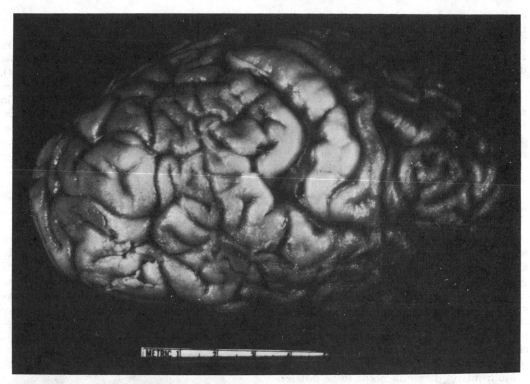

FIGURE 3.   Pick's disease: severe frontal and temporal pole cerebral atrophy with sparing of motor and sensory cortex and first temporal convolutions. (Courtesy of Dr. Thomas Reagan, Mayo Clinic, Rochester, Minnesota.)

the patient often becomes helpless. Death is usually from intercurrent illness.

During the disease, the patient's attempts to adapt to his dementia may lead to an exaggeration of any prior psychopathology. The symptoms then often include depression or paranoid responses. These symptoms are often the ones that bring the patient to the attention of the physician.

The patient must adapt to his dementia, but other serious medical or sociological problems related to his aging may precipitate crises of adaptation. Brain disease may make it impossible for the patient to adapt to these problems. Specific difficulties include the loss of loved ones who may have provided essential intellectual and emotional support, and the onset of other serious illnesses that may necessitate hospitalization and its attendant loss of the familiar home environment.

The diagnosis of Alzheimer's disease is made on the basis of a clinical history of progressive and insidious dementia in middle or late life. A work-up is indicated to exclude other treatable causes of dementia. In many patients, computer-assisted tomography of the head may be helpful in demonstrating cortical atrophy by visualizing

fluid over the surface of the brain and in the dilated ventricles. Computer-assisted tomography of the head has taken the place of pneumoencephalography.

The differential diagnosis must include such reversible metabolic diseases as myxedema and pernicious anemia, such infectious diseases as syphilis, and such tumors as frontal lobe meningiomas. The differential diagnosis must also include all the other causes of dementia described in this section.

It is also important to differentiate normal senescence from primary degenerative dementia. Often, the difference is only one of degree.

At present, no medication is available that will predictably improve cerebral function.

### Multi-infarct Dementia

Disorders affecting small-size and medium-size cerebral vessels generally produce multiple parenchymal lesions, spread over wide areas of the brain. The resultant clinical expression represents a summation of the effects of these multiple lesions and consists of a combination of neurological and psychiatric symptoms. Of all disorders involving these small vessels, the most common—and hence the most important—is the lacunar state.

The lacunar state, as described here, corresponds to the DSM-III diagnosis of multi-infarct dementia (see Table XIX).

The clinical descriptions of this disorder have included a variety of symptoms: headaches, dizziness, faintness, weakness, transient focal neurological symptoms, memory impairment, sleep disturbance, and such personality changes as emotional lability and hypochondriasis.

Both multi-infarct dementia and the primary degenerative dementias are primarily disorders of later life. However, their simultaneous occurrence does not imply a common cause.

The lacunar state is found in hypertensive patients with a stepwise progression of bilateral, sometimes fluctuating motor symptoms. These symptoms are accompanied by pseudobulbar palsy and dementia.

Anticoagulants, vasodilators, and lipotropic enzymes have been proposed as effective in altering the course of vascular disease. However, no controlled studies have been reported that clearly prove the value of any such agent in a series of histologically verified cases.

Multi-infarct dementia needs to be differentiated from transient cerebral ischemic attacks. These episodes of cerebral ischemia may occur in patients consulting a psychiatrist for other reasons. Although these episodes are not the result of cerebral infarction and do not themselves cause mental deterioration, they are of such paramount importance that they merit additional emphasis. The transient ischemic attack (TIA) is a major identifiable risk factor in the profile of patients in whom cerebral infarction subsequently develops.

Transient ischemic attacks are brief episodes of focal neurological dysfunction, lasting less than 24 hours—usually 5 to 15 minutes. Although a variety of mechanisms may be responsible, these episodes are frequently the result of microembolization from a proximal, extracranial arterial lesion that produces transient brain ischemia, and resolves without significant

pathological alteration of the parenchymal tissues.

The clinician should distinguish episodes involving the vertebrobasilar system from those involving the carotid arterial system (see Fig. 4). In general, symptoms of vertebrobasilar disease reflect a transient functional disturbance in either the brain stem or the occipital lobe; carotid distribution symptoms reflect unilateral retinal or hemispheral abnormality. Anticoagulant therapy, antiplatelet agglutinating drugs such as acetylsalicylic acid (aspirin), and reconstructive extracranial and intracranial vascular surgery have been reported to be effective in reducing the risk of infarction in patients with transient ischemic attacks.

About one-third of untreated patients with transient ischemic attacks later develop a brain infarction (see Fig. 5). Since nearly half of the patients with transient ischemic attacks who later develop infarction do so within a few weeks after the transient episodes appear, prompt recognition and treatment are crucial to the pre-

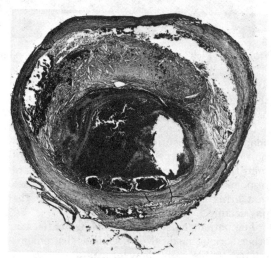

FIGURE 4.   Atherosclerosis. Cross-section of the internal carotid artery. Note the narrowed arterial lumen and the destruction of the intima, with some intraluminal thrombus formation. The media shows marked alteration, with prominent cholesterol clefts.

TABLE XIX
DIAGNOSTIC CRITERIA FOR MULTI-INFARCT DEMENTIA*

A. Dementia.

B. Stepwise deteriorating course (i.e., not uniformly progressive) with "patchy" distribution of deficits (i.e., affecting some functions, but not others) early in the course.

C. Focal neurological signs and symptoms (e.g., exaggeration of deep tendon reflexes, extensor plantar response, pseudobulbar palsy, gait abnormalities, weakness of an extremity, etc.).

D. Evidence, from the history, physical examination, or laboratory tests, of significant cerebrovascular disease that is judged to be etiologically related to the disturbance.

* From American Psychiatric Association: *Diagnostic and Statistical Manual of Mental Disorders*, ed 3. American Psychiatric Association, Washington, DC, 1980. Used with permission.

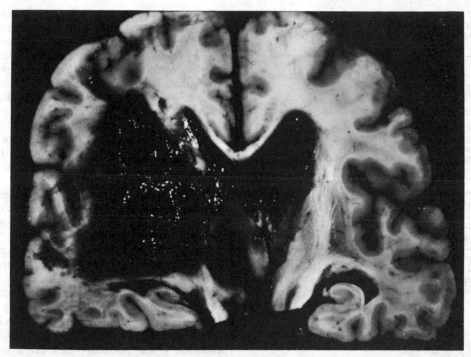

FIGURE 5. Large left intracerebral hemorrhage, with blood extending into the ventricular and subarachnoid spaces.

vention of a major, permanent neurological deficit.

### Substance-induced Organic Mental Disorders

Organic mental disorders may result from the ingestion (intoxication) or reduction in use (withdrawal) of various pharmacological agents (see Table XXVIII).

### Barbiturate or Similarly Acting Sedative or Hypnotic Organic Mental Disorders

Barbiturates, minor tranquilizers, synthetic hypnotics, and bromides constitute this group of drugs. The syndromes most often produced by these drugs include intoxication and withdrawal; amnestic syndrome and delirium are also common. Chronic intoxication may produce symptoms of dementia (see Tables XX through XXIII).

The barbiturates, hypnotics, and minor tranquilizers are all cross-tolerant. In cases of hypnotic or minor tranquilizer addiction, it is often easiest to use the involved drug for the withdrawal period by reducing the dose 10 percent a day. Some authors have advocated substituting pentobarbital for any of the drugs for purposes of gradual withdrawal.

**Barbiturates.** Classified by duration of ac-

TABLE XX
DIAGNOSTIC CRITERIA FOR BARBITURATE OR SIMILARLY ACTING SEDATIVE OR HYPNOTIC AMNESTIC DISORDER*

A. Prolonged, heavy use of a barbiturate or similarly acting sedative or hypnotic.

B. Amnestic Syndrome.

C. Not due to any other physical or mental disorder.

* From American Psychiatric Association: *Diagnostic and Statistical Manual of Mental Disorders*, ed 3. American Psychiatric Association, Washington, DC, 1980. Used with permission.

TABLE XXI
DIAGNOSTIC CRITERIA FOR BARBITURATE OR SIMILARLY ACTING SEDATIVE OR HYPNOTIC WITHDRAWAL DELIRIUM*

A. Delirium within 1 week after cessation of or reduction in heavy use of a barbiturate or similarly acting sedative or hypnotic.

B. Autonomic hyperactivity, e.g., tachycardia, sweating, elevated blood pressure.

C. Not due to any other physical or mental disorder.

* From American Psychiatric Association: *Diagnostic and Statistical Manual of Mental Disorders*, ed 3. American Psychiatric Association, Washington, DC, 1980. Used with permission.

TABLE XXII
DIAGNOSTIC CRITERIA FOR BARBITURATE OR
SIMILARLY ACTING SEDATIVE OR HYPNOTIC
WITHDRAWAL*

A. Prolonged, heavy use of barbiturate or similarly acting sedative or hypnotic, or more prolonged use of smaller doses of a benzodiazepine.

B. At least three of the following due to recent cessation of or reduction in substance use:

(1) nausea and vomiting
(2) malaise or weakness
(3) autonomic hyperactivity, e.g., tachycardia, sweating, elevated blood pressure
(4) anxiety
(5) depressed mood or irritability
(6) orthostatic hypotension
(7) coarse tremor of hands, tongue, and eyelids

C. Not due to any other physical or mental disorder, such as Barbiturate or Similarly Acting Sedative or Hypnotic Withdrawal Delirium.

* From American Psychiatric Association: *Diagnostic and Statistical Manual of Mental Disorders*, ed 3. American Psychiatric Association, Washington, DC, 1980. Used with permission.

TABLE XXIII
DIAGNOSTIC CRITERIA FOR BARBITURATE OR
SIMILARLY ACTING SEDATIVE OR HYPNOTIC
INTOXICATION*

A. Recent use of a barbiturate or similarly acting sedative or hypnotic.

B. At least one of the following psychological signs:

(1) mood lability
(2) disinhibition of sexual and aggressive impulses
(3) irritability
(4) loquacity

C. At least one of the following neurological signs:

(1) slurred speech
(2) incoordination
(3) unsteady gait
(4) impairment in attention or memory

D. Maladaptive behavioral effects, e.g., impaired judgment, interference with social or occupational functioning, failure to meet responsibilities.

E. Not due to any other physical or mental disorder.

* From American Psychiatric Association: *Diagnostic and Statistical Manual of Mental Disorders*, ed 3. American Psychiatric Association, Washington, DC, 1980. Used with permission.

tion, the barbiturates comprise the long-acting types, such as phenobarbital (Luminal); the short-acting types, such as secobarbital (Seconal) and pentobarbital (Nembutal); and the ultra short-acting types most commonly used in general anesthesia, such as thiopental (Pentothal). Acute intoxication produces general depression of the central nervous system, with dizziness, ataxia, confusion, slurred speech, stupor, and coma. Initial excitation may be seen in early intoxication because of the disinhibiting effects on the cortex.

In general, severe intoxication is produced by the ingestion of 200 to 1,000 mg orally; the fatal dose is only slightly higher, about 1,000 to 1,500 mg. In patients with already compromised brain function, or those who have ingested other sedative substances, such as alcohol, much smaller doses may produce severe acute intoxication or death.

Treatment of overdose involves gastric lavage and the support of vital functions. Absorbed barbiturates are best eliminated by the induction of diuresis; peritoneal dialysis or hemodialysis is occasionally necessary.

Chronic intoxication with barbiturates may produce syndromes with characteristics of dementia, affective changes, and organic personality syndrome.

**Minor Tranquilizers.** Diazepam (Valium), meprobamate (Equanil, Miltown), chlordiazepoxide (Librium), oxazepam (Serax), chlorazepate (Tranxene), lorazepam (Ativan), and hydroxyzine hydrochloride (Vistaril), among many others, are minor tranquilizers. Like the barbiturates, the minor tranquilizers are capable of producing acute delirium when given in high doses, but the margin of safety is greater in the minor tranquilizers. Toxic states may be manifested by hyperactivity and rage reactions. Occasionally, acute maniacal behavior—with feelings of depersonalization, hallucinations, and delusions—is seen. Suicide attempts with the minor tranquilizers have been reported, but when they are used alone, extremely high doses are necessary to produce death. When combined with alcohol, however, much smaller doses can lead to a fatal outcome.

**Hypnotics.** Methaqualone (Quaalude), ethchlorvynol (Placidyl), methyprylon (Noludar), glutethimide (Doriden), chloral hydrate (Noctec), and flurazepam (Dalmane) are included in this group of synthetic hypnotics. They are now used about as frequently as barbiturates to induce sleep. Generally, hypnotics are more potent and more hazardous than the minor tranquilizers, and produce toxic symptoms similar to those produced by the barbiturates. From 1.0 to 3.5 percent of hospitalized patients have untoward reactions to the hypnotics. Glutethimide may produce clonic convulsions during the period of coma after an overdose. Methaqualone produces marked respiratory depression associated with convulsions, pulmonary edema, and coma. Withdrawal from many of the substances may produce a syndrome of delirium tremens.

**Bromides.** Four organic mental disorders associated with bromide intoxication have been noted: simple bromide intoxication, bromide delirium, transitory schizophreniform psychosis with paranoia, and bromide hallucinosis. Simple bromide intoxication is characterized by progressive dulling of awareness, forgetfulness, irritability, irregular sluggish pupils, tremors, ataxia, and slowed speech. Bromide delirium, seen in two-thirds of all patients with bromide intoxication, is characterized by disorientation, restlessness, anxiety, insomnia, disturbances of mood, delusions, and hallucinations.

## Amphetamines or Similarly Acting Sympathomimetic Drugs

Organic mental disorders produced by amphetamines, or similarly acting stimulants, include intoxication, delirium, organic delusional syndrome, organic affective syndrome, and withdrawal syndrome.

**Amphetamines.** The amphetamines and methylphenidate (Ritalin) act primarily on the central nervous system. They have marked euphoristic and antifatigue properties. They produce marked tolerance and a mild withdrawal syndrome, characterized by severe fatigue and mental depression, sometimes with suicidal ideation (see Tables XXIV through XXVII).

**Anorectics.** Phenmetrazine (Preludin), diethylpropion (Tenuate), and chlorophentermine (Pre-Sate) are amphetamine derivatives de-

---

TABLE XXIV
DIAGNOSTIC CRITERIA FOR AMPHETAMINE OR SIMILARLY ACTING SYMPATHOMIMETIC DELIRIUM*

A. Delirium within 24 hours of use of amphetamine or similarly acting sympathomimetic.

B. Not due to any other physical or mental disorder.

* From American Psychiatric Association: *Diagnostic and Statistical Manual of Mental Disorders*, ed 3. American Psychiatric Association, Washington, DC, 1980. Used with permission.

---

TABLE XXV
DIAGNOSTIC CRITERIA FOR AMPHETAMINE OR SIMILARLY ACTING SYMPATHOMIMETIC DELUSIONAL DISORDER*

A. Recent use of amphetamine or similarly acting sympathomimetic during a period of long-term use of moderate or high doses.

B. A rapidly developing syndrome consisting of persecutory delusions as the predominant clinical feature and at least three of the following:

   (1) ideas of reference
   (2) aggressiveness and hostility
   (3) anxiety
   (4) psychomotor agitation

C. Not due to any other physical or mental disorder.

* From American Psychiatric Association: *Diagnostic and Statistical Manual of Mental Disorders*, ed 3. American Psychiatric Association, Washington, DC, 1980. Used with permission.

---

TABLE XXVI
DIAGNOSTIC CRITERIA FOR AMPHETAMINE OR SIMILARLY ACTING SYMPATHOMIMETIC INTOXICATION*

A. Recent use of amphetamine or similarly acting sympathomimetic.

B. Within 1 hour of use, at least two of the following psychological symptoms:

   (1) psychomotor agitation
   (2) elation
   (3) grandiosity
   (4) loquacity
   (5) hypervigilance

C. Within 1 hour of use, at least two of the following physical symptoms:

   (1) tachycardia
   (2) pupillary dilation
   (3) elevated blood pressure
   (4) perspiration or chills
   (5) nausea or vomiting

D. Maladaptive behavior effects, e.g., fighting, impaired judgment, interference with social or occupational functioning.

E. Not due to any other physical or mental disorder.

* From American Psychiatric Association: *Diagnostic and Statistical Manual of Mental Disorders*, ed 3. American Psychiatric Association, Washington, DC, 1980. Used with permission.

---

TABLE XXVII
DIAGNOSTIC CRITERIA FOR AMPHETAMINE OR SIMILARLY ACTING SYMPATHOMIMETIC WITHDRAWAL*

A. Prolonged heavy use of amphetamine or a similarly acting sympathomimetic.

B. After cessation of or reduction in substance use, depressed mood and at least two of the following:

   (1) fatigue
   (2) disturbed sleep
   (3) increased dreaming

C. Not due to any other physical or mental disorder, such as Amphetamine or Similarly Acting Sympathomimetic Delusional Disorder.

* From American Psychiatric Association: *Diagnostic and Statistical Manual of Mental Disorders*, ed 3. American Psychiatric Association, Washington, DC, 1980. Used with permission.

---

signed primarily for appetite suppression. Although considered less potent than amphetamines, they are all capable of producing the same side effects, including paranoid psychosis. Certain over-the-counter anorectics, containing phenylpropanolamine (Dexatrim), may produce psychotic symptoms.

**Other Analeptics.** Pemoline (Cylert) is an amphetamine derivative that is particularly long acting and recommended for the treatment of minimum brain damage syndrome and hyperkinesis in children. Although the possibility of toxic effects are considered less than with amphetamines, the potential for amphetamine-like psychosis and overdose exists. Caffeine, the most widely used central nervous system stimulant, is found in coffee, tea, over-the-counter preparations, and cola beverages. Overdoses may produce excitement, flushing, insomnia, diuresis, restlessness, tinnitus, tremors, and convulsions. Usually, large doses are required to produce intoxication, but the syndrome has been seen with as little as 250 mg. of caffeine a day (an average cup of coffee contains 100 mg of caffeine).

### Phencyclidine (PCP) or Similarly Acting Arylcyclohexamine Substances

Phencyclidine (angel dust or Serenyl), ketamine (Ketalar) and the thiophene analogue of phencyclidine (TCP) belong to the group of substances called the arylcyclohexamines.

PCP has become popular as a street drug, and may produce more classical delirium, with isolation, depersonalization, negativism, hostility, apathy, or even a cataleptic state. Phencyclidine seems to have the capability of producing symptoms similar to the primary symptoms of schizophrenia; the other psychedelic agents tend to mimic the secondary symptoms of schizophrenia.

Other hallucinogens, such as marijuana (cannabis), lysergic acid diethylamide (LSD), mescaline, and psilocybin are discussed in detail in Section 19.2.

The treatment of hallucinogen intoxication involves psychological support and calm verbal reassurance to reduce anxiety. Benzodiazepines and butyrophenones, such as haloperidol, reduce the anxiety and may specifically terminate the reaction.

### Psychotropic Agents

**Major Tranquilizers.** Antipsychotic medications produce sedation and tranquilization with minimal narcosis. They inhibit psychomotor activity, reduce anxiety, and inhibit hallucinations and delusional thinking.

Used in large doses, the major tranquilizers may produce somnolence to the point of stupor or coma. Acute delirious reactions have been reported, particularly when major tranquilizers are combined with antiparkinsonian agents or barbiturates. The delirium is apparently an anticholinergic phenomenon, and may respond to treatment with physostigmine salicylate. Preexisting factors, such as advanced age or brain damage, also increase the likelihood of delirium. A depression may be aggravated or precipitated by the major tranquilizers. Dystonic and extrapyramidal reactions are common.

An acute overdose may produce confusion, agitation, and disorientation, often associated with marked postural hypotension, particularly with the phenothiazine derivatives. Extremely large doses produce coma, with hypothermia, shock, and death.

The treatment of an overdose involves gastric lavage, because the anticholinergic effect of the drugs tends to delay gastric emptying, and because they are quite soluble in water. If seizures occur after an overdose, they are treated with intravenous phenytoin (Dilantin). The barbiturates, which may deepen the coma and aggravate the hypotension, should be avoided. Acute dystonic reactions are quickly resolved by slow intravenous injection of 50 to 100 mg of diphenhydramine (Benadryl).

**Antidepressants.** This class of drugs includes the tricyclic antidepressants and monoamine oxidase inhibitors. Adverse effects include fatigue, weakness, unsteadiness, drowsiness, headache, tremor, stimulation, and rarely, grand mal convulsions at therapeutic doses. Psychotic symptoms may be exacerbated in schizophrenic patients. Elderly patients may develop typical symptoms of delirium, disorientation, confusion, paranoia, and hallucinations. In manic-depressive patients, treatment with antidepressants during the depressive phase may result in a rapid swing to hypomania.

**Lithium.** When serum lithium levels are greater than 2 mEq per liter, a toxic confusional state may be produced, with agitation, nausea, diarrhea, thirst, dizziness, blurred vision, slurred speech, weakness, tremor, and impairment of consciousness. With levels above 4 mEq per liter, generalized spasticity and clonic movement of the limbs may be seen, with coma and generalized convulsions. It must be remembered that toxic effects with lithium may be seen even when the blood levels of the drug are within the therapeutic range. Apparently, serum levels of lithium do not accurately reflect intracellular levels in some patients.

### Anticonvulsants

**Hydantoin Derivatives.** Phenytoin (Dilantin), mephenytoin (Mesantoin), and ethotoin (Peganone) are commonly used in the treatment of grand mal, focal, and psychomotor epilepsy. Phenytoin has been found to produce central nervous system disturbances, including drowsiness, ataxia, visual disturbance, and dysarthria in 2 to 3 per cent of hospitalized patients. A host of side effects may be seen associated with these drugs, including blood dyscrasias, dermatological disorders, and hepatitis. The central nervous system effects include drowsiness, irritability, mental depression, tremor, dysarthria, diplopia, nystagmus, and choreiform movements. At high doses, delirium and organic delusional syndrome may be seen.

**Oxazolidinedione Derivatives.** Primidone (Mysoline), trimethadione (Tridione), and paramethadione (Paradione) are all members of this group of anticonvulsants. They are most often used to treat petit mal epilepsy. Their side effects include ataxia and vertigo at therapeutic blood levels; at high blood levels, nausea, vomiting, nystagmus, diplopia, drowsiness, and emotional lability are seen. An overdose of the drugs causes marked sedation, associated with nystagmus, dysarthria, and incoordination.

**Succinimide Derivatives.** Ethosuximide (Zarontin) and phensuximide (Milontin), examples of this type of anticonvulsant medication, are used for petit mal epilepsy. Common side effects include headache, dizziness, irritability, drowsiness, euphoria, and hyperactivity. Psychiatric changes are common, including nightmares, increased aggressiveness, decreased ability to concentrate, and organic delusional states with paranoia.

**Other Anticonvulsant Drugs.** Phenacemide (Phenurone) is a particularly toxic anticonvulsant that is rarely used clinically today because of the attendant hazards. During therapy, marked personality changes, severe depression, suicide attempts, marked aggressiveness, and psychoses are common. Overdosage leads to agitation, manic states, ataxia, and coma.

Clonazepam (Clonopin) is a benzodiazepine-derived antidepressant that is useful in the treatment of petit mal epilepsy and akinetic and myoclonic seizures. Like other benzodiazepines, clonazepam has side effects and a potential for drug dependency; a withdrawal syndrome should be anticipated if the drug is stopped abruptly. The adverse psychiatric effects of clonazepam include drowsiness, ataxia, depression, forgetfulness, confusion, hallucinations, hysterical reactions, psychosis, and suicidal depression.

### Belladonna Alkaloids and Synthetic Anticholinergics

The belladonna alkaloids are widely found in plants, including belladonna and Jimson weed, although most of the compounds used in medicine today are synthetic derivatives. Large doses can produce restlessness, manic behavior, confusion, loss of memory, emotional lability, disorientation, convulsions, and coma. Fatalities are extremely rare, and cases of intoxication with as much as 1 g of atropine have been followed by complete recovery.

A large number of these anticholinergic agents are available. They include tropine and scopine derivatives, such as atropine, scopolamine, and benztropine (Cogentin); quaternary ammonium compounds, such as methscopolamine (Pamine) and propantheline (Pro-Banthine); nonquaternary compounds, such as cyclopentolate (Cyclogyl, Alcon); ethanolamine antihistamines, such as diphenhydramine (Benadryl); piperidine compounds, including trihexyphenidyl (Artane); biperiden (Akineton); and the piperazine antihistamines, such as meclizine (Bonine).

An increasing number of toxic deliriums have been reported to be associated with the ingestion of over-the-counter sleeping preparations. These compounds contain scopolamine, combined with an antihistamine and salicylate. Preparations such as Sominex, Sleep-Eze, Quiet World, and Compoz contain from 0.125 to 0.25 mg of scopolamine in each tablet. They are easily obtainable and are taken by many young people to obtain a high.

Treatment of the anticholinergic delirium involves evacuation of the stomach, and sedation, if necessary, with a minor tranquilizer or barbiturate. Sedation with one of the major tranquilizers, such as chlorpromazine, should be avoided, as it may aggravate the anticholinergic delirium. Intramuscular injection of physostigmine salicylate (Antilirium) in a dose of 1 mg, followed in 15 to 20 minutes by an additional dose if necessary, is indicated. The dose may have to be repeated after an hour.

### L-Dihydroxyphenylalanine (L-Dopa)

Levodopa (Larodopa, Bendopa, Dopar) and a combination drug containing levodopa and carbidopa (Sinemet) are now widely used in the treatment of idiopathic parkinsonism. Levodopa is readily absorbed through the blood-brain barrier and converted to dopamine and norepinephrine. The most common side effects of levodopa are nausea and vomiting, seen in more than half of the treated patients. The symptoms begin with a lessening of parkinsonism symptoms, and are usually controlled by a reduction in the dosage. Psychiatric symptoms are reported in 20 to 30 percent of treated patients, and may occur in association with the dyskinesia. The most common mental side effects are confusion and disorientation, associated with delirium of variable severity. Significant depression, even of suicidal proportions, may be seen in a certain number of patients receiving L-dopa, even though most patients experience an improvement in mood. Psychosis with hallucinations, paranoid delusions, and psychomotor agitation may occur, often associated with delirium but at times in the presence of a clear sensorium. Hypomania may be produced during L-dopa treatment.

## Cardiovascular Agents

The therapeutic and the toxic serum levels of digitalis are unfortunately very close. Delirium with restlessness, nightmares, difficulty in concentration, and apathy may be seen initially. This reaction may gradually evolve into a full-blown delirium, with marked impairment of cognition, irritability, distractability, delusional thinking, and hallucinations. In an unfamiliar environment, relative sensory deprivation and sleep disturbance, such as in an intensive care unit, can increase the susceptibility to digitalis delirium.

Procainamide (Pronestyl) produces mild depression and weakness in moderate doses. High doses may cause severe depression, with psychotic behavior and hallucinations. Propranolol (Inderal), a β-adrenergic blocking agent, commonly produces mild central nervous system effects, including drowsiness, lethargy, and headache.

The thiocyanates have the most notorious reputation among the antihypertension drugs for producing toxic effects on the central nervous system. Thiocyanates cause delirium at blood levels as low as 8 to 12 mg per 100 ml. The drug may accumulate in the body, resulting in sleepiness, weakness, confusion, hallucinations, and delirium. The treatment of thiocyanate toxicity consists of the administration of sodium chloride and hemodialysis in severe cases. Reserpine (Rau-Sed, Ser-Ap-Es, Serpasil) acts by depleting catecholamine stores in body tissues, including the brain, Reserpine often causes depression, frequently severe, closely resembling other endogenous depressions. The patient may present with symptoms of nightmares, marked agitation, and depression of suicidal proportions that may require hospitalization. Methyldopa (Aldomet) commonly causes sedation, and may produce mental depression and nightmares, as seen with reserpine, but the reaction is usually milder and less frequent. Hydralazine (Apresoline) produces a direct vasodilating effect on the vascular smooth muscles. Common effects of hydralazine are headaches, anorexia, and gastrointestinal symptoms. In high doses, hydralazine may produce anxiety, depression, disorientation, confusion, and acute psychotic episodes.

Diuretics cause sodium and potassium depletion and alkalosis, which may produce metabolic abnormalities, with episodes of weakness, disorientation, confusion, and delirium.

## Anesthetics

The volatile anesthetics usually used in general surgical anesthesia are virtually never the cause of an organic brain syndrome.

Toxic reactions may be seen when local anesthetics are injected intravenously to control cardiac arrhythmias, or when they are injected into a vein accidentally during local infiltration. The local anesthetics act as stimulants to the central nervous system, resulting in initial restlessness, tremors, and convulsions. These reactions may be followed by the depression of vital functions and by death resulting from cardiac failure. Cocaine toxicity rapidly causes the patient to become restless, agitated, anxious, and confused. Headache, hyperpyrexia, dilation of the pupils, nausea, vomiting, and abdominal pain are frequently seen. Delirium, with Cheyne-Stokes respiration and convulsions, occurs terminally. Toxicity with cocaine occurs with extreme rapidity, and the patient may collapse and die before the physician realizes what has happened. Procaine (Novocain) in toxic doses may cause central nervous system stimulation and convulsions.

## Hormones

High doses of corticosteroids may result in severe psychotic reactions, characterized by manic behavior and paranoid ideation. Confusion, feelings of depersonalization, and severe depression, with suicidal ideation, may be encountered occasionally. A reduction of the dosage or treatment with a butyrophenone may be of help in managing the psychiatric symptoms related to steroid therapy. Electroshock therapy has been shown to be of benefit in manic states and in severe depressions associated with corticosteroid therapy.

High doses of thyroid hormone may produce symptoms typical of hyperthyroidism, including weakness, fatigue, tachycardia, tremors, headaches, anxiety, agitation, insomnia, and heat intolerance. Overdoses of thryoid preparations may result in symptoms of thyroid storm. Radioactive iodine, propylthiouracil, and carbimazole are antithyroid preparations used in the treatment of thyrotoxicosis. These preparations may precipitate a delirium, an organic delusional syndrome, or hallucinations secondary to the rapid onset of a hypothyroid state.

Hypoglycemia may cause marked changes in psychic function. Irritability, intellectual impairment, confusion, headache, and lethargy may be seen initially. The reaction may progress to full-blown delirium, followed by coma and convulsions. Chronic hypoglycemic states may produce organic personality syndrome or dementia, with epilepsy or focal neurological symptoms.

### Nonnarcotic Analgesics and Antipyretics

The salicylates (aspirin, sodium salicylate) may produce toxic states in high doses, with confusion, agitation, delirium, and hallucinations. Phenacetin has been noted to cause depressed mood, lethargy, dizziness, feelings of detachment, impaired concentration, and toxic delirium with hallucinations. Carbamazepine (Tegretol) is used to treat trigeminal neuralgia and chronic pain states. Because it is closely related chemically to the tricyclic antidepressants, it produces similar side effects. These side effects may include the activation of latent psychosis, depression with agitation, and delirium, particularly in the elderly.

### Anti-ulcer Drugs

Cimetidine (Tagamet) is a histamine $H_2$ receptor antagonist that inhibits both daytime and nocturnal basal gastric acid secretion. It is thus useful in healing and preventing duodenal ulcer. However, reversible confusional states have been reported to occur in elderly or severely ill patients who are treated with cimetidine. Renal insufficiency and existing organic mental disorders predispose to this reaction.

### Anti-inflammatory Drugs

Phenylbutazone (Butazolidin), when given in large doses, may produce a marked delirious state with hallucinations, coma, and convulsions. When lower doses are given, headaches, psychotic reactions, and depression may result. Indomethacin (Indocin) causes headache in about 50 percent of the patients receiving the drug. More severe effects include depersonalization, ataxia, confusion, nightmares, hallucinations, delirium, and convulsions with coma. Prolonged use of indomethacin may cause severe depressive reactions.

### Anti-infection Agents

**Antibiotics.** The sulfonamides have been shown to produce confusion, depression, and acute psychotic reactions. Most often, the sulfa drugs produce minor symptoms, such as drowsiness, dizziness, insomnia, irritability, headaches, and mild mood changes, particularly in children. Penicillin given intravenously may produce an acute psychotic reaction, characterized by severe anxiety, agitation, hallucinations,

and seizures. (This is not a typical anaphylactic reaction because disturbances of the circulatory system, wheezing, and edema are not present.)

**Antituberculosis Agents.** Isoniazid, particularly in the high dose ranges, produces anxiety and restlessness. Prolonged administration may result in irritability, confusion, and paranoid thinking, often with marked belligerence and antagonistic behavior. Schizophrenic symptoms may be reactivated in chronic schizophrenics, or a schizophrenic-like syndrome, with auditory and visual hallucinations, may be induced in apparently normal people. Cycloserine may produce anxiety, irritability, drowsiness, hallucinations, and delirium, and may also activate schizophrenic symptoms in schizophrenic patients. Ethionamide apparently produces some mental depression, together with lethargy, somnolence, and, at times, suicidal ideaton. Iproniazid may produce euphoric states, and has been used as an antidepressant medication. Manic states and agitated delirium may occur secondary to iproniazid administration.

**Antivirus Agents.** Toxic doses of amantadine (Symmetrel) produce an agitated delirium, with aggressive behavior and hallucinations. The drug is also used in the treatment of Parkinson's disease.

**Antiparasite and Antifungus Drugs.** Psychosis, delirium, personality change, and depression have all been related to the use of chloroquine derivatives. Acute psychotic states—with paranoid delusions, aggressive behavior, delirium, and occasionally seizures—may be produced, particularly by high doses. Severe reactions to quinacrine (Atabrine) usually follow large doses used to eradicate tapeworm, although toxic psychoses have been reported when lower doses are used for antimalaria treatment.

Long courses of therapy with Griseofulvin usually cause mild side effects such as drowsiness, headache, fatigue, irritability, and insomnia. However, severe depression and states of confusion sometimes occur.

### Disulfiram

When a patient taking disulfiram ingests alcohol, an unpleasant reaction occurs as a result of acetaldehyde production, making disulfiram a useful agent to encourage alcohol abstinence. Minor side effects of fatigue and decreased libido and potency may be seen with the usual dose of 0.25 g daily. With larger doses, toxic psychoses may be produced, with weakness, difficulty with concentration and memory, disorientation, confusion, and somnolence. The drug may also exacerbate psychotic symptoms in schizophrenic patients. The chronic ingestion of excessive amounts of disulfiram results in a syndrome of carbon disulfide toxicity, characterized by delirium, depression, parkinsonism, and peripheral neuropathy, suggesting an accumulation of the metabolite.

### Antineoplastic Agents

The vinca alkaloids derived from the periwinkle plant, including vinblastine (Velban) and vincristine (Oncovin), have been reported to produce toxic effects—including stupor, hallucinations, and coma—when used in extremely high doses. Somnolence and mental depression, occurring about the second or third day of treatment with the preparations, are common but transient. Methotrexate, a folate antagonist, has been reported to cause progressive confusion, somnolence, irritability, ataxia, and delirium—often with convulsions and coma—and some cases of permanent intellectual deficits have been noted.

### Chemical or Environment-related Organic Mental Disorders, Including Poisons

A variety of gases, noxious vapors, solvents, heavy metals, and insecticides may cause organic mental disorders.

### Gases

When pure oxygen is inhaled at pressures greater than 2 atmospheres, a typical syndrome of oxygen intoxication is observed, with dizziness, muscle twitching, paresthesias, irritability, mood changes, loss of consciousness, and generalized convulsions. The intoxication syndrome is reversible if the oxygen pressure is reduced. Oxygen paradox—with symptoms of confusion incoordination, cardiovascular decompensation, and seizures—may be seen when oxygen is administered after a period of hypoxia, such as after exposure to actual or simulated high altitude.

A carbon dioxide mixture of up to 10 percent produces disagreeable symptoms of dyspnea, restlessness, headache, paresthesias, dizziness, and sweating. Unconsciousness occurs after about 15 minutes of 10 percent carbon dioxide inhalation. At high concentrations of 25 to 30 percent, subcortical areas are activated, resulting in increased cortical excitability and the possibility of convulsions. At levels above 25 percent, humans rapidly develop symptoms of headache, severe mental confusion, and delirium. Chronic exposure to low concentrations of

around 3 percent over several days may produce initial excitation, followed by mental depression.

Acute exposure to large concentrations of carbon monoxide or chronic protracted exposures at lower toxic levels result in permanent brain damage. The most severe neurological symptoms resulting from carbon monoxide poisoning are parkinsonism and seizure disorder. Severe episodic depressions, withdrawal, apathy, and impairment of perception are common psychiatric sequelae. Forgetfulness is common, and is characterized by the retention of critical faculties and the absence of confabulation, but with marked impairment of orientation. The treatment of carbon monoxide intoxication is the immediate administration of oxygen with 5 percent carbon dioxide.

### Noxious Vapors and Solvents

The inhalation of the vapors of solvents used in industrial processes may result in intoxication. An increasing number of intentional intoxications are seen in children and adolescents who sniff the substance for its intoxicating effects.

### Heavy Metals

Chronic lead intoxication occurs when the amount of lead ingested exceeds the ability to eliminate it. It takes several months for toxic symptoms to appear.

The signs and symptoms of lead intoxication depend on the level of lead in the blood. When lead reaches levels above 200 $\mu$g per 100 ml, symptoms of severe lead encephalopathy occur, with dizziness, clumsiness, ataxia, irritability, restlessness, headache, and insomnia. Later, an excited delirium, with associated vomiting and visual disturbances, occurs, progressing to convulsions, lethargy, and coma.

Treatment of lead encephalopathy should be instituted as rapidly as possible, even without laboratory confirmation, because of the high mortality. The treatment of choice to facilitate lead excretion is the intravenous administration of calcium disodium edetate (Calcium Disodium Versenate) daily for 5 days. One gram is given in each dose.

In acute mercury intoxication, central nervous system symptoms of lethargy and restlessness may occur, but the primary symptoms are secondary to severe gastrointestinal irritation, with bloody stools, diarrhea, and vomiting leading to circulatory collapse because of dehydration. Chronic mercury intoxication, resulting from the exposure to small amounts of mercury compounds over extended periods, is more important in the production of central nervous system syndromes. The Mad Hatter in *Alice's Adventures in Wonderland* was a parody of the madness resulting from the inhalation of mercury nitrate vapors, for mercury nitrate was used in the past in the processing of hair for felt hats. Central nervous system symptoms include mental depression, insomnia, fatigue, irritability, lethargy, and hallucinosis. Behavioral changes include excessive ease of embarrassment, timidity, withdrawal, and despondency. Mercury poisoning is best treated as soon as it is recognized with the use of a metal chelating agent, such as penicillamine or dimercaprol.

Early intoxication with manganese produces manganese madness, with symptoms of headache, irritability, joint pains, and somnolence. An eventual picture appears of emotional lability, pathological laughter, nightmares, hallucinations, and compulsive and impulsive acts associated with periods of confusion and aggressiveness. Lesions involving the basal ganglia and pyramidal system result in gait impairment, rigidity, monotonous or whispering speech, tremors of the extremities and tongue, masked facies (manganese mask), micrographia, dystonia, dysarthria, and loss of equilibrium. The psychological effects tend to clear 3 or 4 months after the patient's removal from the site of exposure, but neurological symptoms tend to remain stationary or to progress. There is no specific treatment for manganese intoxication, other than removal from the source of poisoning.

Thallium intoxication initially causes severe pains in the legs, diarrhea, and vomiting. Within a week, delirium, convulsions, cranial nerve palsies, blindness, choreiform movements, and coma may occur. Behavioral changes include paranoid thinking and depression, with suicidal tendencies. Alopecia is a common and important diagnostic clue. Treatment is generally symptomatic.

Severe acute arsenic poisoning results in marked vomiting and diarrhea, followed by dryness of the mucous membranes and severe thirst. Death is the result of shock from fluid loss. Chronic arsenic intoxication has a more insidious onset, with weakness, lethargy, anorexia, diarrhea, nausea, inflammation of the nose and upper respiratory tract, coughing, soreness of the mouth, and dermatitis, with increased pigmentation of the neck, eyelids, nipples, and axillae.

Bismuth subgallate and other insoluble bismuth salts are sometimes prescribed for constipation; they may be changed in the gut to a soluble form, and bismuth may be absorbed into the blood stream, causing encephalopathy. Early symptoms, lasting from days to months, are seen as depression, anxiety, irritability, phobias, and the presence of paranoid delusions. The patient appears weak and at times somnolent, but occasionally he may become agitated. Later, symptoms of ataxia may occur, followed by confusion and a characteristic pseudotremor with myoclonic jerks.

### Organophosphate Insecticides

Mild intoxication produces headache, fatigue, numbness of the extremities, gastrointestinal upset, dizziness, excessive sweating and salivation, tightness in the chest, and abdominal pain. In severe poisoning, the patient feels extremely weak, he has difficulty in walking and talking, and muscle fasciculations are present. Eventually, flaccid paralysis occurs, with decreased respiration, marked miosis, and coma. In severe acute intoxications, a classic picture of delirium is seen, with restlessness, tremulousness, and eventually coma, convulsions, and hyperthermia.

Chronic exposure to organophosphate insecticides is associated with impaired concentration, drowsiness, and confusion. Psychomotor slowing is seen, with a decreased ability to process information rapidly and accurately, and memory is impaired. Speech is slowed, and there is a word-finding disturbance, with slurring and perseveration. There seems to be an increased incidence of depression associated with lethargy.

The treatment of organophosphate poisoning is the administration of atropine sulfate, given parenterally in a dose sufficient to produce atropine side effects.

### Other Organic Mental Disorders

In addition to the previously discussed organic mental disorders, there are many conditions that produce transient or permanent dysfunction of the brain. The characteristic psychological or behavioral signs and symptoms that may accompany these disorders may be recognized by the psychiatrist and be included in the diagnostic process. Some of the more important of these organic mental disorders are described below.

### Epilepsy

The term epilepsy refers to a chronic condition of recurrent or repeated seizures. Almost any pathological process, acquired or genetic, that involves the brain, may cause epilepsy.

A seizure is a transient, paroxysmal, pathophysiological disturbance of cerebral function

TABLE XXVIII
ORGANIC MENTAL DISORDERS AND SYMPTOMS ASSOCIATED WITH SPECIFIC MEDICATIONS

| | Syndromes | | | | | | | | | | Symptoms | | | | | | | | | | | | | | |
|---|---|---|---|---|---|---|---|---|---|---|---|---|---|---|---|---|---|---|---|---|---|---|---|---|---|
| | Delirium | Dementia | Organic Delusional Syndrome | Organic Amnestic Syndrome | Hallucinosis | Organic Affective Syndrome | Organic Depressive Syndrome / Organic Manic Syndrome | Organic Personality Syndrome | Withdrawal Syndrome | Intoxication | Aggression | Agitation | Anxiety | Apathy | Ataxia | Convulsions | Depersonalization | Fatigue | Hallucinations | Headache | Illusions | Insomnia | Irritability | Nightmares | Somnolence |
| Sedatives and hypnotics | X | | | | | | | | X | X | X | * | * | X | X | * | | X | * | | | * | X | | X |
| Barbiturates | X | X | | X | | | | | X | X | X | * | * | X | X | * | | X | * | | | * | X | | X |
| Minor tranquilizers | X | | | X | | | | | X | X | | * | * | X | X | * | | X | * | X | | * | X | | X |
| Hypnotics | X | | | | | | | | X | X | | * | * | X | X | * | | X | X | | | * | X | | X |
| Bromides | | X | | X | | | | X | | | | | | | | | | | | | | | | | |
| Stimulants | | | X | | X | * | | | X | X | X | X | X | * | | X | | * | X | | | X | X | | * |
| Amphetamines | | | X | | | * | | X | X | X | X | X | X | * | | X | | * | X | | | X | X | | * |
| Anorectics | | | X | | | | | X | | X | | X | X | | | X | | | | | | X | | | |
| Aminophyllin | | | | | | | | | | X | | X | X | * | | X | | * | | * | | X | X | | * |
| Caffeine | | | | | | | | | | | | | | | | | | | | | | | | | |
| Psychotropic agents | | | | | | | | | | | | | | | | | | | | | | | | | |
| Major tranquilizers | X | | | | | X | X | | | X | | X | X | X | | X | X | X | X | X | X | X | | X | X |
| Tricyclic antidepressants | X | | | | | | X | | | X | | X | X | | | X | | X | X | X | X | | X | | X |
| Monoamine oxidase inhibitors | | | | | | | | | | | | X | | | | X | | | | | | | | | X |
| Lithium carbonate | X | | | | | | | | | X | | X | | | X | X | | | X | | | | | | X |
| Anticonvulsants | X | | | | | | | | | X | | X | | | X | | | X | | | | | | | X |
| Belladonna alkaloids | X | | X | | | | | | | X | | X | | | | | | | X | | X | | | | X |
| L-Dopa | | | X | | | X | | | | X | X | X | X | X | X | X | X | | X | | X | X | X | X | |
| Cardiovascular drugs | X | | | | | | X | | | X | | X | | | | | | | X | | | | | | X |
| Digitalis | X | | | | | | X | | | X | | X | | | | | | | X | | | | | X | X |
| Antiarrhythmia agents | X | | | | | | | | | X | | X | | | | | | | X | | | | | | X |
| Antihypertension drugs | X | | | | | X | X | | | | | X | X | X | | | | | X | X | | | | X | X |
| Diuretics | X | | | | | | | | | | | X | | | | X | | | | | | | | | |
| Local anesthetics | | | | | | | | | | | | | | | | | | | | | | | | | |
| Hormones | | | | | | | | | | | | | | X | | | | X | | X | | | | | |
| Corticosteroids | | | X | | | X | X | X | X | X | | X | | X | | | X | X | X | | | | X | | |
| Thyroxin | X | | | | | X | | X | | X | | X | X | | | | | X | | | | X | X | | |
| Insulin | X | | | | | X | | | | X | | X | | X | | X | | X | | X | | X | X | X | X |

caused by a spontaneous, excessive discharge of cortical neurons. The clinical manifestation of seizures depends on the site of origin and the pattern of spread of the discharge. Seizures may consist of abnormal movements or an arrest of movement, a disorder of sensation or perception, a disturbance of behavior, or an impairment of consciousness.

Seizures can be classified in several ways (see Table XXIX).

Two additional categories of the international classification system are unilateral seizures, which involve predominantly one side of the body, and unclassified seizures, which cannot be categorized because of incomplete data.

**Generalized Seizures.** The two most common types of generalized seizures are absence and generalized tonic-clonic seizures.

*Absence (Petit Mal) Seizures.* Absence seizures occur predominantly in children. They usually consist of simple absence attacks lasting 5 to 10 seconds, during which there is an abrupt alteration in awareness and responsiveness and an interruption in motor activity. The child often has a blank stare, associated with an upward deviation of the eyes, and some mild twitching movements of the eyes, eyelids, face, or extremities. The petit mal absence seizure is associated with a characteristic generalized, bilaterally synchronous, 3-Hz spike-and wave pattern (see Fig. 6) in the electroencephalogram (EEG) and is often easily induced by hyperventilation. Petit mal is usually a fairly benign seizure disorder, often resolving after adolescence.

*Generalized Tonic-clonic (Grand Mal) Seizures.* The generalized tonic-clonic seizure is the most severe type of seizure. It begins with an abrupt loss of consciousness and generalized tonic stiffening of the body, associated with the epileptic cry caused by forced expiration of air from the lungs through closed vocal cords. In addition, there are dilation of the pupils, cessation of respirations with cyanosis, bladder and fecal incontinence, and biting of the tongue. The initial tonic phase of the seizure is succeeded by a brief period of diffuse trembling of the body lasting several seconds, which is followed by the clonic phase, consisting of generalized, bilaterally synchronous jerks of the body and limbs alternating with periods of relaxation. The clonic movements gradually slow and cease, and are followed by a period of postictal (postseizure) stupor, during which the patient is limp and unresponsive. The actual seizure usually lasts 1 to 2 minutes, and the postictal state may last 5 to 10 minutes. After this stage, the patient may awaken but remain confused and disoriented. If left undisturbed, he may go to sleep for several

Analgesics
Aspirin
Phenacetin
Carbamazepine
Anti-inflammatory drugs
Phenylbutazone
Indomethacin
Anti-infection agents
Antibiotics
Antituberculosis agents
Antivirus agents
Antiparasite drugs
Disulfiram
Antineoplastic

* In withdrawal syndrome.

TABLE XXIX
OUTLINE OF THE INTERNATIONAL CLASSIFICATIONS OF EPILEPTIC SEIZURES*

I.  Partial seizures (seizures beginning locally)
    A.  Partial seizures with elementary symptoms (generally without impairment of consciousness)
        1.  With motor symptoms
        2.  With sensory symptoms
        3.  With autonomic symptoms
        4.  Compound forms
    B.  Partial seizures with complex symptoms (generally with impairment of consciousness) (temporal lobe or psychomotor seizures)
        1.  With impairment of consciousness only
        2.  With cognitive symptoms
        3.  With affective symptoms
        4.  With psychosensory symptoms
        5.  With psychomotor symptoms (automatisms)
        6.  Compound forms
    C.  Partial seizures secondarily generalized
II. Generalized seizures (bilaterally symmetric and without local onset)
    A.  Absences (petit mal)
    B.  Myoclonus
    C.  Infantile spasms
    D.  Clonic seizures
    E.  Tonic seizures
    F.  Tonic-clonic seizures (grand mal)
    G.  Atonic seizures
    H.  Akinetic seizures
III. Unilateral seizures
IV.  Unclassified seizures (because of incomplete data)

* Modified from Gastaut H: Clinical and electroencephalographical classification of epileptic seizures. Epilepsia *11:* 102, 1970.

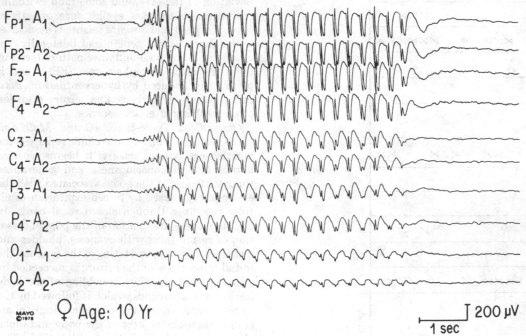

FIGURE 6.   Petit mal absence seizure associated with characteristic generalized, bilaterally synchronous 3 Hz spike-and-wave pattern in EEG.

hours and awaken with a headache and generalized aching and soreness of the muscles.

Generalized tonic-clonic seizures may occur in patients of any age. They may occur as a primary generalized seizure without focal onset, or as a secondary generalized seizure that is initiated from a seizure focus in the cerebral cortex that spreads to involve both cerebral hemispheres and subcortical structures. In primary generalized epilepsy, consciousness is lost at the beginning of the seizure, simultaneous with the onset of generalized convulsion movements. In secondarily generalized seizures, the initial manifestation consists of signs and symptoms associated with the area of the cortex from which the seizure focus initially arises, and is then followed by generalized tonic-clonic movements.

*Myoclonic Seizures.* Myoclonic seizures consist of brief, involuntary jerks of the extremities, face, and body. The jerks are usually bilaterally synchronous and are associated with a generalized spike or spike-and-wave discharge on the EEG. Although myoclonic seizures can occur in patients of any age, they are most frequently seen in children.

*Tonic Seizures.* Tonic seizures consist of brief extension movements of the limbs and are associated with a low-voltage, paroxysmal fast pattern on the EEG, reflecting serial spike discharges. This type of seizure is seen most often in children with the Lennox-Gastaut syndrome.

*Clonic Seizures.* Clonic seizures consist of repetitive clonic movements of the limb and facial muscles, and are often associated with generalized fast spikes or spike-and-wave discharges on the EEG. This type of seizure frequently occurs in children with the Lennox-Gastaut syndrome.

*Atonic and Akinetic Seizures.* Both of these types of seizures are brief, characterized by sudden, abrupt falls to the ground and accompanied by generalized spike-and-wave complexes on the EEG. They are seen most often in children with the Lennox-Gastaut syndrome.

*Infantile Spasms.* Infantile spasms consist of brief episodes of tonic flexion of the neck and body, with the arms flung forward and outward. Less frequently, they consist of extension movements of the body. The episodes usually last 1 to 4 seconds. The EEG accompaniment consists of an initial high-amplitude spike-and-sharp-wave complex, followed by an abrupt decrease in the amplitude of activity, with low-voltage fast rhythms.

**Partial or Focal Seizures.** Partial seizures arise from a localized area of the cerebral cortex; the symptoms of the seizure depend on the site of the seizure focus. On the basis of the symptoms, partial seizures can be divided into two main groups: partial seizures with elementary symptoms and partial seizures with complex symptoms. Partial seizures with elementary symptoms (simple focal seizures) are focal motor or sensory seizures that are often not associated with a loss of consciousness. Partial seizures with complex symptoms (complex partial seizures) are more elaborate, with behavioral, psychic, and emotional components, and usually some impairment of consciousness.

*Partial Seizures with Elementary Symptoms.* These seizures can be subdivided into focal motor seizures, focal sensory seizures, autonomic seizures, and compound seizures.

Focal motor seizures usually originate in the frontal cortex. Seizures arising from the precentral gyrus (the motor strip) are characterized by tonic-clonic movements of the opposite side of the body. These movements can occur in a part of the face, limb, or body or as a march—that is, the Jacksonian seizure.

Another type of motor seizure is the adversive seizure, which arises from a focus in the premotor area of the frontal lobe, and is characterized by deviation of the head, eyes, and body to the opposite side of the seizure focus. Still another type of motor seizure is the postural seizure, in which there is tonic posturing of a part of the body.

Any of the primary sensory areas of the brain can generate focal sensory seizures. Somatic sensory seizures originate in the sensory strip or postcentral gyrus of the parietal lobe, and usually consist of tingling or a pins-and-needles sensation of a part of the body on the side opposite the discharging focus. The seizure may occur in a localized area of the body, face, or extremity, or with a march of symptoms similar to the Jacksonian motor seizure. Visual sensory seizures occur with a seizure discharge in the occipital lobe, and are characterized by unformed visual hallucinations, such as flashing lights or colors, or a dimming of vision in the contralateral visual field. Auditory seizures—usually consisting of sensations of buzzing, ringing, or hissing—occur with a seizure focus in the superior temporal gyrus. Vertiginous seizures are uncommon, but probably arise from a focus in the superior temporal gyrus.

Seizures may be accompanied by autonomic symptoms such as vasomotor changes, flushing, pallor, epigastric sensation, nausea and vomiting, and changes in gastrointestinal motility. Usually, these symptoms are seen with complex partial seizures, and are associated with a discharge in the periinsular or frontotemporal regions.

Compound seizures consist of a combination of symptoms or signs, with involvement of two or more areas of the cortex.

*Partial Seizures with Complex Symptoms (Complex Partial Seizures).* Complex partial seizures are focal seizures that are associated with some impairment of consciousness and, for the most part, arise from the temporal lobe.

Temporal lobe seizures are the most common type of focal seizure. They occur most frequently in adults, and represent about 50 to 55 percent of the seizures that occur in the adult population.

On the basis of the predominant symptoms,

complex partial seizures can be subclassified as those with: (1) impairment of consciousness only, such as transient confusion; (2) cognitive symptoms, such as a sensation of *déjà vu, jamais vu*, distortion of time perception, or a sense of unreality; (3) affective symptoms, such as fear or anxiety; (4) psychosensory symptoms, such as illusions or hallucinations; (5) psychomotor phenomena, such as automatisms and masticatory movements; (6) speech disturbances, such as dysphasia or speech automatisms; and (7) compound forms of the above seizures.

*Partial (Focal Seizures Secondarily Generalized).* A focal seizure may become secondarily generalized. The focal component that precedes the generalized seizure is referred to as an aura. The aura is actually part of the seizure and is an important localizing sign of the focal origin.

**Unilateral Seizures.** In addition to generalized and partial seizures, there is a third type of seizure—the unilateral seizure or hemiconvulsion, which predominates or is restricted to one side of the body. This type of seizure is usually seen in infants and young children.

**Status Epilepticus.** Status epilepticus consists of recurrent or continuous seizures without recovery between the seizures.

*Grand Mal Status.* Grand mal status is characterized by repeated generalized tonic-clonic seizures without recovery of consciousness between the seizures. Anoxia and circulatory collapse occurring as a result of the seizures can cause serious brain damage or death unless the seizures are quickly stopped; thus, this is a true medical emergency, requiring immediate treatment. Grand mal status can be precipitated by a sudden cessation of the use of anticonvulsants, the use of drugs or alcohol, inflammatory processes, metabolic derangements, a head injury, a tumor, hypertensive encephalopathy, and other intercurrent disease processes.

*Absence or Petit Mal Status.* Absence status (also termed "spike-wave stupor") consists of prolonged episodes of a disturbance of mental function in association with continuous or repetitive generalized spike-and-wave discharges on the EEG. Absence status can be manifested as a clouding of consciousness, confusion, apparent psychiatric and cognitive disturbances, automatic behavior, lethargy, somnolence, or amnesia. There may be associated convulsive signs, such as myoclonic jerks, blinking of the eyes, and drooling. Absence status can occur in both children and adults and has been seen in patients older than 60 years of age.

*Temporal Lobe Status.* This rare type of status epilepticus can also present as a prolonged state of confusion with apparent psychiatric and cog-

nitive disturbances, automatic behavior, or amnesia, similar to that of absence status.

*Focal Motor Status.* Focal motor status consists of repetitive or continuous focal motor seizures. It may occur as a result of an acute or subacute disturbance of cerebral function secondary to a vascular disease, encephalitis, an abscess, head trauma, or, less frequently, a tumor. The seizures are often accompanied by periodic lateralized epileptiform discharges in the EEG over the involved area of the brain.

Another type of focal motor status is epilepsia partialis continua, which consists of continuous or recurrent focal motor contractions of the face, limb, or some part of the trunk, and which may continue for days or weeks.

**Differential Diagnosis.** Characteristically, seizures are transient episodes with stereotyped symptoms—usually having an abrupt onset, a brief duration (generally less than 1 to 2 minutes), and a rapid recovery. Seizures must be distinguished from other transient episodes that are nonepileptogenic, including those caused by circulatory disturbances, metabolic disorders, sleep disorders, and psychogenic disturbances mimicking epilepsy.

**Causes.** There are many causes and precipitating factors of seizures. In general, seizures can be classified as primary or secondary, depending on the cause. Primary seizures and seizures caused by extracranial processes are usually generalized, whereas seizures resulting from an intracranial lesion or disease process may be either focal or generalized, depending on whether the disease process is focal or diffuse.

**Evaluation of the Patient.** The diagnostic evaluation should provide answers to the following principal questions: (1) Are the attacks seizures? (2) If they are seizures, what type of seizures are they, and from what area of the brain do they arise? (3) What is the cause of the seizures?

The evaluation should include the history, physical and neurological examinations, certain laboratory studies, and occasionally, psychological testing.

**Treatment.** One should treat the cause of the seizures if possible. Treatment of various underlying neurological or medical conditions and surgical intervention for mass lesions may be necessary. If there are known precipitating factors of seizures, these factors should be avoided if possible.

In most patients, the administration of anticonvulsant drugs is necessary to control the seizures. Currently, the most commonly used anticonvulsant agents are phenobarbital, phenytoin, carbamazepine, primidone, ethosuximide, trimethadione, diazepam, clonazepam, and, most recently, sodium valproate.

The drugs of choice for the various types of seizures are listed in Table XXX.

Status epilepticus should be treated promptly. Respiration and other vital functions should be available because the seizure or the anticonvulsant drugs may affect such functions. If the administration of anticonvulsant agents fails to control the seizures, the use of an anesthetic agent may be necessary.

When an anticonvulsant drug regimen is changed or its use is discontinued, abrupt withdrawal of any drug shold be avoided, as sudden withdrawal may precipitate status epilepticus.

Excision of the epileptogenic focus may be helpful in some patients whose seizures are refractory to the usual forms of therapy. The type of seizure that is most amenable to surgical treatment is temporal lobe epilepsy. Surgical intervention should be considered only after careful evaluation of the patient.

In addition to medical therapy, assistance should be offered to the patient for adjusting to his life situation and coping with the psychological and social consequences of having epilepsy.

**Psychiatric Aspects.** Personality problems and psychiatric symptoms can be seen in patients with epilepsy. These problems and symptoms can result from the patient's inherent personality and his reactions to the disease, the

TABLE XXX
DRUGS OF CHOICE FOR VARIOUS TYPES OF SEIZURES

Generalized tonic-clonic (grand mal) seizures:
  Phenobarbital
  Phenytoin (Dilantin)
  Carbamazepine (Tegretol)
Absence (petit mal) seizures:
  Ethosuximide (Zarontin)
  Sodium valproate (Depakene)
  Trimethadione (Tridione)
Simple partial (focal) seizures:
  Phenobarbital
  Phenytoin (Dilantin)
Complex partial (temporal lobe) seizures:
  Phenytoin (Dilantin)
  Carbamazepine (Tegretol)
  Primidone (Mysoline)
Myoclonic, atonic, akinetic, and atypical absence seizures:
  Clonazepam (Clonopin)
  Diazepam (Valium)
Infantile spasms:
  Adrenocorticotropic hormone
  Corticosteroids
Status epilepticus:
  Diazepam (Valium)
  Phenobarbital
  Amobarbital (Amytal)
  Phenytoin (Dilantin)
  Paraldehyde
  Anesthetic agent

organic brain dysfunction producing the seizures, the response of the patient's personality to the impairment of cerebral function, and the use of medications.

Anticonvulsant medications and other drugs can affect the patient's mental state. Sometimes delirium and psychotic-like reactions can occur with toxic levels of drugs or with abrupt drug withdrawal.

Occasionally, the seizure itself or the postical state is accompanied by psychiatric-like symptoms. Temporal lobe seizures may present with hallucinatory experiences, feelings of fear and anxiety, and confused, altered behavior. Absence status may be associated with prolonged periods of confusion, altered behavior, and slowed mental function. Temporal lobe status, although a rare entity, may present in a similar fashion. During the postictal state the patient can appear to be confused, may have disturbed behavior, and may show primitive reaction patterns.

### Parkinsonism

The clinical disorder is relatively common. The annual prevalence in the Western hemisphere has been reported to be about 200 per 100,000 people. In most cases, the cause of the disorder is obscure. It is commonly a disease of middle life and beyond, although on rare occasions it does affect young adults. It may occur secondary to manganese poisoning, particularly among miners of manganese. It has often complicated the use of phenothiazines and reserpine.

Parkinsonism is a progressive disorder that generally begins in late adult life. Often, the first characteristic sign is a loss of associated movements, with a peculiar immobility of the patient. Tremor may become apparent later; it is most prominent at rest or on assuming a posture and is a characteristic pill-rolling tremor. As with most extrapyramidal disorders, the tremor becomes more prominent with tension and disappears with sleep. In some patients, tremor never becomes an important part of the illness; in others, it may be the most prominent symptom.

Physical examination reveals an impairment of fine movements and a peculiar, cogwheel kind of rigidity that is most apparent in the neck and in the upper extremities. Sucking reflexes, positive Babinski's signs, and other evidence of pyramidal trace involvement are common.

Intellectual impairment is a common component of parkinsonism. Dementia is usually mild, and the patients are able to continue their ordinary activities. However, the dementia tends to increase with the duration and severity of the disease, and may prevent the patient from participating in his usual occupation.

Depression is frequently associated with parkinsonism, concurring in as many as one-third to one-half of all such cases.

The course of parkinsonism is gradually progressive, regardless of therapy. Some patients may have long periods in which the illness appears to show no real progression; others may be completely disabled within a few years of onset.

At present, the treatment of choice is the drug Sinemet, a medication containing a decarboxylase inhibitor and L-dopa at a fixed ratio of 10 parts of L-dopa to 1 part of inhibitor. Most patients with parkinsonism may be started on Sinemet-10/100, four tablets a day; the dosage may be gradually increased to tolerance. Many patients find the optimal dosage to be about 1,000 mg a day.

Amantadine hydrochloride (Symmetrel) has also proved useful and has the advantages of few side effects and a relatively simple therapeutic dose (100 mg twice a day). Its principal use is as an adjunct to therapy with Sinemet.

An unusual disorder with the features of parkinsonism and dementia has been described among the Chamorro people of Guam. The illness is common on Guam, where it accounts for 7 percent of the deaths in the local population.

### Huntington's Chorea

In 1872, Huntington described a hereditary disorder, characterized by choreiform movements and dementia, that began in adult life. Huntington's chorea is rare; it is estimated that there are about 6 such patients in 100,000 persons in the Western hemisphere. The disorder is inherited as an autosomal dominant with good penetrance.

In this disorder, the brain is extensively atrophied, particularly in the caudate and putamen.

The illness eventually progresses to involve the two facets of the disease. The onset is usually insidious; it is often heralded by a personality change that interferes with the patient's ability to adapt to his environment. The disease may begin at any age, but is most common in late middle life. Both sexes are affected in equal numbers. When the movements are first noted, they are frequently misinterpreted as inconsequential habit spasms or tics. As a result, the disease is frequently not recognized for several years, particularly since the family history has often been obscured. Eventually, the choreiform movements or the dementia makes chronic hospitalization imperative. The clinical course then is one of gradual progression, death occurring 10 to 20 years after the onset of the disease. Suicide is frequent in patients with this disorder.

The diagnosis depends on the recognition of the progressive choreiform movements and dementia in a patient with a family history of the disorder.

The only satisfactory treatment at present is prevention of the transmission of the responsible genes.

### Normal Pressure Hydrocephalus

This disorder is a treatable type of dementia in patients with enlarged ventricles and normal cerebrospinal fluid pressure. However, the disorder appears to be relatively uncommon, and, unfortunately, only a few of the many patients who have dementia are found to have the disorder that fits this description.

The disorder is characterized by a progressive dementia that is not unlike that of senile dementia. It occurs for the most part in adults of middle or late life. An associated gait disturbance appears to be more of an apraxia of gait than ataxia. The patient's relatives frequently state that he has had difficulty in bladder control. This sign often seems to be attributable more to a lack of concern than to a true loss of control of the bladder.

Computed axial tomography is now reported to be the only test to differentiate patients likely to improve after surgical diversion of cerebrospinal fluid from those not likely to improve.

If the diagnosis can be established, the treatment of choice is shunting of the cerebrospinal fluid from the ventricular space to either the atrium or the peritoneal space.

### Multiple Sclerosis

Multiple sclerosis is characterized by remission and exacerbations, and by multifocal lesions in the white matter of the central nervous system. In the absence of a known specific cause, it is customarily defined in terms of the diffuseness of the neurological lesions, scattered in both time and space.

It has been estimated that the prevalence of multiple sclerosis in the Western hemisphere is 50 patients per 100,000 population. There is good evidence that the disease is much more frequent in cold and temperate climates than in the tropics and subtropics. It is more common in women than in men, and is predominantly a disease of young adults, the onset in the vast majority of patients being between the ages of 20 and 40 years.

Features suggesting a psychiatric disorder, either as a direct result of the central nervous system lesions or in response to the lesions, are so frequent that they create a diagnostic problem. Mental disturbances are present in at least

50 percent of patients with multiple sclerosis. Often, there is a change in emotional tone, which is usually reported as being one of euphoria, although an instability of mood is reported perhaps as often.

Impairment of cognition is common as the disease progresses and this impairment may lead to gross mental deterioration.

### Amyotrophic Lateral Sclerosis

Amyotrophic lateral sclerosis is a progressive asymmetrical muscular atrophy, beginning in adult life and progressing in months or years to involve all the striated muscles except the cardiac and ocular muscles. In addition to muscular atrophy, the patients have signs of pyramidal tract involvement. The illness is rare, occurring in about 1.6 persons per 100,000 a year.

A few of these patients have concomitant dementia. The relation of dementia to disease of the motor neuron is not clear and may be coincidential. Despite its physical devastation of the patient, the disease is characterized by no other associated psychiatric symptoms.

### Systemic Lupus Erythematosus

Abnormalities in mental function have been reported in many patients with systemic lupus erythematosus. Although the precise incidence of these mental abnormalities in the disease is unclear, it may vary between 15 and 50 percent. The mental disturbances may take one of several forms: The patient may have an acute organic mental disorder, with disorientation, confusion, inattention, delusions, and hallucinations. A chronic progressive dementia may occur, along with a general deterioration of intellectual function and memory. The disease may produce classical, affective, schizophreniform reactions that are indistinguishable from the usual functional psychoses; catatonic and paranoid behavior is not uncommon within this subgroup. Neurotic reactions may occur, including marked anxiety and depression.

### Confusional States after Cardiac Surgery

As many as half of the patients undergoing cardiopulmonary bypass and cardiac surgery may have neurological and psychiatric symptoms. These symptoms include delayed recovery of consciousness, confusion, disorientation, and focal abnormalities.

The acute confusional state after surgery may be related to sensory deprivation during prolonged recovery in a postoperative coronary intensive care unit, and to possible toxic reactions to the medications used at this time. However,

histological studies have suggested that these symptoms have a structural basis. In most patients, this disorder is transient, although some patients complain of impaired memory and dulled intellect for months after surgery.

### Transient Global Amnesia

Transient global amnesia is thought to result from a temporary physiological alteration of the brain. The precise cause of this disorder is unknown. Most clinicians now believe it to be an organic, rather than psychogenic, disturbance, but whether its cause is epileptiform or vascular, or neither, is unclear.

The patient with this syndrome abruptly loses his ability to recall recent events or to record new memories. Events of the distant past are readily recalled. Although the patient is often aware of some disturbance in function during the episode, he may still perform highly complex mental and physical acts.

### Intracranial Neoplasms

Psychiatric symptoms are often the earliest and occasionally the only symptoms of an intracranial tumor. They may precede the more obvious motor or sensory manifestations of brain tumor by weeks or even months.

The mental symptoms of patients who have brain tumors may vary, not only in different patients, but also in the same patient from hour to hour. Brain tumors are usually classified by the most prevalent cell type contained within the tumor.

**Clinical Symptoms and Course.** The patient with a brain tumor suffers a relentless progression in symptoms. The classic neurological symptoms are headache and impaired motor or sensory function. Even when these disturbances are present, they may be obscured by the patient's mental symptoms at first, and may be detectable only after the most careful interrogation and examination. The salient feature of the patient's history is often the unremitting progression of his symptoms, his attempts to adapt producing only temporary periods of respite.

Certain focal brain lesions produce specific intellectual deficits, although most patients with a brain tumor have simultaneous evidence of more generally impaired intellectual function.

*Cognition.* Impaired intellectual functioning often accompanies the presence of a brain tumor, regardless of its type or location.

*Language Skills.* Disorders of language function, particularly if tumor growth is rapid, may be severe. In fact, defects of language function often obscure all other mental symptoms.

*Memory.* Loss of memory is a frequent symptom of brain tumors. Patients with brain tumors may present with Korsakoff's syndrome, retaining no memory of events that occurred since the illness began. Events of the immediate past, even painful ones, are lost. Old memories are retained, however, and the patient is unaware of his recent memory loss.

*Perception.* Prominent perceptual defects are often associated with behavioral disorders, especially when the patient needs to summate tactile, auditory, and visual perception.

*Awareness.* Alterations of consciousness are common late symptoms of increased intracranial pressure due to a brain tumor. Tumors arising in the upper part of the brain stem may produce a unique symptom called akinetic mutism or coma vigil. The patient appears asleep but ready to be aroused.

*Response to Cerebral Loss.* Most mental symptoms in patients with brain tumors result from the patient's response to the destruction of his most valued possession—his cerebral function. These symptoms run the gamut of human complaints. They differ little from those after other catastrophic losses suffered by a person. If the patient becomes aware of the destruction only gradually, the earliest psychiatric symptom is often irritability. Later, the patient usually becomes anxious and depressed. He may finally respond to a progressive cerebral impairment by denial of even the most flagrant loss, with a resultant disappearance of his anxiety and depression.

Often, the severity of the psychological reaction to a brain tumor can best be predicted by the patient's previous ability to adapt to his environment. Inevitably, however, as the tumor progresses, the patient notes his shrinking ability to adapt to his environment. The resulting anxiety and depression are related to the patient's inability to meet the intellectual challenges in his environment. As the deterioration continues, a patient characteristically responds with symptoms of denial, anxiety, depression, and, finally, apathy. Sometimes a patient becomes euphoric, with an increasing sense of well-being, levity, senseless joking, and punning (witzelsucht).

**Diagnosis.** A brain tumor is particularly difficult to diagnose when the presenting symptoms are psychiatric (see Fig. 7). When the onset of psychiatric symptoms is unrelated to situational factors and the clinical course is progressive, the physician should weigh the possibility of a brain tumor.

## Metabolic and Endocrine Disorders

Metabolic encephalopathy is a common cause of organic brain dysfunction, and is capable of producing alterations in mental function, behavior, and neurological function. Such a diagnosis should always be considered whenever recent and rapid changes in behavior, thinking, and consciousness have occurred. The earliest signs are likely to be impairment of memory, particularly recent memory, and orientation. Some patients become agitated, anxious, and hyperactive; others become quieter, withdrawn, and inactive. As metabolic encephalopathies worsen, confusion or delirium gives way to decreased responsiveness, to stupor, and, eventually, to coma.

**Hepatic Encephalopathy.** Severe impairment of liver function from either acute or chronic liver disease, or the shunting of portal venous blood into the systemic circulation, may be attended by disturbances of consciousness, mental changes, asterixis, hyperventilation, and electroencephalographic abnormalities.

Disturbances of consciousness can vary from apathy and drowsiness to coma. The changes in memory, intellect, and personality are nonspecific. Death is very likely in severe cases.

**Uremic Encephalopathy.** Acute or chronic failure of normal renal function leads to serious systemic metabolic changes. Neurological dysfunction—particulary alterations in memory, orientation, and consciousness—is a common accompaniment. Asterixis, similar to that in hepatic encephalopathy, may be seen. A peripheral neuropathy can develop during chronic uremia, with diffuse sensory and motor impairment in the distal portion of the limbs, and reduced or absent deep-tendon reflexes. Restlessness and crawling sensations of the limbs, twitching of muscles singly or in groups, and sometimes persistent hiccups, can be distressing and exhausting to the patient. In severe uremia, generalized convulsions can occur, sometimes in rapid succession, leading to a greater risk of death. Intravenously administered diazepam may be an effective treatment, but the use of barbiturates or even anesthetics may be required for seizure control.

During rapid renal dialysis, in the face of very high blood urea levels, a dialysis dysequilibrium syndrome has been seen, with headache, confusion, alterations in consciousness, and convulsions.

**Hypoglycemic Encephalopathy.** Excessive or inappropriate administration of insulin and hyperinsulinism, caused by a functioning benign adenoma of inlet cells of the pancreas, are the

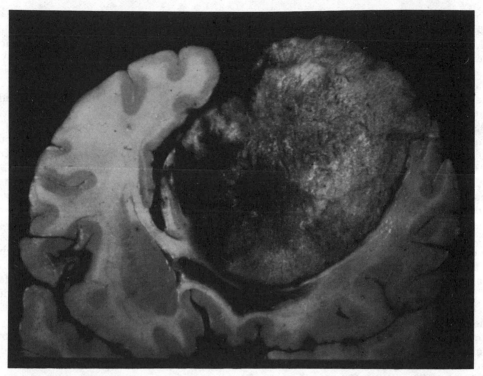

FIGURE 7.  Large parasagittal meningioma. The patient with this tumor presented with depression and later developed hemiplegia.

two most likely causes of hypoglycemia encephalopathy, although hypoglycemia can have a variety of other sources, such as liver necrosis, adrenocortical or pituitary failure, glycogen storage disease of the liver, and insulin coma therapy for schizophrenia.

Hypoglycemic episodes are likely to occur in the early morning hours or after exercise. Premonitory symptoms, which do not always occur in every patient, include nausea, sweating, tachycardia, and feelings of hunger, apprehension, and restlessness. With progressive impairment, disorientation, confusion, hallucinations, pallor, and extreme restlessness or agitation develop. Diplopia, grand mal or focal seizures, myoclonic jerks, and hyperreflexia with clonus and Babinski's responses, can be other features. Stupor and then coma may follow quickly. An occasional patient has no signs or symptoms preceding convulsions.

Many patients with anxiety or other neurotic symptoms are mistakenly thought to have hypoglycemia. When hypoglycemia is thought to be a possible cause of coma or convulsions, blood should be drawn for a blood glucose determination, and then glucose should immediately be given intravenously—at least 25 ml of a 50 percent glucose solution.

**Diabetic Ketoacidosis.** The condition begins with feelings of weakness, easy fatigability and listlessness, and increasing polyuria and polydipsia. Headache and sometimes nausea and vomiting appear. Depending on the severity of the diabetes and the presence of infection, the situation worsens in a matter of hours to several days.

Diabetic coma is a medical emergency. In any unconscious patient who is known or suspected to be diabetic, the differential diagnosis between hypoglycemic coma and diabetic coma must be made. Hypoglycemia as a cause of the coma can be virtually excluded if the patient does not regain consciousness within a few minutes after the intravenous administration of 25 ml of a 50 percent glucose solution.

Diabetic coma without ketoacidosis (nonketotic hyperglycemic coma) may occur, particularly in older persons with adult-onset diabetes mellitus, and it may be the first manifestation of that disease. The principles of treatment include adequate fluid and electrolyte replacement, insulin, and the management of any associated infection or underlying disease.

**Acute Intermittent Porphyria.** This disorder is inherited as an autosomal dominant trait, and its symptoms are most likely to begin after puberty or in the third and fourth decades of life. Women are affected more often than men. A defect exists in the regulation of the liver enzyme, δ-aminolevulinic acid synthetase, important in pyrrole metabolism. The use of barbiturates for any reason is absolutely contraindicated in any person known to have acute intermittent porphyria or to have a relative with the disease.

Symptoms of nervousness and emotional instability are frequently present over a long period. Recurrent abdominal pains, often colicky in nature, are common and sometimes lead to an unnecessary abdominal operation before the true diagnosis is made. Neurological symptoms are also common and may become so severe that death results. Peripheral neuropathy involving all or one of the limbs and cranial nerve signs—such as optic atrophy, facial palsy, ophthalmoplegia, and dysphagia—may all be seen. Confusion, delirium, convulsions, and coma can develop during acute attacks.

There is, as yet, no satisfactory or specific treatment for acute intermittent porphyria. During acute episodes, only careful symptomatic measures can be used.

**Endocrine Disorders.** Changes in personality, mental functions, and memory, as well as neurological abnormalities, occur frequently in endocrine disorders, and they may be prominent manifestations in some instances. Correction of the underlying endocrine problem usually reverses these changes.

Hypothalamic involvement is associated with behavioral disturbances that are sometimes dramatic. Alterations in appetite causing severe inanition or extreme obesity, marked emotional lability, inappropriate rage reactions, and aberrations of the normal sleep pattern are examples of such disturbances.

Thyroid disorders produce hyperthyroidism or myxedema. A sensation of easy fatigability and generalized weakness is felt by most hyperthyroid patients. Insomnia, weight loss in spite of an increased appetite, tremulousness, palpitations, and increased perspiration are all common changes. The patient may appear anxious and restless, and, in the early stages, a neurotic reaction may be mistakenly considered. Prominent mental disturbances develop in a few patients, with impairment of memory, orientation, and judgment, and even manic excitement and schizophrenic-like symptoms with delusions and hallucinations. Occasionally, masked hyperthyroidism, characterized by apathy and mental confusion without tremor and overactivity, occurs, especially in old persons.

The occurrence of hypokalemic periodic paralysis in a patient with hyperthyroidism is the rare association of two distinct diseases; latent until hyperthyroidism develops, the periodic paralysis subsides after treatment of the thyroid disease. Myasthenia gravis can also be associated with hyperthyroidism.

Treatment of hyperthyroidism in most adults consists of the administration of radioactive iodine, although surgical thyroidectomy is still useful in selected patients. Mental symptoms can be expected to improve with adequate treatment of the hyperthyroidism, but, in the occasional patient with severe mental symptoms, hospitalization for their management is needed.

Hypothyroidism (myxedema) arises because of a deficiency of thyroid hormone.

Easy fatigability, feelings of weakness and sleepiness, increased sensitivity to cold, reduced sweating with dryness and thickening of the skin, brittle and thinning hair, and puffy facies are all common manifestations of myxedema. Sometimes the patient is hardly aware of the changes occurring in him, but others note his increased sluggishness, irritability, and slowed, indistinct speech and hoarseness. In some patients, changes in personality, memory, and intellectual function are prominent, and may simulate major psychiatric or organic brain disease. Cerebellar gait ataxia is a feature of some cases.

Parathyroid dysfunction produces derangements of calcium metabolism. Excessive secretion of parathyroid hormone from a parathyroid adenoma or hyperplasia causes hypercalcemia. Common complaints are lassitude, weakness, increased irritability, and anxiety. Some patients display frank disorders of personality and mental function, such as agitation, paranoid thinking, depression, psychotic reactions, confusion, and stupor. Neuromuscular excitability, which depends on a proper calcium ion concentration, is reduced, and true muscle weakness may appear. Occasionally, the weakness is severe enough to prevent the patient from sitting or standing alone or even lifting a limb off his bed.

Lowered serum calcium levels in hypoparathyroidism lead to increased neuromuscular excitability, with transient paresthesias, muscle cramping and twitching, overt tetany with spontaneous carpopedal muscle spasms, and convulsive seizures. Mental symptoms such as confusion, agitation or drowsiness, hallucinations, and depression can also develop.

Adrenal disorders cause changes in the normal secretion of hormones from the adrenal cortex and the adrenal medulla. They are capable of producing significant neurological and psychological changes. Patients with chronic adrenocortical insufficiency (Addison's disease), which is most frequently the result of adrenocortical atrophy or granulomatous invasion due to tuberculous or fungal infection, exhibit mild mental symptoms, such as apathy, easy fatigability, irritability, and depression. Occasionally, psychotic reactions or confusion develops. Cortisone or one of its synthetic derivatives is effective in correcting those abnormalities.

Excessive quantities of cortisol produced by an adrenocortical tumor or hyperplasia (Cushing's syndrome), or the administration of high doses of corticosteroids are likely to produce euphoria, insomnia, restlessness, and increased motor activity. Some patients become anxious and depressed. Psychotic reactions, with schizophrenic or manic-depressive symptoms, are seen in a small number of patients. Suicidal behavior may occur. Psychiatric reactions are more likely to be seen in persons with a previous history of psychiatric illness, but that is not always true.

## Nutritional Disorders

Thiamine (vitamin $B_1$) is required in the formation of the coenzyme thiamine pyrophosphate, which is essential in the intermediary metabolism of carbohydrate. Thiamine deficiency leads to beriberi, characterized chiefly by cardiovascular and neurological changes, and Wernicke-Korsakoff's syndrome, which is most often associated with chronic alcoholism.

**Beriberi.** This disorder occurs primarily in Asia and in areas of famine or poverty; historically, it was an important disease in prisoner-of-war camps in Asia during World War II. Subacute or chronic onset is most common, but it occasionally runs a more rapid acute course. Mental disturbances such as apathy, depression, irritability, nervousness, and poor concentration are frequently seen, but, when more severe changes occur, involving memory and intellectual function, Wernicke-Korsakoff's syndrome is difficult to exclude.

**Central Pontine Myelinolysis.** This disorder is a demyelinating disorder of the brain stem that seems to arise on a nutritional basis. Most patients have been alcoholics, although some have been severely malnourished for other reasons. A single symmetrical focus of demyelination in the center of the base of the pons, with relative preservation of axis cylinders and severe loss of oligodendroglial cells, is characteristic. Quadriparesis with bulbar involvement has occurred in some patients; others have shown no clinical changes, the diagnosis being made on postmortem study.

**Marchiafava-Bignami Disease.** Another uncommon neurological disorder associated with chronic alcoholism, this disease is characterized by the symmetrical degeneration of myelin in the central portion of the corpus callosum. Focal neurological signs and symptoms—such as hemiparesis, aphasia, apraxias, and grand mal seizures—develop, and mental changes are almost always present, with manic, paranoid, and delusional states, depression, or dementia.

**Pellagra.** Dietary insufficiency of nicotinic acid and its precursor, tryptophan, is associated with pellagra, a nutritional deficiency disease of world-wide occurrence. Involvement of the nervous system is important, with headaches, insomnia, apathy, confusional states, delusions, and, eventually, dementia. Cerebellar ataxia can be seen. Peripheral neuropathy is also a frequent feature, but it is probably a manifestation of other associated vitamin deficiencies, particularly thiamine deficiency.

The response of the pellagra patient to treatment with nicotinic acid is rapid, with significant improvement in confusion, abdominal symptoms, and painful swollen tongue being evident in the first 24 hours. However, dementia from prolonged illness may improve slowly and incompletely. If a peripheral neuropathy is present, additional administration of thiamine is important.

Hartnup disease is a familial condition with similarities to pellagra; it is characterized by episodes of cerebellar ataxia, a light-sensitive dermatitis, and mental changes similar to those seen in pellagra. Its pathogenesis is uncertain, but defective absorption and intracellular transport of tryptophan seem to be present. Aminoaciduria and a large urinary output of indolic compounds can be demonstrated. Nicotinic acid and a good diet with protein seem to be helpful.

**Pyridoxine Deficiency.** The clinical syndrome of pyridoxine deficiency is not well defined. Infantile convulsions responsive to pyridoxine administration have been reported in some families, but the specific metabolic defect is unknown, although a disorder of the glutamic acid decarboxylase system has been considered. Isoniazid, used in the treatment of tuberculosis, is an antimetabolite to pyridoxine, inhibiting the formation of its coenzyme form. Patients receiving antituberculosis treatment with isoniazid are prone to develop a peripheral neuropathy; that is especially true of chronic alcoholics and others with poor nutrition, who may rapidly develop a severe disabling neuropathy. The neuropathy responds to pyridoxine, and the occurrence of the neuropathy can be prevented by giving pyridoxine daily to patients receiving isoniazid therapy.

**Vitamin B$_{12}$ Deficiency.** This state arises because of the failure of the gastric mucosal cells to secrete a specific substance, intrinsic factor, required for the normal absorption of dietary vitamin B$_{12}$ from the ileum. The deficiency state is characterized by the development of a megaloblastic anemia (pernicious anemia) and neurological manifestations due to degenerative changes in the peripheral nerves, the spinal cord, and the brain. About 80 percent of patients develop neurological changes; these changes are commonly associated with the megaloblastic anemia, but they occasionally precede the onset of hematological abnormalities.

Mental changes—such as apathy, depression, irritability, and moodiness—are common. In a few patients, confusion, delusions, hallucinations, and dementia, sometimes with paranoid features, are prominent manifestations, presumably related to cerebral involvement with patchy areas of demyelination and degeneration.

The diagnosis can be established by the findings of a low serum B$_{12}$ level, failure to absorb orally administered radioactive vitamin B$_{12}$ (Schilling test), and gastric achlorhydria.

The neurological manifestations of vitamin B$_{12}$ deficiency can be completely and rapidly arrested by the early and continued administration of parenteral vitamin B$_{12}$ therapy.

**Inborn Errors of Metabolism.** Metabolic anomalies affecting the normal handling of lipids (such as lipid storage disease and the leukodystrophies), carbohydrates (such as galactosemia, the mucopolysaccharidoses, and the glycogen storage disease), and protein (such as the aminoacidurias like hepatolenticular degeneration and phenylketonuria) have become much better understood in recent years. These diseases are likely to be heredofamilial; many of them are uncommon or rare, and they are particularly prone to appear in infancy or childhood. Involvement of the central nervous system is frequent, causing mental retardation, convulsive disorders, or progressive neurological deterioration and early death.

Hepatolenticular degeneration (Wilson's disease), inherited as an autosomal recessive defect, is characterized by abnormal copper metabolism, degenerative changes in the brain, cirrhosis of the liver, and the deposition of brownish copper-containing granules of pigment around the corneal margin in Descemet's membrane of the cornea (Kayser-Fleischer ring). Excessive copper deposition also occurs elsewhere in the body, especially in the liver, brain, and kidneys. Although mental symptoms are not promi-

nent in all cases, especially in the early stages, they do occur, and they can become marked. Mild alterations in personality may be present early, with irritability, silliness, difficulty in concentrating, and facile behavior. Memory and intellectual impairment develop in some cases, as do psychotic symptoms, which may be transient and which include hypomanic or paranoid episodes, irritable outbursts, and hallucinations. Untreated, the disease progresses to a stage of total disability and confinement to bed over 3 to 10 years.

D-Penicillamine, a chelating agent that promotes a reduction of total body copper and a marked increase in the urinary excretion of copper, is an effective treatment.

### Brain Trauma

Seven behavioral syndromes ordinarily apply to behavior seen in patients with brain trauma. These categories include delirium, dementia, amnestic syndrome, organic delusional syndrome, hallucinosis, organic affective syndrome, and organic personality syndrome.

Concussion, contusion, hemorrhage, thrombosis, and brain edema are the pathological states usually associated with closed-head injuries (see Fig. 8).

Penetrating wounds may cause local tissue damage, blast effects, tearing of the brain substance and vessels, and possibly infection. Neurosurgical intervention is often required in this type of injury for debridement of the damaged tissue, removal of foreign bodies, and elevation of depressed skull fragments.

**Psychopathology.** The behavioral disorders observed after head trauma are the outcome of several basic causes. The person's personality may undergo changes because of the organic damage itself. A major contributor to personality change after head trauma is impairment of abstract attitude. People with impairment of abstract ability are unable in any given situation to discover its essence, unless it is directly related to their own personalities or something very familiar and preferred by them. The brain-damaged person seems unable to synthesize incoming information and correlate it with action allowing smoothly modulated, goal-directed, selective behavior. Overtly, this behavior results in crude behavior, or the person seems to be acting in a simplistic, stimulus-response manner.

Goal-directed activities for these people are extremely difficult, because the cognitive operations that would successfully lead to a solution disintegrate and are replaced by a series of iso-

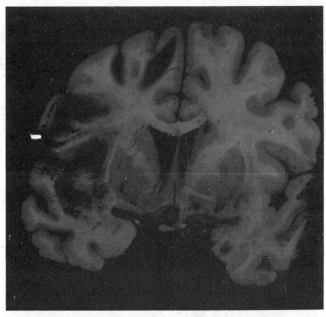

FIGURE 8. Brain section showing coup lesion of the left temporal lobe (smaller contusion) and contrecoup lesion of the right temporal and parietal lobes (larger contusion). This 67-year-old woman died 4 hours after striking the left side of her head and sustaining fractures of the left temporal and parietal bones in an automobile accident.

lated fragmented connections, often not associated with the general plan of action. There is great difficulty in defining a hierarchy or set of priorities to accomplish the task. When the person is unable to organize himself to meet demands made on him by the environment or internal needs, overwhelming anxiety or rage reactions result.

### Infections

Infectious diseases cause brain dysfunction either by directly invading brain tissue or by producing toxic, hypoxic, or allergic effects from an infection elsewhere in the body. Mental and behavioral changes often result, although they are nonspecific and unrelated to the specific pathogen.

Mild effects—such as irritability, insomnia, and restlessness—may appear early in the illness, but subside completely if the infection is overcome rapidly. With progression of the infection, more severe changes can develop, including combativeness, visual hallucinations, impaired memory, and such alterations in consciousness as lethargy, drowsiness, stupor, and coma. Ordinarily, those manifestations disappear as the infection is brought under control, but changes of personality and intellect sometimes persist as sequelae of the infection. For example, viral encephalitis is often followed by subjective symptoms, such as nervousness, irritability, lassitude, and defective memory. Less commonly, meningitis and encephalitis are followed by more severe sequelae, such as mental retardation, dementia, and marked instability of emotions and personality.

Any infection may at some time present itself as intracranial, for the central nervous system offers less resistance to infection than does any other tissue of the body. Intracranial infections are usually classified as being localized in the subarachnoid space (meningitis), involving brain tissue (encephalitis), or being confined to encapsulated regions within the brain or meninges (abscess). Actually, involvement is seldom restricted in that fashion. Meningitis always affects brain tissue to some extent, and encephalitis, early in its course, is usually accompanied by meningitis. A brain abscess begins as a localized cerebritis that only later in its clinical course becomes well localized or encapsulated.

### REFERENCES

Benson F D, Blumer D: *Psychiatric Aspects of Neurological Disease*, vol 1. Grune & Stratton, New York, 1975.

Benson F D, Blumer D: *Psychiatric Aspects of Neurological Disease*, vol 2. Grune & Stratton, New York, 1982.

Karzman R, Terry R: *The Neurology of Aging.* F. A. Davis, Philadelphia, 1983.

Lishman W A: *Organic Psychiatry.* Blackwell Scientific Publications, Oxford, 1978.

Pincus J H, Tucker G J: *Behavioral Neurology,* ed 2. Oxford University Press, New York, 1978.

Seltzer B, Sherwin I: Organic brain syndromes: An empirical study and critical review. Am J Psychiatry *135:* 13, 1978.

Strub R L, Black F W: *Organic Brain Syndromes.* F. A. Davis, Philadelphia, 1981.

Wells C E: Chronic brain disease: An overview. Am J Psychiatry *135:* 1, 1978.

Wells C E: Chronic brain disease: An update on alcoholism, Parkinson's disease, and dementia. Hosp Community Psychiatry *33:* 111, 1982.

Wells C E: Organic mental disorders. In *Comprehensive Textbook of Psychiatry,* ed 4, H I Kaplan, B J Sadock, editors, p 834. Williams & Wilkins, Baltimore, 1985.

Wells C E, Duncan G W: *Neurology for Psychiatrists.* F. A. Davis, Philadelphia, 1980.

# 17

# Neurotic Disorders

## Introduction to Neurotic Disorders

According to DSM-III a neurotic disorder is defined as: "A mental disorder in which the predominant disturbance is a symptom or group of symptoms that is distressing to the individual and is recognized by him or her as unacceptable and alien (ego-dystonic); reality testing is grossly intact. Behavior does not actively violate gross social norms (though it may be quite disabling). The disturbance is relatively enduring or recurrent without treatment, and is not limited to a transitory reaction to stressors. There is no demonstrable organic etiology or factor."

In this book we have included under neurotic disorders the following: anxiety state, which is subdivided into panic disorder, generalized anxiety disorder and obsessive-compulsive disorder; phobic disorder; posttraumatic stress disorder; somatoform disorder; and dissociative disorder. Dysthymic disorder or depressive neurosis may be found in Chapter 14 and psychosexual disorders in Chapter 20.

This organization is consistent with the DSM-III classification of neurotic disorders. In this chapter the terms in parentheses represent the former DSM-II classification and also the current ICD-9 classification. Those terms in parentheses are acceptable as alternative terms to the official DSM-III nomenclature.

---

## 17.1 ANXIETY STATE (ANXIETY NEUROSIS)

### Introduction

Whether it exists alone as the predominant symptom or in conjunction with other manifestations of emotional disorder, anxiety is a central feature of most psychiatric illness, and the clinician must be familiar with its nature and causes.

In anxiety neurosis, the experience of anxiety is the main disturbance. There are two classifications in DSM-III. If it is episodic, it is known as panic disorder; if it is chronic and persistent, it is known as generalized anxiety disorder.

### Definition

DSM-III states that, in panic disorder, the essential feature is recurrent anxiety (panic) attacks and nervousness and the panic attacks are manifested by discrete periods of sudden onset of intensive apprehension, fearfulness or terror often associated with feelings of impending doom (see Table I). In the generalized anx-

iety disorder, the anxiety is persistent for at least 1 month and tends to be chronic in nature (see Table II).

### Epidemiology

Some 5 percent of the population may suffer from acute or chronic anxiety, with women outnumbering men two to one. A few studies indicate that anxiety runs in families, and one investigation of twin pairs suggests the possibility of a genetic basis for the disorder.

### Causes

Any discussion of the causes of anxiety must deal with both psychological and physiological processes.

#### Psychological Aspects

Anxiety is a universal human experience, characterized by a fearful anticipation of an unpleasant event in the future. In psychoanalytic theory, anxiety is differentiated from fear. Anxiety is the person's response to a danger that threatens from within in the form of a forbidden

TABLE I
DIAGNOSTIC CRITERIA FOR PANIC DISORDER*

A. At least three panic attacks within a 3-week period in circumstances other than during marked physical exertion or in a life-threatening situation. The attacks are not precipitated only by exposure to a circumscribed phobic stimulus.

B. Panic attacks are manifested by discrete periods of apprehension or fear, and at least four of the following symptoms appear during each attack:

    (1) dyspnea
    (2) palpitations
    (3) chest pain or discomfort
    (4) choking or smothering sensations
    (5) dizziness, vertigo, or unsteady feelings
    (6) feelings of unreality
    (7) paresthesias (tingling in hands or feet)
    (8) hot and cold flashes
    (9) sweating
    (10) faintness
    (11) trembling or shaking
    (12) fear of dying, going crazy, or doing something uncontrolled during an attack

C. Not due to a physical disorder or another mental disorder, such as Major Depression, Somatization Disorder, or Schizophrenia.

D. The disorder is not associated with Agoraphobia.

* From American Psychiatric Association: *Diagnostic and Statistical Manual of Mental Disorders*, ed 3. American Psychiatric Association, Washington, DC, 1980. Used with permission.

TABLE II
DIAGNOSTIC CRITERIA FOR GENERALIZED ANXIETY DISORDER*

A. Generalized, persistent anxiety is manifested by symptoms from three of the following four categories:

    (1) *motor tension*: shakiness, jitteriness, jumpiness, trembling, tension, muscle aches, fatigability, inability to relax, eyelid twitch, furrowed brow, strained face, fidgeting, restlessness, easy startle
    (2) *autonomic hyperactivity*: sweating, heart pounding or racing, cold, clammy hands, dry mouth, dizziness, light-headedness, paresthesias (tingling in hands or feet), upset stomach, hot or cold spells, frequent urination, diarrhea, discomfort in the pit of the stomach, lump in the throat, flushing, pallor, high resting pulse and respiration rate
    (3) *apprehensive expectation*: anxiety, worry, fear, rumination, and anticipation of misfortune to self or others
    (4) *vigilance and scanning*: hyperattentiveness resulting in distractibility, difficulty in concentrating, insomnia, feeling "on edge," irritability, impatience

B. The anxious mood has been continuous for at least one month.

C. Not due to another mental disorder, such as a Depressive Disorder or Schizophrenia.

D. At least 18 years of age.

* From American Psychiatric Association: *Diagnostic and Statistical Manual of Mental Disorders*, ed 3. American Psychiatric Association, Washington, DC, 1980. Used with permission.

instinctual drive that is about to escape from his control. Fear, on the other hand, is defined as the reaction to a real external danger that threatens the person with possible injury or death. In actuality, this theoretical distinction cannot always be strictly maintained. In phobic disorder, for example, the threatening situation is experienced by the patient as being external, although there may, in reality, be little or nothing dangerous about it. At the same time, an external situation that is genuinely hazardous may arouse instinctual drives that are a function of internally derived anxiety. In any given specific episode, both fear and anxiety may be present in varying proportions; from a practical, clinical point of view, it is probably more relevant to ascertain the causes of the affect than to try to decide whether it is fear or anxiety.

Anxiety is viewed as playing a central role in the functioning of the psychic apparatus. As the ego's reaction to an internal threat arising from forbidden instinctual drives, anxiety is experienced in consciousness as mental pain. The pain, in turn, motivates the ego to defensive maneuvers aimed at controlling the drives, in order to avoid the mental suffering. Anxiety, in other words, is viewed as a signal or indicator to the ego both of the need to erect psychological defenses and of the success of their functioning. In this theoretical scheme, anxiety is not necessarily considered as being pathological.

### Current Psychodynamic Theories

When anxiety occurs, it is a sign of movement within; it is an indication that something is disturbing the internal psychological equilibrium.

Anxiety is a signal to the ego that an unacceptable drive is pressing for conscious representation and discharge; as a signal, it arouses the ego to take defensive action against the pressures from within. If the defenses are successful, the anxiety is dispelled or safely contained, but, depending on the nature of the defenses used, the person may develop a variety of neurotic symptoms. Ideally, the use of repression alone should result in a restoration of psychological equilibrium without symptom formation, since effective repression completely contains the drives and their associated affects and fantasies by rendering them unconscious. More often than not, however, repression is not entirely effective, and it is necessary to call into play auxiliary defenses. Such defenses include conversion, displacement, regression and others, through which the drives achieve a partial, though disguised, expression in the symptoms of hysteria, phobic disorder, or obsessive-compulsive disorder, depending on the defense that predominates.

If repression fails to function adequately and if other defenses are not called into play, anxiety is found as the only symptom; when it rises above the low level of intensity characteristic of its function as a signal, it may emerge with all the fury of a panic attack.

When faced with a patient with anxiety disorder, the therapist must ask himself two questions about the anxiety, both of which have reference to its function in the psychological processes leading to the clinical symptoms: (1) What inner drive is the patient afraid of? (2) What are the consequences he fears from its expression?

Anxiety is seen as falling into four major categories, depending on the nature of feared consequences. These forms of anxiety are: superego anxiety, castration anxiety, separation anxiety, and id or impulse anxiety.

These varieties of anxiety are viewed as having their source—and taking their coloring from—the various points along the continuum of early growth and development. Id or impulse anxiety is seen as related to the primitive, diffuse discomfort of the infant when he feels himself overwhelmed with needs and stimuli over which his helpless state provides him no control. Separation anxiety refers back to the stage of the somewhat older but still preoedipal child, who fears the loss of love or even abandonment by his parents if he fails to control and canalize his impulses in conformity with their standards and demands. The fantasies of castration that characterize the oedipal child, particularly in relation to his developing sexual impulses, are reflected in the castration anxiety of the adult. Superego anxiety is the direct result of the final development of the superego that marks the passing of the Oedipus complex and the advent of the prepubertal period of latency.

Differences of opinion about the nature of anxiety arise in many instances from differences of emphasis, or from focusing on one kind of anxiety to the relative exclusion of others. Otto Rank, for example, traced the genesis of all anxiety back to the processes associated with the trauma of birth. Harry Stack Sullivan placed stress on the early relationship between mother and child and the important role played by the transmission of the mother's anxiety to her infant. Conditioned-reflex theorists use the concept of anxiety or fear in their explanatory schemes, but they tend to see it as an unconditioned, inherent response of the organism to painful or dangerous external stimuli.

### Clinical Description

As mentioned above, anxiety is seen clinically in an acute form and a chronic form. DSM-III takes cognizance of this fact by assigning to each a separate diagnostic label: panic disorder and generalized anxiety disorder, respectively. In what follows, the various manifestations of anxiety are considered together, since, although they show varying degrees of intensity, from the point of view of their phenomenology and causes they share many common features.

#### Onset

Anxiety states may begin slowly and insidiously with general feelings of tension and nervous discomfort, or their onset may be sudden, heralded by the abrupt outbreak of attacks of acute anxiety. Although it is characteristically a disorder of young adults, the initial anxiety attack has been observed to occur at any age from adolescence on.

#### Symptoms

Although anxiety states have numerous somatic manifestations, the central, intensely painful affect predominates in the minds of most patients suffering from the disorder. At times, it reaches a degree of panic and terror that is far more unbearable, for those who have known it, than the worst physical pains they have undergone.

The feeling of panic is hard to define. It often has a peculiar quality that seems to differentiate it from simple fear of a real external danger—a quality that is described by patients as being weird, eerie, or strangely and dreadfully awesome.

Anxiety is forward-looking; the patient is overwhelmed with a sense of some imminent catastrophe about to engulf him. Often the patient's awareness of his heart action forces on him the dreadful anticipation of dropping dead of a heart attack. Just as commonly, he fears only fainting, but the fear is compounded by a terror of being seen by others in that weak and helpless state, a feature that may lead to the development of agoraphobia which is a fear of open spaces and of going outside. Sometimes the patient cannot specify what he dreads, and the mystery about what lies ahead, as well as about what is causing his panic, only adds to his desperation. The anxiety often has an impelling quality: the patient feels that he must do something—run, hide, scream, or get away, although just what he is to do or where he is to go is as undefined as the reason for his terror.

Cardiac symptoms result from the patient's awareness of an actual change in heart function as his heart beats more rapidly and forcefully, as if he had been engaging in strenuous physical exercise. This awareness is often accompanied by a sense of hollow emptiness inside the chest, within which the heart is felt leaping and pounding against the prison of the rib cage.

Generally associated with the cardiac symptoms are a variety of chest pains. Most often, these pains are sharp and sticking in quality and are felt precordially, either at the apex of the heart or a bit higher and more centrally in the upper left quadrant of the chest wall. Frequently, they radiate to the left shoulder, axilla, and arm and, on occasion, even to the right extremity. Less often, the patient complains only of a dull discomfort in the cardiac region, and pains may be felt substernally and in the epigastrium.

Nearly as common as the cardiac manifestations are feelings of discomfort referable to respiration. These feelings are usually described by the patient as a sense of not being able to get enough air into the lungs, accompanied by a feeling of fullness in the chest and of inadequate respiration.

In patients with prolonged hyperventilation because of respiratory discomfort, sufficient carbon dioxide may be blown off to bring on a respiratory alkalosis, which in itself produces additional symptoms. Typically, the patient first notices mild numbness and tingling in his fingers, usually bilaterally but occasionally occurring in one extremity only. With more severe degrees of alkalosis, the numbness and tingling become more widespread, affecting the toes and feet and the face, particularly around the mouth. Much less often, muscle twitching and even tetany result. In addition, the patient often complains of a lightheadedness and a sense of fullness and enlargement of the head.

Dizziness is not unusual and is described as an awareness of an irregular, blurring, and swimming motion of the surroundings. Associated with this symptom is usually a sense of lightheadedness and faintness, which in some 20 per cent of patients results in actual syncope. Flushing of the face, cold perspiration, and goose flesh may be complained of, and patients are often aware of a trembling of their extremities. The trembling can often be observed, but, in addition, patients frequently report a trembling on the inside, which seems to be more a subjective sensation than a visible fact. Gastrointestinal symptoms occur in nearly 40 percent of patients, and are often either epigastric pains or a feeling of a jittery, hollow fluttering in the epigastric region—the familiar sensation of butterflies in the stomach.

## Course and Prognosis

As is often the case with neurotic syndromes, the paucity of studies concerning the natural history and the evolution of anxiety state makes it difficult to speak authoritatively about either its course or its prognosis. General clinical experience suggests that the chronically anxious young adult tends to become less so as he grows older, especially if he has achieved a degree of success and stability in his personal life. The nature of the symptoms alone does not usually help in forecasting the outcome. Prognosis in a patient with anxiety state is guided by a variety of factors—the degree of environmental stress involved in precipitating his disorder, the maturity of his ego, the stability of his personal relationships, his work performance, and the duration of symptoms.

## Diagnosis

The terms "panic disorder" and "generalized anxiety disorder" are reserved for those syndromes in which the characteristic symptoms of acute and chronic anxiety are found without other psychiatric symptoms, such as obsessions and phobias resulting from defense mechanisms used to control the anxiety itself. Panic disorder refers to an anxiety state characterized by acute panic attacks, often in conjunction with less intense, more chronic anxiety that persists in the periods between acute attacks. Generalized anxiety disorder is the term applied to chronic anxiety symptoms not punctuated by intermittent panic attacks.

*Physical Signs and Behavior*

The characteristic signs and behavior of the patient suffering from the extremes of acute anxiety are often obvious. The patient may be pacing anxiously, if not frenetically, or, if he remains seated, moving his arms and legs restlessly about, complaining loudly of his inner turmoil and vociferously demanding help. His facial expression is in keeping with his terror. He may be visibly perspiring, is seen to sigh frequently, and often is obviously hyperventilating. Physical examination discloses no structural abnormalities. The heartbeat is forceful, and pulse and respirations may be elevated, the pulse going as high as 150. The pulse is regular and usually without extrasystoles. Murmurs, if present, are functional, being systolic, soft, and apical or pulmonary in location. Heart size is normal, and elevations of blood pressure, when present, are slight and transient. An area of soreness on the surface of the chest may be discovered on palpation, and a fine tremor of the outstretched hands is often observed. When hyperventilation is present, a positive Chvostek's sign can frequently be elicited, and with severe overbreathing there may be actual tetanic contractions in the extremities.

Patients with chronic and lesser degrees of anxiety show many of the same features as those with the more acute variety, but they are of smaller magnitude. Frequent sighing, restlessness, an anxious mien, pulse in the 80's or 90's, and a degree of jumpiness and irritability mark the anxious patient. A cold, clammy handshake is particularly diagnostic. Patients with chronic anxiety do not usually give physical evidence of respiratory alkalosis, but one may find them to be unusually sensitive to hyperventilation. After 10 to 20 deep breaths taken on the command of the examiner, the patient notices the characteristic symptoms of numbness and tingling in his extremities, and often around his mouth.

*Special Examinations*

In general, special laboratory examinations provide little additional information about the patient and his disorder. Although the electrocardiogram is usually normal, save for a sinus tachycardia, in patients in an acute anxiety attack, depression or inversion of T-waves has been reported in leads II and III and in the precordial lead, especially when the patient is sitting or standing. Likewise, a depression of the S-T segment is occasionally found.

*Differential Diagnosis*

**Other Psychiatric Conditions.** What characterizes panic disorder and generalized anxiety disorder as syndromes is the fact that they manifest the symptoms of acute and chronic anxiety without contamination by other psychiatric symptoms. In certain other psychiatric disorders, anxiety is a prominent feature, but these disorders are rarely to be confused with panic disorder or generalized anxiety disorder. In phobic disorders, the anxiety is characteristically bound to the phobic object or situation, and obsessive-compulsive disorder is easily distinguished by the mental and behavioral phenomena that give the disorder its name. In agitated depression, one finds, in addition to the often prominent and extreme anxiety, the diagnostic psychotic depressive symptoms. Occasionally, an episode of acute schizophrenia is ushered in by the onset of anxiety that is often found to be an intense fear of the dissolution of the self.

**Coronary Artery Disease.** The prominence of cardiac symptoms, chest pain, and respiratory distress in acute anxiety attacks occasionally leads even sophisticated physicians to mistake them for coronary artery disease.

Caution must, of course, be exercised in patients suspected of myocardial infarction; but, when objective evidence for the diagnosis of myocardial infarction is missing, an anxiety state should be suspected, and further positive indications for its existence should be sought. A possible relationship between mitral valve prolapse and panic disorder in some persons has been suggested.

**Hyperthyroidism.** Because of the similarity of many of the symptoms of generalized anxiety disorder and hyperthyroidism, the somatic condition should be considered in patients who complain of anxiety.

**Other Medical Illnesses.** The possibility of a pheochromocytoma must be kept in mind when patients complain of several anxiety-like symptoms. It is, however, a rare disorder, occurring in only 0.1 percent of patients with hypertension, and can usually be differentiated from panic disorder.

The sudden attacks of dizziness in Ménière's disease may occasionally be confused with acute anxiety. Characteristically, the dizziness of Ménière's disease is a true vertigo and is associated with nystagmus, deafness, and other signs of middle-ear disease that are not found in panic disorder.

### Treatment

*Psychotherapy*

**Insight Psychotherapy.** The prognosis of neurotic syndromes, including panic disorder and generalized anxiety disorder, depends not primarily on the nature of the symptoms themselves but on a variety of factors that indicate the ego's degree of strength. The stability of human relationships and of work situations, the ability to bear painful affects and to relate to the therapist, intelligence, motivation for treatment, the capacity for introspection and insight—all must be assessed in determining the chances for a good response to insight psychotherapy.

**Supportive Psychotherapy.** Most patients experience a marked lessening of anxiety when given the opportunity to discuss their difficulties with a concerned and sympathetic physician. Frequently, after the initial hidden precipitants have been determined in the course of a few interviews, the specific supportive technique to be used becomes clear. Reassurance about unrealistic fears, encouragement to face anxiety-provoking situations, and the continued opportunity to talk regularly to the psychiatrist about problems are all helpful to the patient, even if they are not definitively curative.

### Relaxation Therapy

The relaxation techniques used by hypnotists and behavior therapists may prove helpful to many patients, especially those who are suggestible. For those patients with a capacity for hypnotic trance, instruction in the techniques of self-hypnosis may potentiate the effect of the relaxation exercises. Transcendental meditation, and other simpler forms of meditation that do not have religious implications, may be effective in combating the symptoms arising from autonomic nervous system discharge by reversing the processes that lead to autonomic arousal.

### Pharmacotherapy

Drugs, particularly the tranquilizers, may play an important part in symptom control. Generally speaking, the phenothiazines should be reserved for the anxiety associated with schizophrenia and other forms of psychotic illness. Most patients respond adequately to therapeutic doses of the minor tranquilizers, such as chlordiazepoxide (Librium) and diazepam (Valium). The adrenergic blocking agents, such as propranolol, are not yet in regular clinical use, but reports indicate that they may be effective in selected patients.

Imipramine has been used to block panic attacks successfully. When the patient complains of phobias and anxiety, antidepressant medication including monoamine oxidase inhibitors (MAOIs) have been useful. Alprazolam (Xanax) which has both antianxiety and antidepressant actions is also of use in anxiety states.

Finally, it should be emphasized that medication is only an adjunct to, not a substitute for, the doctor-patient relationship. In fact, the effect of the various forms of psychotherapy may be enhanced if the chemical control of painful symptoms allows the patient to direct his attention more freely to the conflicts underlying his anxiety.

### Atypical Anxiety Disorder

The catastrophic quality of panic, the often marked restriction in a person's freedom of action that results from a phobia, and the preoccupation with obsessive-compulsive thoughts that leaves little mental room for anything else—each of these symptoms clearly defines a neurotic disorder that brings significant suffering and disability in its train. Occasionally, however, one sees a patient with neurotic anxiety so mild or transient, or a single morbid fear of such a circumscribed nature, that little or no disability results, and the attending discomfort is minimal. In such cases, one is hardly justified in using a diagnostic category that should be reserved for patients with serious and lasting symptoms, significant morbidity, and a guarded prognosis. Patients with major symptoms of this sort fall into the DSM-III classification of atypical anxiety disorder.

**REFERENCES**

Curtis G C: *Anxiety Disorders: The Psychiatric Clinics of North America.* F E F Larocca, guest editor, W B Saunders, Philadelphia, 1985

Engel G L, Ferris E D, Logan M: Hyperventilation: Analysis of clinical symptomatology. Ann Intern Med *27:* 683, 1947.

Group for the Advancement of Psychiatry (GAP): *Pharmacotherapy and Psychotherapy: Paradoxes, Problems and Progress.* Mental Health Materials Center, New York, 1975.

Klein D, Rabkin J: *Anxiety: New Research and Changing Concepts.* Raven Press, New York, 1981.

Marks I, Lader M: Anxiety states (anxiety neurosis): A review. J Nerv Ment Dis *156:* 3, 1973.

Nemiah J C: Anxiety states (anxiety neuroses). In *Comprehensive Textbook of Psychiatry,* ed 4, H I Kaplan, B J Sadock, editors, p 883. Williams & Wilkins, Baltimore, 1985.

Noyes R, Anderson J, Clancy J, Crouse R, Slymen D, Ghoneim M, Hinrichs V: Diazepam and propranolol in panic disorder and agoraphobia. Arch Gen Psychiatry *41:* 287, 1984.

Pasnau R, editor: *Diagnosis and Treatment of Anxiety Disorders.* American Psychiatric Press, Washington, DC, 1983.

# 17.2  PHOBIC DISORDER (PHOBIC NEUROSIS)

## Introduction and Definition

DSM-III states that the predominant feature in phobic disorders "is persistent avoidance behavior secondary to irrational fears of a specific object, activity or situation. . . . The fear is recognized by the individual as unreasonable and unwarranted by the actual dangerousness of the object, activity or situation. . . . The Phobic Disorders are subdivided into three types: Agoraphobia, the most common and severest form, Social Phobia, and Simple Phobia."

There is a characteristic irrationality to the fear. In phobic disorder, anxiety is a central component—no longer free floating, as in anxiety state disorder, but attached to a specific object, activity, or situation; the anxiety either is not justified by the stimulus that provokes it, or is out of proportion to the real situation; and the sufferer is completely aware of the irrationality of his reaction. Despite the clarity with which one can thus state the features that define phobic disorder, it can at times be difficult to decide whether the response to the external situation is, in fact, justifiable. It is clearly reasonable to experience fear in the face of an enemy charging with a loaded gun; equally clearly, it is completely irrational to experience panic when venturing out onto a peaceful street. In between these two ends of the spectrum lie many situations in which both the absence of a quantitative measure of the degree of the external danger and of the level of anxiety make the assessment of the reasonableness of the response a matter of imprecise clinical judgment.

## Epidemiology

As is so often the case with the less severe emotional disorders, accurate information about the incidence, distribution, and natural history of phobic disorders is not readily available. Agoraphobia seems to be the most common form, constituting some 60 percent of all phobic disorders and having its onset in the patient's late teens or early twenties, although it may first be manifested much later in life. Social phobias are characteristically associated with adolescence. Simple phobia, especially of animals, is a common if transitory phenomenon during the early oedipal phases of growth and development; it may persist into adulthood, or, after a long period of freedom from phobic manifestations, an adult may develop a simple phobia that is often idiosyncratic and determined by inner psychological processes.

Taken as a group, phobic disorders seem to affect less than 1 percent of a given population, and estimates derived from outpatient clinic figures suggest that they constitute less than 5 percent of all neurotic disorders seen in patients over 18.

Agoraphobia and simple phobia are more commonly diagnosed in women than in men; the sex ratio of social phobia is unknown. The family members of patients with agoraphobia show an increased incidence of anxiety disorders in general, and there is an increased prevalence of social phobias in the families of persons suffering from this form of the disorder. Animal phobias similarly tend to run in families, but the family incidence of other simple phobias is unknown.

## Causes

### Current Psychoanalytic Theories

Freud presented a formulation of the phobic neurosis, which has remained in its essentials the analytic explanation of the disorder. Freud took a view that anxiety could be the ego's reactions to danger, and proposed that the quality of being a response was its primary attribute, the response being to a danger arising not only from perilous external situations, but from inner drives and affects that were unacceptable and threatening to the ego. Anxiety had as its major function the task of signaling to the ego the fact that a forbidden unconscious drive was pushing for conscious expression, thus alerting the ego to strengthen and marshal its defenses against the threatening instinctual force.

Freud viewed the phobic disorder—or "anxiety hysteria," as he continued to call it—as resulting from conflicts centered on an unresolved childhood oedipal situation. In the adult, since the sexual drive continued to have a strong incestuous coloring, its arousal tended to arouse anxiety that was characteristically a fear of castration. The anxiety then alerted the ego to exert repression to keep the drive away from conscious representation and discharge, but, repression failing to be entirely successful in its function, it was necessary for the ego to call on auxiliary defenses. In phobic patients, the defenses, arising genetically from an earlier phobic response during the initial childhood period of the oedipal conflict, involved primarily the use of displacement—that is, the sexual conflict was transposed or displaced from the person who evoked the conflict to a seemingly unimportant, irrelevant object or situation, which then had the power to arouse the entire constellation of affects, including signal anxiety. On examination, it can usually be determined that the phobic object or situation thus selected has a direct associative connection with the primary source of the conflict and has thus come naturally to symbolize it. Furthermore, the situation or object is usually such that the patient is able to keep out of its way and, by the additional defense mechanism of avoidance, can escape suffering from serious anxiety. This theoretical formulation of phobia formation, which attributes the phobia to the use of the ego defense mechanisms of displacement and avoidance against incestuous oedipal genital drives and castration anxiety, was first discussed by Freud in his famous case of "Little Hans," a 5-year-old boy who had a fear of horses.

### Conditioned Reflex Theories

In 1920, John B. Watson wrote an article called "Conditioned Emotional Reactions," in which he recounted his experiences with Little Albert, an infant with a phobia of rats and rabbits. Unlike Freud's Little Hans, who had developed symptoms in the natural course of his maturation, Little Albert's difficulties were the direct result of the scientific ingenuity of two experimental psychologists, who dispassionately used techniques that had successfully induced conditioned responses in laboratory animals.

Watson's formulation invokes the traditional Pavlovian stimulus-response model of the conditioned reflex to account for the initial creation of the phobia. That is, anxiety that has been aroused by a naturally and inherently frightening stimulus occurs in contiguity with a second naturally and inherently neutral stimulus. As a result of the contiguity, especially when the two stimuli are paired on several successive occasions, the originally neutral stimulus takes on the capacity for arousing anxiety by itself—that is, it becomes a conditioned stimulus for anxiety production. As a concept, it has a close affinity to Freud's early theoretical model of the displacement of anxiety from one idea to another.

In the classical stimulus-response theory, the conditioned stimulus was seen as gradually losing its potency to arouse a response if it was not reinforced by a periodic repetition of the unconditioned stimulus. In the phobic symptom, this attenuation of the response to the phobic (conditioned) stimulus does not occur, and the symptom may last for years without any apparent external reinforcement. In the more recently formulated operant conditioning theory, however, a model is provided for explaining that phenomenon. In the newer theory, anxiety is viewed as a drive that motivates the organism suffering from it to do what it can to obviate the painful affect. In the course of its random behavior, the animal soon learns that certain actions enable it to avoid the stimulus to anxiety and the consequent experience of pain. The avoidance patterns thus set up remain stable for long periods of time, as a result of the reinforcement they receive from their success in drive reduction—that is, their capacity to diminish anxiety. This model is readily applicable to the phobia in which avoidance of the anxiety-provoking object or situation plays a central part. Such avoidance behavior, clinically observable as the manifestations of phobic neurosis, becomes fixed as a stable symptom, because of its effectiveness in protecting the patient from the phobic anxiety.

Learning theory has a particular relevance to phobic disorders, and supplies simple and intelligible explanations of many aspects of phobic symptoms. In its present form, however, it deals more with the surface mechanisms of symptom formation, and is perhaps less useful in providing an understanding of some of the more complex underlying psychic processes involved—processes to which analytic observations, concepts, and theories are addressed. Nonetheless, phobic disorders provide an important meeting ground for both analytic and learning theorists, and in this clinical area, future clinical investigators from both disciplines should be able to define the significant differences and similarities between the two theoretical models.

### Clinical Features

#### Onset

With the exception of certain simple phobias and the school phobias of childhood, phobic disorders usually begin in the late teens or early adulthood and are generally sudden in onset, heralded by the outburst of an attack of anxiety in the face of what is destined from that time on to be the phobic object or situation. More often than not, the reason for appearance of symptoms is not immediately apparent; only after a period of therapy can one uncover the underlying psychological factors that give clues as to why the circumstances related to the phobia were the source of such seemingly irrational anxiety.

#### Symptoms

The central and diagnostic symptom of a phobic disorder is the phobia. Phobias are characterized by the arousal in the patient of severe anxiety, often mounting to panic, in circumstances specific to each person—circumstances that do not in reality warrant the emotional reactions evoked. Furthermore, in many patients the anxiety may be compounded by a feeling of depersonalization, although this is by no means an essential element of the phobic symptom. As a secondary response to the intense discomfort, the patient does everything in his power to avoid the situation that stimulates his phobic anxiety.

Although the kinds of phobic circumstances that have been described by clinicians are legion, a few are found with great regularity and probably account for the majority of the clinically significant phobic disorders. Fears of streets and open spaces, of crowded and enclosed places (such as churches and theaters), and of vehicles of transportation (most notably the airplane) are the most common phobias. The syndrome's degree of severity and the incapacity resulting from it depend on the practical significance for the patient of the phobic circumstances. A phobia of planes that is a merely unpleasant curiosity to the person who does not have to fly can be a source of great discomfort, if not outright incapacity, to the person whose work requires him to make frequent long trips that necessitate air travel. It is obvious that the patient whose agoraphobia keeps him confined to his house is as incapacitated as if he had a severely crippling physical lesion. Under the best of circumstances, the person with a phobic symptom finds his life to some degree constricted.

### Phobic Circumstances

There are three major categories of circumstances associated with phobic anxiety: phobias of objects, phobias of situations, and phobias of function. This schematization is reflected in the classification in DSM-III of phobias into simple phobia, agoraphobia, and social phobia.

**Simple phobia** (see Table I) is the most common type of phobia and consists of an irra-

tional fear of a specific object such as spiders, snakes, or situations such as heights, darkness, or closed spaces. One of the most common phobias is acrophobia (fear of heights). Simple phobias need to be differentiated from agoraphobia (the fear of open places) and social phobias such as the fear of public speaking. See Table II for a description of the clinical features of simple phobia.

**Agoraphobia** (see Table III) is popularly interpreted as being a fear of open spaces, but it has wider implications, for the agoraphobic patient is generally thrown into a state of trepidation when he is forced into a situation in which he may be subjected to the sense of helplessness or humiliation that results from the eruption of the panic attacks to which he is subject. He is threatened not only by open, public places but by those situations—such as crowded stores, public transportation, elevators, and theaters—from which he can find no ready escape from public view. Although he may feel more comfortable when accompanied by a friend or a relative, he tends to avoid the dangerous situations by restricting his activities and excursions to an increasingly smaller area, and in extreme cases he may be totally confined to his

TABLE II
CLINICAL FEATURES OF SIMPLE PHOBIA*

| Essential Features | Associated Features |
| --- | --- |
| Phobic object is discrete object or situation other than those seen in agoraphobia and social phobia | Anticipatory anxiety may lead patient to seek detailed information before entering situation in which phobic stimulus may be present |
| Anticipatory anxiety leads to avoidance of situation felt to be dangerous | |
| Sudden exposure to phobic stimulus may produce panic attack | |

\* Adapted from American Psychiatric Association: *Diagnostic and Statistical Manual of Mental Disorders*, ed 3. American Psychiatric Association, Washington, DC, 1980.

TABLE I
DIAGNOSTIC CRITERIA FOR SIMPLE PHOBIA*

A. A persistent, irrational fear of, and compelling desire to avoid, an object or a situation other than being alone, or in public places away from home (agoraphobia), or of humiliation or embarrassment in certain social situations (social phobia). Phobic objects are often animals, and phobic situations frequently involve heights or closed spaces.

B. Significant distress from the disturbance and recognition by the individual that his or her fear is excessive or unreasonable.

C. Not due to another mental disorder, such as schizophrenia or obsessive-compulsive disorder.

\* From American Psychiatric Association: *Diagnostic and Statistical Manual of Mental Disorders*, ed 3. American Psychiatric Association, Washington, DC, 1980. Used with permission.

TABLE III
DIAGNOSTIC CRITERIA FOR AGORAPHOBIA*

A. The individual has marked fear of and thus avoids being alone or in public places from which escape might be difficult or help not available in case of sudden incapacitation, e.g., crowds, tunnels, bridges, public transportation.

B. There is increasing constriction of normal activities until the fears or avoidance behavior dominates the individual's life.

C. Not due to a major depressive episode, obsessive-compulsive disorder, paranoid personality disorder, or schizophrenia.

* From American Psychiatric Association: *Diagnostic and Statistical Manual of Mental Disorders*, ed 3. American Psychiatric Association, Washington, DC, 1980. Used with permission.

house. In those occasional instances in which a history of panic attacks is not elicited in a patient suffering from agoraphobic symptoms, the disorder should be classified as "agoraphobia without panic attacks." Table IV lists the clinical features of agoraphobia.

**Social phobia** is perhaps of less clinical significance, since the characteristic manifestations occur less frequently than do those of the other two categories (see Table V). Central to this category is a concern over appearing shameful, stupid, or inept in the presence of others. In particular, the person fears that his behavior—talking or writing in public, for example or one of his bodily functions—such as eating, urinating, or blushing—will be the focus of scornful scrutiny by those around him, a fact that often further impairs his performance. Two particular varieties of this class should be noted—fear of blushing, erythrophobia, and fear of eating (see Table VI).

### Nature of the Anxiety

It was originally thought, particularly by psychoanalytic investigators, that the fear manifested by phobic patients was a form of castration anxiety. On more careful observation, however, it becomes evident that many fears do not fall exclusively into this category. In agoraphobia, for example, separation anxiety clearly plays a leading role, and in erythrophobia the element of shame implies the involvement of superego anxiety. It is perhaps closer to clinical observation to view the anxiety associated with phobias as having a variety of sources and colorings.

### Counterphobic Attitude

Otto Fenichel called attention to the fact that phobic anxiety can be hidden behind attitudes and behavior patterns that represent a denial either that the dreaded object or situation is dangerous, or that one is afraid of it. Basic to this phenomenon is a reversal of the situation in which one is the passive victim of external circumstances, to a position of attempting ac-

TABLE IV
CLINICAL FEATURES OF AGORAPHOBIA*

| Essential Features | Associated Features |
|---|---|
| Central feature is irrational fear of leaving familiar setting of home | Pleading, demanding, manipulative, and infantile behavior is often present |
| Phobic symptoms generally appear after preliminary phase of panic attacks, leading to sense of anticipatory helplessness away from home | Obsessional trends are common |
| Phobic situation includes crowds, closed spaces, and tunnels where access to help is limited | |

* Adapted from American Psychiatric Association: *Diagnostic and Statistical Manual of Mental Disorders*, ed 3. American Psychiatric Association, Washington, DC, 1980.

tively to confront and master what one fears. The counterphobic person, at times with a persistence that is almost obsessional in quality, seeks out situations of danger and rushes enthusiastically toward them—the devotee of dangerous sports like parachute jumping and rock climbing, for example, may be exhibiting counterphobic behavior. Such patterns may be set over against neurotic phobic anxieties, or may be used more normally as a means of dealing with realistically dangerous and anxiety-provoking situations. The play of children may contain counterphobic elements, such as the common game of playing doctor and giving to one's doll the shot one received earlier in the day in the pediatrician's office—a pattern of behavior that also involves the related mechanism of identification with the aggressor.

### Phobias and Obsessions

In the modern classification of the neuroses, phobias are distinguished from obsessive-compulsive ideas. In the strict sense of the term, the phobia is a phenomenon in which the direction of the fantasied action is from an external danger toward the patient. In obsessive and com-

TABLE V
DIAGNOSTIC CRITERIA FOR SOCIAL PHOBIA*

A. A persistent, irrational fear of, and compelling desire to avoid, a situation in which the individual is exposed to possible scrutiny by others and fears that he or she may act in a way that will be humiliating or embarrassing.

B. Significant distress because of the disturbance and recognition by the individual that his or her fear is excessive or unreasonable.

C. Not due to another mental disorder, such as major depression or avoidant personality disorder.

* From American Psychiatric Association: *Diagnostic and Statistical Manual of Mental Disorders*, ed 3. American Psychiatric Association, Washington, DC, 1980. Used with permission.

TABLE VI
CLINICAL FEATURES OF SOCIAL PHOBIA*

| Essential Features | Associated Features |
|---|---|
| Fear of situations in which one is exposed to the scrutiny of others is central feature | Patient is generally aware of fear of exhibiting signs of anxiety in phobic situation to others |
| Marked anticipatory anxiety when confronted with necessity for entering such situations | Anxiety may actually compromise performance, setting up a vicious circle |
| Anxiety predominantly one of acting or performing publicly in a shameful manner | Generalized unfocused anxiety may be present |

* Adapted from American Psychiatric Association: *Diagnostic and Statistical Manual of Mental Disorders*, ed 3. American Psychiatric Association, Washington, DC, 1980.

pulsive ideas, on the other hand, the direction is reversed insofar as a fantasy of action is concerned. The patient is disturbed about some harmful deed he may have done or is impelled to do to others. With a phobia, the patient is passive; with obsessive-compulsive ideas, the patient is active. Furthermore, in the phobia, the patient can quiet his anxiety by avoiding the feared external situation, whereas the obsessive-compulsive idea is characterized by the difficulty the patient has in escaping its persistent, forceful intrusion into his consciousness.

Despite the official diagnostic separation of phobias from obsessive-compulsive ideas, a number of symptoms are not easily assigned to one or the other category, but lie along the middle reaches of the spectrum represented at one end by the pure phobias, and at the other end by pure obsessive-compulsive ideas. In the middle realm the distinction between them is blurred, since the symptoms partake of some of the characteristics of each. The common phobia of knives or other dangerous objects often rests on the patient's fantasy that he will actively hurt someone else, but at the same time he is able to control his anxiety by avoiding the dreaded object. The phobia of dirt or disease, on the other hand, involves the patient's fear that he will be damaged by the external agent, but

the fear has all the intrusiveness of an obsession, and the patient cannot avoid the feared object, since he imagines it as being everywhere around him and as constantly threatening, no matter what he does. Whether the patient with symptoms like these is viewed as having a phobic disorder or obsessive-compulsive disorder is determined by the nature of his other symptoms and by the characteristics of his personality structure, and sometimes one is forced to remain content with placing him in the category of atypical anxiety disorder.

### Secondary Reactions to Phobic Symptoms

Brief mention must be made of certain secondary reactions to phobic symptoms that contribute to the clinical manifestations of phobic disorders. Some patients respond to a capitulation to their phobia by avoiding the feared situation, with a loss of self-esteem experienced as a feeling of being weak, cowardly, or not as effective and capable as they would like to be. That is, a mild element of depression may be added to the phobic symptoms. On the other hand, in those cases in which the patient has been able to master the phobic anxiety and to carry out an action successfully by facing the phobic situation without giving in, he may experience a mild sense of pleasant elation, self-confidence, and emotional freedom.

### Personality Characteristics of the Phobic Patient

A spectrum of character types ranges from the hysterical to the obsessional, and some show passive-dependent features. As a result, some authors view the phobic disorders as falling midway, psychogenetically speaking, between genital hysteria and the anal obsessive-compulsive disorder, and others consider obsessions and phobias as falling within a single nosological category.

### Treatment

Despite the refractoriness of many phobic symptoms to the variety of available treatment techniques, there has always been considerable interest in the therapy of patients with phobic disorders. That interest has recently been heightened by the success of treatment measures based on the learning theory model and on pharmacotherapy.

## Psychotherapy

Early in the development of psychoanalysis and the dynamically oriented psychotherapies, it was felt that these methods were the treatment of choice for phobic neurosis, the genesis of which were seen as lying in the areas of oedipal-genital conflicts. Soon, however, therapists recognized that, despite progress in uncovering and analyzing unconscious conflicts, patients frequently failed to lose their phobic symptoms and, by continuing to avoid the phobic situation, excluded a significant degree of anxiety and its related associations from the analytic process. Both Freud and his pupil, Sandor Ferenczi, had recognized that, if progress in analyzing the symptoms was to be made, therapists had to go beyond their merely analytic roles by actively urging their phobic patients to enter the phobic situation and experience the anxiety involved. There has since been a general agreement among psychiatrists that a measure of activity on the part of the therapist is often required to get at the phobic anxiety. At the same time, a growing body of clinical experience has made it evident that many phobic patients are not readily helped by analytic techniques, especially patients suffering from phobias whose roots lie in serious preoedipal conflicts. The decision to apply the techniques of psychodynamic insight therapy should be based not on the presence of the phobic symptom alone, but on positive indications from the patient's ego-structure and life patterns for the use of this method of treatment.

## Behavior Therapy

In recent years there have been reports of a number of dramatic cures of patients with phobic neurosis through the use of techniques derived from the concepts of learning theory. An increasing number of studies are appearing in the literature reporting favorable results in patients who, after many years of suffering from phobias, despite treatment with more traditional psychotherapies, have been helped by a few sessions in which behavior therapy has been used.

A variety of behavioral treatment techniques have been employed, the most common being imaginal desensitization, a method pioneered by Joseph Wolpe. In desensitization, the patient is exposed serially to a predetermined list of anxiety-provoking stimuli graded in a hierarchy from the least to the most frightening. Each of the anxiety-provoking stimuli is paired with the arousal of another affect of an opposite quality that is strong enough to suppress the anxiety. Specifically, through the use of tranquilizing drugs, hypnosis, and instruction in the art of muscle relaxation, patients are taught how to induce in themselves both mental and physical repose. Once they have mastered these techniques, patients are instructed to employ them in the face of each anxiety-provoking stimulus in the hierarchy as the stimuli are presented to them seriatim from the least to the most potent. As they become desensitized to each stimulus in the scale, the patients move up to the next stimulus until, ultimately, what previously produced the most anxiety is no longer capable of eliciting the painful affect. Other behavioral techniques that have more recently been employed involve intensive exposure to the phobic stimulus either through imagery or in vivo. In imaginal flooding (implosion therapy), patients are exposed to phobic anxiety produced by images of the phobic stimulus for as long as they can tolerate the fear until they reach a point at which they can no longer feel the fear. In vivo flooding requires patients to experience similar anxiety through an exposure to the actual phobic stimulus itself.

Varying degrees of success have been reported in treating phobic disorders by behavioral techniques, although it is not always clear how much the effects are to be attributed to the measures specifically characteristic of behavior therapy and how much to other factors that accompany the effects, such as suggestion or the supportive relationship with an enthusiastic therapist. In general, the simple and social phobias respond best to behavioral methods, whereas patients with agoraphobia, especially when panic attacks are a prominent and continuous feature, fare less well and often run a long and fluctuating course of continuing symptoms and disability. Even in the agoraphobic group, nearly half the patients report sufficient improvement with behavior therapy to enable them to lead reasonably active lives, despite a persistence of their anxiety. It is clear that behavioral therapeutic techniques have added an important dimension to the psychiatrist's therapeutic armamentarium and should be considered for every patient with a phobic disorder.

## Pharmacotherapy

Considerable success in controlling panic attacks, with and without agoraphobia, has been reported in recent years through the use of tricyclic antidepressants, especially imipramine (Tofranil), and monoamine oxidase (MAO) inhibitors, such as phenelzine (Nardil). The dramatic reduction in panic attacks that follows such medication is the central factor in recovery from agoraphobic disorders. Sometimes the mere control of the panic is sufficient to allow patients to resume their customary activities. If anticipatory anxiety persists despite the disappearance of the acute panic attacks, benzodiazepines or behavioral desensitization or both are required to combat this more chronic form of anxiety. In addition, insight psychotherapy should be considered for those patients who fulfill the criteria for this form of treatment; with the acute, disabling symptoms under pharmacological control, such patients may be helped to resolve the psychological conflicts that frequently play a significant role in producing the surface symptoms.

### Hypnosis

Hypnosis is useful not only in enhancing the suggestion that is a part of the therapist's generally supportive approach, but in directly combating the anxiety arising from the phobic situation. The psychiatrist can teach the patient the techniques of autohypnosis, through which he can achieve a degree of relaxation when he is facing the phobic situation that will enable him to tolerate it. Those patients who cannot be hypnotized may be taught techniques of muscular relaxation.

### Supportive Therapy

As in the treatment of any illness, the support afforded patients by a positive relationship with their physicians has a beneficial effect. Beyond this, especially in the more active forms of treatment, such as behavior therapy, psychiatrists must employ active measures of encouragement, exhortation, instruction, and suggestion as they try to help their patients overcome the dread of the phobic situation. In this regard, it is important to keep in mind the fact that the more that patients avoid what they fear, the more they are liable to fear it and, at the same time, to become discouraged and downhearted at their pusillanimity. If they can once be persuaded to face the phobic situation and come through the experience with a measure of success, the increase in their self-esteem and self-confidence will make it easier for them to try it again. Each successful attempt makes the next try less of an ordeal, and the vicious downward cycle of avoidance can at times be reversed to the point where patients either lose their symptoms or so master

them that their lives are no longer seriously constricted by the limitations they had previously imposed on their actions.

### REFERENCES

Fenichel O: The counterphobic attitude. Inter J Psychoanal *20:* 263, 1939.
Freud S: Analysis of a phobia in a five-year-old boy. In *The Standard Edition of the Complete Psychological Works of Sigmund Freud*, vol 10, p 5. Hogarth Press, London, 1955.
Freud S: Inhibitions, symptoms and anxiety. In *The Standard Edition of the Complete Psychological Works of Sigmund Freud*, vol 20, p 87. Hogarth Press, London, 1959.
Freud S: Obsessions and phobias. In *The Standard Edition of the Complete Psychological Works of Sigmund Freud*, vol 3, p 74. Hogarth Press, London, 1962.
Lewin B: Phobic symptoms and dream interpretation. Psychoanal Q *21:* 295, 1952.
Marks I M: *Fears and Phobias*. Wm Heinemann, London, 1969.
Mavissakalian M, Salerni R, Thompson M, Michelson L: Mitral valve prolapse and agoraphobia. Am J Psychiatry *140:* 1612, 1983.
Nemiah J C: Phobic disorders (phobic neuroses). In *Comprehensive Textbook of Psychiatry*, ed. 4, H I Kaplan and B J Sadock, editors, p 894. Williams & Wilkins, Baltimore, 1985.
Nemiah J: A psychoanalytic view of phobias. Am J Psychoanal *41:* 115, 1981.
Prince M: *The Unconscious*. Macmillan, New York, 1924.
Roth M: The phobic anxiety-depersonalization syndrome. Proc R Soc Med *52:* 587, 1959.
Sheehan D: Panic attacks and phobias. N Engl J Med *307:* 156, 1982.

## 17.3 OBSESSIVE-COMPULSIVE DISORDER (OBSESSIVE-COMPULSIVE NEUROSIS)

### Introduction

In the first expansion of his psychological formulations, Freud separated from the somatosensory symptoms of hysteria a group of symptoms characterized by their psychic nature, but he failed initially to differentiate between phobic and obsessive-compulsive phenomena; this differentiation came later in his expanding psychodynamic scheme. There was, however, good reason for that early confusion. Not only do phobic and obsessive-compulsive symptoms have features in common, but the characteristics that are used to differentiate them clinically do not always lead to a clear separation. In fact, the clinical phenomena lie along a spectrum. Although the phenomena at the extremes are clearly differentiated, the forms in the middle of the spectrum are difficult to categorize. Indeed, some contemporary authors still include phobias in the clinical syndrome of the obsessive-compulsive disorder.

## Definition

The word "obsessive" or "obsession" refers to an idea or thought. The word "compulsive" or "compulsion" refers to an urge or impulse to action that, when put into operation, leads to a compulsive act.

Obsessions and compulsions have certain features in common: (1) An idea or an impulse obtrudes itself insistently, persistently, and impellingly into the person's conscious awareness. (2) A feeling of anxious dread accompanies the central manifestation and frequently leads the person to take countermeasures against the initial idea or impulse. (3) The obsession or compulsion is ego-alien—that is, it is experienced as being foreign to and not a usual part of one's experience of oneself as a psychological being; it is undesired, unacceptable, and uncontrollable. (4) No matter how vivid and compelling the obsession or compulsion, the person recognizes it as absurd and irrational; he retains his insight. (5) Finally, the person suffering from the manifestations feels a strong need to resist them.

Most of these characteristics are embodied in the official definition of obsessive-compulsive disorder given in DSM-III: "The essential features are recurrent obsessions and/or compulsions. Obsessions are defined as recurrent, persistent ideas, thoughts, images or impulses which are ego-alien; that is, they are not experienced as voluntarily produced, but rather as ideas that invade the field of consciousness. Attempts are made to ignore or suppress them. Compulsions are behaviors which are not experienced as the outcome of the individual's own volition, but are accompanied by both a sense of subjective compulsion and a desire to resist (at least initially). Obsessions and compulsions are recognized by the individual as foreign to his personality" (see Table I).

## Epidemiology

The exact incidence of obsessive-compulsive disorder is hard to determine. Scattered anecdotal evidence indicates that it has occurred throughout history. Those who have studied the natural history of the disorder have found an incidence that is never higher than 5 percent of all neurotic patients, and its prevalence in the population at large has been estimated at 0.05 percent.

There seems to be no significant sexual difference in the disorder. A large proportion of obsessive-compulsive patients remain unmarried, up to 50 percent in some surveys. Recent studies indicate that the frequency of the disorder is higher in upper-class persons, and in those with higher intelligence levels, than in the general population. The data on familial patterns are meager, but suggest that parents and siblings of patients with obsessive-compulsive disorder have a significantly higher incidence of the condition, as compared with a control population, and that the presence of obsessional traits is similarly increased.

## Causes

### Psychodynamic Factors

Freud described three major psychological defense mechanisms that determine the form and the quality of obsessive-compulsive symptoms and character traits: isolation, undoing, and reaction formation.

TABLE I
DIAGNOSTIC CRITERIA FOR OBSESSIVE-COMPULSIVE DISORDER*

A. Either obsessions or compulsions:

*Obsessions:* recurrent, persistent ideas, thoughts, images, or impulses that are ego-dystonic, i.e., they are not experienced as voluntarily produced, but rather as thoughts that invade consciousness and are experienced as senseless or repugnant. Attempts are made to ignore or suppress them.

*Compulsions:* repetitive and seemingly purposeful behaviors that are performed according to certain rules or in a stereotyped fashion. The behavior is not an end in itself, but is designed to produce or prevent some future event or situation. However, either the activity is not connected in a realistic way with what it is designed to produce or prevent, or may be clearly excessive. The act is performed with a sense of subjective compulsion coupled with a desire to resist the compulsion (at least initially). The individual generally recognizes the senselessness of the behavior (this may not be true for young children) and does not derive pleasure from carrying out the activity, although it provides a release of tension.

B. The obsessions or compulsions are a significant source of distress to the individual or interfere with social or role functioning.

C. Not due to another mental disorder, such as Tourette's Disorder, Schizophrenia, Major Depression, or Organic Mental Disorder.

\* From American Psychiatric Association: *Diagnostic and Statistical Manual of Mental Disorders*, ed 3. American Psychiatric Association, Washington, DC, 1980. Used with permission.

**Isolation.** Isolation is a defense mechanism that protects a person from anxiety-provoking affects and impulses. Under ordinary circumstances, a person experiences in consciousness both the affect and the imagery of an emotion-laden idea, whether it be a fantasy or the memory of an event. When isolation occurs, the affect and the impulse of which it is a derivative are separated from the ideational component and pushed out of consciousness. If isolation is completely successful, the impulse and its associated affect are totally repressed, and the patient is consciously aware only of the affectless idea that is related to it.

**Undoing.** In the face of the constant threat of the impulse to escape the primary defense of isolation and to break free, further secondary defensive operations are required to combat it and to quiet the anxiety that the imminent eruption of the impulse into consciousness arouses in the patient.

The anxiety-allaying function of compulsive acts can readily be noted in the clinical manifestations of obsessive-compulsive disorders. What should be observed here is that the compulsive act constitutes the surface manifestation of a further defensive operation, aimed at reducing anxiety and at controlling the underlying impulse that has not been sufficiently contained by isolation. A particularly important secondary defensive operation of this sort is the mechanism of undoing. As the word suggests, it refers to a compulsive act that is performed in an attempt to prevent or undo the consequences that the patient irrationally anticipates from a frightening obsessional thought or impulse.

**Reaction Formation.** Both isolation and undoing are defensive maneuvers that are intimately involved in the production of clinical symptoms. Reaction formation, a third mechanism closely associated with the obsessive-compulsive disorder, results in the formation of character traits, rather than symptoms. As the term implies, reaction formation involves manifest patterns of behavior and consciously experienced attitudes that are exactly the opposite of the underlying impulses. Often these patterns seem to an observer to be highly exaggerated, and at times quite inappropriate.

### Psychogenetic Factors

One of the striking features of patients with obsessive-compulsive disorder is the degree to which they are preoccupied with aggression or cleanliness, either overtly in the content of their symptoms or in the associations that lie behind them. This and other observations have led to the proposition that the psychogenesis of the obsessive-compulsive disorder lies in disturbances in normal growth and development related to the anal-sadistic phase.

**Regression.** In the classical analytic theoretical formulation, regression is the central mechanism in the formation of obsessive-compulsive neurosis and determines that a person will develop this disorder, rather than conversion disorder. According to psychoanalytic theory, in conversion disorder the person represses oedipal genital libido, the energy from that undischarged impulse being then converted into somatic symptoms. In obsessive-compulsive disorder something different occurs. As with the hysterical patient, the obsessive-compulsive patient may begin with a conflict over the oedipal genital impulse when, for example, it is aroused by an environmental stimulus. However, instead of repressing and converting this impulse, he uses a different maneuver to avoid the anxiety associated with the genital impulse. He abandons the genital impulse and regresses to the earlier anal-sadistic phase of psychosexual development. The return to this earlier stage is facilitated by the fixation points that have remained from the distortions that occurred during his childhood development. By giving up genital urges, the patient is no longer confronted with the conflicts and problems resulting from these urges.

**Ambivalence.** Ambivalence is the direct result of a change in the characteristics of the impulse life. It is an important feature of the normal child during the anal-sadistic developmental phase—that is, toward the same object he feels both love and murderous hate, sometimes seemingly simultaneously; at least, one emotion follows the other in such rapid alternation that they seem temporarily to exist side by side. One finds the obsessive-compulsive patient often consciously experiencing both love and hate toward his object. This conflict of opposing emotions may be seen in the doing-undoing patterns of behavior, and the paralyzing doubt in the face of choices that are frequently found in persons with the emotional disorder.

**Magical Thinking.** In the phenomenon of magical thinking, the regression uncovers earlier modes of thought, rather than impulses—that is, ego functions, as well as id functions, are affected by regression. Inherent in magical thinking is the phenomenon of the omnipotence of thought. The person feels that, merely by thinking about an event in the external world, he can cause that event to occur without intermediate physical actions. This feeling makes having an aggressive thought frightening to obsessive-compulsive patients.

In summary, the psychoanalytic theory of obsessive-compulsive disorder ascribes the appearance of symptoms to a defensive regression of the psychic apparatus to the preoedipal anal-sadistic phase, with the consequent emergence of earlier modes of functioning of the ego, superego, and id. These factors, along with the use of specific ego defenses—isolation, undoing, reaction formation—combine to produce the clinical symptoms of obsessions, compulsions, and compulsive acts.

### Learning Theory

According to learning theory, the obsession represents a conditioned stimulus to anxiety. Because of an association with an unconditioned anxiety-provoking stimulus, the originally neutral obsessional thought gains the capacity to arouse anxiety; that is, a new mode of behavior has been learned. The compulsion is established in a different way: the person discovers that a certain action reduces the anxiety attached to the obsessional thought. The relief brought about when the anxiety, which operates as a negative drive state, is thus reduced by the performance of the compulsive act, reinforces this act. Gradually, because of its usefulness in reducing a painful secondary drive (the anxiety), the act becomes fixed into a learned pattern of behavior. Learning theory provides useful concepts for explaining certain aspects of the obsessive-compulsive phenomena—for example, the anxiety-producing capacity of ideas that are not necessarily frightening in themselves, and the establishment of compulsive patterns of behavior.

## Clinical Description

Because of the relative rarity of the disorder and the paucity of patients adequately studied, it is difficult to make categorical statements about the natural history of obsessive-compulsive disorder. All that can be said must be considered as only tentative and perhaps applicable only to selected patients, rather than to the disorder itself (see Table I).

### Onset

The onset of the disorder occurs predominantly in adolescence or early adulthood. The symptoms first appear in more than two-thirds of the patients by the time they are 15, and frequently before the age of 10. In less than 5 per cent do the symptoms begin for the first time after the fourth decade of life. As compared with patients suffering from hysterical symptoms or anxiety, those with obsessions and compulsions seek professional help at an earlier age. In one series of patients, the average age when they first saw a doctor was 22.0 years for the obsessive-compulsive group, 30.3 for the hysterical patients, and 32.2 for those with anxiety. In more than half the patients a clear environmental precipitating event can be found.

### Symptoms

The fundamental characteristics of obsessive-compulsive phenomena described earlier have a general validity and usefulness in distinguishing them from the manifestations of other emotional disorders. However, in attempting to categorize the various obsessive-compulsive manifestations themselves, one is faced with a complicated task, for the multiplicity of variables makes it difficult to devise a classification that will sharply differentiate one kind of obsessional or compulsive symptom from another.

The phenomena may be manifested psychically or behaviorally; they may be experienced as ideas or as impulses; they may refer to events anticipated in the future or actions already completed; they may express desires and wishes or protective measures against such desires; they may be simple, uncomplicated acts and ideas or elaborate, ritualized patterns of thinking and behavior; their meaning may be obvious to the most unsophisticated observer; or they may be the end result of highly complicated psychological condensations and distortions that yield their secret only to the skilled investigator.

**Obsessional Thoughts.** Perhaps the simplest of the psychic symptoms are those in which thoughts, words, or mental images are obtruded against the patient's will into his conscious awareness.

A young woman of 23 was shocked one day when the mental image flashed into her mind of her father and herself undressing one another and joining in a sexual embrace. From that time on, despite her desperate efforts to erase the image, it recurred with mounting intensity, and she finally fled to the hospital for help. A mother in her late thirties was tortured every time her daughter left the house by images of the child's being hit by a car. Particularly vivid was the mental picture of the little girl's body lying broken and bleeding in the gutter, and nothing she could do would exorcise the tormenting scene. A young law student had the frightening thought every time he turned on a light, "My father will die"; to allay his anxiety, he would have to touch the switch and think to himself, "I take back that thought."

In these examples, the obsessional thought

refers to present or future time. In a minor variation of the theme, the patient is preoccupied with a guilty dread that an action he has performed in the past has or will lead to dreadful consequences.

A special form of forced preoccupation with thoughts is designated by the term "obsessive-ruminative states." As the term implies, the central feature is rumination about a topic or problem, often of a religious or abstrusely philosophical nature. The pros and cons of the questions are repetitively considered, and imponderables are weighed in a prolonged, fruitless, and inconclusive inner dialogue, filled with doubting and despair.

**Compulsions.** In another form of the psychic phenomena, ideas and images may be present, but the central feature is an irrational impulse to some form of action. The impulse, however, remains merely an impulse and is not acted on by the patient, no matter how fearful he may be that he will lose control of his behavior. As earlier defined, this clinical manifestation is known as a compulsion.

The patient may feel the impulse to jump out of the window of a high building or to throw himself in the path of a moving train or car. His aggressions may be aimed at others, rather than himself. A man constantly had the urge to push people down elevator shafts, and he avoided elevators, lest his temptations be too strong. A young mother was beset with the impulse to beat her infant baby when he cried and at times had the urge to pick him up by the heels and bash his head against the wall. Others are driven by impulses to stab those around them with knives, scissors, or other sharp objects. The aggressive compulsion need not be physical, but may be an urge toward an act of defiance or one that is socially inappropriate or shocking, such as shouting obscenities in church. Although these impulses do not lead to action, they frequently arouse strong anxiety in the patient and cause him to avoid the situation or the object that evokes the impulse. Such an avoidance reaction is shared by persons with compulsions of this sort, and by those with typical phobic reactions.

**Behavioral Manifestations.** When the obsessive-compulsive phenomena are psychic, no one knows that anything unusual is going on in the patient unless he chooses to divulge his purely private experiences. The situation is obviously quite different in the case of compulsive acts, in which the phenomena are behavioral and usually visible to anyone who is there to see them, although, often out of shame or embarrassment, the patient tries to restrict his actions

to those times when he is alone. There are two principal types of compulsive acts: (1) those that give expression to the primary urges or impulses that underlie them, and (2) those that are a reaction to or an attempt to control the primary impulse.

Compulsive acts that simply and directly express the underlying urges are rare, although they do occur, as in the case of a young single woman who felt compelled to keep her diaphragm on top of her Bible in her bureau drawer and who did so. In most instances, the compulsion expressing an urge remains in the psychic sphere and is not visible in action, except when it contaminates a compulsive act that began as a controlling maneuver.

In general, compulsive acts are—or, at least, begin as—attempts to control or modify a primary obsession or compulsion, either because the patient fears the consequences of his obsession or because he is afraid that he will not be able to control his impulse. Such defensive compulsive acts are used to contain, neutralize, or ward off the feared results of concurrent obsessions and compulsions, or they may represent a desire to make sure that some action in the past has not led to disaster.

Certain compulsive acts, as has been mentioned, are motivated by a guilty dread on the part of the patient that he has done something bad, and are designed to atone for his sins, or to reassure him that things are, in reality, all right.

At times, however, the patient's compulsive behavior becomes highly elaborate and repetitively stereotyped in the form of compulsive rituals. On going to bed, for example, the process of taking off one's clothes must conform to an exact pattern; they must be placed exactly so on a chair or hanger; the sequence of washing, voiding, and brushing one's teeth is rigidly adhered to; the furniture in the bedroom, the bedclothes, and the pillow must be symmetrically arranged. Any deviation in the pattern arouses anxiety in the patient, and he must be certain that all has been done properly before he can drop off to sleep. Often, the same process must be carried out in reverse when he gets up in the morning and prepares for the day.

### Character Traits

Much has been written about the nature of obsessive-compulsive character traits, and the person who exhibits them has been described variously in the literature as having an obsessional character, an anal personality, or an anancastic personality. All these terms refer to a group of behavioral phenomena characterized by control, in contrast to the histrionic personality, in whom a tendency toward a flamboyant expression of fantasies and feelings predominates.

As he is observed and experienced by others, the person with obsessional personality traits is seen to exercise a marked measure of control over both himself and his environment. He is cautious, deliberate, thoughtful, and rational in his approach to life and its problems, and may seem dry and pedantic when these traits are carried to an extreme. He emphasizes reason and logic at the expense of feeling and intuition, and he does his best to be objective and to avoid being carried away by subjective enthusiasms. As a result, he often appears sober and emotionally distant, but at the same time he is found to be a person with great steadiness of purpose, reliability, and earnest conscientiousness. What he lacks in flexibility, imagination, and inventiveness, he makes up for in a conservative cautiousness about change that provides a salutary balance to the transient but violent enthusiasms of others.

In addition to his need to restrain himself and his emotions, he likes to feel that he has control of his environment as well. He subscribes to the dictum, "A place for everything, and everything in its place," and neatness, orderliness, and tidiness characterize his arrangement of space, as does punctuality his management of time. He likes people and institutions that behave predictably and conform to his predilections. He can be surprisingly obstinate and stubborn when challenged or contradicted. He sets great store by justice and honesty, has a strong sense of property rights, manages his own resources with frugality, and does not easily part with his possessions.

### Course and Prognosis

Accurate statements about the course and the prognosis of obsessive-compulsive disorder are precluded by the lack of detailed knowledge of the natural history of the syndrome. The number of series in which longitudinal studies have been carried out is small, and the figures presented here must be considered as first approximations at best.

On first consulting a physician for their difficulty, two-thirds of obsessive-compulsive patients give a history of prior episodes of obsessive-compulsive symptoms, some 10 to 15 percent having first experienced them before the age of 10. The large majority of patients have had only one such prior attack, although a good number, roughly 30 percent, have experienced two or three episodes. In 85 percent of these attacks, the duration was less than a year, although some attacks lasted 4 to 5 years.

The figures given for the prognosis vary widely from series to series, but the following general statement may be made for patients followed up for anywhere from 1 to 10 years after treatment, excluding leukotomy: some 25 percent are recovered, 50 percent are improved, and 25 percent are unchanged or worse. Those considered improved fall into two groups: (1) patients whose symptoms have lessened to a point at which they are able to work and function socially, and (2) those who run a fluctuating course, often with long periods of complete remission of symptoms.

In general, obsessive-compulsive disorder is chronic, often following a remitting course. The prognosis is better than average (1) the shorter the duration of symptoms before the time the patient is first seen, (2) the greater the element of environmental stress associated with the onset of the disorder, (3) the better the environment to which the patient must return after treatment, and (4) the better his general social adjustment and relationship.

### Diagnosis

*Psychiatric Examination*

The most obvious disturbances in behavior in patients with obsessive-compulsive disorder occur in those whose illnesses are characterized by compulsive acts. The elaborate rituals or stereotyped movements, if they are performed in the public eye, cannot be missed by the observer. Moreover, if the patient divulges the nature of his inner obsessional thoughts and compulsive urges, they are often seen to be irrational and bizarre. At the same time, the patient retains full insight; he recognizes that his pathological thoughts and impulses are quite unreasonable and alien to the mainstream of his personality. Apart from these obviously abnormal phenomena, little else on casual examination seems to be unusual. As one observes more closely and perceptively, however, one becomes aware of behavioral elements, most of which are related to obsessive-compulsive character traits, although they are not invariably present in the obsessive-compulsive patient.

The patient is often neatly dressed and groomed, sometimes with almost fussy tidiness. Reserved and formal in manner, he sits before the examiner stiff and prim, showing little in the way of gestures or facial expression, and his movements are careful and precise, without spontaneity or easy grace. The controlled quality of his posture and movement is matched in his speech. His sentences may be long and involved, and full of stilted phraseology or stereotyped expressions. He characteristically balances one clause against another—"whereas . . . , yet . . ." "on the one hand . . . on the other . . .;" He says the same thing several times in succession, introducing each paraphrase with "Again" or "in other words" or "To put it in another way." He qualifies any direct statement with words like "maybe," "perhaps," or "possibly," to avoid sounding dogmatic or to escape being caught in an error. He relies heavily on rational argument and talks in highly intellectual and intellectualized terms about the simplest matters, interlarding his pronouncements with the copious and needless interjection of words or phrases like "indeed," "to be sure," "be that as it may." He recounts events in infinite detail, with a painful attention to accuracy and completeness, sometimes referring to written notes he has brought with him. It often turns out that he has rehearsed what he plans to say in the interview for hours before it takes place, and has tried to anticipate every move and question the interviewer may introduce. Any attempt to hurry him along, to cut him short, or to switch to another topic is met by the patient's resistance and rigid adherence to his preconceived program of action. Evidence or expression of emotion, save possibly controlled anxiety, is at a minimum or entirely absent. If he is sophisticated about psychiatric theory, and such patients often are, he discourses at length about his "conflicts," his "defenses," his "aggression," or his "libido." But in answer to direct questioning, he denies having any of the feelings related to these words. His self-awareness and self-knowledge, however extensive, are entirely intellectual in nature and quite without emotional correlates.

## Differential Diagnosis

**Phobic Disorder.** Some clinicians classify phobias under the heading of obsessive-compulsive phenomena, and it is often difficult to distinguish sharply between them. In general, the phobic disorder is characterized by anxiety that harm will come to the phobic patient from an external object or situation, and the patient controls his anxiety by avoiding the object. Furthermore, the important mechanisms in phobia formation are displacement and projection, and the underlying conflicts are often oedipal in nature. By contrast, in obsessive-compulsive disorder, the patient fears that he will hurt others, his anxiety is controlled by compulsive acts and by the mechanisms of undoing and isolation, and the underlying conflicts are predominantly preoedipal in nature.

**Depression.** As with the phobic disorder, there are areas of overlap in obsessive-compulsive disorder and the syndrome of depression. Some 20 percent of patients with depressive illness have obsessive-compulsive symptoms, and a third have obsessive-compulsive character traits, the figure being even higher if one restricts one's attention to the midlife agitated or involutional depression that characteristically occurs in obsessional persons.

Patients who for a period of time have manifested the symptoms of obsessive-compulsive disorder may go on to develop a typical depression.

Some patients suffer from obsessive-compulsive symptoms episodically, with seemingly self-limiting periods of marked obsessions and compulsions alternating with periods of remission; in other words, their symptoms run a cyclic course, like the one that characterizes manic-depressive disorder.

The depressed patient tends to retreat from his relationships with others. In the obsessive-compulsive patient, on the other hand, the emotional tie to other people remains intact, but it has all the coloring of the ambivalence that is central to the obsessive-compulsive disorder.

**Schizophrenia.** Because of the eruption into consciousness of magical thinking, the thought content of the obsessive-compulsive patient often has a bizarre quality, which raises the question of whether he is really suffering from schizophrenia. Yet, surprisingly few patients with chronic obsessive-compulsive disorders develop a clearly defined schizophrenic psychosis.

The nature of the clinical evidence shows that there is some relationship between the two syndromes. During the developing phase of schizophrenia, especially in the acute undifferentiated form, one frequently sees transient and varying obsessive-compulsive phenomena, and these phenomena may appear intermittently during the course of a well-established psychosis. Occasionally, a clearly schizophrenic episode appears in the course of a chronic obsessive-compulsive disorder, but it is characteristically mild and transient. The direct transition of an obsessional thought into a delusion is rarely observed.

## Treatment

### Psychotherapy

Obsessive-compulsive patients do respond to the psychotherapeutic maneuvers of the psychiatrist. However, in the absence of adequate studies of psychotherapy in obsessive-compulsive disorder, it is hard to make any valid generalizations about its effectiveness. Individual analyst have seen striking and lasting changes for the better in patients with obsessional personality disorders, especially when they are able to come to terms with the aggressive impulses lying behind their character traits. Likewise, analysts and dynamically oriented psychiatrists have observed marked symptomatic improvement in their patients in the course of analysis or prolonged insight psychotherapy.

Supportive psychotherapy undoubtedly has its place, especially for that group of obsessive-compulsive patients who, despite symptoms of varying degrees of severity, are able to work and make a social adjustment. The continuous and regular contact with an interested, sympathetic, and encouraging professional person may make it possible for the patient to continue to function by virtue of that help, without which he would become completely incapacitated by his symptoms. Occasionally, when obsessional rituals and anxiety reach an intolerable intensity, it is necessary to hospitalize the patient until the shelter of an institution and the removal from external environmental stresses bring about a lessening of the symptoms to a more tolerable level. Nor must it be forgotten that the patient's family is often driven to the verge of despair by the patient's behavior. Any psychotherapeutic endeavors must include attention to family members through the provision of emotional support, reassurance, explanation, and advice on how to manage and respond to the patient.

### Behavior Therapy

Although behavior therapy has been applied extensively to patients with phobias, there are far fewer reports of its use in obsessive-compulsive disorder, and controlled studies of outcomes are rare. The existing literature suggests that desensitization techniques may be helpful to certain patients in removing or reducing the severity of symptoms. Recently, compulsive behavior has been approached through response prevention, in which patients are prevented, forcefully if necessary, from carrying out their compulsive acts and rituals. In at least one follow-up study of this technique, the symptoms were absent or markedly reduced in a majority of patients after treatment. But there are, as yet, insufficient data to enable one to speak with any certainty about the long-term effectiveness of behavior therapy for obsessive-compulsive disorder.

Other techniques such as thought stopping, flooding, implosion therapy, and aversive conditioning have been used.

### Organic Therapies

No drugs have a specific action on the obsessive-compulsive symptoms themselves, although the use of sedatives and tranquilizers as an adjunct to psychotherapy may be helpful when anxiety is excessive.

Tricyclic antidepressants such as imipramine and monoamine oxidase inhibitors have been used with some success in these disorders. When depression is a component factor, there is a greater likelihood of antidepressant medication being successful.

Electric shock treatment seems to have no direct effect on obsessions and compulsions. But if these symptoms are secondary phenomena to a primary mood disorder, physical treatment may improve them, along with the affective disturbance.

Leukotomy has been recommended by some authors as a treatment of obsessive-compulsive disorder. As a general rule, one should avoid irreversible surgical procedures on the brain in patients with psychogenic disorders, particularly when the disorders, as is the case in many patients with obsessive-compulsive disorder, run an intermittent course. However, evidence indicates that leukotomy can lessen the intensity of obsessions and compulsions, and can diminish the suffering they engender, even if it does not necessarily improve the patient's social adjustment. On this basis, it may be considered in those patients who have a chronic, severe, unremitting obsessive-compulsive disorder that has not responded to any of the less drastic forms of treatment.

### REFERENCES

Beech H R: *Obsessional States*. Methuen, London, 1974.

Freud S: Notes upon a case of obsessional neurosis. In *The Standard Edition of the Complete Psychological Works of Sigmund Freud*, vol 3, p 45. Hogarth Press, London, 1955.

Insel T, et al: Obsessive-compulsive disorder. Arch Gen Psychiatry 40: 605, 1983.

Marks I: Review of behavioral psychotherapy; I. Obsessive-compulsive disorders. Am J Psychiatry 138: 584, 1981.

Mellman L A, Gorman J M: Successful treatment of obsessive-compulsive disorder with ECT. Am J Psychiatry 141: 596, 1984.

Nemiah J C: Obsessive-compulsive disorder (obsessive-compulsive neurosis). In *Comprehensive Textbook of Psychiatry*, ed 4, H I Kaplan, B J Sadock, editors, p 904. Williams & Wilkins, Baltimore, 1985.

Pippard J: Rostral leucotomy: A report on 240 cases personally followed up after 1½ to 5 years. J Ment Sci 101: 756, 1955.

Rapoport J. et al: Childhood obsessive-compulsive disorder. Am J Psychiatry 138: 1545, 1981.

Salzman L: *The Obsessive Personality*. Science House,

New York, 1968.

Salzman L, Thaler F: Obsessive-compulsive disorders: A review of the literature. Am J Psychiatry *138:* 286, 1981.

---

# 17.4 POSTTRAUMATIC STRESS DISORDER

## Introduction

Posttraumatic stress disorder is a disorder that has long been recognized in clinical psychiatry, but for which official recognition has been minimal, late in arriving, and long overdue. Acute and chronic stress syndromes occurring after severe physical and emotional traumata are a major public health problem and have significant medicolegal implications.

## Definition and History

Posttraumatic stress disorder is defined in DSM-III as follows: "The essential feature is the development of characteristic symptoms after the experiencing of a psychologically traumatic event or events outside the range of human experience usually considered to be normal. The characteristic symptoms involve reexperiencing the traumatic event, numbing of responsiveness to, or involvement with, the external world, and a variety of other autonomic, dysphoric, or cognitive symptoms."

The characteristic autonomic, dysphoric, and cognitive symptoms include such phenomena as exaggerated startle response, difficulty in concentrating, memory impairment, guilt feelings, and sleep difficulties.

The single classic posttraumatic syndrome—involving recurrent nightmares, anxiety, numbing of responsiveness, insomnia, impaired concentration, irritability, hypersensitivity, and depressive symptoms—has been described in response to an enormous variety of overwhelmingly stressful situations—prisoner-of-war camps, death camps, combat, auto accidents, industrial accidents, such mass catastrophes as Hiroshima, as well as rape, and severe accidents in the home. These various stressors all tend to produce a single syndrome that appears to be the final common pathway in response to severe stress. This syndrome may occur acutely after the disaster, or it may become chronic. Not all victims of disaster are necessarily normal personalities, although the stressor must be of sufficient severity to invoke the syndrome in most normal people. Consequently, the disorder may be diagnosed in persons who have a prior psychiatric diagnosis but who develop the classic posttraumatic syndrome in response to a severe stressor. Some persons who experience the symptoms of posttraumatic stress disorder may also display symptoms of another disorder, such as an organic mental disorder or major depressive disorder.

## Epidemiology

Because posttraumatic stress disorder, by definition, occurs only in response to severe stress, its prevalence can be discussed only in relationship to the occurrence of specific stressors. Because posttraumatic stress disorder is a new category that corresponds only loosely to the older concepts of gross stress reaction and traumatic neurosis, and because traumatic neurosis and gross stress reaction have themselves been defined loosely and variably in the past, no precise epidemiological data are available.

The sex ratio for posttraumatic stress disorder is unknown. The familial pattern is also unknown. No difference in family histories of psychiatric treatment between Vietnam returnees with a depressive syndrome and those without a depressive syndrome has been found. On the other hand, recent studies of the children of Nazi death camp survivors indicate that they may have a high incidence of psychopathology fostered by their parents' survivor guilt and tendency to over-value their children, and to have overly high expectations.

## Causes

The role of the stressor in posttraumatic stress disorder may be compared to the role of force in producing a broken leg. It is normal for a leg to break if enough force is applied, although a broken leg is a pathological condition. Individual legs vary, however, in the amount of force required to produce a break, the amount of time required for healing, and the degree of residual pathology that may remain. In most persons experiencing posttraumatic stress disorder, the stressor is a necessary but not sufficient cause, because even the most severe stressors do not produce a posttraumatic stress disorder in all persons experiencing this stressor. A variety of psychological, physical, genetic, and social factors may also contribute to the disorder.

### Nature of the Stressor

Stressors of various types contribute variable amounts to the development of posttraumatic stress disorder. By definition, the stressor must be severe enough to be outside the range of human experience usually considered to be normal. That is, it does not include stressors such as business losses, marital conflict or divorce, death of a loved one, and chronic illness. Many different kinds of stressors have been described as producing the posttraumatic syndrome. These include natural disasters (floods, earthquakes), accidental man-made disasters (industrial accidents, auto accidents, fires), and deliberate man-made disasters (death camps, torture, bombing). Although the trauma often involves a physical factor, as in the case of rape or accidents involving physical injury, it always involves a psychological component that produces significant emotional trauma. The psychological component involves feelings of intense fear, helplessness, loss of control, and threat of annihilation. The trauma may be experienced alone, as in the case of rape or accidents in the home, or it may be experienced with large groups of people, as in the case of mass catastrophes, military combat, and death camps. These stressors would all be classified as either extreme (industrial accidents, car accidents) or catastrophic (death camps, natural disasters).

### Nature of the Patient

In general, the very young and the very old have more difficulty in coping with traumatic events than do those experiencing them during midlife. For example, about 80 percent of young children experiencing a burn injury show symptoms of posttraumatic stress disorder 1 or 2 years after the initial injury. On the other hand, only 30 percent of adults suffering such injury have a posttraumatic stress disorder after 1 year. Presumably, young children have not yet developed adequate coping mechanisms to deal with the physical and emotional insults of the trauma. Likewise, older people, when compared with younger adults, are likely to have more rigid coping mechanisms and to be less able to develop flexible approaches to dealing with the effects of the trauma. Further, the effects of the trauma may be enhanced by physical disabilities characteristic of late life, particularly disabilities of the neurological or cardiovascular systems, such as decreased cerebral circulation, failing vision, palpitations, and arrhythmias.

Preexisting psychiatric disability, whether in the form of personality disorders or more serious conditions, also increases the impact of particular stressors.

The availability of social supports may also influence the development, severity, and duration of posttraumatic stress disorder. In general, patients who have a good network of social supports are less likely to develop the disorder, or to experience it in its most severe forms. The disorder is more likely to occur in those who are single, divorced, widowed, economically handicapped, or socially deprived.

### Organic Factors

The symptoms that occur immediately after the traumatic event are almost certainly produced, in part, by a massive autonomic discharge occurring in response to fear. The threat of injury or annihilation leads to a massive sympathetic discharge, with its associated symptoms of hyperalertness, increased cardiac rate and output, excessive perspiration, muscular tension, tremulousness, and a subjective sensation of anxiety.

In some instances, the psychological trauma that induces posttraumatic stress disorder is also accompanied by a physical trauma. If a physical injury occurs, it further enhances the likelihood that posttraumatic stress disorder will develop, because a physical injury intensifies the nature of the stress.

### Psychoanalytic Theories

Various psychoanalytic theories have been presented to explain the symptoms occurring after traumatic events. The various symptoms characteristic of posttraumatic stress disorder—such as irritability, insomnia, and fearfulness—are seen as indicative of renascent id drives.

Psychoanalytic theory has stressed the distinction between primary gain and secondary gain in the discussion of neurotic disorders. The primary gain is the reduction of tension and conflict through such neurotic defense mechanisms as regression, repression, and denial. In addition to this internal primary gain, the victim may also receive a secondary gain from the external world. Common forms of secondary gain include monetary compensation, increased attention or sympathy, and the satisfaction of dependency needs. These various forms of secondary gain may further reinforce the patient's disorder and contribute to its persistence.

### Clinical Features

The essential clinical features of posttraumatic stress disorder are summarized in Table I. These features include the occurrence of a stressor that causes significant symptoms of distress in nearly all people, repeatedly reexperiencing the traumatic event, numbing of responsiveness to or involvement with the external world, and at least two from a variety of autonomic, depressive, and phobic symptoms.

TABLE I
DIAGNOSTIC CRITERIA FOR POSTTRAUMATIC STRESS DISORDER*

A. Existence of a recognizable stressor that would evoke significant symptoms of distress in almost everyone.

B. Reexperiencing of the trauma as evidenced by at least one of the following:

(1) recurrent and intrusive recollections of the event
(2) recurrent dreams of the event
(3) sudden acting or feeling as if the traumatic event were reoccurring, because of an association with an environmental or ideational stimulus

C. Numbing of responsiveness to or reduced involvement with the external world, beginning some time after the trauma, as shown by at least one of the following:

(1) markedly diminished interest in one or more significant activities
(2) feeling of detachment or estrangement from others
(3) constricted affect

D. At least two of the following symptoms that were not present before the trauma:

(1) hyperalertness or exaggerated startle response
(2) sleep disturbance
(3) guilt about surviving when others have not, or about behavior required for survival
(4) memory impairment or trouble concentrating
(5) avoidance of activities that arouse recollection of the traumatic event
(6) intensification of symptoms by exposure to events that symbolize or resemble the traumatic event

* From American Psychiatric Association: *Diagnostic and Statistical Manual of Mental Disorders*, ed 3. American Psychiatric Association, Washington, DC, 1980. Used with permission.

The disorder may begin any time after the occurrence of an extreme or catastrophic stress. In many persons, the disorder begins hours or days after experiencing the stressor, but in some persons the reaction may be delayed by months or even years.

A patient experiencing posttraumatic stress disorder is always troubled by unwelcome reexperiencing of the traumatic event in a variety of ways. Recurrent dreams or nightmares, from which the patient often awakes in a state of terror, are perhaps the most common mode of reexperiencing the event. Other patients complain of repeated and intrusive recollections of the event; these recollections persist in spite of attempts to forget and to focus attention and energy on other aspects of life. Some complain of dissociative-like states, during which the patient reacts behaviorally to the experience he is reliving; the reaction may last from a few minutes to several hours or even days.

Patients suffering from posttraumatic stress disorder always experience some form of diminished or constricted responsiveness. This reaction has been referred to as psychic numbing and emotional anesthesia. The patient usually sees this constricted responsiveness as a distinct change from his pretraumatic condition. In mild cases, the patient may complain that he feels detached or estranged from other people, or that he has lost the ability to enjoy activities. When the symptom is more severe, the patient may complain of an inability to feel emotions of any type, especially those associated with intimacy, tenderness, and sexuality.

In addition to painful reexperiencing of the traumatic event and diminished responsiveness,

patients also complain of a variety of other symptoms. At least two of these symptoms are required to make the diagnosis, but many patients complain of more than two. Nearly all patients with posttraumatic stress disorder experience, at some time, symptoms of excessive autonomic arousal, such as hyperalertness, an exaggerated startle response, and difficulty in falling asleep. Others complain of middle or terminal sleep disturbance, often precipitated by their recurrent nightmares, during which the traumatic event is relived. Some patients complain of impaired memory, difficulty in concentrating, or difficulty in completing tasks. These cognitive symptoms are particularly prominent in patients who have experienced both severe physical trauma and psychological trauma, such as may occur in death camp survivors and head injury and accident victims. Patients who have experienced their life-threatening trauma in the company of other people often complain of survivor guilt. That is, they express painful guilt feelings about surviving when so many others have not or about the things that they had to do in order to survive. Some patients report phobic avoidance of activities or situations that may arouse recollections of the traumatic event. The symptoms of posttraumatic stress disorder are often intensified when the patient is exposed to situations or activities that resemble the original trauma, such as hot humid weather or tall grass for veterans who fought in Southeast Asia or the South Pacific.

### Associated Features

Patients with posttraumatic stress disorder may develop a variety of associated features. All types of depressive symptoms are common, including decreased interest, decreased energy, decreased sex drive, loss of appetite, periods of feeling "blue," and crying spells. Symptoms of anxiety are also common and may include restlessness, nervousness, and tremor. Some patients complain of increased irritability, which may be accompanied by sporadic and unpredictable explosions of aggressive behavior, even on minimal or no provocation. Increased irritability and aggressiveness have been described frequently in war veterans. Other patients may display nonviolent impulsive behavior, such as sudden trips, unexplained absences, and changes in life style or residence. Concentration camp survivors may have associated symptoms that reflect an underlying organic mental disorder, such as failing memory, emotional lability, headache, and vertigo. Some patients may begin to abuse alcohol or drugs.

### Complications

Posttraumatic stress disorder may lead to a variety of complications. Psychic numbing may diminish or destroy interpersonal relationships, such as marriage and family life. Phobic avoidance of situations or activities resembling or symbolizing the original trauma may handicap the patient occupationally or recreationally. Patients who have suffered physical injury and who receive pain medication may develop a chemical dependency, particularly if they have a history of alcohol or drug abuse before the injury. Other patients may attempt to cope with their increased autonomic arousal by using central nervous system depressants, such as barbiturates, tranquilizers, and alcohol. This use may lead to a chemical or psychological dependency on such drugs. The emotional lability, depressive symptoms, and guilt feelings may result in self-defeating behavior, suicide attempts, or completed suicide.

### Course and Prognosis

Posttraumatic stress disorder may be either acute or chronic. The DSM-III criteria for subtyping posttraumatic stress disorder appear in Table II. Acute posttraumatic stress disorder occurs in those patients who develop symptoms within 6 months of the initial trauma, or whose symptoms do not last for more than 6 months. In most cases of acute posttraumatic stress disorder, the symptoms develop rather quickly after the traumatic event, usually within hours or days. Most cases of posttraumatic stress disorder are acute, in the sense that the symptoms do not typically persist for longer than 6 months.

TABLE II
DISTINCTION BETWEEN ACUTE AND CHRONIC
POSTTRAUMATIC STRESS DISORDER*

| Acute Posttraumatic Stress Disorder | Chronic Posttraumatic Stress Disorder |
| --- | --- |
| Duration of symptoms for less than 6 months or onset of symptoms within 6 months of the traumatic event | Duration of symptoms for at least 6 months or onset of symptoms at least 6 months after the traumatic event |

\* Table by N. Andreasen, M.D.

In many such cases, the symptoms resolve spontaneously without psychiatric treatment.

Chronic posttraumatic stress disorder is less common but more handicapping. It is defined in DSM-III as a syndrome occurring with a latency greater than 6 months, or a syndrome with symptoms that last for 6 or more months. The more chronic the symptoms, the worse the prognosis.

### Diagnosis

The diagnosis of posttraumatic stress disorder should be made only after all four criteria listed in Table I as essential features are met. The subtype, acute or chronic, should also be specified, using the criteria listed in Table II. A careful history alone is usually adequate to establish the diagnosis.

### Psychiatric Examination

History taking should begin with a detailed examination of the traumatic event and the patient's various reactions to it. If the patient has sought previous medical treatment or legal consultation, his experiences and impressions in these areas should be explored in detail. In addition to collecting information concerning the patient's present illness, the clinician should also evaluate his family history, medical history, and use of alcohol or drugs, because these factors give some indication of the patient's susceptibility to stress. Social, school, occupational, sexual, and marital histories should also be evaluated, because they give an indication of the patient's intellectual and adaptive capacity and the availability of social supports.

A careful mental status examination should also be completed. This examination should focus on other psychiatric syndromes that may accompany posttraumatic stress disorder, such as depression, anxiety, and phobia. Tests of the sensorium should be used to obtain an initial impression concerning the presence of an organic mental disorder.

The clinician should always explore the issue of compensation. The role of compensation in either leading to the development of symptoms or encouraging their persistence may be extremely difficult to evaluate. Nevertheless, the clinician should explore the patient's expectations, past work history, and perception of his degree of disability and its prognosis.

### Differential Diagnosis

In the differential diagnosis, the therapist should consider such diagnoses as major depressive disorder, generalized anxiety disorder, phobic disorder, adjustment disorders, and organic mental disorders. The clinician should also consider a variety of conditions not listed in DSM-III, such as compensation neurosis and postconcussion syndrome.

### Treatment

Treatment of posttraumatic stress disorder should be aimed at reducing the target symptoms, the prevention of chronic disability, and occupational and social rehabilitation. Treatment may consist of behavioral techniques, medication, and various forms of psychotherapy.

### Behavioral Techniques

Behavioral techniques may be of value when anxiety and phobic symptoms are prominent. Relaxation therapy may be useful in decreasing anxiety and inducing sleep. Progressive desensitization may be used to overcome various phobic symptoms.

### Medication

Minor tranquilizers, such as diazepam (Valium) and chlordiazepoxide (Librium), may be useful in decreasing symptoms of anxiety. They should be prescribed with caution, however, for those patients who have a history suggesting a tendency to develop psychological or physical dependency on drugs. Imipramine (Tofranil) may be useful in decreasing phobic or depressive symptoms. These drugs should be used with considerable caution in patients suffering from acute posttraumatic stress disorder after accidents that have led to serious physical illness. Imipramine (Tofranil) in particular may precipitate symptoms of delirium in patients suffering from serious medical illness.

### Psychotherapy

Psychotherapy may be used alone or in conjunction with medication or behavioral methods of treatment. Mild and acute cases of posttraumatic stress disorder often respond simply to supportive psychotherapy. Chronic and severe cases usually require modes of psychotherapy that stress increasing insight, catharsis, and abreaction. Psychotherapy should be kept as brief as possible, however, to minimize the risks of dependency and chronicity.

### Rehabilitation

Patients suffering from chronic forms of posttraumatic stress disorder may benefit from approaches that emphasize rehabilitation—physical, social, or occupational.

### REFERENCES

Andreasen N J C: Posttraumatic stress disorder. In *Comprehensive Textbook of Psychiatry*, ed 4, H I Kaplan, B J Sadock, editors, p 918. Williams & Wilkins, Baltimore, 1985.

Andreasen N J C, Norris A S, Hartford C E: Incidence of long-term psychiatric complications in severely burned adults. Ann Surg *174:* 785, 1971.

Andreasen N J C, Noyes R, Hartford C E, Brodland G, Proctor S: Management of emotional reactions in severely burned adults. N Engl J Med *286:* 65, 1972.

Archibald H C, Long D M, Miller C, Tuddenham R D: Gross stress reaction in combat: A 15-year follow-up. Am J Psychiatry *119:* 317, 1962.

Burchfield S R: *Stress: Physiological and Psychological Interactions,* Hemisphere Publishing Co, Washington, DC, 1984.

Grinker R R, Spiegel J P: *Men Under Stress.* Blakiston, Philadelphia, 1945.

Hoiberg A, McCaughey B G: The traumatic aftereffects of collision at sea. Am J Psychiatry *141:* 70, 1984.

Keiser L: *The Traumatic Neurosis.* J B Lippincott. Philadelphia, 1968.

Norris J, Feldman-Summers S: Factors related to the psychological impacts of rape on the victim. J Abnorm Psychol *90:* 562, 1981.

Ostwald P, Bittner E: Life adjustment after severe persecution. Am J Psychiatry *124:* 1393, 1968.

Scrignar C B: *Posttraumatic Stress Disorder.* Praeger, New York, 1984.

Smith J R: Personal responsibility in traumatic stress reactions. Psychiatr Ann 12: 1021, 1982.

Ursano R J, Boydstun J A, Wheatley R D: Psychiatric illness in U.S. Air Force Vietnam prisoners of war: A 5-year follow-up. Am J Psychiatry *138:* 310, 1981.

---

# 17.5 SOMATOFORM DISORDERS

### Introduction

According to DSM-III, "the essential features of this group of disorders are physical symptoms suggesting physical disorder (hence, Somatoform) for which there are no demonstrable organic findings or known physiological mechanisms and for which there is positive evidence, or a strong presumption, that the symptoms are linked to psychological factors or conflicts. Unlike Factitious Disorder or Malingering, the symptom production in Somatoform Disorders is not under voluntary control, i.e., the individual does not experience the sense of controlling the production of the symptoms. Although the symptoms of Somatoform Disorders are 'physical,' the specific pathophysiological processes involved are not demonstrable or understandable by existing laboratory procedures and are conceptualized most clearly using psychological constructs. For that reason, these disorders are not classified as 'physical disorders.'

"The first disorder in this category is Somatization Disorder, a common and chronic polysymptomatic disorder that begins early in life and that was previously referred to as either Hysteria or Briquet's Syndrome. The second disorder is Conversion Disorder, which, as defined here, is relatively uncommon. This diagnosis is to be used only when conversion symptoms are the predominant disturbance and are not symptomatic of another disorder. Psychogenic Pain Disorder is characterized by psychologically induced pain not attributable to any other mental or physical disorder. Hypochondriasis involves preoccupation with the fear or belief of having a serious disease. Finally, Atypical Somatoform Disorder is the term applied to physical symptoms without an organic basis that do not fit the criteria for any specific Somatoform Disorder."

## Somatization Disorder

### Definition

The term hysteria has been abandoned and a new syndrome, somatization disorder, has been created. As defined by DSM-III: "the essential features are recurrent and multiple somatic complaints for which medical attention is sought: they are not apparently due to any physical illness, begin before early adulthood (prior to age 25), and have a chronic but fluctuating course."

### Epidemiology

Somatization disorder is more common in women than in men, and tends to run in families; it is found to occur in some 20 percent of female parents, siblings, and children of somatization patients. It also seems to be significantly associated with sociopathy and alcoholism in first-degree male relatives of somatization patients.

### Causes

Little can be said about the causes of somatization disorder. The epidemiological data suggest that genetic factors play a role. The frequency with which conversion symptoms are found in patients with somatization disorder indicates that dissociative processes and psychological conflict may contribute to the cause of the disorder, but the absence of any observations relevant to those factors—by those who have proposed that somatization disorder is a distinct psychiatric disorder—precludes further discussion of that possibility.

### Clinical Features

The most characteristic clinical feature of somatization disorder is the presence of multiple, vague somatic complaints (see Table I). The complaints may be referred to any part of the body, but they are most often in the form of headaches, faints, nausea and vomiting, abdominal pains, bowel difficulties, and fatigue. Dysmenorrhea, dyspareunia, and frigidity are frequent, and anxiety and depressive symptoms are common. Briquet described a high incidence of conversion symptoms among the patients he examined. Modern investigators of somatization have similarly found sensorimotor conversion symptoms in their patient population, although the incidence is lower than that reported in the earlier studies.

### Course and Prognosis

Somatization disorder usually begins in the second decade of life, and is often first manifested by complaints referable to the menses. It runs a fluctuating course, but the patient is rarely entirely free of symptoms throughout a lifetime of suffering. Despite the frequency and the persistence with which the patient seeks and receives medical attention, complete relief of symptoms is rare, and the prognosis for cure is poor. Indeed, the patient's medical treatment may complicate and exacerbate her illness, since the somatic nature of many of her symptoms may lead to repeated, generally unnecessary diagnostic studies or surgical procedures that add to her complaints and dysfunction.

### Diagnosis

**Psychiatric Examination.** The most striking behavioral aspect of the psychiatric examination of patients with somatization disorder is the dramatic, exaggerated, and emotional way in which they present themselves and their symptoms. Careful analysis of the behavior pattern reveals a number of elements to which specific adjectives may be applied:

*Dramatic.* The patient tells his or her history and describes symptoms, especially pain, in vivid, colorful language. The patient is often discursive and circumstantial in her account,

TABLE I
DIAGNOSTIC CRITERIA FOR SOMATIZATION DISORDER*

A. A history of physical symptoms of several years' duration beginning before the age of 30.

B. Complaints of at least 14 symptoms for women and 12 for men, from the 37 symptoms listed below. To count a symptom as present the individual must report that the symptom caused him or her to take medicine (other than aspirin), alter his or her life pattern, or see a physician. The symptoms, in the judgment of the clinician, are not adequately explained by physical disorder or physical injury, and are not side effects of medication, drugs or alcohol. The clinician need not be convinced that the symptom was actually present, e.g., that the individual actually vomited throughout her entire pregnancy; report of the symptom by the individual is sufficient.

*Sickly:* Believes that he or she has been sickly for a good part of his or her life.

*Conversion or pseudoneurological symptoms:* Difficulty swallowing, loss of voice, deafness, double vision, blurred vision, blindness, fainting or loss of consciousness, memory loss, seizures or convulsions, trouble walking, paralysis or muscle weakness, urinary retention or difficulty urinating.

*Gastrointestinal symptoms:* Abdominal pain, nausea, vomiting spells (other than during pregnancy), bloating (gassy), intolerance (e.g., gets sick) of a variety of foods, diarrhea.

*Female reproductive symptoms:* Judged by the individual as occurring more frequently or severely than in most women: painful menstruation, menstrual irregularity, excessive bleeding, severe vomiting throughout pregnancy or causing hospitalization during pregnancy.

*Psychosexual symptoms:* For the major part of the individual's life after opportunities for sexual activity: sexual indifference, lack of pleasure during intercourse, pain during intercourse.

*Pain:* Pain in back, joints, extremities, genital area (other than during intercourse); pain on urination; other pain (other than headaches).

*Cardiopulmonary symptoms:* Shortness of breath, palpitations, chest pain, dizziness.

* From American Psychiatric Association: *Diagnostic and Statistical Manual of Mental Disorders*, ed 3. American Psychiatric Association, Washington, DC, 1980. Used with permission.

recounting how her symptoms have affected her life and her relationships with people, rather than giving a description of their nature, character, location, onset, and duration—all of which tend to be overlooked. Her description of previous encounters with doctors is interlarded with recitations of what she said to the doctor and what he said to her.

*Exhibitionistic.* The patient is often overly made-up and overdressed for the occasion, whether it is a visit to the doctor's office or a stay in a hospital bed. She tends to be revealing of her body and, during physical examinations, exposes more of herself than is necessary for the part being examined.

*Narcissistic.* The patient shows a predominant preoccupation with herself and her own concerns and interests, to the exclusion of those of others. She requires and seeks open and direct admiration and praise from other people.

*Emotional.* In tone and intensity of voice, by gestures, and in language, the patient freely expresses the whole gamut of emotions in an often bewildering array, and at times in such a histrionic fashion that she gives the impression of play acting and of not really being capable of experiencing lasting, real, or profound emotions.

*Seductive.* The patient is often coy, flirtatious, and seductive. The impression is gained partly from the quality of exhibitionism mentioned earlier and is reinforced by the patient's facial expression, movements, gestures, verbal innuendos, and even openly seductive invitations to sexual activity.

*Dependent.* Although it may not always be evident in one's initial observation of the patient, it frequently becomes apparent as the doctor-patient relationship develops that the patient is overly dependent, needing not only the gifts of praise and admiration, mentioned as a part of narcissism, but more direct evidence of help, such as advice and medications, which the patient demands with increasing insistence; the patient is capable of anger, at times reaching the proportion of violent temper tantrums, if needs are not being properly satisfied.

*Manipulative.* The patient is skilled in getting what he or she wants from other people by using a variety of artful maneuvers, such as threats to produce a fit of temper; attempts at suicide that are aimed at influencing others, rather than being basically self-destructive; and behavior that otherwise plays on the guilt of others.

**Differential Diagnosis.** The multiplicity of vague somatic symptoms, the dramatic fashion of their presentation, and the chronic course generally distinguish somatization from both anxiety and depression. In depression, the characteristic biological signs and symptoms, the intermittent course, and the family history add further differentiating features.

The eventual emergence in the schizophrenic

patient of delusional phenomena and other evidence of marked disorders in thinking readily establish the diagnosis of a psychotic illness.

Although patients with somatization disorder may include conversion symptoms among their repertoire of complaints, the term conversion disorder should be reserved for those patients in whom conversion symptoms are the primary and predominant manifestations of illness.

## Treatment

In the absence of any systematic studies of the treatment of somatization disorder, it is not possible to speak definitively about therapeutic approaches. Clinical experience suggests that patients with the syndrome are refractory to many of the specific techniques useful in other psychiatric illnesses, a generalization that is confirmed by the observation that, despite extensive medical attention, such patients run a chronic course of morbidity of many years' duration.

Particular attention should be paid to preventing patients from undergoing the multiple unnecessary diagnostic and surgical procedures to which they are subjected by those unfamiliar with the nature of somatization disorder. To this end, the psychiatric consultant needs to inform patients, their families, and their physicians about the clinical characteristics of the syndrome, and about the propensity of many patients to welcome active medical and surgical treatments that, at best, are useless and that may seriously complicate the clinical course and morbidity. At the same time, it must be recognized that patients with somatization disorder, like all other human beings, are subject to serious physical illnesses that require specific somatic treatment. The appearance of new and unusual symptoms should alert the physician to this possibility.

## Conversion Disorder (Hysterical Neurosis, Conversion Type)

### Definition

According to DSM-III, conversion disorder is considered as a subtype of the somatoform disorders, a group of disorders in which the essential features are physical symptoms suggesting physical illness for which there are no demonstrable organic findings to explain the symptoms (see Table II).

Hysteria, dissociative type, is completely divorced from its partner and is considered a totally separate and distinct category, the dissociative disorders, in which, according to DSM-III, the essential feature is a sudden, temporary alteration in the normally integrated functions of consciousness, identity, or motor behaviors, so that some part of one or more of these functions is lost.

In its attempt to be empirical, however, the classification in DSM-III has perhaps overshot the mark by sharply separating conversion disorders from dissociative disorders, and by seeming to ignore the central and common role that the mechanism of dissociation plays in both clinical disorders. In conformity with the DSM-III classification, conversion disorder is discussed here under the somatoform disorders, but the reader would do well to consider it in close conjunction with the description of dissociative disorders, even though they are placed in a separate, apparently unrelated category.

### Epidemiology

It is difficult to speak with precision about the epidemiology of conversion disorder, since the statistical data that underlie epidemiological considerations are neither complete nor accurate. It is important, therefore, to view generalizations about the epidemiology of the disorder

TABLE II
DIAGNOSTIC CRITERIA FOR CONVERSION DISORDER*

A. The predominant disturbance is a loss of or alteration in physical functioning suggesting a physical disorder.

B. Psychological factors are judged to be etiologically involved in the symptom, as evidenced by one of the following:
   (1) there is a temporal relationship between an environmental stimulus that is apparently related to a psychological conflict or need and the initiation or exacerbation of the symptom
   (2) the symptom enables the individual to avoid some activity that is noxious to him or her
   (3) the symptom enables the individual to get support from the environment that otherwise might not be forthcoming

C. It has been determined that the symptom is *not* under voluntary control.

D. The symptom cannot, after appropriate investigation, be explained by a known physcial disorder or pathophysiological mechanism.

E. The symptom is not limited to pain or a disturbance in sexual functioning.

F. Not due to Somatization Disorder or Schizophrenia.

* From American Psychiatric Association: *Diagnostic and Statistical Manual of Mental Disorders*, ed 3. American Psychiatric Association, Washington, DC, 1980. Used with permission.

with reservations, and with the recognition that more systematic observations may require a revision of current ideas.

It is often stated that conversion disorder is less frequently seen in contemporary psychiatric practice than it was 70 or 80 years ago. If by conversion disorder one means the classically described major sensorimotor symptoms of paralyses, anesthesias, convulsions, and so on, there are possibly some grounds for the statement.

Another aspect of the epidemiology of conversion disorder is the tendency of the symptoms to spread from one person to another. This phenomenon is rarely mentioned by contemporary observers. One may occasionally see on a psychiatric ward one patient developing the same hysterical symptom initially manifested by another patient.

*Causes*

An early psychodynamic theory of the causes of hysteria stated that there is a fixation in early psychosexual development at the level of the Oedipus complex. There is a failure to relinquish the incestuous tie to the loved parent, which leads to a conflict in adult life over the sexual drive or libido because it retains its forbidden incestuous quality. The drive is, therefore, subjected to the defensive psychological maneuver of repression. The energy deriving from the drive is converted into the hysterical symptom, which not only protects the patient from a conscious awareness of the drive, but at the same time often provides a symbolic expression of it. In this formulation, hysteria is conceived of as a specific clinical entity arising from specific sexual conflicts originating in the oedipal period of psychosexual development.

Subsequent clinical observations led to a further elaboration of the theory. It was often difficult for patients with hysterical reactions to relinquish their symptoms. This was partly because to do so would subject the patient to experiencing the mental discomfort associated with being aware of the forbidden impulse, which had been a central motivation for the formation of the symptom in the first place. But there were other secondary but important motivations for retaining the symptom once it had resulted from the basic process of conversion. The symptom itself could bring certain advantages to the patient. It defined him as a sick and disabled person, and the people in his environment acted accordingly. Attention, sympathy, and help were focused on him because he was ill, and he was not required, while an invalid, to carry out the duties and responsibilities expected of a healthy adult. Such advantages gratified the dependency needs of the patient and, because of the secondary gains resulting from the gratification, tended to reinforce the perpetuation of hysterical symptoms, which had been produced in the first place by quite different psychological factors—the conflict over oedipal sexuality.

These formulations soon became the standard psychodynamic explanation of conversion hysteria. Even now, the term "conversion" implies to many psychiatrists a psychogenic physical symptom arising from conflicts over sexuality that have their origin in the oedipal phase of psychosexual development. There is no doubt that conversion disorder may arise on this basis alone or that such conflicts may play a part, along with other psychological factors, in producing hysterical symptoms. There is, however, a growing trend in contemporary thinking to expand the concept of conversion to include a wider range of psychological events.

**Expanded Concept.** *Mixed Syndromes.* Hysterical symptoms do not always occur in a circumscribed clinical syndrome. On the contrary, in the mixed neuroses, the hysterical symptom is only one of a repertoire of clinical manifestations—which may include phobias, obsessions, compulsions, and neurotic depression—and in which, according to psychoanalytic theory, the psychogenetic factors are primarily preoedipal and pregenital. A particularly striking instance of the mixture is seen in the transient hysterical symptoms sometimes manifested by patients with schizophrenia.

*Variety of Personality Types.* Hysterical symptoms are not invariably associated with the genital hysterical character. On the contrary, they are found in combination with a variety of personality types—for example, the passive-aggressive, the schizoid, and the paranoid personalities—in which, according to Freudian theory, pregenital conflicts play a predominant role.

*Gratification of Dependency Needs.* It has long been known that hysterical symptoms may result from a frightening physical accident that has produced no bodily injuries. "Railway spine," the name attached to the hysterical sensorimotor phenomena seen in people who had been involved in a railway mishap, was a well-described entity in the 19th century.

Recent interest in the psychological aspects of bodily disease has revealed that oral narcissistic drives are central causal factors in many patients with hysterical symptoms, especially when the conversion process results in pain or in the prolongation or exacerbation of bodily symptoms originally resulting from a local physical lesion. In such patients, the symptoms are motivated by—and provide gratification for—strong, unconscious dependency needs. These needs are a source of conflict for the patient, since they run counter to the image of himself as a strong, self-sufficient person, and he must preserve that image in order to maintain his self-esteem. Since his symptoms seem to the patient to be the result of a bodily illness that has afflicted him without his consent or participation, he can allow himself to become an incapacitated invalid, dependent on others for help and attention. Continuing to believe that he wants to be strong, self-sufficient, and independent, he remains unaware of his underlying dependency needs, and can blame his entire predicament on an accidental, ego-alien sickness that is not his fault.

*Reaction to Environmental Stress.* Psychiatric symptoms are not only pathological adaptations to external stimuli, but may represent learned responses. The learning is reinforced and facilitated by the reduction of the intensity of an inner painful psychological drive that follows the response.

In the case of a hysterical paralysis, for example, the initial episode of paralysis results in a reduction of the painful drive of fear or anxiety. The psychological relief thus obtained reinforces the hysterical response that has produced it and predisposes to a repetition of the same palliative response each time the anxiety occurs. In this way, a pattern of behavior is evolved that may become chronic.

*Psychosomatic Disorders.* Another factor that has had an influence in bringing about changes in the concept of conversion hysteria has been the interest, over the past 4 decades, in psychological factors affecting physical illness, commonly referred to as psychosomatic disorder.

This differentiation is generally made on the basis of two criteria: (1) Hysterical symptoms affect and are mediated by the voluntary sensorimotor system, whereas psychophysiological disorders are the result of autonomic nervous system discharge. (2) The hysterical symptom expresses symbolically an idea or memory that is unconscious. In the psychophysiological disorders, no such symbolism is found. The autonomic response is merely the physiological correlate of an unconscious affect or drive that leads to dysfunction in various organ systems and may, if the dysfunction continues long enough, result in actual lesions in the organ involved.

A number of contemporary investigators have challenged the validity of making such a sharp distinction. Their arguments are based on at

least three observations. (1) Certain symptoms—such as nausea, vomiting, and fainting—that have always been considered part of the classical syndrome of conversion disorder are mediated in part, at least, by the autonomic nervous system. (2) Psychophysiological disorders may, like conversion disorder, represent nonverbal, symbolic communications expressed in body language. (3) In psychophysiological disorders, as well as in hysterical symptoms, an affect or drive that is rendered unconscious by repression seems to be converted into a somatic symptom.

*Symptoms as Communication.* Another and more recent approach to conversion disorder is based on the study of communication in the interpersonal situation. In this framework, the conversion symptom is looked on as a nonverbal communication in body language that has, as its basic purpose, the intent to coerce another person to some action, such as helping or paying attention to the person who is communicating.

Interesting and provocative as some of these propositions have been, they seem to be based primarily on the symbolic and communicative aspects of hysterical symptoms and on their function as a means of expressing dependency needs, either as secondary gain or as arising from a primarily oral organization of the personality structure. As such, they are concepts derived from a limited view of hysterical symptoms and cannot be considered as theories that will ultimately or basically explain all the clinical observations.

**Reappraisal of Conversion Disorder.** In recent years there has been a recrudescence of interest in the mechanism of conversion, and a beginning reappraisal of its nature. The concept of conversion was one of Freud's earliest psychological theoretical formulations, and it arose at a time when he was trying to explain why some neurotic patients developed hysterical sensorimotor symptoms and others fell prey to obsessions or phobias. He recognized that behind all these clinical manifestations there was a splitting off from consciousness—a dissociation—of painful affects and their associated ideas. The theoretical problem was to explain the subsequent choice of symptoms once the basic process of dissociation had occurred. To solve this problem, Freud postulated two further secondary mechanisms: (1) In hysteria, the affect is converted into physical symptoms and discharged over the pathway thus created. (2) In phobias and obsessions, the affect remains in the psychical realm but becomes detached from the unbearable idea that originally provoked it and is displaced to a neutral, unimportant, and innocuous idea, which then provides an avenue for the expression and discharge of the affect.

In this formulation, the concept of conversion carries the idea that it is a special pathological process in which psychic energy is transmuted into a physical neuronal discharge leading to the sensorimotor symptoms. Freud himself was puzzled by the nature of the mechanism and spoke of "the mysterious leap from the mental to the physical" that characterized hysteria. One might, however, ask whether conversion is a unique process, whether it is a mechanism specific to the formation of hysterical symptoms, and whether, indeed, it is any more mysterious than, or different from, the translation of any idea into a volitional motor act. A normal woman in coitus under the influence of consciously felt sexual desire voluntarily and happily performs the bodily movements appropriate to the sexual act. A hysterical woman, without any conscious experience of sexual feelings and wishes, has a hysterical convulsion in which she exhibits all the movements of coitus without being at all aware of their significance. What distinguishes the two is not a difference in the way their sexual desire (a mental phenomenon) leads to the physical movements of coitus (a bodily phenomenon). The difference is that, in the hysterical woman, the process takes place in a dissociated state outside of her conscious awareness. The problem of how the mental phenomenon of volition is related to its corresponding physical bodily movement has been a puzzle to philosophers since Descartes. Conversion is simply that same process taking place in a state dissociated from conscious awareness.

If conversion proves not to be a unique mechanism specific to hysterical symptoms, attention is focused once again on dissociation as the basic psychopathological mechanism, not only for conversion disorders but for dissociative disorders and possibly for all neurotic syndromes as well. The question of symptom choice becomes the problem of explaining not why a dissociated impulse or affect is expressed in a physical, bodily manifestation— which is the normal outcome of unblocked, uncontrolled affects and impulses—but, rather, why these mental events do not show their physical correlates but are shifted (displaced) to other mental phenomena in the form of phobias and obsessions.

## Pathology

There is little to be said about the pathology of conversion disorder. No known neuropathological lesions underlie the symptoms, and the pathology that is associated with the condition is purely secondary to the hysterical paralyses

and contractures. If they are of long duration, muscle atrophy, stiffening, and limitation of motion of the joints of the affected limb or limbs may occur as a result of prolonged disuse.

## Clinical Description

**Motor Disturbances.** There are two kinds of motor disturbances—abnormal movements and paralysis.

*Abnormal Movements.* The abnormal movements may take many forms. Gross, rhythmical tremors of the head, arms, and legs are seen, sometimes when the parts are in use, and the tremors are often worse when attention is called to the movements. A variety of choreiform tics and jerks may be observed; they are usually more organized and stereotyped than the movements of true neurogenic chorea.

Convulsive movements of the entire body are sometimes found; unlike true neurogenic epilepsy, hysterical seizures are characterized not by rhythmical clonic movements of the extremities, but by a wild, disorganized, seemingly unpatterned thrashing and writhing of the body. The patient appears to be completely out of control, his bedclothes are thrown into complete disarray, his arms and legs wave about with abandon, but he rarely hurts himself, bites his tongue, or voids. Such seizures may last many minutes and are accompanied by what appears to be complete unresponsiveness. Careful observation, however, reveals that, in fact, the patient does react to stimuli; he often resists movements of his limbs forced by the examiner; though his eyes are closed, the lids often flutter, and he vigorously resists attempts to open them. When the patient recovers from the seizure and becomes responsive, he can often remember or can be made to remember what was going on around him during the convulsion. This is quite different from the complete amnesia of the patient with neurogenic epilepsy for the events occurring during the period of true physiological unconsciousness. The hysterical patient exhibits an altered state of consciousness, but it is a dissociative state, rather than the unconsciousness accompanying gross disturbances of brain function.

Astasia abasia is also seen. This dramatic disturbance of gait is characterized by gross, irregular, pseudoataxic, jerky movements of the trunk, and by dancing, staggering, drunken steps; also, a wild thrashing and waving of the hands and arms as the patient seems to try to keep his balance or clutches for the support of walls, furniture, or people. He rarely falls; but, if he does, he avoids injury.

*Paralysis.* Paralysis and paresis most often

affect the extremities as a monoplegia, a hemiplegia, or a paraplegia. The affected parts are
flaccid in character or show the result of sustained contractures in antagonistic muscle
groups. The paralysis does not conform to the
pattern resulting from damage to the peripheral
or central nervous system; rather, it follows a
distribution conforming to the conventional idea
of the part affected. The hand is paralyzed from
the wrist down, the forearm from the elbow
down, and the whole arm from the shoulder
down. If the problem is one of paresis, the weakness may be most severe at the proximal portion
of the limb, rather than distally—the opposite
of what occurs in central nervous system disease.
For example, in hysterical hemiplegia, the patient, when walking, drags the affected leg along
limp behind him, rather than swinging it
through at the hip, as in neurogenic hemiplegia.

When the paralyzed or paretic part is examined carefully, it becomes apparent that there is
no genuine deficit in muscle function. If the
patient is asked to move the afflicted member,
one may note a spasm of the antagonist muscles,
and this spasm prevents motion. On passively
flexing the paralyzed limb, the observer may
find a contracture of the muscle groups opposing
the movement. Reflexes remain within the range
of normal, the plantar response is always flexor,
and there is no reaction of degeneration on
electrical stimulation.

A special and localized form of paralysis occurs in the muscles affecting the vocal cords,
leading to hysterical aphonia. In this condition,
the patient is usually able to whisper with no
difficulty but can make no vocalized sound
whatsoever. Examination reveals normal movement of the lips, tongue, pharynx, and vocal
cords during respiration.

**Sensory Disturbances.** Hysterical disturbances of sensation, especially anesthesias, may
go unnoticed unless they are specifically looked
for, since patients do not often complain of
them. This is because of both the complexity of
the clinical ingredients and the refractoriness of
such patients to programs of treatment and rehabilitation. Patients in this category of conversion disorder provide good illustrations of somatic compliance, a common mechanism that
enters into the formation of conversion symptoms. As the term implies, conversion symptoms
tend to appear in locations and organ systems
that are or have previously been the site of
symptom-producing lesions, the existence of the
physical disorder apparently facilitating the subsequent appearance of the conversion symptoms
in the same location.

## Course and Prognosis

Conversion disorder frequently begins in adolescence or early adulthood, but the symptoms
may appear for the first time during middle age
or even in the later decades of life. Like so much
else connected with conversion disorder and the
other neuroses, good observations leading to
valid generalizations about the prognosis in both
treated and untreated patients are hard to find.
From general clinical experience, it is known
that some patients develop transitory hysterical
symptoms that clear without any treatment at
all, whereas others have clinical manifestations
that remain fixed and totally intractable to therapeutic measures for years. Little is known
about the natural history of conversion disorder.
The exact rate of recurrence is unknown, but
clinical experience indicates that hysterical
symptoms tend to come and go in response to
environmental stresses.

Probably the most important factors in determining the prognosis have little to do with the
nature of the manifest symptoms; rather, they
are concerned with the patient's personality
traits and psychological conflicts. Factors that
make for a good prognosis, especially when
skilled psychotherapy is available, are: (1) a
psychological conflict that centers primarily on
genital, oedipal sexuality; (2) evidence of stability in relationships, as indicated by generally
good relationships with family and friends and
a stable work history, when the latter is applicable; (3) the ability to relate to the physician
and to develop a therapeutic alliance; (4) the
capacity to feel and to express emotions without
developing incapacitating anxiety or depression;
(5) the ability to have psychological distance
from consciously experienced emotion; (6) the
capacity for introspection; and (7) symptoms
that are fairly well circumscribed and related to
definite environmental stresses.

## Diagnosis

It is not always easy to establish the diagnosis
of conversion disorder. Generally speaking, the
phenomena of abnormal movements, paralyses,
and anesthesias present few diagnostic problems, since the examiner readily elicits the characteristics that are pathognomonic of the condition. It is when one is dealing with pain and
other symptoms simulating bodily disease—
whether they are entirely hysterical or represent
emotional complications of physical disease—
that difficulties arise.

It is an unsound, though tempting, practice to
consider any symptom as hysterical when all

physical causes have been ruled out by the absence of physical findings and by normal results in laboratory and X-ray examinations. The diagnosis thus arrived at is more indicative of the physician's ignorance than of hysterical mechanisms at work. The diagnosis of conversion disorder must rest on a history, and also on observations positively indicating its existence.

That pain or other local symptoms are wholly or in part the manifestation of conversion disorder is strongly suggested by the presence of all or many of the following additional factors: (1) a history of other symptoms (past or concurrent) that clearly have the characteristics of conversion disorder, such as paralyses and anesthesias; (2) a history of other overtly neurotic symptoms, such as anxiety, depression, obsessions, and phobias; (3) a history of sexual disturbances, with anorgasmia, impotence and a distaste for sexuality playing a prominent role; (4) the presence of *la belle indifférence*; (5) the recent death of a person important to the patient or of other disturbances in personal relationships temporally related to the onset of the symptoms.

The psychiatrist's approach to the patient is of central importance in establishing the diagnosis. Confronting him with direct questions requiring direct answers frequently elicits no information or yields misinformation. The patient is often quite unaware of the relation of difficult environmental situations to the appearance of his symptoms. He may not even be conscious of the fact that he is emotionally upset by what is happening in his life. Only by allowing the patient to talk in his own way about his illness, and by using nondirective forms of interviewing techniques, is the physician able to elicit associations from the patient that give him clues to the presence of problems indicating that hysterical mechanisms are playing a part in the formation of symptoms.

**Psychiatric Examination.** The patient with conversion disorder does not show major abnormalities in his mental status. He is alert, completely oriented, and in good rapport with the examiner. His mood may be variable, but he is not profoundly depressed or retarded, on the one hand, or elated and hyperactive on the other. His thought content is not grossly abnormal, nor is there evidence of a primary-process thought disorder. If he manifests hallucinations, he is aware that they are hallucinations, no matter how vivid and real the sensory images may be to him. In short, the patient's mental status reveals no indications of a psychosis or of a gross physiological disturbance of brain function.

The most characteristic behavioral feature in patients with conversion hysteria is what the French authors of the 19th century called *la belle indifférence*. Despite what appear to be the most extensive and crippling disturbances in function, the patient is completely unconcerned and, indeed, may not spontaneously mention such disturbances, which often results in their being overlooked unless specifically searched for.

**Differential Diagnosis.** The earliest manifestations of central nervous system disease may be confused with conversion disorder. A transitory disturbance of vision in one eye, or a passing weakness of an arm or leg that heralds the onset of multiple sclerosis, leaving no definite neurological sequelae or signs, may lead the unwary to dismiss the complaints as hysterical symptoms. The problem is compounded by the fact that hysterical phenomena may be of short duration, and that patients with early multiple sclerosis may exhibit behavior characteristic of the hysterical personality. In such cases, it is important to follow the patient carefully for subsequent episodes in which the emergence of neurological signs or the lack of them, along with emerging positive indications of hysteria, aids in making a definite diagnosis.

*Schizophrenia.* The fact that hysterical patients sometimes present with hallucinations leads to a diagnostic confusion with schizophrenia. In general, schizophrenic hallucinations are auditory and are often bizarre and vague in content and form. Hysterical hallucinations, on the other hand, are usually visual and represent complex, elaborate scenes that are repeated in a stereotyped fashion. The hysterical patient does not show the gross disturbances of thought and affect that characterize schizophrenia. However, the schizophrenic patient may develop hysterical symptoms. In such cases, the diagnosis is determined by the thought and affective disturbances, rather than by the presence of a hysterical symptom.

*Malingering.* A distinction that is sometimes particularly difficult to make is that between conversion disorder and malingering. The tendency of many hysterical patients to be histrionic, and to use their symptoms as a vehicle of communication and coercion of others, plus the often obvious secondary gain to be derived from symptoms, conspire to convince the observer that the patient is consciously simulating illness to obtain his own ends. Patients with true, conscious malingering seem to be rare; in general, there are more inconsistencies in their histories as they are repeated to various people, and the patient consciously simulating a disease often deliberately produces physical signs and findings, which is a rare pattern of behavior in hysterical patients, in whom one finds, instead, evidence of the use of the mechanism of repression, leading to dissociative phenomena.

## Treatment

Clinical experience suggests that psychoanalysis, as the most extensive and profound of the therapeutic measures, is most likely to make permanent changes for the better in both the symptoms and the personality structure of patients who need techniques involving insight. Good and lasting results, however, may be effected with less protracted methods, and success has been reported with the techniques of hypnoanalysis. However, the removal of symptoms by hypnotic suggestion has little value. Either the symptoms return after a brief period, or others appear in their stead; at the same time, such symptom removal may lead to the development of distressing anxiety or depression.

Those patients who are not candidates for one of the insight psychotherapies are generally suffering from narcissistic character problems in addition to their hysterical symptoms, with predominantly pregenital conflicts, particularly those centering on dependency needs. For such patients, supportive therapy is indicated. The therapy may be a one-to-one relationship, it may be provided in a group therapy setting, or a combination of both therapeutic approaches may be used. Environmental manipulation is often an important and helpful measure, and includes working with the patient's immediate family and other people close to him. Through such supportive techniques, a patient's symptoms may diminish markedly or even disappear, and he may begin to function more effectively in his daily life, maintaining the improvement as long as the supportive relationship remains intact.

Drug therapy is sometimes a useful adjunct to psychotherapy, especially if disabling anxiety is present, but there is no direct pharmacological effect of any of the drugs in current use on the hysterical symptom itself.

**Prevention.** A group of patients develop hysterical symptoms that complicate a physical bodily illness and lead to a psychogenic prolongation of the patient's disability. Such patients—no matter how incapacitated, infantile, demanding, and dependent they may be after they develop symptoms—have frequently been exceptionally hard-working, conscientious, self-sufficient, and independent people before the illness. Psychological observations reveal that their behavior patterns before the onset of their

illnesses represented, in part at least, a reaction formation that kept underlying dependency needs out of the patient's awareness and under control. A new psychological equilibrium may be established, and, even though the physical lesion initially underlying the symptoms of the illness had healed or much improved, the symptoms remain in full force as a means of gratifying the dependency needs that have been grafted into them. Psychological invalidism replaced a physical illness. Prevention is essential if such hysterical reactions are to be avoided, and prevention requires that the physician be aware that they do occur, and that he institute the measures appropriate to blocking their development.

## Psychogenic Pain Disorder

In both somatization disorder and conversion disorder, it is clear that pain, although it may be a prominent symptom, is only one of a number of features that, taken together, characterize and define the specific diagnosis. In a significant group of patients, pain may be the sole or primary complaint. Although the pain is not accompanied by the features characteristic of the other somatoform disorders, it is clearly related to environmental stress—often a significant change in human relationships—and either occurs in the absence of detectable underlying physical disease, or is grossly in excess of what would be expected from whatever physical findings are present.

In DSM-III, such patients are assigned to the diagnostic category of psychogenic pain disorder (see Table III). Although it is presumably a common neurotic condition, it is seen more frequently by internists than by psychiatrists, partly because the somatic nature of the complaint leads the patient to a medical physician and partly because his obtuse, often adamant unawareness of even obvious emotional causative factors causes him more often than not to reject psychiatric consultation.

The mechanisms involved in the production of psychogenic pain are not clearly understood. Researchers who investigated patients suffering from the syndrome, found that many of them exhibit alexithymic (i.e., the inability to express feelings) characteristics. If that can be sustantiated in further clinical studies, it would suggest that symptom production in psychogenic pain is related to major defects in the ego functions underlying the experience and expression of feelings, rather than to the psychological conflicts found in the common neurotic disorders. Emotionally stressful events, in other words, are immediately translated or transduced into so-

TABLE III
DIAGNOSTIC CRITERIA FOR PSYCHOGENIC PAIN DISORDERS*

A. Severe and prolonged pain is the predominant disturbance.

B. The pain presented as a symptom is inconsistent with the anatomic distribution of the nervous system; after extensive evaluation, no organic pathology or pathophysiological mechanism can be found to account for the pain; or, when there is some related organic pathology, the complaint of pain is grossly in excess of what would be expected from the physical findings.

C. Psychological factors are judged to be etiologically involved in the pain, as evidenced by at least one of the following:

(1) a temporal relationship between an environmental stimulus that is apparently related to a psychological conflict or need and the initiation or exacerbation of the pain
(2) the pain's enabling the individual to avoid some activity that is noxious to him or her
(3) the pain's enabling the individual to get support from the environment that otherwise might not be forthcoming.

D. Not due to another mental disorder.

* From American Psychiatric Association: *Diagnostic and Statistical Manual of Mental Disorders*, ed 3. American Psychiatric Association, Washington, DC, 1980. Used with permission.

matic symptoms, without the psychic elaboration in feeling and fantasy that characterizes the mechanisms of neurotic symptom formation.

The treatment of patients with psychogenic pain disorder is notoriously difficult. In most cases, however, the best one can hope for is that the patient will establish a trusting and supportive relationship with a single physician that may bring him some amelioration of his pain, and at the same time keep him from what is called doctor shopping—the needless repetition of diagnostic studies and unnecessary medical and other surgical procedures by one doctor after another.

## Hypochondriasis (Hypochondriacal Neurosis)

### Definition

In DSM-III, the diagnostic term "hypochondriasis" refers to those patients in whom the predominant disturbance is an unrealistic interpretation of physical signs or sensations as abnormal, leading to the preoccupation with the fear or belief of having a disease.

### Epidemiology

The incidence in the population at large is unknown, but is presumably larger than that among a group of psychiatric patients, since many persons with hypochondriacal complaints are seen only by internists and general practitioners and do not appear among the statistics collected by a psychiatric institution.

Hypochondriacal symptoms may first appear at any age, from early childhood on. The peak incidence in men is during the fourth decade and in women during the fifth decade. In a little more than half of patients, no precipitating factors are found. In nearly a third, the hypochondriacal concerns arise from a substrate of symp-

toms referable to bodily disease, and among the remainder a variety of psychological stresses preceded the onset of the hypochondriasis.

### Causes

In any discussion of the causes of hypochondriasis, it must be kept in mind that the diagnosis has had a variety of clinical meanings over the years, and that there never has been and is not now a consensus as to the validity of considering it a syndrome separate and independent from other emotional disorders. The numerous theories that have been proposed as an explanation of hypochondriacal phenomena frequently come from investigators who are concerned with the symptoms, not the syndrome. In what follows no attempt is made to distinguish theories on this basis, and it is assumed that, if an explanation of the formation of hypochondriacal symptoms has any validity, it is of equal clinical relevance whether the symptom appears in pure culture as hypochondriasis, or whether it is merely one manifestation of another psychological disorder.

Freud's concepts of the actual neuroses, with their elaborate parallels between the vicissitudes of object and narcissistic libido, are perhaps more significant as an insight into the orderliness and logic of his thinking than as clinically useful theories, and subsequent analytic investigators have generally ignored the more physiological approach in their attempts to explain the genesis of hypochondriasis. These explanations may be grouped into two major classifications: (1) the theories in which hypochondriacal symptoms are seen as the expression of biological drives and (2) the theories in which they are seen as having ego-defensive functions.

*Biological Drives.* An early group of theoreticians, best represented by Paul Schilder, developed Freud's concept of narcissistic libido along psychological lines. In their views, sexual object libido, through the psychological mechanism of regression, is withdrawn from the object and redirected to the self as narcissistic libido. Sexual pleasure is no longer obtained by direct genital activity with another person but is, to quote Schilder, "experienced on the symbolic genitals in the hypochondriac's organs ... Hypochondriac sensations symbolize the genitals."

*Ego-defensive Functions.* Other clinical investigators see hypochondriacal symptoms as playing primarily a defensive role in the psychic economy. For Sullivan they represented protective substitutive activity that prevents the person from experiencing the pain of directly facing a dangerously low self-esteem. He can, in other words, substitute an image of himself as physically ill or deficient for the far more devastating view of himself as a worthless human being.

One must view all the theoretical explanations of hypochondriasis with cautious reservation. They have been constructed from observations made on a small number of patients who are generally limited in their ability to reveal the kind of psychological introspections on which psychodynamic formulations must be based and tested. Perhaps their major value lies in the fact that they focus attention on the important and still poorly understood problem of narcissism. As most investigators have recognized, hypochondriasis is grounded on a narcissistic personality organization, and the continued investigation of hypochondriacal disorders is essential to a deeper understanding of narcissistic phenomena.

### Clinical Features

The salient features of the manifestations of hypochondriasis are (see Table IV): (1) The symptoms are diffuse and variegated, involving many different areas of the body. The most common sites are the abdominal viscera, the chest, and the head and neck, but they may be related to any part of the anatomy or may consist of a generalized bodily sense of fatigue or malaise. Less often, the patient complains of disturbances in mental functioning that lead him to believe he is losing his mind or going crazy. (2) There is often a curious mixture of the minutely specific and the diffusely vague in the quality of the patient's complaints. (3) The symptoms often arise from the patient's heightened awareness of a bodily sensation (a mild ache, pain, or discomfort), of a normal bodily function (bowel movements, heart beats, peristaltic action, for example), or of a minor somatic abnormality (occasional mucus in the stools, and nasal discharge, or a slightly enlarged lymph node). (4) To the trained medical observer, the symptoms have little pathological significance. Individually, they usually suggest no known or specific malfunction or pathological process in an organ system; taken collectively, they form no pattern that is recognizable as being characteristic of physical disease.

### Course and Prognosis

As is often the case in the clinical study of the neuroses, few data are relevent to the course and the outcome of hypochondriasis. Clinical experience has led to the empirical generalization that depressed patients in whom hypochondriacal symptoms are prominent have a much poorer prognosis for recovery than do those whose symptoms are predominantly affective in nature. Hypochondriasis must be considered a chronic disorder with a poor prognosis for cure.

### Diagnosis

Despite the antiquity of the recognition of hypochondriacal symptoms, the status of hypochondriasis as a diagnostic entity has been far from firmly established. The connection between hypochondriasis and hysteria has been suggested for centuries, and the intimate relation of hypochondriasis to depressive states has been repeatedly commented on in recent times. Many investigators have called attention to the frequent combination of hypochondriacal and

TABLE IV
DIAGNOSTIC CRITERIA FOR HYPOCHONDRIASIS*

A. The predominant disturbance is an unrealistic interpretation of physical signs or sensations as abnormal, leading to preoccupation with the fear or belief of having a serious disease.

B. Thorough physical evaluation does not support the diagnosis of any physical disorder that can account for the physical signs or sensations or for the individual's unrealistic interpretation of them.

C. The unrealistic fear or belief of having a disease persists despite medical reassurance and causes impairment in social or occupational functioning.

D. Not due to any other mental disorder such as Schizophrenia, Affective Disorder, or Somatization Disorder.

* From American Psychiatric Association: *Diagnostic and Statistical Manual of Mental Disorders*, ed 3. American Psychiatric Association, Washington, DC, 1980. Used with permission.

neurasthenic phenomena. Some contemporary clinicians view hypochondriasis merely as the prelude to severe mental illness or fail to find hypochondriacal symptoms occurring apart from other neurotic phenomena, which take diagnostic precedence. The paucity of extensive clinical studies of patients with hypochondriacal disturbances makes it impossible to resolve the conflicting points of view.

**Behavioral Characteristics.** The patient presents his complaints at length, in detail, and with an urgent, insistent pressure of speech that rarely allows the physician to get a word in edgewise. If the physician forcibly interrupts with a question or a comment, it is usually ignored, and the patient continues on his own course as if he were quite unmindful of what the physician had said. The clinical encounter with the hypochondriacal patient is a monologue, not a dialogue, and the traditional procedure of history-taking by the physician succumbs to the history giving of the patient.

The patient frequently punctuates his recitation of symptoms by showing the doctor the parts affected, by demonstrating what he considers a disorder of function, or by pointing out the small, usually insignificant structural lesion that is his major source of concern.

The content of the patient's thought and speech is entirely centered on his bodily complaints, on how they have affected him, and on the saga of his unsuccessful attempts to find help or relief. He rarely speaks spontaneously of human relationships, activities, feelings, or fantasies that are unconnected with his somatic preoccupations. The physician's attempts to get at the grief and discontents that beset most human beings—the frustrations, the fears, the sorrows, the anger, and the anxiety that result from the common disappointments in love or in work aspirations—are either ignored by the patient or arouse his resentment.

The patient often uses medical terms or jargon that he has acquired from his previous contacts with physicians or from his frequently extensive reading of medical texts and articles.

The hypochondriacal patient is characteristically worried, anxious, and concerned about his symptoms–an affective state of mind and behavior that is in contrast to the bland *la belle indifférence* of the patient with conversion disorder. The anxiety is implicit in the patient's preoccupation with the physiological functioning of his body and his somatic complaints, and is visible in his tone of voice, facial expression, and general manner of speaking as he tells his story. The anxiety is often explicitly evident in the patient's expressed fears that he has a serious illness or will develop one if he does not receive the medical help he wants or take preventive measures, which may frequently be elaborate and ritualized.

The hypochondriacal concern may be based on physiological sensations overlooked or unobserved by the normal person, or on symptoms arising from minor physical conditions that the patient exaggerates out of all proportion to their medical significance. It is characteristic of the hypochondriacal patient that, not only are his complaints far more severe than any objective physical findings associated with them, but he persists in his anxious concern, despite being given appropriate medical information and strong reassurance concerning his health by his physician.

Many patients develop a pattern of visiting doctors and clinics that becomes almost a way of life. Some become attached to a single physician, whom they consult repeatedly on the smallest pretext. Others, more fickle in their medical attachments, wander from doctor to doctor and clinic to clinic, undergoing endless examinations and evaluations.

In the patient with hypochondriasis, his fear of and preoccupation with illness does not attain the level of delusional conviction that he has this or that disease, and a mental examination reveals no evidence of psychotic disturbances of thought or affect. However, in many patients the fixity and the intensity of their somatic preoccupations make the line between anxious concern and delusional conviction seem very thin, and it is often difficult to determine the degree to which their reality testing remains intact.

Finally, many hypochondriacal patients arouse in their physicians feelings of frustration and resentment that frequently make it difficult to care for them with compassionate objectivity. The tendency to refer such patients to a colleague or to another clinic no doubt enhances their own natural proclivity for multiple consultations.

**Personality Characteristics.** No personality pattern is specifically characteristic of the patient with hypochondriasis or sets him apart from patients with other emotional disorders. Two characterological features, however, have been stressed by numerous clinical investigators as being common in hypochondriacal patients. (1) Many of them show obsessive-compulsive traits—in particular those of obstinacy, defiance, miserliness, and conscientiousness. (2) In view of the nature of their symptoms, it is not surprising that narcissism is a prominent feature in many hypochondriacal patients. They are variously described as being egocentric, excessively concerned with themselves and their bodies, and unduly sensitive to criticism or slight, or as treating their bodies as libidinal objects. These are all ways of stating the fact central to hypochondriasis, that patients with the disorder focus their interest, attention, and psychic energy on their bodily functions to the almost complete exclusion of a concern for people and objects in the world around them. Hypochondriasis could, in fact, be considered a paradigm of narcissism.

**Differential Diagnosis.** Hypochondriacal symptoms may mask or point to other psychiatric disorders requiring specific form of treatment. In particular, the signs and symptoms of depression and schizophrenia should be looked for in patients who present hypochondriacal complaints. In DSM-III, somatization disorder is differentiated from hypochondriasis by the facts that somatization disorder appears at a much earlier age, and is characterized by a far greater variety and distribution of somatic complaints in the individual patient. Hypochondriacal patients may develop serious bodily illnesses that can be masked not only by the multiplicity and vagueness of their complaints, but by the fact that their tendency to cry wolf about somatic sensations may lull their physicians into a false sense of security that any complaint the patient brings him is psychogenic in origin. In the physician's initial evaluation of a new patient, he must carefully assess the possibility that the patient is harboring a physical illness, even if the symptoms seem hypochondriacal in nature. In a hypochondriacal patient with a long-standing relationship with his physician, any new symptom or change in symptom patterns must be just as critically evaluated.

## Treatment

Hypochondriasis is notoriously refractory to treatment, and many of the clinicians who have written about the disorder either ignore the subject of therapy entirely, or speak in pessimistic tones about the prognosis. Clinical evidence suggests that, unless hypochondriasis is a part of a depressive disorder with an overt affective disturbance, medications and electroconvulsive therapy are without effect.

Generally, the best that one can offer a hypochondriacal patient is an understanding and supportive relationship in which one listens sympathetically to his complaints but refrains from challenging his symptoms or depriving him of the status of an invalid. At the same time, it is important to work with the patient's relatives, especially in the initial phases of treatment, to aid them in understanding the nature of the patient's complaints, to guide them in providing him with a properly supportive relationship, and to help give them the emotional strength to do so. With this kind of management, some patients settle into a stable relationship in which, through regularly scheduled but not necessarily lengthy visits, they can be kept relatively free of anxiety and can be kept from falling into the useless and futile pattern of roaming from doctor to doctor and clinic to clinic. Such a relationship need not be with a psychiatrist; but, if an internist or a social worker is the one who provides it, a psychiatrist should remain available for consultation and advice when the need arises.

Although the character structure of hypochondriacal patients usually precludes the use of insight psychotherapy, on rare occasions it is possible to penetrate the almost impregnable wall of somatic complaints and to bring the underlying affects—commonly anger and depression—into conscious awareness and expression. In such cases, the diminution in somatic symptoms and the general improvement in the patient's functioning can be surprising and gratifying. Such a therapeutic approach must, however, be considered experimental, and more information about its effectiveness and its possible dangers must be accumulated before its true usefulness can be determined.

### Atypical Somatoform Disorder

Sometimes referred to as dysmorphophobia, atypical somatoform disorder includes patients who do not clearly manifest the characteristics of the major somatoform disorders. The patient with an atypical somatoform disorder is preoccupied with an organ or body part. Convinced that he is suffering from a serious disease, either on the basis of a minor local lesion or without any evidence of a pathological process, he relentlessly pursues one physician after another for relief that no amount of reassurance brings. The site chosen for concern may be anywhere in the body, but such patients are often convinced that they have serious heart disease (cardiac neurosis), or they focus their complaints on a putative venereal disease. Of particular importance are persons who are preoccupied with what they think of as disturbances in facial structure, especially the nose, for which they persist in seeking plastic surgery. The plastic surgeon is familiar with such patients, and an essential part of his diagnostic task, often with the help of a psychiatric consultant, is to separate those with legitimate indications for reconstructive surgery from those whose complaints result from an atypical somatoform disorder.

**REFERENCES**

Breuer J, Freud S: Studies on hysteria. In *The Standard Edition of the Complete Psychological Works of Sigmund Freud*, vol 2, p 3. Hogarth Press, London, 1955.

Chodoff P, Lyons H: Hysteria, the hysterical personality and "hysterical" conversion. Am J Psychiatry *114:* 734, 1958.

Goodwin D W, Guze S B: Hysteria (somatozation disorder). In *Psychiatric Diagnosis*, ed 3, D W Goodwin, S B Guze, editors, p 89. Oxford University Press, New York, 1984.

Janet P: *The Major Symptoms of Hysteria.* Macmillan, New York, 1956.

Krohn A: *Hysteria—The Elusive Neurosis.* International Universities Press, New York, 1978.

Ladee G A: *Hypochondriacal Syndromes.* Elsevier, Amsterdam, 1966.

Nemiah J C: Somatoform disorders. In *Comprehensive Textbook of Psychiatry*, ed 4, H I Kaplan, B J Sadock, editors, p 924. Williams & Wilkins, Baltimore, 1985.

Rangell L: The nature of conversion. J Am Psychoanal Assoc *7:* 632, 1959.

Roy A: *Hysteria.* John Wiley & Sons, New York, 1982.

Woodruff R A Jr, Goodwin D W, Guze S B: *Psychiatric Diagnosis.* Oxford University Press, New York, 1974.

## 17.6 DISSOCIATIVE DISORDERS (HYSTERICAL NEUROSIS, DISSOCIATIVE TYPE)

### Psychogenic Amnesia, Psychogenic Fugue, and Multiple Personality

#### Definition

According to DSM-III, the dissociative disorders are characterized by a sudden, temporary alteration in the normally integrated functions of consciousness, identity, or motor behavior, so that some part of one or more of these functions is lost.

#### Epidemiology

No evidence suggests that there has been a diminution in the incidence of most forms of the dissociative disorders. The one exception to this statement is the form manifested as multiple personality. The condition seems to be relatively rare, as compared with the situation 80 years ago. In the absence of adequate statistical studies, however, nothing beyond this can be said about the epidemiology of the disorder.

#### Causes

A variety of psychological factors enter into the production of the symptoms of dissociative disorders. Dependent longings, sexual libido, environmental precipitants, conflict over inner in-stinctual drives, and defensive mechanisms have all been implicated.

The psychological conflicts in the adult patient that lead to dissociative symptoms are viewed as being ultimately the result of earlier disturbances in the course of growth and development.

#### Clinical Description

It is characteristic of the various forms of dissociative disorders that they begin and end abruptly. The patient is seen by observers to slip rapidly into a somnambulistic state, or he is himself suddenly aware that he has lost his memory for a period of time in his immediate past. Or, again, he may "wake up" to find himself in a strange place with no knowledge of how he got there, or what he has been doing in the time that has elapsed from the last thing he can remember.

Although many episodes apparently occur spontaneously, there may be a definite history of a specific, shocking emotional trauma or a situation charged with painful emotions and psychological conflict. Amnesia is at times preceded by a physical head trauma. It may have been so slight as to lead one to doubt its physiological significance, or it may, on the other hand, have been severe enough to have caused unconsciousness, often resulting in considerable difficulty in untangling the element of postconcussional amnesia from psychogenic amnesia. In susceptible persons, treatment with electroshock may lead to psychogenic amnesia.

On occasion, hypnosis may precipitate a limited but sometimes prolonged somnambulistic episode from which the hypnotic subject cannot readily be aroused. Finally, mention should be made of the tendency of intense concentration to induce somnambulistic states in some persons.

The manifestations of dissociative disorders are varied, often complex, and frequently hard to distinguish sharply one from another. One characteristic links them together in a common family: in each, a cluster of recent, related mental events—memories, feelings, fantasies—is beyond the patient's power of conscious recall, but remains capable under given circumstances of returning to his conscious awareness—that is, the mental events are unconscious in the psychodynamic sense of the term. At least three factors, on the other hand, determine the separate natures of the various forms, and stamp them with the characteristics that permit their differentiation into clinical types: (1) the state of consciousness during an episode of hysterical dissociation, (2) the pattern of the amnesia, and

(3) the quality of changes in personality and behavior that may accompany the episode.

**Somnambulism.** It is characteristic of somnambulism that the patient exhibits an altered state of conscious awareness of his surroundings, and often has vivid hallucinatory recollections of an emotionally traumatic event in his past of which he may have no memory during his usual waking state. Somnambulistic episodes may arise either during sleep or during the episodes of sleepwalking commonly seen in children. The somnambulistic episodes produce an altered state of conscious awareness that is usually easy for an observer to detect, but hard to describe. The patient is out of contact with his environment, appears preoccupied with a private world, and is seen to be staring into space if his eyes are open. He may seem emotionally upset, and speaks excitedly in words and sentences that are frequently hard to understand, or he engages in a pattern of seemingly meaningful activities that is repeated every time an episode occurs. It can often be determined that his behavior represents the external manifestations of an inner, hallucinatory reexperiencing of a traumatic event, the memories of which are normally repressed. There is amnesia for the somnambulistic episode, once it is terminated.

**Psychogenic Amnesia.** Patients suffering from psychogenic amnesia, the most common dissociative disorder, are often brought to general hospital emergency wards by police who have found them wandering confusedly around the streets.

The clinical features of psychogenic amnesia are outlined in Table I. Amnesia may take one of several forms: localized amnesia, general amnesia, systematized amnesia, and continuous amnesia.

*Localized and General Amnesia.* In these forms of the disorder, the patient suddenly becomes aware that he has a total loss of memory for the events of a period of time, covering anything from a few hours (localized form) to a whole lifetime of experience (generalized form).

Although psychogenic amnesia for immediate past experience is found in patients with both somnambulism and localized or general amnesia, the state of consciousness of those with amnesia during the time for which they are amnesic is different in character. The somnambulistic patient seems out of touch with his environment and appears as if in a dream. The amnesic patient, on the other hand, usually gives no indication to observers that anything is amiss, and seems entirely alert both before and after the amnesia occurs. The only possible exception to this statement is the evidence provided by some patients that there is a mild, transient disturbance of consciousness immediately surrounding the period of the onset of the amnesia.

*Systematized and Continuous Amnesia.* The other two types of amnesia are rarely seen. In the systematized form, the patient loses memory only for specific and related past events—those concerning the birth of a child, for example—with other memories of simultaneously experienced events being retained in consciousness. The patient with continuous amnesia forgets each successive event as it occurs, although he is clearly alert and aware of what is going on around him. The DSM-III criteria for psychogenic amnesia are listed in Table II.

**Psychogenic Fugue.** There are several features typical of psychogenic fugue (see Table III): (1) As the name implies, the patient wanders, usually far from home and for days at a time. (2) During this period he is completely forgetful of his past life and associations but, unlike the patient with psychogenic amnesia, he is unaware that he has forgotten anything. It is only when he suddenly comes back to his former self that he recalls the time antedating the onset of the fugue, but then he is amnesic for the period covered by the fugue itself. (3) Unlike those in a somnambulistic state, the patient in a psychogenic fugue does not seem to others to be behaving in any way that is out of the ordinary, nor does he, like somnambulistic patients, give evidence of acting out any specific memory of a traumatic event. On the contrary, the fugue patient generally leads a quiet, prosaic, somewhat seclusive existence; works at simple occupations; lives modestly; and does nothing to

TABLE I
CLINICAL FEATURES OF PSYCHOGENIC AMNESIA*

| Essential Features | Associated Features |
|---|---|
| Temporary disturbance in the ability to recall important personal information already registered and stored in the memory without evidence of underlying brain disease | Conflict over sexual or aggressive drives common |
| | May follow physical trauma |
| Sudden onset | Indifference to presence of amnesia frequently present |
| Amnesia generally of localized or systematized form; generalized and continuous amnesias less common | |
| Awareness of disturbance of recall is present | |

* Adapted from American Psychiatric Association: *Diagnostic and Statistical Manual of Mental Disorders*, ed 3. American Psychiatric Association, Washington, DC, 1980.

TABLE II
DIAGNOSTIC CRITERIA FOR PSYCHOGENIC AMNESIA*

A. Sudden inability to recall important personal information that is too extensive to be explained by ordinary forgetfulness.

B. The disturbance is not due to an Organic Mental Disorder (e.g., blackouts during Alcohol Intoxication).

\* From American Psychiatric Association: *Diagnostic and Statistical Manual of Mental Disorders*, ed 3. American Psychiatric Association, Washington, DC, 1980. Used with permission.

TABLE III
CLINICAL FEATURES OF PSYCHOGENIC FUGUE*

| Essential Features | Associated Features |
| --- | --- |
| Loss of identity associated with wandering, often with the assumption of a new identity and life pattern | Heavy alcohol use and conflicts over sexuality, aggression, and money frequently present |
| No evidence of underlying brain disease | |
| Amnesia for events occurring during fugue after its termination | |

\* Adapted from American Psychiatric Association: *Diagnostic and Statistical Manual of Mental Disorders*, ed 3. American Psychiatric Association, Washington, DC, 1980.

draw to himself the attention or suspicion of his neighbors and acquaintances. The DSM-III criteria for psychogenic fugue are listed in Table IV.

**Multiple Personality.** The characteristics of this disorder may be summarized as follows (see Table V): (1) At any given time, the patient is dominated by one of two or more distinct personalities, each of which determines the nature of his behavior and attitudes during the period that it is uppermost in consciousness. (2) The transition from one personality to another is sudden, often dramatic in occurrence. (3) There is generally amnesia during each state for the existence of the others and for the events that took place when another personality was in the ascendancy. Often, however, one personality state is not bound by such amnesia and retains complete awareness of the existence, qualities, and activities of the other personalities. (4) Each personality has a fully integrated, highly complex set of associated memories with characteristic attitudes, personal relationships, and behavior patterns. On examination, the patient generally shows nothing unusual in his mental status, other than a possible amnesia for periods of time of varying duration, and one is unable to tell from a single, casual encounter that the patient leads other lives at other times. Only prolonged contact that enables one to observe the sudden discontinuities in mental functioning discloses this information.

The first appearance of the secondary personality or personalities may be spontaneous, or it may emerge in relation to what seems to be a precipitant. In some patients, the change occurs after an emotional shock or physical trauma, and the initial phase may take the form of a typical episode of amnesia that leads to the development of a secondary personality. The DSM-III criteria for multiple personality are listed in Table VI.

**Other Dissociative States.** A curious and not fully explored or understood form of dissociation is that manifested as the trance states of spirit mediums who preside over spiritual seances. Typically, the medium enters a somnambulistic state, during which the so-called control takes over much of his conscious awareness and influences his thoughts and speech. The control purports to be a real personality from the spirit world who undertakes to be the medium's guide, and to act as an intermediary for the departed spirits of those who wish to communicate with relatives still in the body on earth. In some instances, the control introduces the medium to strange and exotic worlds.

The phenomena associated with automatic writing and crystal gazing are curious but less common manifestations of dissociation. In automatic writing, there is not necessarily an alteration of consciousness, the dissociation affecting only the arm and hand that produce a written message, which often discloses mental contents of which the writer is unaware. Crystal gazing, on the other hand, results in a somnambulistic state in which visual hallucinations are prominent. Both phenomena have been used in the past by investigators studying the nature of unconscious mental processes, and by therapists searching for underlying pathogenic memories, but neither is currently much in vogue as either a clinical or an experimental tool. Phenomena related to crystal gazing are the condition of highway hypnosis and the similar mental states experienced by airplane pilots. In both, the monotony of movements at high speeds through environments that provide little in the way of distractions to the operator of the vehicle leads to a fixation of his attention on a single object— a dial on the instrument panel of a plane, for example, or the never-ending horizon at the end

## 356    Neurotic Disorders

TABLE IV
DIAGNOSTIC CRITERIA FOR PSYCHOGENIC FUGUE*

A. Sudden unexpected travel away from one's home or customary place of work, with inability to recall one's past.

B. Assumption of a new identity (partial or complete).

C. The disturbance is not due to an Organic Mental Disorder.

* Adapted from American Psychiatric Association: *Diagnostic and Statistical Manual of Mental Disorders*, ed 3. American Psychiatric Association, Washington, DC, 1980. Used with permission.

TABLE V
CLINICAL FEATURES OF MULTIPLE PERSONALITY*

| Essential Features | Associated Features |
| --- | --- |
| Domination of the patient by one of two or more distinct personalities at any one time | Conflicts over impulses common |
| Each personality has a full or nearly full range of mental functions, often with different, frequently opposite, characteristics | |
| Transition from one personality to the other is sudden | |
| Amnesic barriers found between one personality and another | |

* Adapted from American Psychiatric Association: *Diagnostic and Statistical Manual of Mental Disorders*, ed 3. American Psychiatric Association, Washington, DC, 1980.

of a road running straight for miles ahead. A trance-like state of consciousness results in which visual hallucinations may occur and in which the danger of serious accident is always present. Possibly in the same order of phenomena are the hallucinations and dissociated mental states described in patients who have been confined to respirators for long periods of time without adequate environmental distractions from the drearily regular sameness of their existence.

The religions of many different cultures have recognized the fact that the practice of concentration may lead to a variety of dissociative phenomena, such as hallucinations, paralyses, and sensory disturbances clearly hysterical in nature.

### Course and Prognosis

The natural history of the dissociative disorders has not received sufficient attention from clinical investigators, and the inadequacy of the data precludes definitive statements about either its course or its prognosis. In general, the outlook for individual episodes of dissociative disorders, such as psychogenic amnesia and psychogenic fugue, is good, particularly if energetic therapeutic measures are applied. On the other hand, the tendency of a person to resort to dissociative mechanisms when he is under either

instinctual or environmental pressures can be a continuing liability for him over long periods of time.

The fortunately rare condition of multiple personality is probably a more serious phenomenon, involving major disturbances of ego function. Partial success in its treatment has been reported in the literature.

### Differential Diagnosis

**Schizophrenia.** To casual observation, a dissociative trance state frequently resembles catatonic stupor, and it may at times be difficult to distinguish between them, especially if the hysterical patient is negativistic, or if it is impossible to establish communication with him while the dissociative mechanisms are at work. The patient in a somnambulistic episode usually gives evidence to indicate that he is engaged in the reliving of a traumatic event, and most dissociative trance states, as contrasted with catatonia, are generally self-limited and of short duration. Furthermore, when contact can be established with the dissociative patient, it is evident that the disorders of thought and affect characteristic of schizophrenia are not present.

**Sleepwalking.** The term somnambulism is used to refer both to the dissociative disorders, and to episodes of activity during sleep that have a different character and significance. Very often in childhood, and less frequently when adulthood has been reached, a person may, during actual sleep, get out of bed and wander around. Such behavior is not necessarily pathological, especially in children, and it differs from dissociative somnambulism in that the nondissociative somnambulism occurs during deep sleep unassociated with dreams, is poorly integrated and nonpurposive in nature, and is characterized by actions that are awkward, fumbling, and show a lack of dexterity. Dissociative somnambulistic episodes may occur at night, but they are as different from normal sleepwalking as hypnosis is from true sleep.

**Postconcussional Amnesia.** Dissociative amnesia may be associated with head injury, and in such cases there may be a combination of dissociative and postconcussional amnesia

TABLE VI
DIAGNOSTIC CRITERIA FOR MULTIPLE PERSONALITY*

A. The existence within the individual of two or more distinct personalities, each of which is dominant at a particular time.

B. The personality that is dominant at any particular time determines the individual's behavior.

B. Each individual personality is complex and integrated with its own unique behavior patterns and social relationships.

* From American Psychiatric Association: *Diagnostic and Statistical Manual of Mental Disorders*, ed 3. American Psychiatric Association, Washington, DC, 1980. Used with permission.

that can be difficult to untangle. In general, the retrograde amnesia after a concussion does not extend beyond a period of one week. Postconcussional amnesia, furthermore, disappears slowly, and memory is usually not completely restored for the events that occurred during the amnesic period, whereas the patient recovers from dissociative amnesia suddenly and with a total restoration of memory. In doubtful cases, hypnosis is sometimes useful as a diagnostic tool. If memories can be retrieved in a hypnotic trance, the evidence is strong that dissociative mechanisms were at least partially responsible for the clinical amnesia.

**Temporal Lobe Epilepsy.** One of the most difficult diagnostic distinctions that the clinician is called on to make is that between a dissociative trance state and an episode of temporal lobe epilepsy. In epilepsy, the patient, like the patient in a psychogenic fugue, may seem to be entirely alert as he skillfully carries out a highly complex pattern of behavior. In some patients with electroencephalographic evidence of temporal lobe dysfunction, their seizure behavior patterns have been shown to have reference to a memory of a significant past event in their lives, as is often the case in patients with dissociative somnambulism. In general, when a trance-like episode occurs in conjunction with evidence of other typical dissociative symptoms and stigmata, and when it is unaccompanied by positive electroencephalographic indications of temporal lobe dysfunction, the episode is a dissociative disorder. On the other hand, when there is positive brain wave evidence of a temporal lobe dysrhythmia, even if the clinical episode has features characteristic of dissociation, it should be considered as being— in part, at least—the result of a gross brain lesion. Such evidence has important implications for further neurological diagnostic studies, and for the possible use of specific anticonvulsant medications.

*Treatment*

It is usually possible to recover the lost memories by various therapeutic interventions. In some patients, one can get at the unconscious mental contents within the span of one or two interviews, simply by allowing the patient to free associate or by encouraging him to give his associations to a specific fragment of the repressed material that has returned in the form of a conscious image dream, or hallucination. At other times, more active measures, such as hypnosis and intravenous thiopental, may be required to mobilize the memories. Once the memories are obtained, the suggestion must be made to the patient that he will retain them in consciousness after awakening.

If there is a significant degree of secondary gain resulting from the presence of the amnesia itself, it may be difficult for the therapist to persuade the patient to abandon his symptoms. When the amnesia is firmly fixed, one must consider the possibility that it is protecting the patient from a continuing difficult situation. At times, there may be an element of malingering in the patient's preservation of symptoms, but, as is true in all forms of hysterical neurosis, this is difficult to ascertain, and one should guard against assuming that the patient is consciously pretending, unless there is strong evidence to support the supposition.

The treatment measures aimed at the immediate symptoms of dissociative disorders should ideally be combined with a therapeutic plan designed to help the patient with the basic conflicts that have resulted in symptom formation.

**Depersonalization Disorder
(Depersonalized Neurosis)**

*Definition*

In DSM-III, depersonalization disorder is considered one of the dissociative disorders and is characterized by "an alteration in the perception of the self so that the feeling of one's own reality is temporarily lost."

Some clinicians distinguish between depersonalization and derealization. They apply depersonalization to the feeling that one's body or one's personal self is strange and unreal; they apply derealization to the experience of perceiving objects in the external world as having the same quality of unreality and estrangement. Strictly speaking, this distinction provides a more accurate description of the phenomena than does lumping them all together under the category of depersonalization. Indeed, if a single term is to be used, derealization is the more appropriate, since it refers to a characteristic change in the perception of objects common to all of them—to self, body, or external world— whereas depersonalization is more limited in scope. In what follows, however, depersonalization disorder is used as the generic label in order to conform to the terminology suggested by DSM-III (see Table VII).

## Epidemiology

As an occasional isolated experience in the life of any person, depersonalization is a common phenomenon and, as such, is not necessarily pathological. Studies of its incidence in normal college students indicate that transient depersonalization may occur in as many as 50 percent of a given population, without any significant difference in incidence between men and women. It is a frequent event in children as they develop the capacity for self-awareness, and adults often undergo a temporary sense of unreality when they travel to new and strange places.

Information about the epidemiology of depersonalization of pathological proportions is scanty. Frequently found as a symptom in association with anxiety states, depression, and schizophrenia, depersonalization is apparently rare as a pure syndrome. In the few studies recently made of the condition, it has been found to occur at least twice as frequently in women as in men, and it is a disorder of young people, rarely being found in those over 40.

## Causes

Depersonalization disorder is, by definition, a condition in which no evidence is to be found for pathological functioning of the brain, such as that associated with epilepsy, brain tumors, and the use of psychotomimetic drugs. Such gross disturbances in the structure and the phys-

iology of the central nervous system are not directly related to the causes of the neurotic disorder. On the other hand, they do point to the possible site of the neuronal structures immediately underlying the phenomena of depersonalization and, therefore, have considerable relevance for the ultimate understanding of the correlative relationships between brain function and psychological symptoms.

## Clinical Features

The central characteristic of depersonalization is the quality of unreality and estrangement that is attached to conscious experience (see Table VIII). Inner mental processes and external events go on seemingly exactly as before, yet everything is different and seems no longer to have any personal relation or meaning to the person who is aware of them. The feeling of unreality affects the person's perception of his physical and psychological self and of the world around him. Parts of one's body or one's entire physical being may appear foreign. All of a person's mental operations and behavior may feel alien to him.

A common and particularly troublesome manifestation is a loss of the capacity to experience emotions, even though the patient may appear

TABLE VIII
CLINICAL FEATURES OF DEPERSONALIZATION DISORDER*

| Essential Features | Associated Features |
| --- | --- |
| Alteration of the perception or experience of the self, with loss of sense of one's own reality and associated changes in body image | Dizziness, anxiety, hypochondriasis, fears of going insane, disturbance in sense of time often associated |
| Onset and disappearance rapid | Derealization—loss of feeling of reality of the world—and perceived changes in size and shape of external objects may be present |
| Feeling of loss of control of one's actions and speech may be present | |
| Episodes last for many minutes to hours and recur frequently | |

* Adapted from American Psychiatric Association: *Diagnostic and Statistical Manual of Mental Disorders*, ed 3. American Psychiatric Association, Washington, DC, 1980.

TABLE VII
DIAGNOSTIC CRITERIA FOR DEPERSONALIZATION DISORDER*

A. One or more episodes of depersonalization sufficient to produce significant impairment in social or occupational functioning.

B. The symptom is not due to any other disorder, such as Schizophrenia, Affective Disorder, Organic Mental Disorder, Anxiety Disorder, or epilepsy.

* From American Psychiatric Association: *Diagnostic and Statistical Manual of Mental Disorders*, ed 3. American Psychiatric Association, Washington, DC, 1980. Used with permission.

externally to express them. Feelings of unreality and strangeness may invade the patient's perceptions of the objects and people in the world around him. Dizziness frequently appears as a symptom. Anxiety is often found as an accompaniment of the disorder, and many patients complain of distortion in their sense of time and space. Especially common is the experience of a change in the patient's body: in addition to his general sense of estrangement from his bodily self, the patient may feel that his extremities are bigger or smaller than usual. An occasional and particularly curious phenomenon is that of doubling; the patient feels that his point of conscious "I-ness" is outside of his body, often a few feet overhead, from where he actually observes himself as if he were a totally other person.

The experience of depersonalization is often accompanied by considerable secondary anxiety, and the patient frequently fears that his symptoms are a sign that he is going insane. It is a curious paradox that, even though the patient complains of being emotionally dead and estranged, he is capable of being emotionally upset by this very sense of loss. Indeed, all the manifestations of depersonalization are acutely unpleasant and not only motivate the patient to seek medical help, but often drive him to vigorous activity, or to inducing intense sensations in himself in order to break through the prison walls of his sense of unreality.

The patient's keen and unfailing awareness of the disturbances in his sense of reality is considered one of the salient characteristics of the syndrome. There seems in depersonalization to be a heightening of the psychic energy invested in the self-observing ego, the mental function on which the capacity for insight rests.

### Course and Prognosis

In the large majority of patients, the symptoms first appear suddenly; only a few patients report gradual onset. The disorder starts most often between the ages of 15 and 30, but it has been seen in patients as young as 10; it occurs less frequently after 30 and almost never in the later decades of life. A few follow-up studies indicate that in more than half the cases, it tends to be a long-lasting, chronic condition. In many patients, the symptoms run a steady course without significant fluctuation of intensity, but they may occur in a series of attacks interspersed with symptom-free intervals. Little is known about precipitating factors, although the disorder has been observed to begin during a period of relaxation after a person has passed through a time of fatiguing psychological stress.

The disorder is sometimes ushered in by an attack of acute anxiety that is frequently accompanied by hyperventilation.

### Differential Diagnosis

It is evident that depersonalization may occur as a symptom in numerous other psychiatric syndromes. The common occurrence of depersonalization in patients with depression and schizophrenia should alert the clinician to the possibility that the patient who initially complains of feelings of unreality and estrangement is actually suffering from these more common disorders. A carefully taken history and the mental status examination should in most cases disclose the characteristic features of these two illnesses. A disturbance of identity as a prominent element in the experience of depersonalization points strongly in the direction of schizophrenia. Because of the frequency with which psychotomimetic drugs induce often long-lasting changes in the experience of the reality of one's self and one's environment, it is important to inquire about the use of these substances. The presence of these other clinical phenomena in patients complaining of unreality should usually take precedence in determining the diagnosis; in general, the label depersonalization disorder is to be reserved for those conditions in which depersonalization constitutes the main and predominating symptom.

The fact that depersonalization phenomena may result from gross disturbances in brain function underlines the necessity for a careful neurological evaluation, especially when the depersonalization is not accompanied by other more common and obvious psychiatric symptoms. In particular, the possibility of brain tumor and epilepsy should be entertained, and the diagnostic studies relevant to epilepsy should be aimed at determining whether the seizures are idiopathic in nature, or the result of a localized alteration of neuronal structures in the temporal area. Since the experience of depersonalization secondary to brain tumor may be an early presenting symptom before there is other detectable evidence of a neoplasm, patients complaining of depersonalization phenomena should be followed carefully.

### Treatment

Little attention has been focused on the treatment of patients with depersonalization disorder. There are insufficient data on which to base a specific pharmacological regimen at this time. Psychotherapeutic approaches are equally untested. As in all patients with neurotic symptoms, the decision to use psychoanalysis or the specific techniques of analytically oriented insight psychotherapy is to be determined not by the presence of the symptom itself, but by a variety of positive indications derived from an assessment of the patient's personality, human relationships, and life situation. The common supportive psychotherapeutic measures are helpful to some patients, but specific recommendations for the management of the disorder await more extensive clinical investigation.

## Atypical Dissociative Disorder

In the diagnostic classification proposed in DSM-III, this category is reserved for individuals who appear to have a dissociative disorder but who do not satisfy the criteria for the more specific forms of the disorder described above. Included here are persons with nonspecific trance-like states, or persons who manifest derealization unaccompanied by depersonalization. This term should be applied to those suffering from more pervasive dissociative states

after being subjected to periods of prolonged and intensive coercive persuasion (brainwashing, thought reform, etc.).

## REFERENCES

Abe K, Amatomi M, Oda N: Sleepwalking and recurrent sleeptalking in children of childhood sleepwalkers. Am J Psychiatry *141:* 800, 1984.
Boor M, Coons P: A comprehensive bibliography of literature pertaining to multiple personality. Psychol Rep *53:* 295, 1983.
Hilgard E R: *Divided Consciousness.* John Wiley & Sons, New York, 1977.
Kiersch T A: Amnesia: A clinical study of ninety-eight cases. Am J Psychiatry *119:* 57, 1962.
Nemiah J: Dissociative amnesia: A clinical and theoretical reconsideration. In *Functional Disorders of Memory,* J Kihlstrom, editor. Erlbaum Associates, Hillsdale, NJ, 1979.
Nemiah J C: Dissociative disorders (hysterical neurosis, dissociative type). In *Comprehensive Textbook of Psychiatry,* ed 4, H I Kaplan, B J Sadock, editors, p 942. Williams & Wilkins, Baltimore, 1985.
Schenk L, Bear D: Multiple personality and related dissociative phenomena in patients with temporal lobe epilepsy. Am J Psychiatry *138:* 1311, 1981.

# 18

# Personality Disorders

## Introduction

No group of emotional disorders is more often encountered in psychiatric practice than the personality disorders. Although until recently psychiatrists were reluctant to acknowledge it, those with personality disorders are functionally more disabled than the neurotics psychiatrists prefer to treat. Personality disorders account for the most irrational elements among the leaders of society.

Those with personality disorders are not easy to understand. The neurotic is often a self-diagnosed sinner who willingly begs for psychiatric help, confesses his problems, and often thereby cures himself. In technical terminology his symptoms are autoplastic (i.e., the process of adapting by changing the self) and experienced as ego-dystonic (i.e., unacceptable to the ego). In marked contrast, someone with a personality disorder is far more likely to refuse psychiatric help, point out the psychiatrist's problems, and, by persisting in his annoying behavior, cause colleagues in other disciplines to scoff at psychiatrists' competence. His symptoms are alloplastic (i.e., the process of adapting by altering the external environment) and ego-syntonic (i.e., acceptable to the ego).

Because those with personality disorders do not routinely acknowledge pain from what society perceives as their symptoms, the person is often regarded as unmotivated for treatment and impervious to recovery—traits unlikely to endear him to mental health personnel.

## Clinical Overview

There are characteristics that all personality disorders share. The first is an inflexible and maladaptive response to stress. The second is a disability in working and loving that is generally more serious and always more pervasive than that found in neurosis. The third is that personality disorders almost always occur in response to a social context. And the fourth characteristic is a peculiar capacity to get under the skin of others.

Personality disorders exhibit repetitious, self-detrimental responses associated with persons who are fatigued, brain damaged, under severe stress, immature, or otherwise regressed. Indeed, DSM-III defines personality disorder as follows: "The essential features are deeply ingrained, inflexible, maladaptive patterns of relating to, perceiving and thinking about the environment and oneself that are of sufficient severity to cause either significant impairment in adaptive functioning or subjective distress. Thus, they are pervasive personality traits and are exhibited in a wide range of important social and personal contexts. The manifestations of Personality Disorders are generally recognizable by the time of adolescence or earlier and continue throughout most of adult life, although often becoming less obvious in middle or old age."

This definition distinguishes personality disorders from personality traits and from personality itself. *Webster's Third New International Dictionary* defines a "personality" as the "totality of an individual's emergent tendencies to act or behave or the organization of the individual's distinguishing character traits, attitudes or habits."

On a continuum of mental health, personality disorders fall between neurosis and psychosis. Those with personality disorders uniformly have trouble with working and with loving. If the clinician is able to penetrate the armor or protective coloring of the personality disorder, he finds anxiety and depression. The adjectives dependent, oral, narcissistic, self-doubting, pessimistic, and passive can be applied to virtually all persons with personality disorders. It is difficult to conceive of a person with a personality disorder using anger or any really strong emotion in a flexible and consistently appropriate manner.

Unlike psychosis and neurosis, personality disorders almost always occur within an interpersonal context. It is difficult to imagine a hypochondriac or paranoiac becoming symptomatic on a desert island. A personality disorder must be seen as a way of making a painful truce with people one can neither live with nor live without. If neurotic symptoms are often the modes by which one copes with unbearable instincts, personality disorders are often the modes by which one copes with unbearable people. Those with personality disorders consistently fail to see themselves as others see them, and they lack empathy with other people. As a result, their behavior consistently annoys other people, and they are labeled bad, or, if they are labeled sick, the label is used pejoratively. Thus, characteristic of personality disorder is the tendency to create a vicious circle in which already precarious interpersonal relationships are made worse by the person's mode of adaptation.

A general characteristic of personality disorders is that they profoundly affect other people, often in the subtle and unconscious way that lovers or mothers and infants affect each other. Thus, a personality disorder often effects a merging of personal boundaries. It induces a breakdown of clear knowledge of what is mine and what is thine.

## History

DSM-III groups the personality disorders into three clusters (see Table I). The first cluster includes the paranoid, schizoid, and schizotypal personality disorders. Persons with these disorders often appear odd and eccentric. The second cluster includes the histrionic, narcissistic, antisocial, and borderline personality disorders. Persons with these disorders often appear dramatic, emotional, and erratic. The second cluster, with the possible exception of the borderline, captures Carl Jung's concept of extroversion. The third cluster includes the avoidant, dependent, compulsive, and passive-aggressive personality disorders. Persons with these disorders often appear anxious or fearful. The third cluster captures Jung's dimension of introversion.

## Etiology

### Genetic Factors

Because personality is clearly molded by social learning, the idea that personality disorders are inherited may seem odd. However, selective breeding of dogs has certainly underscored the remarkable degree to which the desired, stable behavior patterns (personality) can be obtained. Of all the personality traits measured, social introversion was the one in which the importance of heredity seemed most predominant over environment—even more so than intelligence.

The best evidence that genetic factors play a significant role in the genesis of personality disorders, murky as that diagnosis is, comes from the investigations of psychiatric disorder in 15,000 pairs of American twins. Among monozygotic twins the concordance for personality

TABLE I
THREE DOMAINS OF CLASSIFICATION IN THE PERSONALITY DISORDERS

| DSM-III Clusters (Older Terminology in Parentheses) | Genetic, Temperamental, or Constitutional Terms (Used to Understand Causes) | DSM-III Diagnoses (Used to Classify) | Postulated Underlying Defense Mechanisms (Used to Understand Treatment) |
|---|---|---|---|
| Odd, eccentric (oral, prepsychotic, narcissistic) | Schizophrenic continuum, psychoticism | Schizoid, paranoid, schizotypal | Projection, fantasy |
| Dramatic, emotional, erratic (hysterical, extroverted, phallic) | Psychopathic continuum, impulsiveness | histrionic, antisocial, narcissistic, borderline | Dissociation, acting out, splitting, neurotic denial |
| Anxious, fearful, introverted (obsessional, anal, sadomasochistic) | Introversion, neuroticism | Avoidant, dependent, compulsive, passive-aggressive | Isolation, passive aggression, hypochondriasis |

disorder was several times higher than among dizygotic twins.

Most of the convincing work in the heritability of personality disorders has been done on the first cluster in Table I, the so-called schizophrenic spectrum, which includes paranoid and schizotypal personality disorders. Every study indicated an increased incidence of cluster I disorders in the relatives of schizophrenics.

To date, genetic studies have largely concentrated on the evidence for any genetic transmission of the disorder under study. Little attention has been paid to the question of what is inherited. Biochemical and metabolic factors, constitutional predisposition, and temperament are likely areas to scrutinize.

### Constitutional Factors

All forms of neurological insult—especially sedative drug intoxication, postencephalitic states, and temporal lobe epilepsy—increase the incidence and the severity of personality disorders. Neurological soft signs are found more often in adolescents with personality disorders than in the normal adolescent population. Children with minimal brain dysfunction may be predisposed to the later development of personality disorders.

### Cultural and Environmental Factors

Common sense and anecdotal evidence also dictate that sociocultural factors play an important role in personality disorders.

The behavioral model conceives of the persistent maladaptive social behavior exhibited by those with personality disorders as reinforced and maintained by rewards, usually social, present in the environment. This point of view holds that personality disorders are caused by unwitting social reinforcers.

The question also arises whether certain personality disorders arise from a poor fit of temperament to parental expectation and training. It may be important to understand the match between the temperament or personality of a child and that of his parents. For example, a young child on the active side may appear hyperactive if kept in a small, closed apartment, but may appear normal in a larger, middle-class house with a fenced-in yard.

### Epidemiology

Behavior disorders usually begin in childhood or adolescence and are characteristic of most of adult life. However, after age 18, the diagnosis should be changed to the corresponding personality disorder. Using a rural county in Nova Scotia (Stirling County), the Leightons and their co-workers obtained highly reliable information about the prevalence of symptom patterns. The Leightons divided the personality disorders into two broad categories—sociopathic and personality disorder. Sociopathic included antisocial behavior and alcohol abuse; personality disorder included emotionally unstable, compulsive, passive-aggressive, and schizoid personality disorders. They found 18 percent of the men and 11 percent of women so affected. The difference in prevalence between sexes can be attributed in large part to the increased prevalence of alcoholism in the men.

Studying an urban population in the Midtown Manhattan Study, Langer and Michael used different survey instruments but observed roughly the same prevalence. They observed that 10 percent of their population showed frankly paranoid, passive-dependent, or schizoid personalities and some disability. In addition, 16 percent of those surveyed appeared to exhibit patterns of both neuroticism and personality disorder.

The prevalence of personality disorders can be expected to be much higher in any environment in which the socially impaired are concentrated—for example, prisons, welfare offices, and urban areas catering to transients. In the Midtown Manhattan Study, the investigators found that the prevalence of personality trait disorders was three times as high among the lowest socioeconomic stratum as among the highest.

In the Leighton's Stirling County study, social class was not as important as another social variable—social integration versus social disintegration. The proportion of sociopathic disturbances was almost three times as great in the disintegrated areas (31 percent) as in the county as a whole (11 percent). More important, increasing the available social supports and the sources of personal esteem in disintegrated communities, the Leightons observed, diminished the psychopathology and demonstrated that personality disorders are dynamic.

### Course and Prognosis

For a variety of reasons, there is a widespread impression that, once a person has a personality disorder, he always has it. First, a diagnosis of personality disorder is made only when it seems to be an enduring pattern of adaptation and response. One does not expect such disorders to remit rapidly. Second, because of the nature of their psychopathology, those with personality disorders are reluctant to be followed, and clinicians are reluctant to follow them. Third, those who mature out of personality disorders disappear from view entirely, and clinicians are repeatedly confronted by those who grow worse.

The study of prognosis is still further complicated by the fact that, in the past, well-defined diagnostic criteria did not exist for personality disorders. Invariably, therefore, follow-up studies showed a marked instability of diagnosis.

## Differential Diagnosis

To diagnose a personality disorder, the psychiatrist needs to gather objective facts systematically. Because someone with a personality disorder rarely recognizes the need for treatment, and because he seldom complains of the difficulties that he causes others, the diagnosis can rarely be made by listening to the patient alone.

As the first step in the diagnosis, careful medical and neurological examinations are required to rule out organic causation; it is the rule, not the exception, that organic defects of the central nervous system mimic facets of personality disorder. Second, objective records must be obtained from employers, courts, schools, and hospitals; neither the patient's bland minimizing nor the exaggerations of the outraged relative or agency worker who brought the patient to the clinic are reliable. Third, to distinguish a personality disorder from incipient psychosis or from a chance bad break, the psychiatrist must elicit a history of repetition of the disturbing pattern. Therefore, a past social history is a necessity. The past social history also helps the psychiatrist appreciate the anguish underlying the complaints.

Alcoholism must always be considered in the differential diagnosis of personality disorder. Granted, personality disorders and polydrug abuse often go hand in hand, and most chronic opioid abusers also exhibit personality disorders. However, the same cannot be said for the alcohol abuser. Although many persons with personality disorders abuse alcohol, many alcoholics are premorbidly quite normal.

One must understand the current social matrix in which the patient finds himself. A recent shift in personal relationships is likely to have precipitated the crisis, causing an unrecognized personality disorder to become obvious. Social and cultural differences between the patient and the observer are important; personality disorders are always overdiagnosed in patients who are ethnically and culturally different from the diagnostician. In addition, the diagnostician's countertransference toward the patient plays a role.

Finally, in diagnosing a personality disorder,

the clinician must come to terms with the differential diagnosis of malingering.

## Treatment

In its effort to avoid inference and to remain based on objective data, DSM-III ignores the psychodynamic domain of classification of personality disorder. Reliable diagnosis depends on what the psychiatrist can observe with certainty. However, the successful management of patients who insist that nothing is the matter must be based on what he can infer. Therapeutically, the psychiatrist cannot afford to miss the covert dependence concealed behind the insistent isolation of the paranoid character, nor can he afford to ignore the unexpressed fearfulness that manifests itself as the bland affect of the schizoid character. The psychiatrist may not like patients with personality disorders, but he needs to understand why. In treatment, he needs to abandon the pejorative language that fills any description of the personality disorders, for much of what is obnoxious in patients with personality disorders is symptomatic of something else. Just as fever, tachycardia, and cough indicate underlying problems in the infectious diseases, the manifestation of a personality disorder indicates underlying problems. All too often, the psychiatrist treats patients with personality disorders with aspirin and cold showers, as it were, and only in neurotics does he infer treatable underlying mechanisms.

### Defense Mechanisms

Although a patient with a personality disorder may be characterized by his most dominant or rigid mechanism, most patients use several defenses. However maladaptive, the defenses represent solutions to inner problems. Whereas the neurotic may value insight and see the interpretation of his defenses as helpful, confronting the defenses of a patient with a personality disorder is met with anger; breaching his defenses evokes enormous anxiety and depression; and carelessly threatening such a patient's defenses ruptures the therapist-patient relationship. Thus, the loss of a defense should be alleviated with strong social supports—for example, Alcoholics Anonymous—or replaced by an alternative defense—for example, helping the hitherto acting-out Hell's Angel use reaction formation and become a motorcycle policeman.

Typical defense mechanisms include fantasy, dissociation, isolation, projection, displacement, splitting, turning anger against the self, and acting out.

*Other Stereotyped Behaviors*

Narcissism, dependency, and no-win relationships threaten the patient's quest for help.

**Narcissism.** When threatened, many patients with personality disorders see themselves as powerful and all important. To the observer, this behavior may be labeled vanity, grandiosity, entitlement, or narcissism. It may lead the patient to be unusually critical of the therapist. In response, the therapist may become defensive, contemptuous, or rejecting. Clinical progress is facilitated if, instead of belittling the patient or defending himself, the clinician acknowledges that the patient is a person in his own right, offers him a consultation with an expert if that seems appropriate, and matter of factly reassures him of the competence of the treatment team.

**Dependency.** A second stereotyped behavior in personality disorders is dependency, however vehemently denied. Dependency is often manifested first by a sense of entitlement, and then by resentment when unreasonable wants are not met. Pessimism, self-doubt, and immaturity are common, and they lead to a dependent, demanding relationship. Inasmuch as personality disorders are frustrating to begin with, unreasonable wants are met by withdrawal on the part of the physician, and a vicious cycle is begun.

In general, dependent patients are best managed by observing three rules. First, the clinician must protect himself by setting realistic limits. Second, the clinician should never present limits as if they were an expression of impatience and punitiveness. They should never seem to be a withdrawal of interest or consideration; nothing should be taken away from patients without something else being given. Third, at the same time the limits are set, care-givers should convey their readiness to care for the patient as completely as is reasonable.

**No-win Relationships.** The third stereotype that creates therapeutic problems for patients with personality disorders may be summed up by the no-win learning paradigm. A no-win situation is one in which two people take positions that neither will modify; but, without compromise or changes in behavior, both parties must lose what they otherwise could gain if they reached a fair agreement. Those with personality disorders seem perennially entangled in sticky relationships in which there is neither satisfaction nor escape.

*Countertransference*

People with personality disorders get under the skin; their self-defeating behavior provokes compensatory self-defeating patterns in others. Often, the patient directs angry, demanding, or wounding statements toward the therapist, more often than not centered on some real, if minor, limitation or vulnerability in the therapist. A host of natural reactions ensue. The therapist must learn to feel safe in experiencing these reactions, and yet must be trained not to act on them. Getting angry at the patient, feeling on the defensive, denying the truth, wishing to control the patient, and losing one's concentration are common reactions in even the most experienced therapist.

## Individual Personality Disorders

*Paranoid Personality Disorder*

The essential feature of the paranoid personality is his long-standing suspiciousness and mistrust of people in general. Paranoid personalities are further distinguished by the fact that they refuse responsibility for their own feelings and assign responsibility to others. The category includes many of life's least lovable character types—the bigot, the injustice collector, the pathologically jealous spouse, and the litigious crank.

**Definition.** In DSM-III (see Table II), the following criteria are required to make the diagnosis of paranoid personality disorder, and they should characterize the patient's long-term functioning:

1. At least four of the following criteria of pervasive and unwarranted mistrust of others: (1) the expectation of harm or trickery; (2) hypervigilance, injustice collecting, and continual search for signs of external threat; (3) guardedness; (4) refusal of warranted blame; (5) chronic doubting of the fidelity of others; (6) ideas of reference—narrow, focused searching for confirmation of bias; (7) overconcern with hidden motives and special meanings.

2. Evidence of hypersensitivity, as indicated by at least two of the following: (1) chip on shoulder, easily taking offense; (2) making mountains out of molehills; (3) litigiousness, readiness to counterattack any threat; (4) inability to relax.

3. Limited affect, as reflected by at least two of the following: (1) apparently cold, unemotional nature; (2) pride in self as being rational and unemotional; (3) inability to laugh at self; (4) apparent absence of passive, soft, tender, and sentimental feelings.

4. Absence of schizophrenia.

**Epidemiology.** The prevalence of the disorder is not known. Persons with the disorder rarely seek treatment themselves; when referred

TABLE II
DIAGNOSTIC CRITERIA FOR PARANOID PERSONALITY DISORDER*

The following are characteristic of the individual's current and long-term functioning, are not limited to episodes of illness, and cause either significant impairment in social or occupational functioning or subjective distress.

A. Pervasive, unwarranted suspiciousness and mistrust of people as indicated by at least three of the following:

    (1) expectation of trickery or harm
    (2) hypervigilance, manifested by continual scanning of the environment for signs of threat, or taking unneeded precautions
    (3) guardedness or secretiveness
    (4) avoidance of accepting blame when warranted
    (5) questioning the loyalty of others
    (6) intense, narrowly focused searching for confirmation of bias, with loss of appreciation of total context
    (7) overconcern with hidden motives and special meanings
    (8) pathological jealousy

B. Hypersensitivity as indicated by at least two of the following:

    (1) tendency to be easily slighted and quick to take offense
    (2) exaggeration of difficulties, e.g., "making mountains out of molehills"
    (3) readiness to counterattack when any threat is perceived
    (4) inability to relax

C. Restricted affectivity as indicated by at least two of the following:

    (1) appearance of being "cold" and unemotional
    (2) pride taken in always being objective, rational, and unemotional
    (3) lack of a true sense of humor
    (4) absence of passive, soft, tender, and sentimental feelings

D. Not due to another mental disorder such as Schizophrenia or a Paranoid Disorder.

* From American Psychiatric Association: *Diagnostic and Statistical Manual of Mental Disorders*, ed 3. American Psychiatric Association, Washington, DC, 1980. Used with permission.

to treatment by a spouse or an employer, they can often pull themselves together. Because the disorder occurs in the biological relatives of identified schizophrenic patients, there is some evidence that the disorder is part of the schizophrenic spectrum. The disorder is more common in men than in women.

**Etiology.** The early psychoanalytic speculation that paranoid personality was caused by an underlying conflict over homosexuality has been discredited; rather, homosexuals—like minority groups, foreigners, and deviants—serve as foci for the paranoid's projected feelings and conflicts.

**Clinical Features.** The patient is likely to be litigious, moralistic, and a collector of injustices. Although he may have a keen and cutting wit, he is unable to laugh at himself. He externalizes his own emotions but is unusually sensitive to other people's motives and feelings. He is most upset by interpersonal issues involving dependency, and may respond with rage or pathological jealousy. Ideas of reference and logically defended illusions are common.

Two startling observations may be made about the paranoid character. First, his demons often bear a striking similarity to himself; for example, Hitler's inner circle physically resembled the Jews they persecuted, rather than the blond, blue-eyed Aryans they professed to admire. Second, the paranoiac often fears love as

much as hate. In manifestly rejecting intimacy, the paranoid character may exhibit an obsessive overinvolvement with the enemy. At their best, paranoid characters can assume a distant leadership role in movements for social reform. The hypervigilant paranoid personality may be a highly adaptive style in times of war and social disruption.

The paranoid character is often interested in mechanical devices, communication, electronics, and automation. He pays close attention to power and rank, and expresses disdain for the people who are seen as weak, soft, sickly, or defective. In social situations, the hypervigilance of the paranoid character often generates uneasiness, fear, and conflict in others.

On psychiatric examination, the paranoid character may appear business-like and baffled at having been required to seek psychiatric help. Muscular tension, inability to relax, and a need to scan the environment for clues may be evident. His affect is often humorless and serious. Although some of the premises of his arguments may be false, his speech is goal directed and logical. His thought content shows evidence of projection, prejudice, and occasional ideas of reference.

Paranoid patients easily personalize coincidental events and stimuli.

**Course and Prognosis.** Adequate and systematic long-term studies do not exist. In some people, paranoid personality disorder is lifelong. In others, it is a harbinger of schizophrenia. In still others, as they mature or as stress diminishes, paranoid traits give way to reaction formation, appropriate concern with morality, and altruistic concerns.

**Differential Diagnosis.** Paranoid personality disorder can usually be differentiated from the paranoid disorders because fixed delusions are absent in paranoid personality disorder. It can be differentiated from paranoid schizophrenia because hallucinations and formal thought disorder are absent in the personality disorder. Paranoid personality disorder can be distinguished from borderline personality disorder because the paranoid patient is rarely as capable as the borderline patient of overinvolved, if tumultuous, relations with others. Paranoid personality disorder can be distinguished from antisocial personality disorder because the paranoid patient lacks the long history of antisocial behavior of the antisocial character.

**Treatment.** Courtesy, honesty, and respect are the cardinal rules for the treatment of any paranoid patient.

The therapist should be straightforward in all his dealings with the patient. If the therapist is accused of some inconsistency or fault, such as lateness for an appointment, honesty and an apology serve better than a defensive explanation. The therapist must remember that trust and toleration of intimacy are troubled areas for the patient. Individual psychotherapy requires a professional and not overly warm style on the therapist's part. Paranoid patients do not do well in group psychotherapy, nor are they likely to tolerate the intrusiveness of the behavior therapies. Too zealous a use of interpretation—especially interpretation concerning deep feelings of dependency, sexual concerns, and wishes for intimacy—significantly increase the patient's mistrust.

At times, a paranoid patient's behavior becomes so threatening that it is important to control his behavior or set limits on it. Delusional accusations must be dealt with realistically, but gently and without humiliating the patient. It is profoundly frightening for a paranoid patient to feel that those trying to help him are weak and helpless; therefore, a therapist should never threaten to take over control unless he is both willing and in a position to do so.

### Schizoid Personality Disorder

This syndrome is diagnosed in patients who display a lifelong pattern of social withdrawal. Their discomfort with human interaction, their introversion, and their bland, constricted affect are noteworthy. Schizoid personalities are often seen by others as eccentric, isolated, or lonely. Together with paranoid personality disorder and schizotypal personality disorder, it makes up the healthier end of the schizophrenic spectrum.

**Definition.** In DSM-III (see Table III), the following criteria are required to make a diagnosis of schizoid personality disorder, and they should characterize the patient's long-term functioning.

1. Few if any close friends, including family members.

2. Insensitivity to the feelings of others.

3. Cold, aloof, distant nature; no observable warm and tender feelings. Also a lifelong inability to express anger and a tendency to engage in imaginary relationships.

4. No eccentricities of communication, behavior, or thought suggestive of the *forme fruste* of schizophrenia—schizotypal personality disorder.

5. The disturbance is not due to a psychiatric disorder such as schizophrenia or paranoid disorders.

**Epidemiology.** Primarily because of the inconsistent diagnostic criteria used in various

---

TABLE III
DIAGNOSTIC CRITERIA FOR SCHIZOID PERSONALITY DISORDER*

The following are characteristic of the individual's current and long-term functioning, are not limited to episodes of illness, and cause either significant impairment in social or occupational functioning or subjective distress.

A. Emotional coldness and aloofness, and absence of warm, tender feelings for others.

B. Indifference to praise or criticism or to feelings of others.

C. Close friendships with no more than one or two persons, including family members.

D. No eccentricities of speech, behavior, or thought characteristic of Schizotypal Personality Disorder.

E. Not due to a psychotic disorder such as Schizophrenia or Paranoid Disorder.

F. If under 18, does not meet the criteria for Schizoid Disorder of Childhood or Adolescence.

* From American Psychiatric Association: *Diagnostic and Statistical Manual of Mental Disorders*, ed 3. American Psychiatric Association, Washington, DC, 1980. Used with permission.

studies, the prevalence of schizoid personality is not clearly established.

Perhaps 3 percent of the general population fall along the schizophrenic spectrum, with schizoid personality forming the healthiest end. Schizoid disorders may encompass 7.5 percent of the general population. The sex ratio of the disorder is unknown.

**Etiology.** Common sense dictates that early patterns of object relations, familial interactive style, and culture play an important part in the development of the schizoid personality. In retrospective case histories, clinicians have had no trouble in identifying bleak, cold, unempathic childhoods.

**Clinical Features.** The schizoid personality gives an impression of being aloof, and displays a remote reserve and a lack of involvement with everyday events and the concerns of others. He appears quiet, distant, seclusive, and unsociable. He may pursue his own life with remarkably little need or longing for emotional ties with others. He is the last to catch on to changes in popular fashion.

The life history of such a person reflects solitary interests and success at noncompetitive, lonely jobs that others find difficult to tolerate. His sexual life may exist exclusively in fantasy, and he may postpone mature sexuality indefinitely. Usually, he reveals a lifelong inability to express anger directly. A schizoid personality is able to invest enormous affective energy in nonhuman interests like mathematics and astronomy. He is often engrossed in dietary and health fads, philosophical movements, and social improvement schemes, especially those that require no personal involvement.

Although a schizoid personality appears self-absorbed and engaged in excessive daydreaming, he shows no loss of the capacity to recognize reality. Because aggressive acts are rarely included in his repertoire of usual responses, most threats, real or imagined, are dealt with by fantasied omnipotence or resignation. Others experience the schizoid personality as aloof; yet at times, such a person is able to conceive, develop, and give to the world genuinely original, creative ideas.

On initial psychiatric examination, the patient, although not necessarily overtly frigid or anxious, may appear innately ill at ease. Such patients rarely tolerate eye contact. The interviewer may get the impression that the patient is eager for the end of the interview to come. His affect may be constricted, aloof, or inappropriately serious. Underneath the aloofness, the sensitive clinician may recognize fear. The patient finds it difficult to act in a lighthearted

manner; efforts at humor may seem adolescent and off the mark. The patient's speech is goal directed, but he is likely to give short answers to questions and avoid spontaneous conversation. Occasionally, he uses an unusual figure of speech, such as an odd metaphor. His mental content may reveal a sense of unwarranted intimacy with people he does not know well or whom he has not seen for a long time. He may show a fascination with an overvaluation of inanimate objects or metaphysical constructs. The patient's sensorium is intact, his memory functions well, and his proverb interpretations are abstract.

**Course and Prognosis.** The onset of schizoid personality disorder usually begins in early childhood. Like all personality disorders, a schizoid personality disorder is a long-lasting but not necessarily lifelong disorder. The proportion of patients who go on to develop schizophrenia is unknown.

**Differential Diagnosis.** In contrast to schizophrenics and schizotypal personalities, patients with schizoid personality disorders do not have schizophrenic relatives, and they may have very successful, if isolated, work histories. The schizophrenic also differs in exhibiting, at least in the past, thought disorder or delusional thinking. Although he shares many traits with the schizoid, the paranoid personality exhibits more social engagement, a history of aggressive verbal behavior, and a greater tendency to project his feelings onto others. If just as emotionally constricted, the compulsive and avoidant personalities experience loneliness as dysphoric, possess a richer history of past object relations, and do not engage as much in autistic reverie. Theoretically, the chief distinction between the schizotypal personality and the schizoid personality is that the schizotypal shows a greater similarity to the schizophrenic in the oddities of perceptions and communications.

**Treatment.** The treatment of schizoid personalities is similar to the treatment of paranoid personalities. However, the schizoid patient's tendencies toward introspection are consistent with the psychotherapist's expectations, and the schizoid patient may become a devoted if distant patient. As trust develops, the schizoid patient may, with great trepidation, reveal a plethora of fantasies, imaginary friends, and fears of unbearable dependency—even of merging with the therapist.

In group therapy settings, a schizoid patient may be silent for a year or more; nonetheless, involvement does take place. The patient should be protected against aggressive attack by group members on his proclivity for silence. With time, the group may become a meaningful experience for the patient and provide social contact, as well as therapy.

### Schizotypal Personality Disorder

The person with schizotypal personality disorder is someone who, even to the layman's eyes, is strikingly odd or strange. Magical thinking, ideas of reference, illusions, and derealization are part of his everyday world. Although he may never have had a frank psychotic episode, he is the person who in the older nomenclatures was called a borderline, simple, or latent schizophrenic.

**Definition.** In DSM-III (see Table IV) the following criteria are required to make the diagnosis of schizotypal personality disorder.

1. At least four of the following criteria characteristic of the patient's long-term functioning and not limited to episodes of illness: (1) magical thinking, such as superstitiousness, clairvoyance, telepathy, a sixth sense; (2) ideas of reference and self-referential thinking; (3) social isolation, such as no close friends or confidants; (4) recurrent illusions, sensing the presence of a force or person not actually present, depersonalization or derealization not associated with panic attacks; (5) odd communications not clearly due to derailment, loose association, or incoherence, such as speech that is tangential, digressive, overelaborate, or circumstantial; (6) cold, aloof, inadequate rapport in face-to-face interaction; (7) paranoid ideation; (8) undue social anxiety or hypersensitivity to criticism.

2. Absence of schizophrenia.

Largely as a result of recent family studies in schizophrenia, the term schizotypal was introduced into DSM-III. Schizotypal personality disorder has been postulated to include patients who exhibit some traits of schizophrenia but not enough to warrant that diagnosis. The term schizotypal personality disorder is applied to many patients DSM-II would have called simple or latent schizophrenics or schizoid. It encompasses many patients who in the past were labeled ambulatory or pseudoneurotic schizophrenics.

**Epidemiology.** The epidemiology, prevalence, and sex ratio of schizotypal personality disorders are unknown.

**Etiology.** Family and adoption studies of schizophrenics suggest that schizotypal personality disorder is more common in the biological relatives of chronic schizophrenics than in controls.

**Clinical Features.** The clinical features of a schizotypal personality represent the borderland between schizoid personality and schizophrenia. In schizotypal personality disorder, thinking and communicating are disturbed. Like the schizophrenic, the person with schizotypal personality may not know his own feelings, yet he is exquisitely sensitive to detecting the feelings of others, especially negative affects, like anger. He may be superstitious or claim clairvoyance. His inner world may be vividly peopled by imaginary relationships and filled with child-like fears and fantasies. He may believe himself to have special powers of thought and insight. Although frank thought disorder is absent, his speech may often require interpretation. He may admit that he has perceptual illusions or macropsia, or that people appear wooden and alike.

**Course and Prognosis.** The course and the prognosis of the disorder have not been studied. The proportion of these patients who go on to develop schizophrenia is unknown.

TABLE IV
DIAGNOSTIC CRITERIA FOR SCHIZOTYPAL PERSONALITY DISORDER*

The following are characteristic of the individual's current and long-term functioning, are not limited to episodes of illness, and cause either significant impairment in social or occupational functioning or subjective distress.

A. At least four of the following:

    (1) magical thinking, e.g., superstitiousness, clairvoyance, telepathy, "6th sense," "others can feel my feelings" (in children and adolescents, bizarre fantasies or preoccupations)
    (2) ideas of reference
    (3) social isolation, e.g., no close friends or confidants, social contacts limited to essential everyday tasks
    (4) recurrent illusions, sensing the presence of a force or person not actually present (e.g., "I felt as if my dead mother were in the room with me"), depersonalization, or derealization not associated with panic attacks
    (5) odd speech (without loosening of associations or incoherence), e.g., speech that is digressive, vague, overelaborate, circumstantial, metaphorical
    (6) inadequate rapport in face-to-face interaction due to constricted or inappropriate affect, e.g., aloof, cold
    (7) suspiciousness or paranoid ideation
    (8) undue social anxiety or hypersensitivity to real or imagined criticism

B. Does not meet the criteria for Schizophrenia.

* From American Psychiatric Association: *Diagnostic and Statistical Manual of Mental Disorders*, ed 3. American Psychiatric Association, Washington, DC, 1980. Used with permission.

**Differential Diagnosis.** Theoretically, those with schizotypal personality disorder can be distinguished from schizoid and avoidant personalities by the presence of oddities in behavior, thinking, perception, and communication, and perhaps by a clear family history of schizophrenia. Schizotypal personalities may be distinguished from schizophrenics by the absence of psychosis in schizotypal personalities. At present, some patients meet the criteria for both schizotypal personality disorder and borderline personality disorder.

**Treatment.** At present, no evidence indicates that the principles of treatment of schizotypal personality disorder should be different from the principles of treatment of schizoid personality disorder.

### Histrionic Personality Disorder

This disorder is characterized by colorful, dramatic, extroverted behavior in excitable, emotional persons. Alongside of their flamboyant presentation, however, there is often a disturbed ability to maintain deep, long-lasting attachments.

**Definition.** In DSM-III (see Table V), the following criteria are required to make the diagnosis of histrionic personality disorder, and they should characterize the patient's long-term functioning:

1. Behavior that is overly reactive and expressed intensely without reserve, as indicated by at least three of the following: (1) self-dramatization and exaggerated expression of emotions; (2) incessantly drawing attention to oneself; (3) craving for activity and excitement; (4) emotional excitability in response to minor stimuli; (5) irrational, angry outbursts or tantrums; (6) manipulative suicide threats, gestures, or attempts.

2. Characteristic disturbances in interpersonal relationships, as indicated by at least two of the following: (1) seen by others as shallow even if superficial warmth, charm and appeal; (2) demands and lack of consideration for the wishes of others; (3) vanity, egocentricity, and self-absorption; (4) dependence, helplessness, constant seeking of assurance.

**Epidemiology.** Primarily because of the many changes in terminology, nothing is known about the prevalence of histrionic personality disorder.

The diagnosis of histrionic personality disorder is more common in women than in men. The man with histrionic personality disorder is not very different from the woman with the disorder.

**Etiology.** The causes of histrionic personality disorder, like the causes of the trait of extroversion, are unknown but undoubtedly multifactorial. Often, the patients at the sicker end of the histrionic continuum have deprived backgrounds and share many features with antisocial personalities.

**Clinical Features.** In order of importance, the traits associated with the hysterical factor are aggression, emotionality, oral aggression, exhibitionism, egocentricity, sexual protectiveness, and rejection of others.

Because the histrionic patient uses emotional display manipulatively to obtain attention and desired goals, and to evade unwarranted external responsibilities and unpleasant inner affects, there is often a shallow, fraudulent cast to the emotions. The histrionic person is neither con-

TABLE V
DIAGNOSTIC CRITERIA FOR HISTRIONIC PERSONALITY DISORDER*

The following are characteristic of the individual's current and long-term functioning, are not limited to episodes of illness, and cause either significant impairment in social or occupational functioning or subjective distress.

A. Behavior that is overly dramatic, reactive, and intensely expressed, as indicated by at least three of the following:

(1) self-dramatization, e.g., exaggerated expression of emotions
(2) incessant drawing of attention to onself
(3) craving for activity and excitement
(4) overreaction to minor events
(5) irrational, angry outbursts or tantrums

B. Characteristic disturbances in interpersonal relationships as indicated by at least two of the following:

(1) perceived by others as shallow and lacking genuineness, even if superficially warm and charming
(2) egocentric, self-indulgent, and inconsiderate of others
(3) vain and demanding
(4) dependent, helpless, constantly seeking reassurance
(5) prone to manipulative suicidal theats, gestures, or attempts

* From American Psychiatric Association: *Diagnostic and Statistical Manual of Mental Disorders*, ed 3. American Psychiatric Association, Washington, DC, 1980. Used with permission.

stant nor consistent; the lability of emotions and fickleness of belief or affection can exasperate both friend and clinician. A display of negative affect—temper tantrums, tears, or accusations—can often induce a guilty acquiescence in the unwary spouse or companion. Although systematic study reveals anorgasmia and impotence are not as common in histrionic personalities as more impressionistic reports suggest, there may be an indifference to or disgust about adult sexual expression, or its continuation after a brief romantic interlude. Dependent and sexual interests become curiously juxtaposed.

Although sometimes histrionic patients seem naively unaware of their sexual display, their dress is seductive, provocative, or even exhibitionistic. In speaking to others, the person overembellishes a part. A flurry of gestures, extremes of facial expression, and, with age, a heavily lined face are the rule. The patient usually appears intently interested in the examiner, and eye contact is exaggerated. Instead of anxiety or depression, the patient may display naivete or *la belle indifférence*, or follow a painful statement of fact with a dramatic, affect-laden exciting anecdote.

The histrionic patient may appear to blossom while all attention is turned toward him. If someone else holds the stage, there may be marked disppointment. His interview behavior is usually well mannered, and he is eager to please, but extremes of gestures and dramatic punctuation in the conversation are common. The patient may sometimes unconsciously mimic the examiner. The content of his speech may show malapropisms or other slips of the tongue, and, in general, there is a certain colorful inexactness to phrases and words used.

Affective display is common, but, when pressed to acknowledge certain feelings—like anger, sadness, and sexual wishes—the patient may respond with surprise, indignation, or denial. The results of the cognitive examination are usually normal, although lack of perseverance may be shown on arithmetic or concentration tasks, and forgetfulness of affect-laden material may be astonishing. Under stress, histrionic personalities may exhibit impaired reality testing and vivid fantasies about the motives of others. The defenses of repression and dissociation are characteristic of the disorder.

**Course and Prognosis.** The course and the prognosis of histrionic personality disorder have not yet been systematically studied.

**Differential Diagnosis.** The differential diagnosis of histrionic personality disorder is confounded by sex-linked criteria. In some cases, the distinction between histrionic personality disorder and borderline personality disorder is impossible. As a rule of thumb, the histrionic personality does not exhibit the sustained feelings of emptiness, identity diffusion, or display the brief psychotic episodes of the borderline patient. Somatization disorder (Briquet's syndrome) may occur in conjunction with histrionic personality disorder.

Patients with brief reactive psychoses and dissociative disorders may warrant a coexisting diagnosis of histrionic personality disorder.

**Treatment.** Inasmuch as patients with histrionic personality disorder may be surprisingly unaware of their own real feelings, clarification of the patient's inner feelings is an important therapeutic process. Psychoanalytically oriented psychotherapy, whether group or individual, is probably the treatment of choice for this personality disorder. It is important that the therapist not reward sham emotion as he clarifies the correct identification of feelings.

### Narcissistic Personality Disorder

Although a wide psychoanalytic literature exists on narcissism, DSM-III for the first time has suggested that the term be included in the general psychiatric nomenclature as a diagnosis.

**Definition.** In DSM-III (see Table VI), the following criteria are required to make the diagnosis of narcissistic personality disorder.

1. A grandiose sense of self-importance and uniqueness.

2. A preoccupation with fantasies of unlimited success, power, brilliance, beauty, and ideal love.

3. Demands for constant attention and admiration.

4. Indifference to criticism or responses to criticism marked by feelings of rage, humiliation, or emptiness.

5. At least two of the following characteristics in interpersonal relationships: (1) inability to empathize; (2) entitlement, surprise and anger that people do not do what the patient wants; (3) interpersonal exploitiveness; (4) relationships that vacillate between the extremes of overidealization and devaluation.

**Epidemiology.** The incidence, prevalence, sex ratio, and familial pattern of the narcissistic personality disorder have not been investigated.

**Etiology.** Because the criteria for narcissistic personality disorder are general and likely to be found in other personality disorders, it seems likely that the factors leading to personality disorders in general are likely to be the same as those leading to narcissistic personality disorder.

**Clinical Features.** Depressed mood is extremely common in a narcissistic personality.

TABLE VI
DIAGNOSTIC CRITERIA FOR NARCISSISTIC PERSONALITY DISORDER*

The following are characteristic of the individual's current and long-term functioning, are not limited to episodes of illness, and cause either significant impairment in social or occupational functioning or subjective distress:

A. Grandiose sense of self-importance or uniqueness, e.g., exaggeration of achievements and talents, focus on the special nature of one's problems.

B. Preoccupation with fantasies of unlimited success, power, brilliance, beauty, or ideal love.

C. Exhibitionism: the person requires constant attention and admiration.

D. Cool indifference or marked feelings of rage, inferiority, shame, humiliation, or emptiness in response to criticism, indifference of others, or defeat.

E. At least two of the following characteristic of disturbances in interpersonal relationships:

    (1) entitlement: expectation of special favors without assuming reciprocal responsibilities, e.g., surprise and anger that people will not do what is wanted
    (2) interpersonal exploitativeness: taking advantage of others to indulge own desires or for self-aggrandizement; disregard for the personal integrity and rights of others
    (3) relationships that characteristically alternate between the extremes of overidealization and devaluation
    (4) lack of empathy: inability to recognize how others feel, e.g., unable to appreciate the distress of someone who is seriously ill.

*From American Psychiatric Association: *Diagnostic and Statistical Manual of Mental Disorders*, ed 3. American Psychiatric Association, Washington, DC, 1980. Used with permission.

His self-esteem is invariably low, and he is preoccupied with how well he is doing and how well others regard him. In a general sense, the traits of narcissism are often seen in persons who are involved in vocations or avocations preoccupied with dramatic, artistic, athletic, or scholarly excellence. Thus far, the definitions do not appear to be very consistent, perhaps because, in diagnosing narcissism, the clinician makes a moral judgment and sacrifices empathy.

**Differential Diagnosis.** At the present time, differential diagnosis is not possible. To quote DSM-III: "Individuals with this disorder may also meet the criteria for histrionic, antisocial, or borderline personality disorder."

As the disorder is currently defined, the term is likely to serve the role played in the past by "hysteric" and "borderline"—a catch-all term to be applied to any personality disorders that the clinician cannot otherwise categorize.

**Treatment.** In the treatment of personality disorders, the use of the term narcissism may be as ill advised as using narcissism to conceptualize the undeniable self-preoccupation of patients with migraine or pain from phantom limbs.

If the clinician can expunge from his mind the pejorative meanings of the term "narcissism" and replace it with "in pain," therapy will proceed more humanely.

### Antisocial Personality Disorder

Antisocial personality disorder should not be thought of as synonymous with criminality; the disorder reflects continuous and chronic antisocial behavior involving many aspects of the patient's adult adjustment. The antisocial personality is infrequently seen in most clinical settings. Courts, prisons, and welfare departments are more likely places for such a person to appear; when an antisocial personality uses traditional psychiatric settings, it is often as a way of avoiding legal consequences.

**Definition.** In DSM-III (see Table VII), the following criteria are required to make the diagnosis of antisocial personality disorder.

1. Current age of at least 18.

2. Onset before the age of 15, as indicated by a history of four or more of the following, after some adjustment is made for sex and social class: (1) truancy (5 days a year for at least 2 years, not including the last year of school); (2) school expulsion; (3) delinquency (arrested or referred to juvenile court); (4) running away from home overnight at least twice; (5) persistent lying; (6) unusually early or casual sexual behavior, (7) alcohol or substance abuse earlier than one's social peers; (8) persistent thefts; (9) vandalism; (10) school achievement markedly below what is expected on the basis of tested intelligence; (11) chronic violations of home and school rules (excluding truancy); (12) starting fights.

3. At least four of the following since age 18: (1) poor occupational performance (frequent job changes, unemployment, or absenteeism not explicable by economic conditions) or quitting jobs; (2) failure to accept social norms with respect to lawful behavior, repeated thefts, arrests, or a felony conviction; (3) two or more divorces or marital separations; desertions; (4) repeated physical fights or wife or child abuse; (5) irresponsible parent as indicated by any of the following: child ill from malnutrition or ne-

glect, child depends on others for care, leaves child untended for long periods; (6) repeated defaulting on debts or financial responsibilities; (7) sudden desertion of family or traveling from place to place without a clear purpose; (8) multiple speeding or drunk driving offenses; (9) repeated lying, use of aliases, conning for profit. The following are not among the DSM-III criteria but are common in women with antisocial personality disorders; polydrug abuse, multiple suicide attempts, promiscuity without pleasure, and multiple unwanted pregnancies.

4. A history of continuous and chronic antisocial behavior in which the rights of others were violated.

5. Antisocial behavior not explained by severe mental retardation, schizophrenia, alcoholism, or organic mental disorder.

**Epidemiology.** Onset for this disorder is before the age of 15. Usually females develop symptoms before puberty and males develop symptoms even earlier. The disorder is much more common in males than in females. The disorder is most common in highly mobile resi-

TABLE VII
DIAGNOSTIC CRITERIA FOR ANTISOCIAL PERSONALITY DISORDER*

A. Current age at least 18.

B. Onset before age 15 as indicated by a history of three or more of the following before that age:

(1) truancy (positive if it amounted to at least 5 days per year for at least 2 years, not including the last year of school)
(2) expulsion or suspension from school for misbehavior
(3) delinquency (arrested or referred to juvenile court because of behavior)
(4) running away from home overnight at least twice while living in parental or parental surrogate home
(5) persistent lying
(6) repeated sexual intercourse in a casual relationship
(7) repeated drunkenness or substance abuse
(8) thefts
(9) vandalism
(10) school grades markedly below expectations in relation to estimated or known I.Q. (may have resulted in repeating a year)
(11) chronic violations of rules at home and/or at school (other than truancy)
(12) initiation of fights

C. At least four of the following manifestations of the disorder since age 18:

(1) inability to sustain consistent work behavior, as indicated by any of the following: (a) too frequent job changes (e.g., three or more jobs in 5 years not accounted for by nature of job or economic or seasonal fluctuation), (b) significant unemployment (e.g., 6 months or more in 5 years when expected to work), (c) serious absenteeism from work (e.g., average 3 days or more of lateness or absence per month, (d) walking off several jobs without other jobs in sight (Note: similar behavior in an academic setting during the last few years of school may substitute for this criterion in individuals who by reason of their age or circumstances have not had an opportunity to demonstrate occupational adjustment)
(2) lack of ability to function as a responsible parent as evidenced by one or more of the following: (a) child's malnutrition, (b) child's illness resulting from lack of minimal hygiene standards, (c) failure to obtain medical care for a seriously ill child, (d) child's dependence on neighbors or nonresident relatives for food or shelter, (e) failure to arrange for a caretaker for a child under 6 when parent is away from home, (f) repeated squandering, on personal items, of money required for household necessities
(3) failure to accept social norms with respect to lawful behavior, as indicated by any of the following: repeated thefts, illegal occupation (pimping, prostitution, fencing, selling drugs), multiple arrests, a felony conviction
(4) inability to maintain enduring attachment to a sexual partner as indicated by two or more divorces and/or separations (whether legally married or not), desertion of spouse, promiscuity (ten or more sexual partners within one year)
(5) irritability and aggressiveness as indicated by repeated physical fights or assault (not required by one's job or to defend someone or oneself), including spouse or child beating
(6) failure to honor financial obligations, as indicated by repeated defaulting on debts, failure to provide child support, failure to support other dependents on a regular basis
(7) failure to plan ahead, or impulsivity, as indicated by traveling from place to place without a prearranged job or clear goal for the period of travel or clear idea about when the travel would terminate, or lack of a fixed address for a month or more
(8) disregard for the truth as indicated by repeated lying, use of aliases, "conning" others for personal profit
(9) recklessness, as indicated by driving while intoxicated or recurrent speeding

D. A pattern of continuous antisocial behavior in which the rights of others are violated, with no intervening period of at least five years without antisocial behavior between age 15 and the present time (except when the individual was bedridden or confined in a hospital or penal institution).

E. Antisocial behavior is not due to either Severe Mental Retardation, Schizophrenia or manic episodes.

* From American Psychiatric Association: *Diagnostic and Statistical Manual of Mental Disorders*, ed 3. American Psychiatric Association, Washington, DC, 1980. Used with permission.

dents of impoverished urban areas. In prison populations, the prevalence of antisocial personality may be as high as 75 percent.

**Etiology.** In the main, antisocial personality disorder cannot be attributed to cultural conflict, membership in a deviant subgroup, bad associates, social class, organic brain damage, or high-crime neighborhoods. That the disorder frequently arises in a chaotic home environment is well known. A number of early studies suggested a relationship between sociopathy and maternal deprivation in the first 5 years of life.

The work of Lee Robins has been especially useful in distinguishing hereditary from environmental effects. In following up 524 children referred to a child guidance clinic, Robins found that having a sociopathic or alcoholic father was a powerful predictor of antisocial personality disorder in adult life. Surprisingly, this effect was not related to whether the child had actually been reared in the presence of the father. Taken together with the available twin studies and the adoption studies, this finding is consistent in the support of genetic factors.

Other studies present evidence for the importance of environmental factors. Inconsistent care by a mother or mother surrogate—as evidenced by an uncohesive home, a lack of consistent maternal discipline, and a lack of maternal affection—by age 6 was found to allow the prospective identification of children who would be seriously delinquent by age 18.

Studies have repeatedly shown that criminals and antisocial personalities display excessive electroencephalographic abnormalities, and so do their parents. However, these findings have been confounded both by observer idiosyncrasy and by secondary brain damage in delinquent youth. At the present time, although no clear organic basis for antisocial personality disorder is known, a modest statistical relationship exists between hyperactivity and soft neurological signs in childhood and antisocial behavior.

**Clinical Features.** The antisocial personality, often brought to the clinic against his will, may present a normal and even a charming and ingratiating exterior. The diagnosis of antisocial personality disorder depends on the patient's history, not on the results of his mental status examination. Antisocial personalities characteristically have many areas of disordered life functioning. Tatoos are common in men, and scars from self-mutilation are common in women; polydrug abuse is common in both men and women. Often, the antisocial personality impresses the opposite-sex clinician with the colorful, seductive aspects of his personality, but the same-sex clinician may regard him as manipu-

lative and demanding. Antisocial personalities demonstrate a lack of anxiety or depression that may seem grossly incongruous with their situation; their own explanations of their antisocial behavior make it seem mindless. Suicide threats and somatic preoccupations may be common.

Nevertheless, the patient's mental content reveals the complete absence of delusions and other signs of irrational thinking. He often impresses the observer as having good verbal intelligence.

In outpatient settings, clinicians, as their countertransference rescue fantasies give way to fears of persecution, become repelled by the patient's egocentricity and manipulation of others. If, however, the antisocial personality is immobilized or if he is studied in nonclinic settings, then the affects of chronic depression and overwhelming anxiety become visible; in time, his manipulative, antisocial behavior may be seen as symbolic, rather than motiveless.

**Course and Prognosis.** Antisocial personality disorder invariably begins in childhood or early adolescence, and the symptoms are present before the age of 15. The disorder tends to develop earlier in boys, who may show symptoms before the age of 8, than in girls. Besides displaying the childhood antisocial symptoms, a third of all antisocial adults also had persistent enuresis, sleepwalking, and marked irritability as children.

Once antisocial personality disorder develops, it runs an unremitting course, with the height of antisocial behavior usually occurring in late adolescence. The prognosis is variable.

**Differential Diagnosis.** Antisocial personality disorder can be distinguished from illegal behavior, because antisocial personality disorder involves many areas of the person's life. More difficult is the differentiation of antisocial personality disorder from substance abuse disorder. When both substance abuse and antisocial behavior begin in childhood and continue into adult life, both substance abuse disorder and antisocial personality disorder should be diagnosed. When, however, the antisocial behavior is clearly secondary to premorbid alcohol abuse or drug abuse, the diagnosis of antisocial personality disorder is not warranted.

In the diagnosis of antisocial personality disorder, it is important to adjust for the distorting effects of social class, cultural background, and sex on its manifestations. A major reason the differential diagnosis between antisocial personality disorder and borderline personality disorder is obscured is that borderline personality disorder tends to be underdiagnosed in women. Some patients warrant both diagnoses. The diagnosis of antisocial personality disorder is not warranted if mental retardation, schizophrenia, or mania can explain the symptoms.

**Treatment.** If antisocial personalities are immobilized, or if they are approached by understanding peers, then—instead of appearing incorrigible, inhuman, unfeeling, guiltless, and unable to learn from experience—they become only too human. Once an antisocial personality feels that he is among peers, the lack of motivation for change disappears. Perhaps this is why, in alleviating these disorders, self-help groups have been more useful than jails and psychiatric hospitals.

Before treatment can begin, firm limits are critical. The therapist must find some way of dealing with the patient's self-destructive behavior. And, to overcome the antisocial personality's fear of intimacy, the therapist must frustrate the patient's wish to run from tenderness and from the honest pain of human encounter. In doing so, the therapist faces the challenge of separating control from punishment, and separating help and confrontation from social isolation and retribution.

Antisocial personalities are made worse by good defense lawyers. They are not helped by being protected from their own anxiety or from the consequences of their behavior. Antisocial personalities should be encouraged to find alternative defense mechanisms. As with a young child, the therapist does not tell an antisocial personality to stop doing something; he provides the patient with an alternative.

Only group membership, or caring for others, or both, can eventually provide adults with the parenting they never received. Antisocial personalities, so neglected in childhood, need to absorb more of other people than one person, no matter how loving, can ever provide. Membership in altruistic but revolutionary movements, like the Black Panthers, self-help groups, and even marriage to a person as needy as the patient—all seem to be more useful to the antisocial personality than is one-to-one therapy.

### Borderline Personality Disorder

In recent years, the patient with borderline personality disorder has captured professional attention as someone who hovers just across the line from psychosis. Affect, behavior, object relationships, and self-image are extraordinarily unstable, and the person with borderline personality disorder has sometimes been called the personality disorder who decided not to specialize.

**Definition.** In DSM-III (see Table VIII), at least five of the following eight criteria are required to make the diagnosis of borderline personality disorder.

1. Self-detrimental impulsivity in at least two areas, such as extravagance, promiscuity, gambling, overeating, substance abuse, and shoplifting.

2. A pattern of unstable but intense interpersonal relationships, with marked shifts in idealization, devaluation, and manipulation.

3. Inappropriately intense anger or lack of control of anger.

4. Identity disturbance, including uncertainty about self-image, gender identity, friendship patterns and values—for example, "I feel like I am my sister when I am good."

5. Affective instability, as indicated by marked

TABLE VIII
DIAGNOSTIC CRITERIA FOR BORDERLINE PERSONALITY DISORDER*

The following are characteristics of the individual's current and long-term functioning, are not limited to episodes of illness, and cause either significant impairment in social or occupational functioning or subjective distress.

A. At least five of the following are required:

(1) impulsivity or unpredictability in at least two areas that are potentially self-damaging, e.g., spending, sex, gambling, substance use, shoplifting, overeating, physically self-damaging acts
(2) a pattern of unstable and intense interpersonal relationships, e.g., marked shifts of attitude, idealization, devaluation, manipulation (consistently using others for one's own ends)
(3) inappropriate, intense anger or lack of control of anger, e.g., frequent displays of temper, constant anger
(4) identity disturbance manifested by uncertainty about several issues relating to identity, such as self-image, gender identity, long-term goals or career choice, friendship patterns, values, and loyalities, e.g., "Who am I?", "I feel like I am my sister when I am good"
(5) affective instability: marked shifts from normal mood to depression, irritability, or anxiety, usually lasting a few hours and only rarely more than a few days, with a return to normal mood
(6) intolerance of being alone, e.g., frantic efforts to avoid being alone, depressed when alone
(7) physically self-damaging acts, e.g., suicidal gestures, self-mutilation, recurrent accidents or physical fights
(8) chronic feelings of emptiness or boredom

B. If under 18, does not meet the criteria for Identity Disorder.

* From American Psychiatric Association: *Diagnostic and Statistical Manual of Mental Disorders*, ed 3. American Psychiatric Association, Washington, DC, 1980. Used with permission.

shifts from normal mood to depression, irritability, or anxiety, usually lasting only hours, with a return to the patient's normal mood.

6. Problems with being alone.

7. Self-mutilation, recurrent accidents, suicidal gestures, polysurgery, or physical fights.

8. Chronic feelings of emptiness or boredom.

**Epidemiology.** No systematic studies of the epidemiology of borderline personality disorder have been carried out. It is more common in women.

**Etiology.** Most, if not all, theories of the pathogenesis of borderline personality disorder, are based on retrospective clinical impressions and on case histories of patients in psychodynamically oriented treatment. From the start, authors have proposed some constitutional role in the pathogenesis of the disorder. These include a constitutional incapacity to tolerate stress (anxiety intolerance) and a constitutional inability to regulate affects, an inability that predisposes them to psychic disorganization under certain early learning conditions.

Writers on the psychogenesis of borderline personality disorder have uniformly taken a psychoanalytic approach and based their hypotheses on data obtained from patients in treatment.

Kernberg suggested that early pathological object relations are internalized by borderline patients, and that they are maintained by the use of primitive defense mechanisms that healthier people grow out of in normal development. Functionally, the adult borderline patient distorts his present relationships by pigeonholing people into all-good and all-bad categories. People are seen as either nurturant and attachment figures, or hateful and sadistic persons who deprive the patient of security needs and threaten him with abandonment whenever he feels dependent.

As a result of this splitting, the good person is idealized and the bad person is devalued. The patient experiences good feelings only by a flight into omnipotence that requires a defensive denial of past and present feelings and of facts that may contradict his present feelings. At times, however, this vacillation between polar-opposite feeling states is recognized by the patient and is felt as a source of insecurity and self-hatred. Continually feeling deprived and hating those on whom he is dependent, the borderline patient finally disowns these experiences by the use of projective identification and other primitive forms of projection. At the same time, there is a peculiar empathy with the other's situation, expressed like this: "Who wouldn't hate me, since I'm acting so bad?"

**Clinical Features.** When seen in a state of crisis, the borderline patient manifests overwhelming anger. The patient is argumentative and demanding, and tries to make others feel responsible for his troubles. If the patient presents outside of a crisis situation, he may appear to have unremarkable affect, but describes intense moods of anger and depression, both accompanied by chronic feelings of emptiness. Although much of the literature has focused on psychotic symptoms, those with borderline personalities, as a rule, have short-lived psychotic episodes, rather than full-blown psychotic breaks, and their psychotic symptoms are almost always circumscribed, fleeting, or in doubt. In women, episodes of anger and loss of control may be misinterpreted by male clinicians as psychosis.

The behavior of borderline personalities is highly unpredictable; as a consequence, they rarely achieve up to the level of their abilities. The painful nature of their lives is reflected in repetitive self-destructive acts; wrist slashing and other such self-mutilations are performed to elicit help from others, to express anger, and to numb themselves to overwhelming affect.

Because both dependence and hostility are intensely felt, the interpersonal relationships of borderline personalities are tumultuous. They can be clinging—sometimes literally so—and very dependent on those to whom they are close. In contrast to dependent personalities, borderline personalities can express enormous anger at their intimate friends when frustrated. In their capacity to manipulate groups of people, borderline personalities have no peer among the personality disordered. Borderline patients tolerate being alone very poorly and prefer a frantic search for companionship, no matter how unsatisfactory, to sitting with feelings of loneliness and emptiness. This facet of behavior excludes borderline personalities from inclusion in the schizophrenic spectrum.

They often complain about the lack of a consistent sense of identity (identity diffusion) and, when pressed, described how depressed they feel most of the time, despite the flurry of other affects. In therapy, borderline patients frequently regress and become demanding, difficult, and suicidal. Their capacity to evoke therapist countertransference is an exaggeration of what has already been said about countertransference and personality disorders in general.

Most authors agree that borderline patients demonstrate ordinary reasoning abilities on structural tests, such as the Wechsler Adult Intelligence Scale, and demonstrate deviant processes only on unstructured projective tests, such as the Rorschach and the Thematic Apperception Test. On projective tests, they connect unrelated percepts and reason circumstantially, rather than logically; their highly original responses often suggest an excess of affects to which they attribute overwhelming negative content—unlike the equally creative responses shown by artists. In general, those with borderline personalities experience their flamboyant and disturbed thinking as ego-syntonic.

**Course and Prognosis.** Short-term follow-up studies uniformly suggest that borderline patients change little over time.

The long-term outcome of the borderline patient is unknown, but one intriguing observation is that the diagnosis is rarely made in patients over 40. It is unknown whether this phenomenon reflects the fact that those with borderline personalities mature with age or, at least, stop seeking help, or whether their unstable personality patterns evolve into more stable personality disorders.

**Differential Diagnosis.** In up to half of all cases, borderline personality disorders may also meet the criteria for schizotypal personality disorder. Many meet the criteria for histrionic or antisocial personality disorder. The following traits help discriminate borderline personality disorder from other personality disorders: chronic feelings of emptiness, impulsivity, self-mutilation, short-lived psychotic episodes, manipulative suicide attempts, and unusually demanding involvement in close relationships.

Further longitudinal research is required to determine whether borderline personality disorder represents a stable diagnostic subcategory, or whether a majority of patients given that diagnosis can be reclassified as schizotypal, antisocial, or histrionic personalities.

**Treatment.** A study of the long-term psychotherapy for borderline personality disorder reveals it to be fraught with real pain and anger for patient and therapist alike. Regression is an enormous problem in therapy. Borderline patients easily become overwhelmed by intense affects, and deal with these feelings by impulsive behavior. Whether one views such behavior as the result of an acting out of transference states or as a constitutional incapacity to modulate affects matters little in comparison with the real danger the behavior poses to the patient.

In general, two viewpoints have emerged in psychotherapeutic treatment. The first viewpoint suggests that a modified psychoanalytic approach is most useful, and aims at the resolution of pathological internalized representations of interpersonal relationships. Special support systems may be necessary to carry out such a treatment successfully. The second viewpoint maintains that the regressive transference resulting from analytically oriented treatment is rarely constructive, and should be replaced with a more supportive reality-oriented approach. Here the therapist should offer a limited psychotherapeutic relationship to the patient while being indefinitely available. The goal of therapy is not termination but a gradual social adjustment in the context of a realistic therapeutic relationship. This viewpoint merges with a goal-oriented behavioral approach.

### Avoidant Personality Disorder

Because of extreme sensitivity to rejection, the person with this disorder may lead a socially withdrawn life. However, he is not asocial as much as shy; he may show a great desire for companionship, but he needs unusually strong guarantees of uncritical acceptance.

**Definition.** In DSM-III (see Table IX), the following criteria are required to make the diagnosis of avoidant personality disorder.

1. Hypersensitivity to rejection, such as apprehensive alertness to signs of social derogation

TABLE IX
DIAGNOSTIC CRITERIA FOR AVOIDANT PERSONALITY DISORDER*

The following are characteristic of the individual's current and long-term functioning, are not limited to episodes of illness, and cause either significant impairment in social or occupational functioning or subjective distress.

A. Hypersensitivity to rejection, e.g., apprehensively alert to signs of social derogation, interprets innocuous events as ridicule.

B. Unwillingness to enter into relationships unless given unusually strong guarantees of uncritical acceptance.

C. Social withdrawal, e.g., distances self from close personal attachments, engages in peripheral social and vocational roles.

D. Desire for affection and acceptance.

E. Low self-esteem, e.g., devalues self-achievements and is overly dismayed by personal shortcomings.

F. If under 18, does not meet the criteria for Avoidant Disorder of Childhood or Adolescence.

* From American Psychiatric Association: *Diagnostic and Statistical Manual of Mental Disorders*, ed 3. American Psychiatric Association, Washington, DC, 1980. Used with permission.

and interpretation of innocuous events as ridiculing.

2. Unwillingness to enter into relationships unless given unusually strong guarantees of uncritical acceptance.

3. Social withdrawal, such as distancing one's self from close personal attachments and engaging in peripheral social and vocational roles.

4. Desire for affection and acceptance.

5. Low self-esteem, such as devaluing self-achievements and being overly dismayed by personal shortcomings.

**History.** The term avoidant personality disorder is original with DSM-III. Before the advent of DSM-I, such persons would have epitomized Alfred Adler's inferiority complex. In DSM-I and DSM-II, persons with this disorder would probably have been classified as schizoid, dependent, or inadequate personalities.

**Epidemiology.** The prevalence of the disorder is unknown. As defined, it is common. No information is available on its sex ratio and familial pattern.

**Etiology.** Presumably, socialization and temperament play an important role in the causes, but systematic studies are lacking. Some clinicians have suggested that avoidant disorder of childhood and adolescence may precede avoidant personality disorder.

**Clinical Features.** Hypersensitivity to rejection by others is the central clinical feature of this disorder. The person desires the warmth and security of human companionship, but justifies his avoidance of forming relationships by his alleged fear of rejection. When talking with someone, the person expresses uncertainty and a lack of self-confidence, and may speak in a self-effacing manner. He is afraid to speak up in public or to make requests of others, because he is hypervigilant about rejection. He is apt to misinterpret other people's comments as derogatory or ridiculing. The refusal of any request leads the person to withdraw from others and to feel hurt.

The avoidant personality may display an appealing waif-like quality; he may have friends or a spouse who also tends to be introverted but loyal. Often, such friends offer unconditional acceptance of the patient and attempt to bolster him up or mollify his self-denigrating attitude. In the vocational sphere, the avoidant personality often takes a job on the sidelines. He rarely attains much personal advancement or exercises much authority. Instead, at work he may seem simply shy and eager to please.

In the clinical interview, the most striking thing is the patient's anxiety about talking with the interviewer. Nervous and adventitious manners appear to wax and wane with the patient's perception of whether or not the interviewer likes him. He seems vulnerable to the interviewer's comments and suggestions; a clarification or an interpretation may be heard as a criticism.

**Course and Prognosis.** The course and the prognosis of avoidant personality disorder are unknown.

**Differential Diagnosis.** The avoidant personality does not have the demanding quality in his behavior that is characteristic of the dependent person with a borderline, histrionic, or dependent personality disorder. The avoidant personality responds more gratefully to real attention than does the schizoid personality, who alleges that loneliness is his preferred mode. A clinical trial is required to prove that this new diagnosis should remain in the nomenclature.

**Treatment.** Psychotherapeutic treatment must first be directed at solidifying an alliance with the therapist to prevent early termination of therapy. Unlike the schizoid personality, the avoidant personality may find assertiveness training useful. The therapist should be cautious when giving assignments to exercise new social skills outside of therapy, because failure may reinforce the patient's already poor self-esteem. Group therapy may help the patient understand the effect that his sensitivity to rejection has on others.

### Dependent Personality Disorder

Persons with this disorder characterologically subordinate their own needs to those of others, get others to assume responsibility for major areas in their lives, lack self-confidence, and may experience intense discomfort when alone for more than brief periods. As with the borderline personality, many of the behavior patterns of the dependent personality seem to be learned ways of maneuvering other people into accommodating to their style of social interaction.

**Definition.** In DSM-III (see Table X) the following criteria are required to make the diagnosis of dependent personality disorder, and they should characterize the patient's long-term functioning:

1. Getting others to assume responsibility for major areas of the patient's life.

2. Subordinating one's own needs to the needs of persons on whom one depends, such as tolerating an abusive spouse.

3. Marked lack of self-confidence.

**History.** Perhaps the discussion of this disorder begins in the psychiatric literature with the psychoanalytic descriptions of oral character. In the terminology of DSM-I, passive-dependent personality was roughly synonymous

TABLE X
DIAGNOSTIC CRITERIA FOR DEPENDENT PERSONALITY DISORDER*

The following are characteristic of the individual's current and long-term functioning, are not limited to episodes of illness, and cause either significant impairment in social or occupational functioning or subjective distress.

A. Passively allows others to assume responsibility for major areas of life because of inability to function independently (e.g., lets spouse decide what kind of job he or she should have).

B. Subordinates own needs to those of persons on whom he or she depends in order to avoid any possibility of having to rely on self, e.g., tolerates abusive spouse.

C. Lacks self-confidence, e.g., sees self as helpless, stupid.

*From American Psychiatric Association: *Diagnostic and Statistical Manual of Mental Disorders*, ed 3. American Psychiatric Association, Washington, DC, 1980. Used with permission.

with the present term dependent personality disorders. In DSM-II, the diagnosis was not included.

Several studies have validated the finding that there is an oral-dependent dimension to personality; the traits of dependence, pessimism, fear of sexuality, self-doubt, egocentricity, passivity, suggestibility, and lack of perseverance occur as a distinct factor.

**Epidemiology.** In the Midtown Manhattan study, 9.8 percent of their sample showed a personality disorder, and a fourth of them—2.5 percent of the entire sample—were diagnosed as passive-dependent.

Dependent personality is more often diagnosed in women than in men. It is more common in the youngest children of a sibship than in the older children.

**Etiology.** Theories about the causes of dependent personality disorder are largely psychosocial. Cultures often predicate that certain groups—on the basis of gender, ethnicity, or role expectations—should assume a dependent role. Parents may subtly punish the attempts of some children to do things independently, and certain autonomous behavior patterns may never be established because the parent sensitizes the patient to believe that autonomy is related to loss of attachment. In theory, then, such persons may find even abuse or a beating tolerable, as long as it keeps the attachment bond intact.

Some evidence for a genetic contribution comes from the study of personality profiles of monozygotic and dizygotic twins. Identical twins have higher correlations on the scale measuring submissiveness versus dominance than did fraternal twins.

In psychoanalytic theory the trait of dependence is most related to the oral stage of psychosexual development.

**Clinical Features.** Pessimism, self-doubt, passivity, and fears about expressing sexual and aggressive feelings characterize the behavior of the dependent personality. He has learned to externalize many of his problems in such a fash-

ion that in any relationship he becomes the passive member. He avoids positions of responsibility and becomes anxious when forced into them. He may express his helplessness and need for companionship in artful and effective ways. When on his own, he finds it difficult to persevere at tasks for their own benefit, but may find it easy to perform those tasks for someone else— for example, in food preparation, hospitals, and beauty and child care professions. The dependent personality may be seen as storing up credits for the good things done, in order to feel entitled to be attached to another person. Intimate relationships are often distorted by the need to maintain the attachment bond. The dependent person can tolerate more unpleasant feelings in intimate relationships than can most other people. An abusive, unfaithful, or alcoholic spouse may be borne as long as the sense of attachment is not disturbed too greatly, or for too long.

**Course and Prognosis.** The course and the prognosis of dependent personality disorder are unknown.

**Differential Diagnosis.** Because the traits of dependency are present in virtually all psychiatric diagnoses, differential diagnosis is difficult and often noncontributory. Dependency traits are strongly associated with passive-aggressive and borderline personality disorders, and are present in many avoidant, histrionic, schizoid, and even paranoid patients. During periods of community adjustment, persons with chronic schizophrenia frequently present as dependent personalities. Indeed, DSM-II assumed that most patients actually disabled by the traits of dependency can be suitably assigned to other diagnostic categories. The next decade of clinical research, using DSM-III, may provide further guidance.

**Treatment.** The treatment of dependent personality traits can be very successful. Many of the principles have been outlined in the general discussion of the treatment of personality disorders. Sometimes behavior therapies, especially assertiveness training, are the quickest road to interpersonal adjustment for the dependent person.

One pitfall in the treatment of dependent personalities occurs when the therapist challenges a pathological but dependent relationship—for example, when the therapist insists that a wife-beater's wife seek help from the police. The patient may become increasingly anxious and unable to cooperate in therapy, and may feel torn between the therapist and the risk of losing a pathological external relationship. In short, great respect must be shown for a dependent patient's feelings of attachment, no matter how pathological these feelings seem to the observer.

### Compulsive Personality Disorder

The essential features of compulsive personality disorder are emotional constriction, orderliness, perseverance, stubbornness, and indecisiveness. Although the compulsive personality lacks the fear of people that characterizes schizoid personalities, he shows a restricted ability to express warm and tender feelings. Through his stubborn insistence on doing things his own way, and by his preoccupation with order and detail, the compulsive personality often alienates others. Of all the personality disorders, compulsiveness is the most occupationally adaptive, and, because its symptoms are more often autoplastic than alloplastic, it is the personality disorder least often confused with misbehavior.

**Definition.** In DSM-III (see Table XI), the following criteria are required to make the diagnosis of compulsive personality disorder:

1. Emotional constriction such as undue conventionality, seriousness, and formality and stinginess with warm and tender emotions.

2. Orderliness and preoccupation with rules, order, organization, schedules, and lists.

3. Stubbornness, inflexibility, insistence that others submit to the patient's way of doing things.

4. Perseverance and excessive devotion to work and productivity to the exclusion of pleasure and interpersonal relationships.

5. Indecisiveness to the point that decision making is either avoided or postponed because of rumination and fears of making mistakes.

**Epidemiology.** The prevalence of compulsive personality disorder is unknown, because the point at which the compulsive personality, which is common, becomes a disorder, is not clear. Compulsive personalities are found frequently in vocations that value accuracy, orderliness, and moral rectitude more than warmth and sociability.

Many observers have anecdotally noted the tendency for a compulsive personality to be most common in oldest children and more common in men than in women, perhaps reflecting observer bias because of society's differing expectations of men and of women. The earliest psychodynamic hypothesis regarding the development of obsessive personality disorder derives from Freud's theory of psychosexual development. In the anal phase of psychosexual development, ages 2 to 4, the child's libidinal drives were seen to come into conflict with parental attempts to socialize the child, the paradigm learning experience being that of toilet training. Cross-cultural attempts to validate that hypothesis have not upheld the importance of toilet training to personality formation, nor have prospective and cross-sectional studies.

Clinical experience suggests that, whereas the antisocial personality has encountered too little consistent discipline from parental figures, the compulsive personality has often encountered too much discipline.

TABLE XI
DIAGNOSTIC CRITERIA FOR COMPULSIVE PERSONALITY DISORDER*

At least four of the following are characteristic of the individual's current and long-term functioning, are not limited to episodes of illness, and cause either significant impairment in social or occupational functioning or subjective distress.

(1) restricted ability to express warm and tender emotions, e.g., the individual is unduly conventional, serious and formal, and stingy
(2) perfectionism that interferes with the ability to grasp "the big picture," e.g., preoccupation with trivial details, rules, order, organization, schedules, and lists
(3) insistence that others submit to his or her way of doing things, and lack of awareness of the feelings elicited by this behavior, e.g., a husband stubbornly insists his wife complete errands for him regardless of her plans.
(4) excessive devotion to work and productivity to the exclusion of pleasure and the value of interpersonal relationships
(5) indecisiveness: decision-making is either avoided, postponed, or protracted, perhaps because of an inordinate fear of making a mistake, e.g., the individual cannot get assignments done on time because of ruminating about priorities

*From American Psychiatric Association: *Diagnostic and Statistical Manual of Mental Disorders*, ed 3. American Psychiatric Association, Washington, DC, 1980. Used with permission.

In Western societies, compulsive personality traits are heavily reinforced by the Northern European Protestant work ethic, and by the emotional restraint that is necessitated by a high population density, a technological society, and a cold climate.

**Clinical Features.** Unlike most personality disorders, compulsive personality disorder has characteristics that have been consistently described in the literature. Freud described the triad of orderliness, obstinacy, and parsimony as the central features of the anal character. These three traits and six others have been repeatedly cited in the literature of both psychoanalysis and descriptive psychiatry. In rough order of importance, these nine traits are emotional constriction, orderliness, parsimony, rigidity, strict superego, perseverance, obstinacy, indecisiveness, and a lack of sexual provocativeness.

In interactions with others, the compulsive personality shows little give and take. In its stead, he shows a concern with the right way of doing things and with a rigid, just-so personal life. Others see the compulsive person as cold, controlling, and constricted. Rather than share feelings, he seems to attend to details and facts with such assiduousness that the underlying anxiety is often clear enough to the outsider.

Although a stable marriage and occupational success are common, the compulsive person usually has few friends.

Lists, notebooks, and mental notes preoccupy his day; bowel habits, time, and cleanliness seem of special interest. Willful determination characterizes his every action. Because all activities are carried out with seriousness, it is difficult for him to take vacations, admit pleasure, or display the light touch. Fear of making a mistake or a misjudgment contributes to the compulsive personality's indecisiveness. He puts off decisions, demands more evidence, and searches for something factual that will determine which is the only right decision. It was said of the philosopher Immanual Kant that the citizens of Königsberg could set their watches by his passing by, so exact was he as to the time of his evening walk.

In the psychiatric interview, the compulsive personality may present with conventional and meticulous dress. He sits with apparent stiffness or unnaturalness of posture; his hair may be unusually neat. Affect is not blunted or flat, but can best be described as constricted. Real laughter or crying is rare. His mood is usually serious and muted, although on occasion he may appear anxious or depressed. His tone of voice may be droning and monotonous, and his sentences seem to stretch on forever, as he gives very detailed, although often circumstantial, answers to questions. The defenses of isolation, intellectualization, displacement, reaction formation, and undoing are commonly evident.

**Course and Prognosis.** The course of compulsive personality disorder is variable and not predictable. Obsessions or compulsions (obsessive-compulsive disorder) may develop in the course of compulsive personality disorder from time to time. Some highly compulsive adolescents evolve into warm, open, and loving adults; in others, compulsive traits can either be the harbinger of schizophrenia or, decades later, exacerbated by the aging process, of involutional melancholia.

The compulsive personality may do well in positions demanding methodical, deductive, or detailed work, but such persons are vulnerable to unexpected changes, and their personal lives may remain barren. Major depressive disorders, especially those of late onset, are a common occurrence in compulsive personalities.

**Differential Diagnosis.** When recurrent obsessions or compulsions are present, obsessive-compulsive disorder should be noted on Axis I. It may occur with compulsive personality disorder also present. Perhaps the hardest distinction is between the outpatient with some obsessive-compulsive traits, and one with compulsive personality disorder. The diagnosis of compulsive personality disorder is reserved for those patients with a significant impairment in occupational or social effectiveness. In some cases, schizoid and paranoid disorders coexist with compulsive personality disorder; if they do, they should be noted.

**Treatment.** Unlike patients with the other personality disorders, the compulsive personality often knows that he suffers, and he seeks treatment on his own. Free association and nondirective therapy are highly valued by the overtrained, oversocialized compulsive personality. However, treatment in compulsive patients is often long, and countertransference is common.

Group and behavioral therapy occasionally offer certain advantages. In both contexts, it is easy to interrupt the patient in the midst of his maladaptive interactions or explanations. Preventing the completion of his habitual behavior raises his anxiety and leaves him susceptible to new learning. The patient can also experience direct rewards for change, something less often possible in individual psychotherapies.

### Passive-Aggressive Personality Disorder

The passive-aggressive personality expresses his conflicts through retroflexed anger. Since his

TABLE XII
DIAGNOSTIC CRITERIA FOR PASSIVE-AGGRESSIVE PERSONALITY DISORDER*

The following are characteristic of the individual's current and long-term functioning, and are not limited to episodes of illness.

A. Resistance to demands for adequate performance in both occupational and social functioning.

B. Resistance expressed indirectly through at least two of the following:

    (1) procrastination
    (2) dawdling
    (3) stubbornness
    (4) intentional inefficiency
    (5) "forgetfulness"

C. As a consequence of A and B, pervasive and long-standing social and occupational ineffectiveness (including in roles of housewife or student), e.g., intentional inefficiency that has prevented job promotion.

D. Persistence of the behavior pattern even under circumstances in which more self-assertive and effective behavior is possible.

E. Does not meet the criteria for any other Personality Disorder, and if under age 18, does not meet the criteria for Oppositional Disorder.

* From American Psychiatric Association: *Diagnostic and Statistical Manual of Mental Disorders*, ed 3. American Psychiatric Association, Washington, DC, 1980. Used with permission.

anger is often manifested by covert obstructionism, procrastination, stubbornness, and inefficiency, the term passive-aggressive is used in organizational settings, both frequently and pejoratively.

**Definition.** In DSM-III (see Table XII), the following criteria for making the diagnosis of passive-aggressive personality disorder are required:

1. Resistance to demands for adequate activity or performance in both occupational and social areas of functioning.

2. Expression of resistance through at least two of the following: (1) procrastination, (2) dawdling, (3) stubbornness, (4) intentional inefficiency, (5) "forgetfulness."

3. Pervasive and long-standing occupational or social ineffectiveness.

4. Absence of any other personality disorder.

**Epidemiology.** The Stirling County study found that 0.9 percent of their sample exhibited a passive-aggressive or passive-dependent pattern of behavior, but that figure is not necessarily the prevalence of passive-aggressive disorder itself. The sex ratio and the familial pattern of the disorder are unknown.

**Etiology.** Psychosocial rearing is almost certainly of paramount causal importance, and the following learning patterns seem plausible. The child's parents are assertive and perhaps aggressive in their dealings with the child; yet, because of their own conflicts, they punish or block the expression of normal assertiveness in the child and meet his dependency needs only partially and grudgingly. Hence, the child learns to retroflex his anger and, at first glance, appears polite and undemanding, while covertly punishing the oppressor with inefficiency.

Ultimately, a major purpose of turning anger against the self is to protect important relationships. For example, adolescents wish to establish autonomy but do not want to leave parental care. The adolescent learns that certain obnoxious but indirect maneuvers can both procure some attention by the parents, and at the same time discomfort them. Later in life, this paradigm is then unconsciously replayed with all important authority figures.

**Clinical Features.** The passive-aggressive person characteristically procrastinates, resists demands for adequate performance, finds excuses for delays, and finds fault with those he depends on, yet refuses to extricate himself from the dependent relationship. He usually lacks assertiveness and is not direct about his own needs or wishes. He fails to ask needed questions about what is expected of him, and may become anxious when forced to succeed or when his usual defense of turning anger against the self is removed.

In interpersonal relationships, the passive-aggressive personality attempts to manipulate himself into a position of dependency, yet his passive, self-detrimental behavior is often experienced by others as punitive and manipulative. Others must do his errands and carry out his routine responsibilities. Friends and clinicians may become enmeshed in trying to assuage the patient's many claims of unjust treatment, but the close relationships of passive-aggressive personalities are rarely tranquil or happy. Since the passive-aggressive personality is bound to his resentment more closely than he is to procuring a positive satisfaction for himself, he may never even formulate what he wants for himself when it comes to enjoyment.

Several defenses are characteristic of the passive-aggressive patient: turning against the self (broadly interpreted to include sadomasochism), rationalization, and hypochondriasis.

**Course and Prognosis.** In a follow-up study, averaging 11 years, of 100 passive-aggressive inpatients, Small demonstrated that in 54 of them, passive-aggressive personality was the primary diagnosis; 18 were also alcoholic, and 30 could be clinically labeled as depressed. Of the 73 former patients located, 58 (79 percent) had persistent psychiatric difficulties, and 9 (12 percent) were considered symptom free. Most seemed irritable, anxious, and depressed; somatic complaints were numerous. Only 32 (44 percent) were employed full time as workers or homemakers. Although neglect of responsibility and suicide attempts were common, only one patient had committed suicide in the interim. Although hospital readmission occurred in 28 (38 percent), only 3 patients were called schizophrenic.

**Differential Diagnosis.** In the past, women with passive-aggressive personality disorders have been mislabeled as histrionic and borderline; however, the passive-aggressive personality is less flamboyant, dramatic, affective, and openly aggressive than the histrionic and borderline personalities.

**Treatment.** Passive-aggressive patients who receive supportive psychotherapy have better outcomes. However, psychotherapy for the patient with passive-aggressive personality disorder has many pitfalls; to fulfill their demands is often to support their pathology, but to refuse their demands is to reject them. The therapy hour can become a battleground where the patient relieves his feelings of resentment against a therapist on whom he wishes to become dependent. In passive-aggressive patients, it is important to treat suicide gestures as one would any covert expression of anger, and not as one would treat object loss or primary depression. Tricyclic antidepressants should be prescribed only when clinical indications are pressing and the possibility of overdose is seriously taken into account. The therapist must continually point out the probable consequences of passive-aggressive behaviors as they occur. Questions like, "What do you want for yourself?" and "What will happen if you call in sick again?" may be more of an aid in changing the patient's behavior than is a correct interpretation.

### Sadomasochistic Personality

There are personality types characterized by elements of sadism, masochism, or a combination of the two (sadomasochistic). Although not part of the official DSM-III nosology, these personality disorders are of clinical interest.

Sadism (named after Marquis de Sade, who wrote of persons who experienced sexual pleasure when inflicting pain on others) consists of the desire to cause others pain, either through sexual abuse or by being more generally abusive.

Freud believed that the sadist warded off castration anxiety and was able to achieve sexual pleasure only when he was able to do to others what he feared would be done to him.

Masochism (named after Leopold Von Sacher-Masoch, a 19th century Austrian novelist) is characterized by achieving sexual gratification by inflicting pain upon the self. More generally, the so-called moral masochist seeks humiliation and failure rather than physical pain.

Freud believed that the masochist's ability to achieve orgasm is disturbed by anxiety and guilt feelings about sex which are alleviated by his own suffering and punishment.

Clinical observations indicate that elements of both sadistic and masochistic behavior are usually present in the same person. Treatment with insight-oriented psychotherapy including psychoanalysis has been effective in some cases. As a result of therapy, the patient becomes aware of the need for self-punishment secondary to excessive unconscious guilt and also comes to recognize repressed aggressive impulses which have their origins in early childhood.

**REFERENCES**

Akhtar S, Thomsan J A: Overview: Narcissistic personality disorder. Am J Psychiatry *139:* 12, 1982.
Gunderson J G, Siever L J, Spaulding E: The search for a schizotype: crossing the border again. Arch Gen Psychiatry *40:* 15, 1983.
Kendler K S, Gruenberg A M: Genetic relationship between paranoid personality disorder and the "schizophrenic spectrum" disorders. Am J Psychiatry *139:* 1185, 1982.
Kohut H, Wolff E S: The disorders of the self and their treatment: An outline. Int J Psychoanal *59:* 413, 1978.
Lion J R, editor: *Personality Disorders Diagnosis and Management*, ed 2. Williams & Wilkins, Baltimore, 1981.
Morris D, Soroker E, Barruss G: Follow-up studies of shy, withdrawn children. I. Evaluation of later adjustment. Am J Orthopsychiatry, *24:* 743, 1954.
Perry J C, Flannery R B: Passive-aggressive personality disorders: Treatment implications of a clinical typology. J Nerv Ment Dis *170:* 164, 1982.
Presley A S, Walton H: Dimensions of abnormal personality. Br J Psychiatry *122:* 269, 1974.
Robins L N: *Deviant Children Grown Up: A Sociological and Psychiatric Study of Sociopathic Personality*. Williams & Wilkins, Baltimore, 1966.
Shapiro D: *Autonomy and Rigid Character*. Basic

Books, New York, 1981.

Soloff P H, Millward J W: Psychiatric disorders in the families of borderline patients. Arch Gen Psychiat *40:* 37, 1983.

Thomas A, Chess S: *Temperament and Development.* Bruner/Mazel, New York, 1977.

Vaillant G E: *Adoptation to Life.* Little, Brown and Co., Boston, 1977.

Vaillant G E, Perry J C: Personality disorders. In *Comprehensive Textbook of Psychiatry,* ed 4, H I Kaplan, B J Sadock, editors, p 958. Williams & Wilkins, Baltimore, 1985.

# 19

# Drug Dependence

## 19.1 OPIOID DEPENDENCE

### Definitions and Diagnostic Criteria

Over the past 100 years, the terminology used to describe the addictive disorders has been repeatedly revised as concepts about the nature of chronic drug using behavior have evolved. In 1964, the World Health Organizaton Expert Committee on addiction-producing drugs concluded that the term "addiction" was no longer a useful scientific term, and recommended the substitution of the term "drug dependence" for both of the previously used terms, "addiction" and "habituation."

This WHO formulation made it necessary to define dependence on each variety of drug separately, and implied an important distinction between psychic and physical dependency. It was in common use until the publication in 1980 of DSM-III. DSM-III divides opioid use disorders into two major categories, opioid abuse and opioid dependence.

The DSM-III diagnostic criteria for opioid abuse are as follows:

A. *Pattern of pathological use:* inability to reduce or stop use; intoxication throughout the day; use of opioids nearly every day for at least a month; episodes of opioid overdose (intoxication so severe that respiration and consciousness are impaired).

B. *Impairment in social or occupational functioning due to opioid use:* e.g., fights, loss of friends, absence from work, loss of job, or legal difficulties (other than due to a single arrest for possession, purchase, or sale of the substance).

C. Duration of disturbance of at least 1 month.

Diagnostic criteria for opioid dependence require only the presence of either tolerance (the need for increased amount of drug to achieve desired effect), or opioid withdrawal after cessation or reduction in use. Generally, opioid dependence occurs after a period of opioid abuse. However, as defined in DSM-III, opioid dependence does not require antecedent abuse and is synonymous with what has been designated as physical dependence in standard pharmacological textbooks. Technically, to note the presence of both a pattern of pathological use and physical dependence, two diagnoses are required. Current DSM-III criteria make no provision for indicating differences in severity of the dependence syndrome (see Table I).

### Introduction

The drugs discussed in this section—opium, opium alkaloids, and synthetics known together as opioids—produce physical dependence. The characteristics of the drug-dependent state vary, depending on the drug involved.

### Etiology

#### Interpersonal, Familial, Developmental, Psychodynamic Factors

In psychoanalytic literature, the behavior of narcotic addicts was described in terms of libidinal fixation, with regression to pregenital, oral, or even more archaic levels of psychosexual development. Most notably, the oral state was emphasized. The need to explain the relationship between drug abuse, defense, impulse control, affective disturbances, and adaptive mechanisms led to the recent shift in dynamic formulations, emphasizing ego psychology.

Serious ego pathology is often thought to be associated with drug abuse, and is considered to be indicative of profound developmental disturbances. Problems of the relationship between the ego and affects emerge as a key area of difficulty; the problems include affective experiencing, control, intensity, and ambivalence.

There are possible but not definitive warning signs among children who may turn to drugs in later years. These high-risk signs include early health problems, behavioral problems at meal times and in school, mild conduct disorders, and a lack of self-confidence. High-risk children also reflect a self-centered philosophy of life, coupled with antiauthoritarian views.

It seems that the parents themselves are often deeply involved in using prescribed or nonprescribed drugs or alcohol. By and large, the symp-

TABLE I
DIAGNOSTIC CRITERIA FOR OPOID ABUSE AND DEPENDENCE*

*Diagnostic criteria for Opioid Abuse*

A. *Pattern of pathological use:* inability to reduce or stop use; intoxication throughout the day; use of opioids nearly every day for at least 1 month; episodes of opioid overdose (intoxication so severe that respiration and consciousness are impaired).

B. *Impairment in social or occupational functioning due to opioid use:* e.g., fights, loss of friends, absence from work, loss of job, or legal difficulties (other than due to a single arrest for possession, purchase, or sale of the substance).

C. Duration of disturbance of at least 1 month.

*Diagnostic criteria for Opioid Dependence*

Either tolerance or withdrawal:

*Tolerance:* need for markedly increased amounts of opioid to achieve the desired effect, or markedly diminished effect with regular use of the same amount.

*Withdrawal:* development of Opioid Withdrawal after cessation of or reduction in substance use.

* From American Psychiatric Association: *Diagnostic and Statistical Manual of Mental Disorders*, ed 3. American Psychiatric Association, Washington, DC, 1980. Used with permission.

tom of drug taking by the child is derivative or a reflection of the whole family's attitude of inconsistency, self-centeredness, and, very often, inner dishonesty.

Constellations of common characteristics that can be thought of as the addictive personality have been sought, but opioid addicts do not fit into any of the categories of formal nosology.

### Environmental

In recent years, the steady increase in the number of middle-class addicts from privileged homes has cast doubt on any exclusive relation between addiction and socioeconomic status.

Concomitant with the spread of heroin addiction from the minorities to the white population was a drop in the average age of heroin users. The age of initiation of heroin users reaches a peak at 16 to 17. Social situation is most important in initiating drug experimentation and use. The age of initiation has been dropping steadily. Some 10- and 11-year-old children are now experimenting with opioids.

Certain consistent behavior patterns seem especially pronounced in adolescent addicts. These patterns have been called the heroin behavior syndrome: underlying depression, often of an agitated type and frequently accompanied by anxiety symptoms; impulsiveness expressed by a passive-aggressive orientation; fear of failure; use of heroin as an antianxiety agent to mask feelings of low self-esteem, hopelessness, and aggression; limited coping strategies and low frustration tolerance, accompanied by the need for immediate gratification; sensitivity to drug contingencies, with a keen awareness of the relation between good feelings and the act of drug taking; feelings of behavioral impotence counteracted by momentary control over the life situation by means of drugs, with the injection ritual a valued life event, disturbances in social

and interpersonal relations with peer relations maintained by mutual drug experiences.

With authentic engagement not attractive or feasible for many, drug abuse becomes, for a small but growing minority, a form of identification and engagement.

### Iatrogenic

Iatrogenic factors are most common in cases of excessive pain, and in cases in which confirmation of a terminal state has been established. Actually, if the frequency with which opioid analgesics are used in clinical medicine is considered, the incidence of addiction is low. However, the inappropriate prescription of opioids, as well as the continuation of their use long beyond necessity, still does occur.

## Pharmacology

The opioid drug itself is actually capable of inducing dependence in all persons. This statement leads one to explore the pharmacology of specific opioids, and the mechanism of action in terms of dependence and tolerance.

### Opium

Opium (Greek for juice) is produced from the milky exudate of the unripe seed capsules of the poppy plant, *Papaver somniferum*. Dried and powdered, the exudate constitutes official opium with its alkaloids. Only a few alkaloids—morphine, codeine, papaverine, and noscapine—have clinical usefulness. Table II shows the major and naturally occurring alkaloids of opium and the two chemical classes, phenanthrene and benzylisoquinoline. Phenanthrene is the class relevant to this discussion. Morphine is the most important phenanthrene; the most important opium alkaloid of the benzylisoquinoline class is papaverine.

Powdered opium, U.S.P., is a light brown powder supplied for clinical use in capsule, tablet, and pill forms. Pantopon is the proprietary name of a commonly used preparation of purified opium alkaloids. Since the official morphine content of opium is 10 to 10.5 percent by weight, a dose of 0.06 g of opium is equivalent to 6 mg of morphine.

## Morphine

Morphine was isolated and described in 1803 by Serturner, who named the opium alkaloid after the Greek god of dreams. Morphine is by far the most important phenanthrene alkaloid of opium, and it gives to opium its predominant pharmacological characteristics. It is synthesized in the laboratory with great difficulty, yet semisynthetic derivatives have been produced by relatively simple modifications of the morphine molecule, the objective being a potent nonaddicting analgesic.

Codeine is a naturally occurring phenanthrene alkaloid or methylmorphine, the methyl substitution appearing at the phenolic OH at carbon 3. Alterations of hydroxy groups on carbon 3 (phenolic) and carbon 6 (alcoholic) change the pharmacological properties of morphine. Molecular manipulation of the phenolic hydroxy group weakens the analgesic activity. Manipulation of the alcoholic hydroxy group strengthens it. Hydromorphone, oxymorphone, hydrocodone, and oxycodone are all results of modifying the morphine molecule.

Morphine and other semisynthetic derivatives of natural opium alkaloids or opiates, as well as a number of other structurally distinct chemical classes of drugs, also produce analgesia, respiratory depression, gastrointestinal spasm, and physical dependence. These drugs include the semisynthetic derivatives of morphine, the morphinans, benzomorphans, methadones, and phenylpiperidines. Toxic doses of meperidine may produce convulsions. Nalorphine and related antagonists to morphine counteract the analgesic, gastrointestinal, and depressant effects and the convulsions.

The mechanisms whereby morphine and the opiates generally exert their effects remain un-

TABLE II
NATURAL ALKALOIDS OF OPIUM

| Alkaloid | Opium Content (%) |
|---|---|
| Phenanthrene | |
| Morphine | 10 |
| Codeine | 5 |
| Thebaine | 2 |
| Benzylisoquinoline | |
| Papaverine | 1 |
| Noscapine | 6 |

certain. However, the study of opioid receptors for opioids and opioid antagonists promises to clarify the question. Their major areas of activity are in the central nervous system and the bowel. Flushing and itching of the skin result from a release of histamine, and constipation results from a decrease of peristalsis. Most of an injected single dose of morphine appears in the urine within 24 hours, with the remainder appearing in the feces later. Excreted morphine appears as the conjugated glucuronide, but free morphine is also detectable.

Analgesia, drowsiness, changes in mood, and mental clouding are among the central nervous system effects produced by morphine. Small to moderate amounts (5 to 10 mg) produce such analgesia, often without sleep. Other manifestations include a feeling of warmth, with the extremities feeling heavy; the face, particularly the nose, may itch; and the mouth becomes dry. In addition to the relief of distress, some patients experience euphoria, a sense of well-being. If the external situation is favorable, sleep and dreaming ensue. However, the opposite, dysphoria—with mild anxiety or fear, nausea, or vomiting—may occur in the normal, pain-free person. The further psychological effects of morphine may be mental clouding, with drowsiness, inability to concentrate, difficulty in thinking, apathy, and lethargy. These subjective effects tend to become more pronounced with large doses (15 to 20 mg). Idiosyncratic responses—such as insomnia, rather than sedation—have been widely reported, as have allergic reactions, such as urticaria and other skin rashes, wheals at the site of injection, and even anaphylactoid shock, which may be responsible for many of the sudden deaths and episodes of pulmonary edema that occur among heroin addicts.

Morphine analgesia is relatively selective, in that touch, vision, and hearing are not blunted. Morphine and other opioid analgesics do not alter the responsivity or the threshold of nerve endings to noxious stimuli. Neither do they alter the conduction of the nerve impulses along the peripheral nerves. In the clinical situation, morphine and other opioid analgesics are said to act on systems reponsible for affective responses to painful stimuli, thus increasing the patient's tolerance to pain, even though his capacity to perceive the situation may be unchanged. Continuous, dull pain is relieved more effectively than is sharp intermittent pain, such as the pain of renal and biliary colic. Morphine is a primary and continuous depressant of respiration because of its direct effect on the brain stem respiratory centers. In humans, death is nearly always due to respiratory arrest. Changes in blood pressure, heart rate, and cerebral circulation do not seem to be prominent effects of the drug. The depressant effects of morphine and related narcotics may be exaggerated and prolonged by phenothiazines, monoamine oxidase inhibitors, and imipramine-like drugs. An unknown mechanism is the constriction of the pupils caused by morphine. Although morphine greatly enhances the pupillary response to light, some miosis occurs even in total darkness.

Morphine and other analgesic opioids exert both depressant and excitant actions at all levels of the central nervous system. In the spinal cord, polysynaptic reflexes, such as the crossed extensor and ipsilateral flexor reflexes, are depressed by this group of drugs in doses that have little effect on two-neuron reflexes, such as the patellar reflex. This effect implies selective action on multineuronal pathways.

In the higher levels of the cerebral nervous system, it is still unclear which action of morphine produces analgesia, although it has been suggested that it may be related to the alteration of patterns of the cortical recruiting responses to stimulation in a number of sites in the diffuse thalamocortical projection system.

Animal experiments on the pleasure center indicated that the effect of opioids is to increase the threshold stimulus required to produce not only pleasure, but also pain.

Morphine exerts complex actions in the hypothalamus. The opioids cause a release of antidiuretic hormone, producing a decrease in urinary output that is mediated by the hypothalamus. This effect may be important in patients with congestive heart failure, since morphine decreases the effects of diuretics. In human beings, morphine inhibits the release of adrenocorticotrophic hormone (ACTH) and pituitary gonadotropic hormone, and thus decreases plasma and urinary 17-ketosteroid and 17-hydroxycorticosteroid levels.

### Heroin

The most widely abused opiate, heroin (diacetylmorphine), is a simple derivative of morphine, the principal phenanthrene alkaloid of opium. Synthesized in 1890, heroin became commercially available in 1898. Initially, it was thought to be useful in the treatment of morphine dependence; later, it was found that heroin addiction is more intractable than morphine addiction. The chemical synthesis of heroin from morphine involves the acetylation of both the phenolic (carbon 3) and the alcoholic (carbon 6) OH groups.

On the street, the salt, heroin hydrochloride, appears in powdered form, usually white, but varying in color and texture. European heroin is a highly refined white powder, and Oriental heroin consists of fluffy ivory crystals. Mexican heroin is usually darker and more granular. Some Far East brown-rock heroin appears as dark red or maroon chips or looks like Ovaltine granules. Most varieties have a vinegary smell. Pharmacologically, heroin acts like morphine, inducing analgesia, drowsiness, and changes in mood. An initial dose may produce dysphoria, nausea, and often vomiting. In the naive person, this effect is brief; the pleasurable and therapeutic actions of heroin persist for many hours. Heroin is deacetylated and metabolized in a manner similar to the way morphine is metabolized.

The manufacture, sale, and possession of heroin are illegal in the United States. Heroin is more widely used illegally than is morphine, but the reason for this preference is unclear, since the effects of the two drugs are similar. However, in equipotent injectable doses, 1 mg of heroin is equal to 1.80 to 2.66 mg of morphine sulfate. Withdrawn addicts can distinguish between an intravenous dose of morphine and an intravenous dose of heroin, since heroin has greater potency, apparently because of its relatively easier passage through the blood-brain barrier.

Studies have suggested that heroin addiction in women was associated with amenorrhea, anovulation, and infertility. Pregnancy in the addict was associated with a high incidence of maternal complications, and of withdrawal symptoms in the baby born to the addicted mother. However, further studies suggested that these hazards were overemphasized, and that the major hazards are the mother's malnutrition and the infant's prematurity by weight. Switching to methadone in the first two trimesters only is recommended, as are an active counseling program and persistent prenatal care.

### Mechanism of Action

One of the central concerns of modern biochemistry has been to discover what it is about relatively simple chemicals—the opioids—that makes them produce powerful pharmacological effects within the human system.

The two outstanding pharmacological effects are dependence and tolerance. Opinion is divided as to whether there is a single explanation for both phenomena. Some have held that tolerance and physical dependence seemed to be inextricably linked, but others have maintained that the linkage is not valid. Since studies of mechanisms apply to both dependence and tolerance, it is more convenient in the case of the opioids to discuss these two phenomena together.

Dependence has been variously defined. Dependence is a state induced by a drug, the withdrawal of which gives rise to physiological or psychological disturbance, or both, that can be removed by again administering the drug or a drug with which it is cross-dependent. This description allows for the possibility that dependence can arise from a single dose of the drug. If physiological disturbances follow withdrawal, the dependence may be called physical; if the disturbance is psychological, the dependence may be called psychic. In the case of morphine, both physical and psychic dependence occur.

Tolerance is a phenomenon characteristic of the opioids; that is, to continue to maintain the same effect from the opioid that was obtained initially, increasing amounts of opioid will be required. Tolerance to heroin can be increased to levels more than 100 times the initial effective dose. Tolerance can persist in animals for periods of many months without any behavioral signs of abstinence.

Tolerance to heroin occurs fairly rapidly, within days during the periodic administration of the drug. If the tolerant person is challenged with an antagonist such as naloxone, a precipitated withdrawal syndrome follows. Withdrawal signs include restlessness, agitation, rhinorrhea, tearing, gooseflesh, abdominal and muscular cramps, tachycardia, and a rise in temperature, with dilation of the pupils. These signs and symptoms do not often appear after a short exposure to heroin, but they inevitably appear if the drug is continued. An abrupt cessation of drug intake is then followed by the characteristic signs of abstinence. These signs can be reversed by the administration of heroin or another opioid, at lower doses than were previously used by the addict.

Significant changes of narcotic concentration in the blood-brain barrier cannot account for the phenomena of tolerance and dependence, since the rate of absorption of metabolism is not altered significantly in addicted animals, and thus cannot explain the magnitude of tolerance and dependence.

Hypotheses of tolerance and dependence were stimulated by the discovery of specific opiate receptors in 1973, and the subsequent identification of endogenous opioids. It was hypothesized for decades that opioids must bind to specific sites located on the surface of or inside nerve cells in order to exert their effects. These binding sites or receptors were postulated out of necessity, because of the opioids' high degree of structural specificity, high potency, and stereospecificity. Further, the existence of agonist and antagonist forms makes such a conclusion compelling.

With the discovery of the opiate receptors, the question immediately arose as to why receptors for alkaloids, which are of plant origin, exist in the nervous system. The most reasonable conclusion seems to be that similar substances play a physiological role, and thus began the search for an endogenous factor that would bind with the opiate receptor.

In 1974, an endogenous factor with opiate-like effects in an extract of pig brain was discovered. These effects were reversed by naloxone, an opiate antagonist. Purification of this factor identified it as a pentapeptide. The two pentapeptides that were found to be active were termed enkephalins. After this discovery, a number of other peptides with opioid properties were isolated from extracts of the hypothalamus and pituitary glands. All were found to be present in a pituitary hormone, $\beta$-lipotropin. The whole group of endogenous opiate-like peptides were termed endorphins. Although there have been many suggestions, no specific physiological function has been found for the endorphins, but an important role is anticipated, possibly as a novel neural transmitter involved in a natural pain suppression role or in behavioral and emotional functions. The study of the endorphins is expected, not only to clarify many of the problems in neurochemistry and neurophysiology, but also to bring new understanding to the mechanism of action of opioids and to the unsolved problems of addiction, dependence, and tolerance.

## Natural History

Once a person has been initiated into the use of heroin through the social situation, particularly the peer group, his repeated use of narcotics is based on: (1) the pleasurable effects of the drug, (2) their effect in terminating the discomfort of narcotic withdrawal symptoms, and (3) nonpharmacological factors.

The march of events is best understood by the conditioning hypothesis of Abram Wikler. According to this hypothesis, after the first few doses of the drug, accompanied by the development of dependency, the incipient symptoms of the abstinence syndrome generate a homeostatic need for the drug. The patient is aware of tension or discomfort, and seeks and obtains relief in the continued use of opioids. On each occasion, when these symptoms are relieved and the homeostatic need is reduced, there is a reinforcement of the pattern to administer heroin to prevent the development of the abstinence syndrome. Thus, in this period of episodic intoxication, reinforcement occurs with each opportunity for relief by the use of heroin.

After repeated pairings of the narcotic withdrawal syndrome with social and environmental stimuli, the stimuli themselves—the site, the neighborhood, the hustle for the drug, the ambience, the sounds, the smells, the people, and the situation—acquire the potential to precipitate symptoms and signs of withdrawal.

As time passes, heroin reduces tension or discomfort less and less efficiently, as tolerance and physical dependence develop further. There is a constant escalation of the required doses because of tolerance, and the abstinence syndrome is experienced more and more. Sooner or later, the drug is withdrawn; with the supply of opiates gone, the addict is admitted to a hospital, or he is arrested. The addict then enters a phase of physiological disequilibrium and conditioned abstinence. These two stages may exceed the period of simple withdrawal; they often persist for many months or longer. Thus, the principal reinforcements of addiction are the discomforts related to the unfulfilled physiological dependence, and the responses of the addict as he is conditioned to certain aspects and subtle clues of his environment. When the addict is placed again in this environment, the abstinence phenomena recur in him as a conditioned response. Long after the withdrawal of the drug, and for reasons unknown to him, he feels uncomfortable and tense, and seeks narcotics for relief. Thus, the relief of conditioned withdrawal symptoms may be the major motivating factor for the resumption of drug-taking behavior.

This sequence has been recounted on numerous occasions, in case histories in which an addict has been withdrawn and off heroin for many, many months—for example, during incarceration. Such a person recounts that, after his release from prison and on approaching his old neighborhood, he suddenly begins to experience acute withdrawal symptoms, or just acute feelings of discomfort. In any event, he rushes off to obtain heroin and to begin another cycle.

Conditioned withdrawal has been demonstrated experimentally in rats, in monkeys, and in humans.

### Medical Complications and Life Expectancy

Medical complications associated with injection of illicit drugs include a variety of pathological changes in the CNS. Degenerative changes

in globus pallidus and necrosis of spinal gray matter are usually found at autopsy, but sometimes, there are clinical manifestations in those users surviving overdose experiences. Examples of various problems presented by addicts who survive overdoses are transverse myelitis, amblyopia, plexitis, peripheral neuropathy, parkinsonism-like syndromes, intellectual impairment, and personality changes. Pathological changes in muscles and degeneration of peripheral nerves have also been seen.

Because opioid addicts—even physicians who have access to drugs and sterile materials— tend to neglect the hygienic aspects of injecting, infections of skin and systemic organs are quite common. Filtering illicit opioids through cigarette filters or wads of cotton and injection of materials intended for oral use result in starch, talc, and other particulate contaminants entering the bloodstream; these particulates or particles can cause pulmonary emboli, which can eventually result in angiothrombotic pulmonary hypertension and right ventricular failure. Staphylococcal pneumonitis may also be related to septic emboli. The incidence of tuberculosis is higher among heroin addicts than in the general population. Endocarditis and septicemia involving lesions either of the tricuspid or of the aortic and mitral valves are other complications sometimes seen. Less frequent but equally serious complications are meningitis and brain abscess. Other frequently seen infections that are probably related to injecting or sharing of needles include viral hepatitis, malaria, tetanus, osteomyelitis, and syphilis. Although most cases of syphilis are probably acquired in the usual fashion, as is tuberculosis, many opioid addicts who inject have a low-level chronic hepatitis without jaundice and may have abnormal liver function tests and false positive tests for syphilis. In one study, 45 percent of heroin addicts had hepatitis-B antibody levels. Abnormal liver function tests, which are found in about two out of three heroin addicts, may persist long periods after cessation of injection. Excessive use of alcohol may, in some cases, contribute to the liver disease. Drug users who inject are among those persons considered at high risk for acquired immune deficiency syndrome (AIDS). Renal failure secondary to bacterial endocarditis may also occur.

Lymphadenopathy is seen in 75 percent of addicts and may be related to particulate contaiminants; chronic edema of extremities—for example, puffy hand—may be due to lymphatic obstruction caused by contaminants or sclerosis of veins caused by the drugs or their dilutants (see Fig. 1). "Skin popping" may cause wide-

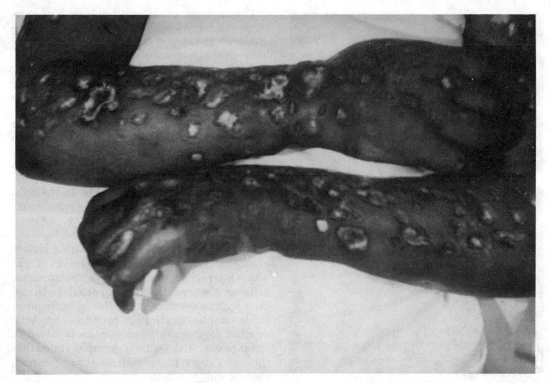

FIGURE 1.    Ulceration of the forearm and nonpitting edema involving the fingers and hands. (Courtesy Michael Baden, M.D.)

spread ulceration and disfigurement as a result of chemical necrosis or infection (see Fig. 2).

What happens to an addict in the course of his life cycle? Vaillant studied 100 male New York City addicts for 20 years after their 1952 hospitalizations. Few of these addicts recovered spontaneously. A significant number remained addicted and in trouble past the age of 40. Vaillant found that, once an addict achieves a stable remission, the remission may be indefinitely maintained.

The number of years addicted and the amount of drugs used before hospitalization do not affect the probability of achieving stable abstinence.

Three variables differentiated the best prognosis—employment of 4 years or more, being raised in the same culture in which parents had been raised, and being married. Opiate-dependent patients who maintain stable heterosexual relationships have a significantly better prognosis with cyclazocine treatment than do patients who are isolated from meaningful relationships.

Voluntary hospitalization or imprisonment alone proves useless; but parole supervision after imprisonment may be surprisingly effective in producing stable abstinence.

In a follow-up study of Vietnam drug users, it was discovered that most of the men who used narcotics extensively in Vietnam stopped when they left Vietnam, and had not begun again. The idea that narcotic addiction is easily acquired and hard to break may have to be revised. Even more surprising was the implication that those who continued to use drugs in civilian life had not become addicted or readdicted. Less than 5 percent of the large sample of Vietnam addicts studied in the United States went back to heavy heroin use.

## Clinical Effects

The clinical effects of morphine may be used as the model for all opiates. The particular setting in which the drug is administered, the person's history of receiving opiates, his particular personality, and the presence or absence of pain contribute to the effects. For the naive user without pain, morphine may produce dysphoria brought about by nausea, giddiness, and a subjective sense of mental clouding. There is no impairment of psychomotor performance, except under stress and the demand for speed. Since morphine relieves pain, a person who is in pain displays a negative euphoria on the injection of morphine, with the pain assuaged.

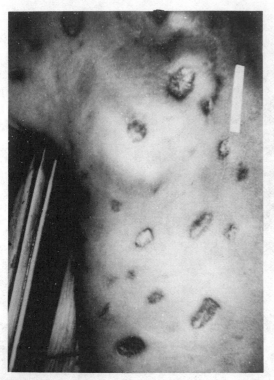

FIGURE 2. "Skin-popper": Circular depressed scars often with underlying chronic abscesses on back of subcutaneous narcotic addict. Thighs are also commonly used skin-popping area. (Courtesy Michael Baden, M.D.)

Apprehension and similar emotional states are assuaged.

For the narcotic addict and for other persons who are not in pain, a single injection usually produces a pleasant state of positive euphoria. But some persons vomit or exhibit an extreme state of pallor. Further, a state of easily aroused semisomnolence (nodding) may be observed. Unaccustomed energy may be displayed. The sensorium remains intact, and skilled acts are not grossly impaired. Increased fantasy, measured by the Rorschach test, has been reported to occur after the parenteral administration of morphine.

Intravenous injection produces some specific phenomena. Although opiates typically decrease sexual activity and potency, addicts occasionally report improved sexual performance, which can be ascribed to a reduction of anxiety and a delay in orgasm.

Flushing and itching of the skin are also common after the intravenous injection of morphine. Pupillary constriction, decreased respiratory rate, a slight lowering of the body temperature, and spasms of smooth muscle sphincters are also seen after single doses of morphine.

The analgesic effect of a single dose of morphine reaches its peak intensity about 20 minutes after an intravenous injection, and about 1 hour after a subcutaneous injection. The analgesic effect persists for 4 to 6 hours.

Morphine and heroin addicts may take varying amounts of those drugs daily. Tolerance to all effects of opiates does not develop equally.

A patient or an addict who is tolerant to one opiate is also tolerant to another, even if the two drugs are chemically dissimilar. Surprisingly large doses—hundreds of milligrams of heroin or as much as 5g of morphine—have been reportedly taken by tolerant addicts. In the nontolerant person, death has been reported after the administration of as little as 60 mg of morphine.

Street heroin is heavily diluted with a variety of substances, particularly large amounts of quinine. Other substances—such as amphetamines, caffeine, phencyclidine (PCP or angel dust), and even sodium cyanide—have also been found in street samples. Death from heroin use has been ascribed to the additional substances added to street heroin. Although it is generally stated that the usual street bag contains 10 mg of heroin, there is wide variation.

The misuse of opioids may result in acute or chronic intoxication or withdrawal, characterized by the abstinence syndrome. In DSM-III, these direct effects on the central nervous system are classified under "substance-induced organic mental disorders." This classification is distinguished from "substance use disorders, opioid abuse and opioid dependence," which deal with the behavior associated with taking opioids.

### Acute Intoxication

Opioid overdose causes marked unresponsiveness, slow and periodic respiration, pinpoint pupils, bradycardia, hypotension, and hypothermia. The pupils may be dilated in cases of severe poisoning; reflexes may be absent, cyanosis marked, and the pulse rapid, weak, and thready. Mild opiate poisoning should be treated vigorously by gastric lavage, if the drug has been taken orally. If necessary, the air passages should be cleared, an airway or trachea cannula inserted, and artificial respiration instituted.

Narcotic addicts are reported to have a high mortality rate due to acute illness associated with drug abuse. Tetanus, acute viral hepatitis, and malaria—diseases that can be causally related to addiction—accounted for less than 2 percent of the 385 deaths of hospitalized narcotic addicts at the Lexington Kentucky Clinical Research Center during the years 1935 to 1966. Heart disease (including bacterial endocarditis), tuberculosis, and carcinoma of the lung accounted for more than half of the deaths. Tuberculosis and nephritis were more frequent causes of addict deaths than might be expected in random samples of the United States population.

Except for overdoses and withdrawal symptoms, medical complications associated with heroin use are caused by contaminants in the injected material or by unsterile injection techniques. In 1972, complications associated with heroin addiction were the leading cause of death in males between the ages of 15 and 35. Most of these deaths were caused by unsterile procedures that produced hepatitis, bacterial endocarditis, tetanus, or pneumonia.

**Treatment.** If a patient is brought unconscious into a hospital as a result of taking a drug overdose, immediate treatment should be instituted. The first and most crucial need is to guarantee an open airway to provide ventilation. At times, intubation or a tracheotomy is required (see Fig. 3). The majority of patients require immediate treatment, since they have taken heroin or a combination of heroin and methadone or other drugs, such as barbiturates. If opioid overdose is suspected, naloxone (Narcan), given intravenously (0.4 to 0.8 mg), may

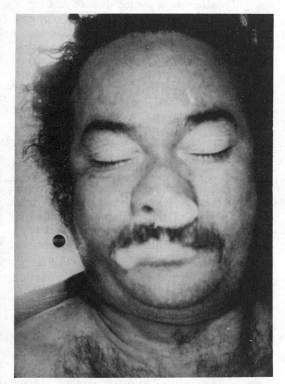

FIGURE 3. Man frothing at the mouth. (Courtesy Michael Baden, M.D.)

be lifesaving and diagnostic. This therapy should lead to an immediate recovery of consciousness, or a lightening of the comatose state if the offending agent is an opioid. If repeated doses of naloxone fail to elicit a response, a nonopioid must be responsible.

A good deal of care should be taken when administering opiate antagonists to physically dependent persons who have taken an overdose, because the antagonist may precipitate violent abstinence symptoms. The action of naloxone is much shorter than that of opioids, and an unconscious patient should be observed carefully while additional doses of 0.4 mg of naloxone are given intravenously or intramuscularly until respiration and other vital signs are at acceptable levels and the patient regains consciousness. The mere regaining of consciousness is not an adequate criterion for discharge. Observation must be continued, with appropriate injections of naloxone, so that certainty is established that there will be no relapse.

A constant infusion of naloxone hydrochloride has been recommended in methadone overdoses. Methadone overdoses have been increasing, as has been the accidental and even fatal ingestion of the drug by children. Methadone may persist at toxic levels for 24 hours; both nalorphine and naloxone remain at therapeutic levels for only a few hours. Therefore, methadone overdose patients may initially respond to the narcotic antagonists, but can subsequently relapse into coma if they are not treated with repeated doses for 24 hours or longer. Accordingly, a patient who continues to have relapses after single-ampule doses of the antagonist drug should be given an intravenous drip of naloxone. The dosage must be established empirically, according to the individual patient's response, paying primary attention to the restoration and maintenance of respiration. No significant side effects of naloxone treatment are known, and it is the recommended treatment.

### Chronic Intoxication

With the continuing use of opioids the manifestations of tolerance are observed. These manifestations include a decline in the relief of pain and anxiety, a diminution in the development of euphoria, little change in the rate of respiration, and a marked decrease in nausea and vomiting. Tolerance does not develop to the constriction of pupils, smooth muscle spasms, constipation, impotence, and amenorrhea. Increasing the dose of the opiate may restore the original effects of the drug, but even enormous doses may not recapture the previous euphoria. Instead, after high degrees of tolerance and physical dependence have occurred, there is the overwhelming feeling of dysphoria, anxiety, and guilt feelings; and, supposedly, the addicted person's predominant motivation is to avoid the abstinence phenomenon. However, this description does not take into account the long-term, irregular uses of morphine or heroin by the so-called weekend addict.

## Withdrawal

The abstinence phenomenon consists of a constellation of signs that reach peak intensity on the second or third day after the last dose of the opiate. These signs subside rapidly during the next 7 days. However, symptoms may persist for 6 months or longer. During the abstinence period, a single dose of an opiate abolishes the abstinence phenomenon, which reappears after the effects of the new drug have worn off. The untreated abstinence syndrome is generally milder than the dramatic depiction of cold-turkey withdrawal. However, the syndrome is dangerous to a person with heart disease, tuberculosis, or other chronic debilitating conditions. The yawning, rhinorrhea, lacrimation, pupillary dilation, sweating, piloerection, and restlessness are observed from 12 to 16 hours after the last dose of an opiate. Later, muscular aches and twitching, abdominal cramps, vomiting, diarrhea, hypertension, insomnia, anorexia, agitation, profuse sweating, weight loss, hyperglycemia, increased output of 17-ketosteroids, and spontaneous ejaculation or profuse menstrual bleeding have been observed as part of the abstinence phenomenon. But there are marked individual differences.

The abstinence syndrome after the withdrawal of heroin is identical to the syndrome of morphine abstinence. Methadone has been found to be more addictive than had been believed, and its withdrawal symptoms last far longer than those encountered with heroin.

An abstinence syndrome may be precipitated by the administration of an antagonist. The symptoms may begin within 60 seconds after an intravenous injection.

## Diagnosis

A history and a physical examination are usually sufficient to make a diagnosis of opioid abuse or dependency. The diagnosis can be made more accurately and can be differentiated from other substance abuse or dependency by means of opioid antagonists and laboratory examinations. As in all medicine, a comprehensive history, including a detailed drug history, is a necessary first step. However, because of the ille-

gality and the stigma attached to opioid use, and because of the deceptions used by addicts in an effort to obtain opioids by prescription, the history obtained may be misleading. Furthermore, a patient may be brought to an emergency room unable to give a history, since he may be in an unconscious state.

Certain physical findings are frequently found in heroin dependency. For example, in the skin there may be needle tracks, bluish phlebitis scars, ulcerating nodules, round punched-out atrophic lesions, brawny subcutaneous edema, and subcutaneous abscesses. Tattoos are often present and are frequently found in the drug-using and drug-abusing population. In the vascular system there may be, in addition to the tracks marks and hyperpigmentation, venous thromboses and silver streaking. Excoriations and perforations of the nasal septum may be found, and the presence of miotic pupils is invariable. Icterus, an enlarged liver, or lymphadenopathy may also be seen.

The typical abstinence syndrome is a good clue to the diagnosis of an addiction. Its observation over a period of 24 to 48 hours in a drug-controlled setting discloses all or some of these signs. A more rapid method of diagnosis is the administration of naloxone, starting with an intramuscular dose of 0.16 mg. If there are no signs of abstinence, a second dose of 0.24 mg is given intravenously. Observations are repeated in 15 minutes.

If opiates have been used in the past 24 hours, they may be detected in the urine. The urine tests for morphine and its analogues include radioimmunoassay (RIA), the free radical assay technique (FRAT test), and the enzyme-multiplied immunoassay technique (EMIT). Thin-layer or gas-liquid chromatography is also used.

## Treatment

No treatment method yet developed has solved all the complex problems involved in drug abuse. In view of the numerous contributing factors to drug abuse, it is clear that a variety of methods must be available, and the modality or program appropriate for a particular patient should be selected.

One of the major considerations in drug treatment is the social cost in terms of treatment programs, damage to society inflicted by untreated addicts, and, especially, the addicts' suffering and self-damage.

## Detoxification

The most widely used method of detoxification is that of methadone substitution, now most often managed on an ambulatory basis. The necessary prerequisites are a complete medical and psychiatric history, and a thorough physical examination.

An initial dose of methadone, large enough to suppress the abstinence syndrome, is administered orally in an orange solution. Various methods may be used to make a rough estimate of the amount of heroin being taken—the amount of money spent a day or the number of bags bought, for instance. Generally, an initial dose of 30 to 40 mg is sufficient. In calculations, 1 mg of methadone can be considered equivalent in its ability to suppress the abstinence syndrome to 1 mg of heroin, and 3 mg of methadone can be considered equivalent to 4 mg of morphine or 0.5 mg of hydromorphone.

After the satisfactory initial suppression of the abstinence syndrome, the methadone is withdrawn progressively over a period of 3 to 7 days. Generally, the rate of withdrawal is 5 mg a day. In this manner, the withdrawal is generally smooth and without complications, except for complaints of weakness, disturbed sleep, or vague pains when the dose of methadone gets low or shortly after its total withdrawal. The judicious use of sedatives or tranquilizers can be beneficial.

Special attention must be paid to the care of patients using barbiturate drugs or alcohol in excess. If there is a history of dependence on barbiturates, alcohol, or other sedatives, appropriate measures for detoxification from these substances must also be taken to prevent the emergence of seizures or delirium tremens.

There are various modifications of the methadone-withdrawal schedule. For example, in some instances, addicts have been allowed to set their own schedules for the gradual reduction of the methadone dose. Alternatively, rapid or precipitated withdrawal has been recommended.

Patients on low-dosage methadone can begin a narcotic antagonist in 48 hours, but the procedure is limited, since its implementation requires inpatient care.

**Other Agents for Detoxification.** Clonidine (Catapres) has been used with reported success in withdrawal from methadone. Clonidine is given orally (0.1 to 0.3 mg, 3 to 4 times per day). The therapy is based on the hypothesis that opiate withdrawal is mediated through a noradrenergic mechanism that is blocked by clonidine.

Lofexindine, another agonist with less sedating effects, is under investigation.

Propoxyphene and dextropropoxyphene (Darvon) have been tried as detoxification agents with some success.

### Therapeutic Communities

Therapeutic communities demanding total commitment from the patients are residential treatment programs that attempt to deal with the psychological causes of addiction by changing the addict's character and personality.

The program goals of therapeutic communities are alleged to be identical with those of the larger society. They aim to eliminate drug use and assume that once abstinence is achieved, the client can become a model citizen. Therapeutic communities share certain common characteristics. A major tenet is that addicts are immature people in flight from reality and responsibility; therefore, they must be given a second chance to grow up. Obstacles are created to enrollment in the programs as a test of the patient's motivation. It is assumed that if the patient can overcome these obstacles, including financial obstacles, his desire to become drug free is genuine. The programs of the therapeutic communities consist largely of harsh group encounters, reeducation, and hard work. Usually, they are nonprofessionally oriented and stress self-help. They are abstinence oriented, and the abstinence is reinforced through intense interaction with others living in the same group. Firm rules of conduct are established and stringently enforced by group confrontation and punishment.

The therapeutic community—whatever its set-up, program, or degree of isolation from the community—adheres to the concept that the abuse of drugs is symptomatic of underlying antisocial personality problems and behavior patterns. The nation's largest therapeutic community for drug-free treatment and rehabilitation of former heroin addicts is Phoenix House.

Therapeutic communities often use group psychotherapy and encounter groups, as well as milieu therapy, in which the addict lives and works within a certain social structure. Through peer influence, behavior modification is encouraged. In a study, it was concluded that "addiction is an aspect of a general sickness dimension which undergoes a positive therapeutic change with time spent in Phoenix House Program."

The problem with therapeutic communities as a treatment method is that they seem to be suitable for very few people. Often as many as three-quarters of those who enter drop out within the first month.

### Methadone Maintenance

The most widely used method of treatment of heroin abuse is that of methadone maintenance, introduced by Vincent Dole and Marie Nyswander in 1964, either in an inpatient setting or on an ambulatory basis.

The pharmacology of methadone is like that of morphine, and its properties are qualitatively identical to morphine's properties. The outstanding properties of methadone, are effective analgesic activity, its efficacy by the oral route, and its extended duration of action in physically dependent individuals. Methadone also causes sedation and respiratory depression; its effect on smooth muscle and the cardiovascular system is like that of morphine. In human beings, methadone is constipating but less so than morphine, and it causes biliary tract spasm.

The typical program operates as follows: The minimum accepted age is 18 years, except in certain experimental adolescent programs. At least a 2-year history of daily heroin use and proof of addiction are usual prerequisites for admission to a methadone-maintenance program. If there is any question of heroin addiction, many clinics verify by using naloxone as a diagnostic procedure. After an interview, which includes the taking of a careful drug history, the patient is checked through a computerized data bank to spot addicts who wish to receive multiple simultaneous treatment. The addict is inducted into treatment after a variable waiting period that depends on the clinic load. Confidentiality is guaranteed by legislation. Induction necessitates a complete medical evaluation, including medical history, a physical examination, and appropriate laboratory tests. Most clinics operate on a 6-day-a-week basis. The patient is initially placed on an oral dose of 20 to 40 mg of methadone a day, depending on the estimate of the amount of heroin taken as determined by the number of bags taken or the amount of money spent a day. These doses are gradually increased up to 80 to 120 mg a day over 6 weeks. During this period, in order to avoid the addict's sale of his tablets or the use of the methadone intravenously, the clinic delivers the methadone to the patient in liquid form, and it is consumed immediately. It may be liquid methadone mixed with synthetic orange juice, a diluted cherry syrup of methadone, or a dissolved tablet of methadone, such as a dissolved Disket or Westadone tablet.

Urine samples may be taken randomly or at each visit; the samples are analyzed for the presence of opioids, barbiturates, amphetamines, or tranquilizers. After 6 to 8 weeks, if the patient is stabilized, a second phase of treatment begins. Daily visits to the clinic continue, with urine monitoring and the administration under observation of the methadone dose.

If the patient remains in the program, is making progress in rehabilitation, and no longer shows any signs of drug abuse or serious abuse of alcohol, he may enter the third phase of treatment. A minimum of 9 months in the second phase is necessary before a patient can be considered for the third phase. In the third phase, the patient must visit the clinic twice a week, at which time he collects supplies for the intervening period. On at least one visit, urine is collected, and the dose of methadone is taken under observation. This phase may continue indefinitely, but there may be attempts at detoxification, either at the patient's request or at the desire of the physician.

The frequency of visits is often cumbersome, particularly for those patients who are employed, and under the best of circumstances there is a great deal of diversion of methadone from patients to the black market. Therefore, the search for longer-acting forms of methadone was instituted. Although the goal was for a drug that would be active for a minimum of 1 week, the most successful thus far has been levo-$\alpha$-acetylmethadol (LAAM). LAAM is effective for 2 or 3 days in the treatment of tolerant and narcotic-dependent patients. Thus, it is possible to set up a schedule of using LAAM three times a week in doses of 30 to 80 mg of LAAM a day. The results with LAAM seem to be similar to those with methadone at a maintenance dose of 80 to 100 mg a day.

**Complications.** One of the unresolved questions in methadone maintenance programs is whether to aim for a therapeutic goal of attaining drug abstinence at some appropriate time, or to opt for the indeterminate administration of methadone, possibly for life. The Food and Drug Administration stated that the administration of methadone to a person in a maintenance program shall be discontinued within 2 years after such treatment began, unless further administration is based on clinical judgment recorded in the patient's clinical record, or unless the patient's status indicates that such treatment should be continued for a longer period of time. The Food and Drug Administration further stated that any patient continuing on methadone for longer than 2 years should be subject to periodic reconsideration for discontinuance of such therapy. Decisions regarding detoxification should be made by the physician on an individual basis after a year or more of successful treatment and after weighing the degree of rehabilitation, the relapse potential, and the patient's wishes.

Unforeseen side effects of methadone maintenance include the accidental ingestion of methadone by children and the presence of methadone in mother's milk, making breastfeeding inadvisable and raising the possibility of withdrawal in the newborn. Nonetheless, methadone-maintenance proponents have compared methadone with insulin for diabetic patients and with digitalis for those with heart disease.

**Heroin vs. Methadone.** Oral methadone has been compared to intravenous heroin at a London clinic in a random assignment study. Those assigned to heroin continued to inject and stayed involved with the drug culture. Some sold part of their prescriptions; others supplemented clinic supplies with opioids from illicit sources. Some of those assigned to oral maintenance refused to participate and left treatment immediately; many others left subsequently. At 12 months, only 29 percent of oral methadone patients were still at the clinic. However, 40 percent of oral methadone patients not at the clinic had become entirely abstinent from opioids. Within the year, more heroin patients than oral methadone patients died or were admitted to hospitals for drug related problems. A strong relationship was found between criminal activity and continued illicit opioid use. Differences in baseline rates of criminality make it difficult to evaluate the net impact of the two types of treatment on crime. As is the case in the United States, at admission, about one-third of patients were mildly depressed, 58 percent had a history of depressive episodes, and 38 percent had made a suicide gesture.

**Advantages.** Methadone maintenance removes the addict from a dependence on injecting himself many times a day with unsterile materials. He no longer needs to engage in illegal practices to obtain the money for his habit. He does not have to deal with criminals to buy his supplies or to sell stolen merchandise. He is not preoccupied during his waking hours with plans to procure his fix.

Although complete abstinence from narcotics is an optional goal, many addicts cannot remain abstinent permanently. For these addicts, a controlled addiction to methadone is preferable to an uncontrolled addiction to heroin. Methadone maintenance is held to be the only realistic mass-treatment modality for the hundreds of thousands of heroin addicts.

The level of certain criminal activities is expected to decrease as significant numbers of people enter methadone maintenance-programs. Some support for this assumption has come from a few metropolitan areas. The methadone-maintenance patient tends to engage in constructive activities. In many instances, he becomes self-supporting. He is capable of driving a car, operating heavy machinery, and performing complex psychomotor tasks. Methadone-maintenance programs are not expensive in comparison with other therapeutic efforts. Between $1,000 and $2,000 a patient-year is sufficient to maintain a well-run program.

**Disadvantages.** The patient remains addicted to a narcotic. He may have to remain on methadone permanently. The amount of methadone given for maintenance may be lethal if consumed by a nontolerant person. The diversion of methadone into the black market by patients or by a member of the clinic staff is a problem, especially in poorly managed programs. Just what happens to the heroin not used by methadone-maintenance patients is not known. It may be a source of supply for new addict populations. The requirement to return to the clinic daily is an inconvenience, especially for the working patient. However, a longer-acting methadone analogue (levo-$\alpha$-acetylmethadol) is now under study. Maintenance may make it unnecessary for a significant number to mature out of drug addiction.

### Opioid Antagonists

Since the 1960s, various antagonists have been used to treat opiate dependence. These agents are useful in heroin and other narcotic addictions, since they block or antagonize the opiates, preventing them from acting. Unlike methadone, the narcotic antagonists do not in themselves exert narcotic effects, nor are they addictive.

The conditioning hypothesis suggests that the extinction of drug-seeking behavior could provide a means to reverse the pathophysiology of addiction. If the relief afforded by narcotics during the period of conditioned abstinence were blocked, the extinction would be accomplished by a substance without narcotic effects that would block the ability of administered opiates to affect the central nervous system. Narcotic antagonists are such substances. Molecular alterations of narcotic analgesics have yielded compounds that antagonize the respiratory effects of narcotics. $N$-Allylnormorphine or nalorphine (Nalline) was extensively studied in 1950, and has been used in the treatment of opiate overdose. Similar chemical substitutions have yielded cyclazocine, naloxone, and naltrexone—three antagonists used for the treatment of opiate dependence.

**Cyclazocine.** This $N$-substitute benzomorphan derivative, chemically similar to nalorphine hydrochloride, is an effective opioid-blocking agent. In addition, cyclazocine is a powerful analgesic but has several side effects, including dysphoria, visual distortions, racing thoughts, anxiety, and sedation.

A typical cyclazocine program operates as follows. Addicts are selected, detoxified from opiates, and permitted a drug-free interval of 7 days. Originally, a period of 40 days was used to induct patients to a maintenance level, but the period has now been reduced to 4 days. This reduction was facilitated by experience with the compound and by the awareness that naloxone (Narcan), a pure narcotic antagonist, antagonizes the side effects of cyclazocine reported by persons during rapid induction.

The present method attains the therapeutic level of 4 mg of cyclazocine a day in 4 days by daily increments of 1 mg; 600 mg of naloxone are available every 4 hours on request. Apparently, the naloxone does not interfere with the antagonistic effects of cyclazocine. Cyclazocine was not acceptable for large-scale clinical trials because of its side effects, in spite of encouraging results in carefully controlled small-series reports.

**Naloxone.** N-Allylnoroxymorphone or naloxone (Narcan) is a narcotic antagonist without agonistic features. It is the substance closest to an ideal opioid antagonist. It is 5 to 8 times as effective as nalorphine in antagonizing opiate effects in animals. The repeated administration of naloxone does not promote the development of tolerance, nor does the withdrawal symptom occur after the abrupt cessation of drug administration. Naloxone has a short duration of action. To obtain a 24-hour blocking action, the therapist must give a single 3-mg oral dose. Thus, naloxone did not prove to be feasible for clinical use in the treatment of opioid addiction.

**Naltrexone.** Naltrexone is an N-cyclopropylmethyl congener of naloxone. About 17 times more potent than naloxone as a morphine antagonist in humans, naltrexone is virtually free of agonist properties and has a duration of action that is significantly longer than that of naloxone. The 80- to 120-mg oral dose produces opiate blockade for as long as 48 hours with few side effects; a dose of 160 to 200 mg produces opiate blockade for 72 hours. Thus, naltrexone seems to be a promising longer-acting form of antagonist for oral use.

### Comparison of Antagonist and Methadone Models

One of the great advantages of methadone is that it is an addicting substance, and patients continue to return; they must do so daily or else be given supplies for self-administration.

The major weakness of the antagonist model is the lack of any mechanism compelling the addict receiving the antagonist to continue. Thus, the addict on cyclazocine may, under personal stress, decide not to take the cyclazocine on a Saturday morning. By Sunday morning it is possible for him to experience a high from heroin if a sufficient amount is available. The withdrawal symptoms from cyclazocine are much milder than those from methadone, and as readily tolerated. The addict can then return to cyclazocine on Monday morning and continue on the program, or he may decide to abandon the whole program. But the addict on methadone maintenance cannot skip or stop without serious consequences. He may trade off on a weekend and sell some of his methadone to obtain some heroin, but he must continue on methadone.

### Treatment of Patients with Special Medical and Surgical Problems

**Opioid Overdose.** The opioid overdose syndrome consists of coma, severely depressed respiration, and pinpoint pupils. In severe cases, gross pulmonary edema occurs with frothing at the mouth, but X-ray evidence of pulmonary changes is seen even in less severe cases. Pulmonary edema is an opioid effect, and is seen with overdoses of oral, medically prescribed opioids. Depending on when the patient is found, there may also be cyanosis, cold clammy skin, and decreased body temperature. Blood pressure is decreased, but only falls dramatically with severe anoxia, at which point pupils may dilate. Cardiac arrhythmias have been reported and may be related either to anoxia or the use of quinine as an adulterant.

The first task is to ensure an adequate airway; tracheopharyngeal secretions should be aspirated. An airway may be inserted. The patient should be ventilated mechanically until naloxone, a specific opioid antagonist, can be given. Naloxone is administered intravenously, slowly (about 0.7 mg per 70 kg initially). Signs of improvement (increase in respiratory rate and pupillary dilation) should occur promptly. In physically dependent addicts, too much naloxone may produce signs of withdrawal as well as reversal of overdosage. If there is no response to initial dosage, naloxone may be repeated after intervals of about 5 minutes; if no response is observed after 4 to 5 mg, the CNS depression is probably not due solely to opioids. Even when the patient responds, additional complications, such as aspiration pneumonia and/or neurological damage, may be found. Pulmonary edema may persist and require positive end-expiratory pressure ventilation and supplemental oxygen. The duration of action of naloxone is short compared to many opioids, such as methadone, and repeated administration may be required to prevent recurrence of opioid toxicity.

**Other Medical and Surgical Problems.** When former opioid addicts and patients maintained on methadone are admitted for medical treatment or surgery, the patient should be told what will be done and that adequate analgesia will be provided. Disclosing the precise dosage is usually unnecessary. It is inappropriate to stress the patient by beginning detoxification before the required medical or surgical treatment has been accomplished. Patients on methadone should be continued on their usual oral dose, or, if oral administration is not possible, should be given their usual dose parenterally in divided doses. Methadone may be omitted on the day of surgery. It is reported that despite their tolerance to the euphorigenic effects of heroin, hospitalized patients maintained on methadone experience satisfactory analgesia with 50 to 100 mg of meperidine given parenterally every 3 to 4 hours.

Opioid addicts who are taking street drugs when admitted should be placed on oral or parenteral methadone to prevent withdrawal; 30 to 40 mg per day in divided doses is usually sufficient. These patients, too, will require additional analgesia depending on the problems and procedures. Patients maintained on methadone should not be given pentazocine, butorphanol, or nalbuphine, since these drugs may precipitate withdrawal.

**The Pregnant Addict.** While opioid withdrawal is almost never fatal for the otherwise healthy adult, opioid withdrawal is hazardous to the fetus and can lead to miscarriage or fetal death. However, maintaining the pregnant addict on high doses of methadone carries the risk of severe withdrawal in the neonate. Maintenance on low doses of methadone may not adequately control the tendency to use illicit opioids, but there is a growing consensus that such low dose maintenance (10 to 20 mg per day) may be the least hazardous course to follow. At such dosage, neonatal withdrawal is usually mild and can be managed with low doses of paregoric. If the pregnancy begins while the patient is on high doses of methadone, reduction to lower dosage should be quite slow (e.g., 1 mg every 3 days) and fetal movements should be monitored.

## Prognosis

Recent research shows that the usual measures of treatment outcome (legitimate work, crime, drug use, family relationships, psychological adjustment) are relatively independent. Fur-thermore, they are predicated on different pretreatment variables. Thus, pretreatment history of high levels of criminal activity predicts posttreatment crime.

## Prevention

In the United States, there is a great preoccupation with drug-treatment programs and legislative controls. Prevention has been largely forgotten. With the constant recruitment of the young at younger and younger ages to drug use, the ultimate futility of treating or jailing established addicts is made clear. Everyone professes a commitment to prevention, but little can be described.

Until the 1960s, primary prevention was achieved by the deterrent force of harsh laws; when that deterrence failed, secondary prevention, through coercive intervention in the life of the user, was implemented. With the manifest failure of that intervention, the emphasis was placed on education and information. The instant expansion of many public information and school programs ended in discouraging evaluations. One fault was in the simple-minded presentation of scare and horror stories that proved at times to be far more fascinating to the young than they were effective in discouraging drug use.

A wiser course seems to be the integration of drug and drug-use information into broad hygiene and problem-solving courses in the schools, rather than the use of exclusive drug courses. The participation of students, faculty, and school administrators in the planning and implementation of these courses, with particular emphasis on students' playing a major and active role, is crucial for success.

Effective prevention also depends on active intervention in those institutions of society that contribute to the genesis of drug abuse. Although such pious hopes are dismissed as visionary or long in the future, the correction of gross inequities in society in regard to housing, race, youth, law, and personal values can only benefit the target population.

## REFERENCES

Berger P A, Akil H, Watson S J, Barchas J D: Behavioral pharmacology of the endorphins. Ann Rev Med *33:* 397, 1982.

Edwards G, Busch C, editors: *Drug Problems in Britain.* Academic Press, London, 1981.

Jaffe J H: Drug addiction and drug abuse. In *The Pharmacological Basis of Therapeutics*, A G Gilman, L S Goodman, A Gilman, editors, ed 6, p 535. Macmillan, New York, 1980.

Jaffe J H: Opioid dependence. In *Comprehensive Textbook of Psychiatry*, ed 4, H I Kaplan, B J Sadock, editors, p 987. Williams & Wilkins, Baltimore, 1985.

Jaffe J H, Martin W R: Opioid analgesics and antagonists. In *The Pharmacological Basis of Therapeutics*, A G Gilman, L S Goodman, A Gilman, editors, ed 6, p 494. Macmillan, New York, 1980.

McLellan A T, Luborsky L, Woody G E, O'Brien C P, Druley K A: Predicting response to alcohol and drug abuse treatments. Arch Gen Psychiatry *40:* 620, 1983.

Meyer R E, Mirin S M: *The Heroin Stimulus: Implications for a Theory of Addiction.* Plenum Medical Book Co., New York, 1979.

Rounsaville B J, Weissman M M, Kleber H, Wilber C: Heterogeneity of psychiatric diagnosis in treated opiate addicts. Arch Gen Psychiatry *39:* 161, 1982.

Senay E C: *Substance Abuse Disorders in Clinical Practice.* John Wright/PSG Inc., Littleton, MA, 1983.

Simpson D D, Joe G W, Bracy S A: Six-year follow-up of opioid addicts after admission to treatment. Arch Gen Psychiatry *39:* 1318, 1982

Verebey K, editor: *Opioids in Mental Illness: Theories, Clinical Observations, and Treatment Possibilities.* The New York Academy of Science, New York, 1982.

Wikler A: *Opioid Dependence: Mechanisms and Treatment.* Plenum Press, New York, 1980.

## 19.2   DRUG DEPENDENCE: NONNARCOTIC AGENTS

### Introduction

For purposes of this section, drug abuse means taking drugs at dose levels, and in circumstances and settings, that significantly augment their potential for harm. The critical issues are *not* whether such use is legal or prescribed by a physician or whether its purpose is therapy, pleasure, or consciousness expansion.

Psychological dependence, a difficult and obscure concept, can be defined as the development of a craving for the drug because of its pleasurable effects. The craving may be quite mild or so severe that it can be called a compulsion. Physical dependence implies a biochemical or physiological change in the body, making the continued presence of the drug necessary to avoid a withdrawal syndrome, which may be merely uncomfortable at one extreme or life-threatening at the other. Tolerance refers to a declining effect of the drug on repeated administration of the same dose, and a consequent necessity to increase the dosage in order to obtain the original euphoric effect.

Because the emphasis in this section is necessarily on the agents, rather than their users and abusers, it should be pointed out that most people can use most of these drugs without abusing them. Those who develop a psychological dependency may have such a make-up that one of the euphoriants becomes essential for them to experience either pleasure or a respite from pain. People with character disorders, anxiety, depression, feelings of inadequacy, or intolerable life situations are susceptible to dependency on any one of a number of these drugs, in addition to alcohol and the opiates.

### Marijuana

Drug preparations from the hemp plant vary widely in quality and potency, depending on the type (there are possibly three species or, alternatively, various ecotypes), climate, soil, cultivation, and method of preparation. When the cultivated plant is fully ripe, a sticky, golden yellow resin with a minty fragrance covers its flower clusters and top leaves. The plant's resin contains the active substances. Preparations of the drug come in three grades, identified by Indian names. The cheapest and least potent, called bhang, is derived from the cut tops of uncultivated plants and has a low resin content. Much of the marijuana smoked in the United States is of this grade. Ganja is obtained from the flowering tops and leaves of carefully selected cultivated plants, and it has a higher quality and quantity of resin. The third and highest grade of the drug, called charas in India, is largely made from the resin itself, obtained from the tops of mature plants. This version of the drug is properly called hashish. Hashish is roughly 5 to 8 times more potent than most of the marijuana regularly available in the United States. Recently, clandestine laboratories have developed, through a refluxing method, a product that is variously referred to as hashish oil, liquid hashish, and "the one"; it is considerably more potent than hashish, and samples have been found that contain more than 60 percent tetrahydrocannabinol.

The effects of cannabis—a general term for the various forms of the psychoactive products of the plant—in animals are confined to the central nervous system. The drug does not noticeably affect the gross behavior of rats or mice, or simple learning in rats; it does, however, calm mice that have been made aggressive by isolation, and in dogs it induces a dreamy, somnolent state reminiscent of the last stage of a human high. In large doses, cannabis produces in animals such symptoms as vomiting, diarrhea, fibrillary tremors, and failure of muscular coordination. Lethal doses have been established for a few animals; given by mouth, the lethal dose for cats, for example, is 3 g of charas, 8 g of ganja, or 10 g of bhang per kg of body weight. Huge doses have been given to dogs without causing death, and there has been no adequately documented case of a fatality from the drug in humans.

Most observers find that the effects from smoking last for 2 to 4 hours, and the effects from ingestion, 5 to 12 hours. For a new user, the initial anxiety that sometimes occurs is alleviated if supportive friends are present. It is contended that the intoxication heightens sensitivity to external stimuli, reveals details that would ordinarily be overlooked, makes colors seem brighter and richer, brings out values in works of art that previously had little or no meaning to the viewer, and enhances the appreciation of music. Many jazz and rock musicians have said they perform better under the influence of marijuana, but this effect has not been objectively confirmed.

The sense of time is distorted; 10 minutes may seem like an hour. Curiously, there is often a splitting of consciousness, so that the smoker, while experiencing the high, is at the same time an objective observer of his own intoxication. He may, for example, be afflicted with paranoid thoughts, yet at the same time be reasonably objective about them and even laugh or scoff at them, and in a sense enjoy them. The ability to retain a degree of objectivity may explain the fact that many experienced users of marijuana manage to behave in a perfectly sober fashion in public even when they are highly intoxicated.

Marijuana is commonly referred to as a hallucinogen. Many of the phenomena associated with lysergic acid diethylamide (LSD) and LSD-type substances can be produced by cannabis. As with LSD, the wave-like aspect of the experience is often reported, as is the distorted perception of various parts of the body, spatial and temporal distortion, and depersonalization. Other phenomena commonly associated with both types of drugs are increased sensitivity to sound, synesthesia, heightened suggestibility, and a sense of thinking more clearly and having a deeper awareness of the meaning of things. Anxiety and paranoid reactions are also sometimes seen as consequences of either drug. However, the agonizingly nightmarish reactions that

even the experienced LSD user may endure are quite rare to the experienced marijuana smoker, not simply because he is using a far less potent drug but also because he has much closer and continuing control over the extent and the type of reaction he wishes to induce. Furthermore, cannabis has a tendency to produce sedation, whereas LSD and the LSD-type drugs may induce long periods of wakefulness and even restlessness. Unlike LSD, marijuana does not dilate the pupils or materially heighten blood pressure, reflexes, and body temperature. On the other hand, it does increase the pulse rate. However, it is questionable whether marijuana in doses ordinarily used in this country can produce true hallucinations. An important difference is the fact that tolerance rapidly develops with the LSD-type drugs, but very little, if at all, with cannabis. Finally, marijuana lacks the potent consciousness-altering qualities of LSD, peyote, mescaline, psilocybin, and so on. These differences, particularly the last, cast considerable doubt on marijuana's credentials for inclusion in this group of drugs.

DSM-III (see Table I) lists a diagnostic category of Cannabis Dependence with the following statement in the text: "The existence and significance of tolerance and withdrawal with regular heavy use of cannabis (Cannabis Dependence) is controversial."

There are those who develop some degree of dependence on cannabis, but this does not appear to have anything to do with tolerance. Furthermore, cannabis produces no withdrawal symptoms (and therefore no physical dependence). Its capacity to lead to psychological dependence is not nearly as strong as that of either tobacco or alcohol.

Only the unsophisticated continue to believe that cannabis leads to violence and crime. Indeed, instead of inciting criminal behavior, cannabis may tend to suppress it. The intoxication induces lethargy that is not conducive to any physical activity, let alone the committing of

TABLE I
DIAGNOSTIC CRITERIA FOR CANNABIS DEPENDENCE*

A. Either a pattern of pathological use or impairment in social or occupational functioning due to cannabis use.

*Pattern of pathologial use:* intoxication throughout the day; use of cannabis nearly every day for at least a month; episodes of Cannabis Delusional Disorder.

*Impairment in social or occupational functioning due to cannabis use:* e.g., marked loss of interest in activities previously engaged in, loss of friends, absence from work, loss of job, or legal difficulties (other than a single arrest due to possession, purchase, or sale of an illegal substance).

B. *Tolerance:* need for markedly increased amounts of cannabis to achieve the desired effect or markedly diminished effect with regular use of the same amount.

* From American Psychiatric Association: *Diagnostic and Statistical Manual of Mental Disorders*, ed 3. American Psychiatric Association, Washington, DC, 1980. Used with permission.

crimes. The release of inhibitions results in fantasy and verbal expressions, rather than behavioral expression. During the high, the marijuana user may say and think things he would not ordinarily, but he generally does not do things that are foreign to his nature. If he is not normally a criminal, he will not commit a crime under the influence of the drug.

There is little evidence that cannabis stimulates sexual desire or power. Nor is there evidence that marijuana weakens sexual desire. Many marijuana users report that the high enhances the enjoyment of sexual intercourse. It is questionable as to whether intoxication with marijuana breaks down moral barriers that are not already broken.

Long-term users of the potent versions of cannabis are typically passive, nonproductive, slothful, and totally lacking in ambition. This finding suggests that chronic use of the drug in its stronger forms may have debilitating effects, as prolonged heavy drinking does. There is a far more likely explanation, however, Many of those who take up cannabis seek to soften the impact of an otherwise unbearable reality. This explanation also applies to many of the "potheads" in the United States. In most situations, one cannot be certain which came first—the drug on the one hand, or the depression, anxiety, personality disorder, or seemingly intolerable life situation on the other.

There is a substantial body of evidence indicating that moderate use of marijuana does not produce physical or mental deterioration. A common assertion made about cannabis is that it may lead to psychosis. There is a vast literature on this subject, and it divides into all shades of opinion.

The explanation for such psychoses is that a person maintaining a delicate balance of ego functioning—so that, for instance, the ego is threatened by a severe loss, a surgical assault or even an alcoholic debauch—may also be overwhelmed or precipitated into a schizophrenic reaction by a drug that alters, however mildly, his state of consciousness. This concatenation of factors—a person whose ego is already over-burdened in its attempts to manage a great deal of anxiety and to prevent distortion of perception and body image, plus the taking of a drug that, in some persons, promotes just these effects—may, indeed, be the last straw in precipitating a schizophrenic break.

Although there is little evidence for the existence of a cannabis psychosis, it seems clear that the drug may precipitate in susceptible people one of several types of mental dysfunction. The most serious and disturbing of these dysfunctions is toxic psychosis. This is an acute state that resembles the delirium of a high fever and is caused by the presence in the brain of toxic substances that interfere with a variety of cerebral functions. Generally speaking, as the toxins disappear, so do the symptoms of toxic psychosis. This type of reaction may be caused by any number of substances taken either as intended or as inadvertent overdoses. The syndrome often includes clouding of consciousness, restlessness, confusion, bewilderment, disorientation, dream-like thinking, apprehension, fear, illusions, and hallucinations. It generally requires a rather large ingested dose of cannabis to induce a toxic psychosis. Such a reaction is apparently much less likely to occur when cannabis is smoked, perhaps because not enough of the active substances can be absorbed sufficiently rapidly or possibly because, in the process of smoking, those cannabinol derivatives that are most likely to precipitate this syndrome are modified in some way as yet unknown (see Table II).

There are people who may suffer what are usually short-lived, acute anxiety states, sometimes with and sometimes without accompanying paranoid thoughts. The anxiety may reach such proportions as properly to be called panic. Such panic reactions, although uncommon, probably constitute the most frequent adverse reaction to the moderate use of smoked marijuana. During this reaction, the sufferer may believe that the various distortions of his perception of his body mean that he is dying or that he is undergoing some great physical catastrophe, and similarly he may interpret the psycho-

TABLE II
DIAGNOSTIC CRITERIA FOR CANNABIS ABUSE*

A. *Pattern of pathological use:* intoxication throughout the day; use of cannabis nearly every day for at least a month; episodes of Cannabis Delusional Disorder.

B. *Impairment in social or occupational functioning due to cannabis use:* e.g., marked loss of interest in activities previously engaged in, loss of friends, absence from work, loss of job, or legal difficulties (other than due to a single arrest for possession, purchase, or sale of the substance).

C. Duration of disturbance of at least 1 month.

\* From American Psychiatric Association: *Diagnostic and Statistical Manual of Mental Disorders*, ed 3. American Psychiatric Association, Washington, DC, 1980. Used with permission.

logical distortions induced by the drug as an indication that he is losing his sanity. Panic states may, albeit rarely, be so severe as to incapacitate, usually for a relatively short period of time.

These reactions are self-limiting, and simple reassurance is the best method of treatment. Perhaps the main danger to the user is that he will be diagnosed as having a toxic psychosis, an unfortunately common mistake. Users with this kind of reaction may be quite distressed, but they are not psychotic, inasmuch as the sine qua non of sanity, the ability to test reality, remains intact, and the panicked user is invariably able to relate his discomfort to the drug. There is no disorientation, nor are there true hallucinations. Sometimes this panic reaction is accompanied by paranoid ideation. The user may, for example, believe that the others in the room, especially if they are not well known to him, have some hostile intentions toward him or that someone is going to inform on him, often to the police, for smoking marijuana. Generally speaking, these paranoid ideas are not strongly held, and simple reassurance dispels them. Anxiety reactions and paranoid thoughts are much more likely in someone who is taking the drug for the first time or in an unpleasant or unfamiliar setting, than in an experienced user who is comfortable with his surroundings and companions; the reaction is very rare where marijuana is a casually accepted part of the social scene.

Rarely, but especially among new users of marijuana, there occurs an acute depressive reaction that resembles the neurotic type. It is generally rather mild and transient, but may sometimes require psychiatric intervention. This type of reaction is most likely to occur in a user who has some degree of underlying depression; it is as though the drug allowed the depression to be felt and experienced as such. Again, set and setting play important parts.

There are accepted medical indications for the use of marijuana. These include treatment of some cases of glaucoma, and the amelioration of side effects, such as nausea, in cancer chemotherapy. Further experimental uses are being evaluated, such as employing marijuana for the relief of spasticity in some instances of multiple sclerosis.

## Amphetamines

Amphetamines are synthetic drugs that produce a sense of increased energy, an enhanced capacity for work, and a feeling of exhilaration.

Amphetamines have accepted therapeutic applications in treating narcolepsy and attention deficit (hyperkinetic) disorders of childhood, and as a short-term adjunct to tricyclic antidepressants in the treatment of depression. They are also prescribed as a short-term therapy for weight reduction, as well as for mild depression and senile withdrawn behavior in the elderly.

With respect to amphetamines, the fourth edition of the AMA's *Drug Evaluation* (1980) states that "no controlled studies exist to support their effectiveness in most depressive illnesses." Many clinicians, however, have observed that the judicious use of these drugs has been most useful in the treatment of some affective disorders. Pressure from regulatory agencies, such as the FDA, DEA, and various state agencies, has seriously curtailed the utilization of amphetamines. The authors feel that this interference with the practice of medicine has prevented the potential value of these drugs from being properly evaluated and utilized by the clinician. More and more reports are appearing in the literature about the positive effects of these drugs in selected cases of depression.

The signs and symptoms of acute amphetamine poisoning and poisoning from chronic use include flushing, pallor, cyanosis, fever, tachycardia, serious cardiac problems, markedly elevated blood pressure, hemorrhage or other vascular accidents, nausea, vomiting, difficulty in breathing, tremor, ataxia, loss of sensory abilities, twitching, tetany, convulsions, loss of consciousness, and coma. Death from overdose is usually associated with hyperpyrexia, convulsions, and cardiovascular shock. When intravenous abuse of amphetamines became increasingly popular in the early 1960s, several new spectra of serious physiological reactions were reported. Since then, severe serum hepatitis, lung abscess, endocarditis and necrotizing angiitis resulting from intravenous abuse of amphetamines have been fairly common occurrences.

Adverse psychological effects are also common. Restlessness, dysphoria, logorrhea, insomnia, some degree of confusion, tension, anxiety, and fear to the point of acute panic have been reported by a large number of authors. Amphetamine psychosis, once considered extremely rare, is another reported effect. Even short-term administration of dextroamphetamine to persons who are nonpsychotic can precipitate a paranoid psychosis (see Table III). Other sympathomimetic drugs, such as phenylpronanoline which is used in over-the-counter decongestant or anorectic agents, have been implicated in producing psychotic like states.

With few exceptions, the symptoms disappear within days or, at the most, weeks after the drug

TABLE III
DIAGNOSTIC CRITERIA FOR AMPHETAMINE OR SIMILARLY ACTING SYMPATHOMIMETIC ABUSE*

A. *Pattern of pathological use:* inability to reduce or stop use; intoxication throughout the day; use of substance nearly every day for at least 1 month; episodes of either Amphetamine or Similarly Acting Sympathomimetic Delusional Disorder or Amphetamine or Similarly Acting Sympathomimetic Delirium.

B. *Impairment in social or occupational functioning due to amphetamine or similarly acting sympathomimetic use:* e.g., fights, loss of friends, absence from work, loss of job, or legal difficulties (other than due to a single arrest for possession, purchase, or sale of the substance).

C. Duration of disturbance of at least 1 month:

* From American Psychiatric Association: *Diagnostic and Statistical Manual of Mental Disorders*, ed 3. American Psychiatric Association, Washington, DC, 1980. Used with permission.

TABLE IV
DIAGNOSTIC CRITERIA FOR AMPHETAMINE OR SIMILARLY ACTING SYMPATHOMIMETIC DEPENDENCE*

Either tolerance or withdrawal:

*Tolerance:* need for markedly increased amounts of substance to achieve the desired effect, or markedly diminished effect with regular use of the same amount.

*Withdrawal:* development of Amphetamine or Similarly Acting Sympathomimetic Withdrawal after cessation of or reduction in substance use.

* From American Psychiatric Association: *Diagnostic and Statistical Manual of Mental Disorders*, ed 3. American Psychiatric Association, Washington, DC, 1980. Used with permission.

has been withdrawn. Distinguishing amphetamine psychosis from paranoid schizophrenia depends heavily on this factor of duration of the symptoms. In some patients, suspiciousness and tendencies toward misinterpretation and ideas of reference may remain for months after the manifest, overt psychosis has disappeared.

The amphetamine psychosis usually occurs while the amphetamine abuser is actually taking amphetamine, usually large amounts of it; but there are also several reports of paranoid psychoses related to the withdrawal process.

Amphetamines produce a high degree of psychological dependence (see Table IV). The craving can be so intense as to be properly called a compulsion. A high degree of tolerance to the euphoric effects also develops in abusers. Amphetamines produce no physical dependence in the sense of a biochemical or physiological need and, therefore, no abstinence syndrome of the kind found in alcohol or heroin addiction. But a letdown or crash occurs when an amphetamine abuser is forced to stop using the drug for a time because it is producing agitation, paranoia, and malnutrition. A debilitating cycle of runs (heavy use for several days to a week) and crashes is a common pattern of amphetamine abuse.

The crash is a kind of withdrawal reaction, and its physical and psychological symptoms can be severe. Extreme lethargy, fatigue, anxiety, and terrifying nightmares are common. The person is often disoriented, bewildered, and confused. He is apt to be extremely irritable and demanding, which drives people away just when he most needs their help. His psychic disruption and loss of self-control may lead to violent acting out of aggressive impulses. His head aches, he sweats profusely, and his body is racked with alternating sensations of extreme heat and extreme cold and with excruciating muscle cramps. He characteristically suffers painful gastrointestinal cramps. Especially if he is alone and despite his sometimes incredible hunger, he often lacks the strength to eat at all, aggravating his condition through malnutrition.

The most characteristic symptom of withdrawal is depression. At times, this depression, which peaks at 48 to 72 hours after the last dose of amphetamine but may persist for several weeks, is so severe that the patient becomes suicidal; repeated suicide attempts have been observed. There is a prominent neurasthenic component to the depression, and these patients appear quite flat and apathetic. Often, a vicious cycle develops: The patient with chronic depression or feelings of inadequacy takes amphetamine for relief or support, and becomes dependent on the drug; subsequent attempts to discontinue its use may result in further depression, which he tries to relieve by renewing his use of amphetamine.

*Treatment*

Because the amphetamine psychosis is generally self-limiting, treatment usually requires little more than supportive measures. The elimination of the amphetamines may be facilitated by acidifying the urine through the use of ammonium chloride. Antipsychotics, either one of the phenothiazines or haloperidol, may be prescribed for the first few days of psychosis; beyond that time there is usually little need for drug treatment. Because the amphetamine psychotic may be assaultive, it may be necessary to treat him in a hospital setting. The withdrawal depression may be treated with tricyclic antidepressants; here, however, symptomatic treatment may require weeks or even a month or so. Ultimately more important than these aspects of treatment is the need to establish the beginnings of a therapeutic alliance, and to make good use of this psychotherapeutic relationship in the treatment of the underlying depression or character disorder, or both. However, inasmuch as many of these patients have become quite dependent on the drug, one can anticipate that psychotherapy will be especially difficult.

## Cocaine

In this country, cocaine is taken by injection or by sniffing, and occasionally it is smoked in pure form known as free-basing. By far the most commonly used route is sniffing or snorting; the average dose is 20 to 50 mg. Street cocaine may be cut with a number of substances, including procaine and amphetamines; its purity may range from as little as 30 percent to as much as 60 or 70 percent. The central stimulant and sympathomimetic effects of cocaine resemble those of amphetamines, but are sometimes thought to be milder, subtler, or less physical. The effects last only about an hour, in contrast to the amphetamines' several hours.

The most common undesirable effect is a feeling of irritability and lassitude after the euphoria subsides, with a desire for more of the drug. Physicians have reported an acute anxiety reaction, with symptoms including high blood pressure, racing heart, anxiety, and paranoia. More severe effects, such as tactile and other hallucinations and delusions, are uncommon but do occur. Hospitals rarely see cases of psychosis, but a few have been reported, mainly in habitual intravenous abusers; cocaine psychosis is qualitatively similar to amphetamine psychosis but lasts a shorter time and for that reason, among others, rarely comes to the attention of psychiatrists (see Table V).

In high doses, cocaine can cause seizures, depression of the medullary centers, and death from cardiac or, more often, respiratory arrest. But, in practice, severe physical poisoning and death from the toxic effects are rare. Deaths from opiates and cocaine in combination are more common than are deaths from cocaine alone.

Because cocaine increases energy and confidence and can produce irritability and paranoia, it has often been said to cause physical aggression and crime. Although it clearly can do so in some circumstances, there is no evidence of any consistent association. However, cocaine is not as conducive to aggression as are other drugs, such as alcohol, barbiturates, and amphetamines.

### Chronic Effects

Taken daily in fairly large amounts, it can disrupt eating and sleeping habits; produce minor psychological disturbances, including irritability and disturbed concentration; and create a serious psychological dependence. Although there is no physical dependence, sometimes withdrawal symptoms, like anxiety and depression, arise. Perceptual disturbances (especially pseudohallucinations), paranoid thinking, and, rarely, psychoses, also occur in chronic users. Runny or clogged noses are common; often, they are treated with nasal decongestant sprays. Less often, noses may become inflamed, swollen, or ulcerated; in the older literature there are reports of perforated septums. All the undesirable effects—except, of course, nasal problems—are much more commonly produced by intravenous injection than by sniffing. In experiments in which unlimited access to intravenous cocaine is provided, animals kill themselves by voluntary injections. Although human beings do not use cocaine in this way, craving can become a serious problem for those who have constant access to it. Users sometimes find it necessary to deny themselves access to cocaine for a few days or weeks; some have been known to try to lock up their bank accounts so that they will not spend all their money on it. Because of this potential for psychological dependence and the accom-

TABLE V
DIAGNOSTIC CRITERIA FOR COCAINE ABUSE*

A. *Pattern of pathological use:* inability to reduce or stop use; intoxication throughout the day; episodes of cocaine overdose (intoxication so severe that hallucinations and delusions occur in a clear sensorium).

B. *Impairment in social or occupational functioning due to cocaine use:* e.g., fights, loss of friends, absence from work, loss of job, or legal difficulties (other than due to a single arrest for possession, purchase, or sale of the substance).

C. Duration of disturbance of at least 1 month.

* From American Psychiatric Association: *Diagnostic and Statistical Manual of Mental Disorders*, ed 3. American Psychiatric Association, Washington, DC, 1980. Used with permission.

panying problems, people familiar with cocaine are aware of the need for caution in using it.

### Treatment

For acute cocaine overdose, the recommended treatment is the administration of oxygen (under pressure, if necessary) with the patient's head down in Trendelenburg's position, muscle relaxants if required to accomplish this, and, if there are convulsions, intravenous short-acting barbiturates, such as 25 to 50 mg of sodium pentothal. For the anxiety reaction with hypertension and tachycardia, 10 to 30 mg of intravenous or intramuscular diazepam has been recommended. An alternative that seems to be a specific antagonist of cocaine's sympathomimetic effects is propranolol (Inderal), a blocker of peripheral adrenergic receptors. Cases have been successfully treated with 1 mg of propranolol, injected intravenously every minute for up to 8 minutes. At this time it is not clear whether propranolol should be regarded as a protection against lethal doses of cocaine.

At present, chronic cocaine abuse does not usually appear as a medical problem, and there is little literature on its treatment. For chronic cocaine abusers who appear at clinics in a state of anxiety, diazepam or chloral hydrate has been recommended. As usual in cases of chronic psychoactive drug abuse, there is often underlying depression, anxiety, or feelings of inadequacy, and the appropriate treatment is psychotherapy combined with anxiolytics or antidepressants.

There has been some limited success in attempting to substitute amphetamine or methylphenidate for cocaine and then withdrawing the patient from the substituted drug slowly. But again, governmental restrictions have inhibited many physicians from utilizing these treatments. This represents yet another example of the interference by governmental agencies in the practice of medicine.

### Barbiturates

The first barbiturate, diethylbarbituric acid or Veronal, was introduced in 1903, but the short-acting barbiturates, such as secobarbital, were developed and came into widespread use only in the past 20 to 30 years; it is these forms of the drug that particularly lend themselves to abuse.

Barbiturates produce psychological dependence, a tendency to increase the dosage to overcome tolerance, and physical dependence when the presence of the drug becomes necessary for the maintenance of homeostasis. The last effect develops only when the drug is taken over a period of 1 to 2 months or longer, at doses above the recommended therapeutic level. Daily dosages of under 0.4 g of secobarbital or pentobarbital do not produce physical dependence.

The three major barbiturates common in the black market are secobarbital ("reds," "red devils," "seggys," "downers"), pentobarbital ("yellow jackets," "yellows," "nembies"), and a combination of secobarbital and amobarbital ("reds and blues," "rainbows," "double trouble," "tooies"). The quality and purity of these drugs are highly uncertain and depend to a large degree on the extent to which they have been tampered with or cut.

### Patterns of Use

Dependence generally occurs in the emotionally maladjusted person seeking relief from unbearable feelings of tension, anxiety, and inadequacy. Like those who become dependent on other psychoactive agents, they can be described as passive-aggressive or passive-dependent types. Almost without exception, persons with a dependence on barbiturates fall into one of three major patterns of use.

The first pattern, that of chronic intoxication, occurs for the most part in 30- to 50-year-old persons who obtain the drug from their physicians, rather than from an illegal source. Often, the drug was initially prescribed in response to their complaints of nervousness or difficulty in falling asleep. Frequently members of the middle or upper classes, they have little difficulty in obtaining refills from their pharmacists, or, now that the number of refills is limited by law, they may choose to visit a number of physicians, obtaining a prescription from each. Their drug dependence may go unidentified by those around them for months or years, until their ability to work becomes impaired, or such physical signs as slurred speech become apparent.

The second pattern of use is episodic intoxication. Users in this category are generally teenagers or young adults who ingest barbiturates for the same reason they use alcohol, to produce a high or experience a sense of well-being. Factors such as the surroundings in which the abuser takes the drug (setting), the psychological make-up of the person, and, most important, his expectations (set) determine whether the effect is regarded as sedative or euphoriant. Like the so-called social drinker, these young people may become so accustomed to the episodic sense of well-being engendered by the drug that barbiturates become a fairly constant aspect of their lives.

The third category is that of intravenous barbiturate use. Users in this category are mainly young adults intimately involved in the illegal drug culture who, sadly, can often be identified by the large abscesses covering accessible areas of their bodies. Their experiences with drugs have often been extensive, ranging from pill-popping to speed and heroin. They may at present be using barbiturates because this drug habit is less expensive to maintain than a heroin habit; even when an abuser is injecting 2,000 mg to 3,000 mg a day, it typically costs him only $10 or so. The drug is injected for its rush effect, which is described as a pleasurable, warm, and drowsy feeling. Like speed freaks, these barb freaks are disliked by the rest of the subculture because of their irresponsibility and occasional tendency to be violent and disruptive.

In addition, some people use barbiturates incidentally to their dependence on other drugs. Barbiturates are sometimes used by heroin addicts to boost the effects of weak heroin; alcoholics are known to consider barbiturates a means of relieving the tremulousness of alcohol withdrawal; and some speed freaks or cocaine abusers inject secobarbital as a downer to help them avoid the paranoia and agitation usually experienced at the end of a trip.

*Effects*

All patterns of use present real dangers to the health of the individual user (see Table VI), and, with the increasingly widespread abuse of these drugs, barbiturate poisoning has become a significant public health problem. Barbiturates are the cause of death in 6 percent of all suicides, and cause more accidental deaths (18 percent) than any other single drug. About 15,000 deaths in the United States are attributed annually to barbiturates. In many cases, one must take cognizance of the factor of drug automatism. Persons whose judgment and memory are already impaired by the drug may forget or disregard previous doses and automatically take an additional dose (overdose) in order to fall asleep, without any conscious intent of committing suicide. Because home medicine cabinets are frequently well stocked with barbiturates, there is a second type of fatal accidental poisoning, one that involves curious children; among drugs, barbiturates rank second only to salicylates as a cause of accidental death in toddlers in the United States.

There is, of course, considerable variance in reports of the amounts of barbiturates taken by addicted users, but an average daily dose of 1.5 g of short-acting barbiturate is common, and some users have been reported to consume as much as 2.5 g daily over a period of months. Although marked tolerance develops to the sedating and intoxicating effects, the lethal dose is not much greater for the chronic abuser than it is for the neophyte. There is always the possibility of accidental death for the addict as he gradually increases his dosage. Once a user has developed tolerance at a specific dose level, he need raise the dosage by as little as 0.1 g to recapture intoxication. However, this process leads the user to a point where his doses are so massive that he may experience cardiovascular failure from the intense depressant effect of the drug. Barbiturate-induced depression of the central nervous system can range from mild sedation to deep coma, depending on the dose and the route of administration, the degree of excitability of the central nervous system at the time the drug is being used, and the degree to which the user has already developed some tolerance to the drug.

The effects of mild barbiturate intoxication, both acute and chronic, resemble intoxication with alcohol. Symptoms include a general sluggishness, difficulty in thinking, poor memory, slowness of speech and comprehension, faulty judgment, narrowed range of attention, emotional lability, and exaggeration of basic personality traits. The sluggishness may wear off after a number of hours, but judgment may be defective, mood distorted, and motor skills impaired for a long time. In a series of multidimensional tests measuring pilot proficiency in simulated

TABLE VI
DIAGNOSTIC CRITERIA FOR BARBITURATE OR SIMILARLY ACTING SEDATIVE OR HYPNOTIC ABUSE*

A. *Pattern of pathological use:* inability to cut down or stop use; intoxication throughout the day; frequent use of the equivalent of 600 mg or more of secobarbital or 60 mg or more of diazepam; amnesic periods for events that occurred while intoxicated.

B. *Impairment in social or occupational functioning due to substance use:* e.g., fights, loss of friends, absence from work, loss of job, or legal difficulties (other than a single arrest due to possession, purchase, or sale of the substance).

C. Duration of disturbance of at least 1 month.

* From American Psychiatric Association: *Diagnostic and Statistical Manual of Mental Disorders*, ed 3. American Psychiatric Association, Washington, DC, 1980. Used with permission.

TABLE VII
DIAGNOSTIC CRITERIA FOR BARBITURATE OR
SIMILARLY ACTING SEDATIVE OR HYPNOTIC
DEPENDENCE*

Either tolerance or withdrawal:

*Tolerance:* need for markedly increased amounts of the substance to achieve the desired effect, or markedly diminished effect with regular use of the same amount.

*Withdrawal:* development of Barbiturate or Similarly Acting Sedative or Hypnotic Withdrawal after cessation of or reduction in substance use.

* From American Psychiatric Association: *Diagnostic and Statistical Manual of Mental Disorders*, ed 3. American Psychiatric Association, Washington, DC, 1980. Used with permission.

flying missions, a dose of 200 mg of secobarbital at bedtime produced performance decrement as much as 10 to 22 hours later. Additional frequent symptoms of barbiturate intoxication are hostility, quarrelsomeness, and moroseness. Occasionally, paranoid ideas and suicidal tendencies surface. Neurological effects include nystagmus, diplopia, strabismus, ataxic gait, positive Romberg's sign, hypotonia, dysmetria, and decreased superficial reflexes. Diagnosis of barbiturate intoxication is based on the presence of at least some of these signs and symptoms, and this diagnosis may be confirmed by a number of laboratory tests (see Table VII).

### Treatment

When a user's tolerance has grown to the point at which he is taking near-lethal doses, it is imperative that he withdraw or be withdrawn from the drug. The withdrawal syndrome can range from rather mild symptoms—such as anxiety, weakness, profuse sweating, and insomnia—to a severe reaction involving grand mal seizures, delirium, and cardiovascular collapse. It is estimated that a dosage of 0.8 g of secobarbital or pentobarbital per day taken for at least 35 days is necessary to produce signs of withdrawal. As one would expect, the greater the user's daily dose, the more severe are his withdrawal symptoms. Users with 400-mg-a-day habits with pentobarbital or secobarbital experience negligible symptoms, whereas those taking 800 mg a day experience orthostatic hypotension, weakness, tremor, anxiety, and considerable discomfort, and about 75 percent have convulsions. Users on even higher doses may experience apprehension, anorexia, confusion, delirium, hallucinations, psychoses, and convulsions. When seizures do occur, they are invariably of the clonic-tonic grand mal type, indistinguishable clinically from those of idiopathic grand mal epilepsy. The psychosis is clinically indistinguishable from that of alcoholic delirium tremens and is characterized by agitation, delusions, and hallucinations that are usually visual but may be auditory. Most of these symptoms appear within a day of the beginning of abstinence; but seizures generally do not occur until the second or third day, and psychosis, if it does develop, starts in the third to the eighth day. The various symptoms may last as long as 2 weeks.

To avoid seizures and sudden death, the physician must institute very conservative treatment of the patient during this period. First, the magnitude of the user's daily habit must be determined; because the patient himself is notoriously unreliable at such times and often underestimates his dosage, family members and druggists should be consulted for some confirmation of this information. The dose level must then be clinically verified. For example, a test dose of 200 mg of pentobarbital may be given by mouth on an empty stomach. This dose should be repeated every hour while the withdrawal or abstinence syndrome is still evident. When a dose level has been attained at which the patient demonstrates a mild degree of intoxication and sedation, he should be stabilized on this dosage for 1 or 2 days. Then, gradually, this dose can be reduced but by no more than 10 percent a day. If, during this gradual withdrawal, the patient again begins to exhibit abstinence symptoms, the daily decrement should be halved. In the case of a patient who, when first seen, is comatose or grossly intoxicated, barbiturates are withheld until these symptoms have cleared.

It has been suggested that long-acting barbiturates such as phenobarbital be substituted in the withdrawal procedure for the more commonly abused short-acting barbiturates. This treatment has definite parallels to the substitution of methadone for heroin. The effects of phenobarbital are of longer duration, and, because there is less fluctuation of barbiturate blood levels, the phenobarbital does not produce the high to which the dependent user is accustomed. It is, therefore, viewed more as a medication than as dope. In addition, phenobarbital has a wider margin of safety between the dose that produces observable toxic signs and a serious overdose. An adequate substitution dosage is 30 mg of phenobarbital for every 100 mg of the short-acting substance. The user should be maintained for at least 2 days at this level before reduction of dosage begins.

After withdrawal is complete, the patient enters a crucial period during which he must overcome his desire to begin once again to take the drug. Although it has been suggested that other nonbarbiturate sedative-hypnotics be substituted for barbiturates as a preventive therapeutic measure, this measure too often turns into substituting one physical dependence for another. If a user is to remain drug free, follow-up treatment, usually involving psychiatric help and the use of community resources, is vital. If this treatment is not forthcoming and successful, the patient will almost certainly return to barbiturates or a drug with similar hazards as a proved means of "adjustment" to his preexisting problems.

## Methaqualone

Methaqualone is a nonbarbiturate sedative-hypnotic whose growth as a drug of abuse, particularly among young people, has accelerated rapidly over the past few years. The drug is no longer available as a prescription drug in this country because of its high abuse level. Abusers take large quantities, which they obtain from illegitimate sources. Street names for methaqualone include "mandrakes" (from the British preparation Mandrax, a combination of methaqualone and diphenhydramine) and "soaps" or "soapers" (from the Arnar-Stone brand name Soper). "Luding out" refers to the common practice of taking the drug with alcohol (usually wine).

Among the undesirable effects reported are dryness of the mouth, headache, urticaria, dizziness, diarrhea, chills, tremors, hangover, paresthesia, menstrual disturbance, epistaxis, and depersonalization. Some users report the feeling that they will lose their minds. Chronic large doses have been reported to lead to epigastric distress, clumsiness, and forgetfulness. Methaqualone stimulates a considerable increase in the activity of the liver microsomal enzymes, more so than do the barbiturates. Furthermore, it is longer acting than amobarbital, secobarbital, and chloral hydrate.

Like the barbiturates, to which it exhibits cross-tolerance, methaqualone is capable of producing a considerable degree of psychological dependence. A withdrawal syndrome has been observed in people using 600 to 3,000 mg of methaqualone daily for prolonged periods of time. The syndrome consists of insomnia, headache, abdominal cramps, anorexia, nausea, irritability, and anxiety. Hallucinations and nightmares have also been reported during withdrawal from very high doses. The withdrawal syndrome generally begins within 24 hours of cessation of drug use and persists for 2 to 3 days. It may be interrupted by giving the patient methaqualone, and this is the basis of treatment, which consists of tapering doses of the drug.

Overdose of methaqualone may result in restlessness, delirium, hypertonia, muscle spasms leading to convulsions, and death. Unlike the severe barbiturate toxic state, cardiovascular and respiratory depression are generally absent from the comparable methaqualone syndrome. Most fatal doses have involved a combination of methaqualone and alcohol. Treatment consists mainly of supportive measures to maintain vital functions. In the case of recently ingested drug in a patient who is still conscious, gastric lavage is indicated.

## Meprobamate

The acute toxic effects of large doses may include ataxia, somnolence, hypotensive reactions, shock, loss of consciousness, respiratory depression, and death. Somnolence is a common symptom of chronic toxicity. Tolerance does develop, and withdrawal symptoms occur in people who have chronically used large doses, usually more than several grams daily. When the drug is withdrawn abruptly, patients experience tremors, ataxia, headache, insomnia, and gastrointestinal disturbances for several days; occasionally, convulsions occur with the cessation of the chronic use of very large doses (3 g or more daily). A delirium tremens-like syndrome may occur within 36 to 48 hours. The symptoms include severe anxiety, tremors, muscle twitching, and hallucinations; grand mal seizures may develop. Control of the convulsions is achieved with the intravenous administration of phenytoin sodium. The over-all treatment involves gradual withdrawal from the drug, but, because there is cross-tolerance with the barbiturates, a regime of a short-acting barbiturate may be started and gradually withdrawn. Alternatively, the meprobamate can be reinstituted and gradually withdrawn over a period of about 10 days. Primarily because of the risk of convulsions, withdrawal is perhaps best accomplished in a hospital setting.

## Benzodiazepines

Like meprobamate, the benzodiazepines are used primarily for the symptomatic treatment of anxiety; in addition, they are commonly used as skeletal-muscle relaxants and in the treatment of alcoholism. The toxicity is relatively low; people who ingest large amounts (more than 2 g) at one time in suicide attempts experience drowsiness, lethargy, ataxia, and sometimes confusion, and manage to depress their vital signs somewhat, but they do not succeed in significantly harming themselves; however, chlordiazepoxide has been taken in doses that have caused comatose states. It now appears that some of the benzodiazepines have a disinhibiting effect that, particularly for people who are subject to environmental frustration, may lead to hostile or aggressive behavior. There is some question as to whether people can become psychologically dependent on the benzodiazepines, because the drugs apparently produce less euphoria, less of a high, than the other drugs mentioned here. But it is clear that those who take the benzodiazepines over long periods of time, usually in large doses (several hundred milligrams daily or more), may experience a withdrawal syndrome when the drugs are withdrawn abruptly. The symptoms may include insomnia, anorexia, agitation, muscle twitching, sweating, and sometimes convulsions. The convulsions may not appear for several weeks after the withdrawal of the drug, and this delayed reaction is thought to be due to the slowness with which the drugs are eliminated. The management of the convulsions is similar to that described for meprobamate.

### Glue and Other Volatile Solvents

Glue sniffing has received a lot of notoriety in recent years, possibly because it is a favorite of the very young—from teenagers to children of 6 or 7 years. The glue is sniffed directly from tubes, from plastic bags, or from smears on pieces of cloth. At first, a few sniffs may lead to a high, but, because tolerance develops over a period of weeks or months, chronic users may have to use up to seven tubes before achieving the desired effect of this central nervous system depressant. The intoxication is characterized by euphoria, excitement, a floating sensation, dizziness, slurred speech, and ataxia. Inebriation is accompanied by a breakdown of inhibitions, which is often reflected in a reckless abandon, and by a sense of greatly increased power and ability. The aggressiveness that accompanies alcoholic inebriation is characteristic of that produced by glue sniffing, and, as in an alcohol drunk, amnesia for the acute intoxication may occur. Visual hallucinations sometimes occur. The duration of the intoxication varies from 15 minutes to several hours. Drowsiness usually accompanies small doses; stupor and even unconsciousness are occasionally sequelae of heavy use. Nausea and anorexia are acute symptoms, and weight loss may accompany chronic use.

Among the abused psychoactive substances, volatile solvents are among the most dangerous. Tolerance to these agents does occur, but it is not clear that there is a physical dependence with a withdrawal syndrome. There is no question, however, that young people may develop a severe psychological dependence. The habit is

dangerous for two reasons. First, there is a risk of tissue damage—particularly to the bone marrow, brain, liver, and kidneys—resulting from high concentrations of toluene and other similar solvents, and the tissue damage may be irreversible; also, overdosage may lead to death from respiratory arrest. Second, young people intoxicated on these solvents are more aggressive and impulsive and at the same time exhibit impaired judgment, a combination that can lead to dangerous and sometimes life-threatening behavior. Toluene appears to be the most wisely used of the agents in this class, but xylene, benzene, lacquers, paint thinners, lighter fluids, and a number of other substances have been used.

### Phencyclidine (PCP)

Phencyclidine, is an arylcycloalkylamine 1-(1-phenylcyclohexyl)piperidine, which was first developed by the Parke-Davis Company in the 1950s, and then patented and marketed in 1963 under the name Sernyl, as both an intravenous surgical anesthetic and as a general preoperative and postoperative analgesic. When it was discovered that the emergency syndrome was frequently characterized by disorientation, agitation, and delirium, investigations of its usefulness as an anesthetic were discontinued, and thenceforth it became available for veterinary use only as an anesthetic for primates. There was also formerly some interest in PCP as a therapeutic drug for psychiatric patients with a variety of diagnoses, but the interest declined along with therapeutic interest in LSD and other psychedelic drugs.

PCP is apparently regarded as something like a cross between a psychedelic drug and a tranquilizer or sedative. Although it may be taken orally, intravenously, or by sniffing, it is usually sprinkled onto joints of parsley or marijuana and smoked, because this mode affords the best means of self-titration. Street names include "angel dust," "crystal," "peace," "peace weed," "super grass," "super weed," "hog," "rocket fuel," and "horse tranks." Much of the PCP available to the illicit market is being sold deceptively; it was found that only a quarter of the street drugs that contain PCP were actually sold as phencyclidine. It is commonly represented as a psychedelic, such as mescaline, psilocybin, or tetrahydrocannabinol (THC). Drugs sold on the street as THC or cannabinol are almost always phencyclidine.

There is great variation in the amount of PCP in a joint; 1 g of phencyclidine may be used to make as few as four or as many as several dozen joints. This kind of variation, together with the extreme variation of PCP content in street samples, makes it difficult to predict the effect, which also depends on the setting and the user's previous experience. Less than 5 mg of phencyclidine is considered a low dose, and doses above 10 mg are considered high. Experienced users report that the effects of 2 to 3 mg of smoked PCP begin within 5 minutes and plateau within ½ hour. In the early phases, users are frequently not communicative, appear oblivious, and report active fantasy production. They experience bodily warmth and tingling, peaceful floating sensations, and occasional feelings of depersonalization, isolation, and estrangement; sometimes there are auditory or visual hallucinations. There is often a striking alteration of body image; a user may believe that his hands or his feet are very small and very distant, and that his body is flattened like paper, shrunken in size or weightless. Distortions of space and time perception are prominent, and delusions may occur. There may also be an intensification of dependency feelings, and confusion and disorganization of thought. The user may be sympathetic, sociable, and talkative at one moment and hostile and negative at another. Euphoria resembling alcohol intoxication is common, and the behavioral toxicity resembles that of alcohol. Anxiety is also sometimes reported; it is often the most prominent presenting symptom in an adverse reaction. Sometimes observed are head-rolling movements, stroking, grimacing, and repetitive chanting speech. The high lasts for about 4 to 6 hours and gradually gives way to a state of mild depression, during which the user may become irritable, somewhat paranoid, and even occasionally belligerent and irrationally assaultive. Users sometimes find that it takes from 24 to 48 hours to recover completely from the high; laboratory tests show that PCP may remain in the blood and urine for more than a week (see Table VIII).

Although the PCP experience is different from that induced by other drugs, with the exception of ketamine (an arylcylcoalkylamine anesthetic) it shares some of the psychedelic qualities of LSD. Like LSD, it is usually pleasant but, especially for those who take the drug for the first time or unknowingly, can be depressing or frightening, with feelings of emptiness, difficulty in thinking, and preoccupation with death. PCP users sometimes describe adverse reactions as "bad trips." It has now been demonstrated that PCP aggravates any underlying psychopathology much more powerfully than does LSD or mescaline. In addition, because the primary symptoms of schizophrenia may be closely approximated by PCP, it is considered a truer schizophrenomimetic than is LSD.

TABLE VIII
DIAGNOSTIC CRITERIA FOR PHENCYCLIDINE (PCP) OR SIMILARLY ACTING ARYLCYCLOHEXYLAMINE INTOXICATION*

A. Recent use of phencyclidine or a similarly acting arylcyclohexylamine.

B. Within 1 hour (less when smoked, insufflated, or used intravenously), at least two of the following physical symptoms:

(1) vertical or horizontal nystagmus
(2) increased blood pressure and heart rate
(3) numbness or diminished responsiveness to pain
(4) ataxia
(5) dysarthria

C. Within 1 hour, at least two of the following psychological symptoms:

(1) euphoria
(2) psychomotor agitation
(3) marked anxiety
(4) emotional lability
(5) grandiosity
(6) sensation of slowed time
(7) synesthesias

D. Maladaptive behavioral effects, e.g., belligerence, impulsivity, unpredictability, impaired judgment, assaultiveness.

E. Not due to any other physical or mental disorder, e.g., Delirium.

\* From American Psychiatric Association: *Diagnostic and Statistical Manual of Mental Disorders*, ed 3. American Psychiatric Association, Washington, DC, 1980. Used with permission.

Mild cases of adverse phencyclidine reaction or overdose usually do not come to medical attention and, when they do, may often be treated as an emergency in the outpatient department. The low-dose symptoms are quite variable and may range from mild euphoria and restlessness to increasing levels of anxiety, fearfulness, confusion, and agitation. Patients with low-dose reactions may demonstrate varying degrees of difficulty in communication, and they may exhibit a blank, staring appearance. Their thought processes may be disordered, and they may exhibit depression and, occasionally, self-destructive behavior. If the symptoms are not severe, and if one can be certain that enough time has elapsed so that all the PCP has been absorbed in those cases in which the drug has been ingested, the patient may be monitored for an hour or so in the outpatient department and, if the symptoms improve, released to his family or friends. However, even at presumably low doses, symptoms on the more disturbed end of this continuum may worsen, requiring hospitalization.

Like the other effects of phencyclidine intoxication, neurological and physiological symptoms are dose related. At low doses there may be dysarthria, gross ataxia, and muscle rigidity, particularly of the face and neck. Increased deep tendon reflexes and diminished responses to pain are commonly observed. Higher doses may lead to agitated and repetitive movement, shivering, clonic jerking of the extremities, and, occasionally, opisthotonic posturing. At even higher dose levels, patients may be drowsy, stuporous with eyes open, comatose, and, in some instances, responding only to noxious stimuli. Clonic movements and muscle rigidity may sometimes precede generalized seizure activity, and status epilepticus has been reported. Cheyne-Stokes breathing has been observed; respiratory arrest may occur and cause death. Elevated blood pressure, particularly systolic pressure, is commonly observed and is usually an early symptom. Vomiting, probably of central origin, may occur, and hypersalivation and diaphoresis are frequent symptoms. Pupillary size and response to light are inconsistent; horizontal, vertical, and rotary nystagmus have been noted by a number of observers. Ptosis, usually bilateral, has also been observed.

Most patients completely recover within a day or two, but some remain psychotic for as long as 2 weeks. Patients who are first seen in coma frequently manifest disorientation, hallucinations, confusion, and difficulty in communication on regaining consciousness. These symptoms may also be seen in noncomatose patients, but they appear to be less severe. A PCP psychotic patient also commonly manifests the following symptoms: staring into space, echolalia, posturing, sleep disturbance, paranoid ideation, depression, and behavior disorder. Sometimes the behavioral disturbance is quite severe; it may include public masturbation and nudity, violence, urinary incontinence, crying, and inappropriate laughing. Frequently, there is amnesia for the entire period of the psychosis.

### Differential Diagnosis and Treatment

Depending on the patient's status at the time of admission, the differential diagnosis may include sedative or narcotic overdose, psychosis as a consequence of the use of other psychedelic drugs, and acute schizophrenic disorder. Laboratory analysis is helpful in establishing the diagnosis, particularly in the many cases in which the drug history is unreliable or unattainable.

Unconscious patients must, of course, be carefully monitored. This care is particularly important in patients who are toxic with PCP, because the excessive secretions may interfere with an already compromised respiration. In the case of an alert patient with a history of recent ingestion of PCP, gastric lavage should be undertaken

TABLE IX
DIAGNOSTIC CRITERIA FOR PHENCYCLIDINE (PCP) OR SIMILARLY ACTING ARYLCYCLOHEXYLAMINE ABUSE*

A. *Pattern of pathological use:* intoxication throughout the day; episodes of Phencyclidine or Similarly Acting Arylcyclohexylamine Delirium or Mixed Organic Mental Disorder.

B. *Impairment in social or occupational functioning due to substance use:* e.g., fights, loss of friends, absence from work, loss of job, or legal difficulties (other than due to a single arrest for possession, purchase, or sale of the substance).

C. Duration of disturbance of at least 1 month.

* From American Psychiatric Association: *Diagnostic and Statistical Manual of Mental Disorders*, ed 3. American Psychiatric Association, Washington, DC, 1980. Used with permission.

only with great caution, because there is a real risk of inducing laryngeal spasm and aspiration of emesis. The frequently encountered muscle spasm is effectively treated with diazepam. The PCP-psychotic patient is best treated in an environment that affords minimal sensory stimulation. Ideally, one person stays with the patient in a quiet, dark room. Diazepam is often effective in reducing agitation, but the PCP-psychotic patient with severe behavioral disturbance may require short-term antipsychotic medication; some clinicians recommend haloperidol, rather than a phenothiazine, because PCP is somewhat anticholinergic. A hypotensive drug may occasionally be needed.

Little is known about chronic effects, but the street term "crystallized" is sometimes used to describe long-term users who suffer from dulled thinking and reflexes, confusion, lethargy, and difficulty in concentration. There is no evidence of permanent brain cell damage, but neurological and cognitive dysfunction have been reported to persist in chronic users even after 2 to 3 weeks of abstinence. Tolerance seems to develop, but no withdrawal syndrome has been described.

See Table IX for the diagnostic criteria for PCP abuse.

### Psychedelics

There are many psychedelic or hallucinogenic drugs, some natural and some synthetic. The best known are mescaline, which is derived from the peyote cactus; psilocybin, derived from several mushroom species; and the synthetic drug lysergic acid diethylamide (LSD), which is related to psychoactive alkaloids found in morning-glory seeds, the lysergic acid amides. Other psychedelic drugs include the natural substances harmine, harmaline, ibogaine, and dimethyltryptamine (DMT), as well as a large number of synthetic drugs with a tryptamine or methoxylated amphetamine structure. A few of these drugs are diethyltryptamine (DET), dipropyltryptamine (DPT), 3,4-methylenedioxyamphetamine (MDA), and 2,5-dimethoxy-4-methylamphetamine (DOM, also known as STP). The average effective dose varies considerably; for example, it is 75 $\mu$g for LSD, about 1 mg for lysergic acid amides, 3 mg for DOM, 6 mg for psilocybin, 50 mg for DTM, 100 mg for MDA, and 200 mg for mescaline. Only LSD, and to some extent MDA, is now available on the illicit market in any quantity, but false labeling is common.

There are some differences among the subjective effects of these drugs, but LSD produces the widest range of effects and can be taken as a prototype. The reaction varies with personality, expectations, and setting even more than does the reaction to other psychoactive drugs, but LSD almost always produces profound alterations in perception, mood, and thinking. Perceptions become unusually brilliant and intense. Colors and textures seem richer, contours sharpened, music more emotionally profound, smells and tastes heightened. Normally unnoticed details capture the attention, and ordinary things are seen with wonder, as if for the first time. Synesthesia or merging of the senses is common, so that colors are heard or sounds seen. Changes in body image and alterations of time and space perception also occur. Intensely vivid dream-like kaleidoscopic imagery appears before closed eyes. True hallucinations are rare, but visual distortions and pseudohallucinations are common. Emotions become unusually intense and may change abruptly and often; two seemingly incompatible feelings may be experienced at one time. Suggestibility is greatly heightened, and sensitivity to nonverbal cues is increased. Exaggerated empathy with or detachment from other people may arise. Other features that often appear are seeming awareness of internal body organs, recovery of lost early memories, release of unconscious material in symbolic form, and regression and apparent reliving of past events including birth. A heightened sense of reality and significance suffuses the experience. Introspective reflection and feelings of religious and philosophical insight are common. The sense of self is greatly changed, sometimes to the point of depersonalization, merging with the external world, separation of self from body, or total dissolution of the ego in mystical ecstasy.

People sometimes maintain that a single psychedelic experience or a few such experiences have given them increased creative capacity, new psychological insight, relief from neurotic and psychosomatic symptoms, or a desirable change in personality.

The most common adverse effect of LSD and related drugs is the bad trip, which resembles the acute panic reaction to cannabis but can be more severe and occasionally produces true psychotic symptoms. The bad trip ends when the immediate effect of the drugs wears off—in the case of LSD, in 8 to 12 hours. Psychiatric help is usually unnecessary; the best treatment is protection, companionship, and reassurance, although occasionally tranquilizers may be required—diazepam or chloral hydrate by preference, but phenothiazines if necessary.

Another common effect of hallucinogenic drugs is the flashback, a spontaneous transitory recurrence of drug-induced experience in a drug-free state. Most flashbacks are episodes of visual distortion, time expansion, physical symptoms, loss of ego boundaries, or relived intense emotion, lasting usually a few seconds to a few minutes but sometimes longer. Probably about a quarter of all psychedelic drug users have experienced some form of flashback. As a rule, the flashbacks are mild, often even pleasant, but occasionally they turn into repeated frightening images or thoughts resembling a traumatic neurosis; in that case they may require psychiatric attention. Flashbacks decrease quickly in number and intensity with time, and it is rare to hear of anyone experiencing one a year after his last previous LSD experience. They are most likely to occur under stress or at a time of diminished ego control; thus, they are often induced by conditions like fatigue, drunkenness, and marijuana intoxication. Marijuana smoking is possibly the most common single source of LSD flashback.

Prolonged adverse reactions to LSD present the same variety of symptoms as bad trips and flashbacks. They have been classified as anxiety disorders, depressive disorders, and psychoses; often, they resemble prolonged and more or less attenuated bad trips. Most of these adverse reactions end after 24 to 48 hours, but sometimes they last weeks or even months. Psychedelic drugs are capable of magnifying and bringing into consciousness almost any internal conflict, so there is no typical prolonged adverse reaction to LSD, as there is a typical amphetamine psychosis. Instead, many different affective, neurotic, and psychotic symptoms may appear, depending on individual forms of vulnerability. This lack of specificity makes it hard to distinguish between LSD reactions and unrelated pathological processes, especially when some time passes between the drug trip and the onset of the disturbance.

TABLE X
DIAGNOSTIC CRITERIA FOR HALLUCINOGEN
ABUSE*

A. *Pattern of pathological use:* inability to reduce or stop use; intoxication throughout the day (possible only with some hallucinogens); episodes of Hallucinogen Delusional Disorder or Hallucinogen Affective Disorder.

B. *Impairment in social or occupational functioning due to hallucinogen use:* e.g., fights, loss of friends, absence from work, loss of job, or legal difficulties (other than due to a single arrest for possession, purchase, or sale of the illegal substance).

C. Duration of disturbance of at least 1 month.

* From American Psychiatric Association: *Diagnostic and Statistical Manual of Mental Disorders*, ed 3. American Psychiatric Association, Washington, DC, 1980. Used with permission.

TABLE XI
DIAGNOSTIC CRITERIA FOR HALLUCINOGEN
AFFECTIVE DISORDER*

A. Recent use of a hallucinogen.

B. Development of an Organic Affective Syndrome that persists beyond 24 hours after cessation of hallucinogen use.

C. Absence of delusions.

D. Not due to any other physical or mental disorder, such as preexisting Affective Disorder.

* From American Psychiatric Association: *Diagnostic and Statistical Manual of Mental Disorders*, ed 3. American Psychiatric Association, Washington, DC, 1980. Used with permission.

The most likely candidates for adverse reactions are schizoid and prepsychotic personalities with a barely stable ego balance and a great deal of anxiety who cannot cope with the perceptual changes, body-image distortions, and symbolic unconscious material produced by the drug trip. There is a very high rate of previous mental instability in people hospitalized for LSD reaction (see Table X).

The treatment for prolonged reactions to psychedelic drugs is the same as the treatment for similar symptoms not produced by drugs: an appropriate form of psychotherapy and, if necessary, tranquilizers, antipsychotics, or antidepressants. Anyone suffering from unpleasant flashbacks should avoid smoking marijuana.

Long-term psychedelic drug use is not very common. There is no physical addiction, and psychological dependence is rare because each LSD experience is different and there is no reliable euphoria. Tolerance to these drugs develops very quickly but also disappears quickly—in 2 to 3 days. Some studies of long-term psychedelic drug users show minor perceptual and thought changes, chiefly less anxiety and more sensitivity to low-intensity visual stimuli. There is no good evidence of organic brain damage, drastic personality change, or chronic psychosis produced by long-term LSD use. However, it is likely that some heavy psychedelic drug users, like other heavy drug users, suffer from chronic anxiety, depression (see Table XI), or feelings of inadequacy. In these cases, the drug abuse is a symptom, rather than the central problem.

## REFERENCES

Ager S A: Luding-out. N Engl J Med *287:* 51, 1972.

Cornelius, J R, Soluff P H, Reynolds C F: Paranoia, homicidal behavior and seizures associated with phenylpropanolamine. Am J Psychiatry *141:* 120, 1984.

Grinspoon L: *Marihuana Reconsidered,* ed 2. Harvard University Press, Cambridge, MA, 1977.

Grinspoon L, Bakalar J B: *Cocaine: A Drug and Its Social Evolution.* Basic Books, New York, 1977.

Grinspoon L, Bakalar J B: *Psychedelic Drugs Reconsidered.* Basic Books, New York, 1979.

Grinspoon L, Bakalar J B: Drug dependence: Nonnarcotic agents. In *Comprehensive Textbook of Psychiatry,* ed 4, H I Kaplan, B J Sadock, editors, p 1003. Williams & Wilkins, Baltimore, 1985.

Grinspoon L, Hedblom P: *The Speed Culture: Amphetamine Use and Abuse in America.* Harvard University Press, Cambridge, MA, 1975.

Institute of Medicine: *Marijuana and Health.* National Academy Press, Washington, DC, 1982.

Petersen L C, Stillman R C, editors: *Phencyclidine (PCP) Abuse: An Appraisal.* N.I.D.A. Research Monograph 21, U.S. Government Printing Office, Washington, DC, 1978.

Zinberg N E: *Drug, Set, and Setting: The Basis for Controlled Intoxicant Use.* Yale University Press, New Haven, CT, 1984.

## 19.3 ALCOHOLISM AND ALCOHOLIC PSYCHOSES

### Introduction

Alcoholism is usually referred to as the country's third most serious public health problem, following cardiovascular disease and cancer. However, in terms of total morbidity, as contrasted to mortality, it is the number one health problem in the United States.

There has been an increase in per capita alcohol consumption in the past two decades. The rate of consumption in the United States began to rise some 15 years ago, and is now 32 percent higher. The figure compares with a 9 percent reduction in alcohol consumption per capita in France, and a 1 percent increase in Italy. During the same time interval, there has been a 61 percent increase in West Germany, a 54 percent increase in Denmark, an 83 percent increase in

The Netherlands, and a 50 percent increase in Finland. Although there is no absolute relationship between alcohol consumption and rates of alcoholism, it is believed that such a relationship does exist.

## Definition

Alcoholism has been described as a chronic behavioral disorder, manifested by the repeated drinking of alcoholic beverages in excess of the dietary and social uses of the community, and which interferes with the drinker's health or his social and economic functioning.

DSM-III identifies two alcohol disorders: alcohol dependence (alcoholism) and alcohol abuse (see Tables I and II). This separation must be viewed as somewhat arbitrary, and has little relevance from a treatment viewpoint. Clinically, patients probably shift back and forth between these two categories.

According to DSM-III, the essential features of alcohol abuse are (1) continuous or episodic use of alcohol for at least 1 month; (2) social complications of alcohol use including impairment in social or occupational functioning—such as arguments or difficulties with family or friends over excessive alcohol use, violence while intoxicated, missed work, being fired—or legal difficulties, such as being arrested for intoxicated behavior and traffic accidents while intoxicated; and (3) either psychological dependence—a compelling desire to use alcohol, an inability to cut down or stop drinking, repeated efforts to control or reduce excess drinking by going on the wagon (periods of temporary abstinence) or restricting drinking to certain times of the day—or a pathological pattern of use—drinking nonbeverage alcohol, going on binges (remaining intoxicated throughout the day for at least 2 days), occasionally drinking a fifth of spirits or its equivalent in wine or beer, or having two or more blackouts (amnesic periods for events occurring while intoxicated).

Alcohol dependence (alcoholism) is described in DSM-III as having these features plus either tolerance—that is, increasing amounts of alcohol are required to achieve the desired effect, or a diminished effect is achieved with regular use of the same dose—or withdrawal symptoms—for example, morning shakes and malaise that are relieved by drinking—after the cessation or reduction of drinking.

TABLE I
DIAGNOSTIC CRITERIA FOR ALCOHOL DEPENDENCE*

A. Either a pattern of pathological alcohol use or impairment in social or occupational functioning due to alcohol use:

*Pattern of pathological alcohol use:* need for daily use of alcohol for adequate functioning; inability to cut down or stop drinking; repeated efforts to control or reduce excess drinking by "going on the wagon" (periods of temporary abstinence) or restricting drinking to certain times of the day; binges (remaining intoxicated throughout the day for at least 2 days); occasional consumption of a fifth of spirits (or its equivalent in wine or beer); amnesic periods for events occurring while intoxicated (blackouts); continuation of drinking despite a serious physical disorder that the individual knows is exacerbated by alcohol use; drinking of nonbeverage alcohol.

*Impairment in social or occupational functioning due to alcohol use:* e.g., violence while intoxicated, absence from work, loss of job, legal difficulties (e.g., arrest for intoxicated behavior, traffic accidents while intoxicated), arguments or difficulties with family or friends because of excessive alcohol use.

B. Either tolerance or withdrawal:

*Tolerance:* need for markedly increased amounts of alcohol to achieve the desired effect, or markedly diminished effect with regular use of the same amount.

*Withdrawal:* development of Alcohol Withdrawal (e.g., morning "shakes" and malaise relieved by drinking) after cessation of or reduction in drinking.

\* From American Psychiatric Association: *Diagnostic and Statistical Manual of Mental Disorders*, ed 3. American Psychiatric Association, Washington, DC, 1980. Used with permission.

TABLE II
DIAGNOSTIC CRITERIA FOR ALCOHOL ABUSE*

A. *Pattern of pathological alcohol use:* need for daily use of alcohol for adequate functioning; inability to cut down or stop drinking; repeated efforts to control or reduce excess drinking by "going on the wagon" (periods of temporary abstinence) or restricting drinking to certain times of the day; binges (remaining intoxicated throughout the day for at least 2 days); occasional consumption of a fifth of spirits (or its equivalent in wine or beer); amnesic periods for events occurring while intoxicated (blackouts); continuation of drinking despite a serious physical disorder that the individual knows is exacerbated by alcohol use; drinking of nonbeverage alcohol.

\* From American Psychiatric Association: *Diagnostic and Statistical Manual of Mental Disorders*, ed 3. American Psychiatric Association, Washington, DC, 1980. Used with permission.

## Etiology

The precise causes of alcoholism are unclear. The presence of a wide range of psychopathology with varying degrees of severity in alcoholic populations has resulted in a number of theories postulating a psychological cause. Alcoholic populations do display significantly more depression, paranoid thinking trends, aggressive feelings and acts, and significantly lower self-esteem, responsibility, and self-control than nonalcoholic populations. Psychological and coping factors play an important causative role in the development of alcoholism.

Biological and physical factors have long been sought as clues to the causes of alcoholism. Although the response of some persons to alcohol differs markedly from the anticipated norm, a causal relationship to alcoholism has not been convincingly demonstrated. Among the aberrant factors are skin-flushing responses, alcohol tolerance, specific blood enzymes, and color-blindness.

Jews and Chinese are known to have very low attack rates, and the Irish have a high rate. These high or low rates persist for some generations in the United States and then move toward a national norm. If the change in rate does occur, it raises questions about the hereditary aspects of alcoholism.

That alcoholism is familial is beyond dispute; various studies of alcoholic groups reveal that up to 50 percent of their fathers, 30 percent of their brothers, 6 percent of their mothers, and 3 percent of their sisters are also alcoholic.

Certain occupations are associated with increased rates of alcoholism, such as acting, medicine, bartending, and corporate management.

A hereditary link is obviously more difficult to demonstrate than a familial link. Some studies have suggested the possibility that some forms of alcoholism have a hereditary component.

Ultimately, researchers may discover that, from a causative viewpoint, alcoholism is not a unitary illness. Rather, it may prove to be a group of disorders with a final common pathway manifested by an inability to refrain from drinking and an inability to drink in a controlled manner.

## Tolerance

Many studies indicate that task impairment begins when blood alcohol levels reach about 0.5 percent. Most persons become quite uncoordinated at blood alcohol levels of 0.10 percent and higher. However, alcoholics demonstrate an obvious tolerance to alcohol and are able to function at blood alcohol levels that would impair nonalcoholics.

Some factors in tolerance may be inborn, rather than acquired, although doubtless both are found in many alcoholics. Some persons cannot drink more than a small amount of alcohol without developing unpleasant sequelae. Others can consume large amounts with little effect.

## Diagnosis

Efforts have been made to establish diagnostic criteria for alcoholism in a number of ways. These efforts have included definitions based on (1) quantity imbibed, (2) degree of loss of control, (3) social consequences, (4) physiological and biochemical criteria, and (5) psychological factors.

Using the quantity of beverage alcohol consumed in a day, a week, or a sitting to make a diagnosis of alcoholism has two major drawbacks. One drawback is the lack of guidelines for the quantity of alcohol that must be consumed before a person can be judged alcoholic.

The second drawback inherent in using quantities of alcohol consumed as a criterion for alcoholism is that the answers given by the alcoholic about quantities tend to be vague, inaccurate, or deceptive. Many alcoholics simply reduce the amount they think they drink when queried; whether they do so by design is sometimes difficult to say.

Clinical observations and psychological tests have found a high incidence of various types of psychopathology in alcoholic populations. The psychopathology includes depression, poor reality testing, impulsivity, struggle with dominance-submission issues, and activity-passivity conflicts. Although many of these factors are present in a high percentage of alcoholics, they are not specific to alcoholic populations. Nor is any combination of psychological factors sufficiently specific to alcoholism to serve as a convincing diagnostic tool. One can only state that a well-adjusted person is unlikely to drink regularly to excess and is even less likely to become an alcoholic.

The best means of detecting alcoholism remains confirming the presence of the most diagnostic and frequently occurring sequelae of alcoholism, with heavy reliance on those sequelae that are a direct consequence of excessive and chronic drinking.

## Alcohol-induced Mental Disorders

### Alcohol Intoxication

The essential features of alcohol intoxication are specific neurological and psychological signs and maladaptive behavioral effects due to the recent ingestion of alcohol, with no evidence suggesting that the amount was insufficient to cause intoxication in most people, as in alcohol idiosyncratic intoxication. The neurological signs include slurred speech, incoordination, unsteady gait, and impairment in attention or memory. The psychological signs include mood lability, disinhibition of sexual and aggressive impulses, irritability, and loquacity. The maladaptive behavioral effects include fighting, impaired judgment, interference with social or occupational function, or failure to meet responsibilities.

Personality traits may be exaggerated or muted. A person who tends to be somewhat suspicious may, while intoxicated, become markedly so. A person who is ordinarily withdrawn and uncomfortable in social situations may become excessively convivial while intoxicated.

Alcohol intoxication sometimes produces amnesia (blackouts) for events occurring while the person was fully alert but intoxicated. Although the phenomenon is frequently reported by alcoholics, it is occasionally reported by nonalcoholics.

**Etiology.** The initial behavioral effects of alcohol intoxication are usually disinhibitory. If the person continues to drink, the inhibitory effects of alcohol supervene. Thus, during a period of intoxication, a person may initially become bellicose, and later become withdrawn.

The length of the intoxication period depends on the amount of alcohol consumed and how rapidly it was consumed, ranging from several hours to 12 hours after the person stops drinking. Alcohol is metabolized at the rate of about 1 ounce of beverage alcohol an hour. The signs of intoxication are more marked when the blood alcohol is increasing than when it is decreasing. In addition, short-term tolerance to alcohol occurs, so that a person may seem less intoxicated after many hours of drinking than after only a few hours. Some people show intoxication with blood levels of 30 mg per 100 ml; others seem unintoxicated at higher levels, irrespective of previous drinking experience. Signs of intoxication are almost always present when blood levels of 200 mg per 100 ml or more are reached. Unconsciousness usually occurs when the blood level is between 400 mg and 500 mg per 100 ml and death usually occurs at between 600 mg and 800 mg per 100 ml, although there is considerable variation. Unconsciousness usually occurs before the person can drink enough to die. When death does occur, it is usually caused by respiratory paralysis or vomiting followed by aspiration.

Medical complications from alcohol intoxication include those that result from falls, such as subdural hematomas and fractures, the consequences of exposure to the elements, such as frostbite or sunburn, and possible suppression of immune mechanisms that may predispose to infection.

**Differential Diagnosis.** Drinkers frequently have taken tranquilizers or other drugs before or simultaneously with drinking. Barbiturate or other sedative hypnotic substances can produce behavior identical to that seen in alcohol intoxication.

Persons suffering from neurological illnesses, such as postictal or postconcussional states, can also appear intoxicated, as can persons with metabolic disorders, such as diabetic acidosis.

In alcohol idiosyncratic intoxication, the person has marked behavioral changes such as aggressive or assaultive behavior, after taking an amount of alcohol that is known to be insufficient to cause alcohol intoxication in most people.

### Alcohol Idiosyncratic Intoxication (Pathological Intoxication)

The essential features of alcohol idiosyncratic intoxication are a marked behavioral change while drinking or shortly thereafter and subsequent amnesia for the period of intoxication in a person in whom there is evidence of the recent ingestion of alcoholic beverage that is known to be insufficient to induce intoxication in most people. The marked behavioral changes usually involve aggressive or assaultive behavior that is atypical of the person who, after a few drinks, becomes belligerent and assaultive. During the episode the person seems out of contact with others. The disorder usually manifests itself early in life.

**Etiology.** The episode usually passes quickly, within hours. The person returns to normal when his blood alcohol levels fall. Fights or criminal behavior occurring during the period of intoxication may be dangerous to the person and to those around him.

**Predisposing Factors.** Although the evidence is still anecdotal, it is thought that people with brain damage lose tolerance for alcohol and behave abnormally after drinking small amounts. The types of brain injury most often associated with the syndrome result from trauma and encephalitis. The loss of tolerance may be temporary or permanent. Another possibility is that the person has been taking tranquilizers, sedatives, or hypnotics that have additive effects with alcohol, and produce behavior that would not occur with alcohol alone. It is also reported that persons who are unusually fatigued or have a debilitating medical illness may have a low tolerance for alcohol and respond inappropriately to small amounts.

When criminal behavior is associated with pathological intoxication, the intoxication is sometimes introduced in court as an extenuating circumstance. A small percentage of people have been reported to have temporal lobe spikes on an electroencephalogram after receiving small amounts of alcohol.

**Differential Diagnosis.** Alcohol idiosyncratic intoxication must be distinguished from other causes of abrupt behavioral change. The history of recent alcohol ingestion is essential to the diagnosis. Other exogenous agents may occasionally produce a somewhat similar syndrome. Certain patients with temporal lobe epilepsy may, as an interictal phenomenon, be prone to fits of destructive rage. These patients, however, usually have a history of previous behavior of the same sort. Furthermore, they were not drinking during those episodes and have a definite history of seizure disorder.

### Alcoholic Withdrawal Sydrome

The alcohol withdrawal syndrome includes a broad spectrum of severity. Most common are the relatively mild withdrawal phenomena that are probably ubiquitous among alcoholics. Cessation of prolonged heavy drinking is often followed by tremors that affect the hands, tongue, and eyelids, and the development of one or more of the following: nausea and vomiting, malaise or weakness, autonomic hyperactivity (such as tachycardia, sweating, and elevated blood pressure), anxiety, depressed mood or irritability, insomnia, grand mal seizures, and orthostatic hypotension after the cessation or reduction of alcohol ingestion in a person who has been doing heavy drinking of alcohol for several days or longer. The clinical picture does not meet the criteria for alcohol withdrawal delirium.

The nausea and vomiting are often associated with a gastritis. Another associated feature is dry mouth that is not due to dehydration. Persons withdrawing from alcohol are not dehydrated unless there has been sufficient vomiting or diarrhea to produce the dehydration. Headache is common. The complexion is often puffy and blotchy, and there may be mild peripheral edema. Frequently, there is restless sleep with dreaming, including nightmares. There may be acute anxiety attacks during withdrawal. The person may also have brief unformed hallucinations—visual, auditory, or tactile—during the withdrawal. Typically, the hallucinations begin 1 or 2 days after the cessation of drinking and are usually transitory, rarely persisting more than 3 days. Tendon hyperreflexia may be present. Myoclonic muscular contractions, spasmodic jerking of the extremities, and bizarre movement patterns may develop within 6 days of the substance cessation. Occasionally, grand mal seizures (rum fits) occur. They are most likely to appear if there has been a history of withdrawal seizures or epilepsy. Withdrawal seizures do not, however, produce epilepsy, and persons who have had alcohol withdrawal seizures normally do not have seizures unless withdrawing, and they have normal sober electroencephalograms. Epileptics are particularly prone to have convulsions due to the seizure threshold-lowering effect of withdrawal from alcohol.

Onset of the syndrome may occur at any age, depending on when the person developed his alcohol addiction. However, the majority of alcoholics begin early in life and have their first withdrawal syndromes in the thirties or forties.

**Etiology.** Withdrawal symptoms begin shortly after the cessation of drinking and almost always disappear in 5 to 7 days. If they persist longer, other causes—medical or psychiatric—should be considered. In the absence of the development of alcohol withdrawal delirium, (delirium tremens) withdrawal from alcohol is usually a benign, self-limiting, transitory event from which the person recovers spontaneously in a few days. However, he should be given prophylactic sedative medication to guard against the possibility of grand mal withdrawal seizures.

After the acute withdrawal syndrome has subsided, the person is usually able to resume normal activities. No specific complications are associated with withdrawal itself.

Malnutrition, fatigue, depression, and medical illness may worsen the syndrome.

**Differential Diagnosis.** If hallucinations occur in alcohol withdrawal, they are transitory and do not persist more than a few days. In contrast, the hallucinations of alcohol hallucinosis are persistent, and present after the symptoms of withdrawal have resolved.

Conditions that may mimic alcohol withdrawal are familial tremor, diabetic acidosis and other metabolic abnormalities, hypoglycemia, and withdrawal from sedative or hypnotic drugs. Barbiturates produce a withdrawal syndrome almost identical to that seen in alcohol withdrawal. Hypoglycemia may result from an insulin reaction or other nonalcohol-related causes or may be a complication of alcohol withdrawal; this complication is rare and usually occurs only if the person has not eaten for several days.

*Alcohol Withdrawal Delirium (Delirium Tremens)*

This is the severest form of the withdrawal syndrome. Among alcoholics who are hospitalized, about 5 percent develop delirium tremens. Predisposing factors to delirium tremens are believed to be the presence of other illnesses, including those to which alcoholics are vulnerable—pneumonia, fractures, head injuries, and liver disease.

The essential feature is a delirium that occurs within 1 week of the cessation or reduction of heavy alcohol ingestion. Additional features include autonomic hyperactivity, such as tachycardia, sweating, and elevated blood pressure; a disturbance of attention, as manifested by an impairment in the ability to sustain attention to environmental stimuli, goal-directed thinking, or goal-directed behavior; disordered memory and orientation; at least two of the following: (1) reduced wakefulness or insomnia, (2) perceptual disturbance (simple misinterpretations, illusions, hallucinations), or (3) increased or decreased psychomotor activity; clinical features that develop over a short period of time and fluctuate rapidly; the presence of no other physical or mental disorder to account for the disturbance.

Tremor is almost always present. Periods of calm and agitation may alternate. The hallucinations are most frequently visual but may also be auditory or tactile. Fever is frequent.

This disorder usually begins in the patient's thirties or forties. In general, the first episode is preceded by 5 to 15 years of heavy drinking, typically of the binge type.

**Course.** The onset typically occurs on the third day after the cessation or reduction of alcohol ingestion. It may occur earlier but rarely later. In the absence of medical illness, the delirium, together with other withdrawal symptoms, has usually resolved by the fifth to seventh day after the cessation of drinking.

The delirious patient is a danger to himself and to others. In his confused, disoriented state, he is highly unpredictable and may, without warning, attack others, leap out of windows, or commit other sudden and violent acts. The delirious patient sometimes acts on his hallucinations and delusional thoughts, responding as if they constituted genuine dangers. Untreated delirium tremens is associated with a significant mortality rate (10 to 15 per cent) usually—but not invariably—from intercurrent medical illness such as heart failure or secondary infection.

**Differential Diagnosis.** Even if there is a history or evidence of heavy drinking, all other causes of delirium must be ruled out as a possibility, since the alcohol may be only a minor factor, and the actual cause of delirium may be another source.

**Treatment.** The best way to deal with delirium tremens is to prevent its occurrence. Patients withdrawing from alcohol who exhibit any withdrawal phenomena should receive 25 to 50 mg of chlordiazepoxide hydrochloride (Librium) every 2 to 4 hours, as necessary, until they seem to be out of danger. Once the delirium has appeared, doses of 50 to 100 mg of chlordiazepoxide should be given every 4 hours orally or intramuscularly. The drug may be used intramuscularly if the patient cannot retain oral medications. Diazepam (Valium) may also be used. A high-caloric, high-carbohydrate diet supplemented by multivitamins is important. Patients with delirium tremens should never be physically restrained since they may fight the restraints to exhaustion. When patients are disorderly and uncontrollable, a seclusion room can be used. Dehydration may be a problem, and can be corrected with fluids by mouth or intravenously. Anorexia, vomiting, and diarrhea often occur during withdrawal. Diaphoresis and fever may also contribute to volume depletion. Nevertheless, dehydration usually does not occur, and excessive fluids given parenterally are distinctly harmful. The use of parenteral fluids must be individualized and titrated.

Phenothiazines should be avoided unless absolutely essential for other reasons. Phenothiazines tend to reduce seizure thresholds and introduce the possibility of a hepatitis superimposed upon preexisting impaired hepatic functioning.

The need for warm, supportive psychotherapy in the treatment of delirium tremens needs to be emphasized. Patients are often bewildered, frightened, and anxious in the face of their tumultuous symptoms. Skillful human and verbal support is imperative.

Grand mal seizures infrequently occur as a complication of alcohol withdrawal with or without delirium tremens. They usually appear within 48 hours of drinking cessation, and are nonfocal and one or two in number. They cease without specific treatment. The emergence of focal neurological symptoms, lateralizing seizures, increased intracranial pressure, skull fracture, nonmidline pineal or other indications of central nervous system pathology obviously calls for further neurological investigation and treatment. It is now generally believed that anticonvulsant medication is ineffectual in preventing or treating alcohol withdrawal convulsions; the use of chlordiazepoxide or paraldehyde is generally effective.

### Alcohol Hallucinosis

The essential feature of alcohol hallucinosis is a hallucinosis, usually auditory, persisting after a person has recovered from the symptoms of alcohol withdrawal and is no longer drinking. The hallucinations are not part of alcohol withdrawal delirium.

Although first episodes have been reported in people in their early to mid-20's, the more typical onset is about age 40, following 10 or more years of heavy drinking. The disorder has been found to be 4 times more common in males than in females. In some cases, the hallucinations last for several weeks; in other cases they last for several months, and in still other cases they seem to be permanent. The condition is very rare.

**Course.** The disorder typically lasts only a few hours or days, but it may persist for a week. Ten percent of cases may last several months. A chronic form of the disorder can occur which is difficult to distinguish from schizophrenia, because of continued hallucinations, delusions, illogical thinking, and inappropriate affect.

**Diagnosis.** The usual case of alcohol hallucinosis differs from schizophrenia by the temporal relation to alcohol withdrawal, the short-lived course, and the absence of a past history of schizophrenia. Alcohol hallucinosis is usually described as a condition manifested primarily by auditory hallucinations, sometimes accompanied by delusions, in the absence of symptoms of an affective disorder or organic mental disorder. Hallucinosis is differentiated from delirium tremens by the absence of a clear sensorium in delirium tremens.

**Treatment.** The treatment of alcohol hallucinosis is much like the treatment of delirium tremens—with chlordiazepoxide or diazepam, adequate nutrition, and fluids if necessary. In the absence of improvement with that regimen, phenothiazines can be used, as described for the treatment of schizophrenia.

### Alcohol Amnestic Syndrome (Wernicke-Korsakoff's Syndrome)

The essential feature of alcohol amnestic syndrome is a short-term, but not immediate, memory disturbance, due to the prolonged heavy use of alcohol. Other complications of alcoholism, such as cerebellar signs, peripheral neuropathy, and cirrhosis may be present.

Since the disorder usually occurs in persons

who have been drinking heavily for many years, it rarely occurs before the age of 35.

**Etiology.** The irreversible memory deficit, known as Korsakoff's psychosis or alcohol amnestic syndrome, often follows an acute episode of Wernicke's encephalopathy, a neurological disease manifested by ataxia, ophthalmoplegia (particularly involving the sixth cranial nerve), nystagmus, and confusion. Wernicke's encephalopathy may clear spontaneously in a few days or weeks, or progress into alcohol amnestic syndrome, in which the sensorium is clear but the patient has an irreversible short-term memory impairment. The early acute Wernicke stage apparently responds rapidly to large doses of parenteral thiamine, which is believed to be effective in preventing the progression into the alcohol amnestic syndrome. However, once the syndrome is established, the course is chronic and impairment is always severe. Lifelong custodial care is often required.

**Predisposing Factors.** Wernicke's encephalopathy and alcohol amnestic syndrome—the two are sometimes combined in the term Wernicke-Korsakoff's syndrome—are believed to be caused by thiamine deficiency. Therefore, malnutrition can be considered a predisposing factor. Heavy alcohol ingestion produces a malabsorption syndrome.

**Prevalence.** The prevalence is unknown, but the condition is apparently rare and may have become rarer in recent years because of the prophylactic effects of thiamine administered almost routinely during detoxification.

**Differential Diagnosis.** All causes other than prolonged and heavy use of alcohol must be ruled out.

**Treatment.** The syndrome is usually irreversible, although various degrees of recovery have been reported with a daily regimen of 50 to 100 mg of thiamine hydrochloride.

### Marchiafava-Bignami Disease

Marchiafava-Bignami disease is a rare disorder associated with alcoholism in which there is degeneration of the corpus callosum. The symptom is severe mental dysfunction. The diagnosis is seldom made before autopsy.

### Dementia Associated with Alcoholism

The essential feature of dementia associated with alcoholism is a dementia that persists at least 3 weeks after cessation of prolonged alcohol use, and for which all other causes of dementia have been ruled out. Other complications of alcoholism—such as cerebellar signs, peripheral neuropathy, and cirrhosis—may be present. Since the disorder occurs in persons who have been drinking heavily for many years, the disorder rarely occurs before the age of 35.

By definition, there is always some impairment in social or occupational functioning. When impairment is severe, the patient becomes totally oblivious to his surroundings and requires constant care.

**Predisposing Factors.** It is not yet known whether dementia associated with alcoholism is a consequence of the primary effect of alcohol or its metabolites on the brain, or an indirect consequence of the malnutrition, frequent head injury, and liver disease that occur with chronic alcoholism.

The disorder is apparently rare.

**Differential Diagnosis.** In the alcohol amnestic syndrome, there may be some features of a dementia. However, in alcohol amnestic syndrome, the most prominent disturbance is impairment in short-term memory, but not in immediate memory.

### Gastrointestinal and Cardiac Pathology

Some 10 percent of alcoholics develop cirrhosis of the liver, an often disabling and sometimes fatal complication correlated with the duration and the amount of alcohol consumption. Among the more serious complications of cirrhosis are esophageal varices, which often rupture, resulting in serious hemorrhage, liver failure, and carcinoma of the liver. With the cessation of alcohol intake and with adequate nutritional intake, cirrhotic patients can improve markedly.

Alcoholics have an abnormally high frequency of cancer of the mouth, throat, esophagus, and stomach. They are almost invariably heavy smokers, which undoubtedly contributes to their higher cancer rate. Gastritis is a common finding in alcoholics, as are gastric ulcers.

Although no specific entity can be identified as alcoholic pancreatitis, a definite association of uncertain mechanism exists. Alcoholic populations seem to be more vulnerable to pancreatitis than is the general population.

Alcoholic cardiomyopathy seems to be a distinct entity that occurs in men with a long history of alcoholism.

### Alcohol, Alcoholism, and Accidents

Most studies indicate that 60 to 80 percent of apprehended drivers are alcoholics.

In addition to having serious problems with alcohol, persons arrested for drunk driving—who thus far have been predominantly male—are significantly different from the general population on a number of personality parameters. They are more apt to have problems with depression, responsibility, self-esteem, paranoid thinking trends, and aggression when apprehended. They are also apt to be very resistant

to accepting the idea that they are alcoholic.

Since some two-thirds of persons arrested for driving while intoxicated are alcoholic, these arrests represent an excellent case-finding method for initiating appropriate treatment procedures—in many cases at a relatively early phase of the person's alcoholic illness.

Alcohol also plays a role in many types of accidents. A majority of fatally injured pedestrians were intoxicated at the time they were struck. Some 47 percent of nonfatal industrial accidents and up to 40 percent of fatal industrial accidents are alcohol related. Alcohol use has been found in 44 percent of pilots killed in general aviation crashes, and its use has been associated with 69 percent of drownings.

Alcohol use and alcoholism have been implicated in the cause of fires and in the failure to detect or escape them. Cigarettes are the major incendiary in alcohol-related burn injuries and deaths.

### Fetal Alcohol Syndrome

Studies of infants with neonatal abnormalities that included the drinking histories of the mothers revealed the possibility that many of the mothers were alcoholics. Mental retardation, growth deficiencies, craniofacial abnormalities, limb anomalies, cardiac defects, and delayed motor development are among the disabling findings.

Although the risk of an alcoholc woman's having a defective child is thought to be high—perhaps as high as 35 percent—it is difficult to generalize from existing studies to entire populations because of the nature of the study groups. The precise mechanism of the damage to the fetus is unknown, although the damage seems to be the result of in utero exposure to ethanol or its metabolites.

### Alcohol-Drug Interactions

The physical and behavioral effects of drugs and alcohol in combination are important considerations, whether patients are moderate drinkers or alcoholics. Of the 100 most frequently prescribed drugs, more than half contain at least one ingredient known to interact adversely with alcohol. Most adverse effects due to alcohol-drug interactions are accidental, but the medical toll is high.

Some alcohol-drug interactions occur only in chronic heavy alcohol users. An example is an increased metabolism rate for phenytoin sodium (Dilantin), requiring larger-than-normal doses to maintain a therapeutic effect. Patients who drink occasionally in small quantities do not suffer this effect.

Tolbutamide is another drug for which there

are distinct differences in effects among alcoholics, as opposed to occasional drinkers. Whereas short-term consumption of large amounts of alcohol increased tolbutamide's half-life, alcoholism causes a significant decrease in the drug's half-life.

Even abstaining alcoholics are reported to need doses different from those required by non-drinkers to achieve therapeutic levels of certain drugs, such as warfarin, phenytoin, tolbutamide, and isoniazid. The half-life of each of these drugs is 50 percent shorter in abstaining alcoholics than in nondrinkers.

An interaction between alcohol and a drug is any alteration in the pharmacologic effects of either due to the presence of the other. Interactions may be one of four general types: antagonistic, additive, supraadditive, and cross-tolerance.

Unpredictable or unexpected effects of alcohol-drug combination can pose serious problems in any of the four categories. For example, in addition to clinically significant enhancement of central nervous system depression from alcohol-chloral hydrate interaction, profound vasodilation can result. Infrequently, vasodilation occurs in persons who have received chloral hydrate for more than 7 days and who then ingest alcohol. They may experience a profound reaction characterized by tachycardia, palpitations, facial flushing, and dysphoria.

### Analgesics

Even when used alone, the salicylates—aspirin and sodium salicylate—commonly cause mild gastrointestinal blood loss and, rarely, severe bleeding. Alcohol also irritates the stomach and the intestines. Their combination can cause increased gastritis and blood loss.

Alcohol combined with salicylates can also predispose patients to delayed clotting and possible hemorrhages. The drugs tend to inhibit blood platelet aggregation, and chronic alcohol use is associated with alterations in red blood cells, granulocytes, and platelets.

### Anesthetics

Both cross-tolerance and synergistic effects can result from alcohol-anesthetic combinations. Patients who have alcohol in their systems require greater than usual amounts of an anesthetic to induce sleep. With chloroform and ether, cross-tolerance has been long observed, and recent reports indicate that alcoholics also need larger than usual doses of the fluorinated anesthetics to reach a desired level of narcosis.

After the initial phase of anesthesia, however, the presence of alcohol results in a supraadditive interaction. A deeper narcosis develops, plus an increase in sleeping time and a fatal outcome may be the result.

### Antianginal and Antihypertensive Agents

As a result of an additive interaction, alcohol may increase the blood pressure-lowering capability of some drugs, leading to postural hypotension, faintness, and loss of consciousness. For example, alcohol has an additive hypotensive effect in combination with reserpine, methyldopa (Aldomet), hydralazine (Apresoline, Dralzine), guanethidine (Esimil, Ismelin), ganglionic blockers, nitroglycerin, and peripheral vasodilators. In addition, propranolol may mask the signs and symptoms—rapid heartbeat, profuse sweating, and so on—of alcohol-caused hypoglycemia.

### Anticoagulants

The interference of alcohol with the metabolism of oral anticoagulant drugs is variable and not predictable, but it can be clinically significant in the case of warfarin (Athrombine-K, Coumadin, Panwarfin).

Acute intoxication can reduce the metabolism of these drugs, leading to increased anticoagulant effects and the danger of hemorrhage. The combination causes blood-warfarin levels to be higher than expected from a given dose. Chronic alcohol abuse, however, can enhance enzyme activity, leading to decreased anticoagulant effects. Because the effects on prothrombin time can change with varying intakes of alcohol, physicians need to monitor closely the prothrombin times in patients who drink.

### Anticonvulsants

A serious interaction between phenytoin sodium (Dilantin) and alcohol is the development of cross-tolerance to the anticonvulsant drug in patients with epilepsy who are also heavy drinkers. Alcohol apparently speeds up the metabolism of phenytoin, causing accelerated removal of the drug and making normal doses inadequate.

### Antidepressants and Stimulants

Tricyclic antidepressants can produce either synergistic or antagonistic interactions with alcohol, depending on the ratio of sedative activity to stimulant activity of the drug. For example, desipramine has a tendency to antagonize the depressant effects of alcohol, whereas amitriptyline can potentiate alcohol's sedative effects.

In addition, the tricyclic antidepressants may increase susceptibility to convulsions and should not be administered until after alcohol withdrawal. Because the drugs may produce hypotension, they should be prescribed only for alcoholics who can be monitored or who are no longer drinking.

Certain alcoholic beverages, such as beer and Chianti wine, contain tyramine and present known hazardous effects in combination with the monoamine oxidase inhibitors, causing hypertensive crises. The drugs also slow the metabolism of alcohol, causing intoxication to be greater than expected.

### Antihistamines

The prominent sedative side effect of antihistamines, experienced as drowsiness, is increased to such an extent in combination with alcohol that it is dangerous to perform any hazardous task while taking the combination.

### Antidiabetic Agents and Hypoglycemics

Tolbutamide and alcohol interact by multiple mechanisms and cause unpredictable fluctuations in serum-glucose levels. The most serious side effects are symptoms of severe hypoglycemia. Another dangerous and severe alcohol-drug interaction with these products is a disulfiram-like reaction. Because of the unpredictability of these reactions, patients should be cautioned about the excessive intake of alcohol when taking tolbutamide (Orinase), chlorpropamide (Diabinese), acetohexamide (Dymelor), and tolazamide (Tolinase).

### Antimicrobials and Antiinfective Agents

In combination with alcohol, some drugs may cause disulfiram-like reactions of nausea, vomiting, headache, and possibly convulsions. In general, these interactions are milder than the reactions to disulfiram and are due to the drugs' inhibition of alcohol metabolism. Antimicrobials with such potential interactions with alcohol include chloramphenicol, furazolidone (Furoxone), griseofulvin (Fulvicin), isoniazid, metronidazole (Flagyl), and quinacrine (Atabrine).

### Barbiturates

The well-known danger to human life from the combined use of alcohol and barbiturates appears to result from a synergistic interaction. The lethal dose for barbiturates is nearly 50 percent lower in the presence of alcohol than it is when the drug is used alone. Blood levels of secobarbital or pentobarbital as low as 0.5 mg per 100 ml can cause death from respiratory depression when combined with blood-alcohol levels of 0.1 percent. In severe alcohol-barbitu-

rate intoxication, the symptoms include vomiting, severe motor impairment, unconsciousness, coma, and death.

In addition to its potential for direct lethal effects, the alcohol-drug combination in sublethal doses can seriously impair skills needed for driving by increasing complex reaction times, and by causing some persons to fall asleep or exhibit impaired motor skills for several hours.

Alcohol abusers who have developed tolerance to alcohol exhibit cross-tolerance to barbiturates.

### Minor Tranquilizers

Many patients use minor tranquilizers in combination with alcohol because they are generally unaware that tranquilizers are central nervous system depressants that can increase the adverse effects of alcohol on performance skills and alertness.

Alcohol acts synergistically with meprobamate (Equanil, Meprospan, Miltown) to depress performance tasks and driving-related skills, such as time estimation, attention, reaction time, body steadiness, oculomotor control, and alertness.

The benzodiazepines (Librium, Valium, Dalmane) are the most frequently used minor tranquilizers. The majority of recent studies have found increased impairment from the alcohol-diazepam combination, and provide clear indications that the combination is dangerous.

### Major Tranquilizers

The major tranquilizers are central nervous system depressants. The most commonly used drugs in the group are the phenothiazines and haloperidol.

The phenothiazines, in combination with alcohol, may produce severe and possibly fatal depression of the respiratory center, and impaired hepatic function that results in toxic manifestations. In addition, hypotension, a side effect of the drugs, can be exacerbated by alcohol. Several studies indicate that alcohol, in combination with any of the major tranquilizers, impairs driving skills.

### Narcotics

Alcohol potentiates the depressant effects on the central nervous system of the narcotic analgesics—hydromorphone (Dilaudid), meperidine (Demerol), morphine, and propoxyphene (Darvon).

Repeated exposure to alcohol appears to increase the sensitivity to morphine and vice versa. Other opiates and propoxyphene have been reported to be frequently involved in deaths due to alcohol-drug combination.

## Alcoholic Women

Women tend to become alcoholic at a later age than do men (45, women; 30, men), but the women move rapidly from social drinking to alcoholism. Both men and women show a decreased incidence after 60.

In general, attempts to establish a female alcoholic personality as a unique phenomenon have not materialized. Clinical observations have indicated an increase in alcoholism in women. The changing societal role of women has been suggested as a possible reason for the increase.

Women are twice as likely as men to associate their alcoholism with specific circumstances or situations.

Women alcoholics are more apt than men to postpone treatment, and their families are more reluctant to force them into treatment. They often have a greater opportunity for remaining closet alcoholics.

## Treatment

### Barriers to Diagnosis and Treatment

A number of barriers interfere with the clinician's ability to diagnose and treat alcoholism.

Making the diagnosis can be hindered by the alcoholic's ability to camouflage his excessive drinking. Although many alcoholics realize that they have a drinking problem, an equally large number are resistant to the idea. This denial may be unconscious, a psychological mechanism designed to protect the alcoholic from the knowledge that he must give up drinking. Unfortunately, the alcoholic's denial is sometimes abetted by the clinician's focusing on some other aspect of his emotional difficulties.

The difficulty in making a diagnosis of alcoholism is compounded by the fact that most alcoholics are respectable citizens who live relatively quiet lives and manage to get to their places of employment each day, although they produce relatively little work after reaching their destinations.

Some 25 to 30 percent of alcoholics in the United States become and remain alcoholic on beer alone.

Although most alcoholics drink heavily and become intoxicated daily, a number are apt to concentrate their drinking on weekends, or drink in episodic or binge fashion.

If the clinician has a drinking problem, he or she is quite likely to minimize, overlook, or dismiss the alcoholism of patients who come for consultation or treatment; what other choice do they have, else find themselves aware of their own drinking problems?

The alcoholic's lack of self-restraint and repeated binges produce mixed feelings, even in those willing to help him. Some clinicians may be so ashamed of their anger at alcoholic patients that they tend to avoid treating them altogether, or hide their anger in an overindulgent attitude that is not conducive to helping the alcoholic toward sobriety.

Although some alcoholics have agreeable personalities, many have one or more personality or behavioral traits that may pose a barrier to those attempting to treat them. Although described separately here, these traits are often clinically melded.

**Dependency.** A dependent, demanding patient may well create anger and, ultimately, anxiety in a member of the healing profession who feels that anger is an unworthy emotion. It may be in the alcoholic's best interest for the clinician to recognize and accept his anger at the patient. It is inimical to the treatment process to evade and avoid anger or, even worse, to pretend good-humored acceptance of the alcoholic's petulant behavior. One must recognize anger in such situations as a logical response to unreasonable attitudes or demands.

**Hostility.** The alcoholic patient frequently feels frustrated and deprived; hence, he is recurrently angry with the world and its inhabitants. Clinicians, accustomed to responsive and grateful patients, may understandably react by becoming angry themselves or by losing interest in such nonconforming patients.

**Self-centeredness.** Alcoholics can be extremely self-centered, with devastating effects on those persons who look to them for the satisfaction of their needs.

**Depression.** The self-destructive tendency of alcoholic populations is well documented, with a suicide frequency ranging from 7 percent to 21 percent. If one includes alcoholics who are often seriously preoccupied with thoughts of suicide, the figure rises to 40 percent.

### Detoxification

Outpatient detoxification requires a cooperative patient and a cooperative significant other person. The patient must be seen as frequently as necessary for continued evaluation of his physical status. An outpatient detoxification regimen may require that the patient be seen as often as every day, or it may require no more than weekly visits. The patient is given chlordiazepoxide hydrochloride (Librium), 20 to 25 mg 4 times daily, with the dose depending on the severity of the withdrawal symptoms, if any. Arrangements are made for the patient to begin taking 250 mg of disulfiram (Antabuse) daily, starting 24 hours after the last drink. Generally, those with intact homes and interested families are the most likely candidates for outpatient detoxification.

Those requiring hospitalization for detoxification are alcoholics who show signs of impending delirium tremens, such as tremors, diaphoresis, hyperirritability, and rising pulse or blood pressure. Alcoholics who are severely depressed, suicidal, psychotic, uncooperative, or uncomprehending also require a hospital setting for detoxification, as do those whose physical illnesses would interfere with their cooperating with an outpatient program. Finally, one must hospitalize those alcoholics whose drinking cannot be interrupted except through an inpatient program. Inpatient detoxification programs are similar to that described for the treatment of delirium tremens. Medication dosages and the length of treatment are based on the severity of the withdrawal syndrome.

### Multiple Treatment Approach

Clinical trials indicate that, when two or more treatment modalities are used in combination, the percentage of patients with a favorable treatment outcome increases significantly. Hence, the development of a multiple treatment approach, in which every alcoholic patient is treated with as many modalities as can be used in logical and consistent fashion. A comprehensive multiple treatment program includes at least psychotherapy, both individual therapy and conjoint therapy if the patient is married, disulfiram, and appropriate minor tranquilizers and antidepressants. Many patients also find Alcoholics Anonymous of value, and all should be urged to explore affiliation with this organization. In addition, selected patients may need assistance from vocational rehabilitation and social service support agencies.

Before the component parts of a multiple treatment approach are described, two issues related to the treatment of alcoholism require clarification—voluntary versus involuntary treatment, and the question of sobriety as a treatment goal. The issue of voluntarism of alcoholic patients for treatment is a specious one. Virtually all alcoholic patients come into treatment as a consequence of some form of coercion. The coercing force may be the patient's spouse, foreman, employer, or the knowledge that continued drinking is imposing a serious health hazard. Rare is the alcoholic who comes to a psychiatrist because he alone has concluded that he is alcoholic. In actual practice, those patients who are coerced into treatment by circumstances or by persons who are meaningful to them are more apt to remain in treatment and to have a successful outcome than are alcoholics who are not coerced into treatment.

The goal of sobriety remains an important principle in the treatment of alcoholism. Since it is impossible to determine which alcoholic will be able to drink in controlled fashion again, or how many years and relapses must occur before he can arrive at this point, absolute abstinence must remain the most important objective—although not the sole objective—in the treatment of alcoholism.

**Psychotherapy.** Intensive psychotherapy designed to expose and interpret unconscious material is usually more deleterious than helpful to the alcoholic. Most alcoholics have a rather frail ego structure, and the interpretation of previously unconscious material may prove extremely anxiety producing, frustrating, or depressing for them, often to the extent that they have to be reassured at great length after the interpretations. Their intolerance of anxiety may result in a premature abandonment of treatment.

The psychotherapy of alcoholism should focus painstakingly on the reasons for the alcoholic's desire for intoxication, and his rejection of the sober state. What is the appeal for that person of being drunk? What are the drawbacks of being sober? Problems should be examined in terms of what the alcoholic feels these problems to be.

As the patient is encouraged to ventilate his thoughts and feelings about various aspects of his life, the therapist has the oportunity to help him determine which factors have contributed to his need to avoid sobriety.

The drinking itself—its past, present, and future consequences—must receive firm emphasis in psychotherapy.

The foregoing psychotherapeutic emphasis on drinking, its causes, and its consequences does not preclude psychotherapeutic exploration of all areas of the patient's psychopathology. Indeed, issues of dependency, hostility, and frustration, among others, often must be dealt with to enhance the alcoholic's chances for recovery.

Psychotherapy of any type is probably all but useless with a patient who is frequently or continually intoxicated.

**Conjoint Therapy.** When an interested and cooperative spouse is available, involving her in the patient's therapy brings many benefits. The vast majority of spouses of alcoholics are quite willing to do everything possible to bring about the alcoholic's recovery.

**Medication.** Two categories of drugs are useful in the treatment of alcoholism—the deterrent drug disulfiram (Antabuse) and psychotropic drugs.

*Disulfiram.* Disulfiram interferes with the metabolism of alcohol so that even a single drink usually causes a toxic reaction due to acetaldehyde poisoning. The patient uses 250 mg daily, first having been warned in detailed fashion by the physician as to the consequences of imbibing alcohol while using the drug or for 4 days thereafter. Nor should the patient start using the drug unless 24 hours have elapsed since his last drink. Those who drink while taking disulfiram experience flushing and feelings of heat in the face, sclera, upper limbs, and chest. They may become pale, hypotensive, and nauseated, and experience serious malaise. There may also be dizziness, blurred vision, palpitations, air hunger, and numbness of the extremities. The most serious potential consequence is severe hypotension. There is no justification for giving the patient a test dose of alcohol.

Most patients who experiment with drinking while taking disulfiram experience no more than unpleasant sensations and malaise. Severe reactions, usually associated with heavy drinking, may result in severe hypotension, and can be treated by placing the patient in shock position and administering intravenous or intramuscular diphenhydramine hydrochloride (Benadryl) or ephedrine sulfate. In rare cases, patients may require the type of treatment reserved for profound hypotension.

Disulfiram has been much maligned, probably because those programs that relied exclusively on its use were largely failures. Properly integrated into a multiple-treatment program, the drug is invaluable.

*Antianxiety Medication.* Inasmuch as anxiety and restlessness may be present for some weeks and even months during the initial stages of treatment of alcoholism, chlordiazepoxide hydrochloride (Librium), 20 mg to 60 mg daily in divided doses, is often helpful. Diazepam (Valium) may also be of use. There has been considerable controversy over the use of anxiolytic medication after alcohol withdrawal symptoms have subsided. Some have contended that the addictive person will substitute one habituating drug for another. At least one study of chlordiazepoxide as an adjunct to the treatment of 108 alcoholics revealed that such fears are largely groundless.

*Antidepressant Medication.* Studies of alcoholic patients indicate that as many as 30 percent may suffer from lasting depression of clinical magnitude. Those patients who remain clinically depressed beyond the detoxification period often benefit from antidepressant medications. Many respond to the tricyclic antidepressants in doses similar to those prescribed for other clinically depressed patients. The antidepressants can be used without difficulty in patients taking disulfiram.

*Sedation.* Long after they are detoxified, but particularly during the immediate postdetoxification period, many alcoholics suffer from sleep disruption, characterized by difficulty in sleep onset and by numerous arousals and awakenings. Even after many months of sobriety, the abstinent alcoholic may awaken more than a 100 times a night, several times the corresponding frequency of arousal found in normal controls. Hence, alcoholics with severe sleep disturbances may require the selective use of sedation from time to time. Chloral hydrate, 500 or 1000 mg, and flurazepam hydrochloride (Dalmane), 15 or 30 mg nightly, are useful for this purpose. Again, the possibility of habituating a patient to the use of these medications must be weighed against the patient's nocturnal distress and daytime fatigue. Furthermore, there is a growing body of data indicating that repeated sedation becomes less effective after several days.

**Alcoholics Anonymous.** AA is a voluntary fellowship of hundreds of thousands of alcoholics that was founded in 1935 by two alcoholics— a stock broker and a surgeon.

The multiple treatment approach to alcoholism should include the suggestion to the patient that he attend meetings of Alcoholics Anonymous, and determine whether membership can assist him toward a sober life. Physicians should not refer an alcoholic to AA except as part of a multiple treatment approach. Frequently, patients who initially object when AA is suggested later derive much benefit from the organization, and become enthusiastic participants.

Al-Anon is an organization for the spouses of alcoholics that is organized along the same lines as Alcoholics Anonymous. The major thrust of Al-Anon is to assist, through group support, the efforts of the spouses to regain self-esteem, give up the feeling of responsibility for their spouses' drinking, and develop a rewarding life for themselves and their families. Alateen has also been developed, for children of alcoholics, so that they may better understand their parents' alcoholism.

**Halfway Houses.** The discharge of alcoholic patients from hospitals often poses serious placement problems. Home or other previous environments may be deleterious or indifferent, or leave the alcoholic with too much time on his or her hands. Clinicians should be aware of the halfway house as an important treatment resource.

### Behavior Therapy

Modern behavior therapy, in its approach to alcoholism treatment, is dedicated to the concept that the alcoholism syndrome can be broken down into component parts that can be isolated, studied, and modified. Behavioral investigators have focused on such phenomena as antecedent cues, emotional factors such as depression and frustration, cognitive factors such as self-derogatory thoughts, and outcome variables such as the consequences of drinking behavior.

Another behavioral approach has been to teach the alcoholic alternatives to excessive drinking. These alternatives have included the teaching of relaxation techniques, assertiveness training, marital and other coping skills, and self-control skills. For example, self-control is not considered a character trait in the sense of will power but, rather, a behavioral skill that can be developed through training and practice. Some of the self-control strategies involve (1) rearranging environmental cues or life routines to decrease the chance of drinking, (2) using thought processes to modify the positive value of drinking, and (3) rearranging the social and environmental consequences of both drinking behaviors and nondrinking alternatives, so that the alternatives become more appealing and more likely than the drinking.

A number of operant conditioning programs have been described in which reward-punishment programs are used to condition the alcoholic to modify or stop his or her drinking. These reinforcers have included monetary rewards, an opportunity to live in an enriched versus an impoverished inpatient environment, and access to pleasurable social interactions.

Although many of the alcoholism behavior modification programs have important research dimensions, it is uncertain whether they will survive in their present form. In any case, interesting treatment ideas and concepts that have originated with behavior modification research have already contributed useful ideas to the therapy of alcoholism and the structuring of alcoholism treatment programs.

### REFERENCES

Fuller R K, Williford W O: Life-table analysis of abstinence in a study evaluating the efficacy of disulfiram. Alcoholism 4: 298, 1980.

Goodwin D W: Genetic component of alcoholism. Annu Rev Med 32: 93, 1981.
Goodwin D W: *Alcoholism: The Facts.* Oxford University Press, New York, 1981.
Goodwin D W: Drug therapy of alcoholism. In *Psychopharmacology Vol 1,* D G Grahame-Smith, H Hippius, G Winokur, editors. Excerpta Medica, Amsterdam, 1982.
Goodwin D W: Alcoholism and alcoholic psychoses. In *Comprehensive Textbook of Psychiatry,* ed 4, H I Kaplan, B J Sadock, editors, p 1016. Williams & Wilkins, Baltimore, 1985.
Grant I, Adams K M, Reed R: Aging, abstinence, and medical risk factors in the prediction of neuropsychologic deficit among long-term alcoholics. Arch Gen Psychiatry 41: 710, 1984.
Jellinek E M: *The Disease Concept of Alcoholism.* College & University Press, New Haven, CT, 1960.
Ryback R S, Eckardt M J, Felsher B: Biochemical and hematological correlates of alcoholism and liver disease. JAMA 248: 2261, 1982.
Turner T B, Bennett V L, Hernandez H: The beneficial side of moderate alcohol use. Johns Hopkins Med J 148: 53, 1981.
Whitfield J B: Alcohol-related biochemical changes in heavy drinkers. Aust NZ J Med 11: 132, 1981.

---

## 19.4  CAFFEINE AND TOBACCO DEPENDENCE

### Introduction

Caffeine and tobacco are two of the most widely consumed psychoactive substances in the world. Disorders stemming from caffeine and tobacco use were not officially included in the psychiatric nomenclature before the publication of DSM-III, since both nicotine and caffeine are commonly considered nondrugs. In actuality, however, both are potent pharmacological agents: both may induce distinct syndromes and modify the clinical manifestations of other psychiatric conditions, and both may pharmacologically interfere with common biological treatments used by psychiatrists. For these reasons, caffeine and tobacco dependence warrant inclusion in a complete nosological system of mental disorders; however, at the present time, only tobacco dependence is included in DSM-III.

### Caffeine

#### Definition

Caffeinism is a pharmacological state of acute or chronic toxicity that results from the ingestion of high doses of caffeine, whether in the form of coffee, tea, cola drinks, cocoa, chocolate, or various medications, including over-the-counter and prescription analgesics, cold preparations, and stimulants. Caffeinism is generally characterized by a constellation of anxiety and

TABLE I
SOME COMMON SOURCES OF CAFFEINE

| Source | Approximate Amounts of Caffeine per Unit* |
|---|---|
| Beverages | |
| Brewed coffee | 80–140 mg per cup |
| Instant coffee | 66–100 mg per cup |
| Tea (leaf) | 30–75 mg per cup |
| Tea (bagged) | 42–100 mg per cup |
| Decaffeinated coffee | 2–4 mg per cup |
| Cola drinks | 25–55 mg per glass |
| Cocoa | 5–50 mg per cup |
| Prescription medications | |
| A.P.C.'s (aspirin, phenacetin, caffeine) | 32 mg per tablet |
| Cafergot | 100 mg per tablet |
| Darvon compound | 32 mg per tablet |
| Fiorinal | 40 mg per tablet |
| Migral | 50 mg per tablet |
| Over-the-counter analgesics | |
| Anacin, aspirin compound, Bromo-Seltzer | 32 mg per tablet |
| Cope, Easy-Mens, Empirin compound, Midol | 32 mg per tablet |
| Vanquish | 32 mg per tablet |
| Excedrin | 60 mg per tablet |
| Pre-Mens | 66 mg per tablet |
| Many over-the-counter cold preparations | 30 mg per tablet |
| Many over-the-counter stimulants | 100–200 mg per tablet |
| Small chocolate bar | 25 mg per bar |

* Cup = 5–6 ounces; cola drinks = 8–12 ounces.

affective symptoms, sleep disruptions, psychophysiological complaints, and withdrawal manifestations.

### Epidemiology

When caffeine consumers ingest billions of kilograms annually, all forms are considered. Table I lists the common sources, with approximate amounts of caffeine in each.

The exact incidence and prevalence of caffeinism are unknown. About 20 to 30 percent of all adult Americans consume more than 500 mg of caffeine a day. Doses exceeding 250 mg a day are considered pharmacologically large. Caffeinism's prevalence is estimated to be at 10 percent for the general population of North Americans. Among hospitalized psychiatric patients, more than 20 percent report caffeine consumption exceeding 750 mg a day from all sources.

### Etiology

Caffeine's typical actions begin after 50 to 200 mg. Of epidemiological significance, this dosage is surpassed daily by millions. For example, five cups of coffee, two headache tablets, and a cola drink amount to a daily intake of about 700 mg. Although tolerance has been disputed, it clearly exists on a clinical basis, explaining why some

persons regularly consume doses exceeding 2 g daily without ostensible problems.

Caffeine is relatively safe, principally because it is markedly diluted. About 8 to 10 g—equivalent to ingesting 75 to 100 cups of brewed coffee—are required for lethality.

### Clinical Features

The only theoretical requirement for the development of caffeinism is the ingestion of toxic doses. Intake exceeding 500 to 600 mg a day significantly increases the risk of developing overt clinical manifestations of caffeinism. Five symptom constellations dominate the clinical presentation. Although discussed separately, these five symptom clusters usually coexist to some degree. They may also fluctuate in severity (see Table II).

**Anxiety Manifestations.** Diuresis, restlessness, tremulousness, hyperactivity, and irritability are most frequently reported. Patients often describe the constellation vaguely—for example, "I've been quite nervous lately."

**Psychophysiological Manifestations.** Physical complaints predominate in general medical patients with caffeinism. In psychiatric patients, moderate users (250 to 750 mg a day) report psychophysiological symptoms more frequently than do either low consumers (up to 250 mg a day) or high consumers (more than 750 mg a day), perhaps because the low consumers ingest nontoxic doses, and the high consumers are innately less sensitive—or develop a tolerance to—caffeine.

**Insomnia.** Sleep disruptions have long been

TABLE II
DIAGNOSTIC CRITERIA FOR CAFFEINE
INTOXICATION*

A. Recent consumption of caffeine, usually in excess of 250 mg.

B. At least five of the following:

    (1) restlessness
    (2) nervousness
    (3) excitement
    (4) insomnia
    (5) flushed face
    (6) diuresis
    (7) gastrointestinal complaints
    (8) muscle twitching
    (9) rambling flow of thought and speech
    (10) cardiac arrhythmia
    (11) periods of inexhaustibility
    (12) psychomotor agitation

C. Not due to any other mental disorder, such as an Axiety Disorder.

* From American Psychiatric Association: *Diagnostic and Statistical Manual of Mental Disorders*, ed 3. American Psychiatric Association, Washington, DC, 1980. Used with permission.

observed in sporadic or moderate users who consume caffeine near bedtime. The heaviest users usually develop a tolerance to this side effect.

**Withdrawal Symptoms.** Caffeine withdrawal headaches can be produced experimentally in laboratory settings, and are reported by as many as one-third of the moderate and high consumers in nonlaboratory settings if their daily intake is interrupted. This headache, which seems to be remarkably consistent in different persons, is described as generalized and throbbing, proceeding from lethargy to a sense of cerebral fullness to a full-blown headache. It occurs about 18 hours after the discontinuation of habitual caffeine intake and responds best to a renewed elevation of caffeine plasma levels, perhaps explaining why many tension headache-prone persons prefer over-the-counter analgesics that contain caffeine. Other withdrawal symptoms include drowsiness and lethargy, rhinorrhea, a disinclination to work, irritability, nervousness, a vague feeling of depression, and occasional yawning and nausea.

**Depression.** Few recent reports have emphasized depression as a central feature of caffeinism. But surveys of psychiatric patients revealed that the highest caffeine consumers (more than 750 mg daily) reported significantly greater scores on the Beck depression scale.

**Other Features.** Caffeine toxicity may induce psychosis in susceptible persons, or exacerbate thinking disruptions in patients previously diagnosed as having schizophrenia.

The symptoms of caffeinism are listed in Table III.

### Course and Prognosis

The longitudinal course of caffeinism is unpredictable. Tolerance may develop at different stages, producing temporary symptom disappearance, but if intake is again increased, the symptoms may reappear.

In the absence of other psychiatric conditions, the prognosis for caffeinism is good. Permanent long-term psychiatric consequences have not been documented, and afflicted persons generally function well in most areas.

### Diagnosis

The diagnosis should be tentative until it is clinically supported by a period of caffeine withdrawal followed by symptom relief and, ideally, by a caffeine challenge to reproduce the symptoms and even more strongly confirm a causative relationship.

TABLE III
CAFFEINISM

Confirmed history of recent caffeine consumption, usually exceeding 250 mg a day, more often exceeding 500 mg a day

Presence of at least five of the following signs and symptoms at a time when caffeine is being consumed:

Restlessness, nervousness, irritability, agitation, tremulousness, muscle twitching, or fasciculation

Insomnia or sleep disruption

Headache

Sensory disturbances (hyperesthesia, ringing in ears, lightheadedness, flashing of light, ocular dyskinesias)

Diuresis

Cardiovascular symptoms (palpitations, extrasystoles, arrhythmias, flushing, tachycardia, increased cardiac awareness)

Gastrointestinal complaints (epigastric pain, nausea, vomiting, diarrhea)

Rambling flow of thoughts and speech, periods of inexhaustability

Persistence of symptoms daily or sporadically for at least 2 weeks in conjunction with caffeine consumption, or consistent development of such symptoms each time higher caffeine consumption occurs

Absence of any disorder that otherwise accounts for the symptoms of caffeinism, such as anxiety, hyperthyroidism, pheochromocytoma, mania, hypomania, and electrolyte disturbances; caffeinism may contribute to and aggravate these conditions

Onset of caffeine withdrawal symptoms following cessation of caffeine consumption after a prolonged period with at least three (probable) or four (definite) of the following signs and symptoms present:

Headache, being relieved by further caffeine intake

Irritability

Inability to work effectively

Nervousness

Lethargy

The differential diagnosis of caffeinism should include anxiety disorders, mania, hypomania, hyperthyroidism, pheochromocytoma, electrolyte disturbances, spontaneously occurring sleep disorders, and intoxication from cocaine, amphetamine, and similarly acting sympathomimetics. Caffeinism may also coexist with and complicate these entities.

### Treatment

Effective treatment depends principally on the discontinuation or reduction of caffeine intake. After intake is stopped or dramatically reduced, troublesome symptoms should begin clearing in 4 to 10 days if they are due to caffeine toxicity. After several days of relief, a caffeine challenge may be worthwhile to help convince the patient of the need to eliminate or moderate the future intake of caffeine.

The substitution of decaffeinated beverages, and the encouragement to consume water when thirsty, may improve the outcome. The use of anxiolytics should be avoided if possible.

The majority of patients gradually resume previous patterns of high consumption and develop a fluctuating pattern of symptom recurrence.

## Tobacco

### Definition

Tobacco dependence is defined as either persistent tobacco use, despite the person's psychological distress at the need for repeated use, or persistent tobacco use whenever a person has developed serious tobacco-related physical disorders—for example, emphysema, bronchitis, coronary artery disease, peripheral vascular diseases, various cancers, and tobacco amblyopia—but continues to be so dependent on the drug that he or she is unable to discontinue its use.

Tobacco withdrawal is defined as a physiological withdrawal syndrome that is precipitated by the cessation of chronic tobacco use, and that is characterized by a strong craving for tobacco, anxiety, irritability, impaired attention, a cognitive preoccupation with actions associated with tobacco use, and mild physiological alterations. Withdrawal from the nicotine contained in tobacco is presumably responsible for most facets of this syndrome.

### Epidemiology

About 55 million Americans smoke cigarettes. These smokers consume an average of 11,000 cigarettes annually, or 1.5 packs daily. Thirty-nine per cent of American men and 29 percent of American women smoke. Although the percentage of smoking adults decreased between 1964 and 1978—from 42 to 32 percent—the percentage of women and teenage smokers increased.

### Etiology

The initiation of tobacco use seems to occur predominantly through social reinforcements. Once smoking is started, nicotine's multiple pharmacological effects promptly produce habituation in most regular users. Tobacco may induce a conditioning of the special senses, especially smell and taste. Instruments of smoking may also function as psychosocial coping mechanisms for some smokers; the physical actions of holding the cigarettes or cigars or pipes, tapping the tobacco, striking the match, inhaling, and exhaling enable some persons to feel comfortable in stressful situations. In addition, many smokers state that they avoid discontinuation of their habit because of their fears of gaining weight.

### Clinical Features

**Tobacco Dependence.** Psychological distress at continued tobacco use usually presents with mild anxiety, subtle guilt or shame, the development of a secretive pattern of tobacco use, or the appearance of an angry counterattacking style that defends the substance and criticizes opponents (see Table IV). If physical disorders exist that may be correlated to tobacco use, diagnosticians are forced to make a judgment as to whether the drug is causative or exacerbating. Consultations with other physicians treating these conditions may be necessary before applying this diagnosis. Because cigarette smoking has now been documented to pose a major health hazard for women who use oral contraceptives, they should be considered a high-risk group.

**Tobacco Withdrawal.** The most common symptoms of tobacco withdrawal are irritability, restlessness, dullness, sleep disturbances, gastrointestinal disturbances, headache, impaired concentration and memory, anxiety, and occasionally an increased appetite. Psychophysiological assessments have confirmed that increased slow rhythms develop in the electroencephalogram after discontinuation of tobacco. Also seen are increased frequency of muscle contractions, decreased heart rate and blood pressure, reduced performance on vigilance tasks, and weight gain. The sense of craving for tobacco steadily increases. If cigarettes, pipes, cigars, or chewing

TABLE IV
DIAGNOSTIC CRITERIA FOR TOBACCO DEPENDENCE*

A. Continuous use of tobacco for at least 1 month.

B. At least one of the following:

(1) serious attempts to stop or significantly reduce the amount of tobacco use on a permanent basis have been unsuccessful
(2) attempts to stop smoking have led to the development of Tobacco Withdrawal
(3) the individual continues to use tobacco despite a serious physical disorder (e.g., respiratory or cardiovascular disease) that he or she knows is exacerbated by tobacco use

* From American Psychiatric Association: *Diagnostic and Statistical Manual of Mental Disorders*, ed 3. American Psychiatric Association, Washington, DC, 1980. Used with permission.

TABLE V
DIAGNOSTIC CRITERIA FOR TOBACCO WITHDRAWAL*

A. Use of tobacco for at least several weeks at a level equivalent to more than ten cigarettes per day, with each cigarette containing at least 0.5 mg of nicotine.

B. Abrupt cessation of or reduction in tobacco use, followed within 24 hours by at least four of the following:

(1) craving for tobacco
(2) irritability
(3) anxiety
(4) difficulty concentrating
(5) restlessness
(6) headache
(7) drowsiness
(8) gastrointestinal disturbances

\* From American Psychiatric Association: *Diagnostic and Statistical Manual of Mental Disorders*, ed 3. American Psychiatric Association, Washington, DC, 1980. Used with permission.

tobacco served as coping mechanism, their discontinuation may also produce a reemergence of symptoms that had previously been modulated by the physical actions of smoking.

Another clinical consequence of nicotine use that clinicians may encounter is acute nicotine poisoning syndrome, consisting of nausea, salivation, abdominal pain, vomiting or diarrhea, headaches, dizziness, a cold sweat, inability to concentrate, mental confusion, and various sensory disturbances. Tachycardia and a weak, rapid pulse are often present.

Clinicians must also consider the fact that tobacco use may complicate prescribed psychiatric treatments. Because the substance increases the function of drug-metabolizing enzymes, lower plasma levels of neuroleptics and tricyclic antidepressants may result. This effect may explain why smokers who take chlorpromazine, for example, have lower rates of sedation and less hypotension than do nonsmokers.

Tobacco use is highly confounded with the use of other psychoactive substances. Alcoholics, for example, smoke significantly more than do nonalcoholics, and there is a high positive correlation between the amount of alcohol consumed and the amount of tobacco used. These correlations begin early; adolescent smokers have been observed to drink more beer, wine, and liquor than do nonsmokers. The essential features for the diagnosis of tobacco withdrawal are listed in Table V.

## Course and Prognosis

Tobacco dependence has no precise age of onset or longitudinal course. Because the deleterious effects of the drug usually appear only after chronic use, the diagnosis is likely to be infrequent among adolescents and young adults. By definition, some tobacco disorders may periodically disappear and reappear, depending on the patient's level of distress.

Most smokers experience significant withdrawal on discontinuation of tobacco use. Symptoms usually appear within several hours and persist from days to weeks. Indeed, some report a strong craving years after quitting. The degree of psychiatric impairment from tobacco disorders is usually minimal, but some persons experience significant impairment during withdrawal. This discomfort certainly contributes to the finding that the return to tobacco use exceeds 50 per cent in the first 6 months, and only about one-quarter of those who attempted to stop smoking have succeeded at the end of 1 year.

## Diagnosis

Although diagnostic accuracy is obviously vital, diagnosticians can realistically anticipate that these diagnoses will often be overlooked or omitted, in view of degree of social acceptance of tobacco use. Incidence and prevalence figures must be examined with caution.

**Differential Diagnosis.** Tobacco disorders need to be differentiated from anxiety, electrolyte disturbances, and various endocrine conditions. The major disorders to be considered before diagnosing a condition as tobacco withdrawal are the withdrawal disorders from other substances.

**Psychological Tests.** Smokers seem to differ from nonsmokers in being somewhat more impulsive and externally oriented, and having a higher degree of extroversion, more antisocial behavior, and greater levels of anger. The highest smoking rates are observed in those who are divorced and separated. The rates are lowest in those with a higher than average education and in the high socioeconomic groups.

## Treatment

The effective treatment of patients who attempt to stop using tobacco depends on accurate information, the avoidance of moralizing and judgmental stances, and the use of an understanding, supportive approach. Written contracts for the discontinuation of tobacco use may be helpful. The substitution of other activities during times when cigarettes are traditionally smoked may provide diversions. Some clinicians have suggested that persons who are trying to stop smoking should learn relaxation techniques and practice them daily. Smoking paraphernalia and all available sources of tobacco should be eliminated. Support from friends who have succeeded in quitting the habit should also be generated. Smokers attempting to quit have reported that positive reinforcement from treating clinicians is very influential. The doctor might also suggest that money previously used for tobacco be allocated for some narcissistic reinforcement, such as a desired vacation or the purchase of a luxury item. Hypnosis, aversive conditioning—for example, rapid puffing to develop nicotine toxicity—and phased withdrawal plans have all been used.

Lobeline sulfate, a nicotine agonist, has been used by some clinicians but probably lacks effectiveness. Nicotine gum and nicotine sprays can be substituted for the nicotine contained in tobacco, but whether they facilitate long-term discontinuation has yet to be determined. Clinicians must anticipate that repeat efforts will be required. Many people who fail to respond to one approach may benefit from another. Most cigarette smokers state that they have never been advised by a physician to discontinue their smoking.

## REFERENCES

Boublik J H, Quinn M J, Clements J A, Herington A C, Wynne K N, Funder J W: Coffee contains potent opiate receptor binding activity. Nature *301:* 246, 1983.

Boulenger J-P, Uhde T W: Caffeine consumption and anxiety: preliminary results of a survey comparing patients with anxiety disorders and normal controls. Psychopharmacol Bull *18:* 53, 1982.

Dreisbach R H, Pfeiffer C: Caffeine-withdrawal headache. J Lab Clin Med *28:* 1212, 1943.

Dunn W L Jr, editor: *Smoking Behavior: Motives and Incentives.* Winston & Sons, Washington D.C., 1973.

Greden J F: Anxiety or caffeinism: a diagnostic dilemma. Am J Psychiatry *131:* 1089, 1974.

Greden J F: Anxiety and depression associated with caffeinism among psychiatric inpatients. Am J Psychiatry *135:* 963, 1978.

Greden J F: Caffeine and tobacco dependence. In *Comprehensive Textbook of Psychiatry*, ed 4, H I Kaplan, B J Sadock, editors, p 1026. Williams & Wilkins, Baltimore, 1985.

Jaffe J H, Kanzler M: Nicotine: tobacco use, abuse and dependence. In *Substance Abuse: Clinical Problems and Perspectives*, J H Levinson, C Ruiz, editors, p 256. Williams & Wilkins, Baltimore, 1981.

Shaffer H, Stimmel B, editors: *The Addictive Behaviors.* Haworth Press, New York, 1984.

United States Public Health Service: *Smoking and Health: Report of the Advisory Committee to the Surgeon General of the Public Health Service.* United States Government Printing Office, Washington D.C., 1964.

# 20

# Psychosexual Disorders

## 20.1 GENDER IDENTITY DISORDERS OF CHILDREN AND ADULTS

### Introduction

Gender identity is a term used for one's sense of masculinity and femininity; it was introduced to contrast with sex, a term that summarizes the biologic attributes adding up to male or female. The essential feature of these disorders is an incongruence between anatomic sex and gender identity. Gender identity is the product of three kinds of forces: biologic, biopsychic, and intrapsychic responses to environment, especially effects due to parents and to societal attitudes.

### Origins

**Biologic.** For mammals, the resting state of tissue is female, and maleness is produced only if an androgen pulse is added. This process of sex differentiation is set off by the Y chromosome. Natural experiments in humans confirm the general rule that maleness and masculinity depend on fetal and paranatal androgens. As one observes animals in an ascending evolutionary scale, however, the general rule of behavior is that the organism is granted greater flexibility of response to a larger spread of environmental stimuli. This is also true for gender behavior—masculinity and femininity as contrasted with maleness and femaleness. No species more than humans so often breaches the rule that maleness and masculine behavior or femaleness and feminine behavior go together.

**Environmental Intrapsychic.** The second category of forces contributing to the development of gender identity is made up of two parts. The first is the effects of shaping—reward and punishment that do not leave deposits of intrapsychic conflict. The second, familiar largely because of Freud's work, is made up of the effects of trauma, frustration, and conflict (at first especially with objects in the outside world and then with one part of oneself attempting to control another), and the efforts the person

makes to resolve these conflicts in order to ensure gratification and tranquility. This prolonged childhood development, eventually leading to masculinity and femininity, is known in psychoanalytic circles as the oedipal conflict and its resolution.

### Disorders

The gender disorders can be divided into two groups. The first group is made up of those aberrations of masculinity and femininity that are not the result of intrapsychic conflict; the latter disorders are the result of intrapsychic conflict. For instance, an aberration due to an unusual core gender identity development is a variant, for it is not the result of intrapsychic conflict, avoidance of trauma, or unconscious (repressed) awareness that one has compromised and erected personality attributes to disguise one's true self. An unexpectedly powerful force—biologic or early postnatal—that shifts the balance in core gender identity development can produce a variant, such as a transsexual male, who chooses an object of the same sex but of opposite gender identity. So, too, any sexual styles that change with cultures and eras produce a variant; for example, women's ankles had great fetishistic power 70 years ago in Western society but have none now. Deprivation may also produce a variant, such as the use of animals *faute de mieux* (literally, for want of something better) in an adolescent.

It is almost universally argued today that the perversions are not created by personality, but by forces outside the psyche.

### Gender Identity Disorders of Childhood

At the extremes of gender disorder in children there are boys who, by the standards of their cultures, are as feminine as the most feminine of girls, and there are girls who are as masculine as the most masculine of boys. The aberrance may start as early as any that can be labeled masculine or feminine: by the second or third year of life. In each situation, everyone—adults and other children—are struck by the femininity of the boys and the masculinity of the girls. Even peers, the most sensitive of all observers, accept the validity of what they observe, so that these most feminine boys are allowed—as more normal boys would not be—by girls into the girls' games and vice versa for very masculine girls into boys' play. With the publicity that is given nowadays to gender disorders, these children know of and want "sex change."

Cross-gender behavior ranges on a continuum from these extreme cases to cases with persistent but mild gentleness, delicacy, lack of interest in rough and tumble play and sports in boys—not to be considered gender disorder—and equivalent to tomboyishness in girls. Prognosis for later gender disorder depends on the age of onset, intensity of the desires, natural appearance of the gender behavior, and resistance to change if the condition is discouraged. Although many children experiment momentarily with cross-gender play, the ones whose interests are persistent and obvious are at risk for later problems. In a long-term prospective study of 42 feminine boys who were first seen at ages 4 to 11, about 60 percent were overtly bisexual or homoerotic by young adulthood, but these problems were not found in the control group of 32 boys who were demographically matched but not preselected because of masculine behavior. Cross-dressing may be part of the syndrome of gender identity disorder. Seventy-five percent of boys who cross-dress begin to do so before their fourth birthday. Females also cross-dress early but usually stop by late childhood or adolescence because of social pressure.

No sharp line can be drawn on the continuum of gender disorder between the children who deserve a formal diagnosis and the ones who do not. Prevalence is therefore unknown. The criteria for diagnosis depend on the observers' discomfort, politicization of gender issues (when shall behavior be considered simply "different" and when is it "disorder"), and studies that will allow prediction of adult outcome, such as how many will become homosexuals, transvestites, transsexuals, or heterosexuals. Table I lists the DSM-III criteria for such disorders in childhood.

### Transsexualism

According to DSM-III, transsexualism is a persistent sense of discomfort about one's anatomic sex and a wish to live as a member of the opposite sex. The disturbance is continuous and should be present for at least 2 years. Persons with this disorder usually show gender identity problems as children. The ratio of males to females suffering from transsexualism varies from as high as 8 to 1 to as low as 2 to 1 (see Table II).

**Male Primary Transsexualism.** In this condition, an anatomically normal male knows he is anatomically normal but nonetheless considers himself to be a female within, and so makes every effort to arrange his body to conform with his gender identity.

The diagnosis is easily made clinically. This anatomically normal male is, at the time of evaluation—whether the patient is 4, 14, 24, 44, or 84—the most feminine (by the clichés of his culture) of any male, has always been so without any episodes—for moments, months, or years—of living, with normal appearance, in roles typical for males of that culture (for example, heterosexual liaisons, marriage, employment in masculine professions, military service, fetishism, or other evidence of valuing one's penis), and has been feminine since the first behavior that can be distinguished as gender behavior (between 1 and 2 years of age). This history—which is confirmed by direct observation of transsexuals from childhood on, by interviews with parents and other members of the family, and by childhood photographs in family albums—has never been reported for anyone in the categories of gender disorders to be described later.

The word "primary" is used in this diagnosis because the condition starts in the patient's earliest years and remains constant throughout life. It can, therefore, be contrasted with secondary transsexualism, a later acquisition.

Feeling as if he were a girl, although not denying the anatomic maleness, the transsexual single-mindedly seeks out "sex change" procedures and, with this desire overriding all other wishes of existence, in time manages to arrange for the following: estrogens to create breasts and otherwise feminize body contours, electrolysis to remove the male hair distribution and surgery to create female-appearing genitals by means of castration of the testes, amputation of the penis, and creation of an artificial vagina. Now, "she" can fully pass in society as a female; in fact, "she" has done so for months or years before these procedures. With no rehearsal, often in their teens, transsexuals are able to go into the world and be accepted by society at large, unsuspectingly, as a female.

*Etiology.* This discussion is retricted to the most feminine of males only, those who have been so since any gender behavior appeared and who have never had a period of masculinity. This is a small but homogeneous group of persons, all with a similar clinical picture, underlying psychodynamics, and etiologic complex.

TABLE I
DIAGNOSTIC CRITERIA FOR GENDER IDENTITY DISORDER OF CHILDHOOD*

*For females:*

A. Strongly and persistently stated desire to be a boy, or insistence that she is a boy (not merely a desire for any perceived cultural advantages from being a boy).

B. Persistent repudiation of female anatomic structures, as manifested by at least one of the following repeated assertions:

    1. That she will grow up to become a man (not merely in role)
    2. That she is biologically unable to become pregnant
    3. That she will not develop breasts
    4. That she has no vagina
    5. That she has, or will grow, a penis

C. Onset of the disturbance before puberty. (For adults and adolescents, see Atypical Gender Identity Disorder.)

*For males:*

A. Strongly and persistently stated desire to be a girl, or insistence that he is a girl.

B. Either (1) or (2):
    1. Persistent repudiation of male anatomic structures, as manifested by at least one of the following repeated assertions:

        (*a*) that he will grow up to become a woman (not merely in role)
        (*b*) that his penis or testes are disgusting or will disappear
        (*c*) that it would be better not to have a penis or testes

    2. Preoccupation with female stereotypical activities as manifested by a preference for either cross-dressing or simulating female attire, or by a compelling desire to participate in the games and pastimes of girls

C. Onset of the disturbance before puberty. (For adults and adolescents, see Atypical Gender Identity Disorder.)

* From American Psychiatric Association: *Diagnostic and Statistical Manual of Mental Disorders*, ed 3. American Psychiatric Association, Washington, DC, 1980. Used with permission.

TABLE II
DIAGNOSTIC CRITERIA FOR TRANSSEXUALISM*

A. Sense of discomfort and inappropriateness about one's anatomic sex.

B. Wish to be rid of one's own genitals and to live as a member of the other sex.

C. The disturbance has been continuous (not limited to periods of stress) for at least 2 years.

D. Absence of physical intersex or genetic abnormality.

E. Not due to another mental disorder, such as schizophrenia.

* From American Psychiatric Association: *Diagnostic and Statistical Manual of Mental Disorders*, ed 3. American Psychiatric Association, Washington, DC, 1980. Used with permission.

The boy's mother is a woman with a strong bisexual component in her personality. In childhood, her femininity was flawed because her mother felt no regard for this girl's femaleness and femininity. The mother (the transsexual's grandmother)—a cold, distant, harsh woman—was unable to give the girl a sense of worth, and so the child, although knowing she was a girl, had the conviction that being a girl was of no value and far inferior to being a boy.

The transsexual-to-be's father is distant and passive; only occasionally do these men have an effeminate tinge.

Although experts speculate that transsexualism must be the result of genetic, hormonal, or central nervous system factors, no such evidence has been found in humans. In fact, no complete gender reversal is found even in anatomically intact animals, except in the laboratory. The only biologic contribution to etiology known at present is the boys' beauty and grace, and very few beautiful boys become transsexuals.

*Treatment.* Although few cases have been reported, one can be cautiously optimistic that treating the very feminine boy may stop the progress of his developing femininity. In essence, the treatment is behavior modification, although the guidelines in some reports are drawn from a more dynamic approach—an understanding of the interplay of forces in the family. In addition to treating the boy, encouraging the pleasures of masculinity and discouraging femininity, the mother is also treated.

So far, no treatment has been reported that will make the adult primary transsexual masculine; with such patients one can either do nothing, or comply with the patient's wish for a sex change. Some have felt that doing the latter is the same as treating delusions by giving a patient what he delusionally demands, but their suggestion that the patient be treated by psychotherapy or psychoanalysis has yet to meet with success (at least none has been reported). On the other hand, when "sex change" procedures are used on these most feminine males (although by no means is this true for all patients receiving such treatment), the results seem uniformly successful; the patients are more content, become employable, and establish sturdier relationships with others.

**Male Secondary Transsexualism.** Anatomically normal males who do not fit the clinical decription for primary transsexualism, but who nonetheless request sex reassignment on the basis of feeling a powerful feminine urge, are classified as secondary transsexuals. This term implies that the manifest condition does not start when gender behavior first appears but, rather, later in life, from childhood on to any age. These males give a history of episodes or periods extending over years in which they appear unremarkably masculine and manage successfully in roles that are typically lived in that culture by males. They show that they are attached to their masculinity and maleness by, for instance, having married, by working as men who are accepted by others as masculine, and by getting gratification from their male genitals (heterosexually, homosexually, or in the practice of such perversions as fetishism and transvestism). In other words, this is a mixed group of men who have little necessarily in common except that they wish to change sex and that they do not fit the description of primary transsexuals.

*Etiology.* Because the category of secondary transsexualism is made up of different clinical states, one would not expect to find causes common to all patients in this class. The literature confirms this position, inasmuch as many different causative factors are reported. The one factor common to all is that no patient whose clinical picture fits the picture described herein had exposure to the family dynamics present in primary transsexualism.

*Treatment.* It is with secondary transsexuals—the patients who make up by far the greatest number of people requesting sex reassignment—that the major issues regarding treatment arise. First, surgical transformation is definitive; there is no turning back if the psychologic results are poor. Second, there are so many different personalities represented in secondary transsexualism that a single treatment approach would be wrong. Third, due to the failure of most of these patients' physicians to publish short-term and long-term follow-ups, physicians still do not know to what risks they expose these patients.

**Female Transsexualism.** Female transsexuals are the most masculine of females. These anatomically normal females have been masculine since early childhood and have not had episodes in their lives when they expressed femininity. Like the males, they are exclusively homosexual if measured by the anatomy of their sex objects, but heterosexual if measured by identity. They, like the males, do not deny their anatomic sex but are, nonetheless, unendingly preoccupied with the sense of really being men and with the desire to have their bodies changed to male. Although males can surgically receive a genital that can function in a female manner—even including, at times, capacity for orgasm—it is not yet possible to give a female functioning testes or a penis. However, with testosterone, mastectomy, and panhysterectomy, the patient can pass as a man.

When a child, this girl refuses to be a girl. She gives herself a boy's name, dresses completely in boys' clothes, and is interested in and skillful in the same activities as are boys. She successfully appears as a male, without rehearsal and the first time out in public, with no one suspecting her true sex. Even before "sex change" the patient has found a partner with whom she lives for a long time, perhaps permanently. This partner is not an overt homosexual but is usually a woman who has not had homosexual relations, who has been married and had children, and who responds to the patient as if she were a man without a penis, not as if she were a homosexual.

*Etiology.* Although the evidence is fragmentary, the following may account for female transsexualism. At the time this infant is born—an infant seen by her parents as not pretty or cuddly but as strong and vigorous—or in the early months of life, her mother is unavailable for mothering. This is usually because the mother is clinically depressed, although in some cases the mother has been absent from her mothering (but not totally physically absent) because of severe physical illness or psychological illness. That she is physically but not psychologically present sets up a poignant situation, more intense than if the mother were completely gone and replaced by an adequate substitute. At this time in the relationship between her parents, the infant's father is either unwilling or unable to move in and by himself carry the burden of his wife's problem. The little girl is used for that; she is to be a comfort and a cure that the father will not provide. Her task, she comes to sense, is to restore her mother. In doing this, she is supported by her father, with whom she may have a close and happy relationship, but, in order to do so, he makes her into his substitute. He encourges her in behavior he considers masculine, and so she spends much time with him successfully learning to be like his little boy. His joy when she is physically adept and then athletically skilled, and his pleasure in having her accompany him when he works around the house or at his hobbies, when he hunts or fishes, augment the encouragement to be masculine she already senses in having been chosen as her father's substitute in her mother's suffering.

This process is furthered from the start by the infant's unlovely appearance. Had she been considered feminine, she would not have served as well for molding into masculinity.

As with male transsexualism, there is no reported evidence of biologic factors in the etiology other than the appearance just noted.

*Treatment.* There are no cases reported in the literature of child, adolescent, or adult female transsexuals successfully treated by any method that would make them feminine. As with the males, it seems that, if one establishes a clearcut core gender identity, it is difficult later in life to instill attributes of an opposite identity. Whether behavioristic techniques in the future will succeed in doing this is still unknown.

### Fetishistic Cross-dressing (Transvestism)

**Clinical Features.** Sexual excitement produced by garments of the opposite sex is found exclusively in males. Although this perversion starts most often in adeolescence, it has been seen in prepubertal boys and may even first manifest itself in adult men in their thirties or forties. There are two groups—those men who prefer a single type of garment, such as shoes, throughout their lives and those who, starting with a single garment, eventually prefer to dress completely as women and who, in addition to the penile gratification, also have the nonerotic pleasure of feeling themselves temporarily to be women with penises.

In DSM-III, transvestism is defined as "recurrent and persistent cross-dressing by a heterosexual male in the absence of the transsexual syndrome." In DSM-III, transvestism is diagnosed when the cross-dressing relieves anxiety or gender discomfort. When sexual arousal is caused by the cross-dressing, the diagnosis of fetishism is added.

Most transvestites are overtly heterosexual and marry. They work in professions requiring masculine interests and behavior; they dress, except when cross-dressed, in masculine clothes, and they have masculine interests and hobbies, and engage in masculine sports. Cross-dressing begins in childhood or early adolescence.

*Etiology.* Although the causative factors are less clear in transvestism than in primary transsexualism, many transvestites or their families, or both, report that the first episode of cross-dressing occurred when a female dressed the boy in girl's clothes in childhood, at which time he was not sexually excited. It was done to humiliate him; that is, it was done by a female attacking an essential of the boy's identity, his masculinity. Years later, however, the fetishism—erotic cross-dressing—surfaced. In all cases of transvestism, as differentiated from primary transsexualism, there is a history of some masculine development and present-day masculinity. One could not humiliate a primary transsexual at any age by putting him into girls' clothes. It is unlikely, however, that a single episode of forced cross-dressing could permanently distort a boy's erotic development unless he had been made susceptible by earlier, continuous pressure (most likely by parents or sisters) that chronically threatened his developing masculinity.

*Treatment.* One report shows that behavior modification techniques can be successful. Although the follow-up time is too short for a final decision about efficacy, the aberrant sexual behavior can be removed in some of those who choose to have it removed. The more purely fetishistic the patient, the better is the prognosis with this treatment. The more his condition consists also of desires to pass in public as a woman, the poorer the results.

### Cross-gender Homosexuality

Many male and female homosexuals (no reports tell how many) have cross-gender qualities. One sees a continuum among homosexuals of each sex, the males ranging from having no effeminate qualities to a marked and persistent effeminacy, the females from being nonmasculine to being in states approaching female transsexualism. The prime feature stressed herein for distinguishing these people from others with gender disorders is that those considered here are overt homosexuals, acknowledging, at least to themselves, that this is the case, and clearly preferring people of the same sex. This last qualification can be underlined by stating that the homosexual feels that he prefers a person of the same sex; the transsexual, in contrast, feels himself heterosexual.

### Psychoses and Borderline States

Although flagrant cross-gender behavior is not typical of schizophrenia and borderline states, it is occasionally seen. The gender disorder is sometimes only a minor element in the patient's style of behavior and at other times dominates it, creating a bizarre picture indeed.

### Intersexuality

Today, the term "intersexuality" is used in discussing persons with gross anatomic or physiologic aspects of the opposite sex.

**Turner's Syndrome.** In this condition, one sex chromosome is missing (XO). The result is an absence (agenesis) or minimal development (dysgenesis) of the gonads; no significant sex hormone, male or female, is produced in fetal life or postnatally. The sexual tissues thus retain a female resting state. Since the second X chromosome, which seems responsible for full femaleness, is missing, these girls are incomplete in their sexual anatomy and, lacking adequate estrogens, develop no secondary sex characteristics without treatment. They often suffer other stigmata, such as web neck. The infant is born with normal-appearing female external genitals, and so is unequivocally assigned to the female sex and thus reared. All these children develop as unremarkably feminine, heterosexually oriented girls, although later medical management is necessary to assist them with their infertility and absence of secondary sex characteristics.

**Klinefelter's Syndrome.** This person (usually XXY) has a male habitus, under the influence of the Y chromosome, but this effect is weakened by the presence of the second X chromosome. Although he is born with a penis and testes, the testes are small and infertile, and the penis may also be small. In adolescence, some of these patients develop gynecomastia and other feminine-appearing contours (see Fig. 1). Sexual desire is usually weak. Sex assignment and rearing should lead to a clear sense of maleness, but these patients often have gender disturbances, ranging from a complete reversal, as in transsexualism, to homosexuality or intermittent desire to put on women's clothes. It seems that, as a result of lessened androgen production, the fetal hypogonadal state in some patients has failed to produce fully the central nervous system organization that should underlie masculine behavior. In fact, in many of these patients, there is a wide spread of psychopathology, well beyond that of gender.

**Andrenogenital Syndrome.** When this condition occurs in females, excessive adrenal fetal androgens cause androgenization of the external genitals, ranging from mild clitoral enlargement to external genitals that look like a normal scrotal sac, testes, and a penis; hidden behind these external genitals are a vagina and a uterus. These patients are otherwise normally female. At birth, if the genitals look male, the child is assigned to the male sex and is so reared. The result is a clear sense of maleness and unremarkable masculinity, but if the child is diagnosed as a female and is so reared, a sense of femaleness and femininity results. If the parents are uncertain to which sex their child belongs, a hermaphroditic identity results. Although these patients show the power of rearing, the resultant gender identity seems to be also the effect of fetal androgens, organizing the fetal brain in a masculine direction; for what results in those children raised unequivocally as girls is a tomboy quality more intense than that found in a control series, but with the girls nonetheless having a heterosexual orientation (see Fig. 2).

**Male Pseudohermaphroditism.** Different conditions can lead to hermaphroditic external genitals in otherwise normal males. The genitals' appearance at birth, not the true biologic maleness, determines the sex assignment, and the core gender identity is male, female, or hermaphroditic, depending on the family's conviction as to the child's sex. See Figure 3 for an example of a true hermaphrodite.

**Androgen Insensitivity Syndrome.** This congenital (probably genetic but not chromosomal) disorder results from an inability of target tissues to respond to androgens. Unable to respond, the fetal tissues remain in their female resting state, and the brain is not organized to masculinity. The infant at birth appears an unremarkable female, although she is later found to have cryptorchid testes, which produce the testosterone to which the tissues do not respond, and minimal or absent internal sexual organs and vagina. Secondary sex characteristics at puberty are female because of the small but sufficient amounts of estrogens typically produced by testes. These patients invariably sense themselves as females, and are feminine (see Fig. 4).

**Temporal Lobe Abnormality.** There are a handful of cases of gender disorders, all in males, associated with temporal lobe dysfunction and that remit when the brain disorder is treated— for example, impulsive cross-dressing. Perhaps related are reports stating that electroencephalograms show dysrhythmias in transsexuals and transvestites more frequently than in control

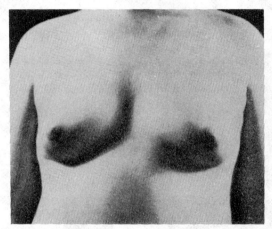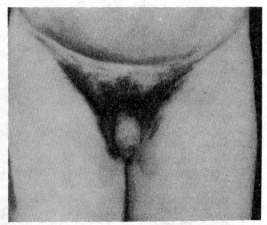

FIGURE 1.   Gynecomastia in a male with Klinefelter's syndrome, with positive Barr bodies and an XXY karyotype. The testes are very small and show typical seminiferous tubule sclerosis. (Courtesy of Robert B. Greenblatt, M.D., and Virginia P. McNamara, M.D.)

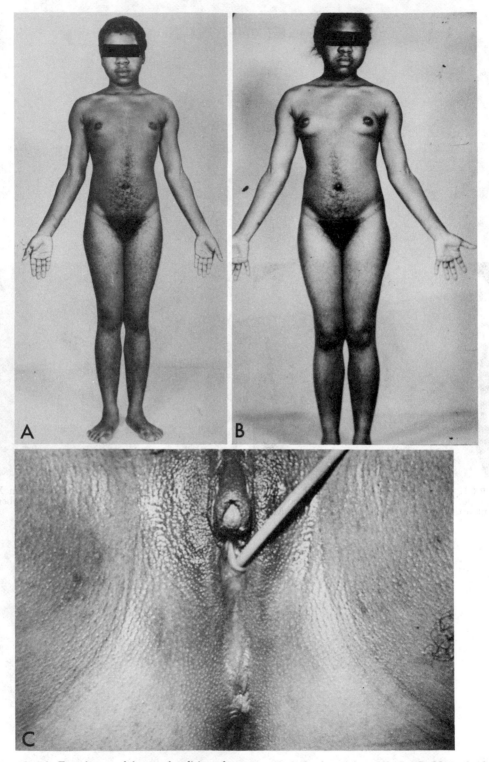

FIGURE 2.   *A.* Female pseudohermaphroditism due to congenital adrenal hyperplasia. *B.* Note the breast development after 6 months of cortisone therapy; normal cyclic menses began within a few months. *C.* Note the enlarged clitoris and urogenital sinus. (Courtesy of Robert B. Greenblatt, M.D., and Virginia P. McNamara, M.D.)

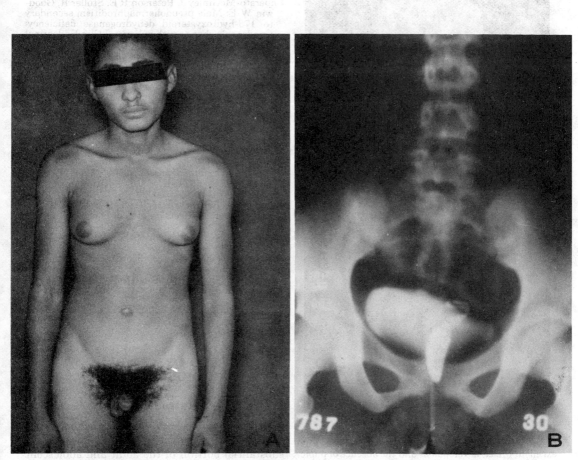

FIGURE 3. A true hermaphrodite. An abdominal ovary and a scrotal testis were found on biopsy of gonadal structures. Menses occurred each month from the urogenital sinus. *A.* Note gynecomastia. *B.* A cystogram and vaginal-uterosalpingogram revealed separate openings for the urethra and vaginal tract. The unicollis uterus and the Fallopian tube are outlined. (Courtesy of Robert B. Greenblatt, M.D., and Virginia P. McNamara, M.D.)

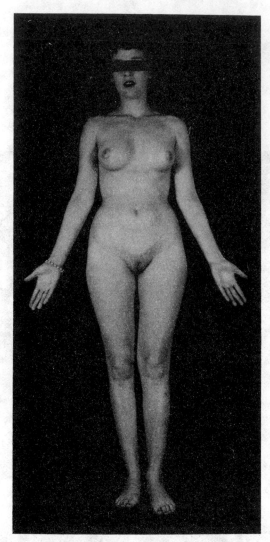

FIGURE 4. A phenotypic female with abdominal testes and an XY chromosomal karyotype. Note the excellent breast development and the absence of pubic hair. A normal blind vagina was present without clitoral enlargement. (Courtesy of Robert B. Greenblatt, M.D., and Virginia P. McNamara, M.D.)

groups. These reports need corroboration before one speculates on the role of the temporal lobes in gender behavior.

**Treatment.** Obviously, these different disorders require different medical and psychiatric management. The first rule, however, is that attempts to change gender orientation should be based on careful investigation of the patient's present gender identity. The somatic state should not cause one to inflict arbitrarily on the patient an attempt at creating a new personality; judgments about the somatic state must be made on the basis of identity.

## REFERENCES

Freud S: Three essays on the theory of sexuality. In *Standard Edition of the Complete Psychological Works of Sigmund Freud*, vol 7, p 135. Hogarth Press, London, 1953.
Green R: *From "Sissy" Boys to "Gay" Men? A Fifteen Year Puzzle.* Yale University Press, New Haven, 1983.
Imperato-McGinley J, Peterson R E, Stoller R, Goodwin W E: Male pseudohermaphroditism secondary to 17β-hydroxysteroid dehydrogenase deficiency: Gender role change with puberty. J Clin Endocrinol Metab *49:* 391, 1979.
Jost A: A new look at the mechanisms controlling sex differentiation in mammals. Johns Hopkins Med J *130:* 38, 1972.
Lothstein, L M: *Female-to-Male Transsexualism.* Routledge and Kegan Paul, London, 1983.
Money J, Ehrhardt A A: *Man and Woman/Boy and Girl.* Johns Hopkins Univerity Press, Baltimore, 1972.
Ohno S: The role of H-Y antigen in primary sex determination. JAMA *239:* 217, 1978.
Person E, Ovesey L: The transsexual syndrome in males: I. Primary transsexualism. Am J Psychotherapy *28:* 4, 1974. II. Secondary transsexualism. Am J Psychotherapy *28:* 174, 1974.
Rubin R T, Reinisch J M, Haskett R F: Postnatal gonadal steroid effects on human behavior. Science *211:* 1318, 1981.
Stoller R J: *Sex and Gender.* Science House, New York, 1968.
Stoller R J: Gender identity disorders in children and adults. In *Comprehensive Textbook of Psychiatry*, ed 4, H I Kaplan, B J Sadock, editors, p 1034. Williams & Wilkins, Baltimore, 1985.

## 20.2   EGO-DYSTONIC HOMOSEXUALITY

### Introduction

Persons with an exclusively or predominantly same-sex sexual partner preference constitute a substantial portion of the adult and adolescent population. Estimates of the occurrence of homosexual and bisexual behaviors vary, as do the definitions. In spite of the contemporary wave of sex surveys, the best data remain those of Kinsey, who reported that 4 percent of adult men were exclusively homosexual throughout their lives and that another 13 percent were predominantly homosexual for at least 3 years between ages 16 and 55. More than one in three men had experienced a sexual interaction leading to orgasm with another male during the postpubertal years. For women, the reported rates were approximately half those for men.

### Terminology

The American Psychiatric Association in April 1974 ruled that homosexuality per se is not a mental disorder and would no longer be listed as such. In its place was created the new category of sexual orientation disturbance.

In DSM-III, sexual orientation disturbance has been omitted and a classification of ego-dystonic homosexuality has been listed under the larger category of psychosexual disorders. Ego-dystonic homosexuality is not listed in the section headed paraphilias. That section includes disorders that "involve gross impairment in the capacity for affectionate sexual activity between adult partners." A lengthy introductory comment to the classification of homosexuality again underscores the fact that homosexuality per se is not a mental disorder, and is not to be classified as such. DSM-III notes, however, that for some persons there is persistent distress associated with a same-sex partner preference and that the person experiences a strong need to change the behavior or, at least, to alleviate the distress associated with homosexuality. These persons experience ego-dystonic homosexuality.

## Definition

The criterion features of ego-dystonic homosexuality are a desire to acquire or increase heterosexual arousal so that heterosexual relationships can be initiated or consummated, and a sustained pattern of overt homosexual arousal that is explicitly unwanted and a persistent source of distress. Diagnosis is reserved for those homosexuals for whom reversal of their sexual orientation is a persistent concern and not simply the product of a disappointing love relationship or of a difficulty in adjusting to a new awareness of homosexual impulse (see Table I). Age of onset is commonly during early adolescence, when the individual becomes aware that he or she is homosexually aroused and has negative feelings about possibly being a homosexual.

## Etiology

An overview of homosexuality is necessary to understand ego-dystonic homosexuality. The causes of homosexual behavior are enigmatic and controversial. Much remains unknown regarding the causes of heterosexual behavior, unless one argues, in a Darwinian sense, for a biologically programmed predisposition required for survival of the species.

Freud viewed homosexuality as an arrest of psychosexual development. When vestiges of the early phase remain, latent (i.e. unconscious) homosexually develops. This latent homosexuality is transformed by sublimation into affectionate behavior toward persons of one's own sex or into passive tendencies in men and aggressive tendencies in women.

Castration fear for the male is prominently mentioned by Freud and subsequent psychoanalytic writers. Others added fear of maternal engulfment in the preoedipal phase of psychosexual development. Early-life situations that can result in male homosexual behavior include a strong fixation on the mother, lack of effective fathering, inhibition of masculine development by the mother, fixation or regression at the narcissistic stage of development, and losing competition with brothers and sisters.

Freud's views on female homosexuality included a lack of resolution of penis envy in association with unresolved oedipal conflicts.

Based on available studies, there is suggestive evidence that genetic and biological components may contribute to homosexual orientation.

Homosexual female patients, as compared with heterosexual female patients, have been reported to have fathers who were close binding and intimate, the converse of that found for male homosexuals. However, the descriptions given of the mothers of female homosexuals were not different from the descriptions given of the mothers of the heterosexuals.

## Clinical Features

The behavioral features of male and female homosexuals are as varied as those of male and female heterosexuals. Sexual practices engaged in by homosexuals are the same as for heterosexuals with the obvious limitations imposed by anatomy. Just as with heterosexuals, homosexuals show individual preferences that may involve kissing, fondling, oral-genital sexuality, manual-genital manipulation, and anal inter-

TABLE I
DIAGNOSTIC CRITERIA FOR EGO-DYSTONIC HOMOSEXUALITY

A. The individual complains that heterosexual arousal is persistently absent or weak and significantly interferes with initiating or maintaining wanted heterosexual relationships.

B. There is a sustained pattern of homosexual arousal that the individual explicitly states has been unwanted and a persistent source of distress.

* From American Psychiatric Association: *Diagnostic and Statistical Manual of Mental Disorders*, ed 3. American Psychiatric Association, Washington, DC, 1980. Used with permission.

course. The patterns of sexual experience between same-sex couples vary from dyad to dyad. Thus, there may be preferences for a particular pattern of sexual expression, but these preferences are typically not stereotyped from relationship to relationship but are, in part, influenced by the preferences of the partners. Significant cross-gender aspects of homosexual experiences are rare, specifically the use of an artificial phallus by female homosexuals and cross-dressing by males.

Varying ongoing relationship patterns exist among homosexuals, as they do among heterosexuals. Some male and female dyads have lived in a common household in either a monogamous or a primary relationship for decades, and other homosexually oriented persons typically have only fleeting sexual contacts. Although more stable male-male relationships exist than were previously thought, it appears that male-male relationships are less stable and more fleeting than are female-female relationships. Many fleeting male relationships are initiated in gay baths and bars, with a smaller number initiated in public restrooms and parks. The comparable female institutions are practically nonexistent. The amount of male homosexual promiscuity has diminished since the onset of autoimmune deficiency syndrome (AIDS) and its transmission in homosexuals through sexual contact.

Homosexual males are subjected to civil and social discrimination and do not have the legal social support system of marriage or the biological capacity for childbearing that is a bond holding some otherwise incompatible heterosexual couples together. Female-female couples, on the other hand, experience less social stigmatization and appear to have more enduring monogamous or primary relationships.

More overlap than was previously thought may exist between heterosexual and homosexual life patterns. The heterosexual singles bar and the homosexual singles bar have much in common with respect to the nature of their social activity. The heterosexual divorce rate at 50 percent, even with the extant social support systems, suggests that many of the unstable characteristics ascribed to homosexuals have been misfixed to homosexual relationships. Further, the gay-bar set is only reflective of a subsample of the larger homosexual population, quite clearly the most visible sample.

## Psychopathology

The range of psychopathology that may be found among homosexuals is parallel to that found among heterosexuals, unless one is wedded to the belief that homosexuality per se is a mental disorder. Much confusion has been rendered by reports in the psychiatric literature of impressions of psychopathology derived from clinical samples.

In DSM-III, under the category psychosexual disorder, is the diagnosis ego-dystonic homosexuality. The features are the "desire to acquire or increase heterosexual arousal so that heterosexual relationships can be initiated or maintained, and a sustained pattern of overt homosexual arousal that the individual explicitly complains is unwanted and a source of distress. Individuals with this disorder may either have no or very weak heterosexual arousal. Typically, there is a history of unsuccessful attempts at initiating or sustaining heterosexual relationships. In some cases, no attempt has been made to initiate a heterosexual relationship because of the expectation of lack of sexual responsiveness. In other cases, the individual has been able to have short-lived heterosexual relationships, but complains that his heterosexual impulses are too weak to sustain such relationships. When the disorder is present in an adult, usually there is a strong desire to be able to have children and family life. Usually individuals with this disorder have had homosexual relationships, but often without satisfaction because of strong negative feelings regarding homosexuality. In some cases, the negative feelings are so strong that the homosexual arousal has been confined to fantasy." Associated features include loneliness, guilt, shame, anxiety, and depression in varying degrees (see Table I).

## Diagnosis

The criteria for ego-dystonic homosexuality, as outlined in DSM-III, include long-standing dissatisfaction with homosexual arousal patterns, weak or absent heterosexual arousal patterns, a desire to increase heterosexual arousal, and strong negative feelings regarding being homosexual. In the absence of distress over being homosexual or the desire to become heterosexual, the diagnosis of ego-dystonic homosexuality cannot be made. With a person who is primarily or exclusively homosexually oriented without the above criteria and who is depressed or anxious or has some other psychiatric symptom, that symptom becomes the key to the diagnosis. Homosexuality per se is not coded as a mental disorder.

Occasional statements to the effect that life would be easier if the person were not homosexual do not warrant the diagnosis of ego-dystonic homosexuality. Also, distress resulting only from conflict between the homosexual and the societal value structure is not classifiable here. If the distress is sufficiently severe to warrant a diagnosis, an adjustment disorder or a depressive disorder is to be considered. Some homosexuals suffering from a major depressive disorder may experience guilt and self-hatred that become directed toward their sexual orientation, but the diagnosis of ego-dystonic homosexuality is not to be made if the desire for sexual reorientation is only a symptom of the depressive disorder.

### Course and Prognosis

Some homosexuals, particularly males, report being aware of same-sex romantic attractions before puberty. According to Kinsey's data, about half of all prepubertal males have some genital experience with a same-sex partner. However, this experience is often of an exploratory nature and typically lacks a strong affective component. Most male homosexuals recall the onset of romantic and erotic attractions to same-sex partners during early adolescence. For females, the age of initial romantic feelings toward same-sex partners may also be preadolescent. However, the clear recognition of a same-sex partner preference typically occurs in mid to late adolescence or not until young adulthood. Early adolescents may be aware of both heteroerotic and homoerotic attractions.

More homosexual women than homosexual men appear to have heterosexual experiences during their primarily homosexual careers. In one study 56 percent of a lesbian sample had heterosexual intercourse before their first genital homosexual experience, compared with 19 percent of a male homosexual sample who had heterosexual intercourse first. Nearly 40 percent of the lesbians had had heterosexual intercourse during the year preceding the survey.

### Treatment

As for treatment of ego-dystonic homosexuality there is some dispute as to the efficacy of various procedures. It has been reported that, with a minimum of 350 hours of psychoanalytic therapy, approximately one-third of about 100 bisexual or homosexually oriented males achieved a heterosexual reorientation at 5 years' follow-up. Behavior therapists' outcome studies report similar figures. Avoidance conditioning techniques have also been used, but a basic problem with behavioral techniques is that, while the behavior may be changed in the laboratory setting, it may not be changed outside of the laboratory, in real life.

Prognostic factors weighing in favor of heterosexual reorientation for men include youthfulness (under 35), some experience of heterosexual arousal, and lack of femininity, plus, of course, high motivation for reorientation.

An alternative style of intervention is directed at enabling the person with ego-dystonic homosexuality to live more comfortably as a homosexual without shame, guilt, anxiety, or depression. Gay counseling centers are engaged with patients in such treatment programs. At present, outcome studies of such centers have not been reported in detail. As for the treatment of women with ego-dystonic homosexuality there are few data, and those are primarily single case studies.

### REFERENCES

Bayer R: *Homosexuality and American Psychiatry: The Politics of Diagnosis.* Basic Books, New York, 1981.
Bell A, Weinberg M, Hammersmith S: *Sexual Preference.* Indiana University Press, Bloomington, 1981.
Ehrhardt A, Meyer-Bahlburg H: Effects of prenatal sex hormones on gender-related behavior. Science *211:* 1312, 1981.
Harry J: Defeminization and adult psychological wellbeing among male homosexuals. Arch Sex Behav *12:* 1, 1983.
Kinsey A, Pomeroy W, Martin C: *Sexual Behavior in the Human Male.* W. B. Saunders, Philadelphia, 1948.
Kinsey, A, Pomeroy W, Martin C, Gebhard P: *Sexual Behavior in the Human Female.* W. B. Saunders, Philadelphia, 1953.
Licata S: The homosexual rights movement in the United States: A traditionally overlooked area of American history. J. Homosex *6:* 161, 1980/1981.
Meyer J K: Ego-dystonic homosexuality. In *Comprehensive Textbook of Psychiatry,* ed 4, H I Kaplan, B J Sadock, editors, p 1056. Williams & Wilkins, Baltimore, 1985.
Spitzer R: The diagnostic status of homosexuality in DSM-III: A reformation of the issues. Am J Psychiatry *138:* 210, 1981.

# 20.3 PARAPHILIAS

### Introduction

Paraphilias are characterized by specialized sexual fantasies, masturbatory practices, sexual props, and requirements of the sexual partner. The special fantasy, with its unconscious and conscious components, is the pathognomonic element, arousal and orgasm being variously dependent on the active elaboration of that illusion. The influence of the fantasy and its elaborations in behavior extend beyond the sexual sphere to pervade the person's life.

Paraphilia, also referred to as perversion and sexual deviation, occupies an important position on the continuum between health and illness. In pure form, paraphilia is clinically distinct and unique. However, at one end of the spectrum it shades into the psychoses and gender identity disorders. At the other end, perversity gradually becomes more and more repressed in the neuroses. Over all, paraphilia shares more common ground with borderline character disorders.

A perversion is not a normal variant or an alternate life style, but is a recognizably human product of an individual developmental pathway. Nevertheless, what is so exaggerated in a perversion as to seem unique is, in fact, built out of common wishes and experiences.

## Definitions

With the advent of DSM-III, the paraphilias have found their place in a new and major classification, psychosexual disorders. This classification also includes gender identity disorders, psychosexual dysfunctions, and ego-dystonic homosexuality. Subcategories of paraphilia recognized in DSM-III are fetishism, transvestism, zoophilia, pedophilia, exhibitionism, voyeurism, sexual masochism, sexual sadism, and atypical paraphilia.

## Epidemiology

Among legally identified cases, pedophilia is far more common than the other perversions. Because a child is the object, the act is taken more seriously, and a greater effort is spent in tracking down the culprit than in other paraphilias. Exhibitionism, since it involves public display to young girls, is also commonly apprehended. Voyeurs may be apprehended, but their risk is not great. Sexual masochism and sadism are underrepresented in any prevalence estimates. Sexual masochism receives most attention when the degree of tolerable suffering, short of permanent harm, is miscalculated, with tragic results. Sexual sadism usually comes to attention only in sensational cases of rape, brutality, or lust murder. The excretory perversions are scarcely reported, since any activity usually takes place between consenting adults, or between prostitute and client. Fetishists ordinarily do not become entangled in the legal system. Transvestites may be arrested occasionally on disturbing-the-peace misdemeanors if they are obviously men dressed in women's clothes, but arrest is more common among the gender identity disorders. Zoophilia, as a true paraphilia, is simply rare.

Completely underrepresented in all samples are those persons who are in equilibrium with their paraphilias. Although there is an active grapevine in many of the paraphilias and a well-structured subculture in some, organizational registers and mailing lists, including the mailing lists of specialty pornography distributors, provide only inadequate and contaminated samples.

At first glance, the sex ratio in the paraphilias is striking. As usually defined, the sexual perversions seem to be largely male conditions. In homosexuality, too, the incidence among men is regarded as higher than that among women. In the gender identity disorders, the ratio of clinically active men to women is about two to one.

Males are preponderant by a wide margin in the overt perversions.

## Causes and Dynamics

Observations of intersex children and iatrogenic manipulations of fetal hormones have failed to show a clear effect of genetic, hormonal, or physiological variables on gender identity or sexual object choice.

It seems probable that constitutional factors are involved in sexual behavior, but most likely as minute feedback loops acting in concert from multiple loci. The data indicate that experimental and psychological factors dominate in the formation of perversions.

In the first few months of life, if external structuring is of poor quality, the child is at the mercy of his internal drives, which are strongly tainted with oral and anal components, and butt against a primitive superego. The drives, along with self and object images, may become or remain split into aggressive and libidinal clusters. Internalized objects are crudely drawn, and identifications are primitive. Sexuality arrested at this level is characterized by perverse trends infiltrated with sadomasochism. Coincidentally, there is exquisite sensitivity to engulfment or abandonment, with an uneasy oscillation in the degree of intimate contact permitted. In an effort to cope, devices such as fetishes, which are simultaneously bridging and distancing part objects, may be incorporated into sexuality.

Since an appreciation of anatomical differences between males and females is being integrated during that period as the psychological basis of sex and reproduction, a disorder here is associated with aberrations in sexual object choice, and in the fabric of maternity or paternity.

A poorly defined and unstable body image is a feature in the pathology of perversion. There is uncertainty about the permanence, position, size, and functioning of the penis and the attributes of the gonads.

Male perversions are external, often flamboyant structures with concrete props that tell the story of triumph over a castration threat. Female perversions are largely unobtrusive, being revealed by a particular willingness to accommodate to male perversion. Fueled by castration resentment, female perversions represent a clandestine insurgence against a sense of genital inferiority. Perversity in the woman is satisfied by an illusory penis, which may be represented by rituals or props or, more often, by the incorporation of the phallus of a man.

### Clinical Features

Clinical features are divisible into two groups: those common to the whole class of disorders and those specific to a particular subclassification. Common to sexual perversion is the obligatory or nearly obligatory dependence of arousal and orgasm on a sexual fantasy featuring objects or acts that attenuate the linkages between sexual expression, genital congress, and human contact. In contrast to the neuroses in which perverse elements are unconscious, the fantasy in the paraphilias is conscious, although unconscious features determine its power, and with regularity it is manifested in overt behavior. The individual paraphilias are characterized by the particular nature of the fantasy and by special behaviors, such as cross-dressing with arousal in transvestism, erotization of pain in sadomasochism, and sepulchral dramas in necrophilia.

Both the expression of clinical features and the ultimate treatability of paraphilias are materially influenced by ego strength. One important hallmark of ego strength is psychological flexibility. The usual sequence is relative flexibility (health), some inflexibility (neurosis), rigidity (borderline character), and brittleness with fragmentation (psychosis). The general principle is that it takes at least a modicum of ego strength to create a perversion. By and large, a perversion both stabilizes and fixes character. With relatively more ego strength, there is complete dependence on the perverse fantasy and its trappings for arousal and orgasm. Greater ego capabilities lessen the servitude to the perversion. At higher levels of ego strength, neurosis is fashioned, and perverse elements in the person's fantasy life are largely unconscious.

Similarly, the various paraphilias show a tendency to arrange themselves along a gradient of preservation of object relations. In fetishism, sadism, masochism, and transvestism, there is the potential for maintaining contact with adult objects. Contact of a sort is maintained in pedophilia, but with immature objects. With exhibitionism and voyeurism, the contact is strained and largely autistic. In urolagnia and coprophilia (pleasure derived from urine or feces, respectively) there may be involvement with a partner, but it is likely that the more meaningful contact is with the excremental part object. In zoophilia and necrophilia, the object is further degraded and displaced.

It has occasionally been suggested that perverse imagery and arousal requirements are sufficiently atypical or bizarre to preclude relations with consensual partners. However, this is true only for the more seriously disturbed perverts who have no choice but to totally dehumanize any partner. Their relationships are tenuous and rapidly rupture. For those less disturbed, who are capable of object attachment, consensual partners are available.

Table I lists the common features of the paraphilias. Care was taken to include all the elements considered essential features in DSM-III, although these elements are not necessarily weighted in the same way. In Table I, an effort was made to include the fundamental dynamic elements under essential features, less significant dynamic elements and important descriptive elements under associated features, and more minor descriptive elements under other features. Features considered essential in the official nomenclature are distinguished by two asterisks (**).

### Fetishism

In fetishism, the sexual focus is on objects—such as shoes, gloves, corsets, or hose—that are intimately associated with the human body, and that are relatively indestructible. The particular fetish is linked to someone closely involved with the patient during his childhood, and has some quality associated with this loved, needed, and traumatizing person. Usually the disorder begins by adolescence, although the fetish might have been established in childhood. Once established, this disorder tends to be chronic.

Sexual activity may be directed toward the fetish itself, such as masturbation with or into a shoe, or the fetish may be incorporated in sexual congress—for example, with the demand that high-heeled shoes be worn.

Fetishization has been viewed as a central process in all sexual arousal, perverse and normal. The fetish may be a concrete means of compensating for the gap in reality sense left by the disavowal of sexual reality—that is, disavowal of the anatomical distinctions between the sexes (see Table II).

### Transvestism

Transvestism is marked by fantasized or actual dressing in female clothes, for purposes of arousal and as an adjunct to masturbation or

TABLE I
COMMON FEATURES IN PARAPHILIAS*

| Essential Features | Associated Features | Other Features |
|---|---|---|
| The nuclear perversion grows out of a blurring of sexual and generational differences and a poor infant-mother demarcation, particularly in the realm of the genitalia. | **There are persistent, repetitive, or intrusive sexual fantasies of an unusual nature. The fantasies are for the most part ego-syntonic, although they are recognized as unusual. | **There may be preferential use of nonhuman objects for sexual arousal. ** There may be repetitive sexual activity involving real or simulated suffering or humiliation. |
| There is impairment in gender and reality sense. | **Sexual arousal and orgasm are dependent in an obligate way on the fantasies. | ** There may be repetitive sexual activity with nonconsenting partners. |
| The paraphilia serves to cover over flaws in the sense of bodily integrity and in the sense of reality. | The perverse fantasy is a powerful organizing motif in the patient's life. | ** The sexual interest is focused on substitutive acts or objects or degraded or distanced objects. |
| The paraphilia protects against both castration anxiety and separation anxiety. | There is general psychopathology characteristic of the spectrum of borderline disorders. | |
| The paraphilia provides an outlet for aggressive drives, as well as sexual drives. | | |
| The perverse fantasy and behavior are symptomatic compromise formations growing out of developmental conflict and distress. | | |

* These features, considered common to all the paraphilias, are not repeated in Tables II through VIII.
** Features considered essential in DSM-III.

TABLE II
FEATURES IN FETISHISM*

| Essential Features | Associated Features | Other Features |
|---|---|---|
| A device with magical phallic qualities is used as a hedge against castration anxiety. | ** There is use of a nonliving, usually inanimate object as the preferred or necessary adjunct to arousal, sexual activity, or orgasm, exclusive of cross-dressing in female clothes. | The preferred fetish or class of fetishes—for example, shoes, gloves, or rubber—is usually constant over time. |
| The device also functions as a bridging object—similar to a transitional object—serving as a hedge against separation anxiety. | ** The fetish is associated, in actuality or in fantasy, with the human environment, most often the human body. | |

* Features common to the paraphilias (Table I) are not repeated here but are understood to characterize fetishism.
** Features considered essential in DSM-III.

coitus (see Table III). Transvestism typically begins in childhood or early adolescence. Some individuals with transvestism, as years pass, want to dress and live permanently as women. Usually, more than one article of clothing is involved; frequently, an entire wardrobe is involved. When a transvestite is cross-dressed, the appearance of femininity may be quite striking, although usually not to the degree found in transsexualism. When not dressed in women's clothes, transvestite men may be hypermasculine in appearance and occupation. Cross-dressing itself exists on a gradient from solitary, depressed, guilt-ridden dressing to ego-syntonic,

sociable membership in a transvestite subculture. Anxiety may be experienced about the acceptability of cross-dressing, but anxiety is seldom associated with cross-dressing itself unless it is failing as a defense.

The overt clinical syndrome of transvestism may begin in latency, but it is more often seen around pubescence or in adolescence. Frank dressing in women's clothes usually does not begin until mobility and relative independence from parents are fairly well established. In other words, cross-dressing does not usually appear until the parents feel comfortable about leaving the child alone.

TABLE III
FEATURES OF TRANSVESTISM*

| Essential Features | Associated Features | Other Features |
| --- | --- | --- |
| Cross-dressing serves to express feminine identification.<br>Arousal and orgasm express the triumph over feminine identification.<br>Transvestism serves to protect against castration and separation anxieties. | Feminine identification is a more dominant factor in early life, middle age, and late life than in adolescence and young adulthood.<br>** In adolescence and young adulthood, the focus is on sexual arousal and release. | ** One focus of the characteristic fantasy is on dressing in clothes of the opposite sex.<br>A second focus of the fantasy is on subjugation by a woman.<br>The diagnosis of transvestism is limited to nonhomosexual, nontranssexual men. |

* Features common to the paraphilias (Table I) are not repeated here but are understood to characterize transvestism.
** Features considered essential in DSM-III.

## Sexual Sadism and Masochism

Since sadism and masochism most often represent two opposite and unintegrated aspects of the self, the two conditions are considered under the same heading. They represent, respectively, the active and the passive poles of the subjugation-humiliation axis. The power of the fantasy derives from a poorly compensated fear of injury, and a reactive narcissistic rage (see Table IV).

In sexual masochism, excitement is linked with the passive experience of physical or emotional subjugation, humiliation, discomfort, danger, abuse, or torture—any of which may be simulated or real. Sexual sadism is the direct reciprocal of sexual masochism. Excitement in sexual sadism is linked to the active infliction, in fantasy or in reality, of humiliation, subjugation, abuse, or torture. Sexual sadism fantasies are likely to be present in childhood, although sexual sadistic activities are common by early adulthood.

Although relatively pure sadists and pure masochists do exist, the most common finding is that the active or passive perversion is preferential but not exclusive. Sadists also indulge in masochistic fantasies or practices, and the subjugated, compliant masochist is often quite able to take the opposite role with arousal and pleasure. Neither condition is exclusively male or female, although masochistic practices are more common among men. These disorders are usually chronic.

## Exhibitionism and Voyeurism

Exhibitionism and voyeurism, like sadism and masochism, are in many respects paired opposites. This disorder may occur at any time from pre-adolescence to middle age. Peak age of onset is the middle 20s. It is reported that this condition becomes less severe after the age of 40.

This condition apparently occurs only in males, and the victims are female children and adults. Exhibitionism involves acts of exposing the genitals to a stranger or an unsuspecting person. Voyeurism, conversely, involves repetitively seeking out situations in which unsuspecting women may be observed while disrobing, grooming, or copulating. In both situations, sexual excitement occurs in anticipation of the exposure or the observation, and orgasm is brought about by masturbation during or after the event (see Table V). The first voyeuristic act has been reported to occur in early childhood.

Exhibitionism and voyeurism—showing and looking—define opposite positions along the same dimensional axis. The dynamics of both acts are related. In exhibitionism, the presence and the power of the phallus is reasserted by watching the reaction—fright, surprise, awe, disgust—of a woman confronted with it. The exhibitionist both identifies with his victim and feels contemptuously superior to her. The voyeur watches a woman to note the true nature of her genitals and identifies with her, but he reassures himself through his masturbation that his penis is intact and that he is superior.

Although exhibitionists and voyeurs frequently marry, the importance of the relationship often lies in their wives' maternal qualities. Sexual performance in the marital bed is usually lackadaisical, with real excitement being confined to the situation of showing or looking. The preferential objects of the perverse act—young girls, women with large breasts, brunettes, and so on—are selected because of attributes associated with the mother. These attributes make them fit substitute objects for reenactment of the struggle over merger and separation.

In other related perversions, the central themes are derivatives of looking or showing. For example, in obscene phone calling, tension and arousal begin in anticipation of phoning, an unsuspecting partner is involved, the recipient of the call listens while the telephoner verbally

TABLE IV
FEATURES OF SEXUAL SADISM AND MASOCHISM*

| Essential Features | Associated Features | Other Features |
|---|---|---|
| Triumph over the fear of injury (equivalent to the fear of feminine identification) and the expression of narcissistic rage (equivalent to the reassertion of bodily integrity) provide the motivation for constant reenactment of situations of power or dominance. | ** The central impelling fantasy involves degradation, humiliation, suffering, or injury either brought about actively or experienced passively. | ** Sexual activity with a partner or in solitary masturbation preferentially involves real or simulated degradation or subjugation, either inflicted actively or experienced passively. |

* Features common to the paraphilias (Table I) are not repeated here but are understood to characterize sexual sadism and masochism.
** Features considered essential in DSM-III.

TABLE V
FEATURES OF EXHIBITIONISM AND VOYEURISM*

| Essential Features | Associated Features | Other Features |
|---|---|---|
| Expression of feminine identification and resistance to it are compulsively repeated through the constant reexamination of genitals and the reactions to seeing them. | ** The central fantasy involves genital exposure to another person either in the active or the passive sense—showing or looking, respectively. Exhibitionism and voyeurism together determine the opposite poles of the scoptophilic perversion. | ** Exposure of the genitals or observing grooming, nudity, or sexual activity is a preferential component of sexual activity and may occur frequently. Exposure or looking is merely one feature of a sequence that includes tension, fantasy, anticipatory arousal, preliminary masturbation, exposure or looking, and masturbation to orgasm. |

* Feature common to paraphilias (Table I) are not repeated here but are understood to characterize exhibitionism and voyeurism.
** Features considered essential in DSM-III.

exposes his preoccupations or induces her to talk about sexual activity, and the conversation is accompanied by masturbation, which is often completed after the contact is interrupted.

### Pedophilia

Pedophilia involves preferential sexual activity with children either in fantasy or in actuality (see Table VI). Adult sexual activities or fantasies involving prepubertal children, the essential behavior in pedophilia, may be exclusively homosexual or exclusively heterosexual, and may occur within the family, among acquaintances, or between strangers. This disorder may begin at any time in adulthood, although it most frequently begins in middle age.

Pedophilic perversions vary in their most conspicuous elements. In some, teasing seduction predominates; the pedophile plays with the child, slowly steering the game into sexual areas. Often, the child is involved in a version of strip poker, leading to the exposure of his genitals. The pedophile ordinarily feels excited and triumphant at this accomplishment, and masturbates surreptitiously while the child is present, or openly once the child has gone. In this form of pedophilia, the game, the stratagems to

overcome the child's hesitation, and the looking are the consciously exciting elements. In other variations, the child is induced to allow manipulation of his genitals or to manipulate the adult's genitals.

Although apparently only a small percentage of pedophilic encounters result in injury or death, aggression and sadism are inherent components in pedophilia. Pedophilia does involve narcissistic and restitutive identifications with the child, but the perversion also involves dominance and power over the child. For the pedophile who is frightened of adult partners, the opportunity to terrify, rather than be terrified, is present with children, and provides the component of erotically tinged aggression that is important in arousal. The aggression may be under conscious control or out of awareness, but it is never far away. In a situation in which the sexual partner is comparatively helpless physically, injury may be inflicted in cold blood, in passion, or in panic.

Although not classifiable as a perversion in the true sense, incest is superficially related to pedophilia by the frequent selection of an immature child as a sexual object, the subtle or overt element of coercion, and the occasionally

TABLE VI
FEATURES OF PEDOPHILIA*

| Essential Features | Associated Features | Other Features |
|---|---|---|
| Identification with and narcissistic investment in immature sexual objects compensate for early deprivation.<br>Control, domination, and seduction of the child compensate for early powerlessness. | ** The central and preemptive fantasy focuses on children as sexual objects. | ** Sexual activity with children is preferential and may occur repeatedly.<br>The object choice may be homosexual or heterosexual, but it is almost always exclusively one or the other. |

\* Features common to the paraphilias (Table I) are not repeated here but are understood to characterize pedophilia.
\*\* Features considered essential in the DSM-III.

preferential nature of the adult-child liaison. The scope and the variability of incest, however, go beyond issues that are relevant to pedophilia.

## Zoophilia

In zoophilia, animals—which may be trained to participate—are preferentially incorporated into arousal fantasies or sexual activities, including intercourse, masturbation, and oral-genital contact (see Table VII). Zoophilia as an organized perversion is rare, even though sensual relations with animals are relatively common. For a number of people, animals provide the major source of relatedness, so it is not surprising that a broad variety of domestic animals are sensually or sexually used.

Sexual relations with animals may occasionally be an outgrowth of availability or convenience, especially in parts of the world where rigid convention precludes premarital sexuality, or in situations of enforced isolation. Masturbation, however, is also available in such situations, so it is reasonable to suspect that some predilection for animal contact is present in opportunistic zoophilia.

## Atypical Paraphilias

An important group of perversions, not specifically catalogued in the nomenclature, are those associated with excretory functions. DSM-III classifies these paraphilias as atypical. They include coprophilia, urolagnia, and defecation and urination on or around sexual partners; the administration of enemas; and derivative practices, such as obscenity during intercourse (see Table VIII). Intrinsic to this closely allied group of perversions are a fascination with dirtiness and soiling and an eroticized overinvestment in excretory processes and the expulsion of body contents. The unifying feature is the incorporation of excretory functions, excreta, or their close substitutes into sexual activity. Although analization is generally characteristic of perversions, it is particularly prominent in this group of paraphilias.

## Diagnosis

Descriptive diagnosis, as called for in DSM-III, is based on the presence of the criterion signs and symptoms outlined and marked by double asterisks in Tables I through VII. In brief, the criteria include the presence of the pathognomonic fantasy and its behavioral elaboration. The fantasy contains unusual sexual material that is relatively fixed and shows only minor variations. The achievement of arousal and orgasm depends on mental elaboration or behavioral playing out of the fantasy. Sexual activity is ritualized or stereotyped, and makes use of degraded, reduced, or dehumanized objects. The patients regularly show earmarks of borderline personality disorder in symptoms and signs.

## Treatment

Psychoanalysis offers the opportunity to trace out and unseat the illness at its core. It is effective through the resurrection of the transference of the passions and relationships condensed in the perversion. The therapeutic power of analysis lies in the opportunity to reexperience, reexamine, and reintegrate pathological elements, with the benefit of an adult observing ego and in the context of a relationship in which the original pathogenic roles are not repeated. In the process of this working through, the freeing of stymied potentials leads to the opportunity for personal renovation.

When less ego strength is available, dynamic psychotherapy is likely to be the most beneficial treatment modality in reducing and stabilizing the pressure from the perversion, and in helping make other aspects of life as free from its interference as possible. Behavior modification techniques have their place in the effort to detoxify the behavior in severe compelling and driven perversions. Psychotropic agents, including major tranquilizers, may also be used in those perversions that are acutely or dangerously compulsive. Antiandrogens, such as cyproterone ace-

TABLE VII
FEATURES OF ZOOPHILIA*

| Essential Features | Associated Features | Other Features |
|---|---|---|
| The animal functions as a substitute, degraded object, serving both to express contempt for and to encourage sexual activity, which is viewed literally as bestial. | ** The central sexual fantasy incorporates an animal as a necessary component of sexual arousal or orgasm. | ** Sexual relations with animals are preferential and may occur frequently. |

\* Features common to the paraphilias (Table I) are not repeated here but are understood to characterize zoophilia.
\*\* Features considered essential in DSM-III.

TABLE VIII
FEATURES OF THE EXCRETORY PARAPHILIAS*

| Essential Features | Associated Features | Other Features |
|---|---|---|
| The focus on excretory functions and products, which are shared by the two sexes, obscures their genital differences.<br>Excretory products are renewable and, in their loss and replenishment, serve as a hedge against castration fear, object loss, and the fear of the loss of bodily integrity. | The central and imperative fantasy involves excretory functions, excreta, or a close substitute, such as compulsory vulgarity during sexual activity. | Sexual activity involving excreta, excretory functions, or close symbolic substitutes is preferential and frequently occurs. |

\* Features common to the paraphilias (Table I) are not repeated here but are understood to characterize the excretory perversions.

tate in Europe and medroxyprogesterone acetate (Depo-provera) in the United States, have been used experimentally in sexually hyperactive perversions. In some carefully selected cases, there have been reports of decreases in the hypersexual behavior. Medroxyprogesterone acetate seems to be of benefit for those patients whose driven hypersexuality—for example, virtually constant masturbation, sexual contact at every opportunity, compulsively assaultive sexuality—is out of control or dangerous.

## REFERENCES

Berlin F, Mieneke C: Treatment of sex offenders with antiandrogenic medication. Am J Psychiatry *138:* 601, 1981.
Edgcumbe R, Burgner M: The phallic-narcissistic phase. Psychoanal Study Child *30:* 161, 1975.
Ehrhardt A, Meyer-Bahlburg H: Effects of prenatal sex hormones on gender-related behavior. Science *211:* 1312, 1981.
Gadpaille W: Biological factors in the development of human sexual identity. Psychiatr Clin North Am *3:* 3, 1980.
Gagne P: Treatment of sex offenders with medroxyprogesterone acetate. Am J Psychiatry *138:* 644, 1981.
Galenson E, Roiphe H: Some suggested revision concerning early female development. J Amer Psychoanal Assoc *25:* 29, 1976.
Galenson E, Roiphe H: The preoedipal development of the boy. J Am Psychoanal Assoc *28:* 805, 1980.
Jaffe D: Some relations between the negative oedipus complex and aggression in the male. J Am Psychoanal Assoc *31:* 956, 1983.
Marks I: Review of behavioral psychotherapy, II: Sexual disorders. Am J Psychiatry *138:* 750, 1980.
Meyer J: The theory of gender identity disorders. J Am Psychoanal Assoc *30:* 381, 1982.
Meyer J K: Paraphilias. In *Comprehensive Textbook of Psychiatry,* ed 4, H I Kaplan, B J Sadock, editors, p 1065. Williams & Wilkins, Baltimore, 1985.

# 20.4    PSYCHOSEXUAL DYSFUNCTIONS AND TREATMENT

## Introduction

The acceptable expression of sexuality varies greatly across time and culture. A historical survey of sexual practices in Western civilization reveals attitudes that oscillate between the liberal and the puritanical, between acceptance and repression of human sexuality. During the past several decades, the prevalent sexual attitudes in American society have changed sufficiently to call the period an era of sexual revolution.

Concurrent with the cultural changes of the sexual revolution has been a growth in scientific research into sexual physiology and sexual dysfunctions. Masters and Johnson published their pioneering work on the physiology of sexual response in 1966 and reported on their program to treat sexual complaints in 1970. Most medical centers now have programs specifically geared to the treatment of sexual dysfunctions.

## Definition

The evolution of the diagnosis and nomenclature of psychosexual dysfunctions reflects the results of research and the social changes that have occurred. In the second edition of the *Diagnostic and Statistical Manual of Mental Disorders* (DSM-II), psychosexual dysfunctions were subsumed under psychophysiological genitourinary disorders or marital maladjustment; in the ninth edition of the *International Classification of Diseases* (ICD-9), there was a separate category for psychosexual dysfunctions, but only frigidity and impotence were listed; in DSM-III, psychosexual dysfunctions constitute a separate category of Axis I disorders and eight distinct syndromes are listed. These syndromes are inhibited sexual desire, inhibited sexual excitement, inhibited female orgasm, inhibited male orgasm, premature ejaculation, functional dyspareunia, functional vaginismus, and atypical psychosexual dysfunction.

In DSM-III, the sexual response cycle is divided into four phases: appetitive, excitement, orgasm, and resolution. The essential feature of the psychosexual dysfunctions is inhibition in one or more of these phases, including disturbance in the subjective sense of pleasure or desire or disturbance in the objective performance. Either type of disturbance can occur alone or in combination. Psychosexual dysfunctions are so diagnosed only when such disturbances are a major part of the clinical picture. They are not diagnosed if such dysfunctions are entirely attributable to organic factors or are symptomatic of other Axis I psychiatric syndromes such as schizophrenia.

In actuality, one rarely finds psychosexual dysfunctions, with the possible exception of premature ejaculation, separate from other psychiatric syndromes. Psychosexual dysfunctions are frequently associated with depression, adjustment reactions, neurotic disorders, or personality disorders. In the first two cases, the psychosexual dysfunctions may exist for too short a period of time to warrant a diagnosis. In the latter two instances, psychosexual dysfunctions may be diagnosed in conjunction with the other psychiatric disorders.

## Normal Sexuality

Normal men and women experience a sequence of physiological responses to sexual stimulation. In the first detailed description of these responses, Masters and Johnson observed that the physiological process involves increasing levels of vasocongestion and myotonia (tumescence) and the subsequent release of the vascular activity and muscle tone as a result of orgasm (detumescence). The process occurs in the four phases of excitement, plateau, orgasm, and resolution (see Tables I and II). DSM-III differs somewhat in its definition of these phases, and these variations are discussed following the physiological discussion.

### Stages of Sexual Response

**Phase I: Excitement.** This phase is brought on by psychological stimulation (fantasy or the presence of a love object), physiological stimulation (stroking or kissing), or a combination of the two. The excitement phase is characterized by penile erection in the man and vaginal lubrication in the woman. The nipples of both sexes become erect, although nipple erection is more common in women than in men. The woman's clitoris becomes hard and turgid, and her labia minora become thicker as a result of venous engorgement. The excitement phase may last several minutes to several hours.

**Phase II: Plateau.** With continued stimulation, the man's testes increase in size 50 percent and elevate. The woman's vaginal barrel shows a characteristic constriction along the outer third known as the orgasmic platform. The clitoris elevates and retracts behind the symphysis pubis. As a result, the clitoris is not easily accessible. As the area is stimulated, however, traction on the labia minora and the prepuce occurs, and there is intrapreputial movement of the clitoral shaft. Breast size in the woman increases 25 percent. Continued engorgement of the penis and vagina produces specific color changes; these color changes are most marked in the labia minora, which become bright or deep red. Voluntary contractions of large muscle groups occur, rate of heartbeat and respiration increases, and blood pressure rises. The plateau stage lasts 30 seconds to several minutes.

**Phase III: Orgasm.** A subjective sense of ejaculatory inevitability triggers the man's orgasm. The forceful emission of semen follows. The male orgasm is also associated with four to five rhythmic spasms of the prostate, seminal vesicles, vas deferens, and urethra. In the woman, orgasm is characterized by three to fifteen involuntary contractions of the lower third of the vagina and by strong sustained contractions of the uterus, flowing from the fundus downward to the cervix. Both men and women

TABLE I
THE MALE SEXUAL RESPONSE CYCLE*

| | I. Excitement Phase (several minutes to hours) | II. Plateau Phase (30 sec. to 3 min.) | III. Orgasmic Phase (3–15 sec.) | IV. Resolution Phase (10–15 min.; if no orgasm, ½-1 day) |
|---|---|---|---|---|
| Skin | No change | Sexual flush: inconsistently appears; maculopapular rash originates on abdomen and spreads to anterior chest wall, face, and neck and can include shoulders and forearms | Well-developed flush | Flush disappears in reverse order of appearance; inconsistently appearing film of perspiration on soles of feet and palms of hands |
| Penis | Erection within 10–30 sec caused by vasocongestion of erectile bodies of corpus cavernosa of shaft. Loss of erection may occur with introduction of a-sexual stimulus, loud noise | Increase in size of glans and diameter of penile shaft; inconsistent deepening of coronal and glans coloration | Ejaculation: marked by 3 to 4 contractions at 0.8 sec. of vas, seminal vesicles, prostate, and urethra; followed by minor contractions with increasing intervals | Erection: partial involution in 5–10 sec. with variable refractory period; full detumescence in 5–30 min. |
| Scrotum and testes | Tightening and lifting of scrotal sac and partial elevation of testes toward perineum | 50 per cent increase in size of testes over unstimulated state due to vasocongestion and flattening of testes against perineum signaling impending ejaculation | No change | Decrease to base line size due to loss of vasocongestion. Testicular and scrotal descent within 5–30 min. after orgasm. Involution may take several hours if there is no orgasmic release |
| Cowper's glands | No change | 2–3 drops of mucoid fluid that contain viable sperm | No change | No change |
| Other | Breasts: inconsistent nipple erection | Myotonia: semispastic contractions of facial, abdominal, and intercostal muscles. Tachycardia: up to 175 per min. Blood pressure: rise in systolic 20–80 mm.; in diastolic 10–40 mm. Respiration: increased | Loss of voluntary muscular control Rectum: rhythmical contractions of sphincter Up to 180 beats per min. 40–100 systolic; 20–50 diastolic Up to 40 respirations per min. Ejaculatory spurt: 12–20 inches at age 18 decreasing with age to seepage at 70 | Return to base line state in 5–10 min. |

\* Table prepared by Virginia A. Sadock, M.D., after Masters and Johnson data. In DSM-III the excitement phase and the plateau phase are combined into one phase called excitement phase.

TABLE II
THE FEMALE SEXUAL RESPONSE CYCLE*

| | I. Excitement Phase (several minutes to hours) | II. Plateau Phase (30 sec. to 3 min.) | III. Orgasmic Phase (3–15 sec.) | IV. Resolution Phase (10–15 min.; if no orgasm, ½–1 day) |
|---|---|---|---|---|
| Skin | No change | Sexual flush inconstant except in fair skinned; pink mottling on abdomen, spreads to breasts, neck, face, often to arms, thighs, and buttocks—looks like measles rash | No change (flush at its peak) | Fine perspiration, mostly on flush areas; flush disappears in reverse order |
| Breasts | Nipple erection in two-thirds of subjects Venous congestion Areolar enlargement | Flush: mottling coalesces to form a red papillary rash Size: increase one fourth over normal, especially in breasts that have not nursed Areolae: enlarge; impinge on nipples so they seem to disappear | No change (venous tree pattern stands out sharply; breasts may become tremulous) | Return to normal in reverse order of appearance in ½ hour or more |
| Clitoris | Glans: half of subjects, no change visible, but with colposcope, enlargement always observed; half of subjects, glans diameter always increased 2-fold or more Shaft: variable increase in diameter; elongation occurs in only 10 per cent of subjects | Retraction: shaft withdraws deep into swollen prepuce; just before orgasm, it is difficult to visualize; may relax and retract several times if phase II is unduly prolonged Intrapreputial movement with thrusting: movements synchronized with thrusting owing to traction on labia minora and prepuce | No change Shaft movements continue throughout if thrusting is maintained | Shaft returns to normal position in 5–10 sec.; full detumescence in 5–30 min. (if no orgasm, clitoris remains engorged for several hours) |
| Labia majora | Nullipara: thin down; elevated; flatten against perineum Multipara: rapid congestion and edema; increases to 2–3 times normal size | Nullipara: totally disappear (may reswell if phase II unduly prolonged.) Multipara: become so enlarged and edematous, they hang like folds of a heavy curtain | No change | Nullipara: increase to normal size in 1–2 min. or less Multipara: decrease to normal size in 10–15 min. |
| Labia minora | Color change: to bright pink in nullipara and red in multipara Size: increase 2–3 times over normal; prepuce often much more; proximal portion firms, adding up to ¾ inch to functional vaginal sidewalls | Color change: suddenly turn bright red in nullipara, burgundy red in multipara, signifies onset of phase II, orgasm will then always follow within 3 min. if stimulation is continued Size: enlarged labia gap widely to form a vestibular funnel into vaginal orifice | Firm proximal areas contract with contractions of lower third | Returns to pink blotchy color in 2 min. or less; total resolution of color and size in 5 min. (decoloration, clitoral return and detumescence of lower third all occur as rapidly as loss of the erection in men) |
| Bartholin's glands | No change | A few drops of mucoid secretion form; aid in lubricating vestibule (insufficient to lubricate vagina) | No change | No change |

TABLE TABLE  II—*Continued*

| | I. Excitement Phase (several minutes to hours) | II. Plateau Phase (30 sec. to 3 min.) | III. Orgasmic Phase (3–15 sec.) | IV. Resolution Phase (10–15 min.; if no orgasm, ½–1 day) |
|---|---|---|---|---|
| Vagina | Vaginal transudate: appears 10–30 sec. after onset of arousal; drops of clear fluid coalesce to form a well-lubricated vaginal barrel (aids in buffering acidity of vagina to neutral pH required by sperm) Color change: mucosa turns patchy purple | Copious transudate continues to form; quality of transudate generally increased only by prolonging preorgasm stimulation (increased flow occurs during premenstrual period) Color change: uniform dark purple mucosa | No change (transudate provides maximum degree of lubrication) | Some transudate collects on floor of the upper two thirds formed by its posterior wall (in supine position); ejaculate deposited in this area forming seminal pool |
| Upper two-thirds | Balloons: dilates convulsively as uterus moves up, pulling anterior vaginal wall with it; fornices lengthen; rugae flatten | Further ballooning creates diameter of 2½–3 inches; then wall relaxes in a slow, tensionless manner | No change: fully ballooned out and motionless | Cervical descent: descends to seminal pool in 3–4 min. |
| Lower third | Dilation of vaginal lumen to 1–1¼ inches occurs; congestion of walls proceeds gradually, increasing in rate as phase II approaches | Maximum distension reached rapidly; contracts lumen of lower third and upper labia to ½ or more its diameter in phase I; contraction around penis allows thrusting traction on clitoral shaft via labia and prepuce. | 3–15 contractions of lower third and proximal labia minora at ⅓-sec. intervals | Congestion disappears in seconds (if no orgasm, congestion persists for 20–30 min.) |
| Uterus | Ascent: moves into false pelvis late in phase I Cervix: passively elevated with uterus (no evidence of any cervical secretions during entire cycle) | Contractions: strong sustained contractions begin late in phase II; have same rhythm as contractions late in labor, lasting 2+ min. Cervix: slight swelling; patchy purple (inconstant; related to chronic cervicitis) | Contractions throughout orgasm; strongest with pregnancy and masturbation | Descent: slowly returns to normal Cervix: color and size return to normal in 4 min; patulous for 10 min. |
| Others | Fourchette: color changes throughout cycle as in labia minora | Perineal body: spasmodic tightening with involuntary elevation of perineum Hyperventilation and carpopedal spasms; both are usually present, the latter less frequently and only in female-supine position | Irregular spasms continue Rectum: rhythmical contractions inconstant; more apt to occur with masturbation than coitus External urethral sphincter: occasional contraction, no urine loss | All reactions cease abruptly or within a few seconds |

\* From *The Nature and Evolution of Female Sexuality*, by Mary Jane Sherfey, Copyright 1966, 1972 by Mary Jane Sherfey. Reprinted by permission of Random House, Inc.

have involuntary contractions of the internal and external sphincter. These and the other contractions during orgasm occur at intervals of 0.8 second. Other manifestations include voluntary and involuntary movements of the large muscle groups, including facial grimacing and carpopedal spasm. Systolic blood pressure rises 20 mm, diastolic blood pressure rises 40 mm, and the heart rate increases up to 160 beats a minute. Orgasm lasts from 3 to 15 seconds and is associated with a slight clouding of consciousness.

The parasympathetic nervous system activates the process of erection. The pelvic splanchnic nerves (S2, S3, and S4) stimulate the blood vessels of the area to dilate, causing the penis to become erect. In ejaculation, the sympathetic nervous system is involved. Through its hypogastric plexus, the sympathetic nervous system innervates the urethral crest and the muscles of the epididymis, vas deferens, seminal vesicles, and prostate. Stimulation of the plexus causes ejaculation of seminal fluid from those glands and ducts into the urethra. That passage of fluid into the urethra provides the man with a sensation of impending climax called the stage of ejaculatory inevitability. Indeed, once the prostate contracts, ejaculation is inevitable. The ejaculate is propelled through the penis by urethral contractions. The ejaculate consists of about 1 teaspoon (2.5 ml) of fluid and contains about 120 million sperm cells.

**Phase IV: Resolution.** Resolution consists of the disgorgement of blood from the genitalia (detumescence), and this detumescence brings the body back to its resting state. If orgasm occurs, resolution is rapid; if it does not occur, resolution may take 2 to 6 hours and be associated with irritability and discomfort. Resolution through orgasm is characterized by a subjective sense of well-being.

**Refractory Period.** After orgasm, men have a refractory period that may last from several minutes to many hours; in that period they cannot be stimulated to further orgasm. The refractory period does not exist in women, who are capable of multiple and successive orgasms.

Sexual response is a true psychophysiological experience. Arousal is triggered by both psychological and physical stimuli, levels of tension are experienced both physiologically and emotionally, and, with orgasm, there is normally a subjective perception of a peak of physical reaction and release. Psychosexual development, psychological attitude toward sexuality, and attitudes toward one's sexual partner are directly involved with and affect the physiology of human sexual response.

### The DSM-III Phases of the Sexual Response Cycle

DSM-III consolidates the Masters and Johnson excitement and plateau phases into a single excitement phase and precedes it with its unique appetitive phase. The orgasm and resolution phase remain the same as originally described by Masters and Johnson.

**DSM-III Phase I: Appetitive.** This phase is distinct from any identified solely through physiology and reflects the psychiatrist's fundamental concern with motivations, drives, and personality. The phase is characterized by sexual fantasies and the desire to have sexual activity.

**DSM-III Phase II: Excitement.** This phase consists of a subjective sense of sexual pleasure and accompanying physiological changes. All the physiological responses noted in Masters and Johnson's excitement and plateau phases are combined under this phase.

**DSM-III Phase III: Orgasm.** This phase consists of a peaking of sexual pleasure, with release of sexual tension and rhythmic contraction of the perineal muscles and pelvic reproductive organs. The phase is identical to Masters and Johnson's Phase III.

**DSM-III Phase IV: Resolution.** This phase entails a sense of general relaxation, well-being, and muscular relaxation. This phase as defined does not differ from the Masters and Johnson resolution phase.

### Psychosexual Dysfunctions

Sexual disorders can be symptomatic of biological problems, intrapsychic conflicts, interpersonal difficulties, or a combination of these factors. The sexual function can be adversely affected by stress of any kind, by emotional disorders, and by a lack of sexual knowledge.

In this section, various sexual dysfunctions are discussed as they apply to heterosexual relationships. The eight sexual dysfunctions listed in DSM-III will be examined.

### Inhibited Sexual Desire

Inhibited sexual desire is experienced by both men and women, who may not be hampered by any dysfunction once they are involved in the sex act. Lack of desire may be expressed by decreased frequency of coitus, perception of the partner as unattractive, or overt complaints of lack of desire (see Table III).

The need for sexual contact and satisfaction varies among individuals, as well as in the same person over time. In a group of 100 couples with stable marriages, 8 percent reported having intercourse less than once a month. In another group of couples, one-third reported lack of sexual relations for periods of time averaging 8 weeks. Masters believes that lack of desire may be a common complaint among married couples; the true incidence, however, is not known.

Desire disorders are not new, although they have recently become the focus of much attention. Patients with desire problems often have good ego strengths and use inhibition of desire in a defensive way to protect against unconscious fears about sex. Lack of desire can also be the result of chronic stress, anxiety, or depression. Abstinence from sex for a prolonged period sometimes results in suppression of the sexual impulse. It may also be an expression of hostility or the sign of a deteriorating relationship.

In one study of young married couples who ceased having sexual relations for periods of 2 months, the reasons stated for this behavior were different for men and for women. The men were influenced by social factors, such as recent immigration, religion, and their wives' employment or lack of it. The women were more influenced by their perceptions about dominance, decision-making, affection, and their husbands' threats to leave home. Both men and women mentioned lack of privacy as a reason for discontinuing sexual relationships. Marital discord, however, was the most frequently given reason for the cessation of sexual activity.

### Inhibited Sexual Excitement

Psychosexual dysfunction with inhibited sexual excitement involves recurrent and persistent inhibition during sexual activity, manifested either by the man's partial or complete failure to attain or maintain an erection until the completion of the sex act or by the woman's partial or complete failure to attain or maintain the lubrication-swelling response of sexual excitement until the completion of the sexual act. The diagnosis is made in the light of clinical judgment that takes into account the focus, intensity, and the duration of the sexual activity in which the patient engages (see Table IV).

**Women.** Women who have excitement-phase dysfunction often have orgastic problems as well. In one series of relatively happily married couples, 33 percent of the women described difficulty in maintaining sexual excitement.

Numerous psychological factors are associated with female sexual inhibition. These conflicts may be expressed through inhibition of excitement or orgasm and are discussed under orgasmic phase dysfunctions. In some women, excitement-phase disorders are associated with dyspareunia or with lack of desire.

Less research has been done on physiological components of dysfunction in women than in men, but some recent work suggests a possible hormonal pattern contributing to responsiveness in women with desire and excitement phase dysfunction. Masters and Johnson found normally responsive women to be particularly desirous of sex premenstrually. In a recent study, dysfunctional women tended to be more responsive immediately following their periods. A third group of dysfunctional women felt the greatest sexual excitement at the time of ovulation.

**Men.** Inhibited sexual excitement in the male is also called erectile dysfunction or impotence. In primary impotence, the man has never been able to obtain an erection sufficient for vaginal insertion. In secondary impotence, the man has successfully achieved vaginal penetration at some time in his sexual life, but is later unable to do so. In selective impotence, the man is able to have coitus in certain circumstances, but not in others; for example, a man may function

TABLE III
DIAGNOSTIC CRITERIA FOR INHIBITED SEXUAL DESIRE*

A. Persistent and pervasive inhibition of sexual desire. The judgment of inhibition is made by the clinician's taking into account factors that affect sexual desire, such as age, sex, health, intensity and frequency of sexual desire, and the context of the individual's life. In actual practice this diagnosis is rarely made unless the lack of desire is a source of distress to either the individual or his or her partner. Frequently, this category is used in conjunction with one or more of the other psychosexual dysfunction categories.

B. The disturbance is not caused exclusively by organic factors, e.g. physical disorder or medication, and is not due to another Axis I disorder.

*From American Psychiatric Association: *Diagnostic and Statistical Manual of Mental Disorders*, ed 3. American Psychiatric Association, Washington, DC, 1980. Used with permission.

TABLE IV
DIAGNOSTIC CRITERIA FOR INHIBITED SEXUAL EXCITEMENT*

A. Recurrent and persistent inhibition of sexual excitement during sexual activity, manifested by:

*In males*, partial or complete failure to attain or maintain erection until completion of the sexual act, or

*In females*, partial or complete failure to attain or maintain the lubrication-swelling response of sexual excitement until completion of the sexual act.

B. A clinical judgment that the individual engages in sexual activity that is adequate in focus, intensity, and duration.

C. The disturbance is not caused exclusively by organic factors, e.g. physical disorder or medication, and is not due to another Axis I disorder.

*From American Psychiatric Association: *Diagnostic and Statistical Manual of Mental Disorders*, ed 3. American Psychiatric Association, Washington, DC, 1980. Used with permission.

effectively with a prostitute, but may be impotent with his wife.

It was estimated by Kinsey that a few men (2 to 4 percent) are impotent at age 35, but 77 percent are impotent at age 80. More recently, it has been found that the incidence of primary impotence in men 35 years old or under is about 1 percent. Masters and Johnson report a fear of impotence in all men over 40, which the researchers believe reflects the masculine fear of loss of virility with advancing age. (As it happens, however, impotence is not a regularly occurring phenomenon in the aged; having an available sexual partner is more closely related to continuing potency in the aging man than is age per se.) More than 50 percent of all men treated for sexual disorders have impotence as the chief complaint. The incidence of psychological as opposed to organic impotence has been the focus of many recent studies. Impotence may be physiologically due to a variety of organic causes (see Table V). Some workers have reported an incidence of organic impotence in a medical clinic outpatient population as high as 75 percent. Other researchers believe that these same populations have not had adequate psychological screening and maintain that in more than 90 percent of cases the causes of impotence are psychological. In addition, the clinician should be aware of the possible pharmacological effects of medication on sexual functioning (see Table VI).

A number of procedures from benign to invasive are used to help differentiate organically caused impotence from functional impotence. These procedures include the monitoring of nocturnal penile tumescence, or erections that occur during sleep, normally in association with rapid eye movement; monitoring tumescence with a strain gauge; measurement of the blood pressure in the penis using an ultrasound (Doppler) flow meter to assess blood flow in the internal pudendal artery; and caversonograms and measurement of pudendal nerve latency time. Other diagnostic tests to delineate organic bases for impotence include glucose tolerance tests; plasma hormone assays; liver and thyroid function tests; prolactin, FH, and FSH determinations; and cystometric examinations.

A good history is of primary importance in determining the etiology of the dysfunction. If a man reports having spontaneous erections at times when he does not plan to have intercourse, having morning erections or only sporadic erectile dysfunction, or having good erections with masturbation or with partners other than his usual one, then organic causes for his impotence can be considered negligible, and costly

TABLE V
DISEASES IMPLICATED IN ERECTILE
DYSFUNCTION*

Infectious and Parasitic Diseases
  Elephantiasis
  Mumps

Cardiovascular Diseases
  Atherosclerotic disease
  Aortic aneurysm
  Leriche syndrome
  Cardiac failure

Renal and Urological Disorders
  Peyronie's disease
  Chronic renal failure
  Hydrocele or variocele

Hepatic Disorders
  Cirrhosis (usually associated with alcoholism)

Pulmonary Disorders
  Respiratory failure

Genetics
  Klinefelter's syndrome
  Congenital penile vascular or structural abnormalities

Nutritional Disorders
  Malnutrition
  Vitamin deficiencies

Endocrine Disorders
  Diabetes mellitus
  Dysfunction of the pituitary-adrenal-testis axis
  Acromegaly
  Addison's disease
  Chromophobe adenoma
  Adrenal neoplasias
  Myxedema
  Hyperthyroidism

Neurological Disorders
  Multiple sclerosis
  Transverse myelitis
  Parkinson's disease
  Temporal lobe epilepsy
  Traumatic or neoplastic spinal cord disease
  Central nervous system tumors
  Amyotrophic lateral sclerosis
  Peripheral neuropathies
  General paresis
  Tabes dorsalis

Pharmacological Contributants (see Table VI)
  Alcohol and other addictive drugs (heroin, methadone, morphine, cocaine, amphetamines, and barbituates)
  Prescribed drugs (psychotropic drugs, antihypertensive drugs, estrogens, and antiandrogens)

Poisoning
  Lead (plumbism)
  Herbicides

Surgical Procedures
  Perineal prostatectomy
  Abdominal-perineal colon resection
  Sympathectomy (frequently interferes with ejaculation)
  Aortoiliac surgery
  Radical cystectomy
  Retroperitoneal lymphadenectomy

Miscellaneous
  Radiation therapy
  Pelvic fracture
  Any severe systemic disease or debilitating condition

*Table by Virginia Sadock, M.D.

Table VI
Pharmacological Agents Implicated in Male Sexual Dysfunction*

| Drug | Impairs Erection | Impairs Ejaculation |
|---|:---:|:---:|
| **Psychiatric Drugs** | | |
| Tricyclic antidepressants† | | |
|   Imipramine (Tofranil, Geigy) | + | + |
|   Protriptyline (Vivactil, Merck Sharpe & Dohme) | + | + |
|   Desmethylimipramine (Pertofran, USV) | + | + |
|   Clomipramine (Anafranil) | + | + |
|   Amitriptyline (Elavil, Merck Sharp & Dohme) | + | + |
| Monoamine oxidase inhibitors | | |
|   Tranylcypromine (Parnate, Smith Kline & French) | + | |
|   Mebanazine (Actomal) | + | + |
|   Phenelzine (Nardil, Parke-Davis) | + | + |
|   Pargyline (Eutonyl, Abbott) | − | + |
|   Isocarboxazid (Marplan, Roche) | − | + |
| Other mood-active drugs | | |
|   Lithium | + | |
|   Amphetamines | + | + |
| Major tranquilizers‡ | | |
|   Fluphenazine (Prolixin, Squibb) | + | |
|   Thioridazine (Mellaril, Sandoz) | + | + |
|   Chlorprothixene (Taractan, Roche) | − | + |
|   Mesoridazine (Serentil, Boehringer Ingelheim) | − | + |
|   Perphenazine (Trilafon, Schering) | − | + |
|   Trifluoperazine (Stelazine, Smith Kline & French) | − | + |
|   Butaperazine (Repoise) | − | + |
|   Reserpine (Serpasil, CIBA) | + | + |
|   Haloperidol (Haldol, McNeil Pharmaceuticals) | − | + |
| Minor tranquilizers§ | | |
|   Chlordiazepoxide (Librium, Roche) | − | + |
| **Antihypertensive Drugs** | | |
|   Clonidine (Catapres, Boehringer Ingelheim) | + | |
|   Debrisoquin (Declinax) | − | + |
|   Methyldopa (Aldomet, Merck Sharp & Dohme) | + | + |
|   Spironolactone (Aldactone, Searle) | + | − |
|   Hydrochlorthiazide (Apresoline, CIBA) | + | − |
|   Arramethidine (Ismelin, CIBA) | + | + |
| **Commonly Abused Drugs** | | |
|   Alcohol | + | + |
|   Barbiturates | + | + |
|   Cannabis | + | − |
|   Cocaine | + | + |
|   Heroin | + | + |
|   Methadone | + | + |
|   Morphine | + | + |
| **Miscellaneous Drugs** | | |
|   Antiparkinsonian agents | + | + |
|   Clofibrate (Atromid-S, Ayerst) | + | − |
|   Digoxin | + | − |
|   Glutethimide (Doriden, UVS) | + | + |
|   Indomethacin (Indocin, Merck Sharp & Dohme) | + | − |
|   Phentolamine (Regitine, CIBA) | − | + |
|   Propranolol (Inderal, Ayerst) | + | − |

* Table by Virginia Sadock, M.D. The effects of drugs on the sexual function of the female have not been extensively evaluated, but women appear to be less vulnerable to pharmacologically induced sexual dysfunction than are men. Oral contraceptives are reported to decrease libido in some women and phenelzine (Nardil, Parke-Davis) impairs the orgasmic reponse in some women. Both increase and decrease in libido have been reported with psychoactive agents. It is difficult to separate those effects from the underlying condition or from improvement of the condition. Sexual dysfunction associated with the use of a drug disappears when the drug is discontinued.

† The incidence of erectile dysfunction associated with the use of tricyclic antidepressants is low.

‡ Impairment of sexual function is not a common complication of the use of major tranquilizers. Priapism has occasionally occurred in association with the use of major tranquilizers.

§ Benzodiazepines have been reported to decrease libido, but in some patients the diminution of anxiety caused by those drugs enhances sexual function.

diagnostic procedures can be avoided. In those cases in which an organic basis for impotence is found, psychological factors often contribute to the dysfunction, and psychiatric treatment may be helpful. In some diabetics, for instance, erectile dysfunction may be psychogenic.

In general, the psychological conflicts that cause impotence are related to an inability to express the sexual impulse because of fear, anxiety, anger, or moral prohibition. Primary impotence is a more serious but less common condition than secondary impotence.

Many developmental factors have been cited as contributing to impotence. Any experience that hinders the ability to be intimate, that leads to a feeling of inadequacy or distrust, or that develops a sense of being unloving or unlovable may result in impotence. In an ongoing relationship, impotence may reflect difficulties between the partners, particularly if the man cannot communicate his needs or his angry feelings in a direct and constructive way.

### Inhibited Female Orgasm (Anorgasmia)

Psychosexual dysfunction with inhibited female orgasm is defined as the recurrent and persistent inhibition of the female orgasm, as manifested by the absence of orgasm after a normal sexual excitement phase that the clinician judges to be adequate in focus, intensity, and duration. It refers to the inability of the woman to achieve orgasm by masturbation or coitus. Women who can achieve orgasm with one of these methods are not necessarily categorized as anorgasmic although some degree of sexual inhibition may be postulated (see Table VII).

Physiological research regarding the female sexual response has demonstrated that orgasms caused by clitoral stimulation and those caused by vaginal stimulation are physiologically identical. Freud's theory that women must give up clitoral sensitivity for vaginal sensitivity in order to achieve sexual maturity is now considered

misleading, although some women say that they gain a special sense of satisfaction from an orgasm precipitated by coitus. Some workers attribute that to the psychological feeling of closeness engendered by the act of coitus, but others maintain that the coital orgasm is a physiologically different experience. Many women achieve orgasm during coitus by a combination of manual clitoral stimulation and penile vaginal stimulation. DSM-III tentatively states that women who are able to experience orgasm during noncoital clitoral stimulation but who are not able to experience orgasm during coitus in the absence of manual clitoral stimulation may warrant the diagnosis of anorgasmia. However, more and more evidence is forthcoming that this exclusively clitoral orgasm is a normal behavioral variation.

Primary nonorgasmic dysfunction exists when the woman has never experienced orgasm by any kind of stimulation. Secondary orgasmic dysfunction exists if the woman has previously experienced at least one orgasm regardless of the circumstances or means of stimulation, whether by masturbation or during sleep while dreaming. Kinsey found that the proportion of married women over 35 years of age who had never achieved orgasm by any means was only 5 percent. The incidence of orgasm increases with age. According to Kinsey, the first orgasm occurs during late adolescence in about 50 percent of women. The rest usually experience orgasm by some means as they get older. Primary anorgasmia is more common among unmarried women than among married women; 39 percent of the unmarried women over age 35 in Kinsey's study had never experienced orgasm. Increased orgasmic potential in women over 35 has been explained on the basis of less psychological inhibition, greater sexual experience, or both.

Secondary orgasmic dysfunction is a common complaint in clinical populations. One clinical treatment facility described nonorgastic women as about 4 times more common in its practice

TABLE VII
DIAGNOSTIC CRITERIA FOR INHIBITED FEMALE ORGASM*

A. Recurrent and persistent inhibition of the female orgasm as manifested by a delay in or absence of orgasm following a normal sexual excitement phase during sexual activity that is judged by the clinician to be adequate in focus, intensity, and duration. The same individual may also meet the criteria for inhibited sexual excitement if at other times there is a problem with the excitement phase of sexual activity. In such cases, both categories of psychosexual dysfunction should be noted.

Some women are able to experience orgasm during noncoital clitoral stimulation, but are unable to experience it during coitus in the absence of manual clitoral stimulation. There is evidence to suggest that in some instances this represents a pathological inhibition that justifies this diagnosis, whereas in other instances it represents a normal variation of the female sexual response. This difficult judgment is assisted by a thorough sexual evaluation that may even require a trial of treatment.

B. The disturbance is not caused exclusively by organic factors, e.g. physical disorder or medication, and is not due to another Axis I disorder.

* From American Psychiatric Association: *Diagnostic and Statistical Manual of Mental Disorders*, ed 3. American Psychiatric Association, Washington, DC, 1980. Used with permission.

than patients with all other sexual disorders. In another study, 46 percent of the women complained of difficulty in reaching orgasm, and 15 percent described inability to have orgasm. The true prevalence of problems in maintaining excitement is not known, but inhibition of excitement and orgastic problems often occur together.

Numerous psychological factors are associated with female sexual inhibition. They include fears of impregnation, rejection by the sexual partner, or damage to the vagina; hostility toward men; and feelings of guilt regarding sexual impulses. For some women, orgasm is equated with loss of control or with aggressive, destructive, or violent behavior. Fear of these impulses may be expressed through inhibition of excitement or orgasm. Cultural expectations and societal restrictions on women are also relevant. Nonorgastic women may be otherwise symptom-free or may experience frustration in a variety of ways, including such pelvic complaints as lower abdominal pain, itching, and vaginal discharge, as well as increased tension, irritability, and fatigue.

### Inhibited Male Orgasm

In inhibited male orgasm, also called retarded ejaculation, the man achieves climax during coitus with great difficulty, if at all. A man suffers from primary retarded ejaculation if he has never been able to ejaculate during coitus. The disorder is diagnosed as secondary if it develops after previous normal functioning (see Table VIII).

Some workers suggest that a differentiation should be made between orgasm and ejaculation. Certainly, inhibited orgasm must be differentiated from retrograde ejaculation, in which ejaculation occurs but the seminal fluid passes backward into the bladder. The latter condition always has an organic cause. Retrograde ejaculation can develop after genitourinary surgery and is also associated with medications that have anticholinergic side effects, such as the phenothiazines.

The incidence of inhibited male orgasm is much lower than that of premature ejaculation and impotence. Masters and Johnson reported only 3.8 percent in one group of 447 sex dysfunction cases. This problem is more common among men with obsessive-compulsive disorders than among others.

Inhibited male orgasm may have physiological causes and can occur after surgery of the genitourinary tract, such as prostatectomy. It may also be associated with Parkinson's disease and other neurological disorders involving the lumbar or sacral sections of the spinal cord. The antihypertensive drug guanethidine monosulfate (Esimil, CIBA), methyldopa, and the phenothiazines have been implicated in retarded ejaculation.

Primary inhibited male orgasm is indicative of more severe psychopathology. The man often comes from a rigid, puritanical background; he perceives sex as sinful and the genitals as dirty; and he may have conscious or unconscious incest wishes and guilt. There are usually difficulties with closeness that extend beyond the area of sexual relations.

In an ongoing relationship, secondary ejaculatory inhibition frequently reflects interpersonal difficulties. The disorder may be the man's way of coping with real or fantasized changes in the relationship. These changes may include plans for pregnancy about which the man is ambivalent, the loss of sexual attraction to the partner, or demands by the partner for greater commitment as expressed by sexual performance. In some men, the inability to ejaculate reflects unexpressed hostility toward the woman.

### Premature Ejaculation

In premature ejaculation, the man recurrently achieves orgasm and ejaculation before he wishes to. There is no definite time frame within which to define the dysfunction. The diagnosis is made when the man regularly ejaculates before or immediately after entering the vagina. DSM-III advises the clinician to consider factors that affect duration of the excitement phase, such as age, novelty of the sexual partner, and

TABLE VIII
DIAGNOSTIC CRITERIA FOR INHIBITED MALE ORGASM*

A. Recurrent and persistent inhibition of the male orgasm as manifested by a delay in or absence of ejaculation following an adequate phase of sexual excitement. The same individual may also meet the criteria for inhibited sexual excitement if at other times there is a problem with the excitement phase of sexual activity. In such cases, both categories of psychosexual dysfunction should be noted.

B. The disturbance is not caused exclusively by organic factors, e.g. physical disorder or medication, and is not due to another Axis I disorder.

*From American Psychiatric Association: *Diagnostic and Statistical Manual of Mental Disorders*, ed 3. American Psychiatric Association, Washington, DC, 1980. Used with permission.

the frequency and duration of coitus (see Table IX). Masters and Johnson conceptualize the disorder in terms of the couple and consider a man a premature ejaculator if he cannot control ejaculation for a sufficient length of time during intravaginal containment to satisfy his partner in at least one-half of their episodes of coitus. This definition assumes that the female partner is capable of an orgastic response. As with the other dysfunctions, this disturbance is not caused exclusively by organic factors, nor is it symptomatic of any other clinical psychiatric syndrome. No separate category of premature orgasm for women is included in DSM-III because of the absence of data on the subject. Also, the presence of a refractory period in the man has obvious consequences that do not necessarily exist for the potentially multiorgasmic woman.

Premature ejaculation is more common today among college-educated men than among men with less education and is thought to be related to their concern for partner satisfaction; the true incidence of this disorder has not been determined, however. About 40 percent of men treated for sexual disorders have premature ejaculation as the chief complaint.

Difficulty in ejaculatory control may be associated with anxiety regarding the sex act or with unconscious fears about the vagina. It may also result from negative cultural conditioning. The man who has most of his early sexual contacts with prostitutes who demand that the sex act proceed quickly or in situations in which discovery would be embarrassing, such as in the back seat of a car or in the parental home, may become conditioned to achieve orgasm rapidly.

In ongoing relationships, the partner has been found to have great influence on the premature ejaculator. A stressful marriage exacerbates the disorder. The developmental background and dynamics found in this disorder and in impotence are similar.

### Functional Dyspareunia

Dyspareunia refers to recurrent and persistent pain during intercourse in either the man or the woman. The dysfunction is related to and often coincides with vaginismus. Repeated episodes of vaginismus may lead to dyspareunia and vice versa, but in either case somatic causes must be ruled out. Dyspareunia should not be diagnosed as such when an organic basis for the pain is found, or when, in a woman, it is associated with vaginismus or with lack of lubrication (see Table X).

The true incidence of dyspareunia is unknown, but it has been estimated that 30 percent of surgical procedures on the female genital area result in temporary dyspareunia. Additionally, of women with this complaint who are seen in sex therapy clinics, 30 to 40 percent have pelvic pathology.

Organic abnormalities leading to dyspareunia and vaginismus include irritated or infected hymenal remnants, episiotomy scars, Bartholin's gland infection, various forms of vaginitis and cervicitis, endometriosis, and other pelvic disorders. The postmenopausal woman may develop dyspareunia resulting from thinning of the vaginal mucosa and lessened lubrication. Dynamic factors are usually considered causative, although situational factors probably account more for secondary dysfunctions. Painful coitus may result from tension and anxiety about the sex act that cause the woman to involuntarily tense her vaginal muscles. The pain is real and makes intercourse unbearable or unpleasant. The anticipation of further pain may cause the woman to avoid coitus altogether. If the partner

TABLE IX
DIAGNOSTIC CRITERIA FOR PREMATURE EJACULATION*

A. Ejaculation occurs before the individual wishes it, because of recurrent and persistent absence of reasonable voluntary control of ejaculation and orgasm during sexual activity. The judgment of "reasonable control" is made by the clinician's taking into account factors that affect duration of the excitement phase, such as age, novelty of the sexual partner, and the frequency and duration of coitus.

B. The disturbance is not due to another Axis I disorder.

* From American Psychiatric Association: *Diagnostic and Statistical Manual of Mental Disorders*, ed 3. American Psychiatric Association, Washington, DC, 1980. Used with permission.

TABLE X
DIAGNOSTIC CRITERIA FOR FUNCTIONAL DYSPAREUNIA*

A. Coitus is associated with recurrent and persistent genital pain, in either the male or the female.

B. The disturbance is not caused exclusively by a physical disorder and is not due to lack of lubrication, functional vaginismus, or another Axis I disorder.

* From American Psychiatric Association: *Diagnostic and Statistical Manual of Mental Disorders*, ed 3. American Psychiatric Association, Washington, DC, 1980. Used with permission.

proceeds with intercourse regardless of the woman's state of readiness, the condition is aggravated. Dyspareunia can also occur in men, but it is uncommon and is usually associated with an organic condition, such as Peyronie's disease.

### Vaginismus

Vaginismus is an involuntary constriction of the outer one-third of the vagina that prevents penile insertion and intercourse. This response may be demonstrated during a gynecological examination when involuntary vaginal constriction prevents introduction of the speculum into the vagina. The diagnosis is not made if the dysfunction is caused exclusively by organic factors or if it is symptomatic of another Axis I psychiatric syndrome (see Table XI). Vaginismus is less prevalent than anorgasmia. It most often afflicts highly educated women and those in the higher socioeconomic groups. The woman suffering from vaginismus may consciously wish to have coitus, but she unconsciously prevents penile entrance into her body. A sexual trauma such as rape may result in vaginismus. Women with psychosexual conflicts may perceive the penis as a dangerous weapon. In some women, pain or the anticipation of pain at the first coital experience causes vaginismus. A strict religious upbringing that associates sex with sin is frequently noted in these cases. For others, there are problems in the dyadic relationship; if the woman feels emotionally abused by her partner, she may protest in this nonverbal fashion.

### Atypical Psychosexual Dysfunctions

This category is for psychosexual dysfunctions that cannot be classified under the seven categories described above. Examples include persons who experience the physiological components of sexual excitement and orgasm but report no erotic sensation or even anesthesia. Women with conditions analogous to premature ejaculation in the man should also be classified here. The orgastic female who desires but has not experienced multiple orgasms can be classified under this heading as well. Also, disorders of excessive rather than inhibited function, such as compulsive masturbation, might be diagnosed under atypical dysfunctions.

Other mastubatory practices have resulted in what has been called autoerotic asphyxiation. This practice involves masturbating while hanging oneself by the neck to heighten erotic sensations and the intensity of orgasm. Although the individual releases himself from the noose after orgasm, an estimated 500 to 1,000 individuals per year unwillingly kill themselves by hanging.

TABLE XI
DIAGNOSTIC CRITERIA FOR FUNCTIONAL VAGINISMUS*

A. There is a history of recurrent and persistent involuntary spasm of the musculature of the outer third of the vagina that interferes with coitus.

B. The disturbance is not caused exclusively by a physical disorder and is not due to another Axis I disorder.

\* From American Psychiatric Association: *Diagnostic and Statistical Manual of Mental Disorders*, ed 3. American Psychiatric Association, Washington, DC, 1980. Used with permission.

TABLE XII
COMMON SEXUAL FANTASIES (MOST FREQUENT, LISTED IN ORDER OF OCCURRENCE)*

| Heterosexual Men | Heterosexual Women |
|---|---|
| 1. Replacement of established partner | 1. Replacement of established partner |
| 2. Forced sexual encounters with woman | 2. Forced sexual encounters with man |
| 3. Observing sexual activity | 3. Observing sexual activity |
| 4. Sexual encounters with men | 4. Idyllic encounters with unknown men |
| 5. Group sex | 5. Sexual encounters with women |

| Homosexual Men | Homosexual Women |
|---|---|
| 1. Images of male anatomy | 1. Forced sexual encounters with women |
| 2. Forced sexual encounters with men | 2. Idyllic encounters with established partner |
| 3. Sexual encounters with women | 3. Sexual encounters with men |
| 4. Idyllic encounters with unknown men | 4. Memories of past sexual experiences |
| 5. Group sex | 5. Sadistic imagery |

\* After Masters W, Schwartz M: Treatment program for dissatisfied homosexual men. Am J Psychiatry *141:* 173, 1984. Copyright 1984 by New York Times Company. Reprinted by permission.

Most persons indulging in this practice are male; transvestism is often associated with the habit, and the majority of deaths occur among adolescents. Such masochistic practices are usually associated with severe mental disorders such as schizophrenia and major affective disorders.

The category of atypical psychosexual dysfunctions also might be used to cover complaints engendered by couple rather than individual dysfunction. An example is a couple where one partner prefers morning sex and one functions more readily at night; another example is a couple with unequal frequencies of desire.

Other atypical disorders are found in persons who have one or more sexual fantasies about which they feel guilty or otherwise dysphoric. As indicated in Table XII, however, the range of common sexual fantasies is broad.

## Treatment

Various corrective therapies are now used to treat psychosexual dysfunctions. Some significant new techniques are available, and psychiatrists are eminently well qualified to incorporate the recently developed techniques of sex therapy into their practices.

In addition to making the determination of which type of therapy to use, the clinician must evaluate whether or not the disorder has a physiological cause. It is assumed that prior to entering psychotherapy the patient will have had a thorough medical evaluation, including a medical history, physical examination, and appropriate laboratory studies when necessary. If an organic cause for the disorder is found, treatment should be directed toward ameliorating the physical cause of the dysfunction.

Prior to 1970, the most common treatment of psychosexual dysfunction was individual psychotherapy. Classic psychodynamic theory considers sexual inadequacy to have its roots in early developmental conflicts, and the sexual disorder is treated as part of a more pervasive emotional disturbance. Treatment focuses on the exploration of unconscious conflicts, motivation, fantasy, and various interpersonal difficulties. One of the assumptions of therapy is that the removal of the conflicts will allow the sexual impulse to become structurally acceptable to the patient's ego and thereby find appropriate means of satisfaction in the environment. Unfortunately, the symptom of sexual dysfunction frequently becomes secondarily autonomous and continues to persist when other problems evolving from the patient's pathology have been resolved. The addition of behavioral techniques is often necessary to cure the sexual problem.

Four treatment modalities, dual-sex therapy, hypnotherapy, behavior therapy, and group therapy, will be discussed, as well as analytically oriented sex therapy, which integrates the tenets of psychoanalysis with behavioral techniques.

### Dual-Sex Therapy

The theoretical basis of the dual-sex therapy approach is the concept of the marital unit or dyad as the object of therapy. The method of dual-sex therapy, the major advance in the diagnosis and treatment of sexual disorders in this century, was originated and developed by William Masters and Virginia Johnson. In dual-sex therapy, there is no acceptance of the idea of a sick half of a patient couple. Both are involved in a relationship in which there is sexual distress, and both, therefore, must participate in the therapy program.

The sexual problem often reflects other areas of disharmony or misunderstanding in the marriage. The marital relationship as a whole is treated, with emphasis on sexual functioning as a part of that relationship. Psychological and physiological aspects of sexual functioning are discussed, and an educative attitude is used. Suggestions are made for specific sexual activity, and those suggestions are followed in the privacy of the couple's home.

The crux of the program is the roundtable session in which a male and female therapy team clarifies, discusses, and works through the problems with the couple. These four-way sessions require active participation on the part of the patients. The aim of the therapy is to establish or reestablish communication within the marital unit. Sex is emphasized as a natural function that flourishes in the appropriate domestic climate, and improved communication is encouraged toward that end.

Treatment is short-term and is behaviorally oriented. The therapists attempt to reflect the situation as they see it, rather than interpret underlying dynamics. An undistorted picture of the relationship presented by the psychiatrist often corrects the myopic, narrow view held individually by each marriage partner. The new perspective can interrupt the vicious cycle of relating in which the couple have been caught, and improved, more effective communication can be encouraged.

Specific exercises are prescribed for the couple to help them with their particular problem. Sexual inadequacy often involves lack of information, misinformation, and performance fear. The couples are, therefore, specifically prohibited from any sexual play other than that prescribed by the therapists. Beginning exercises usually focus on heightening sensory awareness to touch, sight, sound, and smell. Initially, intercourse is interdicted, and couples learn to give and receive bodily pleasure without the pressure of performance. They are simultaneously learning how to communicate nonverbally in a mutually satisfactory way and learning that sexual foreplay is as important as intercourse and orgasm.

During these exercises, which are called "sensate focus exercises," the couple is given much reinforcement to lessen their anxiety. The patients are urged to use fantasies to distract them from obsessive concerns about performance, which is termed "spectatoring." The needs of both the dysfunctional and the nondysfunctional partner are considered. If either partner becomes sexually excited by the exercises, the other is encouraged to bring him or her to orgasm by manual or oral means. This procedure is important to keep the nondysfunctional partner from sabotaging the treatment. Open communication between the partners is urged, and the expression of mutual needs is encouraged. Resistances, such as claims of fatigue or not enough time to complete the exercises, are common and must be dealt with by the therapist. Genital stimulation is eventually added to general body stimulation. The couple are instructed sequentially to try various positions for intercourse, without necessarily completing the act, and to use varieties of stimulating techniques before they are instructed to proceed with intercourse.

Roundtable sessions follow each new exercise period, and problems and satisfactions, both sexual and in other areas of the couple's lives, are discussed. Specific instructions and the introduction of new exercises geared to the individual couple's progress are reviewed in each session. Gradually, the couple gain confidence and learn or relearn to communicate, verbally and sexually. Dual-sex therapy is most effective when the sexual dysfunction exists apart from other psychopathology.

**Specific Techniques and Exercises.** Different techniques are used to treat the various dysfunctions. In cases of vaginismus the woman is advised to dilate her vaginal opening with her fingers or with size-graduated dilators.

In cases of premature ejaculation, an exercise known as the squeeze technique is used to raise the threshold of penile excitability. In that exercise, the man or woman stimulates the erect penis until the earliest sensations of impending ejaculation are felt. At that point, the woman forcefully squeezes the coronal ridge of the glans,

the erection is diminished, and ejaculation is inhibited. The exercise program eventually raises the threshold of the sensation of ejaculatory inevitability and allows the man to become more aware of his sexual sensations and confident about his sexual performance. A variant of the exercise is the stop-start technique developed by J. H. Semans in which the woman stops all stimulation of the penis when the man first senses an impending ejaculation. No squeeze is used. Research has shown that the presence or absence of circumcision has no bearing on a man's ejaculatory control. The glans is equally sensitive in either state.

A man with inhibited desire or inhibited excitement is sometimes told to masturbate to demonstrate that full erection and ejaculation are possible. In cases of primary anorgasmia, the woman is directed to masturbate, sometimes using a vibrator. The shaft of the clitoris is the masturbatory site most preferred by women, and orgasm depends on adequate clitoral stimulation. Men masturbate by stroking the shaft and glans of the penis.

Retarded ejaculation is managed by extravaginal ejaculation initially and gradual vaginal entry after the stimulation to the point of near ejaculation

### Hypnotherapy

Hypnotherapists focus specifically on the anxiety-producing symptom; that is, the particular sexual dysfunction. The successful use of hypnosis enables the patient to gain control over the symptom that has been lowering self-esteem and disrupting psychological homeostasis. The cooperation of the patient is first obtained and encouraged during a series of nonhypnotic sessions with the therapist. These discussions permit the development of a secure doctor-patient relationship, a sense of physical and psychological comfort on the part of the patient, and the establishment of mutually desired treatment goals. During this time, the therapist assesses the patient's capacity for the trance experience. The nonhypnotic sessions also permit the clinician to take a careful psychiatric history and do a mental status examination before beginning hypnotherapy. The focus of treatment is on symptom removal and attitude alteration. The patient is instructed in developing alternative means of dealing with the anxiety-provoking situation, which is the sexual encounter.

Patients are also taught relaxing techniques to use on themselves before sexual relations. With those methods to alleviate anxiety, the physiological responses to sexual stimulation can more readily result in pleasurable excitation and discharge. Psychological impediments to vaginal lubrication, erection, and orgasm are removed, and normal sexual functioning ensues. Hypnosis may be added to a basic individual psychotherapy program to accelerate the impact of psychotherapeutic intervention.

### Behavior Therapy

Behavior therapists assume that sexual dysfunction is learned maladaptive behavior. Behavioral approaches were initially designed for the treatment of phobias. In cases of sexual dysfunction, the therapist sees the patient as phobic of sexual interaction. Using traditional techniques, the therapist sets up a hierarchy of anxiety-provoking situations for the patient, ranging from the least threatening to the most threatening situation. Mild anxiety may be experienced at the thought of kissing, and massive anxiety may be felt when imagining penile penetration. The behavior therapist enables the patient to master the anxiety through a standard program of systematic desensitization. The program is designed to inhibit the learned anxious response by encouraging behaviors antithetical to anxiety. The patient first deals with the least anxiety-producing situation in fantasy and progresses by steps to the greatest anxiety-producing situation. Medication, hypnosis, or special training in deep-muscle relaxation is sometimes used to help with the initial mastery of anxiety.

Assertiveness training is also used and is helpful in teaching the patient to express his or her sexual needs openly and without fear. Exercises in assertiveness are given in conjunction with sex therapy, and the patient is encouraged both to make sexual requests and to refuse to comply with requests perceived as unreasonable. Sexual exercises may be prescribed for the patient to perform at home, and a hierarchy may be established, starting with those activities that have proved most pleasurable and successful in the past.

One treatment variation involves the participation of the patient's sexual partner in the desensitization program. The partner, rather than the therapist, presents the hierarchical items to the patient. In such situations, a cooperative partner is necessary to help the patient carry gains made during treatment sessions to sexual activity at home.

### Group Therapy

Methods of group therapy have been used to examine both intrapsychic and interpersonal problems in patients with sexual disorders. The therapy group provides a strong support system for a patient who feels ashamed, anxious, or guilty about a particular sexual problem. It is a useful forum in which to counteract sexual myths, correct misconceptions, and provide accurate information regarding sexual anatomy, physiology, and varieties of behavior.

Groups for the treatment of sexual disorders can be organized in several ways. Members may all share the same problem, such as premature ejaculation; members may all be of the same sex with different sexual problems; or groups may be composed of both men and women who are experiencing different sexual problems. Group therapy may be an adjunct to other forms of therapy or the prime mode of treatment. Groups organized to cure a particular dysfunction are usually behavioral in approach.

Groups have also been effective when composed of sexually dysfunctional married couples. The group provides the opportunity to gather accurate information, provides consensual validation of individual preferences, and enhances self-esteem and self-acceptance. Techniques such as role playing and psychodrama may be used in treatment. Such groups are not indicated for couples when one partner is uncooperative, when a patient is suffering from a severe depression or psychosis, when there is a strong repugnance for explicit sexual audiovisual material, or when there is a strong fear of groups.

### Analytically Oriented Sex Therapy

One of the most effective treatment modalities is the use of sex therapy integrated with psychodynamic and psychoanalytically oriented psychotherapy. The sex therapy is conducted over a longer than usual time period, and the extended schedule of treatment allows for the learning or relearning of sexual satisfaction under the realities of the patients' day-to-day lives. The addition of psychodynamic conceptualizations to the behavioral techniques used to treat sexual dysfunctions allows for the treatment of patients with sex disorders associated with other psychopathology.

The themes and dynamics that emerge in patients in analytically oriented sex therapy are the same as those seen in psychoanalytic therapy, such as relevant dreams, fear of punishment, aggressive feelings, difficulty with trusting the partner, fear of intimacy, oedipal feelings, and fear of genital mutilation.

For example, a 33-year-old single man with a history of intermittent impotence was referred for therapy. He kept a changeable "harem" of five or six sex partners in addition to a "serious" girlfriend. He was sporadically impotent with all the partners, with sufficient frequency to cause him great distress. In the course of treatment he revealed fears of being engulfed by a woman, or, as he put it, "lost in a long tunnel I could never get out of." He also had an unconscious fear of genital mutilation. His many partners served as a protection from the intimacy he was afraid would overwhelm him. In addition, his multiple sexual experiences reassured him that his genitals remained intact. His girlfriends were also part of a search for the magical partner with whom he would never be impotent. Therapy dealt both with the fear of performance, which contributed to his impotence, and with his deeper psychological problems.

The dynamics and the emotional difficulties evident in this vignette are similar to those seen every day by the psychiatrist. The combined approach of analytically oriented sex therapy can be used by the general psychiatrist, who must carefully judge the optimal timing of sex therapy and the ability of patients to tolerate a directive approach that focuses on their sexual difficulties.

### Other Treatment Methods

Other forms of treatment have limited application. Coexisting physical and psychiatric problems should receive appropriate treatment as necessary. Drug treatment has little application, although intravenous methohexital sodium (Brevital Sodium, Lilly) has been used in desensitization therapy. Antianxiety agents may have limited application in very tense patients, although these drugs can also interfere with sexual response. Sometimes the side effects of such drugs as thioridazine and the tricyclic antidepressants are used to prolong the sexual response in conditions such as premature ejaculation. The use of tricyclics has also been advocated in the treatment of patients who are phobic of sex. The risks of taking such medications are rarely justified, however, and most such problems respond to nonpharmacological means.

Surgical treatment is even more rarely advocated, but improved penile prosthetic devices are available for men with inadequate erectile response who are resistant to other treatment methods or who have organically caused deficiencies. Placement of a penile prosthesis in a male who has lost the ability to ejaculate or have an orgasm due to organic causes will not enable him to recover those functions. Men with prosthetic devices have generally reported satisfaction with their subsequent sexual functioning. Their wives, however, report much less satisfaction than do the men. Presurgical counseling is strongly recommended so that the couple have a realistic expectation of what the prosthesis can do for their sex lives. Some European physicians are attempting revascularization of the penis as a direct approach to treating erectile dysfunction due to vascular disorders. There are limited reports of prolonged success with this technique.

Surgical approaches to female dysfunctions include hymenectomy in the case of dyspareunia in an unconsummated marriage, vaginoplasty in multiparous women complaining of lessened vaginal sensations, or freeing of clitoral adhesions in women with inhibited excitement. Such surgical treatments have not been carefully studied and should be considered with great caution.

### Results of Treatment

The reported effectiveness of various treatment methods for problems of sexual dysfunction varies from study to study. Demonstrating the effectiveness of traditional outpatient psychotherapy is just as difficult when therapy is oriented to sexual problems as it is in general. In some cases the patient improves in all areas except the sexual area. Unfortunately, the more severe the psychopathology associated with a problem of long duration, the more adverse the outcome is likely to be.

The more difficult treatment cases involve couples with severe marital discord. Cases with problems of fear of intimacy, excessive dependency, or excessive hostility are also complex. Other challenges are posed by patients with lack of desire, impulse disorders, unresolved homosexual conflicts, or fetishistic defenses. Patients phobic of sex also present treatment difficulties.

When behavioral approaches are used, empirical criteria that are supposed to predict outcome are more easily isolated. Using these criteria, for instance, it appears that couples who regularly practice assigned exercises have a much greater likelihood of successful outcome than do more resistant couples or couples whose interaction involves sadomasochistic or depressive features or mechanisms of blame and projection. Flexibility of attitude is also a positive prognostic factor. Overall, younger couples tend to complete sex therapy more often than do older couples. Those couples whose interactional difficulties center on their sex problems, such as inhibition, frustration, fear of failure, or fear of performance, are also likely to respond well to therapy.

Masters and Johnson have reported higher positive results for their dual-sex therapy approach. They have studied the failure rates of their patients; failure is defined as the failure to initiate reversal of the basic symptom of the presenting dysfunction. They compared initial failure rates with 5-year follow-up findings for the same couples. Although some have criticized their definition of the percentage of presumed successes, other studies have confirmed the effectiveness of their approach. One therapist, however, seems to be nearly as effective as a dual-sex therapy team.

In general, methods that have proved effective singly or in combination include training in behavioral-sexual skills, systematic desensitization, directive marital counseling, traditional psychodynamic approaches, and group therapy. Although treating a couple for sexual dysfunctions is the mode preferred by most workers, treatment of individuals has also been successful.

## REFERENCES

Bennett H A, Revard O J: Male impotence; New concepts in management. NY State J Med *80:* 1676, 1982.
Brady J P: Behavior therapy and sex therapy. Am J Psychiatry *133:* 896, 1976.
Carmen E H, Rieker P P, Mills T: Victims of violence and psychiatric illness. Am J Psychiatry *141:* 378, 1984.
Diego B L, Magni G: Sexual side effects of antidepressants. Psychosomatics *24:* 12, 1983.
Herman J, LoPiccolo J: Clinical outcome of sex therapy. Arch Gen Psychiatry *40:* 443, 1983.
Masters W H, Johnson V E: *Human Sexual Inadequacy.* Little Brown and Co, Boston, 1970.
Sadock V A: The treatment of psychosexual dysfunctions; An overview. In *Psychiatry 1982, The American Psychiatric Association Annual Review,* L Grinspoon, editor. American Psychiatric Assoc., Washington, DC, 1982.
Sadock V A: Psychosexual dysfunctions and treatment. In *Comprehensive Textbook of Psychiatry,* ed 4, H I Kaplan, B J Sadock, editors, p 1077. Williams & Wilkins, Baltimore, 1985.
Semans J H: Premature ejaculation; A new approach. South Med J *49:* 353, 1956.
Slagg M F, Nelson C J, Nuttall F Q: Impotence in medical clinic outpatients. JAMA *249:* 13, 1983.
Wise N T: Sexual dysfunctions in the medically ill. Psychosomatics *24:* 9, 1982.

---

## 20.5  SPECIAL AREAS OF INTEREST

### Rape

The problem of rape is most appropriately discussed under the heading of aggression. Rape is an act of violence and humiliation that happens to be expressed through sexual means.

Rapes are used to express power or anger. There are rarely rapes in which sex is the dominant issue; sexuality is usually used in the service of nonsexual needs.

A legal definition of rape in the United States is: "The perpetration of an act of sexual intercourse with a female, not one's wife, against her will and consent, whether her will is overcome by force or fear resulting from the threat of force or by drugs or intoxicants; or when because of mental deficiency she is incapable of exercising rational judgment, or when she is below an arbitrary age of consent."

The crime of rape requires slight penile penetration of the victim's outer vulva. Full erection and ejaculation are not necessary. Forced acts of fellatio and anal penetration, although they frequently accompany rape, are legally considered sodomy.

In DSM-III, rape is cautiously considered under the diagnosis of sexual sadism: "Rape or other sexual assault may be committed by individuals with this disorder. In such instances, the suffering inflicted on the victim increases the sexual excitement of the assailant. However, it should not be assumed that all or even most rapists are motivated by sexual sadism. Often the rapist is not motivated by the prospect of inflicting suffering, and may even lose sexual desire as a consequence. These represent two poles of a spectrum, and for cases falling in the middle, it may be very difficult for the clinician to decide if the diagnosis of sexual sadism is warranted."

Studies of convicted rapists suggest that the crime is committed to relieve pent-up aggressive energies against persons toward whom the rapist is in some awe. Although these awesome (to the rapist) persons are usually men, the retaliatory violence is directed toward a woman. This finding dovetails with feminist theory, which proposes that the woman serves as an object for the displacement of aggression that the rapist cannot express directly toward other men. The woman is considered the property or vulnerable possession of men, and is the rapist's instrument for revenge against the men.

Rape often occurs as an accompaniment to another crime. The rapist always threatens his victim with fists, gun, or knife and frequently harms her in nonsexual ways, as well as sexual ways. The victim may be beaten, wounded, and sometimes killed.

Statistics show that 61 percent of rapists are under 25, 51 percent are white and tend to rape white victims, 47 percent are black and tend to rape black victims, and the remaining 2 percent come from all other races. A composite picture of a rapist drawn from police figures portrays a single, 19-year-old man from the lower socioeconomic classes with a police record of acquisitive offenses.

Rape is a highly underreported crime. The estimate is that only 1 out of 4 to 1 out of 10 rapes is reported. If the lowest estimated figure is taken, the reported incidence of 50,000 rapes a year increases to 200,000 rapes a year. The underreporting is attributed to feelings of shame on the part of the victim.

Victims of rape can be any age. Cases have been reported in which the victim was 15 months old and in which she was 82 years old. The greatest danger exists for women aged 10 to 29. Rape most commonly occurs in a woman's own neighborhood, frequently inside her own home. Most rapes are premeditated, and about 50 percent of the rapes are committed by strangers, and 50 percent by men known, to varying degrees, by the victims; 7 percent of all rapes are perpetrated by close relatives of the victim.

The woman being raped is frequently in a life-threatening situation. During the rape she experiences shock and fright approaching panic. Her prime motivation is to stay alive. In most cases, rapists choose victims slightly smaller than themselves. The rapist may urinate or defecate on his victim, ejaculate into her face and hair, force anal intercourse, and insert foreign objects into her vagina and rectum.

After the rape, the woman may experience shame, humiliation, confusion, fear, and rage. The type of reaction and the length of duration of the reaction are variable, but women report effects lasting for 1 year or longer. Many women experience the symptoms of a posttraumatic stress disorder. Some women are able to resume sexual relations with men, particularly if they have always felt sexually adequate. Others become phobic of sexual interaction or develop such symptoms as vaginismus. Few women emerge from the assault completely unscathed. The manifestations and the degree of damage depend on the violence of the attack itself, the vulnerability of the woman, and the support systems available to her immediately after the attack.

The victim fares best when she receives immediate support, and is able to ventilate her fear and rage to loving family members and to believing physicians and law enforcement officials. She is helped when she knows she has socially acceptable means of recourse at her disposal, such as the arrest and conviction of the rapist. Therapy is usually supportive in approach, unless there is a severe underlying disorder, and focuses on restoring the victim's sense of adequacy and control over her life, and relieving the feelings of helplessness, dependency, and obsession with the assault that frequently follow rape. Group therapy with homogeneous groups composed of rape victims is a particularly effective form of treatment.

The rape victim experiences a physical and psychological trauma when she is assaulted. Until recently, she also faced frequent disbelief when she reported the crime, if she had sufficient ego strength to do so, or accusations of having provoked or wanted the assault.

In reality, the National Commission on the Causes and Prevention of Violence found discernible victim precipitation of rape in only 4.4 percent of cases. This statistic was lower than in any other crime of violence.

Such writers as Brownmiller and French depicted the threat of rape as a cultural method of intimidation of all women tacitly supported by all men.

Feminist literature also perceives the myth of the falsely accusing woman—from Potiphar's wife in the Old Testament to the present—as a male projection. The fear of being falsely accused of rape seems particularly irrational in view of the degree of underreporting of actual rapes.

The education of police officers and the use of policewomen in dealing with rape victims have helped increase the reporting of the crime. Rape crisis centers and telephone hot lines are available for immediate aid and information for victims. Volunteer groups work with emergency rooms in hospitals and with physician education programs regarding the treatment of victims.

Legally, women no longer have to prove that they actively struggled against the rapist when they appear in court. Testimony regarding the prior sexual history of the victim has recently been declared inadmissible as evidence in a number of states. Also, penalties for first-time rapists have been reduced, making juries more amenable to considering a conviction. In some states wives cannot prosecute husbands for rape.

### Male Rape

In some states, the definition of rape is being changed to substitute the word "person" for "female." In most states, male rape is legally sodomy. Homosexual rape is much more frequent among men than among women, and it occurs primarily in closed institutions, such as prisons and maximum-security hospitals. The attacks are violent, rather than sexual, and are used to express anger or power. The dynamics are identical to those involved in heterosexual rape. The crime enables the rapist to discharge aggression and to aggrandize himself. The victim is usually smaller than the rapist and may be handsome in a feminine way. He is always perceived as passive and unmanly (weaker), and is used as an object.

The homosexual-rape victim often feels, as does the raped woman, that he has been ruined. In addition, he often fears he will become homosexual because of the attack.

### Statutory Rape

Intercourse is unlawful between a male over 16 and a female under the age of consent. This age varies from 14 to 21, depending on the jurisdiction. Thus, a man of 18 and a girl of 15 may have consensual intercourse, and the man may be held for statutory rape. This type of rape may vary drastically from the crimes described above in being nonassaultive and in being a sexual act, not a violent act. Nor is it a deviant act, unless the age discrepancy is sufficient for the man to be defined as a pedophile—that is, when the girl is 12 years old or less. Charges of statutory rape are rarely pressed by the consenting girl; they are brought by her parents.

### Spouse Abuse

Spouse abuse is estimated to occur in from 3 million to 6 million families in the United States. This aspect of domestic violence has been recognized as a severe problem, largely as a result of recent cultural emphasis on civil rights and the work of feminist groups, although the problem itself is one of long standing.

The major problem in spouse abuse is wife abuse, although some beatings of husbands are reported. In these cases, the husbands complain of fear of ridicule if they expose the problem, fear of charges of counterassault, and inability to leave the situation because of financial difficulties. Husband abuse has also been reported when a frail elderly man is married to a much younger woman.

Wife beating occurs in families of every racial and religious background, and crosses all socioeconomic lines. It is most frequent in families with problems of drug abuse, particularly when there is alcoholism.

Behavioral, cultural, intrapsychic, and interpersonal factors all contribute to the development of the problem. Abusive men are likely to have come from violent homes where they witnessed wife beating, or were abused themselves as children. The act itself is reinforcing. Once a man has beaten his wife, he is likely to do so again. Abusive husbands tend to be immature, dependent, and nonassertive, and to suffer from strong feelings of inadequacy.

Their aggression is bullying behavior, designed to humiliate their wives to build up their own low self-esteem. The abuse is most likely to occur when the man feels threatened or frustrated at home, at work, or with peers. Impatient and impulsive, abusive husbands physically displace aggression provoked by others onto their wives. The dynamics include identification with an aggressor (father, boss), testing behavior (will she stay with me no matter how I treat her?), distorted desires to express manhood, and dehumanization of the woman. As in rape, aggression is permissible when the woman is perceived as property.

Recently, hot lines, emergency shelters for women, and other organizations such as Respond have been developed to aid battered wives and to educate the public. A presidential commission was established to investigate spouse abuse. A major problem for abused women has been where to find a place to go when they leave home, frequently in fear of their lives. Battering is often severe, involving broken limbs, broken ribs, internal bleeding, and brain damage. When an abused wife tries to leave her husband, he often becomes doubly intimidating and threatening, saying: "I'll get you." If the woman has small children to care for, her problem is compounded.

Some men feel remorse and guilt after an episode of violent behavior, and become particularly loving. This behavior gives the wife hope, and she remains until the next cycle of violence, which inevitably occurs.

Change is initiated only when the man is convinced that the woman will not tolerate the situation, and when she begins to exert control over his behavior. She can do so by leaving for a prolonged period, with therapy for the man as a condition of return. Family therapy is effective in treating the problem. With relatively less impulsive men, external controls, such as calling the neighbors or the police, may be sufficient to stop the behavior.

### Incest

Incest is defined as the occurrence of sexual relations between close blood relatives. A broader definition describes incest as intercourse between participants who are related to one another by some formal or informal bond of kinship which is culturally regarded as a bar to sex relations. For example, sexual relations between stepparents and stepchildren or among stepsiblings are usually considered incestuous, even though no blood relationship exists.

The strongest and most universal taboo exists against mother-son incest. It occurs much less frequently than any other form of incest does, and such behavior is usually indicative of more severe psychopathology among the participants than is father-daughter or sibling incest.

Numerous factors have been cited as determining prohibitions against incest. In *Totem and Taboo*, Freud developed the concept of primal horde, in which the younger men collectively murdered the group's patriarch, who had kept all the women of the tribe to himself. The incest taboo arose both out of guilt after the murder, and to prevent a repetition of the act and further rivalry after the murder and subsequent disintegration of the horde.

Sociologists have underlined the role of incest prohibitions as socialization factors. Biological factors also support the taboo. Groups that inbreed risk the unmasking of lethal or detrimental recessive genes, and the progeny of inbreeding groups are generally less fit than other progeny. Anthropologists have observed that the particular form of the incest taboo is culturally determined, and affected by whether the society is patriarchal or matriarchal, and particularly by how property is inherited.

Accurate figures of the incidence of incest are difficult to obtain because of the general shame and embarrassment of the entire family that is involved. Females are victims more often than males. About 15 million women in the United States have been the object of incestuous attention and one-third of sexually abused persons have been molested before the age of 9.

Incestuous behavior is much more frequently reported among families of low socioeconomic status than among other families. This difference may be due to greater contact with reporting officials—such as welfare workers, public health personnel, and law enforcement agents—and is not a true reflection of higher incidence in that demographic group. Incest is more easily hidden by economically stable families than by the poor.

Social, cultural, physiological, and psychological factors all contribute to the breakdown of the incest taboo. Incestuous behavior has been associated with alcoholism, overcrowding and increased physical proximity, and rural isolation that prevents adequate extrafamilial contacts. Some communities may be more tolerant of incestuous behavior than is society in general. Major mental illnesses and intellectual deficiencies have been described in some cases of clinical incest. Some family therapists view incest as a defense designed to maintain a dysfunctional family unit. The older and stronger participant in incestuous behavior is usually male. Thus, incest may be viewed as a form of child abuse, or as a variant of rape.

Father-daughter incest is reported to be more common than either sibling incest or mother-son incest. Many cases of sibling incest are denied by parents, or involve near-normal interaction if the activity is prepubertal sexual play and exploration.

The daughter, in father-daughter incest, has frequently had a close relationship with her father throughout her childhood, and is at first pleased when he approaches her sexually. The onset of incestuous behavior usually occurs when the daughter is 10. As the incestuous behavior continues, however, the abused daughter becomes more bewildered, confused, and frightened. As she nears adolescence, she undergoes physiological changes that add to her confusion. She never knows whether her father will be parental or sexual. Her mother may be alternately caring and competitive. Her relationships with her siblings are also affected as they sense her special position with her father and treat her as an outsider. The incestuous father, fearful that his daughter may expose their relationship and often jealously possessive of her, interferes with the development of her normal peer relationships.

The physician must be aware of the possibility of intrafamilial sexual abuse as the cause of a wide variety of emotional and physical symptoms, including abdominal pain, genital irritations, separation anxiety, phobias, nightmares, and school problems. When incest is suspected, it is essential to interview the abused child apart from the rest of the family.

### Homosexual Incest

In father-son incest, two cultural sanctions are violated: the taboo against incestuous behavior and the sanction against homosexual behavior. The family in which such behavior occurs is usually highly disturbed, with a violent, alcoholic, or psychopathic father, a dependent mother who is unable to protect her children, and an obliteration of the usual family roles and individual identities. Father-son incest is rarely reported. The son is frequently the eldest child, and, if he has sisters, they are sexually abused by the father as well. The father does not necessarily have any other history of homosexual behavior. The sons in the situation may experience homicidal or suicidal ideation, and may first present to a psychiatrist with self-destructive behavior.

### Treatment

The first step in the treatment of incestuous behavior is its disclosure. Once a breakthrough of the denial and collusion or fear by the family members has been achieved, incest is less likely to recur. When the participants suffer from severe psychopathology, treatment must be directed toward the underlying illness. Family therapy is useful to reestablish the group as a functioning unit and to develop healthier role definitions for each member. The external control provided by therapy helps prevent further incestuous behavior, while the participants are learning to develop internal restraints and more appropriate methods of gratifying their needs. Sometimes the revelation of incestuous behavior results in the extrusion of a family member from the group.

### Infertility

It is not one factor or one mate but a combination of several factors in each that contributes to infertility in 80 percent of all cases. A couple is considered infertile if they have had coitus without contraception for a period of 1 year and pregnancy has not occurred. In the United States, 12 percent of all marriages are estimated to be involuntarily childless. Various clinics report that 20 to 50 percent of couples presently facing infertility can be helped.

Until recently, the onus for the failure to conceive was on the woman, and feelings of guilt, depression, and inadequacy frequently accompanied her perception of being barren. Current practice encourages simultaneous investigation of factors preventing conception in both the man and the woman. However, it is still frequently the woman who first presents for an infertility workup.

A thorough sexual history of the couple—including such factors as frequency of contact, erectile or ejaculatory dysfunction, and coital positions—must be obtained. Frequently, conception is less possible simply because the woman rises to void, wash, or even douche immediately after coitus. Preference for coitus with the woman in the superior position is also not conducive to conception because of the lessened retention of semen.

A psychiatric evaluation of the couple may be advisable. Marital disharmony or emotional conflicts around intimacy, sexual relations, or parenting roles can directly affect endocrine function and such physiological processes as erection, ejaculation, and ovulation.

The stress of infertility itself in a couple who want children can lead to emotional disturbance. When a preexisting conflict gives rise to problems with identity, self-esteem, and neurotic guilt, the disturbance may be severe. It may manifest itself through regression; extreme dependency on the physician, the mate, or a parent; diffuse anger; impulsive behavior; or depression. The problem is further complicated if

hormone therapy is being used to treat the infertility, as the therapy may temporarily increase depression in some patients.

People who have difficulty conceiving experience shock, disbelief, and a general sense of helplessness, and they develop an understandable preoccupation with the problem. Involvement in the infertility work-up, and the development of expertise about infertility, can be a constructive defense against feelings of inadequacy and the humiliating, sometimes painful aspects of the work-up itself. Worry about attractiveness and sexual desirability is common. Partners may feel ugly or impotent, and episodes of sexual dysfunction and loss of desire are reported. These problems are aggravated if a couple is scheduling their sexual relations according to temperature charts.

In addition, they are dealing with a narcissistic blow to their sense of femininity or masculinity. An infertile partner may fear abandonment, or feel that the spouse is remaining in the relationship resentfully. Single people who are aware of their own infertility may shy away from relationships for fear of being rejected once their "defect" is known.

Infertile people may have particular difficulty in their adult relationships with their own parents. The identification and the equality that come from sharing the experience of parenthood must be replaced by internal reserves and other generative aspects of their lives.

Professional intervention may be necessary to help infertile couples ventilate their feelings and go through the process of mourning their lost biological functions and the children they cannot have. Couples who remain infertile must cope with an actual loss. Couples who decide not to pursue parenthood may develop a renewed sense of love, dedication, and identity as a pair. Others may need help in exploring the options of husband or donor insemination, laboratory implantation, and adoption.

### Sterilization

Sterilization is a procedure that prevents a man or a woman from producing offspring. In a woman, the procedure is usually salpingectomy or ligation of the Fallopian tubes. It is a hospital procedure with low morbidity and low mortality. A man is usually sterilized by vasectomy, ligation of the vas deferens. It is a simpler procedure than a salpingectomy and is performed in the physician's office. A sperm granuloma may develop at the operative site, but it usually diminishes with time. Fear of serious medical complication associated with autoimmune disease due to the sperm granuloma has not been substantiated.

A small proportion of patients who elect sterilization may suffer a neurotic poststerilization syndrome. It may be manifest through hypochondriasis, pain, loss of libido, sexual unresponsiveness, depression, and concerns about masculinity or femininity. When it occurs, a premorbid psychopathological state can generally be found.

Involuntary sterilization procedures have been performed to prevent the reproduction of traits considered genetically undesirable. There have been statutes allowing for the sterilization of hereditary criminals, sex offenders, syphilitics, the mentally retarded, and epileptics. Some of these statutes have been found unconstitutional. In recent years, human rights and civil liberties groups have been challenging the legality and the ethical standing of such sterilization procedures with increasing vigor.

## The Unconsummated Marriage

### Introduction

Studies by gynecologists, family physicians, and sexual therapy clinics reveal that the unconsummated marriage is not a rare complaint. Couples present with the problem after having been married several months or several years. Masters and Johnson reported an unconsummated marriage of 17 years' duration.

The couple involved in an unconsummated marriage are typically uninformed and inhibited about sexuality. Their feelings of guilt, shame, or inadequacy are only increased by their problem, and they are conflicted by a need to seek help and a need to conceal their difficulty.

Frequently, the couple do not seek help directly, but the woman may reveal the problem to her gynecologist on a visit ostensibly concerned with vague vaginal or somatic complaints. On examining her, the gynecologist may find an intact hymen. In some cases, the wife may have undergone a hymenectomy. This surgical procedure is another stress, however, and often serves to increase the feelings of inadequacy in the couple. The wife may feel put upon, abused, or multilated, and the husband's concern about his manliness is increased. The hymenectomy usually aggravates the situation without solving the basic problem. The physician's questioning, if he is comfortable in dealing with sexual problems, may be the first opening to frank discussion of the couple's distress. Often, the pretext of the medical visit is a discussion of contraceptive methods or, even more ironically, a request for an infertility work-up.

Once presented, however, the complaint can often be successfully treated. The duration of the problem does not significantly affect the prognosis or the outcome of the case.

### Causes

Lack of sexual education, sexual prohibitions overly stressed by parents or society, neurotic problems of an oedipal nature, immaturity in both partners, overdependence on primary families, and problems in sexual identification—all contribute to nonconsummation of a marriage. Religious orthodoxy, with severe control of sexual and social development or the equation of sexuality with sin or uncleanliness, has also been cited as a dominant causative agent.

### Clinical Features

In the unconsummated marriage, the husband frequently has a problem with impotence, and many wives present with vaginismus. It is often difficult to determine which problem arose first, as there has frequently been no premarital sexual experience for either partner. The woman may develop vaginismus after repeated sexual encounters with a dysfunctional man have caused her to feel rejected and frustrated; or the man may develop impotence due to the same feelings after unsuccessful attempts at intercourse with a woman suffering from vaginismus. Occasionally, one partner is able to function outside of the marital situation, and, frequently, either partner would function better sexually with a less dysfunctional mate.

### Treatment

The problem of the unconsummated marriage is best treated by seeing both members of the couple. Dual-sex therapy involving a male-female co-therapy team has been markedly effective. However, other forms of conjoint therapy, marital counseling, traditional psychotherapy on a one-to-one basis, and counseling from a sensitive family physician, gynecologist, or urologist are all helpful.

The couple needs to receive factual sexual information from a sympathetic, accepting, but authoritative source. They need permission and encouragement to function sexually and to build confidence and pride in their own sexuality. Couples who come for treatment with the problem have usually proved to be highly motivated and have responded quickly and positively to therapy.

Many women involved in unconsummated marriages have distorted concepts about their vaginas. There can be a fear of having no opening, a fear of being too small or too soft, or a confusion of the vagina with the rectum, leading to feelings of being unclean. The man may share in these distortions of the vagina and, in addition, perceive it as dangerous to himself. Similarly, both partners may share distortions about the man's penis, perceiving it as a weapon, as too large, or as too small. Many of these patients can be helped by simple education about genital anatomy and physiology, by suggestions for self-exploration, and by corrective information from a physician.

Both partners in an unconsummated marriage contribute to the problem. Thus, it is desirable to see the couple in treatment. Improvement or change in attitude in one partner, however, may be sufficient to enable him or her to help the mate.

Within the appropriate therapeutic milieu, the partners and the couples are often able to achieve a degree of growth and emotional maturity that enable them to start functioning sexually together.

## REFERENCES

Brownmiller S: *Against Our Will: Men and Women, and Rape.* Simon & Shuster, New York, 1975.

Felman Y M, and Nikitas J A: Sexually transmitted diseases and child sexual abuse. NY State J Med *83:* 341, 1983.

Herman J, Hirschman L: Families at risk for father-daughter incest. Am J Psychiatry *138:* 967, 1981.

Hilberman E: "Wife-beater's wife" reconsidered. Am J Psychiatry *137:* 1336, 1980.

Nadelson C C, Notman M T, Zackson H, Gornick J: A follow-up study of rape victims. Am J Psychiatry *139:* 1266, 1982.

Sadock V A: Special areas of interest. In *Comprehensive Textbook of Psychiatry,* ed 4, H I Kaplan, B J Sadock, editors, p 1090. Williams & Wilkins, Baltimore, 1985.

Wells L. Family pathology and father-daughter incest: Restricted psychopathy. J Clin Psychiatry *42:* 5, 1981.

# 21

# Adjustment and Impulse Control Disorders

## 21.1 ADJUSTMENT DISORDERS

### Introduction

Adjustment disorders may be manifested in a variety of ways. Thus, one may find affective reactions—for example, anxiety, depression, anger, aggression, or fear. More severe reactions include melancholias, psychophysiological decompensations, regressions, depersonalizations, and inappropriate impulsive acts. The reactive responses may be marked, specific, repetitive, circumscribed, or diffuse, and can involve behavior, affect, thought, or substance abuse.

Psychiatric disorders that are reactive follow stimuli to the mental system that are of such degree that they cannot be integrated or disregarded, and subsequently cause residual symptoms. When the stress is an ordinary life event or circumstance—for example, loss of a parent, divorce, business difficulties—DSM-III uses the term adjustment disorder. In this case, the ability to participate in the ordinary activities of everyday life is impaired with common symptoms, such as anxiety, depression, irritability, and physical complaints. Symptoms may be delayed for weeks or months, but it is assumed they will disappear with the removal of the stimulus. The basis of the disorder lies in the concept of trauma as psychic overload, with a subsequent partial or complete feeling of helplessness, accompanied by regression and inhibitions. With adjustment disorders, the stressor is within the realm of ordinary human experience, the response is disproportionately intense, and the overload is surprising, but the impairment is moderate and temporary.

### Definition

According to DSM-III, an adjustment disorder is a maladaptive reaction to a clearly identifiable event, stressor or adverse circumstances that occurs within 3 months after the onset of the stressor. It is a pathological response to what a layman might call "bad luck" or "big change"; it is not an exacerbation of a psychiatric disorder meeting other criteria. The disorder is expected to remit eventually, after the stressor disappears, or a new level of adaptation is attained. The response is maladaptive because of an impairment in social or occupational functioning, or because of symptoms or behaviors that are beyond the normal, usual, expectable response to such a stressor. Hence, the diagnostic category should not be used if the patient meets the criteria for a more specific disorder. A concurrent personality disorder or organic impairment may render the patient more vulnerable to an adjustment disorder.

Stressors may be single, such as a divorce or the loss of a job, or multiple, such as the death of an important person occurring at the time of one's own physical illness and loss of a job. Stressors may be recurrent, such as seasonal business difficulties, or continuous, as in the case of chronic illness or having to live in a poverty area. Discordant intrafamilial relationships may produce adjustment disorders with effects on the family system. The disorder may be limited to the patient, however, as when he or she is the victim of a crime or has a physical illness. At times, adjustment disorders occur in a group or community setting, where the stressor involves a broad number of people, as is the case in a natural disaster or in racial, social, or religious persecution. Specific developmental stages—such as beginning school, leaving home, getting married, becoming a parent, failing to achieve occupational goals, the last child's leaving home, and retiring—are often associated with adjustment disorders.

The severity of a stressor is a complex function of degree, quantity, duration, reversibility, and the environment and personal context. As an example, the loss of a parent is quite different in the cases of a 10-year-old and a 40-year-old.

## Epidemiology

Clinicians believe that adjustment disorders are quite common. Because of the recent revision of the definition, there are no statistical data.

## Etiology

As adjustment disorders are currently defined, the existence of a prior personality disorder or organic mental disorder may increase the patient's vulnerability to stress. By definition, also, the severity of the stressor or stressors is not always predictive of the severity of the adjustment disorder. Personality organization and cultural or group norms and values play a role in the disproportionate responses to stressors.

Several psychoanalytic researchers have contributed to the understanding of the capacity of the same stress to produce a range of responses in various normal human beings. Throughout his life, Freud remained interested in why the stresses of ordinary life produced illness in some and not in others, why an illness took a particular form, and why some experiences and not others predisposed to psychopathology. In contrast to a popular misconception, Freud always laid considerable weight on the constitutional factor and saw it as interacting with a person's life experiences to produce fixation.

Psychoanalytic research has emphasized the role of the mother and the rearing environment in a person's later capacity to respond to stress. Particularly important was Winnicott's concept of the "good-enough mother," a person who makes "active adaptation to the infant's needs, an active adaptation that gradually lessens, according to the infant's growing ability to account for failure of adaptation and to tolerate the results of frustration."

In the adjustment disorder, a specific meaningful stress has found the point of vulnerability in a person of otherwise considerable ego strength.

## Diagnosis

Although by definition an adjustment disorder must follow some stressors, symptoms do not necessarily begin immediately, nor do they always subside as soon as the stressor ceases. If the stressor continues, the disorder may be lifelong. The disorder may occur at any age. Symptoms vary considerably, with depressive, anxious, and mixed features most common in adults. Physical symptoms are most common in children and the elderly, but may occur in any age group. Assaultiveness, reckless driving, excessive drinking, defaulting on other legal responsibilities, and withdrawal also occur. See Table I for the DSM-III diagnostic criteria for adjustment disorder.

### Subtypes of Adjustment Disorder

**Adjustment Disorder with Depressed Mood.** Here the predominant manifestations are depressed mood, tearfulness, and hopelessness. One must distinguish between adjustment disorder with depressed mood and a major depressive disorder or uncomplicated bereavement.

**Adjustment Disorder with Anxious Mood.** Here the major differential is with anxiety disorders.

**Adjustment Disorder with Mixed Emotional Features.** This category applies when the predominant symptoms involve combinations of anxiety and depression or other emotions. One must differentiate it from depressive and anxiety disorders.

**Adjustment Disorder with Disturbance of Conduct.** Here the predominant manifestation involves conduct in which the rights of others are violated, or age-appropriate societal

TABLE I
DIAGNOSTIC CRITERIA FOR ADJUSTMENT DISORDER*

A. A maladaptive reaction to an identifiable psychosocial stressor, that occurs within three months of the onset of the stressor.

B. The maladaptive nature of the reaction is indicated by either of the following:
1. Impairment in social or occupational functioning
2. Symptoms that are in excess of a normal and expectable reaction to the stressor

C. The disturbance is not merely one instance of a pattern of overreaction to stress or an exacerbation of one of the mental disorders previously described.

D. It is assumed that the disturbance will eventually remit after the stressor ceases or, if the stressor persists, when a new level of adaptation is achieved.

E. The disturbance does not meet the criteria for any of the specific disorders listed previously or for uncomplicated bereavement.

* From American Psychiatric Association: *Diagnostic and Statistical Manual of Mental Disorders*, ed 3. American Psychiatric Association, Washington, DC, 1980. Used with permission.

norms and rules are disregarded. The major differential that must be entertained is conduct disorders. Examples of behavior in this category are truancy, vandalism, reckless driving, and fighting.

**Adjustment Disorder with Mixed Disturbance of Emotions and Conduct.** This category allows for predominant manifestations that are both emotional, such as depression or anxiety, and disturbances of conduct, such as truancy, vandalism, reckless driving, and fighting.

**Adjustment Disorder with Work Disturbances or Academic Inhibition.** This category is applicable for an inhibition of work or academic functioning in a person who has previously functioned adequately in this area. Frequently, there is anxiety and depression, and the condition must be differentiated from depressive disorder and phobic disorder.

**Adjustment Disorder with Withdrawal.** To be differentiated from depressive disorder, this category is used for cases of social withdrawal without significant depressed or anxious mood.

### Differential Diagnosis

Adjustment disorder must be differentiated from conditions not attributable to a mental disorder. According to DSM-III, conditions not attributable to a mental disorder do not have impairment in social or occupational functioning or symptoms or other behaviors, beyond the normal and expectable reaction to the stressor. Because no absolute criteria are available to aid in the distinction between a condition not attributable to a mental disorder and adjustment disorder, clinical judgment is often necessary.

Although uncomplicated bereavement often contains temporarily impaired social and occupational functioning, the dysfunctioning remains within the expectable bounds of a reaction to the loss of a loved one, and thus is not considered an adjustment disorder.

Other disorders from which an adjustment disorder must be differentiated include major depressive disorder, chronic depressive disorder, brief reactive psychosis, generalized anxiety disorder, somatization disorder, the various substance use disorders, conduct disorders, specific academic or work inhibition, identity disorder, and posttraumatic stress disorder. The guideline is that these diagnoses should be given precedence in all cases that meet their criteria, even in the presence of a stressor or group of stressors that served as a possible precipitant. However, some patients meet the criteria for both an adjustment disorder and a personality disorder.

In a posttraumatic stress disorder, the symptoms develop after a psychologically traumatizing event or events outside of the range of normal human experience. The stressors involved in producing such a syndrome are expected to do so in the average human being. They are outside the realm of ordinary experience. They may be experienced alone, such as rape or assault, or in groups, such as military combat. A variety of mass catastrophes—such as floods, airplane crashes, atomic bombings, and death camps—have been identified as stressors. There is always a psychological component to the stressor, and frequently a concomitant physical component that causes direct damage to the nervous system. Clinicians believe that the disorder is more severe and lasts longer when the stressor is of human origin than when it is not.

### Treatment

Psychotherapy remains the treatment of choice in adjustment disorders. Group therapy for patients who have undergone similar stresses can be particularly useful—for example, a group of retired persons or renal dialysis patients. Individual psychotherapy offers the opportunity to explore the meaning of the stressor to the patient, so that earlier traumas can be worked through. On occasion, after successful therapy, patients emerge from an adjustment disorder stronger than in the premorbid period, although no pathology was evident during that period. Minor tranquilizers are too often prescribed by nonpsychiatrist physicians short on both time and the technique to deal psychotherapeutically with adjustment disorder patients.

The psychotherapy of adjustment disorders rests on the concept that the symptom picture is linked to earlier modes of attempted adaptation. When intensive therapy is indicated because of a recurrent adjustment disorder or the persistence of impairment, the goals should include identification of the stressor's preconscious and unconscious meanings.

The psychiatrist treating an adjustment disorder must be particularly mindful of problems of secondary gain. The illness role may be refreshing to some normal persons who have had little experience with its capacity to free one from responsibility. The therapist's attention, empathy, and understanding, which are necessary for success, can become gratifications in their own right, reinforcing the symptoms. Such considerations must be weighed before intensive psychotherapy is begun. When secondary gain has already established itself, attempts at therapy may be fruitless.

On occasion, minor tranquilizers (benzodiazepines) are useful in treating the anxiety often found in those disorders; less frequently, tricyclic antidepressants are effective with the depression. When one finds oneself thinking of instituting a course of antidepressive medication, one must reconsider the diagnosis and wonder about a depressive disorder. Few if any adjustment disorders are adequately treated by medication alone.

Patients whose adjustment disorder includes conduct disturbance may have difficulties with the law, authorities, or school. It is inadvisable for the psychiatrist to attempt to rescue the patient from the consequences of his actions. Too often, such kindness only reinforces socially unacceptable means of tension reduction, and stands in the way of the acquisition of insight and subsequent emotional growth.

Because a stressor can be clearly delineated in adjustment disorders, the position has often been taken that psychotherapy is not indicated: "It's just an adjustment reaction: he'll get over it." Such thinking neglects the fact that most persons exposed to the same stressor would not develop similar symptoms, that it is a pathological response. Psychotherapy can serve as a source of better adaptation to the stressor if it is not reversible or time limited, and can serve as a preventive intervention if the stressor does remit.

## REFERENCES

Andreasen N C, Hoenk P R: The predictive value of adjustment disorders: A follow-up study. Psychiatry *139:* 584, 1982.

Andreasen N C, Warek P: Adjustment disorders in adolescents and adults. Arch Gen Psychiatry *37:* 1166, 1980.

Frosch J: The relation between acting out and disorders of impulse control. Psychiatry *40:* 295, 1977.

Ginsberg G L: Adjustment and impulse control disorders. In *Comprehensive Textbook of Psychiatry,* ed 4, H I Kaplan, B J Sadock, editors, p 1097. Williams & Wilkins, Baltimore, 1985.

Leicester J: Temper tantrums, epilepsy, and episodic dyscontrol. Br J Psychiatry *141:* 262, 1982.

Lewis D: *Vulnerability to Delinquency.* Spectrum Publications, New York, 1981.

---

# 21.2    DISORDERS OF IMPULSE CONTROL

## Introduction

According to DSM-III, a disorder of impulse control is characterized in the following way:

(1) There is a failure to resist an impulse, drive, or temptation to perform some action that is harmful to the individual or others. There may or may not be a conscious resistance to the impulse. The act may or may not be premeditated or planned. (2) Prior to committing the act, there is an increasing sense of tension. (3) At the time of committing the act, there is an experience of either pleasure gratification, or release. The act is ego-syntonic in that it is consonant with the immediate conscious wish and aim of the individual. Immediately following the act, there may or may not be genuine regret, self-reproach, or guilt.

Pathological gambling, kleptomania, pyromania, intermittent explosive disorder, isolated explosive disorder, and atypical impulse control disorder are specifically mentioned. Other disorders involving impulse control are classified as substance use disorders and paraphilias.

## Etiology

Psychoanalytic notions have proved particularly illuminating in the history of attempts to understand the impulse disorders. Freud conceptualized these disorders in terms of the pleasure principle and the reality principle. Disorders of impulse control can be viewed as a temporary lapse of the control held by the reality principle. Patients who can be diagnosed as having these disorders do tend to function well in other respects—sometimes, in fact, achieving memorable accomplishments. The commonality of the disorders of impulse control lies in the similar source of the tension in each condition— that is, the libidinal and aggressive instinctual drives—and in the similar episodic lapse in the ego's defense against them.

An impulse is a disposition toward action to decrease the heightened tension state caused by the welling up of instinctual drives, or by diminished ego defenses against them.

The term impulse has been defined as the generally unpremeditated welling-up of a drive toward some action that usually has the qualities of hastiness, lack of deliberation, and impetuosity.

The disorder contains both the impulse and the consequent action that may be harmful to the person or others. Those who suffer from powerful impulses that they resist may be normal or obsessional neurotics, or even schizophrenics.

The psychodynamics of persons designated as impulse disorder patients are varied even when the symptoms are similar. Fenichel believed that impulsive actions defend against danger, including depression, and simultaneously bring about a distorted instinctual satisfaction of a sexual or aggressive nature. The actions are directed less toward achieving a goal than toward the negative aim of getting rid of tension; the acquisition of pleasure is less significant than the discontinuance of pain. Several authors have stressed the early, oral stage of fixation or developmental arrest in such patients that leads to a defect in psychic structure. The patients attempt to master anxiety, guilt, depression, and other painful affects by means of action, but these actions aimed at obtaining relief seldom succeed even temporarily.

Biological lesions of the nervous system may underlie these disorders. For example, kleptomania has been reported as a presenting feature of cortical atrophy. Recent work has suggested the continuance of impulse disorder symptoms into adulthood in persons who were classified as suffering from childhood minimal brain dysfunction syndrome. Several studies reported evidence of brain disorders in a significant percentage of patients who exhibited episodic violence. Life long or acquired mental deficiency, epilepsy, and even reversible acute brain syndromes have long been known to be implicated in lapses of impulse control.

The capacity to undermine ego defenses by temporary organic states produced by alcohol and other drug abuse is well known. Stealing and burning "for the fun of it," gambling, and actual physical fighting are common antisocial acts caused by intoxicants.

There are disorders of impulse control in which ego defenses are overwhelmed without actual nervous system pathology. Fatigue, incessant stimulation, and psychic trauma can lower resistance. There is a temporary suspension of the ego's control. Improper models for identification, and parental figures who often suffer from difficulty in impulse control themselves, seem to be important in the formulation of these defective personalities. From the side of the instinctual drives, too long a period without gratification can lead to their relative strengthening, so that ego defenses are overwhelmed. These patients have learned substitute discharge patterns (the symptoms) that disregard temporarily the punishment society will demand.

Usually, there is a compromise in the drive gratification that includes punishment. For example, the kleptomaniac or pyromaniac is caught, the aggressive person is arrested or beaten up, the pathological gambler is disgraced or in legal trouble because of bad debts. It is as if there were a freedom to act on the impulse because the superego will have its eventual moment in court, often literally. With the explosive breakthrough of murderous impulses, one can often see the suicidal impulse of the aggressor. With repeated episodic impulses, the knowledge of past subsequent guilt and pain can often reinforce the behavior. In fact, in some cases the need for punishment is antecedent to the impulse.

## Pathological Gambling

### Definition

As currently defined by DSM-III, pathological gambling's essential features are: A chronic and progressive preoccupation with gambling and urge to gamble, and gambling behavior that compromises, disrupts or damages personal, family and/or vocational pursuits. The gambling preoccupation, urge and activity increase during periods of stress. Problems that arise as a result of the gambling lead to an intensification of the gambling behavior. These include loss of work due to absences in order to gamble, defaulting on debts and other financial responsibilities, disrupted family relationships, borrowing money from illegal sources, forgery, fraud, embezzlement and income tax evasion (see Table I).

TABLE I
DIAGNOSTIC CRITERIA FOR PATHOLOGICAL GAMBLING*

A. The individual is chronically and progressively unable to resist impulses to gamble.

B. Gambling compromises, disrupts, or damages family, personal, and vocational pursuits, as indicated by at least three of the following:
  1. Arrest for forgery, fraud, embezzlement, or income tax evasion due to attempts to obtain money for gambling
  2. Default on debts or other financial responsibilities
  3. Disrupted family or spouse relationships due to gambling
  4. Borrowing of money from illegal sources (loan sharks)
  5. Inability to account for loss of money or to produce evidence of winning money, if this is claimed
  6. Loss of work due to absenteeism in order to pursue gambling activity
  7. Necessity for another person to provide money to relieve a desperate financial situation

C. The gambling is not due to antisocial personality disorder.

* From American Psychiatric Association: *Diagnostic and Statistical Manual of Mental Disorders*, ed 3. American Psychiatric Association, Washington, DC, 1980. Used with permission.

## Epidemiology

Estimates place the number of pathological gamblers at a million or more in the United States. The disorder is thought to be more common in men than in women. The fathers of males with the disorder and the mothers of females with the disorder are more likely to have the disorder than is the population at large.

## Etiology

According to DSM-III: There is some evidence that the following may be predisposing factors for the development of the disorders: loss of parent by death, separation, divorce or desertion before the child is 15 years of age; inappropriate parental discipline (absence, inconsistency or harshness); availability of gambling activities to the adolescent; a high family value on material and financial symbols; and a lack of family values on saving, planning and budgeting.

Freud, in his study of Dostoyevsky, saw his gambling as a substitute for masturbation, and made reference to use of the word "playing" in both gambling and masturbation.

Freud also discussed the role of Dostoyevsky's need for punishment because of his murderous wishes toward his father. Gambling and repeatedly losing everything satisfied this guilt for a while.

Fenichel also described the gambler's conflicts as centered on masturbation, with the excitement of winning corresponding to orgasm or killing, and losing being equated to castration and dying.

Other workers saw the neurotic gambler as also engaged in an oedipal struggle in which the gambling situation may represent (1) a challenge or a testing of the father figure for acceptance or rejection, (2) a battle for supremacy, (3) an expression of extreme submissiveness, (4) an attempt to bribe so that forbidden pleasures might be enjoyed, or (5) an attempt to woo the father.

The wish to lose is based on unconscious aggression toward the authorities of childhood who trained the person away from the pleasure principle and toward the reality principle. The aggression leads to unconscious guilt; hence, the gambling and losing are sexualized.

## Clinical Features

In addition to the essential features described above, DSM-III includes the following:

The pathological gambler most often appears overconfident, somewhat abrasive, very energetic and a free spender, but there are times when there are obvious signs of personal stress, anxiety, and depression. Commonly these individuals have the attitude that money causes all their problems and is also the solution to all of their problems. As the gambling increases, the individual is usually forced to lie in order to obtain money and to continue gambling, while hiding the extent of the gambling behavior. There is no serious attempt to budget or save money. When borrowing resources are strained, the likelihood of antisocial behavior occurs in order to obtain money for gambling. Any criminal behavior is typically nonviolent, such as forgery, embezzlement, or fraud. The conscious intent is to return or repay the money.

The disorder usually begins in adolescence, waxes and wanes, and tends to be chronic.

The disorder is extremely incapacitating and results in a failure to become or maintain financial solvency or provide basic support for oneself or one's family.

Complications include alienation from family and acquaintances, loss of one's life accomplishments and attainments, suicide attempts, and association with fringe and illegal groups. Arrest for nonviolent crimes may lead to imprisonment.

## Course and Prognosis

Researchers have described three phases in the pathological gambler: (1) The winning phase, ending with a big win, equal to approximately a year's salary, which hooks the patient. (2) Losing progressively, with the patient structuring his life around gambling. He moves from being an excellent gambler to a stupid one— taking considerable risks, cashing in securities, owing money, missing work, and losing jobs. (3) The desperate stage, with the patient gambling in a frenzy with larger amounts of money, not paying debts, involving himself with loan sharks, writing bad checks, possibly embezzling. It may take 10 or 15 years to reach the third phase, but, within a year or two of it, the patient is a human wreck.

## Differential Diagnosis

Social gambling is distinguished from pathological gambling by the former being associated with gambling with others, on special occasions, and with predetermined acceptable and tolerable losses.

Gambling symptomatic of a manic episode can usually be distinguished from pathological gambling by the history of marked mood changes preceding the gambling. Mild manic-like mood changes are common in pathological gambling, but always follow winning.

Although individuals with antisocial personality disorder may have problems with gambling, at present it is suggested that pathological gambling not be diagnosed when the criteria for antisocial personality disorder are met.

### Treatment

All those who write about pathological gambling indicate that the gambler seldom comes forward for treatment of his own accord. Legal difficulties, family pressures, or other psychiatric complaints bring the gambler into a treatment situation if and when he does arrive. Gamblers Anonymous (GA) was founded in Los Angeles in 1957 and modeled on Alcoholics Anonymous; it is most accessible—at least in larger cities—and probably most effective in treating gambling. It is a method of inspirational group therapy.

It may be helpful in some cases to hospitalize the patient to get him away from his environment, and to not work to achieve insight until the patient has been away from gambling for 3 months. Then pathological gamblers may become excellent candidates for insight-oriented psychotherapy.

## Kleptomania

### Definition

According to DSM-III, kleptomania's essential feature is: "a recurrent failure to resist impulses to steal objects, not for immediate use or for their monetary value. The objects taken are either given away, returned surreptitiously, or are kept and hidden" (see Table II).

The person usually has the money to pay for the objects he impulsively steals. There is the cycle found in other impulse disorders of mounting tension followed by gratification and of tension reduction with or without guilt, remorse, or depression. Stealing is done without long-term planning and without the involvement of others. There can be guilt and anxiety afterward. When the object stolen is the goal, the diagnosis is not kleptomania; in kleptomania, the act of stealing itself is primary.

### Epidemiology

The incidence and prevalence of kleptomania are unknown. Some workers have found it to be somewhat more common in women.

### Etiology

As with other disorders of impulse control, brain disease and mental retardation are known on occasion to be associated with profitless stealing.

Some psychoanalytic writers have stressed the expression of the aggressive impulses in kleptomania and aggression as far more easily discerned than the libidinal aspect. Those who focus on symbolism see meaning in the act itself, the object stolen, and the victim of the theft. Emphasis is also placed on the underlying personality.

Much attention has been addressed by analytic writers of the past two generations to stealing by children and adolescents. Anna Freud pointed out that first thefts coming from the mother's purse indicate the degree to which all stealing is rooted in the initial oneness between mother and child. One worker established seven categories of stealing in chronically acting-out children: (1) as a means of restoring the lost mother-child relationship, (2) as an aggressive act, (3) as a defense against fears of being damaged, (4) in order to achieve punishment, (5) as a means of restoring or adding to self-esteem, (6) in connection with and as a reaction to a family secret, and (7) for excitement (*Lust Angst*) and as substitute for a sexual act. Undoubtedly, one or more of those dynamic configurations can have a causal role in adult kleptomania.

### Clinical Features

In addition to the essential feature noted in DSM-III of a recurrent failure to resist impulses to steal objects, not for immediate use or their monetary value, several associated features are often present. The patient is often distressed about the possibility or actuality of being apprehended and manifests signs of depression, anx-

---

TABLE II
DIAGNOSTIC CRITERIA FOR KLEPTOMANIA*

A. Recurrent failure to resist impulses to steal objects that are not for immediate use or their monetary value.

B. Increasing sense of tension before committing the act.

C. An experience of either pleasure or release at the time of committing the theft.

D. Stealing is done without long-term planning and assistance from, or collaboration with, others.

E. Not due to conduct disorder or antisocial personality disorder.

* From American Psychiatric Association: *Diagnostic and Statistical Manual of Mental Disorders*, ed 3. American Psychiatric Association, Washington, DC, 1980. Used with permission.

iety, and guilt. Persons with the disorder often have serious problems with interpersonal relationships, but personality function, in general, is fairly sound and intact.

Kleptomania often begins in childhood or adolescence. The great majority of children or adolescents who steal do not become kleptomaniacs in adulthood. Serious impairment and complications are usually secondary to being caught, and more so when linked to being arrested. Many persons seem never to have consciously considered the possibility of being forced to face the consequences of their actions, a feature in line with those writers who have described kleptomaniacs as people who feel they have been wronged and are therefore entitled to do what they do. And, some persons have bouts of incapacity to resist the impulse to steal, and then free periods that last weeks or months.

### Course and Prognosis

The course of the disease waxes and wanes, but tends to be chronic. The spontaneous recovery rate is unknown. Prognosis with treatment can be good, but few patients come for help of their own accord. Often, the disease in no way impairs the person's social or work functioning. New bouts of the illness in quiescent cases may be precipitated by loss or disappointment.

### Diagnosis

Since most patients with the disorder are referred in connection with legal proceedings after apprehension, the clinical picture may be clouded by subsequent symptoms of depression and anxiety.

**Differential Diagnosis.** The major differentiation is between kleptomania and other forms of stealing. For a diagnosis of kleptomania, the stealing must always be subsequent to a failure to resist the impulse and be a solitary act, and the stolen articles must be without immediate usefulness or monetary gain.

### Treatment

Because true kleptomania is rare, reports of treatment tend to be individual case descriptions or small series of cases. Insight-oriented psychotherapy and psychoanalysis have been successful, but depend on the patient's motivation.

No one has adequately isolated the factors that inhibit the impulse to steal, and no treatment is based on such a theory. Behavior therapy, including systematic desensitization, aversive conditioning, and a combination of aversive conditioning, altering social contingencies, and marital therapy has been reported to be successful, even when motivation was lacking. These reports cite follow-ups of up to 2 years.

## Pyromania

### Definition

As defined by DSM-III, pyromania's essential features are recurrent failure to resist impulses to set fires, intense fascination with the setting of fires, and seeing fires burn. Prior to setting the fire, there is a build-up of tension. Once the fire is underway, the individual experiences intense pleasure or release. Although the firesetting results from a failure to resist an impulse, there may be considerable advance preparation in order to get the fire underway.

The diagnosis is not made when firesetting is associated with conduct disorder, antisocial personality disorder, schizophrenia, or an organic mental disorder (see Table III).

### Epidemiology

No information is available on the prevalence of pyromania, except the fact that only a small percentage of those adults who set fires would be classified as having pyromania. The disorder is found far more often in males than in females.

### Etiology

Freud gave unconscious meaning to fire, seeing it as a symbol of sexuality: The warmth that is radiated by fire calls up the same sensation that accompanies a state of sexual excitation, and the shape and movements of a flame suggest a phallus in activity.

Later writers thought that fire may symbolize activities deriving from various levels of libidinal and aggressive development, including oral and anal, both passive and active.

According to one major study, firesetters appear quite normal to the casual observer, work in an organized fashion, and attract little attention. Often, after putting the neighborhood into confusion with a fire and knowing that the fire engines are at work, their tension subsides, and they fall into a peaceful sleep. Some persons experience the impulse episodically, with extended free periods interposed; for others the impulse recurs night after night. Either type of pathological firesetter responds to the impulse almost every time it appears. Researchers found several motives in those who set fires because of irresistible impulses. Associated with an abnormal craving for power and social prestige was a wish to identify with the firemen. Some pyromaniacs were volunteer firemen who set fires to prove themselves brave, or in order to force other firemen into action. Researchers thought

TABLE III
DIAGNOSTIC CRITERIA FOR PYROMANIA*

A. Recurrent failure to resist impulses to set fires.

B. Increasing sense of tension before setting the fire.

C. An experience of either intense pleasure, gratification, or release at the time of committing the act.

D. Lack of motivation, such as monetary gain or sociopolitical ideology, for setting fires.

E. Not due to an organic mental disorder, schizophrenia, antisocial personality disorder, or conduct disorder.

* From American Psychiatric Association: *Diagnostic and Statistical Manual of Mental Disorders*, ed 3. American Psychiatric Association, Washington, DC, 1980. Used with permission.

that the firesetters were not primarily interested in the blaze or destruction, but identified with the power to extinguish a blaze. It was noted that the incendiary act seems to symbolically represent a sexual experience, but in actual fact they saw it, rather, as a means of relieving accumulated rage over the frustration caused by a sense of social, physical, and sexual inferiority.

Further, it was found that the women firesetters, in addition to being much fewer in number, do not make fires to put the firemen into action, as men frequently do. Promiscuity without pleasure and petty stealing, often approaching kleptomania, were frequently noted delinquent trends in firesetting women.

### Clinical Features

In addition to the essential features described above, DSM-III lists the following: Individuals with the disorder are often recognized as regular, watchers at fires in their neighborhoods, frequently set off false alarms and show interest in firefighting paraphernalia. They may be indifferent to the consequences of the fire to life or property, or they may get satisfaction from the resulting destruction. Frequently the individual may leave obvious clues. Common associated features include alcohol intoxication, psychosexual dysfunctions, lower than average I.Q., chronic personal frustrations, and resentment towards authority figures. Cases have been described in which the individual was sexually aroused by the fire.

In discussing differential diagnosis, DSM-III notes:

There should be little trouble distinguishing this disorder from the fascination of many young children with matches, lighters, and fire as part of the normal investigation of their environment. Pyromania must be distinguished from incendiary acts of sabotage carried out by dissident political extremists or by "paid torches."

In conduct disorders and antisocial personality disorders, when firesetting occurs it is a deliberate act rather than failure to resist an impulse.

In schizophrenia, firesetting may be in response to delusions or hallucinations.

In organic mental disorders, firesetting may occur because of failure to appreciate the consequences of the act.

### Treatment

Because of its position as a symptom, rather than a disorder, little has appeared on the specific treatment of pyromania. The treatment of firesetters has been difficult because of their frequent refusal to take responsibility, the use of denial, concurrent alcoholism, and lack of insight.

Firesetting in children should be taken with the utmost seriousness, and intensive interventions when possible should be undertaken, both as therapeutic and as preventive measures. Further research must be undertaken to clarify the causal forces in this highly dangerous disorder of impulse control.

## Intermittent Explosive Disorder

### Definition

According to DSM-III, this diagnostic category describes individuals who have recurrent and paroxysmal episodes of significant loss of control of aggressive impulses. Behavior in these episodes results in serious assault or destruction of property, and are grossly out of proportion to any psychosocial stressors which may have played a role in eliciting the episodes. The symptoms appear within minutes or hours, and regardless of duration, remit almost as quickly. Each episode is followed by genuine regret or self-reproach. Signs of generalized impulsivity or aggressiveness are absent between each attack. The diagnosis is not made if the loss of control can be accounted for by schizophrenia, antisocial personality disorders, or conduct disorder (see Table IV).

Epileptoid personality has been used to convey the seizure-like quality of the outbursts, which are out of character for the patient, and to convey the suspicion of an organic disease process. Episodic dyscontrol has been used to

TABLE IV
DIAGNOSTIC CRITERIA FOR INTERMITTENT EXPLOSIVE DISORDER*

A. Several discrete episodes of loss of control of aggressive impulses resulting in serious assault or destruction of property.

B. Behavior that is grossly out of proportion to any precipitating psychosocial stressor.

C. Absence of signs of generalized impulsivity or aggressiveness between episodes.

D. Not due to schizophrenia, antisocial personality disorder, or conduct disorder.

* From American Psychiatric Association: *Diagnostic and Statistical Manual of Mental Disorders*, ed 3. American Psychiatric Association, Washington, DC, 1980. Used with permission.

describe several types of aggressive behavior used as regulatory devices to forestall extensive personality disintegration. Episodic dyscontrol has come to be applied only to patients who present episodes of violent loss of control characterized by physical attack on property or another person.

### Epidemiology

According to DSM-III, this disorder appears to be more common in males than in females. The males are likely to be seen in a correctional institution, and the females in a psychiatric facility.

There is evidence that intermittent explosive disorder is more common in family members of persons with the disorder. A variety of factors could be contributory, however, and a simple genetic explanation seems unlikely.

### Etiology

Some workers suggest that disordered brain physiology, particularly in the limbic system, is involved in most cases of episodic violence. It is, however, generally believed that an unfavorable environment in childhood is the major determinant. Predisposing factors in childhood are perinatal trauma, infantile seizures, head trauma, encephalitis, and hyperactivity. A childhood environment replete with alcoholism, beatings, threats to life, and promiscuity is frequently seen. Constitutional factors, early developmental experiences, and current stresses all contribute to the efficacy of the control apparatus or to the intensity of the drive.

Those who have concentrated on psychogenesis in the etiology of episodic explosiveness have stressed identification with assaultive parental figures or the symbolic nature of the target of the violence. Early frustration, oppression, and hostility have been noted as factors that make the person vulnerable. Situations that are directly or symbolically reminiscent of these early deprivations, such as persons who directly or indirectly evoke the image of the frustrating parent, become targets for destructive hostility.

Such patients have been described as typically large but dependent men, whose sense of masculine identity is poor. A heightened sense of being useless and impotent, or of being unable to change the environment, often precedes the episode of physical violence.

### Clinical Features

Intermittent explosive disorder may begin at any stage of life. It is most often seen in the second or third decade. The disorder begins to burn out with the onset of middle age, but this is by no means true in all cases.

Essentials of intermittent explosive disorder are exemplified in the following history: A 48-year-old man, thrice married, lost his job as a long-distance truck driver after repeated episodes of violence several years before admission. He had broken each of his 10 fingers at one time or another after bursts of rage in which he would punch the wall to avoid striking a person. He had on occasion destroyed furniture. His third wife supported him, and he functioned marginally until her illness led to increased drinking on his part and admission for alcoholism. Each attempt at discharge from the hospital led to a new outbreak of violence or suicidal behavior.

In addition to the essential features cited above, several associated features are often but not invariably present. According to DSM-III, prodromal affective or autonomic symptoms may signal an impending episode. Subtle changes in sensorium may occur followed by partial or spotty amnesia. The individual and others are often startled by the behavior. Hypersensitivity to sensory input such as loud noises, rhythmic auditory or visual stimuli, and bright light may be reported. Medical history often reveals hyperactive motor behavior and accident proneness.

### Course and Prognosis

In most cases the disorder decreases in severity with the onset of middle age. Heightened organic impairment, however, can lead to more frequent and severe episodes.

## Diagnosis

The history is typically of a childhood in the midst of alcoholism, violence, emotional instability, and a poor work history. The patients themselves report job losses, marital difficulties, and trouble with the law. Most have sought psychiatric help in the past, but to no avail. There is a high level of anxiety, and guilt and depression are usually present after an episode. Neurological examination sometimes reveals soft neurological signs such as left-right ambivalence and perceptual reversal. Electroencephalographic studies are frequently normal in their findings or show nonspecific changes. Psychological tests for organicity are frequently normal.

## Differential Diagnosis

In the rare instances in which a specific underlying organic disorder, such as a brain tumor or epilepsy, is responsible for the syndrome, it must be diagnosed on Axis III. In the vast majority of cases, the physician is dealing with a behaviorally defined condition, and the diagnosis is made on Axis I, despite strong suspicion of disordered brain physiology.

One can differentiate intermittent explosive disorder from antisocial personality disorder, because in the personality disorder, aggressiveness and impulsivity are part of the patient's character and are present between outbursts. In dissociative disorder, a major stress precedes the attack, but in intermittent explosive disorder, the stress is negligible and at times totally absent. In paranoid or catatonic schizophrenia, there may be violent behavior in response to delusions and hallucinations, and there is gross impairment in reality testing.

## Treatment

Few psychiatrists are interested in treating violent patients. Those who do tend to be young and in training. Most of those who have had a special interest in the treatment of patients with the disorder have advocated a combined pharmacological and psychotherapeutic approach. Psychotherapy with violent patients is difficult, dangerous and often unrewarding. Countertransference difficulties and the value of limit setting have been noted. Group psychotherapy with violent outpatients may be of some help. Family therapy may be useful particularly when the explosive patient is an adolescent or a young adult.

Anticonvulsants have long been used in the treatment of explosive patients, with mixed results. Phenothiazines and antidepressants have been effective in some cases, but one must then wonder whether schizophrenia or affective disorder is the actual diagnosis. When there is a likelihood of subcortical seizure-like activity, these medications can lead to a worsening of the situation.

Operative treatments for intractable violence and aggression have been performed by some neurosurgeons, who believe that withholding such treatment from these patients may be depriving them of their only chance for help. To date, evidence is totally lacking that such treatment is effective.

### Isolated Explosive Disorder

## Definition

DSM-III separates a single episode of an explosive disorder with a special category, isolated explosive disorder: This diagnostic category describes individuals who have had a single episode, characterized by failure to resist an impulse that led to a single violent externally directed act, that had a catastrophic impact on others, and for which the available information does not justify the diagnosis of schizophrenia, antisocial personality disorder, or conduct disorder. An example would be an individual who for no apparent reason suddenly begins shooting at total strangers in a fit of rage, and then shoots himself. In the past, this disorder was referred to as catathymic crisis (see Table V).

The catathymic crisis occurs in a patient who develops a tremendous urge to carry out a vio-

TABLE V
DIAGNOSTIC CRITERIA FOR ISOLATED EXPLOSIVE DISORDER*

A. A single, discrete episode in which failure to resist an impulse led to a single, violent, externally directed act that had a catastrophic impact on others.

B. The degree of aggressivity expressed during the episode was grossly out of proportion to any precipitating psychosocial stressor.

C. Before the episode there were no signs of generalized impulsivity or aggressiveness.

D. Not due to schizophrenia, antisocial personality disorder, or conduct disorder.

*From American Psychiatric Association: *Diagnostic and Statistical Manual of Mental Disorders*, ed 3. American Psychiatric Association, Washington, DC, 1980. Used with permission.

lent act against others or himself, and sees it as the only way out. The patient may murder, set fire to a crowded tenement, castrate or blind himself or commit infanticide or suicide.

### Diagnosis

Usually the sudden murderer is a solitary, conforming person who blames others at times when he cannot conform and consequently feels alone and isolated. At times of doing well, when others expect him to be even more conforming and mature than in the past, he becomes most aware of his shortcomings.

More covertly, many traffic accidents and vehicular homicides can be explained as the use of an automobile as a means of tension discharge, with catastrophic results.

## Atypical Impulse Control Disorder

This category is for disorders of impulse control that cannot be classified elsewhere. The older psychiatric literature classified under the term "morbid impulses" persons who cannot resist the impulse to cut off braids, to defecate after committing a crime, to wander, to rub

against other persons, or to run away. Other behaviors can certainly be added.

**REFERENCES**

Alvarez A: *The Biggest Game in Town*. Houghton Mifflin, Boston, 1983.
Bach-y-Rita G, Lion J R, Clement C E, Ervin F R: Episodic dyscontrol: A study of 130 violent patients. Am J Psychiatry *127:* 1473, 1971.
Frosch J: The relation between acting out and disorders of impulse control. Psychiatry *40:* 295, 1977.
Ginsberg G: Adjustment and impulse control disorders. In *Comprehensive Textbook of Psychiatry*, ed 4, H I Kaplan, B J Sadock, editors, p 1097. Williams & Wilkins, Baltimore, 1985.
Goldstein M: Brain research and violent behavior. Arch Neurol *30:* 1, 1974.
Greenberg H R: Psychology of gambling. In *Comprehensive Textbook of Psychiatry*, ed 3, H I Kaplan, A M Freidman, B J Sadock, editors, p 3274. Williams & Wilkins, Baltimore, 1980.
Leicester J: Temper tantrums, epilepsy, and episodic dyscontrol. Br J Psychiatry *141:* 262, 1982.
Lewis D: *Vulnerability to Delinquency*. Spectrum Publications, New York, 1981.
Lewis N D C, Yarnell H: *Pathological Firesetting*. Nervous and Mental Diseases Publishing Co., New York, 1951.
Macht L B, Mack J E: The firesetter syndrome. Psychiatry *31:* 277, 1968.

# 22

# Psychological Factors Affecting Physical Conditions (Psychosomatic Disorders)

## 22.1 HISTORY AND CURRENT CONCEPTS OF PSYCHOSOMATIC MEDICINE

### Introduction

Although psychosomatic (psychophysiological) medicine has only recently, within the past 5 decades, become a specific area of concern within the field of psychiatry, it is impossible to trace the history of it without immediately becoming involved with the idea of mind-body unity, implied by the Greek words psyche (mind) and soma (body). The problem of mind and body, and how they relate, has been considered by all ages. The controversy about the interrelationship can be seen currently in DSM-III, which has deleted the nosological term "psychophysiological disorder," used in DSM-II, and replaced it with "psychological factors affecting physical conditions." This change indicates an ill-advised continued questioning about how psychic and somatic holism is to be defined.

After much debate as to whether "psychophysiological" should be replaced by the original, succinct term "psychosomatic" or by the terms ultimately used, the latter was chosen by the task force that wrote DSM-III because they thought that "psychological factors affecting physical conditions" more aptly described psychosomatic phenomena. The diagnostic criteria given in DSM-III for this category are the following: Psychologically meaningful environmental stimuli are temporally related to the initiation or exacerbation of a physical condition; and the physical condition has either demonstrable organic pathology (e.g. rheumatoid arthritis) or a known pathophysiological process (e.g. vomiting).

### History and Current Concepts

Exactly where and how do psyche and soma interrelate? One reencounters the question of the primitive, of Egyptian and Jew, of Greek and Christian. Representatives from both fields of study, psyche and soma, have agreed for more than 100 years that, in a small body of disorders, emotional and somatic activities overlap. These disorders were first called psychosomatic disorders by Heinroth in 1818, when he used the term in regard to insomnia. The word was later popularized by Jacobi, a German psychiatrist; the disorders other than insomnia that were classed as psychosomatic grew to include conversion hysteria—later excluded because it operates through the voluntary central nervous system, rather than through the involuntary autonomic nervous system—ulcerative colitis, peptic ulcer, migraine, bronchial asthma, and rheumatoid arthritis, etc. (See Table I for a listing of some psychosomatic disorders.)

Treatment of psychosomatic disorders by psychological methods has not produced enough satisfactory results to encourage psychological

TABLE I
SOME PSYCHOSOMATIC DISORDERS*

| | |
|---|---|
| Acne | Nausea |
| Allergic reactions | Neurodermatitis |
| Angina pectoris | Obesity |
| Angioneurotic edema | Painful menstrua- |
| Arrhythmia | tion |
| Asthmatic wheezing | Pruritis ani |
| Bronchial asthma | Pylorospasm |
| Cardiospasm | Regional enteritis |
| Coronary heart disease | Rheumatoid arthritis |
| Diabetes mellitus | Sacroiliac pain |
| Duodenal ulcer | Skin diseases such as |
| Essential hypertension | neurodermatitis |
| Gastric ulcer | Spastic colitis |
| Headache | Tachycardia |
| Hyperinsulinism | Tension headache |
| Hyperthyroidism | Tuberculosis |
| Hypoglycemia | Ulcerative colitis |
| Irritable colon | Urticaria |
| Migraine headache | Vomiting |
| Mucous colitis | Warts |

* Adapted, in part, with permission, from American Psychiatric Association: *Diagnostic and Statistical Manual of Mental Disorders*, ed 3, American Psychiatric Association, Washington, DC, 1980.

treatment alone. Indeed, investigators have raised the question about the validity of the concept of psychophysiological medicine; some have suggested that it is too diffuse a term; others say it is too narrow. The field of psychophysiological medicine is on a threshold. There is a great deal to be known, but until more information is definitive, generalizations are insecure.

In the past, two trends existed in psychosomatic medicine, one suggesting that specific emotions lead to specific cell and tissue damage, and the second holding that generalized anxiety creates the precondition for a number of not necessarily predetermined diseases (so called non-specific theories). Cases of shell shock during World War I and new endocrine studies provided observations for the swell of interest in theory evidenced in the 1930s and 1940s.

### Incorporation of Stress Along Specific Pathways

Franz Alexander (see Fig. 1) believed that if a specific stimulus or stress occurred, it expressed itself in the specific physiological response of a predetermined organ. He applied the fight-flight alert of the body against stress, as reported by W. B. Cannon, to the problem. Alexander saw conflict as a stress and suggested that, when conflict presents itself to a person, he may suppress the stress and produce, through the voluntary nervous system, a reaction such as the conversion reaction described by Freud. On the other hand, after suppressing stress, he may, through the autonomic system, keep his sympathetic responses alert for heightened aggres-

FIGURE 1. Franz Alexander, 1891–1964. (Courtesy of the Franz Alexander Archives of Psychoanalytic History in the Institute for Psychoanalysis of Chicago.)

sion or flight, or his parasympathetic responses alerted for heightened vegetative activity. Prolonged alertness and tension can produce accompanying physiological changes and eventual pathology of the organs of the viscera.

For instance, Alexander, using much of Freudian psychodynamics, postulated that in a passive-dependent person without someone to satisfy his dependence, stress is created. This particular stress may stimulate and keep alert the parasympathetic nervous system (the vagus nerve), which means that too much gastric acid is secreted and that gastric hypermotility results, all of which may lead to a peptic ulcer. Another dependent person with a different genetic set may, in repressing conflict, stimulate the parasympathetic overfunctioning through pathways leading to colitis or asthma. Still other dependent persons, in seeking to move beyond dependency, incorporate the stress; such a move entails overstimulation of the sympathetic system, and the chronic alertness caused thereby produces migraine, hypertension, or arthritis. Alexander called these relationships typical specific conflict constellations. Although many other workers used different specificity approaches, Alexander's Chicago Psychoanalytic Institute group has continued to support his original findings dating back to the 1930s, and in 1968 they published additional supportive data for his theories.

Alexander's studies have been criticized on theoretical and experimental grounds. Theoretically, Alexander discounted the role of the voluntary nervous system in the genesis of psychosomatic disease. He assumed as fact certain hypothetical and questionable psychoanalytic concepts, and proposed a series of fixed unconscious conflictual constellations as causative factors in various diseases. He assumed that certain psychological conflicts or stresses have specific physiological concomitants. This last point has been experimentally challenged, and represents an example of the conceptual confusion that results from mixing concepts from two levels of description.

Although there is some validation of Alexander's studies, there has been considerable disagreement on whether it is possible to demonstrate the same specific conflicts in all cases of the same disease. It is also questionable whether the conflicts postulated for one disease differ from those associated with other diseases; in other words, it has not been possible thus far to predict disease from conflict or vice versa. In addition, it is highly doubtful whether specific psychological conflicts can be correlated clinically or experimentally with specific physiological vegetative changes.

Even though Alexander's theory of the typical unconscious conflict is a major theoretical force in the psychosomatic field, it remains at this time a basically unvalidated hypothesis, resting on questionable underlying assumptions.

A number of investigators have developed the pathway concept of constellations into other theories involving the whole personality. The ambitious, hard-driving man prone to coronary occlusion, as described by Flanders Dunbar in the 1940s, is no longer accepted as having predisposition enough to dictate death by coronary occlusion. But he is not so different from the competitive, restless, time-haunted, and coronary-bound type A person more recently proposed by Friedman and Rosenman. Friedman and others later listed certain physiological characteristics of their type A person: high plasma triglycerides, high cholesterol level, hyperinsulinemic response to glucose challenge, and high levels of noradrenaline present in urine. Some researchers have suggested correlations between cancer proneness and personalities who repress and deny emotional stress, seldom project for defense, and only slowly recover from depression after loss; they hypothesized that depression is somatized as neoplasm. Increased knowledge of such factors as body type, personality type, environmental conditions, and chemical process within a person seems promising for the near future, but these proposals require validation.

## Nonspecific Theories of Psychosomatic Disorders

There are, it seems, four general types of reaction to stress: the normal, in which alert is followed by an action of defense; the neurotic, in which the alert or anxiety is so great that the defense becomes ineffective and neurotic symptoms develop; the psychotic, in which the alarm may be misperceived resulting in psychosis; and the psychosomatic, in which defense by the psyche fails, and the alert is translated into somatic symptoms, causing changes in body tissue. The second trend in psychosomatic medicine has been that of investigating what happens to a person in a nonspecific way when faced with stress; chronic arousal can be studied by itself without being tied to specific pathway reactions or psychic constellations.

Harold Wolff and Stewart Wolf observed that chronic hyperfunction or chronic hypofunction in the vascular and secretory activities of the mucosa of the gastrointestinal and respiratory systems can produce pathology. Overfunctioning of the mucosa was correlated with hostility, and underfunctioning with fear or sadness. The patient's entire reactive patterning and his life history account for whether he reacts to stress by hyperfunctioning or hypofunctioning.

Other workers in the nonspecific group have demonstrated various possible mechanisms by which psychologically induced stress may cause organic disease in humans and animals. Hans Selye thought that the hypophyseal-adrenocortical axis responds to various types of physical and psychic stress with hormonal changes that can ultimately cause a variety of organic diseases, such as rheumatoid arthritis and peptic ulcer. Selye viewed such diseases as a by-product of the body's attempt to adapt to stress from any source. He named this the general adaptational syndrome (GAS).

George Mahl, an experimental psychologist with a learning theory conception of behavior, studied the effect of chronic unrelieved anxiety in humans and animals, and found that gastric hydrochloric acid production increases under such circumstances. Since such acidity is a precursor of peptic ulcer, he concluded that chronic anxiety, derived from any source whatsoever, is the variable intervening between the behavioral and the physical events involved in psychosomatic illness.

Other animal experimenters have successfully produced a variety of psychosomatic symptoms, such as certain respiratory conditions in animals, by experimentally creating stressful situations and inducing conflict. Since it can be assumed that animals do not have a human being's capacity for symbolic thought, but since they do demonstrate psychosomatic phenomena in response to psychogenic stress, one wonders whether it is necessary or practical to postulate the operation of specific psychological conflicts, which can hardly be meaningful to an animal, in the etiology of such disease.

Another non-specific theory is alexithymia, postulated by Peter Sifneos and John Nemiah. Alexithymic persons cannot express feeling tones into words. Instead, they develop psychosomatic symptoms as an expression of affect.

If, on the promise of reward, a person can control his heart rate, systolic blood pressure, temperature, and rhythm frequency, as occurs in biofeedback research—in short, more of the autonomic system's reactions than before supposed—where does the power of control of the body by the will actually end? If human beings show altered electroencephalographic patterns in response to words, and if people who tend to conform to social pressure show a lower level of skin potential than those who do not, what is

TABLE II
MODERN CONCEPTS OF PSYCHOSOMATIC MEDICINE

**Psychological Factors**

| Freud (1900) | Somatic involvement occurs in conversion hysteria, which is psychogenic in origin; for example, paralysis of an extremity. Conversion hysteria always has a primary psychic cause and meaning; that is, it represents the symbolic substitutive expression of an unconscious conflict. It involves organs innervated only by the voluntary neuromuscular or sensory-motor nervous system. |
|---|---|

↓

| Jelliffe; Groddeck (1910) | Clearly organic, such as fever and hemorrhage, were held to have primary psychic meanings; that is, they were interpreted as conversion symptoms, which therefore represented the expression of unconscious fantasies. |
|---|---|

↓

| Ferenczi (1910) | Concept of conversion hysteria applied to organs innervated by the autonomic nervous system; for example, the bleeding of ulcerative colitis might be described as representing a specific psychic fantasy. (Diseases such as colitis are known today as psychosomatic diseases that occur only in organs innervated by the autonomic nervous system.) Ferenczi's interpretation of psychosomatic symptoms as being conversion reactions was the first application of this concept to diseases such as colitis. |
|---|---|

**Somatic Factors**

| Garma (1950) | Peptic ulcer has a specific psychological meaning. This is an extension of Freud's conversion concept to an organ innervated by the autonomic nervous system. Similar to Ferenczi's concept. |
|---|---|

| Cannon (1927) | Cannon demonstrated the physiological concomitants of certain emotions and the important role of the autonomic nervous system in producing those reactions. |
|---|---|

| Dunbar (1936) | Suggested a specific conscious personality picture associated with specific psychosomatic diseases. Similar to type A coronary type, Friedman (1959). |
|---|---|

Deutsch (1939) and Greenacre (1949) believed trauma during birth, infancy, and childhood predisposed to adult psychosomatic disease.

| Alexander (1934) (1968) | Psychosomatic symptoms occur only in organs innervated by the autonomic nervous system and have no specific psychic meaning (as does conversion hysteria), but are end results of prolonged physiological states, which are the physiological accompaniments of certain specific unconscious repressed needs. There are also certain constitutional predisposing factors in addition to the psychic factors involved. |
|---|---|

Genetic and other somatic studies.

Selye (1945) demonstrated that under stress there is the development of a general adaptation syndrome. Adrenal cortical hormones are responsible for this physiological reaction. Rogers (1979) studied role of immune response.

**Cultural Factors**

Ruesch (1958) emphasized the importance of the interaction between persons; that is, communication between the patient and the environment. Disturbance in communication results in psychosomatic illness, which is a regressive type of communication.

Wolff (1943) attempted to correlate life stress (conscious) to physiological response, using objective laboratory tests. Physiological change, if prolonged, may lead to structural change. Margolin (1951) recommended the correlation of unconscious conflicts and physiological response.

Horney (1939), Halliday (1948), and Mead (1947) emphasized the influence of the culture in the development of psychosomatic illness. They felt that influence acted on the mother who, in turn, affected the child in her relationship with the child; for example, nursing, child rearing, anxiety transmission.

Mahl (1949) questioned whether any specific conflict is associated with ulcer. He believed that what is important is chronic anxiety, which may result from any conflict, conscious or unconscious, external or internal. Mahl was influenced by animal experimenters, such as Gantt (1944) and Masserman (1943). Later workers were Brady (1958) and Ader (1971).

**Laboratory Factors**

Grinker (1953) and Lipowski (1970) felt a total approach to psychosomatic disease was necessary. External (ecological, cultural, environmental), internal (emotional), genetic, somatic, and constitutional factors, as well as past and present history, are important and should be studied by multiple investigators, each working in the frame of reference in which they are trained. DSM-III (1980) de-emphasizes psychosomotic holism in nosology.

the exact boundary between an organism and its environment? The control of the autonomic nervous system through such biofeedback was suggested by Neal Miller. Pavlovian conditioning has been studied intensively by Soviet neurophysiologists as a causative agent in psychosomatic disease—for example, the corticovisceral approach of Bykov. There are a multitude of unanswered but basic questions in the field of psychosomatic medicine. Social factors, what one may call the outer psyche, have lately come to the fore as an area of study.

### Social Factors

Jurgen Ruesch, in studying communication between people, proposed that psychosomatic disorders are infantile in nature, since the sick person, like the infant, expresses his somehow unspeakable verbal communication through his own viscera. Rahe and Holmes showed that life crises often precede illness, and that there is some correlation between the intensity of the crisis and the length and the harshness of the illness that follows; the crisis ranked as the most intense by subjects was the death of a spouse. A study by Arthur Schmale and his co-workers William Greene and George Engel isolated a giving-up-given-up complex, in which a person feels powerless to change either his environment or himself and eventually loses the will to try, becoming mentally or physically ill, perhaps because of changes in the immunological and neuroendocrine systems.

### Toward a Clarified Interaction

In recent reports on the disorders now classified as psychosomatic, there is a tendency to isolate what becomes of the stress produced by conflict. The conflicts are often seen as unresolved holdovers from Freud's pregenital period: dependence versus independence and resultant tensions leading to ulcer; riddance versus retention and resultant tensions leading to intestinal disorders; and expression or suppression of anxiety or rage and resulting tensions leading to cardiovascular problems and vascular headache. The panic at feared object loss in a person with a high demand for support leading to asthma, hyperthyroidism, and rheumatoid arthritis is not, strictly speaking, a conflict.

The constellations are set, however, within a matrix of genetic predispositions. A genetic predisposition to physiological exaggeration of normal functioning is related to the excessive pepsinogen production of the potential ulcer patient. A genetic enzyme deficiency is projected. A congenitally high sensitivity to parasympathetic stimulation is noted in cases of irritable

colon. Less well-defined genetic factors are related to obesity and diabetes. To conflict as a source of stress have been added the crises of human chronology, such as puberty, parenthood, and aging, and those of situations, such as success, failure, and loss of key persons.

For a summary of modern concepts of psychosomatic medicine, see Table II.

### REFERENCES

Adler R: Experimentally induced gastric lesions, results and implications of studies in animals. Adv Psychsom Med *6:* 1, 1971.
Alexander F: *Psychosomatic Medicine: Its Principles and Application.* W. W. Norton, New York, 1950.
Dunbar F: *Emotions and Bodily Changes.* Columbia University Press, New York, 1954.
Kaplan H I: History of psychosomatic medicine. In *Comprehensive Textbook of Psychiatry*, ed 4, H I Kaplan, B J Sadock, editors, p 1106. Williams & Wilkins, Baltimore, 1985.
Lipowski Z J, Lipsitt D R, Whybrow P C: *Psychosomatic Medicine: Current Trends and Clinical Applications.* Oxford University Press, New York, 1977.
Mahl G F: The effect of chronic fear on gastric secretion. Psychosom Med *11:* 30, 1949.
Mirsky I A: Physiologic, psychologic, and social determinants in the etiology of duodenal ulcer. Am J Dig Dis *3:* 285, 1958.
Nemiah J C, Sifneos P C: Affect and fantasy in patients with psychosomatic disorders. In *Modern Trends in Psychosomatic Medicine*, O Hill, editor, p 120. Butterworth, London, 1970.
Revensen T A, Wollman C A, Felton B J: Social support as stress buffers for adult cancer patients. Psychosom Med *14:* 4, 1983.
Rose R M: Endocrine responses to stressful psychological events. Psychiatr Clin North Am *3:* 251, 1980.

## 22.2     GASTROINTESTINAL DISORDERS

### Introduction

An impressive body of evidence indicates that the expression of emotion is accompanied by important changes in gastrointestinal functions, and that such effects can be molded by learning. A number of emotional states, including anger and pleasurable excitement, which seem to have in common an active involvement with the environment, seem capable of leading to increased vascular engorgement, motility, and gastric secretion. Depressed withdrawal, on the other hand, has been reported to result in pallor and diminished secretion and motility of the stomach.

### Upper Gastrointestinal Disorders

#### Vomiting and Esophageal Conditions

In psychogenic vomiting, one sees obvious conflicts over the ingestion of food. It has been reported that highly conflicted maternal feeding and nurturing patterns lead to states of unrelieved tension in the young infant, and the development of spontaneous frequent vomiting of psychogenic origin.

In contrast, psychogenic vomiting in adults often occurs in patients who seem to be relaxed and undismayed. Such patients run the diagnostic gamut from psychotic to essentially normal persons with brief episodes of vomiting under great stress.

The symptom pattern represents a borderline between psychophysiological processes and conversion disorder, in which a physiological function assumes a purely symbolic role. Vomiting is a process that, like breathing, is on the borderline between voluntary control and automatic physiological regulation.

Esophageal reflux has some similarities to psychogenic vomiting, but it has been little studied. Although it is most often part of the syndrome of diaphragmatic hernia, many patients have such hernias without significant reflux, and many patients with reflux have no demonstrable hernias. There seems to be a depressive equivalent in some patients with reflux; relief of symptoms follows the unmasking of a hidden depression. The use of biofeedback to increase esophageal sphincter tone has been demonstrated to be effective, raising the possibility of a learned conversion-like process.

Peptic ulcer of the esophagus occurs in ectopic gastric mucosa in the esophagus and is, therefore, a variant of gastric ulcer and relatively poorly understood.

### Peptic Ulcer

Peptic ulcer is a disease or group of diseases of unknown cause and pathogenesis involving chronic ulceration of the digestive mucosa of the esophagus, stomach, or duodenum. The two major groups of peptic ulcer are the gastric ulcers, including ulcer of the esophagus, and the duodenal ulcers. Also, a group of acute ulcers of the upper digestive tract must be distinguished from peptic ulcers—the acute posttraumatic or stress ulcers.

Early efforts to identify an ulcer personality failed. The depiction of an ambitious and hard-driving person was found to result from a selection bias.

The study of conflicts preceding the exacerbation of ulcer disease produced a variety of observations and concepts. Stewart Wolf followed a stress model and proposed that the organism responds to a wide variety of external threats with physiological reaction patterns, some of which involve the stomach.

The psychosomatic theories of ulcer disease have been dominated by Alexander's compelling theory of conflicts specificity. He disagreed with early formulations of the ulcer personality, and thought that the personality traits exhibited were defensive against unconscious dependent longings that were shameful and forbidden, opposed by the patient's ego ideal and kept in a state of repression, although maintaining a continuous pressure toward physiological activation of oral drive activity.

Studies of women with peptic ulcers reveal psychological features having both similarities and differences with men who have peptic ulcers. Women have been described as having more psychopathology than men, but this finding is in dispute. Women also fail to demonstrate an ulcer personality but, rather, fall into distinct personality clusters.

## Intestinal Disorders

Psychosomatic interest in intestinal diseases has centered primarily on ulcerative colitis, regional enteritis, and irritable bowel syndrome. These three diseases have been more extensively studied than other intestinal disorders, and have a certain magnetism for physicians with a psychosomatic interest because the pressure of clinical experience constantly confronts the physician with the impression that a serious psychological component is at work in these patients' illnesses. The elusiveness of this psychological component and the difficulty of making valid and reliable distinctions among the psychological processes at play in particular patients and in groups of patients have been intriguing to clinicians and researchers.

### Ulcerative Colitis

Ulcerative colitis is a serious disease that was first distinguished from infectious dysentery in the late 19th century. It is an inflammatory disease of the mucosa of the colon, primarily affecting the rectum and the sigmoid colon but often also affecting the right side. Extracolonic manifestations are common and may be serious.

This straightforward definition is complicated by the fact that there may be more than a single disease subsumed under the heading. Granulomatous colitis (Crohn's disease of the colon) may coexist with ulcerative colitis, and in some instances be indistinguishable from it. On the other hand, ulcerative colitis on rare occasions occurs in the ileum.

**Ulcerative Colitis and Personality.** There have been fairly uniform descriptions of the personalities of patients with ulcerative colitis. Attempts to identify these factors by standardized psychometric ratings, and to validate findings with control or comparison groups, have had mixed results.

The typical personality traits that have been described include neatness, carefulness, oversensitivity, and a seeming modesty that covers up a grandiose self-concept, egocentricity, passivity, lack of ambition, and a need for love, sympathy, and affection. Typical patients give little and have a naive infantile concept of love. They are deeply attached to their mothers.

The mixture of compulsive traits and underlying narcissistic vulnerability does not create a uniform ulcerative colitis personality but, rather, a range of psychological vulnerabilities and limitations in adaptation that manifest themselves in varying ways and intensities in different patients. Herbert Weiner stated that "ulcerative colitis patients . . . differ from each other in degree, but . . . demonstrate a spectrum of personal sensitivities and vulnerabilities that are brought to the fore in certain life settings or in the face of certain experiences."

In children, too, obsessional, fastidious, unemotional, rigid traits have been described, along with an intense need for approval. They tend to be either compliant and passive, or manipulative and petulant.

**Psychosomatic Theories.** Psychosomatic theories have attempted to bring the psychological and physiological data together into a coherent understanding of the disease process. The major theoretical split is whether symbolic factors are secondary to the emotional and constitutional factors, or are primary in determining the organ in which the disturbance occurs.

It has been postulated that ulcerative colitis represented a pregenital conversion reaction. It has also been suggested that the organ comes to express symbolically the condensed history of the relationship to mother or early key objects.

George Engel shifted attention away from intrapsychic conflict and focused on interpersonal relationships—close dependence on first a parent and later a surrogate object, ambivalence, jealousy, inability to give to others, compliance in order to retain the needed supplies, and sensitivity to the loss of an object of the patient's dependent attachment. However, this same emphasis on early attachment to parental figures has come to dominate dynamic psychiatric views of borderline and narcissistic character features. These features are found in patients with ulcerative colitis, varying widely in the degree of their pervasiveness, and correlating with the severity of the somatic process.

**Psychotherapy.** Psychotherapy for ulcerative colitis has received intensive scrutiny. The most thorough study of psychotherapy in

ulcerative colitis, and perhaps in all of psychosomatic medicine, was that of Aaron Karush and his colleagues. They conducted a 30-year follow-up of patients treated by psychotherapy, along with medical and surgical measures, compared with a control group who received medical and surgical measures alone. Their results, assessed by a team of gastroenterologists, showed a statistically significant advantage for the psychotherapy group except for a subgroup—about one-fourth—of patients who had schizophrenic features. Those patients did poorly no matter what treatment they received.

### Regional Enteritis (Crohn's Disease)

Regional enteritis is an inflammatory disease of the small bowel, and sometimes the colon. The distinctive pathological lesions are granulomata, with inflammation extending through the full thickness of the bowel wall. The bowel frequently presents discontinuous segments of pathology interspersed with normal bowel. Anal or perianal involvement—abscess, ulceration, fissure, fistula—is more common in Crohn's disease than in ulcerative colitis, as are perforation and intraabdominal fistulas.

Systemic manifestations and extraintestinal complications are the same as in ulcerative colitis, but, in addition, granulomata of distant parts of the body—mouth and skeletal muscle—may occur in Crohn's disease.

There is an increased incidence of Crohn's disease and of ulcerative colitis in parents and siblings of patients with Crohn's disease. In fact, they are as likely to have ulcerative colitis as regional enteritis. Genetic, immunological, and slow-virus causes are all hypothesized.

**Psychosomatic Considerations.** Character disturbances in regional enteritis patients are similar to those in patients with ulcerative colitis; they manifest varying degrees of early ego defect, resulting in compulsive or paranoid traits with excessive dependency, compliance, and inhibition or demanding, explosive manipulation. Their mothers are described in identical terms as those of patients with ulcerative colitis— demanding and dominating, giving love only on condition that the child be compliant, inhibited, and industrious. Onset conditions include, as in ulcerative colitis, loss of a significant object, loss of self-esteem, being faced with a task or demand perceived as too great, a significant interpersonal struggle, pregnancy, and retirement. Regression, helplessness, and hopelessness have been described in the patients, too. Even many of those who reject the concept of a psychosomatic factor in the onset of the condition agree that the symptoms and physical pathology increase with emotional disturbances.

**Psychotherapy.** The literature on the psychiatric treatment of patients wtih Crohn's disease is extremely meager, except for a few case reports.

Karush and his colleagues reported on a large number of patients with atypical colitis and granulomatous colitis. They described a psychotherapeutic approach and experiences with these patients similar to those with typical ulcerative colitis patients, including the observation that therapist skill and experience seemed to be related to better improvement rates.

### Irritable Bowel Syndrome

The syndrome has had a variety of names—irritable colon, spastic colitis, mucous colitis, nervous diarrhea, and others. Frequently, the patients are grouped as those with abdominal pain and those with painless diarrhea. Patients present with complaints of diarrhea (nervous diarrhea, mucus colitis), abdominal cramps (spastic colon or spastic constipation), or alternating constipation and diarrhea. They have a chronic, relapsing condition, sometimes with a sudden onset, and sometimes with a gradual onset. Constipation may present as a reduction in the frequency of stools, as the passage of hard pellets, or as pencil stools. Large amounts of mucus may be described by the patients as "worms" or "pus" in the stools. Diarrhea may present as increased frequency of passage of loose, semiformed stools or watery diarrhea.

**Psychological Characteristics.** Patients with irritable bowel syndrome have been described as nervous, hysterical, neurotic, hypochondriacal, neurasthenic, anxious, and depressed. Systematic study has also yielded findings of increased neuroticism, compulsiveness, hysteria, and depression in these patients. The onset of symptoms is generally correlated with demonstrable life changes of a stressful nature, as are exacerbations in the course of the illness. Simple situational manipulations often reduce the intensity of the symptoms.

These findings are clearly different from those reported for patients with ulcerative colitis. The psychological features are more clearly neurotic in irritable bowel patients than in ulcerative colitis patients; the literature reflects this neuroticism in the frequency with which concious reports of distressing events, nervous symptoms, and physical symptoms are elicited from irritable bowel patients, in contrast to the great difficulty patients with ulcerative colitis display in recognizing and reporting troubling events, and in recognizing their disturbed feelings. Clinical descriptions of irritable bowel syndrome patients lack the impression of primitive narcissistic and borderline personality features that repeatedly arise in the clinical descriptions of patients with ulcerative colitis.

**Psychotherapy.** Immediate benefit can be brought to the patient through the identification of current life stresses that precipitate the symptoms. Environmental manipulation, by reducing commitments in appropriate cases, can be of great help. Promoting and aiding in the grieving process is indicated in other cases. Antianxiety agents may be of some immediate benefit in appropriate patients. Antidepressants have been used in the syndrome, but reports of results have been conflicting: some reported benefit, while others showed no significant benefit over the placebo but showed that the placebo itself was fairly effective. Intensive psychotherapy, or psychoanalysis aimed at the alteration of the patient's defensive style and conflict resolution, is of major lasting benefit in patients who are, on overall psychological grounds, candidates for these treatment modalities, but the majority of the patients are satisfied with symptom relief through relatively simple interventions.

### REFERENCES

Alexander F: *Psychosomatic Medicine*. W. W. Norton, New York, 1950.

Alexander F, French T M, Pollack G H: *Psychosomatic Specificity: Experimental Study and Results*. University of Chicago Press, Chicago, 1968.

Drossman D A, Powell D W, Sessions J T Jr: The irritable bowel syndrome. Gastroenterology *73:* 811, 1977.

Engel G L: Studies of ulcerative colitis: III. The nature of the psychological processes. Am J Med *19:* 231, 1955.

Engel G L: *Psychological Development in Health and Disease*. W. B. Saunders, Philadelphia, 1962.

Engel G L, Reichsman F, Siegel H L: A study of an infant with a gastric fistula. Psychosom Med *18:* 374, 1956.

Karush A, Daniels G E, Flood C, O'Connor J F: *Psychotherapy in Chronic Ulcerative Colitis*. W. B. Saunders, Philadelphia, 1977.

Kyle J: *Crohn's Disease*. Heinemann, London, 1972.

Oken D: Gastrointestinal disorders. In *Comprehensive Textbook of Psychiatry*, ed 4, H I Kaplan, B J Sadock, editors, p 1121. Williams & Wilkins, Baltimore, 1985.

Weiner H M: *Psychobiology and Human Disease*. Elsevier, New York, 1977.

Wolf S, Wolff H G: *Human Gastric Function*. Oxford University Press, New York, 1943.

## 22.3  OBESITY

### Definition

Obesity is a condition characterized by excessive accumulations of fat in the body. By convention, obesity is said to be present when body weight exceeds by 20 percent the standard weight listed in the usual height-weight tables.

## Epidemiology

The most striking influence is that of socio-economic status. Obesity is 6 times more common among women of low status than among those of high status. A similar, although weaker, relationship is found among men. Obesity is far more prevalent among lower-class children than it is among upper-class children; significant differences are already apparent by age 6. Social mobility, ethnic factors, and generation in the United States also influence the prevalence of obesity.

Age is the second major influence on obesity. There is a monotonic increase in the prevalence of obesity between childhood and age 50; a three-fold increase occurs between ages 20 and 50. At age 50, prevalence falls sharply, presumably because of the very high mortality of the obese from cardiovascular disease in the older age groups.

Women show a higher prevalence of obesity than do men; this difference is particularly pronounced past age 50 because of the higher mortality rate among obese men after that age.

## Etiology

When the intake of calories is greater than the expenditure of calories, the excess is stored in fat tissue resulting in obesity. Most persons of normal weight seem to regulate their body weight. Thus, their weight tends to be the same year after year, despite the exchange of vast amounts of energy. For example, the average nonobese man consumes about a million calories a year; his body fat stores remain unchanged during this time because he expends an equal number of calories. An error of no more than 10 per cent in either intake or output leads to a 30-pound change in body weight within a year.

### Regulatory Theories

Hunger is theorized as being the consequence of the decreasing strength of a metabolic signal, secondary to the depletion of the critical nutrient.

Four classical theories of the regulation of body weight have been based on this view. They differ from one another only in the nature of the signal to which they ascribe primary importance. The thermostatic theory, for example, proposes that postprandial increases in hypothalamic temperature mediate satiety: hunger results from a decrease in temperature at this site. Lipostatic, aminostatic, and glucostatic theories each assign the critical regulatory role to blood-borne metabolites of fat, protein, or carbohydrate, respectively.

Progress has been made in solving a problem that has long plagued theories of body weight regulation. The problem is how any physiological theory can account for the function of satiety. Satiety occurs so soon after the beginning of a meal that only a small proportion of the total caloric content of the meal can have been absorbed. If satiety were based solely on the limited information about food intake available at that time, it could contribute little or nothing to the regulation of food intake.

If humoral factors do not terminate eating, what does? A full stomach may be a better answer than one would think. Experimental evidence indicates that gastric filling, irrespective of the nutritive value of the meal, is the major determinant of satiety in single-meal experiments.

Although the nutritional value of meals plays little part in satiety in single-meal experiments, humans learn, as do other animals, to change food intake and even meal size in response to changes in energy expenditure and in the nutritive value of the food.

### Determinants of Obesity

**Genetic Determinants.** Although evidence of genetic transmission has been postulated for such rare conditions as the Laurence-Moon-Biedl syndrome and Prader-Willi syndrome, there is essentially no information about the genetic transmission of the obesity that afflicts the vast majority of overweight persons.

Evidence of the heritability of somatotypes may be stronger than the evidence for the heritability of obesity.

**Developmental Determinants.** The increased adipose tissue mass in obesity can result from either an increase in fat cell size (hypertrophic obesity), from an increase in fat cell number (hyperplastic obesity), or from an increase in both size and number (hypertrophic-hyperplastic obesity). A study of experimental obesity in rodents reveals that most of the animals exhibit either hypertrophic or hypertrophic-hyperplastic obesity, and it appears that obese humans also usually fall into one of these two categories. Most persons whose obesity began in adult life suffer from hypertrophic obesity. When they lose weight, it is solely by a decrease in the size of their fat cells; the number of their fat cells does not change. Persons whose obesity began in childhood are more likely to suffer from hyperplastic obesity, usually of the combined hypertrophic-hyperplastic type. They may have up to 5 times as many fat cells as either persons of normal weight or those suffering from pure hypertrophic obesity.

A knowledge of fat cell size and number can clearly be of value in the assessment and treatment of obesity. The availability of these measures for general clinical use would be a major forward step.

**Physical Activity.** The marked decrease in physical activity in affluent societies seems to be the major factor in the recent rise of obesity as a public health problem. Obesity is a rarity in most underdeveloped nations and not solely because of malnutrition; in some rural areas, high levels of physical activity are at least as important in preventing obesity. Such levels of physical activity are the exception in this country.

Restricting physical activity may actually increase food intake. Conversely, when sedentary animals increase their physical activity, their food intake may decrease. The mechanisms involved in this intriguing control are still unclear. Recently, it has been shown that the regulatory effect of activity on food intake is even more potent in obese animals than in those of normal weight.

**Brain Damage.** Brain damage can lead to obesity, although it is probably a rare cause of obesity in humans.

## Clinical Features

The physical signs of obesity are primarily the direct physical consequence of the increase in body weight and the encompassing mass of fatty tissue. The most serious manifestation, and the only one which is (very rarely) life threatening, is caused by pressure on the thorax from the encompassing sheath of fatty tissue, combined with pressure on the diaphragm from below by large intraabdominal accumulations of fat. The resulting reduction in respiratory capacity may produce dyspnea on even minimal exertion. In massively obese persons, this condition may progress to the so-called Pickwickian syndrome, characterized by hypoventilation with consequent hypercapnia and hypoxia and, finally, somnolence.

Many obese persons report that they overeat when they are emotionally upset, often soon thereafter. Unfortunately, many nonobese persons report similar experiences, and it is difficult to ascertain the specificity for obesity of such short-term contingencies. Reports linking emotional factors and obesity over a long range seem more specific. It is common for obese persons to lose large amounts of weight when they fall in love, and to gain weight when they lose a loved one.

The habitual eating patterns of many obese persons seem similar in many ways to those found in different forms of experimental obesity. Impaired satiety is a particularly important problem. Obese persons characteristically complain of being unable to stop eating; it is the unusual obese person who reports being driven to eat or who eats in a ravenous manner. Instead, obese persons seem inordinately susceptible to food cues in their environment, to the palatability of foods, and to the inability to stop eating if food is available.

## Emotional Disturbance

Bulimia, or binge eating, is found in fewer than 5 percent of obese persons and is one of the rare exceptions to the pattern of impaired satiety. It is characterized by the sudden, compulsive ingestion of very large amounts of food in a very short time, usually with great subsequent agitation and self-condemnation. It appears to represent a reaction to stress. Bulimic episodes are followed by induced vomiting. These bouts of overeating are not periodic, and they are far more often linked to specific precipitating circumstances. Binge eaters can sometimes lose large amounts of weight by adhering to rigid and unrealistic diets, but such efforts are almost always interrupted by a resumption of eating binges.

The second form of emotional disturbance specific to obese persons is a disparagement of the body image. Obese persons with this disturbance characteristically feel that their bodies are grotesque and loathesome, and that others view them with hostility and contempt. This feeling is closely associated with self-consciousness and impaired social functioning. It seems reasonable to suppose that all obese persons have derogatory feelings about their bodies. Such is not the case. Emotionally healthy obese persons have no body image disturbances; in fact, only a minority of neurotic obese persons have such disturbances. The disorder is confined to those who have been obese since childhood; even among these juvenile-onset obese persons, fewer than half suffer from it. But in the group with body image disturbances, neurosis is closely related to obesity, and this group contains a majority of obese persons with specific eating disorders.

## Course and Prognosis

The prognosis for weight reduction is poor, and the course of obesity tends toward inexorable progression. There is a three-fold increase in the prevalence of obesity with advancing age, and both individual humans and animals show increasing amounts of body fat with increasing age, even when body weight is constant.

The prognosis is particularly poor for persons who become obese in childhood—the so-called juvenile obese. Juvenile-onset obesity tends to be more severe and is more likely to be associated with emotional disturbance.

### Treatment

The basis of weight reduction is utterly simple—establish a caloric deficit by bringing intake below output. All the many treatment regimens have as their goal this simple task. The simplest way to reduce caloric intake is by means of a low-calorie diet. The best long-term effects are achieved with a balanced diet that contains readily available foods. For most people, the most satisfactory reducing diet consists of their usual foods in amounts determined with the aid of tables of food values available in standard works. Such a diet gives the best chance of long-term maintenance of the weight lost during dieting. But it is precisely the most difficult kind of diet to follow during the period of weight reduction.

### Fasting

Fasting has had considerable vogue as a treatment of obesity in the recent past. Its importance lies primarily in what it has taught about radical dietary restriction in the treatment of obesity. The great virtue of fasting is the rapid weight loss it engenders, usually with minimal discomfort; many obese people find it relatively easy to tolerate fasting. After 2 or 3 days without food, hunger largely disappears, and patients get along well as long as they remain in an undemanding environment. The main problem with fasting as a treatment is the failure to maintain weight loss; most patients regain most of the weight they have lost. Furthermore, although surprisingly safe for such a radical procedure, fasting is not without complications, and deaths have been reported.

### Pharmacological Treatment

Pharmacological treatment of obesity has been profoundly altered by recent directives of the Drug Enforcement Administration, which has responded to the widespread abuse of the amphetamines by progressively restricting their use as appetite suppressants. Various agents are taking the place of the amphetamines; diethylpropion (Tenuate), fenfluramine (Pondimin), and mazindol (Sanorex) are the common examples. Their efficacy and side effects seem comparable to each other, and their potential for abuse is limited. Various over-the-counter appetite supressant drugs are now available with their active ingredient being propanolamine; they are of questionable efficacy at this time.

The use of appetite suppressants is currently out of favor, and there seems little doubt that weight lost with their assistance is readily regained. Nevertheless, their efficacy in weight reduction may have been underestimated, and newer methods of combining pharmacological and behavioral measures may produce greater weight losses than those traditionally achieved by appetite suppressants.

Thyroid or thyroid analogues are indicated for the exceptional obese person with hypothyroidism, and not otherwise. Lowered basal metabolic rate is rarely of importance in obesity. Bulk producers may help control the constipation that follows decreased food intake, but their effectiveness in weight reduction is very doubtful. Controlled studies of chorionic gonadotropin have found it to be ineffective.

### Physical Activity

Increased physical activity is frequently recommended as a part of weight-reduction regimens, but its usefulness has probably been underestimated, even by many of its proponents. Because caloric expenditure in most forms of physical activity is directly proportional to body weight, obese persons expend more calories with the same amount of activity than do persons of normal weight. Furthermore, increased physical activity may actually cause a decrease in the food intake of sedentary persons. This combination of increased caloric expenditure and probably decreased food intake makes an increase in physical activity a highly desirable feature of any weight-reduction program.

### Surgery

Surgical procedures designed to bypass most of the absorptive surface of the intestine have achieved considerable popularity in recent years as treatment for massive obesity. The original rationale was that the jejunoileal bypass would greatly reduce the absorption of nutrients, resulting in a temporary caloric imbalance and consequent weight loss. Careful study has revealed, however, that weight loss is produced primarily by a reduction in food intake.

A very different surgical procedure is gastric bypass which involves the construction of a gastric pouch with a capacity of 50 ml which empties into the intestine via a stoma 1.2 cm in diameter. At this time surgical procedures are of very limited value in the long-term treatment of obesity.

### Group Self-help

Group methods are being used successfully with increasing numbers of obese persons by the burgeoning self-help movement. The two largest organizations are the nonprofit TOPS (Take Off Pounds Sensibly), with more than 350,000 members, and the profit-making Weight Watchers, which is even larger.

### Complications of Weight-reduction Programs

Obese persons with extensive psychopathology, those with a history of emotional disturbance during dieting, and those in the midst of a life crisis should attempt weight reduction cautiously and under careful supervision, if at all. For others, the possibility of complications need not preclude treatment when it is indicated.

### Specialized Psychotherapeutic Techniques

**Psychoanalysis.** In recent years, psychoanalysis and psychoanalytic therapy have fallen from favor for the treatment of obesity and its associated psychological disability. No more than 6 per cent of those obese persons entering treatment by these modalities do so for treatment of their obesity, and analysts themselves have been skeptical of their efficacy.

Although psychoanalysis and psychoanalytic therapy are expensive ways to lose weight, they may be indicated for persons suffering from severe disparagement of the body image. This condition has not been influenced by other forms of treatment, even those that produce weight reduction. Psychoanalysis and psychoanalytic therapy may be indicated also for treatment of bulimia, another particularly resistant condition. Furthermore, obese people may seek psychotherapy for reasons other than their obesity; helping them to cope with their obesity may help them to resolve other problems. It has been noted that many obese people overeat under stress. When psychotherapy can help them live less stressful and more satisfying lives, they are less likely to overeat. As a result, they may reduce and stay reduced. These benefits are not less significant for being nonspecific results of treatment.

**Behavior Therapy.** It is clear that behavior therapy represents an improvement over traditional outpatient treatments for mild and moderate obesity, but that its great early promise has been imperfectly realized.

### REFERENCES

Bennett W, Gurin J: *The Dieter's Dilemma: Eating Less and Weighing More.* Basic Books, New York, 1982.

Bjorntorp P, Carlgren G, Issakson B, Krotkiewski M, Larsson B, Sjostrom L: Effect of an energy-reduced regimen in relation to adipose tissue cellularity in obese women. Am J Clin Nutr 28: 445, 1975.

Bray G: *The Obese Patient.* W. B. Saunders, Philadelphia, 1976.

Bruch H: *Eating Disorders: Obesity and Anorexia Nervosa and the Person Within.* Basic Books, New York, 1973.

Herman C P, Polivy J: Restrained eating. In *Obesity,* A J Stunkard editor. W. B. Saunders, Philadelphia, 1980.

Nisbett R E: Hunger, obesity, and the ventromedial hypothalamus. Psychol Rev 79: 443, 1972.

Rand C S W, Stunkard A J: Obesity and psychoanalysis: Treatment and four-year follow-up. Am J Psychiatry 140: 1140, 1983.

Stern J S, Johnson P R: Size and number of adipocytes and their implications. In *Advances in Modern Nutrition,* H Katzer, R Mahler, editors. vol 2, p 303. John Wiley & Sons, New York, 1978.

Stuart R B: *Act Thin, Stay Thin.* W. W. Norton, New York, 1978.

Stunkard A J: Anorectic agents lower body weight set point. Life Sci 30: 2043, 1982.

Stunkard A J: *The Pain of Obesity.* Bull Publishing Co, Palo Alto, CA, 1976.

Stunkard A J, editor: *Obesity.* W. B. Saunders, Philadelphia, 1980.

Stunkard A J: Obesity. In *Comprehensive Textbook of Psychiatry,* ed 4, H I Kaplan, B J Sadock, editors, 1133. Williams & Wilkins, Baltimore, 1985.

Stunkard A J, Rush A J: Dieting and depression reexamined: A critical review of reports of untoward responses during weight reduction for obesity. Ann Intern Med 8: 526, 1974.

Stunkard A J, Stellar E: *Eating and Its Disorders.* Raven Press, New York, in press.

## 22.4  ANOREXIA NERVOSA

### Introduction

Anorexia nervosa is an eating disorder characterized by self-imposed dietary limitations, behavior directed toward losing weight, peculiar patterns of handling food, weight loss, intense fear of gaining weight, disturbance of body image, and, in women, amenorrhea. It is one of the few psychiatric illnesses that may have a course that is unremitting until death (see Fig. 1).

Other eating disorders which may occur from infancy through young adulthood are bulimia, pica and rumination; they are discussed in Section 35.2 under disorders of infancy, childhood and adolescence.

### Epidemiology and Prevalence

The only incidence study of anorexia nervosa conducted in this country reported an average incidence of 0.37 per 100,000 population per year.

Recent prevalence studies have shown anorexia nervosa to be a common disorder in the age group at risk—12 to 30 years—and in the higher socioeconomic classes.

Anorexia nervosa occurs predominantly in fe-

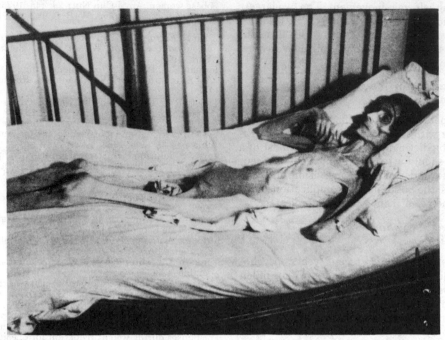

FIGURE 1.   Patient with anorexia nervosa. (Courtesy Katherine Halmi, M.D.)

TABLE I
DIAGNOSTIC CRITERIA FOR ANOREXIA NERVOSA[a]

A. Intense fear of becoming obese, which does not diminish as weight loss progresses.

B. Disturbance of body image, e.g., claiming to "feel fat" even when emaciated.

C. Weight loss of at least 25 percent of original body weight or, if under 18 years of age, weight loss from original body weight plus projected weight gain expected from growth charts may be combined to make the 25 percent.

D. Refusal to maintain body weight over a minimal normal weight for age and height.

E. No known physical illness that would account for the weight loss.

   * From American Psychiatric Association: *Diagnostic and Statistical Manual of Mental Disorders*, ed 3. American Psychiatric Association, Washington, DC, 1980. Used with permission.

males. Various studies report that a range of 4 to 6 percent are males. The morbidity risk for a sister of an anorectic patient is about 6.6 percent, which greatly exceeds normal expectation. Often mothers or fathers had an explicit history of significantly low adolescent weight or weight phobia. At the present time, the evidence available does not permit any conclusions as to the role of heredity in the development of this disorder, because of possibly biased selection and the small numbers in the studies reported.

## Etiology

The psychological theories concerning the causes of anorexia nervosa have centered mostly on phobias and psychodynamic formulations. One investigator postulated that anorexia nervosa constitutes a phobic-avoidance response to food resulting from the sexual and social tensions generated by the physical changes associated with puberty. The resulting malnutrition leads to a reduction in sexual interest, which in turn leads to greater self-starvation.

An early psychodynamic theory was that anorectic patients reject, through starvation, a wish to be pregnant, and have fantasies of oral impregnation. Other dynamic formulations have included a dependent seductive relationship with a warm but passive father, and guilt over aggression toward an ambivalently regarded mother. Others have described disturbances of body image (denial of the emaciation), disturbances in perception (lack of recognition or denial of fatigue, weakness, and hunger), and a sense of ineffectiveness as being caused by false learning experiences.

Adequate studies have not been conducted to establish definite predisposing factors in anorexia nervosa. In the descriptive literature of this illness, several different stressful life situations have been noted to occur shortly before the onset of anorexia nervosa. Above-average scholastic achievement and an unrealistic fear of failure are often characteristics in these patients.

## Clinical Features

The onset of anorexia nervosa occurs between the ages of 10 and 30. Although there are cases reported of this illness developing before age 10, the onset is uncommon before age 10 and after age 30, and often those cases outside this age range are not typical, and so their diagnoses are in question. From the age of 13 years, the frequency of onset increases rapidly, with the maximum frequency at 17 to 18 years of age. About 85 percent of all anorectic patients develop the illness between the ages of 13 and 20 years.

Most of the aberrant behavior directed toward losing weight occurs in secret. The anorectic patients usually refuse to eat with their families or in public places. They lose weight by a drastic reduction in the total food intake, with a disproportionate decrease in high carbohydrate and fat-containing foods.

Unfortunately, the term anorexia is a misnomer, because the loss of appetite is usually rare until late in the illness. Evidence that the patients are constantly thinking about food is their passion for collecting recipes and engaging in elaborate meal preparations for others. Some patients cannot exert continuous control over their voluntary restriction of food intake, and they have eating binges. These binges usually occur secretly and often at night. Self-induced vomiting (bulimia) frequently follows the eating binge. Patients abuse laxatives and even diuretics in order to lose weight. Ritualistic exercising, extensive cycling, and walking are common activities.

Patients with this disorder exhibit peculiar behavior around food. They hide food, especially candies, all over the house, and frequently carry large quantities of candies in their pockets and purses. While eating meals, they try to dispose of food in their napkins or hide it in their pockets. They cut their meat in very small pieces and spend a great deal of time rearranging the food items on their plate. If the patients are confronted about their peculiar behavior, they often deny that their behavior is unusual or flatly refuse to discuss it.

The patient's failure to recognize her starved body as too thin, or to regard it as normal or even overweight in the face of increasing cachexia, has been tested experimentally by several groups of investigators. The degree of body image disturbance appears to be related to the severity of the illness. Patients who overestimate themselves the most are also the most

malnourished and had repeatedly failed to improve during hospitalizations. They also gain less weight during treatment than do those patients who more accurately estimate their various body widths. Those patients who vomit overestimate their size more than do the nonvomiters. Greater denial of illness is associated with greater body image distortion.

An intense fear of gaining weight and becoming obese is present in all patients with this illness. This fear undoubtedly contributes to their lack of interest in, and even resistance to therapy.

Obsessive-compulsive behavior, depression, and anxiety are other psychiatric symptoms in anorexia nervosa most frequently noted in the literature. Somatic complaints, especially epigastric discomfort, are usual. Compulsive stealing, usually of candies and laxatives but occasionally of clothes and other items, is common.

Poor sexual adjustment is frequently described in patients with this disorder. Many adolescent anorectics have delayed psychosocial sexual development, and adults often have a markedly decreased interest in sex with the onset of the illness. An unusual minority subgroup of anorectics have a premorbid history of promiscuity or drug abuse or both. These patients seldom have a decreased interest in sex during the illness.

The patient usually comes to medical attention when weight loss is observable. As the weight loss becomes profound, physical signs such as hypothermia (as low as 35°C), dependent edema, bradycardia, hypotension, and lanugo (the appearance of neonatal-like hair) appear, and a variety of metabolic changes occur.

Many female anorectics come to medical attention because of amenorrhea, which often appears before noticeable weight loss has occurred. Most studies have shown an impaired luteinizing hormone (LH) response to gonadotropin-releasing hormone during the acute stage of emaciation, with an increased response after weight gain.

Abnormalities of thyroid function are found in other malnourished states and cannot be considered a defect specific to anorexia nervosa.

A reduced metabolic clearance rate of cortisol and the incomplete suppression of adrenocorticotrophic hormone (ACTH) and cortisol levels by dexamethasone have been reported in patients with protein calorie malnutrition, as well as in anorexia nervosa.

There is a remarkable variability of fasting growth hormone levels in patients with anorexia nervosa. About one-third have elevated basal growth hormone levels.

Noradrenergic neurotransmitter system is involved both in the control of feeding behavior and in primary depression. A relationship exists between urinary secretion of 3-methoxy-4-hydroxy phenylglycol (MHPG), a major metabolite of brain norepinephrine, and the symptom of depression in anorexia nervosa patients. An increase in urinary MHPG correlates with a decrease in depression ratings after weight gain.

Some anorectic patients engage in self-induced vomiting or abuse purgatives and diuretics, causing unnecessary investigations for hypokalemic alkalosis. Impaired water diuresis may be noted.

Electrocardiographic changes—such as flattening or inversion of the T waves, ST segment depression, and lengthening of the QT interval—have been noted in the emaciated stage of anorexia nervosa. ECG changes may also occur as a result of potassium loss, which may lead to a fatal outcome.

Gastric dilation is a rare complication of anorexia nervosa. In some of these patients, aortography has shown a superior mesenteric artery syndrome.

## Course and Prognosis

The course of anorexia nervosa varies greatly—from spontaneous recovery without treatment, recovery after a variety of treatments, a fluctuating course of weight gains followed by relapses, to a gradually deteriorating course resulting in death due to complications of starvation. The short-term response of patients to almost all hospital treatment programs is good. Studies have shown a range of mortality rates from 5 percent to 21.5 percent.

The most consistent indicator of good outcome is early age onset of anorexia nervosa. The most consistent indicators of poor outcome are late age onset of the illness and number of previous hospitalizations. Such factors as childhood neuroticism, parental conflict, bulimia, vomiting, laxative abuse and various behavioral manifestations—such as obsessive-compulsive, hysterical, depressive, psychosomatic, neurotic, and denying symptoms—have been related to poor outcome in some studies, and have not been significant in affecting outcome in other studies. The expected outcome can vary from complete recovery, with normal weight maintenance and unusually effective functioning, to an inability to maintain weight, with a gradual starvation course and, eventually, inability to function because of extreme weakness and severe interfering preoccupation with losing weight and thoughts of food.

## Diagnosis

The diagnosis of anorexia nervosa should be made only after finding the essential features that are listed in Table II. Patients with this disorder are often secretive, deny their symptoms, and resist treatment. In almost all cases, it is necessary to have a confirmation of the history by relatives or intimate acquaintances. The mental status examination usually shows an alert mind that is very knowledgeable on the subject of nutrition, and is preoccupied with food and weight.

It is necessary that the patient have a thorough general physical and neurological examination. There have been some reported cases of brain tumors stimulating anorexia nervosa. If the patient is vomiting, she may well have a hypokalemic alkalosis. Since most patients are dehydrated, it is necessary to obtain serum electrolytes initially and then periodically throughout the course of hospitalization.

### Differential Diagnosis

It is extremely important to ascertain that the patient has no medical illness that can account for the weight loss.

Weight loss, peculiar eating behavior, and vomiting can occur in several psychiatric disorders. Weight loss frequently occurs in depressive disorders. These disorders and anorexia nervosa have several features in common, such as depressed feeling, crying spells, sleep disturbance, obsessive ruminations, and occasionally suicidal

---

TABLE II
CLINICAL FEATURES OF ANOREXIA NERVOSA*

*Essential features that are always present:*
1. Behavior directed toward losing weight
2. Peculiar patterns of handling food
3. Weight loss
4. Intense fear of gaining weight
5. Disturbance of body image
6. Amenorrhea in women

*Associated features that are common but not invariably present:*
1. Steadfast denial of the illness
2. Disinterest or even resistance to therapy
3. Delayed psychosexual development in adolescence and markedly decreased interest in sex with onset of the illness in adults
4. Mildly overweight (about one-third of the patients) before onset of illness
5. Compulsive behavior other than that related to food and losing weight
6. Higher than expected frequency of urogenital abnormalities and of Turner's syndrome

* Adapted from American Psychiatric Association: *Diagnostic and Statistical Manual of Mental Disorders*, ed 3. American Psychiatric Association, Washington, DC, 1980.

thoughts. There are, however, several distinguishing features between the disorders. Generally, a patient with a depressive disorder has a decreased appetite, whereas an anorectic denies the existence of a normal appetite. It should be emphasized that only in the severe stages of anorexia nervosa does the patient actually have a decreased appetite. In contrast to depressive agitation, the hyperactivity seen in anorexia nervosa is planned and ritualistic—exercising, jogging, and cycling programs. The preoccupation with the caloric content of food, collecting recipes, and preparing gourmet feasts is typical of the anorectic patient that is not present in the patient with a depressive disorder.

Weight fluctuations, vomiting, and peculiar food handling may occur in a somatization disorder. On rare occasions, a patient fulfills the criteria for both a somatization disorder and anorexia nervosa; in such a case, both diagnoses should be made. Generally, the weight loss in a somatization disorder is not as severe as in anorexia nervosa, nor does the patient with a somatization disorder express the morbid fear of becoming overweight, as is common in the anorectic patient. Amenorrhea for 3 months or longer is unusual in a somatization disorder.

Delusions about food in schizophrenia are seldom concerned with the caloric content of food. A patient with schizophrenia is rarely preoccupied with a fear of becoming obese and does not have the hyperactivity that is seen in an anorectic patient.

Anorexia nervosa must be differentiated from bulimia, a disorder in which episodic binge eating, followed by depressive moods, self-deprecating thoughts, and often self-induced vomiting, occurs while the patient maintains his or her weight within a normal range.

## Treatment

The immediate aim of treatment in anorexia nervosa is to restore the patient's nutritional state to normal. This is necessary because the complications of emaciation, dehydration, and electrolyte imbalance may cause death. Usually, a hospitalized treatment program that provides considerable environmental structure is necessary for the weight restoration stage of treatment.

General management of anorexia nervosa patients during a hospitalized treatment program should take into account the following considerations. Each patient should be weighed daily early in the morning after emptying the bladder. The daily fluid intake and urine output should be recorded. If vomiting is occurring, it is especially important to obtain serum electrolytes regularly and to watch for the development of hypokalemia. Since regurgitation of food takes place after meals, it is possible to control the vomiting by making the bathroom inaccessible for at least 2 hours after meals. The constipation of an anoretic is relieved when she begins to eat normally. Occasionally, it may be necessary to give stool softeners, but never laxatives. If diarrhea occurs, it usually means that the patient is surreptitiously taking laxatives. Because of the rare complication of stomach dilation and the possibility of circulatory overload if the patient starts eating an enormous amount of calories immediately, it is advisable to start the patient on about 500 calories over the amount required to maintain her present weight. This usually means that the patient is started on 1,500 to 2,000 calories a day. It is wise to give these calories in six equal feedings throughout the day, so that the patient does not have to eat a large amount of food in one sitting. There may be an advantage in starting a patient out with a liquid food supplement, such as Sustagen. The patient may at first be less apprehensive about gaining weight slowly with the formula than by eating food.

After discharge from the hospital, it is usually necessary to continue some type of outpatient supervision of whatever problems are identified in the patient and in her family.

Most patients are uninterested and even resistant to treatment, and are brought to a doctor's office unwillingly by agonizing relatives or friends. The patient rarely accepts the advice for hospitalization without many arguments and criticisms of the program that is being offered to her. At this time, emphasizing the benefits, such as relief of insomnia or depressive signs and symptoms, may help to persuade the patient to admit herself willingly to the hospital. The relatives' support and confidence in the doctor and the treatment team are essential when firm recommendations must be carried out. The patient's family should be warned that she will resist admission, and for the first several weeks of treatment will have many dramatic complaints to get the family's support for releasing her from the program. Only when the risk of death from complications of malnutrition is likely should a compulsory admission or commitment be obtained. On rare occasions, the patient may demonstrate a gratifying response by proving the doctor's statements about the likelihood of outpatient failure wrong. Such a patient may gain a specified amount by the time of each outpatient visit; however, this behavior is uncommon, and usually a period of inpatient care is necessary.

The patient should be given regular feedings. Russell developed a nursing treatment program that contains many of the positive reinforcements and privileges present in the behavior therapy programs. In the nursing treatment program, total bed rest is instituted and then progressively relaxed through a series of rewards as the patient cooperates and gains weight.

Behavior conditioning has been used along with family therapy. The usefulness of behavioral contingencies in conjunction with other therapies in treating anorexia nervosa has become widely recognized.

The first impressive drug used for anorexia nervosa was chlorpromazine (Thorazine). Although reports suggest amitriptyline is effective in the treatment of anorexia nervosa, no controlled study has been conducted. Another drug that has been used to treat anorexia nervosa is cyproheptadine (Periactin). The only side effect observed with this drug was drowsiness.

Other organic therapies have also been used to treat anorexia nervosa. Electroconvulsive therapy (ECT) in single cases has sometimes been reported to be successful.

The classical psychodynamically oriented therapy approach has not been effective in anorexia nervosa. This form of therapy is not effective in inducing weight gain or in changing the abnormal eating behavior.

Despite the fact that there is a paucity of research on family interaction in anorexia nervosa, family therapy has been used in treating this disorder.

## REFERENCES

Berquist W E: Gastroesophageal reflex in children: A clinical review. Pediatr Ann *11:* 135, 1982.
Danford D E, Smith J C, Huber A M: Pica and mineral status in the mentally retarded. Am J Clin Nutr *35:* 958, 1982.
Darby P L, Garfinkel P E, Garner D M, Coscina D V: *Anorexia Nervosa: Recent Developments.* Allen R. Liss, New York, 1983.
Halmi K A: Anorexia nervosa. In *Clinical Psychopharmacology,* D G Grahams-Smith, H Hippius, G Winokur, editors, p 313, Excerpta Medica, Amsterdam, 1982.
Halmi K A: The state of research in anorexia nervosa and bulimia. In *Psychiatric Development, Advances and Prospects in Research and Clinical Practice.* S Guze, M Roth, editors, vol 1, p 247. Oxford University Press, New York, 1983.
Halmi K A: Anorexia nervosa. In *Comprehensive Textbook of Psychiatry,* ed 4, H I Kaplan, B J Sadock, editors, p 1143. Williams & Wilkins, Baltimore, 1985.
Herzog D B: Bulimia in the adolescent. Am J Dis Child *136:* 985, 1982.
Johnson C, Larson R: Bulimia: An Analysis of Moods and Behavior. Psychosom Med *44:* 341, 1982.
Lacey J H: Bulimia nervosa, binge eating, and psychogenic vomiting: A controlled treatment study and long-term outcome. Br Med J *286:* 1609, 1983.
Pope H G, Hudson J I, Jonas J M, Yurgelun-Todd D: Bulimia treated with imipramine: A placebo-controlled, double-blind study. Am J Psychiatry *40:* 5, 1983.
Stunkard A J, Stellow E: *Eating and Its Disorders.* Raven Press, New York, 1984.

## 22.5   CARDIOVASCULAR DISORDERS

### Introduction

The interactions between cardiovascular physiology and pathology, on the one hand, and mental processes and behavior, on the other, constitute the subject matter of psychosomatic cardiovascular disorders.

### Coronary Heart Disease

*Epidemiology*

Coronary heart disease is the leading cause of death in the United States, which ranks third, after Finland and Scotland, in mortality rate from coronary heart disease among young adult and middle-aged men. However, the age-adjusted death rate from coronary heart disease peaked in 1963, and has declined since then.

Major postulated risk factors for premature development of coronary heart disease involve (1) dietary factors—habitual diet high in saturated fat, cholesterol, and calories; (2) blood chemistry—elevated serum cholesterol and triglycerides, hyperglycemia, hyperuricemia; (3) organ system pathology and dysfunction—hypertension, diabetes mellitus, hypothyroidism, renal disease, gout; (4) living habits—cigarette smoking, physical inactivity, overeating; (5) psychosocial factors—type A behavior pattern, job or marital dissatisfaction, status incongruity, work overload, and disturbing emotions of anxiety and depression; and (6) familial factors—family history of premature atherosclerotic or hypertensive disease and death therefrom.

*Psychosocial Predisposing Factors*

The most influential and widely tested hypothesis linking causal psychological variables and the occurrence of coronary heart disease is that formulated by Friedman and Rosenman. They asserted that a pattern of behavior, designated type A, distinguishes coronary-prone persons, and has predictive value for the development of coronary heart disease and its complications. The type A behavior pattern features aggressiveness, competitiveness, ambition, drive for success, restlessness, impatience, devotion to work, a subjective sense of time urgency, abruptness of speech and gesture, and a tendency to hostility. People relatively lacking these behavior characteristics have been designated as type B. Type A behavior is exhibited by persons who are constantly engaged in a struggle to achieve, to outdo others, and to meet deadlines. It is not synonymous with life stress, nor does it represent a response to life stress. Rather, it constitutes a habitual behavioral state, the precursors of which have been observed in children. Parental attitudes characterized by escalating standards of performance may influence children to develop a chronic type A behavior pattern. Studies have shown that men exhibiting the pattern tend to have elevated plasma triglyceride and cholesterol values, a hyperinsulinemic response to a glucose challenge, and increased diurnal secretion of noradrenalin. Extreme type A persons have an increased serum level of corticotropin and a reduced serum level of growth hormone, and they show accelerated clotting. Preliminary reports indicate that young type A males show more marked heart rate and blood pressure responses to challenging perceptual-motor and cognitive tasks than do type B persons.

Data available at this time indicate that type A behavior pattern may be the final overt manifestation of different motives, and that its role in the development of coronary heart disease may be co-determined by such factors as the degree to which it is at variance with the person's basic personality. Further, the extent to which striving is rewarded with success may also prove to be significant. One must avoid the temptation to oversimplify the results of the investigations carried out to date and mistake promising hypotheses for established facts. There is little doubt that the cause of coronary heart disease is multifactorial, and that certain psychological and social factors represent no more than a set of contributory causal variables, interacting in a still unknown but complex fashion with biological and biochemical factors.

### Behavioral Prevention

Attempts to alter behavior have so far focused mainly on discouraging smoking, on weight reduction, on encouraging physical activity, on dietary modifications, and on compliance with blood pressure control.

Since type A behavior is viewed by some experts as a risk factor, attempts have begun to modify it. The so-called cardiac stress management program is a method, based on principles of behavioral modification, aimed at two objectives: stress management training and change of habitual behavior. Stress management training involves teaching the person how to relax, identify situations inducing stress responses in him or her, and control stimuli evoking such responses and the responses themselves. The type A person is helped to learn to make changes in daily routines to reduce stress, and to avoid situations and persons who induce in him or her competitiveness, time pressure, achievement motivation, hostility, and other components of the type A behavior pattern.

### Myocardial Infarction and Angina

#### Psychosocial Antecedents

Psychosocial factors are believed to precipitate acute cardiac events, such as myocardial infarction, angina pectoris, and sudden death.

Patients with angina pectoris tend to differ psychologically from those who suffer from myocardial infarction. The angina pectoris patients are more likely to exhibit overt anxiety, emotional lability, somatic concerns in response to stress, and a lower pain threshold. By contrast, patients with myocardial infarction are said to be more compulsive, to repress emotions, and to have a poor fantasy life. These alleged personality differences are relative, and have not yet been shown to be of predictive value.

More widely accepted by clinicians are the psychological precipitants of anginal attacks. Anger, fear, anxiety, elation, excitement—emotional states characterized by heightened autonomic arousal—are able to trigger and exacerbate anginal attacks. Nocturnal angina can be precipitated by frightening dreams during rapid eye movement (REM) sleep.

The postulated psychophysiological mediating mechanisms for the role of social and emotional factors in angina include coronary vasoconstriction, increased catecholamine and cortisol secretion leading to myocardial hypoxia, stimulation of the limbic system and the hypothalamus, and increase in cardiac output, heart rate, and blood pressure.

#### Psychological Responses

The most common immediate responses to myocardial infarction are fear and minimization of danger, respectively. Fear implies that the victim realizes that his symptoms signify a heart attack. Intense fear may contribute to the onset of lethal cardiac arrhythmias with electrical instability of the heart. Denial interferes with the decision process to seek immediate help. The resulting delay in initiating treatment may be fatal. Patients with a history of a previous myocardial infarction or angina tend to delay calling for help more than do younger persons having their first experience of chest pain or dyspnea. Education of high-risk patients, such as those with a history of previous infarction, could reduce the tendency to delay seeking help.

Several types of response to and coping with manifest heart disease may be distinguished: (1) realistic acceptance of damage, and judicious attempts at full attainable rehabilitation; (2) excessive dependence—with or without anxiety, depressive, or conversion symptoms—and related perpetuation of the sick role; (3) denial of the significance of the disease, and attempts to live as if it did not exist; and (4) the use of heart disease to manipulate and control others by playing on their sympathy and feelings of guilt.

### Psychological Aspects of Rehabilitation

The rehabilitation of coronary patients has been defined as the sum of activity required to ensure them the best possible physical, mental, and social conditions, so that they may, by their own efforts, regain as normal as possible a place in the community and lead an active, productive life. Postmyocardial infarction invalidism is often needlessly prolonged because of anxiety, depression, or social problems. Health professionals caring for patients with heart attacks should consider rehabilitation from the very beginning.

A heart attack creates an existential crisis for the victim and his or her family. The period of adjustment to this stressful event is often difficult for both.

Brief psychotherapy throughout the hospitalization period has been reported to shorten the hospital stay, relieve excessive anxiety and depression, reduce the frequency of congestive heart failure and supraventricular arrhythmias, and enhance adaptive coping after discharge from the hospital. Group therapy for postmyocardial infarction patients has also been shown to be beneficial, as judged by successful adjustment and coping with the consequences of the heart attack. Marital couple therapy may be helpful in selected cases. Sexual counseling for the patient and spouse should be a routine procedure before discharge. Postinfarction patients may return to sexual activity at the same time they are able to perform ordinary activities without symptoms, cardiac arrhythmias, or electrocardiographic changes.

### Psychological Aspects of Management

Three major innovations in the management of heart disease are coronary care units, the implantation of cardiac pacemakers, and cardiac surgery.

**Coronary Care Units.** Psychophysiological aspects of acute coronary care have attracted much attention in the past decade.

The incidence of adverse reactions to a stay in a coronary care unit varies in different studies, but seems to be low. Delirium occurs in 3 to 10 percent of patients; it may be due to cerebral hypoxia-ischemia or cardiac drugs or both. Sleep deprivation and anxiety seem to facilitate the onset of delirium and to aggravate it. Anxiety or depression may be present in some 80 percent of the patients in the coronary care unit, but these affects are not usually severe and are not in most cases related to the physical setting of the unit. Human contacts can increase heart rate and the frequency of ectopic beats in coronary unit patients.

Any variables, including responses to the sensory input from the physical and social environment of the coronary care unit, that enhance the patient's anxiety, may induce potentially lethal arrhythmias and cause death. These considerations have influenced the design and the routine of the units, and have prompted attempts at reducing anxiety in patients by sedation. Diazepam (Valium) is commonly used for this purpose, and has been claimed to reduce the incidence of malignant arrhythmias and the extension of myocardial injury. Diazepam is reported to cause a significant reduction in catecholamine excretion, and an increase in myocardial blood flow. Excessive anxiety should be looked for and treated in coronary unit patients. Diazepam, 5 to 10 mg orally 4 times a day, is a safe sedative in this situation, and should be used when sedation is indicated.

Nocturnal sleep after a myocardial infarction is markedly disturbed. It is likely that the disruption contributes to the delirium observed in some patients, especially elderly, after a heart attack. Delirium is found in about 10 percent of elderly myocardial infarction patients. The delirium usually starts on the third to the fourth day after the infarction and lasts 2 to 5 days. The markedly agitated delirious patient may be given haloperidol (Haldol), 2.5 to 10 mg orally or intramuscularly every 30 minutes until he is calm, followed by decreasing oral doses. The drug has proved to be remarkably safe in these acutely ill patients.

Regular attendance of a liaison psychiatrist in a coronary care unit helps the staff identify psychiatric problems in the patients and use psychotropic drugs rationally and effectively. A weekly conference with the staff of the unit may help relieve some of the stress commonly present in the nursing staff.

The unit is also the setting in which rehabilitation of the coronary patient should begin. Transfer from a coronary care unit may arouse anxiety and a concomitant increase in catecholamine secretion in some patients. Cardiovascular complications may result and ought to be prevented by preparing the patient for the transfer and by maintaining continuity of care.

**Permanent Cardiac Pacemakers.** Permanently implanted cardiac pacemakers have prolonged the lives of thousands of patients with heart block and other arrhythmias. They are particularly valuable in Stokes-Adams attacks. These attacks are relieved, and the quality of the patient's life is improved as episodes of loss of consciousness or delirium, or both, are eliminated. Some 75 percent of patients report an improved life style after implantation. A minority of patients have difficulty in adjusting to dependence on a mechanical device. Some experience anxiety related to misconceptions and lack of information about the working and reliability of the pacemaker. Education and continued support offered the patients by the cardiac team are important factors in preventing avoidable maladjustment.

**Heart Surgery.** Cardiac surgery, especially open-heart and coronary artery bypass surgery, is followed by psychiatric complications more often than are other major operations. The incidence of delirium varies according to different reports but ranges from about 20 to 40 percent. The incidence of delirium after coronary bypass surgery is comparable to that after open-heart surgery (postcardiotomy delirium), and is about 30 percent. Three other psychiatric syndromes have been reported to follow cardiac surgery: hallucinosis; paranoid-hallucinatory syndrome; and a mixed affective syndrome, with varying combinations and degrees of depression, elation, anxiety, and apathy. Some authors speak only of postcardiotomy delirium when referring to psychiatric complications of open-heart surgery, and fail to mention the other syndromes. The following discussion refers to postcardiotomy delirium unless otherwise specified.

Delirium may have its onset on the first postoperative day, or it may occur after a lucid interval of 2 to 5 days. There is disagreement in the literature as to which mode of onset is more common. The duration of delirium is less than a week in about 90 percent of all cases. The cause of postcardiotomy delirium is multifactorial. Factors predisposing to its development include age over 45 years, evidence of cerebral disease before surgery; acquired, rather than congenital, heart disease that is severe and involves multiple valve-replacement procedures; and preoperative anxiety or depression or both.

The most important variables related to the operation are the duration of the cardiopulmonary bypass and the degree and duration of hypotension, with resulting inadequate cerebral perfusion and ischemia-hypoxia. Microemboli in small cerebral blood vessels, hypotension, metabolic acidosis, and disturbances of fluid and electrolyte balance are among the intraoperative factors responsible for cerebral ischemia-hypoxia and consequent neuropsychiatric complications.

Factors related to postoperative care that are believed by some authors to precipitate or intensify delirium include altered sensory environment—monotony, unfamiliarity, noise—in the intensive care unit and sleep deprivation due to frequent awakening.

The incidence of postcardiotomy delirium has been reduced in recent years by the careful selection of patients, preoperative psychological preparation, improved surgical techniques, the avoidance of hypotension, the provision of a better sensory environment in intensive care units, more sleep, and supportive nursing care. The treatment of severe postcardiotomy agitation and excitement includes the administration of haloperidol (Haldol) parenterally in sufficient doses to achieve tranquilization.

### Cardiac Arrhythmias and Sudden Death

*Psychological Factors*

Psychological factors can predispose to and precipitate disturbances of cardiac rate and rhythm, regardless of whether heart disease is present. Emotional influences are particularly prominent in the commonest arrhythmias, those most likely to occur in the absence of heart disease—sinus tachycardia, paroxysmal atrial tachycardia, and atrial and ventricular ectopic beats. And, some evidence indicates that psychological factors, mediated by enhanced sympathetic activity, may induce ventricular arrhythmias, including ventricular fibrillation.

The repetitive sustained paroxysmal tachycardia—supraventricular or, rarely, ventricular—may occur in the absence of organic heart disease. It usually starts in adolescence or young adulthood, and shows an association with neurosis and psychological stress. Supraventricular tachycardia is only occasionally fatal, but, if organic heart disease develops in such a patient, the prognosis may become grave.

Lethal cardiac arrhythmia, such as ventricular fibrillation or standstill, is a possible cause of sudden death in response to overwhelming emotional arousal or giving up. Ventricular fibrillation is considered responsible for about 450,000 deaths in the United States every year. George Engel proposed that giving up in the face of emotional arousal and psychological uncertainty are factors facilitating vasodepressor syncope and sudden death. Simultaneous activation of the fight-flight and conservation-withdrawal responses is postulated to induce lethal arrhythmias, especially in persons with coronary artery disease. Interviews with patients resuscitated after circulatory arrest indicate that they suffered no anxiety at the time of the attack.

Potentially fatal arrhythmias and sudden death may occur during sleep. A combination of propranolol, a $\beta$-adrenergic receptor blocking agent, and a benzodiazepine drug may be used in patients at risk to reduce sympathetic activity and to improve sleep without increasing rapid eye movement time, respectively.

### Management

Psychological approaches to the treatment of arrhythmias are indicated in two broad categories of patients: (1) those whose recurrent arrhythmias are believed to be related to periods of psychological stress or emotional arousal or both, and (2) those who are frightened by an awareness of even innocuous cardiac irregularity. Therapy should aim at the better management of stress, resolution of conflicts, and relief of anxiety, chronic resentment, indecision, and guilt. The development of more adaptive modes of coping with unavoidable situations that provoke the arrhythmia is another goal. Fear of cardiac disease and of sudden death aroused by benign arrhythmias needs to be explored for its unconscious meaning, which is likely to involve guilt over personally unacceptable impulses and emotions. Psychotherapy with insight as its goal could be helpful in such cases.

Learned voluntary control of premature ventricular contractions with the use of biofeedback has been reported in some cases. This technique is still experimental, but has shown promise of clinical applicability.

Benzodiazepines are useful in reducing anxiety without producing peripheral autonomic side effects. Diazepam is the drug of choice to achieve sedation in cardiac patients. Tricyclic antidepressants and phenothiazine derivatives should be used cautiously or not at all in patients with a history of cardiac arrhythmias, especially if heart disease is known to be present.

### Congestive Heart Failure

#### Psychological Factors

Heart failure connotes a state in which the defective function of the myocardium renders the heart unable to supply enough blood for the metabolic needs of the tissues. The dysfunction may be due to a primary myocardial pathology or chronic cardiac work overload.

Patients with compensated heart disease of any kind may develop heart failure in response to psychosocial factors acting directly or indirectly. Direct effects include intense emotional arousal, such as anxiety or anger, and feelings of depression and hopelessness. Indirect effects result from the patient's deviant illness behavior, which may take the form of noncompliance with medical treatment—for example, failure to take digitalis glycosides or diuretics, failure to follow dietary restrictions, or failure to restrict physical activity.

#### Management

Inquiry into the patient's emotional state and social situation, before the development of unexpected heart failure or when the heart fails to respond to medical treatment, should be routine.

Psychotherapy, usually of a supporting and information-giving type, is best provided by the physician responsible for the patient's continuous medical care. The doctor's awareness of the patient's personality, current cognitive and emotional state, living arrangements, and family relationships helps direct therapy selectively toward the problems most relevant to cardiovascular dysfunction.

Some patients with chronic heart failure cannot cope with the imposed restrictions on physical activity, and require help with finding less strenuous work and leisure pursuits. Attention to sleep is always important. Insomnia is common in heart failure patients, and may be accompanied by frightening dreams, anxiety, hyperventilation, and increased load on the heart. Delirium during the night may further complicate the situation.

### Essential Hypertension

Essential or idiopathic hypertension designates sustained elevation, for multiple causes, of systolic or diastolic blood pressure, or both, above an arbitrarily accepted limit of 160 mm Hg systolic and 95 mm Hg diastolic. Idiopathic hypertension accounts for more than 90 percent of elevated blood pressure cases; another 5 to 10 percent are due to identifiable renal, endocrine, neurogenic, and other disorders. Essential hypertension is a multicausal disorder of homeostasis.

### Psychosocial Predisposing Factors

A positive family history of hypertension, obesity, and spikes of blood pressure in youth have an adverse prognostic significance. Psychosocial variables have engendered a vast literature but equivocal study results. Claims have been advanced that essential hypertension develops in persons possessing a specific personality or intrapsychic conflict between passive-dependent tendencies and aggressive impulses, with repression of chronic anger or resentment or hostility. These hypotheses have achieved wide popularity, rather than adequate empirical support.

Lack of support for specificity hypotheses in essential hypertension must not be taken to imply that psychological and social factors are of no consequence for its cause, pathogenesis, course, and outcome. The available empirical evidence does not support such a sweeping negative conclusion. On the contrary, both clinical studies and experimental work on humans and animals indicate that the opposite is the case. It is highly unlikely, however, that any single psychological factor plays a causal role in essential hypertension.

### Psychophysiology

Episodes of raised blood pressure in labile hypertension are intermittent and readily provoked by emotional and sympathetic nervous system arousal, in response to personally meaningful environmental stimuli eliciting an attitude of vigilance, uncertainty, anger, fear, and physiological preparedness for fight or flight.

### Management

Psychological approaches to the management of essential hypertension have three main objectives: (1) to reduce and control blood pressure; (2) to modify behaviors contributing or predisposing to hypertension; and (3) to encourage compliance with medical treatment. Psychological or behavioral methods have flourished in the past few years, but their effectiveness is still uncertain and their application should be tempered by a cool appraisal of their limitations.

Early detection is essential. Blood pressure determination should be a routine procedure in every health care facility, including psychiatric facilities of all types. All persons with blood pressure elevations of 160/95 or above should be referred for further medical evaluation.

Support of the patient's motivation for and compliance with medical treatment, control of obesity and sodium intake, and other recommended measures are important. Patients with essential hypertension tend to have few symptoms, and this feature contributes to their noncompliance. Drug therapy of hypertension is often complicated by unpleasant side effects, such as sexual dysfunction, that may contribute to poor compliance. A sustained and trusting relationship between the patient and his doctor is essential. The patient's beliefs regarding the seriousness and the potential consequences of his disorder need to be elicited by the physician as a basis for individually tailored education.

Psychotherapy has not been demonstrated by controlled studies to be beneficial in essential hypertension.

Behavioral methods—including biofeedback, relaxation, behavior modifications, and meditation—are increasingly being used for the control of hypertension. Biofeedback is the most often used technique. Varying degrees of reduction of blood pressure have been achieved with these methods.

Psychotropic drugs may be used as an adjunct to other therapies, especially during periods of heightened anxiety and tension, and related increases in sympathetic arousal. Benzodiazepines are most appropriate for sedation at such times, but they do not lower blood pressure, are not recommended as primary drug therapy, and should not be prescribed indiscriminately and for long periods. Depression may occur in patients receiving antihypertensive drugs, and this depression needs to be treated. There is a high prevalence of depression in hypertensives taking such drugs. Patients with a past history of psychiatric disorder are particularly likely to develop mild or moderate depression while they are treated for hypertension. No individual antihypertensive drug has been shown to be associated with especially frequent or severe depressions. Reserpine, methyldopa, clonidine, guanethidine, and propranolol have all been implicated in depression in hypertensive patients, but it has been difficult to establish whether they represent a causal or a coincidental relationship.

## Borderlands of Psychiatry and Cardiology

### Reactive Disorders

Psychiatric disorders may coexist with, complicate, or imitate cardiovascular disease. The onset of a cardiovascular disorder may aggravate preexistent psychiatic disorder, usually a depressive, anxiety, or somatoform disorder; or one of these mental disorders may arise as a maladaptive reaction to the cardiovascular disease.

### Psychogenic Cardiac Nondisease

A different problem is presented by patients who are free of heart disease yet complain of symptoms related to the heart and suggestive of cardiac disease, or who exhibit morbid concern about their heart, or both. Some such patients have an exaggerated fear of heart disease, yet they may not report symptoms suggestive of it. The fear may range from anxious concern, through severe phobia or hypochondriasis, to a delusional conviction.

A larger group of patients complain of symptoms referred to the heart or suggestive of heart disease, but without any evidence of it. In one study of 505 patients seen in a medical clinic for the complaint of chest pain, one-quarter were given a psychiatric diagnosis. Many of those patients suffer from an ill-defined syndrome usually referred to as neurocirculatory asthenia.

First described by DaCosta in 1871 and named by him "irritable heart," neurocirculatory asthenia has some 20 synonyms, such as effort syndrome, DaCosta's syndrome, cardiac neurosis, vasoregulatory asthenia, hyperkinetic heart syndrome, and hyperdynamic $\beta$-adrenergic circulatory state. Psychiatrists tend to view it as a clinical variant of anxiety disorder.

The diagnostic criteria for neurocirculatory asthenia used in the Framingham heart disease epidemiology study were: (1) a respiratory complaint, such as sighing respiration, inability to get a deep breath, smothering and choking, or dyspnea; and (2) one or more symptoms from at least two of the following groups: (a) palpitation, chest pain, or discomfort; (b) nervousness, dizziness, faintness, or discomfort in crowds; (c) undue fatigability or tiredness or limitation of activities. Breathlessness, palpitations, chest pain, fatigue, poor exercise tolerance, and nervousness constitute the core symptoms. In addition, the patient may complain of dizziness, tremulousness, easy startle response, paresthesias, faintness and syncopal attacks, excessive sweating, insomnia, and irritability. The symptoms usually start in adolescence or the patient's early twenties, but may have their onset in middle age. They are twice as common in women as in men and tend to be chronic, with recurrent acute exacerbations.

The management of neurocirculatory asthenia may be difficult, and prognosis is guarded if the condition is chronic, phobic elements are prominent, or the patient derives primary or secondary gains from his or her disability. Psychotherapy aimed at uncovering psychodynamic factors—usually issues relating to hostility, unacceptable sexual impulses, dependence, guilt, and death anxiety—may be effective in some cases, but most patients with the condition tend to shun psychiatric help. The use of propranolol may interrupt the vicious cycle of cardiac symptoms having a positive feedback effect on anxiety, which aggravates the symptoms. Physical training programs aimed at correcting faulty breathing habits and at gradually increasing the patient's effort tolerance may be helpful, especially if the programs are combined with group psychotherapy.

### REFERENCES

Brand R J, Rosenman R H, Sholtz R I, Friedman M: Multivariate prediction of coronary heart disease in the Western Collaborative Group Study compared to the findings of the Framingham Study. Circulation 53: 348, 1976.

Cassem N H: Psychiatric problems in patients with acute myocardial infarction. In Coronary Care, J S Karlinger, G Gregoratos, editors, p 829. Churchill Livingstone, New York, 1981.

Cassem N H: Cardiovascular effect of antidepressants. J Clin Psychiatry 43: 22, 1982.

Friedman M, Thoresen C E, Gill J J, Ulmer D, Thompson L, Powell L, Price V, Elek S R, Rabin D D, Breall W S, Piaget G, Dixon T, Bourge E, Levy R A, Tasto D L: Feasibility of altering type A behavior pattern after myocardial infarction. Recurrent coronary prevention project study: Methods, baseline results and preliminary findings. Circulation 66: 83, 1982.

Glassman A H, Johnson L L, Giardina E V, Walsh T, Roose S P, Cooper T B, Bigger J T Jr: The use of imipramine in depressed patients with congestive heart failure. JAMA 250: 1997, 1983.

Hackett T P, Cassem N H, editors: MGH Handbook of General Hospital Psychiatry. C. V. Mosby, St. Louis, 1978.

Hackett T P, Rosenbaum J F: Emotion, psychiatric disorders, and the heart. In A Textbook of Cardiovascular Medicine, E Braunwald, editor, p 1826. W. B. Saunders, Philadelphia, 1984.

Hackett, T P, Rosenbaum J F, Cassem N H: Cardiovascular disorders. In Comprehensive Textbook of Psychiatry, ed 4, H I Kaplan, B J Sadock, editors, p 1148. Williams & Wilkins, Baltimore, 1985.

Jenkins C D: Recent evidence supporting psychological and social risk factors for coronary disease. N Engl J Med 294: 987, 1976.

Lown B, DeSilva R A: Roles of psychological stress and autonomic nervous system changes in provocation of ventricular premature complexes. Am J Cardiol 41: 979, 1978.

Weiner H: Psychobiology and Human Disease. Elsevier, New York, 1977.

## 22.6   RESPIRATORY DISORDERS

### Introduction

Although the effects of pulmonary disease on its host are many and varied, and although psychological factors may play a role in predisposing, initiating, and sustaining some pulmonary diseases, this section is limited to a discussion of two syndromes: the hyperventilation syndrome and bronchial asthma.

## Hyperventilation Syndrome

The hyperventilation syndrome is a psychosomatic disorder that may be experimentally induced by asking a patient to breathe rapidly and deeply for 2 to 3 minutes, which elicits a series of subjective sensations that may be followed by loss of consciousness. The patient begins to feel lightheaded, then faints; he or she may sense vertigo or giddiness. Feelings of derealization may occur. Buzzing in the ears may be experienced. Vision may be blurred. The patient's extremities may begin to tingle and feel numb. The muscles may stiffen, and carpopedal spasm may develop. The mouth may feel dry. Uncontrollable laughter or crying may occur. Such hyperventilation may be followed by apnea. However, these symptoms may not be mentioned by the patient. Rather, the patient may complain mainly of faintness, loss of consciousness, breathlessness, or fear and apprehension and their multivarious concomitants. Only careful history taking elicits the information that some of the symptoms occur when the patient exercises or runs up several flights of stairs. Other patients are aware of the fact that hyperventilation precedes or is associated with the main presenting symptoms. However, the main symptoms of the syndrome may occur at any time and place, and may characteristically last a considerable amount of time.

### Psychological Considerations

The hyperventilation syndrome may occur in a variety of different persons. Hyperventilation is a physiological concomitant of fear, anxiety, pain, and anger. Therefore, it may occur not only in the neurotic person, but on occasions in which anyone may become afraid or angry or have pain for any reason. On the other hand, in certain hysterical persons, hyperventilation may have special meanings of which the patient is not aware—for instance, when such a patient becomes sexually aroused. Some hysterical patients hyperventilate because of a hysterical identification with a family member who suffered from dyspnea or asthmatic attacks. In the history of some hyperventilating patients, there is a family member who at some time in the past had difficulties in breathing that are analogous to or exactly like the patient's current symptoms.

### Physiological Aspects

Several different physiological mechanisms may be involved in the hyperventilation syndrome. The patient is unusually prone to develop a rapid reduction in alveolar and arterial carbon dioxide tension, but less of a diminution in venous carbon dioxide tension. Respiratory alkalosis ensues, and the concentration of bicarbonate ion in plasma is reduced. The calcium ion in plasma passes out of the alkaline solution. The deionization of calcium is responsible for the depolarization of peripheral nerves, which is, in turn, the basis of the tingling and numbness in the extremities, and ultimately of tetany.

The respiratory alkalosis leads to vasoconstriction, particularly of the medium-sized arteries of the brain and the heart. The cerebral vasoconstriction reduces cerebral blood flow and is associated with the development of synchronized, slow-wave, high-voltage electroencephalographic (EEG) waves.

Patients with the hyperventilation syndrome have normal EEG's at rest and when breathing normally; but, when they voluntarily hyperventilate, they rapidly develop slow, high-voltage EEG waves. The slow EEG pattern seems to be correlated with the symptoms of lightheadedness, dizziness, and faintness.

The symptoms of the syndrome can be averted rapidly by the patient's rebreathing expired air, thus restoring the diminished alveolar and arterial carbon dioxide tension, thereby averting respiratory alkalosis.

In some patients with the hyperventilation syndrome, additional physiological changes may occur. The heart rate may increase, and the blood pressure may fall. If such patients are standing, they may faint.

### Differential Diagnosis

The hyperventilation syndrome should not be difficult to diagnose, except perhaps when loss of consciousness occurs. Fainting patients may be misdiagnosed for epilepsy, hysteria, hypoglycemia, and vasodepressor, vasovagal, or hypoglycemic attacks. Patients with myocardial infarctions, the Adams-Stokes syndrome, and paroxysmal cardiac arrhythmias may feel faint or may actually faint. Anxious patients and those with phobic anxiety or symptoms of depersonalization may remind one of the syndrome. Paresthesias may occur in hypoparathyroid states, peripheral neuropathies, and hysteria.

Nevertheless, once the diagnosis is considered, it is easily confirmed by making the patient hyperventilate.

### Treatment

Many patients respond well to being instructed or educated about the nature of their symptoms. They can then avoid hyperventilating. But other anxious or hysterical patients may need psychotherapy to uncover in what contexts and circumstances they become anxious or begin their hysterical hyperventilation.

## Bronchial Asthma

### Definition

Bronchial asthma is a recurrent, obstructive disease of the bronchial airways, which tend to respond by bronchoconstriction, edema, and excessive secretion to a variety of stimuli. Allergens, pulmonary infections (especially with viruses), psychological stimuli, cold air, odors, exercise, and irritation of the nasal passages may singly or in combination incite bronchoconstriction. Wheezing results from bronchoconstriction; it may be temporary or mild, episodic or paroxysmal, chronic or severe, seasonal or perennial.

At least two main forms of bronchial asthma are recognized—the extrinsic and the intrinsic forms. About 30 to 50 percent of all patients suffer from the extrinsic form. The extrinsic form of bronchial asthma is characterized by allergic mechanisms that are necessary but probably not sufficient to precipitate clinical attacks.

Some additional factors are necessary to account for the usually episodic nature of bronchial asthma. Many experts in this area concede that, in addition to the immunological mechanisms already outlined, patients with bronchial asthma have an innate or acquired tendency to bronchoconstriction. In addition, in at least some patients, psychological factors play a predisposing and initiating role in the disease and its recurrences.

Extrinsic asthma is a multifactorial disease in which psychological, immunological, and physiological factors interact. The extrinsic form most frequently occurs in young people, especially children, some of whom outgrow it. Its incidence is often seasonal, and it tends to run in families. Many asthmatic children have a history of allergic rhinitis, eczema, or food allergies before developing asthmatic attacks.

Patients with intrinsic asthma are usually more than 40 years of age. In them, the influence of hereditary, familial, or preexisting allergic factors is less evident. However, they tend to be sensitive to certain drugs, such as aspirin and indomethacin. Both aspirin and indomethacin are powerful suppressors of prostaglandin synthesis. Some prostaglandins are potent bronchoconstrictors, others are bronchodilators. Patients with intrinsic asthma characteristically have an eosinophilia of blood and nasal polyps that contain eosinophils. Both the drug sensitiv-

ity, the presence of eosinophils in nasal polyps, and the blood are symptomatic of the action of immunological mechanisms that seem to be different from the mechanisms in extrinsic asthma.

These immunological mechanisms in intrinsic asthma may be instigated by a virus, because intrinsic asthma frequently follows a viral infection of the lung, becomes perennial, and is unresponsive or becomes refractory to drugs such as the corticosteroids.

### The Role of Psychological Factors

After the first attack of bronchial asthma, neither viral, allergic, nor psychological factors individually precipitate every attack. One of these factors may predominate, with the others being subsidiary. The predominant factor may interact with the subsidiary ones. In addition, the predominant factor is different in different age groups.

The course of bronchial asthma, especially the extrinsic form in some children, may be radically altered by removing the child from his home; in his new environment the child rapidly remits from asthmatic attacks. Other children, whose attacks were only controlled by the continuous use of steroid medication, become less dependent on the medication when away from home. Still other children have attacks only at home and not at school, even when they are exposed to the same allergen in both locations. These observations provide powerful support to the idea that psychological factors within the child and the social context in which he finds himself do play a role in precipitating asthmatic attacks, and in altering the course of asthma.

But psychological factors interact with other factors. A comprehensive view of the various forms of bronchial asthma must take into account the facts that its extrinsic subform runs in families and that, in some manner, physiological, infectious, immunological, and psychological factors interact to predispose, initiate, and sustain the disease.

### Genetic Factors

Genetic factors play a minor role in the predisposition to bronchial asthma. This conclusion is based on the fact that studies of families with bronchial asthma and other allergic diseases do not by themselves prove the operation of genetic factors. The family aggregation of bronchial asthma could well be a chance occurrence.

More sophisticated studies are needed to prove the role of genetic factors in bronchial asthma.

## Epidemiological Data

In childhood, boys with bronchial asthma outnumber girls by two or three to one. Prevalence rates increase with age in both sexes. After the age of 45, the proportion of men in the intrinsic group increases.

## Psychological Characteristics of Patients

At the present time, clinical research on asthmatic patients, especially children, has been guided by these main principles: (1) No single or uniform personality type has bronchial asthma; (2) many asthmatic patients (about one-half) have strong unconscious wishes for protection and for being encompassed by another person, particularly the mother or her surrogate, on whom they are very dependent. These wishes sensitize some patients to separation from the mother. In other patients, the wish produces such an intense conflict that separation from the mother or her surrogate produces remission from asthmatic attacks; (3) the specific wishes for protection or envelopment are said to be caused by the mother's attitudes toward her asthmatic child. However, studies of asthmatic children and their families have shown that no single pattern of mother-child relationship obtains. The mother may be overprotective and oversolicitous of the child; perfectionistic and overambitious for the child; overtly domineering, punitive, or cruel to the child; helpful and generative. Presumably, these attitudes both antecede the child's illness and are responsible for his conflicts and failure to develop psychologically. However, there is no proof of these assumptions. In fact, the attitude of the mother is more likely related to the child's social adjustment—his or her truancy or invalidism—than to the asthmatic attacks; (4) the asthmatic attack occurs when these wishes are frustrated by the mother or some other person, or when they are activated and produce conflict. In both instances, strong emotions are aroused; and (5) some adult asthmatic patients have various psychological conflicts, other than the ones already described.

Many asthmatic children demonstrate age-inappropriate behaviors and traits, and poor impulse control. Some of them are timid, babyish, and overly polite; others are tense, restless, rebellious, irritable, and explosive in their emotional outbursts. Asthmatic boys, in particular, tend to be passively dependent, timid, and immature, and at times they become irritable when frustrated. The asthmatic girls tend to depend on their fathers more than their mothers, and try to be self-sufficient but are frequently chronically depressed. Asthmatic children are also dominated by a fear of losing parental support. They attempt to defend against this fear by a show of independence, maturity, and masculinity. The mothers of some of the children are seductive; others overemphasize achievement and self-control. Regardless of the quality of the parental attitudes, whenever separation from their parents, particularly the mother, is threatened or actually occurs, the asthmatic children become anxious, lose control, become dependent, or have an asthmatic attack.

Asthmatic attacks are precipitated not only by the frustration of unconscious wishes and separation from or proximity to parents. The seasonal exposure to allergens plays a major role in inciting attacks. In adolescent asthmatics, physical activity (such as dancing), fighting, sexual excitement, fear, and angry outbursts occasioned by disappointment or by jealousy also antecede asthmatic bouts. About 40 percent of all asthmatic attacks occur at night, for reasons not understood.

Also, odors may play a role in precipitating individual attacks. It is the meaning of the odor to the patient, rather than the direct effect of the odor on the olfactory mucosa, that is significant in inciting attacks.

Adult asthmatic patients are poorly attuned to their human environment. Some are shy and sensitive to criticism; some strive to please others; some are timid or seclusive, egocentric, and moody; and some are suspicious and hostile.

Two major factors about bronchial asthma need reemphasis: The name, bronchial asthma, is applied to a syndrome, and at present, two major subforms, the extrinsic and the intrinsic, are recognized, but in all likelihood there are additional subforms.

The heterogeneity of bronchial asthma possibly reflects the fact that in the years since Alexander first formulated his opinion about the specific frustrated dependency conflicts in asthmatic patients, many other observers have described a variety of unconscious conflicts in such patients. In addition, clinical observers have shifted their attention to the moods and feeling states of patients between, during, and immediately after an asthmatic attack. For example adult asthmatic patients are usually poorly adapted to their human environment by virtue of their dependency on others, their immature ways of coping with their environment, and their tendency to become depressed and helpless without the support of other people.

The asthmatic attack occurs when various psychological defenses fail in part and the patient is overwhelmed by the anticipation or actuality of rejection by another person, or when he experiences a profound sense of depletion, occasioned by the rejection, withdrawal, or the actual or anticipated loss of the loved object. Identification with the object as a defense against such loss was inferred by Flanders Dunbar.

Studies indicate that actual or anticipated separation or loss plays an important role in initiating attacks in about 50 percent of all asthmatic patients, regardless of age. Subsequent attacks may be triggered by a variety of situations in which emotions, both pleasant and unpleasant, are aroused. In addition, the failure to fully express these emotions may be an important element in triggering attacks. By the same token, the complete discharge of a strong emotion, such as anger, may relieve the attack. But physical exertion also triggers attacks. Exercise or exertion can produce bronchoconstriction in some asthmatic persons.

### Psychophysiology

Because the pathophysiology of bronchial asthma consists of an increased resistance to airflow at all lung volumes, one may well ask whether psychological factors can, indeed, produce this increased resistance.

Both increases and decreases in airway resistance can be induced by suggestion in some asthmatic patients. These changes can be blocked by atropine, suggesting that the induction of asthmatic attacks is mediated by parasympathetic mechanisms.

Asthmatic attacks can also be conditioned. Asthmatic patients can develop conditioned asthmatic attacks when exposed to pictures of the objects that normally induce attacks. In these experiments, generalization from the conditioned stimulus to the experimental situation also occurs.

### Ameliorating and Sustaining Factors

Some children and adolescents outgrow their asthmatic attacks; some do not. Those who remit in adolescence may have a recurrence of attacks in middle age. The variable course of the disease has so far defied full explanation.

Social and psychological factors influence the course of the disease. Also, having asthma may alter the person's adaptation to school and work, and his relationships with other people. Bronchial asthmatic attacks cause school absences. The child may not be allowed to participate in athletic activities. He may have to be hospitalized. He may fall behind in his studies. His peer relationships may be impaired by his attacks, which frighten away his schoolmates. He may or may not follow a treatment program. Later, he may eschew marriage because of his chronic illness. Some asthmatic children fall behind in their physical maturation. The drugs used in the treatment of asthma may have adverse side effects that affect the child in diverse ways. Some asthmatic patients have frank neurotic or psychotic illnesses, but there is no cyclical relationship between psychosis and asthma and one illness does not prevent the other.

All or any of these complications may depend on the response of parents, siblings, teachers, and peers and may lead to various forms of psychological maladaptation.

The complex interactions between bronchial asthma, the child, his caretakers, his behavior, and his symptoms are attested to in children with rapidly remitting asthma. When sent away from home to a hospital, they become free of asthmatic symptoms and no longer need medication. The term "parentectomy" has been used to describe this separation. A second group of hospitalized children continue to require steroids to treat their asthmatic symptoms.

Between 30 and 45 percent of all children with extrinsic (allergic) asthma outgrow their clinical symptoms. Moreover, 50 percent of all children with asthma that is intractable to drug treatment remit on removal from their homes. Other children lose their symptoms without leaving home.

Of importance is the fact that patients who outgrow clinical asthma remain at risk for the disease.

Very little information is currently available as to why some patients with either form of asthma remit, why the disease follows an intermittent or continuous course in others, why still others repeatedly develop status asthmaticus, and why others die.

### REFERENCES

Alexander F: *Psychosomatic Medicine.* W. W. Norton, New York, 1950.
Boushey H A: Neural mechanisms in bronchial asthma. In *Brain, Behavior, and Bodily Disease,* H Weiner, M A Hofer, A J Stunkard, editors. Raven Press, New York, 1981.
Burrows B: *Respiratory Disorders.* Year Book Medical Publishers, Chicago, 1983.
Edfors-Lubs M-L: Allergy in 7000 twin pairs. Acta Allergol 26: 249, 1971.
Engel G L: *Fainting, Physiological and Psychological Considerations.* Charles C Thomas, Springfield, IL, 1950.
Gold W M: Asthma. Am Thoracic Soc News 1: 12, 1976.
Groen J J: Present status of the psychosomatic approach to bronchial asthma. In *Psychosomatic Medicine,* O W Hill, editor. Butterworth, London, 1976.
Knapp P H, Nemetz S J: Acute bronchial asthma:

Concomitant depression with excitement and varied antecedent patterns in 406 attacks. Psychosom Med 22: 42, 1960.

Stein M: Biopsychosocial factors in asthma. In *Critical Issues in Behavioral Medicine*, L J West, M Stein, editors. J. B. Lippincott, Philadelphia, 1982.

Weiner H: Respiratory disorders. In *Comprehensive Textbook of Psychiatry*, ed. 4, H I Kaplan, B J Sadock, editors, p 1159. Williams & Wilkins, Baltimore, 1985.

Williams D A, Lewis-Faning E, Rees L, Jacobs J, Thomas A: Assessment of the relative importance of the allergic, infective, and psychological factors in asthma. Acta Allergol 12: 376, 1958.

# 22.7   ENDOCRINE DISORDERS

## Introduction

Many of the syndromes associated with endocrine dysfunction may be easily confused with psychogenic disorders—in their early stages with neurotic disorders, and in more advanced stages with dementias and severe psychotic disorders. It is important to differentiate disorders of endocrine functioning early, since in many cases they represent treatable syndromes.

## Thyrotoxicosis

Thyrotoxicosis is the syndrome that manifests the biochemical and physiological changes occurring as a result of a chronic—endogenous or exogenous—excess of thyroid hormone. The terms Graves' disease and diffuse toxic goiter refer specifically to the syndrome of endogenous thyrotoxicosis—that is, thyrotoxicosis resulting from hyperactivity of the thyroid gland.

### Mental Manifestations

Mental changes almost always accompany thyrotoxicosis. The patient feels tense and hyperexcitable and may be emotionally labile, often with inappropriate temper outbursts, crying spells, or euphoria. He may describe himself as "tired from the neck down" but experiencing a need to be doing something despite this feeling of physical fatigue. Distractibility, short attention span, and impaired recent memory may be present. In severe hyperthyroidism or in thyrotoxic storm, there may be frank psychosis, delirium, coma, and death. In contrast, a minority of patients, particularly the elderly, with chronic thyrotoxicosis may be depressed, apathetic, and anorectic.

### Physical Signs and Symptoms

The patient may complain of palpitation, heat intolerance, shortness of breath, increase in appetite with weight loss or only slight weight gain, change in bowel habits (more frequent bowel movements), change in menstrual pattern (disruption of usual pattern progressing to amenorrhea), muscle weakness, and fatigability. Later, generalized weakness, insomnia, greatly increased appetite, and increased sweating may occur; any one of these signs and symptoms may predominate in a particular patient.

The thyrotoxic patient may manifest observable signs of the disorder. Fine rhythmic tremor of the hands, tongue, or tightly closed eyelids may be evident. Eyelid retraction gives the patient a fixed bright stare; in Graves' disease, exophthalmos is also present, and the patient shows lid lag.

### Differential Diagnosis

Thyrotoxicosis may be confused with anxiety disorders, especially in young women who complain of fatigue, palpitation, irritability, and insomnia. In patients with anxiety disorders, the anxiety is often intermittent and related to specific social or psychological stimuli, the fatigue is not accompanied by the need to be active, fatigue is already present on awakening, and the palms are usually cool and moist (clammy), rather than warm and moist. In thyrotoxicosis, tension or anxiety is constant and not as situationally determined; tachycardia persists in sleep. Weight loss in combination with increased appetite and food intake occurs only in thyrotoxicosis and early diabetes mellitus, which is also accompanied by polyuria and polydipsia. Other metabolic disorders—such as pheochromocytoma, diabetes mellitus, and hypermetabolic states—may also be confused with thyrotoxicosis.

Exogenous thyroid excess must be differentiated from thyrotoxicosis caused by overactivity of the thyroid gland itself.

Measurement of serum concentrations of triiodothyronine ($T_3$) and thyroxine ($T_4$), and appraisal of the $T_3$-$T_4$ ratio have replaced both the measurement of protein-bound iodine and basal metabolic rate as initial diagnostic screening tests. Iodine-131 uptake provides a direct test of thyroid function. The TRH test, in combination with the determination of $T_3$ and $T_4$, increases diagnostic sensitivity in early suspected cases.

### Epidemiology

Thyroid disorders are 7 times more frequent in women than in men. In women, goiter often appears during puberty, pregnancy, and menopause. Men usually get thyroid disease at older ages. Hyperthyroidism occurs frequently in members of the same family (sisters and daughters), and is most common in women in their third and fourth decades.

### Etiology

The cause of endogenous thyrotoxicosis is not known. The disease may be precipitated by acute emotional stress or shock, sometimes even developing within hours after an extreme fright or emotional trauma. Several premorbid personality characteristics have been described and agreed on by independent investigators. One often described personality pattern is characterized by premature assumption of responsibility and martyr-like reaction formation to and suppression of dependent wishes and needs, often combined with an exaggerated fear of death and injury.

### Management and Prognosis

The course of untreated Graves' disease may fluctuate and manifest spontaneous remissions and exacerbations. It may progress slowly for months or years and may be exacerbated by stress. Treatment consists of antithyroid drugs, radioactive iodine, or surgical ablation.

An organic deficit may persist in a minority of patients.

Tricyclic antidepressants may induce cardiac arrhythmias, and some phenothiazines may increase tachycardia.

### Hypothyroidism

Hypothyroidism results from the insufficient synthesis of thyroid hormone, either from loss of functioning thyroid tissue or from insufficient stimulation of a normal gland secondary to hypothalamic or pituitary disease, or biochemical suppression of a normal gland.

### Clinical Description

The clinical state is related more to the degree of thyroid deficiency than to the underlying cause. Hypothyroidism develops slowly and insiduously, unless secondary to surgery.

### Mental Manifestations

A high proportion of patients with adult onset show evidence of mental disturbance as part of the syndrome. All mental processes, including speech, slow down. There is decreased initiative, slowness in comprehension, and impaired recent memory. The patient may complain of fatigue, lethargy, and drowsiness. An affective disturbance, predominantly depression, is common. Cognitive deficits may result in dementia. A frank organic mental disorder may develop and progress to stupor or coma. Myxedema madness

is a psychosis in which a wide range of organicity, from minimal to marked, may be manifest. It is often characterized by paranoid suspicions and auditory hallucinations.

### Physical Signs and Symptoms

Neurological manifestations may include peripheral neuropathy, with numbness and tingling in the fingers and involvement of auditory nerves, with hearing loss, or median nerve involvement (carpal tunnel syndrome). Headache, confusional attacks, and syncope may occur. Patients change in appearance; the hypothyroid patient gradually develops thickened edematous skin, leading to coarse features and a dull expression. The skin is pale and may be yellow. There may be puffiness around the eyes. Hair becomes brittle and dry and may fall out; the outer third of the eyebrows may be lost. The voice is husky with slurred speech because of a thickened tongue.

The patient may complain of cold intolerance, stiff and aching muscles, constipation, infertility, and menstrual irregularity. Appetite is decreased, with a slight weight gain in spite of lowered food intake. However, massive obesity is not part of the syndrome.

Body temperature may be lowered, and the heart may be enlarged. Pulse rate and cardiac output are decreased, and electrocardiographic and characteristic changes develop. Skeletal muscle contraction and relaxation are slowed. Mild normocytic, normochromic anemia may be present.

In infancy, hypothyroidism leads to cretinism.

### Differential Diagnosis

As noted above, the onset of hypothyroidism is often slow and insidious except in patients with surgical ablation of the thyroid, and in patients who discontinue replacement therapy, and may be missed by the patient, relatives, and friends. Difficulty in diagnosis may arise in the elderly. In them, hypothyroidism may be confused with dementia. Myxedema is one of the most common causes of potentially reversible dementia. Old age, chronic renal insufficiency, and pernicious anemia may mimic hypothyroidism.

Misdiagnosis of the symptoms and signs accompanying psychogenic disorders as mild hypothyroidism, and inappropriate treatment with thyroid hormone, may lead to the development of iatrogenic thyrotoxicosis.

Measurement of thyroid hormone levels ($T_4$) and thryoid function ($^{131}I$ uptake) help establish the diagnosis.

## Etiology

Most often, hypothyroidism results from the attempt to control hyperthyroidism by the administration of radioactive iodine or subtotal thyroidectomy.

Primary hypothyroidism of unknown cause is uncommon; when it does occur, the incidence is higher in women than in men, and the disease usually appears between the ages of 40 and 60. Thyroid autoantibodies are present in up to 80 percent of the patients with primary hypothyroidism. Other causes of decreased thyroid hormone include the cessation of maintenance thyroid hormone therapy, severe or chronic iodine deficiency, Hashimoto's disease, and tumors of the thyroid gland. Disorders of the hypothalamus or pituitary can lead to hypothyroidism, despite an intact thyroid gland.

## Management and Prognosis

Gradual replacement of thyroid hormone avoids precipitating physiological disturbances, especially heart failure in old patients, and psychological disturbances. Most patients with mental symptoms improve; however, a small proportion may have a residual impairment of intellectual functioning, especially in long-standing disease.

Patients with hypothyroidism have an increased sensitivity to central nervous system depressant drugs, such as morphine and phenothiazines, perhaps as a result of a reduction in metabolic degradation, leading to increased blood levels.

In cretinism, replacement therapy should be instituted at the earliest possible age in order to prevent or minimize the intellectual impairment that will result from the absence or deficiency of thyroid hormone, which is essential for normal brain development.

### Addison's Disease

Diminished functioning of the adrenal glands leading to decreased levels of circulating corticosteroids—aldosterone, cortisol, adrenal androgens—results in a clinical syndrome known as Addison's disease when it is due to primary adrenal insufficiency.

## Mental Manifestations

The development of Addison's disease is often insidious and slowly progressive. Significant changes in personality and behavior almost always occur early in its course. Apathy, fatigue, lack of initiative, depression, and poverty of thought may be evident. Often, the patient becomes seclusive and irritable as the disease progresses; in advanced stages, depressive mood and psychomotor retardation may be marked. Some patients develop mild organic mental disorders with recent memory deficits. Acute exacerbations of adrenal cortical insufficiency (Addisonian crises) may occur, during which an acute brain syndrome may develop, with hallucinations, delusions, and other signs of frank psychosis that may later proceed to stupor and coma. Hypotension may lead to shock and death. Overwhelming weakness, nausea, vomiting, abdominal pain, and apathy are early clinical manifestations of the Addisonian crisis.

## Physical Signs and Symptoms

Physical signs and symptoms of a deficiency of corticosteroids include weakness, fatigability, anorexia, weight loss, and hypotension. The skin may be diffusely pigmented. There is often perceptual dysfunction with a lowered threshold for smell, touch, and hearing, combined with difficulty in recognizing stimuli.

## Differential Diagnosis

In view of its insidious slow onset and the character of the symptoms, it is not surprising that Addison's disease is often misdiagnosed as depression, neurotic fatigue, hypochondriasis, neurasthenia, and chronic anxiety disorder, The combination of weakness, weight loss, anorexia, and hypotension should alert the physician to the possibility of Addison's disease.

## Etiology

In the past, the principal cause of adrenal insufficiency was tuberculosis. Now idiopathic atrophy is the most common cause; it may be an autoimmune disease.

## Management and Prognosis

Treatment consists of replacement therapy by adrenal steroids. The mental symptoms of Addison's disease respond quickly to cortisone. Brain functioning returns to normal with cortisone and other glucocorticoid therapy, whereas treatment with salt and mineral corticoids alone has no effect on the mental symptoms.

Patients with Addison's disease are particularly sensitive to narcotic agents, especially the barbiturates.

### Cushing's Syndrome

Cushing's syndrome results from a chronic excess of circulating cortisol.

## Mental Manifestations

Mental changes often precede the physical signs and symptoms. A wide variety of behavioral symptoms differ according to whether the origin of excess glucocorticoid is endogenous or exogenous. In the past, clinical descriptions of Cushing's disease often failed to distinguish between these two sources, resulting in a confusing variety of clinical descriptions.

Psychiatric difficulties are the presenting complaint in 40 to 50 percent of the patients with spontaneously occurring Cushing's syndrome, endogenous hypercortisolism. The most common problem is depression. The risk of suicide is high. The patient may complain of loss of libido, irritability, and insomnia. There may be brief episodes of disturbed behavior characterized by excitement, acute anxiety, and emotional lability. Memory deficits, especially loss of recent memory and difficulty in concentrating, may appear. Severe manifestations include a nonpsychotic organic mental disorder with confusion, and disorientation that may mimic other organic toxic or metabolic conditions. More rare is a psychotic organic mental disorder with paranoia and hallucinations that may be mistaken for schizophrenia.

Patients receiving exogenous corticosteroids often show alterations in their mental state. In 75 percent euphoria appears, often accompanied by increased appetite and libido. Depression occurs less often but may be severe. Acute toxic psychosis with organic features may develop.

## Physical Signs and Symptoms

Physical signs and symptoms of Cushing's syndrome may be evident later than the early mental symptoms, and can result in marked changes in appearance and function. Characteristic physical signs include increased appetite, truncal and facial obesity (moon facies), heightened facial color, and abdominal striae. The patient may suffer from increased susceptibility to infection, hypertension, osteoporosis, muscle wasting, fragile skin, weakness, and impaired glucose tolerance. The male patient may become impotent; in the female patient, the excess production of adrenal androgens may lead to amenorrhea, hirsutism, and acne. Most patients present with only some of the clinical features described.

## Pathophysiology

Laboratory data in Cushing's syndrome show hypercortisolemia, with loss of diurnal rhythm, increased urinary-free cortisol and 17-hydroxy-

corticosterone, and abnormal resistance to the suppressive influence of small doses of dexamethasone. The large-dose dexamethasone suppression test, along with clinical appraisal for neoplasm and measurement of plasma ACTH, may be necessary to differentiate among the varieties of Cushing's disease.

## Differential Diagnosis

Differential diagnosis must consider exogenous obesity, hepatic disease, and other syndromes related to individual symptoms, such as depression, with which Cushing's syndrome is commonly confused, particularly before physical signs appear.

## Etiology

Excess corticosteroids may be caused by adrenal hyperplasia secondary to hypothalamic dysfunction or an ACTH-secreting tumor, adrenal adenoma or carcinoma, or the exogenous administration of ACTH or glucocorticosteroids.

## Epidemiology

Cushing's syndrome occurs in all races, all ages, and both sexes. It is more common in women between the ages of 20 and 60 than in men.

## Management and Prognosis

Treatment of the underlying cause with a lowering of the levels of excess hormone leads to an improvement in the psychological status and is thus directed to the source of the difficulty; surgery or pituitary irradiation is used if necessary. When psychosis is secondary to exogenous cortisone or ACTH, the effect may be dose related, and the cerebral manifestations may clear when the dose is lowered. A patient may become psychotic on a dose that he can tolerate at another time. Prior mental disease is not a contraindication to steroid therapy. If a patient becomes psychotic, the dose should be lowered and the psychosis actively treated. There have been no reports of increased sensitivity to psychotropic medication.

## Hypopituitarism

### Mental Manifestations

Hypopituitarism can be caused by postpartum necrosis of the anterior pituitary (Sheehan's syndrome) or by other destructive lesions of anterior pituitary tissue, such as infections, head injuries, and tumors. Patients with hypopituitarism show clinical effects of target gland—adrenal, thyroidal, and gonadal—deficiencies. Almost all develop mental disturbances, profound apathy, indifference, inactivity, fatigue, drowsiness, loss of initiative, and depression. Cognitive deficit and delusions may develop. A dramatic loss of libido occurs in both men and women. The disease may progress to an Addisonian-type crisis, with hypothermia, hypertension, delirium, stupor, coma, and death.

### Physical Signs and Symptoms

The appearance of the skin is an early indicator of hypopituitarism. It may become waxy with myxedema; however, in contrast to what is seen in simple hypothyroidism, the skin may be finely wrinkled around the mouth and the eyes, giving a prematurely aged appearance. Pigmentation of the areolae of the breasts is lost, as is the capacity to tan in sunlight. These changes in pigmentation distinguish it from Addison's disease.

### Hypoandrogen Secretion In Men

Psychogenic influence on testicular function is not well understood. It has been observed that stress, such as from acute battle fatigue or officers' training, can decrease urinary secretion of testosterone. Decreased rate of beard growth has been correlated with sexual abstinence and increased rate of beard growth with expectation of sexual activity.

The male climacteric—a syndrome associated with actual androgen deficiency and displaying symptoms of vasomotor and emotional instability—is a rare syndrome that may occur in young men, as well as in old men. Diagnostic tests for gonadal function should be used to determine the degree of testicular deficiency. The male climacteric is not a normal part of the aging process; testosterone secretion is maintained at about the same level in almost all men until the sixth decade. The gradual and slow decline in male sexual vigor that begins to occur after the second decade represents normal maturation and aging of neural and gonadal structures involved in sexual behavior, rather than androgen deficiency. Testosterone therapy has been commonly and erroneously used as a treatment for impotence in men, but impotence is usually due to other factors, such as neurotic conflict—including fears of impotence—depression, fatigue, and poor health. Testosterone acts mainly as a placebo.

If exogenous androgen is given in excess, the side effects are insomnia, increased pressure of thought, and irritability.

### Disorders Associated with Female Endocrine Function

#### Menopausal Distress

Menopause is a natural physiological event. Menopause is usually defined as having occurred after an absence of menstrual periods for 1 year. Usually, menses taper off during a 2- to 5-year span, most often between the ages of 48 and 55; the median age is 51.4 years. Menopause also occurs immediately after surgical removal of the ovaries. The term involutional period refers to advancing age, and climacteric refers to involution of the ovaries.

**Clinical Description.** Many psychological symptoms have been attributed to the menopause, including anxiety, fatigue, tension, emotional lability, irritability, depression, dizziness, and insomnia. There is no general agreement on the relative contribution to those complaints of the psychological and social meanings of the menopause and this developmental era in a woman's life and the relative contribution of physiological changes.

Physical signs and symptoms include night sweats, flushes, and hot flashes. The hot flash is a sudden perception of heat within or on the body that may be accompanied by sweating or color change. The cause of the hot flash is unknown. It may be linked to pulsatile LH secretion. Estrogen-dependent functions are sequentially lost; atrophic changes in mucosal surfaces, accompanied by vaginitis, pruritus, dypareunia, and stenosis, may occur. Changes in calcium and lipid metabolism occur, probably as secondary effects to the lower levels of estrogen, and may be associated with a number of medical problems occurring in the postmenopausal era, such as osteoporosis and coronary atherosclerosis. The physical changes may begin as much as 4 to 8 years before the last menstrual period, often during a time of irregular menstrual periods with variation in menstrual interval and quantity and quality of menstrual flow.

**Hormonal Changes and Their Relation to Clinical Manifestations.** Blood levels of ovarian hormones decline gradually during the climacteric period, usually over a period of several years. For many years, decreasing estrogen levels were thought to be of primary importance in relation to the clinical manifestations of menopause. Both estrogen and progesterone bind directly to brain tissue and were thought to have direct action on brain function. More recently, other hormones, such as androgens and LH, are also considered to be involved. Effects of estrogen on mood may be indirectly moderated through its influence on androgen production. In any case, a significant role for changing hormonal levels is evidenced by the severe physical and psychological symptoms that follow abrupt (surgical) depletion of ovarian hormones. One difficulty in studies that have attempted to assess relationships of changing hormonal levels in the normal female is that the date of the last menstrual period is often difficult to establish, and as does the menarche, that date merely marks a point on a curve of changing hormonal function. Presence or absence of menstrual bleeding is not an exact measure of hormonal status.

The degree of symptomatology at the menopause seems to be related to the rate of hormone withdrawal; the amount of hormone depletion; a woman's constitutional ability to withstand the overall aging process, including her overall health and level of activity; and the psychological meaning of aging for her.

**Psychological and Psychosocial Factors.** Serious, clinically significant psychiatric difficulties may develop during the involutional phase of the life cycle. Women who have experienced prior psychological difficulties, such as low self-esteem and low life satisfaction, are likely to be vulnerable to difficulties during menopause. A woman's response to menopause has been noted to parallel her response to other crucial developmental events in her life, such as puberty and pregnancy. Attempts to link the severity of menopausal distress with the premenstrual tension syndrome have been inconclusive.

Women who have invested heavily in childbearing and child rearing activities are most likely to suffer distress during the postmenopausal years. Concerns about aging, loss of childbearing capacity, and changes in appearance all may be focused on the social and symbolic significance attached to the physical changes of the menopause.

Although in the past it was assumed that the incidence of mental illness and depression would be increased during the menopause, epidemiological evidence casts some doubt on this assumption as an all-inclusive and complete explanation. Epidemiological studies of mental illness showed no increase in symptoms of mental illness or in depression during the menopausal years, and studies of psychological complaints found no greater frequency in menopausal women than in younger women. Obviously, clinical and epidemiological studies vary in respect to such features as diagnostic criteria, sampling methods, and methods of data analysis.

**Treatment.** Treatment programs must be individualized. Postclimacteric women may be asymptomatic for estrogen deprivation or may manifest estrogen excess (dysfunctional uterine bleeding).

The use of estrogen replacement treatment is still controversial. For women with signs of estrogen depletion, recent studies have been more encouraging about the use of long-term combined estrogen and progesterone replacement therapy, both in estrogen depletion syndrome and as a preventive measure of osteoporosis. Topical estrogen cream used for treatment of mucosal atrophy is readily absorbed systematically. Increased risk of cancer, particularly endometrial cancer, has been implicated in use of exogenous estrogen, and the addition of a progestational agent to the replacement estrogen regime is thought to reduce this increased risk.

Exercise, diet, and symptomatic treatment all are helpful in reducing physical discomfort. Psychological distress should be evaluated and treated primarily by appropriate psychotherapeutic and sociotherapeutic measures.

Psychotherapy should include exploration of life stage and the meaning of aging and of reproduction to the patient. She should be encouraged to accept the menopause as a natural life event and to develop new activities, interests, and gratifications. Psychotherapy should also attend to family dynamics and enlist family and other social support systems when necessary.

### Premenstrual Syndrome

Women of childbearing age often are aware of cyclical subjective changes in mood and general sense of physical and psychological well-being correlated with their menstrual cycle.

The premenstrual syndrome (PMS) is composed of a variety of physical, psychological, and behavioral symptoms that may begin soon after ovulation, increase gradually, and reach a maximum of intensity about 5 days before the menstrual period. These symptoms also may intensify around the time of ovulation. The symptoms decline rapidly once menstruation starts, and a peak of well-being and positive feelings occurs during mid- and late-follicular phase. A symptom-free time between menstruation and ovulation helps to establish the diagnosis of PMS. The symptoms vary in severity from mild to incapacitating. Seventy to 90 percent of all women of childbearing age report at least some of these symptoms. Less than a third of these women alter their daily routine in terms of work absence, bed rest or seeing a doctor. The syndrome is rare in teenage girls and tends to in crease in severity with age, particularly in the thirties and forties, ending after the menopause. The syndrome continues in women with intact ovaries after hysterectomy.

It has not been established firmly whether these changes are psychologically or hormonally determined or whether they are a variant of a normal pattern or manifestations of an abnormal process.

**Mental Manifestations.** Mental manifestations include feelings of irritability and depression, emotional lability, anxiety, crying spells, and fatigue. Sensitivity and increased awareness of internal stimuli may contribute to these feelings. Some women experience several days of intense energy and euphoria, followed by lethargy. In the past, questions were raised about occurrence of cognitive changes. There may be a subjective sense of inability to concentrate and increased forgetfulness, but recent studies indicate that performance is not significantly impaired during the premenstrual and menstrual days.

The incidence of a variety of clinically serious behaviors and events—such as criminal acts, suicide attempts and psychiatric admissions—has been reported to increase during the premenstrual period, suggesting that concurrent psychological disorders may be exacerbated by the changes and discomforts of PMS.

**Physical Signs and Symptoms.** Physical signs and symptoms occurring during the premenstrual period include changes in appetite, with craving for sweets or chocolate—some women experience an increase in glucose tolerance—headache; breast engorgement; lower abdominal bloating (only a minority of women with PMS show true premenstrual weight gain and edema); gastrointestinal complaints, particularly constipation and increased sweating. Incidence and severity of physical manifestations vary and are not necessarily correlated with changes in affect.

**Etiology.** Psychological, social, and biological factors have been implicated in the pathogenesis of this syndrome. Estrogen excess, progesterone deficiency, vitamin deficency, hypoglycemia, and fluid retention have all been proposed to contribute to PMS.

Changes in levels of estrogen and progesterone, androgen, adrenal hormones (renin-angiotensin-aldosterone hypothesis), and prolactin have all been hypothesized to be important in the etiology of this syndrome. Recently, it has been proposed that excessive exposure to and subsequent abrupt withdrawal of endogeneous opiate peptides that fluctuate under the influence of gonadal steroids may contribute to PMS. An increase in prostaglandins secreted by the uterine musculature has also been implicated in accounting for the pain associated with PMS.

Explanations, such as difficulty in accepting femininity or learned patterns of disability, have been used to deny the existence of this syndrome. The term premenstrual tension by which the syndrome was known reflects this bias.

**Treatment.** The complaints of PMS, if severe, may be treated symptomatically. Water retention may be relieved by diet or antidiuretic medication. Severity of water retention does not always correlate with psychological symptoms.

Other drugs, including progesterone, lithium carbonate, thiazide diuretics, antidepressants, and antiprostaglandins, have been tried with uncertain success. It is helpful to many women to be made aware that premenstrual symptoms represent a recurring syndrome and can be anticipated. Psychotherapy may be helpful in individual cases.

### Idiopathic Amenorrhea

The cessation of normal menstrual cycles in nonpregnant, premenopausal women with no demonstrable structural abnormalities in brain, pituitary, or ovaries is termed idiopathic amenorrhea.

The diagnosis is made first by exclusion and then, if possible, by identification of primary psychogenic cause. Amenorrhea may occur as one feature of complex clinical psychiatric syndromes, such as anorexia nervosa and pseudocyesis. Other conditions associated with amenorrhea include massive obesity, diseases of the pituitary and hypothalamus, and in some cases, excessive amounts of running (jogging). Drugs such as reserpine and chlorpromazine can block ovulation and so delay menses. Drug-induced amenorrhea is almost always accompanied by galactorrhea and elevated levels of prolactin.

The patterns of hormone defect that result in psychogenic amenorrhea are not well understood.

Disturbed menstrual function with delayed or precipitate menses is a well-known response to stress in healthy women. The stress can be as minor as going away to college or as catastrophic as being put into a concentration camp.

In most women, menstrual cycling returns without medical intervention, sometimes even in continuing stressful conditions. Psychotherapy should be undertaken for psychological reasons, not just in response to the symptom of amenorrhea. However, if the amenorrhea has been protracted and refractory, psychotherapy may be helpful in restoring regular menses.

## Hypoparathyroidism-Hypocalcemia

### Mental Manifestations

A low level of serum calcium may lead to a variety of mental manifestations. The symptoms include emotional lability, irritability, anxiety, fatigue, depression, and, in severe cases, delirium, delusion, or psychosis. Intellectual impairment to the level of mental retardation has been reported, often in association with organic syndromes.

### Physical Signs and Symptoms

In long-standing calcium deficiency, skin changes may occur, including coarseness, scaliness, thin patchy hair, and atrophic or brittle nails.

Attacks of tetany, a common manifestation of hypocalcemia, may be preceded by complaints of muscular weakness, palpitation, and numbness and tingling of the extremities. Later, more classical signs, such as carpopedal spasm and athetoid movements, may appear. Unrelieved tetany may progress to laryngeal stridor and generalized convulsions.

### Differential Diagnosis

The signs and symptoms of hypocalcemia can mimic epilepsy, delirium tremens, brain tumor, and other psychiatric disturbances. Hypocalcemic states with psychiatric symptoms, and tetany due to hypoparathyroidism must be differentiated from hyperventilation syndrome, with its resultant respiratory alkalosis and tetany. In hyperventilation syndrome there is usually a history of similar attacks under stress. During an attack of hyperventilation, respiration is deep, sighing, and rapid. Pseudohypoparathyroidism—tissue unresponsive to parathyroid hormone—is another rare cause of hypocalcemia. Hypocalcemia may also occur as a result of vitamin D deficiency, either nutritional or secondary to malabsorption or renal failure.

### Etiology and Incidence

Surgical hypoparathyroidism damage, due to unintentional damage or loss of parathyroid tissue during a thyroidectomy, is the most common cause. The syndrome may also result from idiopathic hypoparathyroidism—a rare syndrome; only 200 cases have been reported in the literature since 1962. Most cases occur in children, more often in girls than in boys.

### Pathophysiology

Decreased levels of plasma-ionized calcium lead to increased neuromuscular excitability. Parathyroid hormone acts to maintain plasma calcium through the mobilization of calcium and phosphate from bone, the retention of calcium by the kidneys, and decreased calcium absorption from the bowel.

### Treatment

The objective of treatment is to raise and maintain the plasma calcium levels. Purified or synthetic parathyroid hormone is not available for replacement; therefore, therapy consists of vitamin D and oral calcium supplements. The major difficulty in maintenance is the prevention of hypercalcemic episodes.

## Hyperparathyroidism-Hypercalcemia

The symptoms of parathyroid hormone excess result from increased serum levels of calcium.

### Mental Manifestations

Early symptoms of hypercalcemia include poorly defined neurotic symptoms—determined by the patient's personality structure and adjustment—lack of initiative and spontaneity, and depression, sometimes associated with suicidal tendencies. In chronic hypercalcemia, loss of the ability to concentrate and short-term memory deficits develop. Those symptoms may be followed in severe cases by spells of unconsciousness and confusion, with an acute organic psychosis.

### Physical Signs and Symptoms

The patient may complain of renal colic pain, dull back pain, frequent urinary tract infections, vague skeletal pains, and nonspecific gastrointestinal dysfunction—anorexia, nausea, vomiting, constipation, and vague abdominal pains. Physical signs directly related to hypercalcemia include muscular weakness, electrocardiographic changes, and decrease in hearing acuity. There may be evidence of kidney stones and nephrocalcinosis with renal failure or signs associated with bone disease—decalcification with deformity.

### Differential Diagnosis

Hyperparathyroidism is a chronic disease that often begins gradually, manifesting itself by a wide variety of symptoms and signs and showing exacerbations and remissions. It is easily overlooked or confused with primary psychiatric disorders, including neurosis, hypochondriasis, affective disorders, and schizophrenia, However, once hyperparathyroidism has been considered, the diagnosis is relatively easy to make. A serum calcium level is a quick screening device. More specialized tests are available to distinguish the cause of the elevated calcium, including measurement of plasma immunoreactive parathyroid hormone levels.

### Etiology and Incidence

Hypercalcemia can be due either to a defect in the normal feedback control of parathyroid hormone secretion by the plasma calcium concentration, most often due to simple adenoma, or to a disruption in mineral homeostasis—such as in hypervitaminosis D, acute adrenal insufficiency, and neoplasm—leading to a compensatory increase in parathyroid gland function.

Parathyroid adenoma, the most common cause of parathyroid hyperfunction, is rare before puberty and is 2 to 3 times more common in women than in men. In some patients, a genetic factor is operative. Recently, there has been an increased frequency of the diagnosis as awareness of the disorder and the use of routine calcium measurements have become more widespread.

### Pathophysiology

Calcium level acts directly on nervous tissue, the level of calcium determining the alteration in mental function. When calcium blood level is returned to normal, mental abnormalities disappear.

### Management and Prognosis

The underlying disorder should be treated in order to lower the serum calcium level. Symptomatic improvement follows surgical removal of the malfunctioning parathyroid tissue. This surgical procedure is the only well-established treatment of hyperparathyroidism. After surgical excision of a single adenoma, the disease may recur. Therefore, continuing follow-up is of utmost importance.

### Hypoglycemia

Hypoglycemia results from a disturbance in glucose metabolism leading to a depressed plasma glucose concentration and a characteristic clinical syndrome that includes alterations in mental function. Glucose metabolism is regulated by a complex series of interactions between neural and hormonal factors, including insulin, catecholamines, growth hormone, glucocorticoids, and thyroid and gonadal hormones.

Hypoglycemia, like fever, is a symptom of an underlying disorder, rather than a disease.

### Clinical Description

At the onset of an acute attack, the patient may experience a variety of mental symptoms, including restlessness, headache, confusion, hunger, irritability, lightheadedness, and visual disturbances. These symptoms are accompanied or soon followed by signs of epinephrine release—anxiety, palpitation, tremor, pallor, tachycardia, and perspiration. If the attack is unrelieved, confusion may worsen and progress to disorientation and increased sensitivity to sensory stimuli. The patient then manifests signs of severe cortical disturbance—Babinski's sign, myoclonic spasms, ocular deviation, stupor, coma, and death. Prompt administration of glucose early in the attack alleviates the symptoms completely. If attacks have been severe, prolonged, and recurrent over a long period of time, brain damage may result and lead to long-term changes in personality, severe enough sometimes to resemble chronic schizophrenia, depression, or dementia.

### Etiology and Incidence

The commonest cause of hypoglycemia is overdosage of exogenous insulin in patients with diabetes. Functional (reactive) hypoglycemia may also occur spontaneously in otherwise healthy persons. In them, the attacks occur 2 to 4 hours after meals, when blood sugar drops to unusually low levels. Hypoglycemia may also occur in a large number of medical conditions, such as insulin-secreting $\beta$-cell tumors of the pancreas, early diabetes mellitus, postgastrectomy, a variety of endocrine disorders—such as adrenal, thyroid, or pituitary insufficiency—alcoholism, hereditary disorders of carbohydrate metabolism, and extensive liver damage. Alcoholism is an extremely important cause.

It has become fashionable of late to ascribe many mental signs and symptoms to hypoglycemia; but, in fact, this condition is extremely rare and uncommon.

### Differential Diagnosis

Hypoglycemia is easy to misdiagnose and may be confused with a number of psychiatric disorders—in mild cases with anxiety disorders and in severe chronic cases with dementias and depressive or schizophrenic psychoses.

During the acute attack, the level of blood glucose is usually in a diagnostically low range or has fallen precipitously, and administration of glucose intravenously results in prompt recovery. This combination is diagnostic of the condition.

## Pathophysiology

Cortical depression occurs when blood glucose falls. Epinephrine release follows, producing many of the symptoms of an acute attack. A series of changes in functioning occurs, based on the absolute level of blood glucose; symptoms of hypoglycemia usually appear when plasma glucose levels fall below 55 mg per 100 ml.

## Management and Prognosis

Acute episodes of hypoglycemia are treated with glucose, which should completely alleviate the symptoms in the early stages. In chronic hypoglycemia or after a prolonged episode, complete recovery of mental functioning may not occur. The underlying cause of hypoglycemia should then be determined and treated appropriately—for example, by diet, medication, or surgery. Dietary manipulation is the treatment of choice for functional hypoglycemia.

Monoamine oxidase inhibitors probably should not be used in patients with functional (reactive) hypoglycemia, since these drugs lower blood glucose in some diabetic patients and in some persons with normal glucose metabolism.

## Diabetes Mellitus

Diabetes mellitus is a disorder both of metabolism and of the vascular system. Usually believed to involve a genetic predisposition, it manifests itself in disturbances of glucose, lipid, and protein metabolism—presumed to be caused by an absolute or relative functional insufficiency of insulin—and in a variety of serious primarily microarterial vascular lesions, and in accelerated atherosclerosis.

## Clinical Features

Patients with the full manifest disease present a characteristic complex of cardinal symptoms—polydipsia, polyuria, and polyphagia combined with weight loss. In childhood, the disease may be manifest initially by episodes of diabetic acidosis with ketosis and coma. In adult-onset diabetes, prodromal and early symptoms—such as fatigue, lassitude, impotence, and paresthesias—may be incorrectly ascribed to depression or neurosis.

## Differential Diagnosis

Since the diabetic patient may be unconscious when first seen by the physician—for example, in an episode of diabetic acidosis with coma or exogenously induced hypoglycemia—there may be a need to differentiate between diabetic acidosis and (1) psychologically determined unresponsiveness, such as catatonia or hysterical stupor; (2) hypoglycemia; and (3) hyperventilation syndrome.

The most critical and decisive test to be done immediately is to withdraw blood for laboratory tests, including glucose and electrolytes, and inject 50 ml of 50 percent glucose solution intravenously while the venipuncture needle is still in place. This procedure should produce a prompt reversal of the unresponsive state in the patient with hypoglycemia and do no harm to any of the other patients.

## Epidemiology

Diabetes is one of the most common of the chronic diseases. It is thought to affect about 5 percent of the total population, although its exact prevalence and incidence are not known. It is estimated that there are about 200,000 new cases a year in the United States.

## Etiology and Pathogenesis

Although no evidence supports the idea that psychological factors play a specific role in proximal cause of diabetes mellitus, it seems clear that emotional stress may participate in precipitating diabetes or in exacerbating its course by activating the same physiological mechanisms through which other stresses—such as infection, obesity, trauma, and fever—influence the course. These mechanisms include autonomic nervous system pathways, psychoneuroendocrine mechanisms, and direct vagal influences on the pancreas.

Clinical studies have suggested that emotional conflict may exacerbate the clinical course, and psychophysiological studies demonstrated changes in metabolic indices in the direction of ketosis after stress interviews. The exact physiological mechanisms underlying such phenomena have not, however, been demonstrated.

## Somatopsychic and Indirect Influences

Having diabetes constitutes a formidable psychological stress that may exceed the patient's adaptive and coping capacities. This is particularly true of those with juvenile or adolescent onset, in many of whom the metabolic disorder is subject to wide fluctuations (brittle diabetes), thus rendering dietary and medication requirements particularly rigid. These requirements exaggerate the patient's differences from his peer group and render coping very difficult. And, at times of life crises—such as object loss, bereavement, and depression—the diabetic patient has readily available two covert ways, manipulating diet and manipulating insulin, of wittingly or unwittingly acting out suicidal impulses by inducing diabetic acidosis or profound hypoglycemia.

## Treatment

In more difficult situations, psychiatric consultation or treatment—individual, group, or family—may be advisable. Antidepressants—tricyclics or monoamine oxidase inhibitors—may lower blood glucose in patients with diabetes, but they can be used if the physician keeps this effect in mind.

Neuroleptic medication can induce hyperglycemia in controlled diabetes, but should be used if needed to control a psychosis.

## REFERENCES

Martin J B, Reichlin S, Brown G: *Clinical Neuroendocrinology.* F. A. Davis, Philadelphia, 1977.
Reichlin S: Neuroendocrinology. In *Textbook of Endocrinology,* ed 6, R H Williams, editor, p 589. W. B. Saunders, Philadelphia, 1981.
Reid R L. Premenstrual syndrome: A therapeutic enigma. Drug Ther *12:* 33, 1982.
Reiser M F: Changing theoretical concepts in psychosomatic medicine. In *American Handbook of Psychiatry,* M F Reiser, editor, vol 4, p 491. Basic Books, New York, 1975.
Reiser L W, Reiser M F: Endocrine disorders. In *Comprehensive Textbook of Psychiatry,* ed 4, H I Kaplan, B J Sadock, editors, p 1167. Williams & Wilkins, Baltimore, 1985.
Rose R, Sachar E: Psychoendocrinology. In *Textbook of Endocrinology,* ed 6, R H Williams, editor, p 647. W. B. Saunders, Phiadelphia, 1981.
Sachar E J, editor: *Hormones, Behavior, and Psychopathology.* Raven Press, New York, 1976.
Speroff L, Glass R, Kase N: *Clinical Gynecologic Endocrinology and Infertility.* Williams & Wilkins, Baltimore, 1983.
Swigar M E, Naftolin F, DeCherney A H: Psychogenic factors in amenorrhea. In *The Gonadotropins: Basic Science in Clinical Aspects in Females,* C Flamigni, J R Givens, editors, p 259. Academic Press, New York, 1982.
Weiner H: *The Psychobiology of Human Disease.* Elsevier/North Holland, New York, 1977.

# 22.8 SKIN DISORDERS

## Introduction

Psychosomatic skin disorders focus on abnormal skin sensations and skin manifestations emphasizing the relevance of emotional factors to causation, precipitation, and aggravation of skin disease.

## Abnormal Cutaneous Sensations

### Generalized Pruritus

It has been shown that itch, tickle, and pain are all conveyed by the same afferent fibers and are differentiated only by the frequency of impulse.

The itching dermatoses are scabies, pediculosis, bites of insects, urticaria, atopic dermatitis, contact dermatitis, lichen rubor planus, and miliaria among others. Internal disorders that frequently cause itching are diabetes mellitus, nephritis, diseases of the liver, gout, diseases of the thyroid gland, food allergies, Hodgkin's disease, leukemia, and cancer. Itching can also occur during pregnancy and senility.

The term generalized psychogenic pruritus denotes that no organic cause for the itching exists or, at least, no longer exists, and that on psychiatric examination, emotional conflicts have been established that convincingly account for its occurrence.

Individual differences as to the precipitation threshold for skin responses have been demonstrated. Anxious and tense persons, or normally well-adjusted persons at times of anxiety and tension, may be more conscious than usual of itching sensations from a given lesion. Guilt, anger, boredom, irritation, and sexual arousal may all predispose the person to itching and subsequent scratching. Experimental manipulation of the itch threshold with psychic stress has been demonstrated.

The emotions that most frequently lead to generalized psychogenic pruritus are repressed anger and repressed anxiety. An almost irresistible urge to scratch oneself results from the itching impulse. Whenever persons consciously or preconsciously experience anger or anxiety, they scratch themselves, often violently. An inordinate need for affection is a common characteristic of these patients. Frustrations of this need elicit aggressiveness that is inhibited. The rubbing of the skin provides a substitute gratification of the frustrated need, and the scratching represents aggression turned against the self.

### Localized Pruritus

**Pruritus Ani.** The investigation of this disorder commonly yields a history of local irritation—thread worms, irritant discharge, fungal infection—or general systemic factors, such as nutritional deficiencies and drug intoxication. However, after running a conventional course, it often fails to respond to therapeutic measures and acquires a life of its own, apparently perpetuated by scratching and superimposed inflammation. It is a distressing complaint that often interferes with work and social activity. Careful investigation of large numbers of these patients has revealed that personality deviations often precede this condition, and that emotional disturbances often precipitate and maintain it.

**Pruritus Vulvae.** As in pruritus ani, specific physical causes, either localized or generalized, may be demonstrable in pruritus vulvae, and the presence of glaring psychopathology in no way lessens the need for adequate medical investigation. In some patients, pleasure derived from rubbing and scratching is quite conscious—they realize that it is a form of masturbation—but more often than not the pleasure element is repressed. Most of the patients studied gave a long history of sexual frustration, which was frequently intensified at the time of the onset of pruritus.

## Abnormal Cutaneous Manifestations
### Hyperhidrosis

States of fear, rage, and tension can induce an increase of sweat secretion. It has been demonstrated that perspiration in the human is of two distinct forms, thermal and emotional. Emotional sweating appears primarily on the palms, soles, and axillae; thermal sweating is most evident on the forehead, neck, trunk, and dorsum of hand and forearm. The sensitivity of the emotional sweating response serves as the basis for the measurement of sweat by the galvanic skin response (an important tool of psychosomatic research), biofeedback, and the polygraph (lie detector test).

Excessive sweating (hyperhidrosis) may, under conditions of prolonged emotional stress, lead to secondary skin changes, rashes, blisters, and infections, and may thereby underlie a number of other dermatological conditions that are not primarily related to emotions. Basically, hyperhidrosis may be viewed as an anxiety phenomenon mediated by the autonomic nervous system; it must be differentiated from drug-induced states of hyperhidosis.

### Rosacea

This condition is more common in women than in men and usually occurs in the thirties and forties. It features an increased vascularity with papule formation on the blush area of the face and upper chest. Sufferers from rosacea display a heightened vascular responsiveness not only to heat but also to hot drinks, spiced food, hurried meals, and a variety of emotions.

### Urticaria

Many physical, chemical, and biological factors have been incriminated as causative of urticarial eruptions. In acute cases, an allergic basis is often established with some degree of conviction, but in subacute, chronic, and recurrent cases, the most careful examination often fails to elicit an allergic cause. Most dermatologists agree that emotional factors are of enormous relevance to the cause of urticaria.

### Atopic Dermatitis

Of the many diseases in the eczema dermatitis group, atopic dermatitis has long been regarded as the one most strongly influenced by emotional conflict. It is usually accompanied by itching that often appears disproportionate in severity to the visible lesions. Some authors have considered the itching to be primary and the skin lesions a reaction to scratching. For this reason, it is often called neurodermatitis.

This condition is found in both a childhood form and an adult form, both frequently appearing in the same person, with an intervening period of several years. The term atopic signifies that it is regarded as an allergic disorder, but the specific interrelationship of allergic and emotional factors is far from clear.

### Dermatitis Artefacta

Dermatitis artefacta, a disorder easily recognizable by dermatologists, is caused by its sufferers through scratching, usually during sleep at night. Areas affected are commonly the hand, the abdomen, the legs, and sometimes the face.

Analogous conflicts exist in trichotillomania, a compulsive pulling of the hair.

### Psoriasis

Psoriasis is a fairly common disease, affecting about 1.5 percent of the population. This disorder affects all ages and shows a marked fluctuation in severity both from patient to patient, and in the same patient at different periods of time.

Genetic studies have suggested a genetically determined mode of inheritance (recessive), but the primary cause of psoriasis is not known, although a number of aggravating factors have been well established. These factors include systemic infection, an excess or deficiency of sunlight, damp or cold, and emotional stress. Among other factors, emotional upsets may cause psoriasis. Several studies have found that roughly half of the patients observed were emotionally maladjusted; yet a great variety of emotional disorders were recorded. There is no uniformity of personality type or specific conflict constellation. Investigators agree that any severe emotional disturbance may have a precipitating or aggravating effect.

## Alopecia Areata

This disorder has frequently been described by dermatologists as a condition in which the emotional factor plays an important role. A psychodynamic constellation that characterizes the onset in young children with alopecia areata has been described. Characteristic features are (1) symbiotic loss at an early age (a traumatic weaning for example); (2) subsequent management of the loss; and (3) a precipitating event, such as a real or threatened abandonment or the birth of a sibling, leading to the collapse of the management system, precipitating extensive hair loss.

Alopecia areata in adults, especially in women, is frequently associated with severe psychic stress and is often cyclic in nature.

## Acne Vulgaris

Some degree of acne vulgaris is so common at puberty that it may be regarded as a physiological accompaniment. Acne may occur in either sex at puberty if an androgen-estrogen imbalance develops toward a preponderance of androgen.

Various factors predispose to acne formation: the insufficient use of soap and water encourages the accumulation of sebaceous and horny plugs, and the use of greasy cosmetics can cause folliculitis. Acne is often aggravated by a diet rich in fats and carbohydrates, and it is often worse just before and during menstruation.

No claim can be made that acne vulgaris can be explained on psychological grounds alone. But the hypothesis may be submitted that not only the physiological process of maturation but also the emotional disturbances connected with puberty are relevant to its common onset at this period of life, and that retardation of emotional and psychosexual developments is related to its onset and to its persistence beyond the span of life usually allotted to puberty.

## Psychogenic Purpura

The condition is characterized by episodes of painful spontaneous bruising of a particular sort. A sudden pain, usually of some severity, draws the patient's attention to some part of the skin surface; thereupon a lump appears, soon becomes erythematous, and thereafter shows a characteristic ecchymotic change. This last phase lasts a week or longer. The pain is frequently disabling. The patient otherwise experiences normal bruising susceptibility.

This condition was originally described exclusively in female patients, but cases in male patients have been reported.

## Psychiatric Treatment

Psychiatrists are frequently consulted by family physicians and dermatologists on the management of cases in which an emotional factor is suspected. In many cases in which a good relationship exists between the primary physician and the patient, and in cases in which external circumstances, precarious defensive structure, or questionable ego strengths impose limits, the optimal psychiatric role is a return of the patient to the referring physician with a brief, simply stated outline of the basic psychiatric features and guidelines for supportive and directive management.

The relevant issues here may be related both to the psychologial factors influencing the onset and the course of the skin disorders and—in the case of severe, poorly remitting skin conditions—to the devastating effects on the patient and his family of a chronic disabling disease state.

### REFERENCES

Bär L H J, Kuypers B R H: Behavior therapy in dermatological practice. Br J Dermatol 88: 591, 1973.

Engels W D: Dermatologic disorders: Psychosomatic illness review. Psychosomatics 23: 1209, 1983.

Engels W D: Skin disorders. In Comprehensive Textbook of Psychiatry, ed 4, H I Kaplan, B J Sadock, editors, p 1178. Williams & Wilkins, Baltimore, 1985.

Friedman S: A psychophysiological model for the chemotherapy of psychosomatic illness. J Nerv Ment Dis 166: 349, 1978.

Lefebvre P, Leroux R, Crombez J C: Object relations in the dermatologic patient: A contribution to the psychoanalytic theory of psychosomatic disorder. Psychiatr J Univ Ottawa 5: 17, 1980.

Musaph H: Itching and Scratching: Psychodynamics in Dermatology. F. A. Davis, Philadelphia, 1964.

Whitlock F A: Psychophysiological Aspects of Skin Disease. W. B. Saunders, London, 1976.

Wittkower E D, Russell B: Emotional Factors in Skin Disease. Hoeber, New York, 1953.

# 22.9 RHEUMATOID ARTHRITIS

## Introduction

Rheumatoid arthritis is a systemic disorder whose cause is still unknown. Although the prime symptoms and the inflammatory changes are characteristically found in articular and associated structures, there are also a number of extraarticular signs and symptoms.

The term rheumatism comes from the Greek word *rheuma*, which means flowing. The early Greek physicians believed that the joint manifestations were due to a movement of rheum, a humor, into the joints.

## Epidemiology

The syndrome is more common in women than in men, with a ratio of nearly three to one, and for both sexes there is a rise in incidence with increasing age. No difference was found in the incidence between whites and blacks.

Perhaps of significance is the suggestion that, among men in the United States, rheumatoid arthritis has a higher incidence in the married than in the unmarried, whereas among women the incidence is higher in those who have been divorced and in those married women with several children, as opposed to those who have no children.

The disease may begin at any time from infancy through the ninth decade. In the United States, the onset of the disease is most often in the fourth decade.

In about 20 percent of all cases, the onset of the illness is characterized by high fever for several weeks, followed by a return of the patient's temperature to normal or subnormal levels. Most young patients with this type of onset also have a characteristic rash, which can appear anywhere on the body. The rash appears most often during the febrile periods. Iridocyclitis is a complication but in the 50 percent of all cases that begin with a low-grade fever and a polyarticular involvement there is rarely any evidence of eye involvement. However, of the 40 percent of all cases with an onset affecting few joints, about half proceed to acute and chronic iridocyclitis.

## Etiology and Pathogenesis

There may be a genetic predisposition toward immunological abnormalities that is a necessary substrate for the disease. If there is a genetic substrate, it could lead to manifest disease through environmental factors. Some of these environmental factors may prove to be psychological in nature. Thus, psychological factors may lead to the precipitation of the disease and to its exacerbations.

### Immunological Factors

Although the exact role of immunological factors in the causation and continuation of rheumatoid arthritis is still unclear, it seems reasonably certain that immune mechanisms are important, even if they are not fully understood. Present theories suggest that an as yet unidentified antigen stimulates antibody production by the plasma cells in the synovium. The resulting antigen-antibody complexes somehow lead to the alteration of the antibody, so that it is no longer regarded as "self" by the body. The alienated antibody stimulates the production of the rheumatoid factor. The newly formed complex may also fix complement, leading to phagocytosis and the release of lysosomes, which results in tissue damage and inflammation.

### Life Events

A number of investigators have theorized or demonstrated that changes in the psychological and social milieu are important as antecedents of a variety of illnesses. For example, although rheumatoid arthritis may tend to develop in a person with particular identifiable personality traits, the illness tends to develop in the context of stresses associated with life events that are demanding and restricting.

Investigators have suggested that there may be three groups of rheumatoid arthritic patients: those with an illness of acute onset, associated with significant life stress factors and no hereditary predisposition, and two groups of those with an illness of slow onset, with little relationship to conflict situations and a relatively stronger hereditary predisposition. In the slow onset group, the illness develops in two types of patients: those with previous psychiatric disorders associated with and leading to difficult life stress problems and more or less chronic depression; and those patients with exceptionally heavy genetic backgrounds for the disease, especially those patients in whom the disease leads to depressive reactions with poor motivation for rehabilitation—that is, a passive, helpless attitude leading to severe functional disability.

### Psychoimmunological Relationships

Some authors have suggested that stress predisposes patients to the so-called autoimmune disorders by leading to alterations in immunological reactivity. In support of this hypothesis is the finding of increased 19 S protein in stressed prison populations, and reported increased levels of certain types of immunoglobulins in psychiatric patients.

### Psychosocial Findings

Researchers found that women with rheumatoid arthritis tended to come from homes in which there were high discrepancies in social status indicators between the mother and the father. They tended to recall their mothers as being arbitrary, severe, unreasonable, and controlling. Further, their reaction to their mothers was a high degree of covert anger but very little overt aggression and resistance. Nevertheless, in spite of their recollections of their mothers in that negative way, the rheumatoid arthritic women chose them as role models as often as did women without rheumatoid arthritis. Recollections of the father and reactions to the father showed no differences between the arthritics and the nonarthritics. In their current personality functioning, the rheumatoid arthritic women showed a continuation of conflicts over the expression of aggressive impulses. They revealed a high level of anger but wished to control it, and their guilt about expressing it was found to be as strong as in women without rheumatoid arthritis. On a variety of measures of poor mental health, the rheumatoid arthritic women reported a greater number of symptoms than did the nonarthritic women. The arthritic women's marriages were characterized by high discrepancies between their own and their husbands' status variables; they showed high status stress, and they tended to be married to men whose own status variables were incongruent. The rheumatoid arthritic women and their husbands expressed a great deal of anger and aggression toward one another. Husbands of the rheumatoid arthritic women were also found to be more likely to have peptic ulcers than the general population.

The men with rheumatoid arthritis did not reveal the same attitudes toward their mothers as did the rheumatoid arthritic women. Like the women, the men reported more symptoms of poor mental health than did nonarthritic men, but, in contrast to the women, the arthritic men were found to be low on anger and aggression. Because their wives were equally low on this factor, the marriages of the rheumatoid arthritic men and healthy women were low on marital hostility, in contrast to the marriages of rheumatoid arthritic women and healthy men.

## Clinical Features

In some cases the illness begins suddenly, with high fever, extensive polyarticular inflammation, and the rapid development of severe deformities. Usually, however, the onset is slower, with minimal to moderate discomfort and only the gradual development of minimal deformities. Psychological and genetic factors may differ in these differing onsets.

The disease frequently begins with systemic symptoms, such as fatigue, weight loss due to anorexia, and occasional fever. Later, fleeting or more long-lasting pain develops in joints and the muscles near them. Early-morning joint stiffness is a particularly frequent complaint. The joints most often attacked are the knees and the joints in the hands and feet in a sym-

metrical manner. Once attacked, a joint tends to remain involved for long periods of time, and other joints are gradually added to the progressive disability. Tenosynovitis is quite common. A variety of joint deformities occur, caused by the joint disease itself, by a shortening of tendons, or by the muscle imbalance associated with splinting or myositis. Ulnar deviation of the fingers is frequently noted.

## Prognosis

Of the patients who have the symptoms of the illness for less than a year, about 75 percent improve, and as many as 20 percent have a complete remission; the physician in his early interactions with the patient can afford to be cautiously optimistic. Factors related to a poor prognosis in respect to joint function include disease that persists longer than a year in a patient below the age of 30, disease that is sustained rather than evanescent, the presence of subcutaneous nodules, and high titers of the rheumatoid factor. However, even in these cases, observations extending for 15 years reveal that up to 70 percent of all patients remain capable of full employment. In fact, even after about 20 years, the completely incapacitated group consists only of about 15 percent of the patients with the illness.

## Treatment

In considering treatment, the physician should examine more than which drug or which procedure to use. He or she should also consider the patient's entire life situation, habits, hobbies, behaviors, relationships, and personal aspirations.

## Psychotherapy

Any evidence of emotional distress should be met by some attempt to reconstitute healthy personality functioning. The physician should be alert to the kinds of life stresses that may influence exacerbations. Life events of particular significance, such as separation and the loss of loved objects, are particularly important. Psychotherapy is valuable in the management of certain patients with rheumatoid arthritis. One valuable aspect of psychotherapy is its provison of a structured, predictable, and dependable interpersonal relationship. Hypnosis may be useful in cases of rheumatoid arthritis as an aid in muscle relaxation and the control of pain. Psychoanalytically oriented psychotherapy in selected cases can be particularly helpful, especially in understanding the specific idiosyncratic conflicts and psychosomatic solutions of individual patients.

## REFERENCES

Gilliland B C, Mannik M: Rheumatoid arthritis. In *Harrison's Principles of Internal Medicine*, ed 10, R G Petersdorf, R D Adams, E Braunwald, K J Isselbacher, J B Martin, J D Wilson, editors, p 1977. McGraw Hill, New York, 1983.

Hunder G G, Bunch T W: Treatment of rheumatoid arthritis. Bull Rheum Dis *32*(1): 1, 1982.

Kirkpatrick C J, Mohr W, Haferkamp O: Prostaglandins and their precursors in rheumatoid arthritis: Progress and problems. Z Rheumatol *41*(3): 39, 1982.

Laudenslager M L, Ryan S M, Drugan R C, Hyson R L, Maier S F: Coping and immunosuppression. Science *221:* 568, 1983.

Samuelsson B: Leukotrienes: Mediators of immediate hypersensitivity reactions and inflammation. Science *220:* 568, 1983.

Silverman A J: Rheumatoid arthritis. In *Comprehensive Textbook of Psychiatry*, ed 4, H I Kaplan, B J Sadock, editors, p 1185. Williams & Wilkins, Baltimore, 1985.

Solinger A M, Hess E V: The role of collagens in rheumatic diseases. J Rheumatol *9:* 491, 1982.

Solomon G F: Emotional and personality factors in the onset and course of autoimmune disease, particularly rheumatoid arthritis. In *Psychoneuroimmunology*, R Ader, editor, p 159. Academic Press, New York, 1981.

Tan E M: Antinuclear antibodies in diagnosis and management. Hosp Pract *18*(1): 79, 1983.

---

# 22.10 HEADACHES

## Introduction

Headaches are the most common neurological symptom, and one of the most common of all medical complaints. Every year about 80 percent of the population is estimated to suffer from at least one headache, and 10 to 20 percent of the population presents to a physician with headache as their primary complaint. Headaches also are a major cause or excuse given for absenteeism from work or avoidance of other undesired social or personal activities.

The majority of headaches are not associated with significant organic disease. Many individuals have a susceptibility to headaches at times of emotional stress. In fact, many psychiatric disorders, including anxiety and depressive disorders, frequently present with headaches as a prominent symptom. Headache patients are frequently referred to psychiatrists by primary care physicians and neurologists after extensive biomedical work-ups, often including a CT scan of the head. The majority of such work-ups for common headache complaints are negative and negative results after a lengthy search for a cause of the headache may be frustrating for both patient and physician. The psychologically unsophisticated physician may attempt to reassure the patient by telling him there is no disease process. This may often have the opposite of the desired effect, increasing the patient's anxiety and even escalating into a disagreement about whether the pain is real or imagined.

Psychological stresses usually worsen headaches, whether their primary underlying cause is physical or psychological. Psychosomatic headaches are sometimes differentiated from psychogenic (e.g. anxiety, depression, hypochondriacal, delusional) headaches. For example, headaches may be a conversion symptom in patients with hysterical or other types of personality traits. In these patients the headache is symbolically expressing unconscious psychological conflicts and the symptoms are mediated through the voluntary sensorimotor nervous system. In contrast, psychosomatic headaches are defined as autonomic responses to conscious or unconscious conflicts, and are not symbolic in nature. This distinction is important for psychiatrists to make to reach the proper diagnosis, which then allows the most specific treatment to be recommended.

## Evaluation

A large number of biomedical illnesses may cause headaches (see Table I), and these should be considered for all chronic headache patients.

A careful drug history, including prescription and nonprescription drugs, should be elicited. While they are often a result of alcohol, nicotine, and caffeine abuse, headaches are also a frequent side effect of several classes of prescribed medications, including tricyclic antidepressants, monoamine oxidase inhibitors, antiarrhythmics, insulin, several anti-inflammatories (e.g., phenylbutazone, indomethacin), and rarely in recent years, bromides. In evaluating a headache, also determine the exact location; to some, headache may mean any place from the neck up. Is it localized to the eye, ear, back of throat, etc.? Is the quality steady, throbbing, rhythmic, etc.? Does the quantity of discomfort allow the patient to go about his daily activities or lead to incapacitation and restriction to bed? What is the time sequence and progression of symptoms? What are the settings, and time of week or month, in which it tends to occur? What factors make it better or worse? Are there associated symptoms (e.g., dizziness, nausea)? What is the meaning and effect of the symptoms in terms of the patient's job and personal life?

TABLE I
CLASSIFICATION OF HEADACHES

| |
|---|
| Vascular headache (migraine type): |
|     Classic or common migraine |
|     Hemiplegic or ophthalmoplegic migraine |
|     Cluster headache |
|     Lower-half headache |
| Nonmigrainous vascular headache |
| Muscle contraction (tension) headache |
| Combined vascular-muscle contraction headache |
| Nasal vasomotor reaction headache |
| Psychogenic headaches: depression, hypochondriasis, conversion, psychotic (delusional) |
| Traction headache |
| Secondary to cranial inflammation |
| Secondary to disease of other cranial or neck structures: dental, ocular, aural, nasal, sinuses |
| Cranial neuritides or neuralgias |

What secondary gains result? Have family members or someone else the patient knows had similar headaches?

### Psychogenic Headaches

Chronic anxiety and depressive syndromes often result in muscular contraction (tension) headaches. However, headaches are also a common complaint selected by patients with hypochondriasis. Since it is virtually impossible to rule out all potential biomedical causes of headaches, to observe the tissue damage, or objectively quantify the pain, chronic headaches meet the psychological needs that an illness must fulfill for these patients: impossible to disprove, requiring regular reevaluation, and ensuring an ongoing doctor-patient relationship. Often numerous analgesic prescriptions are sought by the patient as a way of proving they are really sick and ensuring ongoing care and followup.

In patients in whom headaches are felt to be due to a conversion disorder, a careful history may reveal recurrent episodes occurring in specific types of situations, especially sexual situations or threatened separations. The head is often selected as the symbolic organ of choice for symptom expression when unconscious conflicts exist concerning intelligence, emotional maturity and adequacy, and psychological problems per se.

Schizophrenics may develop bizarre delusions concerning their brain, psychotic depressives may be convinced their brain is rotting or infected, and demented or delirious patients often are convinced someone is poisoning them with a toxin that causes headaches and brain dysfunction.

### Vascular (Migraine) Headaches

Vascular headaches often are precipitated by emotional conflicts or psychological stress. Some degree of vascular headaches may develop in about 15 to 20 percent of men and 20 to 30 percent of women in response to emotional stress. Two-thirds of those developing migraines have a family history of similar disorders. Although the presence of psychological triggers are universally accepted, evidence for specific personality types and unconscious conflict constellations is unconvincing. Obsessional personalities who are overly controlled, perfectionistic, and who suppress anger may be at risk for numerous stress-related disorders.

Although sometimes developing in childhood, most vascular headaches come to clinical attention between puberty and middle age. Fluctuating estrogen levels, including secondary to birth control pills, greatly increase the risk and probably account for the increased incidence of migraines in females, especially premenstrually. Susceptible individuals may also have attacks triggered by several types of food, including: monosodium glutamate (Chinese restaurant headache syndrome), tyramine-containing foods, and chocolate or other phenylethylamine-containing foods.

Common migraines generally have intense pain that is either one-sided or bilateral and in the temporal or frontal areas. They most commonly begin in the morning or on weekends and are associated with nausea and vomiting, photophobia, red and tearing eyes, moodiness and irritability. Initially the pain is more often unilateral and throbbing but later it becomes more constant and generalized. The duration of most migraines is a few hours to a few days and the frequency is usually 1 to 3 per month, depending upon the presence and intensity of precipitating factors.

Only about 30 percent of vascular headaches are classic migraines. Classic migraines are like common migraines except that they are associated with classic prodromata. The prodromata are most often visual (e.g., flashing lights in a peripheral visual field), other neurological symptoms (e.g., paresthesias, weakness), or a sudden mood disturbance (e.g., sense of dysphoria and strangeness).

Although the exact cause of migraines is not known, they are probably due to disturbances in functioning of the vasomotor centers of the cerebral cortex. The vessels in a branch of the internal carotid artery constrict, leading to ischemia, which may cause the prodromata in classic migraines. External carotid arteries later dilate causing edema, swelling, and tenderness around the artery and the typical throbbing headache. Although migraines tend to be unilateral, if the headache is always on the same side the risk of an underlying arteriovenous malformation or aneurysm is slightly increased.

Migraines are most effectively treated during the prodromal phase by prompt administration of ergotamine tartrate concomitant with analgesics. Prophylactic administration of propranolol phenytoin is recommended if headaches are frequent. Estrogens, including birth control pills, should be immediately discontinued since a higher incidence of permanent neurological deficit (stroke) is present in migraine patients on birth control pills. Methysergide maleate may also be quite effective prophylactically but should be used with caution, and for only as long as absolutely necessary, due to possible side effects including retroperitoneal fibrosis, endocardial lesions, and hematologic toxicity.

## Cluster Headaches

As their name implies, these headaches tend to occur in clusters of one or more daily for a period of several weeks. They are relatively short in duration (i.e., usually 20 minutes to 2 hours), unilateral, almost always occurs on the same side, and are without prodromata. Severe, boring, piercing pain usually occurs in the orbital or forehead areas and may be associated with nasal congestion, tears, and a partial Horner's syndrome (i.e., miosis and ptosis). Patients are often euphoric after an episode. Cluster headaches which may begin just after falling asleep are much more common in males and are often precipitated by alcohol ingestion. Increased serum histamine levels are associated with exacerbations. Prophylactic use of methysergide, propranolol, prednisone, and lithium carbonate has been recommended, but none seem clearly beneficial. Due to the recurrent nature of these painful attacks, the use of opiate analgesics is especially risky because narcotic addiction may result.

## Tension (Muscle Contraction) Headaches

Emotional stress is often associated with prolonged contraction of head and neck muscles, which over several hours may cause constriction of the blood vessels and result in ischemia. A dull, aching pain often begins suboccipitally and may spread over the head, sometimes feeling like a tightening band. The scalp may be tender to the touch and, in contrast to migraines, the headache is usually bilateral and not associated with prodromata, nausea and vomiting. The onset is often toward the end of the work day or in early evening, possibly after the individual has gotten away from stressful job pressures, begun to try to relax, and focused more on somatic sensations. If family or personal pressures are equal or greater than those at work, the headaches may be worse later in the evening, on weekends, or during vacations.

Tension headaches may occur to some degree in about 80 percent of the population during periods of emotional stress. Anxiety and depression frequently are associated with these headaches. Tense, high strung, competitive, type A personality individuals are especially prone to this disorder. They may be treated acutely with antianxiety agents, muscle relaxants and massage or heat application to the head and neck. If an underlying depression is present, antidepressants may be prescribed. However, psychotherapy is usually the treatment of choice for patients chronically afflicted by tension headaches. Learning to avoid or better cope with tension increasing situations or individuals is the most effective long-term management approach. Electromyogram feedback from the frontalis or temporalis muscles may help some tension headache patients. Relaxation associated with the practice periods, meditation, or other changes in a pressured life-style may provide symptomatic relief for some patients.

## Some Other Types of Headaches

Headaches of recent onset in the elderly may be due to temporal (giant cell) arteritis. They are usually unilateral, temporal, throbbing, and are worse at night. The inflamed artery may be palpably tender and show biopsy evidence of arteritis. Diagnosis and treatment, often with steroids, are important because temporal arteritis may lead to ophthalmoplegia or blindness. An unexplained elevation of the sedimentation rate should alert the physician to the diagnosis.

Although only a very small percentage of headaches are due to brain tumors or other types of intracranial masses, many patients will be frightened of the possibility of this diagnosis. The physician should specifically question and reassure the patient if signs and symptoms do not support this diagnosis. Otherwise, worry about potential serious causes of the headaches may produce concomitant tension headaches and complicate differential diagnosis and treatment. With intracranial masses, other symptoms of increased intracranial pressure (e.g., nausea) that typically are worse in the morning, seizures, or focal neurological deficits are seen. The pain is often described as a steady ache and tends to progressively increase in severity over a period of weeks or longer. Tumors, chronic subdural hematomas, or other masses may often be diagnosed by a CT scan of the head.

Headache associated with subarachnoid or intracranial hemorrhage is sudden in onset, severe and associated with altered consciousness or sensory and motor deficits. An unruptured aneurysm or arteriovenous malformation may rarely cause headaches by pressure (mass) effects. Hypertension during a period of acute increase in blood pressure frequently causes headaches but headaches are less common with chronic hypertension. If fever and nuchal rigidity are present in a patient with an acute, new onset headache the physician should attempt to rule out meningitis, encephalitis, or other CNS infectious processes.

Finally, the psychiatrist may be requested to provide an opinion regarding postconcussion or other accident or trauma-related headaches. There may be a significant psychogenic and secondary gain component in many headaches of these types, especially if litigation, workman's compensation, or other forms of secondary gain are pending. It is often impossible to effectively treat such headaches until pending settlements are concluded.

## REFERENCES

Adams R D: Headache. In *Harrison's Principles of Internal Medicine*, ed 8, G W Thorn, R D Adams, E Braunwald, K J Isselbacher, R G Petersdorf, editors, p 20. McGraw-Hill, New York, 1977.

Lance J W, Anthony M: The cephalgias, with special reference to vascular and muscle contraction headache. In *Scientific Approaches to Clinical Neurology*, E S Goldensohn, S H Appel, editors, p 1959. Lea & Febiger, Philadelphia, 1977.

Newland C A, Illis L S, Robinson P K, Batchelor B G, Water W E: A survey of headache in an English city. Res Clin Stud Headache *5:* 1, 1978.

Raskin N H: *Headache*. W. B. Saunders, Philadelphia, 1980.

Ryan R E Sr, Ryan R E Jr: *Headache and Headache Pain: Diagnosis and Treatment*. C. V. Mosby, St. Louis, 1978.

Saper J R: *Headache Disorders: Current Concepts and Treatment Strategies*. Wright-PSG, Boston, 1983.

Thompson T L II: Headache. In *Comprehensive Textbook of Psychiatry*, ed 4, H I Kaplan, B J Sadock, editors, p 1203. Williams & Wilkins, Baltimore, 1985.

Waters W E, O'Conner P J: Prevalence of migraine. J Neurol Neurosurg Psychiatr *38:* 613, 1975.

Ziegler D K: Tension headache. Med Clin North Am *62:* 495, 1978.

---

## 22.11 IMMUNE DISORDERS

### Introduction

Considerable evidence is accumulating that demonstrates a relationship between psychosocial factors, immune function, and health and illness. It seems that psychosocial processes, including a range of life experiences and state and trait characteristics of the person, influence the central nervous system, resulting in the enhancement of the suppression of immune activity.

### *Immune Response*

Immunological responses in vivo can be divided into two types— immediate hypersensitivity and delayed hypersensitivity. An immediate response is exemplified by the wheal-and-flare reaction that takes place 10 to 15 minutes after an extract of pollen is injected into the skin of a person with hay fever. An example of delayed response is the erythema and induration elicited 24 to 48 hours after the injection of tuberculin into the skin of a patient with tuberculosis.

The immediate and delayed hypersensitivity responses may be further distinguished by the ability to produce these responses in immunologically naive recipients. The immediate wheal-and-flare response can be transferred to an apparently healthy person by the serum of a hypersensitive person. In contrast, delayed hypersensitivity may be transferred by cells (lymphocytes) but not by serum. As a result, delayed hypersensitivity is referred to as cell-mediated immunity, and immediate hypersensitivity is referred to as humoral immunity, since it is mediated by antibodies in the serum.

### *Psychosocial Processes and the Humoral Immune Response*

Experimental studies concerning the association between psychosocial situations and humoral immunity reveal a complex interaction. A number of studies have demonstrated that various experiences are associated with depressed humoral immune function.

### Psychosocial Processes and the Cell-mediated Immune Responses

The results of experimental studies of psychosocial effects on cell-mediated immunity are similar to those found in humoral immunity.

Time and frequency of exposure, as well as the nature of the stimulus, seem to play a role in psychosocial effects on cell-mediated immunity, as on humoral immunity. Early studies of resistance to poliomyelitis, a viral infection involving cell-mediated immunity, demonstrated a variable response in different systems that may be related to these parameters.

### Mediation of Psychosocial Influences on Immune Function

The endocrine system is highly responsive to both life experiences and psychological state, and has a significant, although complicated, effect on immune processes. The most widely studied hormones are those of the pituitary-adrenocortical system. A wide variety of stressors associated with the elicitation of emotional changes within the organism induce the classical stress response characterized by the rapid release of adrenocorticotrophic hormone (ACTH), followed by the release of corticosteroids. Corticosteroids have been found to alter various immune functions and usually suppress but, on occasion, may enhance the immune response. The release of corticosteroids subsequent to life events may be associated with the effect of psychosocial factors on immune function and illness.

### Infectious Diseases

Clinical studies have reported that psychological variables influence the rate of recovery from infectious mononucleosis and influenza, and the susceptibility to rhinovirus-induced common cold symptoms and tularemia. Recurrent herpes simplex lesions have been shown to be most frequent in persons who tend to feel depressed, and in patients with clinical depression. Life events and psychological state have been found to decrease resistance to tuberculosis and to influence the course of the illness. Social supports have also been shown to play a role in recovery from tuberculosis. Life experiences that induce anger have been noted to alter the bacterial composition of the intestine. College students who respond to upsetting events with maladaptive aggression or affective changes were found to have a higher incidence of subse-

quent upper respiratory infections. It should be noted that in these studies the primary immune response was cell mediated.

### Allergic Disorders

Considerable clinical evidence suggests that psychological factors are related to the precipitation of many allergic disorders. Bronchial asthma is a prime example of a pathological process involving immediate hypersensitivity that is associated with psychosocial processes. Emotional reactions to life experience, personality patterns, and conditioning have been reported to be involved in the onset and the course of asthma.

### Organ Transplantation

Psychosocial factors seem to play a role in organ transplantation. A number of clinical studies have reported that stressful life events, anxiety, and depression precede some cases of graft rejection. Psychosocial effects on the immune system may play a role in the mechanisms involved in such rejections.

### Autoimmune Diseases

A prime function of the immune system is to distinguish between self and nonself, and to reject foreign antigens (nonself). Occasionally, for reasons that are unclear at the present time, a cell-mediated or humoral immune response develops against a person's own cells. This results in a variety of pathological effects that clinically are known as autoimmune diseases. Disorders in which an autoimmune component has been implicated include Graves' disease, Hashimoto's disease, rheumatoid arthritis, ulcerative colitis, regional ileitis, systemic lupus erythematosus, psoriasis, myasthenia gravis, and pernicious anemia.

### Cancer

A large literature has been accumulating in the area of the relationship between psychosocial factors and cancer. It has been reported that stressful life experiences, particularly experiences of separation and loss, frequently precede the clinical onset of various neoplasms, including cancer of the cervix, leukemia, and lymphoma.

Several studies, in contrast, have found no association between life experience and the onset of cancer of the breast. In one of these studies, however, there was a relationship between life events and benign breast disease. A similar observation was reported in an investigation of benign prostatic hypertrophy, in which a relatively high rate of life change was found to precede the onset of benign prostatic hypertrophy, in contrast to a lower rate of life events before the onset of cancer of the bladder.

Numerous studies have attempted to relate personality traits and susceptibility to cancer. Patients with lung cancer have been reported to exhibit a more restricted ability for emotional discharge than do patients without cancer. In a 30-year prospective study of medical students who developed cancer tended not to express emotions readily. Others reported that patients with cancer used the defense of denial and repression excessively.

If a causal relationship exists between psychosocial factors and the onset and development of neoplasms, a question that has attracted considerable interest is concerned with the nature of the biological processes involved. The growing information on the immunological aspects of cancer raises the possibility that immunological mechanisms play an important role in the mediation of psychosocial influences on the susceptibility and the course of neoplastic disease.

### Immunity and Psychiatric Disorders

Although a number of investigators have found evidence suggestive of altered immunity and autoimmunity in patients with schizophrenia, the specific findings have been difficult to replicate. Whether the immune abnormalities are involved in the pathogenesis of some or all types of schizophrenia, or whether such abnormalities are related to a wide range of factors, including chronic institutionalization and neuroleptic agents, remains to be determined.

Immune phenomena in psychiatric disorders other than schizophrenia have been less extensively studied. Work indicates that psychiatric patients manifest increased IgM and IgA levels. These findings indicate the need for further study. The notion that patients with depression have an increased incidence of autoimmune antibodies has sparked some controversy. The frequency of antinuclear antibodies, commonly found in patients with autoimmune disorders, such as systemic lupus erythematosus, has been reported as increased in patients with depression in some but not all studies.

### REFERENCES

Ader R, editor: *Psychoneuroimmunology.* Academic Press, New York, 1981.
Ader R: Developmental psychoneuroimmunology. Dev Psychobiol *16:* 251, 1983.
Besedovsky H, Del Ray A, Sorkin E, Da Prada M, Burri R, Honegger C: The immune response evokes changes in brain noradrenergic neurons. Science *221:* 564, 1983.
Blecha F, Kelley K W, Satterlee D G: Adrenal involvement in the expression of delayed-type hypersensitivity to SRBC and contact sensitivity to DNFB in stressed mice. Proc Soc Exp Biol Med *169:* 247, 1982.
Keller S E, Weiss J M, Schleifer S J, Miller E, Stein M: Stress induced suppression of lymphocyte stimulation in adrenalectomized rats. Science *221:* 1301, 1983.
Levy S, editor: *Biological Mediators of Stress and Disease: Neoplasia.* Elsevier/North Holland, New York, 1982.
Schleifer S J, Keller S E, Camerino M S, Thornton J, Stein M: Suppression of lymphocyte stimulation following bereavement. JAMA *250:* 374, 1983.
Stein M, Schiavi R C, Camerino M S: Influence of brain and behavior on the immune system. Science *191:* 435, 1976.
Stein M, Schleifer S J, Keller S E: Immune disorder. In *Comprehensive Textbook of Psychiatry,* ed 4, H I Kaplan, B J Sadock, editors, p 1206. Williams & Wilkins, Baltimore, 1985.
Weiner H: *Psychobiology and Human Disease.* Elsevier/North Holland, New York, 1977.

# 22.12 CHRONIC PAIN

### Introduction

Persistent pain is the most frequent complaint of patients, yet it is one of the most difficult symptoms to treat because of differing etiologies and individualized responses to pain. Chronic low back pain is the most common cause of time lost from work in this country.

Pain is affected by a myriad of subjective, unmeasurable factors such as level of attention, emotional state, personality, and past experiences. Pain may simultaneously be a symptom and be serving as a defense against psychological stresses. Psychological factors may cause a person to become somatically preoccupied and magnify even normal sensations into chronic pain. Patients may be excessively responsive to pain for personal, social, or financial secondary gain. Chronic pain may be a way of justifying failure or establishing relationships with others. Cultural, ethnic, or religious affiliations may influence the degree and manner in which individuals express pain and the way in which their families react to the symptoms. Therefore, in evaluating and treating persistent pain, the physician should realize that pain is not a simple stimulus-response phenomenon. The perception of and reaction to pain is multifactorial, simultaneously summating many biopsychosocial variables.

### Pain Threshold and Perception

Peripheral sensations are transmitted via the pain pathways (e.g., lateral spinothalamic tract, posterior thalamus of the diencephalon) to cortical somatosensory regions of the central nervous system for conscious perception. The parietal cortex both localizes pain and perceives intensity. However, psychogenic pain may be entirely of central origin. More complex reactions to pain involve other areas of the cortex, responsible for memory, and conscious and unconscious elements of an individuals personality.

The threshold for perception of pain is the same for most people, but may be decreased by about 40 percent by biofeedback, a positive emotional state, relaxation exercises, physical therapy or other physical activity, meditation, guided imagery, suggestion, hypnosis, placebo, or analgesics. Beneficial response to placebo is sometimes falsely thought to differentiate organic from functional etiologies. In fact about one-third of normal individuals or those with organic causes of pain have at least a transient positive response to a placebo.

Variations in the effectiveness and responsiveness of individuals' endorphin or other neurotransmitter systems may modulate pain perception and tolerance. A gate control theory has been proposed which suggests that large peripheral afferent nerve fibers modulate sensory input by inhibiting hypothetical sensory transmitting neurons (gateway cells) in the substantia gelatinosa of the spinal cord. Relief of pain by transcutaneous or dorsal column electrical stimulators may be from activation of this system.

## Diagnosis

The psychiatrist should independently take a history of pain since the referring physician may have overlooked an important aspect of the history or not have elicited critical clinical data. The exact location, onset, duration and course, quality, severity, aggravating or alleviating factors including circumstances and settings of occurrence, and any associated signs or symptoms may have direct relevance. Some physicians may medically clear patients in haste because the physicians are uncomfortable with the patient. Since many physicians feel that the relief of pain is a fundamental responsibility, a doctor may label a chronic pain patient pejoratively because the patient has caused him to fail. Physicians may also assume the pain has psychic underpinnings as a means of ridding themselves of the responsibility of providing ongoing care for these patients.

A physician should always remember that a psychiatric diagnosis does not preclude the existence of a concomitant medical illness. It may be risky for a known chronic pain patient with a new organic illness to seek medical help because the physician may erroneously assume that the present symptoms are an exacerbation of his long-standing disorder. The medical evaluation should be repeated periodically, especially if chronic pain worsens or changes significantly. About 10 percent of patients (who have had thorough work-ups) referred to pain clinics eventually are found to have a neoplasm or other occult medical condition that slowly became manifest.

Most chronic pain patients attempt to treat themselves before seeking medical help. Billions of dollars are spent annually by people seeking relief through over-the-counter preparations or other nonmedical means. These individuals often become addicted to alcohol and other drugs. Therefore, the physician should be alert for drug toxicity (especially overmedication) and withdrawal symptoms during evaluation and treatment of chronic pain patients. Explanation to the patient and family that sensitivity to pain may greatly increase during drug withdrawal may partially decrease anxiety and increase pain sensitivity caused by weaning.

A large number of emotional states and psychiatric disorders may lead to a chronic pain syndrome. Also, any type of ongoing pain is stressful and will cause some degree of disorganization of the personality because it indicates that the organism is failing to maintain or protect itself in some manner. Chronic, excessive pain may cause a psychological reaction termed pain shock, manifested by chronic irritability, anxiety, depression, fatigue, insomnia, and job and family problems. Ongoing pain results in decreased activity which may lead to atrophy, weakness, and further disability.

Depressed patients are especially prone to develop chronic pain, and if depression is severe, the patients may develop delusions of cancer, rotting, or other metaphors of decay and death to explain the chronic pain. The physician should assume masked depression is present until vigorous clinical trials of treatment for depression (possibly including antidepressants, monoamine oxidase inhibitors, and electroconvulsive treatment) have failed. Some chronic pain patients have been successfully treated in this manner without ever acknowledging that they felt depressed; their depression may have been entirely manifested through somatic equivalents.

The mourning or grieving individual may develop pain similar to that experienced by the lost person as a means of identifying with him and introjecting part of the person in an attempt to deny the loss. Patients with obsessive personalities often recount their history in seemingly endless detail and may develop compulsive rituals to alleviate their discomfort. Schizophrenic, demented, delirious, or psychotic patients develop bizarre forms of pain that are often attributed to some persecuting external force. Psychotic patients are also at risk for incorporating the pain of an organic illness (e.g., myocardial infarction, perforated ulcer) into a delusion and not seeking medical help.

DSM-III classifies chronic pain patients (who do not have a factitious or malingering disorder or an affective, psychotic, or physical disorder accounting for their symptoms) under somatoform disorders. If patients have multiple recurrent pains of at least several years' duration which began before age 30 they are considered to have a somatization disorder. If patients' pain suggests a physical illness but may be attributed to psychological factors alone their diagnosis is conversion disorder or psychogenic pain disorder (if pain is the only symptom). In conversion disorders the distribution and referral of pain are inconsistent with neurophysiological pathways, and the pain often is associated with unusual or bizarre posturing or flexion type deformities of the extremities or spine. Psychogenic pain disorder is often due to major defects in the ego functions of experiencing and expressing emotions. Alexithymia may be an associated symptom. These patients are not psychologically minded which may make effective treatment difficult or impossible. The usual goal is supportive and maintenance treatment by a concerned, psychologically oriented physician.

Patients with ongoing, unrealistic interpretations of minor pains and who become preoccupied with the fear of having a serious disease are diagnosed as having hypochondriasis. A clue to patients with hypochondriasis is that the patients often avoid answering evaluation questions in any detail. Instead they may discourse at great length and bring medical records (often focusing on perceived mistreatments by a long list of physicians and institutions), X-rays, medical journal or magazine articles documenting tests, treatments, and etiologic theories, and demand a specific treatment.

An individual with a stoic or masochistic personality may experience pain without much reaction or even find the experience pleasurable. Pain-prone patients consciously or unconsciously desire to have chronic pain due to a fear of success or sense of guilt. The pain serves as deserved punishment or atonement. The derivation of the word pain from the Latin *poena* and Greek *poine* meaning penalty or punishment is interesting in this light. The infliction of pain as a means of punishing children is common in many families.

Pain may become an acceptable way of receiving attention, love, and having other basic needs met. Chronic pain patients tend to be middleaged or older, to come from a lower socioeconomic group, larger family, to have more siblings, to have more relatives who have had painful illnesses and received disability compensation, and to have a history of more painful injuries and illnesses. Some chronic pain patients previously were hard working, independent individuals who took care of others as a way of dealing with their strong underlying dependency needs and wishes to be taken care of themselves; chronic pain may make fulfillment of those wishes acceptable. However, the price paid may be the threat or actual relinquishment of positions of authority in the family, social network, or at work. Financial stresses may result from a decreased salary and the medical bills necessary to legitimize their sick role.

The malingerer, sociopath, or patient with a compensation neurosis may be especially difficult to treat. Lawsuits, disability hearings, or other potential sources of secondary gain associated with ongoing pain should be resolved if at all possible before heroic efforts are made to treat chronic pain. Interpersonal (e.g., spouse or boss responding in a special manner) or sociopathic (e.g., selling drugs) types of secondary gain may be difficult to recognize, especially if a spouse or other individual is consciously or unconsciously contributing to a patient's illness behaviors. A differential diagnostic point may be that these patients often deny any fluctuation in their pain (i.e., it is always equally bad), when in fact patients with organic, or other psychogenic types of pain typically report some fluctuation.

### Phantom Limb and Phantom Pain

The sensation that an amputated part is still present occurs normally after most amputations. Painful phantom sensations are rare but may arise from abnormalities in nerve endings in the stump or more centrally. Causalgia, a posttraumatic pain syndrome, occurs in 2 to 5 percent of patients following nerve injury and may contribute to phantom pain. The psychological reaction and degree of adjustment to the amputation may also affect the degree of pain experienced.

### Treatment

Patients with bona fide reasons for significant chronic pain are often undermedicated with narcotics. Physicians hesitate to prescribe effective analgesia because of a lack of knowledge of the pharmacology of analgesics, an unrealistic fear of causing addiction (even in terminal patients), and the ethical judgment that only bad physicians prescribe large doses of narcotics. In this regard it is critical to differentiate patients with chronic benign pain (who tend to do much better with psychotherapy and psychotropic drugs) from those with chronic pain due to cancer or other chronic medical disorders. The former often respond to the combination of an antidepressant and a phenothiazine. The latter usually respond better to analgesics, nerve blocks, and neurodestructive procedures. Many cancer patients may be kept relatively active, alert, and comfortable with judicious use of morphine, avoiding costly and incompletely effective surgical procedures such as peripheral nerve section, cordotomy, or stereotaxic thalamic ablations.

A behavior modification, deconditioning program may also be useful. Analgesia should be prescribed at regular intervals rather than only as needed. Otherwise patients must suffer before receiving relief, which only increases anxiety and sensitivity to pain. Standing orders dissociate experiencing pain from receiving needed medication. The deconditioning of needed care from experiencing increased pain should also extend to a patient's interpersonal relationships. Patients should receive as much or more attention for displaying active and healthy behaviors as they receive for passive, dependent, pain-related behaviors. Their spouses, bosses, friends, physicians, health care, or social agencies should not reinforce chronic pain and penalize patients (including threatening to immediately discontinue disability payments) if the patients begin to relinquish their sick role. Patients should be assured of regular, supportive, and ongoing appointments that are not contingent on pain. Hospitalization should be avoided if possible to prevent further regression.

A number of pain clinics with a multispecialty staff have developed to evaluate and treat patients with complex pain disorders (see Table I). These clinics include the early involvement of

TABLE I
SOME OF THE MORE COMMON DISORDERS SEEN IN CHRONIC PAIN CLINICS*

Psychiatric Disorders
1. Depression, "masked" depression
2. Hypochondriasis
3. Psychologically triggered pain (e.g., migraines)
4. Conversion symptoms
5. Compensation neurosis
6. Malingering
7. Delusions due to psychosis (e.g., dementia, schizophrenia)

Musculoskeletal Disorders
1. Low back pain (may be associated with arthritis, spondylitis, failed disk surgery)
2. Rheumatoid arthritis
3. Osteoarthritis
4. Myofascial pain (e.g., frozen shoulder)
5. Paget's disease (due to encroachment on nerves)

Ischemic Disorders
1. Angina pectoris
2. Peripheral vascular disease (e.g., claudication)

Neoplastic Disorders
1. Direct invasion or compression of nerves
2. Metastases causing invasion or compression of other structures

Neurologic Disorders—Nerve Lesions
1. Posttraumatic neuritis
2. Causalgia
3. Postoperative neuromas
4. Amputation stump (phantom) pain
5. Coccydynia
6. Scar pain
7. Nerve entrapments
8. Postherpetic neuralgia (shingles)
9. Trigeminal neuralgia (tic douloureux)
10. Sympathetic dystrophy (e.g., shoulder hand syndrome)
11. Spastic states
12. Thalamic pain

Some Other Disorders
1. Temporomandibular joint syndrome (bruxism) or arthritis
2. Dental, nasal, sinusoidal, ophthalmologic, or otologic pain
3. Gout
4. Chronic pancreatitis

* Adapted in part from Merskey H: Disorders seen in a pain clinic. In *Pain: Meaning and Management.* W L Smith, H Merskey, S C Gross, editors. Spectrum, Jamaica, NY, 1980.

psychiatrists, rather than only after real causes of pain have been ruled out and the patient and physicians are frustrated. The patients are managed without addicting drugs, exploratory, or neurodestructive surgery unless there is evidence to support a specific diagnosis, especially if the patient has a hysterical personality or history of multiple surgical procedures. Pain clinics also recognize that most chronic pain patients experience a vicious cycle of biological and psychosocial factors, so that the most effective treatment involves a systems approach that addresses each relevant biopsychosocial component for the patient.

## REFERENCES

Adams R D: Pain—general considerations. In *Harrison's Principles of Internal Medicine*, ed 8, G W Thorn, R D Adams, E Braunwald, K J Isselbacher, R G Petersdorf, editors, p 13. McGraw-Hill, New York, 1977.
Brena S F, Chapman S L, editors: *Management of Patients with Chronic Pain*. SP Medical and Scientific Books, New York, 1983.
Hackett T P: The pain patient: Evaluation and treatment. In *Massachusetts General Hospital Handbook of General Hospital Psychiatry*, T P Hackett, N H Cassem, editors, p 41. C. V. Mosby, St. Louis, 1978.
Hendler N H, Long D M, Wise T N, editors: *The Diagnosis and Treatment of Chronic Pain*. John Wright-PSG, Boston, 1982.
Luce J M, Thompson T L II, Getto C J, Bynny R L: New concepts of chronic pain and their implications. Hosp Pract *14:* 113, 1979.
Reuler J B, Girard D E, Nardone D A: The chronic pain syndrome: Misconceptions and management. Ann Intern Med *93:* 588, 1980.
Smith W L, Merskey H, Gross S C, editors: *Pain Meaning and Management*. Spectrum, Jamaica, NY, 1980.
Stimmel B: *Pain, Analgesia, and Addiction: The Pharmacologic Treatment of Pain*. Raven Press, New York, 1983.
Thompson T L II: Chronic pain. In *Comprehensive Textbook of Psychiatry*, ed 4, H I Kaplan, B J Sadock, editors, p 1212. Williams & Wilkins, Baltimore, 1985.
Webb W L Jr: Chronic pain. Psychosomatics *24:* 1053, 1983.

# 22.13 TREATMENT OF PSYCHOSOMATIC DISORDERS

## Introduction

The concept of psychomedical treatment—that is, the approach that emphasizes the interrelation of mind and body in the genesis of symptom and disorder—calls for a greatly expanded sharing of responsibility among various professions. If one views disease from a multi-causal point of view, every disease can be considered psychosomatic, since every disorder is affected in some fashion by emotional factors.

Hostility, depression, dependency, and anxiety, in varying proportions, are at the root of most psychosomatic disorders. Psychosomatic medicine is principally concerned with those illnesses that present primarily somatic manifestations. The presenting complaint is usually physical; the patient rarely complains of his anxiety or depression or tension but, rather, of his vomiting or diarrhea or anorexia.

## Types of Patients

Three major groups of medical patients require special evaluation of their psychological and somatic factors.

### Psychosomatic Illness Group

These patients suffer from such classic psychosomatic disorders as peptic ulcer and ulcerative colitis. In these disease processes one cannot posit a strictly psychogenic explanation, since the particular set of emotional factors found, for example, in the typical ulcer case, may also appear in the patient with no history of ulcer.

### Psychiatric Group

Patients in this group suffer from physical disturbances caused by psychological illness. Their somatic disabilities may be real (objective) or unreal. When real, the disability usually involves the voluntary nervous system and is termed a conversion or somatization disorder. Among the unreal disabilities are hypochondriasis and delusional preoccupation with physical functioning, which is often seen in schizophrenics. Patients in this group suffer primarily from a psychological disturbance that requires psychiatric treatment, but auxiliary medical therapy may be necessary.

### Reactive Group

These patients do have actual organic disorders, but they also suffer from an associated psychological disturbance. For example, a patient with heart disease or renal disease requiring dialysis may develop a reactive anxiety or depression regarding his life-threatening condition. This anxiety, in turn, may produce physical manifestations that complicate the somatic situation.

## Combined Psychomedical Treatment Approach

The combined treatment approach, in which the psychiatrist handles the psychiatric aspects of the case and the internist or other specialist treats the somatic aspects, requires the closest collaboration between the two physicians. The purpose of the medical therapy is to build up the patient's physical state so that he may successfully participate in psychotherapy for total care.

Disorders such as bronchial asthma, in which psychosocial processes play a distinct role in the development and the course, may respond well to the combined treatment approach.

Although the asthmatic attacks themselves may be treated successfully by the physician, psychiatric treatment can be useful in the short run by helping to alleviate the anxiety associated with the attacks, and in the long run by helping to uncover the causes of the interdependency involved in the disorder.

In the acute phase of a somatic illness, such as an acute attack of ulcerative colitis, medical therapy is the primary form of treatment; psychotherapy, with its long-range goals, consists at that stage of reassurance and support. As the pendulum of disease activity shifts and the illness progresses to a chronic state, psychotherapy assumes the primary role, and medical therapy the less active position.

Sometimes reassurance is all that is needed in the treatment of psychosomatic syndromes.

The patient, of course, must participate in the process of improving his life situation. The symptoms themselves must be treated by the internist, but the psychiatrist can help the patient focus on his feelings about the symptoms and gain understanding of the unconscious processes involved.

If the patient is handled insensitively or if his illness is regarded unsympathetically, the results can be grave.

### Role of Liaison Psychiatry

The great surge of recent interest in liaison psychiatry parallels what is recommended here. The setting may be on a medical, surgical, gynecological, or neurological service—just as in the combined therapy the psychiatrist may work in any setting with the internist, surgeon, or other physician.

### Indications for Combined Treatment

If during an initial attack of a psychosomatic disorder the patient responds to active medical therapy in association with the superficial support, ventilation, reassurance, and environmental manipulation provided by the internist, additional psychotherapy by a psychiatrist may not be required. Psychosomatic illness that does not respond to medical treatment, or that is in a chronic phase, should receive psychosomatic evaluation by a psychiatrist, and combined therapy, as indicated.

### Goal of Combined Therapy

It is useful to set up a tentative, elastic spectrum of therapeutic goals in the treatment of psychosomatic disorders. The end desired is cure, which means resolution of the structural impairment and reorganization of the personality, so that needs and tensions no longer produce pathophysiological results. Treatment should aim at a more mature general life adjustment, increased capacity for physical and occupational activity, amelioration of the progression of the disease, reversal of the pathology, avoidance of complications of the basic disease process, decreased use of secondary gain associated with the illness, and increased capacity to adjust to the presence of the disease.

## Psychiatric Aspects

Treatment of psychosomatic disorders from the psychiatric viewpoint is a difficult task.

The purpose of therapy should be to understand the motivations and mechanisms of disturbed function and thus help the patient to an understanding of the nature of his illness and of himself and of the implications of his costly adaptive pattern. This insight should result in changed and healthier patterns of behavior.

Psychotherapy based on analytic principles is effective in treating psychosomatic disorders, mainly in terms of the patient's experiences in the treatment, particularly regarding his relationship with the therapist. This type of patient is usually even more reluctant to deal with his emotional problems than are patients with other psychiatric problems. Unlike other neurotics, who are usually able to express their emotional problems in a nonphysical manner, the psychosomatic patient in a sense eschews responsibility for his illness by isolating the diseased organ and presenting it to the doctor for diagnosis and cure. He thus may be satisfying an infantile need to be cared for passively, at the same time denying that he is an adult, with all the stresses and conflicts implied in that state of being.

### Resistance to Entering Psychotherapy

When the psychosomatic patient first becomes ill, he is usually convinced that the illness is purely organic in origin. He rejects psychotherapy as treatment for his sickness, and, in fact, the very idea of emotional illness may be repugnant because of personal prejudices concerning psychiatry.

In the initial phase, physical treatment and psychotherapeutic procedures must be combined subtly. A good arrangement in the early stage is treatment by a psychologically oriented physician, one who is sensitive to unconscious and transference phenomena and who is perhaps working with a psychotherapist.

### Development of Relationship and Transference

Psychotherapy with the psychosomatic patient must often proceed more slowly and cautiously than with other psychiatric patients. Positive transference should be developed gradually. The psychiatrist must be supportive and reassuring during the acute phase of the illness. As the disorder enters a chronic stage, the psychiatrist may make exploratory interpretations, but a strong patient-physician relationship is essential for any such exploration. The psychosomatic patient is very dependent, and this characteristic may be used supportively and interpretatively at crucial periods in the treatment. During therapy, a great deal of hostility appears—first in the form of overt ventilation and then in the framework of the transference. Free and appropriate expression of the patient's hostility is to be encouraged.

### Interpretation

The therapist must pay particular attention to current problems in the patient's immediate life situation, and deal with his reaction to the therapist and to treatment. There should be increased emphasis on evaluation of the patient's characterological difficulties and on his habitual reactions, particularly his reactions to himself (self-esteem, guilt) and his reactions to his environment (dependency, submission, need for affection). The psychiatrist should also analyze the patient's anxieties, such as asking for complete care, always having to be right, refraining from self-assertion, and suppressing all forbidden impulses.

Some investigators have reported dramatic results when unconscious material was interpreted as a drastic measure during an acute phase. Although most Freudian analysts believe that genetic material must eventually be interpreted for a complete cure, many cultural analysts have demonstrated that adequate results can be obtained when psychotherapy is limited to the analysis of characterological and ego defenses associated with disturbed interpersonal relations.

The psychosomatic patient is often involved in a repetitious pattern involving stress in his interpersonal relations. Since he is usually unaware of this pattern, it is helpful to show him that the pattern is not accidental but is determined by factors of which he is unaware, and it is essential to show him how he may change this disturbing pattern and act in a new and healthier manner.

Psychosomatic patients tend to drive toward psychologically regressed mental and physical behavior. Usually, their regression is to a traumatic or highly conflictual period. By reenacting certain specific attitudes of childhood or infancy, they are attempting to master the anxiety and illness first manifested during those earlier stages.

In the treatment of psychosomatic disorders, the key concept is flexibility in technique. Because of the patient's poor motivation and because of his poor physical condition, it may be necessary to make frequent changes in the psychotherapeutic approach.

### Resistance during Therapy

Since psychosomatic patients frequently have a great deal of resistance to entering psychotherapy, it is not surprising that the resistance often continues unabated during therapy. In many patients, the motivation for entering treatment is so poor that they frequently drop out of therapy for minor reasons.

### Interruption of Psychotherapy for a Medical Emergency

During a course of psychotherapy, a patient with a psychosomatic disorder may require medical or surgical treatment for his organic disorder. The psychiatrist should cooperate closely with the surgeon or medical personnel and should maintain contact with the patient—in person or by telephone—during the emergency. Such interest offers valuable emotional support in a time of crisis.

If a patient is hospitalized, the psychiatrist should help other hospital personnel recognize and learn to tolerate the frequently difficult and provocative behavior of certain psychosomatic patients. The preparation can be of use to the patient as well; if he sees his demands being met considerately, he may be less inclined to view his world as hostile and formidable.

### Danger of Psychosis

There are no simple relationships between psychosomatic disorders and psychoses. Some people in whom physiological and psychological processes are poorly integrated manifest both psychosomatic disorders and psychoses. In others, the ego integration is such that stress produces a breakdown of bodily function, rather than a psychotic maladjustment. Some nonpsychotic psychosomatic patients can become psychotic or exhibit symptoms, as a result of too active an interpretation and the removal of defensive elements in the personality structure.

## Medical Aspects

The internist's treatment of psychosomatic disorders should follow the established rules for their medical management. Generally, the internist should spend as much time as possible with the patient, and listen sympathetically to his many complaints. He must be reassuring and supportive. Before he performs a physically manipulative procedure—particularly if it is painful, such as a sigmoidoscopy—he should explain to the patient just what will happen. The explanation allays the patient's anxiety, makes him more cooperative, and actually facilitates the examination.

The patient's attitude toward taking drugs may also affect the outcome of the psychosomatic treatment. For example, a patient suffering from diabetes who does not accept his illness and who has self-destructive impulses of which he is unaware, may purposely not control his diet and, as a result, end up in a hyperglycemic coma. In the case of cardiac patients, some refuse to curtail their physical activity after a myocardial infarction because of a reluctance to admit weakness, or because of a fear that they will somehow be considered less successful. Others use their illness as a welcome punishment for guilt or as a way of avoiding responsibility. Therapy in such cases must strive to help the patient minimize his fears, and to focus on self-care and the reestablishment of a healthy body image.

## Acceptance of Psychomedical Treatment

The advantages of the collaborative approach are that the patient receives the benefit of the efforts of specialists trained in various medical disciplines, each working in the area in which he is best equipped to function. However, some medical specialists have resisted the psychiatric approach because of inadequate training in psychiatry in medical school, unfamiliarity with the specialized language of psychiatry, and a general prejudice based on the high cost of psychotherapy and the alleged unscientific and subjective aspects of psychiatry.

## New Types of Therapy for Psychosomatic Disorders

During recent years, new types of treatment have been introduced for psychosomatic disorders, and several are described below. The first category includes psychotherapies based on psychological insight and change, such as group and family psychotherapy; the second category is composed of behavioral therapies based on Pavlovian principles of learning new behavior, such as biofeedback and relaxation therapy.

### Group Psychotherapy and Family Therapy

Because of the psychopathological significance of the mother-child relationship in the development of psychosomatic reactions, modification of this relationship has been suggested as a likely focus of emphasis in the psychotherapy of psychosomatic disorders. The group approach especially offers greater interpersonal contact, and provides increased ego support for the weak egos of psychosomatic patients who fear the threat of isolation and parental separation. Family therapy offers hope of a change in the relationship between parent and child.

The long-term evaluation of results of the various psychotherapies, individual and group, of psychosomatic disorders remains to be carried out. Some patients with medical disorders may respond positively to psychological treatment, either physically or psychologically. Some medical disorders appear to be more amenable to psychotherapy than other disorders and various therapeutic modalities appear to be more effective than others. Some individuals appear to be more responsive to psychotherapy than others, especially in relation to the nature of their psychopathology, rather than their physical pathology.

### Behavioral Therapies

**Biofeedback.** The application of biofeedback treatment techniques to patients with hypertension, cardiac arrhythmias, epilepsy, and tension headaches has provided encouraging but inconclusive therapeutic results. Controlled studies and outcome studies must still be carried out in the future.

**Relaxation Treatment.** The treatment of hypertension may be accomplished through the use of the relaxation response. Positive results have been published about headache, alcoholism and drug abuse treatment, using the relaxation therapy and transcendental meditation.

**REFERENCES**

Alexander F: *Psychosomatic Medicine*. W. W. Norton, New York, 1950.

Gilbert M M: Reactive depression as a model psychosomatic disease. Psychosomatics *11:* 426, 1970.

Kaplan H I: Treatment of psychosomatic disorders. In *Comprehensive Textbook of Psychiatry*, ed 4, H I Kaplan, B J Sadock, editors, p 1215. Williams &

Wilkins, Baltimore,1985.

Karusu T B: Psychotherapy of the medically ill. Am J Psychiatry *136:* 1, 1979.

Miller L: The mind and the body. Int J Psychiatry *7:* 518, 1967.

Steptoe A, Medville D, Ross A: Behavioral response demands, cardiovascular reactivity, and essential hypertension. Psychosom Med *46:* 33, 1984.

# 23

# Other Psychiatric Disorders

## 23.1 UNUSUAL PSYCHIATRIC DISORDERS, ATYPICAL PSYCHOSES, AND BRIEF REACTIVE PSYCHOSES

### Introduction

At the end of the 19th century, Emil Kraepelin molded a huge collection of functional mental diseases into two clearly defined endogenous psychoses: schizophrenia, or, as he called it then, dementia precox and manic-depressive psychosis. This division neatly categorized most of the functional psychiatric disorders but not all of them. There remained many smaller fragments that had their own special characteristics that could not be fitted easily into Kraepelin's great dual system. These fragments were the unusual psychiatric syndromes—the rare, the exotic, and the atypical mental disorders.

### Classification

The following is a classification of unusual psychiatric syndromes: (1) Situation-specific syndromes or behavioral manifestations that arise from certain specific environmental conditions that are essential factors in the pathogenesis of the syndrome; (2) idiopathic syndromes, in which there is only a postulated constitutional predisposition to the syndrome and certain hypothesized psychodynamic factors; (3) culture-bound syndromes or psychiatric syndromes that are restricted to specific cultural settings; (4) atypical psychoses or psychotic syndromes that seem to belong to a well-known diagnostic entity, but that show certain symptomatic features that cannot be reconciled with the generally accepted typical characteristics of this diagnostic category.

### Situation-specific Syndromes

#### Brief Reactive Psychosis

A group of brief psychotic disorders presents certain characteristic features that distinguish these disorders from other psychotic conditions.

Most important, the symptoms of this type of psychotic breakdown are almost always preceded by stressful life events to which the patient reacts with strong dysphoric affect. In addition to a clear history of such precipitating events, the disorder is further characterized by its acute and florid symptoms, its short duration, and its good prognosis. The patient presents the picture of a severely disturbed person who has lost contact with reality and manifests at least one but frequently all the hallmarks of psychosis—specifically, hallucinations, delusions, formal thought disorder, and grossly aberrant behavior. The patient is often dangerous to himself or to others in his environment.

DSM-III lists the condition under the name brief reactive psychosis. Its diagnostic criteria appear in Table I.

**Epidemiology.** It is probably more frequent in the less developed countries than in industrialized nations. In the more developed countries, the disorder is most frequently seen in adolescents and young adults, and its incidence increases under conditions of war and disaster.

**Etiology.** By definition, the main precipitating factor is a major stress experience, closely related in time to the emergence of symptoms. Unstable personalities seem to be more susceptible than other persons to this kind of psychotic breakdown. No clear genetic links are known at this time, but it seems that the disorder is not one of the spectrum of schizophrenia.

**Treatment and Prognosis.** Symptomatic treatment with antipsychotic drugs and careful observation and nursing assistance are usually effective. Brief hospitalization may be required. Most patients recover within a few days. Follow-up psychotherapy may be indicated to deal with the aftermath of the stressful events and underlying personality problems.

#### Ganser's Syndrome

In 1898, the German psychiatrist Sigbert J. M. Ganser published a report about patients who showed a peculiar hysterical twilight state whenever they were replying to questions. The

TABLE I
DIAGNOSTIC CRITERIA FOR BRIEF REACTIVE PSYCHOSIS*

A. Psychotic symptoms appear immediately following a recognizable psychosocial stressor that would evoke significant symptoms of distress in almost anyone.

B. The clinical picture involves emotional turmoil and at least one of the following psychotic symptoms:
1. Incoherence or loosening of associations
2. Delusions
3. Hallucinations
4. Behavior that is grossly disorganized or catatonic

C. The psychotic symptoms last more than a few hours but less than 2 weeks, and there is an eventual return to the premorbid level of functioning. (Note: The diagnosis can be made soon after the onset of the psychotic symptoms without waiting for the expected recovery. If the psychotic symptoms last more than 2 weeks, the diagnosis should be changed.)

D. No period of increasing psychopathology immediatley preceded the psychosocial stressor.

E. The disturbance is not due to any other mental disorder, such as an Organic Mental Disorder, manic episode, or Factitious Disorder with Psychological Symptoms.

*From American Psychiatric Association: *Diagnostic and Statistical Manual of Mental Disorders*, ed 3. American Psychiatric Association, Washington, DC, 1980. Used with permission.

state was characterized by what he called "passing by" or "passing beside the point" (*vorbeireden*).

The most remarkable feature of this psychiatric disorder is this phenomenon of the patient's giving an utterly incorrect and often ridiculous reply, although it is quite clear that he has understood the sense of the question. Furthermore, although these patients often appear to be disoriented in time and place, their general behavior gives the distinct impression that they are alert. They are not confused in the usual sense.

Auditory and visual hallucinations, hysterical analgesia, true spatial and temporal disorientation, circumscribed amnesia, and lack of insight are often symptoms associated with the Ganser state. Thus, this syndrome frequently bears the marks of a psychosis.

**Epidemiology.** Ganser's syndrome is a rare disease but is observed relatively often in prisoners. The premorbid personality of the patient is often characterized by certain hysterical features. It has been pointed out that this condition has never been observed in persons of superior intelligence.

**Etiology.** Ganser's syndrome is a functional psychiatric disorder that occupies an intermediate position between neurosis and psychosis and between disease and malingering. In order to comply with DSM-III, it should be diagnosed as a type of factitious illness with psychological symptoms (see Table II). It may also be thought of as an unusual dissociative state in which the patient unconsciously attempts to mimic the disorganized behavior and thinking of a psychotic patient, according to the naive and personal mental image he has of madness. The secondary gain for the patient seems to be that

he escapes a threatening or frustrating reality by conveying the impression that he is insane to the people around him.

In almost every case the patient presenting Ganser's syndrome finds himself in a confining situation.

Most authors agree that Ganser's syndrome may occur as an isolated dissociative state or may occasionally be temporarily superimposed on other functional or organic mental disease.

**Treatment and Prognosis.** Like most hysterical twilight states, Ganser's syndrome is usually short lived, and the patient recovers within a few days or weeks. Psychotherapy, tranquilizers, and possibly intravenous injections of amobarbital are usually effective in speeding the patient's recovery.

### Folie à Deux (Double Insanity)

*Folie à deux* or *folie communiquée* was first described by Lasègue and Falret in 1877. Double insanity, psychosis of association, and in DSM-III, shared paranoid disorder, have been proposed as equivalent English terms. The disease is characterized by psychotic symptoms, including delusions shared by two or more persons living in close and intimate association.

### Diagnosis

The following conditions occur in this disorder: (1) One person is the dominant one. He or she is usually more intelligent than the other and gradually imposes his or her delusions on the more passive and originally healthy partner; (2) the two persons have lived a very closely knit existence in the same environment for a long period of time, relatively isolated from the outside world; and (3) the shared delusion is usually kept within the realm of possibility and may be based on past events or certain common expectations (see Table III).

**Epidemiology.** *Folie à deux* is a rare condition. It occurs more frequently in women, but the phenomenon has also been observed in men. It usually flourishes among those living in poverty and economic distress. The condition probably occurs in all ethnic and cultural groups.

Heredity may be a predisposing cause, particularly when the two persons come from the same family.

**Etiology.** A virtually inevitable condition for the occurrence of *folie à deux* is the close physical association and the intimate emotional bond between the two affected people. The mechanism of identification with the aggressor (the dominant person) probably plays a key role. The initiator of induced or shared psychosis is usually a paranoid schizophrenic whose special adjustment to the world is characterized not only by his or her persecutory and grandiose delusions, but also by a deeply rooted relationship with another, usually dependent, person.

The recipient or passive partner in this psychotic relationship has much in common with the dominant partner because of many shared life experiences, common needs and hopes, and, most important, a deep emotional rapport with the partner.

**Prognosis and Treatment.** The key therapeutic recommendation is to separate the recipient partner from the source of his delusions, who is usually schizophrenic. In a number of cases, the passive partner in the psychotic relationship loses his delusions and regains his unimpaired reality testing after he has been separated for some weeks or months from the actively psychotic partner. The dominant partner must be treated like any other patient suffering from a functional psychosis—that is, with pharmacotherapy or electroconvulsive treatment. The passive partner may also require organic treatment to speed his recovery, or he may recover spontaneously over a period of time. He almost certainly requires psychotherapy to help him work through the loss of the other person, and accept the fact that the other one is— and he himself has been—mentally ill.

TABLE II
CLINICAL FEATURES OF FACTITIOUS ILLNESS WITH PSYCHOLOGICAL SYMPTOMS (GANSER'S SYNDROME)*

| Essential Features | Associated Features | Other Features† |
|---|---|---|
| Production of psychological symptoms under the patient's voluntary control | Inconsistent mental symptoms, such as memory loss, hallucinations, dementia | May occur in adolescents |
| Symptoms do not fit any other mental disorder but may be superimposed on one | Suggestibility or negativism and uncooperativeness | Feeling of being caught in an inescapable situation, such as jail or severe threat of disability |
| The patient's goals—in contrast to malingering—are not easily recognized and require careful knowledge of his psychology to be understood | *Vorbeireden*—the giving of approximate answers, talking past the point | Has been observed under the stress of voluntary restraint, as during disulfiram treatment of alcoholism |
| | Substance use | |
| | Manifestations may be present only when patient believes he is being watched | Never observed in persons of superior intelligence |

\* Adapted from American Psychiatric Association: *Diagnostic and Statistical Manual of Mental Disorders*, ed 3. American Psychiatric Association, Washington, DC, 1980.
† Not cited as a clinical feature in DSM-III but may be present in this disorder.

TABLE III
CLINICAL FEATURES OF SHARED PARANOID DISORDER (*FOLIE À DEUX*)*

| Essential Features | Associated Features | Other Features† |
|---|---|---|
| Condition meets the criteria for paranoid disorder—predominance of persistent persecutory delusions and absence of characteristic schizophrenic symptoms—a manic or depressive syndrome, or an organic mental disorder | If the patient can be separated from the other, primarily paranoid person, his delusional beliefs will usually disappear | Whole families have been involved |
| | More than two persons may be involved | Murder and suicide have resulted from this disorder |
| The same delusions are at least partly shared by another person | | Drug abuse, aging, and social isolation may be contributory factors |
| | | Therapeutic results are greatly dependent on the response of the primary paranoiac; simple separation is rarely successful |

\* Adapted from American Psychiatric Association: *Diagnostic and Statistical Manual of Mental Disorders*, ed 3. American Psychiatric Association, Washington, DC, 1980.
† Not cited as clinical feature in DSM-III but may be present in this disorder.

## Idiopathic Syndromes

### Tourette's Disorder

In 1885, Gilles de la Tourette published a description of this autonomous syndrome when he was studying under Charcot at the Salpétrière in Paris. The syndrome is sometimes referred to as *tic convulsif* and in the German literature as *mimische Krampfneurose*. It is called Tourette's disorder in DSM-III (see Table IV).

The symptoms begin in childhood, usually between the ages of 2 and 12 years. Patients exhibit an expanding repertoire of motor tics that involve not only spasmodic grimacing but also violent stereotyped tics. Spasmodic movements of the upper part of the body may finally involve the whole body until the tic-like actions are expressed by hopping, skipping, jumping, grinding of the teeth, and other sudden compulsive motor outbursts that may, nevertheless, also involve a certain amount of coordination. What gives this syndrome its specific flavor and is pathognomonic for it is that the patients are compelled to utter swear words or obscenities, usually repeatedly calling out four-letter words. The patient's compulsive and stereotyped coprolalia, which is present in close to 60 percent of all cases, may be accompanied by compulsive coughing, spitting, blowing, or barking sounds. There may also be echolalia, consisting of the repetition of words or short phrases immediately after the patient has heard them. This strange behavior is exhibited spontaneously and unpredictably by the patient, although it may sometimes be triggered or made worse when he is experiencing emotional stress or fatigue.

**Epidemiology.** The syndrome in its typical form is rare. Males outnumber females in a ratio of three to one, and the parents seem to show paranoid and dominant traits in a higher than expected proportion.

**Etiology.** Organic pathology of the central nervous system has always been suspected of playing a role in the development of the unusually gross physical symptoms these patients display. However, soft neurological signs of central nervous system abnormalities and nonspecific electroencephalographic findings are observed in only about half of the patients. Autopsies of long-standing cases have not revealed any consistent lesions in the brain. Few familial cases of this disorder were reported until recently. The disease may be of functional origin, but most investigators currently consider it to be organic. The meaning of the patient's symptoms may be understood as a desperate attempt to draw attention to himself, and also as the automatized, inhibited rage reaction of a rejected child.

Other researchers concluded that in the cause of Tourette's disorder there is an important organic element involving a neurochemical abnormality of the central nervous system.

**Prognosis and Treatment.** Until recently, no reliable, effective treatment of the condition was known. The outcome was almost always poor. Eventually, many patients had to be institutionalized or live as recluses. None of Gilles de la Tourette's original cases developed favorably.

Haloperidol, a butyrophenone derivative, is the standard treatment. Doses of 6 to 180 mg a day are being prescribed, and most patients show more than a 90 percent reduction of their symptoms after 1 year of treatment. However, there is the everpresent risk that a patient receiving haloperidol may later develop tardive dyskinesia. It is possible that not only haloperidol, but other neuroleptic drugs, will be effective

TABLE IV
CLINICAL FEATURES OF TOURETTE'S DISORDER (GILLES DE LA TOURETTE'S DISEASE)*

| Essential Features | Associated Features | Other Features† |
|---|---|---|
| Presence of involuntary, rapid, repetitive, purposeless movements (tics) involving various muscle groups | Symptoms are aggravated by stress | Symptoms are exacerbated by amphetamine-like drugs and significantly reduced by neuroleptic drugs |
| Multiple vocal tics (coprolalia in 60 percent) | There may be echokinesia (imitation of movements of another person), palilalia (repetition of one's last words), obsessive thoughts, and compulsive impulses to touch | Occasional onset in adulthood carries a poor prognosis |
| The movements can be voluntarily suppressed, vary in intensity over time, and disappear during sleep | | |
| Duration of more than 1 year | Nonspecific EEG abnormalities, soft neurological signs, and psychological test abnormalities occur in about 50 percent of those affected | |
| Age of onset usually before puberty | | |

\* Adapted from American Psychiatric Association: *Diagnostic and Statistical Manual of Mental Disorders*, ed 3. American Psychiatric Association, Washington, DC, 1980.
† Not cited as a clinical feature in DSM-III but may be present in this disorder.

in alleviating the symptoms of Tourette's disorder. In some cases, drug treatment has been reported to be more effective in combination with psychotherapy. Behavior therapy has also been reported to reduce behavioral tics.

### Autoscopic Phenomena

These autonomous phenomena are, as a rule, not symptomatic of any particular mental disorder. They consist of hallucinatory experiences in which all or part of the person's own body is perceived as appearing in a mirror. This specter is usually colorless and transparent, but it is seen clearly, appears suddenly and without warning, and imitates the person's movements.

These phantoms, which have been referred to as dislocated body images, usually appear for only a few seconds and are usually seen at dusk. In addition to the visual perception, there may be hallucinations in the auditory and other modalities. The person usually retains a certain detached insight into the unreality of the experience, and reacts with bewilderment and often with sadness.

**Epidemiology.** Autoscopy is a rare phenomenon. Sex, age, heredity, and intelligence do not seem to be significantly related to its occurrence. Some persons have this experience once in a lifetime, but a few seem to be always close to it.

**Etiology.** The cause of the autoscopic phenomenon, like the cause of other complex hallucinations, is not known. One theory holds that the phenomenon reflects an irritation of areas in the temporoparietal lobes; another holds that it represents the projection of specially elaborated memory traces. Occasionally, but certainly not often, the phenomenon is symptomatic of schizophrenia or depression.

Many authors believe some normal persons with well developed imaginations, a visualizer type of personality structure, and narcissistic character traits may occasionally see their doubles under conditions of emotional stress.

**Prognosis and Treatment.** There is rarely any need for special treatment of this condition, which in most cases is neither incapacitating nor progressive. In certain instances, treatment of the accompanying neurological, neurotic, or psychotic condition may be indicated.

### Capgras' Syndrome

This psychiatric syndrome was described by the French psychiatrist Capgras in 1923 as *illusion des sosies*. Its main characteristic feature is the patient's delusional conviction that other persons in his environment are not their real selves but, instead, their own doubles who, like impostors, assume the role of the persons they impersonate and behave like them.

**Epidemiology.** This is a rare syndrome that occurs somewhat more frequently in women than in men.

No cases are known in which the condition definitely did not occur as a manifestation of another psychosis, usually schizophrenia.

**Etiology.** A necessary condition for the occurrence of this syndrome is the impairment of reality testing that develops only as a result of a psychotic process. Capgras explained the particular nature of this illusion as the result of feelings of strangeness combined with a paranoid tendency to distrust.

The uncoupling of normally fused components of perception and recognition may have a neurophysiological cause that so far remains unknown.

Capgras' syndrome may, on the other hand, be determined psychodynamically. The patient rejects the particular person involved and attributes bad features to him, but he cannot allow himself to become conscious of this rejection because of guilt feelings and ambivalent attitudes. What he really feels about the person with whom he is confronted is displaced to the double, who is an impostor and, therefore, may be safely and righteously rejected.

**Prognosis and Treatment.** The outcome of this condition depends on the success in treating the psychosis with which it is associated. Like other psychotic manifestations, it often responds to electroconvulsive treatment and pharmacotherapy, at least temporarily.

### Cotard's Syndrome

At the time when most current psychiatric classifications crystallized during the last two decades of the 19th century, the French psychiatrist Cotard described several patients suffering from a syndrome he referred to as *délire de négation*. Patients exhibiting *délire de négation* may complain of having lost not only their possessions, status, and strength, but also their heart, their blood, and their intestines. The world beyond them may be reduced to nothingness. The full-blown syndrome may be characterized by a delusion of immortality, which may occur in combination with other megalomanic ideas.

**Epidemiology.** In its pure form, the syndrome is seen most frequently in patients suffering from agitated depression, but occasionally it occurs in acute schizophrenic breakdowns and in certain brain syndromes, particularly of the senile and presenile types.

**Prognosis and Treatment.** This syndrome usually lasts only a few days or weeks, and it responds to any treatment that influences the basic disorder of which it is a part. Chronic forms of the syndrome are today almost exclusively associated with senile psychoses.

## Culture-bound Syndromes

### Amok

The Malayan word amok means to engage furiously in battle, and the amok syndrome consists of a sudden, unprovoked outburst of wild rage that causes the affected person to run madly about, armed with a knife—or today frequently with a firearm or grenade—and to attack and maim or kill indiscriminately any people and animals in his way before he is overpowered or killed himself. An average of 10 victims are involved. This savage homicidal attack is generally preceded by a period of preoccupation, brooding, and mild depression. After the attack the person feels exhausted, has complete amnesia for it, and often commits suicide. The Malayan natives also refer to the attack as *mata gelap* (darkened eye).

**Epidemiology.** The condition used to be almost exclusively associated with Malayan people, where it occurred only among men, but it has also been reported occasionally in African and other cultures in the tropics.

**Etiology.** It has been theorized that a culture that imposes heavy restrictions on adolescents and adults, but allows children free rein to express their aggression, may be especially prone to psychopathological reactions of the amok type. The belief in magical possession by demons and evil spirits may be another cultural factor that has contributed to the development of the amok syndrome in the Malayan people. Shame and loss of face have been proposed as determining factors for the amok behavior.

**Prognosis and Treatment.** The only immediate treatment consists of overpowering the amok patient and getting complete physical control over him. The attack is usually over within a few hours. Afterward, the patient may require treatment for the toxic confusional or the chronic psychotic condition that was the underlying cause.

### Koro

This is an acute anxiety reaction characterized by the patient's desperate fear that his penis is shrinking and may disappear into his abdomen, in which case he will die.

**Epidemiology.** The koro syndrome occurs almost exclusively among the people of the Malay archipelago and among the south Chinese (Cantonese), by whom this reaction is referred to as *suk-yeong*. Corresponding female cases have been described, the affected woman complaining of shrinkage of her vulva, labia and breasts. Occasional cases of a koro syndrome among people belonging to the Western culture have also been reported.

The typical syndrome is rather rare.

**Etiology.** Koro is a psychogenic disorder resulting from the interaction of cultural, social, and psychodynamic factors in specially predisposed personalities. Culturally elaborated fears about nocturnal emission, masturbation, and sexual overindulgence seem to give rise to the condition. Probably all koro patients have been troubled by what they consider sexual excesses and by fears about their virility. The patient's insight into his own condition is usually quite impaired.

**Prognosis and Treatment.** Patients have been treated with psychotherapy, neuroleptic drugs, and, in a few cases, electroshock treatment. As with other psychiatric disorders, the prognosis is related to the premorbid personality adjustment and the associated pathology.

### Latah

This syndrome has been observed mostly among the Malaysian people, and it occurs clinically in two different forms. One is the startle reaction, in which a sudden stimulus provokes the suspension of all normal activity and triggers a set of unusual and inappropriate motor and verbal manifestations, over which the affected person has no voluntary control. The other type of latah is a mimetic or echo reaction, in which a sudden stimulus compels the affected person to imitate any action or words to which he is exposed. In other words, he exhibits sustained and complete echopraxia, echolalia, and often automatic obedience. Although the person affected by the latah reaction cannot control or inhibit his peculiar behavior, he remains aware of the situation and may verbally protest against any unacceptable action he is forced to carry out, such as disrobing in public.

Latah may become a chronic disease that, after years, leads to permanent automatic obedience and echo reactions, forcing the affected person into hiding and inducing marked personality deterioration.

**Epidemiology.** The disorder is found in women of all Malaysian races, especially the Javanese, but it is also observed in a smaller proportion of men in Malaysia.

**Etiology.** It may be an intense fright reaction involving disorganization of the ego and obliteration of the ego boundaries. A sudden fright may provoke inhibition of proper perceptual-motor integration and may, through loosening of the ego boundaries, render the patient powerless to resist any stimuli coming from the environment. As a result, the patient's behavior is determined by echolalia and echopraxia. The coprolalia that is sometimes observed may be a symbolic defensive act.

**Treatment.** As with other periodic psychogenic disorders, the treatment should consist of psychotherapy and pharmacotherapy.

### Piblokto

Occurring among the Eskimos and sometimes referred to as Arctic hysteria, this condition is characterized by attacks lasting from 1 to 2 hours, during which the patient, who is usually a woman, begins to scream and to tear off and destroy her clothing. While imitating the cry of some animal or bird, she may then throw herself on the snow or run wildly about on the ice, although the temperature may be well below zero. After the attack the person appears quite normal and usually has amnesia for it. The Eskimos are reluctant to touch any afflicted person during the attack because they think that it has something to do with evil spirits.

Piblokto is almost certainly a hysterical state of dissociation. It has become much less frequent than it used to be among the Eskimos.

### Wihtigo

Wihtigo or windigo psychosis is a psychiatric illness confined to the Cree, Ojibway, and Salteaux Indians of North America. They believe that they may be transformed into a wihtigo, a giant monster that eats human flesh. During times of starvation a man may develop the delusion that he has been transformed into a wihtigo, and he may actually feel and express a craving for human flesh. Because of the belief in witchcraft and in the possibility of such a transformation, symptoms concerning the alimentary tract, such as loss of appetite or nausea from trivial causes, may sometimes cause the patient to become greatly excited for fear of being transformed into a wihtigo.

### Voodoo and Other Possession States

In North American black ghettos, voodoo is called root work, and patients may appear on any hospital service presenting with organic or psychological symptoms.

The voodoo cult that is practiced in African societies and among native West Indians is particularly widespread in Haiti. A survey of the incidence of psychiatric disorders in that country reveals an increased incidence of hysterical and epileptic disorders.

Aside from the usually short-lasting, voluntary, ritual-induced hysterical or psychotic states, the psychiatric significance of voodoo lies in the widespread belief of the people of these cultures in the possibility of being involuntarily possessed by evil spirits. Because of this belief, chronic hysterical and psychosomatic symptoms may be induced, and appropriate treatment for such conditions and for major psychoses due to other causes may be delayed.

## Atypical Psychoses

### Atypical Cycloid Psychoses

The cycloid psychoses, which are characterized by phasic recurrences, are subdivided into three forms: motility psychoses, confusional psychoses, and anxiety-blissfulness psychoses.

In their hyperkinetic form, the motility psychoses may resemble a manic or catatonic excitement. A hyperkinetic motility psychosis may be distinguished from a manic state by the presence of many abrupt gestures and expressive movements that seem to be the result of autonomous mechanisms and are apparently not responses to environmental stimuli or expressions of the patient's mood. These disorders may be differentiated from catatonic excitement by the absence of stereotyped and bizarre movements.

The akinetic form of motility psychosis seems to be identical with the typical picture of a catatonic stupor. These states are separated from typical schizophrenia mainly on the basis of their rapid and favorable course, which does not lead to any personality deterioration.

The excited confusional psychosis must be distinguished from some confused manic states. The difference can be found mainly in the greater lability of the patient's emotional state, which may be characterized by prevailing anxiety, rather than euphoria. These patients are not so distractible as the manic patients are, they often misidentify persons in their environment, and the incoherence of their speech seems to be independent of a flight of ideas.

The inhibited confusional psychosis shares with the catatonic stupor and the akinetic motility psychosis the symptoms of mutism and greatly decreased motor behavior, but it differs from these states by the preservation of better self-care and greater spontaneity and by the absence of negativism.

The anxiety phase of the anxiety-blissfulness psychosis may very much resemble the picture of what is generally known as agitated depression, but it may also be characterized by so much anxious inhibition that the patient can hardly move. Periodic states of overwhelming anxiety and paranoid ideas of reference are characteristic of this condition, but self-accusations, hypochondriacal preoccupations, and other depressive symptoms, as well as hallucinations, may accompany it.

The blissfulness phase manifests itself most frequently in expansive behavior and grandiose ideas, which are concerned less with self-aggrandizement than with the mission of making others happy and of saving the world. In women the dominant emotion is usually one of passive ecstasy, often the result of fantastic religious delusions.

Within the group of atypical cycloid psychoses, periodic recurrences are most frequent in the motility psychoses; they are less frequent in the anxiety-blissfulness psychoses and are still rarer in the confusional psychoses. Complete recovery of the patient is the rule in all these conditions.

### Atypical Schizophrenias

Patients suffering from affect-laden paraphrenia express manifold delusions, which may be well systematized. They receive their characteristic color through the strong and sustained affect that pervades them. This affect is pathological, although it may be an appropriate reaction to the content of the delusions, and it may be expressed as irritability, anxiety, or ecstasy.

Periodic catatonia, which differs from typical schizophrenic catatonia by the periodicity of its excited or stuporous phases, may sometimes resemble an akinetic or hyperkinetic motility psychosis, but it usually presents distinctive symptoms of stereotypy, bizarreness, grimacing, and a peculiar mixture of akinetic and hyperkinetic manifestations at the same time.

Schizophasia is characterized by a profound thought disturbance that results in a disorder of concept formation and abstract thinking, and expresses itself in marked incoherence of speech. Such patients may at times resemble excited confusional psychotics; at other times they may resemble excited catatonics.

The prognosis is, in general, much poorer for the atypical schizophrenias than for the cycloid psychoses, and it is most guarded for the schizophasic patients, who often remain chronically ill or may recover with a permanent personality defect.

### REFERENCES

Caine E D, Margolin D L, Brown G L, Ebert M H: Gilles de la Tourette's syndrome, tardive dyskinesia, and psychosis in an adolescent. Am J Psychiatry *135:* 241, 1978.
Cannon W B: Voodoo death. Am Anthropol *44:* 169, 1942.
Hajal F, Leach A M: Familial aspects of Gilles de la Tourette syndrome. Am J Psychiatry *138:* 90, 1981.
Lehmann H E: Unusual psychiatric disorders, atypical psychoses, and brief reactive psychoses. In *Comprehensive Textbook of Psychiatry*, ed 4, H I Kaplan, B J Sadock, editors, p 1224. Williams & Wilkins, Baltimore, 1985.
Murphy H B M: History and the evolution of syndromes: The striking case of latah and amok. In *Psychopathology: Contributions from the Social, Behavioral, and Biological Sciences*, M Hammer, K Salzinger, S Sutton, editors, p 33. John Wiley & Sons, New York, 1973.
Reich P, Gottfried L A: Factitious disorders in a teaching hospital. Ann Intern Med *99:* 240, 1983.
Synodinou C, Christodoulou G N, Tzavara A: Capras' syndrome and prosopagnosia. Br J Psychiatry *132:* 413, 1977.
Teicher M: Windigo psychosis: A study of a relationship between belief and behavior among the Indians of northeastern Canada. Proc Am Ethnol Soc *11:* 1, 1961.

---

## 23.2  FACTITIOUS DISORDERS

### Introduction

Factitious disorders are characterized by the repeated, knowing simulation of a physical or mental illness for no apparent purpose other than obtaining immediate medical or psychiatric treatment. To support their history, these patients may feign symptoms suggestive of a disorder, or may initiate the production of symptoms through self-mutilation or interference with diagnostic procedures. For example, body temperature, routinely recorded and presumably an objective measure, may be made to appear elevated through either manipulation or substitution of a thermometer. Similarly, urine collected for laboratory examination may be contaminated with feces or blood, obtained by self-laceration, so as to suggest infection or renal disease.

The unique aspect of these disorders is that the sole objective is to assume the role of a patient. Without an acute emotional crisis or a recognizable motive, as would be evident in an act of malingering, and, indeed, without a need for treatment, many of these patients make hospitalization itself a primary objective and often a way of life.

Three separate categories of factitious disorders are described in DSM-III. Among these, chronic factitious illness with physical symptoms, more commonly known as Munchausen syndrome, is the most frequently recognized and reported subtype. It is the prototype for these disorders. The other two categories are factitious illness with psychological symptoms and other factitious illness with physical symptoms.

### Chronic Factitious Illness with Physical Symptoms

Although this disorder has been designated by a variety of labels (see Table I), the term Munchausen syndrome has proved the most durable. However, the use of the term factitious disorder is preferred because it states more precisely the nature of the disorder.

#### Epidemiology

Data suggest that the true prevalence of this disorder is unknown. In its extreme form it is relatively rare.

There is controversy about the sex ratio, but it seems that this disorder occurs equally in men and women.

#### Etiology

It is currently believed that the disorder represents a final common pathway for certain predisposed persons.

Early investigators considered factitious illness as a form of malingering. Speculated motives for seeking hospitalization included bed and board, evasion of justice, and obtainment of drugs.

Psychological models of factitious illness generally emphasize the etiological significance of childhood deprivation and rejection. The usual history reveals that one or both parents are experienced as rejecting figures who are unable to form close relationships.

The physician is perceived by these patients as a potential source of the sought-for love, and as a person who will fulfill the unmet dependency needs. The physician serves as a substitute father figure and as the object of a father transference. The patient uses the facsimile of genuine illness to recreate the original parent-child interaction. The disorder is a form of repetition compulsion—repeating the basic conflict of needing and seeking acceptance and love, while expecting that it will not be forthcoming. The physician and staff become transformed into rejecting parents.

A frequent occurrence in the history of these patients is a personal history of serious illness, disability, or exposure to genuine illness in a family member or significant extrafamilial figure. A history of prior or current employment as a nurse, laboratory technician, ambulance driver, physician, or other health-related position is so common as to suggest inclusion as a clinical feature, as well as a causal factor. Consistent with the concept of poor identity formation is the observation that these patients oscillate between two separate roles—a health professional and a patient—with momentary confusion as to which role is being played at the time.

The cooperation or encouragement of persons other than the patient in simulating a factitious illness represents a rare variant of the disorder, suggesting another possible causative factor. Although the majority of these patients act alone, there are well-documented instances in which friends or relatives participate in the fabrication of the illness.

#### Clinical Features

The essential feature of factitious illness with physical symptoms, as delineated in DSM-III, is the patient's plausible presentation of factitious physical symptomatology of such a degree that he is able to obtain and sustain multiple hospitalizations. The frequency of hospitalizations will be so extensive that the individual spends the majority of his days either seeking or maintaining hospitalization. DSM-III states that persons with this disorder have voluntary control over their behavior. However, the sense of voluntary control is subjective and can only be inferred by the outside observer. Difficulty arises because the patient, when confronted with evidence of his simulation, often denies the voluntary production of illness.

The patient's ability to manipulate his activities and falsifications so as to avoid detection suggests that he is able, through judgments involving timing and choice of mechanical activity, to conceal the nature of his illness or to change its course. By any definition, some degree of voluntary control is present. A single instance or episode of illness may be accidental, but repeated occurrences suggest voluntary production.

TABLE I
LABELS APPLIED TO FACTITIOUS ILLNESS WITH PHYSICAL SYMPTOMS

| |
| --- |
| Munchausen syndrome |
| Hospital hoboes |
| Hospital addiction |
| Chronic factitious illness |
| Ahasuerus's syndrome |
| Peregrinating patients |
| Hospital vagrants |
| Polysurgical addiction |
| Pathomime |
| Problem patients |
| Professional patients |
| Factitial illness |

This does not mean that strong underlying emotional factors are absent. There is a compulsive quality about these patients and their activities. As in a compulsion disorder, the patient may admit to the behavior but claim that he cannot control himself.

Table II outlines the DSM-III diagnostic criteria of this disorder.

### Course and Prognosis

Onset of the disorder is usually in early adult life, although it may appear during childhood or adolescence. As the course progresses, increasing sophistication about medicine and hospitals is acquired.

These patients often spend time in jail, usually for minor crimes, such as burglary, vagrancy, and disorderly conduct. Intermittent psychiatric hospitalization may also occur.

This disorder is extremely incapacitating to the patient, often producing severe trauma or untoward reactions related to treatment. As may seem obvious, a course of chronic hospitalization is incompatible with meaningful vocational work and sustained interpersonal relationships. Prognosis in most cases is poor.

Although no adequate data are available about the ultimate outcome for these patients, it seems likely that a few of them die as a result of needless medication, instrumentation, or surgery. Given the often expert simulation and risks these patients experience, it is assumed that some patients die without this disorder being suspected.

### Diagnosis

As noted in DSM-III, any combination of the following features suggests a diagnosis of chronic factitious illness with physical symptoms: pseudologia fantastica, with emphasis on the dramatic presentation; disruptive behavior on the hospital ward, including noncompliance

TABLE II
DIAGNOSTIC CRITERIA FOR CHRONIC FACTITIOUS DISORDERS WITH PHYSICAL SYMPTOMS*

A. Plausible presentation of physical symptoms that are apparently under the individual's voluntary control to such a degree that there are multiple hospitalizations.

B. The individual's goal is apparently to assume the "patient" role and is not otherwise understandable in light of the individual's environmental circumstances (as is the case in Malingering).

* From American Psychiatric Association: *Diagnostic and Statistical Manual of Mental Disorders*, ed 3. American Psychiatric Association, Washington, DC, 1980. Used with permission.

with hospital rules and regulations and arguing excessively with nurses and physicians; extensive knowledge of medical terms and hospital routines; continued analgesics for reported pain; evidence of multiple surgical interventions—a "gridiron" abdomen or burr holes; an extensive history of traveling; social isolation, as evidenced by few if any visitors while hospitalized; a fluctuating clinical course, with the rapid production of complications or new pathology once the initial work-up proves to be negative.

The psychiatric interview should be performed in detail, following the outline of the standard history and mental status examination. Great emphasis should be given to securing information from any available friend, relative, or other informant, because interviews with reliable outside sources often reveal the false nature of the patient's illness. Although time-consuming and tedious, verification of all the facts presented by the patient with those hospitals or other facilities he reports having been treated by previously is essential. The value of an independent history cannot be overstated.

**Differential Diagnosis.** Any other disorder in which physical symptoms are prominent should be considered in the differential diagnosis. The possibility of true physical illness must always be explored.

*Somatoform Disorders.* Factitious illness is differentiated from somatization disorder (Briquet's syndrome) by the voluntary production of factitious symptoms, the extreme course of multiple hospitalizations, and the seeming willingness of the patient to undergo an extraordinary number of mutilative procedures.

Patients diagnosed as having a conversion disorder are not usually sophisticated in medical terminology and hospital routines, and their symptoms have a direct temporal relation or symbolic reference to specific emotional conflicts. Conversion symptoms are often amenable to suggestion, hypnosis or psychotherapy. *La belle indifférence* may or may not be present in these patients.

*Hypochondriasis.* In hypochondriasis the essential feature is the patient's fear that he has a disease, and his behavior, including doctor shopping and preoccupation with bodily functions, follows from that fear. Hypochondriasis differs from factitious illness in that the hypochondriacal patient does not voluntarily initiate the symptom production, and hypochondriasis typically has a later age of onset.

*Personality Disorder.* An antisocial personality disorder usually appears at an earlier age than does a factitious illness, and antisocial persons do not usually resort to a way of life marked by chronic hospitalizations and invasive procedures.

Because the behavior of a person with a factitious illness may be interpreted as attention seeking and because some of these persons show a flair for the dramatic, they may be diagnosed as having a histrionic (hysterical) personality disorder. However, not all of these patients present this histrionic flair; many are withdrawn and bland.

Consideration of the person's chaotic life style, past history of disturbed interpersonal relations, identity crises, drug abuse, self-damaging acts, and manipulative tactics may lead to the diagnosis of borderline personality disorder.

These persons do not have the eccentricities of dress, thought, or communication that characterize the DSM-III diagnosis of schizotypal personality disorder.

*Schizophrenic Disorders.* The diagnosis of schizophrenia is most likely made because of the patient's admittedly bizarre life style, but he does not usually meet the specified criteria of schizophrenia. If the patient has the fixed delusion that he is actually ill and acts on that belief by seeking chronic hospitalization, he may meet the criteria for a schizophrenic disorder. However, this seems to be the exception, rather than the rule, for few such patients show such evidence of thought disorder.

*Malingering.* Factitious illness differs from malingering in that no obvious, recognizable environmental goal accounts for the production of the symptoms. Though patients with a factitious illness may have a complicating history of drug abuse, they should not be considered merely as drug addicts, for they do not usually show symptoms of withdrawal if their medication is abruptly discontinued.

## Treatment

Ideas about treatment have ranged from no treatment at all to involuntary long-term psychiatric hospitalizations or custodial care. Such approaches as electroconvulsive therapy, and hypnosis have been suggested but have not proved successful. Case histories of successfully treated patients describe the use of various therapeutic modalities, but all stress initial treatment in a closed-ward setting.

Blacklisting of these patients is frequently advocated.

Some authors reject this view. They think that, even when recognized as presenting with a factitious illness, these patients should be evaluated.

Personal reactions of physicians and staff members are of great significance in the treatment of the patient and in the establishment of a working alliance with the patient. It is almost predictable that these patients evoke feelings of futility, bewilderment, betrayal, hostility, and even contempt.

Further investigation, in the form of controlled treatment and outcome studies, is necessary to determine what therapeutic modalities are most effective.

### Factitious Illness with Psychological Symptoms

Occasionally, a person simulates a mental disorder by presenting factitious psychological symptoms. These patients have in the past been described as presenting hysterical Ganser's syndrome, pseudopsychosis, or pseudodementia. In contrast to the patient who presents factitious physical symptoms, these patients seek admission to mental hospitals.

The clinical picture is often that of a panpsychosis, with features of organic, affective, and schizophrenic disorders exhibited simultaneously. An associated feature is *vorbeireden*, the practice of giving approximate answers or of talking past the point. For example, when asked, "What color is snow?" a patient may answer "Red."

This disorder is extremely difficult to distinguish from malingering, and its occurrence without a coexisting mental disorder has not been established. Persons with factitious illness exhibiting psychological symptoms often present with physical symptoms as well.

Psychodynamic formulations of this disorder resemble those of chronic factitious illness with physical symptoms.

Also observed in this group of patients are transient amnesia and transient loss of personal identity. These patients often take drugs secretly, e.g., LSD, mescaline, cocaine, to produce symptoms.

The DSM-III diagnostic criteria for this disorder are presented in Table III.

### Other Factitious Illness with Physical Symptoms

Some patients may present with a factitious disorder with physical symptoms but not to the extent or with the severity previously described. Provision is made in DSM-III for such a residual category: other factitious illness with physical symptoms. Patients in this group differ from those in the better-studied category in that their factitious symptoms suggest a more benign condition and do not require hospitalization. Com-

TABLE III
DIAGNOSTIC CRITERIA FOR CHRONIC FACTITIOUS
DISORDERS WITH PSYCHOLOGICAL SYMPTOMS*

A. The production of psychological symptoms is apparently under the individual's voluntary control.

B. The symptoms produced are not explained by any other mental disorder (although they may be superimposed on one).

C. The individual's goal is apparently to assume the "patient" role and is not otherwise understandable in light of the individual's environmental circumstances (as is the case in Malingering).

* From American Psychiatric Association: *Diagnostic and Statistical Manual of Mental Disorders*, ed 3. American Psychiatric Association, Washington, DC, 1980. Used with permission.

mon examples of such symptoms include voluntary dislocation of the shoulder and dermatitis artefacta.

**REFERENCES**

Asher R: Munchausen's syndrome. Lancet *1:* 339, 1951.
Black D: The extended Munchausen syndrome: A family case. Br J Psychiatry *138:* 466, 1981.
Bursten D: On Munchausen's syndrome. Arch Gen Psychiatry *13:* 261, 1965.
Evans D L, Hsiao J K, Nemeroff C B: Munchausen syndrome, depression and the dexamethasone suppression test. Am J Psychol *141:* 570, 1984.
Hyler S E, Sussman N: Chronic factitious disorder with physical symptoms (the Munchausen syndrome). Psychiatr Clin North Am *4:* 365, 1981.
Ireland P, Sapira J D, Templeton B: Munchausen's syndrome. Am J Med *43:* 579, 1967.
Phillips M R, Ward N G, Ries R K: Factitious mourning; painless parenthood. Am J Psychiatry *140:* 420, 1983.
Raspe R E: *The Singular Travels, Campaigns, and Adventures of Baron Munchausen*. Cresset Press, London, 1948.
Sparr L, Pankrantz L D: Factitious posttraumatic stress disorder. Am J Psychiatry *140:* 1016, 1983.
Sussman N, Hyler S E: Factitious disorders. In *Comprehensive Textbook of Psychiatry*, ed 4, H I Kaplan, B J Sadock, editors, p 1242. Williams & Wilkins, Baltimore, 1985.

# 23.3 POSTPARTUM DISORDERS

## Introduction

Postpartum disorders are a group of diverse conditions—affective disorders, functional psychoses, or organic-like mental disorders—that occur in the postpartum period. Depressive disorder is the most common of these conditions. Postpartum disorders are believed to result from the stresses undergone during pregnancy and the period from 3 days to approximately 30 days after childbirth. These stresses include: (1) en-docrine changes, (2) changes in body image, (3) activation of unconscious psychological conflicts pertaining to pregnancy, and (4) intrapsychic reorganization of becoming a mother. According to DSM-III, this disorder is classified most often as a brief reactive or schizophreniform psychosis, and is used only when no other psychotic disorder can be diagnosed.

## Epidemiology

Data from studies of normal pregnant women indicate that from 20 to 40 percent of women report emotional disturbance or cognitive dysfunction, or both, in the early postpartum period, the so-called postpartum blues.

Questionnaires exploring psychiatric symptoms to an unselected sample of women up to 1 year after childbirth revealed that 25 percent had more than six symptoms that had apparently arisen postpartum. The most common symptoms were fatigue, irritability, tension, and anxiety. Disturbances of psychotic proportions occur with one to two per 1,000 deliveries.

## Etiology

### Biological Factors

Most of the contributions in this area have focused on the possible interaction of thyroid and adrenal function with the high estrogen and progesterone level of pregnancy, and the abrupt termination of these high levels of sex hormones at parturition.

A state of steroid withdrawal may exist after pregnancy. Cases of psychoses upon withdrawal of large amounts of oral contraceptive steroids have been reported.

There have been some reports on hormone treatment of postpartum syndromes. Treatment with progesterone alone has not been shown to produce a remission of the original illness.

Studies from early pregnancy to the postpartum period revealed that the sleep system is profoundly affected throughout pregnancy and sometimes for several months after delivery.

### Psychosocial Factors

Psychodynamic studies of postpartum mental illness point to conflicting feelings within the mother with regard to her mothering experience, her new baby, her husband (for example, as lover, father, and co-parent), and herself (for example, as mother of her new baby and as a child of her own mother).

## Clinical Features

One of the outstanding features relates to the time of onset of illness. Symptoms are almost never noted before the third day postpartum. Symptoms usually occur from the third to the seventh day. This latent period may be the period during which some kind of chemical or hormonal development related to the childbearing process takes place and leads to later manifestation of illness. Prodromal symptoms include insomnia, restlessness, feelings of fatigue, depression of spirit, irritability, headache, and lability of mood. According to some studies, insomnia was the most distressing symptom. Later symptoms include suspiciousness, evidence of confusion or incoherence, irrational statements, obsessive concern over trivialities, and refusal of food.

The percentages of patients receiving diagnoses of delirium have gone down over the years, presumably due in part to improved obstetrical techniques and lessened toxicity in relation to pregnancy.

The clinical symptoms center on the patient's relationship to the baby and the maternal role. Depressed patients may manifest excessive concern about the baby's health or welfare, or guilt about their lack of love or wish to care for the baby. They may express feelings of inadequacy with regard to the baby's care. When psychosis is present, delusional material may involve the idea that the baby is dead or defective in some way. The birth may be denied, and ideas of being unmarried or virginal, or ideas of persecution, influence, or perverse sexuality may be expressed. Hallucinations may contain similar material and may involve voices telling the woman to kill the baby. Behavior toward the baby may be characterized by avoidance or anxious oversolicitude. Infanticide and suicide are infrequent, but occasionally occur.

### Diagnosis

The cardinal diagnostic feature of these illnesses is their relationship to the postpartum period, with the greater proportion of these illnesses having their onset within the 30-day period after childbirth. Depressive neurosis seems to be the most common occurrence seen in these patients, with schizophrenia or affective disorders being less common but more often resulting in hospitalization. Symptoms of impairment of cognitive functioning—such as disorientation, impaired memory and judgment, and lability of mood—may lead to the diagnosis of an organic affective or delusional syndrome or, more often, a diagnosis of atypical psychosis. Much of the content of these illnesses relates to the ambivalent feelings about motherhood and its attendant child care responsibilities. In addition to the need for routine clinical psychiatric ex-

aminations, the presence of atypical features may necessitate neurological consultations, electroencephalograms, brain scans, and echoencephalograms. Computerized axial tomography scanning may also be indicated. Neuropsychological testing is helpful in assessing the degree of impairment of cognitive functioning and its chronicity.

### Differential Diagnosis

Those women with a prior history of schizophrenia or affective disorders are seen as having a recurrence related to the stresses of pregnancy. Because of its clinical similarity to postpartum depression, hypothyroidism should always be considered. Cushing's syndrome is not uncommon after a pregnancy, and is frequently associated with a depressive state. Drug-induced depression is not uncommon, especially in those receiving antihypertensive or other drugs with known central nervous system-depressant properties. Pentazocine (Talwin), a drug with psychotomimetic properties, is widely used in the postpartum period and has been reported to produce bizarre mental phenomena; those with prominent organic mental symptoms should receive careful evaluation for infection, encephalopathy related to toxemia, and neoplasm.

### Treatment

Electroconvulsive therapy is most often mentioned in the treatment of psychoses, especially depressive illnesses. There has been a decline in the use of this modality with the advent of the use of tricyclic antidepressants, which are the treatment of choice in all but seriously suicidal patients. Failure of pharmacotherapy is an indication for use of electroconvulsive therapy. For patients who suffer manic illnesses, lithium carbonate therapy alone or in combination with phenothiazines during the first 7 days is the treatment of choice. For those with schizophrenic-type psychoses, phenothiazines are indicated. These pharmacological agents are not recommended for use by mothers who are breast feeding.

Psychotherapy is usually indicated for these patients after the period of acute psychosis is past. This therapy is usually directed at the conflictual areas that have become evident during the period of evaluation. Therapy may involve helping the patient to accept the feminine role accentuated by the childbearing experience, or to accept her angry, jealous feelings toward the child occasioned by her own thwarted dependency needs in relation to her own mother. Changes in environmental factors may also be indicated. Increased support from the husband and other persons in the environment may be helpful in lessening stress. Most studies report high rates of recovery from the acute phase of illness.

## REFERENCES

Handley S L, Dunn T L, Baker J M, Cockshott C, Gould S: Mood changes in puerperium, and plasma tryptophan and cortisol concentrations. Br Med J 2: 18, 1977.

Jarrahi-Zadeh A, Kane F J, Jr, Van de Castle R L, Lachenbruch P A, Ewing J A: Emotional and cognitive changes in pregnancy and early puerperium. Br J Psychiatry 115: 797, 1969.

Kane F J Jr: Postpartum disorders. In Comprehensive Textbook of Psychiatry, ed 4, H I Kaplan, B J Sadock, editors, p 1238. Williams & Wilkins, Baltimore, 1985.

Karacan I, Heine W, Agnew H W, Williams R L,

Webb W B, Ross J J: Characteristics of sleep patterns during late pregnancy and the postpartum periods. Am J Obstet Gynecol 101: 570, 1968.

Melges F T: Postpartum psychiatric syndromes. In Psychosomatic Medicine, M F Reiser, editor, vol 30, no 1, p 59. Harper & Row, New York, 1968.

Metz A, Stump K, Cowen P J, Elliot J M, Gelder M G, Grahame-Smith L J: Changes in platelet $\alpha$-2-adrenoceptor binding postpartum: Possible relation to maternity blues. Lancet 1: 495, 1983.

Nott P N: Psychiatric illness following childbirth in Southhampton: A case register study. Psychol Med 12: 557, 1982.

O'Hara M W, Neunaber D J, Zekoski E M: Prospective study of postpartum depression: Prevalence, course and predictive factors. J Abnorm Psychol 93: 158, 1984.

Stein G, Milton F, Bebbington P: Relationship between mood disturbances and free and total plasma tryptophan in postpartum women. Br Med J 21: 457, 1976.

Thuwe I: Genetic factors in puerperal psychosis. Br J Psychiatry 125: 378, 1974.

# 24

# Sleep and Sleep Disorders

## Introduction

Sleep is a regular, recurrent, easily reversible state of the organism that is characterized by relative quiescence and by a great increase in the threshold or response to external stimuli relative to the waking state.

Sleep is both a biological and a behavioral state. Certain electroencephalographic (EEG) and polygraphic characteristics are part of a definition of sleep because of their regular and constant association with sleep.

## Normal Sleep

As a person falls asleep, his brain waves go through certain characteristic changes, classified as stages 1, 2, 3, and 4 (see Fig. 1). The waking EEG is characterized by $\alpha$-waves of 8 to 12 cycles a second and low-voltage activity of mixed frequency. As the person falls asleep, he begins to show a disappearance of $\alpha$-activity. Stage 1, considered the lightest stage of sleep, is characterized by low-voltage, regular activity at 4 to 6 cycles a second. After a few seconds or minutes, this stage gives way to stage 2, a pattern showing frequent spindle-shaped tracings at 13 to 15 cycles a second (sleep spindles) and certain high-voltage spikes known as K-complexes. Soon thereafter, $\delta$-waves—high-voltage activity at 0.5 to 2.5 cycles a second—make their appearance (stage 3). Eventually, in stage 4, these $\delta$-waves occupy the major part of the record. The division of sleep into stages 1 through 4 is a somewhat arbitrary division of a continuous process.

Sleep is cyclical, with four or five periods of emergence from stages 2, 3, and 4 to a stage similar to stage 1 (see Fig. 2). Persons awakened during those periods of emergence frequently— 60 to 90 percent of the time—report that they have been dreaming. Such periods are characterized not only by stage 1 EEG patterns but also by rapid conjugate eye movements, (REM) and a host of other distinguishing factors, including irregularity in pulse rate, respiratory rate, and blood pressure; the presence of full or partial penile erections; and generalized muscular atony interrupted by sporadic movements in small muscle groups. These periods differ markedly from typical stage 1 sleep, as well as from the other three stages. Because of their distinguishing characteristics and specific neurophysiological and chemical character, these periods are now almost universally seen as constituting a separate state of sleep. This view is reinforced by the fact that similar periods differing from the remainder of sleep are found in nearly all mammals and birds studied.

This distinct state of sleep is referred to as D-sleep (desynchronized or dreaming sleep), and the remainder of sleep as S-sleep (synchronized sleep). These two states of sleep are also known as REM sleep (rapid eye movement sleep) and NREM sleep (nonrapid eye movement sleep), as paradoxical sleep and orthodox sleep, and as active sleep and quiet sleep. See Table I for the different terms to describe stages of sleep. In this section, D and REM, and S and NREM, are used interchangeably.

Several important characteristics of the typical night's sleep should be noted (see Fig. 2). First of all, there are four or five D-periods (or REM periods) during the night, and the total time taken up by the periods (D-time) is about 1½ hours, a little more than 20 percent of the total sleep time. The first D-period occurs about 70 to 120 minutes after the onset of sleep; the interval may be longer in some normal persons, but it is significantly shorter only in a few abnormal clinical and experimental conditions, such as D-deprivation and narcolepsy.

The cyclical nature of sleep is quite regular and reliable; a D-period covers about every 90 to 100 minutes during the night. The first D-period tends to be the shortest, usually lasting less than 10 minutes; the later D-periods may last 15 to 40 minutes each. Most D-time occurs in the last third of the night, whereas most stage 4 sleep occurs in the first third of the night.

S-sleep (synchronized, NREM or nondreaming sleep) can be neatly organized according to depth: Stage 1 is the lightest stage, and stage 4

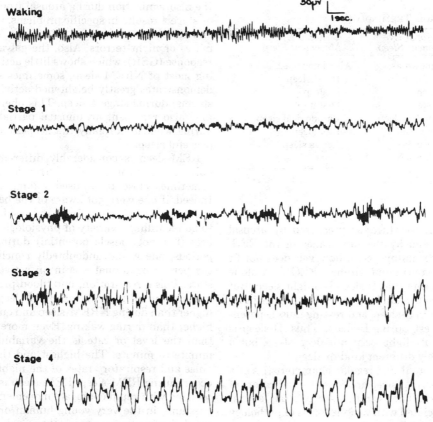

FIGURE 1.   The electroencephalogram of sleep in a human adult. A single channel of recording—a monopolar recording from the left parietal area, referred to the ears as a neutral reference point—is shown for each stage.

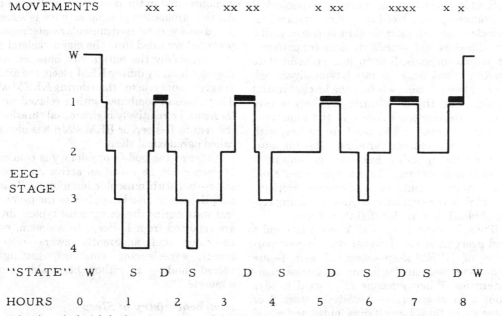

FIGURE 2.   A typical night's sleep in a young adult. W, waking state; S, synchronized or nondreaming sleep, also called non-REM sleep; D, desynchronized or dreaming sleep (REM sleep).

TABLE I
SLEEP STAGE TERMINOLOGY*

| Nonrapid Eye Movement Sleep | Rapid Eye Movement Sleep |
|---|---|
| Also known as: | Also known as: |
| NREM sleep | REM sleep |
| S-sleep | D-sleep |
| S-state | D-state |
| Orthodox sleep | Paradoxical sleep |
| Slow-wave- | Fast sleep |
| sleep | Active sleep |
| Quiet sleep | |

* S = synchronized and D = desynchronized or dreaming.

is the deepest stage, as measured by arousal threshold and by the appearance of the EEG. D-sleep (dreaming sleep), however, does not fit into that continuum. Human EEG data alone might indicate that D-sleep is a light sleep. But the arousal threshold in animals is higher in D-sleep than in S-sleep, and resting muscle potential is lowest during D-sleep. Thus, D-sleep is neither truly light sleep nor deep sleep, but a qualitatively different kind of sleep.

The constant and regular characteristics of a night of normal sleep are sensitive indicators of disturbance. They can be used to study alterations associated with various forms of pathology or produced by various drugs.

Much of the basic work on sleep derives from studies by Eugene Aserinsky, Nathan Kleitman, and William Dement in the 1950s.

Simple recordings of various physiological measures—pulse, blood pressure, respiration, muscle potential, galvanic skin response, penile erections—reveal some fairly clear-cut patterns. In normal persons, S-sleep is a peaceful state relative to waking. Pulse rate is typically slowed, 5 or 10 beats a minute below the level of restful waking, and the pulse during S-sleep is very regular. Respiration behaves in the same way, and blood pressure also tends to be low, with few minute-to-minute variations. Resting muscle potential of body musculature is lower in S-sleep than in waking. There are no or few rapid eye movements and seldom any penile erections. Blood flow through most tissues, including cerebral blood flow, is also slightly reduced.

Thus, in most ways NREM-sleep is a quiet and peaceful sleep. However, the deepest portions of NREM-sleep—stages 3 and 4—are sometimes associated with unusual arousal characteristics. When someone is aroused ½ to 1 hour after sleep onset—usually in stage 3 or stage 4—he finds himself disoriented and would probably do poorly on a formal mental status examination at such a time. In certain persons

the disorganization during arousal from stage 3 or stage 4 results in specific problems, including enuresis, somnambulism, and stage 4 nightmares or night-terrors. Also, the galvanic skin response (GSR), which shows little activity during most of NREM-sleep, sometimes suddenly demonstrates greatly heightened activity (GSR storms) during stage 4 sleep. This phenomenon may also represent an unusual partial arousal during what is normally the deepest and most peaceful sleep.

REM-sleep is considerably different. Many polygraphic measures show irregular patterns sometimes close to aroused waking patterns. Indeed, if one were not aware of the behavioral state of the person or animal and one happened to be recording a variety of physiological measures (but not muscle potential) during REM-periods, one would undoubtedly conclude that the person or animal was in an active waking state. Pulse, respiration, and blood pressure in humans are all high during REM-sleep—much higher than during NREM-sleep and quite often higher than during waking. Even more striking than the level or rate is the variability from minute to minute. The highest and the lowest pulse and respiratory rates of the night usually occur during REM-sleep. REM-sleep is also associated with rapid conjugate movements of the eyes and, in the very young human or animal, rapid phasic movements of other small muscles. Almost every REM-period is accompanied, in the human male, as well as in other species, by a partial or full penile erection; this has been demonstrated in the monkey, as well as in man. All this aroused-appearing activity is superimposed on a very relaxed muscular state: muscular potential recorded from the major skeletal muscles, especially the antigravity muscles, shows the least activity during REM-sleep; the muscles are even more relaxed than during NREM-sleep. That arousal, combined with a relaxed musculature and a relatively high arousal threshold, is the reason D-sleep or REM sleep has also been called paradoxical sleep.

As far as the body's physiology is concerned, D-sleep could be called an active and aroused state—but with muscular immobility. This description could also be applied to the psychological state during dreaming; most typical dreams are reported from D-sleep. In a dream, one is conscious and apparently aware—watching things, experiencing emotions, getting involved—and yet all without being able to move a muscle.

### Neurochemistry of Sleep

A great deal of work has helped to elucidate the basic neurochemistry of sleep. The best evidence involves the monoamines, with cell bodies in the brain stem. The neurohumor most clearly involved is brain serotonin. Studies demonstrated that the administration of the serotonin precursor *l*-tryptophan induces sleep (reduces sleep latency) and tends to increase total sleep and to increase D-sleep time in humans, as well as in animals, without altering the states and stages of sleep.

A large number of studies support the role of serotonin in sleep. One of the best ways to raise brain serotonin levels at its normal sites of occurrence is by the administration of the serotonin precursor *l*-tryptophan. As mentioned, the amino acid *l*-tryptophan, administered at bedtime, can reduce sleep latency in normal persons and in insomniacs. *l*-Tryptophan is being used as a hypnotic medication, and since it is a natural food substance it does not suffer from the many problems of current sleeping medications. It does not work as a successful hypnotic, however, in many persons.

There is also good evidence that dopamine is involved in sleep-waking mechanisms. Pharmacological methods of increasing brain dopamine tend to produce arousal and wakefulness, whereas dopamine blockers, such as pimozide and the phenothiazines, tend to increase sleep time somewhat, without altering the cycles of sleep or the relative amounts of S-sleep and D-sleep.

Norepinephrine may also be involved in the control of sleep. There seems to be an inverse relationship between functional brain norepinephrine and D-sleep. Drugs and manipulations that increase the available brain norepinephrine produce a marked decrease in D-sleep, whereas reducing brain norepinephrine levels increases D-sleep. That action of norepinephrine almost certainly involves $\alpha$-adrenergic receptors, since an $\alpha$-blocker, such as phenoxybenzamine, increases D-time, but a $\beta$-blocker, such as propranolol, has no effect.

There is little question that acetylcholine is also involved in sleep. It has been demonstrated that physostigmine and similar cholinergic agents can trigger D-sleep in humans. Acetylcholine does not occur in well-delineated systems, as do the monoamines, but is extremely widespread in the brain.

## Sleep Disorders

In approaching the sleep disorders, only three basic symptoms or groups of symptoms need be considered: insomnia, difficulty in initiating or maintaining sleep; hypersomnolence, which includes excessive sleep and excessive daytime sleepiness; and episodic sleep disturbances. Insomnia is by far the most common symptom, and it is also the one most frequently encountered by psychiatrists.

In many instances, exploring the causes of insomnia and hypersomnolence leads to well-known medical and psychiatric illnesses as causes; these illnesses are not described in detail in this section. When a symptom leads to a specific sleep-related illness, such as apnea or narcolepsy, this illness is delineated here in detail.

## Insomnia

Insomnia is a symptom that can have many different causes. Some of the causes are beginning to be understood; new ones are being discovered every year (see Table II).

### *Definition*

Insomnia refers to difficulty in sleeping. There are basically only two complaints: difficulty in falling asleep and difficulty in remaining asleep. Insomnia must be clearly differentiated from merely short sleep. Some persons get along well on about 5 hours of sleep a night. Short sleepers should not require medical attention.

Insomnia is an extremely common complaint. In the course of a year, up to 30 percent of the population suffer from insomnia and seek help for it. In many cases, no treatment may be required; in many other cases, a careful diagnostic work-up reveals specific causes of the insomnia, and specific treatment aimed at the cause may be used. Psychological factors account for

TABLE II
CAUSES OF INSOMNIA*

| Sleep-onset Insomnia† | Sleep-maintenance Insomnia‡ |
|---|---|
| Anxiety or tension | Depression |
| Environmental change | Environmental |
| Emotional arousal | change |
| Fear of insomnia | Sleep apnea |
| Phobia of sleep | Nocturnal myoclonus |
| Disruptive environment | Dietary factors |
| Pain or discomfort | Parasomnias |
| Restless legs syndrome | Drugs |
| Caffeine | Alcohol |
| Alcohol | Drug interactions |
| Medications | Drug withdrawal |
| Drug withdrawal | Dream interruption |
| Jet lag | Pain or discomfort |
| Work-shift changes | Disease |
| Delayed sleep phase | Aging |
| Akathisia | Advanced sleep phase |

* The boundaries between the columns are not entirely distinct.

† Difficulty in falling asleep.

‡ Difficulty in staying asleep.

50 percent of all insomnias evaluated in sleep laboratories. The prescription of a sleeping pill as a long-term remedy for insomnia should be a relatively rare occurrence.

### Etiology

The grouping of insomnia by chief complaint is still useful—difficulty in falling asleep (sleep-onset insomnia) versus difficulty in remaining asleep—although there is considerable overlap; some causes can produce either or both symptoms. Some refer to three symptoms—difficulty in falling asleep, frequent awakenings during the night, and early morning awakening. However, the second and third symptoms almost always occur together and are associated with the same probable cause. Thus, they are combined here in the symptom, difficulty in remaining asleep.

Difficulty in falling asleep is certainly more common in the young, and difficulty in remaining asleep is more frequently seen in older people, but there are enough exceptions that the distinction is worth keeping. The prevalence of insomnia is higher in women.

The two columns in Table II represent broad categories of causal factors. The lists are in no way final or static. Growing attention to insomnia in sleep laboratory studies has gradually increased the number of conditions listed and the number of cases of insomnia that can be classified. Not more than 20 percent of insomniac patients now need to be classified as idiopathic.

**Pain or Discomfort.** Any painful or uncomfortable condition can produce insomnia, usually difficulty in falling asleep.

**Sleep Apnea.** Sleep apnea is characterized by multiple apneas during sleep associated with loud snoring and daytime sleepiness. Although not a common cause of insomnia, it is important, since it can be life threatening and is often treatable by nasopharyngeal surgery. This condition is discussed in greater detail below.

**Nocturnal Myoclonus.** Nocturnal myoclonus is a neuromuscular abnormality that manifests itself in sudden, repeated contractions of one or more muscle groups—usually the leg muscle—during sleep. Each jerk lasts less than 10 seconds. Nocturnal myoclonus typically includes extension of the big toe and partial flexion of the ankles, the knee, and, less frequently, the hip. Myoclonus often occurs in both legs simultaneously, but it can occur in either leg alone, without any apparent pattern. Nocturnal myoclonic jerks usually occur in isolation, not as parts of generalized body movements. Partial arousal or a full awakening often follows the myoclonic jerk. Myoclonic jerks usually occur every 20 to 40 seconds in episodes lasting from a few minutes to an hour or more. Between the episodes of nocturnal myoclonus, sleep seems normal.

The patient is usually unaware of his myoclonus but complains either of frequent nocturnal awakenings and unrefreshing sleep or of excessive daytime sleepiness. Sometimes the patient is unaware of any problem, and only the bed partner complains.

Nocturnal myoclonus is seen predominantly in middle-aged and older people. It is extremely rare in children. Estimates of the incidence of nocturnal myoclonus among serious insomniacs range from 1 to 15 percent. There is some suggestion that the myoclonus is worse or appears in some patients at times of stress. A few studies suggest familial patterns for some types of nocturnal myoclonus, but the issue has not yet been explored in depth.

Nocturnal myoclonus is often observed in association with the restless legs syndrome.

**Restless Legs Syndrome.** Restless legs syndrome, a condition closely related to nocturnal myoclonus, is characterized during waking by extremely disagreeable but rarely painful creeping sensations deep inside the calf, occasionally in the feet and the thighs, and in rare instances in the arms. The dysesthesias occur mainly when the person is sitting or lying down—hence, the insomnia—and at other times of inactivity during the day. They cause an almost irresistible urge to move the legs, and the sensations are usually relieved by vigorous exercise. The relief gained from such exercise varies; in severe cases the dysesthesias reappear almost as soon as the exercise is terminated. Although not painful, the disorder may be extremely stressful, occasionally leading to serious depression.

Almost all patients with restless legs syndrome also have nocturnal myoclonus.

Restless legs syndrome is exacerbated by sleep deprivation, often occurs with particular severity during pregnancy, and typically becomes more serious with age. Curiously, the syndrome often disappears with fever.

About one-third of patients with restless legs syndrome show a familial pattern. It has been suggested that the syndrome may be transmitted as an autosomal, dominant trait with reduced penetration. The cause of restless legs syndrome is currently unknown.

**Dietary Factors.** Dietary factors as causes for insomnia may turn out to be important, but have not yet been investigated in depth. General malnutrition can play a role in producing insomnia.

**Episodic Events.** Episodic nocturnal events

of many different kinds are discussed below under episodic sleep disturbances, since the event itself—night-terrors, nocturnal angina, sleepwalking—is often the symptom of chief concern. However, all or most of the episodic events can sometimes produce the symptom of insomnia—difficulty in remaining asleep.

**Direct Drug Effects.** A variety of drugs can produce insomnia, both difficulty in falling asleep and difficulty in remaining asleep. The stimulants such as amphetamine and methylphenidate clearly have this effect. Among the substances of special interest to psychiatry, the monoamine oxidase inhibitors and ethanol are frequently associated with insomnia. Although some persons use a small dose of alcohol in order to relax and get to sleep, continuing the intake of large quantities of alcohol results in great distortions of normal sleep patterns, involving multiple awakenings, and complaint of nonrestorative sleep. Other drugs implicated in insomnia include antimetabolites, thyroid preparations, ACTH, oral contraceptives, and β-blockers.

**Drug Withdrawal Effects.** A frequent and often unrecognized cause of insomnia is drug withdrawal. The difficulty may be either in falling asleep or in remaining asleep. The effect is found in its most dramatic form in withdrawal from hypnotic medication, especially the barbiturates.

Insomnia is quite common, for instance, after withdrawal from phenothiazines and other antipsychotics. Occasionally, withdrawal from minor tranquilizers, such as the benzodiazepines, is associated with insomnia: similarly, insomnia is occasionally reported after the withdrawal of the more sedative antidepressant drugs.

Alcohol in large continued doses produces very disturbed sleep both during its administration and after its withdrawal. The withdrawal period is quite frequently associated with insomnia, vivid dreams, and nightmares, often lasting weeks or longer. Alcohol and drug abuse account for about 12 percent of all cases of reported insomnia.

**Thyroid Dysfunction.** Abnormal thyroid function clearly affects sleep. Hyperthyroidism causes fragmented, short sleep. Hypothyroidism, on the other hand, seems to cause excessive sleepiness.

**Brain Stem and Hypothalamic Lesions.** Neoplastic, inflammatory, vascular, traumatic, or other lesions are rare causes of insomnia.

**Aging.** Normal aging is usually associated with decreased sleep time and an increased number of awakenings during the night. However, there is considerable variation; a sizable minor-

ity of people actually sleep longer with increasing age.

**Anxiety.** Anxiety can sometimes produce insomnia. In a young, medically healthy person, some form of anxiety is probably the chief cause of insomnia.

Simple or transient anxiety is a phenomenon all persons experience before an examination, a difficult meeting, or an interview. It can frequently produce one night or several nights of insomnia—almost always difficulty in falling asleep.

Chronic neurotic anxiety can produce insomnia when the particular psychopathology either involves sleep and dreaming, or becomes especially prominent at night. A diagnosis of insomnia produced by chronic neurotic anxiety should be made only if there is at least a hint of some definite fear of what will happen if the person lets go or, at least, some supporting evidence, such as difficulty in letting go at other times—for instance, inability to relax and daydream, or inability to have orgasms.

Some patients develop anxiety about their dreams or about specific dreams, which can produce either difficulty in falling asleep or awakenings during the night. One specific condition has been described in a small number of patients characterized by an awakening early during each REM-period of the night. This has been called dream interruption insomnia. Patients with this condition may have experienced nightmares during long REM-periods, and have developed the awakenings as a mechanism to avoid the occurrence of nightmares.

Psychotic and prepsychotic anxiety can produce insomnia, usually difficulty in falling asleep. A prepsychotic patient may present with insomnia as his only symptom.

Chronic muscular tension anxiety is common. It is a condition in which there may originally have been a separate cause for anxiety or for insomnia, but the chronic anxiety is then expressed in the muscles, which become so tense as frequently to preclude sleep.

**Depression.** Among middle-aged and older people, depression is a frequent cause of insomnia. At times, the patient may not be experiencing conscious sadness or hopelessness, or may be unwilling to speak of it. In such situations, a probable diagnosis of depression can often be made on the basis of insomnia (difficulty in remaining asleep), combined with such symptoms as weight loss, constipation, loss of energy, and loss of interest in the world.

Patients with dysthymia (depressive neurosis) show normal REM latencies—the time between falling asleep and the first REM period. Major affective disorders produce decreased REM latencies.

**Environment and Phase Shifts.** There are many environmental causes of insomnia, such as noisy or disturbing sleeping environments. One of the frequent causes of insomnia is jet lag which usually disappears spontaneously in 2 to 7 days.

**Habit Insomnia.** In habit insomnia, the assumption is that, whatever causes may have originally produced the insomnia in the past, it is currently maintained by habit or association. The patient's bed is experienced as a place for tossing and turning, a place for the insomnia, rather than as a place for sleep. The conditions should be suspected when an insomniac describes sleeping better when away from home or away from his usual bed.

**Pseudoinsomnia.** By pseudoinsomnia, doctors and sleep researchers mean that a patient complains of insomnia, of hardly sleeping at all, and yet careful observation by nurses in a hospital or sleep laboratory reveals that sleep does occur—quite often 4 to 8 hours of sleep a night.

Some hypochondriacs tend to exaggerate all symptoms for various psychological reasons.

## Treatment

The first step in treating insomnia is careful medical and psychiatric evaluation. When the diagnosis is not clear on the basis of a clinical evaluation, one or several nights of sleep in a sleep laboratory or specialized sleep disorders clinic may be recommended. Conditions such as sleep apnea, nocturnal myoclonus, and a few others can be clearly demonstrated in a sleep laboratory. Sleep patterns in depression are now becoming so well established that sleep laboratory recordings can sometimes help make a diagnosis of endogenous depression when it is not clear on clinical grounds.

**Specific Treatment.** The specific treatment varies with the particular illness or condition producing the insomnia. The painful or uncomfortable conditions listed in the first column of Table II are often amenable to appropriate medical or surgical treatment. Sleep apnea is sometimes found to be secondary to local pathology of the neck and throat, especially of the oral pharynx. In these cases, a tracheotomy, which can be left open at night to ensure proper breathing and closed in the daytime, has often provided dramatic relief. When apnea is due to obesity of local tissues, dieting can be useful. When sleep apnea appears to be related to a brain stem abnormality (central type), stimulant medication has been used successfully.

Nocturnal myoclonus can sometimes be helped by a number of different treatments. Occasionally, muscle relaxation techniques have been helpful. Sometimes simply reassuring the patient that myoclonus is not a dangerous condition can be useful and can decrease the associated awakenings, even if the actual muscle jerks are not significantly reduced. When pharmacotherapy is required, clonazepam is often effective. Vitamin E has also been used successfully.

When an insomniac patient is taking multiple medications for different causes, one of the medications or an interaction between medications may be responsible for the insomnia. Treatment involves carefully withdrawing the medications one by one; it is surprising how often this procedure is successful.

Insomnia that is secondary to psychiatric or environmental conditions usually responds to specific treatment. When anxiety of a psychotic or prepsychotic type is responsible for the insomnia, antipsychotic medication is indicated, and psychotherapy may also be useful. Anxiety related to particular conflicts—for instance, anxiety about letting go and losing control of one's aggressive or sexual impulses—is often treatable by psychotherapy. When the problem is chronic and closely related to the patient's character, long-term nondirective therapy—psychoanalysis—may occasionally be useful. In some cases of anxiety, antianxiety medications (minor tranquilizers) are helpful. When the anxiety is partly muscular, techniques such as relaxation therapy, medication, and biofeedback can be effective. These techniques sometimes help other insomniacs as well. When environmental problems or schedules produce insomnia, a careful evaluation usually reveals some way in which the environmental factors can be altered.

In major depression, an antidepressant medication usually improves the insomnia, along with the depression. Amitriptyline is the medication of choice in a large number of cases.

When no certain, treatable cause of insomnia can be determined, some simple nonpharmacological treatments should be tried before turning to the long-term use of a sleeping medication. The treatments include careful attention to dietary intake; some people are especially sensitive to the effects of certain foods. Difficulty in sleeping after drinking coffee, tea, or carbonated beverages containing caffeine is common, and these beverages can be avoided in the evening. Alcohol in small doses may help certain people get to sleep, but the pharmacological effects of alcohol are quite disruptive to sleep, and some insomniacs can definitely benefit from not drinking any alcohol or, at least, from avoiding alcohol in the evening.

Exercise is often useful in moderate quantities if done regularly, preferably in the afternoon or early evening and not immediately before bedtime. In people whose bedtime, mealtimes, and work times vary considerably, simply regularizing the schedule can considerably improve sleep if done carefully over a period of weeks or months.

In some patients with habit insomnia, the bed is associated with sleeplessness, instead of sleep. In such cases, a form of deconditioning is useful. The patient is instructed to associate his bed only with sleep. If he cannot get to sleep after 5 minutes, he is to get out of bed, read a book, or perform some other activity in another room until he is worn out and really wants to sleep. He can then return to bed but must get up again if he does not fall asleep in a few minutes. As can be imagined, that procedure can be quite painful for the first few days, but it has been successful in helping some severe cases of insomnia.

**Sleeping Pills.** Several groups of insomniacs may require sleeping pills. Certainly, patients with pain or discomfort from medical and surgical conditions sometimes require sleeping medication for a brief period; but analgesics to remove the pain may be preferable to a sleeping medication in those instances. Similarly, persons with insomnia related to environmental changes—changes in occupation, jet lag, and so on—who are unhappy about the loss of a few nights' sleep may sometimes require medication. Patients with such conditions can be given sleeping pills for a period of days or weeks, with the understanding of both patient and doctor that it is to be a short-term measure and that there may be a period of difficult sleep after withdrawal of the medication.

The long-term use of sleeping pills should be restricted to a fairly small group of patients who have severe insomnia for which no clear medical or psychiatric cause has been established, or perhaps when a cause has been established but no adequate or specific treatment has been found.

In patients with the rare metabolic illness porphyria, the administration of barbiturates can be dangerous and life threatening. In patients with sleep apnea, in which respiratory function is borderline in any case, the additional respiratory depression produced by any central nervous system depressant can be life threatening.

Most hypnotic medications lose their effectiveness after long-term administration. Sleep may be worse during the chronic use of hypnotics than after they are withdrawn.

The most highly recommended sleeping medication is flurazepam (Dalmane) which has the advantage of being minimally abused. A more recent medication is triazolam (Halcion). Barbiturates are effective for short-term use; but are often abused and are restricted by governmental agencies who frequently view their use as similar to that of narcotics, the latter being a questionable viewpoint.

## Hypersomnolence

Hypersomnolence includes two groups of symptoms: complaints about excessive amounts of sleep (hypersomnia) and complaints about excessive daytime sleepiness (somnolence). In some situations, the two symptoms are clearly separate, but many of the conditions responsible for hypersomnolence can, at times, produce both symptoms.

Table III describes a causal classification of hypersomnolence. As with the symptom of insomnia, there are borderline conditions and situations hard to classify, as well as idiopathic cases. The main point, however, is the same: Hypersomnolence should be considered a symptom with many causes, and the cause should be sought. It may hardly be necessary to state here that hypersomnolence is not simply an illness for which a stimulant is the cure; it is doubtful that many physicians would ever have considered it in this light, but some patients may have done so in prescribing treatment for themselves.

The most common conditions responsible for hypersomnolence are narcolepsy, alcohol and other drug conditions, depression, and sleep apnea.

### Conditions Producing Chiefly Excessive Sleep

**Kleine-Levin Syndrome.** This condition is characterized by recurrent periods of hypersomnia, usually associated with hyperphagia. The hypersomnia is characterized by prolonged sleep from which the patient is incapable of being aroused. Apathy, irritability, and even confusion may be present during wakefulness, with the patient withdrawing from social contacts and returning to bed as soon as possible in most cases.

Prominent associated features consist of disturbances of appetite and social interaction during the periods of hypersomnia. The patient often voraciously consumes large amounts of food. However, anorexia has been described in a few cases. Bizarre behavior frequently involves

TABLE III
CAUSES OF HYPERSOMNOLENCE*

| | Chiefly Medical | Chiefly Psychiatric or Environmental |
|---|---|---|
| Principal symptom: excessive sleep (hypersomnia) | Kleine-Levin syndrome<br>Menstrual associated<br>Metabolic or toxic conditions<br>Trypanosomiasis or other encephalic conditions | Depression (some)<br>Alcohol<br>Other depressant medications<br>Withdrawal from amphetamines and other stimulants |
| Principal symptom: excessive daytime sleepiness | Narcolepsy<br>Sleep apnea<br>Hypoventilation syndrome<br>Hyperthyroidism<br>Other metabolic and toxic conditions | Depression (some)<br>Medication and medication withdrawal (as above)<br>Phase shift<br>Non-24-hour cycles |

Excessive daytime sleepiness is sometimes a secondary symptom of any of the causes of insomnia (see Table II); in other words, insufficient sleep at night sometimes produces excessive daytime sleepiness.

* The items listed in the two columns are not entirely separable.

loss of sexual inhibitions, inappropriate sexual advances or public exhibitionism, delusions and hallucinations, frank disorientation, memory impairment, incoherent speech, excitation or depression, and truculence. Unexplained fevers have occurred in a few patients.

In most cases, several attacks of hypersomnia, each lasting for one or several weeks, are experienced by the patient in a year. With few exceptions, the first attack occurs between the ages of 10 and 21 years. The disorder appears almost invariably self-limited, with spontaneous, enduring remission occurring before age 40 years in most cases.

Most authors ascribe Kleine-Levin syndrome to an intermittent, organic dysfunction in limbic or hypothalamic structures, without known cause.

Kleine-Levin syndrome is probably relatively uncommon, although its exact prevalence is undetermined.

No specific treatment is available for Kleine-Levin syndrome. Reassurance about the intermittent and usually self-limited course can be useful. Psychotherapy may help when psychological factors appear to precipitate the attacks.

**Menstrual-associated Hypersomnolence.** This category is reserved for women in whom the appearance of intermittent, marked hypersomnolence occurs at or shortly before the onset of the menses. The entity may resemble Kleine-Levin syndrome in other respects, at times involving similar behavioral patterns and voracious eating.

Endocrine factors are probably involved, but specific abnormalities in laboratory endocrine measures have not been reported.

The invariant relationship between menses and the onset of attacks makes this entity distinct from other periodic hypersomnolence syndromes. Care must be taken to establish that interattack intervals are characterized by relatively normal patterns of sleep and arousal, in order to exclude episodic aggravation of continuous hypersomnolence syndromes by menstrual periods.

Premenstrual tension, including some associated depression and increased sleep, is quite common. What is currently called menstrual associated hypersomnolence may simply be an exaggerated form of premenstrual tension.

**Infections and Inflammatory Conditions.** Infectious causes of hypersomnolence as an isolated symptom are extremely rare or nonexistent at present in the United States, but they are common in Africa and have been seen at times in many parts of the world. The best-known such condition is trypanosomiasis, which produces sleeping sickness as classically described by von Economo. The pathology involves lesions in the hypothalamus and the surrounding areas.

**Metabolic and Toxic Conditions.** Hypersomnolence can be a symptom of encephalopathy produced by elevated blood urea nitrogen, as well as many other metabolic abnormalities, and also a symptom of encephalopathies produced by poisons. Usually, other symptoms of encephalopathy are present.

**Alcohol and Other Depressant Drugs.** The sustained use of alcohol or other central nervous system depressants can produce excessive sleep time and daytime sleepiness. Discovering the cause of this kind of hypersomnolence should ordinarily present no problem. However, a patient may consciously suppress or unconsciously repress the extent of his alcohol or drug use. In unclear cases, it may be useful to obtain blood levels of alcohol and other drugs.

In patients taking phenothiazines or other antipsychotics, somnolence occurs when the dose is excessive.

**Tolerance to Stimulant Drugs.** Excessive

sleep and depression are typical symptoms of withdrawal from amphetamines. Withdrawal from other stimulant drugs, including caffeine, can produce similar effects.

**Depression.** Serious depression is almost always associated with some disorder of sleep. Major depression is most often associated with insomnia, especially difficulty in remaining asleep and early morning awakening. However, subgroups of depressed patients definitely show hypersomnia—excessive sleep—during their depressions. This finding may be quite typical in bipolar patients, and it occurs in some unipolar cases as well. In addition, a large number of dysthymic disorders and other mild depressions, even cases of simple mourning, are associated with hypersomnia, especially in young persons.

Some persons have periods of hypersomnia and periods of insomnia associated with different depressive episodes or different stages of the same episode. It seems that hypersomnia, in general, occurs when the patient is in some way worrying about and dealing with his problems, whether he is in therapy or not. This may be related to the high REM time in hypersomnia.

**Other Psychiatric Conditions.** More rarely, hypersomnia occurs in a number of other psychiatric illnesses or conditions. Young schizophrenic patients often go through periods of excessive sleep. It is sometimes associated with depressive mood, and is sometimes more a matter of complete avoidance and withdrawal from the world.

Hypersomnia sometimes forms part of a hysterical condition, in which case the sleep appears to be a means of escape from an intolerable, often sexual, situation. Severely obsessional patients sometimes report hypersomnia for unknown reasons.

### Conditions Producing Chiefly Excessive Daytime Sleepiness

**Narcolepsy.** The essential features of classical narcolepsy are an abnormal tendency to sleep during the day (excessive daytime sleepiness), often disturbed nocturnal sleep, and pathological, virtually undeniable, episodic attacks of REM sleep. D-Sleep abnormalities manifested in narcolepsy include sleep-onset REM periods, hypnagogic hallucinations, cataplexy, and sleep paralysis. The cataplexy and sleep paralysis are abnormally appearing and dissociated REM sleep motor inhibitory processes.

Excessive daytime sleepiness and naps, and the accessory symptoms of cataplexy, sleep paralysis, and hypnagogic hallucinations, are the classically recognized tetrad of narcolepsy. Patients generally first report the onset of daytime sleepiness before the accessory symptoms are noted.

The sleepiness may persist throughout the day, but more often it is periodic and may be relieved by a sleep attack or by a nap from which the patient characteristically awakens refreshed. Thus, there are often refractory periods of 2 or 3 hours of almost normal alertness. The sleep attacks are usually associated with characteristic times of the day, such as after meals, when some degree of sleepiness is quite normal. The attacks are typically irresistible and may even occur while eating, riding a bicycle, or actively conversing and during sexual relations.

Cataplexy, which occurs in two-thirds to 95 percent of the cases, represents the paralysis or the paresis of the antigravity muscles in the awake state. A cataplectic attack often begins during expressions of emotion, such as laughter, anger, and exhilaration. The attacks vary in intensity and frequency; they can consist of a weakening of the knees, a jaw drop, a head drop, or a sudden paralysis of all the muscles of the body—save the eyes and the diaphragm—leading to a complete collapse. Consciousness is usually clear during short cataplectic attacks. However, cataplectic and sleep attacks can occur in combination, and the patient may experience intense sleepiness and possibly hypnagogic hallucinations. In a cataplectic attack merging with a sleep attack, the patient's eyes are closed, and, except for breathing, the patient is immobile, usually lying on the ground or slumped in a chair. As a result, many cataplectic attacks are incorrectly regarded as sleep attacks by observers. However, most frequently, the patient is able to remember events occurring during the cataplectic attacks, particularly brief ones. The frequency of cataplectic attacks varies considerably—from less than once a week in 4 percent of cases to more than four a day in 5 percent of patients.

Sleep paralysis, which occurs in 17 to 57 percent of patients with narcolepsy, occurs during sleep onset or emergence from sleep. The patient is conscious but unable to move; he usually regains the use of his muscles in 30 to 60 seconds, but sometimes not for a period of minutes. The attacks, although often innocuous and self-limited—some patients can force the attack to end by moving their eyes rapidly—can be particularly frightening when accompanied by hypnagogic imagery.

Hypnagogic hallucinations are vivid perceptual dream-like experiences occurring at sleep onset or on awakening. They occur in about 50 percent of the patients. The accompanying affect is usually fear or dread. The hallucinatory imagery is remembered best after a brief narcoleptic sleep attack, when it is often described as a dream.

Patients frequently report memory disturbances or blackouts (lapse of memory) and automatic behaviors. They come to after having performed appropriate or inappropriate complex motor acts lasting 15 minutes to 1 hour, but are then amnesic for the whole episode.

The nocturnal sleep of narcoleptics is usually characterized by rapid sleep onset but with complaints of awakenings during the night.

Other occasionally associated symptoms include ptosis, blurred vision, and diplopia.

*Course, Complications, and Prevalence.* The course in narcolepsy usually involves continuous symptoms at about the same level, except that sleep attacks may begin several years before cataplexy. The age of onset is usually in the decade between 15 and 25 years.

Predisposing factors include the significant disruption of nocturnal sleep that is induced by work schedules. Narcolepsy that is precipitated by shift work or other kinds of disturbances in nocturnal sleep may be compensable.

Complications include automobile accidents, side effects of medications used to treat the disorder, and abuse or habituation to stimulant drugs. The prevalence of narcolepsy has been calculated to be four cases per 10,000. Males and females are affected in equal numbers. A hereditary component is evidenced by the fact that relatives of narcoleptic index cases have a 60-fold greater risk of having narcolepsy than do persons in the general population.

*Differential Diagnosis.* Narcolepsy must be differentiated from all other conditions producing hypersomnolence, particularly sleep apnea.

*Treatment.* The most widely used treatment for narcolepsy involves the use of stimulant medication. This treatment controls sleep attacks and daytime sleepiness dramatically. Doses as high as 40 to 60 mg a day of amphetamine or methylphenidate may be required.

Forced naps are sometimes useful. Quite often, the scheduling of one to four daytime naps, even if the patient's schedule allows only 10 minutes or so for such naps, enables the patient to function normally at other times without the use of medication.

Dietary management can occasionally be useful. A few narcoleptic patients have been especially sensitive to the postprandial drowsiness that everyone experiences at times after large meals, especially large protein meals. In these patients, it is important to advise light meals or vegetarian meals during the day, and to alert the patient not to schedule a heavy meal just before important activities that require alertness.

In the treatment of other symptoms, especially the cataplectic attacks, tricyclic antidepressant medication has been found useful, especially imipramine, protriptyline, and chlorimipramine. Because of their side effects, these drugs must be carefully weighed against the added benefits. At times, antidepressants must be used in combination with small doses of amphetamines or other stimulants.

Psychotherapy and support can sometimes be useful in helping a narcoleptic patient make life adjustments and deal with emotional problems produced by his illness. On the other hand, psychotherapy is not useful and can be potentially harmful if it is undertaken on the basis of a misdiagnosis–that is, if the therapist or the patient, or both, believe that the symptoms are psychological in origin and can be completely cured by psychotherapy.

**Sleep Apnea.** Sleep apnea is a condition characterized by recurrent episodes of breathing stoppage during sleep. The essential feature for diagnosis is apneic episodes recorded in the laboratory. The diagnostic features obtainable by a history in the great majority of patients with sleep apnea syndrome include excessive daytime sleepiness and inordinately loud snoring. The snoring usually occurs throughout the night, but it is intermittently interrupted by prolonged silences. A characteristic pattern of snoring is often noted, in which inspiratory snores gradually increase as obstruction of the upper airway develops. A loud, choking inspiratory gasp then occurs as the patient's respiratory efforts succeed in overcoming the occlusion. The patient is often not aware of his disturbing behavior, or of his accompanying numerous body movements that are at times violent and that disturb his nocturnal sleep. Many patients with sleep apnea flail their arms and sit or stand up without awakening as a manifestation of their physical restlessness. The patient's sleep partner must be questioned closely when excessive daytime sleepiness is a prominent presenting complaint. The patient's respirations are typically normal in the waking state.

Apneic episodes during sleep, defined as the cessation of air flow at the nose and the mouth for 10 seconds or longer, can be readily documented.

*Course.* The course of sleep apnea is generally progressive and chronic; in severe cases it eventually leads to profound impairment and life-threatening complications. Appropriate treatment can significantly control the apneic episodes, and may even reverse the cardiovascular complications. Hemodynamic and cardiac ab-normalities induced by the repetitive sleep apneic episodes only gradually affect the waking period. The time course of the illness depends on a number of factors, such as the severity and the type of apneic episodes, the patient's age, and the presence of obesity or other anatomical aggravating factors. Although excessive daytime sleepiness is most often the presenting complaint, the sequence in which symptoms appear may vary. The appearance of secondary cardiac failure often appears to herald the onset of fulminant worsening, with rapid deteriorations ensuing in many such cases.

Daytime sleepiness is frequently incapacitating and often results in job loss, marital and family problems, poor school performance in children, and being labeled as lazy or as having a primary psychiatric disorder. Secondary anxiety, irritability, depression, and even profound despair are common.

*Complications.* Cardiovascular sequelae are frequently severe and may prove fatal. Gradual development of persistent pulmonary hypertension and right-heart failure may be accompanied by systemic hypertension and left ventricular failure. Cardiac arrhythmias are frequently observed during sleep, and range from premature ventricular contractions and ventricular tachycardia to atrioventricular block and sinus arrest. The sleep apnea syndrome carries an increased risk of sudden death during sleep, and appears to be responsible for at least some cases of sudden infant death.

*Treatment.* The diagnosis of sleep apnea must be made accurately, both because many cases of apnea respond strikingly to the proper treatment, and because misdiagnosis and mistreatment can be dangerous. Respiratory depressants, such as most hypnotic medications and alcohol, can be hazardous in a patient already suffering from the nocturnal respiratory depression of central sleep apnea.

When obstructive sleep apnea is the problem or plays a role, treatment is aimed at relieving the obstructions to the passage of air. The problem usually involves the pharynx. At times, a malfunction of the jaw is responsible and can be corrected. Weight loss can be curative. The treatment of hypothyroidism can reduce an obstruction in appropriate cases. Occasionally, teaching the patient to sleep in certain positions and to avoid others can help in mild cases. When tissue obstruction cannot be relieved in these ways, treatment involves a tracheotomy that can be closed in the daytime and left open at night.

No totally effective treatment for central sleep apnea is available as yet. Caffeine and stimulant drugs can help somewhat. The avoidance of depressant medication and alcohol is essential.

**Hypoventilation Syndrome.** This diagnostic term refers to impaired ventilation, in which the respiratory abnormality appears only during sleep, and in which significant apneic pauses are not present.

The pathogenesis of the condition varies, as sleep-induced hypoventilation can arise from factors within or external to the central nervous system. Individual cases have demonstrated impaired ventilatory drive without apneas as a feature of myotonic dystrophy, narcolepsy, poliomyelitis, other encephalitides, central nervous system neoplasias, ventrolateral cervical spinal cord lesions, and other primary central nervous system disorders. Familial instances with a variety of other sleep-related complaints, ranging from excessive drowsiness to somnambulism and pavor nocturnus, have been identified on rare occasions.

Polysomnographic recordings, with monitoring of arterial oxygen levels, are necessary to confirm the diagnosis, and to exclude significant elements of sleep apnea and partial obstruction of the upper airway. Thorough neurological, neuroradiological, and otolaryngological examination and specialized tests of cardiopulmonary function and ventilatory responsiveness to hypoxia and hypercardia may prove warranted to isolate correctable factors and to provide optimum therapy.

Hypoventilation conditions have been less well studied than sleep apnea, to which they appear to be related.

**Phase Shifts and Unusual Cycles.** Hypersomnolence and insomnia can be produced temporarily by rapid time zone changes, the jet lag syndrome. The condition usually resolves quickly after adjustment to a new time zone several days after an east-west flight.

On rare occasions, a person has cycles of unusual lengths—usually several days in length—partially replacing the normal circadian cycles. This condition can result in several-day periods of insomnia and of somnolence. The symptom of this "free-running" pattern is sleep onset and waking times which become later by about 50 or 60 minutes every day. It has been reported in some blind persons and has been produced experimentally by placing a person in a totally dark environment for long periods.

**Other Rare Causes of Hypersomnolence.** Excessive daytime sleepiness and excessive sleep can occasionally result from trauma. In such cases, the condition develops 6 to 18 months after a head trauma. Hydrocephalus in children and adults can also occasionally be responsible for excessive sleep or excessive daytime sleepiness.

**Hypersomnolence Secondary to Insomnia.** Severe loss of sleep can obviously lead to sleepiness in the daytime. Therefore, any of the causes of insomnia can sometimes secondarily produce hypersomnolence.

### Episodic Nocturnal Events (Dyssomnias and Parasomnias)

A heterogeneous group of conditions may occur during the night. Not all the conditions disturb the sleeper himself; some are disturbing chiefly to the bed partner or to the patient's parents. See Table IV for a list of the stages of sleep associated with a specific nocturnal event.

**Somnambulism (Sleepwalking).** The essential feature of somnambulism is motoric behavior, consisting of rising out of bed and walking about; the behavior is performed by a person of any age during an apparent state of sleep. The activity is often accompanied by other complex behavioral automatisms, such as the opening of doors, dressing, occasionally even driving or going to the bathroom. Sleepwalking attacks usually occur in the first third of the night and last a few minutes to a half-hour, in extreme cases as long as 40 minutes. If awakened in the course of the episode, the person is often confused and temporarily disoriented. Typically

amnesiac for the behavior executed, the person also has no clear remembrance of dreaming associated with the attack (see Table V).

Not all inaugurations of sleepwalking behav-

TABLE V
DIAGNOSTIC CRITERIA FOR SLEEPWALKING
DISORDER*

A. There are repeated episodes of arising from bed during sleep and walking about for several minutes to a half hour, usually occurring between 30 and 200 minutes after onset of sleep (the interval of sleep that typically contains EEG delta activity, sleep stages 3 and 4).

B. While sleepwalking, the individual has a blank, staring face; is relatively unresponsive to the efforts of others to influence the sleepwalking or to communicate with him or her; and can be wakened only with great difficulty.

C. Upon awakening (either from the sleeping episode or the next morning), the individual has amnesia for the route traversed and for what happened during the episode.

D. Within several minutes of awakening from the sleepwalking episode, there is no impairment of mental activity or behavior (although there may initially be a short period of confusion or disorientation).

E. There is no evidence that the episode occurred during REM sleep or that there is abnormal electrical brain activity during sleep.

* From American Psychiatric Association: *Diagnostic and Statistical Manual of Mental Disorders*, ed. 3. American Psychiatric Association, Washington, DC, 1980. Used with permission.

TABLE IV
EPISODIC NOCTURNAL EVENTS (PARASOMNIAS)

| Disorder | Associated Sleep Stage |
| --- | --- |
| Sleepwalking (somnambulism) | NREM sleep, stage 4 |
| Night-terrors (pavor nocturnus) | NREM sleep, in early stages 3 and 4 |
| Bed wetting (enuresis) | NREM sleep, stages 3 and 4 |
| Nightmares | NREM sleep |
| Teeth-grinding (bruxism) | NREM sleep, primarily in stage 2 and transitions |
| Sleeptalking | NREM sleep |
| Jactatio capitus nocturnus (head banging) | Pre-sleep period and sometimes early stage 1 of NREM sleep |
| Erections | REM sleep |
| Familial sleep paralysis | REM sleep, usually first episode of the night |
| Hyperactive gag reflex | Not determined |
| Paroxysmal nocturnal hemoglobinuria | Not determined |
| Nocturnal epileptic seizures | Most frequently occur in the first 2 hours and last 2 hours of sleep |
| Cluster headaches and chronic paroxysmal hemicrania | REM sleep |
| Nocturnal cardiovascular symptoms (angina and dyspnea) | REM sleep (association is inconsistent) |
| Nocturnal asthma | REM sleep most frequently; NREM sleep, stages 3 and 4 least frequently |
| Nocturnal gastroesophageal reflex | Not determined |

ior go on to frank somnambulistic episodes. Sleepwalking-prone children often sit up in bed and first display stereotyped or purposeless movements, such as repetitive picking at the bed covers. In many instances they then lie down and resume normal sleep. In only a small proportion of the episodes do the children progress to leaving bed and the full-blown sleepwalking pattern.

Although the higher cortical functions are inefficient, coordination poor, and the enacted behaviors generally simple, the sleepwalker may exhibit fairly complex coordinated behaviors, including visual inspection, avoidance of objects in the way, and rearranging the furniture. Nevertheless, a parent or an observer finds it no easy task to gain the attention of the sleepwalker, who, despite his open eyes, usually appears dazed or expressionless and seems to behave only in concert with an internally appreciated situation. Attempts to awaken a sleepwalker meet with great difficulty.

It is a myth that sleepwalkers make their rounds in absolute safety. On the contrary, during their episodes they can stumble over objects, lose their balance while climbing through windows and onto fire escapes, and incur injuries while traversing other hazardous routes.

Whereas an attack may terminate spontaneously and the sleepwalker return to responsive contact with his environment, the somnambulist more frequently returns to the bedroom without having reached consciousness, or lies down somewhere in the house other than his bed and is mystified to find himself there in the morning. Children often climb into their parents' bed and continue their sleep.

During sleepwalking episodes, sleeptalking occasionally occurs. Sleeptalking during somnambulistic episodes is almost always of the soliloquy type, and the words are generally difficult to understand. True dialogue with a parent or other persons is not often reported.

Aggressive, violent, or frenzied behavior is rare in somnambulism, although it may occur when night terrors occur in association with somnambulism and when the condition is exacerbated by alcohol.

Sleepwalkers have been shown to be very deep sleepers in that they are more difficult to awaken from sleep than are normal persons, in response to either significant or nonsignificant stimuli. Sleepwalkers also have lower rates of reporting dreams and other mental activity after awakenings from appropriate sleep stages for the elicitation of such material.

Patients who sleepwalk have a higher than normal incidence of other episodic disorders arising from deep sleep, such as nocturnal enuresis, sleep terrors, and sleep drunkenness. The incidence of central nervous system infections, trauma, and waking epileptic patterns is also higher than in the normal population.

*Etiology and Predisposing Factors.* Sleepwalking in children is not believed to be caused by psychological factors and does not even signify the presence of psychopathology, although some tendency exists for emotional tension and stress to increase the incidence of the attacks. The persistence of or a return of somnambulism in adulthood is correlated with diverse forms of psychopathology and personality disturbance. Times of anxiety or conflict in adults who are prone to sleepwalking potentiate the episodes of increased muscular discharge in sleep.

Factors associated with the deepening of nighttime sleep, such as fatigue and prior sleep loss, may increase the probability of sleepwalking episodes in children. Sedative and hypnotic drugs may also increase attacks in patients with repetitive sleepwalking.

*Course.* Childhood somnambulism may occur at infrequent intervals, or be an almost nightly problem. In either case, it is usually present for only a few years, and then it disappears. Most childhood sleepwalkers are free of the disturbance by the third decade. Adult sleepwalking, although much less prevalent than childhood somnambulism, is more often chronic and associated with psychiatric disturbances, and it virtually always occurs in persons who give a history of sleepwalking in late childhood or adolescence.

The age of onset can be at any time after the skill of walking has been learned, but it is most common in childhood, especially from 6 to 12 years of age. Sleepwalking is usually self-limiting and does not directly predispose to other illnesses. The symptom, by definition, occurs during sleep periods, with no resultant impairments of waking mentation or behavior. The course is usually benign unless accidental injury befalls the sleepwalker. Repetitive sleepwalking may lead to secondary problems in family and interpersonal relationships.

*Epidemiology.* Somnambulism is fairly common in children and adolescents. As many as 15 percent of all children have had one or more sleepwalking experiences. The precise prevalence of chronic childhood somnambulism is not known, but it is usually given as 1 to 6 percent. Adult sleepwalking is relatively rare. Somnambulism is considered more common in males than in females.

Sleepwalking definitely shows a strong genetic influence, and has been described in identical twins. Relatives of sleepwalkers show a much higher incidence of sleepwalking and of nocturnal enuresis and sleep terrors than do control populations. The families of sleepwalking patients tend to be deep sleepers.

*Differential Diagnosis.* The differential diagnosis of somnambulism is not usually difficult, but it requires separating somnambulism from nocturnal epileptic seizures, psychomotor epilepsy, fugue states, and difficulties in morning awakening in hypersomniacs. Psychomotor epileptic seizures—usually of temporal lobe, especially amygdalar, or frontal lobe origin—occasionally occur at night and produce episodes of confusional automatic behavior similar to that of sleepwalking. However, psychomotor epileptic patients tend to be totally unreactive to environmental stimuli; automatisms like swallowing and rubbing the hands that are typical of temporal lobe seizures are common, and returning to bed is uncommon in psychomotor epileptics. Patients with convulsive, epileptic, and psychomotor siezures usually manifest them also in wakefulness. Nocturnal epileptic and psychomotor seizures are usually associated with a recordable EEG seizure discharge. In fact, sleepwalking episodes, even in epileptics, are most frequently nonepileptic in mechanism; they lack an EEG seizure discharge, rather than representing nocturnal psychomotor epileptic attacks.

Fugue states of various causes are not difficult to distinguish from somnambulism. The states are rare in children, usually begin in wakefulness, generally last much longer (typically a number of hours or days) than sleepwalking episodes, manifest only occasional difficulties with consciousness, and in psychiatric patients are usually associated with severe psychopathology.

Hypersomnia is often characterized by difficulty in awakening, as well as by prolongation of sleep, and may be associated with a morning form of sleep drunkenness, with the person taking a long time to awaken fully at the termination of sleep. Somnambulism is distinctly a first third of the night phenomenon. Nighttime or morning confusional awakenings with complex automatisms and extensive walking are also rare in the hypersomnias.

*Treatment.* Specific treatment for somnambulism is not often required. However, when the situation is serious, it may be useful to make the room and the house relatively free from dangerous objects, corners, and dangerous places to fall. Alcohol and other central nervous system depressant medications should be avoided. If medication is necessary, benzodiazepines have sometimes been found to be of use.

**Night-terrors.** Night-terrors also called pavor nocturnus are another one of the stage 4 dyssomnias. They occur early during the night, during arousal from stage 3 or stage 4 sleep. The episode usually involves a scream, then sometimes wild and agitated moving about, sometimes talking, and definite physiological activation—tachycardia, tachypnea, and so on. The patient usually awakes and has no dream recall or very little. Often, the sleeper remembers simply a feeling of terror or a feeling of pressure on the chest. Quite often, the sleeper returns to sleep, and there is total amnesia for the event in the morning (see Table VI).

In children, episodes sometimes last 10 or 20 minutes or more. The child may arise out of bed, walk around, and look about him, apparently terrified of something unseen. The parents find it impossible to wake the child, who usually returns to bed and has amnesia for the event the next morning.

Tachycardia and tachypnea are usually present, as well as other signs of autonomic arousal, just before an awakening. Night-terrors are sometimes combined with somnambulism; a patient may scream and then continue in a terrified and somnambulistic state for some minutes.

*Course.* Night-terrors or pavor nocturnus constitute quite a common condition at ages 3 to 5. The incidence decreases rapidly after that, but

TABLE VI
DIAGNOSTIC CRITERIA FOR SLEEP TERROR DISORDER*

A. Repeated episodes of abrupt awakening (lasting 1–10 minutes) from sleep, usually occurring between 30 and 200 minutes after onset of sleep (the interval of sleep that typically contains EEG delta activity, sleep stages 3 and 4) and usually beginning with a panicky scream.

B. Intense anxiety during the episode and at least three of the following signs of autonomic arousal:

1. Tachycardia
2. Rapid breathing
3. Dilated pupils
4. Sweating
5. Piloerection

C. Relative unresponsiveness to efforts of others to comfort the individual during the episode and, almost invariably, confusion, disorientation, and perseverative motor movements (e.g., picking at pillow).

D. No evidence that the episode occurred during REM sleep or of abnormal electrical brain activity during sleep.

* From American Psychiatric Association: *Diagnostic and Statistical Manual of Mental Disorders*, ed 3. American Psychiatric Association, Washington, DC, 1980.

a small number of adults continue to have night-terrors throughout their lives. Terrors also sometimes occur as a posttraumatic condition.

*Differential Diagnosis.* It is important to differentiate night-terrors from ordinary night-mares (D or REM nightmares), since the treatment approaches may be quite different in the two conditions.

Usually, the distinction is quite clear, even without polygraphic recordings, which can make the diagnosis certain. The distinguishing features are (1) time of night—night-terrors occur in the first third of the night, and D-nightmares usually occur in the second half of the night; (2) the quality of the experience—night-terrors are far more terrifying and involve far more autonomic activation than do D-nightmares; (3) the remembered content–night-terrors usually involve no recall of content or only a single frightening image, such as something pressing on the sleeper's chest; nightmares, on the other hand, are long, vivid, frightening dreams.

*Treatment.* Often, no specific treatment is required for night-terrors. Reassurance that the condition is not dangerous and is not a disturbing form of epilepsy can be helpful. When psychological factors appear to exacerbate the condition, psychotherapy is sometimes useful. Abstinence from alcohol can help decrease night-terrors in many persons. If medication is required, diazepam, 5 to 20 mg just before bedtime, often abolishes or greatly reduces night-terror attacks.

**Enuresis.** Enuresis refers to micturition or bed wetting that occurs at any age. Like sleep-walking, it almost always occurs during the first third of the night, and the patient usually returns to sleep and is amnesic for the episode. Enuresis is discussed in greater detail in Section 37.3.

### Episodic Disturbances not Associated with Stage 4 Sleep

**Nightmares.** Nightmares, sometimes called "REM anxiety attacks" are simply long, frightening dreams that are quite different from night-terrors.

Nightmares usually awaken the sleeper during the second half of the sleep period, and there is long, vivid recall of a dream ending in a frightening episode; often, the dreamer is being chased or being attacked, or occasionally some catastrophe is threatening the entire world.

All-night polygraphic recordings clearly establish that nightmares occur during REM-periods, as do most other dreams. Usually, a long REM-period—at least 15 minutes—results in an awakening with a recalled nightmare. The heart rate and the respiratory rate do not show the marked changed characteristic of night-terrors.

Nightmares occur equally in males and females. There is a high incidence of nightmares in children at ages 3 to 7, and generally they gradually decrease during adulthood. However, although few adults report night-terror episodes, a number of adults—perhaps 10 percent of the population—report occasional nightmares.

Definite factors predispose to nightmares. Persons who are especially sensitive or easily hurt appear to have more nightmares than does the general population. A recent study indicated that the incidence may be higher in persons vulnerable to schizophrenia—for instance, first degree relatives of schizophrenics—than in normal persons. Indeed, the prepsychotic period in a schizophrenic is often characterized by severe REM-nightmares. Reserpine, L-dopa in large doses, and, at times, monoamine oxidase inhibitors have all been linked with initiating REM-nightmares. In a population of persons susceptible to REM-nightmares, there were more nightmares after small doses of L-dopa given at night than after a placebo was given.

REM-nightmares themselves do not generally require treatment. However, they may sometimes be a symptom of something going wrong psychologically, of a stressful period, or of an incipient psychotic episode. In certain cases, psychotherapy can help solve the conflicts that give rise to or exacerbate the nightmares. If the studies suggesting a dopaminergic element and a relationship to schizophrenia are correct, dopamine blockers may be a pharmacological treatment for such nightmares if they are ever serious enough to require treatment.

**Bruxism.** Bruxism is a grinding, gnashing, or clenching of the teeth during sleep. Some degree of bruxism is common and has been reported in 13 to 15 percent of normal persons. At times, it is a severe enough condition to produce damage to the teeth, and dentists claim that such damage is not at all rare.

The nature and the strength of the muscle activity are quite striking. The tooth grinding, even though it does not awaken the sleeper, is often intensely disturbing to persons sleeping in the same room and can sometimes be heard several rooms away. It is impossible for the patient to duplicate the intensive tooth gnashing consciously while awake.

Bruxism can occur during any stage of sleep, but it has been reported to occur most often during stages 1 and 2. The condition is associated neither with stage 4 sleep, as are the major dyssomnias discussed above, nor with REM-sleep, as are the REM-nightmares.

The cause of bruxism is not entirely clear. Various neurological abnormalities have been suggested but not proved. Certain organic factors, especially interference or difficulty in occlusion, are often found in persons with bruxism and may be part of the cause. Psychological factors are clearly involved in initiating or, at least, in exacerbating periods of bruxism in many persons. Bruxism patients are more anxious than are normal persons, and, in patients who occasionally have bruxism, periods of tension and perhaps suppressed anger are related to increased bruxism. Alcohol intake often aggravates bruxism.

Bruxism can occasionally be treated by occlusal adjustment when there is difficulty in occlusion. Psychotherapy can be helpful at times, as can abstinence from alcohol. Various medications, especially the benzodiazepines, have been used in the treatment of bruxism.

**Sleeptalking (Somniloquy).** Sleeptalking is quite common in children and adults. It has been studied extensively in the sleep laboratory and is found to arise out of all stages of sleep. The talking usually involves a few words that are difficult to distinguish. Longer episodes of talking involve the sleeper's life and concerns, but the sleeptalker does not relate his dreams during sleep, nor does he often reveal deep secrets.

Episodes of sleeptalking sometimes accompany night-terrors and somnambulism. Sleeptalking in itself requires no treatment.

**Other Episodic Conditions.** Other rare episodic events include jactatio capitus nocturnus (head-banging), painful erections, familial sleep paralysis, hyperactive gag reflex, paroxysmal nocturnal hemoglobinuria, nocturnal epileptic seizures, cluster headaches and chronic paroxysmal hemicrania, nocturnal cardiovascular symptoms, nocturnal asthma, nocturnal gastroesophageal reflux, nocturnal angina, and nocturnal episodes of other illnesses such as asthma.

**REFERENCES**

Cleghorn J M, Bellissimo A, Kaplan R D, Szatmari P: Insomnia: I. Classification, assessment and pharmaceutical treatment. Can J Psychiatry 28: 347, 1983.
Dement W C: *Some Must Watch While Some Must Sleep*. W. H. Freeman, San Francisco, 1974.
Hartmann E: *The Biology of Dreaming*. Springfield, IL, Charles C Thomas, 1967.
Hartmann E: *The Functions of Sleep*. Yale University Press, New Haven, CT, 1973.
Hartmann E: *The Nightmare*. Basic Books, New York, 1984.
Hartmann E L: Sleep disorders. In *Comprehensive Textbook of Psychiatry*, ed 4, H I Kaplan, B J Sadock, editors, p 1247. Williams & Wilkins, Baltimore, 1985.
Hauri P J: A cluster analysis of insomnia. Sleep 6: 326, 1983.
Kleitman N: *Sleep and Wakefulness*. University of Chicago Press, Chicago, 1963.
Reynolds C F, Taska L S, Seivtch D E, Restifo K, Coble P A, Kupfer D J: Persistent psychophysiologic insomnia: Preliminary research diagnostic criteria and EEG sleep data. Am J Psychiatry 141: 804, 1984.
Webb W B, editor: *Biological Rhythms, Sleep, and Performance*. John Wiley & Sons, New York, 1982.

# 25

# Psychiatric Emergencies

## 25.1 SUICIDE

### Introduction

Although some suicidal people may be death seeking, others attempt to communicate pain, mitigate isolation, avoid the sequelae of status change, seek revenge, and transmit a host of other meanings. Suicidal patients are probably the most frequent cause of psychiatric emergencies. The suicidal person is difficult to identify with certainty. He is often unmanageable in an outpatient setting and resistant to hospitalization, and he is subject to recurrent crises in management.

### Demography

About 20,000 to 35,000 suicides are recorded annually in the United States. This figure represents the lethal end of attempted suicides, which are estimated to exceed that number by 8 to 10 times. Lost in the reporting process are the purposeful misclassification of cause of death, accidents of undetermined cause, and what are referred to as forms of chronic suicide—for example, alcoholism, drug abuse, and consciously poor adherence to medical regimens for diabetes, obesity, and hypertension.

Certified suicides constitute a rate of 12.5 deaths per 100,000 population, ranking suicide as the ninth over-all leading cause of death in the country. Out of every 20 attempted suicides, 1 succeeds.

Suicide rates in the United States rank at or near the midpoint of national rates reported to the United Nations by industrialized countries. Internationally, suicide rates range from highs of more than 25 per 100,000 population in Scandinavia, Switzerland, West Germany, Austria, and eastern European countries (the suicide belt) and Japan to fewer than 10 per 100,000 in Spain, Italy, and the Netherlands.

### Sex

Men commit suicide more than 3 times as often as do women, a rate that is stable over all ages. Women, on the other hand, are 3 times as likely to attempt suicide as are men.

### Age

The significance of the midlife crisis is underscored by suicide rates. Among men, suicides peak after age 45; among women, the greatest number of completed suicides occurs after age 55. Rates of 40 per 100,000 population are found in men age 65 and older; the elderly attempt suicide less often than younger people but are successful more frequently, accounting for 25 percent of the suicides, although the elderly make up only 10 percent of the total population. A decline in suicide in men begins between the ages 75 to 85. A peak risk among males is found also in late adolescence, when suicide is the third leading cause of death, exceeded only by death attributed to accidents. It is also the second leading cause of death among college students.

### Race

Suicide among whites is recorded at nearly twice the rate as among nonwhites, but these figures are increasingly called into question since the suicide rate among blacks is increasing. Among blacks, ghetto youth, and certain native American and Alaskan Indian groups, suicide rates greatly exceeded the national rate. Two out of every three suicides are white males.

### Religion

Historically, suicide rates among Catholic populations have been recorded as lower than rates among Protestants and Jews. It may be that the degree of orthodoxy and integration within a religion are a more accurate measure of risk within this category than is simple institutional religious affiliation.

### Marital Status

Marriage, reinforced by children, seems to significantly lessen the risk of suicide. Among

575

married persons, the rate is 11 per 100,000. Single, never married persons register an overall rate of nearly double the married rate. Previously married persons show sharply higher rates: 24 per 100,000 among the widowed; 40 per 100,000 among divorced persons, with divorced men registering 69 suicides per 100,000, as compared with 18 per 100,000 for divorced women. Suicide is more common in persons who have a history of suicide (attempted or real) in the family and who are socially isolated. Serious suicide attempts where the patient has been comatose as a result of the suicide attempt are highly predictive of future attempts.

### Health

The relationship of physical health and illness to suicide is both predictable and inconsistent and, in either case, significant. Prior medical care appears to be a positively correlated risk indicator of suicide; 42 percent of suicides have had medical attention within 6 months of death. Seventy percent of victims have been affected by one or more active—and, for the most part, chronic—illnesses at the time of death. Among suicide attempts studied, more than one-third of the persons were actively ill at the time of the attempt, and more than 90 percent of the attempts were influenced by the illness. In both groups, psychosomatic illnesses constituted the majority of diagnoses. A particular group at risk are patients on renal dialysis.

Highly significant factors in suicide also include the following: alcoholism, other drug abuse, depression, schizophrenia and other mental illnesses.

Factors associated with illness and contributing to both suicides and attempts were loss of mobility among persons for whom physical activity was occupationally or recreationally important; disfigurement, particularly among women; and chronic, intractable pain. In addition to the direct effects of illness, it has been noted that the secondary effects of illness— for example, disruption of relationships and loss of occupational status—are prognostic factors.

### Occupation

Among occupational rankings with respect to risk for suicide, physicians have traditionally been considered to stand out, and, among physicians, psychiatrists are considered to be at greatest risk, followed by ophthalmology and anesthesiology; but the trend is toward an equalization among all specialties. Special at-risk populations are musicians, dentists, law enforcement officers, lawyers, and insurance agents.

### Methods

Drug ingestion is the most common method of suicide and is used more frequently than any other method by women. Men use firearms, which are more likely to be fatal than drugs. Where gun control laws are in effect, the use of guns has decreased as a method of suicide.

## Sociological and Psychological Approaches

### Durkheim

The first major contribution to the study of the problem of suicide was made at the end of the last century by the French sociologist Emile Durkheim. In an attempt to explain the statistical patterns, he divided suicides into three social categories: egoistic, altruistic, and anomic.

Egoistic suicide comprised those who were assumed not to have been strongly integrated into any social group. Family integration or the lack of it could be used to explain why the unmarried were more vulnerable to suicide than the married, and why couples with children were the best protected group of all. Rural communities had more social integration than urban areas and thus less suicide. Protestantism was a less cohesive religion than Catholicism, and Protestants thus had a higher suicide rate than Catholics.

Altruistic suicide described the group whose proneness to suicide stemmed from their excessive integration into a group. Durkheim had in mind the kind of suicide that could be expected of certain classes in Japanese society.

Anomic suicide occurs when a disturbance in the balance of the person's integration with society leaves him without his customary norms of behavior. Anomie could explain the greater incidence of suicide among the divorced as compared with the married, and the greater vulnerability of those who had undergone drastic changes in their economic situation.

Increases in anomic and egoistic suicide were responsible, Durkheim thought, for the rising suicide rates of Europe. With industrial and scientific development, the family, the state, and the church were not the forces for social integration that they had once been, and nothing had been found to replace them. Suicide, like crime, neurosis, and alcoholism, is a factor that measures social pressure and tension. The extremely high rate seen in West Berlin is perhaps the most dramatic manifestation of this principle.

### Freud

The first important psychological insight into suicide came from Freud. He described only one patient who actually made a suicide attempt, but he did see a good number of depressed patients. In his 1917 paper "Mourning and Melancholia," Freud stated that the self-hatred seen in depression originated in anger toward a love object, anger that the person turned back on himself. He regarded suicide as the ultimate form of this phenomenon, and doubted that there would be a suicide without the earlier repressed desire to kill someone else.

### Psychodynamics

The suicide attempt often represents a kind of psychological drama. The communication of suicidal intent is often an integral part of the method employed. Such communication can be coercive, can be a plea for help, and can involve a gamble with death in which another person is empowered to decide whether the potential suicide will live or die. Disorganized or multiple suicidal methods or those carried out in a chaotic manner and lasting several days are usually chosen by disorganized, schizoid patients.

Something of the relationship between suicide and depression can best be understood by the need for atonement that can underlie both. Depressed persons may attempt suicide just as they appear to be recovering from their depression. And a suicide attempt can cause a depression of long standing to disappear. One form of atonement appears to substitute for another. Of equal relevance, many suicidal patients use a preoccupation with suicide as a way of fighting off intolerable depression.

However, a great many suicidal patients do not manifest the clinical features or classic psychodynamics associated with depression. And many depressed patients are not suicidal. Many suicidal patients appear to view their deaths as an internalized murder, and the suicide attempts of others are explained as acts of expiation.

Persons who have survived suicide attempts have provided important clues about psychodynamics of suicide. Edwin Schneidman and Neal Farberow have classified suicides into four groups: (1) patients who conceive of suicide as a means to a better life; (2) patients who commit suicide as a result of psychosis with associated delusions or hallucinations; (3) patients who commit suicide out of revenge against a loved person; and (4) patients who are old and/or infirm for whom suicide is a release.

### Prediction

It remains the task of an individual clinician to assess an individual patient's risk on the basis of a careful clinical examination.

Cognizant of the clinician's dilemma, a num-ber of researchers have engaged in efforts to sharpen the validity and the utility of predictive variables, which are outlined in Table I. The most predictive items associated with high suicide risk are listed first in Table I, and in descending order the first eight are age; presence of alcoholism (the suicide rate is 50 times higher in alcoholics); no recent irritation, rage, or violence; high lethality of prior suicidal behavior; male sex; not accepting help at the time of evaluation; the longer the current suicidal episode the higher the risk; and no prior psychiatric inpatient experience.

Four variables used to predict acute high lethality in a chronically suicidal person are prior psychiatric hospitalization; presence of irritation, rage, or violence; recent loss of health; and a current loss.

The last four items in Table I, variables 12 to 15, showed tendencies in the direction of suicide. Of these variables, by far the most important one to the clinician is depression. Depression—probably one of the best predictors—is most reliably obtained in a clinical interview. All psychiatric examinations, regardless of diagnosis, should always include questions about whether or not the patient ever had thoughts of wanting to harm himself or take his own life. A family history of suicide should be questioned because there is a high familial incidence.

Tuckman and Youngman developed a scale for the assessment of suicide risk (see Table II). Fourteen characteristics were identified as high-risk or low-risk factors, with validity tested against a criterion of subsequent death by sui-

TABLE I
DISCRIMINANT FUNCTION ANALYSES*

| Variable in Rank Order | Content of Item | Direction for Suicide |
|---|---|---|
| 1 | Age | Older |
| 2 | Alcoholism | Yes |
| 3 | Irritation, rage, violence | No |
| 4 | Lethal prior behavior | Higher |
| 5 | Sex | Male |
| 6 | Accept help now | No |
| 7 | Duration of current episode | Longer |
| 8 | Prior inpatient psychiatric treatment | No |
| 9 | Recent loss or separation | No |
| 10 | Depression, somatic | Yes |
| 11 | Loss of physical health | Less |
| 12 | Occupational level | Higher |
| 13 | Depression, affective | No |
| 14 | Repeatedly discarded | No |
| 15 | Family available | Less |

* From Litman R E, Farberow N L, Wold C I, and Brown T R: Prediction models of suicidal behaviors. In *The Prediction of Suicide*, A T Beck, H L P Resnik, D J Lettieri, editors, p 141. Charles Press, Bowie, MD, 1974.

TABLE II
SUICIDE RATES* MEASURED BY HIGH-RISK AND LOW-RISK CATEGORIES OF RISK-RELATED FACTORS
AMONG 1,112 ATTEMPTED SUICIDES†

| Factor | High-risk Category | Suicide Rate | Low-risk Category | Suicide Rate |
|---|---|---|---|---|
| Age | 45 years and older | 40.5 | Under age 45 | 6.9 |
| Sex | Male | 33.8 | Female | 5.3 |
| Race | White | 16.7 | Nonwhite | 9.0 |
| Marital status | Separated, divorced, widowed | 41.9 | Single, married | 12.4 |
| Employment status‡ | Unemployed, retired | 24.8 | Employed§ | 16.3 |
| Living arrangements | Alone | 71.4 | With others | 11.1 |
| Health | Poor (acute or chronic condition in the 6-month period preceding the attempt) | 18.0 | Good§ | 13.8 |
| Mental condition | Nervous or mental disorder, mood, or behavioral symptoms, including alcoholism | 17.6 | Presumably normal, including brief situational reactions§ | 11.7 |
| Method | Hanging, firearms, jumping, drowning | 45.5 | Cutting or piercing, gas or carbon monoxide, poison, combination of methods, other | 13.1 |
| Potential consequences of method | Likely to be fatal¶ | 31.5 | Harmless, illness producing | 6.0 |
| Police description of attempted suicide's condition | Unconscious, semiconscious | 16.3 | Presumably normal, disturbed, drinking, physically ill, other | 13.0 |
| Suicide note | Yes | 22.5 | No§ | 13.7 |
| Previous attempt or threat | Yes | 22.6 | No§ | 13.1 |
| Disposition | Admitted to psychiatric evaluation center | 21.0 | Discharged to self or relative, referred to family doctor, clergyman, or social agency, or other disposition | 11.6 |

* Although mental health statistics generally use rates per 100,000 population, here it is more appropriate to use per 1,000 population because of the small size of the sample.
† From Tuckman J, Youngman W F: Assessment of suicidal risk in attempted suicides. In *Suicidal Behaviors*, H L P Resnik, editor, p 190. Little, Brown, & Co., Boston, 1968.
‡ Does not include housewives and students.
§ Includes cases for which information on this factor was not given in the police report.
¶ Several criteria used in estimating whether the method used was likely to be fatal.

cide. High-risk characteristics included 45 and over in age; male; divorced, widowed, or separated; lived alone; and choice of a highly lethal attempt.

Family disorganization is a risk-related factor. Additional risk-related factors include occupation, precipitants of the attempt, elapsed time between the attempt and its discovery, motivation, and diagnosis of depression. Twenty-five percent of all suicides are alcoholics.

### Evaluation and Management

As mentioned above, any patient who is suspected of being suicidal should be directly asked if he feels so bad that he would like to end it all. Every therapist should feel comfortable with these or similar words of his choice. No clinical evidence suggests that asking a patient this question inserts the thought or provides the psychic momentum needed to act it out. Rather, the contrary occurs. The patient is, by inference, usually relieved by the invitation to talk about his self-destructive feelings; this invitation can reassure the patient that the psychiatrist is com-

fortable with the subject and is experienced and competent in treating suicidal patients.

If the patient's response is affirmative, he should be encouraged to go on. During the interview, phraseology, tone, spontaneity, and concern communicate reassurance. Suicidal thoughts and feelings are likely to require temporary external support. As the patient indicates assent, the therapist should increase the specificity of his questions to ask whether the thoughts involve a plan, the nature of the plan, the timing, and the availability of the means. It is useful to ask whether the suicidal preoccupation is a first-time occurrence, or if the patient has been struggling with such impulses for many years; if so, the therapist should determine whether the patient ever attempted suicide. Typically, the clinician observes a progressive opening up on the part of the patient.

A clinician who begins such an interview with the permissive first question must be prepared to take an active role, to the extent of calling in the patient's family or friends or by directly hospitalizing the patient. Once high suicidal risk is determined, a patient must never be left alone until he is hospitalized.

Before treatment, the patient often experiences a period of evolving suicidal ideation as the ego attempts to come to grips with stresses. The primary phase of treatment begins at the point at which the clinician has made the diagnosis of high suicidal risk and has committed to engage the problem. A variety of therapeutic moves in the primary phase may often be used: (1) a temporary giving in to the patient's infantile, demanding dependency needs, thus providing a strong and loving parent surrogate for support; (2) being direct and authoritarian in order to take over decision making when the patient's decision has been based on faulty and illogical decision making; (3) abandoning customary techniques of reflection, free association, and other nondirective procedures, thus allowing for direct questioning. The clinician should obtain the necessary information about the suicidal plan, the lethality, and, in the event of suicidal communications made by telephone, the patient's whereabouts. It is often useful to note the home and work phone numbers of suicidal patients for emergency reference; occasionally a patient hangs up unexpectedly during a late night call or provides only a name to the answering service.

A straightforward clinical ploy is to ask any patient considered suicidal whether he will agree to call when he reaches a point beyond which he is uncertain of controlling his suicidal impulses. If a patient can commit himself to such an agreement, he is reaffirming his belief that he has sufficient strength to cry out for help. If a patient who is considered seriously suicidal cannot make this commitment, immediate hospitalization may be indicated, and both the patient and his family should be apprised.

In return for the patient's commitment, the clinician should reciprocate. By agreeing to be available 24 hours a day and to be directly accessible during what the patient understands to be usual consultation hours, the clinician reassures the patient. Perhaps the only patients unable to honor such a commitment contract are those who are struggling with alcoholism or drug abuse at the time that they are actively suicidal. These patients should be hospitalized directly.

Once a patient has been identified as a high suicidal risk, the alternatives to immediate hospitalization are limited.

A therapist's anxiety and apprehension may result from fear that the patient will, indeed, kill himself, despite the therapist's efforts. The therapist must remember that the state of suicide prediction and, indeed, of psychiatric care, is such that he cannot take full responsibility for any person's life for long periods of time without that person's eventually accepting a share of the responsibility. In a hospital, the responsibility is shared.

## Hospital Care

Danger to self is one of the few clear-cut indications presently acceptable in all states for involuntry hospitalization. Even among high-risk groups of hospitalized patients, suicide may occur, although it is a rare event. The annual suicide rate among patients in psychiatric hospitals is approximately 0.003 percent.

Although patients classified as acutely suicidal may have favorable prognoses, chronically suicidal patients are difficult to treat, and they exhaust the caretakers. Constant observation by special nurses, seclusion, and restraints do not prevent a determined suicide over time. Only electroconvulsive therapy (ECT) may have this capability for some severely depressed patients, and then not usually without repetition.

Regardless of whether or not the patient is in a hospital, the recovering suicidal patient is at particular risk. As the depression lifts, patients become more energized and are able to put suicidal plans into action. Other depressed patients, with or without treatment, suddenly appear to be at peace with themselves because they have reached a secret decision to commit suicide. The clinician should be especially suspicious of such a dramatic clinical change.

## Legal and Ethical Considerations

Liability issues stemming from suicides in psychiatric hospitals frequently involve questions regarding the rate of deterioration of psychiatric status, the presence of clinical signs during hospitalization indicating risk, and determination of the psychiatrist's and the staff's awareness of and response to the clinical signs.

At present, suicide and attempted suicide are variously viewed as a felony and a misdemeanor; in some states the acts are considered not crimes but unlawful; in other states they are neither crimes nor unlawful under common law and statutes. The role of an aider and abettor in suicide adds another dimension to the legal morass; some court decisions have held that, although neither suicide nor attempted suicide is punishable, one who assists in the act may be punished. As yet unresolved is the culpability of one who prevents a suicidal act and thus possibly infringes on the constitutional rights of the attempter.

Damage to oneself is a legal course for commitment to a mental hospital in all states. A major cause of malpractice suits in psychiatry is suicide.

### Community Organizations

Community organizations seem to have fewer problems than do individual therapists with the ethics and legalities of helping suicidal people. Prevention and crisis listening posts are a clear attempt to intervene and diminish the isolation, withdrawal, and loneliness that have been highlighted. Outreach programs have provided highly motivated lay people to respond to cries for help in a variety of ways in which professionals do not respond. It would be simplistic to believe that such responses do more than diminish an acute crisis; highly suicidal people place fewer than 10 percent of such calls. However, there are instances in which suicidal persons with high-risk characteristics have been hospitalized as a result of these efforts.

### REFERENCES

Arffa S: Cognition and suicide: A methodological review. Suicide Life Threat Behav *13:* 109, 1983.
Beck A T, Resnik H L P, Lettieri D, editors: *The Prediction of Suicide*. Charles Press, Bowie, MD, 1974.
Farberow N L, Shneidman E, editors: *The Cry for Help*. McGraw-Hill, New York, 1961.
Leading Components of Upturn in Mortality for Men, United States—1952–67: *Vital and Health Statistics Series 20*, No. 11, DHEW Publication No. (HSM) 72-1008. U.S. Government Printing Office, Washington, DC, 1971.
Perlin S, editor: *A Handbook for the Study of Suicide*. Oxford University Press, New York, 1975.
Pfeffer C R: Suicidal behavior of children: A review with implications for research and practice. Am J Psychiatry *138:* 154, 1981.
Pfeffer C R, Plutchik R, Mizruchi M S: Suicidal and assaultive behavior in children, measurement, and interrelations. Am J Psychiatry *140:* 12, 1983.
Robins E: Suicide. In *Comprehensive Textbook of Psychiatry*, ed 4, H I Kaplan, B J Sadock, editors, p 1311. Williams & Wilkins, Baltimore, 1985.
Roose S P, Glassman A H, Walsh B T, Woodring S, Vital-Herne J: Depression, delusions and suicide. Am J Psychiatry *140:* 1159, 1983.
Rosenthal P A, Rosenthal S: Suicidal behavior by preschool children. Am J Psychiatry *141:* 520, 1984.

## 25.2 OTHER PSYCHIATRIC EMERGENCIES

### Definition

A psychiatric emergency is a disturbance in thoughts, feelings, or actions for which immediate treatment is deemed necessary. Most often, the patient himself expresses this need.

When questioned in the emergency room, the patient often responds with a long account concerning chronic emotional disturbances. In the course of the recital, the key issue is frequently lost—namely, why does the patient come for help now? The most common cause of acute emotional disturbance is the loss of some crucial person through death, separation, divorce, or abandonment. A related cause is loss of self-esteem due to unemployment, failure in school, mutilating surgery or some other physical impairment, new job responsibilities, retirement, or the birth of a baby. One should not overlook the traumatic impact of separation from the psychiatrist in a chronically ill patient whose physician has gone off on a holiday without having provided proper coverage in his absence.

Because of language barriers or cultural characteristics, the patient may express his cry for help with somatic complaints, thus creating a major responsibility for the psychiatrist. Of all the diagnoses made in the emergency room, psychosis and neurosis are the most fraught with potential error. Head trauma, drug abuse, stroke, metabolic abnormalities, and medication sensitivities may all cause abnormalities of behavior. Follow-up studies of emergency room psychiatric patients consistently show an increased mortality rate.

A state of psychiatric emergency may be declared by family members, teachers, or police. The psychiatric emergency may also be defined by a referring physician at a time when the patient and others may choose to deny the impending danger.

### Doctor-Patient Relationship

The emergency room physician may respond with condemnatory attitudes toward a patient whose psychiatric emergency has been precipitated by alcohol or drug abuse. Chronic mental illness may have led to social deterioration and lack of personal cleanliness. Many acutely disturbed patients are irritable, demanding, hostile, and provocative. For all these reasons, the physician may respond to the patient with negative feelings. These feelings are understandable, but they should sound an alarm for redoubled care in the examination of the patient. The physician must subject himself constantly to self-criticism and self-appraisal, and must alert himself to feelings and attitudes that may adversely affect his relationship with the patient and thus impair his clinical judgment.

### Involuntary Hospital Admission

It is sometimes necessary to get a disturbed patient into safe custody in a hurry and against the patient's wishes.

When the patient presents a clear and immediate danger to himself or others and refuses inpatient treatment, the responsible physician may have no other recourse than to hospitalize the patient against his will. Physicians should decide one issue only—namely, whether mental illness impairs the patient's capacity to make an informed decision regarding treatment. For example, many schizophrenic patients flatly reject the sick role because they reject the intimate human contacts that the role entails. Such patients reject treatment not only for psychiatric illness but for all forms of physical illness. Such patients obviously have no competence to make an informed decision regarding treatment.

## Treatment

Most emergency room patients have a lifelong history of psychopathology, often severe, in spite of which they have managed to adapt. These people seek emergency room help only when that adaptation mechanism has decompensated. Usually, the breakdown results not so much from a change in the patient as from a breakdown in the supportive social network. A parent, a spouse, other key relatives, an employer, or a teacher may have finally experienced an exhaustion of patience and hope. A prompt therapeutic response in the emergency room and a vigorous treatment program in an outpatient setting that is family centered, and that offers supportive environmental change with the aid of social service, can restore the patient's reservoir of social credit, and may delay or even obviate the need for inpatient care. This pattern of care—one that depends on the immediate availability of a treatment team that addresses itself specifically to the current situation responsible for the breakdown, that places the patient's current plight in the context of his life history as ascertained through a careful psychiatric examination, that provides suitable medications for symptomatic relief and renegotiates the patient's role in the family through the family-centered approach to his problem—is what is meant by crisis therapy.

Probably the greatest single limitation of the emergency room psychiatrist is the brief time at his disposal.

To overcome this limitation, he needs a psychiatric holding area in conjunction with the emergency room. The over-all mission of the holding area is to make the best possible disposition for each patient, and preferably to avert hospitalization and to facilitate the patient's return to the community. Holding a patient for a few hours, sedating a patient and keeping him in a bed for 1 to 3 days, beginning crisis intervention with the family while the patient is sheltered for a few days from a traumatic home situation—these measures may make it possible to initiate ideal care at once and to avoid the potentially regressive effects of long-term inpatient care.

If the emergency contact is by telephone, it has been suggested that the following routine be used: The psychiatrist should obtain the number from which the call is made and the exact address. These items are important in case the call is interrupted, and they allow the psychiatrist to direct help, depending on the circumstances.

In case of a drug overdose, the psychiatrist should ask what amount and type of substance was ingested. Unless a caustic has been swallowed, the patient should be encouraged to vomit into a receptacle by inserting a finger in his throat, by drinking soapy water, or by the administration of a tablespoon of syrup of ipecac if it is available; the vomitus should be saved for laboratory analysis.

If the patient is alone, the police should be alerted. If possible, an assistant should call the police on another line while the psychiatrist keeps the patient engaged until help arrives. The patient should not be told to drive alone to the hospital, because he may injure himself or others driving a vehicle. If the telephone call is disconnected, the psychiatrist should try to get to the patient personally. He may arrive before the police emergency crew. In his bag he should carry an airway to assist if breathing is obstructed. Mouth-to-mouth respiration may be neeeded. If the patient is in shock, the foot of his bed should be elevated until emergency help arrives. All psychiatrists should be well trained in cardiopulmonary resuscitation (CPR).

## Emergencies

### Psychological States

Although all clinical conditions are really the outcome of a three-fold input embodied in the biopsychosocial point of view, one can consider first a category of emergency disorders in which psychological factors predominate.

**Depression.** Suicidal depression is the single most important category in emergency psychiatry.

One must be alert to the danger signs— namely, a relatively abrupt onset in a previously competent person, early-morning insomnia and agitation, a loss of all appetites and interests, feelings of hopeless despair, inability to express one's thoughts or feelings, and progressive social withdrawal. The appearance of delusions, such as having committed an unpardonable sin, is a particularly ominous sign, calling for emergency inpatient care under constant nursing supervision, antidepressant medication, and possibly calling for the emergency administration of electroconvulsive therapy (ECT). See Section 25.1 for a more complete discussion of the management of the suicidal patient.

**Violence.** Outwardly directed destructive behavior is relatively rare in mental illness. The fear with which some people regard all psychiatric patients is completely out of proportion to the rather small group representing an authentic danger to others. The best predictors of potential violent behavior are (1) excessive alcohol intake, (2) a history of violent acts, and (3) a history of childhood abuse. As in any other type of case, an attitude of calm objectivity is required. If one takes enough time for a proper history, it will be found that there are many types of potentially violent behavior, each requiring its own treatment. Although violent patients can arouse realistic fear in the psychiatrist, they can also touch off irrational fears that impair clinical judgment, and that may lead to the premature and excessive use of sedation. Violent patients are usually frightened of their own hostile impulses and desperately seek help to prevent loss of control.

*Management.* A patient in the grip of a violent episode pays no attention to the rational intercessions of others, and it is highly probable that he does not even hear them. When armed, he is particularly dangerous and even capable of mass murder. Such a patient should be disarmed by trained law enforcement personnel without harming the patient, if at all possible. If unarmed, such a patient should be approached with sufficient help and with overwhelming strength so that there is, in effect, no contest.

The violent struggling patient is most effectively subdued with an appropriate intravenous (IV) sedative. Diazepam (Valium) may be given slowly IV 5 to 10 mg over 2 minutes. Sodium amobarbital (Amytal sodium), 0.5 g, may also be given slowly intravenously. It is most important to give intravenous medication with great care. It is important that the IV not be injected too rapidly so that respiratory arrest does not occur. If the furor is due to alcohol or is part of a postseizure psychomotor disturbance, the sleep produced by a relatively small amount of intravenous medication may go on for hours. On awakening, such patients are often entirely alert and rational, and typically have a complete amnesia for the violent episode.

Responsibility for violent acts committed during such dissociative states poses a complicated legal problem. In the case of alcohol, at least, it seems proper to hold a person legally responsible for any acts performed by him after he has taken a drink.

If the furor is part of an ongoing psychotic process and it returns as soon as the intravenous medication wears off, continuing parenteral medication may be given. The medication used should be one that the physician knows thoroughly. As a general principle, it is better to use small doses at ½- to 1-hour intervals—for example, haloperidol, 2 to 5 mg, or diazepam, 10 mg—until the patient is controlled, than to use larger doses initially and end up with an overmedicated patient. As the patient's disturbed behavior is brought under control, successively smaller and less frequent doses are used. During the preliminary period of treatment, the patient's blood pressure and other vital signs should be carefully monitored.

In general, intramuscular haloperidol, 2 to 5 mg, is one of the most useful emergency treatments for violent psychotic patients.

ECT has also been used on an emergency basis to control psychotic violence. The administration of one or several ECT treatments within several hours usually ends an episode of psychotic violence.

Violent psychotic patients are sometimes placed in mechanical restraint. The danger of that procedure should be noted. Not only does it create a vicious cycle by intensifying the patient's psychotic terror, but, if prolonged, mechanical restraints can cause hyperthermia, and in some instances of catatonic excitement it can cause death. Mechanical restraints should be used with due regard to local laws—that is, with permission from the proper authorities and with careful monitoring of the patient's physical condition.

Adjustment disorders in all age groups may result in tantrum-like outbursts of rage. These outbursts are seen particularly in marital quarrels. Police are often summoned by neighbors distressed by the sounds of a violent altercation. Such family quarrels should be approached with great caution, because they may be complicated by the use of alcohol and the presence of dangerous weapons. It frequently happens that the warring couple turn their combined fury on the unwary outsider. Wounded self-esteem is a big issue. Therefore, patronizing or contemptuous attitudes must be avoided, and an effort made to communicate an attitude of respect and an authentic peacemaking concern.

In family violence, the special vulnerability of selected close relatives should be noted. A wife or a husband may have a curious masochistic attachment to the spouse in which violence is provoked by taunting and otherwise undermining the self-esteem of the partner. Such relationships often end in the murder of the provoking partner and sometimes in the suicide of the other partner.

Alcohol is a complicating factor in the management of all violent patients.

In evaluating the possibilities of recurrent episodes of violence, one should inquire concerning a history of previous acts of violence by the patient; of violent parental behavior during the patient's developmental years; of a childhood history of fire setting and cruelty to animals; the possession of weapons as a hobby or otherwise; and drug dependency states, involving, most of all, alcohol, but including the barbiturates, amphetamines, lysergic acid diethylamide (LSD) and phencyclidine (PCP). Patients with schizoid personality disorders who harbor paranoid and vengeful obsessional thoughts about authority figures may be future candidates for assassination behavior.

These patients share a low frustration tolerance, and they react violently when crossed. Although violence is usually directed against family members, it may be expressed indiscriminately during periods of acute stress. Such people often come to the emergency room voluntarily, asking for help because of impending loss of control.

As in the case of the suicidal patient, violent patients usually accept the offer of inpatient care gratefully and with a sense of relief. The nonpsychotic violent patient is often an ideal candidate for crisis psychotherapy, by means of which the episode of violent behavior can be effectively resolved.

**Fugue States.** A patient is occasionally brought to an emergency room with an expression of bewilderment on his face. In spite of negative findings on physical and laboratory examinations, the patient describes a total amnesia for the events of the preceding several hours or days. Often, the patient claims to have forgotten all data of personal identification. In military settings, the patient may be an enlisted man found by military police wandering in the streets in an overseas setting without a proper pass, scrutinizing his dog tags in an attempt to discover his identity. These patients are usually suffering from a hysterical dissociative reaction or fugue state.

Such patients should be hospitalized and the life circumstances preceding the fugue state carefully scrutinized. The history so obtained usually reveals that the patient has taken a two-fold flight from an unbearable life situation—a physical flight so that he is usually some distance from his appropriate habitat, and a psychological flight into the dissociative state. The traumatic situation often involves a personal interaction filled with rage and threats to self-esteem, and is fraught with the danger of loss of impulse control. Such patients are often hypnotizable, and in the induced trance state it is possible to reconstruct the missing details in the personal history, including the feelings involved. A history of fainting spells and previous fugue states is often elicited.

The most important aspect of treatment is to assist the patient in relation to the overwhelming environmental trauma from which he has taken flight. If he is discharged to an unchanged home situation, another fugue state will probably supervene, in the course of which the patient may commit murder and suicide.

Related to the fugue state is brief reactive psychosis, a psychotic reaction of acute and dramatic onset, temporally related to a profoundly upsetting event or circumstance. Clinical manifestations include delusions, hallucinations, depersonalization and grossly unusual behavior. The acute episode seldom lasts more than a week or two, and on recovery there is practically no residue.

The essential diagnostic feature of this psychosis is the pressure of an overwhelming environmental trauma. Treatment consists of a brief period of separation from the traumatic environment, and then the provision of appropriate pharmacologic and psychological assistance.

**Homosexual Panic.** This is a term applied to a disorder of adult life characterized by delusions and hallucinations that accuse the patient, in derisive and contemptuous terms, of a variety of homosexual practices. The panic typically occurs in patients with schizoid personality disorders who have successfully protected themselves in the past from physical intimacy. Breakdown occurs in a setting of enforced intimacy, such as a college dormitory or a military barracks. There may be a history of alcohol or drug use preceding the acute episode.

**Other Panic Reactions.** Panic reactions without psychotic content can occur as part of agoraphobia, episodes of acute anxiety occurring in crowded public settings, such as theaters, department stores, and vehicles from which access to an escape route is cut off. These episodes may present clinically as a fear of an impending fatal heart attack. They may be associated with localized inframammary chest pain and sensations of a lump in the throat (globus hystericus).

Typically, there is a history of anxiety and depression during the preceding months, based on an increasingly stressful life circumstance related to difficulties at work, at school, or in the home.

Treatment of the acute episode is by simple reassurance and the use of a mild sedative, preferably a benzodiazepine. Proper long-term treatment depends on a careful diagnostic evaluation. Tricyclic antidepressants and monoamine oxidase inhibitors have been used successfully in agoraphobia.

**Posttraumatic Stress Disorder.** This term is commonly used to designate the acute anxiety symptoms that start after a near escape from death in combat, an accident, or a natural catastrophe.

Usually, the patient retains self-control during the actual period of danger, although a panic reaction can occur, characterized by terror and ineffective efforts at flight, that may precipitate panic reactions in others. Such panic-stricken patients are extraordinarily suggestible and easily hypnotizable, so that reassurance and firm instructions concerning appropriate behavior are usually followed with child-like obedience by the patient.

Typically, gross neurotic symptoms appear only after removal of the patient from the stress has occurred. At such times, one may observe coarse tremors and a variety of symptoms involving sensory and motor abnormalities. Treatment should encourage an immediate return to previous responsibilities. Most of all, prolonged diagnostic and therapeutic inpatient procedures should be avoided, as these encourage regression and chronic invalidism.

**Mania.** Manic excitement occurs in the manic phase of an affective disorder.

In a pathologically elated state, the patient may impoverish himself with extravagant expenditures, engage in inappropriate sexual adventures, and commit traffic violations because of reckless driving. The frantic family often consults a psychiatrist first without the patient. The family should be advised to notify all merchants that the patient is ill and that they run the risk of nonpayment if they injudiciously fill his orders. In communicating with the patient, the family should be encouraged to adopt an attitude of nonpunitive sobriety and firm insistence on the need for a physician's help. For the physician, the most important fact is the degree to which every manic patient teeters on the brink of depression. Careful listening readily reveals a depressive content to the patient's flight of ideas. With appropriate psychothera-

peutic intervention, it is usually possible to quiet the patient down long enough for him to accept medications and hospitalization, if necessary.

If the manic pressure is considerable, it may be necessary to use an intravenous medication, such as diazepam or intramuscular haloperidol. If emergency ECT is available, a schedule of treatments repeated in 5 minutes, 60 minutes, and 24 hours is often an effective way of terminating the attack. As soon as the patient is cooperative, the psychiatrist should start him on lithium carbonate by mouth in sufficient quantity to achieve therapeutic blood levels as determined by laboratory testing.

**Paranoid Schizophrenia.** Paranoid schizophrenics occasionally display psychotic excitement in which they may barricade themselves against imagined enemies or declare themselves the principal figure in some grandiose plot—political, religious, or otherwise.

As in the case of the manic patient, it is usually possible to establish contact with a rational ego core and to talk the patient down to the point where he accepts the need for medication and hospitalization. The initial feeling of no contact that such a patient engenders may discourage the inexperienced physician. Nevertheless, a sober attitude, firmly based in reality, usually reaches the patient and, more often than not, surprises the physician with the degree to which rational cooperation can be mobilized. To accomplish this end, the physician may have to make a house call, personally escort the patient to the hospital, and directly manage the technical details of hospital admission. Depending on the degree of excitement, the psychiatrist may have to administer, in his office or in the patient's home, a suitable intravenous medication, such as diazepam or haloperidol, in sufficient quantity to enlist the patient's cooperation without, at the same time, immobilizing him through overmedication.

**Catatonic Schizophrenia.** Catatonic schizophrenia may present a psychiatric emergency in the stage of either stupor or excitement.

The patient with catatonic stupor usually displays automatic obedience and accepts inpatient care without resistance. Unless there is some physical contraindication, ECT in an inpatient setting is very effective for interrupting an attack of catatonic stupor. When improvement occurs in an inpatient setting, the patient should not be discharged until the environmental precipitating factors are understood and corrected. The major tranquilizers may produce a catatonic stuporous state in some schizophrenic patients. In any case, they may not be effective in the treatment of catatonic stupor. Once the stupor has been relieved, major tranquilizers may be used to help the patient cope more competently with the stresses he faces on leaving the hospital.

Catatonic excitement may be more difficult than catatonic stupor to manage as a psychiatric emergency. Hospital admission is the necessary first step. ECT is one of the safest, swiftest, and most dependable ways of interrupting the condition. However, the psychiatrist can first begin by giving haloperidol, 2 to 5 mg, intramuscularly before trying ECT. As in catatonic stupor, discharge should be delayed until the traumatic environment has been improved and the patient has been started on an appropriate major tranquilizer. Catatonic states, stuporous or excited, may occur as a result of organic brain disease, and this possibility should be excluded by careful physical and laboratory examinations.

**Anorexia Nervosa.** Anorexia nervosa has as a key symptom an obsessional preoccupation with the desire to be thin. It usually occurs in females. The victim of the condition usually shows a wide range of interests and activities that belie the impression of physical fragility and even impending death, communicated by the cachectic appearance from lack of eating. The compulsive avoidance of food may reduce the patient to such an extreme degree of inanition that death by starvation occurs. For this reason, hospitalization and forced feeding may become necessary.

**Acute Psychosomatic Issues.** The value of a psychiatric presence has been proved in intensive care units, coronary care units, surgical recovery rooms, and the hospital admitting room itself, where the presence of the patient's personal physician and a family member reduces complications due to panic. After admission to the hospital, symptoms of severe anxiety may appear on the first or second day of confinement, inability to cooperate in a treatment procedure may appear during the next 2 days, and reactions of depression may appear thereafter. Toxic metabolic problems and impaired cerebral circulation add an organic factor that may precipitate a reaction of psychotic delirium.

Patients who press for elective surgery as a device to escape from unbearable life situations may be detected at times with careful preoperative psychiatric evaluation. In this way, postoperative emotional storms and pathologically prolonged periods of convalescence may be avoided. Cosmetic surgery is often sought when a patient is contemplating a major life change, such as the break-up of a marriage. A properly focused preoperative examination may forestall an ill-advised operation. One of the complications of surgery is a postoperative flare-up of dependency needs.

Patients who are to undergo mutilating surgery—such as amputation, mastectomy, or colostomy—should be psychologically prepared. Often, a surgeon with great technical skill is temperamentally unable to prepare the patient psychologically, and he should be assisted by a psychiatric consultant who is also prepared to participate in the postoperative care of the patient.

**Elective Cosmetic Surgery.** Rhinoplasty is occasionally followed by a psychotic reaction. In view of the frequency with which the procedure is done, postoperative psychosis is relatively rare. Adolescents, in particular, in the midst of an identity crisis, may react to an excellent cosmetic result with ambivalence and psychotic decompensation. Treatment of these cases may require hospitalization, antipsychotic medications, and psychotherapy that focuses on sexual questions and other issues involved in the identity crisis.

**Antihypertension Medications.** Rauwolfia derivatives are particularly apt to precipitate an acute depressive action in a patient undergoing treatment for hypertension.

If depression starts, Rauwolfia should be discontinued and another antihypertensive agent substituted. Once the depression has started, discontinuing the Rauwolfia by itself is usually not enough to relieve the condition. Antidepressant medications are ineffective for several weeks after Rauwolfia is discontinued, and ECT may be necessary in the presence of suicidal danger. If the depression is severe and there is danger of suicide, ECT is the procedure of choice. ECT should be withheld for at least 12 days after the last dose of Rauwolfia.

**Insomnia.** Insomnia may occur as a relatively benign symptom in relation to a period of unusual personal stress. It may mark the onset of a more severe depressive reaction, in which case it is associated with early-morning agitation and other signs and symptoms of depression. There may be a fear of falling asleep because of frightening dreams as part of a traumatic neurosis after a battle, accident, or other personal catastrophe. Insomnia may be part of a hysterical neurotic sleep disorder. The differential diagnosis depends on a careful history. However, the accumulating fatigue of successive sleepless nights can complicate the clinical picture, whatever the diagnosis.

Treatment consists of sedatives of the diazepam class such as triazolam (Halcion), 0.25 to

0.5 mg, at bedtime for up to 2 weeks. Any underlying mental disorder should be treated.

**Headache.** Headache can be the result of so many factors that careful study to rule out organic disease is most important. However, in the absence of positive physical findings, and in the presence of positive signs and symptoms of depression, headache may be treated with appropriate medications as an element in the depressive syndrome, with appropriate caution concerning the dangers of drug dependency or suicide by overdose.

**Dysmenorrhea.** A patient who presents herself at the emergency room with dysmenorrhea, particularly when it is associated with premenstrual depression and hostility, should be carefully evaluated from a suicidal point of view. When there is a history of marital disharmony, sexual difficulty, a variety of medical and gynecological complaints, and actual suicidal attempts in the past, suicidal precautions are particularly indicated.

**Hyperventilation.** Anxious patients may sometimes pant in terror. After a few seconds of overbreathing, a state of alkalosis sets in, due to excess carbon dioxide output. A reduction in consciousness occurs, with giddiness, faintness, and blurring of vision. These symptoms further terrify the already panic-stricken patient. Overbreathing tends to continue automatically and uncontrollably. Peripheral vasoconstriction causes a tingling feeling in the extremities and carpopedal spasm. Electroencephalogram and electrocardiogram changes occur during the attack, reflecting the metabolic derangement.

The classic remedy is breathing into a paper bag. More effective is a behavior modification approach, in which the patient is encouraged to hyperventilate in the doctor's office in the presence of a friend or relative. It is not difficult to convince the patient that hyperventilation is responsible for the symptoms while the patient is in the office. However, lasting results depend on further reinforcement where the attacks usually occur. The patient's understanding of the mechanisms of the symptom lays the best foundation for effective therapy.

**Dying.** The dying patient often creates a complex psychiatric emergency for himself, his physician, and his family. Those about him tend to avoid him. The result is an intensification of despair.

If a psychiatrist is called in to assist with the care of a dying patient, he should encourage the referring physician to accept primary responsibility for comforting the patient and yet respect the referring physician's emotional limitations if his need is to avoid the dying. Elisabeth Kubler-Ross has described 5 stages in the normal response to dying: (1) shock and denial, (2) anger, (3) bargaining, (4) depression, and (5) acceptance. Depending upon the patient and the illness, the psychiatrist may suggest that the patient be told that he is dying. Support, empathy, and taking the lead from the patient are essential therapeutic tasks. It is important to keep the family involved as much as possible.

Sudden infant death syndrome is often followed by a profound emotional upheaval in both parents that requires careful explanation and supportive psychotherapy. Similar problems may arise in relation to the birth of a congenitally malformed child.

**Rape.** In recent years, there has been a growing concern and compassion for the victims of rape. The rape victim fares best when she receives immediate support and is able to ventilate her fear and rage to a believing physician or other professional. She is helped also if family members are supportive of the patient, and the psychiatrist may wish to work with the patient and her family toward that end. Many cities now have rape crisis centers that are listed in the telephone directory and that should be consulted by the patient for further guidance.

**Mental Illness in a Physician.** The mentally ill physician presents a threefold set of problems. The primary responsibility is to ensure safe and competent care to the patient population affected. Parallel to this concern is the welfare of the ill physician and his family. Finally, there is the need to safeguard the reputation of the profession as a whole. Drug dependency and alcoholism are the major diagnostic categories, but other mental illnesses may be involved.

### Organic States

**Delirium.** This psychotic reaction, characterized by disorientation and frightening delusions, can occur in any acute, organically caused disorganization of brain functioning. Both the diagnosis and treatment of delirium are discussed in Chapter 16, "Organic Mental Disorders."

**Alcoholism.** In the emergency room, the alcoholic is often dirty and smells bad. It is easy to recoil from him in distaste. As a result, no other group is more frequently misclassified or mistreated. The chronic alcoholic usually has chronic liver, brain, and heart diseases. He has nutritional deficiencies, is prone to infection, and is even more prone to certain malignancies.

The alcohol may disguise behavioral abnormalities due to schizophrenia, hypoglycemia, or subarachnoid hemorrhage. The analgesic effect of alcohol may obscure the presence of broken bones and other serious injuries.

One should be alert to the problem of mixed addiction, the alcoholic who is also on barbiturates and other minor tranquilizers. In addition, the antidepressants, the phenothiazines, and related psychotropic agents potentiate the effects of alcohol. Thus, a careful drug and medication history is important. A regimen for barbiturate withdrawal may be the primary treatment indicated.

When the possibility of a major physical disease requiring inpatient care has been eliminated, the treatment of the acute alcoholic in the emergency room is aimed at making the patient ambulatory as swiftly as possible.

The emergency room alcoholic can be divided into four classes.

Class I: awake but clinically drunk—slurred speech, ataxic gait, slowed mental activity, belligerent, and totally uncooperative.

Class II: semicomatose—in deep sleep but responsive to painful stimuli; most reflexes intact.

Class III: comatose—no response to painful stimuli but some reflexes still present.

Class IV: comatose—no response to painful stimuli, no reflexes, but usually no respiratory or circulatory impairment.

When the obvious signs of intoxication have subsided, it is necessary to watch for withdrawal symptoms, coarse tremors, hyperreflexia, a tendency to startle in response to minor stimuli, and nausea. Pulse rate and blood pressure tend to be elevated at this time.

The severity of the withdrawal syndrome depends on the chronicity and the severity of the preceding alcoholic state. When there is doubt, the patient should be hospitalized. A benzodiazepine is administered by mouth and repeated in 1 to 6 hours, depending on the patient's condition. There is no need for parenteral medication if the patient is cooperative. When the patient has been stable for 24 to 36 hours, the medication should be gradually discontinued by reducing the dose over a 2-day period. If withdrawal symptoms do not appear but are expected, a benzodiazepine should be administered every 6 hours for 24 hours. If the symptoms have not occurred after 24 hours, the medication should be gradually discontinued over a 2-day period.

**Drug Abuse.** From an emergency psychiatric point of view, heroin overdose is a major problem. Even though treatment involves technical details remote from the usual responsibilities of the psychiatrist, it is helpful to know how to treat heroin overdose, because the patient may well be someone who is chronically under the psychiatrist's care.

The overdosed heroin patient is pale and cyanotic. He has pinpoint pupils and is areflexic. He may not be breathing at all, or he may take three or four shallow gasping breaths a minute. Without a moment's delay, his tongue should be pulled forward and out of the way, and the angles of his jaws should be strongly pushed forward and his mouth wiped free of blood and mucus. Vital signs should be noted—that is, level of consciousness, deep tendon reflexes, pupil size and reactivity, blood pressure, pulse rate, and respiration.

Blood should be drawn for a study of drug levels, and the patient given intravenous naloxone hydrochloride (Narcan), 0.4 mg in a 1-ml dose. Naloxone is a narcotic antagonist that reverses the opiate effects, including respiratory depression, within 2 minutes of the injection. If the desired degree of counteraction and respiratory improvement is not obtained, the dose may be repeated after 2 or 3 minutes. Failure to obtain significant improvement after two or three such doses suggests that the condition may be due partly or completely to other disease processes or to nonnarcotic sedative drugs. If the veins are burned out, the naloxone should be injected into a lingual vein or the jugular vein. Patients who respond to naloxone should be carefully observed, lest they lapse into coma again.

If the overdose is due to methadone, breathing should be monitored for 24 hours because toxicity may last that long, and the naloxone action is quite brief. It may be necessary in methadone overdosage to provide naloxone in the form of a continuous intravenous drip overnight, 2.0 mg of naloxone in 500 ml of 0.45 normal saline, injected at a rate of 0.4 mg every 30 minutes.

The family or friends who bring the patient to the emergency room must remain available to provide pertinent information, such as drug preferences and customary doses. If a sample of the patient's drug is available, it should be forwarded for laboratory assay. A urine analysis should be done as soon as a specimen can be obtained. It is important to consider the possibility of a physical condition that may mimic a drug reaction, such as diabetes or a postseizure state.

*Sedative-Hypnotic Withdrawal.* The use of barbiturates, nonbarbiturates, and the so-called minor tranquilizers is widespread. Hospitalization may be indicated because the addicted person can no longer function competently in the community. In addition, a patient may be hospitalized for medical or surgical reasons, and the withdrawal reaction is precipitated accidentally.

The first symptoms of withdrawal may start about 8 hours after the last pill has been taken, and may consist of anxiety, confusion, and ataxia. In time, gross tremors appear, with headache, nausea, and vomiting. Seizures, including status epilepticus, may occur sometime after the first 12 hours of withdrawal; seizures are a serious complication, since head injuries may be incurred. Whenever seizures occur in a previously nonepileptic adult, withdrawal should be considered in the differential diagnosis.

As the withdrawal continues, a psychotic state erupts, characterized by hallucinations, panic, and disorientation. Nystagmus is almost invariably present. During the delirium, the patient may leap to his death in an attempt to escape from his frightening psychotic experience.

Barbiturates are the most common culprit in the foregoing sequence of events, but any of the nonbarbiturate sedatives, including the minor tranquilizers, may be involved. In any event, the withdrawal process is the same.

The simplest way to institute the withdrawal procedure is to ask the patient directly what was his usual daily drug intake, divide that reported figure in half, and administer it to the patient in four doses every 6 hours. In a case of mixed addiction, the withdrawal procedure is most simply accomplished with a barbiturate, because there is cross-tolerance of all those substances. The patient should be closely observed and the dose decreased if he becomes drowsy and increased if withdrawal signs appear. From then on, the dose is reduced every other day in small steps, using 7 to 10 days for the patient to reach a dose of one pill a day. This dosage is continued for 2 days; then all further sedation is terminated.

If it is not possible to learn from the patient what his customary daily dose is, it has been suggested that the patient receive by mouth a 200-mg test dose of amobarbital sodium and be observed 1 hour later. If the patient is clearly drowsy or asleep, it may be concluded that his intake is minimal, equivalent to 200 mg a day; if there is nystagmus, ataxia, and drooping eyelids without verbal responsiveness, that suggests moderate abuse in the range of 500 mg a day; if the patient is able to speak but is dysarthric, that suggests heavy use in the 600 to 700 mg daily dose range; if the patient shows minimal effects, it may be concluded that there is extremely heavy use in the range of 900 mg or more a day. The withdrawal schedule can then be planned accordingly.

*Sedative Overdose.* If the patient is still awake, whoever finds him should make him vomit. If an attempted suicide or accidental overdose is reported, 15 ml (1 tablespoonful) of ipecac syrup should be administered. However, a patient who is only partially responsive should not be provoked to vomit. In a hospital setting, vomiting can be induced by apomorphine, 6 mg subcutaneously, if the patient is fully alert and cooperative.

Although swallowed barbiturates are usually absorbed in 4 to 6 hours after ingestion, other substances, such as glutethimide (Doriden), are absorbed more slowly. Long-lasting gastric concretions may form if many tablets are swallowed in a short time.

The next step is to institute forced diuresis until the patient's urine output has reached 500 ml an hour. Continued forced diuresis requires the specialized knowledge of how to maintain a proper blood electrolyte balance. An indwelling catheter is necessary to monitor urinary output. Dialysis should be instituted as needed.

Mixed sedative intoxications pose no special problem, since treatment consists of nonspecific supportive measures. However, alcohol accelerates absorption and retards hepatic detoxification, thereby increasing the likelihood of fatal outcome.

*Anticholinergic Drugs.* Atropine, scopolamine, belladonna, and the antihistamines are commonly encountered as the active ingredient in over-the-counter—that is, nonprescription—sleeping pills and in antiparkinsonism medications, including L-dopa. As a result of overdose or drug sensitivity, these so-called anticholinergic substances may produce an acute psychotic reaction. This syndrome may also be caused by antidepressant and antipsychotic medication. Apart from the psychotic symptoms that may be confused with schizophrenia, the patient shows fixed dilated pupils, a flushed dry skin, and urinary retention.

With these telltale signs as a basis, one may administer physostigmine, 4.0 mg intramuscularly, for diagnostic purposes and for swift symptomatic relief. In anticholinergic psychotic states, improvement after a single injection lasts about 2 to 3 hours. In any event, the psychotic reaction usually subsides within 3 days. Perhaps the most important aspect of this psychotic category is the fact that the patients are intolerant of phenothiazines because of their anticholinergic effects, tending to react with more delirium and sometimes with dangerous hypotension. When in doubt, one should avoid the phenothiazines and, instead, use chlordiazepoxide (Librium), diazepam (Valium), or phenobarbital.

*Central Anticholinergic Syndrome.* This emergency consists of delirium, hot skin, fever, blurred vision, and dilated pupils. These anticholinergic symptoms result from an idiosyncratic reaction to neuroleptics or an overdose. Treatment consists of close medical supervision and IV or IM physostigmine (2 mg), which may be repeated in 15 minutes and then every hour. Physostigmine overdose must be watched for (sweating, hypersalivation) and treated with atropine sulfate.

*Hallucinogens.* In this category are included LSD, phencyclidine (PCP), psilocybin, and mescaline. New substances appear sporadically. These drugs produce dilated pupils that react to light, elevated blood pressure, hyperactive reflexes, fever, tachycardia, sweating, and nystagmus. Psychotic reactions are associated with perceptual distortions and hallucinations. Panic may occur, with impulsive flight and suicide. Occasionally, there may be impulsive acts of violence.

Phencyclidine (PCP, angel dust, hog) has become, next to alcohol, the most common cause of psychotic drug-related emergency hospital admissions. The presence of nystagmus (horizontal, vertical, rotary), muscular rigidity, and elevated blood pressure in a patient who is agitated, psychotic, or comatose and whose respirations are not depressed is diagnostic for PCP intoxication. Treatment of the condition with the major tranquilizers is contraindicated. The so-called talking-down process does not help, since the patients are out of contact with reality. The following steps are recommended: (1) Sensory isolation is indicated in a darkened, quiet room with the patient on a floor pad; (2) gastric lavage may recover a significant amount of the drug; (3) diazepam, 10 to 20 mg orally (or 10 mg intramuscularly), should be given to quiet the patient and repeated at 3- to 4-hour intervals if necessary, 2 to 3 mg intravenously if seizures intervene; (4) diazoxide should be given for serious hypertension, 300 mg intravenously, rapidly; (5) ammonium chloride, 0.5 to 1 g every 6 hours by mouth or nasogastric tube, should be administered, and the patient's urine pH (5.5 to 6) should be checked; (6) if the patient is comatose, his nasopharynx should be suctioned frequently, and he should be hydrated carefully and turned often; and (7) full recovery may require long-term treatment.

The flashback or acute recurrence of an LSD-like state in the absence of subsequent LSD use is usually transient and harmless; it is significant primarily from a diagnostic point of view. If necessary, these episodes can be treated safely with a major tranquilizer.

Cannabis intoxication can occur from marijuana, hashish, or tetrahydrocannabinol (THC). In some persons, panic and transient paranoid reactions can occur; these reactions usually subside with simple supportive psychotherapy.

*Amphetamines and Cocaine.* These drugs produce dilated pupils that are reactive to light, elevated blood pressure and temperature, dry mouth, tachycardia and cardiac dysrhythmias, and hyperactive tendon reflexes. The patients are often paranoid, subject to tactile hallucinations, irritable, and capable of violent aggressive behavior. A major tranquilizer is the medication of choice for symptom control and for stabilization of cardiovascular and autonomic irregularities.

### Other Emergency Disorders

**Acute Intermittent Porphyria.** This disorder is a rare cause of an acute psychiatric emergency. A psychotic reaction associated with severe abdominal pain, grand mal seizures, and other evidences of central nervous system involvement characterizes the disease. It is diagnosed by demonstrating the presence of specific abnormal porphyrins in the urine or abnormal blood enzymes characteristic of defective heme production. It is associated with a genetically determined sensitivity to barbiturates, alcohol, tranquilizers, and oral contraceptives, the use of which precipitates an attack. Treatment consists essentially of avoiding the precipitating substances.

**Acute Major Tranquilizer Dyskinesias.** The acute dyskinetic syndrome or hyperkinetic dystonic crisis is an idiosyncratic reaction to phenothiazines and consists of difficulties in speech and swallowing due to hypertonicity of regional muscle groups, perioral spasms, involuntary protrusion of the tongue, torticollis, oculogyric spasms, hyperextension of the neck and trunk, myoclonic movements, and torsion spasms. Consciousness is never impaired. These reactions are usually terrifying to the patient and may be confused with hysteria. Occasionally, respiratory distress occurs because of a dystonic reaction in the laryngeal musculature.

Severe dyskinesias of sudden onset can be relieved by the intravenous injection of antiparkinsonism drugs. Further tranquilizer administration may be tried at a lower dosage, with prophylactic antiparkinsonism medication by mouth. Unfortunately, some patients cannot tolerate even minimal doses and react similarly to all the major tranquilizers.

Akathisia is a condition characterized by restlessness. There is a sense of quivering discomfort in the muscles of the lower extremities that is relieved somewhat when the patient moves about. The patient is unable to sit still. The reaction can be frightening to the patient and can be misinterpreted clinically as an agitated intensification of the basic psychiatric illness. Antiparkinsonism medication usually does not relieve akathisia. However, the patient may be able to tolerate a related phenothiazine derivative.

**Hypertensive Crisis.** This type of emergency can occur in a patient treated for depression with a monoamine oxidase (MAO) inhibitor if he has eaten food with a high tyramine content (strong cheese, smoked or pickled fish, spiced meats, highly seasoned foods, wines and alcohol in general, chicken liver, yeast extract, excessive amounts of coffee, chocolate) or if he has taken sympathomimetic drugs, particularly by injection. The hypertensive crisis is characterized by a severe occipital headache that may radiate frontally, palpitation, neck stiffness and soreness, nausea, vomiting, sweating, photophobia, constricting chest pain, and dilated pupils. Intracranial bleeding, sometimes fatal, has been reported in association with hypertensive crisis.

If a hypertensive crisis occurs, the MAO inhibitor should be discontinued at once, and therapy should be instituted to reduce blood pressure. Phentolamine (Regitine), 50-mg tablet, should be carried by the patient and taken by mouth if a severe headache occurs after a dietary infraction. If the crisis is severe and the patient is brought to a hospital emergency room, he should receive 5 mg of phentolamine intravenously, slowly, to avoid producing an excessive hypotensive effect.

**Postseizure Excitement.** This is an unpleasant reaction occasionally seen after an electroconvulsive treatment. Some patients, particularly men, awaken with terror, become dangerously assaultive, and try to escape. They attack anyone who tries to control them.

If the patient is permitted to sleep quietly after the treatment for as long as he wants and is permitted to awaken spontaneously, the likelihood of postseizure excitement is reduced. In a patient known to be subject to this pattern of postseizure behavior, a needle may be placed in his vein before full awakening and a small quantity of a barbiturate injected very slowly as he starts to stir, in order to prolong the postseizure

sleep period. This treatment also tends to reduce the likelihood of postseizure excitement.

**Heatstroke.** Patients with a history of head injury, alcoholism, or major tranquilizer medication are prone to respond adversely to excessive exposure to hot weather, particularly if the exposure involves physical exertion and direct exposure to the sun. The patient may become mute, stuporous, or delirious. Diagnosis depends on the history, the presence of a hot dry skin, and an elevated pulse and body temperature.

Treatment consists of removal of the patient to a cool place, cold-water sponges to reduce body temperature, and saline, either as tablets by mouth if the patient can swallow or as intravenous saline.

**Agranulocytosis.** This is an occasional hematological side effect of psychotropic medications. Symptoms usually include sore throat, fever, fatigue, lethargy, stomatitis, lymphadenopathy, and other signs of infection. If a patient on medications presents with any of those symptoms or findings, medication should be discontinued at once. If the white count is depressed, proper treatment should be instituted.

**Heimlich Maneuver.** From time to time, institutionalized psychotic patients bolt food and obstruct the airway with a large bolus. Staff knowledge of the Heimlich maneuver—compression of the epigastrium with fist and hand from an *a tergo* position—may be lifesaving.

### Emergencies in Child Psychiatry

Because of the relative shortage of trained child psychiatrists, the burden of diagnosis and treatment falls for the most part on the general psychiatrist, who must be available for emergencies. The actual emergency is usually the last stage in a long history of psychopathology, family disorganization, and physical and emotional exhaustion. The emergency becomes manifest when the significant adults around the child can no longer provide ego support and control.

**Accidental Poisoning.** Many children are poison repeaters. One 4-year-old child, for example, was hospitalized seven times in 1 year with poison ingestions serious enough to warrant repeated gastric lavage. Self-poisoning attempts in children fall into four categories. Accidental occurrences constitute the smallest group. A somewhat larger group are experiments in children looking for a kick or a trip. About 25 percent are real suicidal attempts. The majority, almost 50 percent, are episodes involving complicated pathological mother-child interactions. In the majority of instances of repetitive self-poisoning, the child was locked in a power struggle with the mother, and swallowing the poison was an act of defiance.

In recent years, the treatment of enuresis with tricyclic antidepressants like imipramine (Tofranil) and amitriptyline (Elavil) has led to a great increase in the number of children hospitalized for overdosage with those agents. Similarly, the methadone treatment of heroin addiction has been associated with an increasing number of cases of methadone poisoning in children. Most patients are boys under 5 years of age.

The usual general principles concerning poisoning in children should be followed and can be found in any standard pediatric textbook.

**Hyperkinesis.** Minimal brain dysfunction in the hyperkinetic child is probably the single most common disorder seen by child psychiatrists. It is characterized by overactivity, distractibility, impulsivity, and excitability.

Hyperactivity is a nonspecific symptom and not a total personality disorder. It is comparable to the symptoms of anxiety and depression in adults. It occurs more or less normally in the infant and young preschool child, and frequently appears with fatigue in normal children. It is considered a sign of developmental immaturity only when it persists after age 7 or when it is excessive in degree. At any point, the hyperkinetic child may become a psychiatric emergency if the significant adults about the child can no longer tolerate his behavior. Treatment involves the use of amphetamine or methylphenidate and psychotherapy.

**School Phobia.** School phobia can be a crippling disorder. Without apparent reason, a child may suddenly refuse to go to school. When pressured, he panics unless permitted to stay home. It is a serious psychiatric emergency because of a vicious circle that quickly sets in—the longer the child stays out of school, the more severe are his social and educational impairments and the more difficult is the problem of treatment.

**Adoption.** Adopted children have an increased incidence of mental disorders. The disorders tend to become manifest primarily during adolescence. The identity crisis that erupts normally at that time is typically associated with rebellion and parental rejection. Adopted children may run away from home at that time in search of their natural parents. There may be intense daydreaming, with romantic fantasies concerning one's natural origins. If the adoptive parents are middle-class, there may be sexual acting out with partners from lower social stratums. Overt psychotic reactions may occur.

The adoptive parents need support in relation to their feelings of bewilderment, disappointment, and guilt. The patient needs help in understanding his rejection of the adoptive parents in part, at least, as a normal adolescent quest for identity.

**Battered Child Syndrome.** Perhaps the most important aspect of this problem is its episodic character. There is a premonitory phase, during which the child's parent is struggling actively with the fear of loss of self-control. The mother may bring her normal child to the doctor repeatedly with minor complaints calculated to alert the doctor to her fear that she will injure her child if he does not intervene. The child may show evidence of poor nutrition and hygiene and of general failure to thrive.

In all suspicious cases, even when the injury is not serious, the child should be hospitalized. It is important to avoid accusations or premature confrontations, so as not to cause counterproductive defensive parental reactions. The first priority is to separate the child from a potentially dangerous environment.

The child's parents should be interviewed separately, starting with the mother. One should look for a history of violence in the parents' childhood backgrounds, including a history of parental alcoholism and broken marriage.

The maltreated child is usually different from his siblings in some way to make him more vulnerable than they to abuse. Precocious and hyperactive children, prematures, adopted children, and stepchildren are all abuse prone. In terms of the current crisis, one should inquire into the presence of a major setback in the child's family situation, stemming from parental loss of a job, physical or mental illness, death of a grandparent, and so on. In response to a family crisis, there may be an increased parental alcohol or drug intake that reduces judgment and control. The actual explosion of child battering may take place in a dissociative state for which the guilty parent is amnesic. Recent changes in the child are also important. A febrile condition, for example, causing fretfulness may provoke an already teetering parent to lose control.

Most local governments require the reporting of child abuse. This requirement should be followed and the parents so informed. In most cases, the reporting is all that is done, and the bureau of child welfare is not asked to take particular action.

If the hospitalized child has siblings, their safety must be evaluated. Sometimes one child is the exclusive family scapegoat. In other cases, however, removal of the abused child puts the other children in danger.

It is essential to set up a long-term program of help for the parents, who may be surprisingly cooperative. Local self-help groups under professional guidance have been set up in various parts of the country.

**Anorexia Nervosa.** Anorexia nervosa occasionally presents as an emergency, particularly in boarding school or in travel settings away from home. Weight loss in this condition can be life threatening. It is usually helpful to set a limit, with the understanding that, if the child's weight drops below the agreed-on level, a return to the parental home and possible hospitalization is obligatory. This dictum by itself may bring the progressive weight loss to an end. If it does not, hospital admission and inpatient care are indicated.

**Firesetting.** Firesetting is a dramatic act that understandably frightens parents and authorities. It is often associated with enuresis and hyperkinetic behavior and is most likely an expression of anxiety and depression. At times, a parental role of subtly condoning and encouraging the behavior can be detected. Treatment requires a careful diagnostic evaluation and a family-centered treatment program. The use of amphetamines, tricyclic antidepressants, and other appropriate medications is often of considerable value.

**Sexual Assault.** Sexual assault in childhood can be divided into two separate categories—those involving purely an adult's act of exhibitionism or indecent exposure, and those involving actual physical contact and rape. Exhibitionism is much more common than rape and involves both boys and girls. It is common for these children to be recidivists—that is, they are the victims of repeated episodes of indecent exposure. A study of those youngsters reveals that the child himself often invites these attentions from perverse adults as part of a state of emotional deprivation.

Treatment should be directed at diminishing the reactions of panic and outrage on the part of the parents and at exploring the family pathology that may have contributed to the child's vulnerability. The adult exhibitionist who does not establish physical contact with the child is suffering from a relatively benign disorder that may be safely treated in an outpatient setting.

The child who has been physically molested has suffered a much more serious trauma, particularly if rape has occurred. In most rape cases, the perpetrator is a family member or a family friend. Very often, the adult is under the influence of alcohol at the time of the episode. In short, the family setting may be highly disturbed. In terms of long-range pathological effects, it is worth noting that many prostitutes report a history of rape in childhood. Subsequent promiscuity as an adolescent and prostitution as an adult seem to represent, in part, efforts to overcome the trauma of the early sexual assault, feelings of self-hatred, disillusionment, and contempt for men.

Physical treatment of the rape victim is directed at repair of the injuries, prevention of venereal disease, and prevention of pregnancy. Material must be collected for medicolegal examination. The gynecologist should be experienced in examining children, so as not to further traumatize the child.

From a psychological point of view, a family-centered treatment approach is crucial. If at all possible, hospitalization should be avoided. The child should be kept at home, and the parents should be given the necessary counseling support. Home visiting by trained professionals is most important. The treatment plan aims to permit free ventilation of the child's thoughts and feelings. The usual pattern of suppressing all discussion has the effect of intensifying the child's guilt and sets the stage for long-range chronic psychopathology. If the family pathology is severe, foster home placement may be indicated.

**Newborn Abstinence Syndrome.** Heroin addiction in newborn infants is increasing. In this condition, the incidence of prematurity is high. In general, the newborn infant may appear normal at birth, but, somewhere between 6 and 48 hours after birth, the abstinence syndrome begins. The infant develops a high-pitched, ear-piercing cry that is continuous and far louder than a normal cry. In its mildest form, the infant displays hypertonic muscles, with an exaggerated Moro's reflex and tremulousness. In more severe forms there are, in addition, sweating, salivating, yawning, sneezing, and loose stools. In the most severe reaction, vomiting, diarrhea, and convulsions occur.

Diazepam (Valium) in doses of 1 to 2 mg, depending on the severity of the symptoms and the infant's size, is given by injection every 8 hours until the withdrawal symptoms are fully controlled, then reduced by one-half, and finally tapered off by increasing the time intervals between injections to 12 hours and lowering the dose level to 0.5 mg. The treatment can usually be terminated in about 4 days without a recurrence of the symptoms.

Women receiving barbiturates in the last trimester of pregnancy for the treatment of epilepsy or because of drug abuse may give birth to barbiturate-addicted babies. The abstinence symptoms do not start until 4 to 7 days after birth. The baby's cry is loud, shrill, and continuous. The infant eats voraciously but often gags and vomits, so that pyloric stenosis may be suspected. There is irritability and fitful sleep.

Treatment consists of protecting the baby from extraneous stimuli and the liberal use of a pacifier and, if necessary, sedatives, such as phenobarbital and diazepam. Treatment must be continued for 2 to 6 months before the baby becomes normal. In all cases, the first sign of progress is the infant's ability to sleep for longer periods, up to several hours during the night.

The fetal alcohol syndrome, which occurs in children whose mothers are addicted to alcohol, is discussed in Section 19.3.

**Pediatric Hospitalization as Crisis Intervention.** Much has been written about the traumatic impact of hospitalization on a sick child and his family. Insufficient attention has been paid to the positive therapeutic aspects of the experience. Many children with asthma, persistent vomiting, diarrhea, and failure to thrive improve swiftly and dramatically while in the hospital, only to relapse on discharge. Separation from hypothetical allergens in the home is often cited as an explanation, even though practitioners have observed that "parentectomy" is most likely the chief therapeutic agent in these cases. Such hospital admissions can be lifesaving at times by providing an urgently needed respite from an unendurable home situation. Rational therapy for these cases calls for a careful study of the family and the child and a family-centered treatment program, which should be worked out before the child is returned to his home.

**Bereavement.** Many children seen in emergency psychiatric consultations give a history of the loss of a parent, sibling, or other close relative through illness, hospitalization, or death within weeks of the onset of symptoms. The symptoms include suicidal behavior, acute phobias, hysterical conversion, hypochondriasis with panic-stricken reactions to minor injuries, fear of death and dying, regression in toilet training, firesetting, cruelty to pets, and even psychotic reactions. In teenagers, there may be drug abuse, delinquency, sexual promiscuity, and out-of-wedlock pregnancy.

The disturbance in the child is almost always an expression of a disturbance in the family. Adults caught in the web of their own grief may have scotomata for the emotional needs of the child. The child may feel that a grief-stricken parent has withdrawn his love. Coming on top of guilt based on oedipal or sibling rivalry, the experience may be emotionally crushing to the bereaved child.

**Fatal Illness.** A psychiatric emergency can arise in relation to the parents of a dying child. The child usually suffers much guilt in relation to his illness and is apt to misinterpret his parents' frantic behavior as evidence of the withdrawal of their love. For the dying child, that withdrawal impinges on the greatest fear of all— that he will be abandoned and left to die alone. The parents need support in their grief and in understanding the child's feelings of guilt and fear of abandonment.

### Psychiatric Complications of Encounter Groups

A variety of quasitherapeutic groups are characterized by a lack of any screening procedures for admission to the group; a certain amount of coercion to participate in the group; a failure to obtain informed consent from persons entering the group; a failure to delineate clearly the rules and goals of the group, so that a passive, frightened person may feel unable to voluntarily disengage himself from the group; a lack of available mental health professional consultation; a lack of follow-up concerning the subsequent clinical course of a group member; and, most important, a lack of proper training of the leaders—indeed, a lack of any screening procedure to eliminate persons incapable of providing responsible leadership.

With this spectrum of deficiencies as a background, it becomes understandable why there are increasing reports in the literature of acute psychotic episodes, suicidal acting out, homosexual panic, depression, sexual and aggressive acting out, and ill-advised upheavals in personal life, including the breakup of families and divorce.

A careful psychiatric study of such cases may reveal that a precarious adaptational balance preceded the encounter experience and that drug use contributed to individual instances of breakdown. If these complications occur in settings away from home, such as a college campus or a vacation setting, it is advisable to have the patient return home at once—if possible, accompanied by his parents or responsible relatives. Treatment of the individual case depends on the results of a careful diagnostic study. Perhaps the most urgent issue is to educate the public concerning the dangers of indiscriminate participation in nonprofessional groups led by incompetent leaders.

### REFERENCES

Barton W: *The Psychiatric Emergency*. American Psychiatric Association and National Association of

Mental Health, Washington, DC, 1966.

Blachly P H: Naloxone for diagnosis in methadone programs. JAMA *224:* 334, 1973.

Glick R A, Myeerson A T, Robbins E, Talbott J A, editors: *Psychiatric Emergencies.* Grune & Stratton, New York, 1976.

Herrington R E, Benzer D G, Jacobson G R, Hawkins M K: Treating substance-use disorders among physicians. JAMA *247:* 2253, 1982.

Hillard J R, Ramm D, Zung W W K, Holland J M: Suicide in a psychiatric emergency room population. Am J Psychiatry *140:* 459, 1983.

Kapoor W N, Karpf M, Wieand S, Peterson J R,

Levey G S: A prospective evaluation and follow-up of patients with syncope. N Engl J Med *309:* 197, 1983.

Linn L: Other psychiatric emergencies. In *Comprehensive Textbook of Psychiatry,* ed 4, H I Kaplan, B J Sadock, editors, p 1315. Williams & Wilkins, Baltimore, 1985.

Litovitz T L, Troutman W G: Amoxapine overdose: Seizures and fatalities. JAMA *250:* 1069, 1983.

Mellor C S, Jain V K: Diazepam withdrawal syndrome: Its prolonged and changing nature. Can Med Assoc J *127:* 1093, 1982.

# 26

# Psychotherapies

## 26.1 PSYCHOANALYSIS AND PSYCHOANALYTIC PSYCHOTHERAPY

### Introduction

Psychoanalysis and psychoanalytic psychotherapy both apply psychoanalytic understandings of human behavior; both attempt to modify behavior by such psychological methods as confrontation, clarification, and interpretation; both require introspection by the patient and empathic understanding by the therapist; and both require consistent attention to the countertransference. But psychoanalysis attempts to rely solely on interpretation as its technical modality, and it concentrates on the events of the analytic relationship, tending to treat the relationship as a closed system when a transference neurosis has been established. Psychoanalytic psychotherapy, on the other hand, often minimizes the relationship of the patient and therapist except when they clamorously obstruct the treatment process, and may use supportive measures, advice, environmental manipulation, and other maneuvers in addition to interpretation. At times, the ends of the continuum may be so dissimilar that the two forms of treatment seem to be unrelated. Often, however, it may be quite difficult, if not impossible, to decide whether a particular treatment is psychoanalysis or psychotherapy. Underlying all forms of psychoanalysis and the derivative therapies is the factor of the real relationship of the patient and the therapist. This relationship arises out of the necessity to deal with such matters as schedules and fees, and out of the circumstance that the patient and the therapist are both adults, however troubled the patient may be by the past. The correct handling and weighting of the real relationship may be critical for the successful outcome of both analysis and therapy.

### Psychoanalysis as Therapy

#### The Psychoanalytic Situation

The externals of the psychoanalytic situation—the setting—are little changed from Freud's day. The patient lies on a couch or sofa, and the analyst sits behind him, remaining for the most part outside the patient's field of vision and intruding as little as possible into the patient's thought processes, except through his interpretations. Sessions are usually held four or more times a week, and have an average duration of 45 to 50 minutes. Innovators, such as Jacques Lacan from France, who has introduced decreases in session frequency and length, have caused much controversy; but some analyses are now being conducted in this country with session lengths varying from 20 to 30 minutes and frequency of one to two sessions per week. The patient is guided in his behavior by the so-called basic or fundamental rule, and the analyst endeavors to maintain a kind of evenly suspended attention that is the counterpart to the patient's activity of free association. For the most part, the analyst's activity is limited to timely interpretation of his patient's associations. Although the analyst tries not to impose his own personality and system of values on his patient, he nevertheless must enter into some reality negotiations with his patient. There are schedules and fees to be arranged; and weekends, vacations, and illnesses will interrupt the course of treatment. Realistic aspects of the analyst's personality become apparent to the patient in many ways, and it is neither possible nor desirable for the analyst to maintain the much-misinterpreted blank screen. Thus, a real relationship underlies the analytic setting, and the handling of the real relationship may make the difference between success and failure in the treatment endeavor.

The reclining position of the patient on the couch, with the analyst seated nearby, attending to every word, reproduces symbolically an ancient parent-child situation, the nuances of which vary from patient to patient. This situation is not without the potential to generate anxiety in the patient, who is probably already in an anxious state because of his neurosis when he begins analysis. Preoedipal anxieties derived from the early mother-child dyad may be revived early in the analysis. The patient's difficulties in trusting the analyst, whom he does not see, to maintain this trust in the absence of immediate gratification and response, and to maintain an appreciation of the separateness of the patient from the analyst, may occupy the center of the stage during the opening phases of analysis. The capacity of the patient to call on these ego functions through the analysis is indispensable for its ultimate success, and an estimate of this capacity is one of the important considerations in the assessment of analyzability.

Another aspect of the use of the couch is that it introduces an element of sensory deprivation, because visual stimuli are limited. Also, an analyst's interpretations and interventions tend to be rather sparse, especially in the early phases of an analysis. A relative diminution of both visual and auditory stimuli tends to promote regression. In the analytic situation, however, regression must remain controlled and in the service of the treatment. Almost any verbal input from the analyst tends to counteract regression by its sensory impact.

### Fundamental Rule

The patient's job is indicated in the fundamental rule. As part of the realistic collaborative approach to the cure of his neurosis, the patient agrees to be completely candid with his analyst.

Implicit in the fundamental rule of psychoanalysis are two interrelated principles. First, in psychoanalysis there is a clear emphasis on the value of recognition and verbalization of psychic contents—of ideas, impulses, conflicts, and emotions. Second, psychoanalytic technique emphasizes the principle that action based on impulse without adequate prior consideration is to be avoided.

Some patients may take the fundamental rule so literally that they sabotage their treatment while giving an appearance of meticulously complying with its requirements. They may parody its spirit while obeying its letter. This is particularly likely to occur in some obsessional states, in which the fundamental rule may be used as a weapon against the analyst, rather than against the neurosis. Some analysts, therefore, do not always give their patients explicit statements about the fundamental rule, preferring, instead, to lead them to discover it for themselves through a study of the obstacles they place in the way of communication. Properly observed, however, the fundamental rule leads to the patient's use of the technique of free association.

### Free Association

This term is actually a misnomer, inasmuch as associations are soon seen not to be free at

all, but to be directed by three kinds of unconscious forces: (1) the pathogenic conflicts of the neurosis, (2) the wish to get well, and (3) the wish to please the analyst. The interplay between these factors becomes very complex and at times threatens the progress of the analysis, as when some impulse that is unacceptable to the patient and that is a part of his neurosis comes into conflict with his wish to please his analyst, who, he assumes, also finds the impulse unacceptable.

### Free-floating Attention

The counterpart in the analyst to the patient's free association is a special way of listening that is usually called free-floating attention. In this process, the analyst listens to his patient's associations and temporarily forms an identification with his affects and ideas. At the same time, he pays attention to his own associations, which are for the most part stimulated by his patient's material. Because, in theory at least, the analyst is more receptive to thoughts and feelings that may be warded off by his patient, it is usually possible for him to form some idea about what it is that his patient is struggling not to express.

The longer the patient and the analyst work together—the better the analyst knows his patient—the easier it is to achieve free-floating attention. The analyst's careful attention to his own subjective experiences is an indispensable part of the work of analyzing.

### Rule of Abstinence

In addition to the fundamental rule, there is another rule, the rule of abstinence. This rule does not mean, as it has often been misinterpreted to mean, that a patient must forego instinctual gratifications during the course of analysis. But the patient must be prepared to endure delay of gratification of instinctual wishes so that he can talk about them in the treatment. It is only through the optimal frustration of the patient's wishes in the framework of the analysis that the analytic process is propelled forward, that the patient becomes conscious of his psychic tensions, instead of reducing them in unproductive gratification or keeping them in repression.

### Analytic Process

The process of clinical psychoanalysis is for the most part slow and tedious. The analyst, observing the principle of maintaining an optimal level of anxiety in his patient and the principles of optimal dosages of interpretation and gratification, tends to regard a sudden abreactive breakthrough as unfortunate and poten tially traumatic. Freud called it an "outright mishap."

**Transference.** One criterion by which psychoanalysis can be differentiated in principle from other forms of psychotherapy, including psychoanalytic psychotherapy, is the management of transference. In general psychiatry, the term transference has come to be used as a loose designation for all aspects of the patient's feelings and behavior toward the physician. It includes rational and adaptive aspects, as well as those irrational distortions that arise from unconscious strivings. When it is used in this encompassing sense, it may be more appropriate to refer to transference as a relationship. In contrast, transference in psychoanalysis is conceived of as an endopsychic phenomenon that occurs entirely within the mind.

**Therapeutic Alliance.** Various writers have delineated two additional categories of object relationships within the analytic situation: the therapeutic alliance and the real relationship with the analyst.

The first job of the analyst and of the psychotherapist is to assess the reliability of the therapeutic alliance or, to use another term for the same thing, the working alliance. It is only when the alliance is secure that effective work can be done on the dyadic aspects of the relationship that develop in the transference neurosis.

It would be erroneous to assume that, once the therapeutic alliance has been established, it remains stable. In reality, it must constantly be watched and reintegrated, especially during periods of strong positive and negative transference in which the patient's observing ego is overwhelmed by his experiencing ego and has lost its alliance with the analyst's analyzing ego.

**Real Relationship.** The third form of object relationship between patient and analyst is the real relationship. This term refers to what is realistic and genuine between the analyst and the patient. The term includes that part of the analytic relationship between two adults entering into a joint venture, and the necessity for them to conduct themselves realistically around such matters as fees, illnesses, and interruptions—in short, all the reality arrangements necessary in the analysis.

The real relationship between analyst and patient also includes the patient's realistic perceptions of his analyst. A patient may accurately perceive objectionable character traits in his analyst that make it impossible for the analysis to continue. He may also perceive the analyst's countertransference reactions quite astutely.

**Transference Neurosis.** The central event in a classical therapeutic analysis is the establishment of the transference neurosis and its ultimate resolution by interpretation.

Clinically, the transference neurosis often announces its existence with an increase in the patient's concern and preoccupation with his analysis, which becomes temporarily the most important concern of his life, more important at times than spouse or children.

In contrast to the evanescent transference reactions, the transference neurosis is a somewhat variable but more or less sustained set of transferences, focused on the analyst, in which the patient repeats much of the crucial material from his past.

**Resistance.** Because the undoing of pathological repression is the hub of analytic work, the analyst, by insisting on a recognition of unwanted impulses, may seem to his patient to be siding with these impulses in repression, instead of with his reasonable ego. Sooner or later the patient feels impelled to repeat old ego or superego defenses against threatening impulses, but now these defenses are also directed against the analyst, who appears to stand for such impulses.

The analysis of resistance is at the heart of analytic work, resistance meaning here the defensive operations of the ego as they appear in the analytic process.

The signs of resistance are legion; sometimes their recognition is simple, at other times difficult. Almost any feature of the analytic situation can be used in the service of resistance. For example, the basic rule requires that a patient say whatever comes to his mind. A compulsive talker may enter into the analytic situation with gusto, looking forward to a captive audience. It may be quite difficult to unmask his enthusiastic adherence to the basic rule as a resistance, a phenomenon that gratifies a wish to dominate the listener but that does not lead to insight and to a deepening of the analytic process.

The very reasonableness of the analytic situation, and of the goal of bringing primary process under secondary process influence, may replicate a childhood situation in which reasonable and enlightened parents provided such an affectively sterile environment that a patient in analysis can have great difficulty in facing affects that he had to reject in childhood. Again, any aspect of the analytic situation can become a nidus of resistance.

**Narcissistic Transferences.** To be analyzable, a patient must have achieved a degree of maturation in childhood characterized by a cohesive, stable sense of self.

Heinz Kohut, an important innovator in psychoanalysis, wrote about a large group of patients suffering from narcissistic personality disorders who, he believes, are analyzable but who do not develop typical transference neuroses in the classical sense. Often, these patients are fairly well-adjusted and well-functioning people whose personality disturbances prevent them from achieving a full measure of satisfaction in life. The central pathology does not appear to involve incestuously cathected parental images but, rather, involves the relationship between the self and the archaic narcissistic objects. These archaic narcissistic objects are the grandiose self and the idealized parent imago, the reactivations of which constitute a threat to the patient's sense of integrity of the self.

**Countertransference.** Just as the term transference has often been used to encompass the patient's total range of feelings for and against the analyst, countertransference connotes a broad spectrum of reactions in the analyst. These reactions may be regarded as analogues of the patient's transferences.

For whatever reasons, there are some patients or groups of patients with whom a particular analyst does not work very well, and the analyst should either remove the impediment to his work by further analysis or self-analysis, or else decline to treat these patients. But this is not necessarily the analyst's neurotic problem. For example, the objectivity and detachment required for research—a legitimate analytic pursuit—may make an analyst a mismatch for a patient who requires a fair amount of interaction in order to establish a working relationship.

### Interpretive Process

In the hypothetical classical analysis, the intervention of the analyst in the neurotic conflicts of his patient is virtually limited to the process of interpretation.

**Relation to Transference.** The analyst in psychoanalysis directs the patient's attention primarily to the events within the analysis itself and to intrapsychic events. In psychoanalytic psychotherapy, interpretations focus on the transference only in its general interpersonal sense; in psychoanalysis proper, the transference constitutes the principal frame of reference for interpretation and, according to some, should be interpreted, at least in its here-and-now aspects, from the beginning of the analysis.

**Dream Interpretation.** The paradigm of psychoanalytic interpretation is the interpretation of the dream. Freud demonstrated that, contrary to the prevailing scientific opinion before 1900, dreams are meaningful and can be set into a context of happenings in which their nonsensical elements become sensible ones. A full exploration of the meaning of a dream requires the investigation of both current and past trends, which are combined into a unity in the dream's manifest content.

**Timing.** It is difficult to formulate clearly what constitutes proper timing; often it boils down to the analyst's tact and his empathic understanding of his patient. One danger is the too-deep interpretation. Another is an interpretation that is made prematurely, or that simply misses the point because the patient is not concerned with the subject matter at the time.

### Indications

The primary indication for psychoanalysis is the finding that in all probability the patient has had long-standing conflicts that continue into the present in an active but unconscious form, and that produce signs or symptoms or character problems sufficient to justify extensive treatment. The analytic patient has a conflict not with his environment, although it may manifest itself as such, but within the structure of his own personality. This conflict is inaccessible to consciousness, and the frustrated drives that are part of the conflict repetitively press for discharge or expression, giving rise to a variety of transference phenomena.

### Contraindications

The various contraindications to the use of psychoanalysis, which have been described at length in the literature, seem generally valid: (1) There may be an apparent absence of a moderately reasonable and cooperative ego. Adults over 40, for example, are often believed to lack sufficient flexibility for major personality changes. However, if there are good opportunities for libidinal and narcissistic satisfactions, analysis of patients over 40 or 50 may have a favorable outcome. (2) The neurosis may be so minor that the expenditure of time, effort, and money in a full-scale analysis cannot be justified. (3) A neurosis may have elements of such pressing urgency that there is not enough time to wait for the establishment of a transference neurosis. (4) A patient's life situation may be unmodifiable, on realistic grounds, so that a successful analysis only results in greater difficulties for him.

### Psychoanalytic Psychotherapy

Psychoanalysis is not the treatment of choice for all types of psychiatric illness; nor are other forms of treatment merely second best substitutes. There are situations in which analysis is contraindicated, others in which it is unnecessary, and still others in which some other form of psychiatric therapy is the treatment of choice. For some of these situations, psychoanalytic psychotherapy—that is, therapy that is not classical psychoanalysis but is based on analytic concepts—is a highly respectable set of procedures. This type of therapy is sometimes called insight therapy or in-depth therapy. Psychoanalytic psychotherapy may also be chosen when, for various practical reasons, psychoanalysis cannot be arranged. In any event, psychoanalytic psychotherapy is the treatment of choice in a great number of situations, certainly more frequently than is analysis.

### Basis for Therapeutic Intervention

The effectiveness of psychoanalytic psychotherapy depends in large measure on the validity and depth of the clinical diagnosis. It should consist of a general statement of the dynamics and genetics of the individual patient, based on adequate study of the somatic, intrapsychic, interpersonal, and cultural aspects of his life.

Human behavior may be said to arise from conflict or to be conflict free. Usually, it is the behavior, symptoms, or discomfort arising from intense conflict that brings the patient to a psychiatrist for treatment. Notable exceptions do occur, however. Some patients, for example, do not seem to have enough conflict about carrying their impulses into action. The psychiatrist must be on the alert to distinguish this group from those patients whose seemingly impulsive behavior represents not an absence of conflict, but serious attempts to provoke punishment at the behest of an excessively strict superego.

The basic conflicts of a persistent neurosis are, in general, primarily intrapsychic, an opposition between segments or functions of the personality. The conflict usually rages over some force or drive, biological or psychological, that is occasionally and probably erroneously called an instinctual striving. This drive is unacceptable to other segments of the personality—that is, to other intrapsychic forces. Or, in another type of conflict, two unconscious strivings of a mutually contradictory nature may be seeking simultaneous expression.

### Definition

Psychoanalytic psychotherapy is psychotherapy based on valid psychiatric diagnosis and on psychoanalytic formulations. The diagnostic work-up should give the therapist an understanding of the patient's major conflicts, and permit an evaluation of his areas of ego strength and weakness. Psychoanalytic psychotherapy also takes into consideration, insofar as it is possible to do so, the available information about the patient's historical development, especially his relationship with the crucial figures of his childhood. The frame of reference developed by psychoanalytic theory provides the coordinates by which the patient's behavior may be evaluated.

Unlike analysis, which has as its ultimate concern the uncovering and subsequent working through of infantile conflicts as they arise in the transference neurosis, psychoanalytic psychotherapy generally takes as its focus current conflicts and current dynamic patterns. Unlike psychoanalysis, which has as its technique the use of free association and the analysis of transference neurosis, psychoanalytic psychotherapy uses interviewing and discussion techniques that use free association much less frequently. And, unlike analysis, the work on transference in psychoanalytic psychotherapy is usually limited to a discussion of the patient's relatively superficial transference reactions toward the psychiatrist and others.

Psychoanalytic psychotherapy does not exclude such measures as the use of psychotropic drugs. In fact, the use of such medication is indicated for specific kinds of patients. Nor does it exclude the use of electroshock therapy or other legitimate somatic methods. In fact, psychoanalytic understanding, interdigitated with psychopharmacological and neurophysiological understanding, provides a set of coordinates by which somatotherapeutic methods, as well as psychotherapeutic methods, can be considered in the management of a particular patient. This is in accordance with general trends. As biological and psychobiological understandings are being coordinated with the understanding derived from cultural anthropology and other social sciences, an increasingly reliable basis for theory and for practice is evolving.

Flexibility of technique and adaptability to the patient's needs can be emphasized in psychoanalytic psychotherapy, whereas the analysis of genetic sources is emphasized in psychoanalysis. In this conception, psychoanalytic psychotherapy can range from a single supportive interview centering on a current but pressing problem, to many years of treatment with one or two interviews a week. In contrast to psychoanalysis, psychoanalytic psychotherapy can be used to treat a major portion of the disorders listed in the field of psychopathology.

### Treatment Techniques

Though a requisite in classical analysis, the use of a couch may also be part of psychoanalytic psychotherapy. The stimulation of temporary regressive patterns of feeling and thinking, a necessary development in psychoanalysis, is much less appropriate in psychoanalytic psychotherapy, with its greater focus on more current dynamic patterns.

The handling of regression is one important point of difference between psychoanalysis and its derivative psychotherapies. In analysis, everything possible is done to promote the controlled regression of the transference neurosis, in order to bring to the surface those specific dynamic patterns from the past that are producing the neurosis. The analyst is aided in his efforts by the analytic setting and by his focus on transference phenomena. In contrast, in most psychotherapy an effort is made to avoid inducing any more regression than the patient brings with him into the treatment. It is wise for the psychotherapist to keep in mind that the patient does not seek out the therapist because of his transferences to him; he comes to treatment because of his transferences to other persons or because of some other difficulty with his environment. As long as a patient is working productively on the problems he brings into treatment, and as long as there is some feeling of rapport or of a therapeutic alliance, the therapist generally should not attempt to promote a therapeutic regression by focusing on the transference in some ill-advised attempt to emulate the analytic model.

## Other Types of Psychotherapy

The psychotherapies can be viewed as a sort of continuum, overlapping and complementary. At one end of the continuum is the hypothetical pure, orthodox, classical psychoanalysis, with its emphasis on the undoing of repression and the recovering of past traumatic experiences and feelings. At the other end of the continuum are supportive therapy and perhaps suppressive therapy. The middle of the continuum consists of varying mixtures of insight therapy and ego-oriented exploration of present-day difficulties, of which good psychoanalytic psychotherapy and good psychiatric social case work may be considered paradigms.

See Table I for a comparison and description of various types of psychotherapy.

### Supportive Therapy

This phrase is often used as if it referred to a separate and distinct entity, but it means only that there is greater emphasis on support than on other processes. Probably all psychotherapies have elements of insight, support, and relationship, but they differ chiefly in the relative emphasis and priority that the therapist gives to each element. Supportive psychotherapy, like the other types of therapy, must be individualized and based on an understanding of the specific patient.

The goal of supportive therapy is limited. The therapy offers support by an authority figure during a period of illness, turmoil, or temporary decompensation. It has the goal of restoring or strengthening the defenses and integrative capacities that have been impaired. It provides a period of acceptance and dependence for a patient who is acutely in need of help in dealing with his guilt, his shame, or his anxiety, and in meeting the frustrations or the external pressures that have been too great for him to handle.

Supportive psychotherapy is of value in psychiatric conditions such as these: relatively mature persons with limited symptoms based largely on severe environmental pressures; persons who, in general, have made a rather good adjustment and are in what seems to be only a temporary period of pressure, turmoil, temptation, or indecision; persons who have been fairly responsible and supportive toward others in their life adjustment, but who are now required to give beyond their psychological means and need to be given to, so that they will have more to give in turn; persons who are extremely resistant to expressive or insight psychotherapy, and those who seem too sick to respond to expressive psychotherapy; and patients who have no drive toward a fundamental change in their adjustment, and are interested only in a restoration of a more comfortable previous adjustment.

**Techniques.** Supportive psychotherapy uses such techniques as a warm, friendly, strong leadership; a gratification of dependency needs, if this can be done without evoking undue shame; support in the development of legitimate independence; help in the development of hobbies and of pleasurable but nondestructive sublimations, adequate rest and diversion; the removal of excessive external strain, if this is a productive step; hospitalization when it is indicated; medication that may alleviate symptoms and often does more; and guidance and advice in current issues. It uses these techniques that may make the patient feel more secure, accepted, protected, encouraged, safe, or less anxious and less alone.

A danger in supportive psychotherapy is the possibility of fostering too great a regression and too strong a dependency. From the beginning, the psychiatrist must plan to work persistently and with good timing toward weaning the patient to a resumption of greater independence. But some patients require supportive measures indefinitely, often with the goal of maintaining a marginal adjustment outside a hospital.

In supportive psychotherapy, the verbalization of unexpressed strong emotions may bring considerable relief. The goal of such talking out is not necessarily or primarily that of gaining insight into the unconscious dynamic patterns that may be intensifying the patient's current responses. Rather, the reduction of inner tension and anxiety may result from the expression of emotion and its subsequent discussion, and may lead to greater insight and objectivity in evaluating a current problem.

**Value.** Supportive therapy is often regarded as less exciting, less dramatic, and less interesting to the therapist than therapy directed more toward insight. But support of the patient when it is appropriate is certainly consistent with some of the best traditions of medicine. And, supportive psychotherapy, correctly used, is a rewarding experience for the psychiatrist who uses it. A nonpsychiatrist physician or other mental health professional can often exercise this form of treatment with great effectiveness, even though he is limited in his ability to make an accurate and full diagnostic assessment of the patient's emotional needs.

### Relationship Therapy

This treatment method stands somewhere between supportive therapy and the expressive techniques that characterize psychoanalysis, and other types of insight psychotherapy. Relationship therapy not only aims at a restoration of the status quo ante, but to some extent also aims at a change in personality patterns and at a decrease in vulnerability to external pressures. Relationship therapy contains strong elements of support, and, in a way, it may be considered as a protracted form of supportive therapy, with deeper dimensions. But its methods and its goals are somewhat more complicated than those involved, for example, in supporting a fairly well-adjusted person through some crisis. Relationship therapy may grow out of the therapist's dissatisfaction with supportive therapy and a conviction that his patient may profit from a broader experience. He may want his patient to obtain more from the therapy than dependency gratification and the security and reassurance that come from feeling accepted, supported, and sustained. Consequently, he may choose relationship therapy, including in his psychotherapeutic approach more than support, more of the many attitudes that characterize the helpful, reliable parent or older sibling.

This therapy can be described as a fairly prolonged period of contact between a patient and a therapist, in which the therapist can maintain, without too much conscious effort, a productive psychotherapeutic approach. The patient responds in various ways, and there develops an interplay of feeling, of communication, and of new experience. Certain therapeutic experiences occur for the patient, such as feeling accepted as worthwhile or potentially so; absence of condemnation or rejection because of defensive distortions; identification with some of the more successful achievements and adjustments of the therapist as they may fit his own needs; and spontaneous corrective emotional experiences as a result of the therapist's not responding in the neurotic fashion expected by the patient.

The therapist is interested in the dynamics of a patient's problems, but he is more interested in fostering a good therapeutic relationship. The cornerstone of this relationship is that the therapist's fairly consistent attitudes toward the patient are like a composite of those attitudes of a good, deeply helpful father or mother, or of a good, deeply helpful older brother or sister.

**Advantages.** In this approach, the psychiatrist is not so much treating the patient as he is rearing him or providing a setting in which the patient can rear himself, can grow and develop. For this reason, relationship therapy is often recommended for patients who are in some sort of developmental turmoil, such as the transition from adolescence to adulthood, at whatever chronological age the change occurs.

Relationship therapy provides the therapist with frequent opportunities to behave in a fashion different from the destructive or unproductive portions of the behavior of the patient's parents. At times, such experiences seem to neutralize or to reverse some of the effects of the parents' mistakes. If the patient had overly authoritarian parents, the therapist's friendly, flexible, nonjudgmental, nonauthoritarian, but at times firm and limit-setting attitude provides the patient with opportunities to adjust to, be led by, and identify with a new type of parent figure. In a similar fashion, patients who had overly indulgent, overly seductive, overly passive, or overly inconsistent parents can begin anew, in a sense, brought up again by a parent figure who is not making the old mistakes and who is responding in a way palpably different from the patterns of the parents, or from the patient's fantasies of the patterns of the parents.

**Suitable Situations.** Relationship therapy is suitable for a variety of psychogenic illnesses. For example, it may be useful when a patient is very resistive to psychoanalytic psychotherapy,

TABLE I
PSYCHOANALYSIS AND PSYCHOANALYTIC PSYCHOTHERAPY

| | Psychoanalysis | Psychoanalytic Therapy | Relationship Therapy | Supportive Therapy |
|---|---|---|---|---|
| Basic theory | Psychoanalytic psychology. Reorganization of character structure, with diminution of pathological defenses, integration or ultimate rejection of warded-off strivings and ideation. Understanding rather than symptom relief the objective, but symptom relief usually results. Correction of developmental lags in otherwise relatively mature personalities | Psychoanalytic psychology Resolution of selected conflicts and limited removal of pathological defenses. Understanding the primary goal, usually with secondary relief of symptoms | Psychoanalytic psychology Growth of the relatively immature personality through catalytic relationship with therapist offsets the neurotogenic effects of prior significant relationships | Psychoanalytic psychology Restoration of prior equilibrium, reduction of anxiety and fear in new situations. Help in tolerating unalterable situations |
| Activity of patient and therapist | Freely hovering attention by the analyst, free association by the patient. Interpretation of transference and resistance. Suggestion ultimately interpreted | Freely hovering attention by the therapist but with more focusing than in analysis. Less emphasis on free association, more on discussion by the patient. Suggestion usually eventually interpreted. | Therapist participates as a real person around current issues, becomes a helpful parental figure | Expressive techniques generally avoided except for some cathartic effects. Therapist actively intervenes, advises, fosters discussion, selects focus |
| Interpretive emphasis | Focus on resistance and transference to the analyst | Greater emphasis on interpersonal events, less on transferences to the analyst than in analysis, but transference interpretation often effective. Transferences to persons other than the therapist often effectively interpreted | Discussion and clarification of interpersonal events. Transference may or may not be interpreted | Interpretations of transferences to therapist generally avoided unless significantly interfering with the therapeutic relationship. Strong focus on external events |
| Transference | Transference neurosis fostered on foundation of the therapeutic alliance and the real relationship | Transference neurosis discouraged; therapeutic alliance fostered | Transference neurosis discouraged. Real relationship and therapeutic alliance emphasized | Transference neurosis discouraged. Therapeutic alliance may be firm or weak |

or is considered too ill for such a procedure. It may be chosen when the diagnostic assessment indicates that a gradual maturing process based on the elaboration of new foci for identification is the most promising path toward modification.

Relationship therapy with the addition, when possible, of attempts at psychoanalytic therapy, can form the backbone of the work of many psychiatrists. It may constitute a significant portion of the work of many psychiatric social workers, psychologists, and others. Possibly it can provide the best line of approach for the growing group of internists and other physicians whose psychosomatic and other medical interests call for the development of delimited techniques of psychotherapy.

### Brief Psychotherapy

In recent years, there has evolved a distinct psychiatric treatment modality known as brief

TABLE I—*continued*

|  | *Psychoanalysis* | *Psychoanalytic Therapy* | *Relationship Therapy* | *Supportive Therapy* |
|---|---|---|---|---|
| Confiden- tiality | Absolute. May be compromised by third-party pay- ers | Absolute. May be compromised by third-party payers | Usually absolute but may be abrogated in some situations. May be compro- mised by third- party payers | Usually absolute but may be abrogated in some situations. May be compro- mised by third- party payers |
| Regression | Fostered in the form of the transference neurosis | Generally discour- aged except as necessary to gain access to fantasy material and other derivatives of the uncon- scious | Regression generally discouraged | Generally discouraged but may occasion- ally be fostered for its own sake |
| Adjuncts | Couch | Couch less used. Psychotropic drugs used occa- sionally | Couch contraindi- cated. Group methods, family therapy, or family contacts on a planned basis. Other therapists and agencies may be involved | Couch usually con- traindicated. Psy- chotropic drugs, oc- cupational therapy, hospitalization (in- cluding day hospi- talization). Family contact on planned basis. Other thera- pists and agencies may be involved |
| Frequency and dura- tion | 4 to 5 times weekly, 2 to 5+ years. Sessions usually about 50 min- utes. New modifi- cations, shorter sessions | 1 to 3 times weekly, few sessions to several years. Ses- sions usually from ½ to 1 hour | 1 to 2 times weekly, 1 month to several years. Sessions usually ½ to 1 hour | Daily sessions to once every few months, one session to a life-long process. Sessions may be brief, ranging from a few minutes to an hour |
| Prerequisites | Relatively mature personality, fa- vorable life situa- tion, motivation for long under- taking, capacity to tolerate frus- tration, capacity for stable thera- peutic alliance, psychological mindedness | Relatively mature personality, ca- pacity for thera- peutic alliance, some capacity to tolerate frustra- tion, adequate motivation, and some degree of psychological mindedness | Capacity for thera- peutic alliance, personality capa- ble of growth, real- ity situation not too unfavorable | Personality organiza- tion may range from psychotic to mature, at least some capacity to form a therapeutic alliance |

psychotherapy. Brief psychotherapy is characterized by a limited number of interviews, concentrates on current problems, only rarely touches on transference issues unless they are negative, and dependence and regression are discouraged. The therapist takes a more active role in determining the focus of the interviews than is the rule in open-ended therapies. Brief psychotherapy is discussed in further detail in Section 26.6.

### Miscellaneous Types

In addition to those forms of psychological treatment that use chiefly the techniques of the patient's talking and his nonverbal communications and cues, and the verbal and nonverbal responses, comments, clarifications, and interpretations by the therapist, certain other forms of treatment can be conceptualized according to

psychoanalytic principles, and should occasionally be included in the psychiatrist's prescription for his patient. These forms of treatment use dynamic understanding of the individual patient and his problems, but verbalization and discussion of conflict are not their primary techniques. Rather, they lie in the borderland between psychotherapy—the talking cure—on one side and nonspecific environmental and psychological treatment techniques on the other side. Often, the role of these psychiatric therapies is one of facilitating psychotherapy, but occasionally they may become central in the treatment plan.

**Environmental Manipulation.** At times, the removal of a patient from a stressful environment or the effecting of some change in the environment so that it is less stressful holds the greatest hope for successful treatment, particularly if the patient's condition may deteriorate unless the external stresses are removed or if, at best, the patient will continue in a fruitless stalemate with external forces. Common instances of this treatment adjunct range from direct contact with the patient's family, through the recommendation of a vacation for an overworked patient, to foster home placement for a child.

*Family Contact.* One form of environmental manipulation involves the therapist's contact with the patient's family or, occasionally, other persons associated with the patient, such as an employer. At times, this is a necessary measure, especially if the disturbance is so grave that the patient's relationship with the family and others is threatened. If the contact is limited to helping the family understand what the patient is going through, or to minor bits of advice about ways to help the patient, contact with the family may be useful. Contact should be made only with the patient's consent and participation, unless there is some dire emergency that warrants breaking confidentiality.

*Vacation.* The recommendation for individualization of the treatment cannot be made too strongly. In the case of a vacation, for example, a seemingly innocuous holiday can become a disaster. A patient may be maintaining his dynamic psychic equilibrium only through such mechanisms as overwork, perhaps out of a guilty need to suffer. To remove the external pressures through a vacation is to risk upsetting a precarious equilibrium; the consequence may be a serious and severe regression or depression, instead of the hoped-for restorative respite from the stresses of everyday life.

*Hospitalization.* Hospitalization is a major form of environmental manipulation that may be called for in the course of some psychotherapies. The psychiatrist considers hospitalization when his patient shows unmistakable evidence that his customary manner of dealing with his environment has become impaired to such an extent that he has become a danger to himself or to others around him.

*Foster Home Placement.* Foster home placement for children requires careful consideration of the complete picture. It is usually undertaken only when the child does not have an opportunity to form satisfactory healthy identifications in his own home environment, and when there is a high probability that the environment will not improve sufficiently in the future.

**Activity Therapies.** Various forms of psychotherapy attempt to work with pathogenic conflicts by facilitating their recognition and verbalization and subsequent integration by the patient. This process requires, most of all, the renunciation of immediate gratification of strong psychological strivings.

In all the activity therapies, especially in occupational therapy, there is an increasing awareness that the process, and not the product of the process, is of greatest importance. It is more important that a patient do leatherwork or make a finger painting than that the purse or the picture be of good quality, although that may also be important to the patient. It is possible to have a room full of hospitalized patients silently engaged in dull, repetitive tasks, without a flicker of human interchange among them; such a situation probably has a low therapeutic value. But there is a growing tendency to use occupational therapy for the fostering of better interpersonal relationships among the patients and with the therapists.

In some hospital settings, where the psychiatric staff is in short supply but long demand, the occupational therapist may be the only person who has some consistent interpersonal contact with a patient. The presence of a nondemanding occupational therapist in this setting may be sufficiently therapeutic to bring about a reversal of the regressive forces of a psychosis, serving as a preparation for other forms of psychological treatment, including psychotherapy.

Other forms of activity therapy may serve as expressions of conflict components. Here recreational therapy should be considered; competitive games, for instance, may give acceptable expression to hostile urges. And, dance therapy, in the form of expressive physical movement, may drain off intense drives. But of greater importance in these therapies is the almost inevitable psychological contact with other human beings that helps to reverse regression.

Even food can be conceptualized as therapy. Almost everyone treats himself to some favorite food—usually fattening and forbidden—at times of frustration and stress. An analytic patient may have a rich malted milk before or after an anxiety-laden analytic hour. But the systematic giving of warm drinks and simple foods to a newly hospitalized patient at some time during the admission procedure may be therapeutic in the sense that it helps to establish an interpersonal bridge between the patient and the hospital. It repeats symbolically the earliest mother-child linkage.

**REFERENCES**

Bibring E: Psychoanalysis and the dynamic psychotherapies. J Am Psychoanal Assoc 2: 745, 1954.
Blum H P, editor: *Psychoanalytic Explorations of Technique: Discourse on the Theory of Therapy.* International Universities Press, New York, 1980.
Brenner C: *Psychoanalytic Technique and Psychic*

*Conflict.* International Universities Press, New York, 1976.

Ellenberger H F: *The Discovery of the Unconscious: The History and Evolution of Dynamic Psychiatry.* Basic Books, New York, 1970.

Freud S: *The Standard Edition of the Complete Psychological Works of Sigmund Freud,* 24 vols. The Hogarth Press, London, 1953–1974.

Friedman L: Trends in the psychoanalytic theory of treatment. Psychoanal Q *47:* 524, 1978.

Gray S H: Brief psychotherapy: A developmental approach. J Philadelphia Assoc Psychoanal *5:* 29, 1978.

Greene M A: The self psychology of Heinz Kohut: A synopsis and critique. Bull Menninger Clin *48:* 37, 1984.

Jones E. *The Life and Work of Sigmund Freud,* 3 vols. Basic Books, New York, 1953–1957.

MacLeod J A, Tinnin L W: Special service project. Arch Gen Psychiatry *15:* 190, 1966.

Stewart R L: Psychoanalysis and psychoanalytic psychotherapy. In *Comprehensive Textbook of Psychiatry,* ed 4, H I Kaplan, B J Sadock, editors, p 1331. Williams & Wilkins, Co., Baltimore, 1985.

Weinshel E M: Some observations on the psychoanalytic process. *Psychoanal Q 53:* 63, 1984.

# 26.2 BEHAVIOR THERAPY

## Introduction

In the behavioral approach to clinical problems, emphasis is placed on observable, confrontable events, especially the behavior of the patient, rather than inferred mental states and constructs. The clinician seeks to relate various behaviors, especially those behaviors called symptoms, to other observable events of a physiological or environmental nature.

Behavior therapy derives from learning theory and from classical and operant conditioning techniques. The goal of therapy is to use those techniques to change maladaptive behavior. Behavior modification is sometimes used interchangeably with behavior therapy; but the former term has a pejorative connotation and is falling out of use.

## Indications

Generally, systematic desensitization is applicable when one can identify the stimulus antecedents that elicit anxiety, which, in turn, mediates maladaptive or disruptive behavior. Often, obsessive-compulsive behavior is mediated by the anxiety elicited by specific objects or situations.

Desensitization has been used effectively with some stutterers by deconditioning the anxiety associated with a range of speaking situations. Certain sexual problems are amenable to desensitization therapy. A number of psychophysiological disorders have been treated by desensitization, using a hierarchy of stimuli that elicit anxiety-related physiological reactions. The reactions include such diverse disorders as bronchial asthma and dysmenorrhea.

The techniques have also been used with autistic children to improve social behavior, and for cardiovascular disorders, insomnia, and pain.

## Techniques

### Systematic Desensitization

This is a core procedure in behavior therapy. It is based on a general behavioral principle that may be stated as follows: A person can overcome maladaptive anxiety that is elicited by a class of situations or objects by approaching the feared situations gradually and in a psychophysiological state that inhibits anxiety. Joseph Wolpe originated systematic desensitization.

In treating patients with maladaptive anxiety by systematic desensitization, the therapist uses deep muscular relaxation to induce a psychophysiological state that counterconditions anxiety responses. Rather than use actual situations or objects that elicit fear, the patient and the therapist prepare a graded list or hierarchy of anxiety-provoking scenes associated with the patient's fears. Finally, the learned relaxation state and the anxiety-provoking scenes are systematically paired in the treatment. Thus, systematic desensitization consists of three steps: relaxation training, hierarchy construction, and the pairing of these two steps.

**Relaxation Training.** Most procedures are based on a method called progressive relaxation. It consists of having the patient tense and then relax major muscle groups of the body in a fixed and systematic order, usually beginning at the top of the body and working down. Some clinicians use hypnosis to facilitate relaxation. Tape-recorded procedures offer the advantage of allowing the patient to practice relaxation on his own.

**Hierarchy Construction.** In this step, the clinician determines all the antecedent (stimulus) conditions that elicit inappropriate anxiety in the patient. For example, a polysymptomatic phobic patient may report maladaptive anxiety to heights, to being in closed places, and to being subject to social criticism. For each theme, a list or hierarchy of 10 to 12 scenes is developed and arranged in order of increasing anxiety. For example, the acrophobia hierarchy may begin with "You are on the second floor near a window" if this scene provokes minimal anxiety, and the hierarchy may end with "You are on a roof of a 20-story building, leaning on the guard rail and looking straight down."

**Desensitization Proper.** The deconditioning of the anxiety attached to each class of situation (theme) is accomplished by having the patient vividly imagine each hierarchy scene while in a deeply relaxed state. The deconditioning is done systematically, beginning with the least anxiety-provoking scene and proceeding through the list at a rate determined by the patient's responses. In general, the patient should experience only minimal anxiety with a given scene before proceeding to the next scene. Several repetitions of each scene may be required before the anxiety reaches the minimal level. The expectation is that, when the patient can vividly imagine the highest or most anxiety-provoking scene of the hierarchy with equanimity, he will experience little anxiety in the corresponding real-life situation. The process of carry-over is facilitated by having the patient enter, between treatment sessions, actual anxiety-provoking situations that he has overcome in therapy.

The therapist should respond to the patient's reports of entering situations on his fear hierarchy with enthusiastic approval. Such approval usually constitutes a powerful reinforcer for the patient to continue to confront his fears and, thus, facilitates progress. However, the patient should not be urged to enter high-anxiety situations prematurely. A heroic effort by the patient to do so may result in his fleeing the situation in an intensely fearful state, thereby reinforcing his phobic-avoidance behavior and losing some of the progress he has made.

### Flooding

Flooding is based on a model of the extinction of conditioned avoidance behavior by response prevention. In clinical situations, it consists in having the patient confront the anxiety-inducing object or situation at full intensity for prolonged periods of time, resulting in his being flooded with anxiety. The confrontation may be done in imagination, as in systematic desensitization, but results are better if real-life situations are used.

If, for example, the patient has a fear of heights, he may be brought to the top of a tall building and required to remain there as long as is necessary for the anxiety to dissipate. The groundless anxiety of the phobic tends to diminish to low levels after 5 to 25 minutes, depending on the patient's characteristics and the history of the disorder. In the next treatment session, preferably within a day or two, the initial anxiety is less, and less time is required to reach a state of calm. The process is repeated until there is little or no initial anxiety. Additional sessions are carried out at increasing intervals of time, to avoid the spontaneous recovery of the conditioned anxiety, until the frequency with which the patient encounters heights in his natural environment is sufficient to prevent relapse. The success of the procedure depends on the patient's remaining in the fear-generating situation on each trial until he is calm and feels a sense of mastery. Premature withdrawal from the situation or prematurely terminating the fantasized scene is tantamount to an escape, and both fear conditioning and avoidance (phobic) behavior are reinforced. Depending on some details of the particular case, as few as 5 and seldom more than 20 sessions are required.

### Implosion

Implosion therapy is a variant of flooding. Rather than simply imagine feared objects or situations, the patient is asked to imagine a bizarre image associated with the object—for example, finding a snake in one's bed in the treatment of a snake phobia.

### Graded Exposure

Despite the efficiency and efficacy of flooding, many patients reject it as a treatment because of the psychological discomfort it entails. In addition, flooding is contraindicated in the patient in whom the induction of intense anxiety would be hazardous. Examples are a person who had a coronary thrombosis recently, a patient who is subject to cardiac arrhythmias in high-anxiety situations, and a patient who is judged to be so fragile psychologically that the induction of intense anxiety may precipitate a psychosis.

Graded exposure is a highly effective alternative in which intense anxiety is avoided. The procedure is identical to flooding, except that the phobic object or situation is approached through a series of small steps. Unlike systematic desensitization, however, specific training in relaxation is not involved, and the treatment is usually carried out in a real-life context.

**Graded Participant Modeling.** Much learning occurs by imitation—that is, by observing the behavior of others and its consequences. Irrational fears may be acquired in the same manner. Imitation is seen clearly in the child who learns to fear and, therefore, avoids small animals or heights by observing the fearful appearance and avoidance behavior of a parent, sibling, or other model in those situations.

In modeling, the same principle is used to help the patient overcome phobias. Originally, the procedure was developed to help children overcome maladaptive fears. If the child was afraid of dogs, even small and harmless canines, he would observe a fearless model, perhaps a child his own age and sex who would approach the dog, touch it, and play with it. The phobic child would then be encouraged to do the same through a series of small steps.

Modeling has been elaborated to maximize its efficacy and extend its use to adults, as well as children. The elaborated procedure, called graded participant modeling, consists first of devising a hierarchy of increasingly aversive behavioral performances involving the feared situation or object. For example, with a phobia for dogs, the hierarchy may begin with entering a room in which a small dog is leashed to a chair some distance away. The gradient of approach may then include walking closer to the leashed dog and touching the dog. The final performance may be petting a much larger and livelier dog that is not on a leash.

First, the fearless model, usually the therapist, goes through the entire hierarchy of activities while remaining calm and describing what he is doing and his state of ease. Then the therapist repeats the first or least anxiety-provoking activity, and the patient is encouraged to do the same immediately afterward. If necessary, the therapist and the patient repeat the first activity until the patient reports no uneasiness and appears completely calm. Then the therapist executes the second activity on the hierarchy, and the patient does the same. The process is continued until the patient has completed all the steps on the behavioral hierarchy with equanimity. It can sometimes be accomplished in a single lengthy session, or it may require several sessions. To prevent relapse, the last items on the hierarchy are repeated in several sessions spaced at increasing intervals.

## Positive Reinforcement and Extinction

The procedures described above are best conceptualized as applications of Pavlovian or classical conditioning; unadaptive anxiety is conditioned to certain environmental cues. The next two procedures—(1) positive reinforcement and extinction and (2) contingency contracting—are applications of operant or instrumental conditioning.

The core notion in positive reinforcement and extinction is that behavior is determined in part by its consequences. If a behavioral response is followed by a generally rewarding event—for example, food, avoidance of pain, or praise—it tends to be strengthened and occur more frequently under the same environmental circumstances. If a response is followed by an aversive stimulus (punishment) or by no stimulus at all

(extinction), it tends to be weakened and occur less frequently under the same environmental circumstances.

Aversion therapy with electric shock or nausea being the aversive stimulus has been used in the treatment of paraphilias such as exhibitionism and in substance abuse and alcoholism.

### Applications to Neurotic Behaviors

Principles of operant conditioning have wide application in the treatment of specific neurotic and habit disturbances. The treatment entails five steps with the ultimate goal of increasing the patient's control of his own behavior—that is, self-management.

The general principles and procedures are outlined below.

**Selecting and Specifying the Target Behavior.** The choice of behavior to be modified must follow from a complete behavioral analysis of the clinical problem. It is not always appropriate to focus on the presenting symptom. For example, there may be secondary gain in pain behavior, such as medication as needed, that should be the focus of treatment.

**Measuring the Target Behavior.** This step is crucial, because evidence that the intervention is effective comes from measurable changes in this dependent variable. The college student with a studying problem may be instructed to record in a notebook the minutes he spends studying on every occasion every day.

**Choosing an Adequate Reinforcer.** The therapist and the patient search the environment for an available reinforcer that is sufficiently powerful to shape and maintain new behavior. One general procedure for doing so is to determine what the patient does frequently. Such high-frequency behavior tends to be reinforcing. A college student may report, for example, that he wastes a lot of his time drinking coffee, watching television, talking with classmates, or playing chess.

**Setting up a Contingency.** The patient, with the aid of the therapist, sets up an arrangement in which access to the reinforcer (working on a crossword puzzle) is contingent on first emitting the weak target behavior (studying). Several principles are important in designing the contingency. In general, a reinforcer is maximally effective if it immediately follows the behavior to be strengthened.

### Adjunctive Use of Drugs

Various drugs have been used in an effort to hasten desensitization. The widest experience is with the ultrarapid-acting barbiturate sodium methohexital (Brevital), which is given intravenously in subanesthetic doses. Usually, up to 60 mg of the drug are given in divided doses in a session. Intravenous diazepam (Valium) is also of use in place of Brevital. If certain procedural details are carefully followed, almost all patients find the procedure pleasant, with few detracting side effects. The advantages of pharmacological desensitization are that preliminary training in relaxation can be shortened, almost all patients are able to become adequately relaxed, and treatment itself seems to proceed more rapidly.

## REFERENCES

Ayllon T, Azrin N H: *The Token Economy: A Motivational System for Therapy and Rehabilitation.* Appleton-Century-Crofts, New York, 1968.
Brady J P: Psychiatry as the behaviorist views it. In *Psychiatry: Areas of Promise and Advancement,* J P Brady, J Mendels, M T Orne, W Rieger, editors. Spectrum Publications, New York, 1977.
Brady J P: Social skills training for psychiatric patients: Concepts, methods, and clinical results. Am J Psychiatry *141:* 333, 1984.
Brady J P: Behavior therapy. In *Comprehensive Textbook of Psychiatry,* ed 4, H I Kaplan, B J Sadock, editors, p 1365. Williams & Wilkins, Baltimore, 1985.
Liberman R P: Behavioral modification of schizophrenia: A review. Schizophr Bull No. 6, p. 37, 1972.
Paul G L, Lentz R J: *Psychosocial Treatment of Chronic Mental Patients.* Harvard University Press, Cambridge, MA, 1977.
Pomerleau O F, Brady J P, editors: *Behavioral Medicine: Theory and Practice.* Williams & Wilkins, Baltimore, 1979.
Stuart R B, editor: *Behavioral Self-Management: Strategies, Techniques and Outcomes.* Brunner/Mazel, New York, 1977.
Wolpe J: *The Practice of Behavior Therapy,* ed 2. Pergamon Press, New York, 1973.

# 26.3 HYPNOSIS

## Introduction

The word "hypnosis" (from the Greek root *hypnos,* meaning sleep) is misleading because the phenomenon to which it refers is not a form of sleep; rather, it is a complex process of attentive receptive concentration. Although peripheral awareness is reduced in both sleep and hypnosis, focal awareness, which is diffuse in sleep, is at optimal capacity during the hypnotic trance.

## Definition

Hypnosis can be understood as a form of concentration characterized by attentive, receptive focal concentration with diminished peripheral awareness. All hypnosis is, in essence, self-

hypnosis, but when a person allows this form of concentration to be structured by another, the hypnotic experience is also characterized by an intense and sensitive interpersonal relatedness between the two, with a relative suspension of critical judgment. This intense concentration can be actively initiated and structured for the achievement of agreed-on goals.

## Assessment of Hypnotic Capacity

### Hypnotic Induction Profile

Administration of the hypnotic induction profile can be a routine part of the initial visit and evaluation. The test begins with the eye-roll sign (see Fig. 1), a presumptive measure of biological ability to experience hypnosis. This sign was developed from informal clinical observation, which indicated that persons who turn out to be highly hypnotizable seem to have an impressive capacity to roll their eyes upward while closing them. In contrast, nonhypnotizable persons do not, in general, seem to show this ability.

### Induction Technique

The induction technique is almost inconsequential in the production of the trance. Creating an atmosphere of appropriate security and relaxation is important. But these elements are secondary compared to the expectation of both the patient and the doctor and the relationship between them. The patient is encouraged to make himself comfortable and to concentrate. The therapist may then ask him to gaze at a dot on a card, a spot on the ceiling, or a pencil point; to roll his eyes up, as if he were trying to look at his eyebrows; to concentrate on holding one hand in a raised position; to sway back and forth from a standing position until he falls back into a chair placed behind him, or to perform any one of an almost limitless number of procedures that involve concentration. The hypnotist chooses a technique with which he feels comfortable and confident and that the patient finds acceptable and sometimes expects.

### The Three Phases of Trance Induction

**Patient's Perception of the Aura.** If the pretrance reputation of the hypnotist, his appearance, or his presentation is such that it coincides with the patient's transference predisposition or expectancy, the necessary rapport is comparatively easy to establish. The patient becomes receptive to the physician's signals to enter the trance.

**Psychophysiological Enhancement.** The hypnotist indicates in advance the probable and therefore the predictable psychophysiological

UP-GAZE                          ROLL

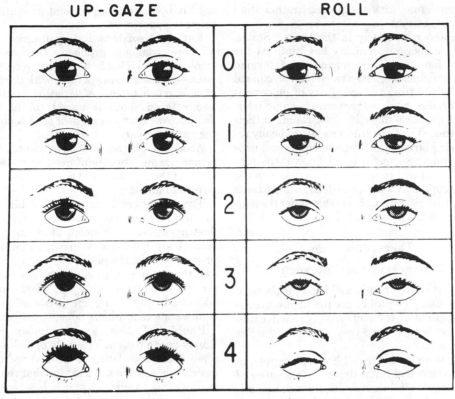

FIGURE 1.    Eye-roll sign for hypnotizability according to H. Spiegel, M.D.

phenomena that will occur. The hypnotist also implies that these phenomena are due to his signals. The patient's suspense accentuates the psychophysiological effect.

**The Plunge.** The patient more or less abandons his executive controls and shows nonrational submission to a dissociated state. The hypnotist has the broad power to structure the nature of the patient's plunge into submission, but he cannot determine either the moment or the manner of the patient's submission.

**Phenomenology.** The specific objective and subjective phenomena that occur can vary widely, depending on the expectations of the subject and the hypnotist. In Western culture the trance state generally exists at one of three levels. The light trance is most readily identified by motor alterations such as hyperkinesis or retardation. The middle range is usually distinguished by these changes plus sensory alterations such as parathesia, analgesia, anesthesia, partial amnesia, and posthypnotic compliance to simple signals. The deep somnambulistic level is characterized by the additional features of posthypnotic compliance, even to bizarre signals; visual, auditory, and tactile hallucinations; time distortion; age regression; hyperamnesia or selective amnesia; profound anesthesia; and the ability to maintain the trance state with the eyes open.

**Compulsive Triad.** While hypnotized, a patient may be told that, when the hypnotist lights a cigarette after the trance, the patient will ask for one, puff at it once or twice, and then put it out. It can be predicted with confidence that after the trance the patient will (1) have an amnesia, more or less, for the instruction, technically called the signal, (2) comply with the instruction compulsively, and (3) rationalize his act of snuffing out the cigarette by saying, "This cigarette is stale" or something along those lines. This triad is most clearly seen when the signal has been planted during a deep trance, but it can also be observed in an attenuated form when the signal has been implanted during a light trance.

### Choice of Psychotherapy

Highly hypnotizable persons are particularly vulnerable to inappropriate therapy, especially because of their proneness to affiliate with new premises while suspending critical judgment. The introspective, analytic approach can lead to confusion for such patients because they emphasize compliance with the process, rather than developing insight.

Recently, particularly in the United States, another induction ceremony has captured the imagination of many clinicians and laymen called acupuncture. Despite claims of clinical relief derived from the specificity of placement of the needles, to date there have been no reliable data available to justify these claims or their implication that Westerners should radically revise their knowledge of neuroanatomy and neurophysiology. So far as is yet known, the patterns of symptom control or dissolution with the use of acupuncture are consistent with patterns of symptom alteration observable under the simpler techniques of hypnotic induction.

### Therapeutic Uses

#### Hypnotic Regression and Abreaction

For psychotherapeutic and legal purposes, it is occasionally helpful to use the highly hypnotizable patient's profound capacity to relive previous events as though they were occurring at the moment.

There is a growing use of hypnotic regression for the purpose of intensifying the memories of witnesses and victims of crime. Information uncovered during hypnotic regression is not necessarily more accurate than any other beliefs and perceptions, but it may be.

#### Symptom-oriented Treatment

The most complex and difficult task for the therapist is developing appropriate treatment strategies for use with hypnosis, because hypnosis is not in itself a treatment but is, rather, a style of concentration. Once the therapist has defined the nature of the problem and has arrived at a working diagnosis, he must turn his attention to the means of treatment.

Restructuring by using self-hypnosis is a collaborative model, in which the therapist is to some extent in the role of a teacher, providing an opportunity to the patient that he can accept or reject.

**Smoking Habit.** The patient who wants to break the smoking habit is told to put himself into the trance state. When he has done this on his own, the therapist presents these three points: (1) For my body smoking is a poison; (2) I need my body to live; and (3) I owe my body this respect and protection. While the patient is still in the trance, the therapist goes through these three points in greater detail, emphasizing the patient's learning to distinguish his desire for a cigarette, from the need to act on the desire as long as he maintains the position that treat-

ing his body with respect and protection is of primary importance.

**Eating Disorders.** Eating disorders provide a more complex problem, because—unlike smoking, in which a habit change recedes as an issue—people are always faced with the problem of how much to eat. A variation of the three points listed above is taught to the patient, emphasizing that an excess of food is poison for the patient's body.

**Anxiety.** The sense of helplessness that accompanies anxiety is reinforced by the snowball effect of the psychological and somatic manifestations of anxiety.

The patient can be taught to put himself into the trance state and allow his body to float; floating, unlike the concept of relaxing, is in a sense body language. While maintaining this physical repose, the patient is taught to picture and think through problems on an imaginary screen. Anxiety-provoking problems are thus addressed while using the dissociation of the trance state to minimize somatic distress.

**Phobias.** Phobias are a complex problem. Rarely does a patient have only one phobia, and often some translating is needed to help the patient understand the message that the phobia is conveying to him. Hypnosis has been useful in reducing the anxiety associated with phobias.

**Pain.** Highly hypnotizable persons are capable of producing complete anesthesia, and major surgery has been performed in this country with hypnosis as the sole anesthetic. For most kinds of acute and chronic pain, however, hypnotic intervention is less dramatic, but can be quite effective.

### Contraindications

In general, hypnosis is remarkably safe when used with sound clinical judgment in a goal-directed setting. Its use entails far fewer side effects than even the most benign psychotropic medications. There are, nonetheless, some precautions to be observed.

The primary precaution is that hypnosis should never be attempted in a threatening or coercive atmosphere. The clinician should explain briefly and directly the nature of hypnosis, emphasize the importance of assessing hypnotizability, state that the patient may discontinue the trance experience at any time, and clarify the goals of the hypnotic intervention.

Certain types of patients should be approached with some caution. Suspicious or paranoid patients usually avoid or resist efforts at hypnosis. An occasional patient may have the trance-induction experience evoke unconscious fears and suspicions. Generally, such patients alleviate the problem by refusing hypnotic induction. Certain fragile, depressed patients who have already suffered many painful failures may be vulnerable if their expectations regarding the rewards to be derived from the hypnotic experience are unrealistic. A discovery that they are not hypnotizable or that they do not achieve symptomatic relief by using hypnosis may constitute an additional failure.

## REFERENCES

Barber T X: Hypnosuggestive procedures in the treatment of clinical pain: Implications for theories of hypnosis and suggestive therapy. In *Handbook of Clinical Health Psychology*, T Millon, editor, p 521. Plenum Press, New York, 1982.
Erickson M H: *Advanced Techniques of Hypnosis and Therapy: Selected Papers of Milton H. Erickson, M.D.*, J Haley, editor. Grune & Stratton, New York, 1976.
Gardner G G, Olness D: *Hypnosis and Hypnotherapy with Children.* Grune & Stratton, New York, 1981.
Spiegel D, Bloom J R: Group therapy and hypnosis reduce metastatic breast carcinoma pain. Psychosom Med *45:* 333, 1983.
Spiegel D, Spiegel H: Hypnosis. In *Comprehensive Textbook of Psychiatry*, ed 4, H I Kaplan, B J Sadock, editors, p 1389. Williams & Wilkins, Baltimore, 1985.
Spiegel H, Spiegel D: *Trance and Treatment: Clinical Uses of Hypnosis.* Basic Books, New York, 1978.
Wain H J: *Clinical Hypnosis in Medicine.* Symposia Specialists, Chicago, 1980.
Wester W C II, Smith A H, editors: *Clinical Hypnosis: A Multidisciplinary Approach.* Lippincott, Philadelphia, 1984.
Williams D T, Spiegel H, Mostofsky D I: Neurogenic and hysterical seizures in children and adolescents: Differential diagnostic and therapeutic considerations. Am J Psychiatry *135:* 82, 1978.

---

# 26.4 GROUP PSYCHOTHERAPY, COMBINED INDIVIDUAL AND GROUP PSYCHOTHERAPY, AND PSYCHODRAMA

## Group Psychotherapy

### Definition

Group psychotherapy is a form of treatment in which carefully selected emotionally ill persons are placed into a group, guided by a trained therapist, for the purpose of helping one another effect personality change. By means of a variety of technical maneuvers and theoretical constructs, the leader uses the group members' interactions to bring about that change.

### Classification

At the present time, there are many approaches to the group method of treatment, and none can be considered superior to the others. Most clinicians work within a psychoanalytically oriented frame of reference. In Table I, the major group therapy approaches are outlined.

### Role of the Therapist

Although opinions differ regarding how active or passive a role the therapist should play, it is generally agreed that his role is primarily a facilitative one. Ideally, group members themselves are the primary source of cure and change.

The climate produced by the therapist's personality is a potent agent of change. He is more than an expert applying techniques; he exerts a personal influence that taps variables such as empathy, warmth, and respect.

### Selection of Patients

To determine a patient's suitability for group psychotherapy, the therapist needs a great deal of information that can be gathered only in individual sessions. In the screening interview, the psychiatrist should take a careful psychiatric history and perform a mental status examination, so that he has certain dynamic, behavioral, and diagnostic factors in hand.

**Dynamic Factors.** The dynamics of the patient, including commonly used defense mechanisms, are important to determine proper selection. Relationship to peers and to authority figures, current and past, should be assessed.

*Authority Anxiety.* Those patients whose primary problem centers on their relationship to authority, and who are extremely anxious in the presence of authority figures, often do better in the group setting than in the dyadic or one-to-one setting. Patients with a great deal of authority anxiety may be blocked, anxious, resistant, and unwilling to verbalize thoughts and feelings in the individual setting, generally for fear of censure or disapproval from the therapist. They may welcome the suggestion of group psychotherapy so as to avoid the scrutiny of the dyadic situation. Conversely, if the patient reacts negatively to the suggestion of group psychotherapy or is openly resistant to the idea, the therapist should consider the possibility of a high degree of peer anxiety.

*Peer Anxiety.* The patient who has destructive relationships with his peer group, or who has been extremely isolated from peer group contact, such as a schizoid personality, generally reacts negatively or with increased anxiety when placed in a group setting.

**Diagnostic Factors.** The diagnosis of the patient's disorder is important in determining the best therapeutic approach and in evaluating his motivation for treatment, his capacity for

TABLE I
COMPARISON OF DIFFERENT TYPES OF GROUP PSYCHOTHERAPY

| Parameters | Supportive Group Therapy | Analytically Oriented Group Therapy | Psychoanalysis of Groups | Transactional Group Therapy | Behavioral Group Therapy |
|---|---|---|---|---|---|
| Frequency | Once a week | 1 to 3 times a week | 1 to 5 times a week | 1 to 3 times a week | 1 to 3 times a week |
| Duration | Up to 6 months | 1 to 3+ years | 1 to 3+ years | 1 to 3 years | Up to 6 months |
| Primary indications | Psychotic and neurotic disorders | Neurotic disorders, borderline states | Neurotic disorders | Neurotic and psychotic disorders | Phobias, passivity, sexual problems |
| Individual screening interview | Usually | Always | Always | Usually | Usually |
| Communication content | Primarily environmental factors | Present and past life situations, intragroup and extragroup relationships | Primarily past life experiences, intragroup relationships | Primarily intragroup relationships; rarely, past history, here and now stressed | Specific symptoms without focus on causality |
| Transference | Positive transference encouraged to promote improved functioning | Positive and negative transference evoked and analyzed | Transference neurosis evoked and analyzed | Positive relationships fostered, negative feelings analyzed | Positive relationships fostered, no examination of transference |
| Dreams | Not analyzed | Analyzed frequently | Always analyzed and encouraged | Analyzed rarely | Not used |
| Dependency | Intragroup dependency encouraged; members rely on leader to great extent | Intragroup dependency encouraged, dependency on leader variable | Intragroup dependency not encouraged, dependency on leader variable | Intragroup dependency encouraged, dependency on leader not encouraged | Intragroup dependency not encouraged; reliance on leader is high |
| Therapist activity | Strengthen existing defenses, active, give advice | Challenge defenses, active, give advice or personal response | Challenge defenses, passive, give no advice or personal response | Challenge defenses, active, give personal response, rather than advice | Create new defenses, active and directive |
| Interpretation | No interpretation of unconscious conflict | Interpretation of unconscious conflict | Interpretation of unconscious conflict extensive | Interpretation of current behavioral patterns in the here and now | Not used |
| Major group processes | Universalization, reality testing | Cohesion; transference, reality testing | Transference, ventilation, catharsis, reality testing | Abreaction, reality testing | Cohesion, reinforcement, conditioning |
| Socialization outside of group | Encouraged | Generally discouraged | Discouraged | Variable | Discouraged |
| Goals | Better adaptation to environment | Moderate reconstruction of personality dynamics | Extensive reconstruction of personality dynamics | Alteration of behavior through mechanism of conscious control | Relief of specific psychiatric symptoms |

change, and the strengths and weaknesses of his personality structure.

Group psychotherapy has been conducted with patients in practically every diagnostic category.

These are no absolute contraindications to group therapy. Antisocial patients generally do poorly because they cannot adhere to group standards. Depressed patients do better after they have established a trusting relationship with the therapist. Manic patients are obviously disruptive; but once under pharmacologic control, they do well in the group setting. Patients who are delusional and who may incorporate the group into their delusional system are best excluded.

## Preparation

Patients who are prepared for the group experience by the therapist tend to continue in treatment longer than those not so prepared. This preparation consists of the therapist explaining the procedure in as much detail as possible and answering any questions the patient may have before the first session attended.

## Structural Organization

The proper organization of the group is crucial if a therapeutic atmosphere conducive to personality change is to occur for all the participants. Therefore, a number of parameters must be considered, which are discussed below.

**Size.** Group therapy has been successful with as few as three members and as many as 15, but most therapists consider 8 to 10 members optimal. With fewer members there may be too little interaction, unless they are especially verbal. With a larger group, the interaction may be too great for the members or the therapist to follow.

**Frequency of Sessions.** Most group psychotherapists conduct group sessions once weekly. It is important to maintain continuity in sessions. When alternate sessions are used, the group meets twice a week, once with the therapist and once without him.

**Length of Sessions.** In general, group sessions last anywhere from 1 to 2 hours, with the average length being 1½ hours. However, the time limit set should be constant.

The fixed time limit to the session has the practical advantage of allowing both the patients and the leaders to adhere to the commitments of their everyday lives. It places an optimum value on the necessity to use the time available for group work as effectively as possible.

Time-extended therapy (marathon group therapy) is a method in which the group meets continuously for 12 to 72 hours. Enforced interactional proximity and, during the longer time-extended sessions, sleep deprivation, produce a breakdown in certain ego defenses, release affective processes, and promote a less-guarded type of communication. However, time-extended groups are not without their dangers in patients with weak ego structures such as schizophrenic or borderline patients. Marathon groups were most popular in the 1970s but are much less used today.

**Homogeneous versus Heterogeneous Groups.** In general, most therapists support the view that the group should be as heterogeneous as possible to ensure maximum interaction. Thus, the group should be composed of members from different diagnostic categories and with varied behavioral patterns; from all races, social levels, and educational backgrounds; and of varying ages and both sexes.

*Diagnostic Factors.* Some schizophrenic patients can be placed in groups with nonschizophrenic patients. The schizophrenic, who is highly vulnerable to the evocation of unconscious processes, can provide the neurotic patient with the necessary stimulation to break through repressive barriers, which are more intact in neurotics than in schizophrenics. Conversely, the neurotic can provide a high degree of reality testing and support for those ego defenses that have become weakened in the schizophrenic.

*Dynamic Factors.* When the therapist has a sound understanding of the psychodynamics of a variety of patients, he can organize a group most efficaciously.

*Behavioral Factors.* An examination of the patients' life styles and behavioral patterns can also help the therapist organize a group effectively. In so doing, the therapist should choose members with a variety of patterns. The patient whose life style is marked by isolation, withdrawal, and a fear of close relationships is ideally suited for group therapy.

*Sexual Factors.* Most patients who present themselves for psychotherapy suffer from some kind of sexual disorder as part of their psychopathology, regardless of diagnosis and regardless of whether the sexual disorder is the primary complaint. Many sexual conflicts stem not only from psychological conflict, but also from educational deficiencies. The interrelationship between the two is exceedingly complex, and the group setting provides a unique opportunity for the patients and the therapist to learn whether a problem is the result of faulty education or psychological problems or a combination of both.

Men and women should be placed in the same group so that attitudes toward sex can be examined more effectively. Even though there may be initial inhibitions to a frank and open discussion of sexual matters in the mixed group, such an exchange does eventually take place, and the anxieties attached to the interchange are fruitfully examined.

*Socioeconomic Factors.* Patients from different socioeconomic levels can be integrated into the same group with salutary effects. Juxtapositions of different social and economic factors can heighten the psychological awareness of the members involved.

Racial, religious, and ethnic variations in

group composition can also be used effectively. When this is done, it is desirable to include more than one member from any given background; two members with similar backgrounds provide mutual support and identification, and so enable each to tolerate the minority position.

*Age.* Adults can be treated in groups with an extremely broad age range. Patients between 20 and 65, in general, can be effectively integrated into the same group. Age differences aid in the development of parent-child and brother-sister models. Patients have the opportunity to relive and rectify interpersonal difficulties that may have appeared insurmountable.

In organizing the adult group, the therapist should be careful not to have only one member representative of the extreme age group.

Both the child and the adolescent are best treated in groups composed of patients in their own age group. Some adolescent patients are quite capable of assimilating the material of the adult group, regardless of content, but they should not be deprived of a constructive peer experience that they might otherwise not have.

### Mechanisms of Group Psychotherapy

**Group Formation.** Each patient approaches the group initially in a way unique to him. In this sense, the group is a microcosm. The patient uses his typical adaptive abilities, defense mechanisms, and ways of relating, which are ultimately reflected back to him by the group, allowing him to become introspective about his personality functioning. But a process inherent in group formation requires that the patient suspend his previous ways of coping. In entering the group, he allows his executive ego functions—reality testing, adaptation to and mastery of the environment, perception—to be taken over to some degree by the collective assessment provided by the total membership, including the leader.

To do this at all, the patient must have developed a sense of basic trust, and must feel that he is able to rely on the outer providers represented by the group as a whole. The patient who has not developed a sense of basic trust, who fears the environment and sees it as hostile, is less willing to suspend his judgments and, accordingly, is less able to allow the group to provide him with new reality-testing devices. With proper group organization, the consensual validation provided by a group can be trustworthy and remarkably objective, even though individually the members may have difficulties in related areas.

**Group Processes.** The commonly agreed on group processes which account for therapeutic change are listed and discussed now.

REALITY TESTING. The group setting serves as a reality-testing forum as each member verbalizes his thoughts and feelings toward the others, and as these verbalizations are examined by the leader and the membership.

TRANSFERENCE. The feelings evoked between members of the group and between members and the therapist are transferential when they are irrational and not consonant with reality.

*Stimulation of Transference.* As patients observe one another's interactions, feelings that may have been repressed or suppressed can emerge. In general, negative feelings are expressed sooner in the group setting than in the one-to-one situation. A group patient may be reassured as he observes the therapist's nonpunitive reaction to another patient's anger, and so be willing to express similar feelings of which he may not have been aware.

*Multiple Transferences.* A variety of group members—each with his own genetic, dynamic, and behavioral patterns—may stand for the people significant in a particular patient's past or current life situation. He may see one co-patient as wife, another as mother, others as father, sibling, employer. The patient can then work through actual or fantasized conflicts with the surrogate figures to a successful resolution. Role-playing techniques make use of this concept extensively.

*Collective Transference.* A member's pathologically personifying the group into a single transferential figure, generally his mother or father, is a phenomenon unique to group therapy. Or, he may see the therapist as one figure and the group as a whole as another. The collective transference may be either positive or negative in feeling tone. The therapist should encourage the patient to respond to members as individuals and to differentiate them, one from the other, in order to work through this particular distortion.

*Transference Neurosis.* When a patient's transferential attachment to the therapist or, in group therapy, to another patient becomes excessively strong, a transference neurosis is said to exist. A strong negative transference by a patient toward the therapist may require an individual psychotherapy session to resolve the distortion. The therapist should not allow one or several patients to attack him in a group but should insist that negative transference be discussed in individual sessions.

IDENTIFICATION. In individual therapy, many patients attempt to learn new modes of adaptation by taking on qualities of the therapist. In the group setting, a variety of other models are available, and patients identify with certain qualities of these other members, a process that may occur consciously by simple imitation or unconsciously, outside of awareness.

Obviously, whether or not identification influences personality growth constructively depends on whom the patient chooses for his model. Most important, the leader must be a suitable model.

UNIVERSALIZATION. In the group, the patient recognizes that he is not alone in having an emotional problem, and that others may be struggling with the same or similar problems. It is generally agreed that the process of universalization is one of the most important in group psychotherapy. The simple sharing of experiences regardless of whether or not they are labeled pathological, is an important human need.

COHESION. All groups, not only psychotherapy groups, are marked by some amount of cohesion. Members feel a "we-ness," a sense of belonging. They value the group, which engenders loyalty and friendliness among them. They are willing to work together and to take responsibility for one another in achieving their common goals. They are also willing to endure a certain degree of frustration to maintain the group's integrity. A cohesive psychotherapy group is one in which members are accepting and supportive, and have meaningful relationships with one another. Cohesion is the single most important factor in group therapy.

The more effectively the therapist can increase a member's cohesion in the group, the more probable is a successful outcome, for the patient will then be more receptive to the mechanisms that group therapy has to offer.

GROUP PRESSURE. Every group member is susceptible to group pressures to alter his behavior, thinking, or feeling; how susceptible he is depends on how attracted he is to the other members of the group and how much he values his group membership.

Much of the effectiveness of the behavioral approach to group psychotherapy rests on the observation that a patient is motivated by the reinforcement of member and therapist approval to embark on a new behavioral pattern.

INTELLECTUALIZATION. This process implies a cognitive awareness of oneself, others, and the various life experiences—both good and bad— that account for current functioning. Feedback, in which each member confronts the others with his immediate responses to events as they occur, serves as a learning device. Each member is helped thereby to evaluate his own defense mechanisms and ways of coping, and those of

his co-patients. Confrontation groups rely on the feedback mechanism extensively.

Interpretation, a derivative of intellectualization, also provides the patient with a cognitive framework within which he can understand himself better, whether this interpretation comes from the therapist or from other group members.

Intellectualization does not necessarily lead to change; experiential factors must be added if effective learning is to take place. The concept of the corrective emotional experience, first formulated by Franz Alexander, combines both these factors, the intellectual and the experiential, into a functional theoretical framework.

VENTILATION AND CATHARSIS. Each group develops its own mix of ventilatory and cathartic processes, the mix depending on the composition of the group, the style of leadership, and the theoretical framework. Some group therapists adhere to a style of leadership that is fixed at the extreme of encouraging emotional release almost exclusively; others, equally rigid in their position, actively suppress the expression of strong affect. It is important that the leader be flexible so as to meet the needs of a particular group, and so that he be able to determine which member will benefit from a greater emphasis on one of these processes. However, both processes should operate within any group.

ABREACTION. Abreaction brings about an awareness, often for the first time, of degrees of emotion previously blocked from consciousness. It is often a highly therapeutic experience, even though it may produce an unavoidable sense of distress in all concerned as the process unfolds.

Techniques geared to release strong emotion must be well timed, and used only when the patient is well integrated into a group capable of providing as much support as is necessary to allow the patient to pass through the abreacted experience. When the experience is not well timed, a serious risk is involved, one that may result in psychological decompensation.

### Therapeutic Considerations

It is necessary to have a clear understanding of the mechanisms capable of effecting therapeutic change, and of the mechanisms beneficial to the particular patient or to the group at a certain point in time. If this conceptual framework is lacking, all techniques, regardless of their seeming appeal or ease of application, are, at best, gimmicks that ultimately have little or no therapeutic effect; at worst, these techniques court disaster.

**Dream Analysis.** The techniques of dream interpretation can be applied to the group setting with only minor changes. Freud outlined several technical procedures: (1) Have the patient associate to elements of his dream in the order in which they occurred; (2) have the patient associate to a particular dream element that he or the therapist chooses; (3) disregard the content of the dream entirely and ask the patient what events of the previous day are associated with his dream; and (4) avoid giving any instructions, and leave it to the dreamer to begin.

In the group setting, all these techniques can be used, but the associations come not only from the dreamer but from the other members as well. In addition, the other members can also give directions. The therapist can use the reverberation of associations produced in the group to provide insight into the psychological processes of the dreamer and his co-patients. For example, if each member is asked to give his interpretation of the dream presented, the various interpretations can be examined collectively.

**Free Association.** The process of free association occurs within the group as one member's thought or feeling is followed by another member's thought or feeling, which may or may not be logically related. The therapist does not direct the group, but encourages spontaneity and a free-floating discussion. His task is to find a common theme in the various productions elicited, and to reflect this theme back to the group. Having done this, he must examine the way the theme applies to each member by eliciting further associations.

**Go-round.** In this technique, the therapist asks each member of the group to respond in turn to a specific thought, feeling, behavioral pattern, topic, or theme introduced by a patient or by the therapist himself. The go-round serves various purposes and can evoke a number of group processes. Since each member must participate and no one is allowed to withdraw, the technique can be especially valuable for the schizoid member, who might not otherwise contribute, and for the passive member, who might be too intimidated to do so. It also helps control the monopolist, who might otherwise dominate a session. When the subject of the go-round is the members' feelings toward a particular member, it provides concentrated feedback and information about transferences. The use of the go-round is especially effective in including a withdrawn member.

**Co-therapy.** Ideally, in co-therapy each therapist becomes actively involved, so that neither is in a position of greater authority or dominance. Co-therapists of different sexes can stimulate the replication of parental surrogates in the group; if the two interact harmoniously, they can serve as a corrective emotional experience for the members. Even if the co-therapists are of the same sex, one often tends to be confrontative and interpretative and is seen as masculine, and the other tends to be evocative of feelings and is seen as feminine. Styles of leadership and the personality characteristics of the co-therapists, regardless of their genders, also elicit transferential reactions.

**New Member.** A new group member, upon being added into a group, may be welcomed and quickly integrated, or he may be the object of overt or covert hostility, irrespective of his personality pattern. It is essential that the group leader discuss the introduction of a new member prior to his arrival and that the therapist help the group resolve any conflicts about the addition of a new member. A new member who is subject to an attack by the group, and who is unprotected by the therapist, rarely returns to the group.

**Acting Out.** A patient may attempt to avoid tension through activity, usually sexual or aggressive. The action gratifies an impulse, and the patient feels relief. But the relief is temporary, providing no lasting solution to the conflicts that contribute to the patient's inability to delay gratification and tolerate frustration. Two people in a group may be sexually attracted to each other and may gratify the impulse by having extragroup activity, which may include sexual intercourse. But if this happens, motivating factors behind their attraction may be inaccessible for examination. For example, the sexual activity may have resulted from a wish by one member to gain an ally and so be protected from real or fantasied hostility from others in the group. Or, one member may attempt to demonstrate sexual prowess to deny feelings of inadequacy, sexual or otherwise, or to achieve a sense of intimacy.

Most group therapists prohibit sexual contact between patients in any situation. When such contact does occur, the therapist attempts to analyze its significance retrospectively and must reconsider whether such patients should remain in the same group. Sexual acting out between group members is divisive to a group.

**Alternate Sessions and Aftersessions.** Alternate sessions are held without the therapist but are specifically organized by him, and all members are expected to attend. The time and the place for the alternate sessions may be left up to the group. A variation of the alternate session is the aftersession, which differs in that it takes place immediately after the session at which the therapist is present. The alternate session is generally held a few days after the regular session. The advantages of aftersessions are that they are better attended than are alternate sessions, and that the themes of the session are still fresh in the minds of the members.

These procedures give the patients more time to get to know one another and to clarify and stimulate their interaction. The members become aware of variations in their behavior related to the presence or the absence of the therapist.

**Electronic Recordings.** Both audiotape and videotape have been used extensively in group psychotherapy. Tapes can be stored and played back at a later date, allowing group members to observe changes over a period of time. Patients may see themselves firsthand on a television monitor while they interact, with dramatic effects on their insight into their own and one another's behavior.

**Movies and Photographs.** Home movies and photographs can be used in group therapy most effectively. A group member may bring in a series of home movies—either from his early childhood or from his current life—to show them to the group as a whole and receive impressions from the other members as to their content. The same can be done with still photographs. What is left out is as important as what is displayed.

**Termination.** The discharge of a patient from group therapy implies that goals have been achieved. Ideally, there should be consensual validation by the patient involved, the therapist, and the other members. The greater the divergence from such consensus, the greater is the likelihood that termination is premature. Usually, however, termination is accompanied by the mutual consent of all concerned.

Although discharge is the goal sought by all the members, it is an event that may cause turmoil and upheaval. Some members become competitive with the departing member. Others are not able to tolerate the loss involved and may feel rejected and abandoned. Some members experience grief. For some members leaving the group, there is also a sense of loss, and a complex array of emotions may be stimulated. The therapist should allow sufficient time prior to termination, generally 2 to 3 months (8 to 12 sessions), for various reactions to be explored, examined, and analyzed.

### Short-term Group Psychotherapy

Short-term group psychotherapy is characterized by a fixed number of sessions, which may vary from as few as 2 or 3 to as many as 50. When group therapy is carried out while the patient is in a hospital, the number of sessions is determined by the patient's length of stay; when the patient is an outpatient, the therapist has greater flexibility. Short-term group psychotherapy in a hospital is useful in increasing the patients' motivation to improve, reducing their dependency ties, and aiding in their adjustment to hospitalization generally.

Short-term groups are most effective when the composition of the group is stable. Effectiveness is also increased when the groups are homogeneous and members have similar disorders or comparable emotional problems. And, groups are most effective when goals are clearly defined for the members and the group as a whole.

The therapist doing short-term therapy in groups must attempt to develop as much cohesiveness as possible, for cohesiveness enables the members to derive the most from the experience. As in long-term groups, the greater the cohesiveness, the more the members benefit.

### Other Types of Groups

**Human Potential Movement.** The human potential movement is composed of growth centers—loosely organized associations of people who gather together in retreats or rural communities to examine behavior through a variety of group approaches. The growth center has a staff who may or may not reside there and whose task is to facilitate the process of personal psychological growth in the participants, who visit for different periods of time from a few days to several weeks.

**Encounter, Sensitivity, and Training Groups.** It is important to differentiate encounter groups, T-groups (the "T" stands for training), and sensitivity training groups from traditional group psychotherapy. The encounter group members seek heightened self-awareness and fulfillment of their human potential. Participants should be free from significant emotional disorders. The psychotherapy group is made up of patients seeking help for their individual problems through the mechanism of group interaction. The participants in an encounter group are learners in an unstructured situation. Most encounter groups use such approaches as physical contact, sensory awareness techniques, and role playing, and some of these practices have been successfully integrated into certain forms of traditional group psychotherapy.

**Self-help Groups.** Groups in this category are composed of persons who are concerned about coping with a specific problem or life crisis. Usually organized with a particular task in mind, the groups do not attempt to explore individual psychodynamics in greath depth, nor do they attempt to change personality functioning significantly. Self-help groups have had a major impact on the emotional health and well-being of a great many people.

A distinguishing characteristic of the self-help group is its homogeneity. Members suffer from the same disorder, and they share their experiences—good and bad, successful and unsuccessful—with one another. By so doing, they educate each other, provide mutual support, and alleviate the sense of alienation that is usually felt by the person drawn to this type of group.

The dynamics involved in self-help groups emphasize the important role that identification plays in facilitating cohesion, which is exceptionally strong in these groups. Because of the shared problems and similar symptoms, a strong emotional bond develops, and the group is seen as possessing characteristics of its own to which magical qualities of healing may be attributed. Examples of self-help groups are Alcoholics Anonymous (AA), Gamblers Anonymous (GA), and Overeaters Anonymous.

The self-help group movement is in its ascendency. The groups meet the needs of their members by providing acceptance, mutual support, and help in overcoming maladaptive patterns of behavior or states of feeling with which traditional mental health and medical professionals have not been generally successful. Increasingly, there is a convergence of the self-help and group therapy movements. The self-help groups have enabled their members to give up a pattern of unwanted behavior; the therapy groups have offered their members an in-depth understanding of why and how they got to be the way they were or are.

## Combined Individual and Group Psychotherapy

In combined individual and group psychotherapy, the patient is seen individually by the therapist, and also takes part in group sessions on a regular basis. The therapist for the group and individual sessions is usually the same.

Groups can vary in size, from 3 to 15 members, but the optimal is 8 to 10. It is extremely important that patients attend all group sessions. Attendance at individual sessions is also important, and failure to attend either group or individual sessions should be examined as part of the therapeutic process.

Combined therapy is a particular treatment modality. It is not a system by which individual therapy is augmented by an occasional group session, nor does it mean that a participant in group therapy meets alone with the therapist from time to time. Rather, it is an ongoing plan in which the group experience interacts meaningfully with the individual sessions, and in which there is reciprocal feedback that helps to form an integrated therapeutic experience. Although the one-to-one, doctor-patient relationship allows for a deep examination of the transference reaction for some patients, it may not provide the corrective emotional experiences necessary for therapeutic change for others. The addition of the group situation provides the patient with a variety of persons toward whom transferential reactions can develop. In the microcosm of the group, the patient can relive and work through the familial and other important influences in his life.

### Selection of Patients

Selecting patients for combined individual and group psychotherapy is much the same as choosing patients for group therapy.

### Dyadic Setting

Much of the work in the dyadic setting consists of examining, in greater depth than is possible in the group, the thoughts and the feelings the patient has toward his fellow group members. Most therapists hold these communications to be confidential, but they encourage the patient to be as open in the group as he is in the dyadic setting. In addition, individual sessions permit the emergence and examination of the transference neurosis, as in classical analysis. The one-to-one, doctor-patient relationship also allows for the easy introduction of a patient into a group for the first time. The presence of the known therapist is reassuring as the patient learns to deal with a group of strangers.

Those patients who experience excessive anxiety in the group are helped by individual therapy, as are extremely shy patients who have difficulty in communicating. The dyadic relationship also gives the therapist an in-depth understanding of the patient; the group experience may not allow the therapist to gather the genetic and dynamic data necessary for true understanding of human behavior. Whereas the group experience may tend to emphasize here-and-now responses, individual therapy is able to delve into the origins, meaning, and implications of these responses, and thus fulfill the requirements of psychoanalytic therapy.

### Group Setting

The group setting superimposes on the dyadic setting all the processes at work in therapy groups, such as support, imparting of information, ventilation, interaction, and reality testing.

The patients in combined therapy have the unique distinction of all sharing the same therapist for individual sessions. This sharing produces groups of high cohesiveness, because patients identify with one another through their common identification with the leader. It is often difficult to integrate someone into a group if he is the only patient with a different therapist for individual sessions. Such a patient may also be deprived of the advantages of having the group therapist know a great deal about him. For these reasons, most workers do not take the patients of other therapists into their own groups. When they do, it is desirable to have frequent communication with the other therapist so that distortions do not occur.

### Therapeutic Process

There is a constant interplay between the group setting and the dyadic setting. One cannot be separated from the other; the two must be viewed as a whole. In a general way, however, the group session focuses on the various defenses used by the patient, whereas the individual session examines the underlying psychic conflict against which the defense was erected in the first place. As the group processes erode a particular defense mechanism, the individual session may serve as a stabilizing force and prevent the patient's anxiety from reaching intolerable levels.

**Resistance.** It is striking at times to see different aspects of the same patient's personality as it appears in the individual setting and in the group setting. For example, a patient may seem withdrawn, timid and shy when alone with the psychiatrist, who may conclude that it is a fixed characterological pattern. When placed in a group, however, the same patient may seem outgoing, friendly, and involved in the problems of his co-patients. What accounts for the disparate behavioral patterns? It may be the high level of authority anxiety that becomes overt when the patient is alone with the therapist, and the low level of peer anxiety when he is with the group. The psychiatrist practicing combined therapy has a better vantage from which to view the full range of the patient's behavior, seeing his strengths in one setting and his weaknesses in another.

Among the advantages of the combined method is the ability of the group to help eliminate resistances. Patients see one another improve, they place pressure on one another to open themselves up for psychic exploration, and they confront each other with interpretations of resistant behavior, such as absences, lateness, withdrawal, and silences.

**Insight.** Just as resistance, which prevents insight, is lessened in combined psychotherapy, insight is frequently facilitated by the combined method. Some workers have felt that insight in the psychoanalytic sense is exclusively the function of individual psychotherapy and that group psychotherapy accomplishes its ends through interaction. In fact, these processes are subtly intertwined. Insight is attained as the patient undergoes changes in both conceptualization and behavior. Formulated concepts can be explored in individual therapy, and experience can be formalized into concepts through the vehicle of group therapy. The group gives the patient opportunities to test and reinforce insights gained in individual therapy.

### Techniques

Various techniques, based on different theoretical frameworks, have been used with the combined therapy format. In general, the same techniques used in combined therapy are used in group therapy.

A particular form of group psychotherapy developed by Harold Kaplan and Benjamin Sadock, structured interactional group therapy, makes good use of the combined method. This form of therapy is based on active leadership and a structured framework in which spontaneous interaction can take place. The combination of group and individual sessions is an integral part of structured interactional group therapy.

**Focal Group Member.** This is a specialized format used in structured interactional group psychotherapy, in which the group focuses on one member at each session. The purpose of the system is to ensure participation by all members, and it is up to the leader to determine who should be up at each session.

**The Go-round.** Psychological exploration and emotional involvement are facilitated by the go-round, also a basic technique of structured interactional group psychotherapy. In this technique, each group member speaks about his personal feelings toward the patient who is focused on or who is up for discussion.

Structured interactional group therapy is discussed more fully in the latest edition of *Comprehensive Group Psychotherapy*.

## Psychodrama

Psychodrama is a method of group psychotherapy originated by Jacob Moreno, M.D., in which personality make-up, interpersonal relationships, conflicts, and emotional problems are explored by means of special dramatic methods. The therapeutic dramatization of emotional problems includes (1) protagonist or patient, the person who acts out his problems with the help of (2) auxiliary egos, persons who enact different aspects of the patient, and (3) director, psychodramatist, or therapist, the person who guides those involved in the drama toward the acquisition of insight.

### Roles

**Director.** The director is the leader or therapist. He must be active and participating. He encourages the members of the group to be spontaneous, and his function is catalytic. The director must be available to meet the needs of the group and not superimpose his values on them. Of all the group psychotherapies, psychodrama requires the most participation and ability to lead from the therapist.

**Protagonist.** The protagonist is the patient in conflict. He chooses the situation to portray in the dramatic scene, or the therapist may choose it for him if the patient so desires.

**Auxiliary Ego.** The auxiliary ego is another group member who represents something or someone in the protagonist's experience. The use of the auxiliary ego helps account for the great range of therapeutic effects available in psychodrama.

**Group.** The members of the psychodrama scene and the audience make up the group. Some are participants, and others are observers, but all benefit from the experience to the extent that they can identify with the ongoing events. The concept of spontaneity in psychodrama refers to the ability of each member of the group, especially the protagonist, to experience the thoughts and feelings of the moment fully, and to communicate emotion in as authentic a manner as possible.

### REFERENCES

American Psychiatric Association: Task Force Report on Encounter Groups and Psychiatry. American Psychiatric Association, Washington, DC, 1970.
Cartright D, Zander A, editors: *Group Dynamics and Research Theory.* Harper & Row, New York, 1960.
Freud S: *Group Psychology and Analysis of the Ego.* Hogarth Press, London, 1962.
Grotjohn M, Freedman C T H, editors: *Handbook of Group Therapy.* Van Nostrand Reinhold, New York, 1983.
Kaplan H I, Sadock B J, editors: *Comprehensive Group Psychotherapy.* Williams & Wilkins, Baltimore, 1980.
Moreno J L: *Psychodrama.* Beacon House, Beacon, NY, 1947.
Olsen P A, Barth P A: New uses of psychodrama. J Operational Psychiatry *14:* 95, 1983.
Pilkonis P A: A comparative outcome study of individual, group, and conjoint psychotherapy. Arch Gen Psychiatry *41:* 431, 1984.
Sadock B J: Group psychotherapy. In *Comprehensive Textbook of Psychiatry,* ed 4, H I Kaplan, B J Sadock, editors, p 1403. Williams & Wilkins, Baltimore, 1985.
Stone W N, Rutan J S: Duration of treatment in group psychotherapy. Int J Group Psychother, 93, 1984.
Wolf A, Schwartz M: *Psychoanalysis in Groups.* Grune & Stratton, New York, 1962.
Yalom I: *The Theory and Practice of Group Psychotherapy,* ed 2. Basic Books, New York, 1975.

## 26.5   FAMILY THERAPY

### General Considerations

Despite differences in specific models, what is unique to family therapy is its family orientation. All the members of the family are interrelated and one part of the family cannot be isolated from the rest. A family's structure and organization must be viewed as a unit and are important factors determining the behavior of the individual family members. Modern day family therapy originated from the pioneering work of Nathan Ackerman, M.D.

### Beginning Treatment

**Initial Consultation.** Family therapy is well-enough known that families with a high level of conflict may request it specifically. When the initial complaint is about an individual, however, pretreatment work may be necessary. Typical fears underlying resistance to a family approach are fear (1) felt by parents that they will be blamed for their child's difficulties, (2) that the entire family will be pronounced "sick," (3) that a spouse will object, and (4) that open discussion of one child's misbehavior will have a negative influence on younger siblings. Refusal by an adolescent or young adult patient to participate in family therapy is frequently a disguised collusion with the fears of one or both parents. An additional complication arises if the referral itself was framed in terms of individual treatment. This situation is challenging for the therapist, demanding patience, flexibility, and a high degree of persuasiveness, even though face-to-face contact has not yet been made. It may be helpful to emphasize consultation, rather than treatment in that situation.

**The Family.** In general, all members of the nuclear household should be included in the initial evaluation unless pressing realities mandate otherwise. Even young children may provide important information through their reports or behavior, despite disclaimers that they are not involved. It may be found that members of the extended family are also relevant, or that certain community members (friends, physicians, ministers, and others) fulfill roles comparable to relatives. In single parent families or stepfamilies, the role of the noncustodial parent should be investigated for the same reason. Some or all of the treatment sessions may require the attendance of these outside figures if they play a significant part in the pattern of the symptoms.

**Interview Technique.** The special quality of the family interview proceeds from two important facts: (1) The family comes to treatment with its history and dynamics firmly in place. To the family therapist it is this established nature of the group, more than the symptoms, that constitute the clinical problem. (2) Family members usually live together and, at some level, depend on each other for physical and emotional well-being. Whatever transpires in the therapy session is known to all. Central principles of technique derive from these facts. For example, catharsis of anger by one family member toward another must be carefully channeled by the therapist. The person who is the object of the anger is present and will react to the attack, either in the interview or at home, running the danger of escalation toward violence, fractured relationships, or withdrawal from therapy. Free association is likewise not appropriate because it would encourage one person to dominate the session. In short, the family interview must always be controlled and directed by the therapist.

**Secrets.** Frequently, a family member who insists on an individual session wishes to impart a personal secret. This situation is delicate, and the therapist must meet it with tact and common sense. Secrets from the past—usually sexual—that are over and done with do not impede treatment and may be left in confidence. Presently active secrets, such as affairs or physical illnesses, pose a more serious problem when confided to the therapist unilaterally. They subtly align the therapist with the secretive family member and thereby weaken efforts at open communication in the treatment sessions. Family therapists should head off these situations before they occur, because they may end in the unpleasant dilemma of forcing a showdown or else terminating therapy. It is often effective to explain the problem in the abstract as soon as one senses the disclosure of a secret is in the offing.

**Transference.** Transference to the therapist is only rarely a tool of family treatment. Instead, therapists work with the actual parent-child relationship or with the transference feelings of family members toward each other. Therapists are therefore free to be their real selves to each family, and they also can make maximum use of direct recommendations.

**Frequency and Length of Treatment.** Unless an emergency arises, sessions are usually held no more than once a week. Each session, however, may require 1½ or 2 hours. Long sessions can include an intermission to give the therapist time to organize the material and plan a response. Flexibility of schedule is especially attractive when geography or personal circumstances make it physically difficult for the family to get together. Length of treatment depends not only on the nature of the problem but also on the therapeutic model. Therapists who use problem-solving models exclusively may accomplish their goals in a few sessions; therapists using growth-oriented models, however, may work with a family for years, with sessions at long intervals.

## Models of Intervention

Family therapy, still young, coalesces around the personal styles and theories of its leaders. Thus different models overlap, and such designations as systemic, strategic, and communications have been claimed by or applied to therapists whose approach varies considerably. The following description indicates the broad distinguishing features, but to some extent, the category titles are arbitrary.

### Psychodynamic/Experiential Models

These models emphasize individual maturation in the context of the family system, free from unconscious patterns of anxiety and projection rooted in the past. Therapists seek to establish an intimate bond with each family member, alternating between their exchanges with the members and the member's exchanges with each other. Clarity of communication and honestly admitted feelings are given high priority; toward this end, family members may be encouraged to change their seats, to touch each other, and to make direct eye contact. Their use of metaphor, body language, and paraphrases are additional data in discovering the unconscious pattern of family relationships. The therapist may also use family sculpting, in which family members arrange each other in tableaux suggesting their personal view of relationships, past or present. The therapist both interprets the sculpture and modifies it as a way of suggesting new forms the relationships might take. In addition, the therapist's subjective responses to the family are given great importance. At appropriate moments they are expressed to the family to form yet another feedback loop of self-observation and change.

**Structural Model.** The family is viewed as a single interrelated system assessed along the following lines: (1) significant alliances and splits between family members; (2) hierarchy of power, i.e. the parents' "in charge" position with regard to the children; (3) the clarity and firmness of boundaries between the generations; and (4) the family's tolerance for conflict without the necessity of either denying it or detouring it to scapegoated individuals. The structural therapist views the origin of symptoms as clustering around developmental transitions or other significant events in the life of the family. This therapy is concerned only with the here-and-now problem; it views excursions into the past or other issues as undesirable detours. The conduct of the session may involve changes of seating and dyadic confrontations, but their aim is to reestablish parental authority, strengthen normal boundaries, or rearrange alliances. Tasks are set to further these goals between the sessions, and the family's performance of them is carefully reviewed. When the initial problem ameliorates, the family is discharged.

**Strategic Models.** In this model, the purpose of the intervention is to propel the resistant family toward a structural shift. As in the structural model, only the present problem is considered, but the interventions are analogous, rather than direct, in order to minimize resistance. A classic intervention is the paradoxical one of prescribing the symptom, provided that it is not dangerous, or else advising that no change take place. This maneuver forces the resistant systems or individuals into one of two positions: (1) Either they must continue to resist the therapist, which would now require abandoning the symptomatic behavior, or (2) they must continue the symptomatic behavior, but now tacitly under the therapist's direction. Paradox differs from reverse psychology in that the choice and framing of the recommendation are only made when the repetitive dysfunctional patterns of the family are clearly understood. In order to be effective, the paradoxical prescription must match the existing paradox in the family's organization.

### Indications and Contraindications

Insofar as family therapy is not a technical maneuver but a way of thinking, it cannot strictly be said to be indicated or contraindicated. This decision will depend on the theoretical preferences and prior experience of the clinician. It has been used successfully—although not necessarily exclusively—in all types of psychiatric problems, including the psychoses, psychosomatic illness, and substance abuse. Certainly it is attractive when the presenting complaint is one of overt family conflict or when patients are mired in real misery within their homes. The practical problems of assembling the family group may place some limitation on the formal aspect of treatment, but even if one is limited to a single individual, it is still possible to think in family systems terms. Exceptional difficulties presented by families are the same as the ones that bedevil any attempt at psychotherapy, such as fixed character pathology, lying, physical violence, lack of motivation, and extreme secrecy. The only true contraindication, however, is lack of adequate training on the part of the therapist, especially when accompanied by the illusion that family therapy can be done by feel and good intentions alone.

### Complications

Every family is meshed with larger systems, including not only the extended family but also society as represented by such systems as schools, medical facilities, welfare departments, and other therapists. The influence of these other systems may be significant in the outcome of therapy. In general, it is easier to start with family therapy and move later to individual sessions than it is to move in the opposite direction.

### REFERENCES

Bloch D, Simon R, editors: *The Strength of Family Therapy: Selected Papers of Nathan W. Ackerman.* Brunner/Mazel, New York, 1982.
Hoffman L: *Foundations of Family Therapy: A Conceptual Framework for Systems Change.* Basic Books, New York, 1981.
Minuchin S: *Families and Family Therapy.* Harvard University Press, Cambridge, MA, 1974.
Morawetz A, Walker G: *Brief Therapy with Single-Parent Families.* Brunner/Mazel, New York, 1984.
Neill J, Kniskern D, editors: *From Psyche to System: The Evolving Therapy of Carl Whitaker.* Guilford Press, New York, 1982.
Selvini-Palazzoli M, Boscolo L, Cecchin G, Prata G: *Paradox and Counterparadox: A New Model in the Therapy of the Family in Schizophrenic Transaction.* Jason Aronson, New York, 1978.
Simon R: Family therapy. In *Comprehensive Textbook of Psychiatry*, ed 4, H I Kaplan, B J Sadock, editors, p 1427. Williams & Wilkins, Baltimore, 1985.
Skynner A C R: Group analysis and family therapy. Int J Group Psychother *34:* 215, 1984.
Walsh F, editor: *Normal Family Processes.* Guilford Press, New York, 1982.

## 26.6 BRIEF PSYCHOTHERAPY AND CRISIS INTERVENTION

### Introduction

During the past decade, brief psychotherapy and crisis intervention have become increasingly popular all over the world. These psychiatric treatment modalities are destined to become one of the most commonly used forms of psychiatric treatment in the near future.

### Crisis Theory

Two major theoretical concepts form the basis of brief psychotherapy: psychoanalytic theory and crisis theory. Most psychiatrists are familiar with psychodynamic assumptions, but unclear as to crisis theory. This theory is reviewed below.

A crisis is a response to hazardous events, and is experienced as a painful state. Because of this, it tends to mobilize powerful reactions to help the person alleviate the discomfort and return to the state of emotional equilibrium that existed before its onset. If this takes place, the crisis can be overcome, but, in addition, the person learns how to use adaptive reactions that can serve him well at a future time. Furthermore, it is possible that by resolving the crisis, he may find himself in a better state of mind, superior to the one that existed before the onset of the psychological difficulties. If, on the other hand, he uses maladaptive reactions, the painful state intensifies, the crisis deepens, and a regressive deterioration takes place, giving rise to psychiatric symptoms. These symptoms, in turn, may crystallize into a neurotic pattern of behavior that restricts his ability to function freely. At times, however, the situation cannot be stabilized, new maladaptive reactions are introduced, and the consequences can be of catastrophic proportions, leading at times to death by suicide.

It is in this sense that psychological crises are painful, and may be viewed as turning points for better or for worse.

A crisis is self-limited, and can last anywhere from a few hours to about 6 weeks. The crisis as such is characterized by an initial phase, in which anxiety and tension rise. This phase is followed by a phase in which problem-solving mechanisms are set in motion. These mechanisms may be successful or not, depending on whether they are adaptive or maladaptive. Conservation of energy is another feature of a person in a state of crisis. All the available resources at one's disposal are used for one and only one purpose—namely, the resolution of the crisis and the diminution of its pain. Such a successful resolution has important mental health implications. The person who has been able to use his resources efficiently, either alone or with the help of another person, not only has learned how to deal with the crisis by becoming acquainted with the ways in which he has gone about resolving it, but has also discovered ways to anticipate future trouble and to avoid its recurrence. In this way, the crisis resolution has also become a preventive intervention.

Patients during a period of turmoil are receptive to minimal help and may obtain meaningful results. All sorts of services, therefore, have been devised for such purposes. Some are open ended; others limit the time available or the number of sessions.

Crisis theory helps one to understand healthy normal people, as well as to develop therapeutic tools aimed at preventing future psychological difficulties. Furthermore, because people in crisis are in a state of flux, a dynamic approach is necessary to help them deal with it. The best such dynamic approach must be based on psychoanalytic principles. Thus, crisis intervention, and the development of brief psychotherapeutic techniques, must be primarily psychodynamic in nature. Despite these facts, however, various short-term therapeutic techniques that have nothing in common with one another except for the brief time interval have been treated as identical, giving rise to considerable confusion.

### Types of Brief Psychotherapies

Because they use entirely different techniques, because they are aimed at helping two entirely different groups of patients, and because they produce entirely different results, psychotherapies of brief duration can be divided into two major categories: anxiety-suppressive or supportive, and anxiety-provoking or dynamic.

### Anxiety-suppressive Techniques

This type of treatment can be subdivided into two varieties: crisis support and brief anxiety-suppressive psychotherapy. Since it is primarily aimed at helping persons in crisis, crisis support lasts whatever time is needed to overcome it—anywhere from a few days to several weeks, with the average being 1 to 1½ months. Brief anxiety-suppressive psychotherapy, on the other hand, may last anywhere up to a year. Obviously, these time elements are not rigid and are used as rough guidelines; anxiety-suppressive techniques can also be used over a long period of time.

**Crisis Support.** This type of intervention is aimed at helping severely disturbed patients in crisis.

*Criteria for Selection.* The patients selected face a hazardous environmental situation, have developed a crisis, are rapidly decompensating, and make a strong appeal for help.

*Requirements and Techniques.* In crisis support, rapidity is of the essence, the hazardous situation must be assessed as to its stressful impact and severity, the precipitating factors that led to the crisis must be identified, the types of maladaptive reactions used by the patient must be evaluated, the potential for rapid regression must be noted, and the focus of the therapy should be on the resolution of the crisis. As soon as this preliminary survey has been made, the therapist must quickly decide on the best therapeutic maneuvers to provide the maximal assistance to the suffering patient.

The supportive techniques are reassurance, suggestion, environmental manipulation, and psychotropic medications. These therapeutic tools may even be combined with brief hospitalization as part of crisis-supportive therapy. All these therapeutic maneuvers are aimed at decreasing the patient's anxiety.

The frequency and the length of the visits for crisis support vary according to the patient's needs and his response to these therapeutic interventions. The intervention may involve a few interviews interspersed over several weeks, or the patient may be seen more frequently—even two or three times a day. Flexibility is of the essence.

*Outcome.* The results that are usually obtained from successful crisis support involve resolution of the crisis, evidence of symptomatic relief, knowledge by the patient of where to turn for help at a time of further difficulties, and a return to the status quo ante.

**Brief Anxiety-suppressive Psychotherapy.** In this type of intervention, one may include a variety of short-term therapeutic techniques that are referred to in the psychiatric literature by a number of terms, such as reeducative or assertive therapies, which aim to overcome behavioral handicaps by the use of relearning or retraining techniques; short sessions in conjunction with medication; short group or family interventions; techniques using suggestion systematically; environmental manipulation; brief hospitalization; and classic brief anxiety-suppressive psychotherapy.

*Criteria for Selection.* Although the literature is not very specific about clear-cut selection criteria for these kinds of brief supportive therapies, there are certain guidelines one may follow to select appropriate patients from a population of severely disturbed persons with character defects who are functioning quite precariously. For brief anxiety-suppressive psychotherapy, these guidelines are: a strong appeal for help, the ability to recognize that their difficulties are psychological in origin, the ability to hold a job, and the willingness to cooperate with a therapeutic plan.

*Techniques.* The most important therapeutic task involves the rapid assessment of the patient's predicament and the evaluation of any existing strengths that can be mobilized and any supports that may be available. The techniques are similar to those used in crisis support and include reassurance, suggestion, environmental manipulation, psychotropic medication, and brief hospitalization.

In addition, an effort should be made to reeducate the patient by helping him to recognize his feelings, anticipate situations that are likely to give rise to similar problems in the future, and learn to avoid their recurrence. This is a modified insight approach.

Because one of the most common character defects of patients who are candidates for brief anxiety-suppressive psychotherapy is their inability to anticipate the situations likely to create difficulties for them, it is important that the therapist make a systematic effort to teach these patients techniques that will help them rehearse and avoid these problem-creating situations.

**Outcome.** The general consensus is that such techniques do not produce a psychodynamic change in the patient but, rather, that they may achieve marked symptomatic improvement; the ability to avoid situations that give rise to the patient's difficulties; a tendency to identify with the institution where the assistance was offered, rather than with the individual therapist; and a tendency to return to the same mental health facility at some future time for more help.

### Anxiety-provoking Techniques

Several terms have been used to describe anxiety-provoking techniques, which has tended to create confusion. These terms include intensive, deep, interpretative, broad focused, and psychoanalytically oriented. However, all these techniques have two basic features in common: (1) a psychodynamic orientation, which implies that the conflicts underlying the patient's difficulties are partially submerged as a result of defense mechanisms, and that anxiety will be aroused when the therapist attempts to deal with them, and (2) the possible occurrence of extensive and lasting psychodynamic change in the patient as a result of these therapies.

All patients who are considered good candidates for brief dynamic psychotherapy share one common feature—they are highly motivated to understand themselves and to change. The dynamic psychotherapies also share certain characteristics—the activity of the therapist in making interpretations, early use of transference clarifications, staying within a specified psychodynamic focus, the use of patient-transference links, problem solving, and early termination after evidence has been obtained that a psychodynamic change has taken place.

Anxiety-provoking psychotherapies of brief duration may be divided into two categories: crisis intervention and brief dynamic psychotherapy.

**Crisis Intervention.** In contrast to crisis support, crisis intervention is offered to persons who had been considered fairly healthy before developing the crisis that has temporarily incapacitated them.

*Criteria for Selection.* The criteria used to select patients are a history of a specific hazardous situation of recent origin that gave rise to anxiety, a precipitating event that intensified this anxiety, clear-cut evidence that the patient is in a state of psychological crisis as already defined, high motivation to overcome the crisis, a potential for making a psychological adjustment equal to or superior to the one that existed before the development of the crisis, and a certain degree of psychological sophistication—ability to recognize psychological reasons for the present predicament.

*Requirements and Techniques.* The length of crisis intervention varies from 1 or 2 sessions, to several interviews over a period of 1 or 2 months. The technical requirements for crisis intervention involve a rapid establishment of rapport with the patient, aimed at creating a therapeutic alliance; a review of the steps that have led to the development of the crisis; a thorough understanding of the maladaptive reactions that the patient uses to deal with the crisis; focusing only on the crisis; learning to use different and more adaptive ways to deal with crises; avoidance of the development of symptoms; use of the predominating positive transference feelings for the therapist so as to transform the work into a learning experience; teaching the patient how to avoid hazardous situations that are likely to give rise to future crises; and ending the intervention as soon as evidence is accumulated that the crisis has been resolved and that the patient has a clear understanding of all the steps that led to its development and its resolution.

**Outcome.** What results can one expect to obtain from crisis intervention that are different from those the patient has derived from receiving crisis support? The most striking aspect, in addition to the resolution of the crisis, has to do with the ability of the patient to become better equipped to avoid or, if necessary, to deal with future hazards as a result of this therapeutic experience. In addition, on the basis of objective observations of some patients, it appears that as a result of this therapeutic experience, they have attained a level of emotional functioning that, as far as they are concerned and in the eyes of their therapists and of society at large, is superior to the one that existed before the onset of the crisis.

**Brief Dynamic Psychotherapy.** This treatment modality has provided a useful model for the study of selection procedures, for the investigation of the process, and for research into outcome.

Within the field of brief dynamic psychotherapy are several types that differ from one another in technical details. Four kinds have been developed: brief psychotherapy at the Tavistock Clinic (Malan), time-limited psychotherapy at Boston University (Mann), broad-focused short-term dynamic psychotherapy at McGill University (Davanloo), and short-term anxiety-provoking psychotherapy at Harvard University (Sifneos).

Neither the chronicity of the illness nor the severity of the pathology has a bearing on the results that have been obtained, but motivation for insight, which is a selection criterion judged during the first few interviews, has proved to be a valuable predictor of successful outcome.

The patients in all these treatment programs need to be well motivated, psychologically sophisticated, capable of responding to interpretation, and able to concentrate on and resolve the conflict around the central issue or focus that underlies their basic problem.

*Sifneos.* The following criteria are used in selecting candidates: a circumscribed chief complaint (this implies an ability to select one of a variety of problems to which the patient assigns top priority and that he wishes to solve as a result of the treatment); one meaningful or give-and-take relationship during early childhood; the ability to interact flexibly with the evaluator and to express feelings appropriately; above-average psychological sophistication (this implies not only an above-average intelligence, but also an ability to respond to interpretations); a specific psychodynamic formulation; a contract between the therapist and the patient to work on the specified focus and formulation of minimal expectations of outcome; and good to excellent motivation for change and not for symptom relief.

*Patient-therapist Encounter.* The therapist establishes a working alliance by using the quick rapport that predominates, and the positive feelings for the therapist that appear, at this phase. Judicious use of open-ended and forced-choice questions enables the therapist to outline and concentrate on a therapeutic focus. The therapist specifies the minimum expectations of outcome to be achieved by the therapy.

*Early Therapy.* In transference, feelings for the therapist are clarified as soon as they appear. This clarification leads to the establishment of a true therapeutic alliance.

*Height of the Treatment.* This phase emphasizes active concentration on the conflicts that have been chosen as the therapeutic focus for this kind of therapy; repeated use of anxiety-provoking questions and confrontations; avoidance of characterological issues, which are used defensively by the patient to avoid dealing with the therapist's anxiety-provoking techniques; avoidance at all costs of the development of a transference neurosis; repetitive demonstration to the patient of his neurotic ways or maladaptive patterns of behavior; concentration on the anxiety-laden material, even before the defense mechanisms have been clarified; repeated demonstration of parent-transference links by the use of properly timed interpretations based on material given by the patient; establishment of a corrective emotional experience; encouragement and support of the patient, who experiences anxiety as he is struggling to understand his conflicts; new learning and problem-solving patterns; and repeated presentation and recapitulation of the patient's pschodynamics, until he clearly understands the nature of the defense mechanisms he uses in dealing with his conflicts.

*Evidence of Change and Termination of Psychotherapy.* This phase emphasizes tangible demonstration of change in the patient's behavior outside of therapy, evidence that more adaptive patterns of behavior are taking place, and initiation of talk about and eventual termination of the treatment.

## REFERENCES

Binder J, Strupp H, Schacht T: Countertransference in time-limited dynamic psychotherapy. Contemp Psychoanal *19:* 605, 1983.
Davenloo H: Short-term dynamic psychotherapy. In *Comprehensive Textbook of Psychiatry*, ed 4, H I Kaplan, B J Sadock, editors, p 1460. Williams & Wilkins, Baltimore, 1985.
Duggan H A: *Crisis Intervention: Helping Individuals at Risk.* Lexington Books, Lexington, MA, 1984.
Malan D H: *A Study of Brief Psychotherapy.* Plenum Publishing Corp., New York, 1976.
Malan D H: *The Frontier of Brief Psychotherapy.* Plenum Publishing Corp., New York, 1976.
Mann J: *Time-Limited Psychotherapy.* Harvard University Press, Cambridge, MA, 1973.
Rogawski, A S: Current status of brief psychotherapy. Bull Menninger Clin *46:* 331, 1982.
Sifneos P E: *Short-Term Psychotherapy and Emotional Crisis.* Harvard University Press, Cambridge, MA, 1972.
Sifneos P E: *Short-Term Dynamic Psychotherapy: Evaluation and Technique.* Plenum Publishing Corp., New York, 1979.

## 26.7    COGNITIVE THERAPY

### Introduction

Cognitive therapy stems from four major theories: psychoanalysis, phenomenological philosophy, cognitive psychology, and behavioral psychology. Several threads emerge from these theories. Perhaps most salient is the recognition of the importance of the subjectiveness of conscious experience, i.e. the experience of reality, rather than objective reality. Another thread is the recognition of the emotional consequences of irrational beliefs.

Aaron Beck, the originator of cognitive therapy, has developed a comprehensive and structured theory of depression. Depression consists of a cognitive triad, specific schemes, and cognitive errors, or faulty information processing.

### Theoretical Roots and Concept of Depression

The cognitive triad consists of negative cognitions regarding oneself, the world, and one's future. First is a negative self percept involving seeing oneself as defective, inadequate, deprived, worthless, and undesirable. Second is a tendency to experience the world as a negative, demanding, and defeating place and to expect failure and punishment. Third is an expectation of continued hardship, suffering, deprivation, and failure.

Schemas are stable cognitive patterns through which one interprets experience. Schemas of depression are analogous to viewing the world through dark glasses. Depressogenic schemas may involve viewing experience as black or white without shades of gray, as categorical imperatives that allow no options, or as expectations that people are either all good or all bad.

Cognitive errors are systematic errors in thinking that lead to persistence of negative schemas in spite of contradictory evidence.

The cognitive theory of depression posits that cognitive dysfunctions are the core of depression and that affective and physical changes, and other associated features of depression, are consequences of the cognitive dysfunctions. For example, apathy and low energy are results of the individual's expectation of failure in all areas. Similarly, paralysis of will stems from the individual's pessimism and feelings of hopelessness.

The goal of therapy is to alleviate depression and to prevent its recurrence by helping the patient (1) to identify and test negative cognitions; (2) to develop alternative, more flexible schemas; and (3) to rehearse both new cognitive and new behavioral responses. The goal is also to change the way an individual thinks and subsequently to alleviate the depressive syndrome.

## General Considerations

Cognitive therapy is a short-term, structured therapy that involves active collaboration between the patient and the therapist toward achieving the therapy goals. It is oriented toward current problems and their resolution. Therapy is usually conducted on an individual basis, although group techniques have been developed and tested. This therapy may be used in conjunction with drugs.

## Strategies and Techniques

As with other psychotherapies, therapist attributes are of fundamental importance to successful therapy. The therapists must be able to exude warmth, be able to understand the life experience of each patient, and be truly genuine and honest with themselves, as well as with the patients. Therapists must be able to relate skillfully to individual patients in their experiential world in a truly interactive way.

As a highly structured therapeutic approach, cognitive therapy involves setting the agenda at the beginning of each session, assigning homework to be performed between sessions, and learning specific new skills. The active collaboration between the therapist and the patient provides a genuine sense of teamwork.

There are three basic components to cognitive therapy: didactic aspects, cognitive techniques, and behavioral techniques.

### Didactic Aspects

Didactic aspects include an explanation to the patient about the nature of the cognitive triad, schemas, and faulty logic. The therapist must explain to the patient that they will formulate hypotheses together and will test them over the course of the treatment. Therapy involves a full explanation of the relationship between depression and thinking, affect, and behavior, as well

as the rationale for all aspects of the treatment. This explanation is in contrast to more psychoanalytically oriented therapies, in which very little explanation is involved.

**Identifying Maladaptive Assumptions.** As the patient and therapist continue to identify automatic thoughts, patterns usually become apparent, representing rules or maladaptive general assumptions that guide the patient's life. Samples of such rules are, "In order to be happy, I must be perfect" or "If anyone doesn't like me, I'm not lovable." Such rules inevitably lead to disappointments and failure and, subsequently, to depression.

**Analyzing the Validity of Maladaptive Assumptions.** Similar to the testing of the validity of automatic thoughts is the testing of the accuracy of maladaptive assumptions. One particularly effective technique for this test is for the therapist to ask the patient to defend the validity of the assumption. For example, when the patient states that he should always work up to his potential, the therapist might ask "Why is that so important to you?"

### Cognitive Techniques

The cognitive approach includes four processes: (1) eliciting automatic thoughts, (2) testing automatic thoughts, (3) identifying maladaptive underlying assumptions, and (4) testing the validity of maladaptive assumptions.

**Eliciting Automatic Thoughts.** Automatic thoughts are cognitions that intervene between external events and the individual's emotional reaction to the event. An example of an automatic thought is the belief that "everyone is going to laugh at me when they see how badly I bowl"—a thought that occurs to someone who has been asked to go bowling and responds negatively. Another example is a person's thought that "he doesn't like me," if someone passes that person in the hall without saying hello.

**Testing Automatic Thoughts.** The therapist, acting as a teacher, helps the patient to test the validity of automatic thought. The goal is to encourage patients to reject inaccurate or exaggerated automatic thoughts after careful examination.

Patients often blame themselves for things that go wrong that may well have been outside their control. The therapist reviews with the patient the entire situation and helps to "reattribute" the blame or cause of the unpleasant events more accurately.

Generating alternative explanations for events is another way of undermining inaccurate and distorted automatic thoughts.

### Behavioral Techniques

Behavioral techniques go hand in hand with cognitive techniques: behavioral techniques are used to test and change maladaptive or inaccurate cognitions. The over-all purpose of such techniques is to help the patients to understand the inaccuracy of their cognitive assumptions and to learn new strategies and ways of dealing with issues.

Among the behavioral techniques that are utilized in therapy are scheduling activities, mastery and pleasure, graded task assignments, cognitive rehearsal, self-reliance training, role playing, and diversion techniques.

Among the first things done in therapy is to schedule activities on an hour by hour basis. A record of these activities is kept and is reviewed with the therapist.

In addition to scheduling activities, patients are asked to rate the amount of mastery and pleasure of their activities. Patients are often surprised at how much more mastery and pleasure they get out of activities than they had otherwise believed.

In order to simplify the situation and allow for mini-accomplishments, tasks are often broken down into subtasks, as in graded task assignments, to demonstrate to patients that they can succeed.

Cognitive rehearsal involves getting the patient to imagine the various steps involved in meeting and mastering a challenge and to rehearse the various aspects of it.

Patients, especially inpatients, are encouraged to become more self-reliant by such simple things as making their own beds, doing their own shopping, or preparing their own meals rather than relying on other people. This is known as self-reliance training.

Role playing is a particularly powerful and useful technique to elicit automatic thoughts and to learn new behaviors.

Diversion techniques are useful in helping patients to get through particularly difficult times and involve the implementation of physical activity, social contact, work, play, or visual imagery.

### Efficacy

Despite the large number of studies that have been reported using cognitive therapy, only a handful used adequate control groups. Over-all, however, cognitive therapy tended to be effective in reducing depressive symptoms. It is one of the most promising psychotherapeutic interventions available currently for depression.

**REFERENCES**

Altshuler K Z: Psychoanalytic and cognitive therapies: A comparison of theory and tactics. Am J Psychother *38:* 4, 1984.
Bandura A: *Social Learning Theory.* Prentice-Hall, Englewood Cliffs, NJ, 1977.
Beck A T: *Depression: Clinical, Experimental, Theoretical Aspects.* Harper & Row, New York, 1967. (Reprinted as *Depression: Causes and Treatment,* University of Pennsylvania Press, Philadelphia, 1972.)
Beck A T: *Cognition Therapy and the Emotional Disorders.* International Universities Press, New York, 1976.
Beck A T: Cognitive therapy. In *Comprehensive Textbook of Psychiatry,* ed 4, H I Kaplan, B J Sadock, editors, p 1432. Williams & Wilkins, Baltimore, 1985.
Beck A T, Emery G: *Anxiety & Phobias, A Cognitive Approach.* Basic Books, New York, 1984.
Beck A T, Rush A J, Shaw B, Emery G: *Cognitive Therapy of Depression.* Guilford, New York, 1979.
Ellis A: *Reason and Emotion in Psychotherapy.* Lyle Stuart, New York, 1962.
Kelly G: *The Psychology of Personal Constructs.* W. W. Norton, New York, 1955.
Mahoney M J: *Cognition and Behavior Modification.* Ballinger, Cambridge, MA., 1974.
Meichenbaum D H: *Cognitive Behavior Modification: An Integrative Approach.* Plenum Publishing Corp., New York, 1977.
Roemy V: *Misunderstandings of the Self.* Jossey-Boss, San Francisco, 1975.

## 26.8 BIOFEEDBACK AND BEHAVIORAL MEDICINE

### Introduction

Although the concepts of biofeedback and behavioral medicine have ancient antecedents in medicine and psychiatry, the terms themselves and their merging and emergent properties are quite recent. Biofeedback is a word first coined in 1969, borrowing the feedback concept formalized by cybernetics during World War II. Biofeedback instrumentation signals a person about normally involuntary or subthreshold biologic processes which he may be able to change by adjusting his behavior or mental processes within limitations set by homeostasis or pathology.

Behavioral medicine merges traditional psychiatric modalities such as psychotherapy and psychopharmacology with biofeedback, self-management skills, and behavioral modification techniques to alter behavior which contributes to the entire spectrum of health problems.

### Theoretical Background

Extensive clinical evidence indicates that primary fear or secondary learned fear, sometimes called anxiety when its source is vague or unknown, plays an important role in many abnormal behaviors. Either primary or acquired fear can be elicited by strange situations, by sudden unexpected strong stimuli, by the removal of social supports and safety signals, by feelings of helplessness, by threats of bodily harm or death, or by the loss of love, respect, prestige, or money. Some people are more susceptible to fear than are others, and animal studies suggest that there are 24-hour circadian variations in the susceptibility to acquisition of acquired fear. Stress reactions to primary or secondary fear run the gamut of virtually all symptoms that have been observed in neurotic and psychotic states, including a pounding heart and rapid pulse; intense feelings of muscular tension, tremor, exaggerated responses, dryness of the throat and mouth, and a sinking feeling in the stomach; perspiration, a frequent need to urinate, irritability, aggression, and an overpowering urge to cry or run and hide; confusion, feelings of unreality, feeling faint, nausea, fatigue, or depression; slowing down of movements and thoughts, restlessness, loss of appetite, insomnia, and nightmares; interference with speech, the use of meaningless gestures, the maintenance of peculiar postures, and sometimes stuttering, mutism, and amnesia. Virtually any psychodynamically based human drive state which previously may have been a relatively neutral stimulus can acquire the psychophysiological manifestations of innate fear through learning. Such drives include guilt, disgust, anger, sex, and the needs for self-esteem, dominance, love, and social approval.

One way of reducing fear is by drugs. Although drugs may be useful, particularly in a therapeutic setting, a number of difficulties warrant closer attention to self-regulation strategies. When a drug is effective in reducing fear, it reinforces the taking of the drug itself, which may not differentiate between realistic and unrealistic fear states. Thus a person who uses alcohol or marijuana to reduce unrealistic fear of normal self-assertiveness at a party may not be cautious when driving home.

In examining lawful principles governing behavior, feedback is, without doubt, one of the most profound and unifying concepts. It is fundamental in biological adaptation, being the basis of natural selection and evolution. Feedback from the environment about the consequences of one's acts provides the rewards and punishment that are an important part of learning. Maintenance of homeostasis and the neurohumoral regulation of behavior also operate

through feedback loops. At whatever level it is studied, the brain is among other things an incredible feedback or servomechanism system. Social psychology also makes use of feedback principles in viewing the interactions of interpersonal reactions; feedback can modify the behavior of each party of a social encounter. Biofeedback is a special case referring to information provided externally to an individual about normally subthreshold bodily processes.

## Biofeedback Methods

### Electromyography (EMG)

Muscle fibers generate electrical potentials which can be measured on an electromyograph. Electrodes placed in or on a specific muscle group, e.g. masseter, deltoid, temporalis, can be monitored for relaxation training.

### Electroencephalograph (EEG)

The evoked potential of the EEG is monitored to determine relaxation. Alpha waves are generally indicative of meditative states; but wave frequency and amplitude are also measured.

### Galvanic Skin Response (GSR)

Skin conductance of electricity is measured as an indicator of autonomic nervous system activity. Stress increases electrical conduction and the GSR; conversely relaxation is associated with lowered autonomic activity and changes in skin response. Similarly, skin temperature as a measure of peripheral vasoconstriction is decreased under stress and can be measured with thermisters (thermal feedback).

## Intrinsic Biofeedback

Incredibly precise intrinsic feedback of neuromuscular responses is available to our conscious brains in learning psychomotor skills, activities involving learning how to read and write, and in tasks such as the test of cerebellar function performed in a neurological examination in which a patient is asked to close his eyes and touch the tip of his finger to the tip of his nose. However, for normally involuntary processes under the control of the autonomic nervous system, conscious feedback is relatively meager except in conditions of malfunction where intrinsic feedback is oftentimes the relatively imprecise sensation of pain.

## Extrinsic Biofeedback

In general, two types of biofeedback application may be distinguished. The first is a specific type in which the patient is provided feedback about the actual condition that needs to be controlled, such as blood pressure or properly timed contraction of the anal sphincters.

The second type of biofeedback application is nonspecific in which the symptom or condition itself is not directly measured on a moment-to-moment basis; rather, a patient is taught a more general skill, such as electromyographic (EMG) reduction or relaxation, that seems to produce a desirable effect. For example, learning to warm the hands may be used to reduce the frequency of migraine headaches, palpitations of anxiety, or the sensations of angina pectoris. A presumptive mechanism would be a lowering of sympathetic activation and voluntary self-regulation of arterial smooth muscle vasoconstrictive tendencies in predisposed persons.

Neal Miller gave credibility to biofeedback and its medical potentials by demonstrating that the normally involuntary autonomic nervous system could be operantly conditioned with appropriate feedback. Miller and his colleagues experimentally challenged a classical doctrine of psychology that instrumental conditioning principles operated only with the voluntary central nervous system and skeletal muscles. The implication seemed clear that instrumental conditioning via enhanced sensory awareness through biofeedback could be the scientific basis underlying a wide spectrum of poorly understood self-regulation techniques including the placebo response (both positive and negative), hypnotic phenomena, meditation, autogenic therapy, relaxation, progressive relaxation, and other variants.

### Biofeedback Applications

**Neuromuscular Rehabilitation**. Mechanical devices or EMG measurement of muscle activity displayed to a patient have increased the effectiveness of traditional therapies, as documented by relatively long clinical histories in peripheral nerve-muscle damage, spasmodic torticollis, selected cases of tardive dyskinesia, cerebral palsy, and upper motor neuron hemiplegias.

**Fecal Incontinence and Enuresis**. The timing sequence of internal and external anal sphincters has been measured using triple lumen rectal catheters providing feedback to selected incontinent patients to reestablish normal bowel habits in a relatively small number of biofeedback sessions. An actual precursor of biofeedback dating to 1938 was the sounding of a buzzer for sleeping enuretic children at the first sign of moisture.

**Raynaud's Syndrome**. Cold hands and cold feet are frequent concomitants of anxiety and are given a formal diagnosis of primary idiopathic Raynaud's disease when vasospasm of arterial smooth muscle produces color changes in the digits or toes not associated by the physical stigmata of Raynaud's phenomenon, which frequently involves an autoimmune process. A number of studies report that thermal feedback from the hand, an inexpensive and benign procedure compared to surgical sympathectomy, is effective in about 70 percent of cases of primary Raynaud's syndrome.

**Migraine Headaches**. The commonest biofeedback strategy with classic or common vascular headaches has been thermal biofeedback from a digit accompanied by autogenic self-suggestive phrases encouraging hand warming and head cooling. The mechanism is thought to be prophylactic in preventing excessive cerebral artery vasoconstriction, often accompanied by an ischemic prodromal symptom, such as scintillating scotomata, followed by rebound engorgement of arteries and stretching of vessel wall pain receptors.

**Tension Headache**. Muscle contraction headaches are most frequently treated with two fairly large active electrodes spaced on the forehead to provide visual or auditory information about levels of muscle tension. This frontal electrode placement with large sensors is sensitive to EMG activity above the first rib and is responsive to both postural bracing and nervous tension overactivity.

**Cardiac Arrhythmias**. Specific biofeedback of the electrocardiogram has permitted patients to nullify the frequency of premature ventricular contractions.

**Idiopathic Hypertension and Orthostatic Hypotension**. A variety of specific (direct) and nonspecific biofeedback procedures, including blood pressure feedback, galvanic skin response, and foot-hand thermal feedback combined with relaxation procedures, have been used to teach patients to increase or decrease blood pressure. Some follow-up data indicate that these changes may persist for at least 2 years and often permit reduction or elimination of antihypertensive medications.

**Myofacial and temperomandibular joint (TMJ) Pain**. Increased levels of EMG activity over the powerful muscles associated with bilateral temporomandibular joints have been decreased using biofeedback in patients diagnosed as being jaw clenchers or demonstrating bruxism.

**Grand Mal Epilepsy**. A number of electroencephalographic biofeedback procedures have been used to suppress seizure activity prophylactically in patients unresponsive to anticonvulsant medication. The procedures permitted patients to enhance the sensorimotor brain wave rhythm or to normalize brain wave activity as computed in real-time power spectrum displays.

**Hyperactivity.** EEG biofeedback procedures have been used on children with attention deficit disorders with hyperactivity to train them to reduce their motor restlessness. Biofeedback for their disorder is still experimental.

**Asthma.** Both frontal EMG and airway resistance biofeedback have been reported as producing relaxation from the panic associated with asthma, as well as improving air flow rate.

As can be seen from the above overview, a wide variety of biofeedback modalities have been used to treat numerous conditions. Many less specific clinical applications, such as treatment of insomnia, dysmenorrhea, speech problems, optimizing athletic performance, treatment of volitional disorders, achieving altered states of consciousness, stress management, and using biofeedback as an adjunct to psychotherapy for anxiety associated with somatoform disorders, use a model in which frontalis muscle EMG biofeedback is combined with thermal biofeedback along with verbal instructions in progressive relaxation or autogenic phrases.

### Biofeedback and Psychotherapy

While many psychiatric patients are able to acquire voluntary self-regulation skills using biofeedback while immersed in the demand characteristics of the treatment milieu, the transfer of such skills outside of the clinical setting is meager and has little direct impact on a number of major psychiatric problems. For example, depression, whether overt or masked, is a major factor for unsuccessful outcome when concomitant somatoform conditions are treated with biofeedback as an adjunct to traditional therapies. Depressed patients tend not to assume responsibility for practicing self-regulation techniques. Many patients have been reported as showing a temporary response to the demand characteristics of the clinic, the biofeedback instrumentation and the extra staff attention, but likely were responding to these as fetish objects rather than realistic transitional objects.

Psychotic patients, particularly those with paranoid and delusional features, tended to show increased confusion and disorganization when exposed to the instrumentation. If biofeedback devices are viewed as auxiliary inanimate therapists, they may provide an opportunity to learn more about the vicissitudes of transitional or facilitating objects in adults with narcissistic and borderline disorders.

Widespread media popularization of biofeedback along with public access to biofeedback instruments and the use of these techniques by lay therapists outside of the context of a supporting professional background are especially worrisome for several reasons. Experienced professionals using biofeedback recognize the need for medical and/or psychiatric screening of patients for conditions better treated by more traditional therapeutic modalities. Lacking such screening, patients may receive an ineffective therapy for their condition (e.g. biofeedback treatment of a tumor or a depression-related headache) and delay seeking appropriate help.

### REFERENCES

Abranowitz S I: Internal-external control and headache response to biofeedback and psychotherapy. Psychosom 41: 57, 1984.

Basmajian J V, editor: *Biofeedback: Principles and Practice for Clinicians.* Williams & Wilkins, Baltimore, MD, 1983.

Blanchard E B: Biofeedback and relaxation training with three kinds of headache: Treatment effects and their prediction. J Consult Clin Psychol 50: 562, 1982.

Gaarder K R, Montgomery S: *Clinical Biofeedback: A Procedural Manual for Behavioral Medicine.* Williams & Wilkins, Baltimore, 1981.

Orne M T, editor: *Task Force Report 19: Biofeedback.* American Psychiatric Association, Washington, DC, 1980.

Pomerleau O F, Brady J P, editors: *Behavioral Medicine: Theory and Practice.* Williams & Wilkins, Baltimore, 1979.

Runck B: *Biofeedback—Issues and Treatment Assessment.* National Institute of Mental Health (DHHS Pub. No. ADM 80-1032), Rockville, MD, 1980.

Stroebel C F, editor: Biofeedback and behavioral medicine and biofeedback in clinical practice. Psychiatr Ann 11: (#2, #3) 1981.

Stroebel C F: Biofeedback and behavioral medicine. In *Comprehensive Textbook of Psychiatry,* ed 4, H I Kaplan, B J Sadock, editors, p 1467. Williams & Wilkins, Baltimore, 1985.

# 27

# Organic Therapies

## 27.1 ANTIPSYCHOTIC DRUGS

### Introduction

Antipsychotic drugs are known also as the major tranquilizers, as represented by chlorpromazine, one of the phenothiazine type of drugs. Although chlorpromazine does not produce a permanent cure in schizophrenia, it does benefit greatly many patients in a way no treatment ever did before. Previously, many mental hospitals had been primarily custodial in character. The fact that clinically significant therapeutic effects could be produced by a drug created an atmosphere that emphasized positive treatment and led to the vigorous application of milieu therapy, psychotherapy, group therapy, and occupational therapy. Some patients were helped so much that they were able to remain out of the hospital and function in the community. Other patients were discharged to nursing homes or halfway houses. For those remaining, the mental hospital became a more humane place. The changes have resulted in a massive reduction in the number of hospitalized schizophrenic patients, a finding all the more remarkable because, up until the introduction of the new drugs, there had been a steady increase in the hospitalized mental patient census.

### Classification

The major classes of antipsychotic drugs are as follows: phenothiazines, butyrophenones, thioxanthenes, dibenzoxazepines, dihydroindolones, and rauwolfia alkaloids (see Tables I and II). Unlike many drugs commonly used in psychiatry, these agents have little or no abuse potential and are thus not classified as controlled substances.

### Efficacy

Studies indicate that antipsychotics are superior to a placebo in the treatment of acute and chronic schizophrenic patients. The magnitude of the improvement produced by the drugs is considerable. About 70 percent of patients significantly improve under phenothiazine therapy; only one-tenth fail to be helped; none show deterioration. Thus, worsening is prevented by phenothiazines. They prevent the emergence of new psychotic symptoms and suppress preexisting symptoms of schizophrenia.

In the case of the average patient, most of the therapeutic gain occurs in the first 6 weeks of phenothiazine therapy, although further treatment gains are made during the subsequent 12 or 18 weeks. Some patients show a rapid improvement in a single day or after a few weeks; other patients show a gradual rate of improvement over several months.

Phenothiazine therapy brings about cognitive restoration—with a decrease in psychotic and paranoid thinking, projection, suspiciousness, pathological hostility, perplexity, and ideas of reference—and a normalization of psychomotor behavior in both retarded and hyperactive patients. There is a reduction of hallucinations, paranoid identification, hostility, belligerence, resistiveness, uncooperativeness, and a reduction in thought disorder, including overinclusive thinking and bizarre, inappropriate response.

The antipsychotic drugs have a normalizing effect. In addition to lessening typical schizophrenic symptoms, such as hallucinations and delusions, they also normalize various other abnormal behaviors. For example, they speed up retarded schizophrenics and slow down excited schizophrenics. Hence, they are not uniformly sedatives in the sense of slowing down all symptoms of all patients.

The drugs are also effective in psychotic depression, mania, and organic psychosis. Since the symptoms that are reduced by the phenothiazines are typical of schizophrenia, in particular, and of psychosis, in general, the agents are best referred to as antipsychotic drugs. They do not, in any real sense, produce a state of tranquility in either normal or psychotic persons. The term tranquilizer is, therefore, inappropriate, and a preferable term is neuroleptic. Normal persons often find the drugs' effects slightly unpleasant. There is a clear-cut difference between their sedative and antipsychotic properties. Furthermore, antipsychotics that are maximally stimulating are just as effective as antipsychotics that are maximally sedating.

### Biological Mechanism of Action

Even though we do not know the biological causation of the schizophrenias, we do know the mechanisms by which the antipsychotic drugs benefit schizophrenia. The most likely common denominator of the antipsychotic drugs is their effect on the central neurotransmitter dopamine. The drugs block dopamine receptors.

Chlorpromazine has a molecular configuration similar to that of dopamine. That similarity may account for chlorpromazine's ability to block dopaminergic receptors. Deviation from the structural characteristics of chlorpromazine—as in promazine hydrochloride, promethazine hydrochloride, and imipramine hydrochloride—results in the loss of antipsychotic activity. In addition to the qualitative receptor association, the potency of dopamine binding measured directly in the test tube correlates exactly to the potency of the agents in treating schizophrenics. Clinical potency and dopamine binding both correlate with pharmacological evidence of dopamine receptor blocking properties.

There is evidence that indicates that the antipsychotic drugs may also benefit schizophrenia patients by blocking the receptors for the catecholamines or interfering with catecholamine storage. They interfere with the storage of many biogenic amines, such as serotonin, norepinephrine, or dopamine, by compromising the integrity of the storage vesicles. One would assume that their beneficial effects on schizophrenia patients are produced by decreasing the levels of biogenic amines, including dopamine, in the brain. Their pharmacological action would, therefore, be consistent with a dopaminergic mechanism of action. If the antipsychotic drugs do benefit schizophrenia through a dopaminergic mechanism by blocking the receptor site, one might assume that, if one could reduce the amount of dopamine in the brain by giving an inhibitor of dopamine synthesis, one could potentiate the action of the antipsychotic drugs.

If decreasing dopaminergic activity benefits schizophrenia patients, perhaps schizophrenia is produced or aggravated by increasing dopaminergic activation. The psychomotor stimulants—such as amphetamine, methylphenidate, and cocaine—are potent releasers of dopamine; they also block the reuptake of dopamine. It is well known that large doses of amphetamine can cause a paranoid schizophrenic episode; that has been shown experimentally in normal volunteers.

Dopa, which is converted to dopamine in the body, can produce a psychosis. Neurologists use a wide variety of agents which directly stimulate dopaminergic receptors. Some of the agents are commercially available and others are experimental. They can produce a paranoid psychosis as a side effect. Amantadine is also a dopaminergic drug, and it can produce paranoid psychosis and other similar mental side effects. A variety of dopaminergic drugs produce paranoid symptoms, hallucination, etc.

The dopamine theory of schizophrenia suggests that certain schizophrenics either have high dopamine levels or supersensitive dopamine receptors. While this theory remains unproven, it is clear that the antipsychotic action produced by these drugs is an antidopaminergic action. What this has to do with the various schizophrenias or psychosis is unknown. Dopamine may be involved in such psychotic processes in a central manner. Alternatively, a dopaminergic system could modulate in some fashion a system which relates to the psychotic process in a manner which is not necessarily absolutely specific.

Understanding the biology of neurotransmission helps explain a wide variety of drug side effects. Many of the autonomic side effects—dry mouth, constipation, blurred vision—are due to these drugs' anticholinergic properties. Parkinsonian side effects may be related to the blockade of central dopamine receptors. Tardive dyskinesia also may be a result of chronic dopamine blockade and increase in dopamine synthesis, leading to a denervation hypersensitivity. Since the antipsychotic drugs can also block the norepinephrine uptake pump, and since guanethidine is concentrated into neurons by the norepinephrine uptake pump, it should not be surprising that chlorpromazine can interfere with the hypotensive action of guanethidine by interfering with guanethidine's reaching its neuronal site of action. Clinical psychiatrists should know something of pharmacology in order to understand the mechanisms involved in side effects.

### Clinical Use

#### Indications

The primary indication for antipsychotics is the presence of psychosis, such as in organic psychosis, paraphrenia, psychotic depression, mania, and the schizophrenic and the schizo-

TABLE I
PHENOTHIAZINE ANTIPSYCHOTIC AGENTS (MAJOR TRANQUILIZERS)

| Name | | | Manufacturer | Structure | Adult Dose Range | | |
| Class | Generic | Trade | | | Acute (mg/day) | Maintenance (mg/day) | Single Dose (mg) |
|---|---|---|---|---|---|---|---|
| Aliphatic | Chlorpromazine | Thorazine | Smith, Kline & French | | 75–400 Oral 25–2,000 IM | 30–75 Oral | 10–25 Oral 10–400 IM |
| | Triflupromazine | Vesprin | Squibb | | 100–150 Oral 60–150 IM | 30–150 Oral | 10–50 Oral 10–50 IM |
| Piperazine | Prochlorperazine | Compazine | Smith, Kline & French | | 30–150 Oral 40–80 IM | 15–40 Oral | 5–25 Oral 10–20 IM |
| | Perphenazine | Trilafon | Schering | | 16–64 Oral 15–30 IM | 12–24 Oral | 2–16 Oral 5 IM |
| | Trifluoperazine | Stelazine | Smith, Kline & French | | 15–40 Oral 4–10 IM | 5–15 Oral | 1–10 Oral 1–2 IM |
| Piperazine | Fluphenazine | Prolixin Permitil | Squibb Schering | | 2.5–20 Oral 2.5–10 IM (HCl) | 1.0–5.0 Oral 25–50 IM (decanoate or enanthate, weekly or biweekly) | 0.5–10 Oral 1.0–5.0 Oral |
| | Acetophenazine | Tindal | Schering | | 40–120 Oral | 20–40 Oral | 20–40 Oral |

| Class | Generic name | Trade name | Manufacturer | Structure | | | |
|---|---|---|---|---|---|---|---|
| | Butaperazine | Repoise | Robins | [structure] | 15–100 Oral | 5–50 Oral | 5–30 Oral |
| | Carphenazine | Proketazine | Wyeth | [structure] | 100–200 Oral | 50–150 Oral | 12.5–50 Oral |
| Piperidine | Thioridazine | Mellaril | Sandoz | [structure] | 200–800 Oral | 100–300 Oral | 20–200 Oral |
| | Mesoridazine | Serentil | Boehringer | [structure] | 100–400 Oral / 25–200 IM | 30–150 Oral | 10–100 Oral / 25 IM |
| | | | | [structure] | 20–160 Oral | 40–80 Oral | 10–60 Oral |

*Table I continued on page 636*

TABLE I
PHENOTHIAZINE ANTIPSYCHOTIC AGENTS (MAJOR TRANQUILIZERS)—continued

| | Available Preparation | | | | | | | | | Equiva-lence* |
|---|---|---|---|---|---|---|---|---|---|---|
| | Oral | | | | Concentrate | Injection | | | Supposi-tory | |
| | Tablet (mg) | Capsule (mg) | Syrup | Elixir | | Ampul | Vial | Syringe | | |
| Chlorpromazine | 10, 25, 50, 100, 200 | Sustained release: 30, 75, 150, 200, 300 | 10 mg/ml | | 30 mg/ml<br>100 mg/ml | 25 mg/ml | 25 mg/ml | | 25, 100 | 100 |
| Trifluopromazine | 10, 25, 50 | | 10 mg/ml | | 100 mg/ml | | 10 mg/ml<br>20 mg/ml | 10 mg/ml<br>20 mg/ml | | 25 |
| Prochlorperazine | 5, 10, 25 | Sustained release: 10, 15, 30, 75 | 5 mg/5 ml | | 10 mg/ml | 5 mg/ml | 5 mg/ml | 5 mg/ml | 2.5, 5, 25 | 15 |
| Perphenazine | 2, 4, 8, 16 | | | | 16 mg/5 ml | 5 mg/ml | | | | 10 |
| Trifluoperazine | 1, 2, 5, 10 | | | | 10 mg/ml | | | | | 5 |
| Fluphenazine | 1, 2.5, 5, 10 | | | 0.5 mg/ml | | | 25 mg/ml HCl (decanoate or enanthate)<br>25 mg/ml (decanoate or enanthate) | | | 2<br>7 |
| Acetophenazine | 20 | | | | | | | | | 25 |
| Butaperazine | 10, 25 | | | | 30 mg/ml | | | | | 10 |
| Carphenazine | 12.5, 25, 50 | | | | 100 mg/ml | | | | | 25 |
| Thioridazine | 10, 15, 25, 50, 100, 150, 200 | | | 25 mg/5ml | | | | | | 100 |
| Mesoridazine | 10, 25, 50, 100 | | | | 25 mg/ml | 25 mg/ml | | | | 50 |
| Piperacetazine | 10, 25 | | | | | | | | | 10 |

* Dose required to achieve therapeutic efficacy of 100 mg. chlorpromazine. All drug enforcement control level "0."

phreniform disorders. Efficacy of antipsychotics for these indications has been established by double-blind studies.

### Goals of Treatment

The aim of drug treatment should be to achieve maximum therapeutic improvement in the patient. In some sense, one should be treating the whole patient or the underlying disease process, rather than a given symptom. That is particularly important for a retarded schizophrenic patient. Those patients often respond dramatically to antipsychotic drugs, even though troublesome target symptoms, such as agitation and aggression, are completely absent. The goals should be maximum cognitive reorganization and lessening of the underlying schizophrenic process, not control of a particular symptom. Evaluation of the severity of typical psychotic symptoms is a convenient benchmark for monitoring drug effects.

### Choice of Antipsychotic Drug

In the hope of developing either a better antipsychotic agent or one with fewer side effects, scientists synthesized a number of new phenothiazine derivatives, including (1) the thioxanthene derivatives (chlorprothixene and thiothixene), close structural analogs of the phenothiazines; (2) the butyrophenones (haloperidol), a class of effective antipsychotic compounds with apparently differing chemical structures; (3) the dibenzoxazepines (loxapine); and (4) the indoles (molindone).

A myth exists in psychiatry that hyperexcitable patients respond best to chlorpromazine because it is a sedating phenothiazine, and that withdrawn patients respond best to an alerting phenothiazine such as fluphenazine (Prolixin) or trifluoperazine (Stelazine). This belief has never been proven true. Despite the lack of clear differential indications for one or another antipsychotic drug in a particular patient or class of patients, psychiatrists continue to observe clinically that patients who fail to respond to one phenothiazine occasionally do show a good response to another. It is unwise to change antipsychotic drugs every few days. One should try to find the optimal dose of a single drug, and allow the drug a reasonable time to exert its behavioral effect. However, at some point—after several days or weeks in the case of a severely disturbed acute patient and after several weeks or months in the case of a less dramatically impaired patient—a trial with a second, maximally different antipsychotic agent is warranted.

### Dosage

Various patients may respond to widely different doses, so there is no set dose for any given antipsychotic agent. There is a wide therapeutic range between effective dose and toxic overdose with the antipsychotic agents. In research studies, patients have been treated safely with 10 to 100 times the therapeutic dose. One can go substantially higher than the prescribed doses without danger. Hence, the physician should not be concerned about a modest increase of dose for a clinical reason.

The most common side effects, sedation and extrapyramidal symptoms, do not usually make a shift to another drug necessary. Sedation can be handled by dose reduction or by administering most of the drug at bedtime (see Table III). However, neurological side effects present a quandary; one can block them with an antiparkinsonian agent, reduce the dose, or both. No clear evidence favors either strategy. The therapeutic decision should probably rest on the patient's level of improvement. If the patient is much better, decrease the dose. If the patient is still psychotic, add an antiparkinsonian drug and raise the dose of the antipsychotic drug if that decision seems clinically necessary.

Most clinicians will gradually reduce the dose of the antipsychotic drug once the patient appears maximally improved, and raise the dose again if symptoms recur. Sometimes a modest prophylactic elevation of dosage is used when the patient is about to undergo a special stress, such as returning home or starting a new job.

The antipsychotic effects are of relatively long duration, on the order of days, but their sedative effects generally last only a few hours. For this reason, the common medical practice of administering medication three times a day may make the patient oversedated when he should be working or learning. The same total dose given at bedtime may well promote better sleep and leave the patient calm but not sedated during the day.

Methods for measuring blood levels of antipsychotic drugs remain technically complex. It may be years before it is possible for psychiatrists to routinely check unresponsive patients to make sure that appropriate antipsychotic drug blood levels have been achieved.

### Treatment of the Acute Psychotic Emergency

It is important to treat the acute emergency with a reasonably high dose of antipsychotic. Intramuscular drug is more rapidly absorbed than oral. When the patient is violent or otherwise dangerously disturbed, IM dosage should

TABLE II
NONPHENOTHIAZINE ANTIPSYCHOTIC AGENTS (MAJOR TRANQUILIZERS)

| Class | Name | | Manufacturer | Structure | Adult Dose Range | | |
| | Generic | Trade | | | Acute (mg/day) | Maintenance (mg/day) | Single Dose (mg) |
| --- | --- | --- | --- | --- | --- | --- | --- |
| Butyrophenones | Haloperidol | Haldol | McNeil | | 1–15 Oral 6–30 IM | 1–15 | 0.5–5 Oral 2–5 IM |
| Thioxanthenes | Chlorprothixene | Taractan | Roche | | 75–600 Oral 75–200 IM | 75 | 25–150 Oral 25–50 IM |
| | Thiothixene | Navane | Roerig | | 6–60 Oral 8–30 IM | 6–60 | 2–20 Oral 4–5 IM |
| Dibenzoxazepines | Loxapine | Loxitane | Lederle | | 20–100 Oral 50–300 IM | 60–100 | 10–60 Oral |
| Dihydroindolones | Molindone | Moban Lidone | Endo Abbott | | 50–225 Oral | 15–225 | 5–75 Oral |
| Rauwolfia alkaloid | Reserpine | Serpasil Rau-sed Sandril Reserpoid | CIBA Squibb Lilly Upjohn | | 0.1–5 Oral 2.5–10.0 IM (after a small initial dose to test patient responsiveness) | 0.1–5 | 0.1–5 Oral |

| Class | Available Preparations | | | | | | Drug Enforcement Administration Control Level | Dose Equivalent* | Side Effects |
|---|---|---|---|---|---|---|---|---|---|
| | Oral | | Elixir | Concentrate | Injection | | | | |
| | Tablet (mg) | Capsule (mg) | | | Ampul | Vial | | | |
| Haloperidol | 0.5, 1, 2, 5, 10 | | | 2 mg/ml | 5 mg/ml | | 0 | 1.6 | Same as for phenothiazine antipsychotic agents |
| Chlorprothixene | 10, 25, 50, 100 | | | 20 mg/ml | 12.5 mg/ml | | 0 | 50 | |
| Thiothixene | | 5, 10, 25 | | 5 mg/ml | | 2 mg/ml | 0 | 5 | |
| Loxapine | | | | 25 mg/ml | | | 0 | 10 | |
| Molindone | 5, 10, 25 | 5, 10, 25, 50 | | | | | 0 | 6–10 | |
| Reserpine | 0.1, 0.25, 1, 2, 5 | 0.25, 0.5 | 0.05 mg/ml | | 2.5 mg/ml | 2.5 g/ml | 0 | | Reserpine is associated with many of the same side effects as the phenothiazine antipsychotic agents. However, in addition, it frequently produces depression. Approximately 6 percent of all patients on reserpine require hospitalization or therapy for depression caused by the drug. |

* Dose equivalent, 100 mg of chlorpromazine.

TABLE III
COMPARISON OF SEDATIVE PROPERTIES AND
ANTIPSYCHOTIC ACTIVITY

| Drug | Sedative Action | Antipsychotic Effect |
|------|-----------------|----------------------|
| Chlorpromazine | 2+ | 4+ |
| Promethazine | 2+ | 0 |
| Phenobarbital | 4+ | 0 |
| Amphetamine | 4− | 0 |
| Trifluoperazine | ± | 4+ |

Key: + to 4+ indicate varying degrees of sedative or antipsychotic activity, with 4+ indicating the greatest and + indicating the least amount of activity; ± indicates that the effect may or may not be sedating, depending on the circumstances; 4− indicates stimulant effect.

be used initially because it acts about 60 minutes faster than oral medication: A peak is reached about 30 minutes after an IM dose, while the peak after a bioequivalent oral dose occurs after about 90 minutes.

Sometimes it can take only a few hours for a patient to decompensate from mild or moderately psychotic to extremely psychotic with loss of control over impulses and severe hostility leading to violence. The clinician should be prepared to diagnose such a decompensation and institute immediate IM therapy with moderately high dosage. Extremely psychotic out-of-control patients often respond to rapid tranquilization within hours. The dose-response curve is such that only minimally more side effects occur with moderately high doses than would have occurred with low-to-moderate doses, and if an episode of violence is prevented or quickly treated, the clinician avoids the serious harm which would be liable to occur if treatment were not speedily and effectively applied. In terms of potential danger in using high doses, it is relevant to note that patients have received several months' of high-dose antipsychotic treatment, such as 1200 mg fluphenazine or 700 mg trifluoperazine, with about the same incidence of side effects as standard dosage and no noteworthy toxicity.

### Maintenance Treatment

After the patient is substantially improved with pharmacotherapy, the next problem is to determine how long a patient should be kept on maintenance antipsychotic drug treatment. Every properly controlled double-blind study from 30 countries has shown that significantly more patients relapsed on a placebo than on continued pharmacotherapy.

The decision to continue on a drug for a long period of time should be arrived at clinically for each individual patient on the basis of a knowledge of his illness and his life situation. It seems reasonable to maintain most patients on anti-

psychotics for 3 months to 1 year after a psychotic episode; however, over longer periods, treatment should be individualized. Since so-called reactive schizophrenics can have one episode and never relapse, such patients should not be treated with long-term maintenance medication.

Obviously, a history of relapse after the discontinuation of antipsychotics is an indication for a longer than usual period of maintenance. Evidence that antipsychotics did not help the patient originally, or that their prior discontinuation did not lead to a relapse, is an indication for the gradual reduction of dosage, leading to the termination of drug treatment. Psychotherapeutic and social interventions during the recovery phase and throughout posthospital care are important in fostering improved social adjustment, and may help to prevent relapses.

### Drug Holidays

Since there is some risk of long-term toxicity with the antipsychotic drugs, it is reasonable to look for ways of maintaining a remission by the use of minimal amounts of antipsychotic drugs.

Empirically, patients have been treated with drug holidays lasting from 1 to 2 days, which did not lead to an increase in relapses. Similarly, knowing the long half-life of the antipsychotics, once-a-day medication is as effective as the conventional three-times-a-day medication.

Intermittent dosage may prove problematic. It is useful in large institutions where staff coverage is low on weekends, but it is poor preparatory training for patients who will be expected to self-administer their own pills after discharge.

### Depot Long-acting Antipsychotics

Because many schizophrenics relapse when they stop taking their oral medication, the development of long-acting depot intramuscular medication represents a major tactical improvement in treatment.

The intramuscular depot forms, fluphenazine enanthate and fluphenazine decanoate, provide a useful treatment approach for patients who do not take their oral medication. The depot intramuscular medication should be considered for patients who do not show optimal response to oral medication or who are suspected of failing to take medication, as evidenced by frequent relapses. The existence of the depot phenothiazines is an important addition to the therapeutic armamentarium—particularly for outpatients—but occasionally for inpatients, as well. Despite their propensity for inducing neurological side effects, depot fluphenazines can be useful in emergency room and home treatment approaches for treating acutely psychotic patients in the community, thereby averting inpatient admission.

## Combined Therapy

### Drug Combinations

It has not been experimentally demonstrated that combining one antipsychotic with another antipsychotic results in treatment that is superior to comparable amounts of a single phenothiazine given alone. Longitudinal studies of single patients that added minor tranquilizers to antipsychotics for patients who appeared to be suffering from anxiety superimposed on the schizophrenic process indicated that the addition seemed to help relieve the anxiety. That finding suggests that the patient may have had two disorders: schizophrenia, which was benefitted to some degree by the antipsychotic, and an anxiety process separate from the schizophrenia, which was abated by the minor tranquilizer. Combining tricyclic antidepressants with phenothiazines suggests that the combination may benefit an occasional schizoaffective patient and patients with catatonic-like symptoms (possibly misdiagnosed atypical affective patients). It is difficult to distinguish profound, mute depression from withdrawn schizophrenia with catatonic features. It is clear that adding a tricyclic does not help the apathetic schizophrenic, but on occasion it can help the patient with a true affective disorder.

### Antipsychotic Drugs and Somatic Therapies

Antipsychotic drugs have replaced insulin coma in the treatment of schizophrenic patients. There are several controlled studies showing that electroconvulsive therapy (ECT) is effective in certain schizophrenics, and several studies find the efficacy comparable to antipsychotics. Some clinicians believe that in the treatment of selected schizophrenics, ECT is helpful when given concurrently with phenothiazine therapy. ECT is not widely used in the United States for schizophrenia where its use is controversial, especially in schizophrenia.

### Psychotherapy in the Aid of Pharmacotherapy

If a patient is doing poorly, the first question to ask is whether or not he is actually taking his medication. A great many patients fail to take their pills as prescribed, often more than 50 percent in an outpatient setting. Liquid suspensions, such as haloperidol in tasteless liquid

form, may adequately ensure that the patient ingests an oral medication. It is important to work psychotherapeutically with the patient so that he will take the drugs as indicated. Failure to take medication may result in a revolving door, repetitive admission phenomenon. Factors involved in the taking and the not taking of medication are the patient's and doctor's feelings about the medication.

## Side Effects

The side effects of the antipsychotic drugs can be classified as follows: autonomic effects, extrapyramidal effects, other central nervous system effects, behavioral toxicity, allergic reactions, agranulocytosis, long-term skin and eye effects, and endocrine effects (see Table IV).

### Autonomic Side Effects

The autonomic side effects are due to the anticholinergic and antiadrenergic properties of the antipsychotic drugs. Autonomic side effects that can occur include dry mouth and throat, blurred vision, cutaneous flushing, constipation, urinary retention, paralytic ileus, mental confusion, miosis, mydriasis, and postural hypotension.

Dry mouth is one of the most frequently occurring side effects of which patients complain. The patient can be advised to rinse his mouth out frequently with water but not to chew gum or candy, since adding sugar to the mouth provides a good cultural medium for fungal infection, such as moniliasis, and, in addition, may increase the incidence of dental caries. Pilocarpine can reduce that side effect, although it may provide only transitory relief. In any case, patients develop tolerance to the dry mouth and to the other autonomic side effects, so that these side effects tend to be troublesome only during the early stages of treatment.

Orthostatic (postural) hypotension occurs most frequently during the first few days of treatment, and patients readily develop a tolerance to it. It is most apt to occur when acute, high doses of intramuscular medications are given, and it can occasionally be troublesome. The chief dangers of the side effect are that the patient may faint, fall, and injure himself, although such occurrences are rare. In susceptible patients—those taking a high dose of parenteral medication—it is sometimes prudent to measure the patient's blood pressure (lying and standing) after the first dose and during the first few days of treatment. Support hose may help. When appropriate, the patient should be warned of the side effect and given the usual instruction: Rise from bed gradually, sit at first with legs dangling,

TABLE IV
REPORTED SIDE EFFECTS OF MAJOR TRANQUILIZERS

Dry mouth and throat
Blurred vision
Cutaneous flushing
Constipation
Urinary retention
Paralytic ileus
Mental confusion
Miosis
Mydriasis
Postural hypotension
Broadened, flattened, or clove T-waves and increased Q-R intervals on electrocardiogram
Parkinsonian syndrome
    Mask-like face
    Tremor at rest
    Rigidity
    Shuffling gait
    Motor retardation
    Drooling
Dyskinesias
    Bizarre movements of tongue, face, and neck
    Buccofacial movements
    Salivation
    Torticollis
    Oculogyric crisis
    Opisthotonos
    Akathisia
Lowered seizure threshold
Convulsive seizures
Sedation
Insomnia
Bizarre dreams
Impaired psychomotor activity
Somnambulism
Confusion
Paradoxical aggravation of psychotic symptoms
Skin eruptions (urticarial, maculopapular, petechial, or edematous)
Contact dermatitis
Photosensitivity reaction
Blue-gray metallic discoloration of the skin over areas exposed to sunlight
Deposits in the anterior lens and posterior cornea (visible only by slit-lens examination)
Retinitis pigmentosa
Abnormal glucose tolerance curve
Breast engorgement and lactation in female patients
Weight gain
Delayed ejaculation
Loss of erectile ability
Agranulocytosis
Eosinophilia
Leukopenia
Hemolytic anemia
Thrombocytic purpura
Pancytopenia
Jaundice

wait for a minute, and sit or lie down if you feel faint. A patient who is severely ill psychiatrically and needs antipsychotic medication can be kept in bed for several days. For a person with a cardiovascular disease, the doses should be increased very slowly, and blood pressure should be very carefully monitored to avoid clinically significant episodes of hypotension. In general, postural hypertension is not troublesome, particularly when the dose is given orally. When it does occur, it can usually be managed by having the patient lie down with his feet higher than his head. On rare occasions, volume expansion or vasopressor agents, such as norepinephrine, may be indicated. Since phenothiazines are α-adrenergic blockers, they block the α-stimulating properties of epinephrine, leaving the β-stimulating properties untouched. Therefore, the administration of epinephrine results in a paradoxical hypotension, and is contraindicated in cases of phenothiazine-induced hypotension.

### Central Anticholinergic Syndrome

This syndrome occurs in patients taking phenothiazine medication or the drugs with strong anticholinergic properties. The syndrome consists of severe agitation, disorientation to time, place, or person, hallucinations, seizures, high fever, and dilated pupils. Stupor and coma may ensue.

Treatment consists of close medical supervision and physostigmine, 2 mg, by slow IV infusion and repeated within 1 hour as necessary. Too much physostigmine is dangerous and is marked by hypersalivation and sweating and can be reversed with small (0.5 mg) doses of atropine sulfate.

### Neuroleptic Malignant Syndrome

This syndrome occurs in some patients taking antipsychotic drugs and has a mortality of 20 percent. The incidence is unknown. The signs and symptoms include: hyperthermia, increased muscle tone, disorientation, respiratory distress, cardiac abnormalities, and labile blood pressure. Treatment consists of the immediate discontinuation of all antipsychotic drugs and supportive medical care to maintain blood pressure and control hyperthermia. The syndrome lasts about 1 week, longer if long-acting depot phenothiazine medication was used. The ergot derivative bromcriptine, has been found to reverse the symptoms by some workers; but there is no other known treatment at this time.

### Cardiac Effects

With cardiac patients, a predrug electrocardiogram for baseline purposes is indicated. An electrocardiogram abnormality consisting of broadened, flattened, or clove T-waves, and increased Q-R intervals of uncertain clinical significance have been described in patients receiving thioridazine at doses as low as 300 mg a day. The abnormality is not associated with any significant clinical problem.

**Sudden Death.** Sudden death has rarely been reported in patients receiving antipsychotic treatment. However, one cannot make an accurate assessment as to whether or not the drugs are causally involved because sudden death in the absence of drugs can occur even in young, apparently healthy persons. Although sudden death can occur because of asphyxia caused by regurgitated food, an endobronchial mucous plug in an asthmatic, shock in patients with acquired megacolon, and complications due to seizures, the most common postulated cause would be ventricular fibrillation. The introduction of antipsychotics did not alter the incidence of sudden death. In the past, it was assumed that sudden death was the result of myocardial infarction. However, with the advent of emergency cardiac resuscitation by paramedics and

laymen, more cardiac patients survived and were available for examination. Upon examination, it appeared that many of the patients may have had ventricular arrhythmias without myocardial infarctions. It has further been suggested that the extremes of stress seen in psychosis can precipitate cardiac arrhythmias. Thus, sudden death might be caused by these stresses of the psychosis, not the drug used to treat the psychosis. Such deaths have been reported in patients on the so-called high-potency, high-extrapyramidal neuroleptics as well as on chlorpromazine. Consequently, no one type of antipsychotic can be implicated. The physician should refrain from falsely attributing sudden death to neuroleptic medication or any other cause until research establishes that there is a causal, not coincidental, link. Whether or not the sudden death that can occur in patients who are coincidentally receiving antipsychotic drug treatment is related to the drug is unknown at the present time.

### Extrapyramidal Effects

The most dramatic and, pharmacologically, the most theoretically important group of side effects shown by all the antipsychotic agents are the extrapyramidal reactions. Among the phenothiazines, thioridazine produces the fewest extrapyramidal effects; haloperidol, thiothixene, butaperazine, trifluoperazine and fluphenazine produce the most extrapyramidal effects; chlorpromazine, chlorprothixene, and acetophenazine occupy an intermediate position.

This family of side effects is typically classified into three arbitrary categories: parkinsonian syndrome, dystonias, and akathisia. The parkinsonian syndrome consists of a mask-like face, tremor at rest, rigidity, shuffling gait, pill-rolling movement of the hand, and motor retardation. In general, the syndrome is quite similar to idiopathic parkinsonism in its symptoms. The dystonias consist of a broad range of bizarre movements of the tongue, face, and neck, including buccofacial movements with salivation, torticollis, oculogyric crisis, and opisthotonos. Akathisia is a motor restlessness in which the patient manifests a great urge to move about, and has considerable difficulty in sitting still.

Although this family of related side effects is fairly characteristic symptomatically, the diagnosis is occasionally difficult. Dystonias can be confused with the bizarre mannerisms of psychotic patients; akathisia can be confused with agitation; and the parkinsonian syndrome, particularly as expressed by motor retardation, can be confused with schizophrenic apathy. The diagnosis is important, for, if one diagnoses these manifestations as an increase in psychosis, the treatment is to increase the dose of the antipsychotic medication; however, if one diagnoses them as extrapyramidal effects, the treatment is to decrease the dose of the antipsychotic medication or to add an antiparkinsonian drug. Particularly helpful in making a correct diagnosis is a therapeutic trial of an antiparkinsonian agent—such as procyclidine (Kemadrin), benztropine (Cogentin), or diphenhydramine (Benadryl)—especially in the dramatic dyskinesias, which respond within minutes to intramuscular or intravenous treatment with antiparkinsonian medication (see Table V).

**Dystonia.** The acute dystonias, which typically occur in the first few days or weeks of treatment, can appear in patients receiving small amounts of phenothiazines, and it is uncommon in children treated with a single dose of prochlorperazine (Compazine) for nausea. The patients sometimes present themselves in emergency rooms, and frequently the patient and his family make no connection between the medication and the symptom. As a result, they often neglect to tell the examining physician that the patient has taken a phenothiazine-type medication. The syndrome is often rather alarming, and can cause considerable concern until the diagnosis is made. Although dystonias can disappear spontaneously, it is generally advisable to treat them with antiparkinsonian medication, since they are often painful and are always psychologically upsetting. Benztropine (Cogentin), 1 mg, or biperiden (Akineton), 2 mg, can be injected IM. The therapeutic trial provides important diagnostic information by confirming the diagnosis with a dramatic response.

Diazepam (valium) up to 10 mg IV or diphenhydramine (Benodryl) up to 50 mg IV can also be safely given and provides dramatic relief.

**Parkinsonian Syndrome.** The parkinsonian syndrome and akathisia can also occur early in treatment, and tend to persist in a fairly constant state if not treated. Diagnosis of parkinsonian symptoms is generally fairly obvious, since the syndrome is quite characteristic, but not invariably so. Sometimes, patients manifest a subtle form of parkinsonian disease, which is seen as an emotional blunting or a zombie-like appearance, rather than a clear parkinsonian. One should be alert to subtle parkinsonian-like symptoms because they can be confused with emotional withdrawal or retardation, and are readily treated by antiparkinsonian medications. Indeed, one should not only watch for the conventional parkinsonian symptoms, such as mask-like facies and shuffling gait, but also be aware that patients who appear apathetic, lacking in spontaneity, relatively unable to participate in social activities, lifeless, zombie-like, or drowsy, may be demonstrating subtle extrapyramidal side effects.

**Akathisia.** The third class of extrapyramidal side effects, the akathisias, can also be confused with psychotic agitation. In akathisia, the patient is driven by motor restlessness and is usually not verbally preoccupied with the psychological content of whatever he is agitated about. The symptoms are primarily motor, and cannot be controlled by the patient's will. Akathisias are worsened by increasing the dose and are benefitted by decreasing the dose and adding an antiparkinsonian medication. The reverse occurs with agitation. Akathisia often responds dramatically to treatment with antiparkinsonian drugs (see Table V); however, sometimes it is resistant to treatment but can be controlled by reducing the dosage or by switching to a different medication. Propranolol may also be effective in treating akathisia. In rare cases, no treatment is effective.

### Tardive Dyskinesia

An extrapyrimidal syndrome called tardive dyskinesia can emerge relatively late during the course of treatment with antipsychotic compounds, particularly when these drugs have been used in high doses over several years. It occurs late in the course of treatment, sometimes appearing several days or weeks after the drug has been discontinued, and may persist for years, although it is absent during sleep. It can be relatively treatment resistant. Tardive dyskinesia is characterized by grimacing and buccofacial-mandibular or buccolingual movements—for example, sucking, smacking movements of the lips, lateral or fly-catching movements of the tongue, and lateral jaw movements—choreiform-like jerky movements of the arms, athetoid movements of the upper extremities or fingers and ankles and toes, and tonic contractions of the neck and back. The symptoms may occur or become intensified a few days to a few weeks after the drug has been stopped or reduced, although they may also appear during drug therapy. Their reappearance or intensification with reduction of the dosage or cessation of drug treatment may be an unmasking of the symptom, since the phenothiazine-induced rigidity can dampen the dystonic movements. Paradoxically, the symptom may be suppressed by putting the patient on large doses of phenothiazines or butyrophenones. The symptoms may persist for long periods of time in some patients; in others, they may disappear weeks or months

TABLE V
ANTIPARKINSONIAN AGENTS

| Class | Name Generic | Name Trade | Manufacturer | Adult Dose Range | Adult Single Dose Range | Oral Tablet (mg) | Oral Capsule (mg) | Oral Concentrate (mg/ml) | Oral Elixir (mg/ml) | Injection Ampul (mg/ml) | Injection Vial (mg/ml) | Injection Syringe (mg/ml) |
|---|---|---|---|---|---|---|---|---|---|---|---|---|
| Piperidines | Biperiden | Akineton | Knoll | 2–6 | 2 | 2 | | | | | | |
| | Procyclidine | Kemadrin | Burroughs Wellcome | 2–20 | 2–5 | 2, 5 | | | | | | |
| | Trihexyphenidyl | Artane Tremin Pipanol | Lederle Schering Winthrop | ?–10 | 1–3 | 2, 5 | Sustained release: 5 | 2 | | | | |
| Ethanolamine Antihistamine | Diphenhydramine | Benadryl | Parke, Davis | 10–400 | 10–50 | | 25, 50 | | 12.5 | 50 | 10 | 50 |
| Tropines | Orphenadrine | Disipal | Riker | 50–150 | 50 | 50 | | | | | | |
| | Benztropine | Cogentin | Merck, Sharpe & Dohme | 0.5–6 | 1–2 | 0.5, 1, 2 | | | | | 1 | |
| Other | Amantadine | Symmetral | Endo | 100–200 | 100 | | | | 50 mg/ml | | | |

Side Effects

Drowsiness
Confusion
Nervousness
Restlessness
Nausea
Vomiting
Diarrhea
Blurred vision
Diplopia
Difficulty in urination
Constipation
Nasal stuffiness
Vertigo
Palpitation
Headache
Insomnia
Tightness of the chest and wheezing
Thickening of bronchial secretions
Dryness of mouth, nose, and throat
Urticaria
Drug rash
Photosensitivity
Hemolytic anemia
Hypotension
Epigastric distress
Anaphylactic shock
Tingling, heaviness, and weakness of hands

after the cessation of treatment. They are not particularly helped by anti-parkinsonian medication; indeed, such treatment aggravates them. Reserpine-like drugs may produce a beneficial effect. Drugs that raise brain acetylcholine—physostigmine, choline, lecithin—may help it. Caution is required in interpreting results, since many patients spontaneously recover when neuroleptics are discontinued after a transient worsening. If a drug was given, the spontaneous improvement may be falsely attributed to the drug. See Table VI for a simple method to determine tardive dyskinesia symptoms.

### Exhaustion and Hyperthermia

Since first reported in 1832, a syndrome known as lethal (or fatal, mortal, or pernicious) catatonia, delirious state, hypertoxic schizophrenia, or exhaustion syndrome is characterized by extreme excitement or catatonia stupor or both, with an elevated temperature, such as 108°F. Such a hyperthermia can quickly progress to death. The violent, hyperagitated state can progress to an exhaustion death in 1½ to 14 days unless effective treatment is given. Electroconvulsive therapy is recommended. The cause of the state is unknown. Since patients are invariably treated with chemotherapy, drugs have been falsely implicated without evidence of a causal connection. The fact that the syndrome occurred before 1952 makes it likely that it is not caused by drug treatment, but rather by a viral or unknown cause.

### Other Central Nervous System Effects

Most of the antipsychotic compounds lower the threshold of seizures in animals. Seizures do occur in humans treated with high doses of antipsychotic compounds, but only rarely. The question therefore arises as to whether phenothiazines are contraindicated in patients with seizure disorders and psychoses. This is important, since schizophrenics frequently show evidence of psychomotor epilepsy or of grand mal epilepsy. In the absence of controlled data, one is left with the clinical opinion that patients with epilepsy generally show an improvement, both of their behavioral disorder and of their seizure disorder, with antipsychotic drug treatment. When seizures do occur, they generally occur with high doses of the drug—that is, they are dose-related—and consist of a single isolated seizure. One can often treat the patient with a slightly lower dose of the drug. On occasion, one can add an anticonvulsant, such as phenytoin (Dilantin) to the treatment regimen and continue antipsychotic drugs with no seizures even at higher doses.

The antipsychotic agents on occasion produce sedation, particularly during the first few days. Patients rapidly develop tolerance to the sedative properties. In addition, the various antipsychotic agents differ in the amount of sedation they produce. Of the phenothiazines, chlorpromazine and thioridazine produce more sedation than fluphenazine, haloperidol, thiothixene, and trifluoperazine. The drowsiness most frequently occurs in the first few days or weeks of treatment. Patients should be warned about driving or operating machinery, although, in general, the drowsiness is not troublesome, since tolerance often develops. Drowsiness can be controlled by reducing the dose, switching to a less sedating antipsychotic, or giving the whole daily dose at bedtime. Antipsychotic drugs, when given to normal persons, may produce sedation that can interfere with mental functioning to a slight degree. However, in the studies of psychotic patients, mental functioning improves because there is an improvement in the underlying schizophrenia.

### Behavioral Toxicity

The term behavioral toxicity has been applied to adverse behavioral change produced by a psychotropic drug. It is often difficult to evaluate such a change in seriously ill schizophrenic patients, since it would be necessary to clearly separate non-drug-related worsening of the schizophrenic state from drug-induced toxicity. Symptoms such as insomnia, bizarre dreams, impaired psychomotor activity, aggravation of schizophrenic symptoms, toxic confusional states, and somnambulism do occur in patients undergoing treatment with psychotropic drugs. Akathisia or an apparent worsening of psychosis, which is thought to be an ideational analogue of extrapyramidal disorder, can be reversed in minutes by intramuscular antiparkinson agents. Some of these effects may be dose related and can be lessened by an alteration in the dose, the addition or depletion of antiparkinsonian drugs, or the use of a different type of antipsychotic agent. Often, treatment requires clinical judgment and flexibility. Some of the confusional states may be related to the anticholinergic properties of the drugs. In addition, patients differ in their rate of metabolism of a specific drug, and slow metabolizers may build up psychotoxic levels of drugs or metabolites.

### Antipsychotic Withdrawal

The antipsychotic drugs do not produce withdrawal symptoms of the barbiturate or opioid type. Patients generally dislike taking neurolep-

TABLE VI
AIMS* EXAMINATION PROCEDURE

---

Patient Identification                              Date

---

Rated by

---

Either before or after completing the examination procedure, observe the patient unobtrusively at rest (eg, in waiting room).

The chair to be used in this examination should be a hard, firm one without arms.

After observing the patient, he may be rated on a scale of 0 (none), 1 (minimal), 2 (mild), 3 (moderate) and 4 (severe) according to the severity of symptoms.

Ask the patient whether there is anything in his/her mouth (ie, gum, candy, etc) and if there is to remove it.

Ask patient about the *current* condition of his/her teeth. Ask patient if he/she wears dentures. Do teeth or dentures bother patient *now?*

Ask patient whether he/she notices any movement in mouth, face, hands or feet. If yes, ask to describe and to what extent they *currently* bother patient or interfere with his/her activities.

| 0 | 1 | 2 | 3 | 4 | Have patient sit in chair with hands on knees, legs slightly apart and feet flat on floor. (Look at entire body for movements while in this position.) |

| 0 | 1 | 2 | 3 | 4 | Ask patient to sit with hands hanging unsupported. If male, between legs, if female and wearing a dress, hanging over knees. (Observe hands and other body areas.) |

| 0 | 1 | 2 | 3 | 4 | Ask patient to open mouth. (Observe tongue at rest within mouth.) Do this twice. |

| 0 | 1 | 2 | 3 | 4 | Ask patient to protrude tongue. (Observe abnormalities of tongue movement.) Do this twice. |

| 0 | 1 | 2 | 3 | 4 | Ask the patient to tap thumb, with each finger, as rapidly as possible for 10–15 seconds; separately with right hand, then with left hand. (Observe facial and leg movements.) |

| 0 | 1 | 2 | 3 | 4 | Flex and extend patient's left and right arms. (One at a time) |

| 0 | 1 | 2 | 3 | 4 | Ask patient to stand up. (Observe in profile. Observe all body areas again, hips included.) |

| 0 | 1 | 2 | 3 | 4 | †Ask patient to extend both arms outstretched in front with palms down. (Observe trunk, legs and mouth.) |

| 0 | 1 | 2 | 3 | 4 | †Have patient walk a few paces, turn and walk back to chair. (Observe hands and gait.) Do this twice. |

*Abnormal Involuntary Movement Scale    † Activated movements tics and do not spontaneously increase the dose and frequently discontinue them without medical advice. Abrupt discontinuance of neuroleptics is associated with its own withdrawal syndrome, which is qualitatively different from that produced by narcotics or barbiturates. It occurs 2 to 7 days after withdrawal and consists of nausea and vomiting, increased sweating, feelings of hot and cold, insomnia, irritation, and headache. Symptoms are generally mild. Patients generally have one or two of such symptoms; rarely do patients develop all of them simultaneously.

### Allergic Reactions

The jaundice induced by chlorpromazine used to be one of the striking side effects of the drug. In the early days of chlorpromazine treatment, the side effect was not unusual, occurring in about one out of every 100 patients treated. More recently, for some unexplained reason, the incidence of chlorpromazine jaundice has dropped considerably; although accurate data are lacking, the incidence is probably in the range of 1 out of every 1,000 patients treated. The jaundice most often occurs 1 to 5 weeks after the initiation of phenothiazine therapy. It is generally preceded, for 1 to 7 days, by a flu-like syndrome, including malaise, abdominal pain, fever, nausea, vomiting, and diarrhea, resembling mild gastroenteritis or infectious hepatitis. Clinical factors that may point toward a diagnosis of a phenothiazine-induced jaundice are the temporal association of the jaundice with the beginning of the phenothiazine therapy, the lack of an enlarged or tender liver, and chemical evidence of choleostasis, such as an increase in direct relation to indirect bilirubin, increased alkaline phosphatase, and a reduction of esterified cholesterol. The aminotransferases are only moderately increased, but often these increases are less impressive than those of the bilirubin and alkaline phosphatase. Peripheral blood smears demonstrate eosinophilia, and liver biopsy shows bile plugs in the canaliculi, with eosinophilic infiltration in the periportal space. The jaundice generally disappears within several weeks. Most cases of chlorpromazine jaundice are benign, and a complete return to normal liver function occurs. Plasma bilirubins generally are only moderately elevated. Occasionally, the much longer-lasting exanthematous biliary cirrhosis can occur, but it is very rare. When it occurs, it eventually clears but often has a chronic course of 6 months to a year. Chlorpromazine jaundice may be, in a broad sense, an allergic phenomenon. Evidence for that hypothesis is its onset in the first few days and weeks

of treatment, its frequent association with other allergic reactions, its association with peripheral eosinophilia and eosinophilic infiltrations in the liver, and the prolonged retention of sensitivity on the challenge test. Patients have developed a second chlorpromazine jaundice as long as 10 years after the first. The significance of the secretion of chlorpromazine by the liver is unclear.

Jaundice has also been reported with promazine, thioridazine, mepazine, and prochlorperazine and vary rarely with fluphenazine and triflupromazine. No convincing evidence indicates that haloperidol or many of the other nonphenothiazine antipsychotics can produce a chlorpromazine-type jaundice. The majority of cases of phenothiazine-induced jaundice reported in the medical literature have occurred with chlorpromazine.

It is occasionally useful to have baseline liver function tests on patients in the unlikely event that they do later develop chlorpromazine jaundice. However, weekly or biweekly liver function tests on a routine basis have never been proven to be useful or necessary.

It is considered good practice to discontinue chlorpromazine if patients develop chlorpromazine jaundice, although the value of this practice has never been proved. Indeed, patients have been maintained on chlorpromazine throughout the illness without adverse effects.

### Agranulocytosis

Agranulocytosis is probably the most serious side effect observed with phenothiazines, but fortunately it is quite rare. It generally occurs within the first 6 to 8 weeks of phenothiazine treatment, its onset being abrupt and consisting of the sudden appearance of sore throat, ulcerations, and fever. When it occurs, the mortality rate is generally high, often 30 percent or more. Phenothiazine medication should be immediately discontinued, and the patient should be transferred to a medical facility for reverse isolation procedure. Energetic treatment of the infection is indicated, although prophylactic antibiotic therapy may not necessarily be indicated because of the danger of propagation of drug-resistant organisms. It is said that the adrenal corticosteroids do not hasten recovery. Cross-sensitivity to other phenothiazines may occur, but hard data are lacking. The incidence of agranulocytosis is said to be low, probably about 1 out of 500,000 patients, but no accurate data exist. On a few occasions, it occurs with promazine, prochlorperazine, mepazine, and thioridazine, although it may occur with almost any phenothiazine.

Phenothiazine-induced agranulocytosis usually occurs in older female patients with other complicating systemic diseases, and it is considerably rarer in young, healthy patients. The value of routine complete blood counts in picking up agranulocytosis is questionable. A baseline count is helpful in evaluating the situation when fever and sore throat occur later, but the agranulocytosis develops so rapidly that daily blood counts would be necessary to pick up an extraordinary rare complication; therefore, they do not appear to be efficacious.

Thrombocytopenic or nonthrombocytopenic purpura, hemolytic anemias, and pancytopenia may also occur occasionally with patients treated with a phenothiazine. Such side effects may be controlled by stopping the drug or by switching to another medication.

Chlorpromazine and other phenothiazines frequently but temporarily reduce the white count by 40 to 80 percent from the normal count. Such a reduction is a different hematological phenomenon from that of agranulocytosis. It is a benign phenomenon, needing neither any special treatment nor a discontinuation of therapy.

### Skin and Eye Effects

A variety of skin eruptions—including urticarial, maculopapular, petechial, and edematous eruptions—have been associated with phenothiazine treatment. These eruptions occur early in treatment, generally in the first few weeks. A contact dermatitis can also occur in personnel who handle chlorpromazine.

A photosensitivity reaction of the phototoxic type that resembles severe sunburn can occur in patients receiving chlorpromazine. When appropriate, patients should be warned of this side effect. Treatment consists of avoidance of sunlight; a sun screen lotion may be helpful.

In the first few years of the chlorpromazine era, phenothiazines were thought to be entirely safe for long-term, high-dose usage; however, patients in whom treatment was initiated 15 years ago are now being seen, so it is now possible for any long-term side effects to be observed.

One such effect consists of a blue-gray metallic discoloration of the skin over areas exposed to sunlight, such as the face, the open neck, and the dorsum of the hands. The skin changes often begin with a tan or golden brown color and progress to such colors as slate gray, metallic blue or purple, or even a marked purple color. Histological examinations of the skin biopsies reveal pigmentary granules that are similar but not histochemically identical to melanin.

In addition, eye changes have been noticed after long-term high-dose chlorpromazine treatment. These changes have been described as whitish brown, granular deposits concentrated in the anterior lens and posterior cornea, visible only by slit-lens examination. They progress to opaque white and yellow-brown granules, often stellate in shape. Occasionally, the conjunctiva is discolored by a brown pigment. These lens changes are quite different from those of senile cataracts, and are in no way related to them.

Statistically, these opacities occur more frequently in patients with skin discoloration than in other patients. Retinal damage is not seen in these patients, and vision is almost never impaired. The occurrence and the severity of the opacities are related to the duration and the total dose of chlorpromazine. The majority of patients who show the deposits are those who ingested 1 to 3 kg of chlorpromazine throughout the therapeutic course. Hospitals differ in their reported prevalence of the skin and eye effects, with estimates varying from less than 1 percent to more than 30 percent.

Sunlight plays a role in both the skin effects and the eye effects; part of the difference between hospitals may relate to the differential exposure of patients to the sun. It has been thought that the condition can be treated by removing the patient from the sun and switching from chlorpromazine to a maximally different antipsychotic.

Thioridazine, in doses about 1600 mg a day, can cause pigmentary retinopathy with consequent visual impairment or even blindness. The condition is sometimes said not to remit when the drug is stopped—or, at least, not to remit fully. Doses of thioridazine of more than 800 mg a day are, therefore, to be assiduously avoided.

### Endocrine Effects

There is extensive basic research literature on the effects of large doses of antipsychotic agents on a wide variety of endocrine systems in obscure species. In practical terms, the clinically important effects are lactation and impotence; the impotence is presumably autonomic in origin. Glucose tolerance curves may also be shifted in a diabetic direction by these drugs, and false-positive pregnancy tests have been reported.

The effect of these drugs in producing breast engorgement and lactation in female patients is well known, although incidence figures are lacking. If every patient were checked for lactation with manual pressure on the breast, an incidence of 20 to 40 percent might be found. Subjective complaints of overt lactation are quite rare—less than 5 percent—and are often adequately handled by dose reduction or by shifting the patient to another drug. Drug-related gyneco-mastia in male patients has also been described.

Clinical studies show small and inconsistent effects of these drugs on other sex hormones and adrenocortical, thyroid, and pituitary hormones. The marked weight gain sometimes associated with phenothiazine treatment has not been explained on any endocrine basis. Molindone does not cause weight gain.

Sexual impotence—beginning with delayed ejaculation, progressing to orgasm without ejaculation, and ultimately ending in a loss of erectile ability—can occur with antipsychotic agents. The area of drug-induced impotence is one in which the psychiatrist may miss a disturbing drug side effect because the patient is too embarrassed to speak of it.

**REFERENCES**

Caffey E M, Diamond L S, Frank T V, Grasberger J C, Herman L, Klett C J, Rothstein D: Discontinuation of reduction of chemotherapy in chronic schizophrenics. J Chronic Dis *17:* 347, 1964.
Cole J O, Goldberg S C, Davis J M: Drugs in the treatment of psychosis: Controlled studies. In *Psychiatric Drugs*, P Solomon, editor. Grune & Stratton, New York, 1966.
Cole J O, Goldberg S C, Klerman G L: Phenothiazine treatment in acute schizophrenia. Arch Gen Psychiatry *10:* 246, 1964.
Greenblatt M, Solomon M H, Evans A S, Brooks G W, editors: *Drug and Social Therapy in Chronic Schizophrenia.* Charles C Thomas, Springfield, IL, 1965.
Hanlon T E , Schoenrich C, Frank W, Turek I, Kurland A A: Perphenazine benzotropine mesylate treatment of newly admitted psychiatric patients. Psychopharmacologia *9:* 328, 1966.
Hogarty G E, Goldberg S C, Scholer N R, Ulrich R F: Drugs and sociotherapy in the aftercare of schizophrenic patients. Arch Gen Psychiatry *31:* 603, 1964.
Hurt S W, Holzman P S, Davis J M: Thought disorder. Arch Gen Psychiatry *40:* 1281, 1983.
May P R: *Treatment of Schizophrenia.* Science House, New York, 1968.
May P R A, Tuma A H, Yale C, Potepan P, Dixon W J: Schizophrenia: A follow-up study of results of treatment. II. Hospital stay over two to five years. Arch Gen Psychiatry *31:* 481, 1976.
May P R A, Tuma A H, Dixon W J: Schizophrenia: A follow-up study of the results of five forms of treatment. Arch Gen Psychiatry *38:* 776–784, 1981.
Spohn H E, Lacousiere P, Thompson K, Coyne L: Phenothiazine effects on psychological and psychophysiological dysfunction in chronic schizophrenics. Arch Gen Psychiatry *34:* 633, 1977.
Stancer H C, Garfinkel P E, Rakoff V M, editors: *Guidelines for the use of Psychotropic Drugs: A Clinical Handbook.* SP Medical and Scientific Books, New York, 1984.

# 27.2  ANTIDEPRESSANT DRUGS

## Introduction

In the late 1950s, two classes of drugs were discovered that proved effective in the treatment of depression—the imipramine-type drugs (tricyclic antidepressants) and the monoamine oxidase inhibitors (MAOI). More recently newer compounds have been developed, which are called heterocyclic antidepressants and which include tricyclics. Their use doubles the chances that a depressed patient will recover within 1 month.

## Pharmacological Activity

The antidepressant drugs do not markedly influence the normal organism in a baseline state but, rather, correct an abnormal condition. The imipramine-type drugs and the MAOI are antidepressants, not necessarily general euphoriants or stimulants. In contrast, amphetamine is a euphoriant and a stimulant, but it is not an antidepressant in the precise sense of the word.

## Tricyclic Drugs

The tricyclic antidepressants—imipramine, amitriptyline, desipramine, nortriptyline, protriptyline—are structurally similar to the phenothiazines, the sulfur atom in the phenothiazine molecule having been replaced by a dimethyl bridge. This similarity emphasizes the importance of minor structural changes in the production of critical differences in pharmacological activity. The drugs all appear to be active antidepressants. Other drugs of this class that are slightly different in structure—such as chlorimipramine, doxepin, trimipramine, and opipramol—also appear to have considerable antidepressant activity. The tricyclic antidepressants are readily absorbed from the gastrointestinal tract. In human beings, imipramine, amitriptyline, and chlorimipramine are partially metabolized to their respective desmethyl derivatives—desmethylimipramine, desipramine, nortriptyline, etc. The great majority of the tricyclic and tricyclic-type drugs work by blocking the reuptake of norepinephrine (NE) or serotonin (5-hydroxytryptamine, 5HT) at the receptor site. A list of the various antidepressant drugs is given in Table I. The mechanism of action for each drug is discussed below.

### Clinical Effects

In normal persons, imipramine and amitriptyline produce slight sedation. However, in se-

TABLE I
ANTIDEPRESSANT DRUGS AND THEIR APPROXIMATE EFFECTIVE DOSE RANGES

| Generic Name | Trade Name | Effective Dose Range (mg/day) | Commercially Available Drug Forms |
|---|---|---|---|
| *Tricyclic drugs* | | | |
| Imipramine | Antipress, Imavate, Janimine, Presamine, SK-Pramine, Tofranil | 150–300 | 10, 25, 50 mg tablets; 75, 100, 125, 150 capsules (Tofranil-PM); 25 mg/2 ml (IM) |
| Amitriptyline | Amitril, Elavil, Endep, SK-Amitriptyline | 150–250 | 10, 25, 50, 75, 100, 150 mg tablets; 10 mg/ml (IM) |
| Desipramine | Norpramin | 75–200 | 25, 50, 75, 100, 150 mg tablets |
| | Pertofrane | | 25, 50 mg capsules |
| Nortriptyline | Aventyl, Pamelor | 30–100 | 10, 25, mg tablets; 10 mg/5 ml (IM) |
| Protriptyline | Vivactil | 15–40 | 5, 10 mg tablets |
| Doxepin | Adapin, Sinequan | 75–300 | 10, 25, 50, 75, 100, 150 mg tablets; 10 mg/ml (IM) |
| *Tricyclic-type drugs* | | | |
| Trimipramine | Surmontil | 75–300 | 25, 50 mg tablets |
| Maprotiline | Ludiomil | 75–150 | 25, 50 mg tablets |
| Amoxapine | Asendin | 50–300 | 50, 100, 150 mg tablets |
| *MAO inhibitors* | | | |
| Tranylcypromine | Parnate | 20–60 | 10 mg tablets |
| Isocarboxazid | Marplan | 20–60 | 10 mg tablets |
| Phenelzine | Nardil | 60–90 | 15 mg tablets |
| Pargyline | Eutonyl | 25–75 | 10, 25 mg tablets |

verely depressed psychotic patients, they produce a striking improvement in behavior and a marked lessening of depression, generally 3 to 10 days after the onset of treatment. Consequently, patients who do not respond after receiving an adequate dose of the drugs for a 3-week period probably will not respond at all. Furthermore, the degree of response in the first 3 weeks of treatment predicts the ultimate therapeutic response: 65 to 80 percent of the depressed patients are substantially benefited by tricyclic antidepressants, in contrast to 30 to 35 percent who are helped by a placebo in the same time period. When examined from the patient's point of view, the patient's chance of recovering after 3 or 4 weeks of treatment is doubled if he receives the tricyclic drugs, instead of a placebo.

## Tricyclic Antidepressant Agents

*Imipramine.* A great number of double-blind studies have shown imipramine to be more effective than a placebo. The statistics indicate that most of the studies presented demonstrate the therapeutic effectiveness of imipramine. The fact that all studies showed a greater improvement produced by imipramine offers proof that there is only an infinitesimal statistical probability that chance alone could explain those results. About 30 percent of the depressive pa-

tients remained unimproved, a fact that certainly indicates the need for improvement in treatment methods. Imipramine inhibits the reuptake of 5HT, but its desmethyl metabolite, desipramine, is a major metabolite in man and inhibits the uptake of NE. Consequently, imipramine is active in both the aminergic systems.

*Amitriptyline and Other Tricyclics.* Most studies that have compared amitriptyline with imipramine have found the drugs to be about equally effective. No studies have shown amitriptyline to be less effective than imipramine.

The desmethyl derivatives of imipramine and amitriptyline—desipramine and nortriptyline—are similar in many pharmacological parameters to their parent compounds, but appear to be more stimulating and may aggravate anxiety and tension.

On the basis of drug-placebo and drug-imipramine comparisons, desipramine and nortriptyline are about comparable to imipramine in efficacy.

Protriptyline is an imipramine-type drug that has been shown to be roughly equivalent to imipramine in outpatient populations, although it is more potent on a milligram-per-kilogram basis. Protriptyline has an unnaturally long half-life, approximately 54 to 124 hours after a single oral 30 mg dose.

These drugs act in a similar fashion to imipramine by both inhibiting the reuptake of 5HT and the uptake of NE.

### Other Antidepressants

*Doxepin.* Doxepin has been found to be superior to a placebo and about equal to tricyclic antidepressants in the treatment of depressed patients. There is also clear evidence of doxepin's usefulness in outpatient anxiety. Doxepin bears a structural resemblance to the tricyclic antidepressants and inhibits the membrane pump for biogenic amines, consequently interfering with the antihypertensive actions of guanethidine. For mixed outpatient anxiety-depression, typical doses of doxepin consist of 100 to 300 mg a day.

*Amoxapine.* Amoxapine is a dibenzoxazepine derivative that is both an NE and 5HT reuptake inhibitor. It has been found to be efficacious in a number of double-blind studies comparing it to standard antidepressants. Amoxapine has a chemical structure similar to that of the antipsychotic agent loxapine, and has effects similar to those of neuroleptics in that it produces dopamine blockade, extrapyramidal side effects, elevated prolactin, transitory suppression of avoidance reaction, and inhibition of stereotyped behavior induced by amphetamines.

*Trazodone* represents a new class of antidepressants that selectively inhibit serotonin reuptake. It also produces a down-regulation of NE receptor sites. Down-regulation can be defined as a receptor subsensitivity to NE, generally a reduction in the density of beta-adrenergic receptors. Though the mechanism of action which produced down-regulation has not been elucidated, down-regulation may be an indication of a functional increase in NE available at the receptor site, and this action would, therefore, be consistent with the NE and 5HT hypotheses. Unlike the standard antidepressants, it has no anticholinergic side effects, though infrequently reported side effects include lethargy, nausea, and headache.

*Trimipramine.* Trimipramine is similar to amitriptyline in its properties.

*Chlorimipramine* has been used in Europe, Canada, and England for a number of years. Chlorimipramine blocks serotonin reuptake in vitro and is metabolized to desmethylchlorimipramine, which blocks the reuptake of norepinephrine. An interesting trend in five placebo-controlled studies of chlorimipramine is that chlorimipramine appears to have an antiobsessive effect.

*Maprotiline.* Maprotiline is exactly equal to imipramine in overall therapeutic effectiveness, and equal to amitriptyline in overall therapeutic efficacy. Maprotiline is a specific norepinephrine reuptake inhibitor.

*Mianserin* is a tetracyclic compound which has some interesting properties. It does not inhibit the uptake of NE, 5HT, or dopamine, nor is it a monoamine oxidase inhibitor. Mianserin appears to act through a presynaptic mechanism to increase norepinephrine turnover. Thus, mianserin is consistent with the norepinephrine theory, even though its mechanism of action is quite different from those of the standard antidepressants.

*Bupropion* has been well studied and has been shown to be an effective antidepressant. It is neither a tricyclic nor an MAOI and has demonstrated none of the anticholinergic, cardiovascular, or sedative side effects common to those agents. It has been found to exert little or no inhibition of the reuptake of serotonin or norepinephrine; however, in rodents, high doses of the drug will produce a significant reduction of noradrenergic $\beta$-receptor density; that is, there is a down-regulation of the noradrenergic receptor sites. Unlike the vast majority of psychotropic drugs, bupropion is nonsedative. This is very important to a patient who values optimal mental functions. It is not a stimulant or euphogenic drug in that it is not self-administered, using the paradigm in which amphetamine-like drugs are self-administered. It is not cardiotoxic and is safe in the overdose situation. It does not cause weight gain. It is not a dysphoric drug and has minimal anticholinergic side effects.

## Clinical Use of Tricyclics

The tricyclic-type drugs are the most effective class of antidepressants. They pose a smaller risk of side effects than the MAOI and are probably the drugs of choice for most depressed patients. First, the patient's psychiatric and medical status is assessed. If the patient is extremely depressed or suicidal, the physician may move rapidly to a higher dosage or use electroconvulsive therapy. If the patient has preexisting cardiovascular disease, a more cautious approach consisting of a lower initial dosage and a less rapid increase is used. Under ordinary circumstances, one starts with a modest dosage, such as 25 to 50 mg of imipramine or amitriptyline two to three times a day; if the dosage is well tolerated, one moves to 150 mg per day within several days. After 1 week, the dose is adjusted up to 200 mg a day or, in some patients, up to 250 mg a day. Occasional patients will need a higher dosage. The systematic recording of the baseline pulse and the postural hypotension with lying and standing blood pressure and the monitoring of therapeutic results and side effects can be helpful in determining dosage adjustments. Initially, twice a day dosing with two-thirds of the dose given at bedtime is recommended; later, once a day dosing is more convenient, proves as satisfactory as dosing two times a day, and is easier for the patient to remember. Once a day dosing produces peak side effects when the patient is asleep; three times a day dosage can be used if toxicity at peak plasma levels is of particular concern. Dosage is reduced by 25 to 50 percent for maintenance treatment—for example, 100 to 150 mg of imipramine; here again, the entire dose can be given at bedtime. Because of the sedative effects of amitriptyline or trazadone, adequate sleep is frequently induced without the necessity of giving a sleeping medication. It is not advisable to administer the less sedating drugs (e.g., protriptyline) any later than 4 hours before bedtime.

### Selection of Patients

Clinical characteristics associated with a good drug response are those indicative of endogenous depression—depression different in quality from normal states of sadness and characterized by feelings of severe guilt and unworthiness, severe psychomotor retardation or agitation, and symptoms such as early morning awakening and weight loss. Patients with neurotic depression whose premorbid personalities showed hysterical, irritable, and hypochondriacal features, along with self-pity, do not demonstrate a clearcut favorable response. Retarded patients tend to do well with tricyclic drugs. Delusional patients do not do well generally on imipramine alone but do respond to electroconvulsive therapy. Although some depressive patients with delusions do respond to imipramine, a fair degree of evidence indicates that some delusional depressives may be less responsive to imipramine than are nondelusional depressives. If the clinician or patient does not want to use ECT, antipsychotic drugs plus tricyclics are helpful in delusional depressives. One should note, however, that 50 percent of nonresponders to tricyclics do recover with electroconvulsive therapy.

### Role of Psychotherapy

Several research studies have shown that both tricyclics and psychotherapy have a greater antidepressant effect than psychotherapy alone. However, both treatments together have greater efficacy than either treatment by itself. The two treatments augment each other and do not interfere with each other.

Much clinical opinion favors psychological interventions to help depressed patients, and certainly those patients who can benefit from psychotherapy should not be neglected. The beneficial effects of drugs are apparent in almost all studies, however, thus providing substantial evidence for their efficacy. The weight of the evidence is such that the clinician should not neglect physical treatment for depression.

### Maintenance Medication

After patients have responded to tricyclic drugs, the next therapeutic decision that faces the clinician is when to discontinue the medication. Since depression is frequently a recurrent disorder, one may wonder whether continued treatment with tricyclic drugs will prevent a relapse.

No data are as yet available for the prediction of which patients required tricyclic drugs to prevent a relapse, except that patients with incomplete remissions are reported to relapse more regularly than patients with complete remissions. When the data from various studies are combined, there is little question that maintenance tricyclics can successfully prevent relapse.

In patients who have a history of multiple relapses, maintenance tricyclics should be considered to prevent their recurrence. Some patients experience only one depressive episode and never have another; obviously, maintenance tricyclics are not indicated in such cases. The decision for prophylaxis should be made on a clinical basis, taking into account the severity of the depressions, the frequency of the depressions, and the risk of suicide. Maintenance lithium is also able to prevent relapses in recurrent unipolar depression.

### Plasma Levels and Therapeutic Window

At least 70 percent of depressed patients are helped by antidepressant drugs. Undoubtedly, some of the patients who are not helped are suffering from a form of depression unresponsive to this class of drugs. However, other patients perhaps do not respond for pharmacological reasons.

There are, for example, wide individual differences in blood level between patients. As the tricyclic drugs are administered, blood levels build up until they reach a fairly constant level in about 2 weeks. From a pharmacological point of view, a lack of response perhaps may be explained by an abnormality in the rate of metabolism of the tricyclic drug. Some patients may metabolize the drug rapidly, fail to build up the blood level adequately, and, hence, have low brain levels and fail to respond. Other patients may have a defect in metabolism; therefore, high plasma levels and high brain levels may accumulate. These patients may have side effects, or fail to improve clinically either because they are receiving toxic doses, or because the drug is less effective at high levels than at low levels. There are, thus, two possible reasons for nonresponse. The pharmacokinetics, uptake and biotransformation of antidepressant drugs should be taken into account in evaluating a particular drugs' therapeutic effect.

The therapeutic window is defined as the lower and upper limit blood level of a drug in which therapeutic effects are observed.

It is expected that there is a lower limit to the therapeutic window with virtually all drugs. That is, if a sufficiently low dose is given, an insufficient quantity of the drug reaches its receptor site to produce a therapeutic response.

Imipramine and amitriptyline have been studied, but there do not appear to be associated curvilinear therapeutic windows.

Neuroleptic medication, as well as methylphenidate, may inhibit the metabolism of tricyclics. Barbiturates speed up metabolism and lower plasma levels. Clinically, many physicians believe that various patients respond to different doses of tricyclics. The available plasma level data indicate that there are wide variations in the rate of metabolism of the drug; this finding is consistent with clinical observations. At this point, a fair degree of evidence suggests that the clinician should make an effort to find the best tricyclic dose for a given patient. At the present time, this effort has to be done purely on a clinical basis.

### Side Effects

Two important properties of the tricyclic antidepressants are (1) their ability to inhibit the reuptake of released norepinephrine, thus potentiating noradrenergic function (norepinephrine remains at the receptor site for a longer period of time because its action is not terminated by the reuptake pump), and (2) anticholinergic blockage, an atropine-like action. Both properties may play roles in producing many of the autonomic side effects. The blockage of the reuptake pump is important in explaining a drug-drug interaction between guanethidine-type drugs and tricyclic antidepressants. The guanethidine-type antihypertensive medication is also pumped up into the peripheral noradrenergic neuron by the membrane pump, and is thereby concentrated in the noradrenergic nerve, where it exerts its hypotensive effect. When the pump is blocked, the uptake of the hypertensive agent, guanethidine, is also

blocked; hence, it cannot get into the neuron where it acts. Therefore, treatment with tricyclic antidepressants, including doxepin, interferes with the therapeutic effects of guanethidine-type and clonidine antihypertensive agents. Phenothiazines also inhibit the membrane uptake pump, and interfere with the antihypertensive effect of guanethidine. When treating depressed patients who suffer from hypertension, these factors should be considered and a careful history obtained.

The tricyclic antidepressants can cause the typical autonomic effects expected as a result of their anticholinergic pharmacological properties—dry mouth, palpitations, tachycardia, loss of accommodation, postural hypotension, fainting, dizziness, vomiting, constipation, edema, and aggravation of narrow angle glaucoma. In rare instances, urinary retention and paralytic ileus have also been observed, and can lead to serious or even fatal complications, particularly if the tricyclic drug has been combined with other drugs with similar anticholinergic effects—for example, a phenothiazine plus an antiparkinsonian drug. Other rare side effects include galactorrhea and profuse sweating. In general, dry mouth is the most notable of the autonomic side effects, and patients should be alerted to its possible occurrence. Falls with broken bones do occur. Common sense precautions are important. Hypotension is not usually a problem, but, in those instances in which it may be troublesome, some physicians advise the use of fluorohydrocortisone (0.025 to 0.05 mg twice a day). The autonomic side effects are, on the whole, very mild, and tend to become less bothersome after the first few weeks of treatment; in any event, they can be controlled by adjusting the dosage of the drug.

Dental caries have been reported in patients receiving anticholinergics when, as a consequence of dry mouth, they ingest hard candy or soda pop. Fluoride lozenges may prove preferable for dry mouth. Bethanechol has been recommended for the treatment of anticholinergic side effects such as urinary retention, although tolerance to it may eventually develop.

The tricyclic drugs differ in their anticholinergic properties. In the case of a patient who has had difficulty with anticholinergic effects—such as urinary retention and constipation—the clinician may wish to consider a tricyclic with the fewest anticholinergic properties. Amitriptyline has the strongest anticholinergic properties, doxepin is intermediate in this respect, and desipramine has the weakest anticholinergic properties. There are techniques for measuring the binding of atropine-like agents to the muscarinic receptor of the brain, the intestine, or other tissue. It is not known to what degree the in vitro preparations correlate with what actually happens in humans. Desipramine is probably slightly less potent in humans on a milligram basis than is amitriptyline. In view of the percentage difference in anticholinergic effects at a given dose and the relative clinical potencies, it is reasonable to conclude that desimipramine has some, but fewer, anticholinergic properties than does amitriptyline. Similarly, doxepin has more anticholinergic properties than does desipramine. Anticholinergic properties should not be confused with cardiac properties. It is true that atropine-like drugs can cause tachycardia. However, the lethal dose of atropine is very high, and atropine is a very safe drug. The more dangerous cardiac properties of the tricyclics are their direct myocardial depressant qualities and quinidine-like characteristics, such as slowing conduction. The safety of the different tricyclics for the heart remains to be determined. Profuse sweating, especially at night, can occur.

**Allergic and Hypersensitivity Effects.** Skin reactions may occur early in therapy, but often subside with reduced dosage. Jaundice, which can occur early, is of the cholestatic type, similar to that attributed to chlorpromazine. Agranulocytosis is a rare complication. Rare cases of leukocytosis, leukopenia, and eosinophilia have also been observed.

**Cardiovascular Effects.** When administered in their usual therapeutic doses, the tricyclic drugs may cause tachycardia, flattened T-waves, prolonged Q-T intervals, and depressed S-T segments in the electrocardiogram. Imipramine has been shown to have a quinidine-like effect at therapeutic plasma levels and, indeed, may reduce the number of premature ventricular contractions. Since these drugs prolong conduction, their use in patients with preexisting conduction defects is relatively contraindicated. The clinician must remain alert to the possibility of impaired conduction. At high plasma levels, the drugs become arrhythmogenic.

Cardiovascular incidents have occurred in patients with preexisting heart disease. However, it is sometimes difficult to separate a side effect causally related to a drug from a cardiovascular incident precipitated by other factors but, by chance, coincident with drug therapy. In predisposed patients, tricyclic drugs should be initiated at low doses, with a gradual dose increment and careful monitoring of cardiac function.

**Central Nervous System Effects.** All the tricyclic drugs produce side effects that are roughly similar, although there are slight quantitative differences—for example, amitriptyline is said to be more sedating and protriptyline less sedating than imipramine. The drugs may cause a persistent, fine, rapid tremor, particularly in the upper extremities, but also in the tongue. The tremor is similar to essential tremor. Twitching, convulsions, dysarthria, paresthesia, peroneal palsies, and ataxia may occur in rare instances. Disturbances of motor functions are rare, but are most likely to occur in elderly patients. Insomnia has also been noted among elderly patients on occasion, but it is transitory and responds well to nightly sedation. From time to time, both amitriptyline and imipramine may cause episodes of schizophrenic excitement, confusion, or mania. Such episodes usually occur in patients with a predisposition to schizophrenia, chronic brain syndrome, or bipolar manic-depressive disorder, rather than neuroses, which suggests that a preexisting substratum of disease must be present for the drug to exert its psychotomimetic properties. Such symptoms usually subside 1 to 2 days after withdrawal of the drug.

It is important to differentiate which type of central nervous toxicity is present, since their treatments may differ. Atropine-like psychosis, the so called central anticholinergic syndrome, produces a characteristic symptom profile of florid visual hallucinations (such as hallucinations of bugs or colors), loss of immediate memory, confusion, and disorientation. Evidence that the syndrome, when observed after the administration of tricyclics, is the central anticholinergic syndrome is indicated by its emergence as the typical symptom picture and, most important, the fact that empirically it is reversible by the administration of physostigmine, an agent that increases brain acetylcholine and pharmacologically overcomes the atropine blockade. Generally, the usual clinical treatment is the discontinuance of anticholinergics, causing the syndrome to subside within a day. In selected cases, physostigmine can be used to produce this dramatic reversal. However, an error in diagnosis, or the use of too much physostigmine, may produce cholinergic toxicity. The conservative course is to treat the patient by withdrawal of anticholinergics. Since tricyclics frequently convert a depression to a mania, one should stay alert to this switch among bipolar patients. Although controlled studies are lacking, some clinicians treat bipolar depressive episodes with lithium-tricyclic combinations. Tricyclics do not typically exacerbate schizophrenia, although on occasion they may do so.

Mild withdrawal reactions have been observed on the abrupt termination of imipramine; the reactions consist of nausea, vomiting, and malaise. Since a gradual reduction in dosage is usually carried out in preference to abrupt withdrawal, these reactions should not pose a clinical problem. The central anticholinergic syndrome can occur, and is best treated by discontinuing the tricyclic drug. The sedation produced by the sedative-type antidepressives may add to the sedation produced by ethyl alcohol. Indeed, empirical studies verify the common sense observation that the sedation caused by different sedative-type drugs, and that caused by alcohol, can combine to produce a greater effect than either agent alone. This does not necessarily apply to all tricyclics, but only to tricyclics with significant sedative properties. Insomnia can occur, especially with protriptyline or MAOI. Table II lists reported side effects of both tricyclics and MAOI.

## Overdosage

An overdose of an imipramine-type antidepressant produces a clinical picture known as the central anticholinergic syndrome or anticholinergic delirium. The syndrome is characterized by temporary agitation, delirium, convulsions, hyperreflexive tendons, bowel and bladder paralysis, orthostatic hypotension and hypertension disturbance of temperature regulation, and mydriasis. The patient then progresses to coma, with shock and respiratory depression. Disturbances of cardiac rhythm—such as tachycardia, atrial fibrillation, ventricular flutters,

TABLE II
SIDE EFFECTS OF ANTIDEPRESSANT AGENTS

Dry mouth
Palpitations
Tachycardia
Heart block
Myocardial infarction
Loss of accommodation
Orthostatic hypotension
Fainting
Dizziness
Nausea
Vomiting
Constipation
Sedation
Agitation
Hallucinations and delusions (in latent psychotics)
Diarrhea
Black tongue
Edema
Aggravation of narrow-angle glaucoma (not chronic
    simple glaucoma)
Urinary retention (caution in benign prostatic hyper-
    trophy)
Paralytic ileus
Peculiar taste
Skin rash
Galactorrhea
Gynecomastia (in males)
Bone marrow depression

and atrioventricular or intraventricular block—can also occur. Coma is generally not protracted for more than 24 hours. All of the above signs and symptoms may be present to some degree or may be absent, depending on the quantity of drugs ingested. The lethal dose of these drugs has been estimated as being from 10 to 30 times the daily dose level.

Treatment of tricyclic overdoses should include vomiting or gastric aspiration and lavage with activated charcoal, the use of intramuscular anticonvulsants (such as paraldehyde or diazepam), coma care, and support of respiration. Activated charcoal is important, since it reduces tricyclic absorption.

Although tricyclic coma is generally of short duration—less than 25 hours—it can result in death due to cardiac arrhythmia; thus, management of cardiac function is critical. If the patient survives this period, recovery without sequelae is probable, and vigorous resuscitative measures—such as cardioversion—continuous electrocardiogram monitoring, and chemotherapy to prevent and manage arrhythmias, should be applied in an intensive care unit. The tricyclics are direct myocardial depressants. Arrhythmias may be mediated, in part, by the tricyclic's quinidine and anticholinergic properties, and the uptake blockade may play a role. The myocardial depressant and quinidine-like properties are particularly important.

Physostigmine (0.25 to 4 mg, intravenously or intramuscularly) is useful to prevent or reverse anticholinergic tachycardia. Physostigmine has a dramatic effect in counteracting anticholinergic toxicity or coma produced by tricyclics. It slows the atropine-induced tachycardia, and wakes the patients from atropine coma. Since this effect can be dramatic, physostigmine can be overused. In a patient thought to have an atropine coma, but actually suffering from other toxicity and not protected by an anticholinergic, physostigmine can produce cholinergic toxicity, such as excess secretions, respiratory depressions, or seizures. In addition, if too much physostigmine is given to reverse the atropine coma, physostigmine toxicity can result. In general, atropine overdose should be treated by benign neglect because it disappears with the metabolism of the atropine-like agent. Physostigmine should be used selectively and judiciously by those who are aware of its toxicity, with proper attention to the use of minimal doses.

The administration of bicarbonate or propranolol is also helpful for preventing arrhythmias.

Late cardiac difficulties can occur even several days after the patient has regained consciousness; thus, patients should be kept under medical supervision for that time period. The average half-life of tricyclics falls between 16 and 24 hours, and in many patients the half-life is substantially longer; hence, the plasma level can be high even as late as 5 days after ingestion. For this reason, cardiac arrhythmias should not be present at that time.

Although the primary care of serious overdosage is usually in the hands of an internist, the psychiatrist should know the seriousness and the problems associated with tricyclic overdose seizures and arrhythmias, facts that are not always well known. Care should be taken so that the suicidal depressed patient does not have access to an excessive number of antidepressant tablets, since several grams—20 to 40 of the 50-mg tablets—can be fatal.

### Monoamine Oxidase Inhibitors

Iproniazid was the first widely prescribed MAOI. The discovery that the drug can produce rare but troublesome liver toxicity led to the synthesis of the other hydrazine MAOI—isocarboxazid, nialamide, and phenelzine—and the nonhydrazine MAOI—tranylcypromine and pargyline. Table I lists the major MAOI and provides approximate dose ranges.

*Results of Treatment*

The therapeutic effect of tranylcypromine is greater than that of a placebo. There is evidence from well-controlled studies that ipronazid, phenelzine, and pargyline are also therapeutically effective. On the basis of the evidence, one may classify the MAOI in terms of their clinical effectiveness as follows: Iproniazid appears to be most effective; isocarboxazid may be least effective; and phenelzine and tranylcypromine occupy an intermediate position.

In recent years, there has been considerable interest in phenelzine (Nardil) as an effective MAOI antidepressant. A number of studies show that phenelzine is effective in treating depression, panic attacks, and agoraphobia. Tranylcypromine has amphetamine-like properties and is, in fact, metabolized to amphetamine. It also inhibits the reuptake of norepinephrine. In a sense, tranylcypromine seems to be almost a combination of amphetamine, tricyclic, and MAOI. Although it has not been extensively studied, the available evidence suggests that tranylcypromine is an effective treatment for depression.

As a class, the MAOI seem less effective than the tricyclic drugs.

Clinical evidence indicates that some patients who do not respond to tricyclics may respond to MAOI, so that a trial period on MAOI for tricyclic nonresponders can be useful. Since tricyclic drugs are usually more effective than MAOI, they become the drugs of choice in most depressions. It has been suggested that endogenous depressions respond best to imipramine, and that phobic anxiety syndromes with secondary depression may respond differentially to MAOI. Well-controlled trials have demonstrated phenelzine to be superior to a placebo in treating outpatient depression and patients with phobic anxiety.

It has been suggested that outpatient depressives who have hysterical symptoms, as well as depression, may be particularly responsive to MAOI. Of course, some cases of endogenous depressions also respond well to MAOI. Recently, however, attention has focused on outpatients with mixed hysterical-phobic symptoms and nonpsychotic depression.

In sum, it is necessary to clearly define the subpopulation of patients for whom phenelzine is indicated. Double-blind studies of suitable populations, such as outpatient depressives, clearly indicate that MAOI are clinically effective for symptomatic relief. In addition, clinical evidence indicates that some patients who fail to respond to tricyclics do respond to MAOI.

The phobic anxiety syndrome also responds to tricyclic drugs. More work is required to identify those patients who are helped by MAOI, since current findings indicate that the MAOI may be useful in treating selected patients.

Improvement with MAOI often occurs from 4 to 8 weeks after the initiation of therapy, its onset frequently being quite dramatic. Since the patients do not generally know when the therapeutic improvement is expected to occur, the phenomenon provides evidence for the efficacy of these drugs.

*Side Effects*

In general, the most common behavioral toxicity with MAOI has been the precipitation of a hypomanic or manic episode, but restlessness, hyperactivity, agitation, irritability, and confusion can also occur. Some cases of paranoid psychosis have been reported.

Severe hepatic necrosis, which occurs very rarely but with a high fatality rate (about 25 percent), was reported initially with iproniazid; the reports led to its withdrawal from general use. Hepatocellular damage, which also occurs very rarely, has similarly been reported to occur in patients treated with other hydrazine MAOI antidepressants—phenelzine and isocarboxazid. Although definitive studies of the incidence of these reactions have not been made, it is believed that they occur much less frequently with those MAOI than with iproniazid; they are, in fact, extremely rare. It is reported that a patient placed on a second trial of MAOI can have a recurrence of jaundice, regardless of whether the same or a different hydrazine MAOI is administered. Consequently, the free hydrazine, rather than the MAO-inhibiting property, is suspected as the causative agent. Jaundice is not reported in association with nonhydrazine MAOI, such as tranylcypromine (Parnate).

The MAOI cause autonomic side effects, such as dry mouth, dizziness, orthostatic hypotension, epigastric distress, constipation, delayed micturition, delayed ejaculation, and impotence.

**Hypertensive Crisis.** A side effect of special importance that may result from the use of the MAOI, particularly tranylcypromine, is the hypertensive crisis, which is occasionally accompanied by intracranial bleeding. Severe occipital headache, stiff neck, sweating, nausea and vomiting, and sharply elevated blood pressure are common prodromal symptoms. It has been estimated that one death in 100,000 patients

treated with tranylcypromine has occurred after such crises. In many instances, these reactions were observed to follow the ingestion of well-ripened cheeses that contain appreciable amounts of tyramine, such as Camembert, Liederkranz, Edam, and cheddar. The pressor effects of indirectly acting sympathomimetic amines in these foods such as tyramine, as well as medicinal amines, are potentiated. Thus, similar attacks may be triggered by epinephrine, cocaine, broad (fava) beans, Marmite or Bovril (both beef boullion concentrates), yogurt, amphetamine, ephedrine and other sympathomimetic agents, such as beer, wine, chicken livers, histamine, and bee venom. The possibility of such side effects as headache, hypertensive crisis, and intracranial bleeding can be substantially reduced by careful attention to diet, and by avoidance of pressor drugs and related substances. Patients should be appropriately warned. See Table III for a sample list given to patients about foodstuffs that should not be ingested while taking MAOI. Should these side effects occur, they can be treated by the admin-

TABLE III
EXAMPLE OF AN INSTRUCTION SHEET GIVEN TO PATIENTS WHO ARE ON MONOAMINE OXIDASE INHIBITOR (MAOI) DRUGS*

The drug you are taking may react to tyramine, a component of certain foods, and may produce unpleasant side effects. Therefore, a diet omitting tyramine-containing foods is necessary. Certain other drugs should also be avoided.

*Omit entirely the following foods containing tyramine:*

Alcohol (particularly beer and wines and especially Chianti). A little pure spirit is permissible, e.g., scotch, gin, or vodka, or a small glass of sherry.
Fava or broad bean pods
Aged cheese. Creamed cheeses and cottage cheeses *are* permitted.
Beef or chicken liver
Orange pulp
Pickled herring or smoked fish
Soups (packaged)
Yeast vitamin supplements
Summer (dry) sausage

*Eat no more than two servings a day of the following foods, which contain smaller amounts of tyramine:*

Soy sauce
Sour cream
Bananas. Green bananas can only be included if cooked in their skins; ordinary peeled bananas are fine.
Avocados
Eggplant
Plums
Raisins
Spinach
Tomatoes
Yogurt

*Take no other medication without informing me. Do not take cough or cold medications or any of the following:*

Pain relievers (especially meperidine or morphine)
Tonics
Stimulants or diet pills
Nasal decongestants
Local anesthetics, e.g. those given by your dentist. First tell him that you are on a MAOI, which can produce side effects with certain local anesthetics that contain added vasoconstrictors.

* Table prepared by Daniel L. Crane, M.D., and Peter M. Kaplan, M.D.

istration of $\alpha$-blockers, such as phentolamine. Chlorpromazine can also be used.

The combination of a MAOI with an imipramine-type drug can lead to restlessness, dizziness, tremulousness, muscle twitching, sweating, convulsions, hyperpyrexia (104° to 109°F), and sometimes death. These reactions can also occur when a MAOI is combined with an imipramine-type drug, dextromethorphan, or meperidine, given in high doses or intramuscularly. Consequently, a washout period of at least 7 days is recommended to allow the MAO enzyme to regain activity before such a substitution is made.

Some clinicians have used a combination of tricyclic-MAOI with reasonable safety by closely supervising their patients. By starting with a tricyclic and then adding the MAIO to the preexisting low-dose tricyclic, while cautiously adjusting dosages where indicated, they have obtained good results without adverse effects. However, these drugs should not be used in combination as a routine measure until their safety, efficacy, and appropriate dosage schedules have been worked out by skilled clinical investigators. The danger is most acute when high doses of an imipramine-type or amphetamine drug are given in cases in which MAO has been inhibited to a considerable degree.

Death can also occur in conjunction with electroconvulsive therapy or tricyclics. The death rate with electroconvulsive therapy is estimated to be in the ratio of one in 10,000 cases; the estimated death rate with iproniazid is one in 10,000 cases and, with tranylcypromine, one in 100,000 cases. For purposes of comparison, death rates from the surgical treatment of peptic ulcer vary from one in 100 to one in 1,000.

The MAOI potentiate a great variety of drugs, including sympathomimetic amines (such as ephedrine), opiates, barbiturates, methyldopa, ganglionic-blocking agents, procaine, anesthetic agents, chloral hydrate, and aspirin.

MAOI can convert a retarded depression into an agitated or anxious one, and can occasionally cause hypomania or an acute schizophrenic psychosis. MAOI can also produce an acute confusional reaction with disorientation, mental clouding, and illusions. The MAOI have been associated with decreased erotic desires, edema, and muscle tremor. In women, they can reduce sexual desire without reducing the ability to have an orgasm. Furthermore, they can cause dizziness, generalized weakness, slurred speech, increased muscle tone, hyperflexia, and clonus. An occasional peripheral neuropathy, similar to that occurring from pyridoxine deficiencies and

observed in connection with isoniazid treatment, can also occur.

The therapeutic hypotensive effect of guanethidine (Esimil, Ismelin) can be antagonized by MAOI tricyclics and chlorpromazine. In some cases MAOI and guanethidine together can produce a parodoxical acute increase in blood pressure.

### Overdosage

Intoxication caused by MAOI is, in general, characterized by agitation that progresses to coma with hyperthermia, an increase in respiratory rate, tachycardia, dilated pupils, and hyperactive deep tendon reflexes. Involuntary movements may be present, particularly in the face and jaw. A major problem is hypertension.

There is a lag period—an asymptomatic period of 1 to 6 hours after the ingestion of the drugs before the general occurrence of toxicity. Acidification of the urine markedly hastens the excretion of tranylcypromine, phenelzine, and amphetamine; dialysis has been used with success in tranylcypromine and amphetamine poisoning. Chlorpromazine, presumably because of its adrenergic blocking action, is a useful drug in the treatment of poisoning with MAOI. In cases of hypertensive crises, $\alpha$-adrenergic blocking agents, such as phentolamine, may be helpful.

### Psychomotor Stimulants

Amphetamine, dextroamphetamine, methylphenidate, deanol, and pipradol are classified as psychomotor stimulants.

Methylphenidate may be of value in treating outpatients with mild depression, particularly patients who drink three or more cups of coffee a day. The effect has been documented in only a few controlled studies, so further work is needed to identify clearly the subtype of patient who is helped by such treatment. No evidence indicates that the drug is beneficial in cases of moderate to severe depression. Some clinicians have noted that a subgroup of mildly depressed patients may be assisted with small (5 to 15 mg) daily doses of methylphenidate.

Uncontrolled clinical evidence indicates that amphetamine may be of value for some outpatients with mild depression, but there is no evidence of its effectiveness in moderate to severe depression. The amphetamine-type drugs can cause jitteriness, palpitations, and psychic dependence. High doses of amphetamines can produce a florid psychosis that usually resembles paranoid schizophrenia. Amphetamine and imipramine may be synergistic in selected cases of depression. A trial period of amphetamines of 3 to 4 days can predict responders to imipramine. The reader is referred to Section 19.2 for a further discussion of amphetamines including the legal implications of its use.

There is evidence that amphetamines and methylphenidate are effective in the reduction and control of hyperkinetic behavior in children, a pharmacological paradox of considerable clinical significance. The stimulants are also effective in postponing the deterioration in psychomotor performance that often accompanies fatigue, a property that may be useful in carefully selected instances. All drugs in the psychomotor stimulant class can cause a paranoid psychosis, as well as psychological dependence.

### Antipsychotics and Antidepressants

Phenothiazine derivatives have proven to be effective antidepressants. Chlorpromazine and imipramine, in one major study, were found to be equally effective, both being superior to a placebo in the treatment of agitated depression; only imipramine proved to be superior to a placebo in the treatment of retarded depression. The antidepressant efficacy of chlorpromazine was verified in a National Institute of Mental Health collaborative study which included schizoaffective patients as well as psychotic depressives. Thioridazine proved to be an effective antidepressant in a Veterans Administration collaborative study. Thioridazine and perphenazine were shown to be effective antidepressants in anxious depression. In these studies, anxious depression refers to mixed anxiety-depression in nonpsychotic depressives.

The addition of antipsychotics to a tricyclic in treating psychosis with depression can be useful. Antipsychotics for anxious depression should be used with more caution, since the anxiety disappears with the tricyclic-induced remission of depression.

In general, it is better to be specific in diagnosis and treat a specific syndrome with a single agent, rather than to use a combination of drugs.

### Anxiety-Depression Syndrome

A common disorder of outpatients is the mixed anxiety-depression syndrome (nonpsychotic). Doxepin, a tricyclic drug having antidepressive and antianxiety properties, has been shown to be superior to a placebo and equal to diazepam (Valium) and to chlordiazepoxide (Librium) in efficacy. Doxepin is about as effective as the conventional tricyclic antidepressants that have also been used to treat the syndrome. Any sedative drug—including amitriptyline,

thioridazine, and the barbiturates—may exert an antianxiety effect.

For depressed patients, with or without anxiety, any of the antidepressants can be effective. Any of the antidepressants are recommended for the treatment of depression with anxiety—namely, the conventional tricyclics, including doxepin and the MAOI. Patients with depression plus associated anxiety should be treated as depressed patients. In cases of anxiety with some secondary depression, doxepin is an effective drug, but so are the minor tranquilizers, the other tricyclics and, for certain patients, the MAOI. Patients with anxiety plus some secondary depression, but with no indication as to which is primary, must be treated by clinical judgment until research more precisely specifies which drug is optimal for which patient. The exception is the panic attack (agoraphobia) syndrome, for which antidepressants are clearly indicated.

The addition of chlordiazepoxide (Librium) to a tricyclic does not interfere with therapeutic action. Some evidence indicates that the combination may be helpful after the first week of treatment. However, other evidence is contradictory. Nevertheless, the addition of an antianxiety agent in the first week does no harm and may have some beneficial effect. More work is needed before definitive conclusions can be made.

### Phobic Anxiety Syndrome

Donald Klein described a syndrome characterized by severe panic attacks—that is, sudden, spontaneous, and unexpected feelings of terror and anxiety, the autonomic equivalence of anxiety, and the desire to flee and return to a safe place. Primary among the symptoms is the panic attack itself. The fear of places where such attacks have occurred, or may possibly occur, is actually a secondary elaboration of the symptom or a reaction to the attacks themselves. For this reason, it is preferable to refer to these behaviors as panic attacks with agoraphobia (see Table IV).

The panic attacks occur when the patient is, in some sense, separated from significant others—for example, when traveling alone in subways, tunnels, or bridges or out in the streets. The patient then begins to show anticipatory anxiety and dread of situations that may get him into the situation of which he is phobic. The patient typically has been a fearful, dependent child with a great deal of separation anxiety.

Antidepressants dramatically halt the panic attacks but do not alter the anticipatory anxiety. Psychological treatment is sometimes useful for

TABLE IV
DIAGNOSTIC CRITERIA FOR PHOBIC ANXIETY
SYNDROME

1. Sudden, spontaneous, unexplained panic attack characterized by feeling of terror, autonomic symptoms of anxiety, and a flight response
2. Symptoms during an attack can be:
   a. Anxiety, terror, helplessness, impending doom
   b. Periods of anxiety with the following physical symptoms:
      1. Smothering or choking feeling, difficulty in getting breath
      2. Dizziness or faintness
      3. Trembling
      4. Tingling, hot or cold spells
      5. Chest pain or discomfort
      6. Nausea
      7. Palpitation and rapid heart beat
      8. Sudden empty feeling in pit of stomach
3. Fear of places where attacks occur:
   a. Public places (restaurants, stores, buses, etc.)
   b. Fear that patient cannot reach secure place, such as home

overcoming the anticipatory anxiety and helping the patient return to the situation in which he experienced the attack, so that he can demonstrate to himself that he no longer experiences it. Antidepressants, particularly MAOI, seem to be specific for the panic attack, as opposed to the anticipatory anxiety. The anticipatory anxiety is helped by the benzodiazepines.

Alprazolam (Xanax) is also effective in preventing panic attacks in doses of 4 to 8 mg per day. Alprazolam also has antidepressant properties.

The syndrome of phobic anxiety is, in many respects, a pharmacologically defined syndrome—that is, defined by its prevention by antidepressants.

A serious complication of the syndrome is the abuse of sedatives and alcohol through self-medication. Patients treated with imipramine do well, and tend not to return to alcohol or to drug abuse. The childhood version of the syndrome, school phobia, is also benefited by imipramine.

## Psychological Tests and Rating Scales

A variety of psychological tests and rating scales are used to evaluate the effects of antidepressant medication in addition to a clinical assessment of the patient performed by the psychiatrist.

The tests are described below. Each has its own strengths and weaknesses and can also be used to monitor and assess illnesses other than depression.

### Measures of Mood

**Zung Scale.** The Zung Self-rating Scale is a 20 item self report scale with normal scoring 34

or less, and depressed 50 or above. This scale provides a global index of the intensity of depressive symptomatology, including the effective expression of depression.

**Raskin Scale.** The Raskin Severity of Depression Scale is a clinician-rated scale measuring severity of depression, as reported by the patient and as observed by the physician on a 5-point scale of three dimensions: verbal report, behavior displayed, and secondary symptoms. It has a range of 3 to 13 with normal scoring 3, and depressed 7 or above.

**Hamilton Depression Scale.** This test is a widely used depression scale with 24 items, each of which are rated 0–4 or 0–2 with a maximum range of 0–76. The ratings are derived from a clinical interview with the patient. Questions about feelings of guilt, suicide, sleep habits, and other symptoms of depression are evaluated by the clinician.

**Clinical Global Impression.** This test consists of 3 global scales (items). Two of the items, Severity of Illness and Global Improvement are rated on a 7-point scale, while the third, Efficacy Index, requires a rating of the interaction of therapeutic effectiveness and adverse reactions.

**Treatment Emergent Symptom Scale.** This test can provide useful information regarding side effects of drugs. For each symptom, three judgments are required: intensity of the symptom, relationship to drug action, and action taken as a consequence of its presence.

## REFERENCES

Baldessarini R J: Biochemical aspect of depression and its treatment. American Psychiatric Association Press, Washington, DC, 1983.

Bunney W E Jr, Davis J M: Norepinephrine in depressive reactions. Arch Gen Psychiatry 13: 483, 1965.

Charney D S, Heninger G R, Sternberg D E: Serotonin function and mechanism of action of antidepressant treatment. Arch Gen Psychiatry 41: 359, 1984

Davis J M: Antidepressant drugs. In Comprehensive Textbook of Psychiatry, ed 4, H I Kaplan, B J Sadock, editors, p 1513, Williams & Wilkins, Baltimore, 1985.

Glassman A H: Cardiovascular effects of tricyclic antidepressants. Ann Rev Med 35: 503, 1984.

Janowsky D, Davis J M, El-Yousef, Sekerkes H: A cholinergic-adrenergic hypothesis of mania and depression. Lancet 2: 632, 1972.

Kay D W K, Fahy T, Garside R F: A seven-month double-blind trial of amitriptyline and diazepam in ECT-treated depressed patients. Br J Psychiatry 117: 667, 1970.

Klerman G L, Cole J O: Clinical pharmacology of imipramine and related antidepressant compounds. Pharmacol Rev 17: 101, 1965.

Maas J W: Biogenic amines and depression: Biochemical and pharmacological separation of two types of depression. Arch Gen Psychiatry 32: 1357, 1975.

Mindham R H S, Howland C, Shephard M: An evaluation of continuation therapy with tricyclic antidepressants in depressive illness. Psychol Med *3:* 5, 1973.

Robinson D S, Nies A, Ravaris C L, Lamborn K R: The monoamine oxidase inhibitor phenelzine in the treatment of depressive-anxiety states. Arch Gen Psychiatry *29:* 407, 1973b.

Schildkraut J J: The cathecholamine hypothesis of affective disorder: A review of supporting evidence. Am J Psychiatry *123:* 509, 1965.

## 27.3    MINOR TRANQUILIZERS, SEDATIVES, AND HYPNOTICS

### Minor Tranquilizers

The term minor tranquilizer, as it is usually applied to drugs like meprobamate and chlordiazepoxide, is a most unfortunate choice. First, it implies that these agents are similar in action to the major tranquilizers, although to a smaller degree. Second, it suggests that large doses of the minor tranquilizers have the same clinical effects as small doses of the major tranquilizers. Neither is the case. The minor tranquilizers do, in fact, resemble the sedative-hypnotic drugs more closely than they do the antipsychotic drugs. All minor tranquilizers can, at high doses, be used as hypnotics, and all hypnotics, at low doses, can be used for daytime sedation. The term anti-anxiety agent is preferred to the term minor tranquilizer.

A sedative dose is that amount, given at one time, sufficient to reduce anxiety without inducing sleep. A hypnotic dose is that amount, given at one time, sufficient to induce sleep.

### Benzodiazepine Derivatives

The first of the benzodiazepine derivatives, synthesized in 1957, was chlordiazepoxide. Eleven other derivatives of this class are now available in the United States: diazepam, oxazepam, clorazepate, lorazepam, prazepam, temazepam, alprazolam, triazolam, halazepam, flurazepam, and clonazepam. Other benzodiazepines are available on foreign markets, and are undergoing study in the United States and elsewhere.

**Pharmacokinetics and Clinical Activity.** To understand the clinical efficacy and the pharmacology of the benzodiazepines, one must understand their metabolism and pharmacokinetics. Chlordiazepoxide, after a series of intermediate changes, is converted to oxazepam, which is conjugated to its glucuronic acid. Diazepam is also converted to oxazepam, which is then converted to its glucuronic acid.

Prazepam, is nearly completely metabolized in a first-pass effect to desmethyldiazepam, suggesting that desmethyldiazepam is the active substance responsible for the antianxiety effect of the drug. Prazepam is essentially a prodrug or precursor of desmethyldiazepam. Clorazepate is also a prodrug and is rapidly and completely converted to desmethyldiazepam.

There are slight pharmacokinetic differences between prazepam and clorazepate—that is, the drugs differ in the rate at which the conversion to diazepam occurs. Clorazepate is rapidly converted in the stomach into desmethyldiazepam which is then rapidly absorbed. This first pass in the liver metabolism of prazepam results in the slower pharmacological appearance of desmethyldiazepam in the blood. That yields a plasma level-time curve similar to the one observed with a sustained release preparation. The more rapid absorption follows the first dose of chlorazepate or diazepam, which yields a more rapid sedative or anxiolytic, and the pharmacokinetic property is relevant when a fast effect is desired after a single tablet. The other benzodiazepines are intermediate in time or onset of therapeutic or side effect after a dose. Rapid absorption is important for a patient who takes a single dose episodically to lessen an episodic burst or simple anxiety. Insofar as diazepam itself may have different pharmacological properties from desmethyldiazepam, there may be differences between diazepam and the other three drugs—in that after diazepam is administered, 40 percent of active plasma benzodiazepine is unchanged diazepam.

From the point of view of clinical efficacy, clorazepate and prazepam are almost identical, since they are products of the same drug. The half-life of desmethyldiazepam in humans ranges from about 30 hours to more than 200 hours in extreme cases. The half-life of chlordiazepoxide is also long. This fact suggests that one daily dose is practical for these drugs.

It often takes from 2 to 3 weeks to achieve steady state for the drugs. Similarly, the long half-lives of chlordiazepoxide and its two principal active metabolites, diazepam and desmethyldiazepam, imply that the pharmacological effects after termination of treatment should persist for a few days.

All drugs accumulate in the body until steady state is achieved, where the rate of entrance into the body equals rate of excretion from the body. Before steady-state is achieved, all drugs accumulate. Therefore, with a drug with a long half-life and in patients who are slow metabolizers, it may take several weeks to reach steady state; hence, drug continues to be accumulated during that time. After a few days, for example, the clinician may think that he has found a reasonable dose, but after 10 days a slow metabolizer may have accumulated still more drug and become toxic. It is not really correct to say that the long half-life drugs accumulate and the short half-life drugs do not; rather, the clinician needs to know the amount of time it takes to reach steady-state and be aware that drug levels are increasing until steady state is achieved. Drug-drug interactions or disease-drug interactions are mediated by impairment of hepatic oxidation that may occur with benxodiazepines. Drugs, such as cimetidine, disulfiram, isoniazid, and estrogens, and diseases or physiological states (cirrhosis, old age) which impair benzodiazepine oxidation can increase plasma levels, so a slightly lower dose might be required.

Lorazepam, temazepam, and oxazepam are pharmacokinetically similar in that they are eliminated primarily through glucuronide conjugation. These drugs have substantially shorter half-lives than do the other benzodiazepines.

Steady state levels are usually arrived at within 4 days with twice or three times a day (b.i.d. or t.i.d.) treatment. However, because the half-life is generally less than 24 hours, two- or even three-times-a-day dosage schedules are indicated. Consequently, drug effects are maintained for a much shorter time after suspension of treatment with those benzodiazepines than with other agents.

**Clinical Efficacy.** The benzodiazepines are used only in simple anxiety and, like other antianxiety agents, cause sedation. Because of this effect, it is wise to start with a small dose before building up to the full therapeutic dose within 3 or 4 days. Patients should be warned against the concurrent use of alcohol and other sedative agents, and should also be cautioned about driving and undertaking other tasks that require an alert state. On the other hand, the benzodiazepines are safe from the standpoint of suicidal risk, and have a relatively low abuse liability when compared with other sedative hypnotic drugs.

When administered orally, the drugs are effective in reducing chronic anxiety. They can also reduce acute anxiety when given intravenously. For example, 10 mg. of diazepam, intravenously infused over 10 minutes, reduces symptoms of anxiety such as jitteriness, shakiness, sick-to-the-stomach feeling, sadness, downheartedness, and a troubled and worried attitude. The maximal effects are observed 20 to 30 minutes after the administration of the drug.

The nature of the improvement produced by minor tranquilizers may go beyond a simple antianxiety effect. For example, they may cause a perceptual alteration, producing a tendency for the patients to regard various occurrences in a positive light. Alternatively, they may provide relief from incapacitating psychiatric symptoms and a secondary increase in vigor, thus allowing the patient to deal with life situations in a constructive manner. It is also possible that the drug has a mild disinhibiting action, similar to that observed socially after modest doses of alcohol.

Typical daily doses for the benzodiazepine minor tranquilizers are: chlordiazepoxide, 15 to 100 mg; diazepam, 4 to 40 mg; oxazepam, 30 to 120 mg; clorazepate, 15 to 60 mg; prazepam, 20 to 60 mg; lorazepam, 15 to 30 mg. When administered intramuscularly, all benzodiazepines except lorazepam are erratically absorbed. Oral administration is effective, but intravenous medication can also be used.

Since the minor tranquilizers do not have antipsychotic properties, it is of the utmost importance to treat incipient schizophrenics with adequate doses of phenothiazines. Furthermore, some patients with depression or panic attacks may do better on one or another of the various antidepressants than on a minor tranquilizer.

Clinical trials show that alprazolam is more effective than placebo in preventing panic attacks, but this drug needs to be used in a dose slightly higher than its simple benzodiazepine antianxiety action (4 to 8 mg/day). This finding is particularly interesting since alprazolam has antidepressant properties. Pure benzodiazepines have no effect in preventing panic attacks. The observation that alprazolam prevents panic attacks implies that these types of agents help depression and also prevent panic attacks. See Table I for an overview of the benzodiazepines. Table II covers the nonbenzodiazepine drugs.

**Indications.** Benzodiazepines are used only in simple anxiety, but the presence of anxiety does not necessarily indicate their use. Mild anxiety might be best treated with psychotherapy. The therapist should determine if the anxiety causes significant dysphoria, is sufficiently crippling, or is otherwise dysfunctional so that its alleviation with drugs will be useful to the patient. There is an inverted "U"-shaped relationship between performance and anxiety: A little anxiety may spur performance, but too much anxiety may interfere with performance. Anxiety is a somewhat nonspecific symptom. Some agitated elderly may do better with antipsychotic agents.

**Other Uses of Benzodiazepines.** One of the most important uses of benzodiazepines is in alcohol detoxification, where a loading-dose

TABLE I
BENZODIAZEPINES*

| Generic Name | Trade Name | Primary Approved Indication | Other Approved Indications | Primary Metabolic Pathway | Rate of Elimination | Elimination Half-life (hr) | Active Metabolites | Commercially Available Dosage Forms | Recommended Total Daily Dose | | |
|---|---|---|---|---|---|---|---|---|---|---|---|
| | | | | | | | | | Pediatric | Adult | Geriatric |
| Diazepam | Valium | Anxiety | Alcohol withdrawal, preoperative sedation, status epilepticus, muscle spasm | Oxidation | Slow | 10–100 | Diazepam, desmethyldiazepam | 2, 5, 10 mg tablets; 5 mg per ml injection; 15 mg sustained release capsules | 3–10 mg | 4–40 mg | 2–5 mg |
| Chlordiazepoxide | Librium | Anxiety | Alcohol withdrawal, preoperative sedation. | Oxidation | Slow | 10–100 | Chlordiazepoxide, desmethylchlordiazepoxide, demoxepam, desmethyldiazepam | 5, 10, 25 mg tablets; injection, 100 mg per ampule; 5, 10, 25 mg capsules | 0.5 mg/kg | 15–100 mg | 10–20 mg |
| Clorazepate | Tranxene | Anxiety | Adjunctive therapy for partial seizures; alcohol withdrawal | Oxidation | Slow | 30–100 | Desmethyldiazepam | 3.75, 7.5, 15 mg tablets and capsules; 11.25, 22.5 mg tablets | 7.5–15 mg (9–12 yr) | 15–60 mg | 7.5–15 mg |
| Halazepam | Paxipam | Anxiety | — | Oxidation | Slow | 15–100 | Halazepam, desmethyldiazepam | 20, 40 mg tablets | —† | 60–120 mg | 20–40 mg |
| Prazepam | Centrax | Anxiety | — | Oxidation | Slow | 30–100 | Desmethyldiazepam | 5, 10 mg capsules; 10 mg tablets | —† | 20–60 mg | 10–15 mg |
| Alprazolam | Xanax | Anxiety | Anxiety-depression | Oxidation | Intermediate | 10–16 | Alprazolam | 0.25, 0.5, 1 mg tablets | —† | 0.75–1.5 mg | 0.25–0.75 mg |
| Lorazepam | Ativan | Anxiety | Anxiety-depression, Preoperative sedation | Conjugation | Intermediate | 10–30 | None | 0.5, 1, 2 mg tablets; 2 mg/ml, 4 mg/ml injection | —† | 2–6 mg | 1–2 mg |
| Oxazepam | Serax | Anxiety | Anxiety-depression, alcohol withdrawal | Conjugation | Intermediate | 5–15 | None | 10, 15, 30 mg capsules; 15 mg tablets | —† | 30–120 mg | 30–45 mg |
| Flurazepam | Dalmane | Insomnia | — | Oxidation | Slow | 47–100 | Hydroxyethylflurazepam, desalkylflurazepam, desmethyldiazepam | 15, 30 mg capsules | —† | 15–30 mg | 15 mg |

| | | | | | | | | | | | |
|---|---|---|---|---|---|---|---|---|---|---|---|
| Temazepam | Restoril | Insomnia | — | Conjugation | Intermediate | 9–14 | None | 15, 30 mg capsules | —† | 15–30 mg | 15 mg |
| Triazolam | Halcion | Insomnia | — | Oxidation | Rapid | 2–3 | None | 0.25, 0.5 mg tablets | —† | 0.25–0.5 mg | 0.125–0.25 mg |
| Clonazepam | Clonopin | Lennox-Gastaut syndrome | Akinetic and myoclonic seizures; petit mal seizures not responsive to other drugs | Oxidation | Intermediate to slow | 20–40 | — | 0.5 1, 2 mg tablets | 0.01–0.03 mg/kg | 1.5 mg | —† |

\* Benzodiazepines have a IV Drug Enforcement Administration control level (D.E.A. IV).
† Dose range recommendation not included by manufacturer. As a rule lower doses are used in children and the elderly.
Side effects: Paradoxical excitement; hypnagogic hallucination; phlebitis; fatigue; drowsiness; somnolence; muscle weakness; nystagmus; ataxia; dysarthria; impaired reaction time, motor coordination, and intellectual function; and central nervous system depression.

technique is useful, since benzodiazepines have a minimal risk of cardiovascular toxicity and respiratory depression. In this situation, administration consists of a single intravenous injection of 20 mg diazepam or oral doses every hour until sedation and/or withdrawal symptom reduction is seen, after which the long half-life of the drug suffices to provide a slow tapering effect. Another important use is in general medicine for surgical or endoscopic procedures and for anesthesic induction. Midazolam, the most lipophilic benzodiazepine, may be particularly useful here, since this lipophilic property results in a rapid passage of drug from plasma into brain (or vice versa), a property necessary for minute-to-minute titration of state of consciousness.

### Meprobamate and Tybamate

Meprobamate was first synthesized in 1950, and now several derivatives of the drug are available on the market. They include tybamate, another antianxiety agent, and carisoprodol (Soma), which has selective properties as a skeletal muscle relaxant but negligible antianxiety effects.

The usual dose of meprobamate is 400 mg, administered three or four times daily. The usual dose of tybamate is two 250-mg capsules, given three or four times a day.

**Side Effects.** About half the patients on meprobamate develop drowsiness as a side effect. Therefore, it is wise to start with a modest dose and build up to a therapeutic dose within 4 days. While on the drugs, patients should be warned against driving or undertaking other tasks that require alertness. The sedative effect of meprobamate is potentiated by alcohol and other central nervous system depressants, so patients should be warned against even the mild use of those agents.

Sudden withdrawal after high doses of meprobamate may cause anxiety, restlessness, weakness, convulsions, and delirium. The dose necessary to produce such symptoms (3.2 g per day) is close to the therapeutic dose. The condition is best treated by slow withdrawal in a supervised setting.

A review of overdosage identified 120 cases of poisoning in which meprobamate was the only drug taken. Of those, 16 were fatalities, with the lowest fatal dose being 12 g—30 of the 400-mg tablets. The benzodiazepines are less toxic drugs than meprobamate.

### Propranolol and Related Drugs

Anxiety is characterized by a number of physical symptoms, such as palpitations, rapid heart

TABLE II
Nonbarbiturate Nonbenzodiazepine Sedatives, Hypnotics, and Antianxiety Agents

| Name | | Adult Dose Range (mg/day) | Adult Single Dose Range (mg) | | Available Preparations | | | | | | | | | D.E.A.‡ Control Level |
| Generic | Trade | | Sedative* | Hypnotic† | Oral | | | | | Injection | | | Suppository (mg) | |
| | | | | | Tablet (mg) | Capsule (mg) | Syrup | Elixir | Am-pul | Ampul | Vial | Syringe | | |
|---|---|---|---|---|---|---|---|---|---|---|---|---|---|---|
| Meprobamate | Equanil Miltown | 1,200–1,600 | 200–400 | | 200, 400, 600 | 400 | | | | | | | | IV |
| Tybamate | Tybatran | 250–2000 | 250–500 | | 250 | 250, 350, 500 | | | | | | | | 0 |
| Ethinamate | Valmid | 500–1000 | | 500–1000 | | 500 | | | | | | | | IV |
| Glutethimide | Doriden | 250–500 | 250–500 | 500 | 125, 250, 500 | 500 | | | | | | | | III |
| Methyprylon | Noludar | 50–400 | 50–100 | 200–400 | 50, 200 | 300 | | | | | | | | III |
| Ethchlorvynol | Placidyl | 500–750 | | 500–750 | | 100, 200, 500, 750 | | | | | | | | IV |
| Methaqualone§ | Mequin Sopor | 75–300 | 75 | 150–300 | 150–300 | | | | | | | | | II |
| Diphenhydramine | Benadryl | 10–400 | 50 | | | 25, 50 | | 12.5 mg/5 ml | | 50 mg/ml | 10 mg/ml | 50 mg/ml | | 0 |
| Hydroxyzine | Vistaril Atarax | 25–400 | 25–100 | | 10, 25, 50, 100 | 25, 50, 100 | 10 mg/5 ml 25 mg/5 ml | | | | | | | 0 |
| Chloral hydrate | Noctec Kessodrate Felsules Aquachloral | 250–750 | 250 | 500–2000 | | 250, 500 | 500 mg/5 ml | | | | | 100 mg/2 ml | 325, 650, 975, 1,300 | IV |
| Promethazine | Phenergan | 12.5–50 | 12.5–50 | 12.5–50 | 12.5, 25, 50 | | 6.25 mg/5 ml 25 mg/5 ml | | | 25 mg/ml 50 mg/ml | | | 12.5, 25, 50 | 0 |
| Paraldehyde | Paral | 4–10 ml | 4–10 ml | 4–10 ml | | | 1000 (1000 mg/= 1 ml) | 30 ml | 5 ml, 10 ml | | | | | IV |

* Sedative dose is that amount given at one time sufficient to reduce anxiety without inducing sleep.
† Hypnotic dose is that amount given at one time sufficient to induce sleep.
‡ D.E.A., Drug Enforcement Administration.
§ Methaqualone is no longer in production.

Side effects: Impaired judgment and performance; drowsiness; lethargy; residual sedation ("hangover"); skin eruptions; nausea; vomiting; paradoxical restlessness or excitement; exacerbation of symptoms of organic brain syndrome; ataxia; atropine psychosis with hypnotic doses of diphenhydramine or hydroxyzine; unpredictable clinical course after glutethimide overdose; high addictive potential and low margin of safety in suicide attempts with glutethimide; and with promethazine, a phenothiazine without antipsychotic activity, side effects of the phenothiazine class may be observed.

beat, tremor, tingling, cold sweats, chest constriction, and twitching. Physiologically, many of these symptoms can be caused by the secretion of epinephrine during stress. This point raises the question of whether one of the components in anxiety is the perception of those internal epinephrine-induced physiological events or, perhaps, a hyperawareness of normal adrenergic functioning.

Many of these peripheral autonomic events can be blocked by a $\beta$-adrenergic receptor blocker. The agent may block the autonomic signals of anxiety and, thereby, benefit a patient with anxiety through a peripheral mechanism.

Propranolol, as well as other $\beta$-blockers, has been compared experimentally with a placebo and with benzodiazepines in the treatment of anxiety and in the treatment of patients in anxiety-provoking situations, such as under stress and before public speaking. In general, propranolol produces an antianxiety effect greater than that produced by a placebo. This is true in most, but not all, of the controlled studies.

The use of $\beta$-blockers for anxiety is still in the investigatory stage, but is theoretically relevant. When used for anxiety, the clinician must be aware of their side effects and contraindications, particularly with asthma and cardiac conditions, for which a slowing of the heart would be detrimental.

### Antihistamines and Over-the-Counter Sedatives

A variety of patent medicines are marketed for the control of nervousness. They usually contain a sedative antihistamine and hydrobromides. Bromism, a toxic psychotic state, can occur as a side effect. One controlled outpatient study of the ingredients in one patent medicine, Compoz, found the drug to be ineffective when prescribed by physicians as a tranquilizer. Antihistamines have sedative side effects in some adults, and one such drug, diphenhydramine, is used as a sedative in children and the elderly; it is found to be most useful for children under 12 years of age. Hydroxyzine, usually used as an antianxiety agent, is also a member of this class.

### Sedatives and Hypnotics

Barbiturates, meprobamate, and the benzodiazepine-type drugs are extensively used as sleeping medications. Controlled studies indicate that all have significant hypnotic properties. At the doses commonly used, barbiturates and nonbarbiturate sedatives are comparable in hypnotic properties to temazepam, triazolam, and flurazepam. The chief advantage of a ben-

zodiazepine is that is has less liability for death in overdose situations and less liability for abuse. This relative freedom from toxicity is an important advantage of all the benzodiazepine drugs. The barbiturates induce the liver microsomal enzymes, which alter, among other things, the metabolism of anticoagulants. The benzodiazepine series has not been shown to alter the metabolism of anticoagulants, thereby simplifying its use. Sedatives should be administered with caution to patients with liver, cardiac, and kidney diseases and diabetes, hyperthyroidism, and congestive heart failure. The nonbarbiturate sedatives, such as glutethimide, have the same side effect liabilities for abuse and overdose as do the barbiturates. They are extremely lethal in overdose; in fact, glutethimide appears to be more lethal than the barbiturates. The nonbarbiturate sedatives have considerable liability for barbiturate-type abuse, and can produce the same withdrawal syndrome.

### Sleep Disorders

Sleep disturbance is a symptom of mental disorder, for which the cause should be identified and treated. Currently, there is a growing body of knowledge in sleep medicine. Patients should be referred to sleep clinics for specialized studies and the identification of specific primary sleep disturbances—such as sleep apnea, hypersomnia, narcolepsy, altered sleep phase cycles, and nocturnal myoclonus. The use of sedatives can create problems in sleep apnea. If the syndrome is secondary to a psychiatric illness, treatment of the underlying disorder is indicated.

Many patients—including those with depression, schizophrenia, and mania—have difficulty with sleep. Sleep disturbance is closely associated with depression, particularly early morning awakening. The primary treatment of depression-related insomnia is treatment of the depression itself, either with tricyclic drugs or with electroconvulsive therapy. Amitriptyline has considerable sedating properties, and the initial two doses or even the third dose can be given at bedtime; doing so should provide ample sedation to ensure a good night's sleep. Sleep disturbance also occurs in mania and schizophrenia, and can be effectively managed by the sedative properties of any antipsychotic compounds given in large doses.

The clinician should identify the underlying psychiatric disorder and treat it specifically, rather than treating the symptom of insomnia. One can use the sedative side effects of a larger-than-normal dose of a psychotherapeutic drug at bedtime. In some cases, one may also have to give a hypnotic agent, but that is rather unusual.

Chronic sleep loss may play a role in precipitating a psychosis, so that the restoration of sleep may be an important phase of the therapeutic process. Of course, if the patients are on a high dose of tricyclic, two-thirds to one-half, but not the whole dose, should be given at bedtime. This avoids an unusually high peak plasma level with potential cardiac toxicity.

### Barbiturates

The first barbiturate to be used in medicine was barbital (Veronal), introduced in 1903. It was followed by phenobarbital (Luminal), amobarbital (Amytal), pentobarbital (Nembutal), secobarbital (Seconal), and thiopental (Pentothal). In all, about 2,500 barbiturates have been synthesized, 50 of which have been used clinically.

It is conventional to divide the barbiturates into four groups on the basis of their duration of action: long acting if they have a duration of action of more than 8 hours (phenobarbital, barbital); medium acting, 5 to 8 hours (butabarbital, pentobarbital, amobarbital); short acting, 1 to 5 hours (secobarbital); and very short acting, less than 1 hour (thiopental) (see Table III). It follows, therefore, that patients who have difficulty in falling asleep, and who then sleep soundly, can be given short-acting barbiturates. Patients who wake up frequently throughout the night may require a medium-acting barbiturate. Long-acting barbiturates are useful as sedatives in chronic anxiety but are relatively poor as hypnotics.

In large doses, the barbiturates produce a depression of the central nervous system; the respiratory center is particularly vulnerable, and respiratory depression is common from barbiturate overdose. This effect may constitute a particular danger in patients with severe pulmonary insufficiency, and a serious respiratory depression can occur when sedatives are given to such respiratory cripples. In anesthetic doses, barbiturates can cause hypotension. Barbiturates have no analgesic action. They do not produce sleep when insomnia is due to pain; instead, they can produce restlessness and confusion.

Phenobarbital deserves special attention. First, it is said to be an excellent anticonvulsant, and, second, it is a potent inducer of hepatic enzymes. Phenobarbital is further known to speed to the body's metabolism of coumarin-type drug in that manner, so that adjustment of anticoagulant dose is often needed if barbiturates are added or discontinued.

### Nonbarbiturate Hypnotics

Now available are drugs such as glutethimide, which are chemically not at all similar to barbiturates but which are either pharmacologically as dangerous as the barbiturates or, in the case of glutethimide, even more dangerous. It is difficult to find a special indication for any of those drugs at the present time.

Chloral hydrate is the oldest hypnotic, having been introduced into medicine in 1869. It is a relatively short-acting drug that is useful in the treatment of initial insomnia, but it has less value as a daytime sedative. Chloral hydrate is an effective, safe, and mild hypnotic. It is rapidly converted to trichloroethanol in the body; that metabolite is also an effective hypnotic. Chloral hydrate's lethal dose is about 5 to 10 times its hypnotic dose of 1 to 2 g. Although physical dependence does occur, it is unusual. It is a good hypnotic but does produce severe gastritis or even ulceration which significantly limits its use.

Paraldehyde is another traditional hypnotic, first introduced into medicine in 1882. When 5 ml are given intramuscularly or 5 to 10 ml are administered orally, it is an old-fashioned treatment for both alcoholic withdrawal symptoms and psychiatric conditions with severely disturbed behavior. Paraldehyde is mostly metabolized, but its excretion by the lungs limits its usefulness because of its offensive taste and ubiquitous odor.

Glutethimide (Doriden) has been widely used as a hypnotic and as a daytime sedative. It should be prescribed with even more vigilance than is exercised in the prescription of barbiturates. Glutethimide is dependency producing and can be lethal is overdose. In glutethimide poisoning, the patient is more likely to go into shock than is the case with barbiturates, and the level of consciousness may show erratic fluctuations. Since the drug is sequestered in tissue, it can be episodically released to the brain. Convulsions can sometimes occur. The drug's anticholinergic properties produce pupillary dilation and may cause glutethimide coma to be misdiagnosed as atropine coma. Detoxification of patients physically dependent on glutethimide is said to be stormier than the treatment of patients dependent on barbiturates. This is a particularly toxic drug, and other drugs are preferable because of the habituating and toxic potentials of glutethimide.

Methyprylon (Noludar) is similar in structure to glutethimide, and, like glutethimide, it is used both as a hypnotic and as a daytime sedative. It is addicting and can be lethal in large doses.

TABLE III
BARBITURATES

| Group | Name | | Manufacturer | Adult Dose Range (mg/day) | Adult Single Dose Range | | Common Therapeutic Uses | | | | D.E.A. Control Level |
|---|---|---|---|---|---|---|---|---|---|---|---|
| | Generic | Trade | | | Sedative (mg) | Hypnotic (mg) | Sedative | Hypnotic | Anticonvulsive | General anesthetic | |
| Long-acting (duration of action, more than 8 hr) | Phenobarbital | Luminal | Winthrop | 15–600 | 15–30 | 100–200 | + | + | + | – | IV |
| | Metharbital | Gemonil | Abbott | 100–300 | – | – | – | – | ++ | – | III |
| | Methobarbital | Mebaral | Breon | 32–400 | 32–100 | – | + | – | ++ | – | IV |
| Intermediate-acting (duration of action, 5 to 8 hr) | Amobarbital | Amytal | Lilly | 65–400 | 65–200 | 100–200 | ++ | ++ | + | + | II |
| | Butabarbital | Butisol | McNeil | 15–120 | 15–30 | 50–100 | ++ | ++ | – | – | III |
| | Pentobarbital | Nembutal | Abbott | 30–120 | 30–40 | 100–200 | + | + | – | + | II |
| Short-acting (duration of action, 1 to 5 hr) | Secobarbital | Seconal | Lilly | 100–300 | – | 100–200 | – | ++ | + | + | II |
| | Talbutal | Lotusate | Winthrop | 120 | | 100–120 | – | ++ | – | – | III |
| Ultrashort-acting (duration of action, less than 1 hr) | Methohexital | Brevital | Lilly | – | – | – | – | – | – | + | IV |
| | Thiamylal | Surital | Parke, Davis | – | – | – | – | – | – | + | III |
| | Thiopental | Pentothal | Abbott | – | – | – | – | – | – | + | III |

Side effects: Residual sedation; vertigo; headache; hebetude; nausea; vomiting; emesis; skin rash; excitement; hypersensivity reactions; confusion; depression; gastric distress; megaloblastic anemia; respiratory depression, including apnea; circulatory depression, psychological dependence; and withdrawal symptoms.

Flurazepam (Dalmane), the first benzodiazepine to be marketed as a hypnotic, is less frequently used since the availability of newer benzodiazepines—temazepam (Restoril) and triazolam (Halcion). Benzodiazepines, unlike the barbiturates, do not alter liver microsomal enzymes. There is no evidence that they are dangerous in suicide atempts. There have been almost no successful well-documented suicides with any benzodiazepines alone. It appears quite likely that benzodiazepines pose much less liability for abuse than do the barbiturates and nonbarbiturate sedatives.

Combination drugs used in psychiatry are listed in Table IV.

## Untoward Drug Effects

### Behavioral Toxicity

In general, most psychotropic drugs, when given in large doses, produce some behavioral impairment in normal volunteers. However, when antipsychotic or antidepressant drugs are used to treat schizophrenia or depression, respectively, an improvement in cognitive functioning is often observed. Presumably, this improvement in the mental disorder results in an improvement in performance on the behavioral task that more than compensates for whatever toxicity the drug may have. It is, of course, possible that severely ill patients tolerate the drugs more effectively than do normal persons.

The sedative drugs and the minor tranquilizers produce a slight impairment on many behavioral tasks, yet they may improve performance on some tasks in certain situations. For example, 30 mg of chlordiazepoxide or 5 mg of diazepam reduces the peak velocity of saccadic eye movements by about 10 percent. Behavioral toxicity is typically dose dependent. Since tolerance to minor tranquilizers or to sedative drug-induced sedation may develop, it is highly desirable to conduct studies of chronic, as well as acute, behavioral toxicity. In the clinical situation, the patient may perform better with than without the drug in cognitive functions related to his work and social life, because the antianxiety effects of the drug free him from the disruptive influence of anxiety; this effect may more than counteract the behavioral toxicity produced by the drug. The behavioral toxicity of the minor tranquilizers is slight and barely measurable at normal doses; but its occurrence should be balanced against the therapeutic benefit in a given case. The sedative effects of different sedative agents can have an additive effect, which may be demonstrated on some tests of behavioral toxicity, such as simulated driving. Thus, when chlordiazepoxide, diazepam, sedative agents, amitriptyline, or phenothiazines are administered in normal doses, together with alcohol, significant behavioral impairment is noted. Sedation is a particular problem in the aged, who may be sensitive to sedatives and become drowsy, mentally confused, and fall down (sundowner syndrome).

Another aspect of the problem is the occurrence of a hangover on the morning after taking a sleeping pill. It has been demonstrated that impairment in cognitive functioning exists the morning after the injestion of 100 mg of pentobarbital. Similar impairments have been noted after the intake of other barbiturates and benzodiazepine sedatives. Thus, behavioral toxicity becomes a key consideration when administering sleeping pills. The clinician should balance the improved performance achieved after getting a good night's sleep with the behavioral toxicity expected. In patients where a drug has a particularly long life, it can take several weeks to reach steady-state drug blood levels.

### Side Effects

The side effects of the minor tranquilizers are usually of only slight importance and generally constitute no more than an inconvenience to the patient. Serious side effects are extremely rare, as those drugs do not cause extrapyramidal effects, autonomic side effects, or liver toxicity. The most common side effect is drowsiness, and patients should be advised not to drive or operate machinery until they can accurately gauge their own reactions to the drug. When used as hypnotics, long half-life drugs produce a slight congitive impairment that is still present the next morning.

Paradoxical excitement can occur with all drugs, but it probably occurs most frequently with the barbiturates. This adverse effect has been particularly noted among hyperkinetic children and in elderly or organically impaired adult patients.

Occasionally, a paradoxical increase in aggression has been noted following diazepam and chlordiazepoxide. This phenomenon, plus the disinhibiting properties that all sedative drugs possess, should caution the clinician to watch for adverse behavioral changes in anxious patients receiving antianxiety drugs.

With meprobamate, urticarial or erythematous rashes, anaphylactoid and other allergic reactions, and angioneurotic edema occur infrequently; even more rarely, cases of dermatitis, blood dyscrasias, gastrointestinal upsets, and extraocular muscular paralysis have been reported. With chlordiazepoxide and diazepam,

TABLE IV
COMBINATION DRUGS USED IN PSYCHIATRY

| Ingredients | Preparation | Manufacturer | Amount of Each Ingredient | Recommended Dosage* | Indications | D.E.A.† Control Level |
|---|---|---|---|---|---|---|
| Perphenazine and amitriptyline | Triavil | Merck, Sharp & Dohme | Tablet—2:25, 4:25, 4:50, 2:10, 4:10 | Initial therapy Tablet of 2:25 or 4:25 q.i.d. Maintenance therapy Tablet 2:25 or 4:25 b.i.d. or q.i.d. | Depression and associated anxiety | 0 |
| | Etrafon | Schering | | | | |
| Meprobamate and benactyzine | Deprol | Wallace | Tablet—400:1 | Initial therapy One tablet q.i.d. Maintenance therapy Initial dosage may be increased to six tablets a day then gradually reduced to the lowest levels that provide relief | Depression and associated anxiety | IV |
| Meprobamate and trihexethyl chloride | Milpath | Wallace | Tablet—400:25, 200:25 | Tablet of 400:25 at mealtimes and two tablets at bedtime One tablet t.i.d. at mealtime, and two tablets at bedtime | Peptic ulcer and irritable bowel syndrome | 0 |
| | Pathibamate | Lederle | | | | |
| Secobarbital and amobarbital | Tuinal | Lilly | Capsule—25:25, 50:50, 100:100 | 50 to 200 mg. at bedtime or 1 hour preoperatively | Insomnia; preoperative sedation | II |
| Dextroamphetamine and amphetamine | Biphetamine‡ | Pennwalt | Sustained release capsule—6.25:6.25 | 1 capsule in the morning | Exogenous obesity | II |
| Chlordiazepoxide and clinidium bromide | Librax | Roche | Capsule—5:2.5 | One or two capsules t.i.d. or q.i.d. before meals and at bedtime | Peptic ulcer, gastritis, duodenitis, irritable bowel syndrome, spastic colitis, and mild ulcerative colitis | 0 |
| Chlordiazepoxide and amitriptyline | Limbitrol | Roche | Tablet—5:12.5, 10:25 | Tablet of 5:12.5 t.i.d. or q.i.d. Tablet of 10:25 t.i.d. or q.i.d. initially, then may increase to six tablets daily as required | Depression and associated anxiety | IV |

* t.i.d., q.i.d., and b.i.d.
† D.E.A., Drug Enforcement Administration.
‡ The United States Food and Drug Administration recommends the use of amphetamine for weight reduction. However, various states (California, New York) allow these medications for short term use as an appetite suppressant and in depression for a 2- to 3-day trial to gauge the effectiveness of certain tricyclics. The authors, based upon their clinical experience, recommend a broader use of amphetamines in selected cases of depression, although such use is controversial.

the major side effects are drowsiness, dizziness, and ataxia.

Although the benzodiazepines are, in general, fairly safe drugs, chlordiazepoxide and diazepam have a low incidence of allergic skin reactions, characterized by the rapid onset of either widespread bilateral maculopapular rashes or hives and generalized itching.

In general, the side effects of the minor tranquilizers do not constitute contraindications for their use. The side effects, such as allergic reactions or gastrointestinal upsets, can usually be effectively controlled by dose reduction or by termination of the medication. Many of the minor complaints may be not pharmacological side effects, but somatic complaints that the patient would experience with a placebo as well. The fact that the minor tranquilizers are relatively safe is an advantage over the antipsychotics and antidepressants, which produce side effects with greater frequency and of somewhat greater severity.

It has been suggested that the ingestion of meprobamate or benzodiazepines during pregnancy, particularly in the first 3 months, may be associated with congenital abnormalities. Not all studies find that to be true, but, until the matter is resolved, physicians should avoid using minor tranquilizers in pregnant patients without a strong warning, since the possibility remains that any drug may be associated with a congenital abnormality. It is also important to avoid alcohol during pregnancy. Alcohol is also known to produce congenital anomalies, the so-called fetal alcohol syndrome.

### Suicide Potential

The possibility of suicide with most of the minor tranquilizers is minimal. Only rarely have successful suicides been reported with meprobamate at high doses; almost no suicides have been linked to benzodiazepines when used alone. It is far easier to commit suicide with the barbiturates. As few as 10 to 20 amobarbital sodium capsules may be fatal; with meprobamate, 20 to 40 g of the drug—50 to 100 of the 400-mg tablets—are required.

There may be a relationship between the prevalence of death by suicide and the availability of lethal amounts of pills.

### Physical Dependence and Tolerance

Of the drugs discussed in this section, the barbiturates, chlordiazepoxide, diazepam, and meprobamate have been clearly shown to produce physical dependence of the barbiturate type, as evidenced by human studies. Gluteth-

imide (Duriden) and methaqualone or Qualude (the latter drug has been withdrawn from the market) clearly have that same property, as documented by cases of patients experiencing the usual withdrawal syndrome. It must be assumed that the other nonbarbiturate hypnotics and the benzodiazepines share that undesirable pharmacological property. Alcohol certainly has shown that property for centuries, as evidenced by delirium tremens. The sedative antihistamines lack this potential, as do phenothiazines and tricyclic antidepressants.

On the basis of limited available information, a dose of 3,200 mg of meprobamate each day for 40 days or 300 mg of chlordiazepoxide for a month can cause clear physical dependence.

Withdrawal from diazepam produces a syndrome starting on the sixth day that peaks on the seventh day and largely disappears by the ninth day and that is characterized by tremor, dysphoric mood, muscle twitches and cramps, facial numbness, insomnia, anorexia, weakness, nervousness, weight loss, and orthostatic hypotension.

Cross-tolerance exists among all those drugs, so one can be used to suppress early withdrawal symptoms induced by the physical dependence of another drug. Cross-tolerance also accounts for the phenomenon of a patient being able to take large amounts of a variety of these drugs, with each drug producing increased tolerance to the others. Although pentobarbital has long been used as a standard detoxification agent, it seems more logical to use a longer-acting drug, such as diazepam; that is a practice already in vogue in some facilities for the detoxification of alcoholics.

Barbiturates are medically indicated for treatment of insomnia and anxiety; however, there is much controversy about their use because of their abuse potential and rapid induction of tolerance. For example, the California Medical Association and the California Board of Medical Quality Assurance recommends that short-acting barbiturates be used only for less than 14 days in the treatment of insomnia, and for short-term use in the treatment of anxiety. In the authors' experience, in selected cases and with careful medical supervision, some patients can be maintained on a low dose of barbiturates as a nightly hypnotic for longer periods, although this is controversial.

### Drug-Drug Interactions

With large numbers of patients taking multiple drugs, the potentialities for drug-drug interactions are considerable. Obviously, such interactions can occur between drugs taken by the patient on his own initiative, by combining over-the-counter medications or borrowed pills with therapeutically administered drugs. It has been shown that information concerning patient consumption of nonspecific drugs—such as antianxiety agents, sedatives, and over-the-counter drugs—is often not well communicated between physicians. That is, a physician may be careful in advising another physician that a patient is receiving a specific therapeutic drug, but he may fail to report that the patient was also provided with a prescription for sleeping pills. A drug-drug interaction occurs when one pharmacological agent influences the action or side effects of another drug, either qualitatively or quantitatively. One must also be aware of the fact that one drug could modify the pharmacokinetics of another drug by altering plasma levels, binding, excretion, absorption, and so forth (see Table V).

Drug interactions can be classified as to whether they involve (1) interactions between drugs on absorption; (2) interactions in the mechanisms by which the drugs reach the receptor site (binding to plasma proteins, displacement or increased binding, drug distribution, or drug transport and release to and from tissue); (3) interactions between drugs on receptor sites; (4) interactions between drugs during their metabolism; or excretion (stimulation of metabolism [induction] or inhibition of metabolism or increased or decreased urinary excretion).

A substantial body of data shows that on the basis of absorption, several types of interactions exist. Antacids can delay the absorption of both chlordiazepoxide and diazepam. Since clorazepate is a prodrug for desmethyldiazepine, being converted to the acid media of the stomach, the coadministration of an antacid slows the rate of absorption of desmethyldiazepam and lowers the rate of absorption.

Antacids may also interfere with the absorption of antipsychotics. Agents that slow gut motilities—such as anticholinergics, alcohol, and food—can potentially interfere with absorption, either by delaying or by impairing absorption.

The clinician should be aware of potential interactions, such as diazepam on muscle relaxants used in anesthesia, benzodiazepine's possible effect on dopa in the treatment of Parkinson's disease, and the influence of loxapine on phenytoin levels.

Drug-drug interactions can be complicated, particularly in drugs with several active metabolites. For example, acute alcohol intoxication can prolong elimination of chlordiazepoxide.

The benzodiazepines can elevate phenytoin levels. Disulfiram can elevate serum phenytoin levels and, furthermore, by interfering with the demethylation of chlordiazepoxide and diazepam, can prolong the half-life of those drugs. Oxazepam, temazepam, and lorazepam are directly conjugated by glucuronide formation; this interaction is not expected to apply to them.

Interactions of distribution include the interference with the hypertensive action of guanethidine by tricyclic antidepressants, such as dox-

TABLE V
DRUG-DRUG INTERACTIONS

| Type | Interaction | Comment |
|------|-------------|---------|
| Absorption | Some antacids may delay or interfere with absorption of benzodiazepines and chlorpromazine. | Since the clinician should adjust dose to clinical effect, he should not see this interaction clinically except when he needs to use a slightly higher dose. |
| Metabolism | 1. Barbiturates plus nonbarbiturate sedative and alcohol speed up metabolism of phenothiazines. | Another reason why the clinician needs to adjust dose to clinical response. |
| | 2. Disulfiram can prolong the half-life of benzodiazepines by interfering with desmethylation. | Oxazepam or lorazepam may be preferred in patients needing disulfiram, since those drugs are directly excreted as conjugates. |
| | 3. Methylphenidate or phenothiazines can increase plasma levels of tricyclics. | |
| | 4. Tricyclics can increase plasma levels of antipsychotics. | |
| Excretion | Acid urine increase and basic urine decrease excretion of amphetamine, phenelzine, tranylcypromine, or PCP. | Applies to any drug or diet that alters urine pH. |
| Distribution | Antipsychotics and antidepressants (including doxepin) interfere with the therapeutic action of guanethidine. | Clinically important, particularly for chlorpromazine and tricyclics, since it can render quanethidine useless for hypertension. |
| Receptor site | Both sedative and anticholinergic side effects of several drugs can produce toxicity. | A simple summation of a common pharmacological effect. |

epin and phenothiazines, as well as the appearance of interference of the hypertensive action of clonidine by tricyclic antidepressants. Interactions at the end organs include the addition of anticholinergic side effects from a number of psychotropic drugs, all of which have anticholinergic properties to produce what, in essence, is an atropine psychosis.

One of the most common drug-drug interactions is the addition of sedative effects on the central nervous system. This can occur with alcohol, sedative hypnotics, sedative tricyclic antidepressants, and, presumably, sedative antipsychotics. It might be expected to involve sedative tricyclics or antipsychotics but not stimulatory tricyclics.

Patients given a hepatocellular dose seem to be particularly sensitive to the sedative properties of a variety of psychotropic drugs. Indeed, the drugs are a common precipitant of hepatic coma. Undoubtedly, the most important cause is that the brains of patients in prehepatic coma may be unusually susceptible to the sedative properties of any sedative agent.

In patients with liver diseases, such as alcoholic cirrhosis, acute viral hepatitis, and hepatic malignancy, the half-life of drugs, such as diazepam, is markedly prolonged and the volume of distribution is increased. Specifically, diazepam's plasma binding is reduced, the volume of distribution is increased, and clearance is decreased. This does not apply to extrahepatic obstructive liver disease. In cirrhosis, the clearance of chlordiazepoxide and the plasma protein binding of that drug are reduced. Lorazepam, temazepam, and oxazepam are relatively unaffected by liver disease, since they are excreted by a different route.

In cirrhosis, there is a small increase in the half-life of lorazepam, because of a small increase in the volume of distribution, probably caused by a reduction in the extent of the drug's plasma binding. A significant change of plasma clearance of lorazepam has been noted. Other drugs excreted by the glucuronic pathway, oxazepam and temazepam, are relatively unaffected by liver disease, vis-a-vis its rate of metabolism.

Since elderly patients seem to be especially sensitive to sedative agents, some investigators have studied the possible mechanism for that effect. The most likely mechanisms are an increased brain sensitivity to the drug and impaired metabolism resulting in elevated brain drug levels.

Age increases the half-life for chlordiazepoxide and diazepam, and also increases the distribution of chlordiazepoxide and diazepam within the body. The plasma clearance of chlordiaze-poxide is reduced; the clearance of diazepam remains normal. There is a lower clearance of desmethyldiazepam in the elderly.

Oxazepam is conjugated, as a lorazepam, and temazepam and the conjugate metabolite is 3-glucuronide. However, the pharmacokinetic parameters of both oxazepam and lorazepam, unlike diazepam, are unaffected by age, and the glucuronidation pathway of metabolism appears to be resistant to aging processes.

Table VI lists the Drug Enforcement Administration's (D.E.A.) control levels of various drugs. Some states require special "triplicate" prescriptions to be used to further control Schedule II drugs. These prescriptions consist of three copies; one copy is sent to the state, which then maintains a computerized list of doctor and patient involved. This practice has been challenged in court on the grounds of a breach of confidentiality. To date, however, the state's position has been upheld.

### Provocative Test Panic Attack Disease

In 1972, it was observed that patients suffering from an anxiety syndrome sometimes called effort syndrome, developed abnormally high lactic acids after running. This led investigators to show that lactate infusions can precipitate anxiety attacks in patients who have the disorder, but not in controls. (There is evidence that chelation is not the mechanism which causes the induced panic). It was observed that effective treatment of the anxiety disorder resulted in patients no longer having lactate-induced panic attacks upon reinfusion. Unsuccessful treatment did not prevent reinfusion panic attacks.

Agoraphobics often respond to lactate with a panic attack, but reinfusion after successful clinical treatment of the agoraphobic fails to produce panic attacks. Since hyperventilation is a type of anxiety attack, clinical observation showed that the tricyclic drug chlorimipramine produced a reduction in hyperventilation attacks in patients after 1 month of treatment. This was followed, a month or two later, by a reduction in the fear that they might have such attacks.

### Mitral Valve Prolapse Syndrome

Mitral valve prolapse syndrome occurs somewhat more frequently in panic attack victims than in controls, but since there is a fairly high incidence in the general population, the possibility of a chance association exists. Since many patients with panic attack syndrome have the mitral valve prolapse syndrome, psychiatrists should be familiar with the syndrome, often

TABLE VI
CHARACTERISTICS OF DRUGS AT EACH DRUG ENFORCEMENT ADMINISTRATION (D.E.A.) CONTROL
LEVEL

| D.E.A. Control Level (Schedule) | Characteristics of Drug at Each Control Level | Examples of Drugs at Each Control Level |
|---|---|---|
| I | High abuse potential No accepted use in medical treatment in the United States at the present time and therefore not for prescription use | LSD, heroin, marijuana, peyote, mescaline, psilocybin, tetrahydrocannabinols, nicodeine, nicomorphine, and others |
| II | High abuse potential Severe physical dependence liability Severe psychological dependence liability | Amphetamine, opium, morphine, codeine, hydromorphine, phenmetrazine, cocaine, amobarbital, secobarbital, pentobarbital, methylphenidate, and others |
| III | Abuse potential less than levels I and II Moderate or low physical dependence liability High psychological liability | Glutethimide, methyprylon, PCP, nalorphine, sulfonmethane, benzphetamine, phendimetrazine, clortermine, mazindol, chlorphentermine, compounds containing codeine, morphine, opium, hydrocodone, dihydrocodeine and others |
| IV | Low abuse potential Limited physical dependence liability Limited psychological dependence liability | Barbital, phenobarbital, benzodiazepines, chloral hydrate, ethchlorvynol, ethinamate, meprobamate, paraldehyde, and others |
| V | Lowest abuse potential of all controlled substances | Narcotic preparations containing limited amounts of nonnarcotic active medicinal ingredients |

referred to as clickmurmur syndrome or Reed Barlow syndrome. It is characterized by a nonejection click with or without a late systolic high pitched murmur, best heard at the apex. The diagnosis can be confirmed by echocardiography. The syndrome is said to be associated with such symptoms as cardiac awareness, atypical chest pain, palpitations, shortness of breath, weakness, fatigue, and dizziness. The syndrome is also associated with musculoskeletal abnormalities such as pectus excavatum, kyphoscoliosis, straight back and tall-thin body habitus.

Irritable heart, or DaCosta's syndrome, has been noted since the Civil War, known by different names and associated with cardiac symptoms and autonomic adrenergic predominance (excess levels of or supersensitivity to peripheral catecholamine). Lactate induces panic attacks in agoraphobics and is associated with elevated epinephrine excretion in comparison to controls. Symptomatic mitral valve prolapse patients excreted elevated urinary epinephrine and norepinephrine. Just how panic attack syndrome, mitral valve prolapse, and a hyperadrenergic predominancy will sort out into cause and effect relationships and disease entities is unknown at this time.

**REFERENCES**

Ameer B: Teratology of psychoactive drugs. In *Psychopharmacology Update. New and Neglected Areas*, J M Davis, D Greenblatt, editors, p 1. Grune & Stratton, New York, 1979.

Cole J O, Altesman R J, Weingarten C H: Beta blocking drugs in psychiatry. McLean Hospital J *4:* 40, 1979.
Davis J M: Minor tranquilizers, sedatives, and hypnotics. In *Comprehensive Textbook of Pyschiatry*, ed 4, H I Kaplan, B J Sadock, editors, p 1537. Williams & Wilkins, Baltimore, 1985.
Greenblatt D J, Shader R I: *Benzodiazepines in Clinical Practice*. Raven Press, New York, 1974.
Greenblatt D J, Shader R I, Abernathy D R: Current states of benzodiazepines. N Engl J Med *309:* 354, 410, 1983.
Klein D F, Davis J M: *Diagnosis and Drug Treatment of Psychiatric Disorders*. Williams & Wilkins, Baltimore, 1969.
Klein D F, Honigfeld G, Feldman S: Prediction of drug effects in personality disorders. J Nerve Ment Dis *156:* 183, 1973.
Lader M, Pertursson H: Rational use of anxiolytic/sedative drugs. Drugs *25:* 514, 1983.
Richels K, Case G, Downing R W, Winokur A: Long-term diazepam therapy and clinical outcome. JAMA *250:* 767, 1983.
Schatzberg A F, Cole J O: Benzodiazepines in depressive disorders. Arch Gen Psychiatry *35:* 1359, 1978.

# 27.4    LITHIUM THERAPY

## Introduction

Lithium carbonate should be considered the treatment of choice for manic depressive illness. It has several advantages over neuroleptics, including a greater degree of specificity and ease of monitoring through plasma levels. In addition, lithium lacks the stigma associated with the antischizophrenic drugs, and does not produce tardive dyskinesia or sedation. From the patient's perspective, therefore, it is a much more acceptable drug. It should be noted, however, that lithium has a slower onset of action (i.e. a 7- to 12-day lag period) which may be a disadvantage in the treatment of highly disturbed manics. Most experts favor treating these cases with a combination of lithium and neuroleptics until the desirable behavioral control is accomplished, and the patient can be safely managed on lithium alone.

## Chemistry and Pharmacokinetics

Lithium is an alkali metal similar to sodium, potassium, magnesium, and calcium. Following ingestion, it is completely absorbed by the gastrointestinal tract. Serum levels peak in 1.5 to 2 hours (lithium carbonate) or 4 to 4.5 hours (slow-release preparation). Lithium does not bind to plasma proteins, and is distributed non-uniformly throughout body water. It reaches equilibrium after about 5 to 7 days of regular intake. Lithium has an elimination half-life of almost 24 hours. Though nonsignificant losses occur through the skin, and in the feces, about one-fifth of the lithium ion is eliminated via renal excretion. During each circulatory phase, plasma sodium levels (resulting from diuretics, excessive sweating, reduced sodium intake, etc.) initiate a compensatory increase in sodium reabsorption accompanied by lithium reabsorption. Considering these pharmacological properties, as well as the well-known potential of lithium to adversely effect CNS, thyroid, heart, and kidneys, it is necessary that candidates for lithium undergo a thorough physical examination in which particular attention is given to the evaluation of the above systems. Aside from well-functioning kidneys, there are no absolute contraindications to lithium therapy.

## Beginning Therapy

Placing a patient on lithium should be preceded by an initial dosage determination. Wide variability exists among patients in the dosage required to attain therapeutic plasma levels. Individual dosage requirements can be more accurately determined based on plasma lithium concentrations, 24 hours after taking a test dose of 600 mg of lithium carbonate.

Optimal therapeutic levels vary from individual to individual, and the physician should be guided primarily by the patient's clinical state and/or the development of side effects. Usually levels below 0.4 meq/l have not been associated with therapeutic response, whereas levels above 1.5 meq/l have been frequently associated with side effects. However, this is extremely variable,

and very low levels of lithium have been known to produce side effects. Based on a large number of studies, most of them retrospective, the recommended therapeutic range for the acute phase is approximately 0.8 to 1.8 meq/l, although deviations from this range (i.e. below or above) have been utilized quite successfully.

For the average healthy young adult in a manic episode, a dosage of 600 mg, three times daily, is recommended as the usual starting dose. However, because our knowledge regarding optimal levels is limited, an appropriate dosage schedule should always be determined on the basis of severity of the clinical condition, body weight, age, concurrent illness, and medication, as well as kidney function. The usual dosage range is between 900 and 2100 mg/day, although at times higher doses have been employed for extremely severe cases of mania without subsequent disturbing side effects. For severely disruptive behavior, intramuscular administration of neuroleptics at frequent time intervals is often considered preferable in order to attain rapid behavioral control and stabilization of the clinical condition. Following stabilization, the neuroleptic, usually haloperidol or chlorpromazine, should be given orally, preferably in liquid form, to prevent eventual covert disposal of the drug by the patient. When the effects of lithium become apparent, the neuroleptic should be gradually discontinued.

## Special Considerations of Lithium Treatment

**Elderly.** In view of the longer elimination half-life found in elderly individuals, these patients are at greater risk for toxicity and require less lithium, usually 900 mg daily, to achieve therapeutic levels.

**Pregnancy.** Due to the potential teratogenic effects of lithium, mainly cardiovascular, lithium should be discontinued during the first 3 or 4 months of pregnancy.

**Negative Fluid Balance.** Due to lithium's well known potential to lower renal concentration with resulting polyuria, polydipsia, and fluid loss, it is essential that patients drink plenty of fluids and have their serum lithium levels closely monitored. Under circumstances during which negative fluid balance is likely to occur (e.g., pre and post surgery), fluids should be given intravenously under close medical monitoring.

## Side Effects and Toxicity

### Central Nervous System Effects

The effects of lithium on the CNS vary and range from mild to severe. The least harmful and usually reversible effects include anxiety, fatigue, lassitude, lethargy, tension, impaired concentration, mild cognitive and memory impairment, decreased motor performance, muscular weakness, and tremor.

**Nerve Effects.** Chronic nephrotoxicity may develop following prolonged exposure to lithium, even when the plasma levels are within the usually accepted therapeutic range. Of the two major renal functional systems, tubular function is the most frequently affected, whereas glomerular function is affected to a much lesser extent. Morphological changes leading to irreversible renal damage have recently raised additional concern.

There are few reported cases of lithium-induced nephrotic syndrome—hypoalbuminemia, proteinuria, edema, and hyperlipidimia—at therapeutic levels. These rare complications, of unknown etiology, are reversible.

At present, it is conceivable that several factors are implicated in glomerular and tubular function defects, including preexistent renal pathology, high plasma lithium levels, and multiple dosing. Affective illness, per se, and concomitant treatment with other drugs may also be associated with changes of kidney morphology and need to be examined in prospective studies.

**Cardiac Effects.** The cardiac effects of lithium resemble hypokalemia on EKG. This is due to displacement of intracellular $K^+$ by the lithium ion. The most common changes on EKG are T-wave flattening or inversion. They are of a benign nature, and disappear after excretion of lithium from the body. Nevertheless, baseline EKG's are essential and should be repeated during maintenance. In rare cases, sinus and atrioventricular nodal arrhythmias, ventricular arrhythmias, edema, and congestive heart failure, have been associated with lithium therapy.

**Thyroid Effects.** Lithium also affects thyroid function, causing a generally benign diminution in the concentration of circulating thyroidal hormones. Reports of goiter (5 percent), benign reversible exopthalmos and hypothyroidism (3 to 4 percent), have also been attributed to lithium. About 50 percent of patients on chronic lithium treatment have abnormal TRH response, and approximately 30 percent have elevated TSH. If laboratory values of thyroid hormone indicate dysfunction, then supplementation can be administered safely. Initial TSH levels are indicated and should be repeated periodically. Hyperthyroidism has rarely been reported.

**Dermatologic Effects.** Several cutaneous side effects, which may be dose-dependent, have been associated with lithium treatment. The more prevalent effects include acneiform, follicular and maculopapular eruptions, pretibial ulcerations and worsening of psoriasis. Most of these respond to the usual dermatological measures. However, worsening of psoriasis and, at times, acneiform eruptions, may require discontinuation of lithium. Concurrent administration of tetracycline, may precipitate lithium toxicity.

## Long-term Treatment

Recent advances in the diagnosis and classification of affective disorders, combined with our improved knowledge of the natural course of the disease process, have contributed to our understanding of the value and problems associated with maintenance treatment. It has long been recognized that affective disorders are episodic. Biopolar episodes usually last about 4 months, while for unipolars the duration of an episode is about 4 to 8 months. Episodes are more frequent for bipolars (around 8) than for unipolars (5 to 6), and the frequency of episodes is greatest during the first 10 years of illness.

Lithium is the drug of choice for maintenance treatment by bipolar affective disorders. It is also effective in maintenance treatment of unipolar depressions. Antidepressants are clearly effective in maintenance treatment of unipolar depressions and are probably the drug of choice following recovery from a severe depressive episode. Their dosage should be decreased to the lowest level required for continued efficacy.

It should be noted, however, that these drugs are not preventive or prophylactic in the true medical sense (i.e. vaccinations in infectious diseases). Rather, their effectiveness is analogous to that of insulin or antihypertensives in medicine (i.e. they allow patients to live productive lives without serious limitations in their functioning).

There is a wide variation of response patterns to lithium maintenance, which ranges from complete abatement of subsequent episodes to no response at all (20 to 30 percent), with several degrees of intensity and frequency attenuation in between. Useful clinical predictors of positive response include: good quality of free intervals, diagnosis of affective disorder, and low frequency of preceding episodes (1 to 2 per year).

## Refractory Manias

Treatment failures usually range between 20 percent and 40 percent. These nonresponders cannot be easily identified on clinical or biochemical grounds. Nevertheless, several factors have been implicated, including family history, inadequate dose, low plasma lithium levels, previous failure of lithium treatment, rapid cycling (four or more episodes of mania per year), and diagnosis (schizophreniform features).

**REFERENCES**

Cade J F J: Lithium salts in the treatment of psychotic excitement. Med J Aust 36: 349, 1949.

Campbell D R, Kimball R R: Replication of "Prediction of antidepressant response to lithium": Problems in generalizing to a clinical setting. Am J Psychiatry, 141: 706, 1984.

Fieve R R, Dunner D L: Unipolar and bipolar affective states. In The Nature and Treatment of Depression, F Flach, S C Drafhi, editors, p 145. John Wiley & Sons, New York, 1975.

Georgotas A: Affective disorders: Pharmacotherapy. In Comprehensive Textbook of Psychiatry, ed 4, H I Kaplan, B J Sadock, editors, p 821. Williams & Wilkins, Baltimore, 1985.

Georgotas A, Gershon S: Lithium in manic-depressive illness: Some highlights and current controversies. In Lithium Controversies and Unresolved Issues, S Gershon, M Schou, N Klein, T Cooper, editors, p 57. Excerpta Medica, Amsterdam, 1979.

Georgotas A, Gershon S: Historical perspectives and current highlights on lithium treatment in manic-depressive illness. J Clin Psychopharmacol 1: 27, 1981.

Jefferson J W, Griest J H, Ackerman D L: Lithium Encyclopedia for Clinical Practice. American Psychiatric Press Inc., Washington, DC, 1983.

## 27.5  OTHER PHARMACOLOGICAL AGENTS

### Narcotherapy

The use of an intravenous injection of a drug that may facilitate the uncovering of emotion-laden material in psychotherapy is known as narcotherapy.

In chemotherapy, the antipsychotic or antidepressant drugs may directly exert their effect by counteracting the presumed biochemical abnormality of the psychotic disorder; that is, they have primarily an antipsychotic or antidepressant action. In narcoanalysis, the therapeutic value of the intervention lies somewhat in the emotional investment of the catharsis, but mostly in the increased insight that may be achieved from psychotherapy and those other psychological changes that may result from the encounter.

Both barbiturates and psychomotor stimulants may facilitate exploration and catharsis. In catharsis the patient psychologically reexperiences the traumatic event.

At present, psychomotor stimulants are used for this purpose in narcoanalysis. For example, 25 to 40 mg of methylphenidate can be slowly injected intravenously to produce a psycho-stimulant-induced narcotherapy session. Another technique is the use of a 10 percent solution of sodium amobarbital given at a rate of about 0.5 to 1.0 ml a minute; the rate and the total dose can be varied and should be adjusted to the clinical state achieved. The total dose may vary between 0.25 and 0.5 g, although occasionally some patients need up to 1.0 g. A combination of sedatives and psychostimulants can also be used. Patients have made dramatic and clinically significant gains after insights were uncovered, while reliving past experiences during the psychotherapeutic working through connected with those interviews.

Intravenous barbiturates have been used, and can still be used to produce rapid hypnosis in disturbed patients. Death from laryngospasm after intravenous barbiturates has occurred in some patients. Because of this, it is recommended that an anesthesiologist be readily available.

Diazepam (Valium) may be used in narcotherapy by slow IV administration. Generally, 10 mg or less are adequate to produce the slight slurring of speech that indicates the reduced level of awareness for suppressed material to be recalled.

### Other Uses

Barbiturates such as sodium amobarbital and sodium pentobarbital can be used as a provocative test to distinguish organic conditions from functional conditions. Neurological symptoms that are normally present in mild degree can become markedly worse after the administration of intravenous barbiturates, and symptoms such as confabulation, denial of illness, and disorientation may appear in blatant form after barbiturate administration when they were present in mild form during the baseline state. Patients with significant organic brain disease may have markedly less tolerance for barbiturate sedation than do other patients. Hence, one must beware of giving a toxic dose to the patient, since even a small dose may result in serious sedation or mild impairment of consciousness.

These agents are also useful in distinguishing catatonic stupor from retarded depression. The depressed patient often becomes sleepy; the catatonic patient sometimes experiences a temporary clearing of the catatonia, with a rational, lucid interval. Patients who do not eat because of catatonia may begin to eat during the lucid interval. Diazepam may prove a slightly safer and slightly more convenient intravenous sedative agent than amorbarbital for such purposes.

**REFERENCES**

Davis J M: Other pharmacological agents. In Comprehensive Textbook of Psychiatry, ed 4, H I Kaplan, B J Sadock, editors, p 1553. Williams & Wilkins, Baltimore, 1985.

Dysken M W, Chang S S, Casper R C, Davis J M: Barbiturate facilitated interviewing: A review. Biol Psychiatry, *14:* 421, 1979.

Dysken M W, Kooser J A, Haraszti J S, Davis J M: Clinical usefulness of sodium amobarbital interviewing. Arch Gen Psychiatry, *36:* 789, 1979.

Weinstein E A, Kahn R L, Sugarman L A, Linn L: The diagnostic use of amobarbital sodium (Amytal Sodium) in brain disease. Am J Psychiatry, *109:* 889, 1953.

Wender P H, Wood D, Reimherr F: Studies in attention deficit disorder, residual type (minimal brain dysfunction in adults). Psychopharmacol Bull *20:* 18, 1984.

---

# 27.6 CONVULSIVE THERAPIES

### History

In Italy during the mid-1930s, a team of neuropsychiatrists led by Cerletti were at work developing an experimental model for epilepsy, using electrically induced seizures. After being suitably impressed with both the effectiveness and the difficulties associated with pharmacoconvulsive therapy, Cerletti and Bini (see Figs. 1 and 2) made a decision to try their experimental technique on an acutely psychotic schizophrenic. Their successful results, reported in 1938, led to an eventual replacement of pharmacoconvulsive therapy with metrazol by its electrical counterpart. This new convulsive treatment modality was initially called electroshock therapy (EST), later being known as electroconvulsive therapy (ECT). By now, pharmacoconvulsive therapy has all but disappeared from psychiatric use, despite a brief period of resurgence beginning in the late 1950s with the development of the convulsive anesthetic gas flurothyl (Indoklon).

From the late 1930s to the present time, a number of modifications in ECT technique have appeared, such as muscular relaxation, anesthesia, oxygenation, unilateral stimulus electrode placement, and low energy stimuli, all of which have been proposed as means to lower morbidity without diminishing therapeutic efficacy. These modifications, along with refinements in the diagnostic utilization of ECT, have led to a contemporary practice of this treatment modality, which most psychiatrists believe still represents an important and appropriate treatment option.

### Electroconvulsive Therapy Technique

**Pretreatment Evaluation.** ECT as it is typically practiced in the United States today involves a series of electrically induced seizures

FIGURE 1. Ugo Cerletti. (Courtesy of New York Academy of Medicine.)

FIGURE 2. Lucio Bini. (Courtesy of New York Academy of Medicine.)

given at a rate of three per week. Because ECT is a major procedure in the sense that acute stresses on the cardiovascular, respiratory, musculoskeletal, and nervous systems are involved, a careful pretreatment evaluation is indicated. Generally, this includes a standard physical exam and medical history; blood and urine tests; electrocardiogram (ECG); spine and skull X-rays; and, in many settings, an electroencephalogram (EEG). The specter of ECT often elicits considerable fear and apprehension on the part of the patients and their significant others. It is important, therefore, as part of the informed consent process, to describe the procedure and all of its potential beneficial and adverse sequelae in as understandable and empathic a manner as possible. The use of involuntary ECT is quite rare today and should be reserved only for cases where the treatments are indicated on an urgent lifesaving basis or where a legally appointed guardian has concurred in its use. Relevant state and federal laws, along with the legal rights of the involved patient, must always be considered. Inasmuch as the very process of informed consent pertaining to severely impaired psychiatric patients may sometimes rest on dubious grounds, a careful record of the justification for the use of ECT, along with the judicious involvement of consultant psychiatric opinions, may be indicated.

**Preparation of the Patient for Treatment.** On completion of the pretreatment evaluation and informed consent procedure, arrangements are made to begin the course of ECT treatments. The patient's ongoing medications should be carefully assessed for possible drug interactions with adjunctive agents used with ECT. This assessment includes the effects of anticholinesterase ophthalmic solutions, phenelzine (Nardil), and lithium on succinylcholine chloride (Anectine) metabolism; other toxic effects, e.g. hypotensive collapse with reserpine, increased CNS sequelae with lithium; and interference with the ability to electrically induce a seizure, e.g. sedative-hypnotics and anticonvulsants. Such medication should be adjusted accordingly, keeping in mind the possibility of a drug withdrawal syndrome.

Thirty minutes prior to treatment an anticholinergic agent, such as atropine or methscopolamine, is injected subcutaneously or intramuscularly (IM) in order to minimize secretions and to create a mild relative tachycardia that will help prevent potential treatment-related bradycardias. Alternatively, this drug may be given intravenously (IV) at the time of the treatment. Atropine, at an IM or subcutaneous dose of 0.6 to 1.0 mg, has traditionally been favored, even though methscopolamine, which does not cross the blood-brain barrier, may be preferable.

**Anesthesia, Muscular Relaxation, and Oxygenation.** Anesthesia has become a necessary concomitant of ECT because of the respiratory paralysis associated with muscular relaxation. The depth of anesthesia should be as light as possible, not only to minimize adverse effects, but also due to the fact that the typical anesthetic agents used with ECT elevate seizure threshold, i.e. require a higher intensity electrical stimulus. In most settings methohexital (Brevital) or thiopental (Pentothal) are used. The former is probably preferable in that the incidence of ECT-associated cardiac arrhythmias appears to be less. The dose of anesthetic, applied either by intravenous bolus or drip, should be titrated to a light anesthetic response at the time of the first treatment session. For methohexital, a typical dose for a medium-sized adult is 60 mg, although a considerable range (30 to 160 mg) occurs.

Following the onset of anesthetic effect, generally within a small fraction of a minute, the muscle relaxant agent is injected intravenously. Succinylcholine, an ultra fast-acting depolarizing blocking agent has gained virtually universal acceptance for this purpose. The optimum succinylcholine dose is that which provides enough relaxation to stop most, but not all, of the major ictal body movements. A typical starting dose is 60 mg for a medium-sized adult. If musculoskeletal or cardiac disease necessitates the use of total relaxation, the addition of curare (3 to 6 mg IV) given several minutes prior to anesthetic induction, along with increased succinylcholine dosage, is indicated. If necessary, a peripheral nerve stimulator can be used to ascertain the presence of complete neuromuscular block. The presence of seizure activity under circumstances of complete relaxation can be monitored either by EEG or by the prevention of succinylcholine flow to one of the forearms, using an inflated blood pressure cuff.

Because succinylcholine is a depolarizing blocking agent, its action is marked by the presence of muscle fasciculations, or fine twitching movements, which move in a rostrocaudal progression. Clinically, this is a very useful phenomenon, as the disappearance of these movements indicates that maximal relaxation has been achieved.

Due to the short half-life of succinylcholine, the duration of apnea following administration generally is not longer than the delays in return to consciousness associated with the combined effects of anesthetic agent and postictal state. In cases of inborn or acquired pseudocholinesterase deficiency, however, or where the metabolism of succinylcholine is disrupted by drug interaction, a prolonged apnea may occur, and the treating physician should always be prepared to manage such an eventuality.

It has long been known that oxygenation protects the brain from seizure-related anoxia. As a result, oxygenation of ECT patients from the onset of anesthesia to the resumption of adequate spontaneous respiration, except for the brief interval of electrical stimulation, is strongly indicated.

**Stimulus Electrode Placement.** There continues to be controversy regarding the optimum location of stimulus electrodes on the scalp. The traditional fashion has been to place the electrodes bifrontotemporally, each with its center approximately 1 inch above the midpoint of an imaginary line drawn from the tragus of the ear to the external canthus of the eye.

The use of unilateral nondominant electrode placement is associated with much less confusion and acute amnesia, but has still not predominated in some countries because of an ongoing controversy regarding its efficacy and its being more difficult to learn to administer properly. For most patients, unilateral ECT is as effective as bilateral ECT, although there remains the possibility that an as yet undefined subgroup of patients may respond either better or quicker to bilateral ECT. To deal with this uncertainty, some clinicians now routinely start patients on unilateral ECT and switch to bilateral placement if no significant improvement is forthcoming after six or more treatments.

With unilateral ECT, one stimulus electrode is typically placed over the nondominant frontotemporal area, as noted above for bilateral placement. Although a number of locations for the second stimulus electrode have been proposed, placement on the nondominant centroparietal scalp, just lateral to the midline vertex, appears to provide a configuration associated with a relatively low seizure threshold in terms of stimulus intensity.

The selection of which cerebral hemisphere is dominant can generally be accomplished by a simple series of performance tasks, i.e. to determine handedness and footedness, along with the patient's stated side of preference. Right body responses correlate very highly with left brain dominance. If the responses are mixed or if they clearly indicate left body dominance, there is no noninvasive way to unequivocally establish the side of brain dominance. In such cases, the clinician should alternate the polarity of unilateral stimulation at successive treatments while monitoring the time that it takes the patient to recover consciousness and to answer simple orientation and naming questions. The side of stimulation associated with less rapid recovery and return of function can be considered dominant.

**The Electrical Stimulus.** Following attainment of muscular relaxation, usually ascertainable by the disappearance of fasciculations from the patient's calf muscles, the stimulus can be delivered. The precise stimulus settings depend on the machine utilized and the individual patient's seizure threshold, but the approach chosen should reflect a desire to achieve a seizure of greater than 25 to 30 seconds by behavioral or electrophysiological criteria. Seizures of more than 60 seconds sometimes indicate that the stimulus is grossly suprathreshold and can be diminished at a later treatment session; at other times even a small decrease in stimulus intensity can lead to no seizure at all. If no seizure is produced after about 20 seconds, restimulation at a higher intensity setting should be carried out. Waiting too long before restimulation may cause the effects of the anesthetic or muscular relaxant agents or both to wear off.

The most commonly used type of U.S. ECT device is the Medcraft B-24. This apparatus allows stimulus voltage and duration to be set by the user, while the current delivered is directly proportional to the voltage and inversely proportional to the scalp impedance between the two stimulus electrodes. Typical starting settings for this device are 140 V rms and 0.6 seconds' duration.

**The Induced Seizure.** The production of a tonic-clonic type of generalized seizure is the mechanism behind both therapeutic and adverse effects associated with ECT. With the advent of muscular relaxation with ECT, it has become clear that it is the neuronal ictal response rather than the behavioral, i.e. convulsive aspects of the seizure, that is essential. As alluded to earlier, there is some evidence indicating that seizures of less than 25 to 30 seconds may not be as effective as longer ones, but as yet, there is no consistent evidence that mean or cumulative seizure length by itself is responsible for therapeutic response.

In order to ensure that a seizure has occurred, the treating physician must be able to either observe some evidence of tonic-clonic movements or to detect electrophysiological evidence of seizure activity from the EEG or EMG. Seizures with unilateral ECT, although typically generalized and bilaterally synchronous, are asymmetrical, demonstrating a higher ictal EEG amplitude over the stimulated hemisphere. Occasionally, however, unilateral seizures may be induced, and for this reason, it is important that at least a single pair of EEG electrodes is placed over the contralateral hemisphere when using unilateral ECT.

Behaviorally, a brief muscular contraction, usually strongest in the jaw and facial muscles, is seen concurrent with the flow of stimulus current, regardless of whether a seizure will occur. The first behavioral sign of ictus is often a plantar extension lasting up to 10 to 20 seconds and marking the tonic phase. This phase is then followed by rhythmic, i.e. clonic, contractions that decrease in frequency and finally disappear. Electroencephalographically, the tonic phase is marked by high-frequency sharp activity on which may be superimposed even higher frequency muscle artifact. During the clonic phase, bursts of polyspike acitivity occur simultaneously with the muscular contractions, but usually persist for at least a few seconds following termination of clonic movements. Postictally there is often some transient suppression and occasionally even an apparent total absence of background EEG activity. Such suppression is much less likely to occur with unilateral ECT, particularly over the nonstimulated hemispheres.

Prolonged seizures (seizures of more than 5 minutes) or status epilepticus are rare and can be terminated either with additional doses of anesthetic agent or with intravenous diazepam (Valium). Management of such complications should be accompanied by intubation, because the oral airway is insufficient to maintain adequate ventilation over an extended apneic period.

**Number and Spacing of ECT Treatments.** Rather than using a fixed number of treatments, the length of the ECT course should be determined on the basis of clinical response. Patients being treated for depression typically show some signs of improvement after the first few treatments, with peak response being attained between 5 and 10 treatments. Manics, catatonics, and some schizoaffective schizophrenics also require an average of 6 to 10 treatments. Other schizophrenics, particularly those with a chronic level of impairment, may not reach a maximal response until after 20 to 25 treatments, for those cases that are ECT-responsive.

**Maintenance Treatment.** It can be categorically stated that an acute course of ECT induces a remission but does not, in itself, prevent relapse. A strong consideration of post-ECT maintenance treatment should always be made. Generally, this maintenance therapy is pharmacological, although a role for maintenance ECT still remains to be clarified.

## Theory of ECT Action

One popular hypothesis for ECT's therapeutic effect involves a potentiation by ECT of monoaminergic pathways leading from diencephalic areas, which are important to seizure generalization, to the hypothalamus, and also to limbic regions. Such an activation would presumably be capable of producing the changes in mood and vegetative symptomatology that are known to reflect a positive response to ECT. Evidence for this hypothesis continues to unfold, with results of recent studies of receptor sensitivity changes suggesting a strong role for heightened

norepinephrine turnover. In addition, neuroendocrine changes consistent with activation of specific hypothalamic nuclei have been reported. In this regard, there is evidence that hypothalamic dysfunction, as indicated by an inability to suppress cortisol response following a dose of dexamethasone, may be a predictor of a good therapeutic response to ECT.

## Indications for ECT

As noted, the most common indication for ECT is the presence of a major depressive episode. It is likely that over 80 percent of ECT patients in the United States now carry such a diagnosis. The closer a patient's presentation fits with a diagnosis of severe major depressive episode with melancholia, the more likely it is that a satisfactory response to ECT will take place. In practice, 80 to 90 percent of such individuals will show marked improvement, a significantly higher figure than with pharmacological intervention. The presence of psychotic symptomatology, usually a poor prognostic sign for antidepressant drug treatment by itself, does not appear to attenuate the changes of a good response to ECT.

Approximately 15 to 20 percent of patients receiving ECT are being treated for schizophrenia. ECT induces a remission in a sizable fraction of such individuals who have an acute presentation, particularly if it is accompanied by catatonic or affective symptomatology. Its efficacy in such cases appears roughly equivalent to neuroleptics. In chronic schizophrenia, only 5 to 10 percent of patients will show a major improvement, although it should be noted that much of these data are based on drug nonresponders.

Although not well established by controlled studies, ECT is quite effective in mania. Because of the high likelihood of response to pharmacological management, however, only around 3 percent of ECT patients carry such a diagnosis.

## Contraindications

There are no absolute contraindications to ECT; only situations for which there is increased risk. Patients with intracranial masses, including tumors, hematomas, and evolving strokes, are likely to undergo profound neurological deterioration with ECT because of an ECT-associated transient breakdown of the blood-brain barrier and increase in intracranial pressure. ECT for such patients should only be done in the presence of measures, such as antihypertensives and steroids, designed to minimize the likelihood and severity of these adverse sequelae. The presence of an acute myocardial infarction raises the risk of further cardiac decompensation with ECT, due to the increased cardiovascular demands associated with the procedure. Severe underlying hypertension can be of concern, because ECT by itself increases blood pressure to a marked degree. Bringing the blood pressure under control, at least at the time of each treatment, is essential.

### Adverse Effects

**Mortality.** The mortality rate with ECT has been variously estimated to be between 1:1,000 and 1:10,000 patients; roughly the same as the rate associated with brief general anesthesia itself. Death is usually on the basis of cardiovascular complications and is more likely to occur in patients whose cardiac status is already compromised.

**Systemic Effects.** The use of anticholinergic premedication, oxygenation, muscular relaxation, and anesthesia have all acted to decrease the presence of adverse effects with ECT. Occasional, although usually quite mild, transient cardiac arrhythmias occur, particularly in patients with ongoing cardiac disease. These arrhythmias are usually a byproduct of the brief postictal bradycardia, and, therefore, they can often be prevented by an increase in the dosage of anticholinergic premedication. At other times arrhythmias may occur secondary to a tachycardia present during the seizure or may occur as the patient returns to consciousness. Prophylactic administration of propranolol (Inderal) can be useful in such cases. As mentioned earlier, a prolonged apneic state may take place under circumstances where succinylcholine metabolism is impaired. Although potentially life-threatening, such cases can usually be managed with supportive care, including intubation and continued positive pressure ventilation. Rarely, toxic or allergic reactions to the pharmacological agents used in the ECT procedure have been reported.

**CNS Effects.** The greatest area of concern on the part of both professional and lay groups regarding ECT has to do with the potential adverse CNS changes. The great majority of objective test data indicate that memory and other forms of cognitive function have returned at least to baseline by 1 to 6 months following ECT. Some ECT patients continue to complain of memory difficulties of a persistent nature. Measures of autobiographical memory function, although usually not objectively verifiable, have suggested the possibility of continued mild, spotty memory losses in some individuals. Because of this fact, the possibility of mild, persistent memory loss should be included in the informed consent procedure.

### Risk-Benefit Considerations

The clinical choice of any form of treatment is predicated on a comparative analysis of the risks and benefits of all available forms of treatment for a given condition. This means that a decision to recommend ECT must follow a consideration of the relative risks and benefits of alternative treatment modalities, typically pharmacotherapy and psychotherapy. Such a comparison will be weighted differently depending on the specific constellation of symptoms and risk factors presented by each individual case. A depressed suicidal patient who refuses to eat and has a history of severe cardiac disease is someone for whom ECT appears more highly indicated than does an initial drug trial. For an uncomplicated depressed outpatient, who, although severely ill, is still working and able to be managed at home, the decision scales shift in the opposite direction.

### REFERENCES

Abrams R, Essman W B, editors: *Electroconvulsive Therapy: Biological Foundations and Clinical Applications.* SP Medical Scientific Books, New York, 1982.
American Psychiatric Association Task Force on ECT: *Task Force Report 14: Electroconvulsive Therapy.* American Psychiatric Association, Washington, DC, 1978.
Crowe R R: Electroconvulsive therapy—a current perspective. N Engl J Med *331:* 163, 1984.
Fink M: *Convulsive Therapy: Theory and Practice.* Raven Press, New York, 1979.
Kalinowsky L B, Hippius H, Klein H E: *Biological Treatments in Psychiatry.* Grune & Stratton, New York, 1982.
Lerer B, Weiner R D, Belmaker R H: *ECT: Basic Mechanisms.* John Libbey, London, 1984.
Palmer R L, editor: *Electroconvulsive Therapy: An Appraisal.* Oxford University Press, London, 1981.
Scovern A W, Kilmann P R: Status of ECT: A review of the outcome literature. Psychol Bull *87:* 260, 1980.
Weiner R D: Does electroconvulsive therapy cause brain damage? Behav Brain Sci *7:* 1, 1984.
Weiner R D: Convulsive therapies. In *Comprehensive Textbook of Psychiatry,* ed 4, H I Kaplan, B J Sadock, editors, p 1558. Williams & Wilkins, Baltimore, 1985.

## 27.7  PSYCHOSURGERY

### Definition

Psychosurgery is the surgical intervention to sever fibers connecting one part of the brain with another or to remove, destroy, or stimulate brain tissue with the intent of modifying or altering disturbances of behavior, thought content, or mood for which no organic pathological cause can be demonstrated by established tests and techniques. Similar neurosurgical procedures are also undertaken for the relief of intractable pain.

This definition encompasses the span of the various therapeutic and research approaches by surgical means to elucidate the intricate relationships of brain anatomy, physiology, and abnormal human behavior.

## Anatomical and Physiological Aspects

Psychosurgery was introduced solely on the basis of the results of animal experimentation, without a theoretical anatomical or physiological rationale. The results were attributed to sectioning the connections of the frontal cortex with other parts of the brain, particularly with the thalamus. Clinical experience soon indicated that the prefrontal operations that avoided the connections of the lateral cortex produced benefits little different from those by more extensive procedures, but eliminated or reduced the severe adverse psychological effects of the extensive procedures (see Fig. 1).

The limbic system plays a major role in regulating the emotions and integrating the functions of cortical and subcortical structures. The reported beneficial outcome of small lesions in different portions of the limbic system is at least as favorable as that of the earlier prefrontal lobotomies. Especially important is the absence of adverse effects, such as intellectual deterioration and personality changes.

The benefits resulting from psychosurgery are all derived by interruption of the interconnecting pathways of areas involved in the regulation of the emotions. Thought disorders, delusions, hallucinations, and obsessive thoughts persist unchanged after the operation, but, because the affective component associated with them is severed, they usually cease to disturb the patient.

## Extent of Psychosurgery

A few years ago, exaggerated charges were leveled that thousands of lobotomies were being performed on hapless patients. The figure of 40,000 to 50,000 lobotomies was cited, with the implication that thousands more were still being carried out each year.

Most techniques in recent years sever fibers in the white matter, and should be called tractotomies. The term lobotomy is frequently but erroneously applied to all psychosurgical procedures, but is accurately used when restricted to the long-abandoned prefrontal operations. Such technical restriction should be observed because

of the negative emotional connotations automatically associated with the word lobotomy, as a result of the highly publicized adverse effects the procedure produced.

The total number of lobotomies that have been performed in the United States is unknown, as is the number of other psychosurgical procedures, but the above figures are clearly exaggerated. In any case, the vast majority of lobotomies were done before 1955. By that time, the serious limitations of the procedure were well recognized, and more limited operations were being pursued. Further, the introduction of the phenothiazines, beginning in 1952, provided pharmacological measures that, in a large majority of cases, were effective in controlling or reducing the disturbed, aggressive, and assaultive behavior in chronically ill patients hitherto not responsive to other available therapeutic efforts except psychosurgery. Also contributing to the rapid decline in psychosurgery in the 1950s was the availability of safe muscle relaxants that, combined with intravenous short-acting barbiturate anesthesia, permitted the more extensive use of electroshock treatment.

## Follow-up Studies

When psychosurgery was first introduced, the primary purpose was the relief of the patient's distressing emotional condition. This has continued to the present as the justification for such an intrusive procedure. The early hope that psychopathology in the cognitive field would also yield to treatment soon faded as follow-up studies were published. Although most reports indicated substantial and comparatively similar improvement rates, the studies were all open to the criticism that they lacked a scientific methodology. That is, to a large extent, understandable in view of the primary purpose for which the operation was originally undertaken. Moreover, emphasis on scientifically constructed investigations is a recent phenomenon in medical research. But, even today, the lack of reliable instruments to measure comprehensive psychological and behavioral change still persists. Follow-up studies are relatively rare in recent United States literature. In Britain, such studies are more frequent and of reasonable quality. Almost all published reports support the conclusion that a majority of chronically ill patients have benefited, although the benefits vary according to the category of the disorder.

One of the major problems in the evaluation of recent psychosurgery arises from the different procedures and sites of the lesions by individual neurosurgeons, resulting in small numbers in comparable groups of patients. The most fre-

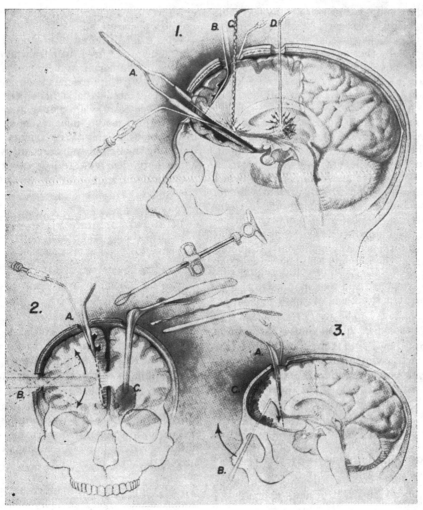

FIGURE 1.    American leukotomy techniques (Scoville. *Diagram 1, A,* Scoville's orbital undercutting; *B,* Scoville's undercutting of superior convexity; *C,* Grantham's electrocoagulation of inferior medial quadrant; *D,* Spiegel and Wycis's stereotoxic electrocoagulation of thalamic nucleus. *Diagram 2, A,* Scoville's cingulate gyrus undercutting; Livingston's cingulate gyrus subcortical sectioning; *B,* Freeman and Watts's "closed" standard lobotomy; *C,* medial inferior quadrant section by McKenzie's eukotome method, Schwartz's nasal speculum method, Grantham's electrocautery method, and Poppen's direct vision suction and spatula method. *Diagram 3, A,* Poppen's "open" standard lobotomy under direct vision; *B,* Freeman's transorbital lobotomy; *arrow* indicates deep frontal cut; *C,* Pool's topectomy operation. (From W Sargant, E Slater: *An Introduction to Physical Methods of Treatment in Psychiatry.* Reprinted with permission of E & S Livingstone, London, 1963.)

quent operation in the United States is anterior cingulotomy.

### Indications

Although some psychiatrists are of the opinion that there are established indications for the procedures, others believe that further research is required. The literature tends to the global conclusion that many patients may benefit, but that specific indications continue to be indefinite. Some psychiatrists believe that these procedures should never be used because of the irreversible damage to the brain. Psychosurgical

treatment of mental illness is one of the most controversial subjects in psychiatry.

There seems to be consensus however, that benefits are derived from operations that interrupt or ablate connections of parts of the brain that alter the patient's affective state. The condition for which the best and most consistent results are obtained is that of long-continued, severe depression that has not responded to other available therapies, including electroshock. Some psychiatrists hold that temporary improvement from electroshock, by evidencing a still intact personality in those chronically depressed patients, is a prognostically favorable indicator for psychosurgery.

There is a consensus that schizophrenic patients, especially those who manifest emotional blunting, do not do well. Moreover, psychosurgery does not seem to reduce the speed of deterioration in schizophrenia and may, in fact, hasten it.

Severe incapacitating anxiety may be relieved, and improvement in phobic states seems to be due to the relief of the affective component. Varying degrees of benefit may be obtained in obsessive-compulsive disorders, especially when psychic distress is concurrently present. Clinical reports on prefrontal lobotomy seem to claim greater success in obsessive-compulsive disorders than is obtained with the recent conservative operations, such as cingulotomy. It should be noted that the patients who have undergone psychosurgery for their conditions are ones who have failed to respond to all other forms of standard treatment.

Even among psychiatrists who believe that psychosurgery has a place in the therapeutic armamentarium, the vast majority believe that it should be considered only after adequate trials of all other available forms of treatment have failed to relieve distress in patients incapacitated by long-standing, severe emotional disorders. It is a treatment of last resort. Disagreements exist with respect to the length of time that should elapse before surgery is performed. From some follow-up studies, it seems that long-standing conditions, including depression, are much less likely to benefit than are recent conditions. Some psychiatrists believe that the sooner the surgery is performed, the better the outcome. When adequate trials of alternative therapies are undertaken, a period of about 1 year or more may pass before psychosurgery is undertaken.

## Complications and Adverse Effects

With early prefrontal lobotomies, serious complications included mortality rates varying from 0.5 to 5 percent. These deaths were often due to hemorrhages from severed, often aberrant, vessels. In up to 15 percent of patients, epilepsy occurred, and might ensue immediately after the operation or after some time had passed. Generally, the epilepsy was well controlled by anticonvulsants. With the more limited operations, especially the stereotactic, these adverse effects have been largely eliminated, with the mortality rate below 0.1 percent and the epilepsy rate at 0.7 percent.

In the past, there have been catastrophic changes in the patient's personality. With operations such as cingulotomy, such outcomes are not now encountered.

With extensive prefrontal lobotomy, intellectual deficits occurred, usually when the lateral surface of the cortex and its connections were involved. With approaches such as orbital undercutting, intellectual deficits, as measured by intelligence tests, were not evident. However, more refined testing may reveal some changes in abstract thinking. With current procedures involving the limbic system, cognitive loss, such as memory, does not seem to occur and, when demonstrated, may be due to preexisting organic changes.

## Ethical and Legal Considerations

In 1974 the United States Congress, partly in response to the charges of abuse of psychosurgery, established a National Commission for the Protection of Human Subjects of Biomedical and Behavioral Research (Public Law 93-384). The commission was charged with investigating the extent and the use of psychosurgery in the 5 years from 1968 through 1972 and with making recommendations to the Congress. The recommendations of the commission, published in 1977, closely paralleled those of an American Psychiatric Association task force on psychosurgery. Both studies found no evidence that the procedures had been used for purposes of political or social control, racism, or sexism or that minority groups had been subjected to psychosurgery because of membership in such categories.

The commission recommended that a national psychosurgery advisory board be established to collect and collate preoperative and postoperative clinical data regarding all patients undergoing psychosurgery; that such surgery be restricted to institutions with institutional research boards approved by the Department of Health, Education, and Welfare and charged with the responsibility of determining the competence of the surgeon and the appropriateness of the procedure; that valid informed consent be given; and that adequate preoperative and postoperative evaluations be performed. Additional protections were recommended with regard to minors, prisoners, involuntarily committed mentally ill patients, incompetent persons, and persons for whom a legal guardian has been appointed. The commission, like the APA task force, rejected the proposal that psychosurgery for therapeutic reasons be prohibited by law.

## Future of Psychosurgery

From the 1974 survey, it was evident that the number of neurosurgeons performing psychosurgery and the number of procedures undertaken were declining by 1973. It is estimated that well under 100 operations are now carried out each year in the United States. Such psychosurgery as is being performed is now done as a treatment of last resort.

In spite of the recent advances in the therapeutic modalities for psychiatric disorders, a relatively small number of severely distressed patients, totally incapacitated both socially and vocationally, are not responsive to any of the currently available forms of treatment, and for them psychosurgery is the only alternative hope. As a result of continuing experience with the disabling adverse effects of the other forms of therapy, it is possible that, in the future, the number of psychosurgical procedures performed may increase.

## REFERENCES

Bartlett J, Bridges P, Kelly D: Contemporary indications for psychosurgery. Br J Psychiatry *138:* 507, 1981.

Corkin S: A prospective study of cingulotomy. In *The Psychosurgical Debate,* E S Valenstein, editor, p 164. W H Freeman & Co, San Francisco, 1980.

Curson D A, Trauer T, Bridges P K, Gillman P K: Assessment of outcome after psychosurgery using the present state examination. Br J Psychiatry, *143:* 118, 1983.

Donnelly J: Psychosurgery, In *Comprehensive Textbook of Psychiatry,* ed 4, H I Kaplan, B J Sadock, editors, p 1563. Williams & Wilkins, Baltimore, 1985.

Kiloh L G, Smith J S: The neural bases of aggression and its treatment by psychosurgery. Aust NZ J Psychiatry *12:* 21, 1978.

Mitchell-Heggs N, Kelly D, Richardson A: Stereotactic limbic leucotomy: A follow-up at 16 months. Br J Psychiatry *128:* 226, 1976.

Sider R C: The ethics of therapeutic modality choice. Am J Psychiatry *141:* 390, 1984.

Teuber H L, Corkin S, Twitchell T: A study of cingulotomy in man. In *Psychosurgery: The Report of the National Commission for the Protection of Human Subjects of Biomedical and Behavioral Research—Appendix,* publication (OS) 77-0002. US Dept of Health, Education, and Welfare, Washington, DC, 1977.

Tippin J, Henn F A: Modified leucotomy in the treatment of intractable obsessional neurosis. Am J Psychiatry *139:* 1601, 1982.

Valenstein E S: The practice of psychosurgery: A survey of the literature (1971–1976). In *Psychosurgery: The Report of the National Commission for the Protection of Human Subjects of Biomedical and Behavioral Research—Appendix,* publication (OS) 77-0002. US Dept of Health, Education, and Welfare, Washington, DC, 1977.

# 27.8　MISCELLANEOUS ORGANIC THERAPIES

## Introduction

Organic therapies are therapies that assume a disturbance of brain functions on the biochemical or neurophysiological level. These therapies—which may use inhalation, invasive procedures, and electricity—are, on the whole, empirical and are being increasingly replaced by psychopharmacology. Some organic treatments, however, claim superior results, without the occasionally crippling side effects, when psychopharmacology has failed, and offer alternative treatment possibilities for drug-resistant psychoses.

## Subcoma Insulin Therapy

The sedative effects of mild hypoglycemia have been largely replaced by tranquilizers; however, a few psychiatrists continue to use small doses of insulin to produce a somnolent state also known as subcoma.

The fasting patient initially receives 20 units of insulin intramuscularly early in the morning and stays in a semidark room. After 3 hours of rest, the patient receives a nutritious meal. The insulin dose is increased daily by 10 units but should not exceed a total of 100 units. If coma inadvertently develops, the patient should receive, intramuscularly, 1 mg of glucagon, which should enable him within 15 minutes to drink a glucose solution. The next insulin dose should be reduced by 10 units. Usually, a dose of 50 units is sufficient. The treatment, which is given on weekdays, with a reduction to 20 units on weekends, can be given on an outpatient basis. This treatment has been used for patients in need of immediate physical rehabilitation, and good results have been reported in posttraumatic stress disorders, exhaustion, postconcussional states, hysterical vomiting, colitis, and gastric ulcer.

Aftershocks, which are hypoglycemic attacks several hours after the meal, and seizures in predisposed patients have been reported. The main goals are sedation and rapid weight gain to ensure an optimal physical and metabolic level. Subcoma insulin therapy has been largely abandoned. Its efficacy cannot be evaluated.

## Insulin Coma Therapy

The development of tranquilizers and emphasis on patient's rights, malpractice suits, cost effectiveness, and short hospitalization have eliminated insulin coma therapy from most American hospitals. The technique was introduced by Manfred Sakel in 1933 following his observation that schizophrenics who went into coma appeared to recover.

**Technique.** The patient initially receives a trial dose of 10 to 15 units of insulin intramuscularly to determine allergy and hypersensitivity. If there is no allergy, this dose should be increased daily by 5 to 10 units until coma is obtained, usually between 100 and 200 units. Treatment is given 5 days weekly for a total of 20 to 60 treatments.

The injection should be given early in the morning to the fasting patient, who should be under careful observation by specially trained nurses and psychiatrists on a properly equipped insulin unit.

The first phase or precoma—characterized by dizziness, somnolence, fatigue, slight confusion, cold sweat, and tremors—lasts about an hour, after which the patient moves into the safe second phase of coma. During the second stage, the patient does not respond to his name or to pain stimuli, is fully unconscious, and may present clonic or tonic twitches, facial contractions, extrapyramidal symptoms, tachycardia, dilated pupils with the light reflex present, and facial flushing. Grand mal convulsions can take place during this stage.

Stage three indicates involvement of the pons and cerebellum. During this phase, tonic spasms and torsion spasms are present, as well as a positive Babinski's sign. There may be extensor spasms and independent eye movements. An important differential sign between the second or safe stage and the third or warning stage is the loss of response to pinprick and to pressure on the supraorbital nerve. The fourth stage involves the medulla and is characterized by pinpoint pupils, loss of the corneal reflex, bradycardia, pallor, slow respirations, decerebrate rigidity, laryngeal spasms, Cheyne-Stokes breathing, cardiac arrhythmia, and abdominal breathing. This stage should be avoided. Most psychiatrists are more comfortable with stage three, which should initially be terminated after 15 minutes, but in subsequent treatments can be prolonged to about 1 hour.

**Termination.** The termination of hypoglycemic coma is effected by the intravenous injection of glucagon in dosages from 0.3 to 1 mg; the dose can be repeated if the patient does not wake up within 20 minutes. After the patient wakes up, he is asked to drink a cup of highly sugared tea or orange juice, and later he is encouraged to have luncheon.

The patient should be watched for aftershock, which may appear after several hours and can be treated by sugar given by mouth or intravenously.

There is no agreement as to the optimal number of comas; however, both the British and the American literature suggests a figure of 40 to 60 comas.

**Indications.** This treatment has been used for those schizophrenics who have not responded to drug treatment and electroshock treatment and whose illness has lasted less than 2 years. Chronic schizophrenia carries a poor prognosis. The treatment is contraindicated in early pregnancy and in patients with advanced cardiac disease, untreated hyperthyroidism, severe diabetes, renal disease, and liver disease. The method carries more risks with increasing age.

The most severe complication is irreversible coma, in which unconsciousness persists despite the administration of adequate intravenous glucose or glucagon. After a protracted coma, the patient may present with marked intellectual impairment, but his intellectual capacity will return over a period of months.

The different methods applied by the investigators and a lack of agreement as to what constitutes schizophrenia make it difficult to evaluate the results. The different elements used in addition to insulin coma—including time, milieu treatment, individualized care, psychotherapy, and at times ECT and drugs—make it difficult to evalute the role of insulin coma treatment properly. Insulin coma is very rarely used in the United States today.

### Atropine Coma Therapy

Atropine sulfate was first used in 1950 to induce coma in mental patients.

The fasting patient receives 15 mg of atropine intramuscularly in the morning. This dosage is increased by 15 mg daily until coma is reached. Rarely is the maximum dose, 250 mg, needed.

The coma lasts 6 to 8 hours. On termination of the coma, the patient should receive warm and cold showers. The treatment takes place daily, including the weekends, for a total of 5 to 15 periods.

Atropine coma starts with the absence of sweating, inhibition of salivary secretion, mydriasis, tachycardia, increased respiratory rate, mild elevation of the blood pressure, decrease in peristalsis, and increase in sphincter tone. The patient shows progressive muscular incoordination, hyperreflexia, and pyramidal signs, with a decrease in pain sensitivity. The patient may experience confusion, with visual hallucinations and affective lability.

It is no longer used in the United States but is used in parts of Europe.

### Carbon Dioxide Therapy

In this method, first used in 1929, the fasting patient inhales a mixture of 30 percent carbon dioxide and 70 percent oxygen through a tight-fitting face mask and a rebreathing bag with an expiratory valve to prevent a rise in pressure. After a few breaths, the patient may feel uncomfortable and experience shortness of breath. The patient should be encouraged to take a few more breaths at every subsequent treatment session. The introductory phase may require up to 24 respirations, whereupon the patient enters into the phase of anesthesia. During this phase, the patient may display motor phenomena, such as struggling movements to escape discomfort, flexor hypertonus, and occasional carpal spasms. After the mask is removed, an abreaction with severe motor excitement takes place. Several modifications have been made dealing with the number of inspirations and differences in the percentages of carbon dioxide and oxygen.

The theoretical aspects assume cerebral stimulation. Other investigators felt that the important part is the cathartic abreaction that occurs. This method was used in the past mostly for neurotic patients and for those with personality disorders. After some initial enthusiasm, several investigators expressed doubt about the efficacy of this treatment. Today, carbon dioxide therapy is used only sporadically and has been largely replaced by psychopharmacology.

### Electrosleep Therapy

During this treatment, which uses a portable battery-powered apparatus, a low-amplitude, pulsating current (0.1 to 0.3 mA) is passed through double electrodes with cathodes placed supraorbitally and anodes placed over the mastoid processes. The treatment, which lasts between 15 and 120 minutes, is given daily for 5 to 30 days. The patients perceives a tingling sensation at the site of the electrodes during this treatment, which does not necessarily induce sleep. The treatment has been given to patients suffering from personality disorders, neuroses, depression, schizophrenia, anxiety, insomnia, migraine headaches, and gastric distress. Some studies showed a transient positive response with improvement of insomnia and anxiety in neurotic patients but with a worsening in depressed patients; other studies noticed an improvement in depressed patients. This treatment is mainly done in Europe.

### Continuous Sleep Treatment

This is a symptomatic method of treatment in which the patient is sedated with any of a variety of drugs in order to induce 20 hours of sleep per day, sometimes for as long as 3 weeks in severely agitated patients. Klaesi introduced the name in 1922 and used barbiturates to obtain a fairly deep narcosis. Other preparations have been used, such as Cloetta's mixture of barbiturates, chloral hydrate, and paraldehyde, usually administered per rectum.

Following the treatment period, whatever drugs have been used are withdrawn slowly in order to avoid withdrawal reactions such as convulsions or delirium.

Best results have been reported in manic excitements, agitated depressions, and acute anxiety disorders. Psychopharmacologic agents are preferred today, although some clinicians advocate the use of some type of narcosis in combination with other treatments—including neuroleptics, antidepressants, and ECT—either routinely or after those treatments have failed to give benefit when used alone. In the U.S.S.R., light narcosis combined with conditioning has been advocated for withdrawn and passive schizophrenics, and in combination with or alternating with insulin coma treatment for agitated or grossly disorganized schizophrenics.

### Sleep Withdrawal Therapy

The withdrawal of sleep for one night as a treatment for depression was first described in 1970. A marked improvement in some patients with unipolar and bipolar depressions after one night of sleep deprivation was observed; some patients improve after two or more treatments, with the addition of 150 mg of amitriptyline. Elderly patients and patients suffering from involutional depression and neurotic depression without vegetative signs did not show any changes. Because depression may be associated with an increase in rapid eye movement (REM) sleep time (antidepressants cause a reduction in REM time), the effectiveness of the treatment may be attributed to a small-scale REM sleep deprivation.

### Orthomolecular Therapy

The treatment of schizophrenia with large doses of niacin is based on two related theories. One theory holds that schizophrenia is the result of a failure in the metabolism of adrenalin, which leads to the production of highly toxic mescaline-like compounds—adrenochrome and adrenolutin. The second theory suggests that nicotinic acid, which converts to nicotinamide (a methyl acceptor), can reduce the potential production of methylated biogenic amines, which possess hallucinogenic properties. A series of carefully controlled collaborative studies, initiated by the Canadian Mental Health Association, did not support the claims of the megavitamin therapists.

Megavitamin therapy nowadays includes other vitamins—ascorbic acid, pyridoxin or $B_6$, folic acid, $B_{12}$—and minerals, diets, and hormones. The designation of $B_3$ as a methyl group acceptor has given way to the concept that schizophrenia is an incipient form of cerebral pellagra and requires large quantities of the B-group vitamins.

Despite the lack of improvement and the occasional severe adverse effects induced by megadoses of vitamins, the orthomolecular movement has had some positive spinoffs. The designation of schizophrenia as a metabolic illness has led to a reduction in guilt and shame in the families of schizophrenic patients and to the institution of self-help groups, like Schizophrenics Anonymous. Today, megavitamin therapy is an unproven and useless modality in psychiatry.

### Propranolol Therapy

Propranolol, a $\beta$-adrenergic blocking agent, is effective in suppressing the cardiac symptoms of anxiety, but not in the control of anxiety itself. Its use is based on the assumption that central manifestations of anxiety lead to peripheral manifestations, which reinforce and perpetuate the central ones. Propranolol has been used in a variety of anxiety-producing situations, including public speaking and examination anxiety. Some success in chronic schizophrenic patients was reported when doses of 500 to 3,500 mg of propranolol were given daily. Today, it is an experimental procedure.

### Acupuncture Therapy

Several investigators in Italy and Australia are exploring the use of acupuncture in the treatment of depression and heroin withdrawal, respectively. Excellent results, with a considerable reduction in drug abuse, in a series of depressed patients were attributed to a possible synergistic mechanism. Acupuncture has also been reported to control successfully the physiological symptoms of heroin withdrawal. During the treatment, battery-attached acupuncture needles are placed in selected sites in both ears, and electrical stimulation at 125 cycles up to 10 volts for 30 minutes daily is given. In spite of these reports, however, there has been no convincing proof that acupuncture is of value in psychiatric treatment.

### Hemodialysis Therapy

On the basis of the improvement of schizophrenic symptoms in a woman who received repeated dialysis for hypertension, trials of dialysis have been used in chronic hospitalized schizophrenics. The patients were dialyzed until improvement was observed, whereupon dialysis was reduced to every 2 weeks or every 3 months. Some patients were able to leave the hospital and showed no evidence of schizophrenia without medications. Some researchers presume that dialysis removes a schizophrenogenic substance, presumably leu-endorphin, an endorphin with leucine. Hemodialysis has not withstood repeated attempts to replicate the initial positive results obtained and is not considered a valid treatment for schizophrenia or any other psychiatric condition.

## REFERENCES

Campbell R J: Miscellaneous organic therapies. In *Comprehensive Textbook of Psychiatry*, ed 4, H I Kaplan, B J Sadock, editors, p 1569. Williams & Wilkins, Baltimore, 1985.
Ferrier I N, Johnston E C, Crow T J, Rincon-Rodriguez I: Anterior pituitary hormone secretion in chronic schizophrenics. Arch Gen Psychiatry *40:* 755, 1983.
Hawkins D, Pauling L: *Orthomolecular Psychiatry. Treatment of Schizophrenia.* W H Freeman, San Francisco, 1973.
Heath R G: Electrical self-stimulation of the brain in man. Am J Psychiatry *120:* 571, 1963.
Kalinowsky L B, Hippius H, Klein H: *Biological Treatments in Psychiatry.* Grune & Stratton, New York, 1982.
Osmond H, Smythies J R: Schizophrenia: A new approach. J Ment Sci *98:* 309, 1952.
Wagemaker H, Cade R: The use of hemodialysis in chronic schizophrenia. Am J Psychiatry *134:* 684, 1977.

# 28

# Child Psychiatry: Introduction

## 28.1 NORMAL CHILD DEVELOPMENT

### Development of the Individual

Significant experiential factors influence intrauterine development in both animals and humans. Intrauterine curare leads to ankylosed joints in sheep; movements of the limbs in utero are important factors in maintaining joint mobility. The administration of androgenic hormones in the effort to prevent miscarriage alters sex differentiation in the infant. Maternal stress, through the production of adrenal hormones, may influence the behavioral characteristics of the newborn. These few examples point to the wide range of potentially significant findings from a still uncharted area of investigation.

### Infant Stage

Table I describes the landmarks of normal behavioral development.

The survival systems—breathing, sucking, swallowing, and circulatory and temperature homeostasis—are relatively functional at birth. But sensory systems are only incompletely developed; sensory impulses register at thalamic levels with no evidence of specific cortical responses. Further differentiation of neurophysiological functions depends on stimulatory reinforcement, and is not an automatic consequence of the genomic structure.

**Stimulus Deprivation.** The developmental process begins with the information encoded in the genome, but its phenotypic expression is continuously modulated by sequential interactions with environmental variables at each stage of development, not excepting circulatory, nutrition, and toxic factors during intrauterine life and the obstetrical characteristics of the birth process itself.

In the child, strabismus not corrected before the fifth or sixth year of life results in amblyopia ex anopsia. The severely limited vision in the unused eye cannot be rectified by optical or surgical procedures. Even relatively restricted interference with access to visual experience has telling effects.

The development of intersensory integration is an active, not an automatic, process. The organism begins with its initial given capacities, and these capacities are differentiated and interrelated by exercise, so that higher order capabilities emerge.

Two fundamental processes are at work: assimilation and accommodation. Assimilation is the process of using and incorporating stimulus aliments in the environment, just as the organism uses foods. Although Piaget used the term "aliment" in a figurative sense, it is remarkably descriptive of the visual experiments in which maintenance of the integrity of the neurons in the optic system depends on external stimulation for alimentation. In assimilation, the organism takes in the new in terms of the familiar, and acts in the present as it did in the past. In the process of accommodation, the organism is modified by the demands—that is, the novelties—of the environment. Accommodation leads to a reorganization of the programs of the organism as it struggles to cope more effectively with the mismatch between its available action patterns and the new requirements of its current environment.

**Development of the Social Bond.** As sensory development progresses, all social organisms have the parallel task of fashioning a tie between the newborn and its species.

The effects of total social isolation in subhuman species are of great interest in studying the socialization process. Puppies isolated in individual cages for 6 months exhibit a peculiar syndrome characterized by overactivity, distractibility, inadequate response to pain, whirling fits, inferiority to pet-reared and colony-reared dogs in problem solving and in food competition, and inability to be effectively socialized thereafter. Monkeys reared as isolated, even when offered surrogate mothers (objects for clinging), are subsequently unable to adjust to a colony existence, and have extraordinary difficulty in learning to mate. When impregnated, isolate-

TABLE I
LANDMARKS OF NORMAL BEHAVIORAL DEVELOPMENT*

| Age | Motor Behavior | Adaptive Behavior | Language | Personal and Social Behavior |
|---|---|---|---|---|
| Birth to 4 weeks | Hand to mouth reflex, grasping reflex, digital extension reflex | Anticipatory feeding approach behavior at 4 days | Crying as a sign of distress<br>Vocal reciprocity between mother and infant | Responsiveness to mother's face, eyes, and voice within first few hours of life |
| Under 4 weeks | Makes alternating crawling movements<br>Moves head laterally when placed in prone position | Responds to sound of rattle and bell<br>Regards moving objects momentarily | Small; throaty, undifferentiated noises | Quiets when picked up<br>Impassive face |
| 4 weeks | Tonic neck reflex positions predominate<br>Hands fisted<br>Head sags but can hold head erect for a few seconds | Follows moving objects to the midline<br>Shows no interest and drops objects immediately | Beginning vocalization, such as cooing, gurgling, and grunting | Regards face and diminishes activity<br>Responds to speech<br>Smiles preferentially to mother |
| 16 weeks | Symmetrical postures predominate<br>Holds head balanced<br>Head lifted 90 degrees when prone on forearm | Follows a slowly moving object well<br>Arms activate on sight of dangling object | Laughs aloud<br>Sustained cooing and gurgling | Spontaneous social smile<br>Aware of strange situations |
| 28 weeks | Sits steadily, leaning forward on hands<br>Bounces actively when placed in standing position | One-hand approach and grasp of toy<br>Bangs and shakes rattle<br>Transfers toys | Vocalizes "m-m-m" when crying<br>Makes vowel sounds, such as "ah" | Takes feet to mouth<br>Pats mirror image |
| 40 weeks | Sits alone with good coordination<br>Creeps<br>Pulls self to standing position<br>Points with index finger | Matches two objects at midline<br>Attempts to imitate scribble | Says "da-da" or equivalent<br>Responds to name or nickname | Separation anxiety manifest when taken away from mother<br>Responds to social play, such as "pat-a-cake" and "peek-a-boo"<br>Feeds self cracker and holds own bottle |
| 52 weeks | Walks with one hand held<br>Stands alone briefly | | Uses expressive jargon<br>Gives a toy on request | Cooperates in dressing |
| 15 months | Toddles<br>Creeps up stairs | | Says three to five words meaningfully<br>Pats pictures in book<br>Shows shoes on request | Points or vocalizes wants<br>Throws objects in play or refusal |
| 18 months | Walks, seldom falls<br>Hurls ball<br>Walks up stairs with one hand held | Builds a tower of three or four cubes<br>Scribbles spontaneously and imitates a writing stroke | Says 10 words, including name<br>Identifies one common object on picture card<br>Names ball and carries out two directions—for example, "put on table" and "give to mother" | Feeds self in part, spills<br>Pulls toy on string<br>Carries or hugs a special toy, such as a doll<br>Imitates some behavioral patterns with slight delay |
| 2 years | Runs well, no falling<br>Kicks large ball<br>Goes up and down stairs alone | Builds a tower of six or seven cubes<br>Aligns cubes, imitating train<br>Imitates vertical and circular strokes | Uses three-word sentences<br>Carries out four simple directions | Pulls on simple garment<br>Domestic mimicry<br>Refers to self by name<br>Says "no" to mother<br>Separation anxiety begins to diminish |

TABLE I—*Continued*

| Age | Motor Behavior | Adaptive Behavior | Language | Personal and Social Behavior |
|-----|----------------|-------------------|----------|------------------------------|
| 3 years | Rides tricycle<br>Jumps from bottom steps<br>Alternates feet going up stairs | Builds tower of nine or 10 cubes<br>Imitates a three-cube bridge<br>Copies a circle and a cross | Gives sex and full name<br>Uses plurals<br>Describes what is happening in a picture book | Puts on shoes<br>Unbuttons buttons<br>Feeds self well<br>Understands taking turns |
| 4 years | Walks down stairs one step per tread<br>Stands on one foot for 5 to 8 seconds | Copies a cross<br>Repeats four digits<br>Counts three objects with correct pointing | Names colors, at least one correctly<br>Understands five prepositional directives: "on," "under," "in," "in back of" or "in front of," and "beside" | Washes and dries own face<br>Brushes teeth<br>Plays cooperatively with other children |
| 5 years | Skips, using feet alternately<br>Usually has complete sphincter control | Copies a square<br>Draws a recognizable man with a head, body, limbs<br>Counts 10 objects accurately | Names the primary colors<br>Names coins: pennies, nickels, dimes<br>Asks meanings of words | Dresses and undresses self<br>Prints a few letters<br>Plays competitive exercise games |

\* Table by S. Chess, M.D.

reared females fail to mother their young. The behavioral peculiarities of these isolates were initially attributed to the lack of mothering in infancy, but Harry Harlow's studies demonstrated that an opportunity for peer interaction between two nonmothered infant monkeys apparently suffices for the development of social behavior.

**Social Deprivation Syndromes.** What happens to the human infant deprived of normal social and cognitive experience? Pediatricians have long known and repeatedly recorded the severe developmental retardation that accompanies maternal rejection and neglect. Infants in institutions characterized by low staff-to-infant ratios and frequent turnover of personnel, even when physical care and freedom from infection are adequate, display marked developmental retardation. The same infants, if placed in adequate foster or adoptive care, undergo a marked acceleration in development. John Bowlby concluded that early separation had persistent and irreversible effects on personality and intelligence.

**Temperamental Differences.** But what of the normal newborn in his own family? Is he a *tabula rasa*, a smooth slate on which characteristics are engraved with ease? Although a definitive answer to this question is not possible with present evidence, there are strong suggestions of congenital differences. Investigators have demonstrated wide individual differences among infants in autonomic reactivity, differences that persist over the newborn period but whose long-range consequences are not yet known. The studies of Alexander Thomas and Stella Chess

demonstrated temperamental characteristics already evident by the third month of life. In a careful longitudinal study of 130 middle-class infants, the researchers were able to identify nine behavioral dimensions on which reliable ratings can be obtained: activity-passivity, regularity-irregularity, intensity, approach-withdrawal, adaptive-nonadaptive, high-low threshold of response to stimulation, positive-negative mood, high-low selectivity, and high-low distractibility. The ratings on individual children showed substantial correlations between 3 months and 2 years, but much lower correlations at 5 years. During this course of the study, 27 of the children presented clinical psychiatric problems.

Clinicians are coming to the view that the infant is an important actor in the family drama, one who in part determines its course. The behavior of the infant serves to control the behavior of his mother, just as her behavior modulates his. The calm, smiling, predictable, good infant is a powerful reward for tender maternal care. The jittery, irregular, irritable infant tries a mother's patience; if her capacities for giving are marginal, his traits may cause her to turn away from him, and thus complicate his already inadequate beginning.

**Cognitive Development.** At birth, all infants have a repertoire of reflex behaviors—breathing, crying, defecating, head turning toward the stimulated cheek, mouthing of a nipple touching the lips, sucking, and swallowing. Studies have indicated that both vision and hearing are more highly developed in the newborn than they had been thought to be. By 1 to 2 weeks of age, the infant smiles; this response is endogenously determined, as evident by smiling in blind infants. By 2 to 4 weeks of age, visual fixation and visual following are evident, behaviors that may be compared to the following movements in subhuman forms. By 4 to 8 weeks, social smiling is elicited by the face or the voice of the caretaker. By 16 to 18 weeks, vocalization or babbling has appeared in the child in a language-rich environment. The persistence and the further evolution of this vocalization depend on rewarding consequences from the human environment. By 18 to 20 weeks, selective social smiling is apparent to familiar faces. This smile has been shaped by the response of adults and is, in turn, a powerful mechanism for controlling the adults. By 6 to 8 months, the child sits; by 9 to 12 months, he stands; and between 12 and 15 months, he usually walks and speaks his first words. Details of the sequence of motor and adaptive behaviors exhibited by the normally developing infant were described by Arnold Gesell, whose scales permit comparison of the accomplishments of a particular infant with normative standards.

In contrast to the normative approach taken by Gesell, who viewed development as the unfolding of a genetically determined sequence, is Piaget's epigenetic theory of intelligence. To Piaget, intelligence was but a special instance of biological adaptation within the context of life, which he viewed as a continuous creative interaction between the organism and its environment. The outer manifestation of this interaction is coping behavior; the inward reflection is the functional organization of the mental apparatus. Adaptive coping continuously reorganizes the structures of the mind.

Piaget divided the development of intelligence into three major periods: sensorimotor, birth to 2 years; concrete operations, 2 to 12 years; and formal operations, 12 years through adult life. The sensorimotor period is one in which the congenital sensorimotor schemata or reflexes are generalized, related to one another, and differentiated to become the elementary operations of intelligence. For a further discussion of Piaget's theories, see Section 3.2.

**Emotional Development.** Parallel to the stages of cognitive development are the stages of emotional development. It is in relation to regular and hence predictable events of caretaking that an affectional tie between infant and caretaker develops; the infant's behavioral repertoire expands as his acts have consequences in the form of social responses from the caretakers.

As perceptual and cognitive maturation occurs, the infant is able to relate these initially disconnected and separate experiences to the person who provides them, and is able to distinguish her from other persons in the environment.

The basis for trust in others begins to emerge from good care in infancy, but trust is in no sense a final acquisition of this first year; it must be continuously reinforced during all of childhood and adolescence if it is to become a prevailing trait.

Emotional development proceeds in an orderly fashion. For example, the capacity for happiness precedes the capacity for sadness. That ordering in the development of emotions continues through the various stages of development, from infancy through adolescence (see Fig. 1).

### Toddler Stage

The second year of life is marked by acceleration of motor and intellectual development. The ability to walk confers on the toddler a degree of control over his own actions that allows him to determine when to approach and when to withdraw. The acquisition of speech profoundly extends his horizons. Typically the child learns to say "no" before he learns to say 'yes." Correspondingly, the infant knows what he does not want long before he is able to formulate what he does want. The negativism of the toddler is a vital stage in individuation.

The second and third years of life are a period of increasing social demands on the child. The clinical observation that toilet training can become a focus of struggle between mother and child has led to the simplistic formulation that toilet training in itself is a critical event for character formation. Toilet training can be elevated to a central issue by a rigid, severe, and restricting mother, but it varies with the culture and with the temperamental characteristics of mother and child. When toilet training problems are associated with clinical psychiatric disorders, it is not necessarily because of the toilet training itself but, rather, because toilet training serves as a paradigm of the general training practices of the family—that is, the mother who is overly severe in this area is likely to be punitive and restrictive in others as well. The child's ability to accommodate himself to social demands by the acquisition of self-control can lead to pride in self and zestful striving for a new accomplishment; if he surrenders to parental coercion with shame at his physiological functions and doubt as to his own worth, he emerges inhibited, fearful, and stereotyped; if he rebels, he may remain stubborn and oppositional.

Parallel to the changing tasks for the child

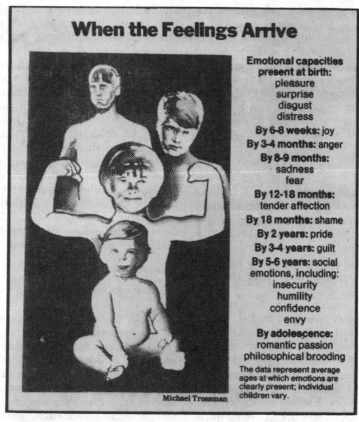

**When the Feelings Arrive**

Emotional capacities
present at birth:
pleasure
surprise
disgust
distress

By 6-8 weeks: joy

By 3-4 months: anger

By 8-9 months:
sadness
fear

By 12-18 months:
tender affection

By 18 months: shame

By 2 years: pride

By 3-4 years: guilt

By 5-6 years: social
emotions, including:
insecurity
humility
confidence
envy

By adolescence:
romantic passion
philosophical brooding

The data represent average
ages at which emotions are
clearly present; individual
children vary.

Michael Trossman

FIGURE 1.   Emotional development from infancy through adolescence. From Joseph Campas at the University of Denver, and other researchers. Used with permission of New York Times Company, 1984.

are changing tasks for his parents. Whereas in the stage of infancy, the major responsibility for parents is to meet the infant's needs in a sensitive and giving fashion, without so anticipating and so fulfilling his needs that he never experiences tension, the parental task at the toddler stage is a requirement for firmness about the boundaries of acceptable behavior and encouragement of the progressive emancipation of the child. The child must be allowed to do for himself insofar as he is able, but he must be protected and assisted when the challenges are beyond him.

In the fourth year of life, there is further augmentation of the youngster's capacities, which, however, still run well behind his aspirations; he often undertakes things he cannot complete successfully. He becomes capable of anticipation as a basis for accepting the postponement of immediate gratification. There is a flowering of imagination, as revealed in controlled fantasy and play. Play is a central psychological activity for the period. It is, to begin with, fun—the sheer pleasure of exercising new executive capacities and acquiring mastery. It

serves the function of releasing tension and energy. After stress, it can provide emotional catharsis. But, perhaps most important of all, the trial roles assumed in dramatic play allow the child to try out the adult identities he will one day have to understand and to assume. It is during this era that sexual identity is firmly established.

The child exhibits active curiosity about anatomical sex. If this curiosity is recognized as healthy and is met with honest and age-appropriate replies, he acquires a sense of the wonder of life, and is comfortable about his own role in it. If the subject is taboo and his questions are rebuffed, he responds with shame and discomfort.

At this stage he is likely to struggle for the exclusive affection and attention of his parents. The struggle includes rivalry both with his siblings and with one or another parent for the star role in the family. Although he is beginning to be able to share, he gives up only with difficulty. If the demands for exclusive possession of love objects are not effectively resolved, the result is likely to be jealous competitiveness in relations with peers and lovers. The fantasies aroused by the struggle lead to fear of retaliation and to displacement of fear onto external objects. These issues are important in elaborating the basis for conscience. In an equitable, loving family, the child elaborates a moral system of ethical rights freely contracted. This system contrasts with conscience based on terror, with fear of retaliation for unchecked cupidity, leading to ritualized and rigid moralism.

### School Period

When the child enters kindergarten and elementary school, the formal demands for academic learning, particularly in Western society, become major determinants of further personality development. So crucial is the task of developing competence, that success or failure in it molds the child's image of himself as a capable and adequate person, or as an inferior and feckless one.

**Intelligence Measurement.** Although the child's intelligence as measured by I.Q. tests is the single variable that correlates most highly with academic success, the coefficient of correlation between I.Q. and grades does not exceed 0.6 to 0.7, thus accounting for no more than a third to a half of the variance. Equally salient are motivation, work habits, creativity, and other traits for which there are as yet no quantitative measures.

Although it is true that I.Q. measures on groups of children show remarkable apparent constancy over a period of several years, the scores for individual children within the group, even of middle-class children, show wide variations.

**Aggressive Behavior.** In the normal child, aggression can be effectively understood in terms of the motives—defense, mastery, curiosity—for which aggressiveness is a suitable mediator. Its greater frequency in the abnormal child can be correlated with defects in the organism, as in the case of brain injury, or with distortions in his environment, as in the case of faulty identification models. Moreover, the frequency of the display of aggressive behavior is a function of the culture in which the child is reared. Aggressive fantasy materials—movies, crime comics, T.V., and so on—rather than affording catharsis for instinctual aggressiveness, generate the very tensions they profess to release.

A central issue is the meaning to be ascribed to the term aggression. If a child is observed taking apart a watch, this behavior can be described as aggressive. In a given instance, it may be—if, for example, the watch belongs to the child's father, and the father has just punished him. On the other hand, if the watch is an old one in his stock of toys, his motive may be curiosity about its mechanism—a belief more readily accepted if his delight as he is able to reassemble it in working order is observed. If he strikes another child, this can be an act of aggression. It well may be if the victim is the baby sister his parents have just embraced. Or, it may be defensive if the victim has made a threatening gesture or has tried to seize a favorite toy. Homely anecdotes serve to make the point, but documented experimental examples are readily available—children emulating adult models, children systematically subjected to frustration, children watching films or T.V. of aggressive behavior—all of which show predictable increases in aggressiveness.

### Adolescence

Adolescence is a period of variable onset and duration, marking the end of childhood and setting the foundation for maturity. Biologically, its onset is signaled by the final phase of acceleration of growth and the beginnings of secondary sexual development, and its termination is marked by epiphyseal fusion and the completion of sexual differentiation. Psychologically, it is marked by an acceleration of cognitive growth and personality formation, and is succeeded by the stage of parenthood and the acquisition of an adult work role. Socially, it is a period of intensified preparation for the assumption of an adult role, and its termination is signaled when the person is accorded full adult perogatives, the timing and nature of which vary widely from society to society. Adolescence is covered in detail in the following section (Section 28.2).

### Development after Adolescence

Development continues as long as life continues. As social roles change, as intellectual and physical capacities first advance and later recede, new challenges demand new adaptations. Studies of sensory deprivation in the normal volunteer have emphasized the role of sensory input in maintaining reality testing and perceptual organization. Social input is necessary for the maintenance of personality organization.

Human personality is always in the making and never complete. One is what he does. One becomes as he decides. One is ever defined by the social world in which he moves.

### REFERENCES

Birch H G, Gussow J D: *Disadvantaged Children.* Harcourt, Brace and World, New York, 1970.

Eisenberg L: The human nature of human nature. Science *176:* 123, 1972.

Eisenberg L: Normal child development. In *Comprehensive Textbook of Psychiatry,* ed 3, H I Kaplan, A M Freedman, B J Sadock, editors, p 2421. Williams & Wilkins, Baltimore, 1980.

Flavell J H: *The Developmental Psychology of Jean Piaget.* D Van Nostrand, New York, 1963.

Greenspan S I: *The Clinical Interview of the Child.* McGraw-Hill, New York, 1981.

Greenspan S I: *Psychopathology and Adaptation in Infancy and Early Childhood: Principles of Clinical Diagnosis and Preventive Intervention.* International Universities Press, New York, 1981.

Greenspan S I: Normal child development. In *Comprehensive Textbook of Psychiatry,* ed 4, H I Kaplan, B J Sadock, editors, p 1592. Williams & Wilkins, Baltimore, 1985.

Greenspan S I, Porges S W: Psychopathology in infancy and early childhood: Clinical perspectives on the organization of sensory and affective-thematic experience. Child Dev 55: 359, 1984.

McCune-Nicholich L: Towards symbolic functioning: Structure of early pretend games and potential parallels with language. Child Dev *52:* 386, 1981.

McDevitt S C, Carey W B: Stability of ratings vs. perceptions of temperament from early infancy to 1–3 years. Am J Orthopsychiatry *51:* 342, 1981.

Rutter M, Hersov L: *Child Psychiatry: Modern Approaches.* J B Lippincott, Philadelphia, 1977.

Rutter M, Tizard J, Whitmore K: *Education, Health and Behavior.* Longmans, Green, London, 1970.

# 28.2  NORMAL ADOLESCENT DEVELOPMENT

## Definition

This section concentrates on the high school years—ages 14 to 18. The reactions of the adolescent to his changing body, his changing emotional needs, and his peer relations are discussed, as are the relationships between parents and the teenager, and the reactions of the culture at large to the adolescent.

The working definition of adolescence here is the stage of life that starts with puberty and ends at the time when the person's independence from his parents has attained a reasonable degree of psychological congruence. Once in high school, the vast majority of teenagers have already undergone the biological changes of puberty. At the end of high school, the majority of middle-class adolescents continue their dependence on their parents. The process is not necessarily the same in different social, ethnic, and cultural groupings.

## Biological Development

The process of biological growth and development is a gradual one, originating at conception and achieving maturity during the high school years. Investigators agree that it is earlier for girls than for boys. Most girls achieve biological maturity at age 15, and boys by their sixteenth birthday (see Table I).

## Psychological Development

Three normative growth patterns—continuous growth, surgent growth, and tumultuous growth—are focused on here, with full recognition that they should serve only as a model for understanding the complexities of normal development of normal adolescents. No single factor in the psychosocial development of the adolescent is responsible for the end product—the adolescent described. Rather, a complex interaction of child-rearing practices, genetic background, experiential factors, cultural and social surrounding, and the coping mechanism that the adolescent used make for a specific growth pattern. Together, the three patterns promise a means of conceptualizing the normal developmental psychology of adolescence among a specific group of normal teenagers.

In describing the normal development of adolescents in the three growth patterns, the following aspects of their psychological development are stressed; the family (background and relationships), interpersonal relationships, emotions (the internal world), coping, and global clinical assessment.

### Continuous Growth

The adolescents described within the continuous-growth grouping are the least commonly encountered. The following description may be considered to be ideal and in its perfection is extremely uncommon. The continuous-growth group progress throughout adolescence with a smoothness of purpose and a self-assurance of their progression toward a meaningful and fulfilling adult life. They are favored by circumstances, and master previous developmental stages without serious setbacks. Their genetic and environmental backgrounds are excellent.

Their family lives do not involve extremely stressful and upsetting events. Their childhoods are unmarked by death or serious illnesses of a parent or sibling.

The parents of this group are able to encourage their children's independence; the parents themselves grow and change with their children.

During the high school years, the parent of the opposite sex is the one who is most important for the healthy development of the adolescent. Through him or her, the teenager tests her or his sexuality, identity, and potential worth as an adult.

TABLE I
PUBERTAL STAGES*

| Stage | Characteristics | | |
|---|---|---|---|
| | Genital development† | Pubic hair development†‡ | Breast development‡ |
| 1 | Testes, scrotum, and penis are about the same size and shape as in early childhood | The vellus over the pubes is not further developed than over the abdominal wall, i.e. no pubic hair | There is elevation of the papilla only |
| 2 | Scrotum and testes are slightly enlarged. The skin of the scrotum is reddened and changed in texture. There is little or no enlargement of the penis at this stage | There is sparse growth of long, slightly pigmented, tawny hair, straight or slightly curled, chiefly at the base of the penis or along the labia | Breast bud stage. There is elevation of the breast and papilla as a small mound. Areolar diameter is enlarged over that of stage 1 |
| 3 | Penis is slightly enlarged, at first mainly in length. Testes and scrotum are further enlarged than in stage 2 | The hair is considerably darker, coarser, and more curled. It spreads sparsely over the function of the pubes | Breast and areola are both enlarged and elevated more than in stage 2, but with no separation of their contours |
| 4 | Penis is further enlarged, with growth in breadth and development of glans. Testes and scrotum are further enlarged than in stage 3; scrotum skin is darker than in earlier stages | Hair is now adult in type, but the area covered is still considerably smaller than in the adult. There is no spread to the medial surface of the thighs | The areola and papilla form a secondary mound projecting above the contour of the breast |
| 5 | Genitalia are adult in size and shape | The hair is adult in quantity and type with distribution of the horizontal (or classically "feminine") pattern. Spread is to the medial surface of the thighs, but not up the linea alba or elsewhere above the base of the inverse triangle | Mature stage. The papilla only projects, with the areola recessed to the general contour of the breast |

* Table by Larry B. Silver, M.D., and Richard W. Brunstetter, M.D.
† For boys.
‡ For girls.

In their interpersonal relationships, these adolescents show a capacity for good object relationships.

Adolescents described by the continuous-growth pattern act in accordance with their consciences, manifesting little evidence of superego problems and developing meaningful ego ideals, often identifying with persons they know and admire within the family or school communities.

These adolescents are able to cope with external trauma, usually through an adaptive action orientation. When difficulties arise, they use the defenses of denial and isolation to protect their egos from being bombarded with affects. They can postpone immediate gratification and work in a sustained manner toward a future goal. They do not experience prolonged periods of anxiety or depression as frequently as other adolescents.

Members of the continuous-growth group share many of the qualities that appear when mental health is viewed in an ideal sense. These adolescents do not portray all these qualities, and they usually have some difficulties in one or another area. What is more distinctive about members of the continuous-growth group is their over-all contentment with themselves and their place in life. They are relatively happy human beings.

### Surgent Growth

The surgent-growth group, although functioning as adaptively as the first group, is characterized by important enough differences in ego structure, in background, and in family environment to constitute a different—although normal—subgroup. Developmental spurts are illustrative of the pattern of growth of the surgent-growth group. This pattern is the most common that adolescents follow.

One of the major differences between the surgent-growth adolescents and those in the continuous-growth group is that the genetic and environmental backgrounds of the surgent-growth adolescents are not as free of problems and traumas; the nuclear families in the surgent-growth group are more likely to have been affected by frequent and common life events such as separation, death, or severe illnesses.

For the adolescents in the surgent-growth category, relationships with parents are marked by conflicts of opinions and values. These adolescents are not as confident as those in the continuous-growth group; their self-esteem wavers. They rely on positive reinforcement from the opinions of important others, such as parents and peers. When this reinforcement is not forthcoming, they often become discouraged about themselves and their abilities. As a group, they are able to form meaningful interpersonal relationships similar to those of the adolescents in the continuous-growth group, but the relationships are maintained with a greater degree of effort.

Some adolescents in this group are afraid of emerging sexual feelings and impulses. For them, meaningful relationships with the opposite sex begin relatively late.

These adolescents differ from the continuous-growth group in the amount of emotional conflict experienced and in their patterns of resolving conflicts. More concentrated energy is directed toward mastering developmental tasks than is obvious for members of the continuous-growth group. A cycle of progression and regression is more typical of this group than of the continuous-growth group. The defenses used, anger and projection, are different than the defenses used by the first group.

Although adolescents in this category are able to cope successfully with their average expectable environment, their ego development is not adequate for coping with unanticipated sources of anxiety. Affects that are usually flexible and available will, at a time of crisis—such as the death of a close relative—become stringently controlled. This, together with the fact that they are not as action oriented as the first group, make them slightly more prone to depression. On some occasions, when their defense mechanisms falter, they experience moderate anxiety and a short period of turmoil. When disappointed in themselves or others, they show a tendency to use projection and anger.

The adolescents work toward their vocational goals sporadically or with a lack of enthusiasm;

but they are able to keep their long-range behavior in line with their general expectations for themselves.

This group as a whole is less introspective than either the first or the third group. The over-all adjustment of these adolescents is often just as adaptive and successful as that of the first group. But the adjustment is achieved with less self-examination and a more controlled drive or surge toward development; suppression of emotionality is characteristic of the adolescents in the surgent-growth group.

### Tumultuous Growth

The third group, the tumultuous-growth group, is similar to the adolescents often described in psychiatric, psychoanalytic, and social science literature. These are the students who go through adolescence with much internal turmoil, which manifests itself in overt behavioral problems in school and in the home.

The adolescents demonstrating tumultuous-growth patterns may come from less stable backgrounds than do the adolescents in the other two groups. Some of the parents of this group have overt marital conflicts, and others may have a history of mental illness in the family. Hence, the genetic and environmental backgrounds of the adolescents in the tumultuous-growth group are decidedly different from those of the other two groups. However, they may have a reasonably normal environmental and family background.

Separation of the adolescent from the family is painful for the parents, and it becomes a source of continuing conflict for the adolescents. That forms much of the basis for the adolescent's identity crisis.

These adolescents are considerably more dependent on peer culture than are their age-mates in the other groups, possibly because they receive fewer gratifications from their relationships within the family.

The tumultuous-growth adolescents begin dating activities at a younger age than their peers described in the first two groups. For these boys in early adolescence, a relationship with a female is that of a dependency relationship, with the female being a substitute for a mothering figure. In later adolescence, for some, their heterosexual relationships gain meaning, and they are able to appreciate the personal characteristics of their female friends.

Many adolescents in the tumultuous-growth group are highly sensitive and introspective. They are usually aware of their emotional need.

As a group, these adolescents may not do as

well academically during their high school years as do adolescents from the first two groups.

These adolescents need and use more energy than usual to cope with the everyday problems that an adolescent has to deal with. If everything goes relatively well, they feel good. When unexpected disappointment comes their way, they have a hard time dealing with it. It takes them longer and they use more psychic energy than the other two groups to get over the disappointment.

Studies that differentiate developmentally between groups of adolescents should help identify the various healthy coping mechanisms and the extent to which these mechanisms and age-specific tasks characterize adolescence as a stage apart. Then, one can look at the patient who needs help with a less limited conceptualization of the possibilities of adolescent development. Or, if the patient belongs in the category of tumultuous development, the therapist will be able to isolate his problems more specifically along his own developmental lines, rather than along the necessities of his age.

**REFERENCES**

Brunstetter R W, Silver L B: Normal adolescent development. In *Comprehensive Textbook of Psychiatry*, ed 4, H I Kaplan, B J Sadock, editors, p 1608. Williams & Wilkins, Baltimore, 1985.

Csikszentmihalyi M, Reed L: *Being Adolescent.* Basic Books, New York, 1984.

Erikson E H: The problem of ego identity. J Am Psychoanal Assoc *4:* 56, 1956.

Freud A: Adolescence. Psychoanal Study Child, *13:* 255, 1958.

Kandel D B: Epidemiologic and psychosocial perspectives on adolescent drug use. J Am Acad Child Psychiatry *21:* 348, 1982.

Kohlberg L: Development of moral character and moral ideology. In *Review of Child Development Research* (Vol. 1), M L Hoffman, L W Hoffman, editors. Russell Sage Foundation, New York, 1964.

Offer D: *The Psychological World of the Teenager: A Study of Normal Adolescent Boys.* Basic Books, New York, 1969.

Piaget J, Inhelder B: *The Psychology of the Child.* Basic Books, New York, 1969.

Tanner J M: Growth and endocrinology of the adolescent. In *Endocrine and Genetic Diseases of Childhood*, L I Gardner, editor. W. B. Saunders, Philadelphia, 1969.

# 29

# Child Psychiatry: Assessment, Examination, and Psychological Testing

## Introduction

The psychiatric examination is the principal instrument for assessment in child psychiatry. It is based on the principle that the child's mental state in disorder, as well as in health, reflects biological (physical), psychodynamic (intrapsychic), and social (interpersonal) forces in transaction.

Healthy mental function in childhood is marked by evidence in the child's everyday behavior that he is maintaining his age-appropriate development and is, by and large, in a satisfied frame of mind as he deals with the feelings, thoughts, and wishes generated, on the one hand, by the physical, psychological, and social experiences that affect him and, on the other hand, by the maturational changes taking place in the course of his growth.

## Examination of the Child

The child is incapable, by virtue of his natural dependency and immaturity, of remembering or communicating some of the facts and experiences essential for the evaluation. These facts include his early development, past physical and psychological stresses, and comparisons of his behavior, emotional states, and course of development with those of siblings and peers.

In all but the more severe derangements, even articulate and cooperative children may conceal, minimize, or deny their problems out of fear and guilt. Children are frequently inarticulate. If they have been coerced, if they are confused, or if they associate the examination with a threat of abandonment and rejection by their parents, they may be counted on to behave as normally and to reveal as little as they know how. They may also be frankly uncooperative, often with ample reason, having been referred in such a way as to rationalize already strong needs to displace the problem from themselves.

Even under the most favorable circumstances, however, there is much that the child cannot provide himself. Family group interviews may be helpful in clarifying areas of disagreement on salient points of the presenting problem. Separate interviews with each of the parents may facilitate any or many of the goals of the examination. Under special circumstances of broken homes, neglect, physical or mental illness, or institutionalization, adults other than the child's parents are of primary importance to the examination and the assessment.

Tables I and II describe suggested outlines for a complete assessment of the child, including the interviewing of the parent or parent surrogate.

## Interview and Direct Observation

It is the clinician's task to provide an emotional setting within which he and the child may interact so that the child can express directly or by implication what he is concerned about and what kind of a person he is. The child's behavior in the interview is observed, appraised, and evaluated in the light of the history and the social milieu. The manner of the interview depends on the child's age. An adolescent may seek help himself and be the principal informant, especially if he is attempting to be independent of his parents.

Advice to parents on how to inform the child and prepare him for the interview ought to be given whenever necessary.

Maximum advantage should be taken of the opportunity provided to observe the child's behavior in the waiting room and his ability to separate from his parents. A child with severe separation problems may have to be examined with a parent in the room.

The child should not be expected to sit quietly in a chair throughout the interview. A conver-

TABLE I
OUTLINE FOR INTERVIEW WITH PARENTS*

Child's history:
  Parents' main concerns about the child (chief complaint or presenting problem)
  Course of symptoms and current adjustment
  Past developmental, medical, social, and psychological history, including peer and school adjustments
  Child's relationships with siblings and each parent
Parents' marital history
Parents' personal history:
  Parents' primary family, past and present
  School and vocational adjustment
  Social and avocational interests and activities
  Review of any specific medical or psychological problems suffered by either parent
Other family problems:
  Other children
  Previous marriages
  In-laws
  Neighbors
Parents' opinions about possible causes and a review of their feelings about various treatments that may be proposed

* Based on Simmons J E: *The Psychiatric Examination of Children.* Lea & Febiger, Philadelphia, 1969.

sational approach should be attempted with all children who are old enough. The examiner will be well-rewarded for any success he can achieve in identifying with the mundane things that preoccupy the child, even or especially when under stress.

Whether in play or in conversation, the child should be allowed and encouraged to take the initiative. The child's self-protective need, out of anxiety, to adapt his communication to the examiner is very strong. It is important, especially at the outset, for the child to perceive the psychiatrist as a responsive human being. Time should be allocated to drawing the child out about his satisfying experiences and interests and to responding empathically to them. The examiner who shows signs of enjoyment in sharing these interests, before focusing attention on less pleasant matters, will be rewarded in the long run. It is virtually useless to push diagnostic questions at a child who is unready or unable to lower his guard.

In the first interview, and as long as the situational or characterological or referral stresses still dominate the atmosphere, it is a good rule to limit one's efforts to change behavior to the interview itself and to refrain from interpretations or suggestions that refer to the child's problem in his outside or real life. Challenging defenses prematurely never facilitates the expression of thoughts, feelings, and wishes for help.

**Limit Setting.** Limits are important to avoid mobilizing excessive anxiety and guilt feelings, with which the child may have no prompt help.

At the outset, therefore, direct but compassionate restraint of destructive or regressive behavior may be unavoidable.

**Confidentiality.** Some degree of mistrust and communication breakdown is inherent in psychopathology. Any child who needs to be examined has to be assumed to have secrets he is afraid to have his parents know. For the most part, the development of trust takes place over time, but a long step forward can be taken, even in the initial interview, if the examiner undertakes to inform the child what communications with his parents are indicated. Absolute confidentiality is unrealistic with young children, but a relationship of reasonable trust can be achieved without it.

**Play.** Through play, the child attempts to regulate the stimuli affecting him. The play of a child with personality problems is directed perforce toward these problems and contains both expressive and defensive reflections. What he says in connection with his play represents the

TABLE II
HISTORY GUIDE*

|  |  | Date:<br>Referral: |
|---|---|---|
| Name: | Sex: | Date of birth: |
| Address: |  |  |
| Father's name: | Mother's<br>name: |  |
| Occupation: | Occupation: |  |
| Siblings: | Sex:<br>Age: | Grade: |

Informants:
Presenting problems:
**Birth and Infancy:**
Parents' ages when child was born:
Length of marriage when child was born:
Planned baby? Problems of conception:
History of pregnancy, labor, and delivery:
Birth weight and neonatal history:
Feeding history:
Daily care of the baby given by:
**Developmental Milestones (Ages Of):**
Sitting: Standing: Walking:
First word: First phrase or sentence:
Toilet training: Time of initiation, mode of procedure:
**Temperament in Infancy:**
**Temperament at Later Stages:**
**Health:**
Operations:
Childhood disease:
Other illnesses:
Accidents:
**School History:**
Nursery:
Kindergarten:
First grade:
Present:
**Interpersonal Relationships:**
**Additional Factors of Importance:**
**Further Development of Behavior**
  **Problems:**
**Impression of Parents:**

* Based on Chess S: *An Introduction to Child Psychiatry,* ed 2. Grune & Stratton, New York, 1969.

partially developed capacity for linguistic abstraction commensurate with his age, personality, and emotional state; it bridges the gap between actions and their meaning, and helps the examiner fathom what is troubling the child and, of equal importance, why he cannot bring it out more directly.

The examining room should be open enough to allow for the physical activity required to reduce tension, but not so large as to attenuate a reasonably intimate contact between the examiner and the patient. Toys and materials should be available to suit children of different ages, sexes, and interests. The room should be furnished and arranged so that toys and materials inappropriate for a particular child can be removed from view. Too great a choice may be overstimulating or distracting; too little may fail to accommodate important fantasies or concerns. Toys and materials made available to the spontaneous interests of the child being examined should not be edited rigidly according to preconceived goals of the examiner. Attempting, for example, to offer boy toys to boys and girl toys to girls may preclude the expression of important elements in the patient's inner life.

Play therapy was initially introduced and developed by the child psychiatrist David Levy.

If the following are included, the range should be adequate for the great majority of children up to the age of 8 or 10 years: facilities for water play, clay, paints and crayons, kitchen equipment, building blocks, a furnished doll house with a doll family, puppets, trains, trucks, cars and planes, a sandbox, dolls with anatomically perceptible body parts, and assorted table games. The play equipment in a well-equipped office-playroom is substantially the same for the diagnostic interview as it is for interviews in the course of play therapy, but certain materials are more strongly associated than others with continuity. The clinician should try to exclude toys that may involve the child in play that cannot come to a comfortable conclusion during a brief diagnostic process.

### Diagnosis and Classification

The Committee on Child Psychiatry of the Group for the Advancement of Psychiatry (GAP) proposed a classification which separates the disorders into 10 major diagnostic categories (see Table III). It is the first system to include healthy responses as a diagnostic category, pointing up the need in diagnostic work to recognize when signs that may cause concern are manifestations of adaptation, and do not indicate failure to maintain mental growth. Whereas the first six categories, arranged more or less in ascending order of seriousness, deal essentially with the total personality, hewing as closely as possible to the unitary view underlying the system, the next three categories reflect end organ or organ system responses, even though the personality of the child with such a disorder may be and almost always is significantly involved.

The system of classification suggested by Anna Freud divides the psychiatric disorders of children into two major groups (see Table IV). Symptoms are defined more narrowly than in the GAP scheme, which gives parity to symptoms of all the specific manifestations of disorder in childhood. For Anna Freud, symptoms are only those manifestations of disorder that result from the failure of an essential step in mental development to take place at the normal time. Symptoms are defined in terms of the

TABLE III
GROUP FOR THE ADVANCEMENT OF PSYCHIATRY CLASSIFICATIONS*

1. Healthy responses
2. Reactive disorders
3. Developmental deviations
4. Psychoneurotic disorders
5. Personality disorders
6. Psychotic disorders
7. Psychosomatic disorders
8. Brain syndromes
9. Mental retardation
10. Other disorders

* Based on Group for the Advancement of Psychiatry: *Psychopathological Disorders in Childhood*, Report No. 62. Group for the Advancement of Psychiatry, New York, 1966.

TABLE IV
ANNA FREUD'S SYSTEM OF CLASSIFICATION

*Symptoms*
　Symptoms resulting from initial nondifferentiation between somatic and psychological processes: psychosomatics
　Symptoms resulting from compromise formation between id and ego: neurotic symptoms
　Symptoms resulting from the irruption of id derivatives into the ego: psychotic or delinquent symptoms if complete irruption, borderline symptoms if partial irruption
　Symptoms resulting from changes in the libido economy or direction of cathexis: symptoms of some personality disorders and hypochondriasis
　Symptoms resulting from changes in the quality or direction of aggression: inhibited or destructive symptoms
　Symptoms resulting from undefended regressions: infantile symptoms
　Symptoms resulting from organic causes
*Other signs of disturbance and other reasons for a child's referral*
　Fears and anxieties
　Delays and failures in development
　School failures
　Failures in social adaptation
　Aches and pains

specific step that failed and at which the child's development took its pathological turn. These true symptoms are viewed as the results of psychopathology, as defined in accord with psychoanalytic theory.

The DSM-III classification of disorders that usually begin in infancy or childhood is outlined in Table V and is the format followed in this textbook. But the reader should be aware that there is much disagreement about the DSM-III classification in childhood among child psychiatrists. For example, some disorders, such as anorexia nervosa, occur in early or later adulthood rather than in infancy, childhood, and adolescence as listed in DSM-III, and the term childhood schizophrenia is subsumed under the term pervasive developmental disorder, with which there is disagreement.

TABLE V
DISORDERS USUALLY FIRST EVIDENT IN INFANCY, CHILDHOOD, OR ADOLESCENCE*

**Mental Retardation**
  Mild mental retardation
  Moderate mental retardation
  Severe mental retardation
  Profound mental retardation
  Unspecified mental retardation
**Attention Deficit Disorder**
  With hyperactivity
  Without hyperactivity
  Residual type
**Conduct Disorder**
  Undersocialized, aggressive
  Undersocialized, nonaggressive
  Socialized, aggressive
  Socialized, nonaggressive
  Atypical conduct disorder
**Anxiety Disorders of Childhood or Adolescence**
  Separation anxiety disorder
  Avoidant disorder of childhood or adolescence
  Overanxious disorder
**Other Disorders of Infancy, Childhood or Adolescence**
  Reactive attachment disorder of infancy
  Schizoid disorder of childhood or adolescence
  Elective mutism
  Oppositional disorder
  Identity disorder
**Eating Disorders**
  Anorexia nervosa
  Bulimia
  Pica
  Rumination disorder of infancy
  Atypical eating disorder
**Stereotyped Movement Disorders**
  Transient tic disorder
  Chronic motor tic disorder
  Tourette's disorder
  Atypical tic disorder
  Atypical stereotyped movement disorder
**Other Disorders with Physical Manifestations**
  Stuttering
  Functional enuresis
  Functional encopresis
  Sleepwalking disorder
  Sleep terror disorder
**Pervasive Developmental Disorders**
  Infantile autism
  Childhood onset pervasive developmental disorder
  Atypical pervasive developmental disorder
**Specific Developmental Disorders**
  Developmental reading disorder
  Developmental arithmetic disorder
  Developmental language disorder
  Developmental articulation disorder
  Mixed specific developmental disorder
  Atypical specific developmental disorder

*From American Psychiatric Association: *Diagnostic and Statistical Manual of Mental disorders*, ed 3. American Psychiatric Association, Washington, DC, 1980. Used with permission.

## Psychological Testing

Psychological test procedures are particularly useful in assessing intelligence level, probing for the presence of significant specific cognitive disabilities, eliciting behavioral evidence of brain dysfunction, and providing indications of the child's emotional development and personality characteristics (see Table VI).

### Intelligence Tests

**Testing the Schoolchild.** Intelligence tests measure primarily those abilities essential for academic achievement. They are often more accurately described as tests of scholastic aptitude.

In America, the most notable adaptation of the original Binet-Simon scale is the Stanford-Binet. Extending from the 2-year level to three superior-adult levels of increasing difficulty, the test yields a mental age and a deviation I.Q. Objects, pictures, and drawings are used largely at the younger ages; printed, verbal, and numerical materials occur increasingly at the older age levels. Oral questions and answers are common throughout the scale.

Another individual test commonly used in the clinical examination of children is the Wechsler Intelligence Scale for Children (WISC). This scale provides separate verbal and performance I.Q.s based on different sets of tests as well as a full scale I.Q.

Both the Stanford-Binet and the WISC are individual tests that must be administered to each subject singly and that require a highly trained examiner. Group tests are designed for rapid mass testing. They enable a single examiner to test a large group during one session and are relatively easy to administer and score. They are useful when a crude index of intellectual level suffices or when facilities for more intensive testing are unavailable.

**Preschool and Infant Testing.** Tests applicable prior to school entrance are subdivided into (1) infant tests designed for the first 18 months of life and (2) preschool tests covering the ages of 18 to 60 months. The infant must be tested while lying down or supported on someone's lap. Speech is of little or no use in giving test instructions, although the child's own

Table VI
Psychological Tests for Children*

| Category | Example |
| --- | --- |
| General scales | Wechsler Scales (WISC-R, WPPSI)<br>Stanford-Binet Scale<br>Columbia Mental Maturity Scale<br>Hiskey-Nebraska Test of Learning Aptitude |
| Speech and language | Peabody Picture Vocabulary Test<br>Illinois Test of Psycholinguistic Abilities (ITPA)<br>Templin-Darley Tests of Articulation |
| Reading and school achievement | Wide Range Achievement Test (WRAT)<br>Durrel Analysis of Reading Difficulty<br>Stanford Diagnostic Reading Test |
| Perceptual and perceptuomotor | Bender-Gestalt<br>Draw-a-Person<br>Benton Visual Retention Test (BVRT)<br>Porteus mazes<br>Trail making<br>Identification of Hidden and Mixed Figures |
| Body schema | Right-Left Orientation<br>Finger Recognition |
| Motor skills | Lincoln-Oseretsky Motor Development Scale<br>Purdue Pegboard<br>Small Parts Dexterity Test<br>Motor Impersistence<br>Imitation-of Gestures (Bergès and Lezine) |
| Social maturity | Vineland Social Maturity Scale<br>AAMD Adaptive Behavior Scales |
| Personality | Rorschach Test<br>Thematic Apperception Test (TAT)<br>Children's Apperception Test (CAT)<br>Missouri Children's Picture Series (Sines)<br>Children's Personality Questionnaire (Cattell)<br>Behavior Problem Checklists (Jenkins: Quay) |

*Table by Arthur L. Benton, Ph.D.

speech development provides relevant data. Most of the tests at this level are actually controlled observations of sensorimotor development: the infant's ability to lift his head, turn over, reach for and grasp objects, and follow a moving object with his eyes. At the preschool level the child can walk, sit at a table, use his hands in manipulating test objects, and communicate by language. The preschool child is also much more responsive to the examiner as a person.

After longitudinal studies of the normal course of development in children, Arnold Gesell and his associates prepared the Gesell Developmental Schedules. Data are obtained by direct observation of the child's responses to standard toys and other stimulus objects and are supplemented by information provided by the mother. The schedules yield separate scores indicating the level of the child's behavioral development in motor, adaptive, language, and personal-social behavior.

A more highly test-oriented approach is illustrated by the Cattell Infant Intelligence Scale. Extending from 2 to 30 months, this scale was developed as a downward extension of the Stanford-Binet and also includes some items from the Gesell Schedules.

**Long-Term Prediction.** Theoretically, if a child maintains the same status relative to his age norms, his I.Q. remains the same at all ages. The I.Q. has, in fact, proved to be fairly constant for most children. But scores on infant tests are virtually useless in predicting intellectual level in late childhood. Infant tests find their chief usefulness in the early detection of severe retardation resulting from organic causes of either hereditary or environmental origin. Infant tests rely heavily on sensorimotor functions, which bear little relation to the verbal and other abstract functions that constitute intelligence in later years.

Even in later childhood, the I.Q. cannot be regarded as rigidly fixed. A major reason for the usual stability of the I.Q. is that most children remain in the same type of environment throughout their development. Another is that their previous experiences determine their level of attainment in intellectual skills needed for learning. An early deficiency thus becomes cumulative unless corrected by special remedial programs.

Large shifts in I.Q. are usually associated with the cultural milieu and emotional climate of the home. Children in disadvantaged environments tend to lose with age; those in superior environments tend to gain. Changes in I.Q. are also related to certain personality characteristics of the child, such as emotional independence and achievement motivation.

*Aptitude Tests*

Since most intelligence tests concentrate on the more abstract verbal and numerical abilities, a need was felt for tests measuring the more concrete and practical intellectual skills. Mechanical aptitudes were among the first for which special tests were developed. Tests of clerical aptitude, measuring chiefly perceptual speed and accuracy, and tests of musical and artistic aptitudes followed.

Multiple aptitude batteries provide a profile of scores on separate tests. An example is the Differential Aptitude Tests (DAT). The DAT yields scores in eight abilities: verbal reasoning, numerical ability, abstract reasoning, clerical speed and accuracy, mechanical reasoning, space relations, spelling, and grammar. Multiple aptitude batteries are most useful in the testing of older children and adolescents.

### Educational Tests

**Readiness Tests.** Readiness tests are designed to assess the child's qualifications for schoolwork. The importance of prior learning is paramount. The acquisition of simple concepts equips the child for learning more complex concepts at any age.

Special emphasis is placed on those abilities found to be most important in learning to read; some attention is also given to the prerequisites of numerical thinking and to the sensorimotor control required in learning to write. Among the specific functions covered are visual and auditory discrimination, motor control, verbal comprehension, vocabulary, quantitative concepts, and general information. A well-known example is the Metropolitan Readiness Tests.

**Tests of Special Education Disabilities.** Reading tests are customarily classified as survey and diagnostic tests. Survey tests indicate the general level of the child's achievement in reading. These tests serve largely to screen children in need of remedial instruction. Diagnostic tests are designed to analyze the child's performance and to identify specific sources of difficulty. These tests yield more than one score, and some include detailed checklists of specific types of errors. Information about possible emotional difficulties and a complete case history are essential.

**Educational Achievement Batteries.** Achievement tests aim to measure the effects of a course of study. Many achievement tests measure the attainment of relatively broad educational goals cutting across subject matter specialties. An outstanding example is the Sequential Tests of Educational Progress (STEP). These tests are available at several levels extending from the fourth grade of elementary school to the sophomore year of college and beyond. At each level there are seven tests: multiple choice tests in reading, writing, mathematics, science, social studies, and listening and an essay-writing test. Major emphasis is

placed on the application of learned skills to the solution of new problems.

**Educational Entrance and Licensure Examinations.** During the past 50 years, there has been increasing use of multiple choice examinations by high schools, colleges, and graduate schools, e.g. the Scholastic Aptitude Test (SAT) given by the Educational Testing Service (ETS); the New Medical College Aptitude Test (MCAT) given by the American College Testing Program and the Association of American Medical Colleges; the Examination of the National Board of Medical Examiners (NBME) for licensure in medicine; and many others.

In the case of the MCAT, for example, the examination is supposed to evaluate science knowledge and reading and quantitative skills. Medical school admission committees are supposed to consider the test along with other information. Some schools weigh the test more, others less.

While all these tests are very useful when proper emphasis on the results is balanced with other information, their utility has been questioned for some of the following reasons: They are not necessarily predictive of later success in school or in later professional practice; the results may be significantly modified by tutoring, anxiety, or cultural background; they have a major influence on curriculum—what students are taught and what they learn in order to pass the examinations; and finally, the organizations producing these examinations tend to follow an inflexible routine with the concentration of authority in a few persons and a complex structure of administrative organization.

The aforementioned criticisms currently represent a national and international problem in achievement, aptitude, and educational testing which has yet to be resolved.

### Creativity Tests

The growing recognition that creative talent is not synonymous with academic intelligence as measured by traditional intelligence tests has been accompanied by vigorous efforts to develop specialized tests of creativity. The tests involve various aspects of fluency, flexibility, and originality. An example of a test that is effective with young children is the improvements test, in which the child is given toys, such as a nurse kit, a fire truck, and a stuffed dog, and is asked to think of ways of changing each toy so that it will be more fun to play with.

### Personality Tests

In comparison with tests of ability, personality tests are much less satisfactory with regard to norms, reliability, and validity. Any information obtained from personality tests should be verified and supplemented from other sources, such as interviews with the child and his associates, direct observation of behavior, and case history.

**Self-report Inventories.** Self-report inventories consist of a series of questions concerning emotional problems, worries, interests, motives, values, and interpersonal traits. Several inventories designed for children and adolescents are basically checklists of personal problems. The questions pertain directly to the information that the examiner wishes to elicit about the child's feelings and actions, and the responses are taken at face value. A clear example of this approach is the Mooney Problem Check List. The problem areas covered in the junior high school form include health and physical development, school, home and family, money, work and the future, boy and girl relations, relations to people in general, and self-centered concerns. Personality inventories find their major usefulness in screening and identifying children in need of further investigation.

**Projective Techniques.** In projective techniques, the subject is assigned an unstructured task that permits an almost unlimited variety of possible responses. The test stimuli are typically vague and equivocal, and the instructions are brief and general. These techniques are based on the hypothesis that the way in which the person perceives and interprets the test materials reflects basic characteristics of his personality. The test stimuli serve as a screen on which the subject projects his own ideas.

One of the most widely used projective techniques is the Rorschach test, in which the subject is shown a set of bilaterally symmetrical inkblots and asked to tell what he sees or what the blot represents. Rorschach norms have been developed for children between the ages of 2 and 10 years and for adolescents between the ages of 10 and 17.

A somewhat more structured test is the Children's Apperception Test (CAT), an adaptation of the Thematic Apperception Test (TAT). In the CAT, pictures of animals are substituted for pictures of people on the assumption that children respond more readily to animal characters. The pictures are designed to evoke fantasies relating to problems of feeding and other oral activity, sibling rivalry, parent-child relations, aggression, toilet training, and other childhood experiences. Another example is the Blacky Pictures, a set of cartoons showing a small dog, his parents, and a sibling (see Fig. 1). Based on a psychoanalytic theory of psychosexual develop-

ment, the cartoons depict situations suggesting various types of sexual conflicts. Still another type of picture test is illustrated by the Rosenzweig Picture-Frustration Study. This test presents a series of cartoons in which one person frustrates another. In a blank space provided, the child writes what the frustrated person would reply (see Fig. 2).

Drawings, toy tests, and other play techniques represent other applications or projective methods. Play and dramatic objects, such as puppets, dolls, toys, and miniatures, have also been used. The objects are usually selected because of their associative value, often including dolls representing adults and children, bathroom and

FIGURE 1.   Sample item from the Blacky Pictures. (Reproduced by permission of Psychodynamic Instruments, Ann Arbor, Michigan.)

FIGURE 2.   Sample item from Rosenzweig Picture-Frustration Study, Form for Children. (Reproduced by permission of Saul Rosenzweig.)

kitchen fixtures, and other household furnishings. Play with such articles is expected to reveal the child's attitudes toward his family, sibling rivalries, fears, aggressions, and conflicts. They are of particular use in eliciting sexual abuse problems in children.

When evaluated as standardized tests, most projective techniques have fared quite poorly. They should be regarded not as tests but as aids to the clinical interviewer.

## REFERENCES

Benton A L, Hamsher K deS, Varney N R, Spreen O: *Contributions to Neuropsychological Assessment: A Clinical Manual.* Oxford University Press, New York, 1983.

Benton A L, Sines J O: Psychological testing of children. In *Comprehensive Textbook of Psychiatry*, ed 4, H I Kaplan, B J Sadock, editors, p 1625. Williams & Wilkins, Baltimore, 1985.

Call J D: Toward a nosology of psychiatric disorders in infancy. In *Frontiers of Infant Psychiatry*, J D Call, E Galenson, R L Tyson, editors, pp 117–128. Basic Books, New York, 1983.

Call J D: Psychiatric evaluation of the infant and the child. In *Comprehensive Textbook of Psychiatry*, ed 4, H I Kaplan, J B Sadock, editors, p 1614. Williams & Wilkins, Baltimore, 1985.

Chess S: *An Introduction to Child Psychiatry*, ed 2. Grune & Stratton, New York, 1969.

Kaufman A S, Kaufman N L: *Kaufman Assessment Battery for Children: Interpretive Manual.* American Guidance Service, Circle Pines, MN, 1983.

Ollendick T H, Heresen M, editors: Handbook of Child Psychopathology. Plenum Press, New York, 1983.

Sattler J M: *Assessment of Children's Intelligence*, ed 2. W B Saunders, Philadelphia, 1982.

Tyson R L, Call J D, Galenson E: *Frontiers of Infant Psychology*, vol 2. Basic Books, New York, 1984.

# 30

# Mental Retardation

## Introduction

The problem of adopting a universally acceptable system of defining and labeling mental retardation has long vexed many individual workers in the field and lately has attracted the attention of national and even international scientific and governmental bodies. The still existing confusion may be attributed primarily to the complexity of the problem of mental retardation, which defies simple conceptualization.

## Definition

The biomedical and sociocultural adaptational models represent the two major approaches to the conceptual definition of mental retardation. The adherents of the biomedical model in the United States insist on the presence of basic changes in the brain as a sine qua non in the diagnosis of mental retardation. The proponents of the sociocultural adaptational model, on the other hand, emphasize the social functioning and general adaptation to accepted norms (see Table I).

The sociopsychological approach focuses on the developmental impairment in infancy and preschool years, on learning difficulties in school age, and on poor social-vocational adjustment in adulthood (see Table II). Table II includes both the DSM-III criteria as well as those of the American Association of Mental Deficiency described below. A broader view is reflected in the definition of mental retardation adopted by the American Association of Mental Deficiency in 1973: Mental retardation refers to significantly subaverage general intellectual functioning (two standard deviations below the normal) existing concurrently with deficits in adaptive behavior and manifested during the developmental period.

According to DSM-III, the essential features of mental retardation are: (1) subaverage general intellectual functioning, (2) resulting in, or associated with, defects or impairments in adaptive behavior, (3) with onset before the age of 18.

## Nomenclature

Mental deficiency is often used interchangeably with mental retardation. However, the World Health Organization has recommended the use of the term mental subnormality, which is divided into two separate and distinct categories: mental retardation and mental deficiency. According to this nosology, mental retardation is reserved for subnormal functioning due to pathological causes. Mental deficiency is often used as a legal term, applied to people with an I.Q. of less than 70. See Table III for DSM-III criteria for mental retardation.

The term feeble-mindedness was often used in American literature in the past and is still in use in Great Britain, where it generally denotes

TABLE I
TWO VIEWS OF MENTAL RETARDATION

| Clinical Perspective | Social Systems Perspective |
| --- | --- |
| Intelligence is an entity that exists independent of cultural setting | Intelligence is relative to the requirements of the particular social system |
| If one is retarded according to standard statistical or medical tools, he is retarded | One can be retarded for some systems (such as school) and normal for others (such as family life) |
| A clinician can detect abnormalities not apparent to laymen. These unseen abnormalities can be proof of retardation. | Retardation cannot be undetected, since a person is retarded only by virtue of being labeled as such in a particular setting |
| The real number of retarded people in an area can be scientifically determined without considering the area's social structure | The number of people labeled retarded in an area is determined by the social structure of that area (What is expected of persons? How much, or how well, is difference tolerated?) |

Table II
Developmental Characteristics of the Mentally Retarded*
This table integrates chronological age, degree of retardation, and level of intellectual, vocational, and social functioning.

| Degree of Mental Retardation | Preschool Age 0–5 Maturation and Development | School Age 6–20 Training and Education | Adult 21 and over Social and Vocational Adequacy |
| --- | --- | --- | --- |
| Profound | Gross retardation; minimal capacity for functioning in sensorimotor areas; needs nursing care; constant aid and supervision required | Some motor development present; may respond to minimal or limited training in self-help | Some motor and speech development; may achieve very limited self-care; needs nursing care |
| Severe | Poor motor develoment; speech minimal; generally unable to profit from training in self-help; little or no communication skills | Can talk or learn to communicate; can be trained in elemental health habits; profits from systematic habit training; unable to profit from vocational training | May contribute partially to self-maintenance under complete supervision; can develop self-protection skills to a minimal useful level in controlled environment |
| Moderate | Can talk or learn to communicate; poor social awareness; fair motor development; profits from training in self-help; can be managed with moderate supervision | Can profit from training in social and occupational skills; unlikely to progress beyond 2nd grade level in academic subjects; may learn to travel alone in familiar places | May achieve self-maintenance in unskilled or semiskilled work under sheltered conditions; needs supervision and guidance when under mild social or economic stress |
| Mild | Can develop social and communication skills, minimal retardation in sensorimotor areas; often not distinguished from normal until later age | Can learn academic skills up to approximately 6th grade level by late teens; can be guided toward social conformity | Can usually achieve social and vocational skills adequate to minimum self-support, but may need guidance and assistance when under unusual social or economic stress |

* Adapted from *Mental Retardation Activities of the U.S. Department of Health, Education, and Welfare*, p. 2. United States Government Printing Office, Washington, DC, 1963. DSM-III criteria are adapted essentially from this chart.

Table III
Diagnostic Criteria for Mental Retardation*

A. Significantly subaverage general intellectual functioning: an I.Q. of 70 or below on an individually administered I.Q. test (for infants, since available intelligence tests do not yield numerical values, a clinical judgment of significant subaverage intellectual functioning)

B. Concurrent deficits or impairments in adaptive behavior, taking the person's age into consideration

C. Onset before the age of 18

* From American Psychiatric Association: *Diagnostic and Statistical Manual of Mental Disorders*, ed 3. American Psychiatric Association, Washington, DC, 1980. Used with permission.

the mild forms of mental retardation. Oligophrenia is in common use in the U.S.S.R., Scandinavia, and other Western European countries. Amentia appears infrequently in modern psychiatric literature and is now referred to as a terminal stage of a degenerative illness.

The choice of the term mental retardation here only reflects the widest preference of all professional groups.

### Classification

The pluridimensional character of mental retardation is also reflected in the various approaches to classification of the condition. Essentially, they all deal with the patient's devel-

opmental characteristics, potential for education and training, and social and vocational adequacy. The degrees or levels of retardation are expressed in various terms. According to DSM-III, the following classification is used: mild mental retardation (I.Q. 50 to 70), moderate mental retardation (I.Q. 35 to 49), severe mental retardation (I.Q. 20 to 34), and profound mental retardation (I.Q. of less than 20).

DSM-III basically follows the American Association on Mental Deficiency's categories of mental retardation, but it adds a new category, borderline intellectual functioning (I.Q. 71 to 84), classified as one of the conditions not attributable to a mental disorder that are a focus of attention or treatment. For a further discussion of borderline intellectual functioning see Section 38.3.

### Epidemiology

The incidence of mental retardation ultimately determines the prevalence of the condition.

About 1 percent of the population are classified as mentally retarded, since only the severe forms of the disorder are recognized on routine examination. The highest incidence is found in school-aged children, with the peak at ages 10 to 14.

The overwhelming majority (80 percent) of the mentally retarded fall into the mild category, moderate is 12 percent, severe is 7 percent and profound is less than 1 percent. The levels of mental retardation by I.Q. range are indicated in Table IV.

### Causes and Syndromes

*Prenatal Factors*

The total of all the known hereditary metabolic defects probably accounts for only a minority of mental defectives. Further biochemical research may bring the number of metabolic disorders to at least 10 percent of the mentally retarded.

Table V lists 30 important syndromes with inborn errors of metabolism, many of which are discussed in more detail below.

**Disorders of Amino Acid Metabolism.** PHENYLKETONURIA. Phenylketonuria (PKU) has become known as the paradigmatic inborn error of metabolism associated with mental retardation.

PKU is transmitted as a simple recessive autosomal Mendelian trait. Its frequency in the United States and various parts of Europe ranges from 1 in 10,000 to 1 in 20,000. Although the disease is reported predominantly in people of North European origin, sporadic cases have been described in blacks, Yemenite Jews, and members of Mongolian races. The frequency among institutionalized defectives is about 1 percent.

The basic metabolic defect in PKU is an inability to convert phenylalanine, an essential amino acid, to paratyrosine, because of the absence or inactivity of the liver enzyme phenylalanine hydroxylase, which catalyzes the conversion.

Recently, two other types of hyperphenylalinemia were described. One is due to a deficiency of an enzyme, dihydropteridine reductase, and the other to a deficiency of a cofactor, biopterin. The first defect can be detected in fibroblasts, and biopterin can be measured in body fluids. Both of these rare disorders carry a high risk of fatality.

The majority of patients with PKU are severely retarded, but some patients are reported to have borderline or normal intelligence. Eczema and convulsions are present in about a third of all cases. Although the clinical picture varies, typical PKU children are hyperactive and exhibit erratic, unpredictable behavior which makes them difficult to manage. They have frequent temper tantrums and often display bizarre movements of their bodies and upper extremities and twisting hand mannerisms, and their behavior sometimes resembles that of autistic or schizophrenic children. Verbal and nonverbal communication is usually severely impaired or nonexistent. Coordination is poor, and there are many perceptual difficulties.

The best-known screening test depends on the reaction of phenylpyruvic acid in the urine with ferric chloride solution to give a vivid green color. This test has its limitations, since it may not become positive until the baby is 5 or 6 weeks old, and since it may be positive in other aminoacidurias. Another commonly used screening method is the Guthrie Test, which measures the phenylalanine level in the blood, using a bacteriological procedure.

Early diagnosis is of extreme importance, since a low phenylalanine diet, in use since 1955, results in significant improvement in both behavior and developmental progress. The best results seem to be obtained with early diagnosis and the start of the dietary treatment before the child is 6 months of age.

Dietary treatment is not without dangers. Phenylalanine is an essential amino acid, and its complete omission from the diet may lead to such severe complications as anemia, hypoglycemia, edema, and even death. Dietary treatment of PKU can often be discontinued at the age of 5 or 6 years, although no alternate meta-

TABLE IV
LEVELS OF MENTAL RETARDATION BY I.Q. RANGE

| Mental Retardation Level | IQ Level* | % of Retarded Population | DSM-III Code |
|---|---|---|---|
| Mild | 50–70 | 80–89 | 317.0x |
| Moderate | 35–49 | 6.0–12 | 318.0x |
| Severe | 20–34 | 3.5–7 | 318.1x |
| Profound | Below 20 | 1.0–1.5 | 318.2x |

* According to DSM-III.

TABLE V
THIRTY IMPORTANT SYNDROMES WITH INBORN ERRORS OF METABOLISM*

| Name of Disorder | Hereditary Transmission† | Enzyme Defect | Prenatal Diagnosis | Mental Retardation | Clinical Signs |
|---|---|---|---|---|---|
| **I. LIPID METABOLISM** | | | | | |
| Niemann-Pick disease | | | | | |
| Group A/infantile / Group B/adult | A.R. | Sphingomyelinase | + | ± | Hepatosplenomegaly |
| Groups C and D/intermediate | | Unknown | - | + | Pulmonary infiltration |
| Infantile Gaucher disease | A.R. | β-Glucosidase | + | ± | Hepatosplenomegaly, pseudobulbar palsy |
| Tay-Sachs disease | A.R. | Hexosaminidase A | + | + | Macular changes, seizures, spasticity |
| Generalized gangliosidosis | A.R. | β-Galactosidase | + | + | Hepatosplenomegaly, bone changes |
| Krabbe disease | A.R. | Galactocerebroside β-Galactosidase | + | + | Stiffness, seizures |
| Metachromatic leukodystrophy | A.R. | Cerebroside sulfatase | + | + | Stiffness, developmental failure |
| Wolman disease | A.R. | Acid lipase | + | - | Hepatosplenomegaly, adrenal calcification, vomiting, diarrhea |
| Farber lipogranulomatosis | A.R. | Acid ceramidase | + | + | Hoarseness, arthropathy, subcutaneous nodules |
| Fabry disease | X.R. | α-Galactosidase | + | - | Angiokeratomas, renal failure |
| **II. MUCOPOLYSACCHARIDE METABOLISM** | | | | | |
| Hurler's syndrome   MPS I | A.R. | Iduronidase | + | + | Varying degrees of bone changes, hepatosplenomegaly, joint restriction, etc. |
| Hunter's disease   II | X.R. | Iduronate sulfatase | + | + | |
| Sanfilippo disease   III | A.R. | Various sulfatases (types A–D) | + | + | |
| Morquio disease   IV | A.R. | N-Acetylgalactosamine-6-sulfate sulfatase | + | - | |
| Maroteaux-Lamy disease   VI | A.R. | Arylsulfatase B | + | ± | |
| **III. OLIGOSACCHARIDE AND GLYCOPROTEIN METABOLISM** | | | | | |
| I-cell disease | A.R. | Glycoprotein N-acetylglucosaminylphospho-transferase | + | + | Hepatomegaly, bone changes, swollen gingivae |
| Mannosidosis | A.R. | Mannosidase | + | + | Hepatomegaly, bone changes, facial coarsening |
| Fucosidosis | A.R. | Fucosidase | + | + | Same as above |
| **IV. AMINO ACID METABOLISM** | | | | | |
| Phenylketonuria | A.R. | Phenylalanine hydroxylase | - | + | Eczema, blonde hair, musty odor |

| | | | | |
|---|---|---|---|---|
| Homocystinuria | A.R. | Cystathionine β-synthetase | + | Ectopia lentis, Marfan-like phenotype, cardiovascular anomalies |
| Tyronsinosis | A.R. | Tyrosine amine transaminase | − | Hyperkeratotic skin lesions, conjunctivitis |
| Maple syrup urine disease | A.R. | Branched chain ketoacid decarboxylase | + | Recurrent ketoacidosis |
| Methylmalonic acidemia | A.R. | Methyl malonyl-CoA mutase | + | Recurrent ketoacidosis, hepatomegaly, growth retardation |
| Proprionic acidemia | A.R. | Proprionyl-CoA carboxylase | + | Same as above |
| Nonketotic hyperglycinemia | A.R. | Glycine cleavage enzyme | + | Seizures |
| Urea cycle disorders | mostly A.R. | Urea cycle enzymes | + | Recurrent acute encephalopathy, vomiting |
| Hartnup disorder | A.R. | Renal transport disorder | − | None consistent |
| **V. OTHERS** | | | | |
| Galactosemia | A.R. | Galactose-1-phosphate uridyltransferase | + | Hepatomegaly, cataracts, ovarian failure |
| Wilson hepatolenticular degeneration | A.R. | Unknown factor in copper metabolism | ± | Liver disease, Kayser-Fleischer ring, neurologic problems |
| Menkes kinky-hair disease | X.R. | Same as above | − | Abnormal hair, cerebral degeneration |
| Lesch-Nyhan disease | A.R. | Hypoxanthine guanine phosphoribosyltransferase | + | Behavioral abnormalities |

* Table by L Syzmanski, MD, and A Crocker, MD, and adapted from: Leroy J G: Heredity, development, and behavior. In *Developmental-Behavioral Pediatrics*, M D Levine et al, editor, p 315. W B Saunders, Philadelphia, 1983.
† A.R. = autosomal recessive transmission. X.R. = x-linked recessive transmission.

bolic pathway capable of keeping the blood phenylalanine levels in the normal range has been discovered as yet.

In untreated older children and adolescents with PKU, a low-phenylalanine diet does not influence the level of mental retardation. However, they do show a decrease in irritability and abnormal EEG changes, and their social responsiveness and attention span increase.

The parents of PKU children and some of these children's normal siblings are heterozygous carriers, and can be detected by a phenylalanine tolerance test, which may be of great importance in genetic counseling of these people.

MAPLE SYRUP URINE DISEASE (MENKES' DISEASE). Maple syrup urine disease is an inborn error of metabolism, transmitted by a rare single autosomal recessive gene. The biochemical defect interferes with the decarboxylation of the branched chain amino acids—leucine, isoleucine, and valine. As a result, these amino acids and their respective keto acids accumulate in the blood, and cause overflow aminoaciduria. The urine has a characteristic odor, which gives the condition its name, and which is due to the derivatives of the keto acids.

The diagnosis can be suspected by the use of ferric chloride or dinitrophenylhydrazine, each of which interacts with the urine to give, respectively, a navy blue color or a yellow precipitate.

The clinical symptoms appear during the first week of life. The infant deteriorates rapidly, and develops decerebrate rigidity, seizures, respiratory irregularity, and hypoglycemia. If untreated, most patients die in the first months of life, and the survivors are severely retarded. Some variants have been reported, with transient ataxia and only mild retardation.

Treatment follows the general principles established for PKU, and consists of a diet very low in the three involved amino acids.

HARTNUP DISEASE. This rare disorder took its name from the family in which it was detected. Like the preceding diseases described, it is transmitted by a single recessive autosomal gene. The symptoms are intermittent and variable, and tend to improve with age. They include a photosensitive pellagra-like rash on extension surfaces, episodic cerebellar ataxia, and mental deficiency. Of particular importance to psychiatrists is the fact that transient personality changes and psychoses may be the only manifestations of the disease, and mild cases do not come to medical attention until late childhood or adolescence.

The metabolic defect involves defective tryptophan transport.

Treatment with nicotinic acid, and antibiotics such as neomycin, may relieve the skin rash and possibly the ataxia, but it does not affect the mental retardation.

UREA CYCLE DISORDERS. *Citrullinuria.* This is one of the rare disorders involving the urea cycle. It involves an enzymatic defect in the conversion of citrulline into argininosuccinic acid because of an argininosuccinate synthetase deficiency. The disorder is accompanied by mental retardation.

*Hyperarginemia.* This disorder, caused by arginase deficiency, is characterized by mental retardation, spastic diplegia, and marked elevation of arginine in the blood, cerebrospinal fluid, and urine.

*Treatment of Urea Cycle Disorders.* Infants who survive the newborn period are sometimes helped by a low-protein diet.

HYPERGLYCINEMIA. Nonketotic hyperglycinemia is an autosomal recessive inborn error of metabolism in which large amounts of glycine are found in body fluids. The clinical picture includes severe mental retardation, seizures, spasticity, and failure to thrive. Ketotic hyperglycinemia is characterized by severe ketosis. The hyperglycinemia is secondary to blood elevation of several amino acids. The clinical picture includes seizures, mental retardation, vomiting, dehydration, ketosis, and coma.

HISTIDINEMIA. This defect in histidine metabolism is transmitted by a single autosomal recessive gene, and involves a block in the conversion of histidine to urocanic acid. The urine gives a positive ferric chloride test (green).

Mild mental retardation and sometimes speech defects are part of the clinical picture.

HOMOCYSTINURA. This disorder comprises a group of inborn errors of metabolism, each of which may lead to the accumulation of homocysteine. The patients are mentally retarded and resemble those with Marfan's syndrome in outward appearance.

LOWE'S OCULORENAL DYSTROPHY. This sex-linked disorder presents a varied clinical picture that includes some of the following eye defects: buphthalmos, microphthalmos, cataracts, and corneal opacities. Renal ammonia production is decreased, and a generalized aminoaciduria is found.

CYSTATHIONINURIA. The metabolic defect in this disease consists of a block at the site of cleavage of cystathionine to cysteine and homoserine. Patients with the disease are mentally retarded. Prolonged administration of pyridoxine may improve intellectual performance.

TYROSINOSIS. The mode of transmission is autosomal recessive. *p*-Hydroxyphenylpyruvic acid (HPA) oxidase deficiency is responsible for the clinical picture, which begins in early infancy. Some believe that the p-HPA deficiency is secondary to an as yet unknown primary defect. The symptoms include vomiting, steatorrhea, sweet odor, vitamin D-resistant rickets, osteoporosis, hepatosplenomegaly, failure to thrive, and mild mental retardation. The serum tyrosine and sometimes methionine are elevated. The ferric chloride test is positive.

HYPERLYSINEMIA. The mode of inheritance in this disorder is not yet defined. There is elevated blood and urine lysine, and elevated urinary homoarginine and homocitrulline. The mental retardation is usually severe, and one finds growth failure, microcephaly, hypotonia, and petit mal seizures.

Several other known aminoacidurias occur very rarely and are, therefore, not included here. The number of known aminoacidurias will, no doubt, continue to increase as more retarded and brain-damaged persons have their blood and urine studied by chromatographic methods.

**Disorders of Fat Metabolism.** It is generally assumed that disturbances in lipid metabolism related to the central nervous tissue are genetically determined, resulting from an enzymatic defect. These disorders can be roughly divided into two groups; the first includes diseases characterized by an increase and storage of lipids in the CNS, and the second involves diseases characterized by a decrease in lipids in the CNS, resulting in demyelination. Specific enzymatic defects have been recently demonstrated in some of these disorders.

CEREBROMACULAR DEGENERATIONS. The cerebromacular degenerations represent a group of disturbances in which there is progressive mental deterioration and loss of visual function. They are all transmitted by an autosomal recessive gene. The four types of cerebromacular degeneration differ as to the age of onset. The earliest one, Tay-Sachs disease, occurs chiefly among Jewish infants, particularly those from Eastern Europe; the others are found in members of all races.

Tay-Sachs disease begins in infants 4 to 8 months of age.

The Jansky-Bielschowsky type, also called the early juvenile or late infantile form of cerebromacular degeneration, has its onset at 2 to 4 years of age.

The juvenile form, Spielmeyer-Stock-Vogt-Koyanagi disease, occurs in early school-aged children.

The late juvenile form, Kufs' disease, is rare and occurs after 15 years of age.

All these variants of cerebromacular degeneration are progressive, and there is no treatment available to date.

*Niemann-Pick Disease.* This disease is transmitted by an autosomal recessive gene and occurs predominantly in Jewish infants.

The biochemical defect involves the storage of sphingomyelins in the neurons, liver, and spleen; the defect can be identified by biopsy of the rectum or the brain.

The clinical picture consists of a developmental arrest and mental regression, accompanied by abdominal enlargement due to hepatosplenomegaly, anemia, general emaciation, and occasionally a cherry-red spot in the retina, similar to that found in Tay-Sachs disease. No treatment is known at present, and death occurs in most cases in early childhood, before the age of 4.

*Gaucher's Disease.* This lipidosis also occurs mostly in Jewish children, and has an autosomal recessive mode of genetic transmission.

Clinically, the illness occurs in two forms. The acute infantile form has its onset in infancy, after several months of normal development, and is characterized by progressive mental deterioration and developmental arrest. Hepatosplenomegaly, abdominal and cranial enlargement, hypotonia, and opisthotonos complete the clinical course, which is usually fatal before the end of the first year of life.

The chronic form has an insidious onset, usually any time before the tenth year of life, but occurs occasionally in adolescents and young adults. The course is chronic, characterized mainly by chronic physical handicaps.

METACHROMATIC LEUKODYSTROPHY. This is a familial disorder, characterized by demyelination and accumulation of metachromatic lipids.

Clinically, the disease is characterized by progressive paralysis and dementia, beginning usually in the second year of life. The disease is usually fatal in 2 to 10 years. Two other rare forms have been defined. In the adult form, psychic disorders and dementia may precede by decades the development of motor dysfunction.

The clinical features include hepatosplenomegaly and mental retardation. No treatment is available.

PROGRESSIVE LEUKOENCEPHALOPATHIES. This group of disorders consists of several clinical syndromes, characterized by a degeneration of the cortical white matter, with the onset varying from infancy to adulthood and even old age.

The genetic mode of transmission is sex linked, except for Krabbe's disease, which is transmitted by an autosomal recessive gene. Schilder's disease may occur sporadically.

The clinical course often begins with ambiguous symptoms, such as irritability or hypersensitivity to external stimuli, but soon progresses to dementia, developmental regression, hypotonia, spasticity, ataxia, cortical blindness and deafness, convulsions, and paroxysmal attacks of laughing. The nature of the clinical symptoms depends on the localization of the degenerative process. The prognosis is usually hopeless, and no treatment is available.

**Disorders of Carbohydrate Metabolism.** GALACTOSEMIA. Galactosemia is transmitted by an autosomal recessive gene.

The urinary findings include the presence of galactose and general aminoaciduria. The reducing substances in the urine may be detected by the use of Clinitest tablets, but not by the use of Tes-Tape, which is specific only for glucose. Heterozygous carriers can be detected by a lower level of transferase in their erythrocytes.

Galactosemia, like PKU, is a fine example of rewarded combined effort in basic and applied research. The pinpointing of the exact location of the enzymatic defect, circumvention by dietary adjustment, and early detection, which allows for a prevention of serious brain damage, are held out as an example and a promise to researchers in other metabolic disorders.

The clinical manifestations begin after a few days of milk feeding and include jaundice, vomiting, diarrhea, failure to thrive, and hepatomegaly. If untreated, the disease may be fatal within a short time, or it may lead to progressive mental deterioration, associated with cataracts, hepatic insufficiency, and occasional hypoglycemic convulsions.

A galactose-free diet, instituted early, prevents all clinical manifestations, and allows normal physical and mental development. Moderate amounts of milk may be reinstituted under careful monitoring at the beginning of school age, since the patients usually develop alternate metabolic pathways of galactose metabolism.

GLYCOGEN STORAGE DISEASES. Type I may begin in the neonatal period, and is characterized by hepatomegaly, doll-like facies, epistagus, hypoglycemia, acidosis, and transient ketonuria.

Type II (Pompe's disease) is a progressive generalized glycogen storage disorder of young infants. Cardiac hypertrophy, skeletal muscle dysfunction, and central nervous system deterioration result in a fatal outcome in the first year of life.

**Miscellaneous Metabolic Disorders.** IDIOPATHIC HYPERCALCEMIA. The pattern of inheritance in this disorder is that of an autosomal recessive trait, and hypersensitivity to vitamin D probably represents the metabolic aberration.

The serum calcium is elevated but may occasionally be normal, and suspicion may be ruled out only after 3 or 4 determinations.

Several therapeutic approaches are in use, of which the maintenance of patients on cortisone is the most commonly used in this country. The more severe form of the illness does not respond to therapy, and often leads to early death or progressive mental deterioration.

HYPOPARATHYROIDISM. The cause of hypoparathyroidism is obscure, but a familial tendency has been reported. The onset in most cases is during childhood. Early diagnosis and early institution of treatment may prevent physical and mental deterioration.

Treatment in early recognized cases consists of the administration of calcium and vitamin D.

GOITROUS CRETINISM. Cretinism as a condition associated with mental retardation has been known since antiquity. Up to the middle of the 19th century, all forms of mental retardation were considered as variants of cretinism.

The classical endemic variety occurs in certain regions as a result of iodine deficiency in the diet.

The clinical signs in all varieties include hypothyroidism, goiter, dwarfism, coarse skin, disturbances in ossification, hypertelorism, and a large tongue. Mental retardation becomes a part of the clinical picture if the disease is unrecognized and untreated in infancy. This fact is explained by the essential role that thyroxin plays in the formation of structural proteins and lipids in the central nervous system during early infancy. Children with the disorder are sluggish, their voices are hoarse, and speech does not develop. Among the laboratory findings are a low basal metabolism rate, depressed protein-bound iodine, and a high cholesterol level. The radioactive iodine uptake is low, except in the varieties inherited. In these familial disorders, the serum thyroid-stimulating hormone is often abnormal.

Treatment with thyroid extract may avert most of the symptoms if instituted early in life. It is not effective in adult cretins. Endemic goitrous cretinism is treated and prevented by the ingestion of small amounts of iodine.

WILSON'S DISEASE (HEPATOLENTICULAR DEGENERATION). This disorder of copper metabolism has a recessive mode of inheritance. The two variants of the disease, the juvenile and the adult forms, are inherited independently as separate entities.

The biochemical changes are similar in both forms, and consist of a diminished blood level of copper-containing ceruloplasmin. The low blood level is accompanied by excessive copper deposits in various tissues, chiefly in the liver and the brain. The resulting liver cirrhosis and degeneration of the lenticular nucleus gave the disease its name. Other laboratory findings include an elevated copper excretion in the urine and aminoaciduria involving primarily the aromatic amino acids (phenylalanine, tyrosine, and threonine). The aminoaciduria is being explained on the basis of kidney damage due to copper deposits, or blamed on a defect in a copper-containing enzyme, tyrosinase.

Heterozygous carriers are asymptomatic, but often manifest abnormal levels of ceruloplasmin in the blood, and a tendency to various hepatic difficulties. A copper-loading test is available for the detection of heterozygous carriers.

Personality changes may precede other clinical manifestations, which include cirrhosis of the liver, progressive emotional and mental deterioration, pseudobulbar palsy, fatuous facial expression, spasticity, and a greenish-brown ring in the iris (Kayser-Fleisher ring). In some cases, there are only manifestations of liver involvement, without neurological symptoms.

The juvenile form begins between the ages of 7 and 15. Inattentiveness in school and dystonia, often with the bizarre wing-flapping movements, are usually the first signs. This form is usually unresponsive to treatment, since the dystonia is related not to copper deposits but to hepatic dysfunction, which causes damage to the basal ganglia of the brain. The nature of the relationship between the hepatic disorder and the brain damage, found also in other liver diseases, is unknown.

The adult form usually begins with tremors and dysarthria, but may begin with psychiatric symptoms. It has a good prognosis. Several treatment methods are available, all aimed at lowering the serum copper level and increasing the urinary copper excretion. Penicillamine, a copper-chelating amino acid derived from penicillin, is presently the most effective therapeutic agent. Penicillin-sensitive patients may require the concomitant administration of steroids. Dimercaprol (British antilewisite, BAL) is also used with fair results. The administration of L-dopa may improve the rigidity and akinesis.

MUCOPOLYSACCHARIDOSES. This group of disorders includes a number of heritable diseases characterized by the storage of dermatan sulfate and heparitin sulfate.

*Hurler's Syndrome—Mucopolysaccharidosis Type I (Gargoylism).* This disorder is transmitted by an autosomal recessive trait. The basic disturbance consists of the accumulation of dermatan sulfate and heparitin sulfate in the urine and tissues, increased levels of gangliosides in

the brain, and decreased activity of $\beta$-galactosidase.

The lymphocytes contain metachromatic inclusions, and X-rays show several characteristic abnormalities, such as elongation of the sella turcica, beaking of the thoracic spine on the lateral view (kyphosis), club-shaped lower ribs, thickening of the long bones, misshapen metacarpal bones and phalanges, and skull malformations.

The clinical course is slow and progressive, and usually starts at a very early age, leading to death before adolescence. The hepatosplenomegaly causes abdominal enlargement. The stature is dwarfed, and the face acquires a peculiar appearance that gave rise to the name of gargoylism. The facial characteristics include bushy confluent eyebrows, thick lips, large tongue, and coarse features. Spade-like hands and sometimes hypertelorism and hydrocephalus complete the picture. There is nearly always a progressive mental deterioration, which often precedes the characteristic facial appearance. No treatment is available (see Fig. 1).

The differential diagnosis may present some problems. The superficial resemblance to cretins

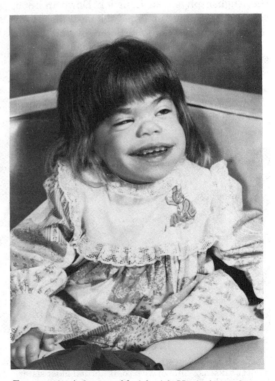

FIGURE 1. A 6-year-old girl with Hurler's syndrome. Her care has involved a class for seriously multihandicapped children, attention to cardiac problems, and special counseling for the parents. (Courtesy of L. S. Syzmanski, M.D., and A. C. Crocker, M.D.)

is easily ruled out by X-ray findings and by the hepatosplenomegaly, as well as by biochemical findings.

*Hunter's Disease—Mucopolysaccharidosis Type II.* This disorder affects only males, and is transmitted as an X-linked recessive trait. The biochemical findings are identical with those of Hurler's syndrome. The clinical picture is milder, however, with only moderate mental retardation and no corneal opacities. Children with the disorder have gargoyle features, dwarfism, and marked skeletal abnormalities (see Fig. 2).

LESCH-NYHAN SYNDROME. This condition occurs mainly in boys, and is X-linked recessive. There is an elevation of uric acid in the blood, due to a deficiency of hypoxanthineguanine phosphoribosyltransferase. In addition to severe mental retardation, there is self-mutilating behavior, such as biting of the fingers and lips, often leading to permanent tissue destruction. Allopurinal lowers the level of uric acid, leading to some improvement of behavior, but not in the mental retardation.

**Chromosomal Aberrations.** AUTOSOMAL DISORDERS. *Down's Syndrome (Mongolism).* Since the classical description of mongolism by the English physician Langdon Down in 1866, this syndrome has remained the most discussed, most investigated, and most controversial in the field of mental retardation (see Fig. 3). Its cause still remains obscure, despite a plethora of theories and hypotheses advanced with variable acclaim in the past 100 years. There is agreement on very few predisposing factors in chromosomal disorders—among them, the increased

FIGURE 2. Two brothers, age 6 and 8 years, with Hunter's disease, shown with their normal older sister. They have had significant developmental delay, trouble with recurrent respiratory infection, and behavioral abnormalities. (Courtesy of L. S. Syzmanski, M.D., and A. C. Crocker, M.D.)

age of the mother and possibly the increased age of the father, and X-ray radiation. The problem of cause is complicated even further by the recent recognition of 3 distinct types of chromosomal aberrations in Down's syndrome:

1. Patients with trisomy 21 (3 of chromosome 21, instead of the usual 2) represent the overwhelming majority of mongoloid patients; they have 47 chromosomes, with an extra chromosome 21. The karyotypes of the mothers are normal. A nondisjunction during miosis, occurring for yet unknown reasons, is held responsible for the disorder.

2. Nondisjunction occurring after fertilization in any cell division results in mosaicism, a condition in which both normal and trisomic cells are found in various tissues.

3. In translocation, there is a fusion of 2 chromosomes, mostly 21 and 15, resulting in a total of 46 chromosomes, despite the presence of an extra chromosome 21. The disorder, unlike trisomy 21, is usually inherited, and the translocation chromosome may be found in unaffected parents and siblings. These asymptomatic carriers have only 45 chromosomes.

The incidence of Down's syndrome in the United States is about 1 in every 700 births. Down, in his original description, mentioned the frequency of 10 percent among all mentally retarded patients. Interestingly enough, the frequency of patients with Down's syndrome in institutions for the mentally retarded today also approximates 10 percent. In a middle-aged mother (more than 32 years old), the risk of having a mongoloid child with trisomy 21 is about 1 in 100, but when translocation is present, the risk is about 1 in 3. These facts assume special importance in genetic counseling.

Amniocentesis (see Fig. 4), in which a small amount of amniotic fluid is removed from the amniotic cavity transabdominally between the 14th and 16th week of gestation, has been of use in diagnosing various infant abnormalities, especially Down's syndrome. Amniotic fluid cells, mostly fetal in origin, are cultured for cytogenetic and biochemical studies. Many serious hereditary disorders can be predicted with this method and then positive therapeutic abortion is the only method of prevention. Amniocentesis is recommended for all pregnant women over the age of 35. Fortunately, most chromosomal anomalies occur only once in a family.

Mental retardation is the overriding feature of Down's syndrome. The majority of patients belong to the moderately and severely retarded groups, with only a minority having an I.Q. above 50. Mental development seems to progress

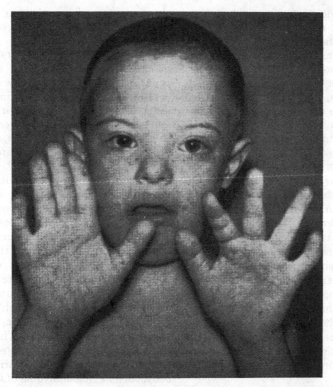

FIGURE 3. Child with Down's syndrome (mongolism). Note the facial features, the single palmar crease, and the short and incurvated little fingers. (Courtesy of Dr. Beale H. Ong, Children's Hospital, Washington, D.C.)

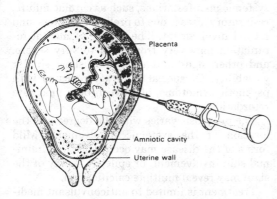

FIGURE 4. Amniocentesis. (From Moment G B, Haberman H M: Biology: A Full Spectrum, Williams & Wilkins, Baltimore, 1973.)

normally from birth to 6 months of age. I.Q. scores gradually decrease from near normal at 1 year to about 30 at older ages. This decline in intelligence may be real or apparent. It could be that infantile tests do not reveal the full extent of the defect, which may become manifest when more sophisticated tests are used in early childhood. According to many sources, patients with Down's syndrome are placid, cheerful, and co-operative, which facilitates their adjustment at home. The picture, however, seems to change in adolescence, especially in institutions, where a variety of emotional difficulties, behavior disorders, and (rarely) psychotic illnesses may be seen.

The diagnosis is made with relative ease in an older child, but is often difficult in newborn infants. The most important signs in a newborn include general hypotonia, oblique palpebral fissures, abundant neck skin, a small flattened skull, high cheek bones, and a protruding tongue. The hands are broad and thick, with a single palmar transversal crease, and the little fingers are short and curved inward. Moro's reflex is weak or absent.

More than 100 signs or stigmata are described in Down's syndrome, but they are rarely all found in one person.

Life expectancy used to be about 12 years. With the advent of antibiotics, few young patients succumb to infections, but most of them do not live beyond the age of 40, when they already have many signs of senescence. Despite numerous therapeutic recommendations, no treatment has proved to be effective.

*Cat-cry (Cri-du-Chat) Syndrome.* This aberration consists of a missing part of the fifth chromosome. The affected children are severely retarded, and show many stigmata often associated with chromosomal aberrations, such as microcephaly, low-set ears, oblique palpebral fissures, hypertelorism, and micrognathia. The characteristic catlike cry—due to laryngeal abnormalities—that gave the syndrome its name gradually changes and disappears with increasing age.

ANOMALIES OF THE SEX CHROMOSOMES. As a group, these disorders are associated with mild forms of mental retardation, and sometimes with normal and even superior intelligence.

*Klinefelter's Syndrome.* The male patients with this disorder have testicular atrophy evident at puberty and signs of feminization, such as gynecomastia. Their karyotypes usually show an XXY pattern. There is a darkly stained Barr chromatin body in the nuclei of the cells on the nuclear membrane; this is a female nucleus pattern dependent on there being two X chromosomes, one of which is genetically active and the other inactive and constituting the nuclear sex chromatin body, according to the Lyon hypothesis.

Other variants with similar physical characteristics have been detected, mostly among the institutionalized mentally retarded. Their sex chromosome patterns show a wide range of aberration, such as XXXY, XXXXY, and XXYY. There are frequent mosaics and associations with autosomal trisomies. There has been a wide-ranging controversy concerning an association between an XYY chromosome complement and tall stature, delinquent behavior, and mental retardation. The evidence linking the disorder with criminal behavior is not firmly established.

The degree of mental retardation may vary from mild to severe, but many patients have normal intelligence. The patients are generally cooperative, but may develop serious social and body image difficulties, leading sometimes to social withdrawal, serious difficulties in adjustment (especially in adolescence), and paranoid tendencies.

*Ovarian dysgenesis (Turner's Syndrome).* The main clinical features of this disorder are small stature, webbed neck, and cubitus valgus. The chromosomal pattern is usually XO, and only a minority of the patients are mentally retarded.

A greater preponderance of mental retardation of mild to moderate degree is found among the so-called superfemales, most of whom have no physical abnormalities, but they do have 3 X chromosomes, giving them a total of 47. A smaller group have 4 X chromosomes, for a total of 48.

AUTOSOMAL DOMINANT DISORDERS. These anomalies are determined by single dominant genes of variable expressivity and penetrance, that vary in frequency. The clinical picture varies greatly, and mild forms, with minimal signs and only mild mental retardation, are often seen. In addition to cerebral defects, ectodermal, visceral, and skeletal anomalies are involved.

*Epiloia (Tuberous Sclerosis).* This autosomal disorder may manifest itself with great variability, probably due to the irregularity of the abnormal gene or to the influence of additional modifying genes. The skin lesions consist of sebaceous adenomata, red on the face and brownish-white on the rest of the body. Vitiligo patches often offer the first diagnostic lead. Throughout the cerebral cortex in the lateral ventricles and in the cerebellum, multiple nodules are found; they are of rubber consistency, composed mainly of glial tissue, with some giant undifferentiated nerve cells. These tumors may cause hydrocephalus, due to obstruction. In addition, tumors are found in various parts of the body, such as rhabdomyoma of the heart, mixed kidney tumors, hepatic fibrolipoma, and retinal nerve tumors.

The clinical picture is often complicated by systemic manifestations, such as cardiac failure, respiratory disease due to preliminary cysts, and retinal involvement. The degree of mental retardation may vary from mild to very severe, and other signs and symptoms show similar variability. Of special interest are cases with psychotic symptoms, often with only moderate retardation.

The prognosis varies with the degree and the location of the systemic involvement. Mild forms of the disease may occur with only minimal skin involvement, or epilepsy. X-ray of the skull may reveal multiple calcification.

Treatment is limited to anticonvulsant medication, which is usually effective in controlling the seizures. The hydrocephalus may often be surgically corrected.

*Neurofibromatosis (Recklinghausen's Disease).* The main features of this disorder are small brown patches distributed over the entire body along the course of the subcutaneous nerves, autonomic nerves, and nerve trunks. Sensory nerves are usually more affected than other nerves. Astrocytomas, ependymomas, and meningiomas may be found in the brain. The skin manifestations usually begin in childhood, and may include large skin polyps and *café au lait* spots over the trunk and the extremities. Acoustic or optic nerve glioma may also occur. Bilateral acoustic neurinomas are almost diagnostic of the disease. In addition to the skin manifestations, epilepsy and, in about 10 percent of cases, mental retardation are also seen.

Anticonvulsant medication and neurosurgery may sometimes be effective because of the benign nature of the tumors.

*Encephalofacial Angiomatosis (Sturge-Weber Syndrome).* This disorder is believed to be due to an irregularly dominant gene, but the exact mechanism of hereditary transmission is not yet clear. In its classical form, the syndrome includes a facial nevus in the distribution of the fifth cranial nerve, buphthalmos, hemiparesis of the contralateral extremities, convulsions, and mental retardation. The convulsions and mental retardation are due to intracranial angiomata, which often become calcified and may be radiologically demonstrated. Neurosurgical intervention has been attempted, but is rarely successful.

*Arachnodactyly (Marfan's Syndrome).* Arachnodactyly is an inheritable disorder, probably transmitted by a single dominant gene of variable expressivity. It involves changes in many parts of the body, chiefly in the skeletal, cardiovascular, and ocular structures. The patients are tall, have long extremities with long spider-like fingers and toes, coloboma, bilateral lens dislocation, and cardiac anomalies. The accompanying mental retardation is usually mild.

*Chondrodystrophy (Achondroplasia).* This disorder is characterized by very short limbs, due to a disturbed ossification of the cartilage. The head is often large, and the accompanying mental retardation is usually mild.

*Craniosynostosis.* This group of disorders includes several conditions characterized by premature closure of cranial sutures, skull deformities, and brain damage, due to increased intracranial pressure. Some include in this group of disorders the formerly separate syndrome of Crouzon's disease (craniofacial dysostosis). The cause of most cases of craniosynostosis is still unknown.

The elongated cranium (dolichocephaly) is most common (see Fig. 5). The broad skull (brachycephaly) represents another variant. Obliteration of all cranial sutures results in a pointed skull (acrocephaly). Several facial and orbital deformities may be associated with various forms of craniosynostosis, such as hypertelorism, shallow orbits resulting in exophthalmos, a beak-shaped nose, choanal atresia, and several others. Syndactyly is often associated with acrocephaly.

*Hypertelorism.* This disorder is characterized by a wide distance between the eyes. Familial occurrence of the disorder indicates a dominant mode of inheritance in most cases, but some cases with a recessive mechanism have been reported.

In addition to the ocular feature, the patients manifest a flat nasal bridge, external strabismus, and sometimes a vertical midline groove in the forehead. The mentality ranges from normal to moderate retardation. Some retarded patients

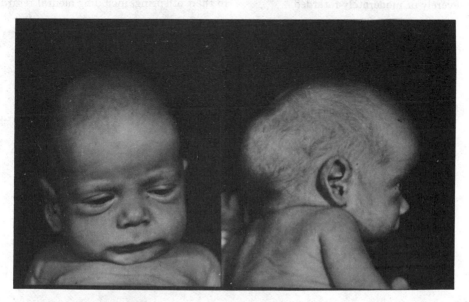

FIGURE 5.   Infant with sagittal synostosis. Note the elongated cranium. (Courtesy of Dr. Michael Malone, Children's Hospital, Washington, D.C.)

with the anomaly have hyperaminoaciduria. Convulsions may occur.

DEVELOPMENTAL ANOMALIES DUE TO RECESSIVE OR UNKNOWN GENETIC MECHANISM. *Anencephaly.* The cause of this lethal anomaly is unknown, but it is believed to be a hereditary polygenic disorder. It is one of the most common congenital brain malformations, and its incidence ranges between 0.5 and 3.7 per 1,000. The anencephalic fetus usually succumbs during delivery, or shortly thereafter. The pathological findings include an absence of the cranial vault and most of the central nervous system or, at least, the absence of both cerebral hemispheres.

*Hydranencephaly.* This condition of unknown cause is characterized by the absence of the cerebral cortex but intact meninges and cranium, which is filled with clear fluid. The infant may live for several weeks or even a few months, and may seem normal at birth. Shortly thereafter, however, he develops spasticity, convulsions, and rigidity of the extremities, and his head enlarges rapidly. Pneumoencephalograms and transillumination of the head are usually diagnostic.

*Porencephaly.* This disorder is characterized by cystic formations in the cerebral hemispheres, communicating sometimes with the ventricular system or subarachnoid space. The defects vary in size and shape, and the clinical picture depends on the amount of remaining functional cortical tissue. The patients who survive early childhood are usually bedridden, have bilateral hemiplegia or tetraplegia, and are either severely or moderately retarded.

*Microcephaly.* Microcephaly is a purely descriptive term, covering a variety of disorders whose main clinical feature is a small, peculiarly shaped head and mental retardation (see Fig. 6).

Microcephaly may be found in 20 percent of the institutionalized mentally retarded population. The causes vary greatly, and include inherited factors, intrauterine influences, and insults in the perinatal or postnatal period.

*Hydrocephalus.* This name covers a number of conditions having in common an increase in the cerebrospinal fluid, resulting in the enlargement of the head or the ventricles. This group of disorders is listed here because one of its variants, usually due to atresia of the aqueduct, has a sex-linked recessive mode of inheritance. Many cases, however, are due to developmental malformations of undetermined origin, including atresias of the foramina of Magendie and Luschka and of the aqueduct Sylvii, and Arnold-Chiari malformation. The Arnold-Chiari malformation is a medullary-cerebellar anomaly, often associated with spina bifida, meningomyelocele, displacement of the medulla into the cervical canal, and occasionally cortical defects. The cases of hydrocephalus that follow viral, bacterial, or aseptic meningitis are due to obstructing fibrosis of the arachnoid tissue.

## Maternal Infections During Pregnancy

### Syphilis

Syphilis in pregnant women used to be a major cause of a variety of neuropathological changes in their offspring, including mental retardation.

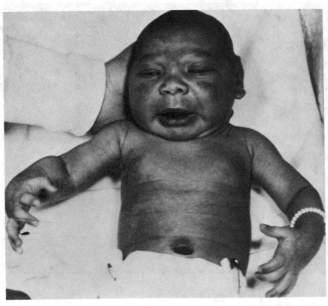

FIGURE 6.  Infant with microcephaly. (Courtesy of Dr. Michael Malone, Children's Hospital, Washington, D.C.)

Today, the incidence of syphilitic complications of pregnancy fluctuates with the incidence of syphilis in the general population. Some recent alarming statistics from several major cities in the United States indicate that there is still no room for complacency.

### Rubella (German Measles)

This disease has replaced syphilis as the major cause of congenital malformations and mental retardation due to maternal infection. The children of affected mothers may present a number of abnormalities, including congenital heart disease, mental retardation, cataracts, deafness, microcephaly, and microphthalmia. Timing is crucial, since the extent and the frequency of the complications are in inverse proportion to the duration of pregnancy at the time of maternal infection. When mothers are infected in the first trimester of pregnancy, 10 to 15 percent of the children will be affected, and the incidence rises to almost 50 percent when the infection occurs in the first month of pregnancy. The situation is often complicated by subclinical forms of maternal infection, which often go undetected.

### Other Diseases

Brain damage due to toxoplasmosis and cytomegalic inclusion body disease transmitted from the pregnant mother to the fetus is another universally recognized but relatively rare complication of pregnancy that often results in mental retardation and a variety of brain malformations. Damage to the fetus from maternal hepatitis has also been reported.

The role of other maternal infections during pregnancy—such as influenza, cold viruses, pneumonia, and urinary tract infections—in the causation of mental retardation is at present under extensive investigation. The results are as yet inconclusive.

### Complications of Pregnancy

Toxemia of pregnancy and uncontrolled maternal diabetes present hazards to the fetus and may sometimes result in mental retardation. Maternal malnutrition during pregnancy often results in prematurity and other obstetrical complications. Vaginal hemorrhage, placenta previa, and premature separation of the placenta may be damaging to the fetal brain by causing anoxia. The same may be said about the prolapse of the cord.

The potential teratogenic effect of pharmacological agents administered during pregnancy was widely publicized after the thalidomide trag-

edy. So far, with the exception of metabolites used in cancer chemotherapy, no usual doses of drugs are known to damage the central nervous system of the fetus, but caution and restraint in prescribing drugs to pregnant women are certainly indicated. Recently, the use of lithium during pregnancy was implicated in some congenital malformations, especially of the cardiovascular system, but the evidence is contested by many as insufficient.

### Effects of Retardation

### Psychiatric Factors

**Personality Development.** Differences in the degree of intellectual functioning in the mentally retarded are compounded by the divergence of causal factors, ranging from clearly demonstrable brain damage—occurring in all phases of prenatal and postnatal development from a multitude of causes—to emotional and cultural deprivation. The resulting extreme heterogeneity of the mentally retarded is probably responsible for the often conflicting and confusing views about their personality development and frequency of psychopathology. What contributes to the existing confusion in the field is the paucity of well-conducted studies and surveys that use similar standardized methods of investigation. Most assumptions are based on studies using residents in state institutions or patients in psychiatric clinics and hospitals. No wonder the views on the personality development of the mentally retarded range widely from the assumption of little or no difference from the normal population in the frequency of emotional disturbance, to the contrasting opinion that assigns to the mentally retarded a very high risk of psychotic illness—up to 40 percent in some studies.

### Diagnosis

### History

Although caution is indicated in taking a history from parents, they often remain the only source of information. The history of the pregnancy, labor, and delivery, the consanguinity of the parents, and the presence of hereditary disorders in their families deserve particular attention. The parents may also provide information about the child's developmental milestones. This area is especially subject to distortions because of parental bias and anxiety. A history is particularly helpful in assessing the emotional climate of the family and their sociocultural background, which play an important part in the evaluation of clinical findings.

### Physical Examination

The physical examination has to include a careful observation of the child's behavior level of activity and the quality of his interaction with his parents, other people, and inanimate objects. Various parts of the body may have certain characteristics commonly found in the mentally retarded due to prenatal causes. The configuration and the size of the head offer clues to a variety of conditions, such as microcephaly, hydrocephalus, and Down's syndrome. The patient's face may have some of the stigmata of mental retardation, which greatly facilitate the diagnosis. Some of the facial signs are hypertelorism, a flat nasal bridge, prominent eyebrows, epicanthal folds, corneal opacities, retinal changes, low-set and small or misshapen ears, a protruding tongue, and a disturbance in dentition. Facial expression, such as dull appearance, may be misleading and should not be relied on without other supporting evidence. The color and the texture of the skin and hair, a high-arched palate, the size of the thyroid gland, the size of the child, and his trunk and extremities are further areas to be explored. Measurement of the head circumference is an essential part of the clinical investigation.

Dermatoglyphics or the handprinting patterns may offer another diagnostic tool, since uncommon ridge patterns and flexion creases are often found in retarded children. Abnormal dermatoglyphics may be found in chromosomal disorders and in children who were infected prenatally with rubella.

Table VI lists the multiple handicaps associated with the syndromes discussed above.

### Neurological Examination

The incidence and the severity of neurological signs generally rise in inverse proportion to the degree of retardation, but many severely retarded children have no neurological abnormalities. Conversely, about 25 percent of all children with cerebral palsy have normal intelligence.

The disturbances in motor areas manifest themselves in abnormalities of muscle tone (spasticity or hypotonia), reflexes (hyperreflexia), and involuntary movements (choreoathetosis). A smaller degree of disability in this area manifests itself in clumsiness and poor coordination.

The sensory disturbances may include hearing difficulties, ranging from cortical deafness to mild hearing deficits. Visual disturbances may range from blindness to disturbances of spatial concepts, design recognition, and concept of body image.

Paine advanced the knowledge of the evolution of postural reflexes in infants, which may help the examining physician in his prognosis. Caution, however, is indicated, since some children who initially present various motor abnormalities later show no abnormal motor signs, and may not be mentally retarded.

Hyperirritable infants, jittery or convulsing with asymmetrical neurological signs, need careful attention, since about half of them may be brain-damaged in later life. The infants with the poorest prognosis are those who manifest a combination of inactivity, general hypotonia, and exaggerated response to stimuli.

In older children, hyperactivity, short attention span, distractibility, and a low frustration tolerance are often hallmarks of brain damage.

In general, the younger the child at the time of investigation, the more caution is indicated in predicting future ability, since the recovery potential of the infantile brain is very good. Following the child's development at regular intervals is probably the most reliable approach.

A pneumoencephalogram is somewhat hazardous and seldom indicated in the evaluation for mental retardation. The occasional findings of internal hydrocephalus, cortical atrophy, or porencephaly in a severely retarded, brain-damaged child are not considered very contributory to the general picture.

Skull X-rays are usually done routinely, but are illuminating only in a relatively few conditions, such as craniosynostosis, hydrocephalus, and several others that result in intracranial calcifications, including toxoplasmosis, tuberous sclerosis, cerebral angiomatosis, and hypoparathyroidism.

The electroencephalogram (EEG) is best interpreted with caution in cases of mental retardation. The most notable exceptions are patients with hypsarrhythmia or grand mal seizures, in whom the EEG may help establish the diagnosis and suggest treatment. In most other conditions, one deals with a diffuse cerebral disorder that produces nonspecific EEG changes, characterized by slow frequencies with bursts of spikes and sharp or blunt wave complexes. The confusion over the significance of the EEG in the diagnosis of mental retardation is best illustrated by the reports of the frequency of EEG abnormalities in Down's syndrome that range from 25 percent to the majority of patients examined.

### Laboratory Procedures

These procedures include examination of the urine and the blood for a host of metabolic disorders. The enzymatic abnormalities in chro-

TABLE VI
THIRTY-FIVE IMPORTANT SYNDROMES WITH MULTIPLE HANDICAPS*

| Syndrome | Diagnostic Manifestations | | | | | |
|---|---|---|---|---|---|---|
| | Craniofacial | Skeletal | Other | Mental Retardation | Short Stature | Genetic Transmission |
| Aarskog syndrome | Hypertelorism; broad nasal bridge, anteverted nostrils, long philtrum | Small hands and feet; mild interdigital webbing; short stature | Scrotal "shawl" above penis | | + | X-linked semidominant |
| Apert syndrome (acrocephalosyndactyly) | Craniosynostosis; irregular midfacial hypoplasia; hypertelorism | Syndactyly; broad distal thumb and toe | | ± | | Autosomal dominant |
| Cerebral gigantism (Sotos syndrome) | Large head; prominent forehead; narrow anterior mandible | Large hands and feet | Large size in early life; poor coordination | ± | | ? |
| Cockayne syndrome | Pinched facies; sunken eyes; thin nose; prognathism; retinal degeneration | Long limbs, with large hands and feet; flexion deformities | Hypotrichosis; photosensitivity; thin skin; diminished subcutaneous fat; impaired hearing | + | + | Autosomal recessive |
| Cohen syndrome | Maxillary hypoplasia with prominent central incisors | Narrow hands and feet | Hypotonia; obesity | + | ± | ? Autosomal recessive |
| Cornelia de Lange syndrome | Synophrys (continuous eyebrows); thin down-turning upper lip; long philtrum; anteverted nostrils; microcephaly | Small or malformed hands and feet; proximal thumb | Hirsutism | + | + | ? |
| Cri-du-chat syndrome | Epicanthic folds and/or slanting palpebral fissures; round facial contour; hypertelorism; microcephaly | Short metacarpals or metatarsals; four-finger line in palm | Catlike cry in infancy | + | + | ? |
| Crouzon syndrome (craniofacial dysostosis) | Proptosis with shallow orbits; maxillary hypoplasia; craniosynostosis | | | | | Autosomal dominant |

TABLE VI—cont.

| Syndrome | Diagnostic Manifestations | | | Mental Retardation | Short Stature | Genetic Transmission |
|---|---|---|---|---|---|---|
| | Craniofacial | Skeletal | Other | | | |
| Down's syndrome | Upward slant to palpebral fissures; mid-face depression; epicanthic folds; Brushfield spots; brachycephaly | Short hands; clinodactyly of 5th finger; four-finger line in palm | Hypotonia; loose skin on back of neck | + | + | 21 Trisomy |
| Dubowitz syndrome | Small facies; lateral displacement of inner canthi; ptosis; broad nasal bridge; sparse hair; microcephaly | | Infantile eczema; high-pitched hoarse voice | ± | ++ | ? Autosomal recessive |
| Fetal alcohol syndrome | Short palpebral fissures; midfacial hypoplasia; microcephaly | | ± Cardiac defect; fine motor dysfunction | + | + | |
| Fetal hydantoin syndrome (Dilantin) | Hypertelorism; short nose; occasional cleft lip | Hypoplastic nails, especially 5th | Cardiac defect | ± | ± | |
| Goldenhar syndrome | Malar hypoplasia; macrostomia; micrognathia; epibulbar dermoid and/or lipodermoid; malformed ear with preauricular tags | ± Vertebral anomalies | | | | ? |
| Incontinentia pigmenti | ± Dental defect; deformities of ears; ± Patchy alopecia | | Irregular skin pigmentation in fleck, whorl, or spidery form | ± | | ? Dom. X-linked ? Lethal in males |
| Laurence-Moon-Biedl syndrome | Retinal pigmentation | Polydactyly; syndactyly | Obesity; seizures; hypogenitalism | + | ± | Autosomal recessive |
| Linear nevus sebaceus syndrome | Nevus sebaceus, face or neck | | +/− Seizures | + | ± | ? |
| Lowe syndrome (oculocerebrorenal syndrome) | Cataract | Renal tubular dysfunction | Hypotonia | + | + | X-linked recessive |

| Syndrome | | | | | | |
|---|---|---|---|---|---|---|
| Möbius syndrome (congenital facial diplegia) | Expressionless facies; ocular palsy | ± Clubfoot; syndactyly | | ± | ± | ? |
| Neurofibromatosis | ± Optic gliomas; acoustic neuromas | ± Bone lesions; pseudarthroses | Neurofibromas; café-au-lait spots; seizures | ± | ± | Autosomal dominant |
| Noonan syndrome | Webbing of posterior neck; malformed ears; hypertelorism | Pectus excavatum; cubitus valgus | Cryptorchidism; pulmonic stenosis | ± | + | ? |
| Prader-Willi syndrome | ± Upward slant to palpebral fissures | Small hands and feet | Hypotonia, especially in early infancy; then polyphagia and obesity; hypogenitalism | + | + | ? |
| Robin complex | Micrognathia; glossoptosis; cleft palate, U-shaped | | ± Cardiac anomalies | | | ? |
| Rubella syndrome | Cataract; retinal pigmentation; ocular malformations | | Sensorineural deafness; patent ductus arteriosus | ± | ± | |
| Rubinstein-Taybi syndrome | Slanting palpebral fissures; maxillary hypoplasia; microcephaly | Broad thumbs and toes | | + | + | ? |
| Seckel syndrome | Facial hypoplasia; prominent nose; microcephaly | Multiple minor joint and skeletal abnormalities | | + | + | Autosomal recessive |
| Sjögren-Larsson syndrome | | Spasticity, especially of legs | Ichthyosis | + | + | Autosomal recessive |
| Smith-Lemli-Opitz syndrome | Anteverted nostrils and/or ptosis of eyelid | Syndactyly 2nd and 3rd toes | Hypospadias; cryptorchidism | + | + | Autosomal recessive |
| Sturge-Weber syndrome | Flat hemangioma of face, most commonly trigeminal in distribution | | Hemangiomas of meninges with seizures | ± | ± | ? |
| Treacher Collins syndrome (mandibulofacial dysostosis) | Malar and mandibular hypoplasia; downslanting palpebral fissures; defect or lower eyelid; malformed ears | | | | | Autosomal dominant |

Table VI—cont.

| Syndrome | Diagnostic Manifestations | | | Mental Retardation | Short Stature | Genetic Transmission |
|---|---|---|---|---|---|---|
| | Craniofacial | Skeletal | Other | | | |
| Trisomy 18 | Microstomia; short palpebral fissures; malformed ears; elongated skull | Clenched hand, 2nd finger over 3rd; low arches on fingertips; short sternum | Cryptorchidism congenital heart disease | + | + | Trisomy 18 |
| Trisomy 13 | Defects of eye, nose, lip, ears, and forebrain of holoprosencephaly type | Polydactyly; narrow hyperconvex fingernails | Skin defects, posterior scalp | + | + | Trisomy 13 |
| Tuberous sclerosis | Hamartomatous pink to brownish facial skin nodules | ± Bone lesions | Seizures; intracranial calcification | ± | | Autosomal dominant |
| Waardenburg syndrome | Lateral displacement of inner canthi and puncta | | Partial albinism; white forelock; heterochromia of iris; vitiligo; +/− deafness | | | Autosomal dominant |
| Williams syndrome | Full lips; small nose with anteverted nostrils; iris dysplasia | Mild hypoplasia of nails | ± Hypercalcemia in infancy; supravalvular aortic stenosis | + | + | ? |
| Zellweger cerebrohepatorenal syndrome | High forehead; flat facies | | Hypotonia; hepatomegaly; death in early infancy | + | + | Autosomal recessive |

* Table by L Syzmanski, MD, and A Crocker, MD and adapted from Smith D W: Patterns of malformation. In *Nelson Textbook of Pediatrics*, ed 11, V C Vaughan III, R J McKay Jr, R E Behrman, editors, p 2035. W B Saunders, Philadelphia, 1979.

mosomal disorders, notably Down's syndrome, promise to become useful diagnostic tools. The determination of the karyotype in a suitable genetic laboratory is indicated whenever a chromosomal disorder is suspected.

### Hearing and Speech Evaluations

These evaluations should be done routinely. The development of speech may be the most reliable single criterion in the investigation of mental retardation. Various hearing impairments are often present in the mentally retarded; on the other hand, the impairments may, in some instances, simulate mental retardation. Unfortunately, the commonly used methods of hearing and speech evaluation require the patient's cooperation and are often unreliable in the severely retarded.

### Psychiatric Examination

The psychiatric examination of mentally retarded children does not differ essentially from such examination of children with normal intelligence. The similarity decreases, however, in direct proportion to the severity of the mental defect. In no other category, except perhaps in psychotic children, is nonverbal communication and careful observation of the patient and his activity of greater importance.

The psychiatrist's contribution should always include a study of the interpersonal aspect of the retarded patient's personality development. The way he reacts to both human and inanimate objects, and how he relates to the examiner and to his mother or caretakers, may tell most about his social maturity. Just as with infants and young children, it may be useful to examine even the older retarded patients with and without a parent or a parent substitute in evaluating dependency status and response to separation.

The child's control over motility patterns should be ascertained, and clinical evidences of distractibility and distortions in perception and memory may be evaluated. The use of speech, reality testing, and the ability to generalize from experiences are important to note.

The nature and the maturity of the child's defenses—particularly the exaggerated or self-defeating uses of avoidance, repression, denial, introjection, and isolation—should be observed. Sublimation potential, frustration tolerance, and impulse control—especially over motor, aggressive, and sexual drives—should be assessed. Also important is self-image and its role in the development of self-confidence, as well as the assessment of tenacity, persistence, curiosity, and the willingness to explore the unknown.

The severely retarded child presents the greatest challenge to the examiner. Bizarre, primitive, and seemingly purposeless behavior is often difficult to interpret. Categorizing the patient's observable behavior in response to the examiner's interaction with him or independent of it, using as a model the developmental examination of infants, may help systematize observations and provide a reasonable estimate of the patient. It is helpful for the psychiatric examiner to combine appropriate components of neurological and psychological examination methods with his own approaches.

In general, in the psychiatric examination of the retarded child, there should be a picture of how the child has solved the stages of personality development. From the areas of failure or regression, it is possible to develop a personality profile of a type that allows for logical planning of management and remedial approaches.

### Psychological Examination

The examining physician may avail himself of several screening instruments that are useful for infants and toddlers. As in many areas of mental retardation, there is a heated controversy over the predictive value of infant psychological tests. The correlation of abnormalities during infancy with later abnormal functioning is reported by some authors as very low, and by others as very high. It is generally agreed that the correlation rises in direct proportion to the age of the child at the time of the developmental examination.

Copying geometric figures may be used as a quick screening test of visual-motor coordination. The same can be said of the Goodenough Draw-a-Person Test, Kohs Block Test, and geometric puzzles.

Psychological testing, performed by an experienced psychologist, must be considered a standard part of an evaluation for mental retardation. The Gesell, Bayley, and Cattell tests are most commonly applied in infants. For children, the Stanford-Binet and the Wechsler Intelligence Scale for Children are most widely used in this country. Both tests have been criticized for penalizing the culturally deprived child, for testing mainly potential for academic achievement rather than for adequate social functioning, and for their unreliability in children with an I.Q. of less than 50. Some people have tried to overcome the language barrier of the mentally retarded by devising picture vocabulary tests, of which the Peabody Vocabulary Test is the most widely used.

The tests often found useful in detecting brain

damage are the Bender-Gestalt and the Benton Visual Retention tests. These tests are also applicable in mildly retarded children. In addition, a psychological evaluation should assess perceptual, motor, linguistic, and cognitive abilities. Of extreme importance also is information on motivational, emotional, and interpersonal factors.

### Differential Diagnosis

A variety of conditions may simulate mental retardation. Children who come from deprived homes that provide inadequate stimulation may manifest motor and mental retardation that is reversible if an enriched, stimulating environment is provided in early childhood. A number of sensory handicaps, especially deafness and blindness, may be mistaken for mental retardation if, during testing, no compensation for the handicap is allowed. Speech deficits and cerebral palsy often make a child seem retarded, even in the presence of borderline or normal intelligence.

Chronic, debilitating diseases of any kind may depress the child's functioning in all areas. Convulsive disorders may give an impression of mental retardation, especially in the presence of uncontrolled seizures.

Chronic brain syndromes may result in isolated handicaps, failure to read (alexia), failure to write (agraphia), failure to communicate (aphasia), and several others that may exist in a person of normal and even superior intelligence.

Emotional difficulties often lead to an apparent retardation. Emotionally disturbed children do poorly in school and often perform far below their actual mental level.

An alert psychiatrist or a pediatrician experienced with normal and abnormal children is usually able to assess properly the child's mental status in most of the above-mentioned conditions.

The most controversial differential diagnostic problem concerns children with severe retardation, brain damage, early infantile autism, childhood schizophrenia, and, according to some, Heller's disease. The confusion stems from the fact that details of the child's early history are often unavailable or unreliable, and, by the time they are evaluated, many children with these conditions manifest similar bizarre and stereotyped behavior, mutism, or echolalia and function on a retarded level. By the time these children are usually seen, it does not matter from a practical point of view whether the child's retardation is secondary to a primary early infantile autism or schizophrenia, or whether the person-

ality and behavioral distortions are secondary to brain damage or retardation on other bases. When ego functions are delayed in development or are atropic on any other basis, the physician must first concentrate on overcoming the child's unrelatedness. The child must be reachable before one can successfully apply remedial educational measures. The diagnostic controversy is aggravated by the fact that many people believe that early infantile autism is accompanied or caused by a brain dysfunction characterized by perceptual and sensory impairments and defects in the arousal system and in language acquisition and comprehension—all of which one often finds in the mentally retarded.

Several differentiating diagnostic criteria have been suggested, such as neurological signs, abnormal electroencephalograms, withdrawal, obsessiveness, better relation to objects than to people, and retention of an intelligent physiognomy. Since these conditions may be interrelated, the diagnosis may be very difficult without an adequate follow-up. Some people use the term "atypical child," implying a common organic matrix for all these conditions. This approach has inherent dangers that always accompany the grouping of medical conditions according to one or several common symptoms. It invites diagnostic complacency and discourages efforts to find more precise diagnostic criteria.

### REFERENCES

Crocker A C: Current strategies in prevention of mental retardation. Pediat Ann *11:* 450, 1982.
Crocker A C: Sisters and brothers. In *Parent-Professional Partnerships in Developmental Disability Services,* J A Mulick, S M Pueschel, editors, p 139. Ware Press, Cambridge, 1983.
Crocker A C, Cushna B: Ethical considerations and attitudes in the field of developmental disorders. In *Developmental Disorders: Evaluation, Treatment and Education,* R B Johnston, P R Magrab, editors, p 495. University Park Press, Baltimore, 1976.
Crocker A C, Nelson R P: Mental retardation. In *Developmental-Behavioral Pediatrics,* M D Levine, M D Levine, W B Carey, A C Crocker, R T Gross, editors, p 756. W. B. Saunders, Philadelphia, 1983.
Edgerton B R, Bollinger M, Herr B: The cloak of competence: After two decades. Am J Ment Defic *88:* 345, 1984.
Featherstone H: *A Difference in the Family: Life with a Disabled Child.* Basic Books, New York, 1980.
Frankenburg W F: Infant and preschool developmental screening. In *Developmental-Behavioral Pediatrics,* M D Levine, M D Levine, W B Carey, A C Crocker, R T Gross, editors, p 927. W. B. Saunders, Philadelphia, 1983.
Grossman F K: *Brothers and Sisters of Retarded Children.* Syracuse University Press, Syracuse, 1972.
Menolascino F J, editor: *Psychiatric Approaches to Mental Retardation.* Basic Books, New York, 1970.
Mercer J R: *Labeling the Mentally Retarded.* University of California Press, Berkeley, 1973.

Pueschel S M, Rynders J E, editors: *Down Syndrome: Advances in Biomedicine and Behavioral Sciences.* Ware Press, Cambridge, 1982.

Sarason B S, Doris J: *Educational Handicap, Public Policy, and Social History.* The Free Press, New York, 1979.

Syzmanski L S, Crocker A C: Mental retardation. In *Comprehensive Textbook of Psychiatry*, ed 4, H I Kaplan, B J Sadock, editors, p 1635. Williams & Wilkins, Baltimore, 1985.

Syzmanski L S, Tanguay P E, editors: *Emotional Disorders of Mentally Retarded Persons.* University Park Press, Baltimore, 1980.

Wolfensberger W: *The Principle of Normalization in Human Services.* National Institute on Mental Retardation, Toronto, 1972.

# 31

# Pervasive Developmental Disorders

## Definition

The classification pervasive developmental disorders of childhood appeared for the first time in DSM-III in 1980. These disorders are characterized by distortions, deviations, or delays in the development of social, language, and motor behaviors, attention, perception, and reality testing.

DSM-III distinguishes among five diagnostic possibilities in this subclass. Two are types of infantile autism, and three are types of childhood-onset pervasive developmental disorders. They include: Infantile Autism, Full Syndrome Present; Infantile Autism, Residual State; Childhood Onset Pervasive Developmental Disorder, Full Syndrome Present; Childhood Onset Pervasive Developmental Disorder, Residual State; and Atypical Pervasive Developmental Disorder. DSM-III criteria for making these diagnoses are given in Table I.

## Infantile Autism

### Introduction

The syndrome of infantile autism was first described by Leo Kanner in 1943 and known as "Kanner's syndrome" in his classic paper "Autistic Disturbances of Affective Contact." He described children who exhibited "extreme autistic aloneness"; failure to assume an anticipatory posture; delayed or deviant language development with echolalia and pronominal reversal (using "you" for "I"); monotonous repetitions of noises or verbal utterances; excellent rote memory; limited range in the variety of spontaneous activity; stereotypies and mannerisms; "anxiously obsessive desire for the maintenance of sameness" and a "dread of change and incompleteness"; and abnormal relationships to people and preference for pictures or inanimate objects. Kanner suspected the syndrome to be more frequent than it seemed—and suggested at least some such children had been confused with mentally retarded or schizophrenic children.

There has been confusion about whether infantile autism was the earliest possible manifes-

tation of schizophrenia, or a discrete clinical entity; but, the evidence weighs very heavily in establishing infantile autism and schizophrenia as separate entities.

### Epidemiology

**Prevalence.** Infantile autism occurs in 2 to 4 children per 10,000 children (or 0.02 to 0.04 percent) under the age of 12 or 15. It begins before 30 months of age, but may not be evident to the parents depending on their acuity and the severity of the disease.

**Sex Distribution.** Infantile autism is found more frequently in boys in all samples studied. Overall, a reasonable estimate would be that 3 to 5 times more boys than girls have autism.

**Social Class.** Many studies report an overrepresentation of the upper classes, while some more recent reports have not found this to be the case. Over the past 20 years, an increasing proportion of cases have been found in the lower social classes. This may well be because of increased awareness of the syndrome and increasing availability of child mental health workers for the lower classes.

### Etiology and Pathology

Infantile autism is a behavioral syndrome. It is generally believed that it is etiologically heterogeneous. Theories run the gamut from the psychodynamic to the organic. Today there is considerable evidence that biological abnormalities underlie the syndrome.

**Psychodynamic Causation.** In his initial report Kanner noted that few parents were "really warmhearted" and that for the most part, the parents and other family members were preoccupied with intellectual abstractions and had little genuine interest in people. Opinions such as parental rage and rejection and parental reinforcement of the development of symptoms were voiced by others without any scientific substantiation. Recent studies, however, comparing parents of autistic children to parents of normal children have not shown significant dif-

TABLE I
PERVASIVE DEVELOPMENTAL DISORDERS OF
CHILDHOOD*

*Diagnostic Criteria for Infantile Autism*
A. Onset before 30 months of age
B. Pervasive lack of responsiveness to other people (autism)
C. Gross deficits in language development
D. If speech is present, peculiar speech patterns such as immediate and delayed echolalia, metaphorical language, pronominal reversal
E. Bizarre responses to various aspects of the environment, e.g., resistance to change, peculiar interest in or attachments to animate or inanimate objects
F. Absence of delusions, hallucinations, loosening of associations, and incoherence as in schizophrenia

*Diagnostic Criteria for Infantile Autism, Residual State*
A. Once had an illness that met the criteria for infantile autism
B. The current clinical picture no longer meets the full criteria for infantile autism, but signs of the illness have persisted to the present, such as oddities of communication and social awkwardness

*Diagnostic Criteria for Childhood Onset Pervasive Developmental Disorder*
A. Gross and sustained impairment in social relationships, e.g., lack of appropriate affective responsivity, inappropriate clinging, asociality, lack of empathy
B. At least three of the following:
 (1) Sudden excessive anxiety manifested by such symptoms as free-floating anxiety, catastrophic reactions to everyday occurrences, inability to be consoled when upset, unexplained panic attacks
 (2) Constricted or inappropriate affect, including lack of appropriate fear reactions, unexplained rage reactions, and extreme mood lability
 (3) Resistance to change in the environment (e.g., upset if dinner time is changed), or insistence on doing things in the same manner every time (e.g., putting on clothes always in the same order)
 (4) Oddities of motor movement, such as peculiar posturing, peculiar hand or finger movements, or walking on tiptoe
 (5) Abnormalities of speech, such as questionlike melody, monotonous voice
 (6) Hyper- or hypo-sensitivity to sensory stimuli, e.g., hyperacusis
 (7) Self-multilation, e.g., biting or hitting self, head banging
C. Onset of the full syndrome after 30 months of age and before 12 years of age
D. Absence of delusions, hallucinations, incoherence, or marked loosening of associations

*Diagnostic Criteria for Childhood Onset Pervasive Developmental Disorder, Residual State*
A. Once had an illness that met the criteria for childhood onset pervasive developmental disorder
B. The current clinical picture no longer meets the full criteria for the disorder, but signs of the illness have persisted to the present, such as oddities of communication and social awkwardness

*Atypical Pervasive Developmental Disorder*
This category should be used for children with distortions in the development of multiple basic psychological functions that are involved in the development of social skills and language and that cannot be classified as either infantile autism or childhood onset pervasive developmental disorder

* From American Psychiatric Association: *Diagnostic and Statistical Manual of Mental Disorders*, ed 3. American Psychiatric Association, Washington, DC, 1980. Used with permission.

ferences or deficits in infant and child-rearing skills, and it appears that psychodynamic causation is not likely to be a major contributor to the etiology of infantile autism.

Of particular import is the inimical influence, through its wide distribution in the popular press, this theory still has on parents. It instills greater guilt and blame than they would otherwise feel. Dispelling guilt is one of the most important matters to be addressed in servicing the family of the autistic child.

**Organic-Neurological-Biological Abnormalities.** Autistic children show more evidence of reproductive complications than comparison groups (schizophrenics, normals, or siblings, particularly those who are free of psychiatric illness). Biological insults peri- and postnatally can at least increase the risk of developing infantile autism. Another possible evidence of complication of pregnancy (first trimester) is the finding that autistics have significantly more minor congenital (physical) anomalies than their siblings or normal controls.

Most reports indicate that at least 10 percent and up to 83 percent of autistics show EEG abnormalities. There is no EEG finding specific to infantile autism; however, there is suggestion that some abnormalities are indicative of failure of cerebral lateralization.

Four to 32 percent of autistics will develop grand mal seizures at some point in life.

About 20 to 25 percent of autistics show ventricular enlargement on computerized tomography scans.

**Biochemical Abnormalities.** In a small sample of patients, a significant correlation was found between high serotonin blood levels and a decrease in cerebrospinal fluid 5-hydroxyindoleacetic acid (5-HIAA), the main serotonin metabolite. 5-Hydroxy-$N,N$-dimethyltryptamine (bufotenin) was found in the urine of autistics and their families, but not in controls, thus implicating genetic influences.

**Genetic Studies.** All reports agree that approximately 2 percent of siblings of autistics are afflicted by infantile autism, a rate 50 times greater than in the general population. Concordance of infantile autism in monozygotic twins is significantly greater than in dizygotic twins. Clinical reports and studies suggest that non-autistic members of families of autistics share various language or other cognitive problems with the autistic individual, although of much lesser severity.

**Sex.** Autism is 3 to 4 times more common in males than in females. There is some suggestion, that females, as a group, might be more impaired (having lower I.Q.'s and brain damage in a greater percent) and have a greater proportion of family members suffering from autism or cognitive or language deficits than the males.

### Clinical Description

**Physical Characteristics.** *Appearance.* Kanner was struck by these children's intelligent physiognomies. While there are exceptions, the large majority of autistic children are not stigmatized and are of average or better looks. Many of these children are, in fact, unusually attractive.

*Height and Weight.* Between the ages of 2 and 7 years, autistic children have been found to be shorter, as a group, than the normal population. Compared to their own siblings in the same age range, there was an excess number of autistic children who were less than the third percentile in height.

*Handedness.* There is a failure of lateralization in the majority of young autistic children which could be a developmental lag. They remain ambidextrous at an age when cerebral dominance is established in their siblings and other normal children.

*Minor Congenital Anomalies.* Autistic children have more minor congenital anomalies than their siblings or controls.

*Dermatoglyphics.* There is a greater incidence of abnormal patterns than in the general population.

*Intercurrent Physical Illnesses.* Of neonatal and early life complications, frequent upper respiratory infections, excessive burping, febrile seizures, constipation, and loose bowel movements were reported. Many autistic children react differently from normal children when ill. Some of this may be the result of an immature or abnormal autonomic nervous system. They may not develop an elevated temperature with infectious illnesses; may not complain of pain either verbally or by gesture; and may not show the malaise of an ill child. Interestingly, their behavior and relatedness may improve to a noticeable degree when ill and this may be a clue to physical illness in some cases.

**Behavioral Characteristics.** *Failure to Develop Relatedness (Autism).* All autistic children fail to develop the usual relatedness to their parents and other people, to a various degree. As infants, many lack a social smile and anticipatory posture for being picked up as an adult approaches. Lack of eye contact, fleeting eye contact, markedly diminished eye contact, or active avoidance of eye contact may be seen in many.

In the first few years of life a lack of attachment to parents is observed. These children often do not seem to recognize or differentiate the most important people in their lives—parents, siblings, or teachers. They may show virtually no separation anxiety upon being left in an unfamiliar environment with strangers.

By school-age, withdrawal may have diminished or not be as obvious, particularly in the higher functioning children. Instead, failure to play with peers, make friends, social awkwardness and inappropriateness, and particularly, failure to develop empathy are observed.

*Disturbances of Communication and Language.* Gross deficits and deviancies in language development are among the cardinal criteria for the diagnosis of infantile autism.

In the first year of life, the amount and pattern of babbling may be reduced or abnormal. Some children emit stereotyped noises, e.g. clicks or sounds, screeches, or nonsense syllables in a stereotyped fashion with no seeming intent at communication.

Unlike normal young children who always have better receptive language skills than expressive skills and understand much before they can speak, verbal autistic children usually say more than they understand. Words or even entire sentences may drop in and out of a child's vocabulary. The child may use a word once, then not use it again for a week, month, or years. Characteristically, speech is usually in the form of echolalia, both immediate or delayed, or perseveration of stereotyped phrases out of context often associated with pronominal reversal; e.g. the child saying "do you want the toy" when he means he wants it. Difficulties in articulation are also noted. Use of peculiar voice quality and rhythm are observed clinically in many cases. About 50 percent of autistic children never develop useful speech.

Some of the brighter children show a particular fascination with letters and numbers. A few literally teach themselves to read at pre-school-age, often astonishingly well. This is, however, in virtually all cases, utterly without any comprehension.

*Abnormalities in Play.* In the first years of life, much of the exploratory play is absent or minimal. Toys and objects are often manipulated differently from their intended use.

*Stereotypies and Ritualistic Behaviors; Insistence on Sameness and Resistance to Change.* The activities and play, if any, of the autistic child are rigid, repetitive, and lack variety. Spinning, banging, and lining up objects are often seen. Attachments to inanimate objects may develop. In addition, many autistic children, particularly those who are more intellectually impaired, exhibit various abnormalities of movements. Stereotypies, mannerisms, and grimacing are more frequent when the child is left to himself and may decrease when placed in a structured situation (see Figs. 1 and 2).

Autistic children are resistant to transitions and changes. Moving to a new house, moving furniture in a room, and serving breakfast before bath, when the reverse was the routine, may result in panic or temper tantrums.

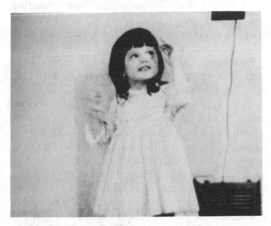

FIGURE 1. A 5-year-old autistic girl showing stereotyped mannerisms. From the film *Looking For Me* by Janet Adler. (By permission of University of California Extension Media Center, Berkeley, and Simons R C, editor: *Understanding Human Behavior in Health and Illness*, ed 3, Williams & Wilkins, Baltimore, 1985.)

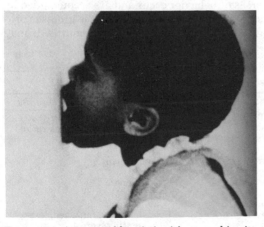

FIGURE 2. A 2-year-old autistic girl engaged in ritualistic behavior. From the film *Looking For Me* by Janet Adler. (By permission of University of California Extension Media Center, Berkeley, and Simons R C, editor: *Understanding Human Behavior in Health and Illness*, ed 3, Williams & Wilkins, Baltimore, 1985.)

*Responses to Sensory Stimuli.* Autistic children may manifest overresponsiveness or underresponsiveness to sensory stimuli, for example to sound or pain. They may selectively ignore spoken language directed at them; because of this, they are often thought to be deaf. However, they may show unusual interest in the sound of a wristwatch. In many, there is a diminished pain threshold or an altered response to pain. They may injure themselves rather severely and not cry.

Many autistic children seem to enjoy music. They frequently will hum a tune, sing a song or commercial before saying words or using speech. Some particularly enjoy vestibular stimulation, spinning, swinging, or up and down movement.

*Other Behavioral Symptoms.* Hyperkinesis is a common behavior problem in young autistic children. Hypokinesis is less frequent; when present, it often alternates with hyperactivity. Aggressiveness and temper tantrums are observed, often for no apparent reason, or are prompted by change or demands. Self-injurious behavior includes head banging, biting, scratching, hair pulling, and so on. Short attention span, or complete inability to focus on a task, insomnia, feeding and eating problems, enuresis, and encopresis are also frequent.

**Intellectual Functioning.** Autistic children may be profoundly retarded to above average in their intellectual functioning. About 50 percent are moderately, severely, or profoundly retarded (with I.Q.'s below 50); about 25 percent are mildly retarded; and 25 percent have I.Q.'s of 70 or more.

Autistic children usually show marked unevenness in their intellectual functioning. Scores on language development and verbal tasks are the lowest. The more seriously retarded children are often virtually untestable on tests requiring verbal ability. The more verbal ones are best at concrete tasks and worst on tasks requiring generalizations, abstract thought, sequencing events, or symbolization.

Unusual or precocious cognitive or visuomotor abilities are present in some autistic children. These may exist even within the overall retarded functioning and are referred to as splinter functions or islets of precocity. Perhaps the most striking examples are the idiot-savants with prodigious rote memories or calculating abilities. Here the specific abilities usually remain beyond the capabilities of normal peers. Other precocious abilities in young autistic children include early ability to read with remarkable fluency (although not able to understand what they read), memorizing and reciting, or musical abilities, singing tunes or recognizing different musical pieces.

### Differential Diagnosis

The major differential diagnoses are childhood onset of schizophrenic disorder; mental retardation with behavioral symptoms; developmental language disorder, receptive type; congenital deafness or severe hearing disorder; psychosocial deprivation; and disintegrative (regressive) psychoses.

**Childhood Onset of Schizophrenic Disorder.** Whereas there is a wealth of literature on infantile autism, only a paucity of data exists on children under age 12 who would meet DSM-III criteria for schizophrenic disorder. Childhood schizophrenia is discussed below.

**Mental Retardation with Behavioral Symptoms.** More than half of autistic children are moderately, severely, or profoundly retarded, and retarded children may have behavioral symptoms including autistic features. DSM-III states that, when both disorders are present, both should be diagnosed. The main differentiating features between infantile autism and mental retardation are as follows. Mentally retarded children usually relate to adults and other children in accord with their mental age; use the language they have to communicate with others; have a relatively even profile of retardedness without splinter functions.

**Developmental Language Disorder: Receptive Type.** There is a subgroup of these children who have autistic-like features and may present a diagnostic problem. Table II summarizes the major differences.

**Congenital Deafness or Severe Hearing Impairment.** Since autistic children often are mute or may show selective disinterest in spoken language in infancy, they are often thought to be deaf. The following may be differentiating features: Autistic children may babble only infrequently, while in deaf infants there is a history of relatively normal babbling which then gradually tapers off and may stop in the second half of the first year of life. Deaf children respond only to loud sounds, whereas autistic children may ignore loud or normal sounds and respond to quite soft sounds if they interest them. Most importantly, audiogram or auditory evoked potentials indicate significant hearing loss in the deaf child. Deaf children usually relate to their parents, seek their affection, and, as infants, enjoy being held.

**Psychosocial Deprivation.** Severe disturbances in the physical and emotional environment (e.g. maternal deprivation, psychosocial dwarfism, hospitalism, or failure to thrive) can cause children to appear apathetic, withdrawn, and alienated. Language and motor skills can be delayed. These children almost always rapidly improve upon being placed in a favorable and enriched psychosocial environment. This is not the case with an autistic child.

**Disintegrative (Regressive) Psychoses.** The disintegrative psychoses usually begin between ages 3 and 5 years. These conditions are even rarer than infantile autism. They are also known as symbiotic psychoses, a term introduced by Margaret Mahler. The child's development in these disorders is usually within normal limits until the onset of illness when severe regression and decline in intelligence and all areas of behavior occur and are accompanied by stereotypies and mannerisms. The illness is progressive over a period of a few months. It may

TABLE II
INFANTILE AUTISM VS. DEVELOPMENTAL LANGUAGE DISORDER: RECEPTIVE TYPE

| Criteria | Infantile Autism | Developmental Language Disorder |
|---|---|---|
| Incidence | 2–4 in 10,000 | 5 in 10,000 |
| Sex ratio (M:F) | 3–4:1 | Equal or almost equal sex ratio |
| Family history of speech delay or language problems | Present in about 25% of cases | |
| Associated deafness | Very infrequent | Not infrequent |
| Nonverbal communication (gestures, etc.) | Absent or rudimentary | Present |
| Language abnormalities (e.g., echolalia, stereotyped phrases out of context) | More common | Less common |
| Articulatory problems | Less frequent | More frequent |
| Level of intelligence | Often severely impaired | Though may be impaired, less frequently severe |
| Patterns of I.Q. tests | Uneven, lower on verbal scores than dysphasics; lower on comprehension subtest than dysphasics | More even, though verbal I.Q. lower than performance I.Q. |
| Autistic behaviors, impaired social life, stereotypies and ritualistic activities | More common and more severe | Absent or, if present, less severe |
| Imaginative play | Absent or rudimentary | Usually present |

follow a mild illness or a known viral infection. In others, at autopsy, a lipoidosis, leukodystrophy, or Heller's disease (dementia infantilis) is found.

### Prognosis and Outcome

Infantile autism has a chronic course and a very guarded prognosis. As a general rule, it is the autistic children with higher I.Q.'s (above 70) and use of communicative language by ages 5 to 7 who have the best prognosis. Perhaps 5 percent of autistics are gainfully employed by their late teens or early adulthood. When compared to normals for age and I.Q., autistics have lower employability. It should be noted that it is unusual for an autistic child to develop into a "normal" adolescent or adult; only 1 or 2% at most achieve this. Prognosis is also better if the environment or home is superior and capable of meeting excessive needs of the child.

The better outcomes are usually "infantile autism, residual state" (DSM-III) with definite social awkwardness and peculiarities of language use persisting. Two-thirds will remain severely handicapped and will have to lead a life of complete dependency. Though decrease of symptoms is noted in many of these cases, in others severe self-mutilation and/or aggressiveness and regression, in general, may develop. Approximately 4 to 32 percent develop grand mal seizures in late childhood or adolescence, and these adversely affect the prognosis.

### Treatment of Infantile Autism

The goals of treatment in autistic children are to decrease behavioral symptoms and to aid in the development of delayed, rudimentary, or nonexistent functions, such as language and self-care skills. In addition, the parents, often distraught, need support and counseling.

Structured classroom training in combination with intrusive behavioral methods is the most effective treatment method for many autistic children and is superior to other types of behavioral approaches. Well-controlled studies indicate that gains in the areas of language and cognition, as well as decreases in maladaptive behaviors, are achieved using this method. Careful parental training, individual tutoring of parents in the concepts and skills of behavior modification, and focusing on individual parent problems and concerns, within a problem solving format, may yield considerable gains in the language, cognitive, and social areas of behavior. However, the training programs are rigorous and a great deal of parental time is involved. The autistic child requires an all day structure and a daily program for as many hours as feasible.

Pharmacotherapy, in addition to the educational/behavioral methods, seems to be a valuable adjunct to the comprehensive treatment programs for many autistic children.

Administration of the potent dopamine antagonist, haloperidol, yields both significant decreases in behavioral symptoms and significant acceleration in learning in the laboratory. The main improvements are as follows: decreases in hyperactivity, stereotypies, withdrawal, fidgetiness, abnormal object relations, irritability, and labile affect. There is supportive evidence that haloperidol, when given judiciously, remains an effective drug on a long-term basis. Under careful clinical monitoring, tardive and withdrawal dyskinesias are not frequent, and in prospective studies to date they always have been reversible.

Fenfluramine, a drug with antiserotonergic properties, has been reported to produce a marked decrease in behavioral symptoms and overall improvement in this disorder and shows promise as an effective treatment.

### Childhood-onset Pervasive Developmental Disorder

As defined in DSM-III, the essential features of the syndrome refer to an extreme and pervasive disturbance in human relations and to a wide range of bizarre behaviors, all becoming the full syndrome after 30 months of age and before the age of 12 years (see Table I).

TABLE III
DIAGNOSTIC CRITERIA FOR SCHIZOPHRENIC DISORDER*

A. *At least one of the following:*
(1) Bizarre delusions
(2) Somatic, grandiose, or other delusions without persecutory or jealous content
(3) Delusions with persecutory or jealous content if accompained by hallucinations
(4) Auditory hallucinations in which either one voice keeps talking about the patient's thoughts or behavior, or more voices converse
(5) Auditory hallucinations heard several times consisting of more than one or two words, with no apparent relation to depressed or elated mood
(6) Incoherent speech, pronounced loosening of associations, and illogical thinking or poverty of content of speech if associated with at least one of the following:
  (a) Blunted, flat, or inappropriate affect
  (b) Hallucinations or delusions
  (c) Catatonic or other grossly disorganized behavior
B. *Deterioration of functioning such as work, self-care and social relations*
C. *Duration:* Continuous manifestation of illness for at least 6 months at some time, with some manifestations currently

* From American Psychiatric Association: *Diagnostic and Statistical Manual of Mental Disorders*, ed 3. American Psychiatric Association, Washington, DC, 1980. Used with permission.

TABLE IV
INFANTILE AUTISM VS. SCHIZOPHRENIC DISORDER

| Criteria | Infantile Autism | Schizophrenic Disorder (with onset before puberty) |
|---|---|---|
| Age of onset | Before 30 months | Not under 5 years of age |
| Incidence | 2–4 in 10,000 | Unknown, possibly same or even rarer |
| Sex ratio (M:F) | 3–4:1 | 1.67:1 (nearly equal, or slight preponderance of males) |
| Family history of schizophrenia | Not raised or probably not raised | Raised |
| Social class | Overrepresentation of upper classes (artifact) | More common in lower classes |
| Pre- and perinatal complications and cerebral dysfunction | More common in autism | |
| Behavioral characteristics | Failure to develop relatedness; absence of speech or echolalia; stereotyped phrases; language comprehension absent or poor; insistence on sameness and stereotypies | Hallucinations and delusions; thought disorder |
| Adaptive functioning | Usually always impaired | Deterioration in functioning |
| Level of intelligence | In majority of cases subnormal, frequently severely impaired (70% ≤ 70) | Usually within normal range, mostly dull normal (15% ≤ 70) |
| Pattern of I.Q. | Marked unevenness | More even |
| Grand mal seizures | 4–32% | Absent or lower incidence |

The disturbance in human relationships is profound and persistent. Emotional interactions with others are inappropriate and inept. There may be a marked absence of social response, or excessive and inappropriate clinging without the achievement of genuine caring or a relationship. Manifestations of conscience are primitive and meager. During the early school years and later, the disordered social behavior is expressed in an absence of friendships, difficulties in participating in a cooperative fashion in play with other children, a pervasive lack of empathy, and a striking insensibility with regard to the feelings of others.

The bizarre behavior varies from child to child, but reflects a number of the seven aberrations listed by DSM-III. Those aberrations include:

1. Acute, excessive, and seemingly illogical anxiety manifested by such symptoms as free-floating anxiety, catastrophic reactions to everyday occurrences, an inability to be consoled when upset, unexplained panics.

2. Diminution, rigidity, distortion and peculiarity of affect, including lack of appropriate fear reactions, unexplained rage reactions and extreme mood lability.

3. Sustained resistance to change in the environment including ritualistic and repetitive behavior.

4. Alterations of behavior consisting of pecu-

liar motility disturbances including hyper- or hypo-activity, peculiar posturing, peculiar hand or finger movements.

5. Abnormalities of speech, such as question-like melody, monotonous voice.

6. Abnormal sensory and perceptual experiences seen in over- or under-sensitivity to sensory stimuli, e.g., hyperacusis.

7. Self-mutilation, e.g., biting, hitting, severe head banging.

Associated with these essential features are many bizarre beliefs and fantasies without insight on the part of the child, as well as strange inner obsessions. There are also abnormal and fixed preoccupations with and use of objects.

For diagnosis, the criteria include a gross and unchanging impairment in relationships, at least three of the seven manifestations of bizarre behavior listed above, and onset of the full syndrome after age 30 months. A formal thought disorder, delusions, and hallucinations are absent.

The syndrome is very rare, and is more common in boys than in girls.

At the present time, childhood-onset pervasive developmental disorder needs to be differentiated from schizophrenia beginning in childhood and from infantile autism. Schizophrenia is likely to be characterized by delusions, hallucinations, formal thought disorders, and incoherence. The childhood-onset disorder may be differentiated from infantile autism by its later age of recognition and onset, and by the absence of the full syndrome of infantile autism.

### Schizophrenia with Onset in Childhood

The evidence weighs very heavily in establishing schizophrenia as a separate entity. Profound disturbances in very young children do have a limited number of ways of being expressed. A small subgroup of autistic children may be early-onset schizophrenics who have not yet reached developmental stages where the symptomatology necessary for the diagnosis of schizophrenic disorder can be expressed. A few cases have been reported of children who, at a young age, fulfilled the criteria for infantile autism and, when older, fit diagnostic criteria for schizophrenia, with the possible exception of lack of deterioration from a previous level of functioning. There is a trend, especially in Europe, to distinctly separate children with infantile autism from those with schizophrenic disorder with onset during childhood and other childhood psychoses.

According to DSM-III, in schizophrenia occurring in childhood there are oddities of behavior; but typically there are hallucinations, delusions, and loosening of associations or incoherence (see Table III). Hallucinations and delusions are disqualifiers for the diagnosis of infantile autism. Particularly important to the DSM-III diagnosis and concept of schizophrenia is that schizophrenia always involves deterioration from a previous level of functioning during some phase of the illness in such areas as work, social relations, and self-care.

Schizophrenia must be differentiated from infantile autism (see Table IV). The majority of autistic children are impaired in all areas of adaptive functioning from early life on. Onset is always before the age of 2½ years, whereas the onset of schizophrenic disorder is usually in adolescence or young adulthood. There are practically no reports of onset of schizophrenia before the age of 5 years, but children under the age of 12 can be diagnosed as schizophrenic.

### Treatment of Childhood-Onset Pervasive Development Disorder

It is clear that the psychotic child requires a broad, ego-educative approach that is precisely attuned to the facilitation of the development of specific adaptive skills in the individual child. Behavior therapy has demonstrated its effectiveness in altering defined and specific behaviors, including social interactions and responses, self-mutilative behavior, imitative behavior, and communication.

The major tranquilizers have been used to influence specific behaviors of psychotic children—for example, chlorpromazine for reducing hyperactivity, and trifluoperazine for overcoming marked apathy and hypoactivity. However, drugs have not in themselves been shown to be effective in reversing the global state of the child that is encompassed by the pervasive developmental disorders or in childhood schizophrenia or in improving ultimate outcomes in life course. Allopurinol combined with a low purine diet in cases manifesting hyperuricosuria has been of use in certain cases.

In planning programs of therapeutic management, the therapist may follow a number of working guidelines. The therapeutic program needs to delineate the specific failures in the development and organization of thought, feeling, and social response of each psychotic child and to direct itself to the improvement of his skills in each area of adaptive failure. Psychotherapy itself needs to pay heed to the facilitation of the child's central need for growth in language, thought, and social response before it can proceed to issues of inner emotional and motivational conflict.

Active, effective education of the adaptive resources of the psychotic child requires clear-cut objectives and a structured therapeutic design throughout the day, every day and for long periods of time. Casual, irregular, or infrequent adult contacts with the children are ineffective. Help for the children and their families should be provided as early as possible.

Changes in therapeutic setting may also be profitable. Thus, residential or inpatient care and separation from the families may be used for varying periods of time. Day treatment and specialized schooling may be helpful at other times.

### REFERENCES

Anderson L T, Campbell M, Grega D M, Perry R, Small A M, Green W H: Haloperidol and infantile autism: Effects on learning and behavior symptoms. Am J Psychiatry *141:* 123, 1984.

Campbell M: Autistic and schizophrenic disorders. In *Psychopharmacology in Childhood and Adolescence,* ed 2, J M Wiener, editor. Basic Books, New York.

Campbell M, Green W H: Pervasive developmental disorders of childhood. In *Comprehensive Textbook of Psychiatry,* ed 4, H I Kaplan, B J Sadock, editors, p 1672. Williams & Wilkins, Baltimore, 1985.

Campbell M, Minton J, Green W H, Jennings S J, Samit C: Siblings and twins of autistic children. In *Biological Psychiatry 1981,* C Perris, G Struwe, B Jansson, editors, p 993. Elsevier/North-Holland, Amsterdam, 1981.

Campbell M, Rosenbloom S, Perry R, George A E, Kricheff I I, Anderson L, Small A M, Jennings S J:

Computerized axial tomography in young autistic children. Am J Psychiatry *139:* 510, 1982.

DeMyer M K, Hintgen J N, Jackson R K: Infantile autism reviewed: A decade of research. Schizo Bull *7:* 388, 1981.

Fish B, Ritvo E R: Psychoses of childhood. In *Basic Handbook of Child Psychiatry*, Vol 2, J D Noshpitz, editor-in-chief, p 249. Basic Books, New York, 1979.

Green W H, Campbell M, Hardesty A S, Grega D M, Padron-Gayol M, Shell J, Erlenmeyer-Kimling L: A comparison of schizophrenic and autistic children. J Am Acad Child Psychiatry *23:* 399, 1984.

*Journal of Autism and Developmental Disorders:* Special Issue on Neurobiological Research in Autism, Volume 12, Number 2, June, 1982.

Kanner L: Autistic disturbances of affective contact. Nervous Child *2:* 217, 1943, and reprinted in Kanner L: *Childhood Psychosis: Initial Studies and New Insights*, pp 1–43. John Wiley & Sons, New York, 1973.

Kolvin I: Psychoses in childhood—a comparative study. In *Infantile Autism: Concepts, Characteristics and Treatment*, M Rutter, editor, p 7. Churchill Livingstone, Edinburgh, 1971.

Rutter M, Greenfeld D, Lockyer L: A five to fifteen year follow-up study of infantile psychosis. II. Social and behavioral outcome. Br J Psychiatry *113:* 1183, 1967.

Rutter M, Schopler E, editors: *Autism: A Reappraisal of Concepts and Treatment.* Plenum Press, New York, 1978.

# 32

# Attention Deficit Disorders

## Definition

Developmentally inappropriate brief attention and poor concentration characterize these disorders according to DSM-III. In the past a variety of names have been attached to these disorders including: hyperkinetic reaction of childhood, hyperkinetic syndrome, hyperactive child syndrome, minimal brain damage, minimal brain dysfunction, minimal cerebral dysfunction, and minor cerebral dysfunction.

Three separate disorders are described in DSM-III: (1) attention deficit disorder without hyperactivity, (2) attention deficit disorder with hyperactivity, and (3) attention deficit disorder—residual type. The relationship between the three disorders is unknown. Attention deficit was previously known as hyperkinetic reaction of childhood.

## Attention Deficit Disorder with Hyperactivity

### Epidemiology

Attention deficit disorder with hyperactivity has been observed in children of varying socioeconomic status and countries. Reports as to the incidence in this country have varied from 4 to 20 percent of school-age children. A conservative figure, and one more likely to be accepted, is that of 3 percent of pre-pubertal elementary school children.

Clinical observation and epidemiological surveys report a greater incidence in boys than in girls, the ratio being 10:1. It is more common in first-born boys.

A significant familial pattern seems to be present, at least in a minority. There is a significant appearance in the parents of hyperkinetics of sociopathy, alcoholism, and hysteria. A correspondence appears in the studies of parents of hyperkinetic children concerning the earlier presence of the hyperkinetic syndrome in the parents.

Onset is usually by the age of 3; but the diagnosis is not generally made until later when the child is in school. The behavioral disturbances must be present for at least 6 months and appear before age 7 for the diagnosis to be made.

### Etiology

**Organic Factors.** There may be a genetic basis in at least some children with the hyperactive syndrome.

Gross structural disease of the cerebrum, cerebellum, or vestibular area can lead to hyperkinesis.

Several attempts have been made to find a biochemical basis for the hyperkinetic syndrome, but a unifying theme has not yet emerged.

Structural alteration of the brain by trauma, epilepsy, or infections like encephalitis can also lead to the hyperkinetic syndrome as a sequel.

Biochemical bases (genetic, food hypersensitivity, environmental toxicity) have been suggested.

**Nonorganic factors.** Time after time, inquiries have shown that some psychic event, a disruption of family equilibrium, or an anxiety-inducing factor seems to diminish the effects of medication. This observation makes it seem reasonable that emotional factors can contribute to the initiation or perpetuation of the syndrome.

A specific emotional constellation of internal anger, both self-directed and outwardly directed, can create the picture of the attention deficit disorder with hyperactivity.

Predisposing factors may include the child's temperament; the genetic-familial factors previously discussed; and the demands of society, as in school systems, for adherence to a routinized way of behaving and performance. Socioeconomic status does not seem to be a predisposing factor in the sense of a particular life style, but may contribute through a greater likelihood of accident. When the attention deficit disorder conditions occur in lower socioeconomic status children, an aggressive component is likely to be present in their behavior.

## Clinical Features

Attention deficit disorder with hyperactivity may have its onset in the earliest days of life. A newborn who is already afflicted with an attention deficit disorder may be unduly sensitive to stimuli, and may respond in an undifferentiated, massive, aversive manner.

Frequently, the converse occurs, and the child is placid, limp, and floppy, sleeping much and developing slowly in the initial months. It is more common, though, for the infant to be active in the crib, have a rapid development schedule, sleep little, and cry much past the traditional first 3 months of colic. The infant often gets out of the crib on his own very early, undissuaded by the parents' attempts to bar his exit. Once out of the crib and able to get about, the infant is apt to do so relentlessly, getting into everything and generally fingering, breaking, or disintegrating objects. As times goes on, his sphere of activity widens and rapidly encompasses the neighboring territory and street.

The toddler phase scarcely exists, but is replaced by a gallop. As the child gets older, the mother often complains that he cannot play ball because he cannot stay at his assigned base; fathers complain that he cannot stay still in line or sit still in his seat.

Although hyperactivity is one of the hallmarks of this state, it does not always mean that quantitatively the degree of activity is greater than that of other children, although this may be so. Rather, the activity may be relatively continuous and not turned off in appropriate situations, such as in school and in church. Hyperkinetic children are far less likely than are normal children to reduce their locomotor activity when their environment is structured by social limits.

Often coupled with hyperactivity is a short attention span or ready distractibility, which may be viewed as involuntary (see Table I). The child is unable, without great and conscious effort, to inhibit his response to any stimulus that comes along, regardless of appropriate meaning or significance. In addition, the child seems incapable of attending to more than one stimulus at a time. Such a child is incapable of attending to any stimulus for more than 10 seconds.

Another set of phenomena, probably related,

TABLE I
DIAGNOSTIC CRITERIA FOR ATTENTION DEFICIT DISORDER WITH HYPERACTIVITY*

The child displays, for his or her mental and chronological age, signs of developmentally inappropriate inattention, impulsivity, and hyperactivity. The signs must be reported by adults in the child's environment, such as parents and teachers. Because the symptoms are typically variable, they may not be observed directly by the clinician. When the reports of teachers and parents conflict, primary consideration should be given to the teacher reports because of greater familiarity with age-appropriate norms. Symptoms typically worsen in situations that require self-application, as in the classroom. Signs of the disorder may be absent when the child is in a new or a one-to-one situation.

The number of symptoms specified is for children between the ages of eight and ten, the peak age range for referral. In younger children, more severe forms of the symptoms and a greater number of symptoms are usually present. The opposite is true of older children.

A. **Inattention.** At least three of the following:

    (1) Often fails to finish things he or she starts
    (2) Often doesn't seem to listen
    (3) Easily distracted
    (4) Has difficulty concentrating on schoolwork or other tasks requiring sustained attention
    (5) Has difficulty sticking to a play activity

B. **Impulsivity.** At least three of the following:

    (1) Often acts before thinking
    (2) Shifts excessively from one activity to another
    (3) Has difficulty organizing work (this not being due to cognitive impairment)
    (4) Needs a lot of supervision
    (5) Frequently calls out in class
    (6) Has difficulty awaiting turn in games or group situations

C. **Hyperactivity.** At least two of the following:

    (1) Runs about or climbs on things excessively
    (2) Has difficulty sitting still or fidgets excessively
    (3) Has difficulty staying seated
    (4) Moves about excessively during sleep
    (5) Is always "on the go" or acts as if "driven by a motor"

D. Onset before the age of 7.

E. Duration of at least 6 months.

F. Not due to schizophrenia, affective disorder, or severe or profound mental retardation.

* From American Psychiatric Association: *Diagnostic and Statistical Manual of Mental Disorders*, ed 3. American Psychiatric Association, Washington, DC, 1980. Used with permission.

consists of impulsiveness and inability to delay gratification. The child is often accident prone. In school, he may rapidly attack a test and do only the first two questions. He may be unable to wait to be called on in school and may answer for everyone else, and at home he cannot be put off for even a minute.

The child is often explosively irritable. This irritability may be set off by relatively minor stimuli, and he may seem puzzled and dismayed over that phenomenon. He is frequently emotionally labile, easily set off to laughter and to tears, and his mood and his performance are apt to be variable and unpredictable.

Not all the phenomena described are always seen together; just one or two of these characteristics may be seen. If so, distractibility is often the only one.

Other manifestations are often seen, including a preoccupation with water play and a fascination with spinning objects. There may be disturbances in left-right discrimination; internal time telling or clock time telling; visual or auditory perception; visuomotor performance and hand-eye coordination; fine motor coordination; figure-background discrimination; the abilities to abstract, conceptualize, and generalize; and the abilities to assimilate, retain, and recall.

Concomitant emotional difficulties are frequent. The fact that other children grow out of this kind of behavior and the hyperkinetic child does not grow out of it at the same time and rate, the variability of performance, the temporary response to pressures, the fact that in most cases the child is not retarded and has no excuse for his behavior, the general nuisance value and inexplicability of his behavior—all may lead to adult dissatisfaction and pressure. The resulting negative self-concept and reactive hostility are worsened by the child's frequent recognition that he is not right inside.

The characteristics most often cited by various authors are, in order of frequency: (1) hyperactivity, (2) perceptual motor impairment, (3) emotional lability, (4) general coordination deficit, (5) disorders of attention (short attention span, distractibility, perseveration, failure to finish things off, not listening, poor concentration), (6) impulsivity (action before thought, abrupt shifts in activity, poor organizing, jumping up in class), (7) disorders of memory and thinking, (8) specific learning disabilities, (9) disorders of speech and hearing, and (10) equivocal neurological signs and electroencephalographic irregularities.

There are frequently associated school difficulties, both learning and behavioral. Sometimes these difficulties come from concomitant developmental language or specific learning disorders. Sometimes they come from the child's distractibility and fluctuating attention, which hamper the acquisition, retention, and display of knowledge. The difficulties superficially resemble specific learning disorders, especially when evaluated on group tests. The adverse reactions of school personnel to the behavior characteristic of the syndrome, and the lowering of self-regard because of felt inadequacies, may combine with the adverse comments of peers to make school a place of unhappy defeat. This, in turn, may lead to acting out antisocial behavior and to self-defeating, self-punitive behaviors.

### Course and Prognosis

The course of the condition is highly variable: Symptoms persist into adolescence or adult life, the symptoms disappear at puberty, or the hyperactivity disappears but attention and impulse problems persist.

Over all, clinical experience suggests that the condition is not likely to remit before the age of 12; in many children, various components, or the total picture but not its complications or sequelae, are likely to have disappeared by 20 years of age. The overactivity is usually the first symptom to remit, and distractibility is the last to remit.

Some children with the condition outgrow the need for medication, achieve adequately in adolescence and adult life, have happy and satisfying interpersonal relationships, and show no significant sequelae. Unfortunately, this is not the most frequent outcome reported in the literature. Hyperactive children may have learning difficulties, along with a tendency to develop sociopathic behavior, personality disorder, schizophrenia, or depression. These effects may persist into adult life, despite the general diminution and final disappearance of the motor hyperactivity in adolescence.

### Diagnosis

By history, observation, or report, the child should have shown excessive motor activity. This activity may be gross and generalized or limited to fidgeting and tapping. It may be generally present, not excessive, but noticeable in that the child cannot seem to respond to the requirement to inhibit the activity when appropriate to do so. It may be seen in some situations, e.g., school, but not others, e.g., the physician's office. It may be less obvious in structured situations than in unstructured situations, or the reverse. It should not be a brief, transient finding under stress, but present for a significant period of time.

Inattentiveness and distractibility represent

other essential features. In schools, they interfere with the capacity to attend to the work at hand and to follow instructions, yet they are often coupled with an insistent demand for attention from the teacher. At home, the child often does not follow through on parental requests; in the neighborhood, he does not follow through in accordance with rules of games. Frequent concomitants are impulsiveness, variability, emotional lability, and explosive irritability.

A neurological examination may show visual-perceptual or auditory-perceptual impairments, problems with coordination and with copying age-appropriate figures, rapid alternating movements, reflex asymmetries, and a variety of soft signs. Sometimes no abnormality at all is seen.

The value of an electroencephalogram in the evaluation of a child with the hyperkinetic syndrome remains in dispute.

A major reason for obtaining an EEG is to recognize the child with frequent bilaterally synchronous discharges resulting in short absence spells. Such a child may react in school with hyperactivity out of sheer frustration. The child with an unrecognized temporal lobe seizure focus can present a secondary behavior disorder. In these instances, several features of the hyperkinetic syndrome are often present. Identification of the focus requires an EEG obtained in drowsiness and in sleep.

Specific developmental disorders—such as those involving reading, arithmetic, language, and coordination—may be found in association with the attention deficit disorders. The history is of great importance. It may give clues to prenatal (including genetic), natal, and postnatal factors that may have affected the central nervous system structure or function. Rates of development and deviations in development may be elicited, along with parental reactions to significant or stressful behavioral transitions. They may help determine the degrees to which parents have contributed to or reacted to the child's inefficiencies and dysfunctions. All this information can be helpful in analyzing how much of the symptom picture is emotional, either primary or secondary, and how much represents an underlying attention deficit disorder.

School history is important in determining whether problems in learning and school behavior are an important component, and in indicating the child's attitude toward school and learning, his resulting self-image, and how these problems have been dealt with. How he has related to siblings and peers, and to free and organized activity, gives diagnostic clues as to the presence of an attention deficit disorder and to complications of the reactions to its presence.

The mental status examination may show a secondarily depressed mood but no thought disturbance, impaired reality testing, or inappropriate affect. There may be great distractibility, even in the office situation, perseverations, and a concrete and literal mode of thinking. As in the neurological examination, there may be indications of visual-perceptual, auditory-perceptual, language, or cognition problems.

There may be evidence of a basic, pervading, organically based anxiety, often referred to as body anxiety.

### Differential Diagnosis.

Anxiety, most likely in the form of an overanxious disorder, must be considered. Anxiety may accompany attention deficit disorder as a secondary reaction; and, by itself, anxiety may manifest overactivity and distractibility.

An entity for possible differentiation is that of depression. As with anxiety, there is the problem whether depression is primary or secondary to the problems created by the psychic consequence of having an attention deficit disorder.

The various forms of conduct disorder may be confused with the attention deficit disorders or, quite commonly, be associated with and secondary to these disorders.

### Treatment

**Medications.** The most common and most controversial method of treatment calls for the use of medications, racemic amphetamine (Benzedrine) or dextroamphetamine sulfate (Dexidrine).

The recommended dosage for children from 3 to 5 years of age starts with 2.5 mg daily in the morning, increasing by a similar amount weekly until satisfactory results are obtained. For children 6 years of age and older, the beginning dose is 5 mg daily, with subsequent increments of 5 mg at weekly intervals until desired results are obtained. It is generally not necessary to exceed a dosage of 40 mg daily. The amount required has been highly variable, but a total of 20 mg has often been sufficient.

There may be a striking specificity, with a particular child responding favorably to one of these drugs and unfavorably to the other, or better to one drug than to the other, or better to one of the medications listed later. There is also great variability as to appropriate dosage.

Initially, for a majority of the children given amphetamines, the drugs are needed day in and day out. As time goes on, the medications are needed only for school, and their use is accordingly limited.

The medication probably most used now is methylphenidate (Ritalin). Recommended dosages for children 6 years of age and older begin with 5 mg daily before breakfast and lunch, increasing by 5 to 10 mg weekly. Daily doses above 60 mg are not recommended, nor is continuation of the medication if no favorable effect has been achieved within a month. Of course, adverse effects call for the reduction of the dose or discontinuance of the medication. As indicated earlier, clinical evidence of the condition and favorable response to medication may persist into adult life.

These drugs are controversial because of the question about possible height and weight suppression from the use of central nervous system stimulants. Some investigators reported a height and weight rebound with abrupt cessation of the medications—some aspects favoring methylphenidate and some favoring amphetamines. It was suggested that these possible adverse effects must be weighed against the favorable effects, case by case. There is also controversy about the habit formation and abuse potential of these drugs; however, if used judiciously and within the above dose range, their use outweighs their chance for abuse.

Another central nervous system stimulant used is pemoline (Cylert). It is supplied in tablets of three strengths—18.75, 37.5 (both chewable and nonchewable), and 75 mg. It is not recommended for children under 6 years. The medication is inherently long acting, which affects the dosage recommendations. It should begin as a single morning dose of 37.5 mg daily and be increased by 18.75 mg weekly until the desired effects are obtained. The average effective daily dose ranges from 56.25 to 75 mg daily, and the maximum recommended daily dose is 115 mg. There is an abuse potential with pemoline but less than that of amphetamine.

Another medication advocated was originally introduced as an antidepressant—imipramine hydrochloride (Tofranil). It is supplied in tablets of 10, 25, and 50 mg. The manufacturer does not recommend it for attention deficit disorders or, for any reason, for children younger than age 6 years. Children have a greater reaction to the cardiac toxic effects than do adults. Favorable effects in patients were shown by the remission of the symptom picture. An advantage of imipramine is that there is no abuse potential with this drug. These drugs work by blocking the reuptake of catecholamines.

Another treatment has been one of eliminating junk food from the diet.

**Psychotherapy.** Only infrequently is the use of medication sufficient to meet the needs of children and their families. Attention must be paid to psychic aspects. At the very least, this involves giving the child the opportunity to explore the meaning of the medication to him or her, helping dispel misconceptions (such as, "I'm crazy") because medication is used, and making it clear that the child has the primary role and that the medication is only an adjuvant to help him play it. He needs to understand that perfection is not the goal and that he has an equal right with all other human beings of being occasionally unpredictable, disagreeable, and difficult. Parents need to be helped not to focus everything on medications; to recognize that they have a child, not a pill; not to respond to any or every deviation by thinking and asking, "Did you take your pill?" Handicaps and potentials need to be discussed freely and an open channel of communication maintained. Sometimes more formal types of therapy are needed.

When the child not only is allowed but helped to structure his environment, his anxiety diminishes. Thus, his parents and teachers need to set up a predictable structure of reward and punishment following a behavior therapy model. This need applies to the physical, temporal, and interpersonal environment, and should be one of the major areas of work with the parents—ranging from informational aspects to an intensive case-work approach in dealing with their feelings of guilt, bewilderment, and hostility. An almost universal requirement is to help the parents recognize that the fashionable permissiveness is not beneficial for their child. They also need to be helped to recognize that, despite their child's deficiencies in some areas, he faces the normal tasks of maturation and attendant problems, including the need to introject standards, and to form a normal, flexible superego. Therefore, he does not benefit from an exemption from the requirements, expectations, and planning applicable to other children.

**Evaluation of Therapy.** Evaluation begins with the use of medication. Since the condition is noted markedly in school, which is often a problem area for children who manifest this condition, special attention is devoted to this area.

Many studies indicate that stimulants reliably reduce overactivity and distractibility and, often, irritability, impulsiveness, and explosive irritability. However, there is no evidence that the medications directly improve any existing impairments in learning.

The stimulants are expected to enable the child to deal with school work more efficiently, not to provide him magically with what he had not previously learned, and certainly not to overcome the developmental learning disorders; tutoring is needed to provide what he had not previously learned, and structured forms of education are needed to overcome developmental learning disorders.

Medication alone may not improve academic performance, but it does provide the preconditions for it. Whether academic performance will actually improve depends much more on what the school has to offer. In most instances, it is not enough to ensure eventual academic success.

The long-term usefulness of stimulant medication cannot be accurately assessed at this time.

## Attention Deficit Disorder without Hyperactivity

### Definition and History·

This syndrome newly appears in the DSM-III classification, and its history is essentially that given earlier for attention deficit disorders and attention deficit disorder with hyperactivity. It is defined in DSM-III as found in children who display, for their age, an impairment in the ability to concentrate, without associated increased gross motor activity.

### Epidemiology

Essentially, little is yet known concerning this syndrome as differentiated from attention deficit disorder with hyperactivity. It is thought to be common, but not generally diagnosed before the age of 4. It is more common in boys than in girls. A familial pattern is not yet known.

### Etiology

Nothing specific is known about its causes. Its etiological aspects may or may not be the same as for attention deficit disorder with hyperactivity.

### Clinical Features

The actual onset seems to be in early childhood, but patients with the disorder are not likely to be seen by a psychiatrist until their school years. When they are seen, there may or may not be a history of earlier overactivity.

The child's essential difficulty in concentration may be shown by not completing tasks, shifting rapidly and unpredictably from one activity to another, seeming to be inattentive or uncomprehending, making careless and impulsive errors in daily school work or in tests, and misperforming work of which the child is entirely capable. This may be the case even when the child is motivated and desires to do well.

These phenomena are more marked in group and unstructured situations in class or out, and less so in one-to-one situations, and where external structure is provided. This translates, in part, to being worse off in open classrooms than in traditional classrooms.

In young children, especially, there may be restless sleep and restless fidgeting, but the children can sit still and not show gross motor activity. Yet their distractibility may hamper their ability to function in organized games.

Impaired academic performance secondary to distractibility may be present, and there may also be associated specific learning disorders.

As described under attention deficit disorders with hyperactivity, soft neurological signs and EEG abnormalities may or may not be present.

### Diagnosis

Essential characteristics of attention deficit disorder without hyperactivity are as follows: (1) difficulty, for the child's age, in sustaining at-

TABLE II
DIAGNOSTIC CRITERIA FOR ATTENTION DEFICIT DISORDER WITHOUT HYPERACTIVITY*

| |
|---|
| The criteria for this disorder are the same as those for attention deficit disorder with hyperactivity except that the individual never had signs of hyperactivity |

* From American Psychiatric Association: *Diagnostic and Statistical Manual of Mental Disorders*, ed 3. American Psychiatric Association, Washington, DC, 1980. Used with permission.

TABLE III
DIAGNOSTIC CRITERIA FOR ATTENTION DEFICIT DISORDER, RESIDUAL TYPE*

A. The individual once met the criteria for attention deficit disorder with hyperactivity. This information may come from the individual or from others, such as family members.

B. Signs of hyperactivity are no longer present, but other signs of the illness have persisted to the present without periods of remission, as evidenced by signs of both attentional deficits and impulsivity (e.g., difficulty organizing work and completing tasks, difficulty concentrating, being easily distracted, making sudden decisions without thought of the consequences).

C. The symptoms of inattention and impulsivity result in some impairment in social or occupational functioning.

D. Not due to schizophrenia, affective disorder, severe or profound mental retardation, or schizotypal or borderline personality disorders.

* From American Psychiatric Association: *Diagnostic and Statistical Manual of Mental Disorders*, ed 3. American Psychiatric Association, Washington, DC, 1980. Used with permission.

tention; (2) more marked difficulties in unstructured situations or in unsupervised performance; (3) disorganized, impulsive aspects manifested by at least two of the following: (a) sloppy work despite intent to perform otherwise; (b) demanding of attention; (c) frequent interruption or inappropriate intrusion into another's activity or conversation; (d) finding it hard to wait one's turn; and (e) poor frustration tolerance; (4) duration of at least 1 year; and (5) absence of excessive gross motor activity (see Table II).

Insufficient data are available to differentiate the syndrome from attention deficit disorder with hyperactivity by means of the psychiatric examination or psychological tests. Only the presence of overactivity in attention deficit disorder with hyperactivity differentiates the two syndromes.

Attention deficit disorder without hyperactivity may be confused with adjustment disorder, but in adjustment disorder there is a clear relationship with a precipitating psychosocial stressor.

## Treatment

The comments made under attention deficit disorder with hyperactivity also apply to attention deficit disorder without hyperactivity. Therapy is fundamentally the same in both disorders.

## Attention Deficit Disorder, Residual Type

In this disorder, the patient must be 18 years of age or older. The history indicates that the patient had an illness during childhood that met the criteria for attention deficit disorder (with or without hyperactivity). Signs of the illness persist, with no period of remission, as demonstrated by signs of both impulsivity and attention deficit; for example, difficulty in organizing and completing work, inability to concentrate, increased distractability, and sudden decision making without thought of consequences. The inattention and impulsive behavior cause impairment in both occupational and social functioning. These patients are sometimes helped by amphetamine or methylphenidate (see Table III).

## REFERENCES

Brunsletter R W, Silver L B: Attention deficit disorders. In *Comprehensive Textbook of Psychiatry*, ed 4, H I Kaplan, B J Sadock, editors, p 1684. Williams & Wilkins, Baltimore, 1985.

Rubinstein R A, Brown R T: An evaluation of the validity of the diagnostic category of attention deficit disorder. Am J Orthropsychiat *54:* 398, 1984.

Rutter M, Graham P, Yule W: A neuropsychiatric study in childhood. Am J Psychiatry *139:* 1, 1982.

Silver L B: A proposed view on the etiology of the neurological learning disability syndrome. J Learn Disabil *4:* 123, 1971.

Trites R L, Lapraed K: Evidence for an independent syndrome of hyperactivity. Child Psychol Psychiatry *24:* 573, 1983.

Wender P H: *Minimal Brain Dysfunction in Children.* Wiley-Interscience, New York, 1971.

# 33

# Specific Developmental Disorders of Childhood and Adolescence

## 33.1 DEVELOPMENTAL READING DISORDERS (ALEXIA AND DYSLEXIA)

### Definition and History

The terms alexia, developmental dyslexia, word blindness, and specific reading disability have been used, variously, to refer to a significant interference with the development of reading proficiency that cannot be explained by inadequate intelligence and poor schooling. Most physicians use the term alexia to refer to reading disabilities, of whatever severity, resulting from brain lesions, whereas they use dyslexia to designate an innate inability to learn to read. Psychologists and educators, on the other hand, use alexia according to its linguistic derivations to refer to a total inability to learn to read.

In general one should confine the definition of dyslexia to the presenting problem, reading failure. The several definitions intersect on the point that in developmental dyslexia, there is a discrepancy between the child's actual reading performance and that expected, given his mental age, schooling and intelligence.

In addition, in school the child's performance on tasks requiring reading skills is below his or her intellectual capacity. Significant impairment differs somewhat with age. A one- to two-year discrepancy in reading skill for ages 8 to 13 is significant; but below that it is difficult to specify how great a discrepancy is significant.

### Epidemiology

Estimates of the incidence of reading disability in the general United States population of schoolchildren generally vary between 3 and 15 percent. Estimates for Canada seem to be in the same range.

The prevalence is higher than average in groups of juvenile offenders. It is also known to be higher than average among the socially disadvantaged.

The incidence of specific reading retardation is higher among boys than among girls, three or four to one. But there is no significant difference in the proportion of males and females among backward readers.

A positive family history of speech, reading, spelling, and writing disability has often been observed by those who work with the reading disabled. The occurrence of a large percentage of affected parents speaks in favor of a dominant mode of inheritance. One study found that 45 percent of first-degree relatives of poor readers showed a history of reading problems. Another study found that the reading and spelling performance of siblings of poor readers was significantly lower than that of controls. Twin studies more conclusively suggest a genetic component, but there is little agreement as to what it is that is inherited.

### Etiology

Reading disorders may result from a lesion of the left occipital lobe, resulting in functional blindness in the right visual field, or from a lesion of the splenum of the corpus callosum that blocks transmission of visual information from the intact right hemisphere to the language areas of the left hemisphere. In one case of alexia, computed tomography revealed damage to the posterior temporal-parietal region of the left hemisphere. It has been suggested that the alexias may fall into three categories—anterior, central, and posterior.

Prenatal and perinatal difficulties, including prematurity, are higher in the histories of children with reading disorders than among those without such histories.

Poor readers, relative to their peer group, show a significantly greater incidence of overt neurological disorders and developmental difficulties, including motor and praxic abnormalities. Children with cerebral palsy show a high rate of reading problems and an elevated incidence of electroencephalographic abnormalities.

Inadequate development of cerebral dominance may result in late development of hand preference and may be responsible for mirror-image and reversal errors that interfere with learning to read. The reversal of cerebral asymmetry may result in language lateralization to a cerebral hemisphere that is structurally less suited to support language function, thus constituting a risk factor for the development of reading disability.

It has also been hypothesized that a specific differentiation of function exists within the higher cortical areas believed to subsume language and that dysfunction in one or several areas may account for subtypes of dyslexia.

Reading disabilities may also represent manifestations of developmental lags.

Findings suggest an association between malnutrition and learning. Children who suffer prolonged early malnutrition may be below average in various cognitive performances and inferior to their siblings who have grown up in the same environment but who are not subject to the same degree of malnutrition.

In some children, reading disabilities may be the direct outgrowth of a primary psychiatric disorder. However, it is hard to distinguish such children from those reading-disabled youngsters whose emotional disturbances are secondary to their academic difficulties.

### Clinical Features

Reading is a complex cognitive process, requiring a delicate balance among relevant components of a support system. These components include a neurological base that is mature and intact enough to integrate information arriving through various processing systems and to relegate disturbing stimuli to the background; the emotional maturity that is necessary for the postponement of immediate gratification for long-term gain; sufficient freedom from conflict to permit the investment of energy into the task, rather than in maintaining defenses against anxiety; and a sociocultural value system that views reading as basic to survival. See Table I for a complete summary of the clinical features of dyslexia.

Reading is language that is segmented into printed symbols and set out along a spatial continuum. Reading and spelling disabilities should be viewed as manifestations of a generalized language disorder.

The most probable conceptualization of reading disability is that the disorders are attributable to irregularities in one or several facets of language functioning, and children who fare less well than their peers in general language ability can be expected to present difficulties in some aspects of reading.

The reading problems exhibited may be observed in terms of the management of printed language units that differ in size—letters, words, sentences, and contextual tests.

Difficulties with the management of letters include problems distinguishing between letter forms, especially those that are different only in spatial orientation and length of line. Letter

TABLE I
CLINICAL FEATURES OF DYSLEXIA*

| Essential Features | Associated Features | Other Features† |
|---|---|---|
| Impaired development of reading skills: faulty oral reading, misreading of graphemes, omissions and additions of words | Poor spelling and dictation; bizarre spelling errors, letter transposals, reversals<br>Poorly formulated compositions<br>Dysgraphia<br>Poor oral language skills: impaired sound discriminations, problems with word sequencing, dysnomia, mildly deficient grammar<br>Comprehension problems in oral and printed language<br>Anomalies of hand-eye preference and impaired left-right discrimination<br>Motor problems: awkwardness, dyspraxia<br>Behavioral problems: impulsiveness, short attention span, immaturity<br>Finger agnosia (less common) | Variability in cognitive efficiency<br>Aversion to reading and writing<br>Soft neurological signs |

* Adapted from American Psychiatric Association: *Diagnostic and Statistical Manual of Mental Disorders*, ed 3. American Psychiatric Association, Washington, D C, 1980.
† Not cited as a clinical feature in DSM-III but may be present in this disorder.

forms may be experienced as shifting randomly both during recall and when confronted on the page–hence, the term strephosymbolia. An associated problem is the stabilization of letter sequences in printed words. The disabled reader may attack a word at the end or in the middle. He may transpose letters because the left-to-right tracking sequence is poorly established. He also finds it hard to compile a repertory of letter-group probabilities. Failures of memory and elicitation include poor recall of letter names and sounds.

Nearly all dyslexics are poor spellers. In observing the pattern of the child's spelling errors, the clinician attempts to answer these questions: (1) How poor is the child's memory for the way the printed word looks? (2) How do errors in the representation of the phonemic pattern interact with poor recall of the printed configuration?

Most dyslexics dislike reading and writing and avoid these activities. Their anxiety is heightened when they are confronted with demands that involve printed language.

## Course and Prognosis

Under the best of circumstances, the child is identified as being at risk during his kindergarten year or early in the first grade. Appropriate remediation is instituted and continued until the child can read and write, adequately and with relative ease.

It is desirable to manipulate the child's grade placement to coincide as closely as possible with his functioning level.

When intervention is instituted early, remediation can sometimes be discontinued by the end of the first or second grade. In more severe cases, and depending on the pattern of deficits and strengths, it may be continued into the middle and high school years.

## Diagnosis

The cardinal features of dyslexia are varying degrees of impairment of reading, spelling, and writing in intelligent, healthy children. Characteristic disorders include difficulties with the recall, evocation, and sequencing of printed letters and words, with the processing of sophisticated grammatical constructions, and with the making of inferences. Clinically, the observer is impressed by the interaction between emotional and specific features. The experience of school failure seems to confirm preexisting doubts some children have had about themselves. The energy of some children is so bound to their conflicts that they are unable to exploit their assets well. The psychiatric evaluation should assess the need for psychiatric intervention and the selection of the preferred treatment.

## Differential Diagnosis

An individually administered intelligence test should be given to rule out the possibility that poor reading is primarily a function of low ability. Hearing and vision should be evaluated. The adequacy of schooling should be investigated. Dyslexia may coexist with a variety of disorders, especially with the attention deficit and conduct disorder syndrome and with emotional problems. When this occurs, multiple diagnoses should be made.

## Psychoeducational Tests

The diagnostic battery may also include a standardized spelling test, the writing of a composition, assessment of the processing and use of oral language, design copying, and a judgment of the adequacy of pencil use. A screening projective battery may include human-figure drawings, a picture-story test, and sentence completion. The evaluation should also include a systematic observation of behavior variables.

## Treatment

There are no universally accepted methods of treating reading disabilities. Most approaches are pedagogic. One frequently used methodology, developed by Samuel Orton, urges therapeutic attention to the mastery of simple phonetic units, followed by the blending of those units into words and sentences. The use of an approach that systematically engages the several senses is recommended. The rationale for this and similar methods is that children's difficulties with the management of letters and syllables are basic to their failures to learn to read; therefore, if they are taught to cope with graphemes, they will learn to read.

Educational therapy of dyslexics is similar to psychotherapy, and like the latter, the therapist-patient relationship is a key to successful treatment.

## REFERENCES

Bender L: Specific reading disability as a maturational lag. Bull Orton Soc 7: 9, 1957.

Benton A: Dyslexia: Evolution of a concept. Bull Orton Soc 30: 10, 1980.

Benton A, Pearl D: *Dyslexia: An Appraisal of Current Knowledge.* Oxford University Press, New York, 1978.

Doehring D, Trites R, Patel P, Fiedorowicz C: *Reading Disabilities.* Academic Press, New York, 1981.

Downing J, Leong C: *Psychology of Reading.* Macmillan, New York, 1982.

Geschwind N: Asymmetries of the brain: New developments. Bull Orton Soc 29: 67, 1979.

Jansky J J: Developmental reading disorder (alexia and dyslexia). In *Comprehensive Textbook of Psychiatry*, ed 4, H I Kaplan, B J Sadock, editors, p 1691. Williams & Wilkins, Baltimore, 1985.

Orton S: *Reading, Writing, and Speech Problems in Children*. W. W. Norton, New York, 1937.

Rutter M, Yule W: Specific reading retardation. In *The First Review of Special Education*, Vol 2, L Mann, D Sabatio, editors, p 1. J.S. E. Press with Buttonwood Farms, Philadelphia, 1973.

Smith S, Pennington B, Lubs H: Specific reading disability: Identification of an inherited form through linkage analysis. Science *219:* 1345, 1983.

## 33.2 DEVELOPMENTAL ARITHMETIC DISORDER

### Introduction

Developmental arithmetic disorder is one of the specific developmental disorders listed in DSM-III. Most people apparently have the ability to tackle elementary mathematics, and there is agreement that the advanced or creative form of mathematics requires specific ability. There is a considerable difference of opinion on whether there is a specific type of mathematical ability necessary to do the elementary level of mathematics very well.

Children who are impaired primarily in mathematical ability are probably not as socially handicapped as are children who are impaired in language or reading ability. However, there are important social consequences for children with arithmetic disorder.

### Definition and History

The official definition of developmental arithmetic disorder in DSM-III (see Table I) includes a serious impairment of the development of arithmetic skills that is not explainable in terms of chronological age, mental age or inadequate schooling. The majority of children with devel-

TABLE I
DIAGNOSTIC CRITERIA FOR DEVELOPMENTAL ARITHMETIC DISORDER*

Performance on standardized, individually administered tests of arithmetic achievement is significantly below expected level, given the individual's schooling, chronological age, and mental age (as determined by an individually administered I.Q. test). In addition, in school, the child's performance on tasks requiring arithmetic skills is significantly below his or her intellectual capacity.

* From American Psychiatric Association: *Diagnostic and Statistical Manual of Mental Disorders*, ed 3. American Psychiatric Association, Washington, DC, 1980. Used with permission.

opmental arithmetic disorder have normal intelligence although performance requiring arithmetic skills is below their intellectual capacity.

### Epidemiology

The prevalence of developmental arithmetic disorder is not known, and opinions differ as to how common it is. One study found that 6 percent of children drawn from a normal population can be expected to have this disorder.

Some researchers suggest that there is a genetic predisposition to mathematical abilities, and hence to disabilities in math. Monozygotic twin studies show a correlation in arithmetic tests that is much higher than the correlations of any other two persons.

The fact that children who are exceptionally gifted in mathematics seem to possess surprising mathematical knowledge from early childhood, irrespective of external influences, suggests that certain persons are born with a predisposition to mathematical ability.

The male-to-female ratio is not known.

### Causes

Developmental arithmetic disorder, as diagnosed in DSM-III, probably has many causes. Some children are probably born with a deficiency in the ability to discriminate and manipulate numerical relationships and spatial relationships. These children lack the fundamental tools necessary for mathematics attainment. However, emotional factors, socioeconomic factors, teaching methods, and other cognitive factors are likely to interact to produce children who have varying degrees of severity of problems with mathematics. Certainly no one cause can be pinpointed for all children with developmental arithmetic disorder.

### Clinical Features

Developmental arithmetic disorder is usually diagnosed when a child's performance falls significantly below age-expected norms in school. Some children may make progress at first in the early years of mathematics by the use of rote memory, but, as the need for discrimination and manipulation of spatial and numerical relationships becomes greater, they encounter difficulties.

Investigators have described certain cardinal characteristics of the child with specific arithmetic disorder: (1) difficulty in learning to count meaningfully, (2) difficulty in mastering cardinal and ordinal systems, (3) difficulty in performing arithmetic operations, and (4) difficulty in envisioning clusters of objects as groups. In addition, they described difficulties in associating auditory and visual symbols, understanding the conservation of quantity, remembering sequences of arithmetic steps, and choosing principles for problem-solving activities. However, these children were presumed to have good auditory and verbal abilities.

It has been suggested that the inability to achieve number concept is particularly prevalent among children with intellectual retardation; when it occurs in children with normal intelligence, it is associated with cerebral palsy.

Although the one essential feature is a serious impairment in the development of arithmetic skills, the child may also have reading and spelling difficulties. But the degree of these deficits is generally not as pronounced as the difficulty in mathematics.

As with other forms of developmental disorders, a number of associated features may be present in some children but certainly not in all. There may be a delay in developmental milestones, as well as secondary problems, such as school difficulties and behavioral and emotional difficulties. These difficulties may often be a presenting complaint, particularly if the child is characterized by inattentiveness and motor disinhibition.

### Course and Prognosis

Due to lack of systematically collected data, definitive statements about the course and the prognosis of developmental arithmetic disorder cannot be made.

Complications include poor school performance, which may lead to misery and low self-esteem, truancy, and the development of a conduct disorder. The association between reading disorder and conduct disorder is much stronger than that between arithmetic disorder and conduct disorder.

### Diagnosis

Careful questioning should reveal the difficulties with mathematics from an early age.

The diagnosis should be established by a performance on an individually administered standardized test of arithmetic achievement that is significantly below what is expected on the basis of the child's chronological age of Full-Scale I.Q.

No psychiatric findings are unique to developmental arithmetic disorder.

### Differential Diagnosis

Developmental arithmetic disorder should be diagnosed only when it is not explainable by general mental retardation.

Attention deficit disorder and conduct disor-

der may be associated with arithmetic problems; in these cases, both diagnoses should be made.

### Treatment

Materials for teaching arithmetic are useful when they fit the pupil, the disability, the diagnosis, and the teaching plan. Project MATH, a multimedia self-instructional or group instructional in-service training program, has been found to be successful for certain children with developmental arithmetic disorder. Poor coordination may accompany the disorder; special physical therapy methods and sensory integration activities may therefore be of help.

Although children with special types of handicaps may need special ways of approaching the problem, essentially the principles of teaching good arithmetic to any child are the ones that work.

### REFERENCES

Badian N A: Dyscalculia and nonverbal disorders of learning. In *Progress in Learning Disabilities*, Vol V, H R Myklebust, editor, pp 235–263. Grune & Stratton, New York, 1983.
Baker L, Cantwell D P: Developmental arithmetic disorder. In *Comprehensive Textbook of Psychiatry*, ed 4, H I Kaplan, B J Sadock, editors, p 1697. Williams & Wilkins, Baltimore, 1985.
Johnson D, Myklebust H: *Learning Disabilities: Educational Principles and Practices*. Grune & Stratton, New York, 1967.
Kosc L: Neuropsychological implications of diagnoses and treatment of mathematical learning disabilities. Top Lang Learn Disord *1:* 19, 1981.
McEntire E: Learning disabilities and mathematics. Top Learn Learn Disabil *1:* 1, 1981.

## 33.3  DEVELOPMENTAL LANGUAGE DISORDER

### Introduction

Developmental language disorder, according to DSM-III, is described as (1) a failure to acquire any language, (2) an acquired language disability as a result of trauma or neurological disorder, and (3) delayed language acquisition. It is the most common of all the disorders affecting language.

Delayed language acquisition is the most common type of developmental language disorder and is divided into two types: expressive type and receptive type. The expressive subtype of the disorder involves an impairment in the encoding or production of language, with the understanding of language remaining relatively intact. The receptive subtype of the disorder which is more serious and inclusive involves impairment of both language production (encoding) and language comprehension (decoding).

## Epidemiology

There have been several studies in which the incidence of developmental language disorder was reported as 1 in 1,000 (0.1 percent) for the expressive type and 1 in 2,000 (0.5 percent) for the receptive type.

The receptive disorder is less common than the expressive disorder.

Developmental language disorder is more common in boys than in girls. The ratio is two to three boys for each girl.

A family history of developmental language disorder is rare, and siblings are usually normal. Nonetheless, a family history of related disorders is common. There is often a history in first-degree relatives of difficulty in the early stage of learning to read and write, a family history of slow speech development, articulation problems, and of difficulties in learning to read and spell. Ambidexterity occurs in a larger number of relatives than might ordinarily be expected.

## Etiology

The cause of developmental language disorder is unknown, although it may be a true cerebral disorder. A major perceptual dysfunction probably underlies the language disorder in the receptive type; the cause of this dysfunction is hypothesized to be either cerebral damage or a lag in cerebral maturation. Evidence for either of these hypotheses is partial and inconclusive. The relatively high incidence of learning disorders in relatives of children with developmental language disorder suggests a role for genetic factors; the nature of this role is unclear at the present time.

Children with the receptive type appear to have an underlying impairment in auditory discrimination. They are more responsive to environmental sounds than to speech sounds.

## Clinical Features

The child with developmental language disorder is slow in developing spoken language, and the existence of this retardation is quite apparent by age 18 months and often earlier. At 18 months, the child with the expressive type fails to utter spontaneously or even to echo words or sounds. Even simple words, such as "Mama" and "Dada," are absent from the child's active vocabulary, and the child points or uses gestures

to indicate his desires, rather than speaking. There are signs of wanting to communicate; he maintains eye contact, relates well to his mother, and enjoys games such as pat-a-cake and peek-a-boo.

At 18 months, the child with the expressive type is able to comprehend simple commands, and is able to point to common objects when they are named. The child with the receptive type is not able to point to common objects or to obey simple commands at 18 months. He frequently appears to be deaf. Actually, the child hears and responds normally to environmental sounds, but does not respond to speech.

When the child finally begins to speak, his language deficit is apparent. Numerous articulation errors are present but inconsistent. Once speech begins, the dysphasic child's language acquisition progresses at a much slower rate than in normal children. Despite these serious disturbances in spoken language, the child is not abnormal in visual perception and visuospatial skills.

School problems are an inevitable complication with developmental language disorder. Reading retardation is the most serious problem, and massive difficuties in all academic subjects result from it.

Emotional problems are another frequent complication. Although some children, generally those with the expressive type, present a reasonably normal picture, many children have emotional and behavioral problems. Symptoms such as hyperactivity, withdrawal, thumb sucking, bed wetting, tantrums, short attention span, and disobedience are common. See Table I and II for the diagnostic criteria of the expressive and receptive types of developmental language disorder.

Neurological abnormalities are associated features that have been reported in a number of children. These features include soft neurological signs, depressed vestibular responses, and EEG abnormalities (see Table III).

## Course and Prognosis

The prognosis for the child with these disorders is generally optimistic. However, the degree of eventual recovery depends on the severity of the disorder and the child's motivation. The prognosis is very good in cases of the simple expressive type, fairly good in cases of the receptive type, and less good in cases of severe receptive types coupled with auditory imperception.

The degree of impairment imposed varies according to the type of disorder. Children with mild expressive types eventually show no im-

TABLE I
DIAGNOSTIC CRITERIA FOR DEVELOPMENTAL LANGUAGE DISORDER, EXPRESSIVE TYPE*

A. Failure to develop vocal expression (encoding) of language despite relatively intact comprehension of language.

B. Presence of inner language (the presence of age-appropriate concepts, such as understanding the purpose and use of a particular household object).

C. Not due to mental retardation, childhood onset pervasive developmental disorder, hearing impairment, or trauma.

* From American Psychiatric Association: *Diagnostic and Statistical Manual of Mental Disorders*, ed 3. American Psychiatric Association, Washington, DC, 1980. Used with permission.

TABLE II
DIAGNOSTIC CRITERIA FOR DEVELOPMENTAL LANGUAGE DISORDER, RECEPTIVE TYPE*

A. Failure to develop comprehension (decoding) and vocal expression (encoding) of language.

B. Not due to hearing impairment, trauma, mental retardation, or childhood onset pervasive developmental disorder.

* From American Psychiatric Association: *Diagnostic and Statistical Manual of Mental Disorders*, ed 3. American Psychiatric Association, Washington, DC, 1980. Used with permission.

pairment, whereas children with severe receptive types may always show moderate impairment. The highest level of adaptive functioning similarly varies between fair and good.

## Diagnosis

A delay in the acquisition of language that is not explainable by a hearing impairment or by general mental retardation characterizes this disorder. The child shows a desire to communicate. Inner language or the appropriate use of toys and household objects is present. If there is any language, it is severely retarded; vocabulary is limited, grammar simplified, and articulation variable. In the receptive type, the child also suffers an impairment in the understanding of language.

Standardized language tests are useful in establishing the degree of the child's impairment. However, for diagnostic purposes, a great deal can be ascertained without the use of standard language tests. The child should be observed at play with objects to determine the child's comprehension, the clinician can ask him to point to each of the objects in turn.

When there is some question of hearing impairment, an audiogram is indicated. When there is some quesion of general intellectual retardation, detailed intelligence testing is useful.

### Differential Diagnosis

When a young child presents with a delay or disorder of language development, a number of possible diagnoses must be considered. These include mental retardation, hearing impairment, infantile autism, elective mutism, developmental articulation disorder, and receptive and expressive dysphonia to brain damage.

The mentally retarded child has normal hearing, and responds appropriately to sounds. The articulation of the mentally retarded child is consistently poor. Motor milestones, only slightly delayed in the dysphasic child, are clearly delayed in the child with mental retardation. Performance intelligence is seriously impaired in the child who is mentally retarded.

An audiogram is the best way to establish the presence of a hearing impairment in a child, although sometimes this diagnosis is clear from the child's behavior.

A differential diagnosis between autism and severe developmental language disorder is generally made on behavioral grounds rather than on linguistic grounds. The most striking feature that distinguishes the two disorders is the lack of interest in communication in the autistic child. The autistic child does not watch the faces of speakers, does not make eye contact, and does not attempt to communicate through the use of gestures. Inner language, slightly impaired in the dysphasic child, is severely impaired or totally absent in the autistic child. In older children who have acquired some language, the child with infantile autism may have inappropriate intonation, delayed echolalia, and stereotyped utterances.

The electively mute child's mother reports that the child had a normal developmental history and can speak normally, but that he is shy, and speaks only to certain persons.

Examination of the language of a child with developmental articulation disorder reveals that comprehension and expression are normal, and that only articulation is disturbed (see Table IV).

Children with developmental language disorder score better on performance intelligence tests than on verbal intelligence tests.

## Treatment

Treatment in the form of language therapy should be instituted as soon as possible. Practice

TABLE III
CLINICAL FEATURES

| Essential Features | Associated Features |
| --- | --- |
| There is retardation of spoken language (expressive dysphasia) or of spoken language and language comprehension | In severe cases there may be an impairment of auditory discrimination |
| The language retardation cannot be accounted for by hearing impairment | An audiogram may show fluctuations and inconsistencies. A partial hearing defect may be present |
| The language retardation cannot be accounted for by general retardation. Performance I.Q. is normal | There may be some delay in reaching motor milestones |
| The child shows a desire to communicate, has eye contact, and uses gestures | |
| Inner language (appropriate use of objects and appropriate play patterns) is present | There may be a slight retardation in make-believe play |
| Articulation is variable Vocabulary is limited Grammar is simplified School problems are inevitable with receptive dysphasia and are common with expressive dysphasia. | |
| | There may be neurological abnormalities |

with vocabulary, sentence construction, speech, and narration are all necessary. For the child with the receptive type, practice in language comprehension, auditory memory, and auditory perception are also needed. The value of psychotherapy for the child is not yet known. Counseling for the family, especially parent training, has proved useful in some cases in helping them cope with the tensions resulting from the child's communication problem. Special classes and tutoring are also of help.

## REFERENCES

Aram D M, Nation J E: *Child Language Disorders*. C. V. Mosby, St. Louis, 1982.

Baker L, Cantwell DP: Developmental language disorder. In *Comprehensive Textbook of Psychiatry*, ed 4, H I Kaplan, B J Sadock, editors, p 1700. Williams & Wilkins, Baltimore, 1985.

Eisenson J: *Aphasia in Children*. Harper & Row, New York, 1972.

Fundudis I, Kolvin I, Garside R F: A follow-up of speech retarded children. In *Language and Language Disorders in Childhood* (book supplement to J Child Psychol Psychiatry 2: 97, 1980).

Holland A, editor: *Language Disorders in Children: Recent Advances*. College Hill Press, San Diego, 1984.

Laney M: *Reading in Childhood Language Disorders*. John Wiley & Sons, New York, 1978.

Morehead D, Morehead A, editors: *Normal and Deficient Child Language*, p 472. University Park Press, Baltimore, 1976.

Myklebust H R: Childhood aphasia: Identification, diagnosis, and remediation. In *Handbook of Speech Pathology and Audiology*, L E Travis, editor. Appleton-Century-Crofts, New York, 1971.

Rutter M, Martin J A, editors: *The Child with Delayed Speech*. Heinemann, London, 1972.

TABLE IV
DIFFERENTIAL DIAGNOSIS*

| | Hearing Impairment | Mental Retardation | Infantile Autism | Expressive Type | Receptive Type | Elective Mutism | Developmental Articulation Disorder |
| --- | --- | --- | --- | --- | --- | --- | --- |
| Language comprehension | − | − | − | + | − | + | + |
| Expressive language | − | − | − | − | − | Variable | + |
| Audiogram | − | + | + | + | Variable | + | + |
| Articulation | − | − | Variable | Variable | Variable | + | − |
| Inner language | + | + (Limited) | − | + | + (Slightly limited) | + | + |
| Uses gestures | + | + (Limited) | − | + | + | + Variable | + |
| Echoes | − | + | + (Inappropriate) | + | + | + | + |
| Attends to sounds | Loud or low frequency only | + | − | + | Variable | + | + |
| Watches faces | + | + | − | + | + | + | + |
| Performance I.Q. | + | − | + | + | + | + | + |

* + = Normal; − = abnormal.

Trantham C R, Pederson J K: *Normal Language Development: The Key to Diagnosis and Therapy for Language-Disordered Children.* William & Wilkins, Baltimore, 1976.

---

## 33.4 DEVELOPMENTAL ARTICULATION DISORDER

### Introduction

Developmental articulation disorder is defined in DSM-III as a functional articulation disorder accompanied by language development that is within normal limits. Although precise epidemiological data are not available, the disorder appears to be a fairly common one, and is reportedly the most frequently occurring articulation disorder in children. Although mild cases may not seriously affect intelligibility and generally show spontaneous recovery, severe cases can result in completely unintelligible speech and require lengthy treatment. Treatment must be offered before the child suffers in his peer relations or at school because of his inability to make himself understood (see Table I).

### Definition

Developmental articulation disorder cannot be accounted for by structural, physiological, or neurological abnormalities. Language is within normal limits. The term actually refers to a number of different articulation problems that range in severity from mild to severe. Only one speech sound or phoneme (the smallest sound unit) may be affected, or many phonemes may be involved. The child may be completely intelligible, partially intelligible, or unintelligible.

Different terms used to describe this disorder have included dyslalia, baby talk, infantile perseveration, lalling, delayed speech, lisping, oral inaccuracy, lazy speech, mild specific developmental speech disorder, and defective articulation.

### Epidemiology

Estimates of the incidence of developmental articulation disorder are few and probably in-accurate. However, preliminary information suggests that the incidence is high.

In various studies, from 1 to 33 percent of school children have been reported to have speech defects. The disorder is more common in boys than in girls. The disorder is present in about 6 percent of males and 3 present of females of school age.

There are reports of articulation defects in parents, aunts, and uncles of children with developmental articulation disorder.

### Etiology

The cause of developmental articulation disorder is unknown. It is commonly believed that a maturational delay in the neurological processes underlying speech may be at fault.

A disproportionately high number of children with developmental articulation disorder are found to be second borns, twins, or of low socioeconomic status. It is now believed that these children, rather than being at risk for the disorder, are the recipients of inadequate speech stimulation and reinforcement.

Constitutional factors, rather than environmental factors, seem to be of major importance in determining whether a child has developmental articulation disorder. The high proportion of children with developmental articulation disorder who have relatives with a similar disorder suggests a genetic component to the disorder.

### Clinical Features

There is a considerable range in the severity with which a child may be affected by developmental articulation disorder. In very mild cases, only one phoneme may be affected. Single phonemes are commonly affected, and these are usually those acquired late in the developmental sequence. The phonemes most commonly affected include r, sh, th (as in "thing"), s, z (as in "scissors"), l, ch, dg (as in "hedge"), g f, th (as in "these"), j (as in "soldier"), and v. In severe cases, even such simple phonemes as p, b, m, t, d, n, and h may be affected. Vowel phonemes are not usually affected.

The child with developmental articulation disorder is not able to articulate certain phonemes correctly, and may distort, substitute, or

---

TABLE I
DIAGNOSTIC CRITERIA FOR DEVELOPMENTAL ARTICULATION DISORDER*

A. Failure to develop consistent articulations of the later-acquired speech sounds, such as r, sh, th, f, z, l, or ch.

B. Not due to developmental language disorder, mental retardation, childhood onset pervasive developmental disorder, or physical disorders.

* From American Psychiatric Association: *Diagnostic and Statistical Manual of Mental Disorders*, ed 3. American Psychiatric Association, Washington, DC, 1980. Used with permission.

even omit the affected phonemes. With omissions, the phonemes are absent entirely—for example "bu" for "blue," "ca" for "car," or "wha a?" for "what's that?" With substitutions, incorrect phonemes are substituted for more difficult ones—for example "wabbit" for "rabbit," "fum" for "thumb," or "whath dat?" for "what's that?" With distortions, the correct phoneme is approximated but is articulated incorrectly. Rarely do additions—usually of the vowel "schwa" or "uh"—occur—for example, "puhretty," for "pretty," "what's uh that uh?" for "what's that?"

It is generally thought that omissions are the most serious type of misarticulation, with substitutions the next most serious type, and distortion is the least serious type.

The articulation of the child with developmental articulation disorder is often inconsistent. A phoneme may be correctly produced in one phonetic environment, and incorrectly produced in another phonetic environment. Errors are most likely to occur in the final consonant of a word, and are least likely to occur in the initial consonant of a word. Another type of inconsistency in the speech of children with developmental articulation disorder is that their articulation of single words in isolation may be normal, whereas articulation of the same word in longer utterances is quite disturbed. Generally, articulation is worse during an increased rate of speech.

Omissions, distortions, and substitutions also occur normally in the speech of a young child learning to talk. However, whereas the young normal child soon replaces these misarticulations, the child with developmental articulation disorder does not. Even as the child with developmental articulation disorder grows and finally acquires the correct phoneme, he may use it only in newly acquired words and may not correct earlier learned words that he has been mispronouncing for some time.

The speech milestone may be somewhat delayed in children with developmental articulation disorders, but, generally, the children begin speaking at the appropriate age.

Most children eventually outgrow developmental articulation disorder by the third grade. After the fourth grade, however, spontaneous recovery is unlikely. It is important to try to remediate the articulation disorder before the development of complications (see Table II).

Recovery from developmental articulation disorder is often spontaneous, particularly in mild cases. Often, the child's beginning kindergarten or school precipitates the improvement. For children who have not spontaneously improved by the fourth grade, speech therapy is

TABLE II
ESSENTIAL AND ASSOCIATED FEATURES OF DEVELOPMENTAL ARTICULATION DISORDER

| Essential Features | Associated Features |
| --- | --- |
| Defective articulation— omissions, distortions, or substitutions—of later acquired speech sounds not attributable to structural or neurological abnormalities | Delay in first beginning to speak |
| | Lack of firmly established laterality |
| | Enuresis |
| | Dysfluencies of speech (stuttering) |
| Language within normal limits | General immaturity, dependency, shyness, or hyperactivity |
| | Problems with school, especially with reading |

necessary. With severely affected children whose intelligibility is affected, and with children who are clearly troubled by their inability to speak clearly, speech therapy is indicated at an early age. Recovery from the articulation disorder is complete with therapy.

## Diagnosis

The cardinal feature of developmental articulation disorder is an articulation defect characterized by omission, substitution, or distortion of phonemes that generally involves the late-learned phonemes. The disorder is not attributable to structural or neurological abnormalities, and it is accompanied by language development that is within normal limits.

### Differential Diagnosis

When a child presents with an articulation disorder, it is essential to determine whether the disorder is a pure articulation disorder, or whether the child's language development is also affected.

Audiometric evaluation is necessary to rule out a hearing impairment.

Children with dysarthria, an articulation disorder caused by structural or neurological abnormalities, differ from children with developmental articulation disorder, in that dysarthria is very difficult and sometimes impossible to remediate. Drooling, slow or uncoordinated motor behavior, abnormal chewing or swallowing, and awkward or slow protrusion and retraction of the tongue are indications of dysarthria. A slow rate of speech is another indication of dysarthria (see Table III).

Children with developmental articulation disorder do not show a characteristic profile on any psychological tests.

TABLE III
DIFFERENTIAL DIAGNOSIS

| Criteria | Articulation Disorder Due to Structural or Neurological Abnormalities (Dysarthria) | Articulation Disorder Due to Hearing Impairment | Developmental Articulation Disorder | Articulation Disorder Associated with Mental Retardation, Infantile Autism, Developmental Dysphasia, Acquired Aphasia, or Deafness |
|---|---|---|---|---|
| Language development | Within normal limits | Within normal limits unless hearing impairment is serious | Within normal limits | Not within normal limits |
| Examination | Possible abnormalities of lips, tongue, or palate; muscular weakness, incoordination, or disturbance of vegetative functions, such as sucking or chewing | Hearing impairment shown on audiometric testing | Normal | |
| Rate of speech | Slow; marked deterioration of articulation with increased rate | Normal | Normal; possible deterioration of articulation with increased rate | |
| Phonemes affected | Any phonemes, even vowels | F, th, sh, and s | R, sh, th, ch, dg, j, f, v, s, and z are most commonly affected | |

## Treatment

Speech therapy is indicated when a child's intelligibility is affected, when a child appears to be disturbed by his articulatory difficulties, or when a child has not spontaneously improved by the third grade.

## REFERENCES

Baker L, Cantwell DP: Developmental articulation disorder. In *Comprehensive Textbook of Psychiatry*, ed 4, H I Kaplan, B J Sadock, editors, p 1705. Williams & Wilkins, Baltimore, 1985.
Bloodstein O: *Speech Pathology: An Introduction.* Houghton Mifflin, Boston, 1979.
Powers M H: Clinical and educational procedures in functional disorders of articulation. In *Handbook of Speech Pathology*, L E Travis, editor, pp 877–910. Prentice Hall, Englewood Cliffs, NJ, 1969.
Sander E R: When are speech sounds learned? J Speech Hear Disord 37: 55, 1972.
Weiss C E, Lillywhite H S: *Communicative Disorders: Prevention and Early Intervention.* C. V. Mosby, St. Louis, 1981.
Wintz H: *Articulatory Acquisition and Behavior.* Prentice Hall, Englewood Cliffs, NJ, 1969.

# 33.5   COORDINATION DISORDER

## Introduction

Coordination disorder is a disorder of development. In developmental sequence, perceptual motor skills are acquired first, then spoken language is acquired, and, with rare exceptions, only after the child has acquired these functions does he learn how to read. Coordination disorder may be considered a subset of the developmental disorders of perceptual motor skills.

## Definition

Although clumsy children or children with coordination disorder have been described for at least the past 15 years, only in the most recent editions of the classification manuals has a specific disorder been so delineated. The operational definition for coordination disorder includes a serious impairment in the development of motor coordination, and the absence of general mental retardation or any neurological disorder that would account for the motor coordination problems. ICD-9 also includes the term coordination disorder as one of its developmental disorders.

## Epidemiology

The exact prevalence of coordination disorder is not known, but it appears to be a relatively common disorder. It is generally accepted that the disorder is more common in boys than in girls, as most developmental disorders are, but the exact boy-to-girl ratio is not known. No evidence suggests that coordination disorder runs in family members of children with this disorder.

## Etiology

Some evidence suggests that children with coordination disorder have an increased frequency of complications before, during, and after birth. Other predisposing factors are thought to include hypoxia during pregnancy, low birth weight, and malnutrition. However, no specific causative factor can be pinpointed for coordination disorder. It is likely that the factors suggested as playing a causative role probably do so in a multifactorial way. They may also lead to other problems. They are not specific for coordination disorder.

## Clinical Features

Coordination disorder begins in infancy. Generally, recognition is early, occurring as soon as the child attempts tasks requiring motor coordination. The one single essential feature is a serious impairment in the development of motor coordination. The manifestations may vary with age and with the severity of the disorder. Generally, a child with motor coordination disorder is looked on as one who has motor learning difficulties. He displays inefficient motor behavior and asynchronous motor behavior when commonly expected movement tasks are carried out. Thus, he may be clumsy, he may drop things, and he may trip over his own feet and fall frequently. Developmental milestones—such as tying shoelaces, buttoning shirts, and zipping up pants—are late in being learned. Most movements are uncoordinated and awkward, leading to difficulties in such things as table games that require putting together puzzles or building models, building blocks, and any type of ball game. Difficulties in handwriting may be noted in a school-age child.

A number of associated features are present in some children with coordination disorder, but not in all these children. For instance, there is a high incidence of speech disorders, and developmental milestones may be delayed in areas other than motor coordination. Secondary problems, such as school difficulties, may often be presenting complaints. Rapid mood swings and inattentiveness may also occur as associated features.

## Course and Prognosis

Solid data on the untreated natural history of children with coordination disorder are not available. There is a suggestion in the literature that children who have an average or above-average intelligence found ways of compensating for their motoric disability. However, not all do so, and clumsiness may persist into adolescence and adult life. Children with below-average intelligence have more difficulty in developing ways to compensate for their problem. In very severe cases that remain untreated, there may be a number of secondary complications. These complications may include repeated failures in school at both nonacademic and academic tasks, repeated problems in attempting to integrate with a peer group, and inability to play games and sports. These problems may lead to low self-esteem, unhappiness, withdrawal, and, in some cases, increasingly severe behavioral problems as reaction to the frustration engendered by the child's disability. All levels of adaptive functioning can be expected in these children.

A variety of treatments have been suggested as being effective for this condition, but the course of the disorder with treatment, as opposed to the untreated natural history, is not known.

## Diagnosis

Diagnosis is made on the basis of the child's history, the clinical picture, examination of the child, and the use of selected tests. The history from the parents reveals impairments in motor coordination ranging from mild to severe, with manifestations as described above. Examination of the child reveals difficulties in coordination, and may reveal fine choreiform movements of unsupported limbs. Mirror movements or the persistence of associated movements, slight abnormalities of reflex, and other neurological signs generally described as soft neurological signs may also be found on examination. The examination also reveals obvious failures on perceptual tasks that require recognizing objects or fitting a box into the appropriately shaped hole.

### Differential Diagnosis

Generalized mental retardation can cause coordination difficulties and must be differentiated from coordination disorder in the absence of generalized retardation. Pervasive developmental disorders, such as infantile autism, are also often associated with coordination problems.

A large number of specific neurological disorders lead to problems of coordination, and these must be ruled out by history, appropriate examination, and testing.

### Treatment

Teaching methods like the Montessori technique may be useful with many preschool children. Developed by Maria Montessori, these techniques emphasize the development of motor skills.

When it comes to the more severe problems, a wide variety of therapeutic approaches have been described. These approaches include physical education, perceptual motor training concepts, and therapeutic exercise techniques for motor dysfunction.

### REFERENCES

Arnheim D D, Sinclair W A: *The Clumsy Child*. C. V. Mosby, St. Louis, 1975.

Breaner M W, Gillman S, Zangwill O L, Farrell M: Visuo-motor disability in school children. Br Med J *4:* 259, 1967.

Cantwell D P, Baker L: Coordination disorder. In *Comprehensive Textbook of Psychiatry*, ed 4, H I Kaplan, F J Sadock, editors, p 1709. Williams & Wilkins, Baltimore, 1985.

Drillien C M: Aetiology and outcome in low-birth-weight infants. Dev Med Child Neurol *14:* 563, 1972.

Gordon N: *Paediatric Neurology for the Clinician*. Heinemann, Philadelphia, 1976.

Prechtl H F, Stemmer C J: The choreiform syndrome in children. Dev Med Child Neurol *4:* 119, 1962.

Stott D H: A general test of motor impairment for children. Dev Med Child Neurol *8:* 523, 1966.

# 34

# Movement and Speech Disorders of Childhood and Adolescence

## 34.1 STEREOTYPED MOVEMENT DISORDERS

### Introduction

The stereotyped movement disorders include transient tic disorder, chronic motor tic disorder, Gilles de la Tourette's disease, and other stereotyped movement disorders, such as head banging and rocking. The common theme for these disorders is the disregulation of gross motor movement.

### Transient Tic Disorder

#### Definition

Transient tics are defined in DSM-III as recurrent, repetitive, rapid, purposeless motor movements. These movements can be voluntarily suppressed for minutes to hours. The total clinical picture usually lasts for weeks or months with varying intensity of symptoms. If the tics last for longer than 1 year, they should be classified as a chronic motor tic disorder.

Leo Kanner first described tics as sudden, quick, involuntary, and frequently repeated movements of circumscribed groups of muscles, serving no apparent purpose. This description has been the standard used by clinicians and is the basis for the DSM-III definition (see Table I).

#### Epidemiology

Transient, tic-like habit movements or nervous muscular twitches are common in children. In many studies, no distinction was made in the length of time a tic had been present; thus, prevalence studies are not always clear.

In two large studies, it was noted that about three boys are affected for every girl. The disorder seems to be more common in family members of those with tics than in the general population.

#### Etiology

It is probable that, with some children or adolescents, tics are a reflection of a psychological conflict, whereas with others they are secondary to an organic difficulty.

**Psychogenic Tics.** Tics may be a reflection of diffuse anxiety or may have a more specific meaning; they may be used as a defense against another motor activity, or may symbolically represent a condensed ego function. Psychogenic tics seem to increase in severity during emotional excitement, decrease as a result of distraction or concentration, and disappear during sleep.

**Organic Based Tics.** Tics may be noted in Gilles de la Tourette's disease and in other organic syndromes discussed later in this section.

Tics and dyskinesias have been noted in children being treated with methylphenidate (Ritalin). These clinical studies suggested the possibility that the development of tics and dyskinesias at relatively low doses of dopaminergic agents, such as methylphenidate, are reflective of denervation hypersensitivity of central dopamine pathways.

#### Clinical Features

The average age of onset of tics is 7 years but may occur as early as 2 years; the great majority of patients have an onset before the age of 10. The face and the neck are the most frequently involved parts of the body. The commonest tics involve the face, and there is a descending gradient of frequency from face to feet.

Types of body movements and types of tics include the following:

(1) Face and head: Grimacing, puckering of forehead, raising eyebrows, blinking eyelids, winking, wrinkling nose, trembling nostrils, twitching mouth, displaying teeth, biting lips and other parts, extruding tongue, protracting lower jaw, nodding, jerking, or shaking the head,

TABLE I
DIAGNOSTIC CRITERIA FOR TRANSIENT TIC DISORDER*

A. Onset during childhood or early adolescence.

B. Presence of recurrent, involuntary, repetitive, rapid, purposeless, motor movements (tics).

C. Ability to suppress the movements voluntarily for minutes to hours.

D. Variation in the intensity of the symptoms over weeks or months.

E. Duration of at least 1 month but not more than 1 year.

* From American Psychiatric Association: *Diagnostic and Statistical Manual of Mental Disorders*, ed 3. American Psychiatric Association, Washington, DC, 1980. Used with permission.

twisting neck, looking sideways, and head rolling.

(2) Arms and hands: Jerking hands, jerking arms, plucking fingers, writhing fingers, and clenching fists.

(3) Body and lower extremities: Shrugging shoulders, shaking foot, knee, or toe, peculiarities of gait, body writhing, and jumping.

(4) Respiratory and alimentary: Hiccoughing, sighing, yawning, snuffing, blowing through nostrils, whistling inspiration, exaggerated breathing, belching, sucking or smacking sounds, and clearing throat.

### Course and Prognosis

By definition, the tics in children with transient tic disorder disappear within 1 year. If they persist beyond a year, they are diagnosed as a chronic motor tic disorder.

### Diagnosis

The criteria for establishing the diagnosis of transient tic disorder are: (1) onset during childhood; (2) the presence of recurrent, involuntary, repetitive, rapid, purposeless motor movements; (3) the ability to suppress such movements voluntarily for minutes to hours; (4) the variability of the intensity of the symptoms over weeks or months; and (5) the duration of the symptoms for at least 1 month, but for not more than 1 year.

### Treatment

The more the child's attention is directed toward the movements, either in a therapeutic effort or by the family or school, the more intense they may become. If the tics persist, an intrapsychic evaluation of the child, a behavioral assessment of the symptom, and a family evaluation may clarify the underlying issues. Psychodynamic, behavioral, or family therapy may be indicated.

In the psychodynamic approach, the therapist may want to make his or her patient fully aware of the tic, not only as a motor movement but also as a reflection of feelings or thoughts.

Behavioral therapy may focus on relaxation techniques in an effort to minimize the use of motor discharges to relieve tension. Another approach has been the use of negative practice. This method involves voluntary repetition of the tic as fast as possible in brief periods of time interspersed with brief rest periods.

One focus in family therapy is to deal with those family dynamics that may contribute to the identified patient's level of anxiety. Another aspect of family therapy is to assist the family members in not focusing on or in any way reinforcing the tic behavior of the identified patient.

Minor tranquilizers have been used in an effort to minimize anxiety. Haloperidol has also been used.

## Chronic Motor Tic Disorder

Much of the clinical and research literature on tics did not differentiate between transient tic disorder and chronic tic disorder. For this reason, much of the information provided above on transient tic disorder is probably also appropriate here.

### Definition

Chronic motor tic disorder is defined in DSM-III as recurrent, involuntary, repetitive, rapid, purposeless motor movements involving no more than three muscle groups at one time. The intensity of the symptoms is constant over weeks or months; the movements can be voluntarily suppressed for minutes to hours; and the disorder lasts for at least 1 year.

### Epidemiology

Data are not available on the prevalence of this disorder. It appears to be rarer than Gilles de la Tourette's disease. Sexual prevalence is not yet clear; however, it appears to be more common in boys. No clear familial patterns are known. The outcome may be significantly worse for those children whose parents had tics that persisted into adult life, and for those children who have a positive family history of tics.

## Etiology

The possible causes of chronic motor tic disorder are similar to those discussed for transient tic disorder.

## Clinical Features and Course

Onset appears to be in early childhood. The tics may persist throughout life. Some tics may first occur after the age of 40. The types of tics and their locations are similar to those in the transient tic disorder.

Vocal tics occur infrequently. When they are present, they are not loud, intense, or noticeable. Often, they are grunts or other noises caused by thoracic, abdominal, or diaphragmatic contractions; they are not primarily from the vocal cords.

Children whose tics start between the ages of 6 and 8 years have a better outcome than do those whose tics started earlier or later. Those children whose tics involve the limbs or the trunk tend to do less well than those with facial tics alone. The onset may be either in childhood or after age 40. Adult-onset tics usually affect a single muscle group.

## Diagnosis

The criteria for establishing the diagnosis of chronic motor tic disorder are: (1) the presence of recurrent, involuntary, repetitive, rapid, purposeless movements involving no more than three muscle groups at any one time; (2) consistent intensity of the tics over weeks or months; (3) the ability to suppress the movements voluntarily for minutes to hours; and (4) the duration of the disorder for at least 1 year (see Table II).

## Treatment

Psychotherapy may be indicated in an effort to focus on what may be the primary emotional conflict or to minimize the secondary emotional problems caused by the tics. Behavioral therapy may minimize the use of motor discharges for anxiety. Minor tranquilizers have not been successful. Haloperidol (Haldol) has been helpful in some cases.

## Tourette's Disorder

### Definition and History

Gilles de la Tourette's disorder (now known simply as Tourette's disorder) is characterized by recurrent, involuntary, repetitive, rapid, purposeless motor movements (tics) and multiple vocal tics. The movements can be voluntarily suppressed for minutes to hours, and the intensity of the symptoms may vary over weeks or months. The motor tics typically involve the head, but frequently also involve other parts of the body—torso, upper and lower limbs. The vocal tics are present in 60 percent of all cases, and include various complicated sounds and words and coprolalia.

### Epidemiology

Coprolalia occurs in only 60 percent of all patients; it may appear an average of 6.3 years after the onset of the disorder, and may spontaneously disappear in some patients an average of 10.3 years after onset. Echolalia occurs in only 35 percent of all patients, and intellectual deterioration is infrequent. Also contributing to this disorder's being underdiagnosed is the fact that physicians may interpret the initial symptoms as transient or habit tics of childhood.

The incidence of cases reported from children's psychiatric clinics varies from 1 case in 1,000 patients, to 1 case in 12,500 patients. Prevalence figures are less available, and reflect the changing diagnostic criteria and the frequency of misdiagnosis. By 1965, which was 80 years after Gilles de la Tourette's paper appeared, only about 50 cases were reported in the literature. Yet the researchers at the Gilles de la Tourette and Tic Laboratory and Clinic at Mt. Sinai School of Medicine found that, with publicity and an effort to establish a diagnosis, 250 patients were identified by them between 1965 and 1976.

Surveys of the sex distribution in Tourette's disorder have consistently reported a greater percentage of males. The lifetime prevalence rate ranges from 0.1 to 0.5 per 1,000. The ratio of males to females is 3 to 1.

TABLE II
DIAGNOSTIC CRITERIA FOR CHRONIC MOTOR TIC DISORDER*

A. Presence of recurrent, involuntary, repetitive, rapid, purposeless movements (tics) involving no more than three muscle groups at any one time.

B. Unvarying intensity of the tics over weeks or months.

C. Ability to suppress the movements voluntarily for minutes to hours.

D. Duration of at least 1 year.

\* From American Psychiatric Association: *Diagnostic and Statistical Manual of Mental Disorders*, ed 3. American Psychiatric Association, Washington, DC, 1980. Used with permission.

Tourette's disorder is found in all social classes. The incidence of this disorder in the same family is higher than statistically expected.

## Etiology

There are three theories about the causes of Tourette's disorder—psychological, neurological, and psychophysiological. The early literature focused primarily on a psychological cause. Patients were described as having schizophrenia, an underlying psychosis, obsessive-compulsive neurosis, or character traits. However, large-sample surveys failed to find evidence of common psychopathological characteristics, schizophrenia, underlying psychosis, or any of the other proposed disorders.

Tourette's disorder is probably caused by a disorder of the central nervous system. This concept is supported by the following data: (1) There is a high incidence of minimal brain dysfunction (57.9 percent) in such patients. (2) Such patients show a high incidence of soft neurological signs. (3) There is a high incidence (50 to 60 percent) of abnormal electroencephalograms. (4) There is a higher than normal incidence of left-handedness. (5) Haloperidol suppresses the tics.

## Clinical Features

The initial symptoms develop between the ages of 2 and 10 years and almost always before the age of 13. A wide range of symptoms may be noted, from a single tic to multiple tics. The most frequent symptom is an eye tic, followed by a head or facial grimace. In one sample, a large number (19.3 percent) began with sounds or words; coprolalia was noted in 6.2 percent of those early patients. Such initial symptoms as tics, stammering, and sniffing may not be diagnosed as Tourette's disorder; the clinical course may need to develop before the diagnosis is clear (see Table III).

The diagnosis is based in part on a lifelong chronic disorder. The initial symptoms may persist or decrease. Old symptoms may be replaced by new ones. The patient has exacerbations and remissions. Voluntary control is usually possible for a limited period of time, but ultimately tension mounts, requiring discharge in tic symptoms.

Coprolalia eventually develops in about 60 percent of the patients. The average age of onset of coprolalia is 13.5 years. As noted, it can also occur as the first symptom.

Untreated, the symptoms persist, and secondary psychological problems develop. Psychotic behavior or intellectual deterioration are not noted with any more frequency than in any other psychiatric population.

## Diagnosis

The diagnosis is often initially difficult; it may be only as the disorder progresses that the disagnosis can be established. The diagnostic criteria include: (1) age of onset between 2 and 15 years; (2) the presence of recurrent, involuntary, repetitive, rapid, purposeless motor movements affecting multiple muscle groups; (3) the possible presence of multiple vocal tics; (4) the ability to suppress the movements voluntarily for minutes to hours; (5) variation of the symptoms' intensity over weeks or months; (6) the disappearance of the symptoms during sleep and orgasm; and (7) duration of the symptoms for more than 1 year; the disorder is lifelong and chronic. Confirmatory but not essential for the diagnosis are coprolalia, coprolagnia, echolalia, and echopraxia. Frequent concomitants of the disorder, but not essential for the diagnosis, are a history of hyperactivity or perceptual problems in childhood or organic stigmata in adulthood, abnormal (nonspecific) electroencephalograms, soft signs of neurological abnormality, and subtle signs of organic dysfunction on psychological testing.

Although the literature suggests that patients with Tourette's disorder have an underlying psychotic process, formal studies do not support

TABLE III
DIAGNOSTIC CRITERIA FOR TOURETTE'S DISORDER*

A. Age at onset between 2 and 15 years.

B. Presence of recurrent, involuntary, repetitive, rapid, purposeless motor movements affecting multiple muscle groups.

C. Multiple vocal tics.

D. Ability to suppress movements voluntarily for minutes to hours.

E. Variations in the intensity of the symptoms over weeks or months.

F. Duration of more than 1 year.

* From American Psychiatric Association: *Diagnostic and Statistical Manual of Mental Disorders*, ed 3. American Psychiatric Association, Washington, DC, 1980. Used with permission.

this concept. Patients with this syndrome do not differ from normal control groups regarding the incidence of schizophrenia and other psychoses.

Patients with Tourette's disorder may have serious emotional problems and difficulty in coping. It is difficult to assess how much these problems are a consequence of their illness, and how much they are caused by subtle central nervous system difficulties that have been present since early life. It is unlikely that such emotional problems are the cause of the disorder. Several studies noted that some patients make good adjustments and show little evidence of psychological problems, despite the presence of a severe chronic illness.

### Differential Diagnosis

Tourette's disorder must be differentiated from various diseases of the central nervous system, schizophrenia and other psychiatric disorders, and the various tic disorders.

### Treatment

Haloperidol (Haldol) is generally acknowledged to be the drug of choice in the treatment of this disorder. Psychotherapy may help the patient cope with his or her illness, but is ineffective as a primary treatment modality. Behavioral therapy has been successful in minimizing some of the symptoms.

An initial daily average dosage is 0.25 mg of haloperidol and 0.5 mg of benztropine mesylate (Cogentin) is given at bedtime. Cogentin is used initially to prevent the occurrence of acute dystonia, which occurs largely in the first 2 weeks of treatment. Cogentin, 0.5 mg a day, will prevent dystonia in most patients. Patients should be advised of the possibility of dystonia, and should be instructed to take 1 mg if it occurs; this should control it within 60 minutes. The dosage of haloperidol is increased 0.25 mg on the fifth day if there is inadequate effect on symptoms. The dosage should be increased 0.25 mg every fifth day until one of three possibilities occurs: The symptoms decrease 70 to 90 percent without side effects; side effects occur with symptomatic benefit; or symptoms decrease, and side effects occur at the same time. The most common response is for the symptoms to begin to decrease with the occurrence of side effects. The dosage may vary from 2 to 40 mg. Because a method of measuring blood levels is not yet available, the correct dosage must be determined clinically. A new drug treatment with pimozide is currently under investigation.

### Other Stereotyped Movement Disorders

### Head Banging

**Definition.** Head banging is characterized by repetitive movement marked by a definite rhythm and monotonous continuity. The head is struck rhythmically against the head board, side railing of the crib, or on other objects.

It is useful to distinguish between autoerotic head banging and tantrum head banging. With the autoerotic head banger, the child's head banging consists of knocking his or her head against a hard surface in a vigorous, noisy, absorbing, rhythmic manner. The child finally exhausts himself and falls asleep. This type of head banging may begin between the ages of 6 and 12 months and continue into latency; it is often associated with severe ego disturbances or developmental disability. It may be seen in association with other self-stimulating activities, such as thumb sucking, rocking, tongue chewing, hair twirling, crib biting, and pica.

Tantrum head banging begins about the time that the child is able to talk. When frustrated, the child throws himself on the ground, arms and legs extended, thrashing, kicking, and banging his head vigorously. Tantrum head banging often results in secondary gains, which may perpetuate the pattern.

**Epidemiology.** In a study of 130 children with rhythmic patterns, about 5 percent more boys than girls were noted. With some of the children, the rhythmic movements were transitory; with others, the movements continued for months or years.

**Etiology.** Head banging has been theorized to be: The result of an insufficient opportunity for physical expression; associated with maternal deprivation; associated with conditions of material neglect; a way to express and relieve tension and anxiety; and a primitive defensive maneuver, aimed at providing the child with immediate gratification.

**Clinical Features.** Four characteristic positions are usually assumed by the patient: on hands and knees, sitting prone, standing, or kneeling.

Most head bangers have shown other evidence of using body rhythmic patterns as a tension release or as self-gratifying behavior. By 2 to 3 months, the infant may rock his head or suck his thumb. With maturation and increased cephalocaudal motor control, head banging may begin.

Many children eventually decide to conform to the wishes of their parents; others substitute another pattern or rhythmic activity, such as rhythmic toe curling, tooth grinding, ear pulling, finger tapping, nose rubbing, and skin scratching. Some develop stereotyped play patterns.

**Diagnosis.** The diagnosis is based on clinical observations. Because head banging may be seen in mentally retarded and other developmentally disabled children, studies should be done to determine whether such a condition exists. Schizophrenic children may spend hours in rhythmic body play. The presence or absence of such a psychotic process should be explored.

Spasmus nutans is an uncommon form of increased motility found in infants after the age of 3 or 4 months. This syndrome is characterized by a nodding spasm and gyrospasm or head rolling, accompanied by nystagmus. Initially, the clinical picture may seem to be head banging, but once the pattern is fully developed, the diagnosis is apparent.

**Treatment.** Increased contact with the child by his or her mother is the treatment of choice. Unfortunately, this approach often fails because mothers of head bangers are often unable to carry out the recommendation. Counseling or therapy with the mother may make her more available to her child. An alternative proposal abandons the concept of treatment, and recommends that the mother find a soft place for her child to bang his or her head.

If mothers are able to pick up a head banger and hold the child for a long enough period of time, the head banging disappears.

### Rocking

**Definition.** Body rocking is characterized by a slow, rhythmic, backward-and-forward swaying of the trunk from the hips, usually while in a sitting position. At times, the rocking is so violent that the child's bed is moved from one side of the room to the other. It may be accompanied by low humming or crooning noises. Some children accelerate the tempo of rocking to a peak of activity, and then decelerate slowly to a calmer pace. These movements are most common in infancy and early childhood, but may persist into adult life. Although such rhythmic habit patterns are more common with children of low intelligence and developmental disabilities, they are also seen in children of normal intelligence and functioning.

**Prevalence.** In some children rhythmic movements are transitory. In others they remain for months or years. In one major pediatric clinic population, 15 to 20 percent of the children had rocked, banged, or swayed in one form or another. Five percent more boys than girls are affected.

**Etiology.** Many explanations have been offered for rocking. The two main groups of theories relate to a developmental disorder and to a psychological basis for the behavior.

**Clinical Features.** The onset of rocking is at about 6 to 10 months of age. Often, there is a history of rhythmic body activity before onset of the rocking. Most children cease the behavior by age 4. Body rocking occurs most frequently at bedtime. Possibly, this is the time of each day when the young child most tries to obtain relaxation, comfort, and the relief of anxiety.

In children without developmental disabilities, the body rocking may, under parental pressure, be controlled; however, other rhythmic forms may appear—rhythmic toe curling, tooth grinding, ear pulling, finger tapping, nose rubbing, skin scratching.

**Differential Diagnosis.** Rocking can be distinguished from tics in that rocking consists of voluntary movements, and it is not spasmodic. Unlike children with a tic disorder, children who rock are not distressed by the symptom; they seem to enjoy the repetitive activities.

Because body rocking is more prevalent among children with mental retardation, perceptual impairments, and other developmental disorders than in otherwise normal children, underlying conditions must be sought.

**Treatment.** Rocking may be seen as a normal or functional symptom. When such behavior is annoying or has reached symptom proportions, several approaches have been tried to stop the behavior. None has been fully successful.

Perhaps the first step in treatment is to understand what underlying developmental, neurological, or psychological issues are operating within the child. Family and other environmental stresses should be noted. Treatment efforts may then be directed toward the underlying difficulties.

### REFERENCES

Cohen D J, Detlor J, Shaywitz B A, Leokman J: Interaction of biological and psychological factors in the natural history of Tourette syndrome: A paradigm for childhood neuropsychiatric disorders. In *Gilles de la Tourette Syndrome*, A J Friedhoff, T N Chase, editors. Raven Press, New York, 1982.

Comings D E, Comings B G: Syndrome and attention deficit disorder with hyperactivity: Are they genetically related? J Am Acad Child Psychiatry 23: 138, 1984.

Kidd K K, Prasoff B A, Cohen D J: The familial pattern of Gilles de la Tourette syndrome. Arch Gen Psychiatry 37: 1336, 1980.

Shapiro A K, Shapiro E: The treatment and etiology of tics and Tourette syndrome. Compr Psychiatry 22: 193, 1981.

Shapiro A K, Shapiro E: Tourette syndrome: History and present status. In *Gilles de la Tourette Syndrome*, A J Friedhoff, T N Chase, editors. Raven Press, New York, 1982.

Shapiro A K, Shapiro E S, Bruun R D, Sweet R D:

*Gilles de la Tourette Syndrome*. Raven Press, New York, 1978.

Shapiro A K, Shapiro E S, Eisenkraft G J: Treatment of Gilles de la Tourette syndrome with pimozide. Am J Psychiatry *140:* 1183, 1983.

Silver L B, Brunstetter R W: Stereotyped movement disorders. In *Comprehensive Textbook of Psychiatry*, ed 4. H I Kaplan, B J Sadock, editors, p 1711. Williams & Wilkins, Baltimore, 1985.

Turpin G, Powell G E: Effects of massed practice and cue-controlled relaxation on tic frequency in Gilles de la Tourette's syndrome. Behav Res Ther *22:* 165, 1984.

# 34.2 SPEECH DISORDERS

## Stuttering

### Definition

Stuttering is a disturbance of rhythm and fluency of speech by an intermittent blocking, a convulsive repetition, or a prolongation of sounds, syllables, words, phrases, or posture of the speech organ. It is believed to be due to tonic and clonic spasms involving respiration, phonation, and articulation. Associated signs—such as eye blinks, tics, tremors of the lips or jaws, and jerking of the head—may also be noted; these signs are considered to be reflective of effort or tension.

The term stammering is considered synonymous with stuttering.

### Epidemiology

About 1 percent of the population are stutterers. The incidence is slightly higher in Europe. About half of all stutterers are children. The incidence of stuttering appears to vary markedly in different cultures. In many primitive societies, it is not seen. There is consistent evidence that the cultures in which relatively large numbers of stutterers are seen are those that are characterized by competitive pressures. In Western cultures, stuttering appears to be more common in certain socioeconomic levels, especially those marked by upward mobility, than in others.

Stuttering is noted more frequently and persists longer in boys than in girls; this ratio increases with age. The ratio of boys to girls appears to vary between 2 to 1 and 5 to 1. Most studies report the ratio of 4 to 1, males to females.

### Etiology

Many theories relate to the cause of stuttering. These theories overlap to interrelate, but they can be grouped into three broad categories: (1) theories related to a conceptual model to explain the stuttering block, (2) theories related to conditions under which the disorder has its onset, and (3) theories that shift the frame of reference to new conceptual orientations.

**Stuttering Block.** Theories related to the stuttering block fall into three groups—genogenic, psychogenic, and semantogenic.

The basic premise in the genogenic models is that the stutterer is biologically different from the nonstutterer. An example is the theory of cerebral dominance, which states that children are predisposed to stutter by a conflict between the two halves of the cerebrum for control of the activity of the speech organs. The current consensus is that there may be some sort of constitutional predisposition toward stuttering, but that environmental stresses work in conjunction with this somatic variant to produce stuttering.

Most psychogenic theories emphasize obsessive-compulsive mechanisms and a variety of psychosocial factors, such as a dysfunctional family. Stuttering is seen as a neurosis caused by the persistence into later life of early pregenital oral-sadistic and anal-sadistic components.

With the semantogenic theories, stuttering is seen as a learned pathological response to the mislabeling of normal early syllable and word repetitions.

**Onset.** There are three groupings—the breakdown, the repressed-need, and the anticipatory-struggle theories.

The breakdown theories view the stuttering as a momentary failure of the complicated coordinations involved in speech. Most such theories regard constitutional or organic factors—that is, the genogenic factors discussed above—as the causes of the breakdown.

The repressed-need theory is based on psychoanalytic concepts, and defines stuttering as a neurotic symptom rooted deeply in unconscious needs. Early theories suggested that stuttering satisfies oral gratifications, or reflects oral-aggressive or anal-aggressive concerns.

The theme with the anticipatory-struggle theory is that the stutterer interferes in some manner with the way he or she talks because of his or her belief in the difficulty of speech. Thus, the stutterer anticipates difficulty with speech.

**New Conceptual Orientations.** In recent years, several new approaches have been proposed to explain stuttering or to understand older theories. These approaches involve the use of learning theory interpretations and of a cybernetic model of stuttering.

*Stimulus-Response.* The stimulus-response theories of learning make use of the relatively precise language of behavior science to define the process by which stuttering is learned and maintained by identifying the motivational factors, stimulus variables, and reinforcing conditions. One of the central problems in the application of learning principles to stuttering is to explain the nature of the reinforcement that causes it to persist in the face of repeated punishment.

*Cybernetic Model.* In the cybernetic model, speech is seen as an automatic process that depends on feedback for regulation. Stuttering may be caused by a breakdown in feedback or in the sensor receptors of this feedback. The observations that stuttering is reduced by white noise, and that delayed auditory feedback produces artificial stuttering in normal speakers, support this view.

### Clinical Features

Stuttering may appear at any age, but it usually starts in childhood. In most cases, stuttering seems to have its onset between the ages of 18 months and 9 years, with peaks at onset between the ages of 2 to 3½ and 5 to 7 years. Stuttering is complex in its development; it does not suddenly happen, but occurs over a period of weeks or months. Even after it develops, stuttering may be absent during oral readings, singing, or talking to pets or inanimate objects.

Four phases in the development of stuttering have been described. These phases evolve continually and gradually.

Phase 1 occurs during the preschool period. Initially, the difficulty tends to be episodic, appearing for periods of weeks or months between long interludes of normal speech. There is a high percentage of recovery from these periods of stuttering. During this phase, the child stutters most when excited or upset, when he or she seems to have a great deal to say, or under other conditions of communicative pressure.

Phase 2 usually occurs in the elementary school years. The disorder is chronic, with few if any intervals of normal speech. The child regards himself or herself as a stutterer. In this phase, the stuttering occurs mainly on the major parts of speech—nouns, verbs, adjectives, and adverbs.

Phase 3 is usually seen after age 8, and up to adulthood. It occurs most often in late childhood and early adolescence. During this phase, the stuttering comes and goes largely in response to specific situations, such as in-class work, speaking to strangers, making purchases in stores, and using the telephone. Certain words and sounds are regarded as more difficult than others.

Phase 4 is typically seen in late adolescence and adulthood. The stutterer shows a vivid, fearful anticipation of stuttering. He or she fears words, sounds, and situations. Word substitutions and circumlocutions are common. The stutterer avoids speech situations, and shows other evidence of fear and embarrassment.

### Diagnosis

Some children pass through a period during the preschool years when speech is not fluent. It is unclear at the time whether this nonfluent pattern is part of normal speech and language development for some children, or whether it represents the initial stage in the development of stuttering. At least 40 percent of young children who stutter outgrow it. It is best to be reassuring, and to minimize any focus on the disfluency during this period.

Many efforts have been made to study the personality of the stutterer. In general, the findings have been inconsistent. There is no one personality type or form of psychological coping or emotional disorder. The results of multiple studies do not indicate that the average stutterer is a distinctly neurotic or severely maladjusted person. Most stutterers perform well within the norms on adjustment inventories. Their responses on projective tests do not show deviations from the normal or any consistent pattern.

Stutterers do show less social adjustment than do nonstutterers. Stutterers tend to have low self-esteem, to be less willing to risk failure, and to be more hostile or anxious than are nonstutterers. Data suggest that stutterers have a low threshold of autonomic arousal and behavioral rigidity of certain types.

The indication for psychotherapy should be based not on the stuttering but on the stutterer's level of emotional and social functioning. If he or she has a poor self-image or feelings of insecurity, anxiety, or depression, or if the stutterer shows evidence of an established neurotic process or other emotional disability, individual therapy may be indicated. Family therapy should also be considered if evidence of family dysfunction, family contribution to the stutterer's symptoms, or family stress, caused by trying to cope with or help the stutterer, is present.

### Differential Diagnosis

As previously noted, at least 40 percent of children who show evidence of difficulty with speech fluency in early childhood develop normal speech. These children probably should not be considered as stutterers. In spastic dysphonia, there is an abnormal pattern of breathing. In cluttering, speech is rapid and fluency breaks down.

## Treatment

The treatment of stuttering goes back to classical antiquity. The most common measures used until the end of the 19th century were distraction, suggestion, and relaxation. Demosthenes' famous use of pebbles, if the story is true, was an example of distraction. More recent approaches using distraction have included teaching the stutterer to talk in time to rhythmic movements of the arm, hand, or fingers. Stutterers have been advised to speak slowly in a sing-song or monotone. These approaches remove the stuttering only temporarily. Suggestion techniques, such as hypnosis, also stop stuttering but, again, only temporarily. Relaxation techniques are based on the premise that it is almost impossible to be relaxed and to stutter in the usual manner at the same time. Because of the lack of long-term benefits, distraction, suggestion, and relaxation approaches as such are not now in use.

Stutterers have been treated by classical psychoanalysis, analytically oriented psychotherapy, group therapy, nondirective therapy, and other varieties of psychotherapy. Although such approaches may improve the patient's self-image and level of anxiety, no form of such therapy has proved successful in producing long-term effects.

Most of the modern treatments of stuttering are based on the view that, essentially, stuttering is a learned form of behavior that is not necessarily associated with a basic neurotic personality or atypical neurology. The objective of this group of approaches has been to work directly with the speech difficulty to minimize the issues that maintain and strengthen the stuttering, to modify or decrease the severity of the stuttering by eliminating the secondary symptoms, and to encourage the stutterer to speak, even if stuttering, in a relatively easy and effortless fashion, avoiding fears and blocks.

One example of this approach is the self-therapy proposed by the Speech Foundation of America. Self-therapy is based on the premise that stuttering is not a symptom of something, but is a behavior that can be modified. The stutterer is told that he can learn to control his difficulty partly through modifying his feelings and attitudes about stuttering, and partly through modifying the deviant behaviors associated with his stuttering blocks. This approach includes desensitization, reducing the emotional reaction to and fears of stuttering, and substi-

tuting positive action to control the moment of stuttering. The basic principle is that stuttering is something one is doing, and that the stutterer can learn to change what he is doing.

Whichever therapeutic approach is used, individual and family assessments and supportive interventions may prove to be helpful. A team assessment of the total child or adolescent and his or her family should be done before any approaches to treatment are initiated.

## Elective Mutism

### Definition

Elective mutism was first reported in the German literature in 1877 by Kussmaul as aphasia voluntaria, to describe mentally sound persons who force themselves into mutism for purposes they refuse to disclose. The term elective mutism describes the behavior of children who are silent among all but a small circle of intimates. These children show no organic basis for this type of mutism. They have normal language skills and comprehend what is said; yet the behavior may persist over many years.

Children with elective mutism may show other evidence of emotional conflicts—excessive shyness, susceptibility to teasing, social isolation and withdrawal, clinging, difficulty in separating from their mothers to go to school, school phobia or refusal, other phobias, encopresis, enuresis, compulsive traits, negativism, and temper tantrums.

### Etiology

Children with elective mutism usually speak freely at home or in another environment; thus, there is no biological disability. There is a psychological inhibition of speech in selected situations. Some children seem to be disposed to develop elective mutism in the presence of early emotional or physical trauma, especially to the mouth; early hospitalization; marital conflict, usually with the affected child closely allied with one parent, usually the mother, while the other parent maintains closeness with the siblings; overprotective yet ambivalent maternal relationships, with the mother needing to control and foster dependence; and families in which silence is used between the parents to express hostility and control. Another predisposing factor can be immigration to a country in which a different language is spoken.

Some children with elective mutism show symptoms in common with neurotics. Those children appear to be either fixated or regressed to the anal stage of development. In addition, there is an intense negativistic and sadistic re-

TABLE I
DIAGNOSTIC CRITERIA FOR ELECTIVE MUTISM*

A. Continuous refusal to talk in almost all social situations, including at school.

B. Ability to comprehend spoken language and to speak.

C. Not due to another mental or physical disorder.

*From American Psychiatric Association: *Diagnostic and Statistical Manual of Mental Disorders*, ed 3. American Psychiatric Association, Washington, DC, 1980. Used with permission.

lationship toward most adults. Muteness is used as a weapon to punish people.

### Clinical Features

The primary clinical picture in elective mutism is the pervasive and persistent refusal to speak in social or school situations. Children with this disorder are able and willing to speak to selected persons, usually family or selected peers. They may communicate via gestures by nodding or shaking their head.

Onset of the mutism is usually between the ages of 3 and 5 years. Before he starts school, the child's reluctance to speak to people outside of the family may be seen as normal shyness; thus, referral often does not occur until the child starts school and his or her failure to speak to anyone is noticed by the teachers and the other children. The child's behavior in school is often in contrast to the parents' report that the child talks and plays freely at home. Most cases last a few weeks or months, but may go on for years. The disorder is rare and found in less than one percent of child guidance clinic referrals. It is more common in girls than boys.

### Diagnosis

The diagnostic criteria for elective mutism are a continuous and persistent refusal to speak in school or in other social situations, an ability to comprehend spoken language, an ability and willingness to speak to at least one person, and no clinical evidence of a mental or physical disorder that would account for the refusal to speak (see Table I).

### Treatment

Individual psychotherapy, counseling, behavior modification techniques, hypnosis, speech therapy, and family therapy have been tried with varying results.

### REFERENCES

Andrews G, Guitar B, Howie P: Meta-analysis of the effects of stuttering treatment. J Speech Hear Disord *45:* 287, 1980.

Brown J B, Lloyd H: A controlled study of children not speaking in school. J Assoc Workers Maladjusted Children, p. 49, 1975.

Fundudis T, Kolvin I, Garside R G: *Speech Retarded and Deaf Children: Their Psychological Development.* Academic Press, London, 1979.

Hayden T L: Classification of elective mutism. J Am Acad Child Psychiat *19:* 118, 1980.

Koller W C: Dysfluency (stuttering) in extrapyramidal disease. Arch Neurol *40:* 175, 1983.

Schwartz M F: *Stuttering Solved.* J. B. Lippincott, Philadelphia, 1976.

Silver L W: Speech disorders. In *Comprehensive Textbook of Psychiatry,* ed 4, H I Kaplan, B J Sadock, editors, p 1716. Williams & Wilkins, Baltimore, 1985.

Speech Foundation of America: *Self-Therapy for the Stutterer: One Approach.* Speech Foundation, Memphis, 1978.

# 35

# Other Disorders of Infancy, Childhood, and Adolescence

## 35.1 ATTACHMENT DISORDERS OF INFANCY

### Introduction

The great majority of these disturbances fall into one of two types. The first separates a normal child from his adequate mother, and the child fails to thrive because of inadequacies in the new environment and caretakers. This has been called, for example, hospitalism, institutional syndrome, anaclitic depression, and maternal deprivation. Some children with reactive attachment disorder of infancy belong to this type. In the second type, there is considered to be something so inimical in the mother-child relationship itself as to cause serious physical and psychological symptoms in the infant or child. This type has been called such names as psychosocial deprivation, nonorganic failure to thrive, and maternal deprivation syndrome, and is the type to which psychosocial dwarfism and most children with attachment disorders belong. Prerequisite to understanding these disorders are the concepts of bonding and attachment.

### Definitions

By bonding is meant the primarily unilateral attachment of the mother to her infant. This more specifically refers to physical contact (usually nude skin-to-skin) between mother and her neonate during a critical period immediately following or soon after delivery that is necessary for the development of optimal attachment of the mother to her infant. This critical period seems to coincide with the observation, first reported in 1959, that normal infants are alert for a remarkably long time immediately after birth. This quiet, relatively alert state of the infant persists for much of the first hour or longer in some cases, and appears ideal to initiate reciprocal responsivity between mother and child. During this time, the baby's eyes are open, eye contact can be made with the mother, and

the infant will usually follow the mother over a 180° range. The infant is able to respond to the environment and will turn toward and move rhythmically with the mother's voice. The baby's nursing also causes an immediate severalfold increase in prolactin secretion and stimulates oxytocin release. The latter causes uterine contraction and reduces postpartum bleeding. It has been reported that each nursing calms the mother and increases her bond to the infant. There has been some speculation these hormonal events may play a causal relation—for example, increased prolactin levels appear to be responsible for the development of the close attachment of the mother bird to her nestlings.

Following this immediate postnatal period of alertness, the infant sleeps most of the time. During the next few days, the infant is similarly alert for relatively brief periods of time—a few minutes at most.

Attachment is the quality of a bilateral, reciprocal affectionate relationship between the infant and parent, especially the mother or primary caretaker, which gradually develops during the first year of life.

John Bowlby has suggested there is an inherent tendency for an infant to attach to one person, which he called monotropy. Although there is clinical evidence that this is usually the case, the primary attachment is not necessarily with the mother, and multiple attachments can occur. Although mother and infant must spend a certain minimum amount of time interacting with each other, after this has been satisfied, it is the intensity and quality of the interaction that appear to be the most important factors in establishing attachment. Appropriate maternal responsiveness in general intensifies attachment, while apathy or indifference toward the child lessens the strength of the infant's attachment to his mother. The ability of the mother to relieve anxiety and fear in her infant also tends to increase attachment. In at least some cases, intermittent mistreatment or abuse may also strengthen attachment, and children may at times develop unusually strong attachments toward abusing parents.

The diagnosis of reactive attachment disorder of infancy appeared for the first time in 1980 in the third edition of the *Diagnostic and Statistical Manual of Mental Disorders* (DSM-III). Psychosocial dwarfism is referred to in the differential diagnosis, but specific criteria for its diagnosis are not given.

### Reactive Attachment Disorder of Infancy

DSM-III criteria for making the diagnosis of attachment disorder are given in Table I. The reader is referred to this table for a summary of the characteristics of this disorder.

### Psychosocial Dwarfism

Criteria for making the diagnosis of psychosocial dwarfism are not specifically given in DSM-III. However, it is noted that in psychosocial dwarfism, there may be "apathy, parental neglect, and disappearance of symptoms with hospitalization. However, psychosocial dwarfism generally has a later onset than reactive attachment disorder of infancy, and the failure of the infant to gain in length with little change or actual increase in weight is the major manifestation." Diagnostic criteria for classical psychosocial dwarfism are presented in Table II.

### Epidemiology

There are no specific data on prevalence, sex ratio, or familial patterns available. In many of the studies, however, there appears to be an increased incidence among the lower classes. This would be congruent with increased psychosocial deprivation, marital instability, disorganization, and economical difficulties reported in families of infants with attachment disorder. Lower social class mothers also have decreased ability to get ancillary help in childrearing, should they wish it, because of financial constraints.

It is important to remember that a woman may be a fully adequate mother for one child while another of her children may develop attachment disorder or psychosocial dwarfism.

### Etiology

#### Contribution of the Infant

Certain qualities of the infant may predispose to the development of attachment disorder because of their selective effects on specific caretakers and which result in a particular mother/

---

TABLE I
DIAGNOSTIC CRITERIA FOR REACTIVE ATTACHMENT DISORDER OF INFANCY*

A. Age at onset before 8 months.

B. Lack of the type of care that ordinarily leads to the development of affectional bonds to others, e.g., gross emotional neglect, imposed social isolation in an institution.

C. Lack of developmentally appropriate signs of social responsivity, as indicated by at least several of the following (the total number of behaviors looked for will depend on the chronological age of the child, corrected for prematurity):

    (1) Lack of visual tracking of eyes and faces by an infant more than 2 months of age;
    (2) Lack of smiling in response to faces by an infant more than 2 months of age;
    (3) Lack of visual reciprocity in an infant of more than 2 months; lack of vocal reciprocity with caretaker in an infant of more than 5 months;
    (4) Lack of alerting and turning toward caretaker's voice by an infant of more than 4 months;
    (5) Lack of spontaneous reaching for the mother by an infant of more than 4 months;
    (6) Lack of anticipatory reaching when approached to be picked up, by an infant more than 5 months of age;
    (7) Lack of participation in playful games with caretaker by an infant of more than 5 months.

D. At least three of the following:

    (1) Weak cry;
    (2) Excessive sleep;
    (3) Lack of interest in the environment;
    (4) Hypomotility;
    (5) Poor muscle tone;
    (6) Weak rooting and grasping in response to feeding attempts.

E. Weight loss or failure to gain appropriate amount of weight for age unexplainable by any physical disorder. In these cases, usually the failure to gain weight (falling weight percentile) is disproportionately greater than failure to gain length; head circumference is normal.

F. Not due to a physical disorder, mental retardation, or infantile autism.

G. The diagnosis is confirmed if the clinical picture is reversed shortly after institution of adequate caretaking, which frequently includes short-term hospitalization.

* From American Psychiatric Association: *Diagnostic and Statistical Manual of Mental Disorders*, ed 3. American Psychiatric Association, Washington, DC, 1980. Used with permission.

TABLE II
DIAGNOSTIC CRITERIA FOR CLASSICAL PSYCHOSOCIAL DWARFISM*

A. Age at onset usually between 2 and 3 years.

B. Severe retardation of growth. Marked linear growth retardation well below the third percentile for age and significantly delayed epiphysical maturation are usually present. (Although not a disqualifier, malnutrition is *not* felt to be contributory in the majority of cases.)

C. Severe disturbances in the mother(ing figure)/child dyad. (Mothers are heterogeneous regarding their psychopathologies.)

D. Emotional disturbance in the child as evidenced by some of the following:
   (1) Bizarre behavior involving abnormal acquisition and intake of food and water (e.g., polyphagia, polydipsia, gorging and vomiting, eating from garbage pails, drinking toilet water);
   (2) Apathy, withdrawal, chronic grief;
   (3) Poor peer relations;
   (4) Accident proneness, self injury, pain agnosia;
   (5) Developmental lags (e.g., psychomotor retardation and delayed language, and I.Q.'s in the borderline or retarded ranges).

E. Abnormal endocrine functioning is present in over 50% of the children (decreased growth hormone (GH) and somatomedin levels and abnormal pituitary-adrenal axis findings).

F. Not due to a physical disorder (e.g., idiopathic hypopituitarism, mental retardation, or infantile autism).

G. The diagnosis is confirmed when growth promptly begins with no medical, hormonal or psychiatric treatment following the child's removal to a new domicile or hospitalization.

\* Adapted from Green W H, et al: *J Am Acad Child Psychiatry 23:* 39, 1984.

infant mismatch. It has been hypothesized that difficult babies, e.g., with irregular rhythmicity of biological functions, negative withdrawal responses to new stimuli, very slow adaptability to changes and intense, frequently negative, moods (Alexander Thomas and Stella Chess' temperamentally difficult child) or a very lethargic, hypoactive child could prove frustrating to the caretaker.

Similarly, infants with serious sensory or physical impairments, such as blindness, deafness, or severe chronic physical illness, may require special modifications of parenting skills to satisfy their basic needs. Several studies, one of which was prospective, showed that nonorganic failure to thrive infants weighed significantly less at birth and/or had shorter gestational ages than infants who grew normally. This may be related to problems in bonding.

### Deficient or Defective Bonding

Bonding theory has resulted in an overall increased early contact between mother and neonate and a humanization of the birth process. While parents clearly can usually develop adequate attachments to their children without such early contact, hospital procedures that make the mother and father less anxious, more comfortable and increase feelings of competence in caring for the newborn baby influence positively the development of both maternal and paternal bonds. Thus, procedures or situations that enhance parental bonding would theoretically protect against the disorder while those which decrease bonding would increase vulner-

ability, e.g., a prolonged period in an incubator following premature birth.

Studies have shown that over three-quarters of mothers held their newborns over the left side of their chest or left shoulder in the days immediately following birth, regardless of their handedness. This was in contrast to mothers of prematures who had a prolonged postpartum separation. They held their infants about equally on either side. This is a piece of evidence that maternal interaction with the neonate in the immediate postnatal period appears to be selectively different from maternal-infant interaction beginning at a later time. It was hypothesized this had to do with the heart's being located on the left side and its calming influence on the infant held in close proximity to it.

### Contribution of the Caretaker

Many factors can potentially interfere with the development of attachment between the mother or primary caretaker and the infant. Only the most important will be addressed here.

**Maternal Psychopathology.** Of particular importance is a postpartum depression or a major depressive disorder so severe as to immobilize the mother and curtail mother-infant interaction, including holding, verbal and sensory stimulation, and adequate physical care and feeding. Alcohol and drug abuse may also interfere enormously with availability of the mother and the quality of her responsivity to the infant and her parenting abilities. Any parental emotional disturbances that interfere with their ability to relate to their infants may be relevant here.

**Psychodynamic Factors.** Psychodynamic factors interfering with the mother's ability to care for and relate to her infant are best determined by a probing, indepth interview by a skilled clinician, although even then some may not be apparent. These would include such factors as the mother's avoidance of her baby because it reminds her of someone she hates; her negative feelings about the gender of her child; anger at the baby's complexion or hair color; avoidance of the infant because it has a physical deformity; feeling the baby has trapped her into a marriage she despises or conversely has caused a man she loves or was dependent upon to abandon her; or resenting the loss of educational or career opportunities. These are intrapsychic conflicts that may be present in mothers even when no diagnosable psychiatric illness is present.

**Lack of Parenting Skills.** Mothering skills may be deficient because of the mother's personal upbringing, social isolation or deprivation, lack of opportunities to learn about maternal behavior, and insensitivity to the infant's cues or mental retardation. Similarly, premature parenthood with an inability to recognize obligations to respond to and care for their infant's needs and where parents' own needs take precedence over their infants' may result in markedly ineffective parenting.

### Lack of a Primary Caretaker

The disastrous effects that institutionalization or prolonged hospitalization may have on infants and young children has been studied and reviewed by René Spitz, John Bowlby, and others. This has been called hospitalism. They have emphasized the need of infants for intimate emotional involvement with their caretakers and adequate sensory stimulation for their physical well-being and resistance to infection as well as their long-term emotional health. Because of this, today, institutions assign more stable or permanent caretakers to specific infants and children, and hospitals encourage increased parental visitation and rooming in. Infants with adequate multiple caretakers do not develop attachment disorders.

### Clinical Description

The clinical presentation of infants and young children is characterized by absent, delayed, or distorted emotional and social development and failure to thrive. The picture then is a deviation from expected developmental norms and varies considerably according to the particular infant's or child's chronological age. In those cases where the infant was born prematurely, chronological age should be corrected for. Likewise, if a child is retarded, developmental expectations should be based on the child's mental age, rather than chronological age.

### Physical Appearance and Characteristics of the Infant

Hypokinesis, dullness, listlessness, or apathy with a poverty of spontaneous activity are usually seen. The children look sad, unhappy, joyless, or miserable. Some infants also appear frightened and an appearance of watchfulness or radar-like gaze has been described. Despite this, these children may exhibit delayed responsiveness to a stimulus that would elicit fright or withdrawal in a normal child.

Some older infants who are psychosocially deprived continue to exhibit infantile postures. They may hold their arms in a characteristic position with elbows flexed to a right angle or more, the upper arm held close to the body but rotated outward and the hands pronated and held up in front of the chest or behind the head. Normally, this posture is not seen in infants over 4 to 5 months of age.

Most of the children appear significantly malnourished, and many have characteristically protruding abdomens (see Figs. 1 and 2). Occasionally, foul-smelling, celiac-like stools are reported. In unusually severe cases, a clinical picture of marasmus may appear (see Fig. 3). Weight is often below the third percentile and markedly below appropriate weight for height. If serial weights are available, it may be noted that weight percentiles have progressively decreased because of actual weight loss or a failure to gain weight as height increases. If strict criteria for weight gain in infants are adhered to, failure to thrive may become evident within the first month as indicated by the infant's failing to regain birthweight by day 14 and by failing to average a weight gain of 18.7 gm/day (0.66 oz/day) from days 15 to 60. Head circumference is usually normal for age. Poor muscle tone may be present. The skin may be colder and more pale or mottled than the normal child's. Laboratory values are usually within normal limits except those abnormal findings coincident with malnutrition, dehydration, or intercurrent illness. Bone age is usually retarded. Growth hormone levels are usually normal or elevated, and pituitary functioning is normal. This is in agreement with suggestions that growth failure in these children is secondary to caloric deprivation and malnutrition. Both physical improvement of the child and concomitant weight gain usually occur rapidly following hospitalization.

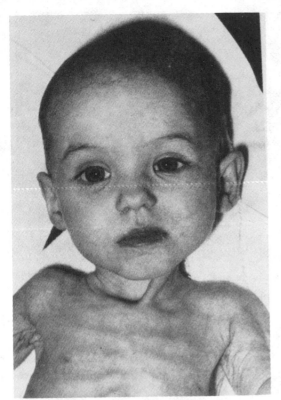

FIGURE 1. A 6-month-old infant with failure to thrive secondary to maternal rejection and caloric deprivation. (Reproduced with permission from Davis J A, Dobbing J, editors: *Scientific Foundations of Paediatrics*, ed 1. William Heinemann Medical Books, Philadelphia, 1974.)

## Socioemotional Characteristics of the Infant/Child

These infants lack age-appropriate behaviors in their social interactions with their caretakers that are also present with the examiner. These behaviors are usually characterized by the infant's lack of spontaneous activity and marked diminution of both social initiative toward others and/or a lack of reciprocity in response to the caretaking adult or examiner. There may be relative indifference shown by both mother and child to their initial separation upon hospitalization or termination of subsequent visits. Frequently, these children show none of the normal upset, fretting, or protest about hospitalization. Rapid or gradual improvement of interest in and relatedness to caretakers in the hospital usually occurs.

Some of these children have increased autostimulatory behaviors, such as rocking, head banging, rumination, and picking at their skin. Others show a decreased interest in their own bodies, and infants less than 6 months of age

may appear to derive no pleasure from such common activities as sucking their thumbs or being tickled playfully. Older infants usually show a decreased interest in the environment and minimal curiosity about their surroundings or exploratory behavior. They may show little interest in playing with toys even if encouraged.

### Differential Diagnosis

Attachment disorders, if particularly severe, can progress to a fatal conclusion. Yet, diagnosis and intervention can, in most cases, completely reverse the clinical picture and result in a child emotionally and physically within the bounds of normalcy. Thus, a rapid and correct differential diagnosis of the infant is of exceptional importance.

### Organic Failure to Thrive

A complete pediatric examination and evaluation is necessary both to identify and treat any intercurrent illnesses to which these children are more vulnerable because of their relatively poor physical health and to eliminate any fail-

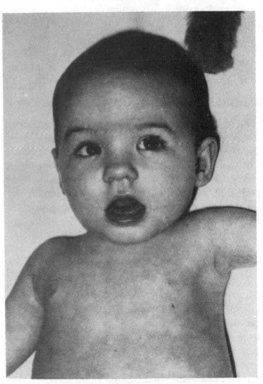

FIGURE 2. The same infant (shown in Figure 1) 3 weeks after hospitalization and showing rapid weight gain on normal full feedings. (Reproduced with permission from Davis J A, Dobbing J, editors: *Scientific Foundations of Paediatrics*, ed 1. William Heinemann Medical Books, Philadelphia, 1974.)

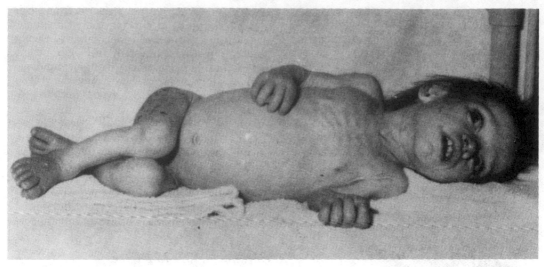

FIGURE 3.   Marasmus precipitated by a mild chest infection in an infant with failure to thrive secondary to maternal deprivation. (Reproduced with permission from Davis J A, Dobbing J, editors: *Scientific Foundations of Paediatrics*, ed 1. William Heinemann Medical Books, Philadelphia, 1974.

ures to thrive of organic etiology. In infants and young children hospitalized for failure to thrive in several series, approximately 40 to 50% had psychosocial (environmental) deprivation and had no evidence of organic disease. Of special relevance, however, is the finding that in 20 to 25% of these children, it was due to a combination of both organic and psychosocial factors.

### Mental Retardation

Failure to thrive does not occur in mentally retarded children unless organic disease or a reactive attachment disorder is also present. Thus, although retarded infants and children may develop more slowly than the normal child, a similar sequence of physical and emotional development should occur that is appropriate for the child's mental rather than chronological age.

### Infantile Autism

Autistic children, 75% of whom are also mentally retarded, usually show no failure to thrive. Although there is a pervasive lack of responsiveness to people, including the parents, these children show, in addition, distortions in behavior that are not normal for children of any developmental stage. Development is also characteristically uneven. Most of these children are not apathetic or listless, and their gross motor development is close to normal or the least affected. There may be unusual or preferential interest in inanimate objects and bizarre responses to environmental stimuli rather than apathy and withdrawal. Infantile autism is discussed in detail in Chapter 31, Pervasive Developmental Disorders and Childhood Schizophrenia.

### Major Affective Episode

DSM-III specifically recommends considering the diagnosis of major depressive episode if a picture clinically similar to attachment disorder develops after 8 months of age. Criteria for this diagnosis in children under 6 years of age differ from those in older children and adults and are given in Table III. The primary differentiating feature would be a history of normal development and attachment behavior up to at least the age of 8 months. The rationale for diagnosing an 8-month-old as major depressive episode and a 7-month-old as attachment disorder is not clear.

### Sensory Deficits

If sensory deficits are present, caretakers may need to be instructed how to give appropriate stimulation and how to facilitate communication. For example, increased kinesthetic and tactile stimulation may be necessary to compensate for decreased visual communication in blind children. This will usually ameliorate any minor attachment disturbances secondary to the sensory impairments.

### Prognosis

Prognosis and outcome are highly dependent upon the severity of the inadequacy in care-

TABLE III
DIAGNOSTIC CRITERIA FOR A MAJOR AFFECTIVE EPISODE IN CHILDREN UNDER SIX YEARS OF AGE*

A. Dysphoric mood which may have to be inferred from a persistently sad facial expression.

B. At least three of the following symptoms present nearly every day for a period of at least 2 weeks:
(1) Poor appetite or significant weight loss or increased appetitie or significant weight gain or failure to make expected weight gains;
(2) Insomnia or hypersomnia;
(3) Psychomotor agitation or retardation or hypoactivity;
(4) Loss of interest or pleasure in usual activities or signs of apathy.

C. Neither bizarre behavior nor preoccupation with a mood-incongruent delusion or hallucination is present before or after the major depressive episode.

D. Schizophrenia, schizophreniform disorder or a paranoid disorder is not present.

E. It is not due to any organic mental disorder or uncomplicated bereavement.

* Adapted from American Psychiatric Association: *Diagnostic and Statistical Manual of Mental Disorders*, ed 3. American Psychiatric Association, Washington, DC, 1980.

taking, the length of time spent in the inimical environment, and the adequacy of corrective measures if the infant remains in or returns home or the new environment and caretakers if the infant is placed elsewhere. Outcomes range from the extreme of death on the one hand to a completely normal development on the other.

There is supporting evidence that with early, completely adequate intervention, often implying a move to a new environment and caretaker, the disorder can be completely reversed. In the usual case, however, the child returns to his family of origin and remains at considerable risk for adverse sequelae. Physical recovery is usually more complete than is emotional or educational. In general, the longer the child stays in the inimical environment without adequate intervention, the worse the prognosis.

### Treatment

Certain general principles of treatment can be enumerated. Often the first decision is whether to hospitalize a child or attempt treatment while the child remains in the home. Usually, the severity of the physical and emotional state of the child will determine this, but occasionally, it may be the state of the caretaker, e.g., a mother who is literally too depressed to care for her infant.

The malnutrition that is usually present must be treated and monitored closely. A greater than normal caloric intake may be required to provide the nutrition and energy necessary for catch-up growth during which growth rates up to 15 times those of normal children their age and 5 times those of normal children of their weight have been recorded. Any intercurrent physical illnesses should be appropriately treated as well.

Intensive sensory and emotional stimulation have been shown to be the sine qua non for inducing psychological recovery in the infant. They must, however, be titrated to the level the specific patient can tolerate and then appropriately modified as the child's capacities to receive attention and stimuli increase. Initially, the infant may be relatively unresponsive and have a poor appetite and reject overtures from the caretaker. However, with improvement, appetite often becomes voracious, and indiscriminate clinging to anyone available may occur.

Concomitantly, with the physical and psychological treatment of the infant, the treatment team must begin to alter the unsatisfactory relationship between caretakers and infant. This will require extensive and intensive long-term psychological therapy with the mother or, in intact households, both parents whenever possible.

### Psychosocial Dwarfism

After infancy and the first year or two of life, growth failure with psychosocial deprivation seen in early childhood (see Fig. 4) may appear.

Most psychosocial dwarfs come to pediatric and/or endocrinologic attention for the first time at ages 2 to 3 or older. While the majority are clearly not malnourished, there are a few who are. And, indeed, the most characteristic abnormal behaviors of PSD revolve around abnormal acquisition and ingestion of food and fluids. Thus, polyphagia and polydipsia are common. Bizarre and voracious appetites with eating of animal foods, jars of condiments, garbage, and drinking of dishwater or water from toilets or rainpuddles are commonly reported.

Other behavioral manifestations include apathy, withdrawal, irritability, and temper tantrums. Some children appear sad or depressed, and sleeping disorders may be present. Poor peer relationships and social indifference are common. While decreased responsivity to pain, self injury, and accident proneness have been reported, some of this could be explained by the increased incidence of child abuse also found in

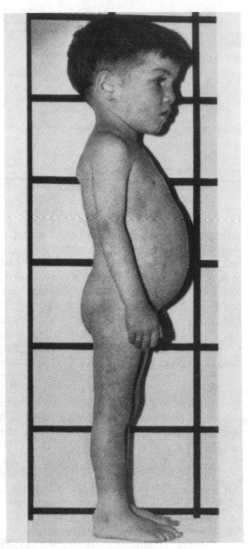

FIGURE 4. A psychosocial dwarf aged 5 years 1 month. Height 89 cm (35 inches). Mean height age 2 years 4 months. Note protuberant abdomen, short legs, normal-sized head, and "infantile" bodily proportions. (Reproduced with permission from Davis J A, Dobbing J, editors: *Scientific Foundations of Paediatrics*, ed 1. William Heinemann Medical Books, Philadelphia, 1974.)

these children. Many have physical and emotional developmental lags, and IQ's frequently fall in the borderline or mildly retarded ranges.

A large majority of psychosocial dwarfs have abnormally low fasting growth hormone (GH) levels at the time of hospitalization. GH levels are also low in about 50 percent of cases following insulin-induced hypoglycemia if measured before growth acceleration begins. GH levels usually normalize within a few days following removal from the inimical psychosocial environ-

ment; the rapidity of this precludes malnutrition's being causative.

In the few cases where somatomedin levels were reported, they were always low. Various, but inconsistent, abnormal functionings of the pituitary-adrenal axis have also been reported. All hormonal abnormalities normalize over time with no specific medical or hormonal treatment. Other abnormal findings include serum lipid abnormalities different from controls and which correlate with parental visits to the hospitalized child.

### Treatment

There is rapid and remarkable recovery of abnormal endocrine and laboratory abnormalities upon change of domicile. Growth usually begins within a few days and often accelerates to catch-up growth rates. There is amelioration of behavioral symptoms although sometimes some abnormalities persist. An increase in IQ has also been reported.

Upon returning home, an alarming number of these children experience a rapid deceleration in growth rate and require rehospitalization or removal from the home. Because of this, there is an almost unanimous consensus among workers in the area that removal to a completely new environment, which at times may mean freeing the child for adoption, is the treatment of choice. Intensive intervention with parents and close monitoring of the child's condition are essential if the child is to return home. Drugs that increase GH secretion, e.g., the $\beta$-adrenergic blocking agent propranolol may eventually prove to be useful as adjunct in the treatment, particularly if the child must remain in a suboptimal environment.

### REFERENCES

Ainsworth M D S: The development of infant-mother attachment. In *Review of Child Development Research*, Vol 3, B M Caldwell, H N Ricciuti, editors, p 1. University of Chicago Press, Chicago, 1973.

Bowlby J: Attachment and Loss, Vol I, II & III. Basic Books, New York, 1969, 1973, 1980.

Campbell M, Green W H, Caplan R, David R: Psychiatry and endocrinology in children: Early infantile autism and psychosocial dwarfism. In *Handbook of Psychiatry and Endocrinology*, P J V Beumont, G D Burrows, editors, p 15. Elsevier Biomedical Press, Amsterdam, 1982.

Campos J J, Barrett K C, Lamb M E, Goldsmith H H, Stonborg C: Socioemotional development. In *Handbook of Child Psychology*, ed 4, Vol II, P H Mussen, editor, p 783. John Wiley & Sons, New York, 1983.

Green W H: Attachment disorders of infancy and early childhood. In *Comprehensive Textbook of Psychiatry*, ed 4, H I Kaplan, B J Sadock, editors, p 1722. Williams & Wilkins, Baltimore, 1985.

Green W H, Campbell M, David R: Psychosocial

dwarfism: A critial review of the evidence. J Am Acad Child Psychiat 23: 39, 1984.

Greenspan S I: *Psychopathology and Adaptation in Infancy and Early Childhood: Principles of Clinical Diagnosis and Preventive Intervention.* International Universities Press, New York, 1981.

Klaus M H, Kennell J H: *Parent-Infant Bonding,* ed 2. C. V. Mosby, St. Louis, 1982.

Osofsky J D, editor: *Handbook of Infant Development.* John Wiley & Sons, New York, 1979.

Rutter M: *Maternal Deprivation Reassessed,* ed 2. Penguin Books, Middlesex, England, 1981.

Taylor P M, editor: *Parent-Infant Relationships.* Grune & Stratton, New York, 1980.

# 35.2 EATING DISORDERS

## Introduction

The eating disorders include bulimia, pica, rumination, and anorexia nervosa. They are characterized by a conspicuous disturbance in eating behavior. Bulimia usually has a chronic, remitting course, whereas the other three disorders most often have a single episode. Anorexia and rumination may have a gradually deteriorating course, leading to death. No familial pattern is known for the eating disorders except anorexia nervosa, which occurs with a higher prevalence in relatives of the afflicted patient than in the general population. Anorexia nervosa and bulimia occur predominantly in females, whereas pica and rumination have no sex preference. The onset of anorexia nervosa and bulimia occurs in adolescence or early adulthood. The onset of rumination is usually in infancy. Pica occurs predominantly in early childhood, but can begin during pregnancy.

The eating disorders must be distinguished from peculiar eating behavior in patients with somatization disorders, affective disorders, and schizophrenic disorders.

## Bulimia

### Definition

Bulimia is an episodic, uncontrolled, compulsive, rapid ingestion of large quantities of food over a short period of time (binge eating). Physical discomfort, such as abdominal pain or feelings of nausea, terminates the bulimic episode, which is followed by feelings of guilt, depression, or self-disgust. A few current reports indicate that bulimia may be far more prevalent, especially in young women, than previously was thought. The official definition of bulimia from DSM-III is presented in Table I.

### Epidemiology and Prevalence

No epidemiological survey has been done of this disorder. The prevalence is not known but appears to be common in adolescents and young adults.

Bulimia occurs predominantly in adolescent females and young women. No studies investigating a familial pattern in this disorder have been reported to date, but obesity may be found in other family members.

### Etiology

There is no substantive evidence to support any causative hypothesis for this disorder.

### Clinical Features

The onset of the illness is usually in adolescence or early adult life. The usual course is chronic over a period of many years, with occasional remission. Bulimia is seldom incapacitating, except in a few persons who spend their entire day in binge eating and self-induced vom-

TABLE I
DIAGNOSTIC CRITERIA FOR BULIMIA*

A. Recurrent episodes of binge eating (rapid consumption of a large amount of food in a discrete period of time, usually less than 2 hours).

B. At least three of the following:
   (1) Consumption of high-caloric, easily ingested food during a binge
   (2) Inconspicuous eating during a binge
   (3) Termination of such eating episodes by abdominal pain, sleep, social interruption, or self-induced vomiting
   (4) Repeated attempts to lose weight by severely restrictive diets, self-induced vomiting, or use of catharthics or diuretics
   (5) Frequent weight fluctuations greater than 10 pounds due to alternating binges and fasts

C. Awareness that the eating pattern is abnormal and fear of not being able to stop eating voluntarily.

D. Depressed mood and self-deprecating thoughts following eating binges.

E. The bulimic episodes are not due to anorexia nervosa or any known physical disorder.

* From American Psychiatric Association: *Diagnostic and Statistical Manual of Mental Disorders,* ed 3. American Psychiatric Association, Washington, DC, 1980. Used with permission.

iting. Electrolyte imbalance and dehydration can occur in persons who vomit excessively.

Definite precipitating factors are unknown, but the onset of binge eating often occurs during the senior year in high school, when the patient is having to make a decision about leaving home, getting a job, or going on to further schooling.

Bulimics are concerned about their body image and their appearance, they worry about how others see them, they are concerned about sexual attractiveness, and they fear getting obese. During a binge, these patients eat food that is sweet, high in calories, generally of smooth texture or soft, such as cakes or pastry. The binge episodes are usually planned, and the food is eaten secretly, rapidly, and sometimes not even chewed.

Once the binge starts, the patient may be unable to stop until vomiting is induced. The patient feels better after having vomited, and abdominal fullness or pain is relieved. The patient may then begin to binge again or may terminate bingeing temporarily. Depression often follows the episode, which has been called post-binge anguish.

The essential and associated clinical features of bulimia are summarized in Table II.

TABLE II
CLINICAL FEATURES OF BULIMIA*

*Essential features that are always present:*
1. Episodic pattern of binge eating—rapid consumption of a large amunt of food in a discrete period of time, usually less than 2 hours.
2. Fear of not being able to stop eating voluntarily.
3. Awareness of the eating disorder and great concern about weight demonstrated by repeated attempts to control weight by diet, vomiting, or use of cathartics.
4. Food eaten as inconspicuously as possible or secretly during a binge; rapid eating with little chewing; consumption of high-caloric, sweet-tasting food with a texture that facilitates rapid eating.
5. Termination of a binge with abdominal pain, sleep, social interruption, or induced vomiting.
6. Disparaging self-criticism and depressive mood after episodes of binge eating.
7. Dieting, often quite severe between episodes of bingeing.
8. Weight fluctuations within a range of mildly underweight to mildly overweight.

*Associated features that are commonly but not invariably present:*
1. History of intermittent substance abuse; substances most frequently abused: barbiturates, amphetamines, alcohol.
2. Disturbed sexual adjustment ranging from promiscuity to a restricted sexual life.
3. Manifest concern with body image and emphasis on appearance, with often intense concern as to how others see and react to the patient.

* Adapted from American Psychiatric Association: *Diagnostic and Statistical Manual of Mental Disorders,* ed 3. American Psychiatric Association, Washington, DC, 1980.

### Diagnosis

Bulimic episodes may occur in anorexia nervosa; but bulimia is not due to anorexia nervosa. A diagnosis of bulimia cannot be made if anorexia nervosa is present, but episodic bulimic symptoms can occur in anorexia nervosa. If a patient meets all the criteria for the diagnosis of anorexia nervosa, then a diagnosis of anorexia nervosa should be given. Severe weight loss does not occur in bulimia, and amenorrhea seldom occurs. These two symptoms are necessary for the diagnosis of anorexia nervosa.

Bulimia should not be diagnosed if the patient meets positive criteria for schizophrenia. It is necessary to ascertain that the patient has no neurological disease state, such as epileptic-equivalent seizures, central nervous system tumors, Klüver-Bucy-like syndromes, and Kleine-Levin syndrome. The pathological features manifested by the Klüver-Bucy syndrome are visual agnosia, compulsive licking and biting, examination of objects by the mouth, inability to ignore any stimulus, placidity, altered sexual behavior (hypersexuality), and altered dietary habits, especially hyperphagia. This syndrome is exceedingly rare, and is unlikely to cause a problem in differential diagnosis. Kleine-Levin syndrome consists of periodic hypersomnia, lasting for periods of 2 to 3 weeks, and hyperphagia. As in bulimia, the onset is usually during adolescence, but this syndrome has a male predominance.

### Treatment

There is a paucity of published information about the treatment of bulimia. The treatment of bulimia in obese patients by psychotherapy is frequently stormy and always prolonged, although some obese bulimics who had prolonged psychotherapy did surprisingly well. Effective positive reinforcement, informational feedback, and contingency contracting with bulimic women with anorexia nervosa have been reported. A program of desensitization to the thoughts and feelings a bulimic patient has just before binge eating, in conjunction with a behavioral contract, may be a promising approach to the treatment of bulimia.

Several investigators have reported good results with imipramine. Pharmacotherapy requires further study.

## Pica

### Definition

Pica is the persistent ingestion of nonnutritive substances, such as dirt, clay, plaster, and paper. The consequences of pica lead poisoning, in testinal obstruction, intestinal parasites, and other medical complications—can be exceedingly detrimental to the patient.

DSM-III gives the diagnostic criteria for pica as evidence of regular eating of non-nutritive substance(s) for at least 1 month and not due to another mental disorder. (see Table III).

### Epidemiology and Prevalence

Of 200 randomly selected pregnant patients in an obstetrical service in Georgia, it was found that geophagia (eating earth) was present in 55 percent of the patients; but it is a rare disease. There is a slight preponderance of black children with pica compared with white children. The prevalence of pica and the range of articles ingested decrease with increasing age. Investigators have reported that pica affects both sexes equally, and age of onset can be from 12 to 24 months or even earlier. It is rare in adults.

Some studies have found that the siblings of children with pica were more likely to have pica than are the siblings of unaffected children.

### Etiology

There are two commonly expounded theories about the causes of pica. One states that a specific nutritional deficit is present in the patient, and this deficit causes the indiscriminate ingestion of nonnutritive substances. The other theory postulates that the inadequate relationship with the patient's mother produces unmet oral needs, which are expressed in the persistent search for inedible substances. Poor supervision and neglect of the child are often found.

### Clinical Features, Course, and Prognosis

Generally, the practice of eating nonedible substances is regarded as abnormal after the age of 12 months. Pica occurs most frequently between the ages of 12 to 24 months and 6 years, but it can occur in any age group. Typically, young children ingest paint, plaster, string, hair, and cloth; older children have access to dirt, animal feces, stones, and paper.

Different forms of pica with varying complications and outcomes have been described. Lead poisoning is a major hazard for children who eat plaster and can result in mental retardation.

Parasitic infestations are common in children who eat contaminated soil. Geophagia has been associated with anemia and zinc deficiency. Amylophagia—the ingestion of large quantities of starch, such as Argo starch—has been associated with severe iron deficiency anemia. Rare forms of pica—such as trichophagia (hair ingestion) and stone or gravel ingestion (lithophagia)—have been associated with intestinal obstruction, such as hair-ball tumors. Low serum iron levels have been found in patients who have pagophagia, or who ingest large amounts of ice. A life-threatening hyperkalemia and chronic renal failure were described in five patients who had geophagia. In summary, the deleterious effects of pica are related to the type and the amount of ingested materials.

The pica of childhood usually remits by the time of adolescence. The pica associated with pregnancy remits with the termination of the pregnancy.

### Diagnosis

Eating nonnutritional substances may be a symptom of infantile autism or a schizophrenic disorder. In such instances, pica should not be given as an additional diagnosis.

### Treatment

Pica may be treated from several approaches—environmental, behavioral, and directive guidance or family counseling. For children who are eating lead plaster, it is obviously necessary to do some altering of the physical environment. In some patients, correction of an iron or zinc deficiency has resulted in the elimination of pica behavior. Several behavior therapy techniques have been effective in stopping pica. Aversion therapy has consisted of using mild electric shock, unpleasant noise, or an emetic drug. Positive reinforcement, such as social recognition or object rewards, has been effective, but it usually produces slower results compared with aversion therapy. Behavior shaping, having the child imitate the preferred behavior from a model, also produces behavioral changes more slowly than do negative reinforcements. Involving parents in a positive reinforcement behavior therapy program may allow the

TABLE III
DIAGNOSTIC CRITERIA FOR PICA*

A. Repeated eating of a nonnutritive substance for at least 1 month.

B. Not due to another mental disorder, such as infantile autism or schizophrenia, or a physical disorder, such as Kleine-Levin syndrome.

*From American Psychiatric Association: *Diagnostic and Statistical Manual of Mental Disorders*, ed 3. American Psychiatric Association, Washington, DC, 1980. Used with permission.

children to get attention that was previously lacking from their parents.

An overcorrection treatment approach has been advocated. In this treatment approach, the patient is educated to accept responsibility for misbehavior through restitutional overcorrection procedures that require the patient to restore the disturbed situation to a vastly improved state, and to practice appropriate modes of responding in the situations in which the patient normally misbehaves through positive practice overcorrection procedures.

## Rumination (Merycism)

### Definition

Rumination is an extremely rare but fascinating illness that has been recognized for hundreds of years. This regurgitation disorder, which is potentially fatal, occurs predominantly in infancy, and seldom in adults. An awareness of the disorder is important so that it may be correctly diagnosed, and so that unnecessary surgical procedures or inappropriate treatment can be avoided.

Rumination is derived from the Latin word ruminare, which means to chew the cud. The Hellenic equivalent is merycism, which describes the act of regurgitation of food from the stomach into the mouth, chewing the food again, and reswallowing.

The association of this behavior with malnutrition and death in children has been reported for many years. Usually, adults with this affliction maintain a normal weight. The DSM-III criteria are specific for the diagnosis of rumination in children The essential feature according to DSM-III is repeated regurgitation of food, with weight loss or failure to gain expected weight developing after a period of normal functioning (see Table IV).

### Epidemiology and Prevalence

Rumination is a very rare disorder that has been reported equally in males and females. Although familial cases, including rumination in five generations and in a man and his six children, have been reported, the bias of selective case reporting does not allow any conclusion as to the existence of a familial pattern in this disorder.

### Etiology

Theories of causation of rumination have ranged from autonomic nervous system dysfunction to a disturbed parent-infant interaction. The latter theory observed that the mothers of these infants were usually immature, involved in a marital conflict, and unable to give to the baby at a time when the infant was developing visual maturation. This resulted in insufficient gratification in the form of visual and probably auditory stimulation; thus, the infant sought gratification from within. Since the infant's greatest source of gratification, even though incomplete, had been through feeding, the infant developed the rumination process, which was interpreted as an effort to recreate the feeding process.

Some patients suffering from rumination have had repeated negative esophagrams, before recognition of a hiatal hernia by a radiologist experienced in the gastrointestinal roentgenological patterns of infants and children. The hernia in those cases was responsible for the disorder.

### Clinical Features, Course, and Prognosis

Rumination usually begins between 3 and 12 months of age. In the early stages, it is difficult to distinguish it from the normal regurgitation seen in most infants. However, in the fully developed case, the diagnosis is obvious. Partially digested food is brought up into the infant's mouth without nausea, retching, or disgust. Some infants appear to enjoy the activity. It is then either ejected from the mouth or reswallowed. The behavior appears to be voluntary in that the infants are observed to strain vigorously to bring food back to their mouths. There may be an associated head rolling, head banging, body rocking, arched back, or hair pulling. The infants are usually referred to the doctor because of failure to thrive, and the diagnosis is then made on the basis of the history and personal observation. Serious medical problems—such as

TABLE IV
DIAGNOSTIC CRITERIA FOR RUMINATION DISORDER OF INFANCY*

A. Repeated regurgitation without nausea or associated gastrointestinal illness for at least 1 month following a period of normal functioning.

B. Weight loss or failure to make expected weight gain.

* From American Psychiatric Association: *Diagnostic and Statistical Manual of Mental Disorders*, ed 3. American Psychiatric Association, Washington, DC, 1980. Used with permission.

malnutrition, dehydration, and lowered resistance to disease—may cause a life-threatening condition.

The mechanism of rumination in children is the same as in adults, in whom it has been possible to do more careful cinefluorography. From these studies, it has been postulated that rumination is the result of an increase of the normal pleuroperitoneal pressure gradient across the diaphragm, with an abrupt relaxation of the intrahiatal and intraabdominal sphincteric vestibular segment, which allows the gastric contents free access into the esophagus.

Table V contains a summary description of infantile rumination. Very little information is available on long-term behavioral disturbances after rumination has ceased. Spontaneous remissions are thought to be common; however, of those cases referred to medical centers, a mortality rate of up to 25 percent has been reported due to malnutrition. Growth failure or failure to thrive can occur with this disorder, and concomitant developmental delays are often present. The mother or caretaker is often discouraged by failure to feed the infant successfully, and may become alienated, if she is not already alienated, from the child. Further alienation occurs as the noxious odor of the regurgitated material leads to avoidance of the infant, with resulting understimulation.

### Diagnosis

Rumination must be differentiated from congenital anomalies or infections of the gastrointestinal system. Pyloric stenosis is usually associated with a projectile vomiting, and is evident before 3 months of age.

TABLE V
CLINICAL FEATURES OF RUMINATION*

*Essential features that are always present:*
1. Regurgitation of food with failure to thrive after a period of normal functioning.
2. Food brought up to the mouth without nausea, retching, or disgust, and then rejected from the mouth or chewed and reswallowed.
3. Characteristic position of straining and arching the back with the head held back.
4. Sucking movements of the tongue; infant gives impression of gaining considerable satisfaction from the activity.

*Associated feature that is commonly but not invariably present:* Irritability and hunger between episodes of rumination.

* Adapted from American Psychiatric Association: *Diagnostic and Statistical Manual of Mental Disorders*, ed 3. American Psychiatric Association, Washington, DC, 1980.

### Treatment

Many therapies have been advocated for treating rumination. Treatment includes fostering a loving relationship between parent and infant and parental training. There are case reports of ruminating infants who gradually gave up this behavior as they were given love and attention from an attentive nurse. Various devices have been invented to keep the mouth securely closed. However, this form of treatment has seldom been successful, nor has thickening the infant's formula met with dramatic results. In three ruminating children with hiatus hernias, one was treated successfully by feeding the child in an upright position, and by maintenance of this upright position for prolonged periods of time. The other two were successfully treated with surgical repair of the hernias.

Behavior therapy techniques have been reported to be successful in stopping rumination. Aversive conditioning with electric shock has been able to eliminate rumination within a 3- to 5-day period. In all the above aversion conditioning reports on rumination, the infants were doing well at 9- or 12-month follow-ups, with no recurrence of the rumination, and with weight gains, increased activity levels, and greater general responsiveness to people. Another form of aversive conditioning reported was that of squirting a small amount of lemon juice into the mouth of an infant whenever rumination activity was detected. This approach was as effective as electric shock therapy.

It is extremely difficult to evaluate the variety of treatments that have been used for rumination, since most are single case reports and since none of the treatments has been evaluated by a randomly assigned controlled study.

### Anorexia Nervosa

Anorexia nervosa is characterized by behavior directed toward losing weight, peculiar patterns of handling food, weight loss, intense fear of gaining weight, disturbance of body image, and, in women, amenorrhea. It is one of the few psychiatric illnesses that may have a course unremitting until death. Anorexia nervosa is discussed in Section 22.4.

### REFERENCES

Berquist W E: Gastroesophageal reflex in children: A clinical review. Pediatr Ann *11:* 135, 1982.
Danford D E, Smith C J, Huber A M: Pica and mineral status in the mentally retarded. Am J Clin Nutr *35:* 958, 1982.
Darby P L, Garfinkel P E, Garner D M, Coscina D V: *Anorexia Nervosa: Recent Developments.* Allen R. Liss, New York, 1983.

Davis P K, Cuvo A J: Chronic vomiting and rumination in intellectually normal and retarded individuals: Review and evaluation of behavioral research. Behav Res Severe Dev Disabil *1:* 31, 1980.

Halmi K A: Anorexia nervosa. In *Clinical Psychopharmacology*, D G Grahams-Smith, H Hippius, G Winokur, editors, p 313. Excerpta Medica Foundation, The Hague, 1982.

Halmi K A: Eating disorders. In *Comprehensive Textbook of Psychiatry*, ed 4, H A Kaplan, B J Sadock, editors, p 1731. Williams & Wilkins, Baltimore, 1985.

Herzog D B: Bulimia in the adolescent. Am J Dis Child *136:* 985, 1982.

Johnson C, Larson R: Bulimia: An analysis of moods and behavior. Psychosom Med *44:* 341, 1982.

Lacey J H: Bulimia nervosa, binge eating, and psychogenic vomiting: A controlled treatment study and long-term outcome. Br Med J *286:* 1609, 1983.

Pope H G, Hudson J I, Jonas J M, Yurgelun-Todd D: Bulimia treated with imipramine: A placebo-controlled, double-blind study. Am J Psychiatry *40:* 5, 1983.

Pope H G, Jr, Hudson J I: *New Hope for Binge Eaters: Advances in the Understanding and Treatment of Bulimia.* Harper & Row, New York, 1984.

# 35.3   SCHIZOID DISORDER

## Definition

Schizoid disorder of childhood is described in DSM-III as a defect in the capacity to form social relationships, introversion, and bland or constricted affect that cannot be attributed to another disorder. Children with this disorder show little desire for social involvements, prefer to be loners, and have few, if any friends. When placed in social situations, they are inept and awkward. Their friendships tend to be with younger, or other poorly functioning youngsters.

They often appear reserved, withdrawn, seclusive, and pursue solitary interests or hobbies. They may seem vague about their goals, indecisive in their activities, absentminded, and detached from their environment ("not with it" or "in a fog"). They do not appear distressed by their isolation.

Children with this disorder usually lack the capacity for emotional display and are unable to express aggressiveness or hostility. They usually appear cold, aloof, and distant, though attachment to a parent or other adult is not unusual. They especially avoid competitive activities and sports.

## Epidemiology

There is uncertainty about the frequency of the disturbance. When the term is used rigorously, it is said to be rare. When schizoid disorder overlaps with anxiety, sensitivity, and shyness, it is found to be common at times of stress, such as early latency, when the child enters school, and in early adolescence.

It can be differentiated as a syndrome as early as 5 years of age. The disorder is more common in boys than in girls.

## Etiology

A constitutional tendency is frequently mentioned with regard to the schizoid child, the result of noting similar features in the parents and the early tendencies to withdraw that are noticeable in some children; the latter may overlap with the slow-to-warm-up child. A combination of such temperamental traits as slow adaptiveness, low activity level, initial withdrawal to strange stimuli, low level of intensity of emotional reactions, and high level of negative moods predisposes to a withdrawal tendency in response to new situations. Infants who are irritable or sensitive to stress are likely to be upset by strangers. Such family factors as social isolation, illness, frequent separations, and being the first or only child may result in limited social interaction in early life, or social patterning on a deviant parental image. Children who are little exposed to strangers show more anxiety than do others. They may have greater difficulties with the separation-individuation phase.

The onset of symptoms may be related to the pressure of a new developmental phase, such as separation from family at school onset, or the strong impulses of early puberty. A sudden increase in aggressive or sexual impulses previously unmastered may lead to compensatory defensive withdrawal.

## Clinical Features

The clinical picture has as its central feature the avoidance of warm and meaningful relationships, and the withdrawal from the real world to fantasies, preoccupation with daydreams, and autistic thinking (see Table I). As children with schizoid disorder do not check their experiences with outside reality, their thinking becomes idiosyncratic. They show minor deviations in thought processes, although they do not develop a true thought disorder. To the outside, they present a picture of listlessness, apathy, lack of initiative, changeable moods, and peculiarities that may result in their being considered queer. They are generally unobtrusive in social situations—appearing shy, sensitive, and passive—but may have outbursts of aggressive or destructive impulses that are seemingly without provocation, but are actually a response to their inability to handle aggression and hostility. The continued withdrawn behavior jeopardizes the

TABLE I
DIAGNOSTIC CRITERIA FOR SCHIZOID DISORDER OF CHILDHOOD OR ADOLESCENCE*

A. No close friend of similar age other than a relative or a similarly socially isolated child.

B. No apparent interest in making friends.

C. No pleasure from usual peer interactions.

D. General avoidance of nonfamilial social contacts, especially with peers.

E. No interest in activities that involve other children (such as team sports, clubs).

F. Duration of the disturbance of at least 3 months.

G. Not due to pervasive developmental disorder; conduct disorder, undersocialized, nonaggressive; or any psychotic disorder, such as schizophrenia.

H. If 18 or older, does not meet the criteria for schizoid personality disorder.

*From American Psychiatric Association: *Diagnostic and Statistical Manual of Mental Disorders*, ed 3. American Psychiatric Association, Washington, DC, 1980. Used with permission.

development of ego functions. They fail to learn social skills or to achieve academically and seem incompetent to cope with the requirements of the environment. They may be scapegoated by their peer group.

## Course and Prognosis

The vicissitudes of the symptom of withdrawing are considerable. In some children, the introversion is a temporary protective restriction of the ego. In others, it progresses to the development of a lifelong pattern of isolation, without, however, the relinquishing of reality. A relatively small number develop an adult schizoid personality or eventually become schizophrenic, as their capacity to cope with the external environment is reduced.

## Diagnosis

The diagnosis depends on the presence of a relatively prolonged emotional withdrawal from family and peers, based on a preference for the isolated state. Although the child may show tolerance for and even satisfaction in some intrafamilial activities, he shows little pleasure in the usual activities with friends on either an individual basis or a group basis. Irritability at being forced into painful or frightening social contact may provoke temper tantrums, but the youngsters are not antisocial in the delinquent sense. They may seem odd or queer, compared with their age-mates, but they have no bizarre features, delusions, hallucinations, breaks with reality, or disorders of thinking. The disorder should be present for at least 3 months before the diagnosis is made.

## Differential Diagnosis

Schizoid disorder must be differentiated from several conditions. In avoidant disorder, the anxious, inhibited child shows extreme shyness, submissiveness, inhibition of initiative, and con-

striction of personality functions, including speech, under selected circumstances. He may enjoy relationships at home or with familiar persons, and may give evidence of desiring social interaction when it is available under nonthreatening conditions, enjoying it once it has been established. He expresses doubts about his abilities and is dependent on others. His behavior is more responsive to environmental shift than is that of the schizoid child.

In adolescence and, less often, in childhood, there is often some overlap between withdrawal and depression, and often the two conditions coexist. Both may show inhibition and isolation. Diagnosis is especially difficult in cases in which the affective components of the depression are masked by alienation. The depressed adolescent is likely to have had better relationships in the premorbid state than the schizoid adolescent had. However, the differential diagnosis can be extremely difficult, and may ultimately depend on outcome or response to medication.

Psychotic children and adolescents tend to demonstrate a greater break with reality, have wider affective swings, and show more bizarre qualities than do schizoid children and adolescents.

Adjustment disorder with withdrawal is a response to an identified stressor that remits when the stress ceases.

Aggressive conduct disorder, undersocialized type, is marked by persistent antisocial behavior, such as lying or manipulation. Children with this disorder, unlike schizoid children, at one time or another become attached to antisocial groups.

## Treatment

Inasmuch as withdrawal and schizoid are terms describing behavior, rather than implying underlying mechanisms, it is necessary, before intervening to remediate the symptom, to understand the origins and the dynamics of the behavior. In young children especially, retreat into the self may be a reaction to negative environmental factors. In such cases, attempts to change the family situation to a more benign one by means of parental support or substitute support systems are important. This strategy is worth trying in all cases, but it is not apt to be effective in fixed personality patterns. Withdrawal based on temperamental tendencies is best treated preventively in early childhood by helping parents to adapt their expectations to the child's capacities. Patience, consistency, flexibility, and persistence aid the child in overcoming handicaps to socialization. Efforts to increase social interaction, such as involving children in social groups or advising parents to increase their social experiences, generally have little success, partly because many parents have similar problems.

Within a therapeutic relationship, the child or adolescent is drawn out of his autistic fantasies to the outside world, so that he can, with support, begin to tolerate the anxieties of his negative affects, of competition, and of the average expectable stresses of reality. Through support and graduated experiences, the ego becomes able to carry out activities without characteristic withdrawal. With older children and adolescents, the direct communication of knowledge to reduce anxiety and to modulate aggression and superego severity has been useful.

As the child attempts more social interaction, the therapist should coordinate these efforts with the responses of significant environmental persons, such as parents and teachers, to maximize the opportunity for successful extrapolations of gains. Psychotherapy has been combined with behavior modification techniques. Assertive interactional responses are fostered, and relaxation techniques are used to facilitate healthier responses. Modeling has been found effective with very young children, although reinforcement is needed to maintain improvement. Group therapy can be used, provided the group is carefully selected and continues uninterruptedly over a period of time. A behavior modification approach that works on the group reaction to the withdrawn child consists of making him more attractive to the group by, for example, having him distribute food. Desirable behavior is naturally reinforced and thus maintained.

**REFERENCES**

Chick J, Waterhouse L, Wolff S: Psychological construing in schizoid children grown-up. Br J Psychiatry 135: 425, 1979.

Group for the Advancement of Psychiatry: *Psychopathological Disorders in Childhood: Theoretical Considerations and a Proposed Classification*, Group for the Advancement of Psychiatry, New York, 1966.

LaVietes R L: Schizoid disorder. In *Comprehensive Textbook of Psychiatry*, ed 4, H I Kaplan, B J Sadock, editors, p 1744. William & Wilkins, Baltimore, 1985.

McConville B J, Boag L: Dropouts without drugs: A study of prolonged withdrawing reactions in younger adolescents. J Am Acad Child Psychiatry 12: 333, 1973.

Wolff S, Barlow A: Schizoid personality in childhood: A comparative study of schizoid, autistic, and normal children. J Child Psychol Child Psychiatry 20: 29, 1979.

Wolff S, Chick J: Schizoid personality in childhood: A controlled follow-up study. Psychol Med 10: 85, 1980.

## 35.4    OPPOSITIONAL DISORDER

### Introduction

Oppositional disorder is of interest for its resemblance to normal periods of development in early childhood, and for its relationship to the passive-aggressive and compulsive personality disorders in adulthood. Oppositional disorder can be seen as an interim diagnostic phase between a period of greater plasticity and one of fixity.

### Definition

Oppositional disorder is defined in DSM-III as follows: The essential features are a pervasive opposition and disobedience to all in authority regardless of self-interest, a continuous argumentativeness, and an unwillingness to respond to reasonable persuasion. Children with this disorder express their aggressiveness by oppositional patterns of behavior, especially toward parents and teachers. The oppositional behavior should be present for at least 6 months before the diagnosis is made.

### Epidemiology

Oppositional negativistic behavior in children is fairly common, but because a good deal of it is normative, temporarily reactive, cultural, or a symptom of another disorder, its presence is not diagnostic. Epidemiological studies of the trait of negativism in nonclinical populations indicate an incidence of between 16 and 22 percent in the over-all school-age population. The disorder can begin at 3 years of age, but is more common during late childhood or early adolescence.

Both the trait of negativism and the diagnosis of oppositional disorder are much more common in boys than in girls, with estimates of the occurrence in boys ranging from twice to 10 times the occurrence in girls.

There are no distinct family patterns, but almost all parents of oppositional children are themselves overconcerned with issues of power, control, and autonomy. Some families contain a large number of obstinate characters, a larger number of controlling and depressed mothers, and fathers who tend to be passive-aggressive. In many cases, the patients were unwanted children.

### Etiology

The capacity to oppose the will of others is crucial to normal development. It is related to separating from the parent, assuming individuality, autonomy, and establishing inner standards and controls. Thus, opposition at certain periods is both normal and healthy. Pathology begins when this developmental phase is prolonged, or when the environment overreacts.

The most prominent instance of normal oppositional behavior is the period between 18 and 36 months, peaking between 18 and 24 months, when the toddler behaves negativistically as an expression of growing autonomy. He insists on doing things his way, and demonstrates strong opposition to interference with his will. The child's need at this time to validate his separateness and mastery is so great that his behavior seems provoked less by a perception of his requirements than by a need to oppose what others ask of him. Still earlier instances of opposition occur around 10 or 11 months with the battle of the spoon, which is the infant's insistence on feeding himself, and in episodes of perseverative motor acts in defiance of parents.

A certain percentage of children, estimated at about 10 percent, exhibit these behaviors in a more intense form than do others. Possibly there is a constitutional predisposition to strong will or strong preferences that are reported by parents either complainingly or admiringly. Such children seem to be at higher than normal risk for the development of oppositional disorder under certain environmental conditions.

Some parents interpret average or increased levels of developmental oppositionalism as hostility and a deliberate effort on the part of the child to be in control. If power and control are issues for parents, or if they exercise authority for their own needs, a power struggle can be established between the parents and the child that sets the stage for the development of the oppositional disorder. What begins for the infant as an effort to establish self-determination becomes transformed into a defense against overdependency on the mother and as a protective device against intrusion into the autonomy of the ego.

A second normative oppositional stage occurs in adolescence as an expression of the need to separate from the parents and to establish an autonomous identity. If older children or adolescents perceive a danger in the overt expression of aggression, it may be expressed in passive resistance, which becomes a characteristic and unconscious method of coping with stress. In some, the symptom may be a defense against overcompliance and submissive tendencies. Opposition in a group setting can be face saving or serve to establish a role among peers.

### Clinical Features

Inasmuch as aggression is the focal issue in oppositionalism, it may be evidenced in various ways at different times. When aggression is expressed indirectly or passively, the symptoms of obstinacy, procrastination, disobedience, carelessness, negativism, dawdling, provocation, resistance to change, violation of minor rules, blocking out communications from others, and resistance to authority are prominent (see Table I). Enuresis, encopresis, elective mutism, running away, school avoidance, school underachievement, and eating and sleeping problems may be the major complaints. More overt manifestations are quarrelsomeness, rebelliousness, teasing, temper tantrums, fighting, and delinquent acts.

The oppositional attitude is seen toward family members and particularly toward the parents. The most striking feature is the persistence of the oppositional attitude even when it is destructive to the interests and well-being of the child or adolescent. For the most part the oppositional patterns appear as ingrained and pervasive. Usually the child or adolescent does not complain of being oppositional but sees the problem as arising from other people and those who are making unreasonable demands upon them. The disorder appears to cause more distress to those around the individual than within the individual himself.

Chronic oppositionalism almost always interferes with interpersonal relationships and school performance. These children are often friendless, perceiving human relationships as unsatisfactory. Despite adequate abilities, they do poorly in school, as they withhold participation, resist external demands, and need to solve problems without others' help. Being held back in school may result.

## Diagnosis

In order to diagnose oppositional disorder, the onset should be between the ages of 3 and 18. The oppositional behavior should be preponderant, demonstrable both at home and in school, and persistent even when it is contrary to the child's best interest. According to DSM-III, five of the following must be present on a continuing basis for at least 6 months: (1) pervasive oppositional behavior; (2) continuous argumentativeness; (3) lack of response to reasonable persuasion; (4) learning problems in spite of cognitive ability; (5) poor peer relationship with "bossy" negative quality toward peers; (6) provocative behavior; (7) stubbornness; (8) dawdling; (9) rebel aggressiveness; (10) passive resistance; (11) persistence of behavior in spite of attempts at correction or discipline; (12) belligerence in the face of corrective efforts by others (see Table I).

## Course and Prognosis

The onset may be sudden, in response to an abrupt increase in environmental stress to which the child or adolescent responds by erecting a barrier of opposition between himself and external pressures. More often, however, the disorder develops gradually as an exaggeration and continuation of a normal developmental period, or as a prolongation beyond the point of usefulness of an originally adaptive reaction. Some instances are reported by parents as beginning as early as the first year of life. Many children who are perceived as independent and strong willed during the toddler and preschool period are seen as negative and contentious as they reach school age.

The prognosis for resolution with or without treatment is better when the disorder is reactive than when it appears characterological. Without treatment and in an aggravating environment,

this disorder can culminate in a personality disorder. Passive-aggressive or obsessional features, varying from mild and adaptive to rigid and self-destructive, may characterize the eventual functional level. After the age of 18, the diagnosis is passive-aggressive personality, if symptoms persist.

## Differential Diagnosis

Because oppositional behavior is both normal and adaptive at specific developmental stages and in response to situational crises, these periods of negativism must be distinguished from the disorder itself. The major difference is in the duration of the opposition. Developmental stage behavior is transient, rather than prolonged. Its intensity and extent are less significant than in the disorder, although conspicuous manifestations may be the harbinger of the full-blown syndrome.

Oppositional behavior of a temporary nature in reaction in life stress should be classified as an adjustment disorder. Oppositional behavior may occur as a symptom in pervasive developmental disorders, in which it does not constitute the majority disability, and in conduct disorder, in which case serious antisocial behavior dominates the picture. Negativism is also found in chronic brain disease and mental retardation. Whether a concomitant diagnosis of oppositional disorder is warranted in these illnesses depends on how ubiquitous or prolonged the behavior is, and on how it interdigitates with other symptoms.

Because oppositional disorders can be diagnosed only on the basis of a chronic reaction, there is frequently a fine line to be drawn between this diagnosis and that of a passive-aggressive personality disorder. Age itself may influence the choice, personality disorder being preferred in longer-standing instances, but this is not always the case. If the syndrome is well

TABLE I
DIAGNOSTIC CRITERIA FOR OPPOSITIONAL DISORDER*

A. Onset after 3 years of age and before age 18.

B. A pattern, for at least 6 months, of disobedient, negativistic, and provocative opposition to authority figures, as manifested by at least two of the following symptoms:
 (1) Violations of minor rules
 (2) Temper tantrums
 (3) Argumentativeness
 (4) Provocative behavior
 (5) Stubbornness

C. No violation of the basic rights of others or of major age-appropriate societal norms or rules (as in conduct disorder); and the disturbance is not due to another mental disorder, such as schizophrenia or a pervasive developmental disorder.

D. If 18 or older, does not meet the criteria for passive-aggressive personality disorder.

* From American Psychiatric Association: *Diagnostic and Statistical Manual of Mental Disorders*, ed 3. American Psychiatric Association, Washington, DC, 1980. Used with permission.

developed and chronic, the diagnosis of personality disorder is justified even in childhood.

## Treatment

The therapeutic intervention of choice is individual psychotherapy of the child and counseling of the parents. Altering the child's environment may be helpful at times, but, because the patients' pattern is both fixed and provocative, it is difficult to arrange a positive shift that will endure without concomitant changes in the child.

Family therapy may be used diagnostically or to clarify ongoing stressors, but family patterns are generally too rigid to shift unless the child himself experiences a new type of object relationship with the therapist, one that depends on individual contact.

The therapist must anticipate opposition to the idea of therapy and to its procedures, and limits must be set when the rights of others are compromised. The child defends himself with characteristic maneuvers, automatically resisting actively or passively what he perceives is expected of him. Missing sessions is frequently used as a form of resistance.

Within the therapeutic relationship, the child can relive the autonomy-threatening experiences that have produced his defense system. In the safety of a noncontrolling relationship, he can understand the self-destructive nature of his behavior and venture to assert himself openly, instead of in disguised forms. Self-esteem, based on his real worth, needs to rise before automatic defenses against being externally controlled can be relinquished. In this way, independence replaces habitual efforts to resist intrusion and control. Once a therapeutic relationship has been formed on the basis of respect for the patient's separateness, the patient is ready to understand the source of his defenses and to assay new ways of coping.

**REFERENCES**

American Psychiatric Association: *Diagnostic and Statistical Manual of Mental Disorders*, ed 3. American Psychiatric Association, Washington, DC, 1980.
Anthony E J, Gilpin D C, editors: *Three Clinical Faces of Childhood*. Spectrum, New York, 1976.
Group for the Advancement of Psychiatry: *Psychopathological Disorders in Childhood. Theoretical Considerations and a Proposed Classification*. Group for the Advancement of Psychiatry, New York, 1966.
LaVietes R L: Oppositional disorder. In *Comprehensive Textbook of Psychiatry*, ed 4, H I Kaplan, B J Sadock, editors, p 1744. Williams & Wilkins, Baltimore, 1985.
Levy D M: Oppositional syndromes and oppositional behavior. In *Psychopathology of Childhood*, P Hoch,

J Zubin, editor, p 204. Grune & Stratton, New York, 1955.
Spitzer R L, Skodol A E, Gibbon M, Williams J B W: *The DSM-III Case Book*, Case 192, p 292. American Psychiatric Association, Washington, DC, 1981.
Werry J S, Methuen J, Fitzpatrick J, Dickson H: The DSM-III diagnosis of New Zealand children. In *International Perspectives on DSM-III*, R L Spitzer, J B Williams, A E Skodol, editors. American Psychiatric Association Press, Washington, DC, 1983.

---

# 35.5 ANXIETY DISORDERS

## Introduction

The concept of anxiety forms a central core for the understanding of developmental difficulties, symptom formation, and the major clinical psychiatric syndromes of childhood. This category, anxiety disorders, includes three disorders of childhood or adolescence in which anxiety is the predominant clinical feature. In the first two, separation anxiety disorder and avoidant disorder of childhood or adolescence, the anxiety is focused on specific situations. In the third category, overanxious disorder, the anxiety is generalized to a variety of situations. See Table I for a description of the various anxiety disorders discussed in this section.

## Definition of Anxiety

Anxiety is the term used to describe any of a large variety of affective, motor, or physiological responses to the nonspecific perceptions of danger by the human organism. It is an affect or feeling of dread, apprehension, discomfort, or fear that something ominous or terrible will happen in the future. Understanding of the anxiety states in children requires familiarity with four underlying concepts: (1) character structure and the determinants of character distortions, (2) the interactions and the complications of interaction between the child and his parents, (3) present stresses or trauma in the child's life, and (4) the entire social environment of the child, including siblings, other relatives, peers, educational situation, and recreational activities.

### Infancy

If the infant's needs were met perfectly by a mothering figure, presumably no discomfort or anxiety would ever be experienced. But such a situation never occurs, and all infants must endure discomfort from the beginning of life. This lack of perfect satisfaction of needs results in discomfort, but also acts as a stimulus for the

TABLE I
COMMON CHARACTERISTICS OF ANXIETY DISORDERS*

| Criteria | Separation Anxiety Disorder | Avoidant Disorder | Overanxious Disorder |
|---|---|---|---|
| Minimum duration to establish diagnosis | More than 2 weeks | More than 6 months | At least 6 months |
| Age of onset | Infancy to adolescence | 2½ years or older | 3 years or older |
| Precipitating stresses | Separation from significant parent figures, other losses, travel | Pressure for social participation | Unusual pressure for performance, damage to self-esteem, feelings of lack of competence |
| Peer relations | Good when no separation involved | Tentative, overly inhibited | Overly eager to please, peers sought out and dependent relationship established |
| Sleep | Difficulty in falling asleep, fear of dark, nightmares | Difficulty in falling asleep at times | Difficulty in falling asleep |
| Psychophysiological symptoms | Stomachaches, nausea, vomiting, flu-like symptoms, headaches, palpitations, dizziness, faintness | Blushing, body tension | Stomachaches, nausea, vomiting, lump in the throat, shortness of breath, dizziness, palpitations |
| Differential diagnosis | Overanxious disorder, schizophrenic disorder, depressive disorder, conduct disorder with school refusal, phobic disorders, attention deficit disorder | Adjustment disorder with withdrawal, overanxious disorder, separation anxiety disorder, introverted disorder of childhood, schizotypal disorder | Separation anxiety disorder, attention deficit disorder, avoidant disorder, adjustment disorder with anxious mood, obsessive-compulsive disorder, depressive disorder, schizophrenia |

* Table by Sidney Werkman, M.D.

infant to attempt to satisfy his own needs—at first, through an increasing ability to delay gratification through an inner, confident perception, mediated by memory, that his mother will be available in the future; later, through the ability to incorporate concepts of mother and others that allow the infant to feel comforted internally; and, finally, through efforts to master the environment and seek independent satisfactions. Thus, a concept of the need-satisfying possibilities of the future is built incrementally into the infant's psychic apparatus.

### Developmental Basis of Anxiety

In the course of development, various stresses were conceptualized by Freud as triggers for the occurrence of anxiety in the child.

Each period of the individual's life has its appropriate determinant of anxiety. Thus, the danger of psychical helplessness is appropriate to the period of life when his ego is immature; the danger of loss of object, to early childhood when he is still dependent on others; the danger of castration, to the phallic phase; and the fear of his superego, to the latency period. Nevertheless, all these danger situations and determinants of anxiety can persist side by side and cause the ego to react to them with anxiety at a period later than the appropriate one; or, again,

several of them can come into operation at the same time.

These views have been elaborated conceptually and clinically by a number of workers. During the period of symbiosis described by Margaret Mahler as occurring at about 3 to 18 months of age, the mother functions as an auxiliary ego and helps the infant develop ego boundaries that define and delimit reality testing, frustration tolerance, and impulse control. The traumatic loss of a mothering figure, or the rejection of the infant by the mothering figure early in life, may result in a fear of total annihilation, followed later by a fear of the loss of the mothering figure or object. These anxieties must border on panic and be among the most powerful and terror-ridden ones experienced by a human. Anna Freud emphasized the concept of anxiety in the recognition of the strength of the instincts of the infant. In this dim, early developmental period, the strength of his rage and destructive impulses may leave the infant with a feeling of overwhelming anxiety.

During the maximal development of early self-awareness or object constancy, the 2-year-old child has internalized experiences of goodness and badness from the mother, and is able to retain an internalized memory of the mothering figure and of others in a rudimentary way.

Under stress, the child may regress and lose this sense of self-awareness or object constancy, resulting in terror and panic. These fears of the loss of self boundaries and of annihilation are in many ways similar to the overwhelming adult anxiety at loss of identity and loss of impulse control.

A fear of loss of body parts and loss of body functions, often conceptualized as castration fears, can be demonstrated most clearly in the child who is 3 to 6 years old.

As the sense of self develops, the 3- to 6-year-old child, under the stress of dealing with oedipal transformations, gradually encompasses a beginning sense of personal responsibility. An internalized superego develops, and the child becomes prone to anxiety and dread at the internalized anger and harsh thoughts directed toward the self.

### Separation Anxiety Disorder

#### Definition

Separation anxiety disorder is a clinical syndrome in which the predominant disturbance is excessive anxiety on separation from the major attachment figures or from home or other familiar surroundings. When separation occurs, the child may experience anxiety to the point of panic which is beyond that expected at the child's developmental level.

#### Etiology

The young child, immature and dependent on a mothering figure, is particularly prone to the anxiety experiences related to separation. Because the child undergoes a series of developmental fears—fear of annihilation, fear of the loss of his mother, fear of the strength of his impulses, fear of the loss of his body parts and of body integrity, and fear of the punishing anxiety of the superego and of guilt—it is an unusual child who does not have transient experiences of separation anxiety based on one or another of these fears. However, well-defined separation anxiety disorders are most frequently seen in early infancy, when they are defined as anaclitic depression or depression due to loss of the mothering figure. At the point of necessary separation from the parent to enter school, the syndrome of school phobia or school refusal occurs.

Thus, the syndrome is common in childhood, especially in mild forms that do not reach the physician's office. It is only when the symptoms have become set, and disturb the child's general adaptation to family life, peers, and school, that they come to the attention of professionals.

When girls are taught to take passive, somewhat helpless roles in society, they become prone to separation anxiety disorders. Girls who have had unusually tense relationships with their mothers are at great risk for the development of separation anxiety. Boys, because of the greater intensity of the oedipal struggle, are more likely to show clinically important separation anxiety at ages 3 to 6, when superego development and internalized anxiety and guilt become important issues.

Phobic anxiety may be communicated from parents to children by direct modeling. As women, more than men, have in the past shown a greater tendency to fear small animals, thunderstorms, and open places without even recognizing such reactions to be clinical problems, they may communicate the phobic anxiety stemming from such reactions to their children. In the past, boys were more likely than girls to manipulate their genitals and, therefore, were more prone to develop concerns leading to castration anxiety on an overt basis.

Anxiety can be traced to two major roots—the fear of not being cared for and the exaggerated anticipation of future dangers in the reality situation, or the internalization of such dangers in the personality. There is probably a genetic basis for the intensity with which separation anxiety is experienced by individual children. However, the major determinants of separation anxiety appear to be the transactions between the child and a parent with separation conflicts. Some parents seem to teach their children to be anxious by overprotecting them from expectable dangers, or by exaggerating the dangers of the present and the future. The parent who cringes in a room during a lightning storm teaches a child to do the same. The parent who is frightened of mice or insects conveys the affect of fright to the child. Conversely, the parent who becomes angry at a child during an incipient phobic concern about animals may inculcate a phobic concern in the child by the very intensity of the anger expressed.

#### Epidemiology

The disorder is ubiquitous in early childhood and occurs equally in both sexes. It is more common in family members than in the general population. The onset may be as early as preschool years; but most cases begin around 11 or 12 years, especially the most extreme form of the disorder involving school refusal.

## Clinical Features

**Essential Features.** The major disturbance is expressed as an exaggerated distress when separation from parents, home, or other familiar surroundings becomes necessary (see Table II). When the child is separated, anxiety may be experienced to the point of terror or panic. The reaction is greater than that normally expected for the child's developmental level, and is not accounted for by any other disorder. In many cases, the disorder is a kind of phobia, although the phobic concern is a general one and not directed to a particular symbolic object. Because the disorder is associated with childhood, it is not included among the phobic disorders of adulthood, which imply a much greater structuralization of the personality.

Morbid fears, preoccupations, and ruminations are characteristic of this disorder. The child becomes fearful that someone close to him will be hurt, or that something terrible will happen to him when he is away from important caring figures. Many children worry that accidents or illness will befall their parents or themselves. Fears about getting lost and about being kidnapped and never again finding their parents are common. Young children express less specific, more generalized concerns because their immature cognitive development precludes the formation of well-defined fears. In older children, fears of getting lost may include elaborate fantasies around kidnappings, being harmed, being raped, or being made slaves.

When separation from an important figure is imminent, children show many premonitory signs, such as irritability, difficulty in eating, and complaining and whining behavior. Physical complaints, such as vomiting or headaches, are common when separation is anticipated or actually happens. These difficulties increase in intensity and organization with age, because the older child is able to anticipate anxiety in a more structured fashion. Thus, there is a continuum between mild anticipatory anxiety before a threatened separation and pervasive anxiety after the separation has occurred.

Animal and monster phobias are common, as are concerns about dying. The child, when threatened with separation, may become fearful that events related to muggers, burglars, car accidents, or kidnapping may occur.

An adolescent may not directly express any anxious concern about separation from a mothering figure. Yet behavior patterns often reflect a pattern of separation anxiety in that the adolescent may express discomfort about leaving home, engage in solitary activities, and continue to use the mothering figure as a helper in buying clothes and entering social and recreational activities.

The separation anxiety disorder in a child often manifests itself at the thought of travel or in the course of travel away from the child's house or his familiar situation. The child may refuse to attend camp, sleep at a friend's home, or move to a new school. When geographic relocation is necessary, the child may refuse to

TABLE II
DIAGNOSTIC CRITERIA FOR SEPARATION ANXIETY DISORDER*

A. Excessive anxiety concerning separation from those to whom the child is attached, as manifested by at least three of the following:

   (1) Unrealistic worry about possible harm befalling major attachment figures or fear that they will leave and not return

   (2) Unrealistic worry that an untoward calamitous event will separate the child from a major attachment figure, e.g., the child will be lost, kidnapped, killed, or be the victim of an accident

   (3) Persistent reluctance or refusal to go to school in order to stay with major attachment figures or at home

   (4) Persistent reluctance or refusal to go to sleep without being next to a major attachment figure or to go to sleep away from home

   (5) Persistent avoidance of being alone in the home and emotional upset if unable to follow the major attachment figure around the home

   (6) Repeated nightmares involving theme of separation

   (7) Complaints of physical symptoms on school days, e.g., stomachaches, headaches, nausea, vomiting

   (8) Signs of excessive distress upon separation, or when anticipating separation, from major attachment figures, e.g., temper tantrums or crying, pleading with parents not to leave (for children below the age of 6, the distress must be of panic proportions)

   (9) Social withdrawal, apathy, sadness, or difficulty concentrating on work or play when not with a major attachment figure

B. Duration of disturbance of at least 2 weeks.

C. Not due to a pervasive developmental disorder, schizophrenia, or any other psychotic disorder.

D. If 18 or older, does not meet the criteria for agoraphobia.

* From American Psychiatric Association: *Diagnostic and Statistical Manual of Mental Disorders*, ed 3. American Psychiatric Association, Washington, DC, 1980. Used with permission.

stay in a room alone, cling to his parents, and follow his parents everywhere. Often, when a family move has occurred, the child displays separation anxiety by intense clinging to the mother figure.

At times, geographic relocation anxiety expresses itself in feelings of acute homesickness or psychophysiological symptoms that break out when the child is away from home or in transit to a new country. The child yearns to return home and becomes preoccupied with fantasies of how much better his old home was. Integration into the new life situation may become extremely difficult.

Sleep difficulties occur frequently, and may require that someone remain with the child until sleep occurs. Children often go to their parents' bed or even sleep at the parents' door when the bedroom is barred to them. Nightmares and morbid fears are further expressions of this anxiety.

**Associated Features.** Fear of the dark and imaginary, bizarre worries may develop. Children may see eyes staring at them and become preoccupied with mythical figures or monsters reaching out for them in their bedrooms.

Many children are demanding and intrusive in adult affairs and require constant attention to allay their anxieties. Symptoms emerge when separation from an important parent figure becomes necessary. If separation is not threatened, many children with this disorder do not experience interpersonal difficulties. They may, however, look sad and cry easily. They sometimes complain that they are not loved, express wishes that they die, or complain that siblings are favored over them. They frequently develop gastrointestinal symptoms of nausea, vomiting, or stomachaches and have pains in various parts of the body, sore throats, and flu-like symptoms. In older children, typical cardiovascular and respiratory symptoms of palpitations, dizziness, faintness, and strangulation are reported.

**Other Features.** Nostalgia for a lost way of life is often seen in children on their return after having lived intense lives away from the United States, or in unusually exotic situations in this country. When confronted with a move to a new situation, they find everything in the new place to be boring, anxiety provoking, or distasteful. Typically, they dismiss everything in the new place as uninteresting, worthless, or harmful, and find themselves unwilling to integrate into a new school or participate in sports and the challenges of making friends. Instead, they cling to memories that are exquisitely pleasing, precisely because these memories do not need to be tested against the reality of what actually happened.

### Course and Prognosis

Typically, there are periods of exacerbation and remission over a period of several years. The course of this disorder is fundamentally dependent on the presence or absence of a reliable mothering figure. When the mothering figure is absent in infancy for a short period of time, separation anxiety disorder may manifest itself, only to be reversed on the return of the mothering figure. In later childhood, symptoms of separation anxiety disorder are not so easily reversed, even with the return of the mothering figure. However, the availability of an adequate substitute caring figure may minimize or reverse the expression of symptoms.

When a reliable mothering figure is not available for a period of months, or when the internalized representation of a rejecting or unavailable mothering figure has become crystallized, the separation anxiety disorder may persist over a long period of time or be exacerbated by specific stresses. Once established, both the separation anxiety and the symptoms developed to avoid this anxiety may be sustained for many years by the child. In severe cases, the child may be unable to attend school or function independently in a variety of areas of his life. In a very few cases, inpatient care may be necessary to offer the child an opportunity to escape noxious influences in the home and to profit from a supportive, reliable environment.

**Complications.** Children with this syndrome are often subjected to numerous physical examinations because of somatic complaints. School refusal, inaccurately described in the past as school phobia, is a common complication. Not all school refusal is due to separation anxiety. However, when separation anxiety results in school refusal, the child experiences difficulty in separating from home or family for a variety of reasons. School attendance is only one of the issues involved in the difficulty in separation. In a true school phobia, which is a rare syndrome, the child fears the school situation whether or not the parent is present. When school refusal occurs as a result of separation anxiety, the child typically avoids many other social situations. In severe cases, a child may become violent toward anyone attempting to force a separation.

### Predisposing Factors

The character structure pattern seen in many children who develop this disorder includes conscientiousness, eagerness to please, and a tendency toward conformity. Family structures tend to be close knit and caring, and such children often seem to be spoiled or the objects of parental overconcern.

External life stresses often coincide with the development of the disorder. The death of a relative, illness in the child, change in the child's environment, or a move to a new neighborhood or new school are frequently noted in the histories of children with this disorder.

### Diagnosis

The diagnosis is based on the child having at least three of the following: (1) Unrealistic worry about possible harm befalling major attachment figures or fear that they will leave and not return; (2) unrealistic worry that an untoward calamitous event will separate the child from a major attachment figure, e.g., the child will be lost, kidnapped, killed, or be the victim of an accident; (3) persistent reluctance or refusal to go to school in order to stay with major attachment figures or at home; (4) persistent reluctance or refusal to go to sleep without being next to a major attachment figure or to go to sleep away from home; (5) persistent avoidance of being alone in the home and emotional upset if unable to follow the major attachment figure around the house; (6) repeated nightmares involving theme of separation; (7) complaints of physical symptoms on school days, e.g., stomachaches, headaches, nausea, vomiting; (8) signs of excessive distress upon separation, or when anticipating separation, from major attachment figures, e.g., temper tantrums or crying, pleading with parents not to leave (for children below the age of six, the distress must be of panic proportions); or (9) social withdrawal, apathy, sadness, or difficulty concentrating on work or play when not with a major attachment figure.

The diagnosis is made when any of these primary symptoms and signs are present for at least 2 weeks, and the disturbance is not accounted for by any other mental disorder. The disorder is considered to be mild when the child shows more than occasional concerns about separating from parents or home but can function in a new situation, despite evidence of anxiety. The disorder is considered to be moderate when the child has panic reactions to separation but can perform adequately for a while, although acute symptoms develop intermittently; for example, the child may have to be picked up from school or camp or be accompanied on errands. In severe separation anxiety disorder, the child has panic reactions to threatened or actual separation and refuses to go to school or to stay home alone.

The history frequently reveals important episodes of separation in the child's life, particularly because of illness and hospitalization, illness of the parent, parent loss, or geographic relocation. The period of infancy should be scrutinized carefully for evidence of separation-individuation disorders or lack of an adequate mothering figure. The use of fantasies, dreams, play material, and observation of the child are of great help in making the diagnosis. Not only the content of thought but the way in which thoughts are expressed should be examined. For example, a child may express fears that his parents will die, even when his behavior does not show evidence of motor anxiety. Similarly, the difficulty a child has in describing events or the bland denial of obviously anxiety-provoking events may indicate the presence of a separation anxiety disorder. Difficulty with memory in the expression of separation themes, or patent distortions in the recital of such themes, may give clues to the presence of the disorder.

### Differential Diagnosis

Transient experiences of separation anxiety are quite frequent, and, as the organism cannot tolerate anxiety for any length of time, the anxiety tends to crystallize into other kinds of disorders. The transformation of anxiety into compulsive mechanisms, phobias, and other symptoms occurs frequently. Therefore, a mixed picture of neurotic symptoms and free anxiety is often seen. Many habit disturbances—such as nail biting, thumb sucking, temper tantrums, eating problems, masturbation, and stuttering—stem from a common base of separation anxiety. Hyperactivity and minimal brain dysfunction must be considered. The characteristic symptoms of these disorders determine the presence of a primary or a secondary anxiety disorder. Childhood depression is separated on the basis of the content of thought and the child's intense concern with separation. Highly structured phobias are typically related to persistent, symbolic objects, and do not show the same amount of diffuse anxiety. Although enuresis may be present in separation anxiety disorder, it is only one of a number of symptoms noted, in contrast to the primary diagnosis of enuresis, in which a disturbance in urination is a central and often solitary symptom.

### Treatment

Of major importance is insistence that the child attend school, if only to be in the school building, inasmuch as there is no medical reason for the child not attending school. It is a true crisis. Often, a definitive change in the pattern of organization of sleeping arrangements, rewards, limits, and means of gaining approval can be of great help. Many developmental phobias can be effectively treated by a gradual desensitization procedure, in which the child is encouraged to talk about the phobic object, to draw pictures of it, to see the object of the phobia, and to gradually become more intimately involved with the object with the help of a supportive person. Behavior modification approaches to separation anxiety offer a similar rationale of graded contact with the object of anxiety under the tutelage of a benevolent adult.

At times sedative drugs such as diphenhydramine (Benadryl) can be useful to break a dangerous cycle of sleep disturbances. Antianxiety agents and antidepressant drugs have similarly been used in conjunction with graded desensitization experiences for children. Psychotherapeutic work should be directed toward helping parents understand the child's need for consistent, supportive love, and the importance of preparation for any important change in life, such as illness, an operation, or a geographic relocation, by family therapy. Efforts should be made to increase the child's sense of competence and autonomy. Premature infants are at particular risk for developmental anxieties. The importance of separation from the mother, feeding, and toilet-training patterns and the vicissitudes of the oedipal period need to be well understood by the parent. Psychotherapeutic work is directed toward support in the development of increasing autonomy, and the exploration of the unconscious meaning of symptoms. Individual psychotherapy of the parents with the child, especially the mother and child, is helpful.

Clinical experience suggests that this frequent disorder is quite effectively treated by a variety of supportive therapies and, when school refusal is a component, by consultation and cooperation among parents, therapist, and teachers. Many children overcome the acute symptoms, only to carry the predisposition to anxious responses to stresses in the future, unless a thorough treatment plan has unearthed and resolved the bases of their concerns. Treatment follow-up studies have established that behavior modification methods are of particular value in school refusal syndromes.

## Avoidant Disorder

### Definition

This syndrome is characterized by a persistent and excessive shrinking from contact with strangers that is of sufficient severity to interfere with social functioning in peer relationships, coupled with a clear desire for affection and acceptance and relationships with family members that are warm and satisfying.

### Epidemiology

This uncommon syndrome is clinically observed more frequently in girls than in boys, possibly because of the socially sanctioned role models of passivity and withdrawal in girls. The syndrome may develop as early as 2½ years of age, after stranger anxiety or a normal developmental phenomenon should have disappeared. Modeling of a shy, retiring parent is frequently noted in such situations, and girls may go through many years of avoiding social situations without overt anxiety if parents support their shyness. Boys, on the other hand, are frequently expected to be more independent and aggressive. Therefore, if shyness is a predominant characteristic in their personality make-up, boys begin to suffer symptoms earlier than girls.

### Etiology

Temperamental differences may account for some of the predisposition to this disorder, particularly if the parent supports the shyness and withdrawal of the child. Devastating losses early in childhood, or sexual traumas of various kinds, may also contribute to the onset and development of avoidant disorder. Children who have chronic medical problems in childhood, such as rheumatic fever or orthopaedic handicaps, may not learn the age-related social skills shared by their age-mates because they have not been involved in typical social interactions with their peers. Children who have grown up in foreign countries or have moved a great deal may not learn the necessary peer social skills that allow them to integrate effectively into the social world of their peers.

### Clinical Features

**Essential Features.** Children with avoidant disorder demonstrate an excessive holding back from the establishment of interpersonal contacts or satisfactory relationships with strangers, to an extent that noticeably interferes with their peer functioning (see Table III). The avoidance of involvement with strangers persists even after prolonged exposure to new relationships. These children are slow to warm up, although many of them participate actively in social groups that offer considerable support and structure. Typically, these children relate warmly and naturally in their home situation. However, they may be clinging, whining, and overly demanding with caretakers, making great demands on those who are with them. At times they are even demanding and dictatorial with close caretakers.

TABLE III
DIAGNOSTIC CRITERIA FOR AVOIDANT DISORDER OF CHILDHOOD OR ADOLESCENCE*

A. Persistent and excessive shrinking from contact with strangers.

B. Desire for affection and acceptance, and generally warm and satisfying relations with family members and other family figures.

C. Avoidant behavior sufficiently severe to interfere with social functioning in peer relationships.

D. Age at least 2½. If 18 or older, does not meet the criteria for avoidant personality disorder.

E. Duration of the disturbance of at least 6 months.

* From American Psychiatric Association: *Diagnostic and Statistical Manual of Mental Disorders*, ed 3. American Psychiatric Association, Washington, DC, 1980. Used with permission.

Embarrassment and timidity are conveyed in their voices, and they may demonstrate a tendency to whisper and stand behind people or hide behind furniture in an attempt not to be noticed. Blushing, difficulties in speech, and easy embarrassment are characteristic. Underneath these behaviors—and often expressed in close relationships—are anger, sullen resentment, rage, or grandiosity. There is no evidence of a pattern of intellectual impairment or fundamental difficulty in communication, even when such children seem most inarticulate.

**Associated Features.** When pressured into social participation, children with this disorder may become tearful and anxious. They may cling to caretakers and refuse to become involved in new activities. In adolescence, the long delay in the development of psychosexual maturity may be evidenced by difficulty in peer relationships, and in the establishment of appropriate social, sexual, and aggressive adolescent activities. Extreme inhibition in recreational activities is seen, and a great deal of support is necessary to encourage participation. At times, shyness and inhibition complicate the learning process. In such cases, the true abilities of a child become apparent only under extremely favorable educational conditions.

**Other Features.** In educational, athletic, or creative situations, children with avoidant disorder show marked perfectionistic and self-condemning trends that result in their shrinking from involvement in competitive activities. Any child who refuses competitive activities, and who uses ego restriction as a major character defense, should be considered as having a potential case of avoidant disorder. Seemingly paradoxical trends are often noted in these children once they are known intimately. Grandiose fantasies of great and unrecognized capabilities, feelings that their true worth is unappreciated, and diffuse athletic, creative, and social ambitions proliferate. Frequently, they invent imaginary companions, with whom they share intimate fantasies and concerns.

This diagnosis is not made before the age of 2½, when the normal stranger anxiety phase has passed. The time of onset may be difficult to determine, as many children are able to function adequately through the mechanism of ego restriction. Thus, their underlying disorder may escape notice for a considerable period of time. Many children recover spontaneously from this disorder, particularly when they experience pleasure or success in school, social situations, or camp experiences. Moving to a new school or acquiring some special social or creative skill often facilitates entrance into a social group. If the disorder is not recognized and treated, it may shade off into the various types of inhibited life-styles and schizoid or borderline personality adjustments. These individuals may never make attachments outside their immediate family. Impairment may be seen only when the child's usual life situation that protects him against the anxiety of new situations is disrupted. Typically, the impairment is noticed when a child moves to a new school, attempts to develop heterosexual relationships, or becomes increasingly independent of parents in adolescence.

### Predisposing Factors

The character structure of a child with avoidant disorder is often molded by an equally shy and inhibited parent, a highly dominating and overbearing parent, or a situation in which the child is consistently belittled or devalued in the family situation. A Cinderella complex may be an example of avoidant disorder.

### Complications

The most serious complications are the failure to make social relationships beyond the family, with resulting feelings of isolation, depression, and difficulty in thinking. A lack of self-confidence is typically present in such children, and they are unable to make reality decisions about their own abilities or the activities necessary for them to find a place in society. Lack of assertiveness is a frequent problem.

## Diagnosis

Avoidant disorder is diagnosed on the basis of a persistent shrinking from contact and involvement with strangers, and on avoidance behavior that interferes with peer functioning. These symptoms must be present for at least 6 months in a child at least 2½ years of age who has generally warm and satisfying relationships with his family members. In the mild disorder, there may be an ability to function comfortably with a few close friends, but some impairment in general peer functioning without any adverse effect on school performance. In the moderate disorder, there is difficulty in participation in class activities and some impairment in school work, together with alienation from friends due to inability to join them in other activities. Severe cases evidence marked interference with the development of peer relationships, and serious impairment in class work or social participation.

Children with avoidant disorder show great difficulty in separating from a parent figure. Often, the parent must come into the examination room at the beginning of the session, and the child demands to know exactly where the parent is during the session. Such children make minimal use of the diagnostic room, often sitting in a chair and waiting passively throughout the session for the examiner's directions. Typically, their play patterns are developmentally regressive, and they show a great interest in nurturing figures, food, and animals—mother dolls, mother animals, baby animals. When comfortable in the playroom, such children often demonstrate a great interest in aggression and destructiveness; they break dolls and become involved in symbolic killing play, and messy or destructive play with clay or blocks.

## Differential Diagnosis

Avoidant disorder often shades into the realm of schizoid character, avoidant personality disorder, adjustment disorder with withdrawal, and borderline characters. The adjustment disorder with withdrawal is clearly related to a recent psychosocial stressor, in contrast to avoidant disorder, which tends to be a long-term situation with no acute, overt stress precipitating it. Overanxious disorder of childhood is a situation in which the anxiety is not limited to contact with strangers, as in avoidant disorder. In the separation anxiety disorder, the anxiety is due to separation from the primary caretaker, rather than to forced contact with strangers. The avoidant personality disorder is diagnosed only

after the behavior pattern has persisted for many years, and the patient is at least 20 years old. The schizoid and borderline syndromes show more serious character pathology and a greater and more diffuse variety of symptoms, which are not characterized primarily by the avoidance of contact with strangers and new situations.

## Treatment

Psychotherapy with the explicit approval of the parent figure is the treatment of choice at the start. The child is helped to increase assertiveness both in the therapeutic situation and in school. Psychotherapy with the child, e.g. play therapy or family therapy, is indicated. Appropriate rewards and encouragement aid in the process of developing assertiveness. A great deal of work is directed toward helping the child separate from the parent and recognize that independent activity can be safe and fulfilling. In the work with parents, it is important to show in an empathic and sensitive way how the child is controlling the parent by his shyness. The parent can then give the child opportunities to experience manageable anxiety, and thus be able to give up some of the secondary gains of shyness. The development of skills in dancing, music performance, singing, or writing may be valuable ego supports for such children.

Antianxiety and sedative medications are sometimes indicated in this disorder; typically their use reinforces passivity and withdrawal. Because of the enduring nature of shyness, it becomes part of the child's characteristic pattern of response. Medication usually deepens the pattern of response, rather than promoting the emergence of a healthier response; however, on occasion medication on a short-term basis may decrease anxiety so that avoidant behavior is overcome. What is needed is a restructuring of relationships in a supportive therapeutic environment that directs the child toward facing new situations and mastering anxiety in order to achieve a higher level of independent functioning.

When parents can help in reversing the great overdependence of the child on the parent and of the parent on the child, healthy development can occur. However, these problems are typically long-standing ones involving parental character structure and the character structure of the child, both of whom are entwined in a regressive, dependent relationship. Frequently, it is only when the child is able to become independent from the parent by moving to a new school, moving away from the family, or engaging in an athletic or social activity that he can begin to examine his situation and change it.

In long-standing cases, these personality traits crystallize into schizoid, highly inhibited character structures that are difficult to treat effectively. Prolonged therapeutic intervention is then indicated. Parents and teachers must set goals combining sensitive appreciation of the child and emphasis on the necessity for individuation and the development of increased autonomy.

## Overanxious Disorder

### Definition

This disorder presents a picture of excessive worrying and fearful behavior that is not focused on a specific situation or object (such as separation from the parents) and is not due to a recent acute stress.

### Epidemiology

The onset may be sudden or gradual, with exacerbations associated with stress. Some clinical evidence suggests that overanxious disorder is most common in small families of upper socioeconomic status, in first children, and in situations in which there is unusual concern about performance, even when the child is functioning at an adequate level. In such families, children who develop the overanxious disorder come to feel that they must earn their acceptance in the family by high-level, conforming behavior. They tend to be goody-two-shoes children. Although both boys and girls develop this disorder, it has been seen more frequently in boys than in girls.

### Clinical Features

**Essential Features.** The main presenting problems are excessive worrying and fearful behavior (see Table IV). The child with overanxious disorder characteristically worries about future events, such as examinations, the possibility of injury, and meeting the expectations of a social group. The child is greatly concerned with competence and external performance. Worries about being judged and found wanting occur in a ruminative or obsessional pattern. A general habit pattern of tension, bodily contortions, and thumb sucking or nail biting may be noted in such children.

Sleep disturbances, particularly related to falling asleep, are common. Worries about anticipated events for the next day—wearing the right clothes, playing with desired children, being accepted in a group, doing well on a test—preoccupy such children.

Psychophysiological symptoms—including lump in the throat, sore throat, palpitations, respiratory distress, gastrointestinal distress, headaches, dizziness, and pains throughout the body—are common.

These children typically complain of being put down or ignored by peers and excluded from activities, even when they are well accepted in their social groups. Older children with this disorder may feel that they are left out of athletic activities or social clubs, and that they are the butt of mean or critical children and teachers.

**Associated Features.** Many children with overanxious disorder are extremely verbal and seem unusually intelligent. They show evidence of precocious ego development and are considered hypermature. They may refuse to depend on adult help at the same time that they take on unusual, strenuous projects and challenges. When in need of advice or help, they find themselves unable to call on available support systems. They inaccurately evaluate their true worth, and saddle themselves with perfection-

TABLE IV
DIAGNOSTIC CRITERIA FOR OVERANXIOUS DISORDER*

A. The predominant disturbance is generalized and persistent anxiety or worry (not related to concerns about separation), as manifested by at least four of the following:

  (1) Unrealistic worry about future events
  (2) Preoccupation with the appropriateness of the individual's behavior in the past
  (3) Overconcern about competence in a variety of areas, e.g., academic, athletic, social
  (4) Excessive need for reassurance about a variety of worries
  (5) Somatic complaints, such as headaches or stomachaches, for which no physical basis can be established
  (6) Marked self-consciousness or susceptibility to embarrassment or humiliation
  (7) Marked feelings of tension or inability to relax

B. The symptoms in A have persisted for at least 6 months.

C. If 18 or older, does not meet the criteria for generalized anxiety disorder.

D. The disturbance is not due to another mental disorder, such as separation anxiety disorder, avoidant disorder of childhood or adolescence, phobic disorder, obsessive-compulsive disorder, depressive disorder, schizophrenia, or a pervasive developmental disorder.

* From American Psychiatric Association: *Diagnostic and Statistical Manual of Mental Disorders*, ed 3. American Psychiatric Association, Washington, DC, 1980. Used with permission.

istic demands and obsessional self-doubts. Approval seeking and excessive conformity are frequent. Many show evidence of unusual motor restlessness, thumb sucking, nail biting, or hair pulling.

Such patients are often overtalkative and may seem overbearing in their domination of conversations. They have a great wish to please, but rarely feel satisfied with their efforts. In their estimation, others always seem to do better. They depend greatly on the evaluations of others, and react with painfully hurt feelings when they do not get the appreciation and acceptance they seek. Many of these youngsters are accident prone and seem to exaggerate the extent of pain, deformity, or potential handicap that may result from illness or accidents. This disorder is typically the result of the gradual development of a character pattern, although it is occasionally of sudden onset. The diagnosis should not be made before the age of 3 years, although tension and fearfulness may be seen earlier.

### Course and Prognosis

Because of the high level of verbal and intellectual abilities of many children with overanxious disorder, the relatively effective preoedipal experiences in their lives, and their infectious wishes to relate, the course is often benign. However, unusually stressful life experiences may contradict such a prognosis. Rarely does the disorder result in an inability to meet at least the minimal demands of school, home, and social life, but the youngster with such a disorder may experience a great deal of inner stress. It persists in adult life as an anxiety disorder such as generalized anxiety disorder or social phobia.

### Diagnosis

The symptoms include the presence of persistent anxiety and worrying about future events, together with a concern about competence in a variety of areas. Difficulty in falling asleep, combined with frightening dreams, and somatic complaints—such as headaches, gastrointestinal symptoms, and respiratory symptoms for which no medical basis can be established—are typically noted. The disorder must be present for at least 6 months and must be shown not to be a symptom of another disorder, such as separation anxiety disorder, avoidant disorder, phobic disorder, obsessive-compulsive disorder, depressive disorder, schizophrenia, or a pervasive developmental disorder.

In separation anxiety disorder, the anxiety is clearly related to specific stressful situations surrounding separation. Children with attention deficit disorders (minimal brain dysfunction) may show anxiety, but they also have characteristic symptoms of visual-motor impairment and do not show the same degree of exquisitely painful self-consciousness noted in children with overanxious disorder. In avoidant disorder, the anxiety breaks out only in new social situations. In adjustment disorder with anxious mood, the anxiety is always related to a recent psychosocial stress. Whenever symptoms of a more pervasive disorder—such as obsessive-compulsive disorder, depressive disorder, or schizophrenia—are present, these diagnoses should take precedence over the overanxious disorder.

Overanxious disorder is considered to be mild when the child continues to master experiences effectively and to function well in school, although he shows more than normal concerns about himself, injuries, his performance at school, or acceptance by his peers. In the moderate disorder, the child worries chronically and shows difficulty in functioning effectively in school, particularly when there is unusual pressure, such as occurs at examination time. However, the child continues to be able to function appropriately with peers. The disorder is considered to be severe when the child's anxiety level is so high that his school and social functioning are impaired. In such cases, the child cannot study for examinations, and performs badly or seeks reassurance so persistently that he becomes an irritant to friends and relatives.

Children with overanxious disorder typically relate immediately and with considerable warmth. They use the entire playroom easily. They start many activities and rarely need to look to the examiner for direction. They show little separation difficulty at the end of a session, and are typically very appreciative of the examiner. In the course of a session, many themes of death, disaster, accidents, and loss of body parts may be played out in symbolic ways. The child does not become panicked or incapacitated by the traumatic aspects of these themes; rather, he is able to continue to move from one to another in an overtly comfortable fashion.

Drawings are typically well conceptualized, cover the entire sheet of paper, and demonstrate considerable inventiveness and a variety of colors, and dramatic responses. Anxiety is demonstrated by the large amount of shading, heaviness of line, and the diffuseness of themes developed in a drawing.

### Treatment

These children are excellent candidates for insight therapy, either individually or in conjunction with their families. Themes of sibling rivalry, wishes to excel, and oedipal struggles tend to be in the forefront. Many children show a great need to deny their childishness and prefer to talk or play structured games, such as chess and checkers. Because they are fearful of lack of control, the therapist must pay particular attention to issues of consistency, acceptance of the patient, and firmness. Under such conditions, these children may allow themselves to give up their need to be in control and, instead, experiment with paints, playdough, or other messy and childish things. In the course of such regressions, they can experience the pleasure of participation in a trusting relationship, and begin to free themselves of perfectionistic, achievement-driven strivings.

Antianxiety medications such as diazepam (Valium) may be of particular use in acute situations, when accompanied by an adequate discussion of their use and concomitant psychotherapeutic involvement of parents. Acute anxiety accompanied by insomnia can be effectively treated by the short-term use of such sedatives as diphenhydramine (Benadryl) or sedating antianxiety agents.

When such children complain of psychophysiological symptoms, they should be given the benefit of one thorough medical or pediatric examination. If the findings of such an examination are normal, their symptoms should be discussed in the therapeutic situation, and treated as somatic equivalents of anxiety. The patient should be assured that such symptoms will disappear when the basis for anxiety is resolved.

Children with overanxious disorder—because of their advanced level of character development, great motivation to please and perform well, and frequent ability to understand and deal effectively with unconscious themes—do exceedingly well in psychotherapy. Because of their many attractive qualities, these children tend to bring out highly positive expectations on the part of the therapist; they exemplify the maxim that it is easy to love the lovable.

**REFERENCES**

Anthony E J: Communicating therapeutically with the child. J Am Child Psychiatry *3:* 106, 1964.
Bowlby J: *Attachment and Loss.* Basic Books, New York, 1969.
Compton A: A study of the psychoanalytic theory of anxiety. J Am Psychoanal Assoc *20:* 3, 1972.
Freud S: Introductory lectures on psychoanalysis. In *Complete Psychological Works of Sigmund Freud,* Vol 16, p 393. Hogarth Press, London, 1963.
Gittleman-Klein R: Pharmacotherapy and management of pathological separation anxiety. Int J Ment Health *4:* 255, 1975.
Hersen M: The behavioral treatment of school phobia: Current techniques. J Nerv Ment Dis *153:* 90, 1971.
Kandel B R: From metapsychology to molecular biol-
ogy: Explorations into the nature of anxiety. Am J Psychiatry *140:* 1277, 1983.
O'Brien J: School problems: School phobia and learning disabilities. Psychiatr Clin North Am *5:* 297, 1982.
Thomas A, Chess S, Birch H S: *Temperament and Behavior Disorders in Children.* New York University Press, New York, 1968.
Werkman S L: A heritage of transience: Psychological effects of growing up overseas. In *The Child and His Family,* E J Anthony, C Chiland, editors, pp 117. John Wiley & Sons, New York, 1978.
Werkman S L: Anxiety disorders. In *Comprehensive Textbook of Psychiatry,* ed 4, H I Kaplan, B J Sadock, editors, p 1746. Williams & Wilkins, Baltimore, 1985.
Werry J S: An overview of pediatric psychopharmacology. J Am Acad Child Psychiatry *21:* 3, 1982.

# 35.6 CONDUCT DISORDERS

## Introduction

DSM-III divides the conduct disorders into four major types: aggressive conduct disorder, undersocialized type; unaggressive conduct disorder, undersocialized type; unaggressive conduct disorder, socialized type; and aggressive conduct disorder, socialized type. Youngsters who cannot be fitted into one of the specific categories of conduct disorder because of lack of information or a mixed symptom picture may be classified as having an atypical conduct disorder.

## Definition

DSM-III defines conduct disorders as follows: The essential feature of this group of disorders is repetitive and persistent patterns of antisocial behavior that violates the rights of others, beyond the ordinary mischief and pranks of children and adolescents. The diagnosis is only given to individuals below the age of 18 years.

## Epidemiology

The conduct disorders are extremely common, especially in boys. Some general population surveys have suggested that 5 to 15 percent of all children show conduct problems serious enough to alarm some adult, although not all these youngsters fit the diagnostic criteria of DSM-III. In America, the prevalence of antisocial behavior seems to have important socioeconomic linkages.

## Etiology

Faulty parental attitudes and child-rearing practices are a major contributing element to the development of conduct disturbances. DSM-

III notes that the conduct disorders are much more frequent in children of adults with anti-social personality disorder. Early extremes of temperament, especially those severe enough to be characterized as an attention deficit disorder, also appear to play an important role in the development of conduct disorders. Longitudinal studies suggest that many behavioral deviations are initially a straightforward response to a poor fit between, on one hand, a child's temperament and emotional needs and, on the other hand, parental attitudes and practices.

Organic brain disease, learning disability, and other factors may play a role in some cases.

## Types of Conduct Disorders

### Conduct Disorder, Undersocialized, Aggressive Type

**Description.** The essential features are a failure to establish a normal degree of affection, empathy, or bonding with others; a pattern of aggressive antisocial behavior; and behavior difficulties at school (see Table I).

The failure to develop social attachments is manifested by the lack of sustained peer relationships, although the youngster may befriend a much older or younger person or have superficial relationships with other antisocial youngsters. Characteristically, the child does not extend himself for others even if there is an obvious immediate advantage for him. Egocentrism is shown by readily manipulating others for favors without any effort to reciprocate. There is a lack of concern for the feelings, wishes, and well-being of others, manifested by callous behavior. Appropriate feelings of guilt or remorse are absent. Such a child may readily inform on his companions and try to place blame on them.

The aggressive antisocial behavior may take the form of bullying, physical aggression, and cruel behavior toward peers. Toward adults the child may be hostile, verbally abusive, impudent, defiant, and negativistic. Persistent lying, frequent truancy, and vandalism are common. In severe cases, there is often destructiveness and stealing, accompanied by physical violence.

The undersocialized aggressive child is likely to be a boy with well-developed musculature who has experienced severe parental rejection, often alternating with unrealistic overprotection, especially shielding against the consequences of unacceptable behavior. Not only has the under-socialized aggressive child encountered unusual frustration, particularly of his dependency needs, but he has also escaped any consistent pattern of discipline. His deficient socialization is revealed not only in his excessive aggressiveness, but in a lack of sexual inhibition that is frequently expressed aggressively and openly. His general behavior is unacceptable in almost any social setting. He is generally viewed as a bad kid, and is frequently dealt with in a punitive way. Unfortunately, punishment almost invariably increases his maladaptive expression of rage and frustration, rather than ameliorating the problem.

Persistent enuresis, even to advanced ages, is a common finding in this diagnostic group.

In evaluation interviews, the undersocialized aggressive child is typically hostile, provocative, and uncooperative. He rarely volunteers information regarding his personal difficulties and, even if confronted with them, may deny their occurrence. If he is cornered, he may blandly justify his behavior, go into a suspicious rage regarding the source of the examiner's information, or even bolt from the room. The under-

TABLE I
DIAGNOSTIC CRITERIA FOR CONDUCT DISORDER, UNDERSOCIALIZED, AGGRESSIVE*

A. A repetitive and persistent pattern of aggressive conduct in which the basic rights of others are violated, as manifested by either of the following:
   (1) Physical violence against persons or property (not to defend someone else or oneself), e.g., vandalism, rape, breaking and entering, firesetting, mugging, assault
   (2) Thefts outside the home involving confrontation with the victim (e.g., extortion, purse-snatching, armed robbery)

B. *Failure to* establish a normal degree of affection, empathy, or bond with others as evidenced by *no more than one* of the following indications of social attachment:
   (1) Has one or more peer-group friendships that have lasted over 6 months
   (2) Extends himself or herself for others even when no immediate advantage is likely
   (3) Apparently feels guilt or remorse when such a reaction is appropriate (not just when caught or in difficulty)
   (4) Avoids blaming or informing on companions
   (5) Shares concern for the welfare of friends or companions

C. Duration of pattern of aggressive conduct of at least 6 months.

D. If 18 or older, does not meet the criteria for antisocial personality disorder.

* From American Psychiatric Association: *Diagnostic and Statistical Manual of Mental Disorders*, ed 3. American Psychiatric Association, Washington, DC, 1980. Used with permission.

socialized aggressive child is usually so maladaptive in his responses that he is unable to disguise his pathology even temporarily, or to elicit the examiner's sympathy by concocting feasible explanations of his misbehavior. Most often, he becomes angry at the examiner and expresses his resentment of the examination procedure with open belligerence or sullen withdrawal. His hostility is not limited to adult authority figures but is expressed with equal venom toward his age-mates and younger children. In fact, he often bullies those who are smaller and weaker than he. Boasting and lying, with little interest in the response of the listener, reveal his profoundly narcissistic orientation.

Evaluation of the family situation often reveals severe marital disharmony, which initially may center on disagreements over management of the child but which, on closer examination, reveals itself to be pervasive. Because of a tendency toward family instability, there is often a stepparent or stepparents in the picture. Many undersocialized aggressive youngsters are only children who were unplanned and unwanted. The parents, especially the father, are often diagnosed as having antisocial personality disorders.

In brief, the undersocialized aggressive child and his family demonstrate a stereotyped pattern of impulsive and unpredictable verbal and physical hostility. The child's aggressive behavior rarely seems directed toward any definable goal and provides him with little pleasure, success, or even sustained advantages with his peers or authority figures. He strikes out wildly at the world, grabbing and slashing, with very little idea of what he would like to gain through his behavior.

**Treatment.** Successful treatment of the undersocialized aggressive disorder is very difficult. Most therapists find it difficult to be patient and sympathetic with these youngsters in the face of their bristling hostility and provocativeness. The age at which treatment is begun is an important determining factor in success, not only because of the tendency of this behavioral pattern to become increasingly internalized and fixed in the face of the counterhostility that these youngsters engender in others but also because of the greater practical ease with which overt aggressiveness can be managed in the younger child.

Involvement of the family is essential. Unless the parents can come to feel some acceptance and warmth for the youngster and provide consistent guidelines for acceptable behavior, there is small likelihood that the most intensive work with the child will be helpful. Conjoint marital therapy and family therapy with these families is extremely demanding. The therapist often feels overwhelmed by the intensity of the hostile interactions in the family group, and frustrated by the parental inability to reach and persist in firm decisions regarding child management. The therapist is often faced with a confusing barrage of accusations, verbal attacks, and manipulations aimed at forcing him into an alliance with one family member against another. Countertransference reactions of irritation, confusion, and helplessness are understandable. Firmness and impartiality are essential but difficult to maintain in the atmosphere of mutual recrimination and contradictory accounts of family interactions. Occasionally, the entire family achieves a temporary united front, but all too often it is based on a shared desire to attack the therapist.

It is often necessary to separate the child from his home to treat him effectively. Even in a placement outside the home, the youngster can be expected to continue his extraordinary aggressiveness, testing of limits, and provocation. Those who are entrusted with the care of the undersocialized aggressive child must be prepared to offer acceptance and affection for long periods of time with very little positive feedback. Expectations for more socialized behavior from the youngster are initially minimal, and are only gradually increased.

Medications, especially the phenothiazines, may be of temporary value in some undersocialized aggressive children. But medication cannot substitute for the consistent and affectionate socializing experiences that the child needs for the development of internal controls and new adaptational skills. Therefore, great care must be taken not to overuse drugs as a convenient management tool.

## Conduct Disorder, Undersocialized, Nonaggressive Type

**Description.** The essential features are a failure to establish a normal degree of affection, empathy, or bonding with others; a pattern of nonaggressive antisocial behavior; and behavior difficulties at school (see Table II).

The failure to develop social attachments is manifested by the lack of sustained peer relationships, although the youngster may befriend a much older or younger person or have superficial relationships with other antisocial youngsters. Characteristically, the child does not extend himself for others unless there is an obvious immediate advantage for him. Egocentrism is shown by readily manipulating others for favors without any effort to reciprocate. There is a lack

TABLE II
DIAGNOSTIC CRITERIA FOR CONDUCT DISORDER, UNDERSOCIALIZED, NONAGGRESSIVE*

A. A repetitive and persistent pattern of nonaggressive conduct in which either the basic rights of others or major age-appropriate societal norms or rules are violated, as manifested by any of the following:
  (1) Chronic violations of a variety of important rules (that are reasonable and age-appropriate for the child) at home or at school (e.g., persistent truancy, substance abuse)
  (2) Repeated running away from home overnight
  (3) Persistent serious lying in and out of the home
  (4) Stealing not involving confrontation with a victim

B. *Failure to* establish a normal degree of affection, empathy, or bond with others as evidenced by *no more than one* of the following indications of social attachment:
  (1) Has one or more peer-group friendships that have lasted over 6 months
  (2) Extends himself or herself for others even when no immediate advantage is likely
  (3) Apparently feels guilt or remorse when such a reaction is appropriate (not just when caught or in difficulty)
  (4) Avoids blaming or informing on companions
  (5) Shows concern for the welfare of friends or companions

C. Duration of pattern of nonaggressive conduct of at least 6 months.

D. If 18 or older, does not meet the criteria for antisocial personality disorder.

*From American Psychiatric Association: *Diagnostic and Statistical Manual of Mental Disorders*, ed 3. American Psychiatric Association, Washington, DC, 1980. Used with permission.

of concern for the feelings, wishes, and well-being of others, manifested by callous behavior.

Two patterns are found. In one, the children are fearful and timid. They do not assert themselves boldly. Self-protective lying is usual, and manipulative lying is common. The children are likely to become hangers-on or fringe members of a delinquent group. Typical are very childish behavior and emotional immaturity, such as whining, demandingness, and temper tantrums. The children invariably feel rejected and unfairly treated, and are mistrustful of others. Self-esteem is very low. These children are frequently victimized, and submissive sexual behavior, heterosexual or homosexual, is fairly common, either under pressure or in an effort to achieve protection, favor, or maternal gains.

In the other pattern of the disorder, the youngsters act ingratiatingly and casually friendly because of exploitative, extractive goals. If no payoff is imminent, the children quickly abandon all efforts to please and lose interest in those toward whom a superficially friendly attitude was expressed.

Invariably, there are behavior problems at school that may include all the above behaviors.

This group of undersocialized unaggressive youngsters contrasts with the aggressive group primarily in that they respond to their frustration and anger with devious techniques and flight, rather than direct aggression. These youngsters are likely to be less physically robust than the openly aggressive undersocialized youngsters. They are also significantly less likely to have siblings than are the youngsters demonstrating socialized conduct disorder. The result of these two characteristics is that the youngster with unaggressive conduct disorder, undersocialized type, is likely to feel weak, abandoned, mistreated, worthless, helpless, and hopeless.

These youngsters may associate with a delinquent gang, but they remain on the fringe of the group, because they lack the courage and loyalty to gain genuine acceptance.

The youngsters are often timid and inept socially. Many of them appear to be what they eventually turn into as adults—born losers. Adult prison populations contain large numbers of these youngsters who were unable to develop more socially acceptable adaptive skills.

**Treatment.** Treatment of these youngsters is extremely difficult because of their lack of empathy, trust, and capacity to develop emotional attachments.

It is difficult to provide the broad range of services necessary to even hope for success. Because the basic cause is rejection in the home, some form of family therapy is indicated. However, this therapy is extremely difficult to arrange and continue, in view of the parent's usual lack of emotional investment in the youngster. Most of these youngsters are chronic school failures and, therefore, detest and avoid traditional classroom learning. They often require skilled special educational help to experience any academic success. This portion of the treatment is essential, however, inasmuch as some degree of improvement in learning skill is useful in raising self-esteem, and may encourage appropriate socialization in the school.

Active efforts to provide the youngster with pleasant and safe social experiences in other areas are also an important part of treatment.

Supportive group therapy, organized social clubs, and supervised recreational experiences may help to reverse the pattern of hopelessness, defeat, and surrender that characterizes these youngsters.

Because of the youngster's proclivity toward acting-out defenses, it is often necessary to provide treatment in a sheltered environment, such as an inpatient unit or residential treatment center. The therapist, parents, and residential staff must be prepared to accept maladaptive behaviors as inevitable if they are to guard against becoming even more angry at the youngster.

And, because the symptoms of the conduct disorders are primarily reactions to faulty parental training and represent, to a large extent, learned behavior, various techniques of behavior modification play an important role in their treatment.

### Socialized Conduct Disorders

The essential features are a pattern of antisocial behavior; affection, empathy, or bond with others; and behavior difficulties at school. There are two types described in DSM-III, a socialized, aggressive type (see Table III) and a socialized, nonaggressive type (see Table IV).

The antisocial behavior, by definition, involves violation of the rights of others. At the mild level it may involve lying, bullying, abusive language, minor thievery or vandalism, or behavior indicating a disregard for the comfort of others. This conduct is beyond the ordinary mischief and pranks of children and adolescents. At the moderate level, there may be physical

TABLE III
DIAGNOSTIC CRITERIA FOR CONDUCT DISORDER, SOCIALIZED, AGGRESSIVE*

A. A repetitive and persistent pattern of aggressive conduct in which the basic rights of others are violated, as manifested by either of the following:

    (1) Physical violence against persons or property (not to defend someone else or oneself), e.g., vandalism, rape, breaking and entering, fire-setting, mugging, assault
    (2) Thefts outside the home involving confrontation with a victim (e.g., extortion, purse-snatching, armed robbery)

B. Evidence of social attachment to others as indicated by at least two of the following behavior patterns:

    (1) Has one or more peer-group friendships that have lasted over 6 months
    (2) Extends himself or herself for others even when no immediate advantage is likely
    (3) Apparently feels guilt or remorse when such a reaction is appropriate (not just when caught or in difficulty)
    (4) Avoids blaming or informing on companions
    (5) Shows concern for the welfare of friends or companions

C. Duration of pattern of aggressive conduct of at least 6 months.

D. If 18 or older, does not meet the criteria for antisocial personality disorder.

*From American Psychiatric Association: *Diagnostic and Statistical Manual of Mental Disorders*, ed 3. American Psychiatric Association, Washington, DC, 1980. Used with permission.

TABLE IV
DIAGNOSTIC CRITERIA FOR CONDUCT DISORDER, SOCIALIZED, NONAGGRESSIVE*

A. A repetitive and persistent pattern of nonaggressive conduct in which either the basic rights of others or major age-appropriate societal norms or rules are violated, as manifested by any of the following:

    (1) Chronic violations of a variety of important rules (that are reasonable and age-appropriate for the child) at home or at school (e.g., persistent truancy, substance abuse)
    (2) Repeated running away from home overnight
    (3) Persistent serious lying in and out of the home
    (4) Stealing not involving confrontation with a victim

B. Evidence of social attachment to others as indicated by at least two of the following behavior patterns:

    (1) Has one or more peer-group friendships that have lasted over 6 months
    (2) Extends himself or herself for others even when no immediate advantage is likely
    (3) Apparently feels guilt or remorse when such a reaction is appropriate (not just when caught or in difficulty)
    (4) Avoids blaming or informing on companions
    (5) Shows concern for the welfare of friends or companions

C. Duration of patterns of nonagressive conduct of at least 6 months.

D. If 18 or older, does not meet the criteria for antisocial personality disorder.

*From American Psychiatric Association: *Diagnostic and Statistical Manual of Mental Disorders*, ed 3. American Psychiatric Association, Washington, DC, 1980. Used with permission.

aggression, traffic violations for reckless driving, serious stealing, breaking and entering, extortion, or larceny of motor vehicles. At the severe level, there is repeated serious physical aggression or assault against others, such as mugging, gang fighting, and beating. The presence or absence of aggressive behavior depends primarily on the nature of the gang or peer groups which the youngster joins.

The antisocial behavior invariably occurs outside the home and, on occasion, may be displayed at home. In addition, there are invariably behavior difficulties at school, such as repeated truancy, destructiveness, and aggression.

Children with this disorder have age-appropriate friendships. Such a child is likely to show concern for the welfare of his friends or companions, and is unlikely to blame them or inform on them. However, there is a callousness toward those whose rights he has violated.

**Epidemiology.** National and international statistics on juvenile delinquency do not distinguish between socialized conduct disorder and undersocialized conduct disorder, or distinguish whether legal delinquents are normal, neurotic, or psychotic.

In the United States at the present time, socialized conduct disorders appear to be very common, accounting for a major proportion of convicted delinquents, especially in the lower socioeconomic classes.

**Etiology.** Various etiological factors have been implicated in socialized conduct disorder. They encompass biological, temperamental, psychological, and sociological influences.

Sociological theories of socialized delinquency view the problem as an essentially normal reaction to socioeconomic conditions. Because many youngsters become neither delinquent nor emotionally ill, even in communities where juvenile crime is most rampant, there are obvious weaknesses in a purely sociological explanation. Some sociologists have dismissed this finding as chance, but recent thinking has considered individual differences in the family and in the child.

It is likely that contrasting theories and findings reflect a failure to distinguish youngsters with socialized conduct disorder from undersocialized and mentally ill delinquents.

In the youngster who is incompletely socialized, early family experiences, especially with the mother, have been satisfactory, but later training is inadequate, usually because of paternal indifference or abuse in the father-child relationship. The father may be inept because of illness, absence, or alcoholism. The family is often poorly adapted to the social mores of the dominant society, and often lacks status in the social hierarchy because of minority prejudice or immigration from rural to urban areas or from foreign countries.

Regardless of the specific reasons, the delinquent gang takes over the adolescent or late childhood socialization of the child. The youngster brings to the peer gang the capacity for warmth, loyalty, courage, and commitment, even though these positive feelings may be directed toward some gang members who do not deserve them and cannot reciprocate.

**Clinical Features.** The longitudinal history does not describe a difficult, angry youngster who has never conformed to parental wishes. Instead, there is a history of adequate or even excessive conformity that ended when the youngster became a member of the delinquent peer group, usually in preadolescence or early adolescence. There may have been evidence of other problems, such as marginal or poor school performance, mild behavior problems, and even neurotic symptoms or shyness.

Some degree of family pathology in the social or psychological area is usually evident. Patterns of paternal discipline are rarely ideal, and may vary from harshness and excessive strictness to inconsistency or relative absence of supervision and control. The mother has often protected the child from the consequences of early mild misbehaviors, but does not seem to actively encourage delinquency, as do the parents of the youngster with superego lacunae. There is usually evidence of a relatively warm relationship between the mother and the child, especially in infancy and early childhood. Some degree of marital disharmony may be present, and there is typically an absence of genuine family cohesion and comfortable interdependence. The socialized delinquent is likely to be from a large family living under poor economic circumstances.

The youngster himself is rarely guilty of criminal or antisocial acts alone. His misdeeds usually occur in the company of his peer group. The parents often recognize the role of the peer group in the youngster's difficulties, and complain of his wish to spend all his time with his friends. Frequently, the parents use this accurate observation to discount the predisposing factors within the family and the community that underlie the child's selection of unsuitable companions. Still, it is important that the examiner not dismiss this diagnostic information simply because of its similarity to the rationalizations that the parents of undersocialized and antisocial youngsters use to deny more severe psychopathology in their families and offspring.

The specific delinquent acts likely to be performed by the youngster with socialized conduct disorder, and the conditions under which they occur, may give clues to the diagnosis. Stealing and other minor delinquencies are the rule, not violent crimes against persons or even severely destructive acts of vandalism. Stealing in the home is relatively rare. Some of the gang's misdeeds seem bold and almost playful—cops and robbers in reality.

The important constant in this diagnostic category is the influence of the group on the youngster's behavior, and his extreme dependency on maintaining membership in the gang.

**Course and Prognosis.** The long-term prognosis for the youngster with socialized conduct disorder seems to be relatively favorable, certainly in comparison with the youngsters with undersocialized conduct disorders or antisocial personalities. Although no figures are obtainable, clinical experience suggests that many of the youngsters with socialized conduct disorder are not totally committed to a delinquent pattern, and give it up even during adolescence. This change may occur in response to fortuitous positive occurrences, such as academic or athletic successes or romantic attachments, or in response to the influence of one or more interested adults. Many other youngsters seem to be dissuaded from the pattern through the unpleasantness of arrest and appearance in a juvenile court. Such occurrences may also awaken the family to their responsibilities for the child.

**Diagnosis.** Socialized conduct disorder is a descriptive diagnosis, based on the finding of repetitive minor delinquencies occurring in a group matrix within which the youngster is capable of attachment, social interaction, and loyalty.

Viewing the youngster's internal psychopathology in isolation is generally insufficient for diagnosis or appropriate treatment planning. The child himself may be basically normal, excessively inhibited, or incompletely socialized. The prognostic implications and therapeutic indications vary widely across this range. The degree of aggressiveness exhibited by the gang may also influence outcome by dictating the severity of legal response to the youngster.

In a youngster with socialized conduct disorder, there is a relative absence of the hostile, belligerent callousness and lack of empathy characteristic of the undersocialized delinquent. This difference may not be readily apparent if the socialized youngster regards the examiner as hostile, punitive, or judgmental, or if the exam-

ination is conducted in a legal setting, such as juvenile court. However, with tact and patience it is usually possible to elicit evidence of cooperative and affectionate potential, even when the youngster shows little evidence of remorse for the pain his behavior may have caused other people. Although rationalization and self-justification occur, there is less deliberate distortion and denial than is usually encountered in interviews with the more narcissistic undersocialized delinquent. A capacity for trust and openness may be apparent if the examiner can demonstrate fairness and a desire to help. Genuine affection and concern for peers may be evident.

Evidence of neurotic conflict may be apparent, especially in the form of depressive tendencies. These self-doubts are not as malignant as those seen in undersocialized delinquents, and are not usually accompanied by the periods of grandiosity seen at other times in that group. A history of anxiety episodes is common. The anxiety is not always related to external danger, such as fear of detection during a delinquent act or the likelihood of punishment. However, the pattern of repeated delinquencies, the comfortable gang membership, and the absence of a structured neurotic illness remove the youngster from the diagnostic category of the neurotic reactions. Psychotic signs and symptoms generally remove a youngster from this diagnostic category, although episodes of extreme panic with somewhat bizarre behavior may occur in situations of stress or danger.

Maintenance of peer relationships is often more important than any other goal in the youngster's life. Spontaneous verbalizations often show a preoccupation with the youngster's friends and his duty to protect them. There is often an insistence that these fellow delinquents understand and care for the patient in a way that his parents and other adults never have.

In the face of betrayal, neglect, and even physical abuse, the youngster defends and justifies his cronies, apparently determined to maintain his fantasy of secure dependence on his companions. This extraordinarily forgiving outlook is especially marked in passive, withdrawn, overly inhibited youngsters who have discovered their first social acceptance in a delinquent group and are willing to pay a dear price to maintain it. The distinction from the youngster with undersocialized conduct disorder who clings to the fringes of a gang for safety may not be apparent initially, but can usually be made once the examiner is better acquainted with the case.

The developmental history is often relatively normal during early childhood. Although marital discord and family difficulties may be apparent, there is usually evidence of adequate maternal care, at least during infancy. Overt rejection and hostility are not as apparent as in the history of the child with an antisocial personality. Parental sins are more those of omission, and may be related to such reality factors as family size, death of the father, parental alcoholism, poverty, and simple social ineptitude, rather than severe personal maladjustment leading to overt hostility toward the child, or to a neurotic need to sanction delinquent behavior.

Maternal hostility toward the child, if present, tends to be recent in origin and clearly related to the child's misbehavior and the real problems it has caused. The father is usually more remiss in his parental duties than the mother. For a variety of reasons, he has been unable to provide the affection, control, and desirable model that the youngster requires. The mother may complain that he is uninterested in the family.

**Treatment.** Treatment approaches to delinquency may be divided into preventive efforts and treatment methods designed for youngsters already officially declared delinquent.

One element of the preventive approach to delinquency is the variety of general welfare programs that have been mounted over the years, in an effort to ameliorate the sociological conditions that seem to produce a high incidence of delinquent behavior. It is obvious that delinquency continues in spite of such programs, but the programs' proponents can argue with justification that efforts have been inadequate and, at any rate, may have prevented the delinquency statistics from being worse than they are.

Experiments in which potential delinquents received traditional individual psychotherapy have produced disappointing results. Individual outpatient psychotherapy appears to be relatively ineffective in problems of this kind, although it should be noted that the psychotherapy was brief and relatively superficial in these studies.

Only a small percentage of delinquent youngsters respond favorably to the typical permissive, dynamically oriented counseling approach. There is some evidence that reality therapy may be most effective in a group setting, either in self-help groups or in professionally directed groups. Basically, these groups use a core of reformed delinquents who understand the rationalizations, denials, and self-justifications of the gang member, and vigorously confront the youngster with the realities of his predicament and the inevitability of eventual negative consequences to him if he persists in delinquency.

Although the evidence to this point is anecdotal and inconclusive, the consensus in the literature seems to favor various forms of group therapy for the youngster with socialized conduct disorder. Group-oriented approaches capitalize on the gang member's natural proclivity to turn to peers for direction and emotional support. The crucial task is to convert the group orientation toward more conventional values. This conversion may require separation from the previous peer group, and transplantation to an entirely new environment, as in training schools, Outward Bound, and therapeutic camping programs.

Many youngsters with socialized conduct disorder do not receive psychiatric treatment at all, but are, instead, remanded to training schools or reformatories. A high percentage of these youngsters improve spontaneously as they become interested in heterosexual relationships, assume family responsibilities, and secure employment. Because their basic capacity for human relatedness is intact, they often discover their own passage out of delinquency.

The evaluative comment that seems consonant with the present state of knowledge is that therapeutic optimism is very much warranted in this group of youngsters. Any approach that alters the attitudes of the entire group, or that separates the youngster from the delinquent peer group and offers him contact with strong adult male leaders and less delinquently oriented peers, is quite likely to improve the group's delinquent behavior.

### Atypical Conduct Disorders

This is a category where the predominant disturbance involves a conduct pattern violating either the rights of others or societal rules or norms but cannot be classified as one of the aforementioned conduct disorders.

### REFERENCES

Bender L: The concept of pseudopsychopathic schizophrenia in adolescents. Am J Orthopsychiatry 29: 491, 1959.
Farrington D P: The family backgrounds of aggressive youths. In *Aggression and Antisocial Behavior in Childhood and Adolescence*, L Herzov, M Berger, D Shaffer, editors. Pergamon, Oxford, England, 1978.
Glueck S, Glueck E: *Unraveling Juvenile Delinquency*. Commonwealth Fund, New York, 1950.
Hewitt L, Jenkins R L: *Fundamental Patterns of Maladjustment: The Dynamics of Their Origin*. State of Illinois, Springfield, IL, 1946.
Hutchings B, Mednick S A: Registered, criminality on the adoptive and biological parents of registered male criminal adoptees. In *Genetics, Environment and Psychopathology*, S A Madnick, F Schlesinger, J Higgins, B Bell, editors. North Holland/Elsevier, Amsterdam, 1974. Lewis D O, editor: *Vulnerabilities to Delinquency*. Spectrum Publications, New York, 1981.
Lewis D O: Conduct disorder and juvenile delinquency.

In *Comprehensive Textbook of Psychiatry*, ed 4, H I Kaplan, B J Sadock, editors, p 1754. Williams & Wilkins, Baltimore, 1985.

Lewis D O, Shanok S S, Grant M, Ritvo E: Homicidally aggressive young children: Neuropsychiatric and experiential correlates. Am J Psychiatry *140:* 148, 1983.

Lewis D O, Shanok S S, Lewis M L, Unger L, Goldman C: Conduct disorder and its synonyms: Diagnosis of dubious validity and usefulness. Am J Psychiatry *141:* 514, 1984.

Martinson R, Palmer T, Adams S: *Rehabilitation, Recidivism, and Research*. National Council on Crime and Delinquency, Hackensack, NJ, 1976.

Mednick S A, Christiansen K O: *Biosocial Bases of Criminal Behavior*, A Sarnoff, S A Mednick, K O Christiansen, editors. Gardner Press, New York, 1977.

Quay H C: Classification in the treatment of delinquency and antisocial behavior. In *Issues on the Classification of Children*, Vol 1, N Hobbs, editor. Jossey-Bass, San Francisco, 1975.

Robins L: *Deviant Children Grown Up*. Williams & Wilkins, Baltimore, 1966.

Wolfgang M E, Figlio R M, Cellin T: *Delinquency in a Birth Cohort*. University of Chicago Press, Chicago, 1972.

---

# 35.7 ADJUSTMENT AND IDENTITY DISORDERS OF ADOLESCENCE

## Adolescent Adjustment Disorder

### Definition

According to DSM-III, this disorder is characterized by impairment in social or academic functionng and is a maladaptive reaction to a stressor such as moving away from home and parental supervision. The symptoms are in excess of a normal and expectable response to the stressor.

### Epidemiology

A conservative estimate is that 10 to 15 percent of the adolescent population, at some point in their development, manifest an adjustment reaction requiring a psychological contact.

### Etiology

The main cause of reactive and adjustment conflicts is found in the failure to adequately process challenges to the mental mechanisms of the psychic structure, the ego. In the disorders described in this section, the intensity of the stress overwhelms the ego solutions available, resulting in symptomatic states affecting emancipation efforts, identity resolution, and learning. These are clearly developmental lags, because no serious mental disorder accompanies the states described, and the reactive nature of the disorder suggests that the therapeutic approaches facilitate correct resolution of the conflict, rather than demanding the restructuring of underlying characterological states.

## Clinical Features of Adolescent Adjustment Disorder

Acute regressive states manifested by anxiety, depression, eating and sleeping disorders, clinging to peers or parents, psychosomatic disorders, or impulsive acting out may be present in the youth who is reacting to a recent demand or separation from home or school, or the anticipation of such a separation. The main feature of this problem is that the conflict over independence follows the expected assumption of a more expectant role for adult, independent behavior. Other features include erratic and pseudoindependent behavior, homesickness, and impulsive major decisions concerning work or education.

The following features are characteristic of adolescent adjustment disorders: (1) recent assumption of a life situation in which the person is more independent of parental control or supervision; (2) the person's regarding the change as desirable; (3) symptomatic expression of a conflict over independence manifested by two or more of the following: (a) difficulty in making independent decisions commensurate with a new situation, (b) increased dependence on parental advice, (c) newly developed and unwarranted concern about parental possessiveness, (d) adoption of values deliberately in opposition to parents, (e) rapid development of markedly dependent peer relationships, (f) homesickness that the person finds inconsistent with a conscious wish to be away from home; and (4) not secondary to other mental disorder.

## Differential Diagnosis of Adolescent Problems

**Schizophrenia.** Only one-third of hospitalized adolescents eventually labeled schizophrenic present no diagnostic difficulty, with clear findings of thinking disorder, anhedonia, diminished capacity to experience pleasure, characterological dependency, impairment in competence, and a vulnerable sense of self-regard. Two-thirds of the schizophrenics may initially present clinical pictures of severe adjustment reaction of psychotic proportions or severe personality disorders.

**Personality Disorders.** These disorders manifest lifelong patterns of behavior demonstrating developmental defect and fixation. A careful past history and a mental status examination are necessary to reveal the true nature of the personality disturbances manifested by one of the personality disorders: schizoid, passive-aggressive, paranoid, schizotypal, borderline, narcissistic, histrionic, avoidant, dependent, compulsive, or antisocial.

**Neuroses.** Anxiety, depression, phobias, conversion symptoms, and other symptoms experienced as subjective distress are common features in neurotic disorders. Patients tend to be cooperative and to give frank, reliable histories. Many manifest personality traits—compulsive, hysterical, schizoid—that seem uninfluenced by the adjustment disorder.

## Treatment of Adolescent Problems

Mild adjustment disorders usually respond well to reassurance or short-term psychotherapy. Support given to parents, teachers, and other concerned adults that the reactions are in the service of ego mastery usually provides enough of a moratorium for eventual integration and synthesis to occur.

## Identity Disorder

The term ego identity denotes the results of certain gains the person has achieved by the end of adolescence. These derivatives of preadult experiences, accomplished to become ready for the tasks of adulthood, eventually connote a persistent sameness within oneself (self-sameness) and a continuing sharing of some kind of essential character with others.

## Definition

DSM-III defines identity disorders as severe subjective distress over an inability to reconcile aspects of the self into a relatively coherent and acceptable sense of self. The disturbance is manifested by uncertainty about a variety of issues relating to identity, including long-term goals, career choice, friendship patterns, values, and loyalties. These symptoms last for at least 3 months. The diagnosis is not valid if the reaction is symptomatic of another mental disorder, such as borderline personality disorder, affective disorder, or schizophrenic disorder. In DSM-II, identity disorder was included in transient situational disturbances.

## Causes

The clinical picture of acute identity disorder is recognized in young people who are unable to use the social or intrapsychic moratoriums provided. The normal intrapsychic transformations necessary in ego mastery result in persistent regressive phenomena leading to crisis formation and, if not relieved by adequate growth responses, identity diffusion.

## Clinical Features

The clinical features of identity disorder are summarized in a serious struggle with the question: "Who am I?" The resulting transitory regression is manifested by being unable to make decisions, a sense of isolation and inner emptiness, an inability to achieve relationships and sexual intimacy, a distorted time perspective resulting in a sense of great urgency and a loss of consideration for time as a dimension of living, an acute inability to work, and, at times, choosing of a negative identity, one that is a hostile parody of the usual roles in one's family or community (see Table I).

The uncertainty regarding long-term goals may be expressed as inability to choose a life pattern (material success versus service to the community) and conflict regarding career choice. Conflict regarding friendship patterns may manifest itself as attraction to particular groups characterized by uncommon interests or styles (revolutionary or drug-oriented move-

TABLE I
DIAGNOSTIC CRITERIA FOR IDENTITY DISORDER*

A. Severe subjective distress regarding uncertainty about a variety of issues relating to identity, including three or more of the following:

    (1) Long-term goals
    (2) Career choice
    (3) Friendship patterns
    (4) Sexual orientation and behavior
    (5) Religious identification
    (6) Moral value systems
    (7) Group loyalties

B. Impairment in social or occupational (including academic) functioning as a result of the symptoms in A.

C. Duration of the disturbance of at least 3 months.

D. Not due to another mental disorder, such as affective disorder, schizophrenia, or schizophreniform disorder.

E. If 18 or older, does not meet the criteria for borderline personality disorder.

* From American Psychiatric Association: *Diagnostic and Statistical Manual of Mental Disorders*, ed 3. American Psychiatric Association, Washington, DC, 1980. Used with permission.

ments or cults). Conflict regarding values and loyalties may include concerns over religious identification, patterns of sexual behavior, and moral issues.

The associated features frequently found in identity disorder include a marked discrepancy between the person's view of himself and the view that others have of him; moderate anxiety and depression, usually related to inner preoccupation rather than external events; self-doubt and doubt about the future, with either difficulty in making choices or impulsive experimentations; and choice of negative or oppositional self-patterns in an attempt to establish an independent identity.

### Course and Prognosis

Identity disorder, now recognized as a continuing dilemma throughout life, has its origins in late adolescence as the person becomes detached from his family's value systems and attempts to establish his own identity. The particular stress varies, but the conflict develops around the demand or assumption of a status in which the youth is more independent of parental control or supervision.

The onset may be acute, but there is usually evidence of a gradual onset of anxiety, depression, regressive phenomena—such as loss of interest in friends, school, or activities—irritability, sleep difficulties, and changes in eating habits.

If the symptoms are not recognized and resolved, a full-blown identity crisis may develop. As described by Erikson, the youth manifests severe doubting and an inability to make decisions (abulia), a sense of isolation and inner emptiness, a growing inability to relate to others, disturbed sexual function, a distorted time perspective with a sense of urgency, and the assumption of a negative identity.

The course of the disorder is usually brief, as developmental lags are very responsive to support, acceptance, and the provision of a psychosocial moratorium. If more than 1 year passes, further diagnostic evaluation should be considered in a search for additional psychopathology. An extensive prolongation of adolescence with continued identity disorder may lead to the chronic state of identity diffusion that usually indicates disturbance of early developmental stages and the presence of borderline personality organization, affective disorder, or schizophrenia.

### Diagnosis

The following features are emphasized in the formulation of identity disorder in DSM-III: (1)

severe subjective distress derived from conflicts about the assumption of an identity, the final results of gains achieved by the end of adolescence including a definition of long-term goals, career choice, friendship patterns, values, and loyalties and resulting in a persistent sameness within the self and a persistent sharing of some kind of essential character with others; (2) not secondary to affective disorder, schizophrenic disorder, pervasive developmental disorder, borderline personality disorder, or any other mental disorder; and (3) age of onset at least 14 years or in late adolescence. The disorder usually resolves by the patient's mid-twenties. If it becomes chronic, the individual may be unable to make career commitments or lasting attachments.

Identity disorder should not be diagnosed if the identity problems are secondary to another mental disorder. Identity disorder must also be differentiated from the ordinary conflicts associated with maturing.

### Treatment

Therapeutic efforts in identity disorder are directed toward encouraging growth and development. Adolescents, particularly in the regressed state of an identity disorder, react like borderline personalities and respond well to the technique in which the transference is permitted to develop in the context of a controlled regression without gratifying or infantilizing the patient. Feelings and wishes are recognized, and the patient is encouraged to examine his longings and feelings of deprivation and to try to understand, with the emphatic help of the therapist, what is happening to him.

## Specific Academic or Work Inhibition

Specific academic or work inhibition, like identity disorder, is an adjustment disorder reflective of conflicts related to transitions from adolescence to adulthood. Instead of affecting only the ego tasks of separation-individuation and identity formation, specific academic or work inhibition involves the cognitive functions of the ego. A student may see the threat of failing an examination in relationship to total failure in life objectives and, consequently, develop a response leading to an inhibition of cognitive processing.

### Definition

The essential feature of specific academic or work inhibition is a clinical picture dominated by an inability to function adequately when intellectual capacity, skills, and previous academic or work performance have been at least adequate.

The associated features may include sleep disturbances, compulsive rituals, disorganization of daily routine, eating disturbances, and the excessive use of drugs, alcohol, or tobacco.

## Causes

In general, the causes of specific academic or work inhibition are similar to the causes of the other disorders of late adolescence.

## Clinical Features, Course, and Prognosis

Specific academic or work inhibition may manifest itself in an acute or a chronic form (see Table II).

One common feature found in many patients with inhibitions of studying or work is the general problem of loneliness. Many adolescents with this difficulty have intense, clinging relationships with their peers or parents. A reluctance to leave these symbiotic-like contacts to go to class or study reveals an essential inability to be alone, a failure to complete the tasks of separation-individuation. In these cases, the cognitive recognition is an affective-cognitive link, rather than the cognitive-affective perception of loss mentioned earlier.

As in the previously described disorders of late adolescence, the course of specific academic or work inhibition is relatively brief and responds to support and opportunities for moratoriums. If more than 1 year passes without resolution of the problem, further diagnostic evaluation should be carried out.

## Diagnosis

The following features are emphasized in specific academic or work inhibition: (1) severe distress interfering significantly with any of the following academic or work tasks and manifested by: (a) anxiety related to examinations or other tests, (b) inability to write papers, prepare reports, or perform in studio arts activities, (c) difficulty in concentrating on studies or work, (d) avoidance of studying or work that does not seem to be under the person's conscious control; (2) distress not present when the person is not thinking about the academic or work task; (3) adequate intellectual and academic or work skills present; (4) adequate previous academic or work functioning; and (5) intended academic or work effort, even if secondarily extinguished by one of conditions included in (1) above.

The differential diagnosis of specific academic or work inhibition is the same as in identity disorder. On occasion, psychological testing exposes a borderline intelligence that was not uncovered in school testing, particularly in a highly socialized person who has been pushed through school.

## Treatment

The treatment plan in specific academic or work inhibition should encourage growth and development. The provision of a period of time away from studies or work allows a moratorium that, along with psychotherapy, provides a support system to discourage further and continued regression, and encourages resolution and synthesis.

TABLE II
CLINICAL FEATURES OF SPECIFIC ACADEMIC OR WORK INHIBITION*

| Essential Features | Associated Features |
|---|---|
| Severe stress interfering significantly with any of the following academic or work tasks and manifested by: | Anxiety and depression |
| | Sleep disturbances |
| | Compulsive behavior |
| | Disorganization of daily routine |
| Anxiety related to examinations or other tests | Eating disturbances |
| | Abuse of drugs, alcohol, or tobacco |
| Inability to write papers, prepare reports, or perform in studio arts activities | Loneliness |
| Difficulty in concentrating on studies or work | |
| Avoidance of studying or work that does not seem to be under conscious control | |
| Distress not present when the person is not thinking about the academic or work task | |
| Adequate intellectual and academic work skills present | |
| Adequate previous academic or work functioning | |
| Intended academic or work effort, even if secondarily extinguished by above symptoms | |

* Based on American Psychiatric Association: *Diagnostic and Statistical Manual of Mental Disorders*, ed 3. American Psychiatric Association, Washington, DC, 1980.

## REFERENCES

Blos P: *On Adolescence.* Free Press of Glencoe, New York, 1962.

Erikson E H: The problems of ego identity. J Am Psychoanal Assoc 4: 428, 1956.

Feinstein S C: Identity and adjustment disorders of adolescence. In *Comprehensive Textbook of Psychiatry*, ed 4, H I Kaplan, B J Sadock, editors, p 1760.

Williams & Wilkins, Baltimore, 1985.

Freud A: Adolescence. Psychoanal Study Child *13:* 225, 1958.

Gardner G E: Psychiatric problems of adolescence. In *American Handbook of Psychiatry*, S Arieti, editor, p 870. Basic Books, New York, 1959.

Geleerd E R: Some aspects of ego vicissitudes in adolescence. J Am Psychoanal Assoc *9:* 394, 1961.

Gittelson M: Character synthesis: Psychotherapeutic problems of adolescence. Am J Orthopsychiatry *14:* 522, 1948.

Goldberg A: On the prognosis and treatment of narcissism. J Am Psychoanal Assoc *22:* 243, 1974.

Grinker R, R, Holzman P S: Schizophrenic pathology in young adults. Arch Gen Psychiatry *28:* 168, 1973.

Henderson A S, Krupinsky J, Stoller A: Epidemiological aspects of adolescent psychiatry. In *Modern Perspectives in Adolescent Psychiatry*, J Howells, editor, p 183. Brunner/Mazel, New York, 1971.

Josseln I M: *Adolescence*. Harper & Row, New York, 1971.

Kohut H: The psychoanalytic treatment of narcissistic personality disorders. Psychoanal Study Child *23:* 86, 1968.

Mahler M S: On the first three subphases of the separation-individuation process. Int J Psychoanal *53:* 333, 1972.

Masterson J F: *The Psychiatric Dilemma of Adolescence*. Little, Brown, Boston, 1967.

Offer D, Offer J B: Three developmental routes through normal male adolescence. In *Adolescent Psychiatry*, Vol 4, S C Feinstein, P L Giovacchini, editors, p 121. Jason Aronson, New York, 1976.

Stierlin H, Levi L D, Savard R J: Centrifugal versus centripetal separation in adolescence. In *Adolescent Psychiatry*, Vol 2, S C Feinstein, P L Giovacchini, editors, p 211. Basic Books, New York, 1973.

# 36

# Child Psychiatry and Psychiatric Treatment

## 36.1 INDIVIDUAL PSYCHOTHERAPY

### Theoretical Assumptions

The choice of intervention with an individual youngster should be based on the clinician's understanding of the child's problem and should stem from an individualized assessment of the child and his family. But, regardless of how individualized such an evaluation is, any rational assessment requires that the data of observation be organized within a coherent framework. Typically, such systematizing schemata are derived from the therapist's preferred theory of personality development and organization, rendering it vital that the clinician be vigilant that these theories not distort the clinical observations or inappropriately influence the therapeutic interventions. Currently, four major theoretical systems underlie the bulk of child psychotherapy: (1) psychoanalytic theories of the evolution and resolution of emotional disturbance, (2) social-learning-behavioral theories, (3) family systems-oriented transactional theories of psychopathology and treatment, and (4) developmental theories.

### Classical Psychoanalytic Theory

Classical psychoanalytic theory conceives of exploratory psychotherapy's working, with patients of all ages, by reversing the evolution of psychopathological processes. A principal difference noted with advancing age is a sharpening distinction between psychogenetic and psychodynamic factors. The younger the child, the more the genetic and the dynamic forces are intertwined.

The development of these pathological processes is generally thought to begin with experiences that have proved to be particularly significant to the patient, and have affected him adversely. Although in one sense the experiences were real, in another sense they may have been misinterpreted or imagined. In any event, for the patient they were traumatic experiences that caused unconscious complexes. Being inaccessible to conscious awareness, these unconscious elements readily escape rational adaptive maneuvers, and are subject to a pathological misuse of adaptive and defensive mechanisms. The end result is the development of distressing symptoms, character attitudes, or patterns of behavior that constitute the emotional disturbance.

Increasingly, the psychoanalytic view of emotional disturbances in children has assumed a developmental orientation. Thus, the maladaptive defensive functioning is directed against conflicts between impulses that are characteristic of a specific developmental phase and environmental influence, or the child's internalized representations of the environment. In this framework, the disorders are the result of environmental interferences with maturational time tables or conflicts with the environment engendered by developmental progress. The result is difficulty in achieving or resolving developmental tasks and achieving the capacities specific to later phases of development, which can be expressed in various ways, such as Anna Freud's lines of development and Erikson's concept of sequential psychosocial capacities.

Psychoanalytic psychotherapy is a modified form of psychotherapy which is expressive and exploratory and endeavors to reverse this evolution of emotional disturbance, through a reenactment and desensitization of the traumatic events by free expression of thoughts and feelings, in an interview-play situation. Ultimately, the therapist helps the patient understand the warded-off feelings, fears, and wishes that have beset him.

Whereas the psychoanalytic psychotherapeutic approach seeks improvement by exposure and resolution of buried conflicts, suppressive-supportive-educative psychotherapy works in an opposite fashion. It aims to facilitate repression. The therapist, capitalizing on the patient's desire to please, encourages the patient to substitute new adaptive and defensive mechanisms. In this type of therapy, the therapist uses interpretations minimally; instead, the therapist emphasizes suggestion, persuasion, exhortation, operant or classical reinforcement, counseling, education, direction, advice, abreaction, environmental manipulation, intellectual review, gratification of the patient's current dependent needs, and similar techniques.

### Learning-Behavioral Theories

All behavior, regardless of whether it is adaptive or maladaptive, is a consequence of the same basic principles of behavior acquisition and maintenance. It is either learned or unlearned, and what renders behavior abnormal or disturbed is its social significance.

Although the theories and their derivative therapeutic intervention techniques have become increasingly complex over the years, it is still possible to subsume all learning within two global basic mechanisms. One is classical respondent conditioning, akin to Pavlov's famous experiments, and the second is operant instrumental learning, which is to be associated with Skinner's name, even though it is basic to both Thorndike's law of effect regarding the influence of reinforcing consequences of behavior, and to Freud's pain-pleasure principle. Both of these basic mechanisms assign the highest priority to the immediate precipitants of behavior, deemphasizing those remote underlying causal determinants that are important in the psychoanalytic tradition. The theory asserts quite simply that there are but two types of abnormal behavior. On the one hand, there are the behavioral deficits that result from a failure to learn, and, on the other hand, there is deviant maladaptive behavior that is a consequence of learning inappropriate things.

Such concepts have always been an implicit part of the rationale underlying all child psychotherapy. Intervention strategies derive much of their success, particularly with children, from rewarding previously unnoticed good behavior, thereby highlighting it and making it more frequent.

### Family Systems Theory

Although families have long been an interest of children's psychotherapists, their understanding of transactional family processes has been greatly enhanced by conceptual contributions from cybernetics, systems theory, communications theory, object relations theory, social role theory, ethology, and ecology.

The bedrock premise entails the family's functioning as a self-regulating open system that possesses its own unique history and structure. Its structure is constantly evolving as a consequence of the dynamic interaction between the family's mutually interdependent subsystems and individuals who share a complementarity of needs. From this conceptual foundation, a wealth of ideas has emerged under rubrics such as the family's development, life cycle, homeostasis, functions, identity, values, goals, congruence, symmetry, myths, rules, roles (spokesperson, symptom bearer, scapegoat, affect barometer, pet, persecutor, victim, arbitrator, distractor, saboteur, rescuer, breadwinner, disciplinarian, nurturer), structure (boundaries, splits, pairings, alliances, coalitions, enmeshed, disengaged), double bind, scapegoating, pseudomutuality, and mystification. Increasingly, it is being noted that appreciation of the family system sometimes explains why a minute therapeutic input at a critical junction may result in farreaching changes, whereas in other situations huge quantities of therapeutic effort appear to be absorbed with minimal evidence of change.

### Developmental Theories

Underlying child psychotherapy is the assumption that in the absence of unusual interferences, children mature in basically orderly, predictable ways that are codifiable in a variety of interrelated psychosociobiological sequential systematizations. The central and overriding role of a developmental frame of reference in child psychotherapy distinguishes it from adult psychotherapy. The therapist's orientation should entail something more than knowledge of age-appropriate behavior derived from such studies as Gesell's descriptions of the morphology of behavior. It should encompass more than psychosexual development with ego-psychological and sociocultural amendments, exemplified by Erikson's epigenetic schema. It extends beyond familiarity with Piaget's sequence of intellectual evolution as a basis for acquaintance with the level of abstraction at which children of various ages may be expected to function or for assessing their capacity for a moral orientation.

## Types of Psychotherapy

Among the common bases for classification of child therapy is identification of the element presumed to be helpful for the young patient.

Isolating a single therapeutic element as the

basis for classification tends to be somewhat artificial, because most, if not all, of the factors are present in varying degrees in every child psychotherapeutic undertaking. For example, there is no psychotherapy in which the relationship between therapist and patient is not a vital factor; nevertheless, child psychotherapists commonly talk of relationship therapy to describe a form of treatment in which a positive, friendly, helpful relationship is viewed as the primary, if not the sole, therapeutic ingredient. Probably one of the best examples of pure relationship therapy is to be found outside of a clinical setting in the work of the Big Brother Organization.

Remedial, educational, and patterning psychotherapy endeavors to teach new attitudes and patterns of behavior to children who persist in using immature and inefficient patterns, which are often presumed to be due to a maturational lag.

Supportive psychotherapy is particularly helpful in enabling a well-adjusted youngster to cope with the emotional turmoil engendered by a crisis. It is also used with those quite disturbed youngsters whose less than adequate ego functioning may be seriously disrupted by an expressive-exploratory mode or by other forms of therapeutic intervention. At the beginning of most psychotherapy, regardless of the patient's age and the nature of the therapeutic interventions, the principal therapeutic elements perceived by the patient tend to be the supportive ones, a consequence of therapists' universal efforts to be reliably and sensitively responsive. In fact, some therapy may never proceed beyond this supportive level, whereas others develop an expressive-exploratory or behavioral modification flavor on top of the supportive foundation.

Release therapy, described initially by David Levy, facilitates the abreaction of pent-up emotions. Although abreaction is an aspect of many therapeutic undertakings, in release therapy the treatment situation is structured to encourage only this factor. It is indicated primarily for preschool-age children who are suffering from a distorted emotional reaction to an isolated trauma.

Pre-school-aged children are sometimes treated indirectly through the parents. The therapist using this strategy should be alert to the possibility that apparently successful filial treatment can obscure a significant diagnosis.

Psychotherapy with children is often psychoanalytically oriented, which means that it endeavors through the vehicle of self-understanding to enable the child to develop his potential further. This development is accomplished by liberating for more constructive use the psychic energy that is presumed to be expended in defending against fantasied dangers. The child is generally unaware of these unreal dangers, his fear of them, and the psychological defenses he uses to avoid both the danger and the fear. With the awareness that is facilitated, the patient can evaluate the usefulness of his defensive maneuvers and relinquish the unnecessary ones that constitute the symptoms of his emotional disturbance.

This form of psychoanalytic psychotherapy is to be distinguished from child psychoanalysis, a more intensive and less common treatment, in which the unconscious elements are interpreted systematically from outside in, resulting in the orderly sequence of affect-defense-impulse. Under these circumstances, the therapist anticipates unconscious resistances and allows transference manifestations to mature to a full transference neurosis, through which neurotic conflicts are resolved.

Although interpretations of dynamically relevant conflicts are emphasized in psychoanalytic descriptions, this does not imply the absence of elements that are predominant in other types of psychotherapies. Indeed, in all psychotherapy, the child should derive support from the consistently understanding and accepting relationship with the therapist, while varying degrees of remedial educational guidance and emotional release are inevitably present.

### Interrelationship of Behavioral and Psychodynamic Therapies

Probably the most vivid examples of the integration of psychodynamic and behavioral approaches, even though they are not always explicitly conceptualized as such, are to be found in the milieu therapy of child psychiatric residential and day treatment facilities. Behavioral change is initiated in the residential setting, and its repercussions are explored concurrently in individual psychotherapeutic sessions, so that the action in one arena and the information stemming from it augment and illuminate what transpires in the other arena.

### Other Types of Psychotherapy

Cognitive therapy has been used with children, adolescents, and adults. This approach attempts to correct cognitive distortions, particularly negative conceptions of oneself and is used mainly in depression.

EST (Erhard Seminars Training), a type of therapy utilized with adolescents and adults, attempts to change behavior using consciousness altering techniques, such as evoking strong emotional states, and abreaction in groups. Utilizing a combination of encounter, zen, positive thinking, gestalt, and Taoism, it is apparently of no therapeutic value and may in fact be harmful even though many adolescents are drawn to this adult-like approach.

### Differences between Children and Adults

Logic suggests that psychotherapy with children, who generally are more flexible than adults and have simpler defenses and other mental mechanisms, should consume less time than comparable treatment of adults. Experience does not usually confirm this expectation, because of the relative absence in children of some elements that contribute to successful treatment.

A child, for example, typically does not seek help. As a consequence, one of the first tasks for the therapist is to stimulate the child's motivation for treatment. Children commonly begin therapy involuntarily, often without the benefit of true parental support. Although the parents may want their child helped or changed, this desire is often generated by frustrated anger with the child. Typically, this anger is accompanied by relative insensitivity to what the therapist perceives as the child's need and the basis for a therapeutic alliance. Thus, whereas adult patients frequently perceive advantages in getting well, children may envision therapeutic change as nothing more than conforming to a disagreeable reality, which heightens the likelihood of perceiving the therapist as the parent's punitive agent. This is hardly the most fertile soil in which to nurture a therapeutic alliance.

Children tend to externalize internal conflicts in search of alloplastic adaptations and to find it difficult to conceive of problem resolution except by altering an obstructing environment. The passive, masochistic boy who is the constant butt of his schoolmates' teasing finds it inconceivable that this situation could be rectified by altering his mode of handling his aggressive impulses, rather than by someone's controlling his tormentors, a view that may be reinforced by significant adults in his environment.

The tendency of children to reenact their feelings in new situations facilitates the early appearance of spontaneous and global transference reactions that may be troublesome. Concurrently, the eagerness that children have for new experiences, coupled with their natural developmental fluidity, tends to limit the intensity and therapeutic usefulness of subsequent transference developments.

Children have a limited capacity for self-ob-
servation, with the notable exception of some obsessive children who resemble adults in this ability. These obsessive children, however, usually isolate the vital emotional components. In the exploratory-interpretative psychotherapies, development of a capacity for ego splitting—that is, simultaneous emotional involvement and self-observation—is most helpful. Only by means of identification with a trusted adult, and in alliance with that adult, are children able to approach such an ideal. The therapist's sex, or the relatively superficial aspects of the therapist's demeanor, may be important elements in the development of a trusting relationship with a child.

Regressive behavioral and communicative modes can be wearing on child therapists. Typically motor-minded, even when they do not require external controls, children may demand a degree of physical stamina that is not of consequence in therapy with adults. The age appropriateness of such primitive mechanisms as denial, projection, and isolation hinders the process of working through, which relies on a patient's synthesizing and integrative capacities, both of which are immature in children. Also, environmental pressures on the therapist are generally greater in psychotherapeutic work with children than in work with adults.

Although children compare unfavorably with adults in many of the qualities that are generally considered desirable in therapy, children have the advantage of active maturational and developmental forces. The history of psychotherapy for children is punctuated by efforts to harness these assets and to overcome the liabilities. Recognition of the importance of play constituted a major forward stride in these efforts.

### The Playroom

The structure, design, and furnishing of the playroom suitable for child psychotherapy is most important. The number of toys should be few, simple, and carefully selected to facilitate the communication of fantasy. Others suggest that a wide variety of playthings be available, to increase the range of feelings that the child may express. These contrasting recommendations have been attributed to differences in therapeutic methods. Some therapists tend to avoid interpretation even of conscious ideas, whereas others recommend the interpretation of unconscious content directly and quickly. Therapists tend to change their preferences in equipment as they accumulate experience and develop confidence in their abilities.

Although special equipment—such as genital dolls, amputation dolls, and see-through anatomically complete (except for genitalia) models—has been used in therapy, many therapists have observed that the unusual nature of such items risks making children wary and suspicious of the therapist's motives. Until the dolls available to the children in their own homes include genitalia, the psychic content that these special dolls are designed to elicit may be more available at the appropriate time with conventional dolls.

Although individual considerations should be decisive, the following equipment can constitute a well-balanced playroom or play area: multigenerational families of flexible but sturdy dolls of various races; additional dolls representing special roles and feelings, such as policeman, doctor, soldier; dollhouse furnishings with or without a dollhouse; toy animals; puppets; paper, crayons, paint, and blunt-ended scissors; clay or something comparable; tools like rubber hammers, rubber knives, and guns; building blocks, cars, trucks, and airplanes; and eating utensils. These toys should enable children to communicate through play. It is wise to avoid mechanical toys because they break readily and thereby contribute to children's guilt feelings and to clutter.

A special drawer or box should be available to each individual child in which to store items the child brings to the therapy session or to store projects, such as drawings and stories, for future retrieval. Of course, limits have to be set, so that this private storage capacity is not used to hoard communal play equipment, depriving the therapist's other patients. Some therapists assert that an absence of such arrangements evokes material about sibling rivalry; however, others feel that this is a rationalization for not respecting the child's privacy, inasmuch as there are other ways of facilitating the expressions of such feelings.

### Initial Approach

A variety of approaches can be derived from the therapist's individual style and perception of the child's needs. The range extends from those in which the therapist endeavors to direct the child's thought content and activity—as in release therapy, some behavior therapy, and certain educational patterning techniques—to those exploratory methods in which the therapist endeavors to follow the child's lead. Even though the child determines the focus, it remains the therapist's responsibility to structure the situation. Encouraging a child to say whatever he wishes and to play freely, as in exploratory psychotherapy, establishes a definite structure. The therapist has created an atmosphere

in which he hopes to get to know all about the child—the good side, as well as the bad side, as children would put it. The therapist may communicate to the child that he does not intend to get angry or to be pleased in response to what the child says or does, but that the therapist will try to understand him. Such an assertion does not imply that therapists do not have emotions, but it assures the young patient that the therapist's personal feelings and standards are subordinate to understanding the youngster.

### Therapeutic Interventions

Therapeutic interventions with children encompass a range comparable to those used with adults in psychotherapy. If the amount of therapist activity is used as the basis for a classificatory continuum, at the least active end are the questions posed by the therapist requesting elaboration of the patient's statements or behavior. Closely aligned is the process of clarification of the patient's manifest productions by means of questions, recapitulation, and reorganization that can arrange the child's productions in a logical, temporal sequence, so frequently neglected by children. Also, clarification can serve as a preliminary step toward the specific goal of the therapy by recapitulating the child's productions so as to highlight motivational possibilities, target behaviors, or whatever may be appropriate for the particular type of therapy. Next on the continuum of therapeutic activity are the exclamations and confrontations in which the therapist more pointedly directs attention to some data of which the patient is cognizant. Then there are interpretations, designed to expand the patient's conscious awareness of himself by making explicit those elements that have previously been implicitly expressed in his thoughts, feelings, and behavior. Beyond interpretation, the therapist may educatively offer the patient information that is new because the patient has not been exposed to it previously. At the most active end of the continuum there is advising, counseling, and directing, designed to help the patient adopt a course of action or a conscious attitude.

Nurturing and maintaining a therapeutic alliance may require some education of the child regarding the process of therapy. Another educational intervention may entail assigning labels to affects that have not been part of the youngster's past experience. Rarely does therapy have to compensate for a real absence of education regarding acceptable decorum and playing games. Usually, children are in therapy not because of the absence of educational efforts, but because repeated educational efforts have failed.

Therefore, therapy generally does not need to include additional teaching efforts, despite the frequent temptation to offer them.

Adults' natural educational fervor with children is often accompanied by a paradoxical tendency to protect them from learning about some of life's realities. In the past, this tendency contributed to the stork's role in childbirth, the dead having taken a long trip, and similar fairytale explanations for natural phenomena about which adults were uncomfortable in communicating with children. Although adults are more honest with children today, therapists can find themselves in a situation in which their overwhelming urge to protect the hurt child may be as disadvantageous to the child as was the stork myth.

The temptation to offer oneself as a model for identification may stem also from helpful educational attitudes toward children. Although there are instances in which this may be an appropriate therapeutic strategy, therapists should not lose sight of the pitfalls in this apparently innocuous strategy.

### Parents

Psychotherapy with children is characterized by the need for parental involvement. This involvement does not necessarily reflect parental culpability for the youngster's emotional difficulties, but is a reality of the child's dependent state. This fact cannot be stressed too much because of what could be considered an occupational hazard shared by many who work with children. This hazard is the motivation to rescue children from the negative influence of their parents, sometimes related to an unconscious competitive desire to be a better parent than the child's or one's own parents.

There are varying degrees of parental involvement in child psychotherapy. With pre-school-aged children, the entire therapeutic effort may be directed toward the parents, without any direct treatment of the child. At the other extreme, children can be seen in psychotherapy without any parental involvement beyond the payment of fees and perhaps transporting the child to the therapeutic sessions. Most therapists agree that only relatively rare neurotic children who have reached the oedipal phase of development can sustain therapy by themselves. Even in such instances, however, the majority of practitioners prefer to maintain an informative alliance with the parents for the purpose of obtaining additional information about the child.

Probably the most frequent arrangements are those that were developed in child guidance clinics—that is, parent guidance focused on the child or on the parent-child interaction, or therapy for the parents' own individual needs concurrent with the child's therapy. The parents may be seen by the child's therapist or by someone else. In recent years, there have been increasing efforts to shift the focus from the child as the primary patient, to the concept of the child as the family's emissary to the clinic. In such family therapy, all or selected members of the family are treated simultaneously as a family group. Although the preferences of specific clinics or practitioners for either an individual or family therapeutic approach may be unavoidable, the final decision as to which therapeutic strategy of combination to use should be derived from the clinical assessment.

### Confidentiality

Consideration of parental involvement highlights the question of confidentiality in psychotherapy with children. There are advantages to creating an atmosphere in which the child can feel that his words and actions will be viewed by the therapist as simultaneously both serious and tentative. In other words, the child's communications do not bind him to a commitment; nevertheless, they are too important to be communicated to a third party without the patient's permission. Although such an attitude may be conveyed implicitly, there are occasions in which it is wise to explicitly discuss confidentiality with the child. It can be risky to promise a child that the therapist will not tell parents what transpires in therapeutic sessions. Although the therapist has no intention of disclosing such data to the parents, the bulk of what children do and say in psychotherapy is common knowledge to the parents. Therefore, should the child be so motivated, it is easy for him to manipulate the situation so as to produce circumstantial evidence that the therapist has betrayed his confidence. Accordingly, if confidentiality requires specific discussion during treatment, the therapist may not want to go beyond indicating that he is not in the business of telling parents what goes on in therapy, as his role is to understand children and to help them.

It is also important to try to enlist the parents' cooperation in respecting the privacy of the child's therapeutic sessions. This respect is not always readily honored, as parents quite naturally not only are curious about what transpires, but may also be threatened by the therapist's apparently privileged position.

Routinely reporting to children the essence of all communications with the third parties regarding the child underscores the therapist's reliability and his respect for the child's autonomy. In certain types of treatment, this report may be combined with soliciting the child's guesses about these transactions. Also, it may be fruitful to invite children, particularly older ones, to participate in discussions about them with third parties.

### Evolving Legal Issues

Although the recent legal reassessment of the traditional parental right and responsibility to speak on behalf of their children's therapeutic needs has tended to focus on cross-sibling organ transplantations and the hospitalization of the severely mentally ill or retarded, both the legal and the dynamic issues involved appear to be pertinent to psychotherapy. The pendulum is swinging from yesteryear's extreme of the courts' tendency to rely on the psychotherapeutic professions to care for all troubled children, to the apparently opposite position of legally protecting children from psychotherapeutic ministrations by a growing tendency on the part of the courts to question and overrule parental decision making. Recently, some state legislatures have enacted statutes formalizing the traditional common law permitting emancipated minors living apart from parents and managing their own affairs to consent to medical care of all types. Increasingly, children above a designated age, often 12 years, may independently obtain treatment for venereal disease and drug dependency. Although legislatures and courts are not granting children younger than these specified ages the right to speak for themselves in therapeutic matters, their parents' rights to do so are being limited increasingly. This limitation has taken the form of the interposition of third parties empowered either to replace the parents as decision makers, or to review parental decisions. The most evident effect has been on the parents' and guardians' traditional right to seek hospitalization for their disturbed children.

Thus far, in outpatient psychotherapy the major effect has been on the nebulous issue of who is the rightful owner of the therapist's recorded notes, and who should have access to them. At this time, it appears that the clinician still owns the chart, but the trend of the law is toward the subject of this record, the patient, being entitled to see his record. Whether this right of access pertains to the child patient or to his parent or to both remains an uncertainty. This uncertainty is not confined to the legal issues; the developmental lines regarding the child's and the adolescent's expanding rights to privacy have been insufficiently explored and explicated in all contexts.

### Indications and Contraindications for Psychotherapy

The present level of knowledge does not permit the compilation of a meaningful list of the multifaceted indications for child psychotherapy. Existing diagnostic classifications cannot serve as the basis for such a list because of invariable deficiencies in nosological specificity and comprehensiveness. In general, psychotherapy is indicated for children with emotional disorders that appear to be permanent enough to impede maturational and developmental forces. Psychotherapy may also be indicated when the child's development is not impeded, but is inducing reactions in the environment that are considered pathogenic. Ordinarily, such disharmonies are dealt with by the child with his parents' assistance, but, when these efforts are persistently inadequate, psychotherapeutic interventions may be indicated.

Psychotherapy should be limited to those instances in which there are positive indicators pointing to its potential usefulness. If psychotherapy, despite its limitations, is invariably the recommended therapeutic intervention after every child psychiatric evaluation by a particular therapist or clinic, this fact suggests not only unsatisfactory professional practice and a disservice to patients, but also an indiscriminate demeaning of psychotherapy.

Psychotherapy is contraindicated if the emotional disturbance is judged to be an intractable one that will not respond to treatment. This is an exceedingly difficult judgment, but one that is essential, considering the excess of the demand for psychotherapy over its supply. Because the potential for error in such prognostic assessments is so great, therapists should bring to them both professional humility and a readiness to offer a trial of therapy. There are times when the essential factor in intractability is the therapist. Certain patients may elicit a reaction from one therapist that is a contraindication for psychotherapy with this therapist, but not necessarily with another.

Another contraindication is evidence that the therapeutic process will interfere with reparative forces. A difficult question is posed by suggestions that the forces mobilized as a consequence of psychotherapy may have dire social or somatic effects. An example is the circumstance in which psychotherapy may upset a precarious family equilibrium, thereby causing more difficulty than the original problem posed.

### REFERENCES

Adams P L: *A Primer of Child Psychotherapy.* Little, Brown, Boston, 1974.

Anthony E J: Communicating therapeutically with children, J Am Acad Child Psychiatry 3: 106, 1964.

Carek D M: *Principles of Child Psychotherapy.* Charles C Thomas, Springfield, IL, 1972.

Group for the Advancement of Psychiatry: *From Diagnosis to Treatment: An Approach to Treatment Planning for the Emotionally Disturbed Child.* Group for the Advancement of Psychiatry, New York, 1973.

Group for the Advancement of Psychiatry: *The Process of Child Therapy,* Group for the Advancement of Psychiatry, New York, 1982.

Harrison S I, editor: *Therapeutic Interventions,* Vol. III of J D Noshpitz: *Basic Handbook of Child Psychiatry.* Basic Books, New York, 1979.

Harrison S I: Individual psychotherapy. In *Comprehensive Textbooks of Psychiatry,* ed 4, H I Kaplan, B J Sadock, editors, p 1766. Williams & Wilkins, Baltimore, 1985.

Karasu T B, chairman: APA Commission on Psychiatric Treatment. Psychotherapy Research: Methodological and Efficacy Issues, APA, Washington, DC, 1982.

Karasu T B: Recent developments in individual psychotherapy. Hosp Community Psychiatry 35: 29, 1984.

Looney J G, Blockty M J: Special perspectives on treatment planning for children, Chapt. 6, pp. 289–336, in J M Lewis, G Usdin, editors, *Treatment Planning in Psychiatry,* APA, Washington, DC, 1982.

McDermott J F, Harrison S I, editors: *Psychiatric Treatment of the Child.* Jason Aronson, New York, 1977.

## 36.2 GROUP THERAPY WITH CHILDREN

### Introduction

The characteristics of developmental stages have influenced the growth of group psychotherapy techniques perhaps more than any other factor.

### Preschool and Early School-age Groups

Work with the preschool group is usually structured by the therapist through the use of a particular technique, such as puppets or artwork, or it is couched in terms of a permissive play atmosphere. In therapy with puppets, the children project onto the puppets their fantasies in a way not unlike ordinary play. The main value lies in the cathexis afforded the child, especially if he shows difficulty in expressing his feelings. Here the group aids the child less by interaction with other members than by action with the puppets.

In play group therapy, the emphasis rests on the interactional qualities of the children with each other and with the therapist in the permissive playroom setting. The therapist should be a person who can allow the children to produce fantasies verbally and in play, but who also can use active restraint when the children undergo excessive tension. The toys are the traditional ones used in individual play therapy. The children use the toys to act out aggressive impulses and to relive with the group members and with the therapist their home difficulties. The children catalyze each other, and obtain libido-activating stimulation from this catalysis and from their play materials. The therapist interprets a child to the group in the context of the transference to the therapist and to other group members.

The children selected for group treatment show in common a social hunger, the need to be like their peers and to be accepted by them. Usually, the therapist excludes the child who has never realized a primary relationship, as with his mother, inasmuch as individual psychotherapy can better help this child. Usually, the children selected include those with phobic reactions, effeminate boys, shy and withdrawn children, and children with primary behavior disorders.

Modifications of these criteria have been used in group therapy for autistic children, along with parent group therapy and art therapy.

A modification of group therapy was used for physically handicapped toddlers who showed speech and language delays. This experience of twice-a-week group activities involved the mothers and their children in a mutual teaching-learning setting. The experience proved effective to the mothers, who received supportive psychotherapy in this group experience; their formerly hidden fantasies about the children emerged, to be dealt with therapeutically.

### Latency-age Groups

Activity group therapy assumes that poor and divergent experiences have led to deficits in appropriate personality development in the behavior of children; therefore, corrective experiences in a therapeutically conditioned environment will modify them. Because some latency-age children present deep disturbances, involving neurotic traits (fears, high anxiety levels, and guilt), an activity-interview group psychotherapy modification evolved. This format uses interview techniques, verbal explanations of fantasies, group play, work, and other communications.

In this type of group therapy, as with pubertal and adolescent groups, the children verbalize in a problem-oriented manner, with the awareness that problems brought them together, and that the group aims to change them. They report dreams, fantasies, and day dreams, as well as traumatic and unpleasant experiences. Both these experiences and the group behavior undergo open discussion. Therapists vary in their use of time, of co-therapists, and of food and materials. Most groups are after school and last at least 1 hour, although some leaders prefer 90 minutes. Some therapists serve food in the last 10 minutes, and others prefer serving times when the children are more together for talking. Food, however, does not become a major feature, never becoming central to the group's activities.

### Pubertal and Adolescent Groups

Similar group therapy methods can be used with pubertal children, who are often grouped monosexually, rather than mixed. Their problems resemble those of late latency-age children, but they are also beginning, especially the girls, to feel the impact and pressures of early adolescence. In a way, these groups offer help during a transitional period. The group appears to satisfy the social appetite of preadolescents, who compensate for feelings of inferiority and self-doubt by the formation of groups. This form of therapy puts to advantage the influence of the process of socialization during these years. Because children of this age experience difficulties in conceptualizing, pubertal therapy groups tend to use play, drawing, psychodrama, and other nonverbal modes of expression. The therapist's role is active and directive, as opposed to the older, more passive role assigned him.

Activity group psychotherapy has been the recommended type of group therapy for latency-age and pubertal children who do not have significantly neurotic personality patterns. The children, usually of the same sex and in groups of not more than eight, freely act out in a setting especially designed and planned for its physical and milieu characteristics. Samuel Slavson, one of the pioneers in group psychotherapy, pictured the group as a substitute family in which the passive, neutral therapist becomes the surrogate for parents. The therapist assumes different roles, mostly in a nonverbal manner, as each child interacts with him and with other group members. Recent therapists, however, tend to see the group as a form of peer group, with its attendant socializing processes, rather than as a reenactment of the family. Late adolescents, from 16 years of age and up, may be included in groups of adults when indicated. Group therapy has been very useful in the treatment of substance abuse problems. Combined therapy (the use of group and individual therapy) has also been used successfully with adolescents.

### Parent Groups

In the group treatment, as with most treatment procedures for children, parental difficul-ties present obstacles. Sometimes uncooperative parents refuse to bring a child or to participate in their own therapy. The extreme of this situation reveals itself when severely disturbed parents use the child as their channel of communication in working out their own needs. In such circumstances, the child finds himself in the intolerable position of receiving positive group experiences that seem to create havoc at home.

Parents groups, therefore, can be a valuable aid to the group therapy of their children. The parent of a child in therapy often has difficulty in understanding the nature of his child's ailment, of discerning the line of demarcation between normal and pathological behavior, in relating to the medical establishment, and in coping with feelings of guilt. A parents' group assists them in these areas, and helps the members formulate guidelines for action.

### Other Group Therapy Situations

Some residential and day treatment units frequently use group therapy techniques in their work. Group therapy in school for underachievers and for the underprivileged has relied on reinforcement and on modeling theory, in addition to traditional techniques, and has been supplemented by parent groups.

With the opportunity for more controlled conditions, residential treatment units have been used for specific studies in group therapy, such as behavioral contracting. Behavioral contracting with reward-punishment reinforcement provides positive reinforcements among preadolescent boys with severe concerns in basic trust, with low self-esteem, and with dependency conflicts. Somewhat akin to formal residental treatment units are social group work homes. The children undergo many psychological assaults before placement, so that supportive group therapy offers ventilation and catharsis, but more often it succeeds in letting these children become aware of the enjoyment of sharing activities and developing skills.

Public schools—also a structured environment, although usually considered not the best site for group therapy—have been used by a number of workers. Group therapy as group counseling readily lends itself to school settings. One such group used gender and problem-homogeneous selection for groups of six to eight students, who met once a week during school hours over a time span of 2 to 3 years.

From the foregoing, one can gather that there are many indications for the use of group psychotherapy as a treatment modality. Some indications can be described as situational; the therapist may work in a reformatory setting, where group psychotherapy has seemed to reach the adolescents better than does individual treatment. Another indication is time economics; more patients can be reached within a given time span by the use of groups than by individual therapy. Using groups best helps the child at a given age and developmental stage, and with a given type of problem. In the young age group, the child's social hunger and his potential need for peer acceptance help to determine his suitability for group therapy. Criteria for unsuitability are controversial, and have been progressively loosened.

## REFERENCES

Abramowitz C V: The effectiveness of group psychotherapy with children. Arch Gen Psychiatry 33: 320, 1976.
Bandura A: Modeling and vicarious processes. In *Principles of Behavior Modification*, p 118. Holt Rinehart Winston, New York, 1969.
Berkowitz I H, editor: *Adolescents Grow in Groups.* Brunner/Mazel, New York, 1972.
Epstein Y M, Borduin C M: The children's feedback game: An approach for modifying disruptive group behavior. Am J Psychotherapy 38: 63, 1984.
Ginott H G: *Group Psychotherapy with Children.* McGraw-Hill, New York, 1961.
Kraft I A: Some special considerations in adolescent group psychotherapy. Int J Group Psychotherapy 11: 196, 1961.
Kraft I A: Group therapy with children and adolescents. In *Comprehensive Textbook of Psychiatry*, ed 4, H I Kaplan, B J Sadock, editors, p 1785. Williams & Wilkins, Baltimore, 1985.
Rose S D: *Treating Children in Groups.* Jossey-Bass, San Francisco, 1972.
Sands R M, Blank R, Brandt B, Golub S, Joelson R, Klappersack B, Levin E, Rothenburg E: Breaking the bonds of tradition: Reassessment of group treatment of latency children in a community mental health center. Am J Orthopsychiatry 43: 212, 1973.
Slavson S R, Schiffer M: *Group Psychotherapies for Children.* International Universities Press, New York, 1975.

---

# 36.3 ORGANIC THERAPIES

## Introduction

Organic therapy in children and adolescents still lies within the shadow of adult psychiatry but is gradually emerging. Ethical considerations, nonrecognition of the existence of adult psychiatric disorders in children, the lack of a descriptive tradition, as well as inadequate research support, have limited this field.

Since the 1980s, organic therapy in child psychiatry has been gradually differentiating itself from adult psychiatry. More elaborate attention to cognitive variables and more extensive psy-

chostimulant research with children have, for the first time, begun to influence and contribute the parent field. On the other hand, recognition and treatment of disorders like major depression, once considered to be limited to older age groups, have extended conceptions from general psychiatry to the pediatric area.

## The Therapeutic Process of Organic Therapy in Childhood and Adolescence

First a thorough diagnostic assessment needs to be made (see Table I). Does the child have a disorder of type and severity that warrants this type of intervention? Other medical or social conditions causing such symptoms need to be considered. Equally important are evaluation and understanding of the social and family context of the patient, which may influence the choice of therapy in a major way: Psychiatric disorders in one or both parents may require intervention simultaneously or even prior to medicating the child. Parental or school opposition to medication can prevent its use and careful evaluation must take this into account. Preexistent causal attributions held by the family and child may be powerful features that influence attitudes about medicating. Thus social and psychological factors are important parts of this determination. The history of drug response in other family members may be helpful in assessing the risk-benefit ratio as well as being helpful in selecting which member of a particular class of drugs to choose.

## Pharmacokinetic Considerations in Childhood

Children appear to be more efficacious metabolizers of psychoactive drugs. They may require or tolerate slightly higher doses on milligram per kilogram body weight basis than adults. This is clearly the case with lithium, which may reflect greater renal clearance. A possible explanation for other differential effects is the greater liver/body weight ratio present in childhood (e.g. 30 percent greater for a 6-year-old compared to an adult). Stimulants seem to have a somewhat shorter half-life in children compared with adults. Children convert imipramine to des-

TABLE I
STEPWISE PROCESS OF ORGANIC THERAPY

| |
|---|
| 1. Diagnostic evaluation |
| 2. Symptom measurement |
| 3. Risk/benefit ratio analysis |
| 4. Establishment of a contract of therapy |
| 5. Periodic reevaluation |
| 6. Termination/tapered drug withdrawal |

methylimipramine more actively than do adults. In children, it is expected that the desmethylated metabolite is the predominant active moiety. Although children clear imipramine more rapidly via demethylation, their clearance of the sum of imipramine and desmethylimipramine following imipramine is at a rate similar to that of adults.

Studies of serum levels of both of these different classes of drugs demonstrate wide variability of serum levels among subjects receiving the same milligram per kilogram dose. Similarly, this same variation has been seen in adults with the above mentioned drugs as well as with most other psychotherapeutic agents as well. At least with imipramine, another similarity with adult pharmacology is seen; depressed children require the same plasma levels associated with a favorable response in adults.

## Indications

### Attention Deficit Disorder with and without Hyperactivity

The most well-documented indication for pharmacologic treatment in child psychiatry is attention deficit disorder with hyperactivity. The symptoms usually prompting therapy are developmentally inappropriate inattention and impulsivity which respond insufficiently to social control. Although research has focused upon those with motoric excess, clinically it is probably that those who have a pure attention disorder who are likely to benefit from stimulant drugs as well.

The clear first choice among organic therapies is a stimulant. (For dosage see Table II.) The dosage of the stimulant can be titrated upward about every 3 to 5 days (every week in the case of pemoline) until either therapeutic benefit is achieved or side effects prohibit further increase.

This is done with the aim of using the lowest dose that is efficacious. Doses are usually limited to the day with frequency based upon the drugs half-life. All of the stimulants are short acting when compared to the long half-lives of the antidepressants and neuroleptics. Of the three drugs, methylphenidate has the shortest half-life (2.5 hours is about the mean). As a consequence it is frequently administered twice daily. Amphetamines half-life is intermediate and pemoline has the longest (about 12 hours).

Decreased restlessness and impulsivity as well as increased attention span, concentration, and compliance with commands are hallmarks of treatment response. About three quarters of patients with the diagnosis will respond to either amphetamine or methylphenidate. Some children will respond to one stimulant but not to another. The mechanism of action has not been elucidated although many pharmacologic properties of these drugs are known. It should be emphasized that the actions of stimulants are not specific to hyperactive children. Normal children show similar behavioral responses, and so stimulant responsiveness does not confirm a diagnosis of attention deficit disorder.

Stimulants are contraindicated in children with thought disorder or psychosis as they may exacerbate those conditions. These drugs are relatively contraindicated for mental retardates, ticquers, and highly anxious children. Stimulants have been associated with precipitation or aggravation of Tourette's disorder. The common side effects of stimulants are listed in Table III.

A second line of drugs, if stimulants are ineffective or if side effects severe, is the tricyclic antidepressants. Those who respond do so rapidly (e.g. within 1 to 2 days); however, the response may be short lived, and not as striking as that with stimulants. The dosage utilized has been lower than that for antidepressant activity.

TABLE II
STIMULANT DRUG DOSAGE

| Drug | Manufacturer's Recommended Dose | | Author's Recommended Range per Single Dose of Short-acting Preparation | Comments |
|------|---------|----------------------|-----------------------------------------------------------------------|----------|
| | Initial | Maximum daily dose | | |
| | | (mg) | (mg/kg) | |
| Methylphenidate (Ritalin, CIBA) | 5 mg b.i.d. | 60 | 0.3–1 | Sustained release preparation is available |
| d-Amphetamine (Dexedrine, Smith, Kline & French) | 2.5 mg q.d. (3–5 yr) 5 mg (q.d. or b.i.d. (≥6 yr) | 40 | 0.15–0.5 | Sustained duration form is available |
| Pemoline (Cyclert, Abbott) | 37.5 mg q.d. | 112.5 | 0.5–2 | 3–4 weeks may be required to see treatment effect |

TABLE III
COMMON DOSE-RELATED SIDE EFFECTS OF
STIMULANTS

1. Insomnia
2. Decreased appetite
3. Irritability or nervousness
4. Weight loss

Dietary management of hyperactivity has received a great amount of public attention, but controlled studies have not substantiated notable benefit. Similarly, caffeine was not found superior to placebo for attention deficit disorder in most controlled studies.

### Tourette's Disorder

This disorder, characterized by both multiple skeletal muscle tics and multiple vocal tics, is one of the clearest indications for pharmacotherapy. Although patients have some ability to voluntarily suppress these movements, most obtain significant additional relief from haloperidol (Haldol). Haloperidol has gained a reputation as the treatment of choice in this condition because most patients will experience a significant reduction in symptoms with this drug. The suggested dose range for 3- to 12-year-old children is 0.05 to 0.075 mg/kg/day. Despite the excellent clinical reputation this treatment has, it has been established without the benefit of a large double blind controlled trial. Nonetheless, haloperidol is now the standard treatment against which other proposed treatments should be compared. Hazards and side effects of neuroleptics are listed below.

### Pervasive Developmental Disorders

**Infantile Autism.** Drugs can provide only symptomatic behavioral management. Hyperactivity, agitation, crying, screaming, and lability of mood make care of these children very difficult. The main symptoms of gross deficits in communication and social unresponsiveness, however, will not be relieved by neuroleptics. Low doses of relatively less sedating neuroleptics (e.g. haloperidol 2 mg/day) seem to best ameliorate the secondary symptoms.

Fenfluramine, a sympathomimetic amine, has been claimed to be useful in uncontrolled trials, but this has not yet been demonstrated in double blind controlled studies.

**Schizophrenic Disorders.** Children having signs and symptoms comparable with those found in adult schizophrenia probably benefit from neuroleptics, but there have been no controlled studies in this area. There is evidence that the same toxic side effects neuroleptics cause in adults are seen in children, including tardive dyskinesia. Consequently, the risk benefit ratio is high and great care to determine the need for continued neuroleptics is needed. Schizophrenia with onset in late adolescence is treated like the adult disorder.

### Sedative, Alcohol and/or Opiate Withdrawal

These conditions, although infrequent, can occur in adolescents and children. They are treated in a manner like that used in adults with symptom suppression using a cross tolerant compound and gradual tapered withdrawal.

### Affective Disorders

Major depression has recently been recognized to occur in childhood and adolescence, and not just limited to adults. The role of pharmacologic therapy in this disorder is not entirely sorted out. Depressed children with endogenous features may respond to imipramine in dosage ranging from 1.5 to 5 mg/kg/day with improvement in mood. The side effects are similar to those experienced by adults. The margin of benefit over placebo does not appear to be as clear as it is in adults. Whether MAO inhibitors are any better remains to be determined. There is no current indication for ECT in children. Thus, a clear indication for organic therapy in childhood depression remains to be established.

Bipolar patients' retrospective accounts indicate that a sizeable minority (30 percent) experience the onset of their illness in adolescence or earlier. Although lithium has had very limited study, a trial is warranted in those who meet DSM-III criteria for the disorder and have not responded to more conservative management. Administration to achieve blood levels of 0.6 to 1.2 meq/l, similar to adult patients, are suggested and doses may approximate adult dose to achieve this. Side effects and complications similar to those seen in adults can occur.

### Conduct Disorder

Little is known about organic treatment in this area. There is considerable overlap between conduct disorder and attention deficit disorder. It is thus unclear in many studies who was responding to the drug treatment. The role of organic therapy in pure conduct disorders remains to be defined. Lithium is the only agent for which efficacy has been shown, but this is limited to a handful of studies.

Older anticonvulsants do not appear beneficial even in those who also have seizure disorders. Some claims for efficacy of carbamazepine (Tegretol) and propranolol (Inderal) have been made but need further study. Stimulants may have some beneficial effects upon aggressiveness in those with attention deficit disorder, but may not be sufficiently helpful in severe conduct disorder, and compliance and/or abuse is a problem in this group.

Antipsychotics decrease severity of aggression but their utility is limited by sedation and possible cognitive impairment.

### Enuresis

Tricyclic antidepressants, in particular imipramine, control enuretic symptoms, but do not provide a cure. They are indicated as adjunctive therapy in children 6 years or older in some appropriate situations. Initially, an oral dose of 25 mg/day given 1 hour before bedtime should be tried. Dosage may be increased to 50 mg in those children under 12 and 75 mg in those over 12, but should not exceed 2.5 mg/kg day. The mechanism of action that provides symptom relief is unknown. What is known is that the anticholinergic effect is irrelevant to enuresis control as other peripherally acting anticholinergics are not efficacious. By the end of a week of adequate amount of the drug, 60 percent or more of the children will have experienced success, but wearoff or tolerance may occur in half of these responders. However, the use of bell and pad conditioning is preferable as the risk is minimal, and produces long-lasting results.

## Mental Retardation

Recent surveys have found roughly half of institutionalized mental retarded persons to be receiving antipsychotic drugs, which most likely reflects overutilization of these agents. Mental retardation by itself is not an indication for psychotropic drug use. Some behaviors such as hyperactivity or stereotypy may benefit from stimulants or neuroleptics. Low doses of haloperidol appear to offer the greatest benefit with the least cognitive impairment.

Thioridazine and haloperidol may have some usefulness in decreasing unwanted behavior such as self-stimulation, aggression, and motor activity. However, in addition to the risk of tardive dyskinesia, there are other risks as well: antipsychotics appear to impair the effectiveness of behavioral training in a dose dependent fashion and of other rehabiliative effects such as workshop performance.

## Anxiety Disorders of Childhood or Adolescence

Imipramine has been shown to be useful as an adjunct in the treatment of school phobic children, and it may be useful in separation anxiety in general. Anecdotal reports of school phobic children benefiting from chlordiazepoxide and from amphetamine are insufficient to justify their adaptation in clinical practice. Minor tranquilizers are overprescribed in relation to the absence of evidence for their efficacy.

### Sleep Terror

Sleep terror disorder consists of repeated episodes of abrupt awakening with intense anxiety marked by autonomic arousal. It occurs during stage IV sleep. Usually the child, who appears confused and disoriented, will not respond to comfort measures during the episode. Diazepam, in 2- to 5-mg doses, by decreasing the proportion of stage IV sleep, has been shown to be helpful.

### Obsessive-Compulsive Disorder

This is a rare condition in childhood marked by obsessive thoughts and compulsive actions which can be very disabling. Chlorimipramine, not currently available in the United States, appears to benefit obsessive compulsive symptoms whether or not there is coexisting depression.

### Specific Developmental Disorders

No pharmacologic agent has been shown to effect clinically significant improvement in any specific developmental disorder. However, many children with psychiatric disorders have learning disabilities and many who have learning disabilities have behavioral problems. Because of this, as well as the importance of school and learning in children's lives, questions about cognitive effects of psychotropics arise. Table IV summarizes drug effects on cognitive tests of learning functions.

In children with learning disabilities but no other psychiatric diagnosis, methylphenidate has been shown to facilitate performance on several standard cognitive, psycholinguistic, memory, and vigilance tests but there was no improvement in academic achievement ratings or teacher ratings. Cognitive impairment from psychotropic drugs, especially neuroleptics, may be an even greater problem in mentally retarded persons.

### Bulimia

This disorder is characterized by compulsive binge-eating episodes that are not due to anorexia nervosa. Reports have begun to appear indicating that antidepressant drugs are beneficial. Controlled studies limited to adolescents or younger children have yet to be done.

TABLE IV
EFFECTS OF PSYCHOTROPIC DRUGS ON COGNITIVE TESTS OF LEARNING FUNCTIONS*†

| Drug Class | Continuous Performance Test (Attention) | Matching Familiar Figures (Impulsivity) | Test Function Paired Associates (Verbal Learning) | Porteus Maze (Planning Capacity) | Short Term Memory‡ | WISC (Intelligence) |
|---|---|---|---|---|---|---|
| Stimulant | ↑ | ↑ | ↑ | ↑ | ↑ | ↑ |
| Antidepressants | ↑ | 0 | | 0 | 0 | 0 |
| Neuroleptics | ↑↓ | | ↓ | ↓ | ↓ | 0 |

* Adapted from M G Aman: Drugs, learning and the psychotherapies. In *Pediatric Psychopharmacology. The Use of Behavior Modifying Drugs in Children*, J S Werry, editor, Bruner/Mazel, New York, 1978.
† ↑ Improved, ↑↓ inconsistent, ↓ worse, and 0 no effect.
‡ Various Tests: digit span, word recall, etc.

## Medication Effects and Complications

### Antidepressants

The side effects seen are usually similar to those reported in adults, and result from imipramine's anticholinergic properties. Dry mouth, constipation, palpitations, tachycardia, loss of accommodation, and sweating may be noted. The most serious side effects are cardiovascular, although in children diastolic hypertension is more common than in adults, and postural hypotension occurs more rarely. ECG changes are more apt to be seen in those on high doses. Slowed cardiac conduction (PR interval >0.20 seconds or QRS interval >0.12) may necessitate lowering the dose. FDA guidelines limit doses to a maximum of 5 mg/kg/day. The drug can be very toxic in overdose and in small children ingestions of 200 to 400 mg can be fatal. When the dose is lowered too rapidly, withdrawal effects are manifested mainly by gastrointestinal symptoms: cramping, nausea, and vomiting. Apathy and weakness may also occur. The treatment is slower tapering of dosage.

### Neuroleptics

The best studied of these compounds in pediatric age groups are chlorpromazine (Thorazine) and thioridazine (Mellaril) and haloperidol (Haldol). It is widely held in adult psychiatry that high and low potency neuroleptics differ in their side effect profiles. The phenothiazine derivatives named above (chlorpromazine and thioridazine) have the most pronounced sedative and atropinic actions, whereas the high potency neuroleptics are more commonly thought to be associated with extrapyramidal reactions, such as parkinsonian symptoms, akathisia, and acute dystonias. Caution is warranted in assuming this to be true in children. Particularly when comparisons are made at low dosage levels of equivalent potency, differences may not be seen.

Even if the frequency of these side effects differs between the different medications, these side effects can be seen with any neuroleptic. Demonstrations in children of impairment of cognitive function and most importantly, of tardive dyskinesia, call for great caution in their use. Tardive dyskinesia, characterized by persistant abnormal involuntary movements of the tongue, face, mouth, or jaw which may also involve the extremities, is a known hazard of neuroleptic administration in patients of all age groups. There is no known effective treatment. Tardive dyskinesia has not been reported for patients having a total cumulative neuroleptic ingestion of less than 375 or 400 g of chlorpromazine equivalents. Nonpersistant choreiform movements of the extremities and trunk, on the other hand, are very frequent following abrupt discontinuation of antipsychotics in children, and need to be followed to distinguish them from the persistent dyskinesias.

Because of the seriousness of this complication, as well as overutilization of neuroleptics, litigation has arisen from several pediatric cases with tardive dyskinesia. The first case to be settled in court was that of *Clites* v. *Iowa*. In awarding damages, the court offered guidelines about the legal constraints on neuroleptic prescription. While the decision indicated major tranquilizers use might be justified to curb severe aggression and self-abuse, use for staff convenience of expediency is substandard medical conduct. Furthermore, the court indicated that all major tranquilizers require some form of informed consent.

It is recommended that, whenever clinically feasible, children on constant neuroleptics should be periodically withdrawn in order to assess current clinical need and the possible development of tardive dyskinesia.

## Use of Other Organic Therapies

There is little convincing evidence for dietary manipulation as a treatment for childhood psychiatric disorders, but it is premature to dismiss dietary measures entirely in the absence of good research. Studies of starvation and/or protein caloric malnutrition emphasize the importance of adequate nutrition to growth and development and suggest that behavioral sequelae of infant malnutrition exist. Concepts such as dietary self-selection as a reflection of metabolic differences and oligoantigenic diets are under study.

Electroconvulsive therapy has been used in the past with children and adolescents. Little, if any, benefit has been reported. Most reports have been confined to children with psychotic disorders rather than children with affective disorders. Whether there is any indication for ECT in this age group has not been documented with controlled trials. No side effects or complications unique to childhood have been documented.

Psychosurgical techniques, including lobotomy, have been applied to children, but there is no accepted indication in child psychiatry for psychosurgery.

**REFERENCES**

Abrams R, Essman W B, editors: *Electroconvulsive Therapy: Biological Foundation and Clinical Applications.* SP Medical Scientific Books, New York, 1982.
American Psychiatric Association Task Force on ECT: *Task Force Report 14: Electroconvulsive Therapy.* American Psychiatric Association, Washington, DC, 1978.
Fink M: *Convulsive Therapy: Theory and Practice.* Raven Press, New York, 1979.
Kalinowsky I B, Hippius H, Klein H E: *Biological Treatments in Psychiatry.* Grune & Stratton, New York, 1982.
Lerer B, Weiner R D, Belmaker R H: *ECT: Basic Mechanisms.* John Libbey, London, 1983.
Palmer R L, editor: *Electroconvulsive Therapy: An Appraisal.* Oxford University Press, London, 1981.
Rapaport J L, Kruesi M J P: Organic therapies. In *Comprehensive Textbook of Psychiatry,* ed 4, H I Kaplan, B J Sadock, editors, p 1793. Williams & Wilkins, Baltimore, 1985.
Scovern A W, Kilmann P R: Status of ECT: A review of the outcome literature. Psychol Bull *87:* 260, 1980.
Small J G, Small I F: Electroconvulsive therapy update. Psychopharmacol Bull *17:* 29, 1981.
Weiner R D: Does electroconvulsive therapy cause brain damage? Behav Brain Sci 1984.

---

# 36.4  RESIDENTIAL AND DAY TREATMENT

## Residential Treatment

### Definition and Indications

Residential treatment consists of a structured living environment, in the context of which strong attachments and commitment by the staff to the child are essential. Special education for the child and treatment of the family are expressions of this commitment.

Children who are likely to benefit from residential treatment include children with antisocial and aggressive behaviors, such as stealing, truancy, running away, fire setting, bed wetting, and destructive behavior. The child may have psychotic symptoms, including loose associations, hallucinations, and precipitous, severe regression. Most, if not all, children referred for residential treatment have severe learning disabilities.

### Staff and Setting

Staffing patterns include various combinations of child care workers, teachers, social workers, psychiatrists, pediatricians, nurses, and psychologists, making the cost of residential treatment very high. Yet the setting and the staff are vital to a good residential treatment program.

### Referral and Intake

Most children who are referred for residential treatment have been seen previously by one or more professional persons, such as a school psychologist or pediatrician, or by members of a child guidance clinic, juvenile court, or state welfare agency. Unsuccessful previous attempts at outpatient treatment and foster home or other custodial placement often precede residential treatment. The age range of the children varies from institution to institution, but most children are between 5 and 15 years of age. Boys are referred more frequently than girls.

An initial review of the data enables the intake staff to determine whether a particular child is likely to benefit from their particular treatment program. It is common to find that, for every child accepted for admission, three are rejected. The next step usually involves interviews with the child and his parents by various staff members, such as a therapist, a group living worker, and a teacher. Psychological testing and neurological examinations are performed when indicated, if these have not already been done. The child and his parents should be prepared for these interviews.

### Group Living

By far the largest amount of time in the child's life in a residential treatment setting is spent in group living. The group living staff consists of child care workers who offer a structured environment that constitutes a therapeutic milieu. Tasks are defined within the limits of the child's abilities; incentives, such as increased privileges, encourage the child to progress, rather than regress.

A child often selects one or more staff members with whom to form a relationship through which the child expresses, consciously and unconsciously, many of his feelings toward his parents. The child care staff should be trained to recognize such transference reactions, and to respond to them in a way that is different from the child's expectations, based on his previous or even current relationship with his parents.

To maintain consistency and balance, the group living staff must communicate freely and regularly with each other and with the other professional and administrative staff members of the residential setting, particularly the child's teacher and his therapist.

The child care staff members must recognize any tendency toward being the good (or bad) parent in response to the child's splitting behavior. This tendency in a staff member may become manifest as a pattern of blaming other staff members for the child's disruptive behavior. Similarly, the child care staff must recognize and avoid such individual and group countertransference reactions as sadomasochistic and punitive behavior toward a child.

The structured setting should offer a corrective emotional experience and opportunities for facilitating and improving the adaptive behavior of the child, particularly when such deficiencies as speech and language deficits, intellectual retardation, inadequate peer relationships, bed wetting, poor feeding habits, and attention deficits are present. Some of these deficits are at the base of the child's poor school academic performance and unsocialized behavior, including temper tantrums, fighting, and withdrawal.

Behavior modification principles have also been applied, particularly in group work with children. Behavior therapy is an adjunct to the total therapeutic effort of the residential center.

### Education

Children in residential treatment frequently have severe learning disabilities, as well as disruptive behavior, and usually they cannot function in a regular community school. Consequently, a special on-grounds school setting is required. The educational process in residential treatment is complex. Table I shows some of the components of the process.

A major goal of the on-grounds school is to motivate the child to learn.

### Therapy

Traditional modes of psychotherapy have a definite place in residential treatment. These modes include intensive, individual psychotherapy with the child; group therapy with selected children; individual or group therapy or both for parents; and, in some cases, family therapy. However, several modifications need to be kept in mind.

The child relates to the total staff of the setting and, therefore, needs to know that what transpires in the therapist's office is shared with all professional staff members. The therapist informs the child that what they discuss and do in individual therapy will not be revealed to other family members or to other children in the residential center, but will be shared with professional staff members within the setting itself.

### The Parents

Concomitant work with the parents is essential. The child usually has a strong tie with the parent, no matter how disturbed this parent is. Sometimes the parent is idealized by the child, but repeatedly fails the child. Sometimes the parent has an ambivalent or unrealistic expectation that the child will return home. In some instances, the parent must be helped to enable the child to live in another setting when this is in the best interests of the child. Most residential treatment centers offer individual or group therapy with the parents, couples therapy, and, in some cases, conjoint family therapy.

### Day Treatment

When psychiatrically ill children require varying combinations of intensive psychotherapy, therapeutic environment, and therapeutically oriented or remedial education, they often need not and should not be away from their families overnight. So that the children may have the appropriate treatment, education, and care during the day, while retaining and protecting their primary relationships with parents and siblings at home, day-long programs in psychiatric and school settings have been developed. The essence of a day hospital treatment program is that it maintains the family, avoids total removal of the child, treats all members of the family, and conveys to the child and the family the idea that the child belongs with his or her family. In order to facilitate such a program, the home must be safe for the child, and there must be some possibility of change within the family.

Day treatment should not refer to programs that are either primarily custodial or primarily educational, since each day treatment center requires a blend of these factors, as well as the child care activities that do not fit under therapy or education. In fact, the concept of therapeutic

TABLE I
THE EDUCATIONAL PROCESS IN RESIDENTIAL TREATMENT

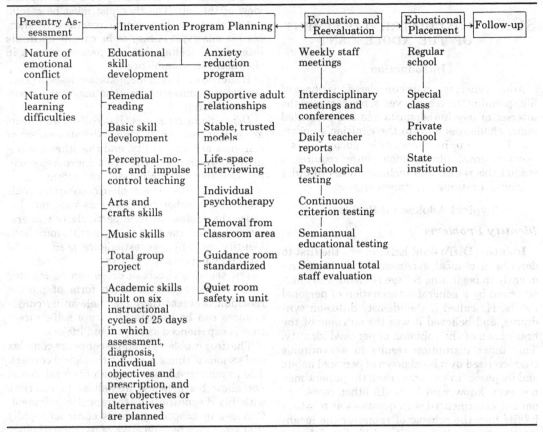

| Preentry Assessment | Intervention Program Planning | | Evaluation and Reevaluation | Educational Placement | Follow-up |
|---|---|---|---|---|---|
| Nature of emotional conflict | Educational skill development | Anxiety reduction program | Weekly staff meetings | Regular school | |
| Nature of learning difficulties | Remedial reading | Supportive adult relationships | Interdisciplinary meetings and conferences | Special class | |
| | Basic skill development | Stable, trusted models | Daily teacher reports | Private school | |
| | Perceptual-motor and impulse control teaching | Life-space interviewing | Psychological testing | State institution | |
| | Arts and crafts skills | Individual psychotherapy | Continuous criterion testing | | |
| | Music skills | Removal from classroom area | Semiannual educational testing | | |
| | Total group project | Guidance room standardized | Semiannual total staff evaluation | | |
| | Academic skills built on six instructional cycles of 25 days in which assessment, diagnosis, indivdiual objectives and prescription, and new objectives or alternatives are planned | Quiet room safety in unit | | | |

environment is as crucial for day treatment as for residential programs for children.

Children who are likely to benefit from day treatment may have a wide range of diagnoses, including infantile autism, borderline conditions, personality disorders, minimal brain dysfunction, and mental retardation.

The lessons learned from day treatment programs have moved the mental health disciplines in the direction of having the services follow the children, rather than discontinuities of care. An increasing number of residential treatment centers have added day treatment programs.

Day treatment programs have become increasingly valuable for children with chronic physical illnesses. Psychological and economic factors converge advantageously in promoting effective treatment with the child remaining in his family.

**REFERENCES**

Colligan R C, Roberts M D, Miner R A: An organizational grid for residential staff conferences. Milieu Ther 1: 41, 1981.

Ferguson R: The role of university child care training programs in the development of a professional career ladder for child care workers. J Child Care 1: 67, 1982.

Haley J: Leaving Home. McGraw-Hill, New York, 1980.

Johnson S: Staff cohesion in residential treatment. Child Care Q 11: 204, 1982.

Lewis M: Day treatment. In Comprehensive Textbook of Psychiatry, ed 4, H I Kaplan, B J Sadock, editors, p 1803. Williams & Wilkins, Baltimore, 1985.

Lewis M: Residential treatment. In Comprehensive Textbook of Psychiatry, ed 4, H I Kaplan, B J Sadock, editors, p 1798. Williams & Wilkins, Baltimore, 1985.

Lewis M, Brown T E: Child care in the residential treatment of the borderline child. Child Care Q 9: 41, 1980.

Lewis M, Lewis D O, Shanok S S, Klatskin E, Osborn J R: The undoing of residential treatment. J Am Acad Child Psychiatry 19: 160, 1980.

Lewis W W: Etiological factors in successful residential treatment. Behav Disord 7: 149, 1982.

Northrup G: The direct care worker in residential treatment. Milieu Ther 2: 32, 1982.

Rick F, Charlesworth J: Role and function of child care working. J Child Care 1: 35, 1982.

## 36.5    PSYCHIATRIC TREATMENT OF THE ADOLESCENT

### Introduction

Adolescence, typically considered the phase of life spanning the teenage years, has captured the interest of psychotherapists and has presented many challenges both to the clinician's understanding and to his therapeutic endeavors. As a developmental phase, adolescence requires a special theoretical and technical focus in order to devise a rational treatment regime.

### Typical Adolescent Problems

#### Identity Problems

**Identity Diffusion.** Erikson was the first to describe a clinical syndrome found most frequently in beginning college students and characterized by a general deterioration of personal habits. He called it the identity diffusion syndrome, and believed it was the outcome of the breakdown of the cohesion of personal identity. This inner disruption results in a syndrome characterized by a breakdown of personal habits and by panic. In extreme cases, the patient may not even know who he is. In other cases, the patient is tormented with questions as to where he fits into the scheme of things or the meaningless, purposeless quality of his life. In spite of symptoms so severe that these patients are often diagnosed as schizophrenic, the identity diffusion syndrome responds well and quickly to supportive psychotherapy. The most severely disturbed patients may have to be returned to their homes, where they usually recover.

**Withdrawal and Suicide.** Withdrawal ranges from severe withdrawal to social shyness, because of some of the inherent disadvantages of adolescence—acne, social clumsiness due to lack of experience, and many other causes—that can be attributed to the formative elements of this stage.

Sometimes, clinicians encounter adolescent patients whose withdrawal can be counted as schizoid. These are seemingly apathetic youngsters who have only a minimal contact with the external world. They lack the adaptive techniques to cope with what for them is an incomprehensible environment. Inasmuch as it is incomprehensible, it is also terrifying, and they have to withdraw from it. This withdrawal naturally affects the quality of a therapeutic relationship.

The most extreme and final withdrawal is suicide. Suicide often represents an attempt to obtain relief from the misery of a contemptible view of the self. The therapist must be careful not to reinforce the patient's reactions by sharing his misery; it is easy to be caught up in the intensity of feeling that the patient infuses in the therapeutic ambience.

**Rebellion.** The rebellious adolescent constructs a counterculture that may take many different forms.

*Dependence on Drugs.* Basically, two effects are sought from drugs. One is the attainment of calmness and tranquility, and the other is stimulation, which is supposed to achieve hyperacuity, sensitive discrimination, and erotic excitement and thrills. These pharmacological goals are found in other age groups as well, but, because the adolescent feels particularly vulnerable and suffers the torments of a still amorphous identity, an affective experience seems to be especially important.

The sedative effects of drugs can be equated with defensive withdrawal, a form of passive rebellion, whereas their mood-elevating consequences can be used to vitalize a self-concept that is experienced as empty and lifeless.

The drug problems of adolescence are complex and serious within a psychopathological context. The psychiatrist has to keep an open mind and not allow his personal prejudices to interfere with his diagnostic and therapeutic judgment. Changes in adaptive patterns occur so rapidly that what may be indicative of psychopathology at one time becomes culturally syntonic later, and then has little meaning as a symptomatic manifestation of emotional illness.

*School Dropouts.* Dropping out of school can often represent a form of rebellion. Discontinuing school may represent an attempt to frustrate parents. This dropping out usually occurs in families who value education, perhaps as a steppingstone toward material success, but, in any case, academic achievement represents status. Frequently, the parents' self-esteem depends on their child's achievement. The student may sense the parents' involvement and resent it. He may see it as an intrusion upon his autonomy that threatens his identity.

#### Affective Problems

**Depression.** The depressed adolescent looks depressed. He is visibly sad and withdrawn from activities and peers. Motorically, he may be retarded, or, by contrast, he may be restless and agitated. Similar to adult patients, the adolescent can have a variety of somatic symptoms—tension headaches, insomnia, anorexia or bulimia, easy fatigability, and all the other symptoms and signs that have become linked to the melancholic syndrome.

Another depressive symptom is feeling depleted. The depressed patient complains of having no energy. Consequently, relating to the outer world and mastering problems may be inordinately difficult. Everything becomes complex and burdensome, and the patient's sense of inadequacy intensifies.

**Manic Disorders.** Psychotherapy alone—because of the manic's short attention span, hyperactivity, euphoria, and scattered behavior—is difficult to conduct. Treatment with lithium carbonate has been immensely useful in controlling disruptive manic or hypomanic behavior and has made many such patients amenable to psychotherapy.

The diagnosis of mania, however, is not always easy to make. Agitated states are often misdiagnosed as mania.

**Anorexia Nervosa.** Anorexia nervosa occurs primarily in girls, the age of onset usually coinciding with the onset of menses. Less frequently, it begins during prepuberty or in later adolescence. It is rarely seen in boys, and, when it does occur in boys, it usually begins before puberty.

This disorder is discussed more fully in Section 22.4.

### Schizophrenic Disorders

From a psychological perspective, psychoses among adolescents usually consist of schizophrenic breakdowns, characterized by withdrawal from the world of reality. The patients replace the world from which they have withdrawn by their private reality, a delusional and distorted one from our viewpoint. Thinking reverts to archaic and primitive modes of operation, an understandable consequence of the profound regression these youngsters have undergone, one based on a fragile and vulnerable character structure that is unable to cope with the exigencies of the world they have to face without adaptive resources.

The affective psychoses rarely occur during adolescence. Patients exhibiting the symptoms of a psychotic depression or a hypomanic or manic state frequently reveal an underlying schizophrenic process.

### Special Problems Causing Treatment Difficulties

#### Noncommunicativeness

Within the psychotherapeutic framework, silence or inhibition of expression has various meanings. Many therapists immediately assume it is a resistance and bend their efforts to get the patient to talk. Others, who may also acknowledge the resistive qualities of silence, prefer to deal with it as part of the patient's adaptations and a manifestation of psychopathology. With this in mind, they attempt to create a setting in which the patient can be comfortably silent.

#### Antisocial Behavior, Acting Out, and Violence

The propensity for certain forms of acting out to stimulate untoward reactions in the therapist must always be kept in mind. Frequently, if the therapist recognizes his behavior in terms of his own sensitivites and perhaps irrational responses, he can relax and resume a therapy that is headed in the direction of progressive structuralization.

The most extreme form of acting out is violent behavior, and it is easy to give examples of adolescent violence that preclude any treatment based on a communicative relationship between two persons. Some patients with very traumatic backgrounds have learned to cope with an assaultive world that is full of hatred. They deal with new situations in a suspicious, mistrusting fashion, and their level of control is low. In a treatment relationship, it may be especially difficult to keep their hostility suppressed, and this hostility may make it impossible to conduct therapy in the usual fashion. In these instances, safety may be the primary concern, and the therapist has to create a setting that is directed toward vigilance to prevent the patient from hurting himself or others.

The therapist's response can often be very influential in preventing violence from getting out of hand. If he is relatively comfortable and knows his limits of tolerance, he may create an atmosphere that the patient finds reassuring.

The ability to express anger in an organized, controlled fashion, rather than through violent outbursts, is one of the goals of psychotherapy. This taming of feelings is of considerable value to the patient and has adaptive significance. Purposeless attacks are equivalent to the screaming and kicking of temper tantrums, and do not really lead to any benefits. Such attacks do not enhance self-esteem, whereas aggression can enhance it, as the patient uses aggression to master problem situations in the external world.

### Therapeutic Approaches and Mechanisms

#### Diagnosis

In middle-class groups, a surprising number of adolescents know about psychoanalysis and seek it for themselves. There seems to be increasing sophistication among youth that causes them to feel curious about the working of their minds. Although many adolescents are action oriented, the growing tendency toward introspection makes many of them suitable for psychoanalytic treatment.

In these circumstances, diagnostic distinctions recede into the background. The analyst may make what can be considered a characterological diagnosis. He reaches tentative conclusions about the patient's capacity to become involved in a relationship that may require tolerance of tension and anxiety, and the ability to regress and reintegrate. Whether the patient can operate in a psychological frame of reference—that is, whether he is able to use mental constructs and focus on intrapsychic factors—is much more significant than any formal diagnostic criteria. The extent of the patient's self-observing function is the crucial indicator of therapeutic feasibility.

The way the patient relates and the course the treatment takes are the chief variables that determine a therapeutic diagnosis. The clinician does not make predetermined judgments about the treatment, and it has been the happy experience of many psychiatrists that this relaxed attitude, in itself, creates an atmosphere of security in which the patient can relax, making him therapeutically accessible.

### Symptom Alleviation and Behavioral Change

By far the majority of therapeutic approaches to adolescent psychopathology are directed toward psychic reintegration and not toward the unearthing and resolution of unconscious conflicts. However, this is a matter of emphasis, because often supportive or educative types of treatment also become involved with deeper layers of the personality. Contrary to what is frequently taught, supportive or educative approaches, which also involve some environmental manipulation, can be very difficult to conduct, and demand the skill of the experienced practitioner rather than the beginning therapist who is often assigned such tasks.

Many therapies are included in this group. For heuristic purposes, one can construct a spectrum ranging from psychotherapy based on psychodynamic principles but whose purpose is to reestablish defensive equilibrium, to therapies exclusively based on phenomenology, such as behavioral modification, drugs, and other somatic therapies. In between are included Gestalt therapy, group therapy, family therapy, and transactional analysis. There are other types of treatment, new ones springing up frequently but fading just as quickly. The ones enumerated seem to have achieved some durability.

All these treatment modalities can be pursued either in the hospital or on an outpatient basis.

**Group Psychotherapy.** Adolescent patients often react well in groups and become intensely involved. They seem to acquire tolerance and understanding that helps them accept an outer world that had previously been alien to them. Many narcissistically constricted adolescents may develop compassion for those less fortunate than themselves, and even view the frailties of society with a benign perspective as a result of a successful group interaction. The milieu can create a setting in which the members' minimal supplies of self-esteem are replenished and perhaps a collective ego ideal is constructed. This is a psychically integrative experience.

**Family Therapy.** A patient's improvement may stir the parents to sabotage the treatment, even to the point of terminating it. Consequently, some therapists believe that the family has to be included in the treatment plan. Not only is this arrangement helpful in dealing with the family's resistance to improvement, but much can be learned about the subtle interactions between siblings and parents that have contributed to and sometimes encouraged the patient's emotional problems.

**Drug and Somatic Therapies.** Drugs are prescribed for disturbed affective states and thought processes. Their function is to help control disruptive symptoms, and in some instances to make the patient more amenable to psychotherapy. Anxiety, depression, hyperactive behavior, and such specific symptoms as tics and enuresis usually respond well to medication.

There does not seem to be much difference in the psychopharmacological approaches to the adolescent and to the adult.

From a psychological viewpoint, the clinician must be aware of the adolescent's sensitivities, which center on distrust of adult authority and particular preoccupation with physical functioning. Consequently, drug complications and side effects may be unusually distressing.

Somatic treatments, such as electroconvulsive therapy, are extreme forms of treatment and are usually restricted to severe psychotic disorders.

### REFERENCES

Blos P: *On Adolescence: A Psychoanalytic Interpretation.* Free Press of Glencoe, New York, 1962.
Feinstein S C, Miller D: Psychoses of adolescence. In *Basic Handbook of Child Psychiatry,* J D Noshpitz, editor. Basic Books, New York, 1979.
Gadpaille W J: Psychiatric treatment of the adolescent. In *Comprehensive Textbook of Psychiatry,* ed

4, H I Kaplan B J Sadock, editors, p 1805. Williams & Wilkins, Baltimore, 1985.

Group for the Advancement of Psychiatry: *Normal Adolescence: Its Dynamics and Impact*, GAP Report No. 68. Group for the Advancement of Psychiatry, New York, 1968.

Group for the Advancement of Psychiatry. *Power and Authority in Adolescence: The Origins and Resolutions of Intergenerational Conflict*, GAP Report No. 101. Group for the Advancement of Psychiatry, New York, 1978.

Holmes D J: *The Adolescent in Psychotherapy*, Little, Brown, Boston, 1964.

Malmquist C P: *Handbook of Adolescence*. Jason Aronson, New York, 1978.

Masterson J F: *The Psychiatric Dilemma of Adolescence*. Little, Brown, Boston, 1967.

Meeks J E: *The Fragile Alliance: An Orientation to the Outpatient Psychotherapy of the Adolescent*. Williams & Wilkins, Baltimore, 1971.

Miller D: *Adolescence: Psychology, Psychopathology, and Psychotherapy*. Jason Aronson, New York, 1974.

# 37

# Child Psychiatry: Special Areas of Interest

## 37.1 CHILD MALTREATMENT AND BATTERED CHILD SYNDROME

### Introduction

The disease of the maltreatment of children is one aspect of social violence, and is symptomatic of an illness that is insidiously creeping into society. Child abuse is a medical-social disease that is assuming epidemic proportion, and that encompasses a child-rearing pattern that is becoming more entrenched in the population. It is a disease that is not a time-limited phenomenon but, rather, the cause and effect of a cyclical pattern of the violence reflected in all statistics on crime.

### Incidence

The National Center on Child Abuse and Neglect in Washington, D.C., has estimated that there are more than 300,000 instances of child maltreatment reported to central registries throughout the country every year, and about 2,000 deaths from abuse annually.

Not all neglected and abused children are taken to physicians or hospitals for medical attention. Many maltreated children who are seen by physicians go unrecognized, undiagnosed, and, hence, not reported. With all the statistics, probably only the upper portion of a submerged iceberg is seen.

### Diagnosis

A maltreated child often presents no obvious signs of being battered, but has multiple minor physical evidences of emotional and, at times, nutritional deprivation, neglect, and abuse. In these cases, the diagnostic ability of the physician, coupled with community treatment and preventive child abuse programs, can prevent the more serious injuries of inflicted battering that are significant causes of childhood deaths.

The maltreated child is often taken to a hospital or private physician with a history of failure to thrive, malnutrition, poor skin hygiene, irritability, a repressed personality, and other signs of obvious psychological and physical neglect. The more severely abused children are seen in hospital emergency rooms with external evidences of body trauma, bruises, abrasions, cuts, lacerations, burns, soft tissue swellings, and hematomas (see Figs. 1–3). Hypernatremic dehydration, after periodic water deprivation by psychotic mothers, has been reported as a form of child abuse. Inability to move certain extremities, because of dislocations and fractures associated with neurological signs of intracranial damage, can be additional signs of inflicted trauma. Other clinical signs and symptoms attributed to inflicted abuse may include injury to viscera. Abdominal trauma may result in unexplained ruptures of stomach, bowel, liver, or pancreas, with manifestations of an acutely injured abdomen. Children manifesting the maltreatment syndrome give evidence of one or more of these complaints. Those with the most severe maltreatment injuries arrive at the hospital or physician's office in coma or convulsions, and some arrive dead. The signs and symptoms indicating the maltreatment of children, therefore, range from the simple undernourished infant, reported as failure to thrive, to the battered child, which is often the last phase of the spectrum of the maltreatment syndrome.

Actual cases of murder, battering, torture, starvation, sexual abuse, and life-ruining neglect are recorded in the medical literature. The accounts range from accidents to discipline. The maltreating parents come from all stratums of society.

Sexual abuse and exploitation of children have become an increasingly important type of child abuse with psychosocial, legal, and medical implications. The children's division of the

American Humane Association reports more than 5,000 cases of incest annually. However, most cases of sexual abuse involving children are never revealed because of the victim's guilt feelings, shame, ignorance, and tolerance, compounded by the resistance of some physicians to recognize and report sexual abuse, the court's insistence on strict rules of evidence, and the families' fears of dissolution if discovered.

Sexual abuse has been reported in schools, day-care centers and group homes where the adult caretakers have been found to be the major offenders. The incidence of sexual abuse and child pornography is much higher than previously assumed.

### Maternal Deprivation Syndrome

It has been established that prolonged maternal deprivation of a child can have a serious and lifelong impact on the child's future character structure. There is clinical evidence that this type of impaired relations between mother and child in the early period of infancy causes a variety of psychological disorders during adulthood. In addition, inadequate mothering or child neglect stemming from maternal deprivation

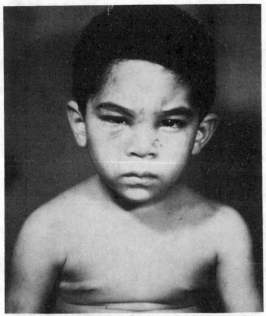

FIGURE 1. A 5-year-old boy was admitted with abrasions and bruises in various stages of healing and evidence of recent trauma to right eye and face. History of periodic beatings by sadistic, mentally retarded mother facilitated diagnosis of child battering.

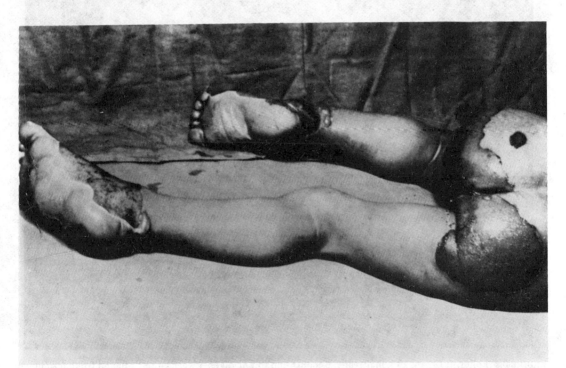

FIGURE 2. A 3½-year-old male child, brought into emergency room by mother, with second degree burns of the buttocks, perineum, hands, and feet. Mother related story that child accidentally fell into tub of hot water while preparing to take a bath. Physical examination revealed burns of the buttocks, hands, and feet without any evidence of burns along the body area. Location of the burns led physicians to suspect that child was forced into boiling water involving the buttocks, and in an attempt to keep himself from being submerged, he extended his feet and hands into the water. Scalding injury to feet, perineum, and buttocks caused burn areas corresponding to the child's posture on dunking. Mother later admitted to the child's placement into tub of hot water by a boyfriend while she was out shopping.

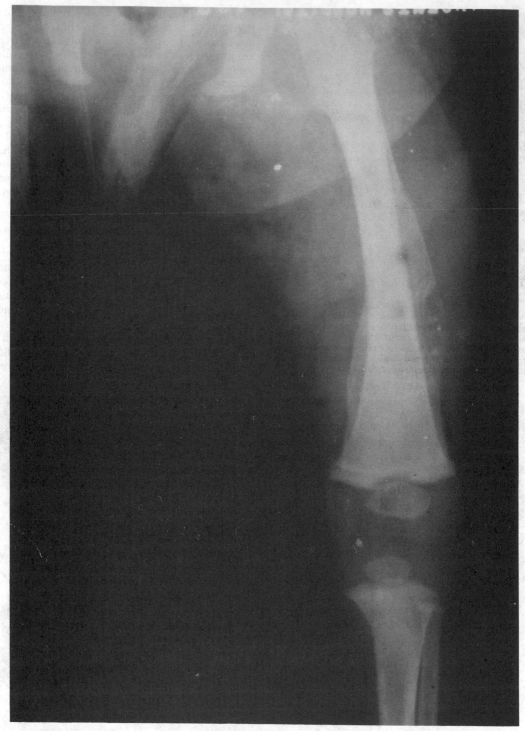

FIGURE 3.    Follow-up X-ray of a maltreated 6-month-old infant taken 4 weeks after inflicted trauma to upper thigh. Extensive reparative changes are noted in association with new bone formation, external cortical thickening, and "squaring" of the metaphysis—diagnostic evidence of bone changes following trauma. The layer of calcification around the shaft of the bone and presence of bone fragments at the ends of the bone should be evidence for suspicion of inflicted trauma and should prompt further investigations into the etiological causes of the X-ray findings. These X-ray changes may be diagnostic when correlated with other manifestations of child abuse.

can result in growth failure, autistic behavior, and retarded mental development in the child.

Although several investigations suggest that the level of mothering is inadequate, and that there is evidence of neglect, the symptoms of growth failure, emotional defects, and developmental lags may be effects of organic brain damage or genetic defects coincident with the neglect syndrome. The only way to establish an unchallengeable cause and effect relationship between the infant's mothering and his symptoms is to demonstrate significant recovery when the mothering is altered. This single criterion can make the diagnosis of maternal deprivation syndrome, and calls for the development of a treatment plan based on immediate intervention and continued persistent surveillance. All infants diagnosed as markedly deprived should have an investigation of the social-environmental condition of the family and the psychological status of the mother to determine the factors responsible for inefficient mothering.

Many of these maltreated children are not taken to a physician or hospital for medical care unless the child is in acute distress or the parents fear impending death or because the parents fear legal entanglements. If the infant or child is taken to a physician or hospital, the history related by the parents is often at variance with the clinical picture and the physical findings noted on examination of the child. The physician often discovers that the mother has taken the child to various hospitals and doctors in an effort to negate any suspicions of parental abuse. Difficulty in obtaining any type of history is often encountered, and diagnosis depends on the physical examinations, X-ray findings, and a high index of suspicion on the part of the physician (see Table I).

## Epidemiology

### Children

Many investigators have observed that the children involved in the incidence of abuse and neglect tend to be very young. Parental neglect and abuse may occur at any age, with an increase of incidence in children under 3 years of age. Several surveys have indicated that the children on whom severe physical injuries were inflicted tended to be younger than those on whom less severe injuries were inflicted.

Older children are often physically abused because they are found to be unacceptable and offer a threat to the viability of the family unit. The mother justifies her actions on the basis of the child's imperfections, using disciplinary ac-

TABLE I
PHYSICIAN'S INDEX OF SUSPICION

*History*
   Characteristic age—usually under 3 years
   General health of child—indicative of neglect
   Characteristic distribution of fractures
   Disproportionate amounts of soft tissue injury; evidence that injuries occurred at different times, with lesions in various stages of resolution
   Cause of recent trauma not known
   Previous history of similar episodes and multiple visits to various hospitals
   Date of injury prior to admission to hospital—delay in seeking medical help
   Child brought to hospital for complaint other than one associated with abuse or neglect, such as cold, headache, stomachache, etc.
   Reluctance of parents or caretaker to give information
   History related by parents or caretakers is usually at complete variance with the clinical picture and the physical findings noted on examination of the child
   Parents' inappropriate reaction to severity of injury
   Family discord or financial stress, alcoholism, psychosis, drug addiction, and inconsistent social history that varies according to intake worker
*Physical Examination*
   Signs of general neglect, failure to thrive, poor skin hygiene, malnutrition, withdrawal, irritability, repressed personality
   Bruises, abrasions, burns, soft tissue swellings, bites, hematomas, ocular damage, old healed lesions
   Evidences of dislocation or fractures of the extremities
   Unexplained symptoms of an acute abdomen—ruptured viscera
   Neurological findings associated with brain damage
   Coma, convulsions, death
   Symptoms of drug withdrawal or drug intoxication
*Differential Diagnosis*
   Scurvy and rickets
   Infantile cortical hyperostosis
   Syphilis of infancy
   Osteogenesis imperfecta
   Neurological, organic brain damage
   Accidental trauma
*Radiological Manifestations*
   Subperiosteal hemorrhages
   Epiphyseal separations
   Periosteal shearing
   Metaphyseal fragmentation
   Previously healed periosteal calcifications
   Squaring of the metaphysis

tions that often lead to battering. Sexual abuse has been reported in children as young as 6 months to 1 year of age.

Many abused children are perceived by their parents as being different, slow in development or mentally retarded, bad, selfish, or hard to discipline. There appears to be a group of children whose defiant behavior or hyperactive behavior makes them particularly vulnerable to abuse. Child abuse and neglect may be suspected when several of the following factors are in evidence: the child seems unduly afraid, especially of his parents; the child is kept confined—as in a crib, playpen, or cage—for overlong periods of time; the child shows evidence of repeated skin or other injuries; the child's injuries are inappropriately treated in terms of bandages and medication; the child appears undernourished; the child is given inappropriate food, drink, or medicine; the child is dressed inappropriately for the weather conditions; the child shows evidence of over-all poor care; the child cries often; the child takes over the role of a parent and tries to be protective or otherwise to take care of parent's needs.

### Parents

The perpetrator of the battered child syndrome is more often the woman than the man. One parent is usually the active batterer, and the other parent passively accepts the battering. Of the perpetrators, 80 percent were regularly living in the homes of the children they abused. More than 80 percent of the children reported in a survey were living with married parents or with the parents' substitutes; approximately 20 percent were living with a single parent. The average age of the mother who inflicted abuse on her children has been reported to be around 26 years; the average age of the father is 30.

The abusive parents show inappropriate expectations of their children, with a reversal of dependency needs. The parent deals with the child as if the child were older than the parent. The parent often turns to the child for reassurance, nurturing comfort, and protection, and expects a loving response. These parents had experienced severe abuse in the form of physical abuse from their own mothers or fathers. Sexual abuse is usually done by men; although women acting in concert with men or alone have also been involved, especially in child pornography.

### Physician's Responsibility

In suspected cases of child abuse and neglect, the physician should (1) make a diagnosis of suspected maltreatment; (2) intervene and admit the child to the hospital; (3) make an assessment—history, physical examination, skeletal survey, and photographs; (4) report the case to the appropriate department of social service and child-protection unit or central registry; (5) request a social worker's report and appropriate surgical and medical consultations; (6) confer within 72 hours with members of the child abuse committee; (7) arrange a program of care for the child and the parents; and (8) arrange for social service follow-up.

### Treatment

Ideally, each patient should have an intervention plan developed for him or her based on an assessment of a number of factors, including (1) the factors responsible for the parent's dysfunction; (2) the severity of the parent's psychopathology; (3) the over-all prognosis for achieving adequate parenting experiences; (4) the time estimated to achieve meaningful change in the parent's ability to parent; (5) whether the parent's dysfunction is confined to this child or involves other children; (6) the extent to which the mother's malfunctioning extends to her other roles—wife, homemaker, housekeeper; (7) the extent to which the parent's over-all malfunctioning, if this is the case, is acute or chronic (reflects a lifelong pattern); (8) the extent to which the mother's malfunctioning is confined to infants, as opposed to older children (the incidence of abuse is inverse to the child's age); (9) the parent's willingness to participate in the intervention plan; (10) the availability of personnel and physical resources to implement the various intervention strategies; and (11) the risk of the child's sustaining physical abuse by remaining in the home.

On the basis of the information obtained, several options can be selected to improve the parent's functioning: (1) eliminate or diminish the social or environmental stresses; (2) lessen the adverse psychological impact of the social factors on the parent; (3) reduce the demands on the mother to a level that is within her capacity through day care placement of the child or provision of a housekeeper or baby sitter; (4) provide emotional support, encouragement, sympathy, stimulation, instruction in maternal care, and aid in learning to plan for, assess, and meet the needs of the infant (supportive case work); (5) resolve or diminish the parent's inner psychic conflict (psychotherapy).

In general, child abuse preventive and treatment programs should include the following objectives: (1) to prevent the separation of parents and child whenever possible; (2) to prevent the placement of children in institutions; (3) to encourage the attainment of self-care status on the part of the parents; (4) to stimulate the attainment of self-sufficiency for the family unit; and (5) to prevent further abuse and neglect by removing children from families who show an unwillingness or inability to profit from the treatment program.

In the areas of sexual abuse, the licensing of day-care centers and the psychological screening of those who work in them should be mandatory to prevent further abuses from occurring.

**REFERENCES**

Fontana V J: *Somewhere a Child Is Crying.* Macmillan, New York, 1973; Mentor (paperback), New York, 1983.
Fontana V J: A multidisciplinary approach to the treatment of child abuse. Pediatrics *57:* 760, 1976.
Fontana V J: *The Maltreated Child: The Maltreatment Syndrome in Children,* ed 4, Charles C Thomas, Springfield, IL, 1979.
Fontana V J: Child maltreatment and battered child syndrome. In *Comprehensive Textbook of Psychiatry,* ed 4, H I Kaplan, B J Sadock, editors, p 1816. Williams & Wilkins, Baltimore, 1985.
Fontana V J, Schneider C: Help for abusing parents. In *Helping Parents Help Their Children.* E Arnold, editor, p 259. Brunner/Mazel, New York, 1978.
Gray J, Culter C, Dean J, Kempe C H: Prediction and prevention of child abuse and neglect. Child Abuse Neglect *1:* 45, 1977.
Kaplan S J, Zitrin A: Psychiatrists and child abuse. J Am Acad Child Psychiatry *22:* 253, 1983.
Kempe C H, Helfer R, editors: *Helping the Battered Child and His Family.* J. B. Lippincott, Philadelphia, 1972.
Kempe C H, Helfer R, editors: *Child Abuse and Neglect: The Family and the Community.* Ballinger Press, Cambridge, MA, 1976.
Kempe C H, Silverman F N, Steele B N, Droegemueller W, Silver H K: The battered child syndrome. JAMA *251:* 3288, 1984.

# 37.2　CHILDREN'S REACTIONS TO ILLNESS, HOSPITALIZATION, AND SURGERY

## Introduction

Whether a child's illness or injury produces a deleterious effect on his adaptation or the family equilibrium depends on (1) the developmental level of the child; (2) the child's previous adaptive capacity; (3) the prior nature of the parent-child relationship; (4) the existing family equilibrium; (5) the nature of the illness or injury, including the organ system affected, the degree of prostration or pain, the type of treatment or home care, and any residual defect or handicap; and (6) the meaning of the illness to the child and his family in terms of immediately antecedent events and their actual or fantasied connection, the previous experience with such illness, the effect on the child's social, academic, and athletic capacities, and the reverberations on siblings.

## Acute Illness or Injury

Certain broad patterns of response are characteristic of children in general, with some differences related to individual variations and to developmental level.

### Direct Effects

Malaise, discomfort, or pain may produce listlessness, prostration, disturbances in sleep and appetite, and irritability in children, much as in adults. However, restlessness is more common in children, and hyperactivity with mild illness is frequently seen, particularly in preschool children. Anorexia and refusal of food may be marked in young children; well-meaning but anxious parents may urge food, and the child's negativistic responses often lead to feeding problems that persist long after the illness subsides. Difficulties in falling asleep, nightmares, and night-terrors are common; sleeping problems also may continue as struggles for control between young children and parents.

### Reactive Effects

In addition to such direct effects, which may closely resemble or overlap disturbances in behavior from primarily psychological or interpersonal sources, other reactive responses may occur.

**Regression.** A ubiquitous pattern in children is that of emotional or behavioral regression, seen most strikingly in older infants and preschool children but encountered also in school-age children and adolescents and, for that matter, in adults to a lesser degree.

**Depression.** Another pattern of response to illness is depression, which takes different forms in infants, children, and adolescents from those seen in adults. Other emotional responses, often related to regressive trends, include the reemergence of primitive fears and feelings of helplessness or inadequacy. Stereotyped behavior of a compulsive or ritualized nature may be seen, as may transient hypochondriacal concerns.

**Misinterpretation.** Misinterpretation of the meaning of illness or injury is a common phenomenon. It is related to the child's limited capacity for intellectual understanding and testing of reality, and his tendency toward magical or animistic thinking, particularly in the young child. Fears are more intense when sensitive areas, such as the head or the genital organs, are involved.

**Physiological Reactions.** Psychological conflicts about the meaning of illness, enhanced by regressive trends, may result in the appearance of the physiological concomitants of anxiety. Tachycardia, palpitation, hyperventilation, diarrhea, or other signs and symptoms may be exhibited.

**Conversion Reactions.** Other psychological reactions, seen frequently in school-age children or adolescents in relation to physical illness, include conversion reactions. These disturbances affect the voluntarily innervated striated musculature and the somatosensory apparatus, with their unconsciously symbolic expression of emotional conflict. They are to be distinguished from psychophysiological disorders, which affect involuntarily innervated systems and visceral end organs, without symbolic significance.

**Dissociative Reactions**. Dissociative reactions—such as amnesia, somnambulism, fugue states, and pseudodelirious states—may also occur. These reactions may compound or be compounded by an actual delirium, which is often of a subclinical nature.

**Perceptual-motor Lags**. Other effects on behavior may be manifest in the convalescent phase. Some children exhibit lags in perceptual-motor functions after a systemic illness, such as pneumonia. The lags may persist for several weeks or months without apparent damage to the central nervous system.

### Chronic Illness or Handicap

Many of the considerations mentioned for acute illnesses and injuries are applicable to chronic illness and handicapping injury. Although serious repercussions on the child's personality development and family functioning are frequent, many children with chronic disease or with congenital or acquired handicaps make a surprisingly adequate adaptation to or compensation for their disabilities. These variables relating to the child's previous adaptive capacity and the parent-child-family balance appear to be of more importance than is the nature of the specific disease or handicap.

#### Effects on Personality

The personality pictures seen in children with various diseases or handicaps appear to fall along a continuum, ranging from overdependent, overanxious, and passive or withdrawn patterns—with strong secondary gains from illness—to over-independent, aggressive modes of behavior—with strong associated tendencies to deny illness, even to markedly unhealthy extremes. A middle group of children show realistic dependence and acceptance of their limitations, with adequate social patterns and compensatory outlets, and with no more denial than is consistent with the maintenance of hope.

Parental reactions also fall along a continuum, ranging from overanxiety, overprotectiveness, and overindulgence—often with difficulties in setting limits on the child's demands—to problems in acceptance of the child's disability—frequently with denial of its extent, projec-

tion of guilt onto the medical staff, reluctance to accept recommended treatment, and occasional rejection or isolation of the child within the family unit. A middle group of parents can, after the initial phases of response, comfortably accept the child's limitations, permit him appropriate dependency, and help him constructively exploit his capacities and strengths.

#### Effects on Body Image

Difficulties in the establishment or maintenance of the body image are present for most children with a chronic illness or handicap, but these difficulties may also be seen in children without physical disfigurement. Size, strength, and attractiveness do play some role in the child's confidence and social adjustment, but only in special cases or in individual family situations do these factors appear to be of great importance.

### Juvenile Diabetes Mellitus

Juvenile diabetes is a good example of a chronic illness with which the child must deal. Like its adult counterpart, it is a chronic condition resulting from a disturbance in carbohydrate metabolism. Insulin is not secreted properly by the pancreas, and presumably this problem has prominent genetic factors.

**Psychophysiology**. It has long been recognized that emotional trauma may precipitate the onset of overt juvenile diabetes. The type of trauma is not specific, but a thorough history often reveals some emotional upset. These children do not appear to have any particular personality type, nor are they grossly abnormal from a psychiatric stand-point.

In a child with diabetes, the most difficult emotional problems often arise after the diagnosis is made. How this occurs varies with the age of the child, but begins with the reaction of the family. Parents often react initially with disbelief. They may go doctor shopping in the hope of proving the diagnosis incorrect. A thorough physical workup, usually in the hospital, and parent education are essential. It is only when the parents accept the fact that their child has diabetes, and when they understand the condition, that they can become necessary team members in its management.

The child who is diagnosed as diabetic usually resents the idea that he has a chronic condition that makes him different from his peers. He may become depressed and may regress or, more often, openly rebel. The rebellion can be dangerous, because the youngster often tries to avoid adhering to the regimen established for him. He sneaks candy and cheats on his diet, as if to prove that he does not have the disorder. This cheating can result in diabetic coma, hospitalization, and even brain damage. The youngster needs to emotionally accept the diabetes, understand the limitations it imposes, and, most important, feel that his parents love and accept him. Depending on his age, he becomes a team member with his parents and his physician in the management of his disease. As soon as he is able, he takes the responsibility for administering his insulin and testing his urine. This, of course, is a gradual process and should not be hurried.

The child whose diabetes appears before or during grade school has usually adapted to it by adolescence; however, when it appears during the teenage years, it is apt to cause considerable emotional upheaval. Adolescents are sensitive about their bodies, and the idea of being damaged is hard to accept. Conformity in eating habits is important in this age group, as is conformity in dress and behavior, and his difference can become a problem for the diabetic teenager. Parental and medical counseling are extremely important during these years. The juvenile diabetic who lives in a strife-ridden home may reflect some of his emotional turmoil in hard to control diabetes. Emotional crises, parental disunity and sibling rivalry may all make the disorder more difficult to stabilize. Some youngsters use their condition to gain special favors or to control emotional unrest in the family.

**Management.** Most juvenile diabetics and their families can receive adequate assistance from the family physician, many of whom are extremely adept at dealing with parents and children with regard to not only the physical but also the emotional aspects of diabetes. It is most important, especially in the early stages, that the physician make ample time available to the family to answer questions and form a trusting relationship.

A useful experience for many children is a diabetic summer camp, where there is not only the camping experience, but an opportunity to meet other children with the same disorder. Some physicians allow the child a free day every couple of months; during this free day the child is free to choose his diet and his activities. The insulin dosage is adjusted appropriately, and most children do not abuse this privilege.

The primary physician may find a need on occasion for consultants, one of whom may be a child psychiatrist. This need arises when there is chronic and relatively severe psychopathology in the child or his family. In such cases, the child psychiatrist should follow the usual procedure of a thorough history of the child and his family, and should also discuss the physical problems with the primary physician. Both physicians should become aware of how emotional factors are involved. A child may feel, sometimes correctly, that he is the target of parental rejection, and that he is considered less than adequate. In other cases, the child may have been overprotected and infantilized, or perhaps the parents are divided in their approach. Emotional problems in diabetic children stem from the same family troubles as emotional problems in any child. The diabetes only adds fuel to the fire. Some parents can accept a chronic physical handicap in their child and help him develop normal self-esteem, but others cannot.

At some point questions usually arise as to the genetic aspects of diabetes. Too often, one parent blames the other. The older adolescent wonders about the chances of his or her children's having diabetes. Unless the family physician or the child psychiatrist is knowledgeable in such matters, a consultation with a geneticist can be useful.

## Hospitalization

Hospitalization, with its separation from home and family and various treatment procedures, may cause various reactions related to the child's developmental level and other factors.

### Short-term Hospitalization

Most, if not all, infants and children show some reaction to the experience of hospitalization. Infants in the first half year of life exhibit temporary and rather global responses, arising from different methods of feeding and handling. Infants in the latter part of the first year experience stranger anxiety and separation anxiety, often with some regression and depression.

Children under 4 years of age are most vulnerable to separation from the mother. This separation is often misinterpreted as punishment or desertion, resulting in feelings of helplessness or fears of attack related to the child's limited capacities for reality testing.

For the child from 4 years through the early school-age period, the psychological meaning of the illness and its treatment appear to have greater potential effects than the actual separation from the parents. Fears of bodily mutilation and the tendency to misinterpret painful treatment procedures as punishment often invoke anxiety, regression, and the other manifestations mentioned earlier; boys ordinarily exhibit more aggressive responses than do girls.

Older school-age children, who can comprehend the reality of the hospital experience more fully, may show mild regression and anxiety over the functioning of certain organs; these reactions are related to incomplete body images. Fears of genital inadequacy, muscular weakness, and loss of body control or mastery contribute to the feelings of anxiety and inferiority characteristic of this stage. In adolescents, many of the same trends are seen in more muted fashion. There are also struggles to establish a sense of identity and independence, and these struggles sometimes interfere with the teenager's cooperation in treatment programs.

Parental reactions show some similarity to the patterns seen during acute illness. Denial and disbelief are less marked with less serious illness, with significant exceptions. Many parents fear criticism from the hospital staff regarding their role in the illness or their effectiveness as parents. Some parents may show strong rivalry with nurses or physicians, misinterpreting professional competence in handling the child as a threat to their own parental capacities. Feeling left out or unwanted is also common among parents. A few may project their own guilt onto the hospital staff and blame them for minor difficulties. Difficulty in accepting recommended treatment occasionally leads to their signing the child out of the hospital against advice, or not complying with posthospitalization treatment plans.

Parents who have newborn infants in high-risk nurseries are in a special situation. They have not had a chance to assume responsibility for the care of their infant, and must delegate this care to the hospital staff.

The need to delegate care, and the paucity of communication between parents and staff members, may have a significant detrimental effect on the eventual emotional adjustment and bonding between the child and his parents. There is a growing concern that hospital care practices that do not take into consideration the importance of the early contacts between infants, parents, and hospital staffs could be contributing to the onset of parent-child relationships that lead to the syndromes of battered child, failure to thrive, and the vulnerable child.

### Posthospitalization

Posthospitalization reactions may occur, even in children who have been able to maintain control through the hospital experience. Regressive tendencies, outbursts of anxiety, and fears of doctors or needles may appear in children after they return home. When parents are unprepared for such behavior, overprotective or overrestrictive tendencies may cause significant

interpersonal reverberations within the family unit.

Although some reactions of the types described are virtually universal, the majority of children are able to adapt successfully to the experience of hospitalization, showing self-limited reactions that ordinarily subside after several weeks to several months. But the possibility of emotionally traumatic reactions is great enough, particularly in preschool children and in previously disturbed children, to require careful thought about the indications for hospitalization, and to warrant the use of psychological preventive measures.

### Long-term Hospitalization

With modern treatment measures, a long-term hospitalization or institutionalization is rarely necessary for the chronically ill or handicapped child. In large institutions especially, children exhibit chronic depression and detachment, often leading to shallow social relationships, distorted time concepts, limited capacities for learning, lowered resistance to disease, and rebellious or antisocial behavior. A few children, because of especially appealing qualities, can reach out to the often limited staff in such settings to meet their emotional needs, but significant personality distortions have resulted for many from such hospitalization.

### Hospitalism

Hospitalism or anaclitic depression (the latter term coined by René Spitz) refers to the syndrome manifested by infants separated from their mothers for long time periods, usually because the child was placed in an institution where children were given inadequate individual attention and where they were rarely held or played with.

At first they show distress and crying; after 3 months of separation, weepiness subsides and stronger stimuli are necessary to provoke it. The children sit with expressionless eyes, unresponsive, and retarded in motor, cognitive, and language development. They act as if in a daze, not aware of their environment. Spitz studied children who were 6 to 8 months old who had been separated from their mothers for at least 3 months.

Hospitalism occurs in inadequate institutions with a rapid turnover in caretakers who do not become emotionally involved with the children. The syndrome is also associated with listlessness, pallor, emaciation, and absence of sucking habits. It is reversible if the child is returned to the mother within 3 months.

In DSM-III, hospitalism is called reactive attachment disorder of infancy if the onset is before 8 months of age, since attachments are formed by that time if there has been adequate caretaking. The same clinical picture with onset past the eighth month is diagnosed as major depression.

For a further discussion of this entire subject, see Section 35.1 on attachment disorders of infancy.

### REFERENCES

Azarnoff P, Woody P D: Preparation of children for hospitalization in acute care hospitals in the United States. Pediatrics 68: 361, 1981.

Bauman S: Physical aspects of the self: A review of some aspects of body image development in childhood. Psychiatr Clin North Am 4: 455, 1981.

Freud A: The role of bodily illness in the mental life of children. Psychoanal Study Child 7: 69, 1952.

Mayhew J F: Parents in the recovery room. Anesth Analg 62: 124, 1983.

Pfeffer C R: Children's reactions to illness, hospitalization, and surgery. In Comprehensive Textbook of Psychiatry, ed 4, H I Kaplan, B J Sadock, editors, p 1836. Williams & Wilkins, Baltimore, 1985.

Prugh D G, Staub E M, Sands H H, Kirschbaum R M, Lenihan E A: A study of the emotional reactions of children and families to hospitalization and illness. Am J Orthopsychiatry 23: 78, 1953.

Ravenscroft K: Psychiatric consultation to the child with acute physical trauma. Am J Orthopsychiatry 52: 298, 1982.

Rutter M: Stress, coping, and development: Some issues and some questions. J Child Psychol Psychiatry 22: 323, 1981.

Sherman M: Pediatric consultation-liason. Psychiatr Clin North Am 5: 1982.

Tarnow J D, Gutstein S E: Children's preparatory behavior for elective surgery. J Am Acad Child Psychiatry 22: 365, 1983.

# 37.3 FUNCTIONAL ENURESIS

### Introduction

Enuresis is manifested as a repetitive, inappropriate, involuntary passage of urine. Operationally, enuresis can be defined as bed wetting or clothes wetting in persons over the age of 5 who fail to inhibit the reflex to pass urine when the impulse is felt during waking hours, and those who do not rouse from sleep of their own accord when the process is occurring during the sleeping state (see Table I).

### Epidemiology

Boys are twice as likely as girls to be enuretic. Boys cease their wetting later than girls. Further, at all ages boys are more wet than girls. In

TABLE I
DIAGNOSTIC CRITERIA FOR FUNCTIONAL
ENURESIS*

A. Repeated involuntary voiding of urine by day or at night.

B. At least two such events per month for children between the ages of 5 and 6, and at least one event per month for older children.

C. Not due to a physical disorder, such as diabetes or a seizure disorder.

* From American Psychiatric Association: *Diagnostic and Statistical Manual of Mental Disorders*, ed 3. American Psychiatric Association, Washington, DC, 1980. Used with permission.

general by age 5 the prevalence of enuresis in girls is 3 percent and in boys 7 percent. By age 10 the figure is 2 percent for girls and 3 percent for boys. At age 18 the figure is almost nonexistent in girls and about 1 percent in boys. The concordance rate is higher in monozygotic than in dizygotic twins, 75 percent of enuretics have a first degree relative with the disorder.

### Etiology

Over the years, observers have noted a number of psychosocial associations with enuresis. Enuresis seems to be more common in the winter than in the summer. It occurs in cold rooms more than in better-heated quarters. Enuretics may form a disproportiontely large number of delinquents. The time of wetting in an enuretic is a variable that complicates treatment. Sometimes enuretics wet before 1 A.M.; other times they wet after 1 A.M. Similarly, enuretics may or may not wet more than once in a night or in a 24-hour cycle.

Compared with controls, those who persist with enuresis into adolescence show a greater frequency in combinations with one or more of the following disturbances: (1) passive-aggressive or -dependent reactions; (2) past history of sleepwalking; (3) family history of sleepwalking; (4) inferior dentition, as measured by decayed, filled, or missing index; (5) chronic genitourinary tract complaints (urgency, frequency, nocturia); and (6) family history of enuresis.

However, in general, no known psychiatric diagnosis is associated with enuresis. Further, as a group, enuretics in childhood and adulthood function as well in ordinary pursuits as do the general population.

Traditionally, the symptom has been thought to be due to one or a combination of influences from psychological, sociological, and biological sources. Psychosocial stressors include hospitalization between the ages of 2 and 4 especially, entering school and the birth of a sibling.

Maturation delay or developmental abnormalities are alleged to be involved in many instances of reported bladder function abnormality in enuretics. This finding calls forth reinforcement for the critical role of genetic determinants.

Even though urological abnormalities such as infection or anatomical defects are found in enuretics, the correction of the abnormality may not cure bed wetting.

## Clinical Features

There are two general categories of enuretics—the primary, also called persistent, enuretic and the secondary, also called transient or neurotic, enuretic. Four-fifths of all enuretics are primary, which means that a period of sustained dryness has never developed before the age of 5 and that the patient has never known the confident feeling of retiring without the worry of enuresis. The secondary enuresis appears after a person has stopped wetting usually between 5 and 8 years of age. At least two enuretic events per month in children between the ages of 5 and 6 and at least one event per month are needed to make the diagnosis.

During infancy, enuretics have more fever convulsions than do other children. The genitourinary tract disturbances, such as frequency and urgency and nocturia, are present early in life in a number of children who are diagnosed as enuretic.

By age 6 there is evidence that the mother of the enuretic evaluates the child poorly. Further, she gives a history of poor marital adjustment, and may have relatively few social contacts. Many enuretic children avoid camp or overnight visits to friends because they are embarrassed and ashamed about their condition.

Studies of adolescent enuretics verify that the teenager has grown up in a household in which there was conflict and bickering.

Female enuretics have a strong attachment to their fathers. While the male enuretic may often be a mother's boy, the female enuretic may be a father's girl. Unlike her male counterpart, however, the girl is found to be a leader of her peers in social and scholastic achievements and interests. According to Freud, the female enuretic may resort to bed wetting as a means of reducing penis envy problems, which are prominent.

Relapses occur in enuretics who are becoming dry spontaneously, as well as in those who are being treated. The enuretic may have variable periods of dryness, then have episodic or isolated bouts of wetness. If he has suffered wetting, say, 5 nights a week and then is dry for a couple of weeks, a night of wetting can be viewed as harrowing evidence of intractability.

## Course and Prognosis

The time-honored counsel to parents is that the enuresis will cease when the child grows up. With certain exceptions, this appears to be true. Although most children are dry by age 10, any child who is enuretic should be treated early, since, at present, it is impossible to distinguish the child who will continue to suffer enuresis into adolescence and adulthood. Enuretics have a higher risk for mental illness than the general population.

## Differential Diagnosis

Most cases of enuresis are psychogenic but organic causes must be ruled out.

Bed wetting may be the presenting symptom in children with obstructive uropathy. Urinary infections are often associated with enuresis.

The combination of nocturnal and diurnal enuresis, especially in the patient with frequency and urgency, should signal the high possibility of an organic basis for the complaint.

Another possibility to be ruled out is epilepsy. Many enuretics are sleepwalkers, and they attempt to urinate during somnambulism. Therefore, sleepwalking must be differentiated from both enuresis and epilepsy.

In young children, the sudden development of enuresis is a common presentation of diabetes mellitus.

Spinal tumors have a low incidence in childhood, but the loss of sphincter control in a child with progressive weakness, clumsiness, pain, and gait disturbance should alert the doctor to the possibility.

Other diagnoses to be considered when a child presents with enuresis include diabetes insipidus, spina bifida, lumbosacral myelodysplasia, sickle-cell anemia, foreign body, calculus, paraphimosis, vaginitis, mental retardation, and the presence of intestinal parasites.

In adolescents who develop enuresis after a period of dryness, the most likely cause is a transient emotional stress, such as homesickness or examination anxiety. However, all the diseases mentioned in regard to young children must be considered.

In young adulthood and in later life, the appearance of bed wetting must first necessitate a consideration of epilepsy and other central nervous system disorders. If there seems to be scanty reason to pursue such diagnostic efforts, the physician should look for a genitourinary tract disorder.

## Treatment

No treatment method is so successful as to win universal endorsement. The clinician is faced with a disorder whose cause is not understood, and whose differential diagnosis is deceptively complex. The management of a case of enuresis is difficult. In the subsequent discussion, it is assumed that any basic underlying problem of organicity has been located and treated. This leaves the following array of approaches in the armamentarium of the psychiatrist: (1) hypnosis, (2) conditioning devices, (3) psychotherapy, (4) placebos, (5) bladder training, (6) sleep interruption, and (7) drugs. The selection of the appropriate method depends on the individual circumstances as comprehended by the diagnostician. Usually, the clinician elects a combination of methods.

**Placebos.** In the literature marvelous successes are reported by using placebos. Since treatment of any sort depends largely on the ability of the therapist to promote a climate of mutual trust, confidence, and respect, the use of placebo methods runs the great risk of destroying such a relationship should the hoax be discovered.

**Conditioning Devices.** The most effective way of banishing the symptom of bed wetting is to use a conditioning device that awakens the patient by an alarm bell, buzzer or mild electric shock as soon as a drop of urine contacts a wire pad on which he is sleeping. The conditioning process quickly leads to cessation of bed wetting, since the patient learns to awaken and void before the stimulus of the bell or buzzer. Although no substitute symptoms develop after conditioning, adjunctive psychotherapy is often helpful to correct serious family psychopathology when conditioning devices are used.

**Psychotherapy.** Critical to the management of any case of enuresis is psychotherapy. The doctor must be supportive and must be capable of promoting and sustaining feelings of confidence and hope in the patient. Behavior therapy with reward and punishment has been used.

The largest barrier to successful psychotherapy is the wish by the patient (often with the psychological encouragement of his parents or spouse) that he continue the symptom. The therapist, by indicating explicitly and implicitly that he has confidence that the patient can cease his habit, may be the factor causing the patient to wish to correct his problem. The therapist must get the parents, too, to indicate genuinely to the patient that they wish him to stop bed wetting.

**Drugs.** The only drug used is the antidepressant anticholinergic drug imipramine hydrochloride. The usual dosage for 6 to 12 year olds is 25 mg, although some children may require as much as 75 mg. Imipramine is not used in children under the age of 6 and when used the dose should be no higher than 3 mg/kg/day. Cardiac monitoring is mandatory. Deaths have resulted from higher doses. Since imipramine reduces stage IV sleep during which enuresis occurs, that may be one of its mechanisms of action.

A number of side effects can result from the use of tricyclic antidepressants. These side effects can be handled by reduction or elimination of the drug. Among the common side effects are dysuria, retention, and loss of appetite. On especially high doses, erythematous maculopapular rashes may occur.

At the present time, antidepressants are the drugs of choice in the treatment of enuresis. Often, drug therapy is most efficacious when used in conjunction with other management methods.

**Bladder Training.** Enuretics have small functional bladder capacities. In bladder training (which stretches the bladder) the patient is asked to quantify his ability to drink measured volumes of fluid and to withhold urination for as long as possible. The desired result is that the patient becomes able to withhold increasingly larger volumes of fluid over greater periods of time. At night the patient's heightened threshold for retention eliminates the problem of bed wetting. Water is restricted at bedtime.

**Sleep Interruption.** Parents sometimes wake up the child to have him void during the night. Favorable responses may be due to the focused concern by the parents and the child as well as to positive behavioral reinforcement.

**Hypnosis.** Success with hypnosis may be related to the special quality of the treatment dyad in the hynotherapeutic process.

### REFERENCES

Ambrosini P J, Nurnberg H G: Enuresis and incontinence occurring with neuroleptics. Am J Psychiatry *137:* 1278, 1980

Attenburrow A: Nocturnal enuresis: A study. Practioner *228:* 98, 1984.

Berg I, Forsythe I, McGuire R: Response of bedwetting to the enuresis alarm: Influence of psychiatric disturbance and maximum functional bladder capacity. Arch Dis Child *57:* 394, 1982.

Brooksbank D: The conditioning treatment of bedwetting in secondary school aged children. J Adolesc *2:* 239, 1979.

May H J, Colligen R C, Schwartz M S: Child enuresis: Important points in assessment, trends, and treatment. J Postgrad Med *74:* 111, 1983.

Mikkelsen E J, Rapoport J L, Nee L, Gruenau C, Mendelson W, Gillin J C: Childhood enuresis. I. Sleep patterns and psychopathology. Arch Gen Psychiatry *37:* 1139, 1980.

Pierce C M: Enuresis. In *Comprehensive Textbook of Psychiatry,* ed 4, H I Kaplan, B J Sadock, editors, p 1842. Williams & Wilkins, Baltimore, 1985.

Rapoport J L, Mikkelsen E J, Zavadil A, Nee L, Gruenau C, Mendelson W, Gillin J C: Childhood enuresis. II. Trycyclic concentration in plasma and antienuretic effect. Arch Gen Psychiatry *37:* 1152, 1980.

Schmitt B D: Daytime wetting (diurnal enuresis). Pediatr Clin North Am *29*: 9, 1982.

Yeates W K: In *Pediatric Urology,* D I Williams, J H Johnston, editors, p. 317. Butterworth Scientific, London, 1982.

## 37.4     FUNCTIONAL ENCOPRESIS

### Introduction

Encopresis is a symptom marked by fecal soiling past the time that bowel control is physiologically possible and after toilet training should have been accomplished, between the ages of 2 and 3 years.

### Definition

Encopresis is defined as the repeated, involuntary passage of stool into clothing without the presence of any organic cause to explain the symptom. It denotes an uncontrolled defecation of an emotional origin. Some authorities believe that an essential component of encopresis is its inappropriateness—that is, the passage of stool takes place at inappropriate times and places. In this wider definition, a child who leaves stool habitually in such places as a cupboard or the doorstep is considered encopretic.

DSM-III defines primary encopresis as that beginning before the age of 4 and secondary encopresis as that developing between 4 and 8 years of age. In the latter case, the child had achieved bowel control for at least 1 year by the age of 4; but then the symptoms appeared.

### Epidemiology

Encopresis is found much more frequently in boys than in girls. The ratio is about five to one. Even so, in terms of large samples of the general population, the malady is found in relatively few persons. About 1 percent of 5-year-old children are encopretic.

Cases of encopresis are found throughout Western civilization. There seem to be no social or class barriers to encopresis.

About one-fourth of all encopretics have an associated constipation, which results in an overflow encopresis. Most cases of encopresis are not associated with voluminous fecal impaction.

### Etiology

Although by definition encopresis excludes any known organicity, recent studies suggest that an encopretic child may suffer from lifelong inefficient and ineffective gastrointestinal motility. Many psychodynamic and developmental theorists believe that the mother-child interaction is crucial. Frequently, the mother is thought to be too coercive or primitive or both in her toilet-training efforts. Inadequate, inconsistent or coercive toilet training may have occurred. Stressors such as the birth of a sibling or entering school may precipitate encopresis.

Neurodevelopmental problems include easy distractibility, short attention span, low frustration tolerance, hyperactivity, and poor motor coordination. The child seems slow in acquiring bowel control. Such a situation may initiate grievances between the mother and the child, and these grievances may later compound the intractability of the symptom.

### Clinical Features

Encopresis is characterized by the passage of stool at inappropriate times and places, seemingly on an involuntary basis but it may be voluntary. Children may be both enuretic and encopretic. The stool-passage accidents usually form no definite pattern as to their frequency, their location, their volume, or their association with life events (see Table I).

Features of abdominal pain, constipation, and fecal impaction demand medical assessment. In those patients without constipation, there is a likelihood of accompanying emotional disturbance.

Encopretic episodes are probably never exclusively or even predominantly nocturnal. However, nearly half of those encopretics who are also enuretic have both nocturnal and diurnal enuresis. The patient's history reveals that the usual times for encopretic episodes are in the late afternoon or early evening. Yet the rarer situation of encopretic accidents at school is often the motivation for a parent to seek medical help.

### Course and Prognosis

The child who fails to attain bowel control may soon suffer from hostile behavior by one or

TABLE I
DIAGNOSTIC CRITERIA FOR FUNCTIONAL ENCOPRESIS*

A. Repeated voluntary or involuntary passage of feces of normal or near-normal consistency into places not appropriate for that purpose in the individual's own sociocultural setting.

B. At least one such event a month after the age of 4.

C. Not due to a physical disorder, such as aganglionic megacolon.

* From American Psychiatric Association: *Diagnostic and Statistical Manual of Mental Disorders,* ed 3. American Psychiatric Association, Washington, DC, 1980. Used with permission.

more family members. As the child associates with others outside the home, there is ridicule by peers and alienation from teachers.

Many encopretics seem to lack the sensory cues as to when they need to defecate. Psychologically, the patient remains blunted to the effect the disorder has on other people. Nevertheless, the child comes to feel unwanted and to have a low self-concept. Dynamically, the mother is frequently depressed, often dissatisfied with her marriage and maternal roles, compulsive, and emotionally unavailable. In such a household, the father is found to be critical, emotionally distant, and often absent physically or psychologically or both.

A rash of mechanical problems may result in organic defects in the lower gastrointestinal tract as the condition continues. The sufferer may require treatment for fissures, rectal prolapse, rectal excoriations, or impaction.

Neverthless, the child who is encopretic can be obedient and tractable and is frequently well liked by adults. This attitude is important, since the disorder may last for years. It usually disappears by adolescence. The natural history of the disorder seems to be self-limited.

### Differential Diagnosis

A chief differential problem is to be certain that the child is not suffering from Hirschsprung's disease (true aganglionic megacolon). The encopretic may have an overflow of feces secondary to impaction. Anal fissures may sometimes be present.

The patients the psychiatrist sees may be encopretics who, at the same time, have infantile autism, childhood schizophrenia, or mental retardation. Also, the encopretic may have an associated enuresis. That occurs in 25 percent of cases.

### Treatment

All who treat encopresis emphasize the importance of banishing punitive methods and the need to reassure the parents that the child's odious action is not willful. All agree that the family climate must be made warmer for the encopretic.

No one claims constant success with encopresis. It seems that the best results for symptom elimination involve the use of reinforcers that reward the child for continence after the therapist has taken pains to include the family and the child in the treatment plan. With symptom reduction or elimination, the therapist can proceed with any necessary psychotherapy. Whether the patient and the parents require psychotherapy or only help in better and more tolerant training methods, it seems important for all concerned to be aided in being less punitive and more relaxed about the symptom. Stool softeners may be useful if constipation becomes a problem and leakage occurs around an impaction.

### REFERENCES

Arnold L E: In *Psychiatry: Essentials of Clinical Practice*, I Gregory, D J Smeltzer, editors, p 259. Little, Brown, Boston, 1977.
Bemporad J R, Pfeifer C, Gibbs L, Cortner R, Bloom W: Characteristics of encopretic patients and their families. J Am Acad Child Psychiatry *10:* 272, 1971.
Cavanaugh R M Jr: Encopresis in children and adolescents. Am Fam Physician *27:* 107, 1983.
De Ajuriaguerra J: *Handbook of Child Psychiatry and Psychology.* Translated and edited by R P Lorion. Masson Publishing, New York, 1980.
Levine , D, Bakow H: Children with encopresis: A study of treatment outcome. Pediatrics *58:* 845, 1976.
Levine M D, Mazonson P, Bakow H: Behavioral symptom substitution in children cured of encopresis. Am J Dis Child. *134:* 663, 1980.
Pierce C M: Encopresis. In *Comprehensive Textbook of Psychiatry,* ed 4, H I Kaplan, B J Sadock, editors, p. 1847. Williams & Wilkins, Baltimore, 1985.
Roy C C, Silverman A, Cozzeto F J: *Pediatric Clinical Gastroenterology,* ed 2. C. V. Mosby, St. Louis, 1975.
Schoengold M: The relationship between father absence and encopresis. Child Welfare *56:* 386, 1977.

## 37.5 OTHER DEVELOPMENTAL DISORDERS: NAIL BITING AND THUMB SUCKING

### Introduction

Nail biting, thumb sucking, and finger sucking are common, everyday symptoms. Thumb sucking and finger sucking may do considerable damage to dentition. These conditions are not included in DSM-III.

### Epidemiology

Nail biting may begin as early as 1 year of age. From this point on, it shows a steadily increased incidence until about age 12. Even so, at age 17 to 18 in a select population of military recruits, as many as one of four persisted in the habit. By age 37, one of 12 persons continues to bite his nails.

Finger sucking is still present in about 31 per cent of children around 12 years old. The habit is more common in girls than in boys. There seems to be some coincidence of finger sucking and nail biting.

## Etiology

In psychoanalytic theory, nail biting is thought to be caused by intense or competitive impulses toward a parent. If such impulses were actualized, the child would destroy his source of dependency gratification. To resolve the conflict, the child bites his nails, thus denying his hostility, injuring himself, and demonstrating his punishment. At the same time, he is able to express aggression but spare the object of his aggression.

Finger sucking and thumb sucking are thought to be the result of regression to oral satisfactions when the person is placed under the duress of tension or fatigue.

Learning theorists have satisfied themselves that the symptoms are the result of simple learned habits. Most investigators agree that no particular personality features characterize a person who is troubled with nail biting or finger sucking.

There is a spirited debate as to the relationship of inadequate or unsatisfactory breast-feeding and later development of finger sucking. However, the general surroundings and social conditions that are present when an infant goes to sleep may exert an influence. Rocking, lullabies, or story telling by a loving adult seem to be positive factors.

Significantly more finger sucking is prevalent in girls and in white children than in boys and black children.

## Pathology

Nail biting, thumb sucking, and finger sucking are considered socially offensive. In a few cases, nail biting or finger sucking is so severe as to cause physical discomfort or even finger necrosis. Thumb sucking after age 3½ should elicit concern relative to the possibility of damage to dentition. Similarly, a child past age 7 who continues to finger suck may adversely affect his teeth, particularly in the anterior region.

In cases so severe that the child has physical discomfort, meets frequent social disapproval, or damages his bite, there may be psychological damage to the child's image of himself.

## Clinical Features

Nail biting is an active process. Finger sucking and thumb sucking are more passive processes.

Although nail biting may be an oral-aggressive, tension-reducing impulse that is most likely to occur when the patient is bored or anxious, the habit is often present in persons in whom there is no obvious emotional disturbance.

Finger sucking and thumb sucking are present in nearly all babies in the first year of life. Such sucking should cause no concern. By age 2 to 5, children may resort to finger sucking when under emotional stress. The persistence of the habit may be associated with general immaturity, characterized by such habits as baby talk and bed wetting.

## Treatment

With young children who do not bite their nails severely, treatment techniques relying on suggestibility and self-reliance have been successful. The child recognizes that the family members are interested in him, and that they have confidence he can master a large problem. The physician should help the family reduce tension on the child by being more tolerant and consistent. The child may participate in the treatment by means of placebo tasks, such as taking the responsibility of soaking his nails daily in olive oil.

In the case of adults or children who have obvious emotional illness, the therapist must attend to the urgent and pressing life stresses.

Behavior therapy is widely used to treat the symptoms of finger sucking and nail biting. Positive rewards for eliminating the habit have been successful with children and adults.

When sucking becomes a problem in the interaction between the environment and the patient, psychotherapy is indicated. Besides securing task-oriented help by the patient, the physician directs major efforts toward the patient's general emotional problems. In many instances, unexpected help comes from the patient's regard for his peer status.

## REFERENCES

Cerny R: Thumb and finger sucking. Aust Dent J 26: 167, 1981.
De La Cruz M, Geboy M: Elimination of thumbsucking through contingency management of behavior. J Dent Child 50: 39, 1983.
Modéer T, Odenrick L, Lindner A: Sucking habits and their relation to posterior cross-bite in 4-year-old children. Scand J Dent Res 90: 323, 1983.
Norton L A: Nail disorders. J Am Acad Dermatol 2: 451, 1980.
Ottenbacher K, Ottenbacher M: Symptom substitution: A case study. Am J Psychoanal 41: 173, 1981.
Pierce C M: Other developmental disorders. In Comprehensive Textbook of Psychiatry, ed 4, H I Kaplan, B J Sadock, editors, p 1849. Williams & Wilkins, Baltimore, 1985.
Slaughter W G, Cordis C: Covert maternal deprivation and pathological sucking behavior. Am J Psychiatry 134: 1152, 1977.

# 37.6   AFFECTIVE DISORDERS

## Introduction

In contrast to a decade ago, the evidence available to support the validity of the diagnosis of depressive disorders in children and adolescents is substantial, if not definitive. This is not only true for major depressive disorders, but also for dysthymia. Mania and hypomania are also found in this age group, although they are much more frequent among adolescents than among prepubertal children, who rarely exhibit bipolar clinical pictures.

## Major Depression

The DSM-III diagnosis of major depressive disorder is made when a child presents sufficient evidence of a persistent depressive mood and/or almost complete inability to either derive pleasure from the usual activities in his life (pervasive anhedonia) and/or almost total loss of interest in them. In addition, the child should have shown persistent evidence of at least four symptoms out of the eight clusters (described below) in the depressive syndrome during the duration of the current episode of illness. The episode should not be diagnosed if, when the affective syndrome has remitted, the clinical picture is dominated by either bizarre behavior, or preoccupation with a delusion or hallucination thematically inconsistent with depressive mood; if the depressive episode is superimposed on a preexisting nonaffective nonorganic psychotic disorder; if it is due to any organic cause; if it follows the death of a loved one; or if it has lasted less than 14 days.

The symptom clusters in the depressive syndrome are: appetite and/or weight changes corrected for normal growth; sleep difficulty or sleeping too much; psychomotor agitation or retardation; loss of interest or pleasure in usual activities, including sexual drive in adolescents; fatigue, tiredness; thoughts of self-reproach, feelings of guilt which are excessive and/or inappropriate, low self-esteem; difficulty concentrating and/or slowed down thinking; and morbid preoccupation with death, suicidal ideation, and/or behavior.

## Mania and Hypomania

The diagnostic criteria for mania in children are no different than in adults. DSM-III requires that at least one distinct period characterized by relatively persistent elevated, elated, expansive, or irritable mood be present. In addition, a minimum of three symtpoms in the manic syndrome should also be present (four if the mood is only irritable); once the affective symptomatology remits there should be neither bizarre behavior, nor a prominent preoccupation with a psychotic symptom the content of which was incongruous with manic mood; and the episode should not be due to any organic cause nor should it follow a preexisting nonorganic, nonaffective psychotic disorder.

## Dysthymia and Minor Depression

In a similar way as with mania/hypomania, some youngsters with depressive symptomatology do not quite meet criteria for major depression. If the episode has persisted for at least 12 months in either a chronic or intermittent fashion (symptom-free intervals are no more than a few months at a time, so that the child has been suffering from these symptoms all or most of the time), such episode is highly likely to fit criteria for DSM-III's dysthymic disorder. For this diagnosis to be made, there should be evidence that the child has presented persistent depressed mood, or marked loss of interest or pleasure in almost all usual activities and pastimes, no psychotic symptoms whatsoever, and other signs such as functional impairment at home, in school or with peers, pessimism or brooding, crying or tearfulness, irritability/anger, social withdrawal, and low self-esteem or feelings of inadequacy. It is probably a mistake to deemphasize psychomotor agitation in children as it is relatively frequent.

It is not infrequent to find that a youngster presents a clinical picture which does not fit criteria for major depression but could be diagnosed as dysthymia, except that the duration of the episode is under 1 year. Sometimes there are two or three episodes, each lasting anywhere between 2 weeks to 11 months, but the symptom-free interval is simply too long (over 2 or 3 months) for the dysthymic diagnosis to be applicable on strict grounds. DSM-III classifies these and other clinical presentations under the overall rubric of atypical depression. When such episodes follow a significant stressful life event by less than 3 months the diagnoses of adjustment disorder with depressive mood or uncomplicated bereavement should be made. As the expressivity of the genetic predisposition to affective disorders is highly likely to be negatively correlated with age, minor affective presentations in children are likely to have high predictive value for future more severe affective disorder episodes.

## Cyclothymia

In the same way that in bipolar illness episodes of major depression and mania or hypomania occur in the same patient either separately, alternating, intermixed or simultaneously, some adolescent patients present full hypomanic and dysthymic symptomatic pictures in any of the above temporal combinations. These patients receive a diagnosis of cyclothymia if the duration of the disorder exceeds 24 months, if there have been no psychotic symptoms whatsoever, and if there have been at least several ill periods, even with the symptom-free intervals lasting for months. It is likely that adolescents with a cyclothymic picture lasting for at least a year should also receive the cyclothymia diagnosis. It is also likely that a majority of cyclothymic adolescents will go on to develop a full fledged bipolar illness on follow-up.

## Psychotic Affective and Schizoaffective Disorders

Children and adolescents with major depressive disorder, which is not superimposed on a preexisting, nonaffective, nonorganic psychotic disorder, will not infrequently be found to suffer from hallucinations and delusions. In the wide majority of cases these psychotic symptoms are thematically consistent with depressive mood, occur within the depressive episode and not outside it (usually during the times the depression is at its worst), and do not include types of hallucinations which are somewhat specific to schizophrenia like conversing voices or a commenting voice. These cases are referred to as psychotic depressions. Depressive hallucinations usually consist of a single voice speaking to the subject from outside his head, with derogatory or suicidal content when the youngster is most depressed. Depressive delusions are centered on themes of guilt, physical disease, death, nihilism, deserved punishment, personal inadequacy, or sometimes persecution if related by the patient to his own imagined or exaggerated fault. They are very rare in prepuberty, probably because of cognitive immaturity, but present in about half of the psychotically depressed adolescents. Depressive hallucinations are almost the sole psychotic depressive symptom presented by prepubertal children, and are also quite frequent in adolescents with psychotic depression.

A parallel description can be made for psychotic mania. It is characterized by delusions and hallucinations thematically consistent with manic mood (i.e., involving grandiose evaluation of the patient's own power, worth, knowledge, family or relationships, or even persecutory delusions if related to the youngster's grandiosity), or flight of ideas with gross impairment of reality testing, which occur at the same time as frank mania, and usually during the worst periods. Conversing and commenting hallucinations are not included.

In a subgroup of youngsters with major depression or mania plus psychotic symptoms, the latter do not strictly conform to the pattern described and cannot be characterized as clearly depressive. For example, when any of the following are present: conversing or commenting voices, delusions of persecution not related to guilt or grandiosity, of thought insertion, broadcasting or withdrawal, of being controlled, or catatonia. For another example, psychotic symptoms are present when mood disorders are no longer manifest, especially if they are not mood congruous. Such cases are usually diagnosed as schizoaffective disorder. Adolescents, and probably also children, who fit criteria for schizoaffective disorder do exist but little is known at present about their natural course, family history, psychobiology, and treatment.

Another subtype of major depression which merits special attention is endogenous or melancholic. There is little question that endogenous subtypes are frequent presentations of major depression during childhood and adolescence.

## Epidemiology

The prevalence rate among 10-year-olds for the combined DSM-III diagnoses of major depression and dysthymic disorder, using a detailed semistructured interview with the child, has been found to be 1.7 percent. No similar study exists in adolescents, but there are good reasons to expect it will be higher. In surveys which utilized modern assessment techniques and diagnostic criteria, a conservative consensual figure for affective disorders of all types on general child psychiatric services in a general hospital would be 10 percent of intakes: approximately 5 percent of children before puberty and 15 percent of adolescents. It should be obvious that affective disorders constitute a relatively frequent clinical set of psychiatric diagnoses in youngsters and a sizeable public mental health problem to be considered in policy making.

## Etiology

Affective disorders in children, adolescents, and adult patients tend to cluster in the same families. The more densely and more deeply (second degree relatives) a family is loaded with affective disorders, the higher the proportion of offspring likely to be affected and the younger their age of onset is likely to be. The current consensus is that having one depressed parent probably doubles the risk to the offspring of developing an affective episode before age 18 years, over the risk in children from two non-depressed parents. In addition, at least four times as many children from two depressive parents as those from normal parents are likely to present an affective disorder during the same time period. The studies which have investigated the effects of dual parental matings in pedigrees of adult depressive probands have found results very consistent with those in children. It should be noted that the timing of such parental depressive episodes is irrelevant to the analyses. Even if the parent had had a major depressive episode before the children were conceived, the results of these analyses would not change. There is some evidence to indicate that the number of recurrences of parental depression do increase the likelihood of the children being affected, but this may be related, at least in part, to affective loading of that parent's own side of the family. Similarly, of the most severe major depressive disorders in children, the endogenous subtype has shown evidence of denser and deeper familial aggregation for major depression than the nonendogenous major depressive proband group.

Among prepubertal children with major depression, in contrast to the unremarkable characteristics of familial structure, substantial deficits in the child's relationship with the parent, with peers, and with siblings have been demonstrated. Sustained recovery from the depressive episode was followed by a general improvement in all these areas of psychosocial functioning. The improvement was partial in the areas which were more severely affected before the affective episode was treated and complete in those where the impairment was originally less profound. In addition, duration of the depressive episode before treatment was positively correlated with the depth of some of the psychosocial deficits. This pattern, instead of supporting a causal role for environmental influences in affective disorders, suggests that psychosocial impairments are likely to be secondary to the depressive episode itself, and that they are compounded by the long duration in this age group of most dysthymic or depressive episodes, during which poorly or unaccomplished developmental tasks progressively accumulate. There is little doubt, but also little evidence, that the level of the child's psychosocial function before the onset of the depression must be related to environmental familial influences.

It is likely that among preschoolers, in whom depressive-like clinical presentations are beginning to be described, the role of environmental influences will receive more experimental support.

It has been found in some studies that male children whose fathers died before the children were 13 years of age are more predisposed to depression than controls.

## Psychobiology

As in adult affective disorders, biological abnormalities have been found in children and adolescents with major affective illness.

### Neuroendocrine Markers

Prepubertal children in an episode of major depression have been shown to secrete significantly more growth hormone during sleep than normal children and than those with nondepressed emotional disorders. They also secrete significantly less growth hormone in response to insulin-induced hypoglycemia than the latter group. Both abnormalities have been found to remain abnormal and basically unchanged after at least 4 months of full, sustained clinical response, the last month in a drug-free state. Similar work in adolescents is ongoing.

In contrast, although occasional cases of cortisol hypersecretion are found among prepubertal children in a major depressive episode, when compared to themselves after recovery, the majority of these children have normal cortisol secretion during and after the depressive episode.

Other putative neuroendocrine markers are being studied at the present time. These include growth hormone responses to desmethylimipramine and clonidine, thyrotropin response to thyrotropin-releasing hormone, and cortisol response to $d$-amphetamine.

Investigators have reported recently on an inherited biochemical trait which may be present in some children born of parents who suffer from bipolar or unipolar depression. There may be a receptor abnormality—specifically a supersensitivity—to the neurotransmitter acetylcholine in those children who would then be at risk for developing a major affective disorder later in life.

The test consists of demonstrating that skin cells, especially fibroblasts grown in vitro, show an increased density of muscarine cholinergic receptors which are then shown to be sensitive to acetylcholine.

The test needs to be validated by further studies but is important because 25 percent of children with a manic depressive parent develop either a bipolar or unipolar disorder later in life. Early detection would target this subgroup and enable the clinician to more easily differentiate depression from substance abuse and antisocial behavior which often mask or are confused with depression. In addition, clinicians are reluctant to use medications such as antidepressants in children or adolescents unless there is a clear indication for their use, and this test would provide such an indication.

The reader is referred to Chapter 13 on affective disorders for further information on neuroendocrine and genetic markers in depression.

## Polysomnography

In spite of frequent subjective sleep complaints, prepubertal children do not show polysomnographic abnormalities during a major depressive episode.

In adolescents, rapid eye movement (REM) latency is shortened during major depressive episodes, like in adults. It is not known at present if this abnormality persists in the drug-free recovered state.

## Clinical Description

The onset of major depressive disorder in children tends to be insidious and retrospectively difficult to pinpoint.

Patients who do not develop their first depressive episode until adolescence are more likely than those with prepubertal onset of affective illness to present episodes with more clearly delineated or acute onset. Nevertheless, a dysthymic course of illness can also occur in adolescent onset affective illness. Typically, mania, hypomania, and cyclothymia begin in or after puberty, although the onset of affective illness (depressive or dysthymic) is likely to have occurred in prepuberty in a substantial proportion of these youngsters.

Adolescent onset of affective disorder may be very difficult to diagnose when the patient is first seen, if there have been attempts at self-medication with either illicit drugs or alcohol. In a recent study, 17 percent of the affective youngsters first presented to medical attention as substance abuse disorders. Only after detoxification can the patient's psychiatric symptoms be properly assessed and the correct affective diagnosis can be made.

A child's negative reply to a question about feeling sad is unlikely to be tantamount to absence of depressed mood. Children may refer to dysphoria with a variety of labels which often may not include sadness. Thus, it is advisable to inquire about feeling sad, empty, low, down, blue, very unhappy, like crying, or having a bad feeling inside which is with him most of the time and he "cannot get rid of." Depressed children

will usually identify one or more of these terms as the persistent dysphoric feeling they have had no name for. The duration and periodicity of depressive mood throughout the day and week should be carefully assessed in order to differentiate relatively universal, short-lived, sometimes frequent periods of sadness, usually following a frustrating event, from true, persistent depressive mood. The younger the child, the more imprecise time estimates are likely to be.

It is clinically sound to use a minimum duration of 3 consecutive hours of reported dysphoria at least three times a week. This cut-off usefully separates true depressive mood from sad affect.

Contrary to common wisdom, children are in fact reliable reporters about their own behavior, emotions, relationships, and difficulties in psychosocial functions. What neither children nor adolescents can even attempt to do is to talk freely, without direction, almost like free-associating, about their troubles, difficulties, and inner feelings. But in a semistructured interview, where the clinician asks direct questions, in a professional yet sensitive manner, youngsters can and do provide the information needed for a psychiatric diagnosis.

### Suicide

Suicide and more commonly suicidal ideas occur frequently in children and adolescents. The third leading cause of death in adolescence is suicide. The suicide rate is higher among male children and in children whose families have recently moved or been dislocated. In one major study of 100 children referred for psychiatric hospitalization, one-third had threatened or attempted suicide.

## Associated Features

Children and adolescents with major depressive or dysthymic disorders rarely present a pure clinical picture. The two main symptom complexes associated with affective illness in this age group are neurotic symptoms or disorders, especially separation anxiety, and conduct disorder.

Childhood onset affective illness, compared with its adult onset counterpart, tends to follow a generally more chronic course, appears in families with higher pedigree density for affective illness and alcoholism, and is more likely to develop secondary complications (conduct disorder, alcoholism, substance abuse, and antisocial personality) in the short and the long run. Such very early onset disorders may represent the most severe forms of affective illness.

Functional impairment associated with depressive disorders in childhood extends to practically all areas of the child's psychosocial world: school performance and behavior, peer relationships, and family relations. Only highly intelligent and scholastically oriented children with no more than moderate depression can compensate their difficulty in learning by substantially increasing time and effort. Otherwise school performance is invariably affected by a combination of concentration difficulty, slowed down thinking, lack of interest and motivation, tiredness, sleepiness, depressive ruminations and preoccupations. Thus, it is not surprising that academic failure is one of the presenting complaints of children with major depression. A misdiagnosis of learning disorder in a depressed child is not an uncommon occurrence. It usually indicates that no symptom-oriented interview with the child was carried out. Learning problems secondary to depression, even when longstanding, always correct themselves quickly after recovery from the affective episode.

In a recent study, children's relationships with their parents, peers, and siblings were found to be markedly abnormal during a major depressive episode. In contrast, the rate of marital breakups or the satisfactoriness of marital relationships among the parents of depressed children was no different from those of control families. Upon sustained recovery from the depressive episode, the child's relationships slowly improve, while no changes could be detected in the parental marital relationship. As a general rule, considerable impairment in social skills is still evident after 4 months of complete recovery from major depression in prepubertal children, and this is probably related to the duration of the prior episode(s) of depression/dysthymia.

### Differential Diagnosis

Psychotic forms of depression and mania and schizoaffective disorders should be differentiated from schizophrenia. The diagnoses of mania and hypomania are very rare in prepuberty. This may be due to the fact that prepubertal children only very rarely will experience elation.

Anxiety symptoms and conduct-disordered behavioral patterns not infrequently coexist with depression and can pose problems in differentiating these cases from nondepressed emotional and conduct disorders. The differentiation of depression or mania from different forms of delirious drug intoxication and substance abuse most frequently will have to await inpatient detoxification for affective assessment to be possible.

More clinically relevant is the differentiation between agitated depression and attention deficit disorder with hyperactivity. Prepubertal children do not present classical forms of agitated depression with handwringing and pacing. Instead, inability to sit still and frequent temper tantrums are the most common symptoms of agitation when the latter is present. On the basis of these signs alone, it is not possible to differentiate agitation from hyperactivity. In dysthymic or depressive disorders, it is frequently impossible to determine if the hyperactivity preceded and coexists with the affective disorder or if, simply, agitation was noted by the parents before the other symptoms of mood disorder. Sometimes the correct answer only becomes apparent after successful tricyclic antidepressant treatment is discontinued. If the child has no difficulty concentrating and is not hyperactive while recovered from the depressive episode in a drug-free state, it is highly likely he or she had never suffered from attention deficit disorder with hyperactivity.

### Prognosis

As indicated earlier, affective disorders with childhood or adolescent onset are likely to be recurrent and, if not properly treated, will produce considerable short- and long-term difficulties and complications: poor academic achievement, arrest in psychosocial developmental patterns, complicating negative reinforcement, suicide, drug and alcohol abuse as a means of self-treatment, and development of conduct disorder. Long-term follow-up studies have not been long enough for the subjects to reach adulthood. The follow-up studies so far do, on the whole, indicate continued liability for affective disorder as predicted.

### Treatment

The treatment methods of depressive episodes in children and adolescents include the following:

#### *Hospitalization*

Immediate protection is made against the patient's own self-destructive impulses or behaviors. If the patient is suicidal, hospitalization is indicated.

#### *Pharmacotherapy*

There is substantial evidence that the antidepressant response of prepubertal children with major depressive disorder treated with imipramine is dependent on maintenance plasma levels.

The imipramine dose can be as high as 6 mg/kg/day, preferably administered in three roughly equal daily doses. Dosage can be increased relatively quickly, beginning at 1.5 mg/kg/day and going up to 3, 4, 5 and 6 mg/kg/day every third or fourth day. Before treatment begins, and also immediately before any dose increase, the following measures are recommended: lying and standing blood pressure, ECG, and systematic inquiry for side effects. If at any point PR intervals reach 0.22 second, or QRS is prolonged over 130 percent of baseline, or pulse rate goes up to 130/minute or blood pressure reaches 140/90 mm Hg, or other side effects become intolerable, the dose is not increased any longer or is adjusted slightly downward. Drowsiness is an exception. During titration upward, children frequently feel sleepy when the dose is raised, but if the dose is not changed this symptom will fade away until the next dose increase to repeat the pattern again. Systematic assessment of clinical response is done 5 weeks after the beginning of treatment. The imipramine-sensitive symptoms are the symptom criteria for major depression and depressive hallucinations.

### Psychotherapy

Child psychotherapy as generally practiced does not appear to be very effective in treating the depressive symptomatology, or any other aspect of the child's psychopathology as long as the youngster is severely depressed.

Based on work with ambulatory adult depressives and on clinical experience with child affective patients, it appears sensible to defer a decision for psychotherapeutic intervention until after the youngster has recovered from major depressive disorder. The best indication for individual or group treatment is the lack of spontaneous gradual improvement in relationships after the affective picture remitted. Other times familial crises are precipitated by the child's recovery indicating that the patient's depression had taken a dysfunctional significance to several family members. The indication for family therapy in such cases is obvious.

### Treatment Maintenance

It is advisable to continue successful antidepressant treatment at the same dose for 3 to 4 months after initial recovery in prepubertal depressives. Following this guideline only about one of every five cases will present a relapse in the 30 days after the last pill. There are two exceptions to this: (1) When during psychopharmacological maintenance a patient receives also a course of any modality of psychotherapy, it is probably well to continue the medication until the end of the psychotherapeutic trial as there is some suggestion from adult work that a depressive relapse could erase psychotherapeutic gains during the course of treatment; and (2) When a child has been found to be prone to relapses in the past, it is advisable to treat him for longer time periods. Discontinuation of tricyclic antidepressants in children should be done on a progressive schedule over a 10-day period in order to avoid a withdrawal syndrome.

### Long-term Follow-up

The long-term aim should be to keep the patient free of any affective periods. The safest way to come closest to this ideal goal for non-bipolar youngsters is to educate them and their families to recognize future episodes and report them immediately to their treating physician. Then, treatment can proceed without delay.

### REFERENCES

Akiskal H S: The bipolar spectrum: New concepts in classification and diagnosis. In: *Psychiatry '83: The American Psychiatric Association Annual Review*, Vol II, L Grinspoon, editor, pp 271–292. American Psychiatric Association, Washington, DC, 1983.

Kovacs M, Feinberg T L, Crouse M A, Paulaskas S, Finkelstein R: Recovery in childhood depressive disorders: A longitudinal prospective study. Arch Gen Psychiatry (in press).

Nurnberger J I, Jimerson D C, Bunney W E Jr: A risk factor strategy for investigating affective illness. Intelligence Rep Psych Disorders 3: 4, 1984.

Poznanski E O: The clinical characteristics of childhood depression. In: *Psychiatry '82: The American Psychiatric Association Annual Review*, Vol I, L Grinspoon, editor, pp 296–307. American Psychiatric Association, Washington, DC, 1982.

Puig-Antich J: Affective disorders in childhood: A review and perspective. Psychiatr Clin North Am 3: 403, 1980.

Puig-Antich J: Major depression and conduct disorder in prepuberty. J Am Acad Child Psychiatry 21: 118, 1982.

Puig-Antich J: Affective disorders. In *Comprehensive Textbook of Psychiatry*, ed 4, H I Kaplan, B J Sadock, editors, p 1850. Williams & Wilkins, Baltimore, 1985.

Puig-Antich J, Weston B: The diagnosis and treatment of depression in children. Ann Intern Med 34: 231, 1983.

# 38

# Conditions Not Attributable to a Mental Disorder

## 38.1 MALINGERING

### Introduction

Malingering is a long-recognized behavior, traditionally thought of in association with the military, criminals, and, in recent history, fraudulent attempts to obtain unwarranted compensation. But it may also be a relatively benign manipulation and occur in a great variety of settings and situations.

Malingering is classified in DSM-III as a condition not attributable to a mental disorder, that is, a focus of attention or treatment. The essential feature is the voluntary production and presentation of false or grossly exaggerated physical or psychological symptoms.

### Characteristics

#### Incidence

Malingering occurs most frequently in settings where there is a preponderance of men—for example, in the military, prisons, and industry. It seems logical that the incidence would, therefore, be proportionately greater in men than in women. However, there is no evidence that there is any real sexual difference in incidence, if the sexual ratios of employees is considered. Similar factors pertain to age, resulting in low incidence in those outside the window of employment age, roughly 16 to 65 years of age.

On the other hand, personality predisposition is of great importance. Although malingering is occasionally adaptive coping behavior and socially acceptable, as for prisoners of war, it is most commonly a manifestation of an unmotivated or misfit personality, such as an antisocial, immature, or substance-abusing person. Most malingerers have a history of drifting from town to town and from job to job and often of alcoholism, drug abuse, criminal records, and military problems. Malingering is seldom detected in persons with a history of adequacy, competency, and success.

### Goals

Motives or goals generally fall into one of four categories: to avoid difficult or dangerous situations, responsibilities, or punishment; to receive compensation, free hospital room and board, a source of drugs, or haven from the police; to prevent the loss of dependent relationships or of a possible job that demands good health; and to retaliate when the victim feels guilt or suffers a financial loss, legal penalty, or job loss. The presence of a clearly definable goal is the main factor that differentiates malingering from a factitious illness.

### Diagnosis

The artifice disorder may follow a planned or accidental event, usually resulting in a complaint, request, or claim. Malingerers seeking compensation often choose an event that commonly results in disability. Timing is important. Many express vague, ill-defined symptoms that are mostly subjective—for example, headache; pains of the neck, lower back, chest, or abdomen; dizziness; vertigo; amnesia; anxiety and depression; and symptoms often having a family history, in all likelihood not organically based but incredibly difficult to refute. Malingerers may complain bitterly, describing how much the symptoms impair normal function, and how much they are disliked. They may use the very best doctor who is most trusted (and perhaps most easily fooled), and promptly and willingly pay all bills, even if excessive, to impress him with their integrity. To seem credible, they must invariably give the same report of symptoms, but tell the physician as little as possible. But often they complain of misery without objective signs or other symptoms congruent with recognized diseases or syndromes; if symptoms are described, they come and go. Malingerers are often preoccupied with cash, rather than cure, and have a knowledge of the law and precedents relative to their claims.

Malingering should be suspected if the patient

states that he is involved in a medicolegal case; if there are no or bizarre objective manifestations of disease; if the patient does not follow a treatment program; or if an antisocial personality disorder is present or antisocial behavior is shown. In malingering, the action is conscious, voluntary, and goal directed. There is always secondary gain. Self-esteem is usually intact.

To differentiate malingering from neurosis, several criteria can be used:

1. Past history of irresponsibility, dishonesty, or inadequacy.

2. Unwilling to accept alternate employment for which capable.

3. Reluctant to have psychiatric hospitalizations, surgery or other treatment.

4. Symptoms are present only during observation known to patient.

5. Resists reexamination, especially by groups of doctors.

6. Poor compliance with therapy and symptoms not influenced by suggestion.

7. Typical psychological testing.

8. Lack of preoccupation with the event in dreams, thoughts, or speech.

9. Preserved capacity for play.

Psychological testing may reveal suspiciously bizarre responses and inconsistencies throughout.

Often, the physician experiences the malingerer as being hostile or unfriendly or even suspicious and may, in turn, feel hostile, especially if the patient is uncooperative with the evaluation and noncompliant with attempted treatment. Thus, the physician's emotional reaction to such behavior may be a diagnostic clue.

### Management

The element of deception often angers the examining clinician. Often, a confrontation occurs, with two consequences: (1) The doctor-patient relationship is disrupted, and no further positive intervention is possible; and (2) the patient is even more on guard, and proof of deception may become virtually impossible. If the patient is accepted and not discredited, subsequent observation, while he is hospitalized or an outpatient, may reveal the versatile nature of the symptoms, which are consistently present only when the patient knows he is being observed. Preserving the doctor-patient relationship is often essential to the diagnosis and long-term management of the patient. Careful evaluation usually reveals the relevant issue without the need for a confrontation. It is usually best to use an intensive treatment approach, as though the symptoms were real. The symptoms can then be given up in response to treatment, without the patient's losing face.

A careful, open-minded clinical interview may often be as revealing as the most intricate examination and observation. Nonetheless, a patient suspected of malingering should be thoroughly and objectively evaluated while the physician refrains from demonstrating his suspicion or disapproval. Objective tests—such as audiometry, brain stem audiometry, auditory and visually evoked potentials, galvanic skin response, electromyography, and nerve conduction studies—may be helpful in sorting out auditory, labyrinthine, ophthalmological, neurological, and other problems.

Careful exploration of the patient's motivation may lead to an understanding of the situation leading to the behavior. Attention may be turned to these more relevant issues, while simply ignoring or minimizing the simulation, thus removing or altering the motive and allowing the patient to be successfully treated by standard means for his "illness."

### REFERENCES

Aduan R P, Fauci A S, Dale D C, et al: Factitious fever and self-induced infection: A report of 32 cases and review of the literature. Ann Intern Med *90*: 230, 1979.

Albert S, Fox H M, Kahn M W: Faking psychosis on the Rorschach: Can expert judges detect malingering? J Pers Assess *44*: 115, 1980.

Bash I Y, Alpert M: The determination of malingering. Ann NY Acad Sci *347*: 86, 1980.

Gorman W F: Defining malingering. J Forensic Sci *27*: 401, 1982.

Reich P, Gottfried L A: Factitious disorders in a teaching hospital. Ann Intern Med *99*: 240, 1983.

Riley T C, Brannon W L: The recognition of pseudoseizures. J Fam Pract *10*: 213, 1980.

Woodyard J E: Diagnosis and prognosis in compensation claims. Ann R Coll Surg Engl *64*: 191, 1982.

Yudosky S C: Malingering. In *Comprehensive Textbook of Psychiatry*, ed 4, H I Kaplan, B J Sadock, editors, p 1862. Williams & Wilkins, Baltimore, 1985.

## 38.2 ANTISOCIAL BEHAVIOR

### Definition

As defined in the third edition of the *Diagnostic and Statistical Manual of Mental Disorders* (DSM-III), this category can be used for "adult antisocial behavior that is apparently not due to a mental disorder." The introduction to the DSM-III chapter, "Conditions Not Attributable to a Mental Disorder That Are a Focus of Attention or Treatment," states clearly that, although in some instances, no mental illness will be found after thorough diagnostic evaluations, in other instances the scope of the diagnostic evaluation has not been adequate to determine the presence or absence of a mental disorder. The category of adult antisocial behavior, except perhaps in the case of certain racketeers, embezzlers, forgers, and others who have made crime an organized profession, is usually an interim designation on the way to a more useful diagnosis. The category of adult antisocial behavior is intended to be distinct from the DSM-III diagnosis of antisocial personality disorder.

There are at least two difficulties with the designation of adult antisocial behavior. First, persons so designated may have manifested diverse behaviors, ranging from repeated cheating, lying, forgery, and embezzlement to arson, rape, and murder. Second, the term gives no indication of whether it is being used to convey the absence of mental illness in the antisocial person or that the person has not yet been adequately evaluated.

Antisocial behaviors in childhood and adulthood are characteristic of persons with a variety of psychopathology, ranging from the psychotic to the characterological. Moreover, antisocial behavior is often characteristic of persons whose functioning is on the border of several other kinds of disorders, including psychosis, organic brain syndromes, and retardation. A comprehensive neuropsychiatric assessment of antisocial persons usually reveals a myriad of more and less serious, potentially treatable psychiatric and neurological impairments that can easily be overshadowed by offensive behaviors and thus be overlooked. When the clinician leaves the patient in the category "antisocial behavior," it is usually because the time has not been taken to complete a thorough evaluation, rather than because, in a comprehensive assessment, the clinician has found no significant disturbance other than the antisocial behavior itself. Because of the negative connotations of any designation that includes the term "antisocial" in its name, be it antisocial personality or simply antisocial behavior, it is imperative that no patient be left in these categories simply for want of a careful assessment. Only in the absence of evidence of organic, psychotic, neurotic, or intellectual impairment should the patient be so categorized.

## Epidemiology

In 1981, in the United States with a population of over 200 million persons, there were over 10 million arrests. Although the nation has focused attention on youth crime, over 80 percent of arrests were of persons 18 years of age or older. Adults 18 years of age or older accounted for 81.5 percent of violent crime, but only 62.6 percent of property crime. That males in today's society are more violent than females is clear from the fact that they commit 8 times the number of violent crimes and 4 times as many property crimes, according to federal arrest data. Violent crime in cities is 10 times as frequent as it is in rural areas. The incidence of violent crime in suburbia falls somewhere between the incidence in cities and in rural areas.

It is noteworthy that, within cities, the crime rate for males between 1980 and 1981 increased 4.7 percent, whereas the rate for females increased 7.9 percent. Thus crime, in general, has been increasing, especially crime committed by females.

Statistics regarding crime, however, are not necessarily synonymous with statistics either on antisocial personality or on antisocial behavior. Clearly, many intelligent, devious, well-functioning criminals do not appear in these statistics, whereas a fair number of psychotic, neurologically impaired, and retarded persons do add to them.

Estimates of the prevalence of the disorder of antisocial personality, which, until the new classification in DSM-III, included those persons currently classified as having antisocial behavior (and which was often called sociopathic personality), have ranged from 5 to 15 percent of the population, depending on criteria and sampling. Even within the prison population, different investigators have reported prevalence figures of between 20 and 80 percent. The higher percentage is most likely due to using previous arrests and incarcerations as important criteria for diagnosing a person as having an antisocial personality.

## Etiology

### Constitutional Factors

There are significantly more abnormalities during the prenatal and perinatal periods of children who subsequently developed cerebral palsy, behavior disorders, and speech difficulties. There is also a significant correlation between hyperactive behavior and antisocial behavior. It is postulated that the relationship of hyperactivity and antisocial behavior may represent a subgroup of the syndrome of hyperactivity, and related possible physiological and genetic factors are important.

The basic data supporting the genetic transmission of antisocial behavior are based on twin studies and adoption studies. Twin studies demonstrate at least 60 percent concordance in monozygotic twins and about 30 percent concordance in dizygotic twins.

Adoption studies show that there is a higher rate of antisocial behavior in the biological relatives of adoptees identified for antisocial behavior and a higher incidence of antisocial behavior in the adopted offspring of those with antisocial behavior.

### Environmental Factors

Studies note that the sons of unskilled workers brought up in neighborhoods in which families of this socioeconomic class predominate are more likely to commit more numerous and more serious criminal offences than are the sons of middle-class or skilled working-class parents, at least during adolescence and early adulthood. These data are not as clear for females, but the findings are generally similar in studies from many different countries. Areas of family training that have been particularly cited as differing by social class from the techniques seen in middle-class parents are the use of more love-oriented techniques in disciplining, the withdrawing of affection versus physical punishments, parental attitudes toward aggressive behavior and attempts to curb it, parental values in general, and the verbal ability to communicate the various reasons for the values and proscriptions of behavior.

One aspect of the family that does emerge as particularly important in delinquent children is the occurrence of serious psychopathology. Several studies have noted that the parents of delinquents, when compared with the parents of nondelinquents, manifest more severe psychopathology. These studies raise questions about the quality of the parenting in the development of delinquent children; however, antisocial behavior in such patients may be a manifestation of a genetic schizophrenic tendency. There is a higher incidence of broken homes in delinquent children. The critical factor seems to relate more to the quality of the home life; homes broken by divorce or separation seem to produce higher rates of delinquency than do homes disrupted by the death of a parent. Thus, the important factor seems to be family discord and disharmony, rather than parental absence.

### Psychological Factors

The psychological theories pertaining to antisocial behavior have focused on two major themes: (1) the quality of the parental experience, particularly the quality of the mothering, and (2) the development of conscience. The psychological theories are as follows: (1) the child feels significant emotional deprivation and strongly resents it; (2) the child cannot establish his own range of skills because his parents have

not set limits for him; (3) the parents, especially the mother, are very often overstimulating and inconsistent in their attitudes toward the child; and (4) the child's behavior usually represents a vicarious source of pleasure and gratification for a parent, and is often an expression of the parent's unconscious hostility toward the child, as the behavior is either overtly or covertly self-destructive to the child.

### Diagnosis

Perhaps the most important clinical point to emphasize in the designation of antisocial behavior is that this is a diagnosis based primarily on the historical description of behavior. Hervey Cleckley, one of the major investigators of antisocial behavior, described the clinical picture of antisocial behavior which is summarized in Table I.

### Childhood Symptoms

The childhood behaviors most predictive of antisocial behavior are theft, incorrigibility, truancy, runaway behavior, bad associates, and staying out late at night; they were present in half of the adults who later developed antisocial personalities. The greater number of symptoms present in childhood also make the later antisocial behavior more likely but not obligatory; however, the presence of greater numbers of symptoms is also indicative of the development of other psychiatric illnesses in adult life.

### Adult Symptoms

The adult symptoms detailed by Leo Robins (see Table II) indicate that the antisocial behavior continues in almost an age-related develop-

TABLE I
CLINICAL PROFILE OF ANTISOCIAL BEHAVIOR*

Superficial charm and good intelligence
Absence of delusions and other signs of irrational thinking
Absence of nervousness and psychoneurotic manifestations
Unreliability
Untruthfulness and insincerity
Lack of remorse or shame
Inadequately motivated antisocial behavior
Poor judgment and failure to learn by experience
Pathological egocentricity and incapacity for love
General poverty in major affective reactions
Specific loss of insight
Unresponsiveness in general interpersonal relations
Fantastic and uninviting behavior with drink and sometimes without
Suicide rarely carried out
Sex life impersonal, trivial, and poorly integrated
Failure to follow any life plan

* Data from H Cleckley: *The Mask of Sanity*, ed. 4. C. V. Mosby, St. Louis, 1964.

TABLE II
ADULT SYMPTOMS OF ANTISOCIAL BEHAVIOR*

| Life Area | Percentage of Antisocials with Significant Problems in This Area |
|---|---|
| Work problems | 85 |
| Marital problems | 81 |
| Financial dependency | 79 |
| Arrests | 75 |
| Alcohol abuse | 72 |
| School problems | 71 |
| Impulsiveness | 67 |
| Sexual behavior | 64 |
| Wild adolescence | 62 |
| Vagrancy | 60 |
| Belligerency | 58 |
| Social isolation | 56 |
| Military record (of those serving) | 53 |
| Lack of guilt | 40 |
| Somatic complaints | 31 |
| Use of aliases | 29 |
| Pathological lying | 16 |
| Drug abuse | 15 |
| Suicide attempts | 11 |

* Data from L Robins: *Deviant Children Grown Up: A Sociological and Psychiatric Study of Sociopathic Personality.* Williams & Wilkins, Baltimore, 1966.

mental progression; most of the difficulties manifested by the adult center on work, marriage, financial difficulties, conflicts with various authorities, and alcohol and drug abuse, thus changing the focus but not the behaviors from school to work, and from parents to other authority figures and spouses.

**Course and Prognosis**

Antisocial behavior begins before the age of 15. In boys, there tends to be an earlier onset than in girls. In girls, the symptoms usually occur around the time of puberty. When these behaviors occur before the age of 15, they may be the prodromata of other psychopathology, such as schizophrenic conditions. However, the greater the incidence of these behaviors in childhood and the greater the variety, frequency, and seriousness, the more likely they are to progress into adult life.

Usually, the antisocial behavior leads to markedly incapacitating results, manifesting as failure to become an independent, self-supporting adult, with frequent institutionalizations, more often penal than medical. It is highly unusual for people displaying antisocial behavior to attain successful careers, particularly those in whom a definite diagnosis can be made. Robins noted that, in their third decade, 40 percent of the adults followed were either significantly improved or recovered. However, in 60 percent the behavior continued unabated.

*Differential Diagnosis*

The intertwining of alcoholism and drug dependence in the descriptive behaviors of antisocial behavior often makes it difficult to distinguish antisocial behavior, related primarily to drug abuse or alcoholism, from disordered behavior that occurred before the drug abuse or alcoholism, or that occurred during episodes unrelated to alcoholism or drug abuse.

During manic phases of cyclothymic disorder, certain aspects of behavior can be similar to antisocial behaviors, such as wanderlust, sexual promiscuity, and financial difficulty. The early onset of antisocial behavior and acts before the age of 15 are most often absent in cyclothymic disorder. The episodic and cyclic nature of cyclothymic disorder is also characteristic and discernible; the mental status symptoms noted in the manic patient of flight of ideas, pressure of speech, grandiosity, and euphoria are most often absent in antisocial behavior. Schizophrenia, especially in childhood, may often manifest as antisocial behavior. However, in the adult schizophrenic, episodes of antisocial behavior may occur, but the symptom picture is usually clear, especially with regard to thought disorders, delusions, and hallucinations on the mental status examination.

Neurological conditions may cause antisocial behavior. EEG's, CT scans, and a complete neurological examination should be done. Temporal lobe epilepsy is often considered in the differential diagnosis. When a clear-cut diagnosis of temporal lobe epilepsy or encephalitis can be made, that may account for the antisocial behavior.

Conduct disorder, which should be differentiated from antisocial disorder, is discussed in Section 35.6. Antisocial personality disorder is discussed in Section 18.

**Treatment**

In general, great therapeutic pessimism surrounds the term antisocial behavior. It is difficult for a therapist not to feel that he has little hope of changing a pattern of behavior that has been present almost throughout the patient's life. In part, the literature bears out this therapeutic pessimism.

There have been no major breakthroughs with biological treatments. There has not been any overwhelming success with the use of medications.

More enthusiasm has been expressed for various therapeutic communities and group treatment of delinquents and adult criminals. However, the data provide little basis for enthusiasm.

Treatment of outpatients with antisocial behavior is extremely difficult, and such patients should be treated individually, primarily in an institutional center, where they can be prevented from running away. Once the patient is immobilized in an institutional setting, he becomes less alien to the therapist and less difficult to understand.

The natural history of violence and of criminal and antisocial behavior seems to decrease after age 40, and recidivism also decreases after age 40. Several authors have suggested that perhaps one way of treating these patients is to isolate them from society until after age 40. Although this position may be overly pessimistic, it is important to recognize that this is a repetitive pattern of behavior that seems to limit itself after age 40, and that has been unresponsive to most therapeutic interventions.

**REFERENCES**

Lewis D O, editor: *Vulnerabilities to Delinquency.* Spectrum Publications, New York, 1981.
Lewis D O: Adult antisocial behavior and criminality. In *Comprehensive Textbook of Psychiatry,* ed 4, H I Kaplan, B J Sadock, editors, p 1865, Williams & Wilkins, Baltimore, 1985.
Lewis D O, Shanok S S, Lewis M, Unger L, Goldman C: Conduct disorder and its synonyms: Diagnoses of dubious validity and usefulness. Am J Psychiatry *141:* 514, 1984.
Mark V H, Ervin F: *Violence and the Brain.* Harper & Row, New York, 1970.
Martinson R, Palmer T, Adams S: *Rehabilitation, Recidivism, and Research.* National Council on Crime and Delinquency, Hackensack, NJ, 1976.
Mednick S A, Christianson K O: *Biosocial Bases of Criminal Behavior.* Gardner Press, New York, 1977.
Pincus J H, Tucker G J: *Behavioral Neurology.* Oxford University Press, New York, 1978.

# 38.3  ACADEMIC PROBLEM AND BORDERLINE INTELLECTUAL FUNCTIONING

## Academic Problem

The term academic problem is listed in DSM-III as a condition in which the focus of attention or treatment is an academic problem that is apparently not due to a mental disorder. According to the manual, this code is to be cited in cases in which a person with adequate intellectual capacity develops a pattern of failing grades or significant underachievement in the absence of a specific developmental disorder, or any other mental disorder that accounts for the problem.

Appropriate use of the category for diagnostic purposes is limited to one of the following three circumstances: (1) the absence of evidence of a mental disorder that accounts for the academic problem, as determined by a complete and adequate psychiatric evaluation; (2) the absence of evidence of a mental disorder that accounts for the academic problem, as determined by an incomplete and inadequate psychiatric evaluation, but one in which some notation is required stating the reason for contact with the mental health care system; (3) the presence of a mental disorder is noted, but it is felt that the focus of attention or treatment—the academic problem—is not caused by that disorder.

### Etiology

Academic problems may result from a variety of causes and may arise at any time in life. They occur most often between the ages of 5 and 21, a span that includes the school years.

During this period, the school setting occupies a major portion of the person's time. It serves as an important social instrument, as well as educational instrument, being interconnected with the major developmental issues of childhood, adolescence, and young adulthood. A boy or girl must cope with the process of separation, adjustment to new environments, adaptation to social contacts, competition, assertion, intimacy, and a myriad of other issues. There is often a reciprocal relationship between how well these developmental tasks are mastered, and the level of school performance.

Ultimately, school performance may be conceptualized as an issue of role performance. Students who are disposed to academic achievement, finding it gratifying and believing it to result in a satisfying and productive life, generally do well in that role. Yet, even among this group, some students fail to fully understand the complexities and realities involved in school work. This problem is especially prevalent among children from homes in which appropriate models for learning are absent. In those cases, the cause of an academic problem may simply be poor preparation and study habits.

Academic problems related to social and cultural deprivation could be considered in this category. In these cases, difficulties arise because education is distant from the immediate experiences of daily life or even offers models that conflict with the conduct of life at home. School is not seen as valuable or meaningful.

Achievement-related anxiety represents a significant source of academic problems. In psychoanalytic psychodynamic terms, some students exhibit evidence of inner conflict believed to be connected with the Oedipus complex. Described by Freud as "those wrecked by success," such persons fear the consequences that are imagined to accompany the attainment of success. Behaviorists may interpret the conflict as a learned disposition to fear success outcomes. An example might be a woman whose motive to avoid success in school is linked to a fear of social rejection or loss of femininity or both, especially when success necessitates aggression and competition with males.

Anxiety may manifest itself primarily in test-taking situations. Test anxiety may, in fact, be the sole presenting complaint and the primary source of scholastic difficulties. Test anxiety is a situation-specific form of self-preoccupation that is accompanied by cognitive difficulties. Students with test anxiety characteristically complain of increased self-awareness, self-doubt, and self-depreciation. Their ability to encode and transform information is disturbed, as is the ability to plan effectively. Moreover, time spent anxiously anticipating a test contributes to inadequate preparation.

The loss of parent-substitute teachers, and the diminished role of the parents themselves as a primary reference group, may undermine academic efforts. Studies revealed that boredom in school is often the result of identity diffusion. Lacking any real and stable sense of themselves and their goals, students become bored and unable to perform their student role.

Girls are more often found to develop scholastic difficulties on entering junior high school than are boys. Boys with school problems generally show a consistent pattern of underachievement from the first grade through high school. The sudden change among girls on entering the ninth grade has been ascribed to two factors—the increased influence of peers and peer values that may be incongruent with scholastic performance, and the increased awareness of sex roles.

Teacher expectations concerning student performance influence performance. The teacher serves as a causal agent whose varying expectations can shape the differential development of student skills and abilities. Such conditioning early in school, especially if negative, can have a strongly disturbing effect on academic performance. Thus, a teacher's affective response to a child can prompt the appearance of academic problems. Most important is the humane approach of the teacher to the student. This applies to all levels of education, including medical school.

Student-teacher mismatching may also involve such nonaffective components as cognition. Cognitive style relates to the processes involved in how a student perceives, thinks, learns, solves problems, and relates to others, as well as personal dimensions. When the cognitive styles of the student and the teacher clash, scholastic impairment may follow. Some persons, called field-dependent, are better at learning and remembering incidental social material, are more affected by external reinforcement in the form of praise or criticism, and are more likely to have difficulty with relatively unstructured academic material than are field-independent persons. An atmosphere in which teachers are aware of cognition and its implications can influence student performance in a positive direction.

## Treatment

Academic problems, although not a diagnosable psychiatric disorder, can best be alleviated through use of psychological means. Psychotherapeutic techniques can be used successfully for scholastic difficulties, including those related to poor motivation, poor self-concept, and underachievement.

Early efforts at the relief of the problem should outweigh all other considerations, since sustained problems in learning and school performance frequently compound themselves and precipitate more severe difficulties. Feelings of anger, frustration, shame, loss of self-respect, and helplessness—emotions that most often accompany school failures—have an emotionally and cognitively damaging effect on self-esteem, disabling future performance and clouding expectations for success.

Tutoring is an extremely effective technique in dealing with academic problems, and should be considered for use in all cases. In dealing with the stigma attached to having a tutor—for many students, having a tutor is a humiliating concession to their perception of being dumb—the therapist may find it helpful to explain to the student that he or she probably holds to the self-serving hypothesis of academic performance—the concept that success in school work is due to internal factors but that failure is due to chance or other forces. Thus, success is attributed to ability or disposition, and failure is attributed to extenuating circumstances. That attitude is exemplified by the saying "good students are born, not made" and by the general reluctance of students to admit that they study hard. Clarification of this outlook, if present, is often important in getting a student to accept tutoring. Tutoring is of special proven value in preparing for objective multiple choice examinations such as the SAT, MCAT, and National Boards. Diminishing anxiety by repetitively taking such type questions is a behavioral deconditioning technique. A therapist may also emphasize the student's hidden strengths, qualities that the student perceives as a legitimate aspect of himself.

### Borderline Intellectual Functioning

In DSM-III, borderline intellectual functioning is considered under the classification conditions not attributable to a mental disorder that are a focus of attention or treatment. As described in DSM-III, the category may be used when a focus of attention or treatment is on a deficit in adaptive functioning associated with borderline intellectual functioning—that is, an I.Q. in the 71 to 84 range. The problem is often masked when a mental disorder is present which comes to the attention of the psychiatrist.

Only about 6 to 7 percent of the population are found to have a borderline I.Q., as determined by the Stanford-Binet test or the Wechsler scales. The premise behind the inclusion of this category is that these persons may experience difficulties in their adaptive capacities, which may ultimately produce impaired social and vocational functioning. Thus, in the absence of specific intrapsychic conflicts, developmental traumas, biochemical abnormalities, or other factors that are linked to mental disorders, they may experience severe emotional distress. Frustration and embarrassment over their difficulties may shape life choices and lead to circumstances warranting psychiatric intervention.

Once the underlying problem is known to the therapist, psychiatric treatment can be quite useful. Many persons with borderline intellectual functioning are able to function at a superior level in some areas, while being markedly deficient in others. By directing them to appropriate areas of endeavor, by pointing out socially acceptable behavior, and by teaching living skills, the therapist can act as a force that improves their self-esteem.

### REFERENCES

Gittleman R, Feingold I: Children with reading disorders. I. Efficacy of reading remediation. J Child Psychol Psychiatry 24: 167, 1983.

Karabenick S A: Fear of success, achievement and affiliation dispositions and the performance of men and women under individual and competitive conditions. J Pers 45: 117, 1977.

Levin J, Arluke A, Smith M: The effects of labeling students upon teachers' expectations and intentions. J Soc Psychol 118: 207, 1982.

Sussman N: Academic problem and borderline intellectual functioning. In *Comprehensive Textbook of Psychiatry,* ed 4, H I Kaplan, B J Sadock, editors, p 1870. Williams & Wilkins, Baltimore, 1985.

Waller J D, Rothchild G: Comparison of need for achievement versus need for affiliation among music students. Psychol Rep 53: 135, 1983.

Wood D, Bruner J S, Ross G: The role of tutoring in problem solving. J Child Psychol Psychiatry 17: 89, 1976.

Zatz S, Chassin L: Cognitions of test-anxious children. J Consult Clin Psychol 51: 526, 1983.

## 38.4   OTHER CONDITIONS NOT ATTRIBUTABLE TO A MENTAL DISORDER

### Introduction

As defined in DSM-III, these conditions have led to contact with the mental health care system, but without sufficient evidence to justify a diagnosis of any of the mental disorders noted previously. In some instances, one of these conditions will be noted because, following a thorough evaluation, no mental disorder is found to be present. In other instances, the scope of the diagnostic evaluation was not such as to adequately determine the presence or absence of a mental disorder, but there is a need to note the primary reason for contact with the mental health care system.

In some cases a mental disorder may eventually be found; but the focus of attention or treatment is on a condition that is not due to the mental disorder. For example, a patient with an anxiety disorder may receive treatment for a marital problem that is unrelated to the anxiety disorder itself.

### Marital Problem

There is a higher percentage of marriages in this country now than ever before, but one of four marriages in the United States ends in divorce. This fact does not necessarily indicate psychiatric illness in one or both of the partners. Remaining in a disruptive marriage creates significant stress, frequently leading to anxiety and depression. It is the task of the psychiatrist to help the patient deal with his own conflicts. When a patient presents with specific marital problems, the result of consultation and treatment may be a happier, more fulfilling marriage or a divorce.

Indeed, one of the evaluations that the physician must make is specifically whether the presenting complaint is engendered by the marriage, or is part of a greater disturbance. The development, family, sexual, personal, and occupational history, as well as the marital history, should be enlightening in this regard.

Marriage involves many stressful situations that tax the adaptive capacities of the partners. If the partners are of different backgrounds and have been raised within different value systems, conflicts are more likely to arise than if they came from similar backgrounds. The areas to be explored include sexual relations; attitudes toward contraception, childbearing, and child rearing; handling of money; relation with inlaws; and attitudes toward social life.

A problem period in a marriage is often precipitated by the birth of children, especially the first child. It is a stressful time for both parents.

Economic stresses, moves to new areas, unplanned pregnancies, and abortions may upset a seemingly healthy marriage. Differing attitudes toward religion can also present a problem.

Complaints of anorgasmia or impotence by marital partners are usually indicative of deeper disturbances, although sexual dissatisfaction is involved in most cases of marital maladjustment. Some marriages can survive without sexual relations, but poor sexual functioning frequently reflects disturbances in other areas of the relationship.

The institution of marriage is itself being stressed by cultural changes. Some workers feel that the family is being scapegoated because of pressures from other rapid changes in the social system.

### Phase-of-Life Problem or Other Life Circumstance Problem

Psychological development throughout the life cycle has been studied and conceptualized by numerous workers. Specific attention is currently focused on the relationship between life stresses and illness to determine what brings people without a mental disorder into the mental health care system.

Emerging from this research is the concept that specific life events in and of themselves do not necessarily produce a mental disorder. A person's adaptive style evolves and matures throughout life, but its evolution is more dependent on internal growth than on the interpersonal environment.

External events are most likely to overwhelm the person's adaptive capacities if they are unexpected, if they are overwhelming in number—that is, a number of stresses occurring within a short time span—if the strain is chronic and unremitting, or if one loss actually heralds a myriad of concomitant adjustments that strain a person's recuperative powers.

T. Holmes quantified life events, assigning a point value to life changes that require adaptation (see Table I). His research indicated a critical level at which too many of these events happening during a 1-year time span to one person put that person at great risk of illness. Of those people who accumulated 300 points in

1 year, about 80 percent were at risk of illness in the near future; with 150 to 299 points, about 50 percent became ill in the near future; of those with fewer than 150 stress points, about 30 percent became ill shortly after the life events. This research was done with persons presenting with physical complaints.

Another survey focused on which life strains are most likely to produce anxiety and depression, and pinpointed situations related to marriage, occupation, and parenthood. The life changes affected both men and women, but women, the poor, and minority groups seemed particularly vulnerable to them. Again, the change created significant strain when it was unexpected and when it involved not only adjustment to a loss (spouse or job), but the need to adjust to a new status that entailed further hardships and problems.

In general, people have demonstrated ability to adjust to life changes if they have mature defense mechanisms, such as altruism, humor, and the capacity for sublimation. Flexibility, reliability, strong family ties, regular employment, adequate income and job satisfaction, a pattern of regular recreation and social participation, realistic goals, and a history of adequate performance—in short, a full and adequately satisfying life—create resilience to deal with life changes.

There is some suggestion that periods of cultural transition, with changing mores and fluidity of role definition, increase individual vulnerability to life strain. Extreme cultural transition can create a condition of severe distress. This problem, also called culture shock, occurs when a person is suddenly thrust into an alien culture, or has divided loyalties to two different cultures.

On a less extreme basis, it occurs when young men enter the army, when people change jobs, when families move or experience a significant change in income, when children experience their first day in school, and when black ghetto children are bused to white middle-class schools.

The person undergoing culture shock experiences a variety of emotions—isolation, anxiety, and depression, often accompanied by a sense of loss close to mourning. The degree of adjustment that such persons can make to their new environment is dependent on their underlying personality structure and strengths.

### Occupational Problem

An occupational history is part of the total psychiatric interview. On occasion, dissatisfaction with work is the presenting complaint. Since some work situations can be stressful and

TABLE I
THE SOCIAL READJUSTMENT RATING SCALE*

| Life Event | Mean Value |
|---|---|
| 1. Death of spouse | 100 |
| 2. Divorce | 73 |
| 3. Marital separation from mate | 65 |
| 4. Detention in jail or other institution | 63 |
| 5. Death of a close family member | 63 |
| 6. Major personal injury or illness | 53 |
| 7. Marriage | 50 |
| 8. Being fired at work | 47 |
| 9. Marital reconciliation with mate | 45 |
| 10. Retirement from work | 45 |
| 11. Major change in the health or behavior of a family member | 44 |
| 12. Pregnancy | 40 |
| 13. Sexual difficulties | 39 |
| 14. Gaining a new family member (through birth, adoption, oldster moving in, etc.) | 39 |
| 15. Major business readjustment (merger, reorganization, bankruptcy, etc.) | 39 |
| 16. Major change in financial state (a lot worse off or a lot better off than usual) | 38 |
| 17. Death of a close friend | 37 |
| 18. Changing to a different line of work | 36 |
| 19. Major change in the number of arguments with spouse (either a lot more or a lot less than usual regarding child rearing, personal habits, etc.) | 35 |
| 20. Taking on a mortgage greater than $10,000 (purchasing a home, business, etc.) | 31 |
| 21. Foreclosure on a mortgage or loan | 30 |
| 22. Major change in responsibilities at work (promotion, demotion, lateral transfer) | 29 |
| 23. Son or daughter leaving home (marriage, attending college, etc.) | 29 |
| 24. In-law troubles | 29 |
| 25. Outstanding personal achievement | 28 |
| 26. Wife beginning or ceasing work outside the home | 26 |
| 27. Beginning or ceasing formal schooling | 26 |
| 28. Major change in living conditions (building a new home, remodeling, deterioration of home or neighborhood) | 25 |
| 29. Revision of personal habits (dress, manners, associations, etc.) | 24 |
| 30. Troubles with the boss | 23 |
| 31. Major change in working hours or conditions | 20 |
| 32. Change in residence | 20 |
| 33. Changing to a new school | 20 |
| 34. Major change in usual type or amount of recreation | 19 |
| 35. Major change in church activities (a lot more or a lot less than usual) | 19 |
| 36. Major change in social activities (clubs, dancing, movies, visiting, etc.) | 18 |
| 37. Taking on a mortgage or loan less than $10,000 (purchasing a car, TV, freezer, etc.) | 17 |
| 38. Major change in sleeping habits (a lot more or a lot less sleep or change in part of day when asleep) | 16 |
| 39. Major change in number of family get-togethers (a lot more or a lot less than usual) | 15 |
| 40. Major change in eating habits (a lot more or a lot less food intake or very different meal hours or surroundings) | 15 |
| 41. Vacation | 15 |
| 42. Christmas | 12 |
| 43. Minor violations of the law (traffic tickets, jaywalking, disturbing the peace, etc.) | 11 |

* From T Holmes: Life situations, emotions, and disease. J Acad Psychosom Med *19*: 747, 1978.

unpleasant in themselves, since there is evidence that mental effort under such conditions can produce neurotic disorders, and since economic necessity may force people to accept work essentially distasteful to them, it is possible for someone with this complaint to be otherwise psychiatrically normal.

Whereas a healthy adaptation to work provides an outlet for creativity, satisfying relationships with colleagues, pride in accomplishment, and increased self-esteem, maladaptation can lead to dissatisfaction with one's self and the job, insecurity, decreased self-esteem, anger, and resentment at having to work.

In reviewing a patient's past work history, a psychiatrist should explore how and why the occupation was chosen. Was it a childhood goal? Was it chosen in emulation of a model and hero? Was it forced or encouraged by the patient's family? Was it an outgrowth of a special talent? Was it well prepared for? Was it arrived at by trial and error? Was it an impulsive decision? Was it forced by financial need? With a young patient, what are the expectations regarding advancement? Are they realistic? With an older patient, what is the record of success? What is the frequency of changing employment? What are the frequency and the duration of unemployment?

Maladaptation at work may, of course, arise from psychodynamic conflicts. These conflicts can be reflected in the patient's inability to accept the authority of competent superiors or, conversely, in an overdependency on authority figures to fulfill infantile needs. People with unresolved conflicts over their competitive and aggressive impulses may experience great difficulty in the work area. They may suffer from a pathological envy of success of others, or fear success for themselves because of their inability to tolerate envy from others. These conflicts are manifest in other areas of the patient's life as well, and the maladaptation is not limited to occupation.

Recent research suggested that job related stress is most likely to develop when work objectives are not clear, when workers are pressured by conflicting demands, when they have too much or too little to do, and when they are responsible for the professional development of others and have little control over decisions that affect them.

Special problems to be considered are the adjustments of those about to face retirement, the dissatisfaction of the housewife, and the minority group member blocked from position or advancement because of sex, race, religion, or ethnic background.

### Role of Socioeconomic Status in Mental Health

Education and occupation are the most important indications of social status in the United States, and social status relates to incidence, prevalence, diagnosis and treatment of mental illness. Because neuroses have been reported to be more prevalent in urban areas, it has been commonly accepted that neurotic behavior is characteristic of urban living. However, neurotic behavior has been found in members of all societies that have been rigorously studied.

**New Haven Study.** Hollingshead and Redlich conducted a survey of New Haven, Connecticut, and its surrounding region during parts of 1950 and 1951.

The project was primarily concerned with determining the relation of social class to the prevalence of treated illness.

The data accumulated by the study proved the following:

Position in the class structure is related to the prevalence of treated mental illness.

Position in the class structure is related to the types of diagnosed psychiatric disorders.

Position in the class structure is related to social and psychodynamic factors in the development of psychiatric disorders.

Mobility in the class structure is related to the development of psychiatric difficulties.

Analysis of the data revealed definitive relationships between social class and various aspects of the psychiatric process, beginning with the nature of the initial referral for treatment. Among those persons classified as neurotics entering treatment for the first time, for example, the referrals by private physicians were much greater in classes I and II (52.5 percent) than in class V (13.9 percent). The police and the courts referred no one from classes I and II, but they referred 13.9 percent of class V.

It was found that an inverse relationship existed between social class and psychosis; that neuroses were more prevalent in classes I and II and fell as the class level fell, but psychoses were most markedly increased among the lower classes; that social class was related to the site, duration, and nature of psychiatric therapy; and that observed relations between sociocultural variables and the prevalence of treated disorders do not establish that sociocultural variables are essential and necessary conditions in the causation of mental disorders. Table II describes the cultural characteristics of each class.

The prevalence of neurotics receiving psychoanalytic psychotherapy is highest among the upper classes (class I) and the incidence of psychosis is highest among the lowest class (class V). The latter receive treatment or custodial care in state mental hospitals, that care being chronic and often inadequate.

In addition, members of the lower class mistrust caretakers and avoid psychiatric treatment until an emergency arises. In the treatment of neurotics, the upper classes are chosen for long-term treatment because of cultural origin, high intelligence, ability to verbalize, and the ability to afford treatment. Even the smaller number of class V neurotics that are actually seen present in clinics and are poorly motivated for psychotherapy.

**Midtown Manhattan Study.** A team under the direction of a psychiatrist, Thomas A. C. Rennie, designed and conducted a survey involving a sample of 1,660 adults drawn from a specific section of New York City. The general objectives of the study were to estimate the mental health of a geographically defined population, the majority of whom had never been psychiatric patients, and to determine the possible influence of demographic factors and social and personal experiences on mental health and mental illness. In contrast to the New Haven study, the sample population in the Midtown project were not necessarily persons under past or present psychiatric care. Moreover, the Midtown project made a major effort to estimate reliably and objectively the mental health of each respondent. The vehicle for obtaining a

Table II
Class Status and Cultural Characteristics of Subjects in the New Haven Study

| Class | Class Status and Cultural Characteristics |
|-------|-------------------------------------------|
| I | Class I, containing the community's business and professional leaders, has two segments: a long established core group of interrelated families and a smaller upward-mobile group of new people. Members of the core group usually inherit money along with group values that stress tradition, stability, and social responsibility. Those in the newer group are highly educated, self-made, able, and aggressive. Their family relations often are not cohesive or stable. Socially, they are rejected by the core group, to whom they are, however, a threat by the vigor of their leadership in community affairs. |
| II | Class II is marked by at least some education beyond high school and occupations as managers or in the lesser-ranking professions. Four of five are upward mobile. They are joiners at all ages and tend to have stable families, but they have usually gone apart from parental families and often from their home communities. Tensions arise generally from striving for educational, economic, and social success. |
| III | Class III males for the most part are in salaried administrative and clerical jobs (51 percent) or own small businesses (24 percent); many of the women also have jobs. Typically, they are high school graduates. They usually have economic security but little opportunity for advancement. Families tend to be somewhat less stable than in class II. Family members of all ages tend to join organizations and to be active in them. There is less satisfaction with present living conditions and less optimism than in class II. |
| IV | In class IV, 53 percent say they belong to the working class. Seven of 10 show no generational mobility. Most are content and make no sacrifices to get ahead. Most of the men are semiskilled (53 percent) or skilled (35 percent) manual employees. Practically all the women who are able to hold jobs do so. Education usually stops shortly after graduation from grammar school for both parents and children. Families are much different from those in class III. Families are larger, and they are more likely to include three generations. Households are more likely to include boarders and roomers. Homes are more likely to be broken. |
| V | Class V adults usually have not completed elementary school. Most are semiskilled factory workers or unskilled laborers. They are concentrated in tenement and cold-water-flat areas of New Haven slums or in suburban slums. There are generally brittle family ties. Very few participate in organized community institutions. Leisure activities in the household and on the street are informal and spontaneous. Adolescent boys frequently have contact with the law in their search for adventure. There is a struggle for existence. There is much resentment, expressed freely in primary groups, about how they are treated by those in authority. There is much acting out of hostility. |

mental health rating was a questionnaire-guided interview conducted by nonpsychiatrists. However, determinations made by psychiatrists during examinations of clinical patients were incorporated into the data. In this fashion a compre-hensive mass of information was obtained, so that the presence or absence of psychiatrically significant symptoms could be determined.

**Findings.** It was observed that there is a rise in mental disorder or poor mental health as age increases. Respondents in their fifth decade of life were, collectively, 15 percent well and 31 percent impaired. The youngest persons studied, from age 20 to 29, were judged 24 percent well and 15 percent impaired. Perhaps the most dramatic conclusions of the project were that, overall, only 19 percent of the study population was considered well and that only 18 percent displayed no symptoms of mental disorder. On the continuum, the largest number (36 percent) suffered from mild symptom formation, with 34 percent categorized as being a probable neurotic type.

Another specific finding was related to socioeconomic status, which was calculated from occupation, education, income, and rent. The highest stratum showed about six times as many members in the well group and less than a quarter as many in the impaired group as did the lowest stratum. Socioeconomic status appeared to be the most important single variable. In the study, the presence of symptoms was not taken as an indication of a disorder. It was observed, however, that those with the largest number of symptoms would most likely be diagnosed as having a mental disorder if they were seen by a psychiatrist.

It has been hypothesized that the upper class, which looks to the past and attempts to maintain the status quo, is unhappy with the present. They tend to feel failure and have the highest frequency of depression and suicide. The middle class emphasizes the future, delays gratifying immediate impulses (pain-pleasure-reality principle) and develops neurotic conflict and anxiety disorders. The lower class is preoccupied with present survival and expresses immediate sexual and aggressive impulses. They have the highest incidence of antisocial behavior.

It was also found that mental health is best among individuals with parents of high socioeconomic status, occupational stability and upward mobility. Children whose parents are of low socioeconomic status, occupational instability and downward mobility have the highest frequency of psychiatric disability.

**Stirling County Study.** Alexander H. Leighton headed a psychiatric epidemiological study of Stirling County, a Canadian county of 20,000 persons. Unlike the New Haven and Midtown Manhattan surveys, the Stirling County population was primarily rural, being mostly scattered in small villages of a few hundred, with one town of 3,000 and a good many isolated farms.

The study found that communities in Stirling County showed a significant correlation between disintegration and prevalence of psychiatric symptoms. The conditions of poverty, secularization, and cultural confusion were three criteria used to identify community disintegration.

Like the Midtown Manhattan study, the Stirling County study found that only about 20 percent of the population could be said with certainty to be free of symptoms of mental disorder. Women showed considerably more psychiatric disorder than did men. In terms of symptom categories, the survey found that 66 percent of the men and 71 percent of the women suffered from psychophysiological symptoms. Psychoneurosis was found in 44 percent of the men and 64 percent of the women. Age was found to be a factor, with psychiatric disorders increasing with age. The study also disclosed a linear relation between mental health and economic position.

**Faris and Dunham.** The pioneer study of Faris and Dunham has been particularly influential. This survey reported that first hospital admissions for schizophrenia were highest among persons from the central sections of Chicago, the lowest socioeconomic sections of the city. It was also reported that rates of admission decreased as one moved away from the central areas and into the more affluent and prestigious communities. These findings gave rise to what is termed the drift hypothesis. According to this theory, the environment in the central city does not produce the disease but, rather, acts as a magnet, drawing schizophrenics who are in the process of decompensating. By the time the illness is most severe and hospitalization is required, they have drifted into the core city.

**Poverty.** Poverty is conventionally defined in terms of a family's financial resources. However, most workers agree that this arbitrary form of definition is inadequate and unrealistic. The related variables of low income, family size, age, low occupational level, high unemployment rate, local cost of living, and geographic location have come to be used in measuring poverty.

Mental health workers have attempted to describe those personality traits and mental disorders that are most frequent among the poor. The poor are said to be (1) physical and visual, rather than aural; (2) content-centered, rather than form-centered; (3) externally oriented, rather than introspective; (4) problem-centered, rather than abstract-centered; (5) inductive, rather than deductive; (6) spatial, rather than temporal; (7) slow, careful, patient, perservering

(in areas of importance), rather than quick, facile, clever; (8) games-and-action-oriented, rather than test-oriented; (9) expressive-oriented, rather than instrumental-oriented; (10) geared to one-tract thinking and unorthodox learning, rather than other-directed flexibility; and (11) prone to use words in relation to action, rather than being word-bound.

The poor are also characterized as being impulsive; oriented in terms of time to the present and, to a lesser extent, the immediate past, a fact that manifests itself in failure to plan for the future and to delay gratification; and resigned and fatalistic, a fact that results in a tolerance of somatic and psychological pathology far in excess of that accepted by the more affluent.

Other findings are that psychiatric hospitalization, depression and suicide decrease during times of war, affluence and high employment. Conversely, during times of peace and high unemployment, psychiatric hospitalization and suicide increase.

All the above studies confirm the close correlation between mental illness, socioeconomic status, and occupation.

### Parent-Child Problem

Difficulties can arise in a variety of situations that stress the usual parent-child interaction beyond the adaptations necessary for individual developments that occur throughout life and those required to cope with expected life events.

For instance, in a family in which the parents are divorced, parent-child problems may arise in the relationship with the custodial parent or the noncustodial parent. The child may vent all his or her anger on the parent with custody—that is, the parent who is there most of the time. The presence of only this parent in the home represents the reality of the divorce, and makes her or him a target for the child's distress. At the same time, this parent, stressed by adjustments of his or her own, may not be able to deal with the child's increased needs and anger at just that time.

The noncustodial parent must cope with the strains of a Sunday relationship and the loss of the day-to-day gratification, as well as the responsibilities, of parenting. Both parent and child usually respond to the physical separation with emotional distress.

The solution of joint custody offers some advantages, but also precipitates some problems. Joint-custody agreements require a high degree of maturity on the part of the parents, who must separate their child-rearing practices from post-divorce resentments and must develop a spirit of cooperation regarding the rearing of the child; they must have the ability to tolerate frequent communication with an ex-spouse.

Remarriage of a divorced or widowed parent can also lead to a parent-child problem. Resentment of a stepparent and favoritism for a natural child are usual in the initial phases of adjustment of a new family.

Other situations that may cause a parent-child problem include the development of a fatal, crippling, or chronic illness in either parent or child—leukemia, epilepsy, sickle-cell anemia, spinal cord injury, and the birth of a child with congenital defects, e.g., cerebral palsy, blindness, deafness. Although these situations are not rare, they challenge the emotional resources of the people involved. The parents and the child have to face present and potential loss and adjust their day-to-day lives on a physical, economic, and emotional level. These situations can stress the healthiest families and give rise to problems in parent-child interaction, not just with the affected child but with unaffected siblings as well. These siblings may be resented, preferred, or neglected because the ill child requires so much time and attention.

### Other Specified Family Circumstances

This category applies to conditions that produce sufficient stress to necessitate contact with the mental health care system, but that are not the outcome of a prior mental disorder, and that are not covered under marital problem or parent-child problem.

For instance, a particular stress arises in dual-career families. The mothers in these families—defined as families in which both spouses have careers, rather than jobs—are found to be particularly vulnerable to guilt and anxiety regarding their maternal role. These women usually accept middle-class or upper middle-class values that emphasize the individual development and psychological health of the child as very important. They espouse middle-class child-rearing practices that use sensitivity and verbal communication in imparting values to the child, rather than using physical punishment to enforce demands to behave and conform. The middle-class family system is particularly demanding of the wife and mother, and it is especially stressful for the career wife and mother who has significant time commitments outside the home.

Another stressful family situation may develop when adults must care for aging parents. Adults often assume this responsibility while they are still caring for their children. Adaptation involves adjustment to a reversal of former roles, recognition of the aging and potential loss

of the parent, and coping with evidence of one's own mortality.

Other circumstances that overlap the categories of marital problem and parent-child problem include families with step-relations, adoptive families, families with special children, and families whose members have significantly differing values—in which there are immigrant parents and native-born children, or in which family members belong to different religious groups.

### Other Interpersonal Problem

This category covers interpersonal problems not attributable to a mental disorder, and not covered under marital, parent-child, or occupational problem. Problems causing sufficient strain to bring a person into contact with the mental health care system may arise in relations with romantic partners, co-workers, in-laws, neighbors, teachers, students, friends, and social groups. The stress-inducing circumstances, coping mechanisms, and symptoms that have brought someone to seek consultation or treatment must be individually evaluated.

### *Other Conditions*

Other conditions not attributable to a mental disorder according to DSM-III are listed here but are discussed elsewhere in this textbook. They include the following: Malingering (Section 38.1); Academic Problem and Borderline Intellectual Functioning (Section 38.3); Childhood, Adolescent and Adult Antisocial Behavior (Section 38.2); and Noncompliance with Medical Treatment (Section 39.2).

**REFERENCES**

American Psychiatric Association: *Diagnostic and Statistical Manual of Mental Disorders,* ed 3. American Psychiatric Association, Washington, DC, 1980.
Blumstein P, Schwartz P: *American Couples.* Morrow, New York, 1983.
Grant I, Yager J, Sweetwood H, Olshen R: Life events and symptoms. Arch Gen Psychiatry *39:* 598, 1982.
Holmes T: Life situations, emotions, and disease. J Acad Psychosom Med *19:* 747, 1978.
Levinson D: *The Seasons of a Man's Life.* Alfred A. Knopf, New York, 1978.
Lidz T: *The Person.* Basic Books, New York 1968.
Lieberman M, Pearlin L: Life stresses. Am J Community Psychol *6:* 1, 1978.
Neugarten B L: Time, age and the life cycle. Am J Psychiatry *136:* 887, 1979.
Roeske N: New forms of family structure. Psychiatr Ann *12:* 830, 1982.
Sadock V A: Other conditions not attributable to a mental disorder. In *Comprehensive Textbook of Psychiatry,* ed 4, H I Kaplan, B J Sadock, editors, p 1872. Williams & Wilkins, Baltimore, 1985.
Vaillant G: *Adaptation to Life.* Little, Brown, Boston, 1977.

# 39

# Community Psychiatry

## 39.1 COMMUNITY PSYCHIATRY AND HEALTH CONCEPTS

### Introduction to Community Psychiatry

Community psychiatry uses the same specific techniques of treatment as are found in a number of other settings. The differences relate to a number of factors, including a commitment to a population, rather than to a patient who has come for treatment.

The characteristics listed below fit the federal requirements for the definition of a community mental health center (CMHC), but there is a diversity among community programs, and the federal requirements have been achieved by only some of the programs.

### Characteristics of a CMHC

**Responsibility to a Population.** Commitment to a population implies a responsibility for planning. It suggests that the plan should identify all the mental health needs of this population, inventory the resources available to meet these needs, and organize a system of care, using existing resources and planning new ones to serve the population. It also suggests a responsibility for carrying on the planning with the citizens and political figures involved, and suggests that prevention is at least as important as direct treatment; and it suggests that the responsibility is to all persons in this population, including children, the aged, minorities, the chronically ill, the acutely ill, and those who live in geographically distant areas.

**Treatment Close to the Patient.** The requirement that mental health services be located close to the patient's residence or place of work makes it easier for people to get to a treatment site, and suggests that illness be identified earlier, making it more likely that hospitalization, when required, would be brief.

**Comprehensive Services.** Viewing community mental health as a total system, rather than a single service, suggests that the system needs a number of services to meet the needs of

a total population. The community mental health movement proposes a series of services suited to the needs of those served. The original legislation called for five required services—emergency services, outpatient services, partial hospitalization, inpatient services, and consultation-education services. Public Law 94-63 required the addition of services for children, services for the aged, screening before hospitalization, follow-up services for those who had been hospitalized, transitional housing services, alcoholism services, and drug abuse services.

**Multidisciplinary Team Approach.** The community mental health team includes psychiatrists (including child psychiatrists), clinical psychologists, psychiatric social workers, psychiatric nurses, necessary administrative help and clerical staff, and occupational and recreational therapists for inpatient and partial hospitalization programs.

**Continuity of Care.** In line with the concern about fragmentation of care and the tendency to keep patients hospitalized or unnecessarily restricted to one type of service, community mental health programs require continuity of care. This continuity of care may be provided by having a single therapist follow a given patient through emergency services, hospitalization, partial hospitalization as a transition to the community, and outpatient treatment as follow-up. It may also be provided by an exchange of information and team responsibility for the patient when different therapists, for reasons of convenience or economy, treat the patient in several different settings. Each center must provide for the free transference of clinical information, and provide a liaison between different agencies that are part of the total system of care.

**Consumer Participation.** Consumer participation suggests that a community should participate in decisions about its mental health care needs and program, instead of having them defined only by professionals. It also suggests that mental health services will be more relevant and sensitive to the needs of those serviced if the public participates. The expectation is that mental health services are more likely to be used when knowledgeable persons interpret and educate the community about their availability.

**Prevention.** One of the basic aspects of a community mental health program is a commitment to prevention (indirect services), as well as treatment (direct services). The commitment to prevention evolved from the public health model, which describes three types of prevention: primary prevention, which consists of the elimination of factors that cause the disease; secondary prevention, which is early detection and prompt treatment at the beginning of the disease process; and tertiary prevention, consisting of rehabilitation or eliminating disability after the acute phase of an illness.

**Mental Health Consultation.** Consultee-centered work focuses on the person receiving the consultation, and varies all the way from attention to or even treatment of the emotional problems of the consultee, to using knowledge about human behavior to help the consultee achieve his or her professional goals with the program and its patients. Program-centered consultation focuses on the total system or program, offering whatever assistance the mental health professional can give in regard to programs, systems, and agencies.

**Evaluation and Research.** Evaluation focuses on the total community mental health program, and is now a required activity on which federally funded centers have to spend at least 2 percent of their budgets. Evaluation refers to the process of obtaining information about the operation and its effect on persons, institutions, and communities. The program evaluation should also provide feedback to the planners and decision makers, so that the operating programs can be modified and new ones planned.

Research may focus more specifically on key issues, rather than on the total program. The problem addressed may be specific disorders or special treatment methods.

**Avoidance of Unnecessary Hospitalization.** The motivation for avoiding hospitalization is in part economic, because 24-hour hospital care is the most expensive of all services. Another reason for avoiding unnecessary hospitalization relates to the tendency of those who are hospitalized to acquire a label—mental patients—and to regress in the hospital more than in other mental health treatment settings.

**Linkages to Health and Human Services.** Community mental health centers need to develop linkages to a wide variety of human services and community support services if they are to discharge their responsibilities to a total population. These linkages include an alliance with welfare workers, clergy, family service agencies, schools, and the large group of health agencies for diagnosis, treatment, and rehabilitation of physical disorders.

## Community Psychiatry in Action

By 1978, the community mental health movement had made a major impact on mental health services and on the practice of psychiatry and the other mental health professions. As of 1976, there were 549 operating centers; an estimated 750 centers were in action in 1978.

The community mental health centers are 58 percent in urban areas, 17 percent in rural areas, and 18 percent in intercity settings; 19 percent are general hospital based, and 5 percent are private or state hospital based.

### Problems Associated with the CMHC

**Neglect of the Chronically Ill.** In 1978, the American Psychiatric Association co-sponsored a conference which made a series of recommendations of specialized services for chronically ill patients. The recommendations proposed a focus on public sensitivity and financial commitment to a system of opportunities and services. The services should include an active outreach program, medical and mental health care, functional evaluation, subsistence, an array of special living arrangements, crisis stabilization services, assistance to families, socialization programs, meaningful and feasible work opportunities, training in the skills of daily living, monitoring, and case management services.

**Accessibility and Availability for the Underserved.** In mental health, the underserved are children, the aged, rural populations, and minority groups. Quality direct services for children are often lacking, in large part because of the absence of qualified child psychiatrists, though there are now promising areas and even hard data on a number of preschool prevention programs.

Community mental health centers also neglect the elderly. As a consequence of negative attitudes toward the aged and a false belief that psychiatric conditions in the elderly are untreatable, mental health centers do not give the elderly a high priority, and so they are significantly underrepresented in terms of service delivered. Many elderly persons could be maintained in the community within their own families or with minimal supervision; instead, large numbers are relegated to nursing homes and institutional care.

Rural populations present other types of problems, predominantly because of geography and the lack of mental health professionals in thinly populated areas. Minority groups are also significantly underserved, because the professional staffs of community mental health centers have few minorities, and these few are all too often paraprofessionals.

**Governance Issues.** Although community mental health programs require the participation of the community, some have translated "participation" to mean community control or governance. In the minds of many, the community mental health centers are a grassroots response to a need, and they must be organized and operated by local citizen groups; to others, citizen participation is guaranteed by the concept of advisory groups that represent consumer and citizen interests.

The President's Commission on Mental Health in 1978 acknowledged this problem, and suggested that there should be evidence of a governance or advisory board with adequate consumer and citizen representation. It was recommended that the National Institute of Mental Health seek changes in current laws to permit differences in board and governance arrangements to properly reflect existing local circumstances.

**Financial Problems.** The funding available to community mental health centers has been small. Many programs are approved but unfunded. In 1975, federal funds accounted for 30 percent of the income of community mental health centers, the states provided 29 percent, other government funds provided 9 percent, and a variety of sources provided the remaining 32 percent. This funding has consistently been diminishing annually and has contributed to the relatively poor performance of the CMHC's.

**Staff Problems.** Community mental health centers have had a number of staffing problems, in part the consequence of a mental health personnel shortage in all disciplines, and in part the consequence of the way in which multidisciplinary mental health teams were organized. The principal staff problem has been the role of the psychiatrist. Although the number of psychiatrist's full-time equivalents for each center has been reduced by nearly 50 percent between 1970 and 1976, the number of psychologists has nearly doubled, and the full-time equivalents of social workers for each center has increased by nearly 50 percent.

**Catchment Area Problems.** The concept of the catchment area (a designated geographic area, having between 75,000 and 200,000 people) as an artificial community has produced a number of problems. Often, the catchment area does not reflect political boundaries, natural communities, and realistic geographic-political definitions. The size of the catchment area has been a problem in thinly populated and rural regions. In cities, the requirement for totally separate catchment areas ignores the realistic political requirements of government. The President's Commission on Mental Health recommended flexibility in delineating catchment area boundaries, sharing of cross-catchment area programs, and flexibility in delineating required services in a community mental health program.

**Prevention Problems.** Primary prevention was generally defined as the avoidance of the development of illness, but mental health staff members have regarded it as population-wide intervention before the onset of symptoms. Prevention was directed at persons or groups not defined as patients, and at those with mental and emotional problems not defined as illnesses. It was also directed at groups thought to be at risk, and was designed to maintain adaptive functioning, rather than to improve pathology. Its targets were institutions, as in caretaker training and program consultation, and individuals, as in developmental crisis and situational problems.

**Health and Social Service Problems.** The majority of community mental health leaders remain convinced that community mental health programs are part of the total health system. They see the need for financial support of health care services and the dangers of relying on social system services at the same time, yet are convinced of the need for close linkages with community support systems, especially for the chronically ill, and with social service groups necessary for the effective management of all mental health services. There is some contradiction in this point of view.

**Second-class Services.** A series of charges have been made about treatment, especially psychotherapy, in community mental health centers. The attraction charge is that mental health professionals cannot create clinical settings that attract the poor; even if they could, the poor would not use them for help with mental or emotional problems. The duration charge states that, even if the poor seek treatment, they receive fewer sessions than do more affluent groups. The elitism charge states that the poor receive second-class services, such as medication clinics, rather than elite services, such as individual, group, and family psychotherapy; poor are treated by nurses and social workers, rather than by psychiatrists and psychologists. The effectiveness charge states that, even if the poor seek treatment and are offered the same quantity and quality of treatment, they benefit less than do the more affluent. These charges have merit and have yet to be resolved.

**Low Profile.** Too few persons know about the resources and the services of community mental health centers. The centers have been encouraged to make their programs and services more visible and better known, and some have responded successfully. Others have been fearful of massive demands for treatment services that they could not meet. They prefer the low profile to avoid the possibility of being overwhelmed.

### Introduction to Psychiatric Health Concepts

Psychiatry is a branch of medicine and a major medical specialty. Because of this, the psychiatrist must be aware of the problems of all medicine with regard to regulatory, organizational, and reimbursement issues, which are discussed below.

### Regulation and Organization of Hospital Standards and Programs

There is a series of agencies such as the American Medical Association Council on Medical Education and the Joint Commission on Accreditation of Hospitals (JCAH) who influence the standards of hospital care and performance. In addition to city and state health rules with which hospitals must comply, the Council on Medical Education and the JCAH inspect hospitals every 2 years. However, JCAH accreditation is on a voluntary basis.

Currently, there is a trend toward monitoring all the hospitals in a community as a single health entity and community resource. That means that each unit does not have the prerogative to develop new facilities without concern for the services offered by the other hospitals in the area. See Table I for an overview of important aspects of hospital organization.

#### Professional Standards Review Organization (PSRO)

The PSRO was set up by the federal government to review and monitor the care received by patients which was paid for with government funds.

PSROs have been established by local medical associations and serve several functions: They attempt to ensure high quality care, control cost, determine maximum length of stay by patients in hospitals, and censure physicians who do not adhere to established guidelines. The PSRO is made up of doctors elected by local medical societies.

The PSRO may conduct a medical audit to retrospectively evaluate the quality of care by carefully examining charts. They may perform a utilization review to determine whether a particular admission was really indicated and if the hospital stay was longer than necessary.

#### Health Maintenance Organizations (HMO)

The HMO is a multispeciality association of physicians who provide both inpatient and outpatient care in all specialities including psychiatry. Physicians are paid a salary by the HMO and patients pay a prepayment fee for all health care services provided for a fixed period of time. Primary prevention is emphasized by HMOs of which there are about 300 in the United States at this time.

#### Health Systems Agency (HSA)

These are nonprofit organizations mandated by the federal government to promote or limit the development of health services and facilities depending on the needs of a particular area of the country. HSAs are made up of consumers. HSAs have much power in medicine. To build a new hospital, for example, the HSA must approve a certificate of need (CON); thereby, they control the availability of medical care.

### Reimbursement Programs

#### Blue Cross Association (BCA)

This is an association of over 80 independent insurance plans around the country which pay primarily for inpatient hospital services. Blue Shield pays for physician services during the patient's hospital stay. BCA is a nonprofit organization and is regulated by state insurance agencies. Psychiatric benefits are limited compared to other medical illnesses. Inpatient psychiatric care is less curtailed than outpatient psychiatric care, the latter being the most constricted.

#### Self-Pay

Persons contract with commercial insurance agencies to cover both in-hospital and out-of-hospital costs including physicians' fees. Self-pay patients pay a premium for this type of insurance which may cover most of the costs incurred.

#### Medicare (Title 18)

Medicare provides both hospital and medical insurance under the Federal Social Security Act. It applies to persons 65 or older in addition to

TABLE I
ASPECTS OF HOSPITAL ORGANIZATION*

| Criteria | Voluntary Hospital | Investor-owned Hospitals | State Mental Hospital System | Municipal Hospital System | Federal Hospital System | Special Hospital |
|---|---|---|---|---|---|---|
| Patient population | All illnesses | All illnesses, although hospital may specialize | Mental illness | All illnesses | All illnesses | 70 percent of facility must be for single diagnosis |
| Number of hospitals | 6,000 | 750 | 280 (200,00 beds nationally) | Variable per city | See below | 150 |
| Profit orientation | Nonprofit | For profit | Nonprofit | Nonprofit | Nonprofit | For profit or nonprofit |
| Ownership | Private management board | Private corporation; may be owned by MDs | State | City government | Federal government | Private or public |
| Affiliation | 1200 church-affiliated; remainder are privately owned or university sponsored | May be owned by large chains such as Hospital Corporation of America or Humana Corporation | Free-standing or affiliated with various medical schools | Voluntary teaching hospitals and medical schools | Department of Defense (190); Public Health Service, Coast Guard, Prison, Merchant Marine, Indian Health Service; Veterans Administration (129) | Optional affiliation with medical schools |
| Other | Provide bulk of care in U.S. | Increasing in importance nationally | Deinstitutionalization—number of patients has been reduced | Most physicians at municipal hospitals are employed by their affiliated medical school | V.A. Hospitals usually have affiliations with medical schools | Less regulated than other types of hospitals (see note 5) |

* *Notes.* (1) To be designated a teaching hospital, at least four types of approved residencies must be provided, and an affiliation with a medical school must be maintained. (2) As of 1982, there were 364 state-operated facilities and approximately 60,000 community facilities for the mentally retarded. (3) In 1981, there were 139 investor-owned for profit hospitals for psychiatric patients in the United States. That number is growing. The total number of psychiatric hospitals (public and private) is about 600. (4) Short-term hospitals have an average patient stay of less than 30 days; long-term, an average of longer duration. (5) Special hospitals include obstetrics and gynecology; eye, ear, nose, and throat; etc. They do not include psychiatric hospitals or substance abuse hospitals.

certain disabled persons such as the blind and those needing renal dialysis. There are two parts to Medicare: Part A covers hospital care, extended care (after care), and home health services. Part B is an option to cover physicians fees, purchased by the patient. Medicare is an insurance program with money coming from federal trust funds. Standards of Medicare are uniform throughout the United States.

### Medicaid (Title 19)

Medicaid is a program financed by both the federal and state governments which provides comprehensive medical care (including psychiatric services) to needy and low-income persons. It is an assistance rather than insurance program and each state defines the requirements for eligibility; consequently, Medicaid services vary from state to state.

### Costs of Health Care

Approximately 10 percent of the United States gross national product of approximately 300 billion dollars is spent for health care (see Fig. 1). Mental illness makes up a large proportion of that figure. In general, hospital costs and general medical care services have risen at a far greater rate than physician's fees (see Fig. 2).

### Claims Review

This method of peer review consists of the examination of claims for the reimbursement of treatment after it has been rendered. It has the disadvantage of being a decision to pay or not

pay after the treatment has been given. Both hospitals and practitioners are even more dissatisfied at being turned down for treatment already given than at being turned down for treatment that has not yet been given. However, it is administratively more realistic to do claims reviews than to establish committees for concurrent review in all areas of the United States. Insurance companies and governments have been doing claims reviews for many years. Traditionally, it has consisted of the examination of a claim by a clerk, with determination of eligibility by nonprofessionals. When a claim for psychiatric treatment payment is turned down and appealed or when a claim is for a large amount, the claim used to be reviewed by a single psychiatric consultant who was an employee of the insurance company concerned. That system resulted in idiosyncratic decisions that may or may not have reflected local quality practice. In many instances, guidelines for insurance companies were developed without any input from practicing psychiatrists. As a result, psychiatric societies are now willing to help develop criteria for claims review and have been willing to nominate committees to serve as claims reviewers (peer reviewers) for insurance plans and government systems.

The first level of claims review generally consists of a clerical examination to determine whether the bill shows the necessary administrative information and whether the claimant is, indeed, insured. There is no determination of appropriateness of care. The second level of claims review is generally done by trained per-

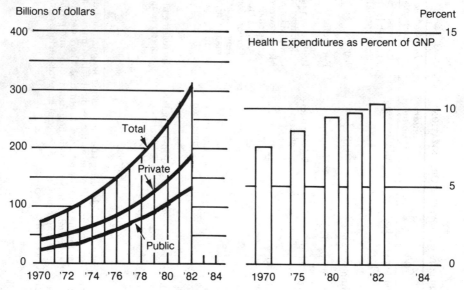

FIGURE 1.    National health expenditures: 1970 to 1982. (Source: Chart prepared by U.S. Bureau of the Census.)

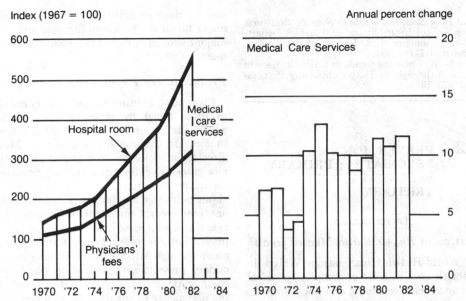

FIGURE 2.    Indexes of medical care prices: 1970 to 1982. (Source: Chart prepared by U.S. Bureau of the Census.)

sons—often nurses. Here the claims reviewer compares the treatment rendered with previously established criteria of treatment that have been agreed on as appropriate for the condition. The second-level reviewer may approve payment for the claim. If the second-level reviewer has questions or if the treatment is considered inappropriate according to the criteria, the claim is reviewed by a third-level group or a true peer review committee. Here there is a professional determination of the appropiateness of care. The peer review committee—onc or more psychiatrists review each claim—may approve or disapprove. There are levels of appeal for the practitioner who is dissatisfied with the committee determination. The appeals process often goes to a special committee of the county or state medical society.

The most extensive system of claims review has been developed by the American Psychiatric Association under a contract with CHAMPUS (Civilian Health and Medical Plans for United States Armed Forces) of the Department of Defense. A national advisory group developed criteria and procedures for the review of both inpatient and office treatment. The criteria and procedures provide for all three levels of review. Peer review committees have been established throughout the United States to function through the central office of the American Psychiatric Association. Claims are reviewed initially by clerks and then by second-level trained reviewers. They go to a committee of peers when

professional determinations about the appropriateness of treatment are needed. Only a peer review committee can deny a claim on the basis of professional necessity for that care, but clerks and second-level reviewers can deny a claim for administrative reasons.

The claims review system is a poor and inequitable one leading to clerical bureaucracy and interference in the doctor-patient relationship which may result in poor medical care.

### REFERENCES

Barton W, Sanborn C J, editors: *An Assessment of the Community Mental Health Movement.* D. C. Health, Lexington, MA, 1977.

Beigel A: The future of community mental health care. In *Current Psychiatric Therapies, 1981,* J Masserman, editor, p 357. Grune & Stratton, New York, 1981.

Berlin R M, Kales J D, Humphrey F J, Kales A: The patient care crisis in community mental health centers; a need for more psychiatric involvement. Am J Psychiatry *138:* 450, 1981.

Joint Commission on Mental Illness and Health: *Action for Mental Health.* Basic Books, New York, 1961.

Langsley D G: The community mental health center: Does it treat patients? Hospital Community Psychiatry *31:* 815, 1980.

Langsley D G: Community psychiatry. In *Comprehensive Textbook of Psychiatry,* ed 4, H I Kaplan, B J Sadock, editors, p 1878. Williams & Wilkins, Baltimore, 1985.

Langsley D G, Berlin I N, Yarvis R M: *Handbook of Community Mental Health.* Medical Examination Publishing Co., Garden City, NY, 1981.

Mollica R F: From asylum to community; the threatened disintegration of public psychiatry. N

Engl J Med *308:* 367, 1983.

*National Data Book and Guide to Sources: Statistical Abstracts of the United States,* ed. 104, U.S. Department of Commerce, U.S. Bureau of the Census, Washington, D.C., 1984.

Winslow W W: Changing trends in CMHC's: Keys to survival in the eighties. Hosp Community Psychiatry *33:* 273, 1982.

## 39.2   PREVENTION IN PSYCHIATRY; PRIMARY, SECONDARY, AND TERTIARY

### Introduction

#### Definition of Physical and Mental Health

The World Health Organization (WHO) defines health as: The state of complete physical, mental and social well being and not merely the absence of disease.

Major factors in the cause of death and illness in the United States are related to life-style, which accounts for about 70 percent of the causes of all illness, mental and physical. Obesity for example, is related to both heart disease and diabetes and a person's weight bears a direct relation to habit patterns.

The socioeconomic status of the patient also influences attitudes toward physical and mental health as illustrated in Table I.

The use of all health care services is influenced by age. For example, young adults (20 to 30 years) and persons over 65 have more illness than persons in middle adulthood. Among the elderly, chronicity of illness is a major factor, and heart disease, arthritis, and cancer are the three major chronic conditions of old age. Regardless of age, women seek health care more often than do men.

The causes of death have varied through the years, with pneumonia, tuberculosis, and gastrointestinal disease being the three leading causes of death at the beginning of the twentieth century. In 1983, the three leading causes of death were heart disease, cancer, and stroke. While psychiatric illness does not play a major

role in the mortality rate, it is probably the major factor in the morbidity rate and is also a major factor in days lost from work and employment.

### Prevention in Psychiatry

Prevention measures in psychiatry are similar to those faced by other medical specialties, which is to diminish the incidence of illness and to diminish the prevalence of illness. Measures directed at incidence aim at the prevention of new cases. Measures directed at prevalence are intended to diminish the number of persons ill at one point in time (point prevalance) or in any one year (yearly prevalence). Reducing the incidence of new cases of the disorder (primary prevention), decreasing the duration of the disorder through effective early intervention (secondary prevention), preventing the long-term complications (tertiary prevention)—all reduce the prevalence of the disorder in a population.

About 15 percent of the general population suffer from mental illness according to President Carter's Commission on Mental Health. In addition, 6 million persons are mentally retarded. Mental illness causes an economic loss of over 10 percent of the gross national product and when combined with alcoholism and drug abuse accounts for 75 billion dollars per year.

### Primary Prevention

Primary prevention is the prevention of a specific undesirable state, whether it is a state of disturbed feelings, a state of disturbed thoughts, a reaction pattern that is undesirable, a stress reaction, a formal illness, or a disease state.

#### Primary Prevention Techniques

Primary prevention techniques may be roughly classified into two broad groups. One group consists of biotechnical methods. The second group consists of psychosocial methods. Biotechnical methods emphasize such things as somatic interventions, engineering, blood tests, removal of toxic substances, and vitamin supplementation. Psychosocial methods require

TABLE I
ATTITUDES TOWARD HEALTH ISSUES

| *Lower Class* | *Upper-Middle Class* |
|---|---|
| Look for immediate solutions | More able to delay gratification |
| Negative view on life | More positive view of life |
| Low contraceptive use | High contraceptive use |
| Seek health care later | Seek health care earlier |
| Longer hospital stays | Shorter hospital stays |
| See pregnancy as time of crisis | Pregnancy seen as normal event |

changes in individual habits or life styles, group interventions, family interventions, and the development of community support systems.

**Biotechnical Interventions.** The major successes in prevention have resulted from biotechnical interventions. The dietary supplementation that led to the virtual elimination of pellagra, the serological testing and penicillin treatment that led to the sharp reduction in tertiary syphilis, the lead control programs that resulted in the reduced incidence and prevalence of lead encephalopathy—all these were related to specific biotechnical prevention methods.

Table II contains a partial listing of disorders and prevention-intervention methods that may limit the prevalence of disorders. Full implementation of all the recommended prevention measures could produce substantial savings, not only in terms of human suffering but also in terms of the cost of chronic psychiatric hospitalization and care facilities for developmental disabilities.

**Psychosocial Prevention Techniques.** The key to effective psychosocial intervention is specificity—specificity of target populations, specificity of goals and purposes, and specificity of interventions and action programs.

Psychosocial intervention techniques are intended to mitigate human misery, emotional distress, dysphoric affect, maladaptation, relational breakdown, and maladjustment. It seems unlikely that these interventions will alter the base rate of schizophrenia. Secondary and tertiary prevention programs are much more likely to affect the prevalence of this major psychosis. For purposes of prevention approaches, crisis theory, crisis intervention activities, knowledge of small-group process, experimental learning, and anticipatory guidance assume particular importance.

No community mental health center can do all the programs. The staff must select those target populations who seem to be at highest risk in their community, and for whom programming is most important.

Rarely is a psychosocial prevention-intervention program carried out in isolation from other agencies. Ultimately, interagency coordinating councils are needed to avoid duplication of effort and unpleasant competitive atmospheres.

## Secondary Prevention

Secondary prevention decreases the prevalence of psychiatric illness by shortening the course of the illness. This level of prevention is often characterized as therapeutic or curative medicine or psychiatry. Early and effective secondary intervention may reduce not only the duration but also the severity of the morbidity

and the mortality from the disorder. In general medicine, early and effective intervention in infections, neoplasms, cardiovascular disease, shock, hemorrhage, and numerous other states reduces risk, complications, duration of illness, and discomfort. No evidence indicates that psychiatric disorders respond any differently to secondary prevention. In fact, considerable evidence indicates that secondary prevention is one of the most effective techniques for lowering the prevalence of psychiatric disorders. Providers at this level are almost always psychiatrists; but psychologists, social workers, and other mental health workers are also involved.

### Utilization of Health Care Services

Rates of hospitalization for all illness increase with age and within the last decade 75 percent of adults have been in a hospital at one time or another, with women being hospitalized more often than men. Twenty-five percent of hospital costs are made up of laboratory and x-ray bills, and the remaining costs are for management, nursing, drugs, and other support services.

Physician services account for 20 percent of every health dollar spent (within or out of a hospital) and 50 percent of physician fees are covered by some form of health insurance except in the case of psychiatry. At present there is a 10 percent oversupply of hospital beds in this country which must be paid for even though they remain empty. The average general hospital stay is just over 8 days in all specialties.

### Effects of Early Intervention

**Positive Results.** Early intervention in depressive illness with a combination of tricyclic drugs and psychotherapy may decrease the duration of the illness by one-half and lower the suicide death rate. A 20 percent reduction in the point prevalence of depressive illness would be achieved if 40 percent of depressions were caught early in their course and interrupted through a good secondary-prevention program. The cost effectiveness of such a program would be difficult to match with any currently available primary-prevention technology.

Secondary prevention of phobic disorders may forestall severe constrictions in the phobic's social range of actions. As the disorder remains untreated, it becomes increasingly harder to limit. The school phobias of children can best be cured if the phobias are diagnosed early and treated by pressing the child to return to school, with a supportive environment being provided in the school.

**Toxic Responses.** Early intervention poorly

TABLE II
PSYCHIATRIC DISORDERS AND DISABILITIES POTENTIALLY PREVENTABLE THROUGH EFFECTIVE
BIOTECHNICAL INTERVENTIONS

| Disorder | Source and Use | Prevention-Intervention |
|---|---|---|
| *Poisoning* | | |
| Lead encephalopathy | Paint and environmental pollutants | No lead in paint; repaint inner city |
| Mercury poisoning | Industrial (felt hats) | Industrial control |
| Thallium poisoning | Industrial and rat poison, etc. | Poison control |
| Arsenic poisoning | Rat poison, etc. | Poison control |
| Organophosphates | Insecticides | Poison control, natural insect control |
| Carbon monoxide | Auto pollutants | Reduce pollutants |
| Manganese poisoning | Battery manufacture, etc. | Industrial control |
| Carbon disulfide | Rayon and rubber industries, etc. | Industrial control |
| *Deficiency disorders* | | |
| Wernicke's encephalopathy | Vitamin B deficiency; alcoholics | Vitamin-fortified alcohol |
| Korsakoff's psychosis | Vitamin B deficiency, alcoholics | Vitamin-fortified alcoholic beverages |
| Pellagra psychosis | Niacin deficiency | Dietary |
| Pernicious anemia madness | $B_{12}$ deficiency | $B_{12}$ shots |
| Beriberi psychosis | Thiamin deficiency | Dietary |
| Cretinism | Iodine deficiency | Iodized salt |
| *Infection* | | |
| Neurosyphilis | *Treponema pallidum* | Serological testing, treatment with penicillin |
| Sydenham's chorea | β-Hemolytic streptococcus | Treatment of strep throat |
| African sleeping sickness | Trypanosomiasis | Public health measures |
| Chagas' disease | Trypanosomiasis | Public health measures |
| *Head trauma* | | |
| Postconcussion syndrome | Auto accidents | Passive restraint system; driver education; drunken-driver prevention device; car and road safety |
| Traumatic encephalopathy | | |
| Traumatic convulsive disorder | | |
| Accident neurosis | | |
| Amnesic-confabulatory syndrome | | |
| *Medications and surgery* | | |
| Bromism | Over-the-counter prescriptions | Ban bromides |
| Barbiturate abuse | Illicit drugs and prescriptions | Decrease use and production |
| Amphetamine psychoses | Illicit drugs and diet pills | Limit use and production |
| Reserpine depression | Hypertension control | Physician education |
| Methyldopa depression | Hypertension control | Physician education |
| Levodopa toxicity | Control of parkinsonism | Physician education |
| Isoniazid confusion | Tuberculosis treatment | Physician education |
| Griseofulvin depression | Fungicide | Physician education |
| Black-patch delirium | Eye surgery, patching | Preoperative preparation |
| Postcardiotomy psychosis | Open-heart surgery | Preoperative preparation |
| *Prenatal and perinatal* | | |
| Malnutrition-related disorders | Maternal malnutrition | Adequate diet |
| Rubella-caused brain damage | Rubella | Immunization |
| Congenital syphilis | Maternal syphilis | Serological test and treatment |
| Cretinism | Hypothyroidism | Thyroid extract |
| Erythroblastomatosis fetalis | Rh incompatibility | Early diagnosis, treatment |
| *Inborn errors of metabolism* | | |
| Phenylketonuria | Error: phenylalanine metabolism | Genetic counseling; amniocentesis |
| Maple syrup urine disease | Error: decarboxylation | Urine screening |
| Galactosemia | Error: carbohydrate metabolism | Dietary control |
| *Chromosomal disorders* | | |
| Mongolism | Trisomy, mosaicism, translocation | Childbearing before late thirties, amniocentesis |
| Klinefelter's syndrome | XXY | Amniocentesis |
| Turner's syndrome | XO | Amniocentesis |
| *Genetic disorders* | | |
| Huntington's chorea | | Genetic counseling |
| Acute remittant porphyria | | Genetic counseling |

handled can produce numerous toxic responses. Inappropriate labeling of a patient in a stigma-ridden community may render recovery more difficult, not less so. Programs that triage early

without providing a treatment backup may be worse than nothing at all. The key to secondary prevention is early intervention, not merely early diagnosis. If the diagnostic system is inadequate, or if the treatment system includes dehumanizing environments, a negative effect can be expected.

**Compliance.** One of the major problems of the therapeutic tasks involved in secondary prevention is that of compliance, which refers to the patient's ability to understand the nature of his illness and to follow the physician's instructions regarding treatment. The major cause of relapse in schizophrenia is noncompliance with regard to the taking of psychotropic medication.

In general, noncompliant patients tend to come from lower socioeconomic groups. Men are more compliant than women, and patients with acute illnesses are more compliant than patients with chronic illnesses. Compliance is increased when there is a good doctor-patient relationship and if the patient is not transferred from one doctor to another at every visit.

Compliance in taking medication is decreased if more than one medication has to be taken. A single daily dose of a medication has a higher compliance rate than multiple doses.

### Tertiary Prevention

Tertiary prevention is directed at reducing the residual defect of chronic mental illness in two related ways. One way is through the prevention of the complications of the disorders. The other way is through an active program of rehabilitation. In the care of the chronically mentally ill, the two are closely interrelated.

#### Complications

The primary complication in the care of the chronically mentally ill is the social breakdown syndrome. Psychiatric patients who are kept in hospitals for long periods of time, or who experience other forms in which their social roles are markedly disrupted, develop a new social role. As patients lose their social skills, they enter a dependent patient role and eventually become permanently disabled.

#### Rehabilitation

Rehabilitation goes hand in hand with the prevention of complications. Rehabilitation is directed toward the achievement of the maximum level at which each individual patient can function. In psychiatry, it is directed at the relearning of socially appropriate adult role behaviors. Such a rehabilitation approach can minimize or mitigate the effects of the social breakdown syndrome. The main focus of rehabilitation is not on the disease, but on the residual assets that help the patient achieve a role in the community. Rehabilitation must begin at the time of the initial diagnosis and treatment planning.

#### Causes of Disabling Chronicity

**Nature of the Chronic Illnesses.** The emphasis on acute illness and cures in American medicine has resulted in deficient long-term care and humane maintenance programs for the chronically ill. A good rehabilitation program mobilizes the person's assets to work around the continuing liability of the disease process. Denying the disease process and ignoring the presence of impairment are not effective approaches to rehabilitation.

**Lack of Good Clinical Treatment.** The most common cause of disabling chronicity in communities that have modern mental health care systems is no longer the hospital-induced social breakdown syndrome. The most common cause is lack of adequate clinical treatment. Sound public health practice calls for the dissemination of the most effective intervention to the population at large. The most effective approach is the widespread use of psychiatric care and phenothiazine medication.

**Socialization into Chronic Institutional Roles.** Social breakdown syndrome and chronic institutionalization are the products of total institutions. Goffman listed five rough groupings of total institutions: (1) institutions for the care of persons who are incapable and harmless—that is, homes for the aged or the indigent; (2) institutions for persons who are both incapable of looking after themselves and potentially a threat to the community, albeit an unintended one—that is, mental hospitals and tuberculosis hospitals; (3) institutions organized to protect the community against intentional dangers—that is, prisoner-of-war camps and jails; (4) institutions established to pursue some work-like task—that is, Army barracks and boarding schools; and (5) retreats from the world—that is, monasteries and convents.

#### Care of the Long-term Chronically Ill Patient

There are multiple levels of care for patients with chronic impairments. When self-care rehabilitation is not yet possible, it is important to provide long-term facilities that do not produce a social breakdown syndrome.

What is needed is a designed chronic institution in which constant clinical care is possible, but complication-inducing total institution features are minimized. About 30 percent of all hospital beds in this country are occupied by the mentally ill.

**Transitional Housing.** Transitional housing can be developed within two broad categories. In one category the patient continues to receive high-intensity clinical care. Psychiatrists and other mental health professionals are readily available within the housing environment. The other category is premised on professional consultation to the facility; physician care is separate from the facility.

**Transitional Work Arrangements.** Because work is reasonably structured, many chronic schizophrenic patients are able to maintain jobs, even when they cannot maintain effective interpersonal relationships. Researchers have found that even the sickest patients in their labor union project could retain their jobs with the help of union committeemen and the labor union mental health clinic.

## Costs of Health Service

Costs of all types of health care, including the care of the mentally ill, continue to rise with the federal and state governments picking up almost 50 percent of all health care costs.

Approximately 85 percent of persons have some form of health insurance, and 75 percent of hospital costs for most patients are covered by health insurance. Only 50 percent of physician services, however, are covered by insurance.

## Health Manpower

There are approximately 30,000 psychiatrists among the 450,000 physicians in the United States and although this number is adequate, there is a problem in their distribution. High physician-patient ratios exist in the Northeast and California; but low concentrations exist in the Southern and Mountain States. Twenty percent of all physicians licensed to practice in the United States are graduates of a foreign medical school. Psychiatrists tend to be concentrated in major urban areas.

Primary care physicians number about 35 percent of all doctors and are usually defined as general practitioners, family practitioners, internists, and pediatricians.

Because primary care has been defined as a type of medical care delivery which emphasizes first contact care and assumes ongoing responsibility for the patient in both health maintenance and therapy of illness, many believe that psychiatry should also be classified as a primary care specialty. The latter is not currently the case.

When projections are made through the 1990s, there are shortages, balances, and surpluses in the number of physicians in various specialties. For example, by 1990 it is estimated that 48,000 psychiatrists will be needed in the United States, but there will only be 38,000 trained. The only other fields in which there will be a shortage include emergency medicine and preventive medicine. Other specialties will be in surplus, e.g., 24,000 surgeons will be needed in 1990, and there will be 35,000 available. Other fields in which there will be a similar surplus are neurology, ophthalmology, obstetrics and gynecology, internal medicine, and neurosurgery.

Fields in which supply will equal demand in 1990 include dermatology, family practice, otolaryngology, and pediatrics.

Physician services tend to be underutilized, with 40 percent of the population not seeing a physician at all in a given year. Of the 60 percent who do see a physician, most are either very young or old, or women, and they average about 5 visits per year.

## REFERENCES

Bachrach L L: Model programs for chronic mental patients. Psychiatry *137:* 1023, 1980.
Berlin I N: Prevention in community mental health. In *Handbook of Community Mental Health,* D G Langsley, I N Berlin, R M Yarvis, editors, p 121. Medical Examination Publishing Co., Garden City, NY, 1981.
Bond G R: An economic analysis of psychosocial rehabilitation. Hosp Community Psychiatry *35:* 356, 1984.
Caplan G: *Principles of Preventive Psychiatry.* Basic Books, New York, 1964.
Chafetz L, Goldman H H, Taube C: Deinstitutionalization in the United States. Int J Ment Health *11:* 48, 1983.
Davis J A: *Education for Positive Mental Health: A Review of Existing Research and Recommendations for Future Studies.* Aldine Publishing Co., Chicago, 1965.
Klein D C, Goldston S E: *Primary Prevention: An Ideal Whose Time Has Come.* U.S. Government Printing Office, Washington, DC, 1977.
Langsley D G: The community health center: Does it treat patients? Hosp Community Psychiatry *31:* 815, 1980.
Langsley D G: Prevention in psychiatry: Primary, secondary, and tertiary. In *Comprehensive Textbook of Psychiatry,* ed 4, H I Kaplan, B J Sadock, editors, p 1885. Williams & Wilkins, Baltimore, 1985.
Langsley D G, Machotka P, Flomenhaft K: Avoiding mental hospitalization: A Follow-up study. Am J Psychiatry *127:* 1391, 1971.
Rutter M: Prevention of children's psychosocial disorders: Myth and substance. Pediatrics *70:* 883, 1982.
Talbott J A, editor: *The Chronic Mentally Ill: Treatment, Programs, Systems.* Human Sciences Press, New York, 1981.

# 40

# Geriatric Psychiatry

## Introduction

Psychological changes accompany the passing of years. These changes include well known features like slowness of thinking, mild nonprogressive impairment of recent memory, reduction of surgency of enthusiasm, an increase in cautiousness, changes in sleep patterns with a tendency to daytime naps, and a relative libidinal shift from genitality to the alimentary tract and interior of the body.

## Definition

Agedness, if one may use this term as denoting the psychopathology of and attending to the later period of life, is a crisis in slow motion. Most changes are gradual and progressive. From ages 30 to 40, the change in nerve conduction velocity and cardiac output, for example, are quantitatively the same as from ages 60 to 70. In terms of the theory of aging, the body dies a little every day.

Old age may be considered as yet another of the developmental phases in the life-span of the person, developmental in the sense that it is not static; the defensive responses to the deficits, physical and psychosocial, may be both old and new. Every phase in the human life cycle has specific traumatic elements that are germane and unique to that particular age group. The aged, however, have accumulated multiple scarring through their exposure to all the sources of human suffering.

The elderly tend to become defined in terms of their separateness from the mainstream of humanity, rather than in terms of their continuity. By its very nature, old age is visible, thus easily labeled into a diagnostic entity for which remedies may be denied and neglect begun.

## Diagnosis

Psychiatric diagnosis in the elderly, in order to be precise, may not be at all simple. Psychiatric illnesses may manifest themselves by physical symptoms and signs, such as loss of weight, constipation, dry mouth, changes in heart rate and blood pressure, and tremors. Disorders of awareness, mood, perception, thinking, and thought content are usually present and prominent.

### Medical Assessment

A number of common and important physical conditions should be kept in mind when examining an elderly psychiatric patient, because these conditions are known to cause mental symptoms. Toxins of bacterial and metabolic origins are common in old age. Bacterial toxins usually originate in occult or inconspicuous foci of infection, such as suspected pneumonic conditions and urinary infections. The commonest metabolic intoxication causing mental symptoms in the aged is uremia; mild diabetes, hepatic failure, and gout may easily be missed as causative agents. Alcohol and drug misuse cause many mental disturbances in late life, but these abuses, with their characteristic effects, are easily determined by the history taking.

Cerebral anoxia, resulting from cardiac insufficiency or emphysema, or both, often precipitates mental symptoms in old people. Anoxic confusion may follow surgery, a cardiac infarct, gastrointestinal bleeding, or occlusion or stenosis of the carotid arteries. Nutritional deficiencies may not only be symptomatic of emotional illness, but also cause mental symptoms. Vitamin deficiencies may occur, but they are not frequent. All in all, various deficiencies need to be taken into consideration in the physical assessment of the aged.

### Mental Assessment

In obtaining a psychiatric history from the elderly, the psychiatrist should stress a number of components particularly germane to this age group.

Overt behavior may manifest itself in the patient's motor activity, his walk, his expressive movements, and the form of his talk. It can be observed by the examining physician, and the history can be obtained from meaningful others.

Mood disorder may be inferred from the patient's movements. But one must be aware of the presence of euphoria, sadness, despair, anxiety, tension, loss of feelings, and a paucity of ideation. The patient often complains of somatic sensations that may, in a sense, be substitutes for an expression of emotional state.

The evaluation of the mental content should be extensive and detailed. One should obtain the patient's own description of his feelings and account of the onset.

Abnormalities of cognitive functioning may be the result of many depressive or schizophrenic disturbances, but they are most often due to some cerebral dysfunctioning or deterioration. In many instances, intellectual difficulties are not obvious. A searching evaluation is necessary.

## Psychiatric Conditions

Mental disorders in old age are quite common. The causes are multiple, complex, and complicated by the frequent presence of organic brain involvement.

### Organic Mental Disorders

The organic mental disorders are mental states associated with impairment in function or the death of brain tissues. The disorders manifest distinct features: disorientation for time, place, and persons; impairment of intellectual functioning; disturbances and impairment of memory; impairment of judgment; defects in comprehension or grasp; evidence of impaired immediate recall; and emotional lability.

Alzheimer's disease patients constitute 50 percent of the 1.3 million people in nursing homes. It is a common type of senile brain disorder, affecting millions of people throughout the world, and is associated with more than 100,000 deaths in the United States each year. Manifesting symptoms of the above-mentioned organic mental disorders, the confusion and memory disturbances lead to total incapacity. The most serious symptom of Alzheimer's disease closely correlates with the accumulation within neuronal cells of abnormal protein structures known as neurofibrillary tangles that are destroyed and replaced by neuritic plaques which are the replacement of the dead nerve cell. Recently, scientists have analyzed nerve cells in long-frozen brains and studied their abnormal molecular structure. They have demonstrated large DNA molecules in the nuclei of nerve cells that produce RNA which in turn controls the cell metabolism and ability to manufacture new protein, a process interfered with in Alzheimer's disease. This latter neuro-biochemical defect leads to markedly diminished production of new protein in cells damaged by Alzheimer's disease and produces the symptoms of the disorder.

The damage is confined to the hippocampus according to most recent evidence. Experimental destruction of the hippocampus has been linked to a profound and lasting memory impairment that affects all types of learning. Alzheimer's disease and the organic mental disorders are discussed in Chapter 16 in this textbook.

A great variety of drugs used in medicine can cause psychiatric symptoms in all classes of patients—but especially among the elderly. These symptoms may result if the drug is prescribed in too large a dose, if the patient is particularly sensitive to the medication, or if the user does not follow instructions for its use. Common symptoms include confusion, delirium, disorientation, and depression. A schizophrenia-like picture may appear if the patient begins to hallucinate or becomes paranoid.

Recent reports by several investigators have implicated certain drugs as producing psychiatric symptoms in the elderly. These symptoms are most often depression, agitation, and delirium. Some of the medications involved include the following: transdermal scopolamine; eye drops containing atropine; cimetidine (Tagamet); ibuprofen (Motrin, Advil); indomethacin (Indocin); levodopa (Dopar); timolol (Timoptic); trazodone (Desyrel) and rantidine (Zantac).

Psychiatric symptoms usually cease after the drug is withdrawn, but the clinician must also be aware that withdrawal reactions to a drug may occur, especially if the drug is stopped abruptly.

For a more extensive list of drugs and classes of drugs that can produce specific mental symptoms the reader is referred to Table XXVIII on page 300 in Chapter 16 on organic mental disorders.

### Schizophrenic Disorders

Much confusion exists about the late-appearing schizophrenias in the elderly. This confusion is due to the fact that the relation of paraphrenic, paranoid, and schizophrenic disorders has been disputed. No view, at the present time, commands general acceptance. Late paraphrenia is used by European authors for those patients with a paranoid symptom complex in which signs of organic dementia or sustained confusion are absent. Delusional and hallucinatory symptoms do not seem to be due to major affective disorders.

On the whole, paranoid symptoms seem to be

a defense against the gradual loss of mastery that the patients experience. Thus, elderly men, especially those with prostatism or postoperative conditions, express delusions about their wives' infidelity. Women often complain about being spied on, subjected to stimulation by concealed electrical appliances, or poisoned by fumes. The symptoms represent face-saving devices against the gradual loss of control and the fear that is experienced. Implicit within all of them is the cry for help.

Aged schizophrenics respond quite well to the phenothiazines; however, as in all medication for the elderly, it should be judiciously administered. One should begin with small doses and gradually work up to tolerance of the individual patient, remembering all the time that the metabolism and the detoxifying aspects of the organism are not as adequately functional in the elderly as in the younger schizophrenic.

Schizophrenic and paranoid symptoms in the elderly almost always respond to phenothiazine medications. Chlorpromazine or thioridazine, beginning with 10 mg three times a day and working up to 50 mg four times a day, may be sufficient to reduce excitation, restlessness, and agitation.

### Affective Disorders

Depressions are unusually common in later life. Late-onset depressives, in comparison with early-onset depressives, had better adjusted personalities emotionally, socially, and psychosexually. The majority of first depressive attacks, especially severe attacks, appear in the second half of life. The highest first incidence occurs between 55 and 65 in men, and between 50 and 60 in women. Regardless of the presence of predominantly neurotic or psychotic symptoms, the onset follows closely the occurrence of some traumatic event. These precipitating events can all be classified as various kinds of loss, such as bereavement, the moving away of children, loss of status, retirement from a job, threatened loss through physical illness, and the illness of the spouse. The precipitants occur more frequently in late-onset depression than in early-onset depression.

The following differential points are important in distinguishing an affective depressive disorder from depression associated with an organic mental disorder.

1. In the history, the depressed patient does not usually show evidences of memory loss or disorientation, nor is there habit deterioration, such as incontinence, self-exposure, or masturbation.

2. In the mental status examination, the de-pressed patient does remain oriented, if one can only make contact with him, in contrast to the patient with chronic organic mental disorder.

3. In the depressed patient, the mood disturbance is primary and is often accompanied by irritability and hostility. The depressed patient rejects questions with "I don't know!" or "Leave me alone!" in contrast to the organically ill patient, who makes some attempt to respond to questions, even though his replies may be irrelevant, confabulatory, or nonsensical.

4. The depressed patient ordinarily does not show signs of a clear neurological deficit or abnormal primitive reflexes, as may the patient with an organic disorder.

5. In general, the depressed patient tends to have a better integrated electroencephalogram, with preservation of basic rhythms.

6. The depressed patient may respond to a therapeutic trial of antidepressant medication; the organically ill patient is likely to react with an increase of confusion because of the central anticholinergic effect.

7. Psychological testing may be helpful in difficult cases. The Bender (Visual-Motor) Gestalt Test, the Wechsler Adult Intelligence Scale, and the Weschsler Memory Scale may all be used.

Antidepressant drugs, particularly the tricyclics, are useful in the treatment of depressive disorders. Those cases resistant to drugs may benefit from a course of electroconvulsive therapy.

Amitriptyline hydrochloride or imipramine hydrochloride should be started with 10 mg three times a day and gradually increased to 150 mg a day. A useful procedure is to provide the largest dose at night—that is, 75 mg before bedtime and smaller doses during the day. This procedure allows for better rest at night and greater alertness during the day.

**Manic and Hypomanic Disorders.** These disorders are less frequent than are depressions. Nevertheless, they may make an appearance in late life. The patient and his family may fail to recognize the hypomanic phase of a bipolar disorder. It may be ascribed to the aggressiveness, overactivity, and poor judgment of a senile brain. It usually follows a depressive disorder, which may have been so brief as to have escaped the attention of those about the patient. Hostile or paranoid behavior is usually present. The response to treatment is usually good. Lithium has been used successfully in these conditions in the elderly.

**Neuroses.** There is a widespread belief to the effect that most neuroses and personality disorders improve with increasing age. Certainly, old people are less often referred by their physicians and their families to psychiatrists or clinics. Community mental health centers report that the elderly make up only a small percentage of their patient load.

Nevertheless, the neuroses occupy a conspicuous place in the disorders of later life. The incidence of neuroses is far greater than that of the psychoses, yet little attention is being paid to them because, in the neuroses, there is no total break with reality.

**Hypochondriasis.** Hypochondriasis is the inordinate preoccupation with one's bodily functions, and it is an especially common disorder in the aged.

Hypochondriacal overconcern is often mitigated by the reeducation in the range of activities permitted by one's own physical limitations, and by conventions in certain socioeconomic groups that accept an excessive concern with bodily functions as normal behavior. However, with fewer worthwhile things than in the past to hold the attention and to divert one from self-concern, it becomes easier to notice and to talk about minor ailments and accidents. In general, the older a person grows, the more experience he has had with illness, operations, and accidents, whether his own or those of other people, and the easier it is for him to feel himself to be ill or in danger. Then too, bodily concern helps to save face when one is beset by failures. "I am ill and, therefore, cannot . . . " is a rationalization that is more universally acceptable than the truthful but prestige-shattering "I cannot."

**Anxiety Disorders.** Anxiety disorders are not entirely new experiences for old people. In all probability, they experienced similar reactions, perhaps rather frequently, whenever their security was threatened, or whenever they faced emotional deprivation. Since insecurity and realistic anxiety-producing situations are common in later life, anxiety states can easily arise.

**Obsessive-Compulsive Disorders.** Obsessive-compulsive disorders and patterns in later life are similar to those occurring in earlier life. The compulsive person can be recognized by his overconscientiousness, perfectionism, orderliness, overattention to details, and doubts about himself and his adequacy. Some of these character traits may be considered praiseworthy, but they can readily become symptoms that undermine the patient's efficiency and immobilize him. Such symptoms may take the form of excessive cleanliness and orderliness, and inflexible rituals to guard against mistakes, danger, or evil thoughts. There may be endless counting; the compulsion to do certain things over and over again—checking and rechecking of gas jets,

locks, or faucets—rituals in food, dress, excretion, and evacuation; and excessive washing of hands.

Any attempt to stop these compulsive acts may arouse acute and intolerable anxiety. These symptoms constitute an effort on the part of the patient to ward off complete disintegration. Therapy, therefore, should be directed at the environment and not at the symptoms themselves.

**Hysterical Neuroses.** Such neuroses are not common in later years. The classical hysterical picture of the giving up of the function of a bodily part—as in hysterical paralysis, blindness, or deafness—so that the rest of the organism can continue to function unimpaired is relatively rare in the elderly. What one does see is an exaggeration of minor physical symptoms.

**Sleep Disturbances.** Contrary to the popular myth, elderly persons need as much if not more sleep than they did in their earlier mature years. However, complaints about sleeplessness are common. To some extent, these complaints can be traced to sleep disturbances, rather than to sleeplessness. The sleep disturbances may be due to the need for more frequent visits to the bathroom, with resulting problems in again falling asleep. Furthermore, many of the elderly—retired, unemployed, not active, and noninvolved—succumb to the practice of taking catnaps during their waking hours, a habit that may interfere with what they describe as a good night's sleep.

When insomnia does occur and is unaccompanied by delirium or a psychotic reaction, it usually responds to standard hypnotics. When insomnia is accompanied by a psychotic or depressive reaction, phenothiazine or tricyclic medication often induces sleep.

Insomnia may also be treated with a bedtime dose of benzodiazapene medication such as diazepam (Valium) or triazolam (Halcion).

## Therapy

### Psychotherapy

Remedial measures for most difficulties can be gratifying. One must make due allowances for the reduced vigor, agility, and learning capacity of the elderly patient. Beyond that, therapy can be conducted along the lines of therapy at any age level.

The type of therapy to be used in treating the older patient depends on a number of factors. First of all, one should assess the physical state of the patient in order to determine how much the aging organism will be able to take. Second, one must evaluate the patient's suitability for therapy from the viewpoint of his earlier adaptation and maladjustments, his capacity for establishing a workable relation with the therapist, and the degree to which these characteristics are modifiable. And, one must determine whether the presenting symptoms are something new in life of the patient, or a continuation of a long-existing neurotic personality structure. Obviously, all these determinations require the services of a trained psychiatrist. It is the psychiatrist's responsibility to decide what type of treatment is to be instituted, and who is to do the therapy.

The over-all treatment goals with the geriatric patient are to maximize his mental, physical, and social capacities. Remotivation techniques challenge the patient's desire to withdraw from life or to die. He is encouraged to establish new social relations and reestablish old ones, and to develop and redevelop former interests in church, recreation, games, and household activities in close proximity with other people. He is encouraged to engage in mutual helping relations, and to take an active interest in the lives of others.

*Pharmacotherapy*

The following principles are useful guidelines regarding the use of psychotropic drugs for the elderly.

Before prescribing a psychotropic drug, the physician should perform a comprehensive evaluation that includes a review of the patient's medical and psychiatric history, current stress factors, use of prescribed and over-the-counter medications, mental status and physical examination results, and other test results as indicated. It is especially useful to have the elderly patient or his family bring to the physician all currently used medications because multiple drug usage may be contributing to his symptoms. If the patient is taking psychotropic drugs at the time of the comprehensive evaluation, it is helpful, whenever possible, to discontinue those medications and to reevaluate him during a drug-free baseline period. The psychotropic drugs, alone or in combination with other drugs, may be contributing to his symptoms.

The comprehensive evaluation may reveal a recent stress, such as a death in the family, that may account for a change in the patient's behavior. The patient's symptoms may, therefore, respond better to environmental support or psychotherapy, than to a major tranquilizer.

Most psychotropic drugs should be given in equally divided doses 3 or 4 times over a 24-hour period, because elderly patients may be intolerant of a sudden rise in drug blood level resulting

from one large daily dose. There should be careful monitoring for changes in blood pressure, pulse rate, and other side effects. For patients with insomnia, however, giving the major portion of a tranquilizer or antidepressant at bedtime takes advantage of its sedating and soporific effect. Liquid preparations are useful for elderly patients who cannot or who refuse to swallow tablets.

The patient should be reassessed at frequent intervals to determine the need for maintenance medication, changes in dosage, and the development of side effects. An antiparkinsonian drug to counteract the extrapyramidal side effects of a major tranquilizer should be used only as needed and not prophylactically; it may further aggravate the anticholinergic side effects of the major tranquilizer and other medications. If an antiparkinsonian drug is used, it should be discontinued on a trial basis after 4 to 6 weeks, since only 18 to 20 percent of patients whose antiparkinsonian drug is discontinued have a recurrence of the extrapyramidal side effects. If the extrapyramidal side effects are mild, decreasing the dosage of the neuroleptic may circumvent the need for an antiparkinsonian drug.

If a major tranquilizer is indicated for such symptoms as agitation, delusions, and hallucinations, it is best to choose a drug that is least likely to further aggravate concurrent medical problems. For example, an elderly psychotic patient whose cardiovascular system is impaired may be particularly sensitive to the hypotensive side effect of a phenothiazine drug, such as chlorpromazine. Haloperidol, because it produces less hypotension and sedation than a phenothiazine drug, may be preferable for the patient. A phenothiazine, rather than haloperidol, is preferable for the elderly patient who has difficulty in motor coordination, because haloperidol produces more extrapyramidal side effects than does a phenothiazine.

The elderly person, particularly if he has an organic brain disease, is especially susceptible to the side effects of the major tranquilizers. Two side effects merit discussion here. The first, tardive dyskinesia, is characterized by disfiguring and involuntary buccal and lingual masticatory movements. Akathisia, choreiform body movements, and rhythmic extension and flexion movements of the fingers may also be present. Examination of the patient's protruded tongue for fine tremors and vermicular movements is a useful diagnostic procedure.

The second side effect of psychotropic drugs is a toxic confusional state, resulting from the anticholinergic properties of a single drug or a combination of psychotropic drugs, such as a neuroleptic, an antiparkinsonian drug, and a tricyclic antidepressant. Also referred to as the central anticholinergic syndrome, it is characterized by a marked disturbance in short-term memory, impaired attention, disorientation, anxiety, visual and auditory hallucinations, increased psychotic thinking, and peripheral anticholinergic side effects. The syndrome is sometimes difficult to recognize, particularly in patients who are psychotic, confused, and agitated before they develop the side effect. The onset may be signaled by a worsening of the preexisting psychotic symptoms. The syndrome may be incorrectly attributed to a worsening of the psychosis, which leads the physician to increase the medication, resulting in a predictable increase of the symptoms. The anticholinergic properties of the antiparkinsonian agent may be a major causative factor. Since many elderly patients receiving a neuroleptic and an antiparkinsonian drug may no longer require the antiparkinsonian drug, the most efficacious treatment may be to discontinue the antiparkinsonian drug, or to reduce or discontinue the neuroleptic or both. The confusional state usually clears within 1 or 2 days after discontinuation of the drug or drugs.

The elderly patient with mild to moderate anxiety may be a candidate for a mild tranquilizer. The effective dosage is usually less than in other adult patients. Chlordiazepoxide or diazepam, in doses of 5 or 10 mg, two or three times a day, is often effective. A mild tranquilizer can also be used at bedtime for its hypnotic effect. Compared with the barbiturates, the minor tranquilizers have a higher ratio of therapeutic effectiveness to side effects and are considered safer. However, the minor tranquilizers, although to a lesser extent than the barbiturates, can also be addictive and can produce paradoxical reactions characterized by confusion, disorientation, excitement, and the exacerbation of psychiatric symptoms.

Depression is the most common psychiatric disorder of the elderly. Elderly white men have the highest suicide rate of any group. Depressions are fairly common among the elderly and are generally responsive to psychotherapy. The tricyclic antidepressants, such as amitriptyline and imipramine, can be used in initial doses of 50 to 75 mg a day, and be gradually increased according to patient response and the development of side effects. Doxepin is believed to be the safest tricyclic antidepressant to use in patients with heart disease because it is the least cardiotoxic. Careful cardiac monitoring is, nevertheless, mandatory. The tricyclic antidepressants, like other psychotropic drugs, have more side effects in old patients than in younger patients. The side effects include anticholinergic side effects: exacerbation of psychotic symptoms, extrapyramidal symptoms, and tremors; the central anticholinergic syndrome; and cardiotoxicity. Elderly patients show considerable variability with regard to the optimal dosage and the development of side effects. Patients unresponsive to one tricyclic antidepressant may respond to another. If a patient is still significantly depressed, despite intensive psychotherapy and a trial on one or more antidepressants, hospitalization should be considered. In the hospital, a monoamine oxidase inhibitor, such as phenelzine, or electroconvulsive therapy may be considered.

## REFERENCES

Bergener M: *Geropsychiatric Diagnostics Treatment: Multidimensional Approaches.* Springer Publishers, New York, 1983.

Birren J E, Sloan R B, editors: *Handbook of Mental Health and Aging.* Prentice Hall, Englewood Cliffs, NJ, 1980.

Butler R N: Geriatric psychiatry. In *Comprehensive Textbook of Psychiatry,* ed 4, H I Kaplan, B J Sadock, editors, p 1953. Williams & Wilkins, Baltimore, 1985.

Butler R N, Lewis M I: *Aging and Mental Health,* ed 3. C. V. Mosby, St. Louis, 1982.

Costa P T Jr, McCrae R R, Arenberg D: Enduring dispositions in adult males. J Pers Soc Psychol *38:* 793, 1980.

Katzman R, Terry R D, Bick K L, editors: *Alzheimer's Disease: Senile Dementia and Related Disorders.* Raven Press, New York, 1978.

Lewis M I, Butler R N: Life review therapy: Putting memories to work in individual and group psychotherapy. Geriatrics *29:* 165, 1974.

Popkin M K, Mackenize T B, Callies A L: Psychiatric consultation to geriatric medically ill inpatients in a University Hospital. Arch Gen Psychiatry *41:* 703, 1984.

Shanas E, Sussman B M, editors: *Family, Bureaucracy, and the Elderly.* Duke University Press, Durham, NC, 1977.

# 41

# Forensic Psychiatry

## Introduction

The intermix of law and psychiatry, called forensic psychiatry, includes problems of credibility of witnesses, culpability of accused persons, competency to make a will, contract, or to take care of one's self or one's property, or to stand trial, compensation of injured persons, and custody of children.

Other notable areas involve assisting in the process of jury selection and preparing presentencing evaluations for probationary status. In addition, the issue of professional negligence, or malpractice, has become an important concern for psychiatrists and other physicians.

## The Judicial Process

Before considering the specific issues that arise with respect to psychiatry and the law, it is helpful to review the rules of procedure and evidence that apply to all matters in the judicial system.

First, the legal process is adversarial, not cooperative, in contrast to medicine. Under the adversary system each side is expected to put its best foot forward, with the judge or jury deciding between them on the basis of the evidence offered. The issues are polarized. In effect, an attorney is a salesman selling a case. Likewise, once an expert decides to engage himself in the undertaking, he, too, is a proponent of a cause, although he may couch his language in an air of neutrality. An attorney puts an expert or other witness on the stand only if he will represent the interest of his client.

The rules of evidence are, generally speaking, rules of exclusion. An objection can be made either as to the form in which the question is asked, or as to the substance of the evidence sought to be elicited. A witness is considered to belong to one side or the other. Hence, an attorney may ordinarily not ask leading questions—questions that suggest the answer desired—of a person he calls as a witness, but the opposing attorney on cross-examination may ask leading questions, since the witness is assumed to be unfriendly. Thus, in a cross-examination of a psychiatrist, the cross-examiner usually tries to impugn the psychiatric method of gathering information and forming conclusions.

## The Psychiatrist in Court

The most common role of the psychiatrist in court proceedings is that of an expert, a medical specialist on mental disorders. He may be asked to testify on issues of competency, testamentary capacity, diagnosis, treatment, or criminal responsibility.

### The Psychiatrist as Expert Witness

**Opinion Witness versus Fact Witness.** According to the so-called opinion exclusion rule, it is the responsibility of the judge or jury to determine the facts of a case, to form opinions, and to thus arrive at a verdict. The function of the ordinary witness is therefore restricted to the statement of the facts, not opinions. The witness is to present only his sensory impressions; the fact finder draws any necessary inference from them to form his own opinion as to the legal consequences of the acts perceived.

On the other hand, if scientific, technical, or other specialized knowledge will assist the trier of fact to understand the evidence or to determine a fact in issue, a witness qualified as an expert by knowledge, skill, experience, training, or education may give opinion testimony in his area of expertise. The opinion may embrace an ultimate issue to be decided by the trier of fact. When psychiatrists testify, they usually do so as experts, although they may also be summoned as fact witnesses.

When a psychiatric expert testifies, he should present his information in three clearly distinguishable portions. First, he should present and discuss his psychological theories as they relate to the legal question at hand. Second, he should describe his data base totally, including such things as exact quotations of things the patient has said, the information about him that has been revealed in documents, and data obtained from his family and significant persons who

887

know him. Third, the diagnostic and legal inferences drawn in relation to the issue at trial should stand clearly apart, so that their logic may be tested thoroughly and without confusion by the fact finders.

During the pretrial conferences with counsel, the psychiatrist should help him prepare to deal with the opposition expert. In addition, the confusion of seemingly disparate expert views can be diminished by taking steps to have them join in their examination and report-writing process.

On direct examination, counsel asks the expert to present the basis of his opinion so that it is convincing. Conclusive labels standing alone are not persuasive, even if from the lips of a highly touted expert.

The trial court may appoint its own neutral expert witnesses, and can reveal to the jury the fact of their appointment, thereby questioning the witnesses' objectivity. Incidentally, an expert need not accept the court's appointment. Should he consent, he may be compelled to testify by any party to the proceeding or called to the stand by the judge himself. Unlike the situation when he is serving one side or the other, the report of the court-appointed expert goes to both parties.

**Hearsay.** The law of evidence bars hearsay—that is, an out-of-court statement offered to prove the truth of the matter asserted.

But there are exceptions to the hearsay rule. One such exception allows a treating physician to repeat a patient's statement to him about the patient's medical history or symptoms. But conventional doctrine has excluded from the exception, as not within its guarantee of truthfulness, statements made to a physician who is consulted solely for the purpose of enabling him to testify as an expert witness.

Another exception to the bar on hearsay covers records kept in the course of a regularly conducted business activity. However, the Federal Rules of Evidence and similar rules adopted in many states specifically include diagnoses, opinions, acts, events, and conditions as proper subjects of admissible entries. Thus, an evaluation report on a disability claimant may be offered in evidence without the examiner's appearing at the hearing.

**Character Evidence.** A basic principle in law is that evidence of a person's character is irrelevant to the merits of a case.

The rationale is that in the ordinary case, be it civil or criminal, character evidence has but a remote bearing as to whether or not the act in question has been committed.

What the law on character testimony bars at one door, however, it invites through another.

What remains of the character evidence exclusion rule is largely consumed by exceptions that shift the orientation from act to person, requiring an evaluation of the whole person viewed as a social being. Character evidence is admissible not only when character is an issue—for example, in actions for defamation, child custody, and the negligent entrustment of a vehicle—but also for the purpose of suggesting an inference that, on the occasion in question, the person acted consistently with his character.

Evidence of character may also be offered for the ascertainment of damages in personal injury or wrongful death actions. Under some wrongful death statutes, evidence may be received to show the nature and the quality of the relationship that had existed between the plaintiff and the decedent and to show the decedent's moral character.

In criminal cases, the character of the accused often comes to the attention of the attorney for consideration in plea bargaining, and may be considered by the judge in a presentencing or probation report. Ironically, testimony that may have been inadmissible at the trial may find its way into a presentencing report.

**Evaluation of Credibility of Witnesses.** It is within the discretion of the trial judge whether a psychiatric examination requested by one of the parties to the action should be granted. Before ordering such an examination, the trial judge requires a substantial showing that the examination is necessary to determine the merits of the case properly and that the imposition on or inconvenience to the witness does not outweigh the value of the examination. Many courts limit psychiatric examination to complaining witnesses in rape and other sex offense cases, in which corroborative proof is nearly always circumstantial. In incest cases, for example, the father and the daughter may jointly deny the incest that the mother persistently alleges; the father may steadfastly deny the act, and in some cases, the mother may support his denial; or, after accusing her father, the daughter may retract the accusation. Psychiatrists say that only a thorough psychiatric examination of the family can eliminate such confusion. Recognizing that false sex charges may stem from the psychic complexes of a victim who appears normal to the layman, courts have permitted psychiatrists to expose mental defects, hysteria, and pathological lying in complaining witnesses. The liberal attitude in the area is probably due to the gravity of the charge, to the general lack of corroborating evidence, and perhaps to a popular feeling that sex is peculiarly within the ken of psychiatrists.

**Testimonial Privilege.** Testimonial privilege is the right to maintain secrecy or confidentiality in the face of a subpoena. The privilege belongs to the patient, not to the physician, and it is waivable by the patient. Currently, 38 of the 50 states have statutes providing some kind of physician-patient privilege. Psychiatrists, licensed in the practice of medicine, fall under the medical privilege, but they have come to find that it is so riddled with qualifications that it is practically meaningless. In purely federal cases, there is no psychotherapist-patient privilege. Moreover, the privilege does not exist at all in military courts, regardless of whether the physician is military or civilian, or whether the privilege is recognized in the state where the court-martial is sitting. The exceptions to the privilege, often viewed as implied waivers, are numerous. In the most common exception, the patient is said to waive the privilege by injecting his condition into the litigation, making his condition an element of his claim or defense. Another exception involves proceedings for hospitalization, in which the interests of both patient and public are said to call for a departure from confidentiality. Yet another exception is made in child custody and child protection proceedings, out of regard for the best interests of the child. Furthermore, the privilege does not apply in actions between a therapist and a patient. Thus, in a fee dispute or a malpractice claim, the complainant's lawyer can obtain the therapists's records necessary to the resolution of the dispute.

In the last analysis, the confidentiality of a physician-patient or psychotherapist-patient communication is protected from disclosure in a courtroom only by showing that the communication would have no relevancy or materiality to the issues in the case.

## Confidentiality

A long-held premise of medical ethics binds the physician to hold secret all information given him by a patient. This obligation is what is meant by confidentiality. Nevertheless, there are innumerable instances where the psychiatrist may be asked to divulge information imparted by the patient. Although it is a court demand for information that worries psychiatrists most, the demand that occurs most frequently is made by one such as an insurer, who cannot compel disclosure but who can withhold a benefit without it. Apart from statutory disclosure requirements and judicial compulsion, there is no legal obligation to furnish information, even to law enforcement officials.

In the usual case, the person himself makes disclosures or authorizes his psychiatrist to make them so as to receive a benefit, such as employment, welfare benefits, or insurance.

### Third-Party Payers, Supervision, and Research

Increased insurance coverage for health care is precipitating the concern with confidentiality and the conceptual model of psychiatric practice. Today, insurance covers about 70 percent of all health care bills. To provide coverage, an insurance carrier must be able to obtain information with which it can assess the administration and the cost of programs.

In regard to supervision, confidentiality considered as an absolute would impede the quality control of care. Quality control necessitates a review of individual patients and therapists and involves discriminate disclosure. The therapist in training must breach the confidence of his patient to discuss the case with his supervisor. Judicially ordained right-to-treatment envisions individualized treatment for institutionalized patients based on a program submitted for review to a mental health board.

### Writing about Patients

In general, a professional has multiple loyalties: He has a loyalty to his client and also to society and his profession. By writing, he shares acquired knowledge and experience, providing information that may be of value to other professionals and to the public generally. However, it is not easy to write about a psychiatric patient without breaching the confidentiality of this relationship. Unlike physical ailments, which can be discussed without anyone's recognizing the patient, a psychiatric history usually entails a discussion of distinguishing characteristics.

### Disclosure to Safeguard the Patient or Others

In some situations, the psychiatrist becomes an informer in order to protect the patient or others.

There are times, albeit few in number, when reporting by a psychotherapist may be crucial. Conflict may arise between the therapist's responsibility to an individual patient and to others.

In a number of situations, reporting by the physician to the authorities is specifically required by law. The classic example of mandated reporting is of a patient having epilepsy who operates a motor vehicle. Another example of mandated reporting, one in which penalities are imposed for failure to report, involves child abuse. By law, therapists are obliged to report suspected cases of child abuse to public authorities. Expanded definitions of what constitutes child abuse under the law have been amended in some jurisdictions to include emotional as well as physical child abuse. Under this legislation a practitioner who learns that his patient is engaged in sexual activity with his child would be obliged to report it although nothing may be gained by notifying the authorities.

Other notable examples of mandated reporting include dangerous or contagious diseases, firearm and knife wounds, and the reporting on patients in drug abuse treatment programs.

In the absence of a specific statute that mandates reporting, the making of a report is optional under prevailing law. As a general principle, a person has no duty to come to the aid of another unless there is a special relationship giving rise to this duty.

Does the establishment of a therapist-patient relationship present sufficient involvement by the therapist to impose on him an obligation of care for the safety not only of the patient, but also of others? This issue was clearly raised in the case of *Tarasoff* v. *Regents of University of California* in 1966. In this case, Prosenjit Poddar, a student and a voluntary outpatient at the mental health clinic of the University of California, related to his therapist his intention to kill a girl readily identifiable as Tatiana Tarasoff. Realizing the seriousness of the intention, the therapist, with the concurrence of a colleague, concluded that Poddar should be committed for observation under a 72-hour emergency psychiatric detention provision of the California commitment law. The therapist notified the campus police both orally and in writing that Poddar was dangerous and should be committed.

Concerned about the breach of confidentiality, the therapist's supervisor vetoed the recommendation and ordered all records relating to Poddar's treatment destroyed. At the same time, the campus police temporarily detained Poddar, but released him on his assurance that he would "stay away from that girl." Poddar stopped going to the clinic when he learned from the police of his therapist's recomendation to commit him. Two months later, he carried out his previously announced threat to kill Tatiana. The girl's parents thereupon brought a suit in negligence against the university.

Because of this, the California Supreme Court, which deliberated the case for the unprecedented time of some 14 months, ruled that a physician or a psychotherapist who has reason to believe that a patient may injure or kill another must notify the potential victim, his relatives, his friends, or the authorities.

The discharge of the duty imposed on the therapist to protect the intended victim against such danger may take one or more various steps, depending on the nature of the case. Thus, said the court, it may call for the therapist to warn the intended victim or others likely to apprise the victim of the danger, to notify the police, or to take whatever other steps are reasonably necessary under the circumstances.

As a matter of practice, the Tarasoff decision does not drastically affect the psychiatrist. It has long been the practice to warn appropriate persons or law enforcement authorities discreetly when a patient presents a distinct and immediate threat to someone. According to the American Psychiatric Association, confidentiality may, with careful judgment, be broken in the following ways: (1) A patient will probably commit murder; the act can be stopped only by the intervention of the psychiatrist. (2) A patient will probably commit suicide; the act can be stopped only by the intervention of the psychiatrist. (3) A patient, such as a bus driver or airline pilot, who is charged with serious responsibilities shows marked impairment of judgment.

The Tarasoff ruling does not require a therapist to report a fantasy. It simply means that when he is realistically convinced that a homicide is in the making, it is his duty to exercise good judgment.

## Laws Governing Hospitalization

### Civil Commitment

It is preferable to have a patient enter a mental hospital or the psychiatric inpatient service of a general hospital voluntarily, for the same reason that his prognosis is better if he enters psychotherapy as an outpatient through his own decision: Because he wants to help himself.

All of the states provide for some form of involuntary hospitalization. Such action is usually taken when the psychiatric patient presents a danger to himself and to others in his environment to the degree that his urgent need for treatment in a closed institution is evident.

The statutes governing hospitalization of the mentally ill have generally been designated as commitment laws. However, psychiatrists have long considered the term an undesirable one because commitment, legally, means a warrant for imprisonment. The American Bar Association and the American Psychiatric Association recommended that the term be replaced by the less offensive and more accurate term hospitalization, and this has been done by most states. Although change in terminology will not correct attitudes of the past, emphasis on hospitalization and treatment is more in keeping with the views of psychiatrists toward this process.

## Procedures of Admission

There are four procedures of admission to psychiatric facilities that have been endorsed by the American Bar Association as safeguarding civil liberties and ensuring that no individual can be railroaded into a mental hospital. While each of the 50 states has the power to enact its own laws regarding psychiatric hospitalization, the procedures outlined are gaining much acceptance.

**1. Informal Admission.** This form of admission operates on the general hospital model in which the patient is admitted to a psychiatric unit of a general hospital precisely on the same basis as a medical or surgical patient might be admitted. Under such circumstances, the ordinary doctor-patient relationship applies with freedom on the part of the patient to enter and freedom to leave, even against medical advice.

**2. Voluntary Admission (Operates in Psychiatric Hospitals).** Under this procedure, the patient applies for admission to any psychiatric hospital in writing. He may come to the hospital on the advice of his personal physician, or he may seek help on the basis of his own decision. In either case, the patient is examined by a psychiatrist on the staff of the hospital, and is admitted if that examination reveals the need for hospital treatment.

**3. Temporary Admission (Emergency Admission or Certificate of One Physician).** This category is used for patients who are so senile or confused that they require hospitalization and are not able to make decisions of their own, or for patients who are so acutely disturbed that they must be immediately admitted to a psychiatric hospital on an emergency basis.

Under this procedure, a person is admitted to the hospital on the written recommendation of one physician. Once having been brought to the psychiatric hospital, the need for hospitalization must be confirmed by a psychiatrist on the hospital staff.

This procedure is temporary, in that the patient cannot be hospitalized against his will for a period exceeding 15 days.

**4. Involuntary Admission (Certificate of Two Physicians).** Involuntary admission involves the question of whether or not the patient is a danger to himself, such as in the suicidal patient, or a danger to others, such as in the homicidal patient. Because these individuals do not recognize their need for hospital care, application for admission to a hospital may be made by a relative, or friend.

Once the application is made, the patient must be examined by two physicians and, if they confirm the need for hospitalization, the patient can then be admitted.

There is an established procedure for written notification to the next of kin whenever involuntary hospitalization is involved. Furthermore, the patient has access at any time to legal counsel, who can bring the case before a judge. If hospitalization is not felt to be indicated by the judge, he can order the patient's release from the hospital.

Involuntary admission allows the patient to be hospitalized for 60 days. After this time, the case must be reviewed periodically by a board consisting of psychiatrists, nonpsychiatric physicians, lawyers, and other citizens not connected with the institution, if the patient is to remain hospitalized. In New York State this board is called the mental health information service. The power of the state to involuntarily commit mentally ill persons in need of care is known as *parens patriae* and sometimes police power in that it prevents mentally ill persons from doing harm to themselves or to others.

In spite of the clear-cut procedures and safeguards for hospitalization available to the patient, to his family, as well as to the medical and legal profession, involuntary admissions are being viewed by some as an infringement of civil rights.

A person who has been involuntarily hospitalized and who believes that he should be released has the right to file a petition for a writ of *habeas corpus*. And, under law, a writ of *habeas corpus* may be proclaimed on behalf of anyone who claims he is being deprived of his liberty illegally. This legal procedure asks a court to decide whether hospitalization has been accomplished without due process of the law and must be heard by a court at once, regardless of the manner or form in which it is filed. Hospitals are obligated to submit these petitions to the court immediately.

## Right to Treatment

Among the rights of patients, that of the standard of quality of care is fundamental. It has been litigated in much publicized cases in recent years under the slogan right to treatment.

In 1966, Judge David Bazelon, speaking for

the District of Columbia Court of Appeals in *Rouse* v. *Cameron*, noted that the purpose of involuntary hospitalization is treatment and concluded that the absence of treatment draws into question the constitutionality of the confinement. Treatment in exchange for liberty is the logic of the ruling. In that case the patient was discharged on a writ of *habeas corpus*, the basic legal remedy to assure liberty.

Federal District Court Judge Frank Johnson, sitting in Alabama, was more venturesome in the decree he rendered in 1971 in *Wyatt* v. *Stickney*. The *Wyatt* case was a class action proceeding, brought under newly developed rules, that sought not release but treatment. Judge Johnson ruled that persons civilly committed to a mental institution have a constitutional right to receive such individual treatment as will give each of them a reasonable opportunity to be cured or to improve his or her mental condition.

He set out minimum requirements for staffing, specified physical facilities and nutritional standards, and required individualized treatment plans. Shortly thereafter, Federal District Judge William Justice, sitting in Texas, set out standards for state training schools.

The new codes, more detailed than the old, include the right to be free from excessive or unnecessary medication, the right to privacy and dignity, the unrestricted right to be visited by attorneys and private physicians, the right not to be subjected to experimental research, the right to wear one's own clothes, and the right not to be subjected to lobotomy, electroshock treatments, or other procedures without fully informed consent. Patients can be required to perform therapeutic tasks but not hospital chores unless they volunteer for them and are paid the federal minimum wage. This is an attempt to eliminate the practice of *peonage*, in which psychiatric patients were forced to work at menial tasks for the benefit of the state, without payment.

In a number of states today, medication or electroshock therapy cannot be administered to a nonvoluntary patient without first obtaining court approval, which may take as much as 10 days. The right to refuse treatment is a legal doctrine which holds that a person cannot be forced to have treatment against his will unless a life and death emergency exists.

In the 1976 case of *O'Connor* v. *Donaldson*, the Supreme Court ruled that harmless mental patients cannot be confined against their will without treatment if they can survive outside. A finding of mental illness alone cannot justify a state's confining a person in a hospital against his will according to the Court. Instead, patients

must be considered dangerous to themselves or others. The question was raised of the psychiatrists' ability to accurately predict dangerousness and the risk to the psychiatrist who might be sued for monetary damages if a person is deprived of civil rights as a result of this difficulty in accurately assessing dangerousness in some cases.

Ethical controversy over applications of the law to psychiatric patients came to the fore through Thomas Szasz, a professor of psychiatry at the State University of New York. In his book, *The Myth of Mental Illness*, Szasz developed the thesis that the various psychiatric diagnoses are totally devoid of significance. He went further to argue that psychiatrists have no place in the courts of law and that all forced confinement of people because of mental illness is unjust. Szasz's thesis against suicide prevention and the imposition of treatment, with or without confinement, is stimulating but is viewed by the psychiatric community with strong misgivings.

## Informed Consent

Lawyers representing an injured claimant now invariably add to a claim of negligent performance of procedures (malpractice) an informed consent claim as another possible area of liability. Significantly, it is one claim under which the requirement of expert testimony may be avoided. The usual claim of malpractice requires the litigant to produce an expert to establish that there was a departure from accepted, proper medical practice. But in a case in which there was no informed consent, the fact that the treatment was technically well performed and effected a complete cure is immaterial. However, as a practical matter, unless there are adverse consequences, a complainant will not get very far with a jury in an action based only on an allegation that the treatment was without consent.

Under classical tort (a tort is a wrongful act) theory, an intentional touching to which one has given no consent is a battery. Thus, the administration of electroshock therapy or chemotherapy, though it may be therapeutic, is a battery when done without consent. Indeed, any unauthorized touching outside of conventional social intercourse constitutes a battery. It is an offense to the dignity of the person, an invasion of his right of self-determination, for which punitive and actual damages may be imposed. Justice Cardozo wrote: "Every human being of adult years and sound mind has a right to determine what shall be done with his own body; and a surgeon who performs an operation without his patient's consent commits [a battery] for which he is liable in damages."

Under Cardozo's formulation, it is not the effectiveness or the timeliness of the treatment that allows taking care of another but the consent to it. Thus, a mentally competent adult may refuse treatment, though effective and of little risk. But when, for example, gangrene sets in and the patient is psychotic, treatment, even of such momentous proportions as amputation—though more costly, less effective, and more intrusive than earlier intervention might have been—may be ordered to save the patient's life. The state is said to have a compelling interest in preventing its citizens from committing suicide.

In the case of minors, the parent or guardian is the person legally empowered to give consent to medical treatment. However, most states by statute list specific diseases or conditions that a minor can consent to have treated—venereal disease, pregnancy, contraception, drug dependency, alcoholism, and contagious diseases. And in an emergency situation, a physician can treat a minor without parental consent. The trend is to adopt what is referred to as the mature minor rule, allowing minors to consent to treatment under ordinary circumstances. As a result of the *Gault decision*, the juvenile must now be represented by counsel, must be able to confront witnesses, and must be given proper notice of any charges. The emancipated minor has the rights of an adult when it can be demonstrated that he is living as an adult with control over his own life.

Traditionally, to obviate a claim of battery, the physician needed only to relate what he proposed to do and obtain the patient's consent thereto. However, simultaneously with the growth of product liabilty and consumer law generally, the courts began to require that the physician also relate sufficient information to allow the patient to decide whether such a procedure is acceptable in light of its risks and benefits and the available alternatives, including no treatment at all. This duty of full disclosure gave rise to the phrase informed consent. However, uninformed consent or coercive consent is no consent. In general, informed consent requires that there be (1) an understanding of the nature and foreseeable risks and benefits of a procedure, (2) a knowledge of alternative procedures, (3) the consequences of withholding consent, and (4) that the consent is voluntary.

## Child Custody

The action of a court in a child custody dispute is now predicated on the best interests of the child. The maxim reflects the idea that a natural parent does not have an inherent right to be named custodial parent, but the presumption, although a bit eroded, remains in favor of the mother in the case of young children. The courts, by a rule of thumb, presume that the welfare of a child of tender years is generally best served by maternal custody when the mother is a good and fit parent. The best interest of the mother may be served by naming her custodial parent, since a mother may never resolve the impact of the loss or death of a child, but her best interest is not to be equated *ipso facto* with the best interest of the child. Care and protection proceedings refer to the court's intervening in the welfare of the child when the parents are unable to do so.

As has been widely reported, more and more fathers are asserting custodial claims. In about 5 percent of the cases, they are named custodians. The movement supporting women's rights is also enhancing the chances of paternal custody. With an increasing number of women going outside the home to work, the traditional rationale for maternal custody has less force than in the past.

The best-interests test is obviously loose and vague, but the proposition is clear that the better psychological parent may be given preference over the biological parent, even in the absence of a showing of parental unfitness.

Every state today has a statute allowing a court, usually a juvenile court, to assume jurisdiction over a neglected or abused child and to remove the child from parental custody under broad standards. Most states provide several grounds for assuming jurisdiction, such as parental abuse, an environment injurious to the child's welfare, and a child in danger of being brought up to lead an idle, dissolute, or immoral life. If the court removes the child from parental custody, it usually orders that the care and custody of the child be supervised by the welfare or probation department. In turn, that department places the child with relatives or foster parents or in an institution. After removal, the natural parent may seek the return of the child, and the social welfare department or foster parents may object.

## Testamentary and Contractual Capacity

The psychiatrist may be called upon to evaluate a patient's *testamentary capacity*, i.e., his competency to make a will. Three psychological abilities are necessary to demonstrate this competency; the patient must know: (1) The nature and extent of his bounty (property); (2) that he is making a will; and (3) who his natural beneficiaries are—that is, his wife, children, and relatives.

Quite often, when a will is being probated, one of the heirs or some other person challenges the validity of the will. A judgment in such cases must be based on a reconstruction of what the testator's mental state was at the time the will was written. The evidence used to make this reconstruction comes from persons who knew the testator at the time he wrote the will and from expert psychiatric testimony. The expert needs to examine all the data from documents and from the witnesses and then make a reconstruction.

An incompetency proceeding and the appointment of a guardian may be considered necessary when a member of the family is dissipating the family's assets. The guardianship process may be used when property is in danger of dissipation in the case of, say, the aged, the retarded, alcoholics, and psychotics. The issue is whether the person is capable of managing his own affairs. However, a guardian appointed to take control over property of one deemed incompetent cannot make a will for the ward. When one is unable or does not exercise his right to make a will, the law in all states provides for the distribution of one's property to the heirs; if there are no heirs, the estate goes to the public treasury. Witnesses at the signing of the will, which may include a psychiatrist, may attest that the testator was rational at the time of the execution of the will. In unusual cases the lawyer may videotape the signing to safeguard the will from attack.

*Competency* is determined on the basis of the person's ability to have sound judgment. The diagnosis of a mental disorder is not, in and of itself, sufficient to warrant a finding of incompetency. The mental disorder must cause an impairment in judgment regarding the specific issues involved. Once declared incompetent, the individual is deprived of certain rights: he cannot make contracts, marry, start a divorce action, drive a vehicle, handle his own property, or practice his profession. Incompetency is decided at a formal courtroom proceeding and the court usually appoints a guardian who will best serve the interests of the patient. Once declared incompetent, another hearing is necessary to declare the patient competent. It should be noted that admission to a mental hospital does not automatically mean the individual is incompetent. A separate hearing is usually required.

In reference to contracts, competency is essential since a contract is an agreement between parties to do some specific act. The contract will be declared invalid if, when it was signed, one of the parties was unable to comprehend the nature of his act. The marriage contract is subject to the same standard and will be voidable if either party did not understand "for want of understanding" the nature, duties, obligations, and other characteristics entailed. In general, courts are unwilling to declare a marriage void on the basis of incompetency.

Whether the competence relates to wills, contracts, or the making or breaking of marriages, the fundamental concern is the person's state of awareness and his capacity to comprehend the significance of the specific subject of the particular commitment he was making—at the time he made it.

A conservator handles the fiscal or contractual affairs of the person under his control; but not with respect to medical or surgical treatment.

## Criminal Law and Psychiatry

### Criminal Responsibility

According to criminal law, a socially harmful act does not represent the sole criterion of a crime. The objectional act must have two essential components: (1) voluntary conduct (*actus reus*) and (2) evil intent (*mens rea*). There cannot be a *mens rea* if the offender's mental status is so deficient, so abnormal, so diseased as to have deprived him of the capacity for rational intent. The law can be invoked only when an illegal intent is implemented. Neither behavior, however harmful, nor the intent to do harm are, in themselves, grounds for criminal action.

In most American jurisdictions until quite recently, a person could be found not guilty by reason of insanity if he suffered from a mental illness, did not know the difference between right and wrong, and did not know the nature and consequences of his acts.

**M'Naghten Rule.** The precedent for determining legal responsibility was established in the British courts during 1843. The so-called M'Naghten rule, which has, until recently, determined responsibility in most of the United States, holds that a man is not guilty by reason of insanity if he labored under a mental disease such that he was unaware of the nature, quality, and consequences of his act, or if he was incapable of realizing that his act was wrong. Moreover, to absolve a man from punishment, a delusion has to be one which if true, would be an adequate defense. If the deluded idea does not justify the crime then presumably the man is to be held responsible, guilty, and punishable. The M'Naghten rule is known commonly as the right-wrong test.

The M'Naghten rule derives from the famous

FIGURE 1. Daniel M'Naghten. His 1843-murder trial led to the establishment of rules still generally observed in legal insanity pleas. (Courtesy of Culver Pictures.)

M'Naghten case dating back to 1843. At that time Edward Drummond, the private secretary of Sir Robert Peel, was murdered by Daniel M'Naghten (see Fig. 1). M'Naghten had been suffering from delusions of persecution for several years. He had complained to many people about his delusional persecutors and finally he decided to correct the situation by murdering Sir Robert Peel. When Drummond came out of Peel's home. M'Naghten shot Drummond, mistaking him for Peel. He was later adjudged insane and committed to a hospital. The case aroused great interest causing the House of Lords to debate the problems of criminality and insanity. In response to questions about what guidelines could be used to determine whether a person should plead insanity as a defense against criminal responsibility, the English judiciary wrote:

1. To establish a defense on the ground of insanity it must be clearly proved that, at the time of committing the act, the party accused was laboring under such a defect of reason, from disease of the mind, as not to know the nature and quality of the act he was doing, or if he did know it, he did not know he was doing what was wrong.

2. Where a person labors under partial delusions only and is not in other respects insane and as a result commits an offense he must be considered in the same situation as to respon-

sibility as if the facts with respect to which the delusion exists were real.

The jury, as instructed under the prevailing law, found the defendant not guilty by reason of insanity.

The M'Naghten rule does not ask whether the accused knows the difference in general between right and wrong; it asks if the defendant understood the nature and quality of his act and if he knew the difference between right and wrong with respect to his act. It asks specifically whether he knew he was doing what was wrong or, perhaps, thought he was right—that is, whether he was under a delusion causing him to act in legitimate self-defense.

Another part of the M'Naghten rule stipulates, with reference to what it calls partial delusions, that the lawbreaker "must be considered in the same situation as to responsibility as if the facts with respect to which the delusion exists were real." That is, it must be asked whether a person would be liable to punishment if it were true that his victim had spread vicious rumors about him. See Figures 2 and 3 for other important criminal law cases.

**Irresistible Impulse.** In 1922, a committee of jurists in England reexamined the M'Naghten

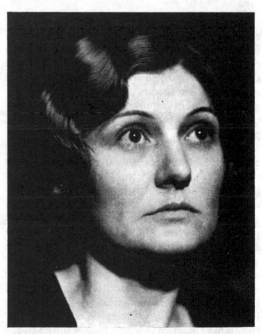

FIGURE 2. Winnie Ruth Judd. Known as the "trunk murderess" of the early 1930s, Judd was saved from execution by a sanity hearing. She was committed to an Arizona state hospital from which she made her seventh escape in 1962. She was found in 1969 working as a receptionist. An Arizona Board of Pardons and Parole recommended her freedom. (Courtesy of United Press International, Inc.)

FIGURE 3.    William Heirens. The 17-year-old University of Chicago student who pleaded guilty to three murders in 1946 was ruled legally insane by Joliet prison psychiatrists and moved to a state mental institution. (Courtesy of United Press International, Inc.)

rule and suggested broadening the concept of insanity in criminal cases to further include the concept of the irresistible impulse. This meant that a person charged criminally with an offense is irresponsible for his act when the act is committed under an impulse which the prisoner was by mental disease in substance deprived of any power to resist. The courts have chosen to interpret this law in such a way that it has been called the "policeman-at-the-elbow" law. In other words, the court will grant the impulse to be irresistible only if it is determined that the accused would have gone ahead with the act even if he had a policeman at his elbow. To most psychiatrists this is an unsatisfactory law because it covers only a small and a very special group of those who are mentally ill.

**Durham Rule.** In 1954, the case of *Durham* v. *United States*, a decision was handed down by Judge David Bazelon who was a pioneering jurist in forensic psychiatry in the District of Columbia Court of Appeals that resulted in the product rule of criminal responsibility: An accused is not criminally responsible if his unlawful act was the product of mental disease or defect.

Judge Bazelon in the *Durham* case expressly stated that the purpose of the rule was to get good and complete psychiatric testimony. He sought to break the criminal law out of the theoretical strightjacket of the M'Naghten test. However, judges and juries in cases using the Durham rule became mired in confusion over the term "product" and over the terms "disease" and "defect." In 1972, some 19 years after its adoption, the Court of Appeals for the District of Columbia in *United States* v. *Brawner* discarded it. The court—all nine members, including Judge Bazelon—decided in a 143-page opinion to throw out its Durham rule and to adopt in its place the test recommended in 1962 by the American Law Institute in its Model Penal Code, which is the law in the federal courts today.

**Model Penal Code.** The American Law Institute in its Model Penal Code recommended the following test of criminal responsibility: (1) A person is not responsible for criminal conduct if at the time of such conduct as a result of mental disease or defect he lacks substantial capacity either to appreciate the criminality [wrongfulness] of his conduct or to conform his conduct to the requirement of the law; (2) As used in this Article, the terms "mental disease or defect" do not include an abnormality manifested only by repeated criminal or otherwise antisocial conduct.

There are five operative concepts in subsection (1) of the American Law Institute rule: (1) mental disease or defect, (2) lack of substantial capacity, (3) appreciation, (4) wrongfulness, and (5) conformity of conduct to the requirements of law. The second subsection of the rule, stating that repeated criminal or antisocial conduct is not of itself to be taken as mental disease or defect, aims to keep the sociopath or psychopath within the scope of criminal responsibility.

The test of criminal responsibility and other tests grading criminal liability refer to the time of the commission of the offense, while the test of competency to stand trial refers to the time of trial.

Although much has been written on the theory of the insanity plea, it is actually asserted as a defense in only a small percentage of cases, and it is upheld in only a fraction of those. Juries are usually skeptical. It is, in the operation of the criminal law, a last-ditch defense, one used when all else fails.

The verdict of a District of Columbia jury in 1982 finding the would-be assassin of President Ronald Reagan, John W. Hinckley, Jr., not guilty by reason of insanity ignited moves to limit or abolish the special plea of insanity. The trial by jury of Hinckley also turned out to be a trial of law and psychiatry. The psychiatrists and the law allowing their testimony were made the culprits for the unpopular verdict. "The psychiatrists spun sticky webs of pseudo-scientific jargon," wrote a prominent columnist, "and in these webs the concept of justice, like a moth, fluttered feebly and was trapped." The American Bar Association (ABA) and the American Psychiatric Association (APA) were prompted to quickly issue statements calling for a change in the law. Over two score bills were introduced in the Congress to amend the law; but none were passed. They helped to defuse the public criticism. At present Hinckley is hospitalized indefinitely at the federal Saint Elizabeth Hospital in Washington, D.C.

The ABA and the APA in their statements of 1982 recommend a defense of nonresponsibility which focuses solely on whether the defendant, as a result of mental disease or defect, was unable to appreciate the wrongfulness of his conduct. These proposals would limit evidence of mental illness to cognition and exclude it on control (but there would apparently still remain defenses available under a not-guilty plea, such as extreme emotional disturbance, automatism, provocation, or self-defense, that may be established without psychiatric testimony on mental illness). The APA also urges that "mental illness" be limited to "severely" abnormal mental conditions. The proposals remain a subject of controversy.

### Competence to Stand Trial

It has long been accepted that a person who lacks the capacity to understand the nature and the object of the proceedings against him, to consult with counsel, and to assist in preparing his defense is not competent to stand trial.

The Supreme Court has said that "the prohibition [against trying a mental incompetent] is fundamental to an adversary system of justice." Accordingly, the Court has approved a test of incompetence that seeks to ascertain whether a criminal defendant "has sufficient present ability to consult with his lawyer with a reasonable degree of rational understanding—and whether he has a rational as well as factual understanding of the proceedings against him."

The failure to observe procedures adequate to protect a defendant's right not to be tried or convicted while incompetent to stand trial deprives him of his due-process right to a fair trial.

### Malpractice

Malpractice is the term commonly used to refer to professional negligence. It is the law of the bungle. It has also been loosely used to cover intentional or willful invasion of another's le-

gally protected interest, such as battery, or treatment without consent. An action based on negligence, whatever the specific situation, involves basic problems of relation of the parties, risk, and reason.

In negligence: (1) a standard of care requisite under the particular circumstances must exist, (2) a duty must have been owed by the defendant or by someone for whose conduct the defendant is answerable, (3) the duty must have been owed to the plaintiff, and (4) a breach of the duty is the legal cause of the plaintiff's asserted damage or injury.

The requisite standard of care under the circumstances may be established in the federal or state constitution, statutes, administrative regulations, court decisions, or the custom of the community. However, the law, with exceptions, does not define particular duties with any degree of definiteness. It is not possible to define the way a person ought to act under myriad circumstances and conditions. As a general rule, a professional person has the duty to exercise the degree of skill ordinarily used under similar circumstances by the members of his profession in good standing. That standard applies to every professional person—whether physician, lawyer, or engineer. Thus a physician's performance is essentially evaluated in terms of what other physicians would do under the circumstances.

The complainant in a malpractice action, as in cases of willfully caused damage, must prove his allegations by a preponderance of the evidence. To sustain the burden of proof, the plaintiff must show, because he is urging the court to action on his behalf: (1) an act or omission on the part of the defendant or of someone for whose conduct he is answerable, (2) a causal relation between the conduct and the damage or injury allegedly suffered by the plaintiff, and (3) the negligent quality of the conduct. Since most professional conduct is not within the common knowledge of the lay person, there must usually be a resort to expert testimony to prove what is the practice and the defendant's conformity or lack of conformity with it.

In relative frequency of malpractice suits, psychiatry ranks eighth among medical specialties, and, in almost every suit for psychiatric malpractice in which liability was imposed, tangible physical injury was demonstrated. The number of suits against psychiatrists is said to be small because of the patient's reluctance to expose a psychiatric history, the skill of the psychiatrist in dealing with the negative feelings of the patient, and the difficulty in linking injury with treatment. Psychiatrists have been sued for malpractice mainly for faulty diagnosis or screening, improper certification in commitment, suicide, harmful effects of convulsive treatments and psychotropic drugs, improper divulgence of information, and sexual intimacy with patients.

Sexual intimacy with patients is a significant problem in the case of all psychotherapists and is both illegal and unethical. Serious legal and ethical questions extend to psychotherapist's even dating or marrying a patient after discharging them from therapy.

## Consultation

Because of the many legal problems with which psychiatrists must deal, the APA in 1982 established a Prepaid Legal Consultation Program. Under the program, for an annual fee, members can take advantage of an unlimited number of telephone consultations and legal memoranda provided by a Washington, D.C., law firm. Various state psychiatric societies have also initiated such programs. In its operation to date, the most frequently raised issues fall into three major areas: (1) malpractice (risks of particular drugs or forms of therapy, commitment and voluntary hospitalization, liability for acts of others, consent forms, insurance coverage, suicide, and duty to warn); (2) business-related matters (billing and bill collection, employment contracts with hospitals or clinics, staff privileges, and advertising); and (3) confidentiality and privilege. Other areas in which members sought advice were with regard to patient access to records, professional incorporation, tax matters, relationships with nonphysician health care providers, office sharing and leases, record keeping, serving as a witness or expert witness, the meaning of various legal standards, third-party issues (most involving private insurance), and referrals to attorneys.

## REFERENCES

Barton W E, Sanborn C F, editors: *Law and the Mental Health Professions: Friction at the Interface.* International Universities Press, New York, 1978.

Blinder M: *Psychiatry in the Everyday Practice of Law.* Lawyers Co-operative Publishing, Rochester, NY, 1982.

Bloch S, Chodoff P, editors: *Psychiatric Ethics.* Oxford, New York, 1981.

Ciccone R J, Clemens C: Forensic psychiatry and applied clinical ethics: theory and practice. Am J Psychiatry *141:* 395, 1984.

Grob G N: *Mental Institutions in America: Social Policy to 1857.* Free Press, New York, 1973.

Gutheil T G, Appelbaum P S: *Clinical Handbook of Psychiatry and the Law.* McGraw-Hill, New York, 1982.

Halleck S L: *Law in the Practice of Psychiatry.* Plenum, New York, 1980.

Modlin H C, Sadoff R L, Slovenko R: *Career Directions: Psychiatry and the Law.* Sandoz, East Hanover, NH, 1976.

Peszke M A: *Involuntary Treatment of the Mentally Ill.* Charles C Thomas, Springfield, IL, 1975.

Sadoff R L: *Forensic Psychiatry: A Practical Guide for Lawyers and Psychiatrists.* Charles C Thomas, Springfield, IL, 1975.

Simon R I: *Psychiatric Interventions and Malpractice.* Charles C Thomas, Springfield, IL, 1982.

Slovenko R: *Psychiatry and Law.* Little, Brown, Boston, 1973.

Slovenko R: Law and psychiatry. In *Comprehensive Textbook of Psychiatry,* ed 4, H I Kaplan, B J Sadock, editors, p 1960. Williams & Wilkins, Baltimore, 1985.

Szasz T: *Law, Liberty and Psychiatry.* Macmillan, New York, 1963.

Winslade W J, Ross J W: *The Insanity Plea.* Scribner's, New York, 1983.

Ziskin J: *Coping with Psychiatric and Psychological Testimony.* Law and Psychology Press, Beverly Hills, CA, 1981.

# Index

Page numbers in **boldface** type indicate major discussions; those followed by "*t*" or "*f*" denote tables or figures, respectively.

Aarskog syndrome, 725*t*
Abortion, in adolescence, 5
Abraham, Karl, 1–2, 244, 268
Abreaction, 67
  in analysis, 596
  in group therapy, 615
  hypnotic, 610
  in release therapy, 815
Abstinence syndrome, 164
Abstract attitude, 278
Abulia, 810
Academic failure, and childhood affective disorders, 853
Academic inhibition, 477
  in adolescence, **810–811**
  differential diagnosis, 478
Academic problem, **860–862** (*see also* School performance)
  DSM-III classification, 185*t*, 860
  etiology, 860–861
  treatment, 861–862
Acceptance, of dying, 268–269
Accident proneness, 485
Accidents
  and alcohol, 421
  traffic, 487
Accommodation, 691
Acetohexamide (Dymelor), alcohol interaction, 423
Acetophenazine (Tindal), 643
  adult dose range, 634*t*
  available preparations, 636*t*
  structure, 634*t*
Acetylcholine, 19
  in depression, 242
  inactivation, 24
  in sleep, 561
Acetylcholinesterase, 24
Achondroplasia, **721**
Acidemia
  methylmalonic, 712*t*
  proprionic, 712*t*
Acne vulgaris, **527**
Acoholics Anonymous, **426**
Acquired immune deficiency syndrome (AIDS), 390
Acrocephalosyndactyly, 725*t*
Acrocephaly, 721
Acrophobia, 151*t*, 323
  definition, 179
Acting out
  adolescent, 831
  in group therapy, 616
Action-specific energy hypothesis, 45–46

Activity therapy, 604
*Actus reus*, 894
Acupuncture, **690**
Adams-Stokes syndrome, 511
Adaptation
  Jung's view of, 103
  Piaget's theory, 35
  to reality
    vs. adjustment, 78
    Freudian theory, 78
Adaptive functioning, 185–187
  rating, 189*t*
Addiction (*see* Drug dependence; Substance abuse)
Addison's disease, 250*t*, 311, **517** (*see also* Adrenal cortical insufficiency)
Adjustment, 78
Adjustment disorder(s), **476–479**, 785, 788
  adolescent, **808–809**
  with anxious mood, 477
    DSM-III classification, 184*t*
  with atypical features, DSM-III classification, 185*t*
  causes, 477
  vs. condition not attributable to mental disorder, 478
  definition, 476
  with depressed mood, 477
    DSM-III classification, 184*t*, 192
  diagnosis, 477
  diagnostic criteria, 477
  differential diagnosis, 478
  with disturbance of conduct, 477–478
    DSM-III classification, 184*t*
  DSM-III classification, 476, 478
  epidemiology, 477
  with mixed disturbance of emotions and conduct, 478
    DSM-III classification, 184*t*
  with mixed emotional features, 477
    DSM-III classification, 184*t*
  psychopathology, 476
  subtypes, 477
  symptoms, 476, 477
  treatment, 478–479
  violence in, 582
  with withdrawal, 478, 797
    DSM-III classification, 184*t*
  with work disturbance or academic inhibition, 478
    DSM-III classification, 184*t*
Adjustment reaction

ICD-9 classification, 187*t*
  with mixed disturbance of emotions and conduct, ICD-9 classification, 187*t*
  with predominant disturbance of conduct, ICD-9 classification, 187*t*
  with predominant disturbance of other emotions, ICD-9 classification, 187*t*
Adler, Alfred, **104–105**, 378
  theory
    of life style, 104
    of motivation, 104
    of personality, 104–105
    of psychopathology, 105
    of social context and social feeling, 104–105
    of unity of individual, 104
  therapeutic techniques, 105
Adolescence, 2, **5**, **90**, **99–100**
  atypical bipolar disorder in, 263
  atypical depression in, 262–263
  definition, 697
  development after, **696**
  development during, **696**, **697–700**
  disorders usually first evident in, DSM-III classification, 182*t*–183*t*, 187–189
  early phase, 2, 5
  growth in
    continuous, 697–698
    surgent, 698–699
    tumultuous, 699–700
  judgment impairment in, 154
  late phase, 2, 5
  middle, 5
  oppositional stage, 787
  other disorders of, DSM-III classification, 182*t*
  pregnancy in, 5
  problems, 830–831
Adolescent(s) (*see also* Child(ren))
  acting out, 831
  affective disorders, 830–831
  antisocial behavior, 831
  combined therapy, 821
  drug dependence, 830
  family therapy, 832
  group therapy, 821, 832
  noncommunicativeness, 831
  organic therapy, 832
  preschizophrenic, 213
  psychotherapy, **830–833**
    behavioral change, 832
    diagnosis for, 831–832

**899**